LITERATURE FOR COMPOSITION

The steaming horses think it queer
To
The ... to think it queer
To stop without a farm house near
Between the woods and a frozen lake
The darkest evening of the year

She
He gives harness bells a shake
To ask if there is some mistake
The only other sounds the sweep
Of easy wind and downy flake.

The woods are lovely dark and deep
But I have promises to keep
That bid me on ... and there are miles
And miles to go before I sleep
And miles to go before I sleep

Manuscript of Robert Frost's "Stopping by Woods on a Snowy Evening"
(Special Collections, The Jones Library, Inc., Amherst, MA.)

Literature for Composition

Essays, Fiction, Poetry, and Drama

FOURTH EDITION

Edited by

Sylvan Barnet
Tufts University

Morton Berman
Boston University

William Burto
University of Lowell

Marcia Stubbs
Wellesley College

HarperCollinsCollegePublishers

Acquisitions Editor: Lisa Moore
Developmental Editor: Judith Leet
Project Editor: Robert Ginsberg
Text Design: Mary Archondes
Cover Designer: Kay Petronio
Cover Art: *Interior* by Joaquin Torres-Garcia, 1923.
    Private Collection, Barcelona
Art Studio: FineLine, Inc.
Photo Researcher: Sandy Schneider
Electronic Production Manager: Valerie A. Sawyer
Manufacturing Manager: Helene G. Landers
Electronic Page Makeup: American–Stratford Graphic Services, Inc.
Printer and Binder: RR Donnelley & Sons Company
Cover Printer: The Lehigh Press, Inc.
Insert Printer: The Lehigh Press, Inc.

Literature for Composition: Essays, Fiction, Poetry, and Drama, 4th Edition

Library of Congress Cataloguing-in-Publication Data

Literature for composition : essays, fiction, poetry, and drama /
    edited by Sylvan Barnet . . . [et al.].—4th ed.
        p.   cm.
    Includes indexes.
ISBN 0-673-52344-6
        1. College readers. 2. English language—Rhetoric. I. Barnet,
Sylvan
PE1417.L633 1996   95-14186
808'.0427—dc20   CIP

4 5 6 7 8 9 10 -DOC-01 00 99 98

Contents

Part Two   Up Close: Thinking about Literary Forms

12 *Thinking Critically about Poetry* 379

Part Three Standing Back: Thinking Critically about
Literature and Approaches to Literature

13 *What, Then, Is Literature?* 393

Part Four A Thematic Anthology

20 *Art and Life*   *850*

Essays   *853*

Fiction   *859*

Appendix B *Writing a Research Paper* 1305

Alternate Contents

Arranged by Literary Genre

Fiction

Poetry

Drama

Preface

This book is based on the assumption that students in composition or literature courses should encounter—if not at the start, then certainly by the midpoint—first-rate writing. By this we mean not simply competent prose but the powerful reports of experience that have been recorded by highly skilled writers past and present. We assume that the study of such writing yields pleasure and insight into life, and that it also yields a sense of what the best words in the best places can do.

Literature for Composition, Fourth Edition, is in large part an anthology of literature, but it is more: It also offers instruction in writing.

Part One, "Getting Started," consists of four chapters with six very short works of literature. The aim of all of the chapters in Part One is to help students to read and to respond—in writing—to literature. The first two chapters discuss such procedures as annotating, free writing, listing, and keeping a journal; the third chapter discusses writing an analysis and an explication; the fourth discusses other kinds of writing, including parody and a story based on a story.

Part Two, "Up Close: Thinking about Literary Forms," is concerned with four literary kinds—the essay, fiction, drama, and poetry. These chapters not only include advice about reading and writing; they also include works of literature (7 essays, 7 short stories, 4 plays, 23 poems). Suggested topics for discussion and writing help students to think critically and to develop arguments about this material. Part Two thus offers a small anthology of literature, organized by genre, as well as guidance in writing about literature. Part Two contains four casebooks—on an essay, a story, a play, and a poem—in which a work of literature is followed by some published critical commentaries, thereby allowing students to think about kinds of criticism, and about evaluating conflicting interpretations. (We talk a bit more about the casebooks later in this preface, in the note on the fourth edition.)

Part Three, "Standing Back: Thinking Critically about Literature and Approaches to Literature," consists of four chapters concerned with the nature of literature and with interpretation, evaluation, and critical approaches. Our idea is this: If instructors have begun by assigning some or all of the chapters in Parts One and Two, the students by now have read enough literature to be in a good position to think further about the assumptions underlying interpretations and evaluations.

Part Four is "A Thematic Anthology" of literature (including essays). Although the earlier chapters include generous samples of literature, most of the literature appears in Part Four, where it is arranged into chapters on six themes: "Parents and Children"; "Innocence and Experience"; "Love and Hate"; "Art and Life"; "The Individual and Society"; and "Men, Women, God, and Gods." Here, as earlier, all of the essays, stories, poems, and plays are followed by questions that are meant to stimulate critical thinking and writing.

The book concludes with two appendices, one on manuscript form and one on the research paper, and a glossary of terms. The material on manuscript form may seem to be yet another discussion of writing, and some readers may wonder why it is put toward the back of the book. But manuscript form is chiefly a matter of editing rather than of drafting and revising. It is, so to speak, the final packaging of a product that develops during a complicated process, a process that begins with reading, responding, and finding a topic, a thesis, and a voice, not with worrying about the width of margins or the form of citations. The last thing that one does in writing an essay, and therefore the last thing in our book, is to set it forth in a physical form fit for human consumption.

And now a few additional words about the literature in this book. Writers write about something. Of course they write essays or stories or poems or plays, but these are *about* something, for instance about love, which comes in many varieties. We arranged the works thematically so that we can give, if not responses to the whole of life, at least a spectrum of responses to large parts of it. By grouping the works according to themes, and by beginning each group with essays that help to set the reader to thinking about the theme, we hope to call attention not only to resemblances but also to important differences, even between superficially similar works such as, say, two sonnets by Shakespeare. Obviously one work is not "right" and another "wrong." There is, after all, no one correct view of, say, love or happiness.

We trust that these multiple views are welcome, though we uneasily recall the Ballyhough railway station, which has two clocks that differ by six minutes. When an irritated traveler asked an attendant what was the use of having two clocks that didn't tell the same time, the attendant replied, "And what would we be wanting with two clocks if they told the same time?"

But works of literature are not clocks; we hope that each work will be valued for itself and will also be valued for the light it throws on other works of literature, and on life. Behind this hope, of course, is the assumption that good writing—the accurate report of powerful thinking and feeling—is a response to and an interpretation of life, and that it is therefore nourishing. We cannot do better than to quote Coleridge on this point:

> The heart should have fed upon truth, as insects on a leaf, till it be tinged with the color and shows its food in every minutest fiber.

WHAT IS NEW IN THE FOURTH EDITION?

Instructors familiar with earlier editions will notice major changes in this edition, some of which have just been mentioned, though we did not specify that they were new. Here, for the convenience of instructors who have used an earlier edition, we will list the major changes:

- We have amplified the material on writing, for instance with new pages on outlining a draft, on using technical language, on using a word processor, and on locating research materials through a computer. We have also increased the number of sample essays by students, and we have added checklists that will aid writers when they are drafting their essays.
- We have made more visible our emphasis on critical thinking and on arguing a thesis. To this end we have, for instance, added a chapter on arguing an interpretation and another on arguing an evaluation, and we have also added material on a variety of critical approaches, such as archetypal criticism, biographical criticism, deconstruction, formalist criticism, gender criticism, historical scholarship, the New Historicism, and psychological criticism.
- We have added four casebooks, that is, works of literature accompanied by critical essays, thereby enabling students to hear a range of views, and to think about what criteria govern interpretation and evaluation. The casebooks are on Francis Bacon's "Of Parents and Children," William Faulkner's "A Rose for Emily," William Shakespeare's *The Tempest,* and Emily Dickinson's "I heard a Fly buzz—when I died—."
- We have greatly increased the number of essays, stories, poems, and plays, for a total of 28 essays, 57 stories, 11 plays, and 158 poems. Two of the six themes are new, "Parents and Children" and "Art and Life"; the second of these includes eight color plates of works of art that are the subjects of poems.

These extensive revisions have been made in the light of our own experience and the experience of many other instructors who have taught *Literature for Composition.*

Note: An Instructor's Manual, with suggestions for teaching each selection, is available from the publisher. In addition, for qualified adoptors an impressive selection of videotapes and HarperCollins audiotapes is also available to enrich students' experience of literature. Instructors are invited to learn more about the HarperCollins video- and audiotape library and to request a complimentary copy of the Instructor's Manual from their HarperCollins representative or from the publisher.

ACKNOWLEDGMENTS

In preparing the first three editions of *Literature for Composition* we were indebted to Margaret Blayney, Bertha Norman Booker, John P. Boots, Pam Bourgeois, Robin W. Bryant, Kathleen Shine Cain, Diana Cardenas, Walter B. Connolly, Linda Cravens, Donald A. Daiker, Bill Elliott, Leonard W. Engel, William Epperson, Elinor C. Flewellen, Kay Fortson, Marie Foster, Donna Friedman, Loris Galford, Chris Grieco, Sandra H. Harris, Sally Harrold, Maureen Hoag, Clayton Hudnall, Joyce A. Ingram, Bill Kelly, Michael Johnson, William McAndrew, Kathleen McWilliams, JoAnna S. Mink, Charles Moran, Patricia G. Morgan, Nancy Morris, Christina Murphy, John O'Connor, James R. Payne, Don K. Pierstorff, Gerald Pike, Louis H. Pratt, Bruce A. Reid, Linda Robertson, Terry

Santos, Jim Schwartz, Robert Schwegler, William Shelley, Janice Slaughter, Judith Stanford, Jim Streeter, Beverly Swan, Leesther Thomas, Raymond L. Thomas, Susan D. Tilka, Dorothy Trusock, Billie Varnum, Mickey Wadia, Nancy Walker, Kathy J. Wright, and Gary Zacharias,

In preparing this latest edition we have been greatly aided by the suggestions of the following reviewers:

In preparing this latest edition we have been greatly aided by the suggestions of the following reviewers: Dennis Ciesielski, Southern Illinois University at Carbondale; Arlene Clift-Pellow, North Carolina State University; Stanley Corkin, University of Cincinnati; Beth DeMeo, Alvernia College; Ren Draya, Blackburn College; Larry Frost, Henderson State University; Sydney Harrison, Manatee Community College; Craig Johnson, Hillsborough Community College; Angela Jones, University of Kansas; Cynthia Lowenthal, Tulane University; Timothy Martin, Rutgers University; Zack Miller, Brookhaven College; Dorothy Minor, Tulsa Junior College; Richard Nielsen, University of South Dakota; Martha Smith, Brookhaven College; Tija Spitsberg, University of Michigan–Dearborn; Darlene Strawser, Lakeland Community College; Mary Trachsel, University of Iowa; John Venne, Ball State University; Linda Woodson, University of Texas, San Antonio; and Dennis Young, James Madison University. All of these people have given us valuable advice.

We must especially mention William Cain, the student of one editor and the colleague of another. Bill has treated us as we hope we have treated our students; his extended annotations are always on the mark, and they are offered in such a way that as readers we almost believe that if we had written just one more draft we would have said something pretty much along the suggested lines.

At HarperCollins, Judith Leet and Lisa Moore carefully watched over this project. We wish also to thank Kathy Mullins, who secured copyright permission—even for our last-minute and way-beyond-the-deadline inclusions—and Bob Ginsberg and Mary Archondes, who converted a manuscript into a book.

Sylvan Barnet
Morton Berman
William Burto
Marcia Stubbs

PART ONE

Getting Started

CHAPTER 1

The Writer as Reader: Reading and Responding

*Interviewer: Did you know as a child you wanted
to be a writer?*
Toni Morrison: No. I wanted to be a reader.

Learning to write is in large measure learning to read. The text you must read most carefully is the one you write, an essay you will ask someone else to read. It may start as a jotting in the margin of a book you are reading or as a brief note in a journal, and it will go through several drafts before it becomes an essay. To produce something that another person will find worth reading, you yourself must read each draft with care, trying to imagine the effect your words are likely to have on your reader. In writing about literature, you will apply some of the same critical skills to your reading; that is, you will examine your responses to what you are reading and will try to account for them.

Let's begin by looking at a very short story by Kate Chopin (1851–1904). (The name is pronounced in the French way, something like "show pan.") Kate O'Flaherty, born into a prosperous family in St. Louis, in 1870 married Oscar Chopin, a French-Creole businessman from Louisiana. They lived in New Orleans, where they had six children. Oscar died of malaria in 1882, and in 1884 Kate returned to St. Louis, where, living with her mother and children, she began to write fiction.

 KATE CHOPIN

Ripe Figs

Maman-Nainaine said that when the figs were ripe Babette might go to visit her cousins down on the Bayou-Lafourche where the sugar cane grows. Not that the ripening of figs had the least thing to do with it, but that is the way Maman-Nainaine was.

It seemed to Babette a very long time to wait; for the leaves upon the trees were tender yet, and the figs were like little hard, green marbles.

But warm rains came along and plenty of strong sunshine, and though Maman-Nainaine was as patient as the statue of la Madone, and Babette as restless as a humming-bird, the first thing they both knew it was hot summertime. Every day Babette danced out to where the fig-trees were in a long line against the fence. She walked slowly beneath them, carefully peering between the gnarled, spreading branches. But each time she came disconsolate away again. What she saw there finally was something that made her sing and dance the whole long day.

When Maman-Nainaine sat down in her stately way to breakfast, the following morning, her muslin cap standing like an aureole about her white, placid face, Babette approached. She bore a dainty porcelain platter, which she set down before her godmother. It contained a dozen purple figs, fringed around with their rich, green leaves.

"Ah," said Maman-Nainaine arching her eyebrows, "how early the figs have ripened this year!"

"Oh," said Babette. "I think they have ripened very late."

"Babette," continued Maman-Nainaine, as she peeled the very plumpest figs with her pointed silver fruit-knife, "you will carry my love to them all down on Bayou-Lafourche. And tell your Tante Frosine I shall look for her at Toussaint—when the chrysanthemums are in bloom."

[1893]

READING AS RE-CREATION

If we had been Chopin's contemporaries, we might have read this sketch in *Vogue* in 1893 or in an early collection of her works, *A Night in Acadie* (1897). But we are not Chopin's original readers, and, since we live in the late twentieth century, we inevitably read "Ripe Figs" in a somewhat different way. And this gets us to an important truth about writing and reading. A writer writes, sets forth his or her meaning, and attempts to guide the reader's responses, as we all do when we write a letter home saying that we're thinking of dropping a course or asking for news or money or whatever. To this extent, the writer creates the written work and puts a meaning in it.

But the reader, whether reading that written work as a requirement or for recreation, *re-creates* it according to his or her experience and understanding. For instance, if the letter-writer's appeal for money is too indirect, the reader may miss it entirely or may sense it but feel that the need is not urgent. If, on the other hand, the appeal is direct or demanding, the reader may feel imposed upon, even assaulted. "Oh, but I didn't mean it that way," the writer later protests. Nevertheless, that's the way the reader took it. The letter is "out there," a physical reality standing between the writer and the reader, but its *meaning* is something the reader as well as the writer makes.

Since all readers bring themselves to a written work, they each bring something individual. For instance, although many of Chopin's original readers knew that she wrote chiefly about the people of Louisiana, especially Creoles (descendants of the early French and Spanish settlers), Cajuns (descendants of the French whom the British had expelled from Canada in the eighteenth century), African-Americans, and mulattoes, those readers must have varied in their attitudes about such people. And many of today's readers do *not* (before they read a work by Chopin) know anything about her subject. Some readers may know where Bayou-Lafourche is, and they may have notions about what it looks like but most readers will not; indeed, many readers will not know that a bayou is a sluggish, marshy inlet or outlet of a river or lake. Moreover, even if a present-day reader in Chicago, Seattle, or Juneau knows what a bayou is, he or she may assume that "Ripe Figs" depicts a way of life still current, whereas a reader from Louisiana may see in the work a depiction of a lost way of life, a depiction of the good old days (or perhaps of the bad old days, depending on the reader's point of view). Much depends, we can say, on the reader's storehouse of experience.

To repeat: Reading is a *re*-creation; the author has tried to guide our responses, but inevitably our own experiences, including, for instance, our ethnic background and our education, contribute to our responses. You may find useful a distinction that E. D. Hirsch makes in *Validity in Interpretation* (1967). For Hirsch, the *meaning* in a text is the author's intended meaning; the *significance* is the particular relevance for each reader. In this view, when you think about meaning you are thinking about what the author was trying to say and to do—for instance, to take an old theme and treat it in a new way. When you think about significance, you are thinking about what the work does for you—it enlarges your mind, offends you by its depiction of women, or whatever.

MAKING REASONABLE INFERENCES

Does this mean, then, that there is no use talking (or writing) about literature, since all of us perceive it in our relatively private ways, rather like the seven blind men in the fable? One man, you will recall, touched the elephant's tail (or was it his trunk?) and said that the elephant is like a snake; another touched the elephant's side and said the elephant is like a wall; a third touched the elephant's leg and said the elephant is like a tree, and so on. This familiar story is usually told in order to illustrate human limitations, but notice, too, that each of the blind men *did* perceive an aspect of the elephant—an elephant is massive, like a wall or a tree, and an elephant is (in its way) remarkably supple, as you know if you have given peanuts to one.

As readers we can and should make an effort to understand what an author seems to be getting at. For instance, we should make an effort to understand unfamiliar words. Perhaps we shouldn't look up every word that we don't know, at least on the first reading, but if certain unfamiliar words are repeated and thus seem especially important, we will probably want to look them up. It happens that in "Ripe Figs" a French word appears: "*Tante* Frosine" means "*Aunt* Frosine." Fortunately, the meaning of the word is not crucial, and the context probably makes it clear that Frosine is an adult, which is all that we really need to know about her. But a reader who does not know, for instance, that chrysanthemums bloom in late summer or early autumn will miss part of Chopin's meaning. The point is this: the writer is pitching, and she expects the reader to catch.

On the other hand, although writers tell us a good deal, they cannot tell us everything. We know that Maman-Nainaine is Babette's godmother, but we don't know exactly how old Maman-Nainaine and Babette are. Further, Chopin tells us nothing of Babette's parents. It rather *sounds* as though Babette and her god-mother live alone, but readers' opinions may differ. One reader may argue that Babette's parents must be dead or ill, whereas another may say that the status of her parents is irrelevant and that what counts is that Babette is supervised by only one person, a mature woman. In short, a text includes **indeterminacies** (passages that careful readers agree are open to various interpretations) and **gaps** (things left unsaid in the story, such as why a godmother rather than a mother takes care of Babette). As we work our way through a text, we keep reevaluating what we have read, pulling the details together to make sense of them, in a process called **consistency building.**

Whatever the gaps, careful readers are able to draw many reasonable infer-ences about Maman-Nainaine. What are some of these? We can list them:

> She is older than Babette.
> She has a "stately way," and she is "patient as the statue of la Madone."
> She has an odd way (is it exasperating, or engaging, or a little of each?) of connecting actions with the seasons.
> Given this last point, she seems to act slowly, to be very patient.
> She apparently is used to being obeyed.

You may at this point want to go back and reread "Ripe Figs," to see what else you can say about Maman-Nainaine.

And now what of Babette?

> She is young.
> She is active and impatient ("restless as a humming-bird").
> She is obedient.

And at this point, too, you may want to add to the list.

If you do add to the list, you might compare your additions with those of a classmate. The two of you may find that you disagree about what may reasonably be inferred from Chopin's words. Suppose, for instance, that your classmate said that although Babette is outwardly obedient, inwardly she probably hates Maman-Nainaine. Would you agree that this assertion is an acceptable inference? If you don't agree, how might you go about trying to convince your classmate that such a response is not justified? We are speaking here of an activity of mind called **critical thinking,** a topic discussed in the next chapter.

READING WITH PEN IN HAND

It's probably best to read a work of literature straight through, enjoying it and let-ting yourself be carried along to the end. But then, when you have an overall view, you'll want to read it again, noticing (for example) how certain innocent-seeming details given early in the work prove to be especially important later.

Perhaps the best way to read attentively is, after a first reading, to mark the text, underlining or highlighting passages that seem especially interesting, and to jot notes or queries in the margins. (*Caution:* Annotate and highlight, but don't get so carried away that you highlight whole pages.) Here is "Ripe Figs" once more, this time with the marks that a student added to it during and after a second reading.

KATE CHOPIN

Ripe Figs

Maman-Nainaine said that when the figs were ripe Babette might go to visit her cousins down on the Bayou-Lafourche where the sugar cane grows. Not that the ripening of figs had the least thing to do with it, but that is the way Maman-Nainaine was.

It seemed to Babette a very long time to wait; for the leaves upon the trees were tender yet, and the figs were like little hard, green marbles.

But warm rains came along and plenty of strong sunshine, and though Maman-Nainaine was as patient as the statue of la Madone, and Babette as restless as a humming-bird, the first thing they both knew it was hot summer-time. Every day Babette danced out to where the fig-trees were in a long line against the fence. She walked slowly beneath them, carefully peering between the gnarled, spreading branches. But each time she came disconsolate away again. What she saw there finally was something that made her sing and dance the whole long day.

When Maman-Nainaine sat down in her stately way to breakfast, the following morning, her muslin cap standing like an aureole about her white, placid face, Babette approached. She bore a dainty porcelain platter, which she set down before her godmother. It contained a dozen purple figs, fringed around with their rich, green leaves.

"Ah," said Maman-Nainaine arching her eyebrows, "how early the figs have ripened this year!"

"Oh," said Babette. "I think they have ripened very late."

"Babette," continued Maman-Nainaine as she peeled the very plumpest figs with her pointed silver fruit-knife, "you will carry my love to them all down on Bayou-Lafourche. And tell your Tante Frosine I shall look for her at Toussaint—when the chrysanthemums are in bloom."

[Marginal annotations:]

strange!

contrast between M-N and B

check ? this

nice echo contrast like a song

is M-N herself like a plump fig?

another contrast

ceremonious

time passes fast for M-N slowly for B

B entrusted with a message of love

opens with figs; ends with chrys. (autumn)

fulfillment? Equivalent to figs ripening?

RECORDING YOUR FIRST RESPONSES

Another useful way of getting at the meaning of a work of literature is to jot down your initial responses to it, recording your impressions as they come to you in any order—almost as though you're talking to yourself. Since no one else is going to read your notes, you can be entirely free and at ease. You can write in sentences or not; it's up to you. You can jot down these responses either before or after you annotate the text. Some readers find that annotating the text helps to produce ideas for further jottings, but others prefer to jot down a few thoughts immediately after a first reading, and then, stimulated by these thoughts, they reread and annotate the text.

Write whatever comes into your mind, whatever the literary work triggers in your own imagination, whatever you think are the important ideas or values of your own experience.

Here is a student's first response to "Ripe Figs":

> This is a very short story. I didn't know stories were this short, but I like it because you can get it all quickly and it's no trouble to reread it carefully. The shortness, though, leaves a lot of gaps for the reader to fill in. So much is <u>not</u> said. Your imagination is put to work.
>
> But I can see Maman-N sitting at her table-- pleasantly powerful--no one you would want to argue with. She's formal and distant--and definitely has quirks. She wants to postpone Babette's trip, but we don't know why. And you can sense B's frustration. But maybe she's <u>teaching</u> her that something really good is worth <u>waiting</u> for and that anticipation is as much fun as the trip. Maybe I can develop this idea.
>
> Another thing. I can tell they are not poor-- from two things. The pointed silver fruit knife and the porcelain platter, and the fact that Maman sits down to breakfast in a "stately" way. They are the leisure class. But I don't know enough about life on the bayous to go into this. Their life is different from mine; no one I know has that kind of peaceful rural life.

AUDIENCE AND PURPOSE

Now, suppose that you are beginning the process of writing about "Ripe Figs" for someone else, not for yourself. The first question to ask yourself is: "For whom am I writing?" That is, who is your *audience?* (Of course you probably are writing because an instructor has asked you to do so, but you must still imagine an audience. Your instructor may tell you, for instance, to write for your class-mates, or to write for the readers of the college newspaper.) If you are writing for people who already are familiar with some of Chopin's work, you won't have to say much about the author, but if you are writing for an audience who per-haps has never heard of Chopin, you may want to include a brief biographical note of the sort we gave. If you are writing for an audience who, you have reason to believe, has read several works by Chopin, you may want to make some com-parisons, explaining how "Ripe Figs" resembles or differs from Chopin's other work.

In a sense, the audience is your collaborator; it helps you to decide what you will say. You are also helped by your sense of *purpose.* If your aim is to intro-duce readers to Chopin, you will make certain points. If your aim is to tell peo-ple what you think "Ripe Figs" means to say about human relationships, or about time, you will say some different things; if your aim is to have a little fun and to entertain an audience that is already familiar with "Ripe Figs," you may decide to write a parody (a humorous imitation) of the story.

🖉 A WRITING ASSIGNMENT ON "RIPE FIGS"

The Assignment

Let's assume that you want to describe "Ripe Figs" to someone who has not read it. You probably will briefly summarize the action, such as it is, and will mention where it takes place, who the characters are, including what their relationship is, and what, if anything, happens to them. Beyond that, you will probably try to explain as honestly as you can what makes "Ripe Figs" appealing or interesting—or trifling, or boring, or whatever. That is, you will *argue* a thesis, even though you almost surely will not say anything as formal as "In this essay I will argue that . . ." or "This essay will attempt to prove that. . . ." Your essay nevertheless will essentially be an argument because (perhaps after a brief summary of the work) you will be pointing to the evidence that has caused you to respond as you did.

Here is an essay that a student, Marilyn Brown, wrote for this assignment.

Sample Essay

Ripening

Kate Chopin's "Ripe Figs" describes a growing season in a young girl's life. Maman-Nainaine agrees to allow young Babette to visit relatives away from home, but Babette must delay her trip until the figs ripen. Babette watches the signs of the natural world, impatiently observing, straining to have time pass at her own speed. At last, Babette finds that the figs have ripened, and she presents them to her godmother, Maman-Nainaine, who gives Babette her leave to go on the journey to Bayou-Lafourche.

Chopin sets the action within the context of the natural world. Babette, young and tender as the fig leaves, can't wait to "ripen." Her visit to Bayou-Lafourche is no mere pleasure trip but represents Babette's coming into her own season of maturity.

Babette's desire to rush this process is tempered by a condition that Maman-Nainaine sets: Babette must wait until the figs ripen, since everything comes in its own season. Maman recognizes in the patterns of the natural world the rhythms of life. By asking Babette to await the ripening, the young girl is made to pay attention to these patterns as well.

In this work, Chopin asks her readers to see the relationship of human time to nature's seasons. Try as we may to push the process of maturity, growth or ripening happens in its own time. If we pay attention and wait with patience, the fruits of our own growth will be sweet, plump, and bountiful. Chopin uses natural imagery effectively, interweaving the young girl's growth with the rhythms of the seasons. In this way, the reader is connected with both processes in a very intimate and inviting way.

✏️ OTHER POSSIBILITIES FOR WRITING

But of course one might write a paper of a very different sort. Consider the following possibilities:

1. Write a sequel, moving from fall to spring.
2. Write a letter from Babette, now at Bayou-Lafourche, to Maman-Nainaine.
3. Imagine that Babette is now an old woman, writing her memoirs. What does she say about Maman-Nainaine?
4. Write a story based on your own experience of learning a lesson in patience.

CHAPTER 2

The Reader as Writer: Drafting and Writing

All there is to writing is having ideas. To learn to write is to learn to have ideas.

Robert Frost

PRE-WRITING: GETTING IDEAS

How does one "learn to have ideas"? Among the methods are these: reading with a pen or pencil in hand, so that (as we have already seen) you can annotate the text; keeping a journal, in which you jot down reflections about your reading; talking with others (including your instructor) about the reading. Let's take another look at the first of these, annotating.

Annotating a Text

In reading, if you own the book don't hesitate to mark it up, indicating (by highlighting or underlining or by making marginal notes) what puzzles you, what pleases or interests you, and what displeases or bores you. Later, of course, you'll want to think further about these responses, asking yourself, on rereading, if you still feel that way, and if not, why not, but these first responses will get you started.

   Annotations of the sort given on page 7, which chiefly call attention to contrasts, indicate that the student is thinking about writing some sort of analysis of the story. That is, she is thinking of writing an essay in which she will examine the parts of a literary work either in an effort to see how they relate to each other or in an effort to see how one part relates to the whole.

More About Getting Ideas: A Second Story by Kate Chopin

Let's look at a story that is a little longer than "Ripe Figs," and then we'll discuss how in addition to annotating one might get ideas for writing about it.

The Story of an Hour

Knowing that Mrs. Mallard was afflicted with a heart trouble, great care was taken to break to her as gently as possible the news of her husband's death.

It was her sister Josephine who told her, in broken sentences, veiled hints that revealed in half concealing. Her husband's friend Richards was there, too, near her. It was he who had been in the newspaper office when intelligence of the railroad disaster was received, with Brently Mallard's name leading the list of "killed." He had only taken the time to assure himself of its truth by a second telegram, and had hastened to forestall any less careful, less tender friend in bearing the sad message.

She did not hear the story as many women have heard the same, with a paralyzed inability to accept its significance. She wept at once, with sudden, wild abandonment, in her sister's arms. When the storm of grief had spent itself she went away to her room alone. She would have no one follow her.

There stood, facing the open window, a comfortable, roomy armchair. Into this she sank, pressed down by a physical exhaustion that haunted her body and seemed to reach into her soul.

5 She could see in the open square before her house the tops of trees that were all aquiver with the new spring life. The delicious breath of rain was in the air. In the street below a peddler was crying his wares. The notes of a distant song which some one was singing reached her faintly, and countless sparrows were twittering in the eaves.

There were patches of blue sky showing here and there through the clouds that had met and piled above the other in the west facing her window. She sat with her head thrown back upon the cushion of the chair quite motionless, except when a sob came up into her throat and shook her, as a child who has cried itself to sleep continues to sob in its dreams.

She was young, with a fair, calm face, whose lines bespoke repression and even a certain strength. But now there was a dull stare in her eyes, whose gaze was fixed away off yonder on one of those patches of blue sky. It was not a glance of reflection, but rather indicated a suspension of intelligent thought.

There was something coming to her and she was waiting for it, fearfully. What was it? She did not know; it was too subtle and elusive to name. But she felt it, creeping out of the sky, reaching toward her through the sounds, the scents, the color that filled the air.

Now her bosom rose and fell tumultuously. She was beginning to recognize this thing that was approaching to possess her, and she was striving to beat it back with her will—as powerless as her two white slender hands would have been.

10 When she abandoned herself a little whispered word escaped her slightly parted lips. She said it over and over under her breath: "Free, free,

free!" The vacant stare and the look of terror that had followed it went from her eyes. They stayed keen and bright. Her pulses beat fast, and the coursing blood warmed and relaxed every inch of her body.

She did not stop to ask if it were not a monstrous joy that held her. A clear and exalted perception enabled her to dismiss the suggestion as trivial.

She knew that she would weep again when she saw the kind, tender hands folded in death; the face that had never looked save with love upon her, fixed and gray and dead. But she saw beyond that bitter moment a long procession of years to come that would belong to her absolutely. And she opened and spread her arms out to them in welcome.

There would be no one to live for her during those coming years; she would live for herself. There would be no powerful will bending her in that blind persistence with which men and women believe they have a right to impose a private will upon a fellow creature. A kind intention or a cruel intention made the act seem no less a crime as she looked upon it in that brief moment of illumination.

And yet she had loved him—sometimes. Often she had not. What did it matter! What could love, the unsolved mystery, count for in face of this possession of self-assertion which she suddenly recognized as the strongest impulse of her being.

15   "Free! Body and soul free!" she kept whispering.

Josephine was kneeling before the closed door with her lips to the keyhole, imploring for admission. "Louise, open the door! I beg; open the door—you will make yourself ill. What are you doing, Louise? For heaven's sake open the door."

"Go away. I am not making myself ill." No; she was drinking in a very elixir of life through that open window.

Her fancy was running riot along those days ahead of her. Spring days, and summer days, and all sorts of days that would be her own. She breathed a quick prayer that life might be long. It was only yesterday she had thought with a shudder that life might be long.

She arose at length and opened the door to her sister's importunities. There was a feverish triumph in her eyes, and she carried herself unwittingly like a goddess of Victory. She clasped her sister's waist, and together they descended the stairs. Richards stood waiting for them at the bottom.

20   Some one was opening the front door with a latchkey. It was Brently Mallard who entered, a little travel-stained, composedly carrying his gripsack and umbrella. He had been far from the scene of accident, and did not even know there had been one. He stood amazed at Josephine's piercing cry; at Richards' quick motion to screen him from the view of his wife.

But Richards was too late.

When the doctors came they said she had died of heart disease—of joy that kills.

[1894]

Brainstorming for Ideas for Writing

Unlike annotating, which consists of making brief notes and small marks on the printed page, "brainstorming"—the free jotting down of ideas—asks that you jot down whatever comes to mind, without inhibition. Don't worry about spelling, about writing complete sentences, or about unifying your thoughts; just let one thought lead to another. Later you can review your jottings, deleting some, connecting with arrows others that are related, expanding still others, but for now you want to get going, and so there is no reason to look back. Thus you might jot down something about the title:

> Title speaks of an hour, and story covers an hour, but maybe takes five minutes to read.

And then, perhaps prompted by "an hour," you might happen to add something to this effect:

> Doubt that a woman who got news of the death of her husband could move from grief to joy within an hour.

Your next jotting might have little or nothing to do with this issue; it might simply say

> Enjoyed "Hour" more than "Ripe Figs" partly because "Hour" is so shocking.

And then you might ask yourself

> By shocking, do I mean "improbable," or what? Come to think of it, maybe it's not so improbable. A lot depends on what the marriage was like.

Focused Free Writing

Focused, or directed, free writing is a method related to brainstorming that some writers use to uncover ideas they may want to write about. Concentrating on one issue—for instance, a question that strikes them as worth puzzling over (What kind of person is Mrs. Mallard?)—they write at length, nonstop, for perhaps five or ten minutes.

Writers who find free writing helpful put down everything they can think of that has bearing on the one issue or question they are examining. They do not stop at this stage to evaluate the results, and they do not worry about niceties of sentence structure or of spelling. They just pour out their ideas in a steady stream of writing, drawing on whatever associations come to mind. If they pause in their writing, it is only to refer to the text, to search for more detail—perhaps a quotation—that will help them answer their question.

After the free-writing session, these writers usually go back and reread what they have written, highlighting or underlining what seems to be of value. Of course they find much that is of little or no use, but they also usually find that some strong ideas have surfaced and have received some development. At this point the writers are often able to make a scratch outline and then begin a draft.

Here is an example of one student's focused free writing:

> What do I know about Mrs. Mallard? Let me put everything down here I know about her or can figure out from what Kate Chopin tells me. When she finds herself alone after the death of her husband, she says, "Free. Body and soul free" and before that she said, "Free, free, free." Three times. So she has

suddenly perceived that she has not been free; she
has been under the influence of a "powerful will." In
this case it has been her husband, but she says no
one, man nor woman, should impose their will on
anyone else. So it's not a feminist issue--it's a
power issue. No one should push anyone else around is
what I guess Chopin means, force someone to do what
the other person wants. I used to have a friend that
did that to me all the time; he had to run
everything. They say that fathers--before the women's
movement--used to run things, with the father in
charge of all the decisions, so maybe this is an
honest reaction to having been pushed around by a
husband. I think Mrs. Mallard is a believable
character, even if the plot is not all that
believable--all those things happening in such quick
succession.

Listing

In your preliminary thinking you may find it useful to make lists. In the previous
chapter we saw that listing the traits of the two characters was helpful in thinking about Chopin's "Ripe Figs":

    Maman-Nainaine
        older than Babette
        "stately way"
        "patient as the statue of la Madone"
        connects actions with seasons
        expects to be obeyed
    Babette
        young
        active
        obedient

For "The Story of an Hour" you might list Mrs. Mallard's traits; or you might list
the stages in her development. (Such a list is not the same as a summary of the
plot. The list helps the writer to see the sequence of psychological changes.)

    weeps (when she gets the news)
    goes to room, alone
    "pressed down by a physical exhaustion"
    "dull stare"
    "something coming to her"
    strives to beat back "this thing"
    "Free, free, free!" The "vacant stare went . . . from her eyes"
    "A clear and exalted perception"
    rejects Josephine
    "she was drinking in a very elixir of life"

gets up, opens door, "a feverish triumph in her eyes"
sees B, and dies

Of course, unlike brainstorming and annotating, which let you go in all directions, listing requires that you first make a decision about what you will be listing—traits of character, images, puns, or whatever. Once you make the decision, you can then construct the list, and, with a list in front of you, you will probably see patterns that you were not earlier fully conscious of.

Asking Questions

If you feel stuck, ask yourself questions. (You'll recall that the assignment on "Ripe Figs" in effect asked the students to ask themselves questions about the work—for instance, questions about the relationship between the characters—and about their responses to it: "You'll probably try to explain as honestly as you can what makes 'Ripe Figs' appealing or interesting—or trifling, or boring, or whatever.")

If you are thinking about a work of fiction, ask yourself questions about the plot and the characters—are they believable, are they interesting, and what does it all add up to? What does the story mean *to you?* One student found it helpful to jot down the following questions:

```
Plot
    Ending false? Unconvincing? Or prepared for?
Character?
    Mrs. M. unfeeling? Immoral?
    Mrs. M. unbelievable character?
    What might her marriage have been like? Many
        gaps.
    (Can we tell what her husband was like?)
    "And yet she loved him--sometimes." Fickle?
        Realistic?
    What is "this thing that was approaching to
        possess her"?
Symbolism
    Set on spring day = symbolic of new life?
```

You don't have to be as tidy as this student. You may begin by jotting down notes and queries about what you like or dislike and about what puzzles or amuses you. What follows are the jottings of another student, Janet Vong. They are, obviously, in no particular order—the student is "brainstorming," putting down whatever occurs to her—though it is equally obvious that one note sometimes led to the next:

```
Title nothing special. What might be a better
    title?
Could a woman who loved her husband be so
    heartless?
Is she heartless? Did she love him?
```

```
What are (were) Louise's feelings about her
    husband?
Did she want too much? What did she want?
Could this story happen today? Feminist
    interpretation?
Sister (Josephine)--a busybody?
Tricky ending--but maybe it could be true.
"And yet she had loved him--sometimes. Often she
    had not."
    Why does one love someone "sometimes"?
Irony: plot has reversal. Are characters ironic
    too?
```

These jottings will help the reader-writer think about the story, find a special point of interest, and develop a thoughtful argument about it.

Keeping a Journal

A journal is not a diary, a record of what the writer did during the day ("today I read Chopin's 'Hour'"). Rather, a journal is a place to store some of the thoughts you may have inscribed on a scrap of paper or in the margin of the text, such as your initial response to the title of a work or to the ending. It is also a place to jot down further reflections, such as thoughts about what the work means to you, and what was said in the classroom about writing in general or specific works.

You will get something out of your journal if you write an entry at least once a week, but you will get much more if you write entries after reading each assignment and after each class meeting. You may, for instance, want to reflect on why your opinion is so different from that of another student, or you may want to apply a concept such as *character* or *irony* or *plausibility* to a story that later you may write about in an essay. Comparisons are especially helpful: How does this work (or this character, or this rhyme scheme) differ from last week's reading?

You might even make an entry in the form of a letter to the author or from one character to another. You might write a dialogue between characters in two works or between two authors, or you might record an experience of your own that is comparable to something in the work.

A student who wrote about "The Story of an Hour" began with the following entry in his journal. In reading this entry, notice that one idea stimulates another. The student was, quite rightly, concerned with getting and exploring ideas, not with writing a unified paragraph.

```
     Apparently a "well-made" story, but seems clever
rather than moving or real. Doesn't seem plausible.
Mrs. M's change comes out of the blue--maybe some
women might respond like this, but probably not most.
     Does literature deal with unusual people, or
with usual (typical?) people? Shouldn't it deal with
typical? Maybe not. (Anyway, how can I know?) Is
"typical" same as "plausible"? Come to think of it,
prob. not.
```

```
        Anyway,  whether  Mrs.  M  is  typical  or  not,  is  her
    change  plausible,  believable?  Think  more  about  this.
        Why  did  she  change?  Her  husband  dominated  her
    life  and  controlled  her  actions;  he  did  "impose  a
    private  will  upon  a  fellow  creature."  She  calls  this
    a  crime,  even  if  well-intentioned.  Is  it  a  crime?
```

Critical Thinking: Arguing with Yourself

In our discussion of annotating, brainstorming, free writing, listing, asking questions, and writing entries in a journal, the emphasis has been on responding
freely rather than in any highly systematic or disciplined way. Something strikes
us (perhaps an idea, perhaps an uncertainty), and we jot it down. Maybe even
before we finish jotting it down we go on to question it, but probably not; at this
early stage it is enough to put onto paper some thoughts, rooted in our first responses, and to keep going.

The almost random play of mind that is evident in brainstorming and in the
other activities already discussed is of course a kind of thinking, but the term
critical thinking is reserved for something different. When we think critically,
we skeptically scrutinize our own ideas—for example, by searching out our underlying assumptions, or by evaluating what we have quickly jotted down as evidence. We have already seen some examples of this sort of analysis of one's own
thinking in the journal entries, where, for instance, a student wrote that literature should probably deal with "typical" people, then wondered if "typical" and
"plausible" were the same, and then added "probably not."

Speaking broadly, critical thinking is rational, logical thinking. In thinking
critically,

- One scrutinizes one's assumptions.
- One tests the evidence one has collected, even to the extent of looking
  for counterevidence.
- One revises one's thesis when necessary, in order to make the argument
  as complete and convincing as possible.

Let's start with assumptions. If, for instance, I say that a story is weak because it
is improbable, I ought at least to think about my assumption that improbability is
a fault. I can begin by asking myself if all good stories—or all the stories that I
value highly—are probable. I may recall that among my favorites is *Alice in Won-
derland* (or *Gulliver's Travels* or *Animal Farm*)—so I probably have to withdraw my assumption that improbability in itself makes a story less than good. I
may of course go on to refine the idea and decide that improbability is not a fault
in satiric stories but is a fault in other kinds, but that is not the same as saying
bluntly that improbability is a fault.

The second aspect of critical thinking that we have isolated—searching for
counterevidence within the literary work—especially involves rereading the
work to see if we have overlooked material or have taken a particular detail out
of context. If, for instance, we say that in "The Story of an Hour" Josephine is a
busybody, we should reexamine the work in order to make sure that she indeed
is meddling needlessly and is not offering welcome or necessary assistance. Perhaps the original observation will stand up, but perhaps on rereading the story

we may come to feel, as we examine each of Josephine's actions, that she cannot reasonably be characterized as a busybody.

Of course different readers may come to different conclusions; the important thing is that all readers should subject their initial responses to critical thinking, testing their responses against all of the evidence. Remember, your instructor probably expects you to hand in an essay that is essentially an **argument,** a paper that advances a thesis of your own, and therefore you will revise your drafts if you find counterevidence. The thesis might be that the story is improbable, or is typical of Chopin, or is anti-woman, or is a remarkable anticipation of contemporary feminist thinking. Whatever your thesis, it should be able to withstand scrutiny. You may not convince every reader that you are unquestionably right, but you should make every reader feel that your argument is thoughtful. If you read your notes and then your drafts critically, you probably will write a paper that meets this standard.

One last point, or maybe it's two. Just as your first jottings probably won't be the products of critical thinking, your first reading of the literary work probably *won't* be a critical reading. It is entirely appropriate to begin by reading simply for enjoyment. After all, the reason we read literature (or listen to music, or go to an art museum, or watch dancers) is to derive pleasure. It happens, however, that in this course you are trying (among other things) to deepen your understanding of literature, and therefore you are *studying* literature. On subsequent readings, therefore, you will read the work critically, taking careful note of (for instance) the writer's view of human nature and the writer's ways of achieving certain effects.

This business of critical thinking is important, and we will discuss it again, on page 409, in talking about interpretations of literature.

Arriving at a Thesis, and Arguing It

If you think critically about your early jottings and about the literary work itself, you probably will find that some of your jottings lead to dead ends, but some will lead to further ideas that hold up under scrutiny. What the **thesis** of the essay will be—the idea that will be asserted and *argued* (supported with evidence)— is still in doubt, but there is no doubt about one thing: A good essay will have a thesis, a point, an argument. You ought to be able to state your point in a **thesis sentence.**

Consider these candidates as possible thesis sentences:

1. *Mrs. Mallard dies soon after hearing that her husband has died.*

True, but scarcely a point that can be argued or even developed. About the most the essayist can do with this sentence is amplify it by summarizing the plot of the story, a task not worth doing unless the plot is unusually obscure. An essay may include a sentence or two of summary to give readers their bearings, but a summary is not an essay.

2. *The story is a libel on women.*

In contrast to the first statement, this one can be developed into an argument. Probably the writer will try to demonstrate that Mrs. Mallard's behavior is despicable. Whether this point can be convincingly argued is another matter; the thesis may be untenable, but it is a thesis. A second problem, however, is this: Even if the writer demonstrates that Mrs. Mallard's behavior is despicable, he or she will have to go on to demonstrate that the presentation of one despicable woman constitutes a libel on women in general. That's a pretty big order.

   3. *The story is clever but superficial because it is based on an unreal character.*

Here, too, is a thesis, a point of view that can be argued. Whether or not this thesis is true is another matter. The writer's job will be to support it by presenting evidence. Probably the writer will have no difficulty in finding evidence that the story is "clever"; the difficulty probably will be in establishing a case that the characterization of Mrs. Mallard is "unreal." The writer will have to set forth some ideas about what makes a character real and then will have to show that Mrs. Mallard is an "unreal" (unbelievable) figure.

   4. *The irony of the ending is believable partly because it is consistent with earlier ironies in the story.*

It happens that the student who wrote the essay printed on page twenty-six began by drafting an essay based on the third of these thesis topics, but as she worked on a draft she found that she couldn't support her assertion that the character was unconvincing. In fact, she came to believe that although Mrs. Mallard's joy was the reverse of what a reader might expect, several early reversals in the story helped to make Mrs. Mallard's shift from grief to joy acceptable.

WRITING A DRAFT

After jotting down notes and then adding more notes stimulated by rereading and further thinking, you'll probably be able to formulate a tentative thesis. At this point most writers find it useful to clear the air by glancing over their preliminary notes and by jotting down the thesis and a few especially promising notes—brief statements of what they think their key points may be. These notes may include some brief key quotations that the writer thinks will help to support the thesis.

   Here are the selected notes (not the original brainstorming notes, but a later selection from them, with additions) and a draft (p. 21) that makes use of them.

```
title? Ironies in an Hour (?) An Hour of Irony (?)
    Kate Chopin's Irony (?)
thesis: irony at end is prepared for by earlier
    ironies
chief irony: Mrs. M. dies just as she is beginning
    to enjoy life
smaller ironies: 1. "sad message" brings her joy
                 2. Richards is "too late" at end;
                 3. Richards is too early at start
```

These notes are in effect a very brief **outline.** Some writers at this point like to develop a fuller outline, but probably most writers begin with only a brief outline, knowing that in the process of developing a draft from these few notes additional ideas will arise. For these writers, the time to jot down a detailed outline is *after* they have written a first or second draft. The outline of the written draft will, as we shall see, help them to make sure that their draft has an adequate organization, and that main points are developed.

Sample Draft

Now for the student's draft—not the first version, but a revised draft with some of the irrelevancies of the first draft omitted and some evidence added.

The digits within the parentheses refer to the page numbers from which the quotations are drawn, though with so short a work as "The Story of an Hour," page references are hardly necessary. Check with your instructor to find out if you must always give citations. (Detailed information about how to document a paper is given on pages 1314-1326.)

Ironies in an Hour

After we know how the story turns out, if we reread it we find irony at the very start, as is true of many other stories. Mrs. Mallard's friends assume, mistakenly, that Mrs. Mallard was deeply in love with her husband, Brently Mallard. They take great care to tell her gently of his death. The friends mean well, and in fact they do well. They bring her an hour of life, an hour of freedom. They think their news is sad. Mrs. Mallard at first expresses grief when she hears the news, but soon she finds joy in it. So Richards's "sad message" (12), though sad in Richards's eyes, is in fact a happy message.

Among the ironic details is the statement that when Mallard entered the house, Richards tried to conceal him from Mrs. Mallard, but "Richards was too late" (13). This is ironic because earlier Richards "hastened" (12) to bring his sad message; if he had at the start been "too late" (13), Brently Mallard would have arrived at home first, and Mrs. Mallard's life would not have ended an hour later but would simply have gone on as it had before. Yet another irony at the end of the story is the diagnosis of the

doctors. The doctors say she died of "heart disease--
of joy that kills" (13). In one sense the doctors are
right: Mrs. Mallard has experienced a great joy. But
of course the doctors totally misunderstand the joy
that kills her.

The central irony resides not in the
well-intentioned but ironic actions of Richards, or
in the unconsciously ironic words of the doctors, but
in her own life. In a way she has been dead. She
"sometimes" (13) loved her husband, but in a way she
has been dead. Now, his apparent death brings her new
life. This new life comes to her at the season of the
year when "the tops of trees . . . were all aquiver
with the new spring life" (12). But, ironically, her
new life will last only an hour. She looks forward to
"summer days" (13) but she will not see even the end
of this spring day. Her years of marriage were
ironic. They brought her a sort of living death
instead of joy. Her new life is ironic too. It grows
out of her moment of grief for her supposedly dead
husband, and her vision of a new life is cut short.

[New page]

Work Cited

Chopin, Kate. "The Story of an Hour." Literature for
    Composition. 4th ed. Ed. Sylvan Barnet et al.
    New York: HarperCollins, 1996. 12-13.

Revising a Draft

The draft, although thoughtful and clear, is not yet a finished essay. The student
went on to improve it in many small but important ways.

First, the draft needs a good introductory paragraph, a paragraph that will
let the **audience**—the readers—know where the writer will be taking them. (In

Chapter 4 we discuss introductory paragraphs.) Doubtless you know from your own experience as a reader that readers can follow an argument more easily—and with more pleasure—if early in the discussion the writer alerts them to the gist of the argument. (The title, too, can strongly suggest the thesis.) Second, some of the paragraphs could be clearer.

In revising paragraphs—or, for that matter, in revising an entire draft—writers unify, organize, clarify, and polish.

1. **Unity** is achieved partly by eliminating irrelevancies. Notice that in the final version, printed on page 26, the writer has deleted "as is true of many other stories."
2. **Organization** is largely a matter of arranging material into a sequence that will assist the reader to grasp the point.
3. **Clarity** is achieved largely by providing concrete details and quotations to support generalizations and by providing helpful transitions ("for instance," "furthermore," "on the other hand," "however").
4. **Polish** is small-scale revision. For instance, one deletes unnecessary repetitions. In the second paragraph of the draft, the phrase "the doctors" appears four times, but it appears only three times in the final version of the paragraph. Similarly, in polishing, a writer combines choppy sentences into longer sentences and breaks overly long sentences into shorter sentences.

Later, after producing a draft that seems close to a finished essay, writers engage in yet another activity. They edit.

5. **Editing** includes checking the accuracy of quotations by comparing them with the original, checking a dictionary for the spelling of doubtful words, and checking a handbook for doubtful punctuation—for instance, whether a comma or a semicolon is needed in a particular sentence.

Outlining a Draft

Whether or not you draw up an outline as a preliminary guide to writing a draft, you will be able to improve your draft if you prepare an outline of what you have written. (If you write on a word processor it is probably especially important that you make an outline of your written draft. Writing on a word processor is—or seems—so easy, so effortless, that we just tap away, filling screen after screen with loosely structured material.) For each paragraph in your draft, jot down the gist of the topic sentence or topic idea, and under each of these sentences, indented, jot down key words for the idea(s) developed in the paragraph. Thus, in an outline of the draft we have just looked at, for the first two paragraphs the writer might make these jottings:

```
story ironic from start
    friends think news is sad
    Ms. M. finds joy
some ironic details
    Richards hastened, but "too late"
    doctors right and also wrong
```

An outline of what you have written will help you to see if your draft is adequate in three important ways. The outline will show you

1. The sequence of major topics
2. The degree of development of these topics
3. The argument, the thesis

By studying your outline you may see (for instance) that your first major point (probably after an introductory paragraph) would be more effective as your third point, and that your second point needs to be further developed.

An outline of this sort is essentially a brief version of your draft, perhaps even using some phrases from the draft. But consider making yet another sort of outline, an outline indicating not what each paragraph says but what each paragraph *does*. An attempt at such an outline of the three-paragraph draft of the essay on "The Story of an Hour" might look like something like this:

1. The action of the friends is ironic.
2. Gives some specific (minor) details about ironies.
3. Explains "central irony."

One ought to see a red flag here. The aim of this sort of outline is to indicate what each paragraph *does,* but the jotting for the first paragraph does not tell us what the paragraph does; rather, it more or less summarizes the content of the paragraph. Why? Because the paragraph doesn't *do* much of anything. Certainly it does not (for example) clearly introduce the thesis, or define a crucial term, or set the story in the context of Chopin's other work. An outline indicating the function of each paragraph will force you to see if your essay has an effective structure. We will see that the student later wrote a new opening paragraph for the essay on "The Story of an Hour."

Peer Review

Your instructor may encourage (or even require) you to discuss your draft with another student or with a small group of students. That is, you may be asked to get a review from your peers. Such a procedure is helpful in several ways. First, it gives the writer a real audience, readers who can point to what pleases or puzzles them, who make suggestions, who may often disagree (with the writer or with each other), and who frequently, though not intentionally, *misread.* Though writers don't necessarily like everything they hear (they seldom hear "This is perfect. Don't change a word!"), reading and discussing their work with others almost always gives them a fresh perspective on their work, and a fresh perspective may stimulate thoughtful revision. (Having your intentions *misread* because your writing isn't clear enough can be particularly stimulating.)

The writer whose work is being reviewed is not the sole beneficiary. When students regularly serve as readers for each other, they become better readers of their own work and consequently better revisers. As we said in Chapter 1, learning to write is in large measure learning to read.

If peer review is a part of the writing process in your course, the instructor may distribute a sheet with some suggestions and questions. Here is an example of such a sheet.

QUESTIONS FOR PEER REVIEW   ENGLISH 125a
Read each draft once, quickly. Then read it again,
   with the following questions in mind.
  1. What is the essay's topic? Is it one of the
     assigned topics, or a variation from it? Does
     the draft show promise of fulfilling the
     assignment?
  2. Looking at the essay as a whole, what thesis
     (main idea) is stated or implied? If implied,
     try to state it in your own words.
  3. Is the thesis plausible? How might the argument
     be strengthened?
  4. Looking at each paragraph separately:
     a. What is the basic point? (If it isn't clear
        to you, ask for clarification.)
     b. How does the paragraph relate to the essay's
        main idea or to the previous paragraph?
     c. Should some paragraphs be deleted? Be
        divided into two or more paragraphs? Be com-
        bined? Be put elsewhere? (If you outline the
        essay by jotting down the gist of each para-
        graph, you will get help in answering these
        questions.)
     d. Is each sentence clearly related to the
        sentence that precedes and to the sentence
        that follows?
     e. Is each paragraph adequately developed?
     f. Are there sufficient details, perhaps brief,
        supporting quotations from the text?
  5. What are the paper's chief strengths?
  6. Make at least two specific suggestions that you
     think will assist the author to improve the
     paper.

THE FINAL VERSION

Here is the final version of the student's essay. The essay that was submitted to the instructor had been retyped, but here, so that you can easily see how the draft has been revised, we print the draft with the final changes written in by hand.

Ironies of Life in Kate Chopin's "The Story of an Hour"
~~Ironies in an Hour~~

Despite its title, Kate Chopin's "The Story of an Hour" ironically takes only a few minutes to read. In addition, the story turns out to have an ironic ending, but on rereading it one sees that the irony is not concentrated only in the outcome of the plot—Mrs. Mallard dies just when she is beginning to live—but is also present in many details.

After we know how the story turns out, if we reread it we find irony at the very start. / ~~as is true of many other stories.~~ Because Mrs. Mallard's friends and her sister assume, mistakenly, that ~~Mrs. Mallard~~ she was deeply in love with her husband, Brently Mallard. They take great care to tell her gently of his death. ~~The friends~~ They mean well, and in fact they do well. ~~They~~ bringing her an hour of life, an hour of joyous freedom. but it is ironic that They think their news is sad. True, Mrs. Mallard at first expresses grief when she hears the news, but soon (unknown to her friends) she finds joy in it. So Richards's "sad message" (12), though sad in Richards's eyes, is in fact a happy message.

Among the small but significant ironic details is the statement near the end of the story that when Mallard entered the house, Richards tried to conceal him from Mrs. Mallard, but "Richards was too late" (13). This is ironic because ~~earlier~~ almost at the start of the story, in the second paragraph, Richards "hastened" (12) to bring his sad message; if he had at the start been "too late" (13), Brently Mallard would have arrived at home first, and Mrs. Mallard's life would not have ended an hour later but would simply have gone on as it had before. Yet another irony at the end of the story is the diagnosis of the doctors. The doctors say she died of "heart disease-- of joy that kills" (13). In one sense ~~the doctors~~ they are right: Mrs. Mallard for the last hour experienced a great joy. But of course the doctors totally misunderstand the joy that

kills her. *It is not joy at seeing her husband alive, but her realization that the great joy she experienced during the last hour is over.*

All of these ironic details add richness to the story, but ∧ ~~T~~he central irony resides not in the well-

intentioned but ironic actions of Richards, nor in the

unconsciously ironic words of the doctors, but in ~~her~~ *Mrs. Mallard's*

own life. ~~In a way she has been dead.~~ She "sometimes"

(13) loved her husband, but in a way she has been
a body subjected to her husband's will
dead/, Now, his apparent death brings her new life.
Appropriately
∧This new life comes to her at the season of the year

when "the tops of trees . . . were all aquiver with

the new spring life" (12). But, ironically, her new
She is "free, free, free"—but only until her husband walks through
life will last only an hour.∧She looks forward to *the doorway.*

"summer days" (13) but she will not see even the end
If
of this spring day∧~~H~~er years of marriage were
bringing
ironic/, ~~They brought~~ her a sort of living death
not only because
instead of joy/, ~~H~~er new life is ironic too/, ~~I~~t grows

out of her moment of grief for her supposedly dead
but also because her vision of "a long progression of years"
husband,∧ ~~and her vision of a new life~~ is cut short/

within an hour on a spring day.

[New page]

Work Cited

Chopin, Kate. "The Story of an Hour." <u>Literature for

Composition</u>. 4th ed. Ed. Sylvan Barnet et al.

New York: HarperCollins, 1996. 12-13.

A Brief Overview of The Final Version

Finally, as a quick review, let's look at several principles illustrated by this essay.

- The **title of the essay** is not merely the title of the work discussed; rather, it gives the reader a clue, a small idea of the essayist's topic. Because your title will create a crucial first impression, make sure that it is interesting.
- The **opening or introductory paragraph** does not begin by saying "In this story . . ." Rather, by naming the author and the title, it lets the reader know exactly what story is being discussed. It also develops the writer's thesis so readers know where they will be going.

- The **organization** is effective. The smaller ironies are discussed in the second and third paragraphs, the central (chief) irony in the last paragraph. That is, the essay does not dwindle or become anticlimatic; rather, it builds up from the least important to the most important point. Again, if you outline your draft you will see if it has an effective organization.
- Some **brief quotations** are used, both to provide evidence and to let the reader hear—even if only fleetingly—Kate Chopin's writing.
- The essay is chiefly devoted to **analysis** (how the parts relate to each other), not to summary (a brief restatement of the happenings). The writer, properly assuming that the reader has read the work, does not tell the plot in great detail. But, aware that the reader has not memorized the story, the writer gives helpful reminders.
- The **present tense** is used in narrating the action: "Mrs. Mallard dies"; "Mrs. Mallard's friends and relatives all assume."
- Although a **concluding paragraph** is often useful—if it does more than merely summarize what has already been clearly said—it is not essential in a short analysis. In this essay, the last sentence explains the chief irony and therefore makes an acceptable ending.
- Documentation is given according to the form set forth in Appendix B.
- There are no typographical errors. The author has proofread the paper carefully.

THE ADVANTAGES OF WRITING WITH A WORD PROCESSOR

If possible, write your paper on a word processor. Writing a first draft on a word processor is physically somewhat easier than writing by hand or by typewriter, and revising the draft is incomparably easier. (You can almost effortlessly move material around or insert new material.) Further, for many people the screen is less intimidating than a sheet of paper, and when you do put words down, they look a lot better than handwritten or typed material. And if your paper includes footnotes or endnotes and a list of works cited, your software probably will automatically format them.

A word processor probably will not save you time, but it will allow you to use your time efficiently. In the past, writers had to spend a great deal of time on the tedious job of typing a clean copy. The more they revised, the more they doomed themselves to hours of retyping. With a word processor, you can spend all of your time reading, writing, and rewriting, and you can virtually leave to the printer the job of retyping.

Pre-writing

Your first notes probably will be in the margins of your text, but once you go beyond these, you can use a word processor, for instance to brainstorm. By means of *free association*—writing down whatever comes to mind, without fretting about spelling, punctuation, or logic—you will probably find that you can generate ideas, at least some of which will lead to something. Or you can try *listing*, jotting down key terms (for instance, the names of characters in a play, or technical terms such as *meter, imagery, stanza* for a poem) and then inserting further thoughts about each of these. Produce a printout, and then start *linking* or *clustering* (with circles and connecting lines) related items. Then return to your screen and reorganize the material, moving *this* word or phrase over to connect it with *that* one.

Many students find *dialoguing* helpful. After writing a sentence or two, they imagine a somewhat skeptical critic who asks questions such as "What examples can you give?," "What counterevidence might be offered?," and "Have you defined your terms?" In answering such questions, writers get further ideas.

Back up your material. Don't run the risk of losing your work. Write on a hard drive (it's faster), and keep a floppy disk nearby for making backups at the close of each work session.

Taking Notes

Write into one file all of your notes for a paper. If the notes are for a paper on (say) Zora Neal Hurston, you will probably name the file "Hurston." The name doesn't matter, so long as you remember it.

Put all bibliographic references in one place. If you are using written sources, you will want to keep a record of each source. Some programs, for instance *Fifty-Third Street Writer,* will automatically alphabetize entries. But even if your program doesn't alphabetize bibliographic entries, you can easily insert a new entry by scrolling down through the existing references to the appropriate alphabetic place, then adding the new reference, last name first.

In taking notes, be sure to **check the accuracy of your transcription.** If you quote directly, make certain that you have quoted exactly. Use an ellipsis (three spaced periods) to indicate an omission within a quotation, and use square brackets to enclose any additions you make within a quotation. (See p. 1311.) As we will see in a moment, when you are drafting your paper you may want to block some of this material and move it into the draft.

It's a good idea to **print out all of your notes before you prepare a first draft.** The screen shows you very little of the material that constitutes your notes; print it all out, so that you can survey it as a whole. Cut apart the various notes, and discard material that no longer seems helpful. Next, arrange the surviving material into a tentative sequence, just as you would arrange index cards with handwritten notes. (The word processor is a great help, but don't hesitate to produce hard copy at various stages and to work with the printed material. The screen is too small to give you a feel of the whole.)

Many writers find it helpful to put this selection of material, now in a sequence, back into the computer. They do this by *blocking* and moving the useful material. Do *not* delete the unused material; as you work on the essay you may realize that you can use some of this material in the final version. It's advisable to copy this selected and arranged material into a new file, headed "Draft" or some such thing. If you simply add it to the end of the file containing all of the notes, you may sometimes find yourself working with the extra material when you meant to be working with your selected notes.

Writing a First Draft

Even if you did not take notes on a computer, you can of course **write your drafts and ultimately the final paper on a word processor.** Set the line spacing at double spacing, to allow space for handwritten additions on a printed version of the draft, and start writing.

Some writers find it useful to start writing on the computer by setting down a rough outline—perhaps phrases, in a sequence that at least for the moment seems reasonable. They then go back and fill in the outline, expanding words or phrases into detailed sentences and paragraphs. Of course, as they write they may find that they want to rearrange some of the material, which they can easily do by moving blocks of text.

Let's assume, however, that you do have notes in the word processor, and that you have arranged them into a sequence. You may want to begin by looking at the first note and writing an opening paragraph that will lead into it, and then go on to the next note. Of course, as you work you will find that some of the notes are unneeded. Don't delete them, since they may come in handy later. Just block them and move them to the end of the file.

Because it is so easy to produce a clean final copy—with a keystroke or two you can tell the printer to print the file—don't hesitate to incorporate comments into your draft that you know you won't retain in the final version, such as "CHECK QUOTATION" or "GET BETTER EXAMPLE." (Use capitals or boldface for such comments, so that you will focus on them when you read the draft, and so that you cannot overlook them when the time comes to delete them.)

When you think you have come to the end of your draft, you will probably want to read it on the screen, from the beginning, to correct typographical errors and to make other obvious corrections. That's fine, but remember that the computer screen cannot give you a good sense of the whole. You won't be able to see, for instance, if a paragraph is much too long; even when you scroll through the draft you will not experience the material in the same way the reader of a printed copy will experience it. What you need to do at this stage is to print your draft.

Revising a Draft

Read the printed draft, making necessary revisions in pen or pencil. Probably you will find that some of the material you have quoted can be abridged, or even deleted, and that in some places better transitions are needed. It is also likely that you will see the need to add details and to reorganize some of the material. Try to read the draft from the point of view of someone new to the material. Keep asking yourself, "Will my reader understand *why* I am making this point at this stage in the essay?" If you ask this question, you probably will find yourself not only adding helpful transitions ("An apparent exception is . . . ") but also occasionally reorganizing. Make these changes on the printed copy, then incorporate them into your computer file, and then print the revised version.

Read the revised version with a critical eye; you probably will find that you can extensively revise even this version. You may get some help from a computer program. For instance, if you are using *Fifty-Third Street Writer,* which includes the *Scott, Foresman Handbook,* and you are uncertain about, say, the use of the semicolon, you can consult the index to the handbook and then bring up the material on semicolons. Similarly, if you are writing a book review, you can find the material on reviews by consulting the index, and you can then bring to the screen the discussion of the qualities that make for a good review. Among other software programs that many writers find useful are *Grammatik, Word, RightWriter,* and *Writer's Workbench.* Some of these will alert you to such matters as spelling errors, clichés, split infinitives, overuse of the passive voice, and certain kinds of grammatical errors. For instance, *Writer's Workbench* (and some of the others) will let you check troublesome pairs of words (*affect/effect*), will flag words and phrases that are potentially sexist, will detect most split infinitives and misspellings, and will (among other things) give you help with transitions. You cannot rely entirely on these programs, but they do offer considerable help.

When you get a version that seems to you the best that you can do without further assistance, ask a friend to read it. **Prepare a copy for peer review.** Print your text—double-spaced and letter-quality, of course—and give it to your reader, along with a copy of the sample peer review sheet on page 25, or with a comparable sheet issued by your instructor.

When the paper is returned to you, respond to the suggestions appropriately and then print out this new version. Don't rely on reading the paper on the screen.

The Final Version

After you print out the version you have prepared in response to the comments by your reviewer, read it to see if you can make any further improvements. (Even at this late date you may think of a better title, or you may sense that a quotation doesn't sound quite right.) You can make small changes by hand, in ink, but if you make a substantial number of changes, print out a clean copy. Your paper will be neater—and there is no labor involved.

✔ A Checklist for Writing with a Word Processor

Pre-writing

- Take notes. Brainstorm; try listing, then linking and clustering your ideas. Use an outline if you find it helpful.
- Check that your transcriptions are accurate if you quote.
- Keep your notes together in one file.
- Organize your sources in a bibliography.
- *Always back up your material.*
- Print out your notes.

Preparing a First Draft

- Use your notes—move them around in blocks. Expand on your ideas.
- Incorporate notes to yourself in your first draft.
- Read your draft on the screen to check for errors.
- Print out a copy of your first draft.

Working with Your Draft

- Revise your printed draft with pen or pencil. Incorporate these changes into your computer file.

- Read your corrected draft on the screen; then print out a fresh copy.
- Repeat these steps as many times as necessary.

Responding to Peer Review

- Give a copy to a peer for comments and suggestions.
- Respond appropriately to your reviewer, making changes in your computer file.
- Print out your revised version and reread it.

Preparing a Final Copy

- If there are only a few changes, make them on your printed copy. Otherwise, incorporate your changes in your computer file and print out your final copy.

A THIRD STORY BY KATE CHOPIN

Here is one more of Chopin's stories. It is followed by some suggestions for writing.

The Storm

I

The leaves were so still that even Bibi thought it was going to rain. Bobinôt, who was accustomed to converse on terms of perfect equality with his little son, called the child's attention to certain sombre clouds that were rolling with sinister intention from the west, accompanied by a sullen, threatening roar. They were at Friedheimer's store and decided to remain there till the storm had passed. They sat within the door on two empty kegs. Bibi was four years old and looked very wise.

"Mama'll be 'fraid, yes," he suggested with blinking eyes.

"She'll shut the house. Maybe she got Sylvie helpin' her this evenin'," Bobinôt responded reassuringly.

"No; she ent got Sylvie. Sylvie was helpin' her yistiday," piped Bibi.

5   Bobinôt arose and going across to the counter purchased a can of shrimps, of which Calixta was very fond. Then he returned to his perch on the keg and sat stolidly holding the can of shrimps while the storm burst. It shook the wooden store and seemed to be ripping great furrows in the distant field. Bibi laid his little hand on his father's knee and was not afraid.

II

Calixta, at home, felt no uneasiness for their safety. She sat at a side window sewing furiously on a sewing machine. She was greatly occupied and did not notice the approaching storm. But she felt very warm and often stopped to mop her face on which the perspiration gathered in beads. She unfastened her white sacque at the throat. It began to grow dark, and suddenly realizing the situation she got up hurriedly and went about closing windows and doors.

Out on the small front gallery[1] she had hung Bobinôt's Sunday clothes to air and she hastened out to gather them before the rain fell. As she stepped outside, Alcée Laballière rode in at the gate. She had not seen him very often since her marriage, and never alone. She stood there with Bobinôt's coat in her hands, and the big rain drops began to fall. Alcée rode his horse under the shelter of a side projection where the chickens had huddled and there were plows and a harrow piled up in the corner.

"May I come and wait on your gallery till the storm is over, Calixta?" he asked.

"Come 'long in, M'sieur Alcée."

His voice and her own startled her as if from a trance, and she seized Bobinôt's vest. Alcée, mounting to the porch, grabbed the trousers and snatched Bibi's braided jacket that was about to be carried away by a sudden gust of wind. He expressed an intention to remain outside, but it was soon apparent that he might as well have been out in the open: the water beat in upon the boards in driving sheets, and he went inside, closing the door after him. It was even necessary to put something beneath the door to keep the water out.

"My! what a rain! It's good two years sence it rain' like that," exclaimed Calixta as she rolled up a piece of bagging and Alcée helped her to thrust it beneath the crack.

She was a little fuller of figure than five years before when she married; but she had lost nothing of her vivacity. Her blue eyes still retained their melting quality; and her yellow hair, dishevelled by the wind and rain, kinked more stubbornly than ever about her ears and temples.

The rain beat upon the low, shingled roof with a force and clatter that threatened to break an entrance and deluge them there. They were in the dining room—the sitting room—the general utility room. Adjoining was her bed room, with Bibi's couch along side her own. The door stood open, and the room with its white, monumental bed, its closed shutters, looked dim and mysterious.

Alcée flung himself into a rocker and Calixta nervously began to gather up from the floor the lengths of a cotton sheet which she had been sewing.

"If this keeps up, *Dieu sait*[2] if the levees goin' to stan' it!" she exclaimed.

"What have you got to do with the levees?"

"I got enough to do! An' there's Bobinôt with Bibi out in that storm—if he only didn' left Friedheimer's!"

"Let us hope, Calixta, that Bobinôt's got sense enough to come in out of a cyclone."

She went and stood at the window with a greatly disturbed look on her face. She wiped the frame that was clouded with moisture. It was stiflingly hot. Alcée got up and joined her at the window, looking over her shoulder.

---

[1]**gallery** porch, or passageway along a wall, open to the air but protected by a roof supported by columns   [2]*Dieu sait* God only knows

The rain was coming down in sheets obscuring the view of far-off cabins and enveloping the distant wood in a gray mist. The playing of the lightning was incessant. A bolt struck a tall chinaberry tree at the edge of the field. It filled all visible space with a blinding glare and the crash seemed to invade the very boards they stood upon.

20   Calixta put her hands to her eyes, and with a cry, staggered backward. Alcée's arm encircled her, and for an instant he drew her close and spasmodically to him.

"*Bonté!*"[3] she cried, releasing herself from his encircling arm and retreating from the window, "the house'll go next! If I only knew w'ere Bibi was!" She would not compose herself; she would not be seated. Alcée clasped her shoulders and looked into her face. The contact of her warm, palpitating body when he had unthinkingly drawn her into his arms, had aroused all the old-time infatuation and desire for her flesh.

"Calixta," he said, "don't be frightened. Nothing can happen. The house is too low to be struck, with so many tall trees standing about. There! aren't you going to be quiet? say, aren't you?" He pushed her hair back from her face that was warm and steaming. Her lips were as red and moist as pomegranate seed. Her white neck and a glimpse of her full, firm bosom disturbed him powerfully. As she glanced up at him the fear in her liquid blue eyes had given place to a drowsy gleam that unconsciously betrayed a sensuous desire. He looked down into her eyes and there was nothing for him to do but to gather her lips in a kiss. It reminded him of Assumption.[4]

"Do you remember—in Assumption, Calixta?" he asked in a low voice broken by passion. Oh! she remembered; for in Assumption he had kissed her and kissed and kissed her; until his senses would well nigh fail, and to save her he would resort to a desperate flight. If she was not an immaculate dove in those days, she was still inviolate; a passionate creature whose very defenselessness had made her defense, against which his honor forbade him to prevail. Now—well, now—her lips seemed in a manner free to be tasted, as well as her round, white throat and her whiter breasts.

They did not heed the crashing torrents, and the roar of the elements made her laugh as she lay in his arms. She was a revelation in that dim, mysterious chamber; as white as the couch she lay upon. Her firm, elastic flesh that was knowing for the first time its birthright, was like a creamy lily that the sun invites to contribute its breath and perfume to the undying life of the world.

25   The generous abundance of her passion, without guile or trickery, was like a white flame which penetrated and found response in depths of his own sensuous nature that had never yet been reached.

When he touched her breasts they gave themselves up in quivering ecstasy, inviting his lips. Her mouth was a fountain of delight. And when he possessed her, they seemed to swoon together at the very borderland of life's mystery.

He stayed cushioned upon her, breathless, dazed, enervated, with his heart beating like a hammer upon her. With one hand she clasped his head,

[3]***Bonté!*** Heavens!   [4]**Assumption** a church feast on 15 August celebrating Mary's bodily ascent to Heaven

her lips lightly touching his forehead. The other hand stroked with a soothing rhythm his muscular shoulders.

The growl of the thunder was distant and passing away. The rain beat
softly upon the shingles, inviting them to drowsiness and sleep. But they
dared not yield.

The rain was over; and the sun was turning the glistening green world
into a place of gems. Calixta, on the gallery, watched Alcée ride away. He
turned and smiled at her with a beaming face; and she lifted her pretty chin
in the air and laughed aloud.

III

30   Bobinôt and Bibi, trudging home, stopped without at the cistern to
make themselves presentable.

"My! Bibi, w'at will yo' mama say! You ought to be ashame'. You
oughtn' put on those good pants. Look at 'em! An' that mud on yo' collar!
How you got that mud on yo' collar, Bibi? I never saw such a boy!" Bibi was
the picture of pathetic resignation. Bobinôt was the embodiment of serious
solicitude as he strove to remove from his own person and his son's the
signs of their tramp over heavy roads and through wet fields. He scraped the
mud off Bibi's bare legs and feet with a stick and carefully removed all traces
from his heavy brogans. Then, prepared for the worst—the meeting with an
over-scrupulous housewife, they entered cautiously at the back door.

Calixta was preparing supper. She had set the table and was dripping
coffee at the hearth. She sprang up as they came in.

"Oh, Bobinôt! You back! My! but I was uneasy. W'ere you been during
the rain? An' Bibi? he ain't wet? he ain't hurt?" She had clasped Bibi and was
kissing him effusively. Bobinôt's explanations and apologies which he had
been composing all along the way, died on his lips as Calixta felt him to see
if he were dry, and seemed to express nothing but satisfaction at their safe
return.

"I brought you some shrimps, Calixta," offered Bobinôt, hauling the can
from his ample side pocket and laying it on the table.

35   "Shrimps! Oh, Bobinôt! you too good fo' anything!" and she gave him a
smacking kiss on the cheek that resounded. *"J'vous reponds,*[5] we'll have a
feas' to night! umph-umph!"

Bobinôt and Bibi began to relax and enjoy themselves, and when the
three seated themselves at table they laughed much and so loud that anyone
might have heard them as far away as Laballière's.

IV

Alcée Laballière wrote to his wife, Clarisse, that night. It was a loving letter,
full of tender solicitude. He told her not to hurry back, but if she and the babies liked it at Biloxi, to stay a month longer. He was getting on nicely; and
though he missed them, he was willing to bear the separation a while
longer—realizing that their health and pleasure were the first things to be
considered.

---

[5]*J'vous reponds* Take my word; let me tell you

V

As for Clarisse, she was charmed upon receiving her husband's letter. She and the babies were doing well. The society was agreeable; many of her old friends and acquaintances were at the bay. And the first free breath since her marriage seemed to restore the pleasant liberty of her maiden days. Devoted as she was to her husband, their intimate conjugal life was something which she was more than willing to forego for a while.

So the storm passed and everyone was happy.

[1898]

WRITING ABOUT "THE STORM"

As we said earlier, what you write will depend partly on your audience and on your purpose, as well as on your responses (for instance, pleasure or irritation). Consider the *differences* among these assignments:

1. Assume that you are trying to describe "The Storm" to someone who has not read it. Briefly summarize the action, and then try to explain why you think "The Storm" is (or is not) worth reading.
2. Assume that your readers are familiar with "The Story of an Hour" and "The Storm." Compare the implied attitudes, as you see them, toward marriage.
3. Write an essay arguing that "The Storm" is (or is not) immoral, or (a different thing) amoral. (By the way, because one of her slightly earlier works, a short novel called *The Awakening,* was widely condemned as sordid, Chopin was unable to find a publisher for "The Storm.")
4. In Part IV we are told that Alcée wrote a letter to Clarisse. Write his letter (500 words). Or write Clarisse's response (500 words).
5. You are writing to a high school teacher, urging that one of the three stories by Chopin be taught in high school. Which one do you recommend, and why?
6. Do you think "The Storm" would make a good film? Why? (And while you are thinking about Chopin and film, think about what devices you might use to turn "Ripe Figs" or "The Story of an Hour" into an interesting film.)

A NOTE ABOUT LITERARY EVALUATIONS

One other point—and it is a big one. Until a decade or two ago, Chopin was regarded as a minor writer who worked in a minor field. She was called a "local colorist," that is, a writer who emphasizes the unique speech, mannerisms, and ways of thinking of the charming and somewhat eccentric characters associated with a particular locale. Other late-nineteenth-century writers who are widely regarded as local colorists are Bret Harte (California), Sarah Orne Jewett and Mary E. Wilkins Freeman (New England), and Joel Chandler Harris (the old South). Because of the writers' alleged emphasis on the uniqueness and charm of a region, the reader's response is likely to be "How quaint" rather than "This is life as I feel it, or at least as I can imagine it."

Probably part of the reason for the relatively low value attributed to Chopin's work was that she was a woman, and it was widely believed that "serious and important literature" was (with a very few exceptions) written by men. In short, judgments, including literary evaluations, depend partly on cultural traditions.

A question: On the basis of the three stories by Chopin, do you think Chopin's interest went beyond presenting quaint folk for our entertainment? You might set forth your response in an essay of 500 words—after you have done some brainstorming, some thinking in a journal, and some drafting, revising, and editing.

CHAPTER 3

Two Forms of Criticism: Explication and Analysis

WHY WRITE? PURPOSE AND AUDIENCE

In Chapter 1 we briefly talked about audience and purpose, but a few further words may be useful. People write not only to communicate with others but also to clarify and to account for their responses to material that interests or excites or frustrates them. In putting words on paper you will have to take a second and a third look at what is in front of you and at what is within you. And so the process of writing is a way of learning. The last word is never said about complex thoughts and feelings, but when we write we hope to make at least a little progress in the difficult but rewarding job of talking about our responses. We learn, and then we hope to interest our reader because we are communicating our responses to material that for one reason or another is worth talking about.

When you write, you transform your responses into words that will let your reader share your perceptions, your enthusiasms, and even your doubts. This sharing is, in effect, teaching. Students often think that they are writing for the teacher, but this is a misconception. When you write, *you* are the teacher. An essay on literature is an attempt to help someone to see something as you see it.

If you are not writing for the teacher, for whom are you writing? For yourself, of course, but also for others. Occasionally, in an effort to help you develop an awareness that what you write depends partly on your audience, your instructor may specify an audience, suggesting that you write for high school students or for the readers of *The Atlantic* or *Ms.* But if an audience is not specified, write for your classmates. If you keep your classmates in mind as your audience, you will not write, "William Shakespeare, England's most famous playwright," because such a remark seems to imply that your reader does not know Shakespeare's nationality or trade. On the other hand, you *will* write, "Sei Shōnagon, a lady of the court in medieval Japan," because you can reasonably assume that your classmates do not know who she is.

EXPLICATION

A line-by-line or episode-by-episode commentary on what is going on in a text is an **explication** (literally, unfolding or spreading out). It takes some skill to work one's way along without saying, "In line one . . . , in the second line . . . , in the third line. . . ." One must sometimes boldly say something like, "The next stanza begins with . . . and then introduces. . . ." And, of course, one can discuss the second line before the first line if that seems to be the best way of handling the passage.

An explication does not deal with the writer's life or times, and it is not a paraphrase, a rewording—though it may include paraphrase. Rather, an explication is a commentary revealing your sense of the meaning of the work. To this end it calls attention, as it proceeds, to the implications of words, the function of rhymes, the shifts in point of view, the development of contrasts, and any other contributions to the meaning.

A Sample Explication: Langston Hughes's "Harlem"

The following short poem is by Langston Hughes (1902–67), an African-American writer who was born in Joplin, Mississippi, lived part of his youth in Mexico, spent a year at Columbia University, served as a merchant seaman, and worked in a Paris nightclub, where he showed some of his poems to Dr. Alain Locke, a strong advocate of African-American literature. When he returned to the United States, Hughes went on to publish fiction, plays, essays, and biographies; he also founded theaters, gave public readings, and was, in short, an important force.

Harlem

What happens to a dream deferred?

> Does it dry up
> like a raisin in the sun?
> Or fester like a sore—   4
> And then run?
> Does it stink like rotten meat?
> Or crust and sugar over—
> like a syrupy sweet?   8
>
> Maybe it just sags
> like a heavy load.
>
> *Or does it explode?*

[*1951*]

Different readers will respond at least somewhat differently to any work. On the other hand, since writers want to communicate, they try to control their readers' responses, and they count on their readers to understand the denotations of words as they understand them. Thus, Hughes assumed that his readers knew that Harlem was the site of a large African-American community in New York City. A reader who confuses the title of the poem with Haarlem in the Netherlands will wonder what this poem is saying about the tulip-growing center in northern Holland. Explication is based on the assumption that the poem contains a meaning and that by studying the work thoughtfully we can unfold the meaning or meanings. (The point—which has been disputed—will be brought up again at the end of this discussion of explication.)

Let's assume that the reader understands Hughes is talking about Harlem, New York, and that the "dream deferred" refers to the unfulfilled hopes of African-Americans who live in a society dominated by whites. But Hughes does not say "hopes," he says "dream," and he does not say "unfulfilled," he says "deferred." You might ask yourself exactly what differences there are between these words. Next, after you have read the poem several times, you might think about which expression is better in the context, "unfulfilled hopes" or "dream deferred," and why.

Working toward an Explication of "Harlem"

In preparing to write an explication, first write on a computer, or type or hand-write, the complete text of the work that you will explicate—usually a poem but sometimes a short passage of prose. *Don't* photocopy it; the act of typing or writing it will help you to get into the piece, word by word, comma by comma. Type or write it *double-spaced,* so that you will have plenty of room for annotations as you study the piece. It's advisable to make a few photocopies (or to print a few copies, if you are using a word processor) before you start annotating, so that if one page gets too cluttered you can continue working on a clean copy. Or you may want to use one copy for a certain kind of annotations—let's say those concerning imagery—and other copies for other kinds of notes—let's say those concerning meter or wordplay. If you are writing on a word processor, you can highlight words, boldface them, put them in capitals (for instance to indicate accented syllables), and so forth.

Let's turn to an explication of the poem, a detailed examination of the whole. Here are the preliminary jottings:

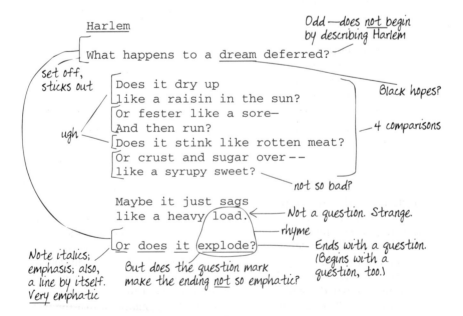

These annotations chiefly get at the structure of the poem, the relationship of the parts. The student notices that the poem begins with a line set off by itself and ends with a line set off by itself, and he also notices that each of these lines is a question. Further, he indicates that each of these two lines is emphasized in other ways: The first begins farther to the left than any of the other lines—as though the other lines are subheadings or are in some way subordinate—and the last is italicized.

Some Journal Entries

The student who made these annotations later wrote an entry in his journal:

Feb. 18. Since the title is "Harlem," it's obvious that the "dream" is by African-American people. Also, obvious that Hughes thinks that if the "dream" doesn't become real there may be riots ("explode"). I like "raisin in the sun" (maybe because I like the play), and I like the business about "a syrupy sweet"--much more pleasant than the festering sore and the rotten meat. But if the dream becomes "sweet," what's wrong with that? Why should something "sweet" explode?

Feb. 21. Prof. McCabe said to think of structure or form of a poem as a sort of architecture, a building with a foundation, floors, etc., topped by a roof--but since we read a poem from top to bottom, it's like a building upside down. Title is foundation (even though it's at top); last line is roof, capping the whole. As you read, you add layers. Foundation of "Harlem" is a question (first line). Then, set back a bit from foundation, or built on it by white space, a tall room (7 lines high, with 4 questions); then, on top of this room, another room (lines, statement, not a question). Funny; I thought that in poems all stanzas are the same number of lines. Then--more white space, so another unit--the roof. Man, this roof is going to fall in-- "explodes." Not just the roof, maybe the whole house.

Feb. 21, p.m. I get it; one line at start, one line at end; both are questions, but the last sort of says (because it is in italics) that it is the most likely answer to the question of the first line. The last line is also a question, but it's still an answer. The big stanza (7 lines) has 4 questions: 2 lines, 2 lines, 1 line, 2 lines. Maybe the switch to 1 line is to give some variety, so as not to be dull? It's exactly in the middle of the poem. I get the progress from raisin in the sun (dried, but not so terrible), to festering sore and to stinking meat, but I still don't see what's so bad about "a syrupy sweet." Is Hughes saying that after things are very bad they will get better? But why, then, the explosion at the end?

<u>Feb. 23</u>. "Heavy load" and "sags" in next-to-last stanza seem to me to suggest slaves with bales of cotton, or maybe poor cotton pickers dragging big sacks of cotton. Or maybe people doing heavy labor in Harlem. Anyway, very tired. Different from running sore and stinking meat earlier; not disgusting, but pressing down, deadening. Maybe <u>worse</u> than a sore or rotten meat--a hard, hopeless life. And then the last line. Just one line, no fancy (and disgusting) simile. Boom! Not just pressed down and tired, like maybe some racist whites think (hope?) blacks will be. Bang! Will there be survivors?

Drawing chiefly on these notes, the student jotted down some key ideas to guide him through a draft of an analysis of the poem. (The organization of the draft posed no problem; the student simply followed the organization of the poem.)

> 11 lines; short, but powerful; explosive
> Question (first line)
> answers (set off by space and also indented)
> "raisin in the sun": shrinking ⎫
> "sore"   ⎬ disgusting
> "rotten meat"   ⎭
> "syrupy sweet": relief from disgusting comparisons
> final question (last line): explosion?
>   explosive (powerful) because:
>   short, condensed, packed
>   in italics
>   stands by self-like first line
>   no fancy comparison; very direct

The Final Draft

Here is the final essay:

Langston Hughes's "Harlem"

"Harlem" is a poem that is only eleven lines long, but it is charged with power. It explodes. Hughes sets the stage, so to speak, by telling us in the title that he is talking about Harlem, and then he begins by asking, "What happens to a dream deferred?" The rest of the poem is set off by being indented, as though it is the answer to his question. This answer is in three parts (three stanzas, of different lengths).

In a way, it's wrong to speak of the answer, since the rest of the poem consists of questions, but I think Hughes means that each question (for instance, does a "deferred" hope "dry up / like a raisin in the sun?") really is an answer, something that really has happened and that will happen again. The first question, "Does it dry up / like a raisin in the sun?," is a famous line. To compare hope to a raisin dried in the sun is to suggest a terrible shrinking. The next two comparisons are to a "sore" and to "rotten meat." These comparisons are less clever, but they are very effective because they are disgusting. Then, maybe because of the disgusting comparisons, he gives a comparison that is not at all disgusting. In this comparison he says that maybe the "dream deferred" will "crust over-- / like a syrupy sweet."

The seven lines with four comparisons are followed by a stanza of two lines with just one comparison:

> Maybe it just sags
> like a heavy load.

So if we thought that this postponed dream might finally turn into something "sweet," we were kidding ourselves. Hughes comes down to earth, in a short stanza, with an image of a heavy load, which probably also calls to mind images of people bent under heavy loads, maybe of cotton, or maybe just any sort of heavy load carried by African-Americans in Harlem and elsewhere.

The opening question ("What happens to a dream deferred?") was followed by four questions in seven lines, but now, with "Maybe it just sags / like a heavy load," we get a statement, as though the poet at last has found an answer. But at the end we get one more question, set off by itself and in italics: "Or does it explode?" This line itself is explosive for three reasons: It is short, it is italicized, and it is a stanza in itself. It's also interesting that this line, unlike the earlier lines, does not use a simile. It's almost as though Hughes is saying, "O.K., we've had enough fancy ways of talking about this terrible situation; here it is, straight."

☐ TOPIC FOR CRITICAL THINKING

The student's explication suggests that the comparison with "a syrupy sweet" deliberately misleads the reader into thinking the ending will be happy, and it thus serves to make the real ending even more powerful. In class another student suggested that Hughes may be referring to African-Americans who play Uncle Tom, people who adopt a smiling manner in order to cope with an oppressive society. Which explanation do you prefer, and why? What do you think of combining the two?

Does some method or principle help us decide which interpretation is correct? Can one, in fact, talk about a "correct" interpretation, or only about a plausible or implausible interpretation and an interesting or uninteresting interpretation?

Note: Another explication (of W. B. Yeats's "The Balloon of the Mind") appears in Chapter 11.

ANALYSIS

Explication is a method used chiefly in the study of fairly short poems or brief extracts from essays, stories, novels, and plays. Of course, if one has world enough and time, one can set out to explicate all of *The Color Purple* or *Hamlet;* more likely, one will explicate only a paragraph or at most a page of the novel or a speech or two of the play. In writing about works longer than a page or two, a more common approach than explicating is **analyzing** (literally, separating into parts in order to better understand the whole). An analysis of, say, *The Color Purple* may consider the functions of the setting or the uses that certain minor characters serve; an analysis of *Hamlet* may consider the comic passages or the reasons for Hamlet's delay; an analysis of *Death of a Salesman* may consider the depiction of women or the causes of Willy Loman's failure.

Most of the writing that you will do in college—not only in your English courses but in courses in history, sociology, economics, fine arts, and philosophy—will be analytic. **Analysis** is a method we commonly use in thinking about complex matters and in attempting to account for our responses. Watching Steffi Graf play tennis, we may admire her serve, or her backhand, or the execution of several brilliant plays, and then think more generally about the concentration and flexibility that allow her to capitalize on her opponent's momentary weakness. And of course when we want to improve our own game, we try to analyze our performance. When writing is our game, we analyze our responses to a work, trying to name them and account for them. We analyze our notes, looking for ideas that connect, searching for significant patterns, and later we analyze our drafts, looking for strengths and weaknesses. Similarly, in peer review, discussed in Chapter 2, we analyze the draft of a fellow student, seeing how the parts (individual words, sentences, whole paragraphs, the tentative title, and everything else) relate to one another and fit together as a whole.

To develop an analysis of a literary work, we tend, whether consciously or not, to formulate questions and then to answer them. We ask such questions as

What is the function of the setting in this story or play?
Why has this character been introduced?
What is the author trying to tell us?
How exactly can I describe the tone?
What is the difference in the assumptions between this essay and that one?

This book contains an anthology of literary works for you to respond to and then write about, and after most of the works we pose some questions. We also pose general questions on essays, fiction, drama, and poetry. These questions may stimulate your thinking and thus help you write. Our concern as teachers of writing is not so much with the answers to these questions; we believe and we ask you to believe that there are in fact no "right answers," only more or less persuasive ones, to most questions about literature—as about life. Our aim is to help you to pose questions that will stimulate your thinking.

The Judgment of Solomon

A brief analysis of a very short story about King Solomon, from the Hebrew Bible, may be useful here. Because the story is short, the analysis can consider all or almost all of the story's parts, and therefore the analysis can seem relatively complete. ("*Seem* relatively complete" because the analysis will in fact be far from complete, since the number of reasonable things that can be said about a work is almost as great as the number of readers. And a given reader might, at a later date, offer a rather different reading from what the reader offers today.)

The following story about King Solomon, customarily called "The Judgment of Solomon," appears in the Hebrew Bible, in the latter part of the third chapter of the book called 1 Kings or First Kings, probably written in the mid-sixth century BCE. The translation is from the King James version of the Bible (1611). Two expressions in the story need clarification: (1) The woman who "overlaid" her child in her sleep rolled over on the child and suffocated it; and (2) it is said of a woman that her "bowels yearned upon her son," that is, her heart longed for her son. (In Hebrew psychology, the bowels were thought to be the seat of emotion.)

Then came there two women, that were harlots, unto the king, and
stood before him. And the one woman said, "O my lord, I and this
woman dwell in one house, and I was delivered of a child with her in

the house. And it came to pass the third day after that I was delivered, that this woman was delivered also: and we were together; there was no stranger in the house, save we two in the house. And this woman's child died in the night; because she overlaid it. And she arose at midnight, and took my son from beside me, while thine handmaid slept, and laid it in her bosom, and laid her dead child in my bosom. And when I rose in the morning to give my child suck, behold, it was dead: but when I considered it in the morning, behold, it was not my son, which I did bear."

And the other woman said, "Nay; but the living is my son, and the dead is thy son." And this said, "No; but the dead is thy son, and the living is my son." Thus they spake before the king.

Then said the king, "The one saith, 'This is my son that liveth, and thy son is dead': and the other saith, 'Nay; but thy son is the dead, and my son is the living.'" And the king said, "Bring me a sword." And they brought a sword before the king. And the king said, "Divide the living child in two, and give half to the one, and half to the other."

Then spake the woman whose the living child was unto the king, for her bowels yearned upon her son, and she said, "O my lord, give her the living child, and in no wise slay it." But the other said, "Let it be neither mine nor thine, but divide it."

5 Then the king answered and said, "Give her the living child, and in no wise slay it: she is the mother thereof."

And all Israel heard of the judgment which the king had judged; and they feared the king, for they saw that the wisdom of God was in him to do judgment.

Analyzing the Story

Let's begin by analyzing the *form* or the shape of the story. One form or shape that we notice is this: The story moves from a problem to a solution. We can also say, still speaking of the overall form, that the story moves from quarreling and talk of death to unity and talk of life. In short, it has a happy ending, a form that (because it provides an optimistic view of life and also a sense of completeness) gives most people pleasure.

In thinking about a work of literature, it is always useful to take notice of the basic form of the whole, the overall structural pattern. Doubtless you are already familiar with many basic patterns, for example, tragedy (joy yielding to sorrow) and romantic comedy (angry conflict yielding to joyful union). If you think even briefly about verbal works, you'll notice the structures or patterns that govern songs, episodes in soap operas, political speeches (beginning with the candidate's expression of pleasure at being in Duluth, and ending with "God bless you all"), detective stories, westerns, and so on. And just as viewers of a western film inevitably experience one western in the context of others, so readers inevitably experience one story in the context of similar stories, and one poem in the context of others.

Second, we can say that "The Judgment of Solomon" is a sort of detective story: There is a death, followed by a conflict in the testimony of the witnesses, and then a solution by a shrewd outsider. Consider Solomon's predicament. Ordinarily in literature characters are sharply defined and individualized, yet the essence of a detective story is that the culprit should *not* be easily recognized as wicked, and here nothing seems to distinguish the two petitioners. Solomon is confronted by "two women, that were harlots." Until late in the story—that is, up to the time Solomon suggests dividing the child—they are described only as "the one woman," "the other woman," "the one," "the other."

Does the story suffer from weak characterization? If we think analytically about this issue, we realize that the point surely is to make the women as alike as possible, so that we cannot tell which of the two is speaking the truth. Like Solomon, we have nothing to go on; neither witness is known to be more honest than the other, and there are no other witnesses to support or refute either woman.

Analysis is concerned with seeing the relationships between the parts of a work, but analysis also may take note of what is *not* in the work. A witness would destroy the story, or at least turn it into an utterly different story. Another thing missing from this story is an explicit editorial comment or interpretation, except for the brief remark at the end that the people "feared the king." If we had read the story in the so-called Geneva Bible (1557-60), which is the translation of the Bible that Shakespeare was familiar with, we would have found a marginal comment: "Her motherly affection herein appeareth that she had rather endure the rigour of the lawe, than see her child cruelly slaine." Would you agree that it is better, at least in this story, for the reader to draw conclusions than for the storyteller explicitly to point them out?

Solomon wisely contrives a situation in which these two claimants, who seem so similar, will reveal their true natures: The mother will reveal her love, and the liar will reveal her hard heart. The early symmetry (the identity of the two women) pleases the reader, and so does the device by which we can at last distinguish between the two women.

But even near the end there is a further symmetry. In order to save the child's life, the true mother gives up her claim, crying out, "Give her the living child, and in no wise slay it." The author (or, rather, the translator who produced this part of the King James Version) takes these very words, with no change whatsoever, and puts them into Solomon's mouth as the king's final judgment. Solomon too says, "Give her the living child, and in no wise slay it," but now the sentence takes on a new meaning. In the first sentence, "her" refers to the liar (the true mother says to give the child to "her"); in Solomon's sentence, "her" refers to the true mother: "Give her the living child. . . . " Surely we take pleasure in the fact that the very words by which the mother renounces her child are the words that (1) reveal to Solomon the truth, and that (2) Solomon uses to restore the child to its mother.

This analysis has chiefly talked about the relations of parts, and especially it has tried to explain why the two women in this story are *not* distinct until Solomon finds a way to reveal their distinctive natures: If the story is to demonstrate Solomon's wisdom, the women must seem identical until Solomon can show that they differ. But the analysis could have gone into some other topic. Let's consider several possibilities.

A student might begin by asking this question: "Although it is important for the women to be highly similar, why are they harlots?" (It is too simple to say that the women in the story are harlots because the author is faithfully reporting a historical episode in Solomon's career. The story is widely recognized as a folktale, found also in other ancient cultures.) One possible reason for making the women harlots is that the story demands that there be no witnesses; by using harlots, the author disposed of husbands, parents, and siblings who might otherwise be expected to live with the women. A second possible reason is that the author wanted to show that Solomon's justice extended to all, not only to respectable folk. Third, perhaps the author wished to reject or at least to complicate the stereotype of the harlot as a thoroughly disreputable person. The author did this by introducing another (and truer?) stereotype, the mother as motivated by overwhelming maternal love.

Other Possible Topics for Analysis

Another possible kind of analytic essay might go beyond the structure of the individual work, to the relation of the work to some larger whole. For instance, one might approach "The Judgment of Solomon" from the point of view of gender criticism (discussed in Chapter 17): In this story, one might argue, wisdom is an attribute only of a male; women are either deceitful or emotional. From this point one might set out to write a research essay on gender in a larger whole, certain books of the Hebrew Bible.

We might also analyze the story in the context of other examples of what scholars call Wisdom Literature (the Book of Proverbs, and Ecclesiastes, for instance). Notice that Solomon's judgment leads the people to *fear* him—because his wisdom is great, formidable, and God-inspired.

It happens that we do not know who wrote "The Judgment of Solomon," but the authors of most later works of literature are known, and therefore some critics seek to analyze a given work within the context of the author's life. For some other critics, the larger context would be the reading process, which includes the psychology of the reader. (Biographical criticism and reader-response criticism are discussed in Chapter 17.)

Still another analysis—again, remember that a work can be analyzed from many points of view—might examine two or more translations of the story. You do not need to know Hebrew in order to compare this early seventeenth-century translation with a twentieth-century version such as the New Jerusalem Bible or the Revised English Bible. One might seek to find which version is, on literary grounds, more effective. Such an essay might include an attempt, by means of a comparison, to analyze the effect of the archaic language of the King James Version. Does the somewhat unfamiliar language turn a reader off, or does it add mystery or dignity or authority to the tale, valuable qualities perhaps not found in the modern version? (By the way, in the Revised English Bible, Solomon does *not* exactly repeat the mother's plea. The mother says, "Let her have the baby," and Solomon then says, "Give the living baby to the first woman." In the New Jerusalem Bible, after the mother says, "Let them give her the live child," Solomon says, "Give the live child to the first woman." If you prefer one version to the other two, why not try to analyze your preference?)

Finally, it should be mentioned (or, to be more truthful, it must be confessed) that an analysis of the structure of a work, in which the relationships of the parts to the whole are considered, allows the work to be regarded as independent of the external world ("autonomous," to use a word common in criticism). If we insist, say, that literature should in all respects reflect life, and we want to analyze the work against reality as we see it, we may find ourselves severely judging "The Judgment of Solomon." We might ask, for instance, if it is likely that a great king would bother to hear the case of two prostitutes quarreling over a child, or if it is likely that the false claimant would really call for the killing of the child. Similarly, to take an absurd example, an analysis of this story in terms of its ability to evoke laughter would be laughable. The point: An analysis will be interesting and useful to a reader only insofar as the aim of the analysis seems reasonable.

Comparison: An Analytic Tool

Analysis frequently involves comparing: Things are examined for their resemblances to and differences from other things. Strictly speaking, if one emphasizes the differences rather than the similarities, one is contrasting rather than comparing, but we need not preserve this distinction; we can call both processes *comparing.*

Although your instructor may ask you to write a comparison of two works of literature, the *subject* of the essay is the works; comparison is simply an effective analytic technique to show some of the qualities in the works. You might compare Chopin's use of nature in "The Story of an Hour" (page 12) with the use of nature in another story, in order to reveal the subtle differences between the stories, but a comparison of works utterly unlike can hardly tell the reader or the writer anything.

Something should be said about organizing a comparison, say between the settings in two stories, between two characters in a novel (or even between a character at the end of a novel and the same character at the beginning), or between the symbolism of two poems. Probably, a student's first thought after making some jottings is to discuss one half of the comparison and then go on to the second half. Instructors and textbooks (though not this one) usually condemn such an organization, arguing that the essay breaks into two parts and that the second part involves a good deal of repetition of categories set up in the first part. Usually, they recommend that the students organize their thoughts differently, somewhat along these lines:

1. First similarity
   a. First work (or character, or characteristic)
   b. Second work
2. Second similarity
   a. First work
   b. Second work
3. First difference
   a. First work
   b. Second work
4. Second difference
   a. First work
   b. Second work

and so on, for as many additional differences as seem relevant. If one wishes to compare *Huckleberry Finn* with *The Catcher in the Rye,* one may organize the material thus:

1. First similarity: the narrator and his quest
   a. Huck
   b. Holden
2. Second similarity: the corrupt world surrounding the narrator
   a. Society in *Huck*
   b. Society in *Catcher*

 3. First difference: degree to which the narrator fulfills his quest and escapes from society
    a. Huck's plan to "light out" to the frontier
    b. Holden's breakdown

Another way of organizing a comparison and contrast:

 1. First point: the narrator and his quest
    a. Similarities between Huck and Holden
    b. Differences between Huck and Holden
 2. Second point: the corrupt world
    a. Similarities between the worlds in *Huck* and *Catcher*
    b. Differences between the worlds in *Huck* and *Catcher*
 3. Third point: degree of success
    a. Similarities between Huck and Holden
    b. Differences between Huck and Holden

A comparison need not employ either of these structures. There is even the danger that an essay employing either of them may not come into focus until the essayist stands back from the seven-layer cake and announces in the concluding paragraph that the odd layers taste better. In one's preparatory thinking, one may want to make comparisons in pairs (good-natured humor: the clown in *Othello,* the clownish grave-digger in *Hamlet;* social satire: the clown in *Othello,* the grave-digger in *Hamlet;* relevance to main theme: . . . ; length of role: . . . ; comments by other characters: . . .), but one must come to some conclusions about what these add up to before writing the final version. This final version should not duplicate the thought processes; rather, it should be organized so as to make the point—the thesis—clearly and effectively. After reflection, one may believe that although there are superficial similarities between the clown in *Othello* and the clownish grave-digger in *Hamlet,* there are essential differences; then in the finished essay one probably will not wish to obscure the main point by jumping back and forth from play to play, working through a series of similarities and differences. It may be better to discuss the clown in *Othello* and then to point out that although the grave-digger in *Hamlet* resembles him in A, B, and C, the grave-digger also has other functions (D, E, and F) and is of greater consequence to *Hamlet* than the clown is to *Othello.* Some repetition in the second half of the essay ("The grave-digger's puns come even faster than the clown's . . . ") will bind the two halves into a meaningful whole, making clear the degree of similarity or difference. The point of the essay presumably is not to list pairs of similarities or differences but to illuminate a work or works by making thoughtful comparisons.

Although in a long essay one cannot postpone until page 30 a discussion of the second half of the comparison, in an essay of, say, fewer than ten pages nothing is wrong with setting forth one half of the comparison and then, in light of it, the second half. The essay will break into two unrelated parts if the second half makes no use of the first or if it fails to modify the first half, but not if the second half looks back to the first half and calls attention to differences that the new material reveals. Students ought to learn how to write an essay with interwoven comparisons, but they ought also to know that a comparison may be written in another, simpler and clearer way.

Finally, a reminder: The purpose of a comparison is to call attention to the unique features of something by holding it up against something similar but significantly different. You can compare Macbeth with Banquo (two men who hear a prophecy but who respond differently), or Macbeth with Lady Macbeth (a husband and wife, both eager to be monarchs but differing in their sense of the consequences), or Hamlet and Holden Caulfield (two people who see themselves as surrounded by a corrupt world), but you can hardly compare Holden with Macbeth or with Lady Macbeth—there simply aren't enough points of resemblance to make it worth your effort to call attention to subtle differences. If the differences are great and apparent, a comparison is a waste of effort. ("Blueberries are different from elephants. Blueberries do not have trunks. And elephants do not grow on bushes.") Indeed, a comparison between essentially and evidently unlike things can only obscure, for by making the comparison the writer implies that significant similarities do exist, and readers can only wonder why they do not see them. The essays that do break into two halves are essays that make uninstructive comparisons: the first half tells the reader about five qualities in Alice Walker, the second half tells the reader about five different qualities in Toni Morrison.

A Sample Comparison

A student in an introductory class was asked to compare any two of the three stories by Kate Chopin ("Ripe Figs," p. 3; "The Story of an Hour," p. 12; "The Storm," p. 32). She settled on "The Story of an Hour" and "The Storm." We print the final version of her essay, preceded by a page of notes (a synthesis of earlier notes) that she prepared shortly before she wrote her first draft.

```
Resemblances or differences greater?

Resemblances

Theme: release from marital bonds; liberated women
Setting: nature plays a role in both; springtime
    in "Hour," storm in "Storm"
Characterization: in both stories, no villains
    forces of nature compel;
    Clarisse presumably happier without husband
    both seem to emphasize roles of women


Differences

Ending: "Hour" sad (LM unfulfilled); "Storm"
    happy; all characters seem content
But endings different in that "Hour" ends
    suddenly, surprise; "Storm" not surprising at
    very end.

Overall view (theme?)

"Hour" very restricted view; only one person is of
    much interest (LM); Josephine interesting only
    in terms of LM (contrast).
```

In "Storm," Cal. and Alc. interesting; but also
interesting are simple Bobinot and even the
child, and also even Clarisse, who sort of has
the last word

Possible titles

Two Women
New Women
Tragic Louise, Comic Calixta
Louise, Calixta, and Clarisse

Two New Women

It is not surprising that two stories by an
author somewhat resemble each other. What is
especially interesting about Kate Chopin's "The Story
of an Hour" and "The Storm" is that although they
both deal with women who achieve a sense of new life
or growth outside of the bonds of marriage, the
stories differ greatly in what we call tone. "The
Story of an Hour" is bittersweet, or perhaps even
bitter and tragic, whereas "The Storm" is romantic
and in some ways comic.

The chief similarity is that Louise Mallard in
"The Story of an Hour" and Calixta in "The Storm"
both experience valuable, affirming, liberating
sensations that a traditional moral view would
condemn. Mrs. Mallard, after some moments of deep
grief, feels a great sense of liberation when she
learns of the death of her husband. She dies almost
immediately after this experience, but even though
she is never physically unfaithful to her husband,
there is a sort of mental disloyalty, at least from a
traditional point of view. Calixta's disloyalty is
physical, not merely mental. Unlike Louise Mallard,
Calixta does go to bed with a man who is not her

husband. But Calixta, as we will see, is treated just
about as sympathetically as is Mrs. Mallard.

Louise Mallard is sympathetic because she does
grieve for her husband, and because Chopin suggests
that Mallard's sense of freedom is natural, something
associated with the spring, the "delicious breath of
rain," and "the tops of trees that were all aquiver
with the new spring life" (12). Furthermore, Chopin
explicitly says that Mallard loved her husband. But
Chopin also tells us that one aspect of the marriage
was a "powerful will bending her" (13). For all of
these reasons, then--Mrs. Mallard's genuine grief,
the association of her new feeling with the power
of nature, and the assertion that Mrs. Mallard loved
her husband but was at least in some degree subject
to his will--the reader sympathizes with Mrs.
Mallard.

In her presentation of Calixta, too, Chopin
takes care to make the unfaithful woman a sympathetic
figure. As in "The Story of an Hour," nature plays a
role. Here, instead of nature or the outside world
being a parallel to the woman's emotions, nature in
the form of a storm exerts pressure on the woman. We
are told that "the water beat in upon the boards in
driving sheets" (33), and a bolt of lightning causes
Calixta to stagger backward, into Alcée's arms.
These forces of outside nature are parallel to a
force of nature within Calixta. Chopin tells us that
during the sexual union Calixta's "firm, elastic
flesh . . . was knowing for the first time its
birthright" (34). And in one additional way, too,

Chopin guards against the reader condemning Calixta. We learn, at the end of the story, that Alcée's wife, Clarisse, is quite pleased to be free from her husband for a while:

> And the first free breath since her marriage seemed to restore the pleasant liberty of her maiden days. Devoted as she was to her husband, their intimate conjugal life was something which she was more than willing to forego for a while. (36)

Since Clarisse is portrayed as somewhat pleased to be relieved of her husband for a while, we probably do not see Alcée as a villainous betrayer of his wife. The story seems to end pleasantly, like a comedy, with everybody happy.

In Louise Mallard and in Calixta we see two women who achieve new lives, although in the case of Louise Mallard the reader is surprised to learn in the last sentence that the achievement lasts only a few moments. By "new lives" I mean emancipation from their husbands, but what is especially interesting is that in both cases Chopin guides the reader to feel that although in fact both women behave in ways that would be strongly condemned by the codes of Chopin's day, and even by many people today, neither woman (as Chopin presents her) is blameworthy. Mrs. Mallard is presented almost as a tragic victim, and Calixta is presented almost as a figure in a very pleasant comedy.

[New page]

Work Cited

Barnet, Sylvan, et al., eds. <u>Literature for

Composition</u>. 4th ed. New York: HarperCollins,

1996.

EVALUATION IN EXPLICATION AND ANALYSIS

When we evaluate, we say how good, how successful, how worthwhile, something is. If you reread the student's essay on "Harlem," you'll notice that he implies that the poem is worth reading. He doesn't say "In this excellent poem," but a reader of the essay probably comes away with the impression that the student thinks the poem is excellent. The writer might, of course, have included a more explicit evaluation, along these lines:

> In "Harlem," every word counts, and every word
> is effective. The image of the "heavy load" that
> "sags" is not as unusual as the image of the raisin
> in the sun, but it nevertheless is just right, adding
> a simple, powerful touch just before the explosive
> ending.

In any case, if an essay argues that the parts fit together effectively, it almost surely is implying a favorable evaluation. But only "*almost* surely." One might argue, for instance, that the parts fit, and so on, but that the work is immoral, or trivial, or unpleasant, or untrue to life. Even though one might grant that the work is carefully constructed, one's final evaluation of the work might be low. Evaluations are based on standards. If you offer an evaluation, make certain that your standards are clear to the reader.

Notice in the following three examples of evaluations of J. D. Salinger's *The Catcher in the Rye* that the writers let their readers know what their standards are. Each excerpt is from a review that was published when the book first appeared. In the first, Anne L. Goodman, writing in *The New Republic* (16 July 1951), began by praising Salinger's earlier short stories and then said of the novel:

> But the book as a whole is disappointing, and not merely because it is a reworking of a theme that one begins to suspect must obsess the author. Holden Caulfield, the main character who tells his own story, is an extraordinary portrait, but there is too much of him. He describes himself early on and, with the sureness of a wire recording, he remains strictly in character throughout.

Goodman then quotes a longish passage from *The Catcher,* and says,

> In the course of 277 pages the reader wearies of this kind of explicitness, repetition, and adolescence, exactly as one would weary of Holden himself.

Goodman lets us know that, in her opinion, (1) a book ought not simply to re-peat a writer's earlier books, and also that, again in her opinion, (2) it's not enough to give a highly realistic portrait of a character; if the character is not a sufficiently interesting person, in the long run the book will be dull.

Another reviewer, Virgilia Peterson, writing in *New York Herald Tribune Book Review* (15 July 1951), found the book realistic in some ways, but un-realistic and therefore defective because its abundant profanity becomes uncon-vincing:

> There is probably not one phrase in the whole book that Holden Caulfield would not have used upon occasion, but when they are piled upon each other in cumulative monotony, the ear refuses to believe.

Ms. Peterson concluded her review, however, by confessing that she did not think she was in a position to evaluate a book about an adolescent, or at least *this* adolescent.

> . . . it would be interesting and highly enlightening to know what Holden Caulfield's contemporaries, male and female, think of him. Their opinion would constitute the real test of Mr. Salinger's validity. The question of authenticity is one to which no parent can really guess the reply.

Notice that here again the standard is clear—authenticity—but the writer con-fesses that she isn't sure about authenticity in this matter, and she defers to her juniors. Peterson's review is a rare example of an analysis offered by a writer who confesses an inability to evaluate.

Finally, here is a brief extract from a more favorable review, written by Paul Engle and published in the *Chicago Sunday Tribune Magazine of Books* (15 July 1951):

> The book ends with Holden in a mental institution, for which the earlier events have hardly prepared the reader. But the story is an en-gaging and believable one for the most part, full of right observations and sharp insight, and a wonderful sort of grasp of how a boy can cre-ate his own world of fantasy and live form.

The first sentence implies that a good book prepares the reader for the end, and that in this respect *The Catcher* is deficient. The rest of the paragraph sets forth other standards that *The Catcher* meets (it is "engaging and believable," "full of right observations and sharp insight"), though one of the standards in Engle's last sentence ("live form") strikes us as obscure.

CHOOSING A TOPIC AND DEVELOPING A THESIS IN AN ANALYTIC PAPER

Because Hughes's "Harlem" is very short, the analysis may discuss the entire poem. But a short essay, or even a long one, can hardly discuss all aspects of a play or a novel or even of a long story. If you are writing about a long work, you'll have to single out an appropriate topic.

What is an appropriate topic? First, it must be a topic that you can work up some interest in or your writing will be mechanical and dull. (We say "work up some interest" because interest is commonly the result of some effort.) Second, an appropriate topic is compassable—that is, it is something you can cover with reasonable attention to detail in the few pages (and few days) you have to devote to it. If a work is fairly long, almost surely you will write an analysis of some part.

Unless you have an enormous amount of time for reflection and revision, you cannot write a meaningful essay of five hundred words or even a thousand words on "Shakespeare's *Hamlet*" or "The Fiction of Alice Walker." You cannot even write on "Character in *Hamlet*" or "Symbolism in Walker's *The Color Purple.*" And probably you won't really want to write on such topics anyway. Probably *one* character or *one* symbol has caught your interest. Think of something in your annotations or "response" notes (described in Chapter 1) that has caught your attention. Trust your feelings; you are likely onto something interesting.

In Chapter 1 we talked about the value of asking yourself questions. To find an appropriate topic, ask yourself such questions as the following:

1. *What purpose does this serve?* For instance, why is this scene in the novel or play? Why is there a comic grave digger in *Hamlet?* Why are these lines unrhymed? Why did the author call the work by this title?
2. *Why do I have this response?* Why do I feel that this work is more profound (or amusing, or puzzling) than that work? How did the author make this character funny or dignified or pathetic? How did the author communicate the idea that this character is a bore without boring me?

The first of these questions, "What purpose does this serve?," requires that you identify yourself with the author, wondering, for example, whether this opening scene is the best possible for this story. The second question, "Why do I have this response?," requires that you trust your feelings. If you are amused or puzzled or annoyed, assume that these responses are appropriate and follow them up, at least until a rereading of the work provides other responses. If you jot down notes reporting your responses and later think about them, you will probably find that you can select a topic.

A third valuable way to find a thesis is to test a published comment against your response to a particular work. Perhaps somewhere you have seen—for instance, in a textbook—a statement about the nature of fiction, poetry, or drama. Maybe you have heard that a tragic hero has a "flaw." Don't simply accept the remark. Test it against your reading of the work. And interpret the word *published* broadly. Students and instructors publish their opinions—offer them to a public—when they utter them in class. Think about something said in class; students who pay close attention to their peers learn a great deal.

Given an appropriate topic, you will find your essay easier to write and the finished version of it clearer and more persuasive if, at some point in your preparation, in note taking or in writing a first draft, you have converted your topic into a *thesis* (a proposition, a point, an argument) and constructed a *thesis statement* (a sentence stating your overall point).

Let's dwell a moment on the distinction between a topic and a thesis. It may be useful to think of it this way: A topic is a subject (for example, "The Role of Providence in *Hamlet*"); to arrive at a thesis, you have to make an arguable assertion (for example, "The role of Providence in *Hamlet* is not obvious, but it is crucial").

Of course some theses are more promising than others. Consider this thesis:

The role of Providence in *Hamlet* is interesting.

This sentence indeed asserts a thesis, but it is vague and provides little direction, little help in generating ideas and in shaping your essay. Let's try again. It's almost always necessary to try again and again, for the process of writing is in large part a process of trial and error, of generating better and better ideas by evaluating—selecting or rejecting—ideas and options.

The role of Providence is evident in the Ghost.

This is much better, and it could stimulate ideas for an interesting essay. Let's assume the writer rereads the play, looking for further evidence, and comes to believe that the Ghost is only one of several manifestations of Providence. The writer may stay with the Ghost or may (especially if the paper is long enough to allow for such a thesis to be developed) alter the thesis thus:

> The role of Providence is not confined to the Ghost but is found also in
> the killing of Polonius, in the surprising appearance of the pirate ship,
> and in the presence of the poisoned chalice.

Strictly speaking, the thesis here is given in the first part of the sentence ("The role of Providence is not confined to the Ghost"); the rest of the sentence provides an indication of how the argument will be supported.

Every literary work suggests its own topics for analysis to an active reader, and all essayists must set forth their own theses, but if you begin by seeking to examine one of your responses, you probably will soon be able to stake out a topic and to formulate a thesis.

A suggestion: With two or three other students, formulate a thesis about Kate Chopin's "The Storm" (in Chapter 2). By practicing with a group you will develop a skill that you will use when you have to formulate a thesis on your own.

AN ANALYSIS OF A STORY

If a story is short enough, you may be able to examine everything in it that you think is worth commenting on, but even if it is short you may nevertheless decide to focus on one element, such as the setting, or the construction of the plot, or the connection between two characters, or the degree of plausibility. Here is a story by James Thurber (1894–1961), the American humorist. It was first published in 1939.

 JAMES THURBER

The Secret Life of Walter Mitty

"We're going through!" The Commander's voice was like thin ice breaking. He wore his full-dress uniform, with the heavily braided white cap pulled down rakishly over one cold gray eye. "We can't make it, sir. It's spoiling for a hurricane, if you ask me." "I'm not asking you, Lieutenant Berg," said the Commander. "Throw on the power lights! Rev her up to 8,500! We're going through!" The pounding of the cylinders increased: ta-pocketa-pocketa-pocketa-*pocketa-pocketa*. The Commander stared at the ice forming on the pilot window. He walked over and twisted a row of complicated dials.

"Switch on No. 8 auxiliary!" he shouted. "Switch on No. 8 auxiliary!" repeated Lieutenant Berg. "Full strength in No. 3 turret!" shouted the Commander. "Full strength in No. 3 turret!" The crew, bending to their various tasks in the huge, hurtling eight-engined Navy hydroplane, looked at each other and grinned. "The Old Man'll get us through," they said to one another. "The Old Man ain't afraid of Hell!" . . .

"Not so fast! You're driving too fast!" said Mrs. Mitty. "What are you driving so fast for?"

"Hmm?" said Walter Mitty. He looked at his wife, in the seat beside him, with shocked astonishment. She seemed grossly unfamiliar, like a strange woman who had yelled at him in a crowd. "You were up to fifty-five," she said. "You know I don't like to go more than forty. You were up to fifty-five." Walter Mitty drove on toward Waterbury in silence, the roaring of the SN202 through the worst storm in twenty years of Navy flying fading in the remote, intimate airways of his mind. "You're tensed up again," said Mrs. Mitty. "It's one of your days. I wish you'd let Dr. Renshaw look you over."

Walter Mitty stopped the car in front of the building where his wife went to have her hair done. "Remember to get those overshoes while I'm having my hair done," she said. "I don't need overshoes," said Mitty. She put her mirror back into her bag. "We've been all through that," she said, getting out of the car. "You're not a young man any longer." He raced the engine a little. "Why don't you wear your gloves? Have you lost your gloves?" Walter Mitty reached in a pocket and brought out the gloves. He put them on, but after she had turned and gone into the building and he had driven on to a red light, he took them off again. "Pick it up, brother!" snapped a cop as the light changed, and Mitty hastily pulled on his gloves and lurched ahead. He drove around the streets aimlessly for a time, and then he drove past the hospital on his way to the parking lot.

5   . . . "It's the millionaire banker, Wellington McMillan," said the pretty nurse. "Yes?" said Walter Mitty, removing his gloves slowly. "Who has the case?" "Dr. Renshaw and Dr. Benbow, but there are two specialists here, Dr. Remington from New York and Dr. Pritchard-Mitford from London. He flew over." A door opened down a long, cool corridor and Dr. Renshaw came out. He looked distraught and haggard. "Hello, Mitty," he said. "We're having the devil's own time with McMillan, the millionaire banker and close personal friend of Roosevelt. Obstreosis of the ductal tract. Tertiary. Wish you'd take a look at him." "Glad to," said Mitty.

In the operating room there were whispered introductions: "Dr. Remington, Dr. Mitty, Mr. Pritchard-Mitford, Dr. Mitty." "I've read your book on streptothricosis," said Pritchard-Mitford, shaking hands. "A brilliant performance, sir." "Thank you," said Walter Mitty. "Didn't know you were in the States, Mitty," grumbled Remington. "Coals to Newcastle, bringing Mitford and me up here for a tertiary." "You are very kind," said Mitty. A huge, complicated machine, connected to the operating table, with many tubes and wires, began at this moment to go pocketa-pocketa-pocketa. "The new anesthetizer is giving way!" shouted an interne. "There is no one in the East who knows how to fix it!" "Quiet, man!" said Mitty, in a low, cool voice. He sprang to the machine, which was now going pocketa-pocketa-queep-pocketa-queep. He began fingering delicately a row of glistening dials. "Give me a fountain pen!" he snapped. Someone handed him a fountain pen. He pulled a faulty piston out of the machine and inserted the pen in its place. "That will hold for ten minutes," he said. "Get on with the operation." A nurse hurried over and whispered to Renshaw, and Mitty saw the man turn pale. "Coreopsis has set in," said Renshaw nervously. "If you would take over, Mitty?" Mitty looked at him and at the craven figure of Benbow, who drank, and at the grave, uncertain faces of the two great specialists. "If you wish," he said. They slipped a white gown on him; he adjusted a mask and drew on thin gloves; nurses handed him shining. . . .

"Back it up, Mac! Look out for that Buick!" Walter Mitty jammed on the brakes. "Wrong lane, Mac," said the parking-lot attendant, looking at Mitty closely. "Gee. Yeh," muttered Mitty. He began cautiously to back out of the lane marked "Exit Only." "Leave her sit there," said the attendant. "I'll put her away." Mitty got out of the car. "Hey, better leave the key." "Oh," said Mitty, handing the man the ignition key. The attendant vaulted into the car, backed it up with insolent skill, and put it where it belonged.

They're so damn cocky, thought Walter Mitty, walking along Main Street; they think they know everything. Once he had tried to take his chains off, outside New Milford, and he had got them wound around the axles. A man had had to come out in a wrecking car and unwind them, a young, grinning garageman. Since then Mrs. Mitty always made him drive to the garage to have the chains taken off. The next time, he thought, I'll wear my right arm in a sling; they won't grin at me then. I'll have my right arm in a sling and they'll see I couldn't possibly take the chains off myself. He kicked at the slush on the sidewalk. "Overshoes," he said to himself, and he began looking for a shoe store.

When he came out into the street again, with the overshoes in a box under his arm, Walter Mitty began to wonder what the other thing was his wife had told him to get. She had told him, twice, before they set out from their house for Waterbury. In a way he hated these weekly trips to town— he was always getting something wrong. Kleenex, he thought, Squibb's, razor blades? No. Toothpaste, toothbrush, bicarbonate, carborundum, initiative and referendum? He gave it up. But she would remember it. "Where's the what's-its-name?" she would ask. "Don't tell me you forgot the what's-its-name." A newsboy went by shouting something about the Waterbury trial.

10   . . . "Perhaps this will refresh your memory." The District Attorney suddenly thrust a heavy automatic at the quiet figure on the witness stand. "Have you ever seen this before?" Walter Mitty took the gun and examined it expertly. "This is my Webley-Vickers 50.80," he said calmly. An excited buzz ran around the courtroom. The Judge rapped for order. "You are a crack shot with any sort of firearms, I believe?" said the District Attorney, insinuatingly. "Objection!" shouted Mitty's attorney. "We have shown that the defendant could not have fired the shot. We have shown that he wore his right arm in a sling on the night of the fourteenth of July." Walter Mitty raised his hand briefly and the bickering attorneys were stilled. "With any known make of gun," he said evenly, "I could have killed Gregory Fitzhurst at three hundred feet *with my left hand.*" Pandemonium broke loose in the courtroom. A woman's scream rose above the bedlam and suddenly a lovely, dark-haired girl was in Walter Mitty's arms. The District Attorney struck at her savagely. Without rising from his chair, Mitty let the man have it on the point of the chin. "You miserable cur!" . . .

"Puppy biscuit," said Walter Mitty. He stopped walking and the buildings of Waterbury rose up out of the misty courtroom and surrounded him again. A woman who was passing laughed. "He said 'Puppy biscuit,' " she said to her companion. "That man said 'Puppy biscuit' to himself." Walter Mitty hurried on. He went into an A. & P., not the first one he came to but a smaller one farther up the street. "I want some biscuit for small, young dogs," he said to the clerk. "Any special brand, sir?" The greatest pistol shot in the world thought a moment. "It says 'Puppies Bark for It' on the box," said Walter Mitty.

His wife would be through at the hairdresser's in fifteen minutes, Mitty saw in looking at his watch, unless they had trouble drying it; sometimes they had trouble drying it. She didn't like to get to the hotel first; she would want him to be there waiting for her as usual. He found a big leather chair in the lobby, facing a window, and he put the overshoes and the puppy biscuit on the floor beside it. He picked up an old copy of *Liberty* and sank down into the chair. "Can Germany Conquer the World through the Air?" Walter Mitty looked at the pictures of bombing planes and of ruined streets.

. . . "The cannonading has got the wind up in young Raleigh, sir," said the sergeant. Captain Mitty looked up at him through tousled hair. "Get him to bed," he said wearily. "With the others. I'll fly alone." "But you can't, sir," said the sergeant anxiously. "It takes two men to handle that bomber and the Archies are pounding hell out of the air. Von Richtman's circus is between here and Saulier." "Somebody's got to get that ammunition dump," said Mitty. "I'm going over. Spot of brandy?" He poured a drink for the sergeant and one for himself. War thundered and whined around the dugout and battered at the door. There was a rending of wood and splinters flew through the room. "A bit of a near thing," said Captain Mitty carelessly. "The box barrage is closing in," said the sergeant. "We only live once, Sergeant," said Mitty, with his faint, fleeting smile. "Or do we?" He poured another brandy and tossed it off. "I never see a man could hold his brandy like you, sir," said the sergeant. "Begging your pardon, sir." Captain Mitty stood up and strapped on his huge Webley-Vickers automatic. "It's forty kilometers through hell, sir," said the sergeant. Mitty finished one last brandy. "After all," he said softly, "what isn't?" The pounding of the cannon increased; there was the rat-tat-tatting of machine guns, and from somewhere came the menacing pocket-pocketa-pocketa of the new flame-throwers. Walter Mitty walked to the door of the dugout humming "Auprès de Ma Blonde." He turned and waved to the sergeant. "Cheerio!" he said. . . .

Something struck his shoulder. "I've been looking all over this hotel for you," said Mrs. Mitty. "Why do you have to hide in this old chair? How did you expect me to find you?" "Things close in," said Walter Mitty vaguely. "What?" Mrs. Mitty said. "Did you get the what's-its-name? The puppy biscuit? What's in that box?" "Overshoes," said Mitty. "Couldn't you have put them on in the store?" "I was thinking," said Walter Mitty. "Does it ever occur to you that I am sometimes thinking?" She looked at him. "I'm going to take your temperature when I get you home," she said.

15   They went out through the revolving doors that made a faintly derisive whistling sound when you pushed them. It was two blocks to the parking lot. At the drugstore on the corner she said, "Wait here for me. I forgot

something. I won't be a minute." She was more than a minute. Walter Mitty
lighted a cigarette. It began to rain, rain with sleet in it. He stood up against
the wall of the drugstore, smoking. . . . He put his shoulders back and his
heels together. "To hell with the handkerchief," said Walter Mitty scornfully. He took one last drag on his cigarette and snapped it away. Then, with
that faint, fleeting smile playing about his lips, he faced the firing squad;
erect and motionless, proud and disdainful, Walter Mitty the Undefeated, inscrutable to the last.

[1939]

Some Journal Entries

Before reading the following entries about "The Secret Life of Walter Mitty,"
write some of your own. You may want to think about what (if anything) you
found amusing in the story, or about whether the story is dated, or about some
aspect of Mitty's character or of his wife's. But the choice is yours.

A student wrote the following entry in her journal after the story was discussed in class.

> March 21. Funny, I guess, especially the business
> about him as a doctor performing an operation. And
> that "pocketa-pocketa," but I don't think that it's
> as hysterical as everyone else seems to think it is.
> And how could anyone stand being married to a man
> like that? In fact, it's a good thing he has her to
> look after him. He ought to be locked up, driving
> into the "Exit Only" lane, talking to himself in the
> street, and having those crazy daydreams. No wonder
> the woman in the street laughs at him.
> March 24. He's certainly a case, and she's not nearly
> as bad as everyone was saying. So she tells him to
> put his overshoes on; well, he ought to put them on,
> since Thurber says there is slush in the street, and
> he's no kid anymore. About the worst I can say of her
> is that she seems a little unreasonable in always
> wanting him to wait for her, rather than sometimes
> the other way around, but probably she's really
> telling him not to wander off, because if he ever
> drifts away there'll be no finding him. The joke, I
> guess, is that he's supposed to have these daydreams
> because he's henpecked, and henpecked men are
> supposed to be funny. Would people find the story
> just as funny if she had the daydreams, and he
> bullied her?

List Notes

In preparation for writing a draft, the student reread the story and jotted down
some tentative notes based on her journal and on material that she had high-

lighted in the text. (At this point you may want to make your own list, based on your notes.)

> Mitty helpless: he _needs_ her
>   chains on tires
>   enters Exit Only
>   ~~Waterbury~~
>   cop tells him to get going
>   fantasies
> wife a nag? → causes his daydreams? Evidence?
>   makes him get to hotel first
>   overshoes
>   backseat driver?
> "Does it ever occur to you that I am sometimes
>   thinking?" Is he thinking, or just having dreams?
> M. confuses ~~Richthoven~~ with someone called Richtman.
> Funny—or anti-woman? Would it be funny if he nagged her, and
> she had daydreams?

Next, the student wrote a draft; then she revised the draft and submitted the revision (printed here) to some classmates for peer review. (The number enclosed within parentheses cities the source of a quotation.) Before reading the student's draft, you may want to write a draft based on your own notes and lists.

Sample Draft

Walter Mitty Is No Joke

James Thurber's "The Secret Life of Walter Mitty" seems to be highly regarded as a comic story about a man who is so dominated by his wife that he has to escape through fantasies. In my high school course in English, everyone found Mitty's dreams and his wife's bullying funny, and everyone seems to find them funny in college, too. Everyone except me.

If we look closely at the story, we see that Mitty is a pitiful man who <u>needs</u> to be told what to do. The slightest glimpse of reality sets him off on a daydream, as when he passes a hospital and immediately begins to imagine that he is a famous surgeon, or when he hears a newsboy shouting a headline about a crime and he imagines himself in a courtroom. The point seems to be that his wife nags him, so he escapes into daydreams. But the fact is that she needs to keep after him, because he needs someone to tell him what to do. It depends on what one considers nagging. She tells him he is driving too fast, and (given the date of the story, 1939) he probably is, since he is going 55 on a slushy or snowy road. She tells him to wear overshoes, and he probably ought to, since the weather is bad. He resents all of these orders, but he clearly is incompetent, since he delays when the traffic light turns from red to green, and he enters an "Exit Only" lane in a parking lot. We are also told that he can't put chains on tires.

In fact, he can't do anything right. All he can do is daydream, and the dreams, though they are funny, are proof of his inability to live in the real world. When his wife asks him why he didn't put the overshoes on in the store, instead of carrying them in a box, he says, "Does it ever occur to you that I am sometimes thinking?" (61). But he doesn't "think," he just daydreams. Furthermore, he can't even get things straight in his daydreams, since he gets everything mixed up, confusing Richthoven with Richtman, for example.

Is "The Secret Life of Walter Mitty" really a funny story about a man who daydreams because he is henpecked? Probably it is supposed to be so, but it's also a story about a man who is lucky to have a wife

who can put up with him and keep him from getting
killed on the road or lost in town.

Work Cited

Thurber, James. "The Secret Life of Walter Mitty."
    <u>Literature for Composition</u>. 4th ed. Ed. Sylvan
    Barnet et al. New York: HarperCollins, 1996.
    58-62.

INTRODUCTIONS, MIDDLES, ENDINGS

Introductory Paragraphs

As the poet Byron said, at the beginning of a long part of a long poem, "Nothing so difficult as a beginning." Woody Allen thinks so, too. In an interview he said that the toughest part of writing is "to go from nothing to the first draft."

We can give two pieces of advice. Unfortunately, they are apparently contradictory.

1. *The opening paragraph is unimportant.* It's great if you can write a paragraph that will engage your readers and let them know where the essay will be taking them, but if you can't come up with such a paragraph, just put down anything in order to prime the pump.
2. *The opening paragraph is extremely important.* It must engage your readers, and probably by means of a thesis sentence it should let the readers know where the essay will be taking them.

The contradiction is, as we said, only apparent, not real. The first point is relevant to the opening paragraph of a *draft;* the second point is relevant to the opening paragraph of the *final version.* Almost all writers—professionals as well as amateurs—find that the first paragraphs in their drafts are false starts. Don't worry too much about the opening paragraphs of your draft; you'll almost surely want to revise your opening later anyway. (Surprisingly often your first paragraph may simply be deleted; your second, you may find, is where your essay truly begins.)

When writing a first draft you merely need something—almost anything may do—to break the ice. But in your finished paper the opening cannot be mere throat-clearing. The opening should be interesting.

Among the commonest ***un*interesting openings** are these:

1. A dictionary definition ("Webster says . . . ").
2. A restatement of your title. The title is (let's assume) "Romeo's Maturation," and the first sentence says, "This essay will study Romeo's maturation." True, there is an attempt at a thesis statement here, but no information beyond what has already been given in the title. There is no information about you, either, that is, no sense of your response to the

topic, such as is present in, say, "*Romeo and Juliet* covers less than one week, but within this short period Romeo is impressively transformed from a somewhat comic infatuated boy to a thoughtful tragic hero."

3. A platitude, such as "Ever since the beginning of time men and women have fallen in love." Again, such a sentence may be fine if it helps you to start drafting, but because it sounds canned and because it is insufficiently interesting, it should not remain in your final version.

What is left? What *is* a good way for a final version to begin? Your introductory paragraph will be at least moderately interesting if it gives information, and it will be pleasing if the information provides a focus—that is, if it goes beyond the title in letting the reader know exactly what your topic is and where you are headed.

Let's assume that you agree: An opening paragraph should be *interesting* and *focused.* Doubtless you will find your own ways of fulfilling these goals, but you might consider using one of the following time-tested methods.

1. *Establish a connection between life and literature.* We have already suggested that a platitude (for instance, "Ever since the beginning of time men and women have fallen in love") usually makes a poor beginning because it is dull, but you may find some other way of relating the work to daily experience. For instance:

   Doubtless the popularity of Romeo and Juliet (the play has been with us for almost four hundred years) is partly due to the fact that it deals with a universal experience. Still, no other play about love is so much a part of our culture that the mere mention of the names of the lovers immediately calls up an image. But when we say that So-and-so is "a regular Romeo," exactly what do we mean? And exactly what sort of lover is Romeo?

2. *Give an overview.* Here is an example:

   Langston Hughes's "Harlem" is about the destruction of the hopes of African-Americans. More precisely, Hughes begins by asking "What happens to a dream deferred?" and then offers several possibilities, the last of which is that it may "explode."

3. *Include a quotation.* The previous example illustrates this approach, also. Here is another example:

> One line from Langston Hughes's poem "Harlem"
> has become famous, "A raisin in the sun," but its
> fame is, in a sense, accidental; Lorraine Hansberry
> happened to use it for the title of a play.
> Doubtless she used it because it is impressive, but
> in fact the entire poem is worthy of its most
> famous line.

4. *Use a definition.* We have already suggested that a definition such as "Webster says . . ." is boring and therefore unusable, but consider the following:

> When we say that a character is the hero of a
> story, we usually mean that he is the central
> figure, and we probably imply that he is manly. But
> in Kafka's "The Metamorphosis" the hero is most
> unmanly.

5. *Introduce a critical stance.* If your approach is feminist, or psychoanalytic, or Marxist, or whatever, you may want to say so at the start. Example:

> Feminists have called our attention to the
> unfunny sexism of mother-in-law jokes, comments
> about women hooking men into marriage, and so
> forth. We can now see that the stories of James
> Thurber, long thought to be wholesome fun, are
> unpleasantly sexist.

Caution: We are not saying that these are the only ways to begin, and we certainly are not suggesting that you pack all five into the opening paragraph. We are saying only that after you have done some brainstorming and written some drafts, you may want to think about using one of these methods for your opening paragraph.

An Exercise: Write (either by yourself or in collaboration with one or two other students) an opening paragraph for an essay on one of Kate Chopin's stories and another for an essay on Hughes's "Harlem." (To write a useful opening paragraph you will, of course, first have to settle on the essay's thesis.)

Middle Paragraphs

The middle, or body, of your essay will develop your thesis by offering support-ing evidence. Ideas for the body should emerge from the sketchy outline that emerged from your review of your brainstorming notes or your journal.

1. *Be sure that each paragraph makes a specific point* and that the point is sufficiently developed with evidence (a brief quotation is often the best evidence).
2. *Be sure that each paragraph is coherent.* Read each sentence, starting with the second sentence, to see how it relates to the preceding sen-tence. Does it clarify, extend, reinforce, add an example? If you can't find the relationship, the sentence probably does not belong where it is. Rewrite it, move it, or strike it out.
3. *Be sure that the connections between the paragraphs are clear.* Transi-tional words and phrases, such as "Furthermore," "On the other hand," and "In the next stanza," will often give readers all the help they need in seeing how your points are connected.
4. *Be sure that the paragraphs are in the best possible order.* A good way to test the organization is to jot down the topic sentence or topic idea of each paragraph, and then to see if your jottings are in a reasonable se-quence.

Concluding Paragraphs

Concluding paragraphs, like opening paragraphs, are especially difficult, if only because they are so conspicuous. Readers often skim first paragraphs and last paragraphs to see if an essay is worth reading. With conclusions, as with open-ings, try to say something interesting. It is not in the least interesting to say, "Thus we see that Mrs. Mitty . . ." (and here you go on to echo your title or your first sentence).

What to do? When you are revising a draft, you might keep in mind the fol-lowing widely practiced principles. They are not inflexible rules, but they often work.

1. *Hint that the end is near.* Expressions such as "Finally," "One other point must be discussed," and "In short," which alert the reader that the end is nigh, help to prevent the reader from feeling that the essay ends abruptly.
2. *Perhaps reassert the thesis, but put it in a slightly new light.* Not, "I have shown that Romeo and Hamlet are similar in some ways," but:

```
These similarities suggest that in some

respects Romeo is an early study for Hamlet. Both

are young men in love, both seek by the force of

their passion to shape the world according to their

own desires, and both die in the attempt. But
```

compared with Hamlet, who at the end of the play understands everything that has happened, Romeo dies in happy ignorance; Romeo is spared the pain of knowing that his own actions will destroy Juliet, whereas Hamlet dies with the painful knowledge that his kingdom has been conquered by Norwegian invaders.

3. *Perhaps offer an evaluation.* You may find it appropriate to conclude your analysis with an evaluation, such as this:

Romeo is as convincing as he needs to be in a play about young lovers, but from first to last he is a relatively uncomplicated figure, the ardent lover. Hamlet is a lover, but he is also a good deal more, a figure whose complexity reveals a more sophisticated or a more mature author. Only five or six years separate Romeo and Juliet from Hamlet, but one feels that in those few years Shakespeare made a quantum leap in his grasp of human nature.

4. *Perhaps include a brief significant quotation from the work.* Example:

Romeo has won the hearts of audiences for almost four centuries, but, for all his charm, he is in the last analysis concerned only with fulfilling his own passion. Hamlet, on the other hand, at last fulfills not only his own wish but that of the Ghost, his father. "Remember me," the Ghost says, when he first appears to Hamlet and asks for revenge. Throughout the play Hamlet does remember the Ghost, and finally, at the cost of his own life, Hamlet succeeds in avenging his dead father.

✔ A Checklist for Revising Paragraphs

- Does the paragraph *say* anything? Does it have substance?
- Does the paragraph have a topic sentence? If so, is it in the best place? If the paragraph doesn't have a topic sentence, might one improve the paragraph? Or does it have a clear topic idea?
- If the paragraph is an opening paragraph, is it interesting enough to attract and to hold a reader's attention? If it is a later paragraph, does it easily evolve out of the previous paragraph, and lead into the next paragraph?
- Does the paragraph contain some principle of development, for instance from general to particular?
- Does each sentence clearly follow from the preceding sentence? Have you provided transitional words or cues to guide your reader? Would it be useful to repeat certain key words, for clarity?
- What is the purpose of the paragraph? Do you want to summarize, or tell a story, or give an illustration, or concede a point, or what? Is your purpose clear to you, and does the paragraph fulfill your purpose?
- Is the closing paragraph effective, and not an unnecessary restatement of the obvious?

REVIEW: WRITING AN ANALYSIS

Each writing assignment will require its own kind of thinking, but here are a few principles that usually are relevant:

1. Assume that your reader has already read the work you are discussing but is not thoroughly familiar with it—and of course does not know what you think and how you feel about the work. Early in your essay name the author, the work, and your thesis.
2. Do not tell the plot (or, at most, summarize it very briefly); instead, tell your reader what the work is about (not what happens, but what the happenings add up to).
3. Whether you are writing about character or plot or meter or anything else, you will probably be telling your reader something about *how* the work works, that is, how it develops. The stages by which a work advances may sometimes be marked fairly clearly. For instance (to oversimplify), a poem of two stanzas may ask a question in the first and give an answer in the second, or it may express a hope in the first and reveal a doubt in the second. Novels, of course, are customarily divided into chapters, and even a short story may be printed with numbered parts. Virtually all works are built up out of parts, whether or not the parts are labeled.
4. In telling the reader how each part leads to the next, or how each part arises out of what has come before, you will probably be commenting on such things as (in a story) changes in a character's state of mind—marked perhaps by a change in the setting—or (in a poem) changes in the

speaker's tone of voice—for instance from eager to resigned, or from cautious to enthusiastic. Probably you will in fact not only be describing the development of character or of tone or of plot, but also (and more important) you will be advancing your own thesis.

A WORD ABOUT TECHNICAL TERMINOLOGY

Literature, like, say, the law, medicine, the dance, and, for that matter, cooking and baseball, has given rise to technical terminology. A cookbook will tell you to boil, or bake, or blend, and it will speak of a "slow" oven (300 degrees), a "moderate" oven (350 degrees), or a "hot" oven (450 degrees). These are technical terms in the world of cookery. In watching a baseball game we find ourselves saying, "I think the hit-and-run is on," or "He'll probably bunt." We use these terms because they convey a good deal in a few words; they are clear and precise. Further, although we don't use them in order to impress our hearer, in fact they do indicate that we have more than a superficial acquaintance with the game. That is, the better we know our subject, the more likely we are to use the technical language of the subject. Why? *Because such language enables us to talk precisely and in considerable depth about the subject.* Technical language, unlike jargon (pretentious diction that needlessly complicates or obscures), is illuminating—provided that the reader is familiar with the terms.

In writing about literature you will, for the most part, use the same language that you use in your other courses, and you will not needlessly introduce the technical vocabulary of literary study—but you *will* use this vocabulary when it enables you to be clear, concise, and accurate.

✔ Editing Checklist: Questions to Ask Yourself

- Is the title of my essay at least moderately informative and interesting?
- Do I identify the subject of my essay (author and title) early?
- What is my thesis? Do I state it soon enough (perhaps even in the title) and keep it in view?
- Is the organization reasonable? Does each point lead into the next without irrelevancies and without anticlimaxes?
- Is each paragraph unified by a topic sentence or a topic idea? Are there adequate transitions from one paragraph to the next?
- Are generalizations supported by appropriate concrete details, especially by brief quotations from the text?
- Is the opening paragraph interesting and, by its end, focused on the topic? Is the final paragraph conclusive without being repetitive?
- Is the tone appropriate? No sarcasm, no apologies, no condescension?
- If there is a summary, is it as brief as possible, given its purpose?
- Are the quotations adequately introduced, and are they accurate? Do they provide evidence and let the reader hear the author's voice, or do they merely add words to the essay?
- Is the present tense used to describe the author's work and the action of the work ("Shakespeare *shows*," "Hamlet *dies*")?

- Have I kept in mind the needs of my audience, for instance, by defining unfamiliar terms or by briefly summarizing works or opinions that the reader may be unfamiliar with?
- Is documentation provided where necessary?
- Are the spelling and punctuation correct? Are other mechanical matters (such as margins, spacing, and citations) in correct form? Have I proofread carefully?
- Is the paper properly identified—author's name, instructor's name, course number, and date?

TWO SHORT STORIES

 ## ALICE WALKER

Alice Walker was born in 1944 in Eatonton, Georgia, where her parents eked out a living as sharecroppers and dairy farmers; her mother also worked as a domestic. Walker attended Spelman College in Atlanta, and in 1965 she finished her undergraduate work at Sarah Lawrence College near New York City. She then became active in the welfare rights movement in New York and in the voter registration movement in Georgia. Later she taught writing and literature in Mississippi, at Jackson State College and Tougaloo College, and at Wellesley College, the University of Massachusetts, and Yale University.

Walker has written essays, poetry, and fiction. Her best known novel, The Color Purple *(1982), won a Pulitzer Prize and the National Book Award. She has said that her chief concern is "exploring the oppressions, the insanities, the loyalties, and the triumphs of black women."*

Everyday Use

For your grandmama

I will wait for her in the yard that Maggie and I made so clean and wavy yesterday afternoon. A yard like this is more comfortable than most people know. It is not just a yard. It is like an extended living room. When the hard clay is swept clean as a floor and the fine sand around the edges lined with tiny, irregular grooves, anyone can come and sit and look up into the elm tree and wait for the breezes that never come inside the house.

Maggie will be nervous until after her sister goes: she will stand hopelessly in corners homely and ashamed of the burn scars down her arms and legs, eyeing her sister with a mixture of envy and awe. She thinks her sister had held life always in the palm of one hand, that "no" is a word the world never learned to say to her.

You've no doubt seen those TV shows where the child who has "made it" is confronted, as a surprise, by her own mother and father, tottering in weakly from backstage. (A pleasant surprise, of course: What would they do if parent and child came on the show only to curse out and insult each other?) On TV mother and child embrace and smile into each other's faces. Sometimes the mother and father weep, the child wraps them in her arms and leans across the table to tell how she would not have made it without their help. I have seen these programs.

Sometimes I dream a dream in which Dee and I are suddenly brought together on a TV program of this sort. Out of a dark and soft-seated limousine I am ushered into a bright room filled with many people. There I meet a smiling, gray, sporty man like Johnny Carson who shakes my hand and tells me what a fine girl I have. Then we are on the stage and Dee is embracing me with tears in her eyes. She pins on my dress a large orchid, even though she has told me once that she thinks orchids are tacky flowers.

5   In real life I am a large, big-boned woman with rough, man-working hands. In the winter I wear flannel nightgowns to bed and overalls during the day. I can kill and clean a hog as mercilessly as a man. My fat keeps me hot in zero weather. I can work outside all day, breaking ice to get water for washing. I can eat pork liver cooked over the open fire minutes after it comes steaming from the hog. One winter I knocked a bull calf straight in the brain between the eyes with a sledge hammer and had the meat hung up to chill before nightfall. But of course all this does not show on television. I am the way my daughter would want me to be: a hundred pounds lighter, my skin like an uncooked barley pancake. My hair glistens in the hot bright lights. Johnny Carson has much to do to keep up with my quick and witty tongue.

But that is a mistake. I know even before I wake up. Who ever knew a Johnson with a quick tongue? Who can even imagine me looking a strange white man in the eye? It seems to me I have talked to them always with one foot raised in flight, with my head turned in whichever way is farthest from them. Dee, though. She would always look anyone in the eye. Hesitation was no part of her nature.

"How do I look, Mama?" Maggie says, showing just enough of her thin body enveloped in pink skirt and red blouse for me to know she's there, almost hidden by the door.

"Come out into the yard," I say.

Have you ever seen a lame animal, perhaps a dog run over by some careless person rich enough to own a car, sidle up to someone who is ignorant enough to be kind to him? That is the way my Maggie walks. She has been like this, chin on chest, eyes on ground, feet in shuffle, ever since the fire that burned the other house to the ground.

10   Dee is lighter than Maggie, with nicer hair and a fuller figure. She's a woman now, though sometimes I forget. How long ago was it that the other house burned? Ten, twelve years? Sometimes I can still hear the flames and feel Maggie's arms sticking to me, her hair smoking and her dress falling off her in little black papery flakes. Her eyes seemed stretched open, blazed open by the flames reflected in them. And Dee. I see her standing off under the sweet gum tree she used to dig gum out of; a look of concentration on her face as she watched the last dingy gray board of the house fall in toward the red-hot brick chimney. Why don't you do a dance around the ashes? I'd wanted to ask her. She had hated the house that much.

I used to think she hated Maggie, too. But that was before we raised the money, the church and me, to send her to Augusta to school. She used to read to us without pity; forcing words, lies, other folks' habits, whole lives upon us two, sitting trapped and ignorant underneath her voice. She washed us in a river of make-believe, burned us with a lot of knowledge we didn't necessarily need to know. Pressed us to her with the serious way she read, to shove us away at just the moment, like dimwits, we seemed about to understand.

Dee wanted nice things. A yellow organdy dress to wear to her graduation from high school; black pumps to match a green suit she'd made from an old suit somebody gave me. She was determined to stare down any disaster in her efforts. Her eyelids would not flicker for minutes at a time. Often I fought off the temptation to shake her. At sixteen she had a style of her own: and knew what style was.

I never had an education myself. After second grade the school was closed down. Don't ask me why: in 1927 colored asked fewer questions than they do now. Sometimes Maggie reads to me. She stumbles along good-naturedly but can't see well. She knows she is not bright. Like good looks and money, quickness passed her by. She will marry John Thomas (who has mossy teeth in an earnest face) and then I'll be free to sit here and I guess just sing church songs to myself. Although I never was a good singer. Never could carry a tune. I was always better at a man's job. I used to love to milk till I was hoofed in the side in '49. Cows are soothing and slow and don't bother you, unless you try to milk them the wrong way.

I have deliberately turned my back on the house. It is three rooms, just like the one that burned, except the roof is tin; they don't make shingle roofs any more. There are no real windows, just some holes cut in the sides, like the portholes in a ship, but not round and not square, with rawhide holding the shutters up on the outside. This house is in a pasture, too, like the other one. No doubt when Dee sees it she will want to tear it down. She wrote me once that no matter where we "choose" to live, she will manage to come see us. But she will never bring her friends. Maggie and I thought about this and Maggie asked me, "Mama, when did Dee ever *have* any friends?"

15   She had a few. Furtive boys in pink shirts hanging about on washday after school. Nervous girls who never laughed. Impressed with her they worshiped the well-turned phrase, the cute shape, the scalding humor that erupted like bubbles in lye. She read to them.

When she was courting Jimmy T she didn't have much time to pay to us, but turned all her faultfinding power on him. He *flew* to marry a cheap gal from a family of ignorant flashy people. She hardly had time to recompose herself.

When she comes I will meet—but there they are!

Maggie attempts to make a dash for the house, in her shuffling way, but I stay her with my hand. "Come back here," I say. And she stops and tries to dig a well in the sand with her toe.

It is hard to see them clearly through the strong sun. But even the first glimpse of leg out of the car tells me it is Dee. Her feet were always neat-looking, as if God himself had shaped them with a certain style. From the other side of the car comes a short, stocky man. Hair is all over his head a foot long and hanging from his chin like a kinky mule tail. I hear Maggie suck in her breath. "Uhnnnh," is what it sounds like. Like when you see the wriggling end of a snake just in front of your foot on the road. "Uhnnnh."

20   Dee next. A dress down to the ground, in this hot weather. A dress so loud it hurts my eyes. There are yellows and oranges enough to throw back the light of the sun. I feel my whole face warming from the heat waves it throws out. Earrings, too, gold and hanging down to her shoulders. Bracelets dangling and making noises when she moves her arm up to shake the folds of the dress out of her armpits. The dress is loose and flows, and as she walks closer, I like it. I hear Maggie go "Uhnnnh" again. It is her sister's hair. It stands straight up like the wool on a sheep. It is black as night and around the edges are two long pigtails that rope about like small lizards disappearing behind her ears.

"Wa-su-zo-Tean-o!" she says, coming on in that gliding way the dress makes her move. The short stocky fellow with the hair to his navel is all grinning and he follows up with "Asalamalakim, my mother and sister!" He moves to hug Maggie but she falls back, right up against the back of my chair. I feel her trembling there and when I look up I see the perspiration falling off her chin.

"Don't get up," says Dee. Since I am stout it takes something of a push. You can see me trying to move a second or two before I make it. She turns, showing white heels through her sandals, and goes back to the car. Out she peeks next with a Polaroid. She stoops down quickly and lines up picture after picture of me sitting there in front of the house with Maggie cowering behind me. She never takes a shot without making sure the house is included. When a cow comes nibbling around the edge of the yard she snaps it and me and Maggie *and* the house. Then she puts the Polaroid in the back seat of the car, and comes up and kisses me on the forehead.

Meanwhile Asalamalakim is going through the motions with Maggie's hand. Maggie's hand is as limp as a fish, and probably as cold, despite the sweat, and she keeps trying to pull it back. It looks like Asalamalakim wants to shake hands but wants to do it fancy. Or maybe he don't know how people shake hands. Anyhow, he soon gives up on Maggie.

"Well," I say. "Dee."

25   "No, Mama," she says. "Not 'Dee,' Wangero Leewanika Kemanjo!"

"What happened to 'Dee'?" I wanted to know.

"She's dead," Wangero said. "I couldn't bear it any longer being named after the people who oppress me."

"You know as well as me you was named after your aunt Dicie," I said. Dicie is my sister. She named Dee. We called her "Big Dee" after Dee was born.

"But who was *she* named after?" asked Wangero.

30   "I guess after Grandma Dee," I said.

"And who was she named after?" asked Wangero.

"Her mother," I said, and saw Wangero was getting tired. "That's about as far back as I can trace it," I said. Though, in fact, I probably could have carried it back beyond the Civil War through the branches.

"Well," said Asalamalakim, "there you are."

"Uhnnnh," I heard Maggie say.

35   "There I was not," I said, "before 'Dicie' cropped up in our family, so why should I try to trace it that far back?"

He just stood there grinning, looking down on me like somebody inspecting a Model A car. Every once in a while he and Wangero sent eye signals over my head.

"How do you pronounce this name?" I asked.

"You don't have to call me by it if you don't want to," said Wangero.

"Why shouldn't I?" I asked. "If that's what you want us to call you, we'll call you."

40   "I know it might sound awkward at first," said Wangero.

"I'll get used to it," I said. "Ream it out again."

Well, soon we got the name out of the way. Asalamalakim had a name twice as long and three times as hard. After I tripped over it two or three times he told me to just call him Hakim-a-barber. I wanted to ask him was he a barber, but I didn't really think he was, so I didn't ask.

"You must belong to those beef-cattle peoples down the road," I said. They said "Asalamalakim" when they met you, too, but they didn't shake hands. Always too busy: feeding the cattle, fixing the fences, putting up salt-lick shelters, throwing down hay. When the white folks poisoned some of the herd the men stayed up all night with rifles in their hands. I walked a mile and a half just to see the sight.

Hakim-a-barber said, "I accept some of their doctrines, but farming and raising cattle is not my style." (They didn't tell me, and I didn't ask, whether Wangero [Dee] had really gone and married him.)

45   We sat down to eat and right away he said he didn't eat collards and pork was unclean. Wangero, though, went on through the chitlins and corn bread, the greens and everything else. She talked a blue streak over the sweet potatoes. Everything delighted her. Even the fact that we still used the benches her daddy made for the table when we couldn't afford to buy chairs.

"Oh, Mama!" she cried. Then turned to Hakim-a-barber. "I never knew how lovely these benches are. You can feel the rump prints," she said, running her hands underneath her and along the bench. Then she gave a sigh and her hand closed over Grandma Dee's butter dish. "That's it!" she said. "I knew there was something I wanted to ask you if I could have." She jumped up from the table and went over in the corner where the churn stood, the milk in it clabber by now. She looked at the churn and looked at it.

"This churn top is what I need," she said. "Didn't Uncle Buddy whittle it out of a tree you all used to have?"

"Yes," I said.

"Uh huh," she said happily. "And I want the dasher, too."

50   "Uncle Buddy whittle that, too?" asked the barber.

Dee (Wangero) looked up at me.

"Aunt Dee's first husband whittled the dash," said Maggie so low you almost couldn't hear her. "His name was Henry, but they called him Stash."

"Maggie's brain is like an elephant's," Wangero said, laughing. "I can use the churn top as a centerpiece for the alcove table," she said, sliding a plate over the churn, "and I'll think of something artistic to do with the dasher."

When she finished wrapping the dasher the handle stuck out. I took it for a moment in my hands. You didn't even have to look close to see where hands pushing the dasher up and down to make butter had left a kind of sink in the wood. In fact, there were a lot of small sinks; you could see where thumbs and fingers had sunk into the wood. It was beautiful light yellow wood, from a tree that grew in the yard where Big Dee and Stash had lived.

55   After dinner Dee (Wangero) went to the trunk at the foot of my bed and started rifling through it. Maggie hung back in the kitchen over the dishpan. Out came Wangero with two quilts. They had been pieced by Grandma Dee and then Big Dee and me had hung them on the quilt frames on the front porch and quilted them. One was in the Lone Star pattern. The other was Walk Around the Mountain. In both of them were scraps of dresses Grandma Dee had worn fifty and more years ago. Bits and pieces of Grandpa Jarrell's paisley shirts. And one teeny faded blue piece, about the piece of a penny matchbox, that was from Great Grandpa Ezra's uniform that he wore in the Civil War.

"Mama," Wangero said sweet as a bird. "Can I have these old quilts?"

I heard something fall in the kitchen, and a minute later the kitchen door slammed.

"Why don't you take one or two of the others?" I asked. "These old things was just done by me and Big Dee from some tops your grandma pieced before she died."

"No," said Wangero. "I don't want those. They are stitched around the borders by machine."

60   "That's make them last better," I said.

"That's not the point," said Wangero. "These are all pieces of dresses Grandma used to wear. She did all this stitching by hand. Imagine!" She held the quilts securely in her arms, stroking them.

"Some of the pieces, like those lavender ones, come from old clothes her mother handed down to her," I said, moving up to touch the quilts. Dee (Wangero) moved back just enough so that I couldn't reach the quilts. They already belonged to her.

"Imagine!" she breathed again, clutching them closely to her bosom.

"The truth is," I said, "I promised to give them quilts to Maggie, for when she marries John Thomas."

65   She gasped like a bee had stung her.

"Maggie can't appreciate these quilts!" she said. "She'd probably be backward enough to put them to everyday use."

"I reckon she would," I said. "God knows I been saving 'em for long enough with nobody using 'em. I hope she will!" I didn't want to bring up how I had offered Dee (Wangero) a quilt when she went away to college. Then she had told me they were old-fashioned, out of style.

"But they're *priceless!*" she was saying now, furiously; for she has a temper. "Maggie would put them on the bed and in five years they'd be in rags. Less than that!"

"She can always make some more," I said. "Maggie knows how to quilt."

70   Dee (Wangero) looked at me with hatred. "You just will not understand. The point is these quilts, *these* quilts!"

"Well," I said, stumped. "What would *you* do with them?"

"Hang them," she said. As if that was the only thing you *could* do with quilts.

Maggie by now was standing in the door. I could almost hear the sound her feet made as they scraped over each other.

"She can have them, Mama," she said, like somebody used to never winning anything, or having anything reserved for her. "I can 'member Grandma Dee without the quilts."

75   I looked at her hard. She had filled her bottom lip with checkerberry snuff and it gave her face a kind of dopey, hangdog look. It was Grandma Dee and Big Dee who taught her how to quilt herself. She stood there with her scarred hands hidden in the folds of her skirt. She looked at her sister with something like fear but she wasn't mad at her. This was Maggie's portion. This was the way she knew God to work.

When I looked at her like that something hit me in the top of my head and ran down to the soles of my feet. Just like when I'm in church and the spirit of God touches me and I get happy and shout. I did something I never had done before: hugged Maggie to me, then dragged her on into the room, snatched the quilts out of Miss Wangero's hands and dumped them into Maggie's lap. Maggie just sat there on my bed with her mouth open.

"Take one or two of the others," I said to Dee.

But she turned without a word and went out to Hakim-a-barber.

"You just don't understand," she said, as Maggie and I came out to the car.

80   "What don't I understand?" I wanted to know.

"Your heritage," she said. And then she turned to Maggie, kissed her, and said, "You ought to try to make something of yourself, too, Maggie. It's really a new day for us. But from the way you and Mama still live you'd never know it."

She put on some sunglasses that hid everything above the tip of her nose and her chin.

Maggie smiled; maybe at the sunglasses. But a real smile, not scared. After we watched the car dust settle I asked Maggie to bring me a dip of snuff. And then the two of us sat there just enjoying, until it was time to go in the house and go to bed.

[1973]

🖉 TOPICS FOR CRITICAL THINKING AND WRITING

1. Alice Walker wrote the story, but the story is narrated by one of the characters, Mama. How would you characterize Mama?
2. At the end of the story, Dee tells Maggie, "It's really a new day for us. But from the way you and Mama still live you'd never know it." What does Dee mean? And how do Maggie and Mama respond?
3. In paragraph 76 the narrator says, speaking of Maggie, "When I looked at her like that something hit me in the top of my head and ran down to the soles of my feet." What "hit" Mama? That is, what does she understand at this moment that she had not understood before?

4. In "Everyday Use" why does the family conflict focus on who will possess the quilts? Why are the quilts important? What do they symbolize?

JOSÉ ARMAS

Born in 1944, José Armas has been a teacher (at the University of New Mexico and at the University of Albuquerque), publisher, critic, and community organizer. His interest in community affairs won him a fellowship, which in 1974–75 brought him into association with the Urban Planning Department at the Massachusetts Institute of Technology. In 1980 he was awarded a writing fellowship by the National Endowment for the Arts, and he now writes a column on Hispanic affairs for The Albuquerque Journal.

El Tonto del Barrio[1]

Romeo Estrado was called "El Cotorro"[2] because he was always whistling and singing. He made nice music even though his songs were spontaneous compositions made up of words with sounds that he liked but which seldom made any sense. But that didn't seem to bother either Romero or anyone else in the Golden Heights Centro where he lived. Not even the kids made fun of him. It just was not permitted.

Romero had a ritual that he followed almost every day. After breakfast he would get his broom and go up and down the main street of the Golden Heights Centro whistling and singing and sweeping the sidewalks for all the businesses. He would sweep in front of the Tortillería America,[3] the XXX Liquor Store, the Tres Milpas[4] Bar run by Tino Gabaldon, Barelas' Barber Shop, the used furniture store owned by Goldstein, El Centro Market of the Avila family, the Model Cities Office, and Lourdes Printing Store. Then, in the afternoons, he would come back and sit in Barelas' Barber Shop and spend the day looking at magazines and watching and waving to the passing people as he sang and composed his songs without a care in the world.

When business was slow, Barelas would let him sit in the barber's chair. Romero loved it. It was a routine that Romero kept every day except Sundays and Mondays when Barelas' Barber Shop was closed. After a period of years, people in the barrio got used to seeing Romero do his little task of sweeping the sidewalks and sitting in Barelas' Barber Shop. If he didn't show up one day someone assumed the responsibility to go to his house to see if he was ill. People would stop to say hello to Romero on the street and although he never initiated a conversation while he was sober, he always smiled and responded cheerfully to everyone. People passing the barber shop in the afternoons made it a point to wave even though they couldn't see him; they knew he was in there and was expecting some salutation.

---

[1]**El Tonto del Barrio** the barrio dummy (in the United States, a barrio is a Spanish-speaking community)   [2]**El Cotorro** The Parrot   [3]**Tortillería America** America Tortilla Factory   [4]**Tres Milpas** Three Cornfields

When he was feeling real good, Romero would sweep in front of the houses on both sides of the block also. He took his job seriously and took great care to sweep cleanly, between the cracks and even between the sides of buildings. The dirt and small scraps went into the gutter. The bottles and bigger pieces of litter were put carefully in cardboard boxes, ready for the garbage man.

5   If he did it the way he wanted, the work took him the whole morning. And always cheerful—always with some song.

Only once did someone call attention to his work. Frank Avila told him in jest that Romero had forgotten to pick up an empty bottle of wine from his door. Romero was so offended and made such a commotion that it got around very quickly that no one should criticize his work. There was, in fact, no reason to.

Although it had been long acknowledged that Romero was a little "touched," he fit very well into the community. He was a respected citizen.

He could be found at the Tres Milpas Bar drinking his occasional beer in the evenings. Romero had a rivalry going with the Ranchera songs on the jukebox. He would try to outsing the songs using the same melody but inserting his own selection of random words. Sometimes, like all people, he would "bust out" and get drunk.

One could always tell when Romero was getting drunk because he would begin telling everyone that he loved them.

10   "I looov youuu," he would sing to someone and offer to compose them a song.

"Ta bueno, Romero. Ta bueno, ya bete,"[5] they would tell him.

Sometimes when he got too drunk he would crap in his pants and then Tino would make him go home.

Romero received some money from Social Security but it wasn't much. None of the merchants gave him any credit because he would always forget to pay his bills. He didn't do it on purpose, he just forgot and spent his money on something else. So instead, the businessmen preferred to do little things for him occasionally. Barelas would trim his hair when things were slow. The Tortillería America would give him menudo[6] and fresh-made tortillas at noon when he was finished with his sweeping. El Centro Market would give him the overripe fruit and broken boxes of food that no one else would buy. Although it was unspoken and unwritten, there was an agreement that existed between Romero and the Golden Heights Centro. Romero kept the sidewalks clean and the barrio looked after him. It was a contract that worked well for a long time.

Then, when Seferino, Barelas' oldest son, graduated from high school he went to work in the barber shop for the summer. Seferino was a conscientious and sensitive young man and it wasn't long before he took notice of Romero and came to feel sorry for him.

15   One day when Romero was in the shop Seferino decided to act.

"Mira, Romero. Yo te doy 50 centavos por cada día que me barres la banqueta. Fifty cents for every day you sweep the sidewalk for us. Qué te parece?"[7]

---

[5]**Ta bueno, ya bete** OK, now go away   [6]**menudo** tripe soup   [7]**Qué te parece?** How does that strike you?

Romero thought about it carefully.

"Hecho! Done!" he exclaimed. He started for home right away to get his broom.

"Why did you do that for, m'ijo?"[8] asked Barelas.

20   "It don't seem right, Dad. The man works and no one pays him for his work. Everyone should get paid for what they do."

"He don't need no pay. Romero has everything he needs."

"It's not the same, Dad. How would you like to do what he does and be treated the same way? It's degrading the way he has to go around getting scraps and handouts."

"I'm not Romero. Besides you don't know about these things, m'ijo. Romero would be unhappy if his schedule was upset. Right now everyone likes him and takes care of him. He sweeps the sidewalks because he wants something to do, not because he wants money."

"I'll pay him out of my money, don't worry about it then."

25   "The money is not the point. The point is that money will not help Romero. Don't you understand that?"

"Look, Dad. Just put yourself in his place. Would you do it? Would you cut hair for nothing?"

Barelas just knew his son was putting something over on him but he didn't know how to answer. It seemed to make sense the way Seferino explained it. But it still went against his "instinct." On the other hand, Seferino had gone and finished high school. He must know something. There were few kids who had finished high school in the barrio, and fewer who had gone to college. Barelas knew them all. He noted (with some pride) that Seferino was going to be enrolled at Harvard University this year. That must count for something, he thought. Barelas himself had never gone to school. So maybe his son had something there. On the other hand . . . it upset Barelas that he wasn't able to get Seferino to see the issue. How can we be so far apart on something so simple, he thought. But he decided not to say anything else about it.

Romero came back right away and swept the front of Barelas' shop again and put what little dirt he found into the curb. He swept up the gutter, put the trash in a shoe box and threw it in a garbage can.

Seferino watched with pride as Romero went about his job and when he was finished he went outside and shook Romero's hand. Seferino told him he had done a good job. Romero beamed.

30   Manolo was coming into the shop to get his hair cut as Seferino was giving Romero his wages. He noticed Romero with his broom.

"What's going on?" He asked. Barelas shrugged his shoulders. "Qué tiene Romero?[9] Is he sick or something?"

"No, he's not sick," explained Seferino, who had now come inside. He told Manolo the story.

"We're going to make Romero a businessman," said Seferino. "Do you realize how much money Romero would make if everyone paid him just fifty cents a day? Like my dad says, 'Everyone should be able to keep his dignity, no matter how poor.' And he does a job, you know."

"Well, it makes sense," said Manolo.

---

[8]m'ijo (mi hijo), my son   [9]Qué tiene Romero? What's with Romero?

35   "Hey. Maybe I'll ask people to do that," said Seferino. "That way the poor old man could make a decent wage. Do you want to help, Manolo? You can go with me to ask people to pay him."

"Well," said Manolo as he glanced at Barelas, "I'm not too good at asking people for money."

This did not discourage Seferino. He went out and contacted all the businesses on his own, but no one else wanted to contribute. This didn't discourage Seferino either. He went on giving Romero fifty cents a day.

After a while, Seferino heard that Romero had asked for credit at the grocery store. "See, Dad. What did I tell you? Things are getting better for him already. He's becoming his own man. And look. It's only been a couple of weeks." Barelas did not reply.

But then the next week Romero did not show up to sweep any sidewalks. He was around but he didn't do any work for anybody the entire week. He walked around Golden Heights Centro in his best gray work pants and his slouch hat, looking important and making it a point to walk right past the barber shop every little while.

40   Of course, the people in the Golden Heights Centro noticed the change immediately, and since they saw Romero in the street, they knew he wasn't ill. But the change was clearly disturbing the community. They discussed him in the Tortillería America where people got together for coffee, and at the Tres Milpas Bar. Everywhere the topic of conversation was the great change that had come over Romero. Only Barelas did not talk about it.

The following week Romero came into the barber shop and asked to talk with Seferino in private. Barelas knew immediately something was wrong. Romero never initiated a conversation unless he was drunk.

They went into the back room where Barelas could not hear and then Romero informed Seferino, "I want a raise."

"What? What do you mean, a raise? You haven't been around for a week. You only worked a few weeks and now you want a raise?" Seferino was clearly angry but Romero was calm and insistent.

Romero correctly pointed out that he had been sweeping the sidewalks for a long time. Even before Seferino finished high school.

45   "I deserve a raise," he repeated after an eloquent presentation.

Seferino looked coldly at Romero. It was clearly a stand-off.

Then Seferino said, "Look, maybe we should forget the whole thing. I was just trying to help you out and look at what you do."

Romero held his ground. "I helped you out too. No one told me to do it and I did it anyway. I helped you many years."

"Well, let's forget about the whole thing then," said Seferino.

50   "I quit then," said Romero.

"Quit?" exclaimed Seferino as he laughed at Romero.

"Quit! I quit!" said Romero as he walked out the front of the shop past Barelas, who was cutting a customer's hair.

Seferino came out shaking his head and laughing.

"Can you imagine that old guy?"

55   Barelas did not seem too amused. He felt he could have predicted that something bad like this would happen.

Romero began sweeping the sidewalks again the next day with the exception that when he came to the barber shop he would go around it and continue sweeping the rest of the sidewalks. He did this for the rest of the week. And the following Tuesday he began sweeping the sidewalk all the way up to the shop and then pushing the trash to the sidewalk in front of the barber shop. Romero then stopped coming to the barber shop in the afternoon.

The barrio buzzed with fact and rumor about Romero. Tino commented that Romero was not singing anymore. Even if someone offered to buy him a beer he wouldn't sing. Frank Avila said the neighbors were complaining because he was leaving his TV on loud the whole day and night. He still greeted people but seldom smiled. He had run up a big bill at the liquor store and when the manager stopped his credit, he caught Romero stealing bottles of whiskey. He was also getting careless about his dress. He didn't shave and clean like he used to. Women complained that he walked around in soiled pants, that he smelled bad. Even one of the little kids complained that Romero had kicked his puppy, but that seemed hard to believe.

Barelas felt terrible. He felt responsible. But he couldn't convince Seferino that what he had done was wrong. Barelas himself stopped going to the Tres Milpas Bar after work to avoid hearing about Romero. Once he came across Romero on the street and Barelas said hello but with a sense of guilt. Romero responded, avoiding Barelas' eyes and moving past him awkwardly and quickly. Romero's behavior continued to get erratic and some people started talking about having Romero committed.

"You can't do that," said Barelas when he was presented with a petition.

60   "He's flipped," said Tino, who made up part of the delegation circulating the petition. "No one likes Romero more than I do, you know that Barelas."

"But he's really crazy," said Frank Avila.

"He was crazy before. No one noticed," pleaded Barelas.

"But it was a crazy we could depend on. Now he just wants to sit on the curb and pull up the women's skirts. It's terrible. The women are going crazy. He's also running into the street stopping the traffic. You see how he is. What choice do we have?"

"It's for his own good," put in one of the workers from the Model Cities Office. Barelas dismissed them as outsiders. Seferino was there and wanted to say something but a look from Barelas stopped him.

65   "We just can't do that," insisted Barelas. "Let's wait. Maybe he's just going through a cycle. Look. We've had a full moon recently, qué no?[10] That must be it. You know how the moon affects people in his condition."

"I don't know," said Tino. "What if he hurts. . . . "

"He's not going to hurt anyone," cut in Barelas.

"No, Barelas. I was going to say, what if he hurts himself. He has no one at home. I'd say, let him come home with me for a while but you know how stubborn he is. You can't even talk to him any more."

"He gives everyone the finger when they try to pull him out of the traffic," said Frank Avila. "The cops have missed him, but it won't be long before they see him doing some of his antics and arrest him. Then what? Then the poor guy is in real trouble."

70   "Well, look," said Barelas. "How many names you got on the list?"

[10]**qué no?** right?

Tino responded slowly, "Well, we sort of wanted you to start off the list."

"Let's wait a while longer," said Barelas. "I just know that Romero will come around. Let's wait just a while, okay?"

No one had the heart to fight the issue and so they postponed the petition.

There was no dramatic change in Romero even though the full moon had completed its cycle. Still, no one initiated the petition again and then in the middle of August Seferino left for Cambridge to look for housing and to register early for school. Suddenly everything began to change again. One day Romero began sweeping the entire sidewalk again. His spirits began to pick up and his strange antics began to disappear.

75   At the Tortillería America the original committee met for coffee and the talk turned to Romero.

"He's going to be all right now," said a jubilant Barelas. "I guarantee it."

"Well, don't hold your breath yet," said Tino. "The full moon is coming up again."

"Yeah," said Frank Avila dejectedly.

When the next full moon was in force the group was together again drinking coffee and Tino asked, "Well, how's Romero doing?"

80   Barelas smiled and said, "Well. Singing songs like crazy."

[1982]

 ## TOPICS FOR CRITICAL THINKING AND WRITING

1. What sort of man do you think Barelas is? In your response take account of the fact that the townspeople "sort of want" Barelas "to start off the list" of petitioners seeking to commit Romero.
2. The narrator, introducing the reader to Seferino, tells us that "Seferino was a conscientious and sensitive young man." Do you agree? Why, or why not?
3. What do you make of the last line of the story?
4. Do you think this story could take place in almost any community? If you did not grow up in a barrio, could it take place in your community?

CHAPTER 4

Other Kinds of Writing about Literature

SUMMARY

The essay on "The Story of an Hour" in Chapter 3 does not include a *summary* because the writer knew that all of her readers were thoroughly familiar with Chopin's story. Sometimes, however, it is advisable to summarize the work you are writing about, thus reminding a reader who has not read the work recently, or even informing a reader who may never have read the work. A review of a new work of literature or of a new film, for instance, usually includes a summary, on the assumption that readers are unfamiliar with it.

A summary is a brief restatement or condensation of the plot. Consider this **summary** of Chopin's "The Story of an Hour."

> A newspaper office reports that Brently Mallard has been killed in a railroad accident. When the news is gently broken to Mrs. Mallard by her sister Josephine, Mrs. Mallard weeps wildly and then shuts herself up in her room, where she sinks into an armchair. Staring dully through the window, she sees the signs of spring, and then an unnameable sensation possesses her. She tries to reject it but finally abandons herself to it. Renewed, she exults in her freedom, in the thought that at last the days will be her own. She finally comes out of the room, embraces her sister, and descends the stairs. A moment later her husband--who in fact had not been in the accident--enters. Mrs. Mallard dies-- of the joy that kills, according to the doctors' diagnosis.

Here are a few principles that govern summaries:

1. A summary is **much briefer than the original.** It is not a paraphrase—a word-by-word translation of someone's words into your own. A paraphrase is usually at least as long as the original, whereas a summary is rarely longer than one-fourth of the original and is usually much shorter. A novel may be summarized in a few paragraphs, or even in one paragraph.

2. A summary **usually achieves its brevity by omitting almost all of the concrete details of the original** and by omitting minor characters and episodes. Notice that the summary of "The Story of an Hour" omits the friend of the family, omits specifying the signs of spring, and omits the business of the sister imploring Mrs. Mallard to open the door.

3. A summary is **as accurate as possible,** given the limits of space. It has no value if it misrepresents the point of the original.

4. A summary is **normally written in the present tense.** Thus "A newspaper office reports . . . , Mrs. Mallard weeps . . . ."

5. If the summary is brief (say, fewer than 250 words), it **may be given as a single paragraph.** If you are summarizing a long work, you may feel that a longer summary is needed. In this case your reader will be grateful to you if you divide the summary into paragraphs. As you draft your summary, you may find **natural divisions.** For instance, the scene of the story may change midway, providing you with the opportunity to use two paragraphs. Or you may want to summarize a five-act play in five paragraphs.

6. The writer of a summary **need not make the points in the same order as that of the original.** If the writer of an essay has delayed revealing the main point until the end of the essay, the summary may rearrange the order, stating the main point first. Occasionally, for instance if the original author has presented an argument in a disorderly or confusing sequence, one writes a summary in order to disengage the author's argument from its confusing structure.

7. Because a summary is openly based on someone else's views, it is usually **not necessary to use quotation marks** around key words or phrases from the original. Nor is it necessary to repeat "he says" or "she goes on to prove." From the opening sentence of a summary it should be clear that what follows is what the original author says.

Summaries have their place in essays, but remember that a summary is not an analysis; it is only a summary.

Paraphrase

A **paraphrase** is a restatement—a sort of translation in the same language—of material that may in its original form be somewhat obscure to a reader. A native speaker of English will not need a paraphrase of "Thirty days hath September," though a non-native speaker might be puzzled by two things, the meaning of *hath* and the inverted word order. For such a reader, "September has thirty days" would be a helpful paraphrase.

Although a paraphrase seeks to make clear the gist of the original, if the original is even a little more complex than "Thirty days hath September" the paraphrase will—in the process of clarifying something—lose something, since the substitution of one word for another will change the meaning. For instance, "Shut up" and "Be quiet" do not say exactly the same thing; the former (in addition to asking for quiet) says that the speaker is rude, or perhaps it says that the speaker feels little respect for the auditor, but the paraphrase loses all of this.

Still, a paraphrase can be helpful as a first step in helping a reader to understand a line that includes an obsolete word or phrase, or a word or phrase that is current only in one region. For instance, in a poem by Emily Dickinson (1830–86), the following line appears:

The sun engrossed the East. . . .

"Engrossed" here has (perhaps among other meanings) a special commercial meaning, "to acquire most or all of a commodity; to monopolize the market," so a paraphrase of the line might go thus:

The sun took over all of the east.

(It's worth mentioning, parenthetically, that you should have at your elbow a good desk dictionary, such as *The American Heritage Dictionary of the English Language,* third edition. Writers—especially poets—expect you to pay close attention to every word. If a word puzzles you, look it up.)

Idioms, as well as words, may puzzle a reader. The Anglo-Irish poet William Butler Yeats (1865–1939) begins one poem with

The friends that have it I do wrong. . . .

Because the idiom "to have it" (meaning "to believe that," "to think that") is unfamiliar to many American readers today, a discussion of the poem might include a paraphrase—a rewording, a translation into more familiar language, such as

The friends who think that I am doing the wrong thing. . . .

Perhaps the rest of the poem is immediately clear, but in any case here is the entire poem, followed by a paraphrase:

The friends that have it I do wrong
When ever I remake a song,
Should know what issue is at stake:
It is myself that I remake.

Now for the paraphrase:

The friends who think that I am doing the wrong thing when I revise one of my poems should be informed what the important issue is; I'm not just revising a poem—rather, I am revising myself (my thoughts, feelings).

Here, as with any paraphrase, the meaning is not translated exactly; there is some distortion. For instance, if "song" in the original is clarified by "poem" in the paraphrase, it is also altered; the paraphrase loses the sense of lyricism that is implicit in "song." Further, "Should know what issue is at stake" (in the original) is ambiguous. Does "should" mean "ought," as in (for instance) "You should know better than to speak so rudely," or does it mean "deserve to be informed," as in "You ought to know that I am thinking about quitting"?

Granted that a paraphrase may miss a great deal, a paraphrase often helps you, or your reader, to understand at least the surface meaning, and the act of paraphrasing will usually help you to understand at least some of the implicit meaning. Furthermore, a paraphrase makes you see that the original writer's words (if the work is a good one) are exactly right, better than any words we might substitute. It becomes clear that the thing said in the original—not only the rough "idea" expressed but the precise tone with which it is expressed—is a sharply defined experience.

LITERARY RESPONSE

Of course anything that you write about a work of literature is a response, even if it seems to be as matter-of-fact as a summary. It's sometimes useful to compare your summary with that of a classmate. You may be surprised to find that the two summaries differ considerably—though when you think about it, it isn't really surprising. Two different people are saying what they think is the gist of the work, and their views are inevitably shaped, at least to some degree, by such things as their gender, their ethnicity, and their experience (including, of course, their *literary* experience).

But when we talk about writing a response, we usually mean something more avowedly personal, something (for instance) like an entry in a journal, where the writer may set forth an emotional response, perhaps relating the work to one of his or her own experiences. (On journals, see pp. 17–18.)

Writing a Literary Response

You may want to rewrite a literary work, for instance by giving it a different ending or by writing an epilogue in which you show the characters 20 years later. (We have already talked about the possibility of writing a sequel to Chopin's "Ripe Figs," or writing a letter from Babette to Mama-Nainaine, or writing Babette's memoirs.) Or you might want to rewrite the work by presenting the characters from a somewhat different point of view. The student who in an essay on Thurber's "The Secret Life of Walter Mitty" argued that Mitty *needed* someone very much like Mrs. Mitty might well have rewritten Thurber's story along those lines. The fun for the reader would of course reside largely in hearing the story reinterpreted, in (so to speak) seeing the story turned inside out.

A Story Based on a Story

Here is an example, written by Lola Lee Loveall for a course taught by Diana Muir at Solano Community College. Ms. Loveall's story is a response to Kate Chopin's "The Story of an Hour" (p. 12). Notice that Loveall's first sentence is close to her source—a good way to get started, but by no means the only way; notice, too, that elsewhere in her story she occasionally echoes Chopin—for instance, in the references to the treetops, the sparrows, and the latchkey. A reader enjoys detecting these echoes.

What is especially interesting, however, is that before she conceived her story Loveall presumably said to herself something like, "Well, Chopin's story is superb, but suppose we shift the focus a bit. Suppose we think about what it would be like, *from the husband's point of view,* to live with a woman who suffered from 'heart trouble,' a person whom one had to treat with 'great care' " (Chopin's words, in the first sentence of "The Story of an Hour"). "And what about Mrs. Mallard's sister, Josephine—so considerate of Mrs. Mallard? What, exactly, would *Mr.* Mallard think of her? Wouldn't he see her as a pain in the neck? And what might he be prompted to do? That is, how might this character in this situation respond?" And so Loveall's characters and her plot began to take shape. As part of the game, she committed herself to writing a plot that, in its broad outline, resembled Chopin's by being highly ironic. But read it yourself.

Lola Lee Loveall

English 6

The Ticket

(A Different View of "The Story of an Hour")

Knowing full well his wife was afflicted with heart trouble, Brently Mallard wondered how he was going to break the news about the jacket. As he strode along his boots broke through the shallow crust from the recent rain, and dust kicked up from the well-worn wagon road came up to flavor his breathing. At least, the gentle spring rain had settled the dusty powder even as it had sprinkled his stiffly starched shirt which was already dampened from the exertion of stamping along. The strenuous pace he set himself to cover the intervening miles home helped him regain his composure. Mr. Brently Mallard was always calm, cool, and confident.

However, he hadn't been this morning when he stepped aboard the train, took off his jacket and folded it neatly beside him, and settled in his seat on the westbound train. He had been wildly excited. Freedom was his. He was Free! He was off for California, devil take the consequences! He would be his old self again, let the chips fall where they may. And he would have been well on his way, too, if

that accursed ticket agent hadn't come bawling out,
"Mr. Mallard, you left your ticket on the counter!"
just when Mallard himself had spied that nosy Jan
Ardan bidding her sister goodbye several car lengths
down the depot. How could he be so unfortunate as to
run into them both twice this morning? Earlier, they
had come into the bank just as the banker had
extended the thick envelope.

"You understand, this is just an advance against
the estate for a while?"

Only Mallard's persuasiveness could have
extracted that amount from the cagey old moneybags.
Mallard had carefully tucked it into his inside
pocket.

This was the kind of spring day to fall in
love--or lure an adventurer to the top of the next
hill. Sparrows hovered about making happy sounds.
Something about their movements reminded Mallard of
his wife--quick, fluttering, then darting away.

He had loved her at first for her delicate
ways. They had made a dashing pair--he so dark and
worldly, she so fragile and fair--but her delicacy
was a trap, for it disguised the heart trouble, bane
of his life. Oh, he still took her a sip of brandy
in bed in the morning as the doctor had suggested,
although, of course, it wasn't his bed anymore. He
had moved farther down the hall not long after
her sister, Josephine, came to help, quick to come
when Mrs. Mallard called, even in the middle of
the night. After one such sudden appearance one
night--"I thought I heard you call"--he had given up

even sharing the same bed with his wife, although
there had been little real sharing there for some
time.

   "No children!" the doctor had cautioned.

   Mallard concentrated harder on the problem of
the missing jacket. What to say? She would notice.
Maybe not right away, but she would be aware. Oh, he
knew Louise's reaction. She would apparently take the
news calmly, then make a sudden stab toward her side
with her delicate hands, then straighten and walk
away--but not before he observed. A new jacket would
cost money. Discussing money made the little drama
happen more often, so now Mr. Mallard handled all the
financial affairs, protecting her the best he could.
After all, it was her inheritance, and he took great
care with it, but there were the added costs:
doctors, Josephine living with them, the medications,
even his wife's brandy. Why, he checked it daily to
be sure it was the proper strength. Of course, a man
had to have a few pleasures, even if the cards did
seem to fall against him more often than not. He
manfully kept trying.

   Everyone has a limit, though, and Mr. Mallard
had reached his several days ago when the doctor had
cautioned him again.

   "She may go on like she is for years, or she may
just keel over any time. However, the chances are she
will gradually go downhill and need continual care.
It is impossible to tell."

   Mallard could not face "gradually go downhill."
His manhood revolted against it. He was young, full

of life. Let Josephine carry the chamber pot! After Louise's demise (whenever that occurred!) the simple estate which she had inherited reverted to Josephine. Let her earn it. Also, good old friend Richards was always about with a suggestion here or a word of comfort there for Louise. They'd really not care too much if Mallard were a long time absent.

As he drew nearer his home, Mallard continued to try to calm his composure, which was difficult for he kept hearing the sound of the train wheels as it pulled away, jacket, envelope, and all, right before his panic-stricken eyes: CALIFORNIA; California; california; california.

DUTY! It was his duty not to excite Louise. As he thought of duty he unconsciously squared his drooping shoulders, and the image of Sir Galahad flitted across his mind.

The treetops were aglow in the strange afterlight of the storm. A shaft of sunlight shot through the leaves and fell upon his face. He had come home.

He opened the front door with the latchkey. Fortunately, it had been in his pants pocket.

Later, the doctors did not think Mr. Mallard's reaction unusual, even when a slight smile appeared on the bereaved husband's face. Grief causes strange reactions.

"He took it like a man," they said.

Only later, when the full significance of his loss reached him, did he weep.

PARODY

One special kind of response is the **parody**, a comic form that imitates the original in a humorous way. It is a caricature in words. For instance, a parody may
imitate the style of the original—let's say, short, punchy sentences—but apply
this style to a subject that the original author would not be concerned with.
Thus, because Ernest Hemingway often wrote short, simple sentences about
tough guys engaged in butch activities such as hunting, fishing, and boxing, par-
odists of Hemingway are likely to use the same style, but for their subject they
may choose something like opening the mail or preparing a cup of tea.

We once heard on the radio a parody of an announcer doing a baseball
game. It went something like this:

> Well, here's Bill Shakespeare now, approaching the desk. Like so
> many other writers, Bill likes to work at a desk. In fact, just about every
> writer we know writes at a desk, but every writer has a particular way
> of approaching the desk and sitting at it. Bill is sitting down now; now
> he's adjusting the chair, moving it forward a little. Oh, he's just pushed
> the chair back an inch or two. He likes his chair to be just right. Now
> he's picking up a pen. It's a gray quill. I think it's the pen he uses when
> he writes a tragedy, and he's due for a tragedy—of his last five plays,
> only one was a tragedy, and two were comedies and two were history
> plays. But you never can tell with Bill, or "The Bard" as his fans call him.
> Some people call him "The Swan of Avon," but I'm told that he really
> hates that. Well, he's at the desk, and, you know, in circumstances like
> these, he might even sneak in a sonnet or two. Oh, he's put down the
> gray quill, and now he's trying a white one. Oh boy, oh boy, he's writ-
> ten a *word. No,* he's going for *a whole sentence!"*

Parodies are, in a way, critical, but they are usually affectionate too. In the best
parodies one feels that the writer admires the author being parodied. The distinguished sociologist Daniel Bell wrote a deliberate parody of sociological writing.
It begins thus:

> The purpose of this scene is to present a taxonomic dichotomiza-
> tion which would allow for unilinear comparison. In this fashion we
> could hope to distinguish the relevant variables which determine the
> functional specifities of social movements.

H. L. Mencken, who had a love-hate relationship with what he called the Great
American Booboisie, wrote a parody in which he set forth the Declaration of Independence as it might have been written (or spoken) by Joe Sixpack in the
mid twentieth century. Here the target is not the original document but the
twentieth-century American. The original document, you will remember, begins
in this way:

> When in the Course of human events, it becomes necessary for one
> people to dissolve the political bands which have connected them with
> another, and to assume among the Powers of the earth, the separate
> and equal station to which the Laws of Nature and of Nature's God en-
> title them, a decent respect to the opinions of mankind requires that
> they should declare the causes which impel them to the separation.

Now for Mencken's version:

> When things get so balled up that the people of a country got to cut loose from some other country, and go it on their own hook, without asking no permission from nobody, excepting maybe God Almighty, then they ought to let everybody know why they done it, so that everybody can see they are not trying to put nothing over on nobody.

REVIEWING A DRAMATIC PRODUCTION

A review, for instance of a play or of a novel, also is a response, since it normally includes an evaluation of the work, but at least at first glance it may seem to be an analytic essay. We'll talk about a review of a production of a play, but you can easily adapt what we say to a review of a book.

A review requires analytic skill, but it is not identical with an analysis. First of all, a reviewer normally assumes that the reader is unfamiliar with the production being reviewed, and unfamiliar with the play if the play is not a classic. Thus, the first paragraph usually provides a helpful introduction, along these lines:

> Marsha Norman's recent play, 'night, Mother, a tragedy with only two actors and one set, shows us a woman's preparation for suicide. Jesse has concluded that she no longer wishes to live, and so she tries to put her affairs into order, which chiefly means preparing her rather uncomprehending mother to get along without her.

Inevitably some retelling of the plot is necessary if the play is new, and a summary of a sentence or two is acceptable even for a familiar play, but the review will chiefly be concerned with

1. Describing,
2. Analyzing, and, especially,
3. Evaluating.

(By the way, don't confuse description with analysis. Description tells what something—for instance, the set or the costumes—looks like; analysis tells us how it works, what it adds up to, what it contributes to the total effect.) If the play is new, much of the evaluation may center on the play itself, but if the play is a classic, the evaluation probably will be devoted chiefly to the acting, the set, and the direction.

Other points:

1. **Save the playbill;** it will give you the names of the actors, and perhaps a brief biography of the author, a synopsis of the plot, and a photograph of the set, all of which may be helpful.
2. **Draft your review as soon as possible,** while the performance is still fresh in your mind. If you can't draft it immediately after seeing the play, at least jot down some notes about the setting and the staging, the acting, and the audience's responses.

3. If possible, **read the play**—ideally, before the performance and again after it.

4. **In your first draft, don't worry about limitations of space;** write as long a review as you can, putting down everything that comes to mind. Later you can cut it to the required length, retaining only the chief points and the necessary supporting details. But in your first draft try to produce a fairly full record of the performance and your response to it, so that a day or two later, when you revise, you won't have to trust a fading memory for details.

A Sample Review

If you read reviews of plays in *Time, Newsweek,* or a newspaper, you will soon develop a sense of what reviews do. The following example, an undergraduate's review of a college production of *Macbeth,* is typical except in one respect: Reviews of new plays, as we have already suggested, customarily include a few sentences summarizing the plot and classifying the play (a tragedy, a farce, a rock musical, or whatever), perhaps briefly putting it in the context of the author's other works. Because *Macbeth* is so widely known, however, the writer of this review chose not to risk offending her readers by telling them that *Macbeth* is a tragedy by Shakespeare.

Preliminary Jottings   During the two intermissions and immediately after the end of the performance, the reviewer made a few jottings, which the next day she rewrote thus:

```
Compare with last year's Midsummer Night's Dream
Set: barren;
    pipe framework at rear. Duncan exits on it.
      Useful?
witches: powerful, not funny
 stage: battlefield? barren land?)
    costume: earth-colored rags
      they seduce--even caress--Mac.
Macbeth
   witches caress him
    strong; also gentle (with Lady M)
Lady Macb.
    sexy in speech about unsexing her
    too attractive? Prob. ok
Banquo's ghost: naturalistic; covered with blood
Duncan: terrible; worst actor except for Lady
    Macduff's boy
costumes: leather, metal; only Duncan in robes
pipe framework used for D, and murder of Lady Macduff)
forest; branches unrealistic; stylized? or cheesy?
```

The Finished Version   The published review appears below, accompanied by some marginal notes in which we comment on its strengths.

Title implies thesis

An Effective *Macbeth*

Opening paragraph is informative, letting the reader know the reviewer's overall attitude

Macbeth at the University Theater is a thoughtful and occasionally exciting production, partly because the director, Mark Urice, has trusted Shakespeare and has not imposed a gimmick on the play. The characters do not wear cowboy costumes as they did in last year's production of *A Midsummer Night's Dream*.

Reviewer promptly turns to a major issue

Probably the chief problem confronting a director of *Macbeth* is how to present the witches so that they are powerful supernatural forces and not silly things that look as though they came from a Halloween party. Urice gives us ugly but not absurdly grotesque witches, and he introduces them most effectively. The stage seems to be a bombed-out battlefield littered with rocks and great chunks of earth, but some of these begin to stir—the earth seems to come alive—and the clods move, unfold, and become the witches, dressed in brown and dark gray rags. The suggestion is that the witches are a part of nature, elemental forces that can hardly be escaped. This effect is increased by the moans and creaking noises that they make, all of which could be comic but which in this production are impressive.

First sentence of this paragraph provides an effective transition

The witches' power over Macbeth is further emphasized by their actions. When the witches first meet Macbeth, they encircle him, touch him, caress him, even embrace him, and he seems helpless, almost their plaything. Moreover, in the scene in which he imagines that he sees a dagger, the director has arranged for one of the witches to appear, stand near Macbeth, and guide his hand toward the invisible dagger. This is, of course, not in the text, but the interpretation is reasonable rather than intrusive. Finally, near the end of the play, just before Macduff kills Macbeth, a witch appears and laughs at Macbeth as Macduff explains that he was not "born of woman." There is no doubt that throughout the tragedy Macbeth has been a puppet of the witches.

Paragraph begins with a broad assertion and then offers supporting details.

Stephen Beers (Macbeth) and Tina Peters (Lady Macbeth) are excellent. Beers is sufficiently brawny to be convincing as a battlefield hero, but he also speaks the lines sensitively, so the audience feels that in addition to being a hero, he is a man of gentleness.

Reference to a particular scene

One can believe Lady Macbeth when she says that she fears he is "too full o' the milk of human kindness" to murder Duncan. Lady Macbeth is especially effective in the scene in which she asks the spirits to "unsex her." During this speech she is reclining on a bed and as she delivers the lines she becomes increasingly sexual in her bodily motions, deriving excitement from her own stimulating words. Her attachment to Macbeth is strongly sexual, and so is his attraction to her. The scene when she persuades him to kill Duncan ends with their passionately embracing. The strong attraction of each for the other, so evident in the early part of the play, disappears after the murder, when Macbeth keeps his distance from Lady Macbeth and does not allow her to touch him. The acting of the other performers is effective, except for John Berens (Duncan), who recites the lines mechanically and seems not to take much account of their meaning.

Description, but also analysis

The set consists of a barren plot, at the rear of which stands a spidery framework of piping of the sort used by construction companies, supporting a catwalk. This framework fits with the costumes (lots of armor, leather, heavy boots), suggesting a sort of elemental, primitive, and somewhat sadistic world. The catwalk, though effectively used when Macbeth goes off to murder Duncan (whose room is presumably upstairs and offstage), is not much used in later scenes. For the most part it is an interesting piece of scenery but not otherwise helpful. For instance, there is no reason why the scene with Macduff's wife and children is staged on it. The costumes are not in any way Scottish—no plaids—but in several scenes the sound of a bagpipe is heard, adding another weird or primitive tone to the production.

Concrete details to support evaluation

Summary

This *Macbeth* appeals to the eye, the ear, and the mind. The director has given us a unified production that makes sense and that is faithful to the spirit of Shakespeare's play.

Documentation

Work Cited

Macbeth. By William Shakespeare. Dir. Mark Urice. With Stephen Beers, Tina Peters, and John Berens. University Theater, Medford, MA. 3 Mar. 1990.

The marginal notes call attention to certain qualities in the review, but three additional points should be made:

1. The reviewer's feelings and evaluations are clearly expressed, not in such expressions as "furthermore I feel," and "it is also my opinion," but in such expressions as "a thoughtful and occasionally exciting production," "excellent," and "appeals to the eye, the ear, and the mind."
2. The evaluations are supported by details. For instance, the evaluation that the witches are effectively presented is supported by a brief description of their appearance.
3. The reviewer is courteous, even when (as in the discussion of the cat-walk, in the next-to-last paragraph) she is talking about aspects of the production she doesn't care for.

PART TWO

Up Close:

*Thinking
about
Literary
Forms*

CHAPTER 5

Reading (and Writing about) Essays

The word *essay* entered the English language in 1597, when Francis Bacon called a small book of ten short prose pieces *Essays*. Bacon borrowed the word from Michel de Montaigne, a French writer who in 1580 had published some short prose pieces under the title *Essais*—that is, "testings," or "attempts," from the French verb *essayer,* "to try." Montaigne's title indicated that his graceful and personal jottings—the fruit of pleasant study and meditation—were not fully thought-out treatises but rather sketches that could be amplified and amended.

If you keep a journal, you are working in Montaigne's tradition. You jot down your tentative thoughts, perhaps your responses to a work of literature, partly to find out what you think and how you feel. Montaigne said, in the preface to his book, "I am myself the subject of my book," and in all probability you are the real subject of your journal. Your entries—your responses to other writers and your reflections on those responses—require you to examine yourself.

SOME KINDS OF ESSAYS

If you have already taken a course in composition (or even if you haven't), you are probably familiar with the chief kinds of essays. Essays are usually classified—roughly, of course—along the following lines: meditation (or speculation or reflection), argument (or persuasion), exposition (or information), narration, and description.

Of these, the **meditative** (or **speculative** or **reflective**) **essay** is the closest to Montaigne. In a meditative essay, the writer seems chiefly concerned with exploring an idea or a feeling. The organization usually seems casual, not a careful and evident structure but a free flow of thought—what the Japanese (who wrote with brush and ink) called "following the brush." The essayist is thinking, but he or she is not especially concerned with arguing a case, or even with being logical. We think along with the essayist, chiefly because we find the writer's tentative thoughts engaging. Of course the writer may in the long run be pressing a point, advancing an argument, but the emphasis is on the free play of mind, not on an orderly and logical analysis.

In the **argumentative** (or **persuasive**) **essay,** the organization probably is apparent, and it is reasonable: for instance, the essay may announce a problem, define some terms, present and refute solutions that writer considers to be inadequate, and then, by way of a knockdown ending, offer what the writer considers to be the correct solution.

The **expository essay,** in which the writer is chiefly concerned with giving information (for instance on how to annotate a text, or how to read a poem, or how to use a word processor), ordinarily has an equally clear organization. A clear organization is necessary in such an essay because the reader is reading not in order to come into contact with an interesting mind that may keep doubling back on its thinking (as in a meditative essay), and not in order to come to a decision about some controversial issue (as in an argumentative essay), but in order to gain information.

Narrative and **descriptive essays** usually really are largely meditative essays. For instance, a narrative essay may recount some happening—often a bit of autobiography—partly to allow the writer and the reader to meditate on it. Similarly, a description, let's say of a spider spinning a web or of children playing in the street, usually turns out to be offered not so much as information—it thus is unlike the account of how to annotate a text—but rather as something for the writer and reader to enjoy in itself, and perhaps to think further about.

Of course most essays are not pure specimens. For instance, an informative essay, let's say on how to use a word processing program on a computer, may begin with a paragraph that seeks to persuade you to use this particular software. Or it might being with a very brief narrative, an anecdote of a student who switched from program X to program Y, again in order to persuade the reader to use this software (Y, of course). Similarly, an argument—and probably most of the essays that you write in English courses will be arguments advancing a thesis concerning the meaning or structure of a literary work—may include some exposition, for instance a very brief summary in order to remind the reader of the gist of the work you will be arguing about.

THE ESSAYIST'S PERSONA

Many of the essays that give readers the most pleasure are, like entries in a journal, chiefly reflective. An essay of this kind sets forth the writer's attitudes or states of mind, and the reader's interest in the essay is almost entirely in the way the writer sees things. It's not so much *what* the writers see and say as *how* they say what they see. Even in essays that are narrative—that is, in essays that recount events, such as a bit of biography—our interest is more in the essayists' *responses* to the events than in the events themselves. When we read an essay, we almost say, "So that's how it feels to be you," and "Tell me more about the way you see things." The bit of history is less important than the memorable presence of the writer.

When you read an essay in this chapter or in a later chapter, try to imagine the kind of person who wrote it, the kind of person who seems to be speaking it. Then slowly reread the essay, noticing *how* the writer conveyed this personality or persona or "voice" (even while he or she was writing about a topic "out there"). The writer's persona may be revealed by common or uncommon words, for example, by short or long sentences, by literal or figurative language, or by familiar or erudite examples.

Let's take a simple, familiar example of words that establish a persona. Lincoln begins the Gettysburg Address with "Four score and seven years ago." He might have said "Eighty-seven years ago"—but the language would have lacked the biblical echo, and the persona would thus have been that of an ordinary person rather than that of a man who has about him something of the tone of an Old Testament prophet. This religious tone is entirely fitting, since President Lincoln was speaking at the dedication of a cemetery for "these hallowed dead" and was urging the members of his audience to give all of their energies to ensure that the dead men had not died in vain. By such devices as the choice of words, the length of sentences, and the sorts of evidence offered, an author sounds to the reader solemn or agitated or witty or genial or severe. If you are familiar with Martin Luther King's "I Have a Dream," you may recall that he begins the piece (originally it was a speech, delivered at the Lincoln Memorial on the one-hundredth anniversary of Lincoln's Emancipation Proclamation) with these words: "Five score years ago. . . ." King is deliberately echoing Lincoln's words, partly in tribute to Lincoln, but also to help establish himself as the spiritual descendent of Lincoln and, further back, of the founders of the Judeo-Christian tradition.

Tone

Only by reading closely can we hear in the mind's ear the writer's tone— friendly, or bitter, or indignant, or ironic (characterized by wry understatement or overstatement). Perhaps you have heard the line from Owen Wister's novel *The Virginian:* "When you call me that, smile!" Words spoken with a smile mean something different from the same words forced through clenched teeth. But while speakers can communicate, or, we might say, can guide the responses of their audience, by body language and by gestures, by facial expressions and by changes in tone of voice, writers have only words in ink on paper. As a writer, you are learning control of tone as you learn to take pains in your choice of words, in the way you arrange sentences, and even in the punctuation marks you may find yourself changing in your final draft. These skills will pay off doubly if you apply them to your reading, by putting yourself in the place of the writer whose work you are reading. As a reader, you must make some effort to "hear" the writer's tone as part of the meaning the words communicate. Skimming is not adequate to that task. Thinking carefully about the works in this book means, first of all, reading them carefully, listening for the sound of the speaking voice, so that you can respond to the persona—the personality or character the author presents in the essay.

Consider the following paragraph from the middle of "Black Men and Public Space," a short essay by Brent Staples. Staples is talking about growing up in a tough neighborhood. Of course the paragraph is only a small example; the tone depends, finally, on the entire essay, which we will print in a moment.

As a boy, I saw countless tough guys locked away; I have since buried several, too. They were babies, really—a teenage cousin, a brother of twenty-two, a childhood friend in his mid-twenties—all gone down in episodes of bravado played out in the streets. I came to doubt the virtues of intimidation early on. I chose, perhaps unconsciously, to remain a shadow—timid, but a survivor.

Judging only from these few lines, what sense of Staples do we get? Perhaps you will agree that we can probably say something along these lines:

1. He is relatively quiet and gentle. We sense this not simply because he tells us that he was "timid" but because (at least in this passage) he does not raise his voice either in a denunciation of white society for creating a system that produces black violence or in a denunciation of those blacks of his youth who engaged in violence.
2. He is perceptive; he sees that the "tough guys," despite the fact that some were in their twenties, were babies; their bravado was infantile and destructive.
3. He speaks with authority; he is giving a firsthand report.
4. He doesn't claim to be especially shrewd; he modestly says that he may have "unconsciously" adopted the behavior that enabled him to survive.
5. In saying that he is a "survivor" he displays a bit of wry humor. The usual image of a "survivor" is a guy in a Banana Republic outfit, gripping a knife, someone who survived a dog-eat-dog world by being tougher than the others. But Staples almost comically says he is a "survivor" who is "timid."

If your responses to the paragraph are somewhat different, jot them down and in a few sentences try to explain them.

Pre-writing

Identifying the Topic and Thesis   Although we have emphasized the importance of the essayist's personality, essayists also make a point. They have a thesis or argument, and an argument implies taking a specific viewpoint toward a topic. In reading an essay, then, try to identify the topic. The topic of "Do-It-Yourself Brain Surgery" can't really be brain surgery; it must be do-it-yourself books, and the attitude probably will be amused contempt for such books. Even an essay that is largely narrative, like Brent Staples's, recounting a personal experience or a bit of history, probably will include an attitude toward the event that is being narrated, and it is that attitude—the interpretation of the event rather than the event itself—that may be the real topic of the essay.

It's time to look at Staples's essay. (Following the essay you will find a student's outline of it and another student's version of its thesis.) Staples, born in 1951, received a bachelor's degree from Widener University in Chester, Pennsylvania, and a Ph.D. from the University of Chicago. After working as a journalist in Chicago, he joined *The New York Times* in 1985, and he is now on the newspaper's editorial board, where he writes on politics and culture. His essay was first published in *Ms.* magazine in 1986 and reprinted in a slightly revised form—the form we give here—in *Harper's* in 1987.

 **BRENT STAPLES**

Black Men and Public Space

My first victim was a woman—white, well dressed, probably in her late twenties. I came upon her late one evening on a deserted street in Hyde Park, a relatively affluent neighborhood in an otherwise mean, impoverished section of Chicago. As I swung onto the avenue behind her, there seemed to be a discreet, uninflammatory distance between us. Not so. She cast back a worried glance. To her, the youngish black man—a broad six feet two inches with a beard and billowing hair, both hands shoved into the pockets of a bulky military jacket—seemed menacingly close. After a few more quick glimpses, she picked up her pace and was soon running in earnest. Within seconds, she disappeared into a cross street.

That was more than a decade ago. I was twenty-two years old, a graduate student newly arrived at the University of Chicago. It was in the echo of that terrified woman's footfalls that I first began to know the unwieldy inheritance I'd come into—the ability to alter public space in ugly ways. It was clear that she thought herself the quarry of a mugger, a rapist, or worse. Suffering a bout of insomnia, however, I was stalking sleep, not defenseless wayfarers. As a softy who is scarcely able to take a knife to a raw chicken— let alone hold one to a person's throat—I was surprised, embarrassed, and dismayed all at once. Her flight made me feel like an accomplice in tyranny. It also made it clear that I was indistinguishable from the muggers who occasionally seeped into the area from the surrounding ghetto. That first encounter, and those that followed, signified that a vast, unnerving gulf lay between nighttime pedestrians—particularly women—and me. And I soon gathered that being perceived as dangerous is a hazard in itself. I only needed to turn a corner into a dicey situation, or crowd some frightened, armed person in a foyer somewhere, or make an errant move after being pulled over by a policeman. Where fear and weapons meet—and they often do in urban America—there is always the possibility of death.

In that first year, my first away from my hometown, I was to become thoroughly familiar with the language of fear. At dark, shadowy intersections, I could cross in front of a car stopped at a traffic light and elicit the *thunk*, thunk, thunk, thunk of the driver—black, white, male, or female— hammering down the door locks. On less traveled streets after dark, I grew accustomed to but never comfortable with people crossing to the other side of the street rather than pass me. Then there were the standard unpleasantries with policemen, doormen, bouncers, cabdrivers, and others whose business it is to screen out troublesome individuals *before* there is any nastiness.

I moved to New York nearly two years ago and I have remained an avid night walker. In central Manhattan, the near-constant crowd cover minimizes tense one-on-one street encounters. Elsewhere—in SoHo, for example, where sidewalks are narrow and tightly spaced buildings shut out the sky—things can get very taut indeed.

5   After dark, on the warrenlike streets of Brooklyn where I live, I often see women who fear the worst from me. They seem to have set their faces

on neutral, and with their purse straps strung across their chests bandolier-style, they forge ahead as though bracing themselves against being tackled. I understand, of course, that the danger they perceive is not a hallucination. Women are particularly vulnerable to street violence, and young black males are drastically overrepresented among the perpetrators of that violence. Yet these truths are no solace against the kind of alienation that comes of being ever the suspect, a fearsome entity with whom pedestrians avoid making eye contact.

It is not altogether clear to me how I reached the ripe old age of twenty-two without being conscious of the lethality nighttime pedestrians attributed to me. Perhaps it was because in Chester, Pennsylvania, the small, angry industrial town where I came of age in the 1960s, I was scarcely noticeable against a backdrop of gang warfare, street knifings, and murders. I grew up one of the good boys, had perhaps a half-dozen fistfights. In retrospect, my shyness of combat has clear sources.

As a boy, I saw countless tough guys locked away; I have since buried several, too. They were babies, really—a teenage cousin, a brother of twenty-two, a childhood friend in his mid-twenties—all gone down in episodes of bravado played out in the streets. I came to doubt the virtues of intimidation early on. I chose, perhaps unconsciously, to remain a shadow—timid, but a survivor.

The fearsomeness mistakenly attributed to me in public places often has a perilous flavor. The most frightening of these confusions occurred in the late 1970s and early 1980s, when I worked as a journalist in Chicago. One day, rushing into the office of a magazine I was writing for with a deadline story in hand, I was mistaken for a burglar. The office manager called security and, with an ad hoc posse, pursued me through the labyrinthine halls, nearly to my editor's door. I had no way of proving who I was. I could only move briskly toward the company of someone who knew me.

Another time I was on assignment for a local paper and killing time before an interview. I entered a jewelry store on the city's affluent Near North Side. The proprietor excused herself and returned with an enormous red Doberman pinscher straining at the end of a leash. She stood, the dog extended toward me, silent to my questions, her eyes bulging nearly out of her head. I took a cursory look around, nodded, and bade her good night.

10   Relatively speaking, however, I never fared as badly as another black male journalist. He went to nearby Waukegan, Illinois, a couple of summers ago to work on a story about a murderer who was born there. Mistaking the reporter for the killer, police officers hauled him from his car at gunpoint and but for his press credentials would probably have tried to book him. Such episodes are not uncommon. Black men trade tales like this all the time.

Over the years, I learned to smother the rage I felt at so often being taken for a criminal. Not to do so would surely have led to madness. I now take precautions to make myself less threatening. I move about with care, particularly late in the evening. I give a wide berth to nervous people on subway platforms during the wee hours, particularly when I have exchanged business clothes for jeans. If I happen to be entering a building behind some people who appear skittish, I may walk by, letting them clear the lobby before I return, so as not to seem to be following them. I have been calm and extremely congenial on those rare occasions when I've been pulled over by the police.

And on late-evening constitutionals I employ what has proved to be an excellent tension-reducing measure: I whistle melodies from Beethoven and Vivaldi and the more popular classical composers. Even steely New Yorkers hunching toward nighttime destinations seem to relax, and occasionally they even join in the tune. Virtually everybody seems to sense that a mugger wouldn't be warbling bright, sunny selections from Vivaldi's *Four Seasons.* It is my equivalent of the cowbell that hikers wear when they know they are in bear country.

[1986]

Summarizing

Summary should be clearly distinguished from analysis. The word *summary* is related to *sum,* the total something adds up to. (We say "adds *up* to" because the Greeks and Romans counted upward and wrote the total at the top.)

A summary is a condensation or abridgement; it briefly gives the reader the gist of a longer work. It boils down the longer work, resembling the longer work as a bouillion cube resembles a bowl of soup. A summary of Staples's "Black Men and Public Space" will reduce the essay, perhaps to a paragraph or two or even to a sentence. It will not call attention to Staples's various strategies, and it will not evaluate his views or his skill as a writer; it will merely present the gist of what he says.

Summary and Analysis   If, then, you are asked to write an analysis of something you have read, you should not hand in a summary. On the other hand, a very brief summary may appropriately appear within an analytic essay. Usually, in fact, the reader needs some information, and the writer of the essay will briefly summarize this information. For example, a student who wrote about Staples's essay is *summarizing* when she writes

> Staples says that he is aware that his presence frightens many whites, especially women.

She is summarizing because she is reporting, without personal comment, what Staples said.

On the other hand, she is *analyzing* when she writes

> By saying at the outset, "My first victim was a woman--white, well dressed, probably in her late twenties," Staples immediately catches the reader's attention and sets up expectations that will be undermined in the next paragraph.

In this sentence the writer is not reporting *what* Staples said but is explaining *how* he achieved an effect.

In Chapter 4 we discussed a few principles that govern summaries (see the list on p. 86). Here is a summary of our comments on "summary":

A summary is a condensation or abridgment. Its chief characteristics are that (1) it is rarely more than one-fourth as long as the original;

(2) its brevity is usually achieved by leaving out most of the concrete details of the original; (3) it is accurate; (4) it may rearrange the organization of the original, especially if a rearrangement will make things clearer; (5) it normally is in the present tense; and (6) quoted words need not be enclosed in quotation marks.

Preparing a Summary   If you are summarizing an essay, you may find that the essay includes its own summary, perhaps at the start or more likely near the end. If it does, you're in luck.

If it doesn't, we suggest that on rereading you jot down, after reading each paragraph, a sentence summarizing the gist of the paragraph. (A very long or poorly unified paragraph may require two sentences, but make every effort to boil the paragraph down to a dozen or so words.) Of course if a paragraph consists merely of a transitional sentence or two ("We will now turn to another example") you will lump it with the next paragraph. Similarly, if for some reason you encounter a series of very short paragraphs—for instance, three examples, each briefly stated, and all illustrating the same point—you probably will find that you can cover them with a single sentence. But if a paragraph runs to half a page or more of print, it's probably worth its own sentence of summary. In fact, your author may summarize the paragraph in the paragraph's opening sentence or in its final sentence.

Here is a student's paragraph-by-paragraph summary of Staples's "Black Men and Public Space." The numbers refer to Staples's paragraphs.

1. "First victim" was a white woman in Chicago, who hurried away.
2. Age 22, he realized--to his surprise and embarrassment--that he (a "youngish black man") could be perceived by strangers as a mugger. And, since his presence created fear, he was in a dangerous situation.
3,4,5. At intersections he heard drivers of cars lock their doors, and elsewhere he sensed hostility of bouncers and others.
    In NY, lots of tension on narrow sidewalks. Women are esp. afraid of him; he knows why, but that's "no solace."
6. He's not sure why it took him 22 years to see that others fear him, but prob. because in his hometown of Chester, Pa., there was lots of adolescent violence, though he stayed clear of it.
7. As a boy, he saw young toughs killed, and he kept clear, "timid, but a survivor."
8,9,10. Though he is gentle, he looks fearsome. Once, working as a journalist, he was mistaken for a burglar. Another time, in a jewelry store, the clerk brought out a guard dog. Another black journalist was covering a crime, but the police thought the journalist was the killer. Many blacks have had such experiences.

11. He has learned to smother his rage--and he
    keeps away from nervous people.
12. Walking late at night, he whistles familiar
    classical music, trying to reassure others
    that he is not a mugger.

When you have written your sentence summarizing the last paragraph, you may have done enough if the summary was intended simply for your own private use, for example, to help you review material for an examination. But if you are going to use it as the basis of a summary within an essay you are writing, you probably won't want to include a summary longer than three or four sentences, so your job will be to reduce and combine the sentences you have jotted down. Indeed, you may even want to reduce the summary to a single sentence.

A Suggested Exercise: Assuming that you find the sentences summarizing "Black Men and Public Space" acceptable, reduce them to a summary no longer than four readable sentences. Then compare your version with the versions of two other students and, working as a group, produce a summary.

Stating the Thesis of an Essay   Summarizing each stage of the essay forces a reader to be attentive and can assist the reader to formulate a **thesis sentence,** a sentence that (in the reader's opinion) sets forth the writer's central point. If an essay is essentially an argument—for example, a defense of (or an argument against) capital punishment—it will probably include one or more sentences that directly assert the thesis. "Black Men and Public Space," chiefly a narrative essay, is much less evidently an argument, but it does have a point, and some of its sentences come pretty close to summarizing the point. Here are three of those sentences:

> And I soon gathered that being perceived as dangerous is a hazard
> in itself. (2)
> The fearsomeness mistakenly attributed to me in public places
> often has a perilous flavor. (8)
> I now take precautions to make myself less threatening. (11)

We asked our students to formulate their own thesis sentence for Staples's essay. One student came up with the following sentence after first drafting a couple of tentative versions and then rereading the essay in order to modify them:

In "Black Men and Public Space" Staples recognizes
that because many whites fear a young black man and
therefore may do violence to him, he may do well to
try to cool the situation by making himself
unthreatening.

Notice, again, that a thesis sentence states the *point* of the work. Don't confuse a thesis sentence with a summary of a narrative, such as "Staples at the age of twenty-two came to realize that his presence was threatening to whites, and he has since taken measures to make himself less threatening." This sentence, though true, doesn't clearly get at the point of the essay, the generalization that can be drawn from Staples's example.

Look again at the student's formulation of a thesis sentence (*not* the narrative summary sentence that we have just given). If you don't think that it fairly represents Staples's point, you may (if you are writing an essay about Staples's essay) want to come up with a sentence that seems more precise to you. Whether you use the sentence we have quoted or a sentence that you formulate for yourself, you can in any case of course disagree very strongly with what you take to be Staples's point. Your version of Staples's thesis should accurately reflect your understanding of Staples's point, but you need not agree with the point. You may think, for instance, that Staples is hypersensitive or (to mention only one other possibility) that he is playing the Uncle Tom.

A thesis sentence, then, whether the words are your own or the author's, is a very brief summary of the argument (not of the narrative) of the work. If you are writing an essay about an essay, you'll probably want to offer a sentence that reminds your reader of the point of the work you are discussing or gives the reader the gist of an unfamiliar work:

> Black males, however harmless, are in a perilous situation because whites, especially white women, perceive them as threatening.

Or:

> In "Black Men and Public Space" Staples recognizes that because many whites fear a young black man and therefore may do violence to him, a black man may do well to try to cool the situation by making himself nonthreatening.

Drafting a Summary   Sometimes, however, a fuller statement may be useful. For instance, if you are writing about a complex essay that makes six points, you may help your reader if you briefly restate all six. The length of your summary will depend on your purpose and the needs of your audience.

The following principles may help you to write your summary:

1. First, after having written sentences that summarize each paragraph or group of paragraphs, formulate the essay's thesis sentence. Formulating the sentence in writing will help you to stay with what you take to be the writer's main point.
2. Next, write a first draft by turning your summaries of the paragraphs into fewer and better sentences. For example, the student who wrote the paragraph-by-paragraph summary (page 108) of Staples's essay turned her first five sentences (on Staples's first paragraphs) into this:

> Staples's "first victim" was a white woman in Chicago. When she hurried away from him, he realized--to his surprise and embarrassment-- that because he was large and black and young he seemed to her to be a mugger. And since his presence created fear, he was in a dangerous situation. Other experiences, such as hearing drivers lock their cars when they were waiting at an intersection, have made him aware of the hostility of others. Women are especially afraid of him, and although he knows why, this knowledge is "no solace."

The student turned the remaining sentences of the outline into the following summary:

> Oddly, it took him twenty-two years to see that others fear him. Perhaps it took this long because he grew up in a violent neighborhood, though he kept clear, "timid, but a survivor." Because he is black and large, whites regard him as fearsome and treat him accordingly (once a clerk in a jewelry store brought out a guard dog), but other blacks have been treated worse. He has learned to smother his rage, and in order to cool things he tries to reassure nervous people by keeping away from them and (when he is walking late at night) by whistling classical music.

3. Write a lead-in sentence, probably incorporating the gist of the thesis sentence. Here is an example:

> Brent Staples, in "Black Men and Public Space," tells how his awareness that many white people regarded him as dangerous caused him to realize that <u>he</u> was in danger. His implicitly recommended solution is to try to cool the anxiety by adopting nonthreatening behavior.

After writing a lead-in, revise the draft of your summary, eliminating needless repetition, providing transitions, and adding whatever you think may be needed to clarify the work for someone who is unfamiliar with it. You may rearrange the points if you think the rearrangement will clarify matters.

4. Edit your draft for errors in grammar, punctuation, and spelling. Read it aloud to test it once more for readability. Sometimes only by reading aloud do we detect needless repetition or confusing phrases.

☞ SOME WRITING ASSIGNMENTS

1. In a paragraph or two set forth what you take to be Staples's *purpose.* Do you think he was writing chiefly to clarify some ideas for himself—for instance, to explore how he came to discover the "alienation that comes of being ever the suspect"? Or writing to assist blacks? Or to assist whites? Or what? (You may of course conclude that none of these suggestions, or all, are relevant.)

2. If you think the essay is effective, in a paragraph or two addressed to your classmates try to account for its effectiveness. Do certain examples strike you as particularly forceful? If so, why? Do certain sentences seem especially memorable? Again, why? For example, if the opening and concluding paragraphs strike you as effective, explain why. On the other hand, if you are unimpressed by part or all of the essay, explain why.

3. The success of a narrative as a piece of writing often depends on the reader's willingness to identify with the narrator. From an examination of "Black Men and Public Space," what explanations can you give for your willingness (or unwillingness) to identify yourself with Staples? (Probably you will want to say something about his persona as you sense it from the essay.) In the course of a 500-word essay explaining your position, very briefly summarize Staples's essay and state his thesis.

4. Have *you* ever unintentionally altered public space? For instance, you might recall an experience in which, as a child, your mere presence caused adults to alter their behavior—for instance, to stop quarreling.

   After a session of brainstorming, in which you produce some possible topics, you'll want to try to settle on one. After you have chosen a topic and produced a first draft, if you are not satisfied with your first paragraph—for instance, if you feel that it is not likely to get and hold the reader's attention—you may want to imitate the strategy that Staples adopted for his first paragraph.

5. If you have ever been in the position of one of Staples's "victims," that is, if you have ever shown fear or suspicion of someone who, it turned out, meant you no harm (or if you can imagine being in that position), write an essay from the "victim's" point of view. Explain what happened, what you did and thought. Did you think at the time about the feelings of the person you avoided or fled from? Has reading Staples's essay prompted further reflections on your experience? (Suggested length: 750 words.)

✔ A Checklist: Getting Ideas for Writing about Essays

Persona and Tone

1. What sort of *persona* does the writer create?
2. How does the writer create this persona? (For example, does the writer use colloquial language or formal language or technical language? Short sentences or long ones? Personal anecdotes? Quotations from authorities?)
3. What is the *tone* of the essay? Is it, for example, solemn, or playful? Is the tone consistent? If not, how do the shifts affect your understanding of the writer's point or your identification of the writer's persona? Who is the *audience?*

Kind of Essay

1. What kind of essay is it? Is it chiefly a presentation of facts (for example, an exposition, a report, a history)? Or is it chiefly an argument? Or a meditation? (Probably the essay draws on several kinds of writing, but which kind is it primarily? How are the other kinds related to the main kind?) What is the overall *purpose* of the essay?

2. What does it seem to add up to? If the essay is chiefly meditative or speculative, how much emphasis is placed on the persona? That is, if the essay is a sort of thinking-out-loud, is your interest chiefly in the announced or ostensible topic, or in the writer's mood and personality? If the essay is chiefly a presentation of facts, does it also have a larger implication? For instance, if it narrates a happening (history), does the reader draw an inference—find a meaning—in the happening? If the essay is chiefly an argument, what is the thesis? How is the thesis supported? (Is it supported, for example, by induction, deduction, analogy, or emotional appeal?) Do you accept the assumptions (explicit and implicit)?

Structure

1. Is the title appropriate? Propose a better title, if possible.
2. Did the opening paragraph interest you? Why, or why not? Did the essay continue more or less as expected, or did it turn out to be rather different from what you anticipated?
3. Prepare an outline of the essay. What effect does the writer seem to be aiming at by using this structure?

Value

1. What is especially good (or bad) about the essay? Is it logically persuasive? Or entertaining? Or does it introduce an engaging persona? Or (if it is a narrative) does it tell a story effectively, using (where appropriate) description, dialogue, and commentary, and somehow make you feel that this story is worth reporting?
2. Does the writer seem to hold values that you share? Or cannot share? Explain.
3. Do you think that most readers will share your response, or do you think that for some reason—for example, your age, or your cultural background—your responses are unusual? Explain.

SEVEN ESSAYS

 JONATHAN SWIFT

Jonathan Swift (1667–1745) was born in Ireland of an English family. He was ordained in the Church of Ireland in 1694, and in 1714 he became dean of St. Patrick's Cathedral, Dublin. He wrote abundantly on political and religious topics, often motivated (in his own words) by "savage indignation." It is ironic that Gulliver's Travels, *the masterpiece by this master of irony, is most widely thought of as a book for children.*

From the middle of the sixteenth century the English regulated the Irish economy so that it would enrich England. Heavy taxes and other repressive legislation impoverished Ireland, and in 1728, the year before Swift wrote "A Modest Proposal," Ireland was further weakened by a severe famine. Swift, deeply moved by the injustice, the stupidity, and the suffering that he found in Ireland, adopts the disguise or persona of an economist and offers an ironic suggestion on how Irish families may improve their conditions.

A Modest Proposal

For Preventing the Children of Poor People in Ireland from Being a Burden to Their Parents or Country, and for Making Them Beneficial to the Public

It is a melancholy object to those who walk through this great town or travel in the country, when they see the streets, the roads, and cabin doors, crowded with beggars of the female sex, followed by three, four, or six children, all in rags and importuning every passenger for an alms. These mothers, instead of being able to work for their honest livelihood, are forced to employ all their time in strolling to beg sustenance for their helpless infants: who as they grow up either turn thieves for want of work, or leave their dear native country to fight for the pretender in Spain, or sell themselves to the Barbadoes.

I think it is agreed by all parties that this prodigious number of children in the arms, or on the backs, or at the heels of their mothers, and frequently of their fathers, is in the present deplorable state of the kingdom a very great additional grievance; and, therefore, whoever could find out a fair, cheap, and easy method of making these children sound, useful members of the commonwealth, would deserve so well of the public as to have his statue set up for a preserver of the nation.

But my intention is very far from being confined to provide only for the children of professed beggars; it is of a much greater extent, and shall take in the whole number of infants at a certain age who are born of parents in effect as little able to support them as those who demand our charity in the streets.

As to my own part, having turned my thoughts for many years upon this important subject, and maturely weighed the several schemes of our projectors,[1] I have always found them grossly mistaken in their computation. It is true, a child just dropped from its dam may be supported by her milk for a solar year, with little other nourishment; at most not above the value of 2s.,[2] which the mother may certainly get, or the value in scraps, by her lawful occupation of begging; and it is exactly at one year old that I propose to provide for them in such a manner as instead of being a charge upon their parents or the parish, or wanting food and raiment for the rest of their lives, they shall on the contrary contribute to the feeding, and partly to the clothing, of many thousands.

5   There is likewise another great advantage in my scheme, that it will prevent those voluntary abortions, and that horrid practice of women murdering their bastard children, alas! too frequent among us! sacrificing the poor innocent babes I doubt more to avoid the expense than the shame, which would move tears and pity in the most savage and inhuman breast.

---

[1]**projectors** persons who devise plans   [2]**2s.** two shillings. Later "£" is an abbreviation for pounds and "d" for pence.

The number of souls in this kingdom being usually reckoned one million and a half, of these I calculate there may be about 200,000 couple whose wives are breeders; from which number I subtract 30,000 couple who are able to maintain their own children (although I apprehend there cannot be so many, under the present distress of the kingdom); but this being granted, there will remain 170,000 breeders. I again subtract 50,000 for those women who miscarry, or whose children die by accident or disease within the year. There only remain 120,000 children of poor parents annually born. The question therefore is, how this number shall be reared and provided for? which, as I have already said, under the present situation of affairs, is utterly impossible by all the methods hitherto proposed. For we can neither employ them in handicraft or agriculture; we neither build houses (I mean in the country) nor cultivate land; they can very seldom pick up a livelihood by stealing, till they arrive at six years old, except where they are of towardly parts; although I confess they learn the rudiments much earlier; during which time they can, however, be properly looked upon only as probationers; as I have been informed by a principal gentleman in the county of Cavan, who protested to me that he never knew above one or two instances under the age of six, even in a part of the kingdom so renowned for the quickest proficiency in that art.

I am assured by our merchants, that a boy or a girl before twelve years old is no salable commodity; and even when they come to this age they will not yield above 3£. or 3£. 2s. 6d. at most on the exchange; which cannot turn to account either to the parents or kingdom, the charge of nutriment and rags having been at least four times that value.

I shall now therefore humbly propose my own thoughts, which I hope will not be liable to the least objection.

I have been assured by a very knowing American of my acquaintance in London, that a young healthy child well nursed is at a year old a most delicious, nourishing, and wholesome food, whether stewed, roasted, baked, or broiled; and I make no doubt that it will equally serve in a fricassee or a ragout.

10   I do therefore humbly offer it to public consideration that of the 120,000 children already computed, 20,000 may be reserved for breed, whereof only one-fourth part to be males; which is more than we allow to sheep, black cattle, or swine; and my reason is, that these children are seldom the fruits of marriage, a circumstance not much regarded by our savages; therefore one male will be sufficient to serve four females. That the remaining 100,000 may, at a year old, be offered in sale to the persons of quality and fortune through the kingdom; always advising the mother to let them suck plentifully in the last month, so as to render them plump and fat for a good table. A child will make two dishes at an entertainment for friends; and when the family dines alone, the fore or hind quarter will make a reasonable dish, and seasoned with a little pepper or salt will be very good boiled on the fourth day, especially in winter.

I have reckoned upon a medium that a child just born will weigh 12 pounds, and in a solar year, if tolerably nursed, will increase to 28 pounds.

I grant this food will be somewhat dear, and therefore very proper for landlords, who, as they have already devoured most of the parents, seem to have the best title to the children.

Infant's flesh will be in season throughout the year, but more plentiful in March, and a little before and after: for we are told by a grave author, an eminent French physician, that fish being a prolific diet, there are more children born in Roman Catholic countries about nine months after Lent than at any other season; therefore, reckoning a year after Lent, the markets will be more glutted than usual, because the number of popish infants is at least three to one in this kingdom: and therefore it will have one other collateral advantage, by lessening the number of papists among us.

I have already computed the charge of nursing a beggar's child (in which list I reckon all cottagers, laborers, and four-fifths of the farmers) to be about 2s. per annum, rags included; and I believe no gentleman would repine to give 10s. for the carcass of a good fat child, which, as I have said, will make four dishes of excellent nutritive meat, when he has only some particular friend or his own family to dine with him. Thus the squire will learn to be a good landlord, and grow popular among the tenants; the mother will have 8s. net profit, and be fit for work till she produces another child.

15   Those who are more thrifty (as I must confess the times require) may flay the carcass; the skin of which artificially dressed will make admirable gloves for ladies, and summer boots for fine gentlemen.

As to our city of Dublin, shambles[3] may be appointed for this purpose in the most convenient parts of it, and butchers we may be assured will not be wanting: although I rather recommend buying the children alive, and dressing them hot from the knife as we do roasting pigs.

A very worthy person, a true lover of his country, and whose virtues I highly esteem, was lately pleased in discoursing on this matter to offer a refinement upon my scheme. He said that many gentlemen of this kingdom, having of late destroyed their deer, he conceived that the want of venison might be well supplied by the bodies of young lads and maidens, not exceeding fourteen years of age nor under twelve; so great a number of both sexes in every country being now ready to starve for want of work and service; and these to be disposed of by their parents, if alive, or otherwise by their nearest relations. But with due deference to so excellent a friend and so deserving a patriot, I cannot be altogether in his sentiments; for as to the males, my American acquaintance assured me from frequent experience that their flesh was generally tough and lean, like that of our schoolboys by continual exercise, and their taste disagreeable; and to fatten them would not answer the charge. Then as to the females, it would, I think, with humble submission be a loss to the public, because they soon would become breeders themselves: and besides, it is not improbable that some scrupulous people might be apt to censure such a practice (although indeed very unjustly), as a little bordering upon cruelty; which, I confess, has always been with me the strongest objection against any project, how well soever intended.

But in order to justify my friend, he confessed that this expedient was put into his head by the famous Psalmanazar,[4] a native of the island Formosa, who came from thence to London about twenty years ago: and in

---

[3]**shambles** slaughterhouses   [4]**Psalmanazar** George Psalmanazar (c. 1679-1763), a Frenchman who claimed to be from Formosa (now Taiwan); wrote *An Historical and Geographical Description of Formosa* (1704). The hoax was exposed soon after publication.

conversation told my friend, that in his country when any young person happened to be put to death, the executioner sold the carcass to persons of quality as a prime dainty; and that in his time the body of a plump girl of fifteen, who was crucified for an attempt to poison the emperor, was sold to his imperial majesty's prime minister of state, and other great mandarins of the court, in joints from the gibbet, at 400 crowns. Neither indeed can I deny, that if the same use were made of several plump young girls in this town, who without one single groat to their fortunes cannot stir abroad without a chair, and appear at the playhouse and assemblies in foreign fineries which they never will pay for, the kingdom would not be the worse.

Some persons of a desponding spirit are in great concern about the vast number of poor people, who are aged, diseased, or maimed, and I have been desired to employ my thoughts what course may be taken to ease the nation of so grievous an encumbrance. But I am not in the least pain upon that matter, because it is very well known that they are every day dying and rotting by cold and famine, and filth and vermin, as fast as can be reasonably expected. And as to the young laborers, they are now in as hopeful a condition: they cannot get work, and consequently pine away for want of nourishment, to a degree that if at any time they are accidentally hired to common labor, they have not strength to perform it; and thus the country and themselves are happily delivered from the evils to come.

20   I have too long digressed, and therefore shall return to my subject. I think the advantages by the proposal which I have made are obvious and many, as well as of the highest importance.

For first, as I have already observed, it would greatly lessen the number of papists, with whom we are yearly overrun, being the principal breeders of the nation as well as our most dangerous enemies; and who stay at home on purpose to deliver the kingdom to the Pretender, hoping to take their advantage by the absence of so many good Protestants, who have chosen rather to leave their country than stay at home and pay tithes against their conscience to an Episcopal curate.

Secondly, The poor tenants will have something valuable of their own, which by law may be made liable to distress and help to pay their landlord's rent, their corn and cattle being already seized, and money a thing unknown.

Thirdly, Whereas the maintenance of 100,000 children from two years old and upward, cannot be computed at less than 10s. a-piece per annum, the nation's stock will be thereby increased £50,000 per annum, beside the profit of a new dish introduced to the tables of all gentlemen of fortune in the kingdom who have any refinement in taste. And the money will circulate among ourselves, the goods being entirely of our own growth and manufacture.

Fourthly, The constant breeders beside the gain of 8s. sterling per annum by the sale of their children, will be rid of the charge of maintaining them after the first year.

25   Fifthly, This food would likewise bring great custom to taverns, where the vintners will certainly be so prudent as to procure the best receipts for dressing it to perfection, and consequently have their houses frequented by all the fine gentlemen, who justly value themselves upon their knowledge in good eating; and a skilful cook who understands how to oblige his guests, will contrive to make it as expensive as they please.

Sixthly, This would be a great inducement to marriage, which all wise nations have either encouraged by rewards or enforced by laws and penalties. It would increase the care and tenderness of mothers toward their children, when they were sure of a settlement for life to the poor babes, provided in some sort by the public, to their annual profit instead of expense. We should see an honest emulation among the married women, which of them would bring the fattest child to the market. Men would become as fond of their wives during the time of their pregnancy as they are now of their mares in foal, their cows in calf, their sows when they are ready to farrow; nor offer to beat or kick them (as is too frequent a practice) for fear of a miscarriage.

Many other advantages might be enumerated. For instance, the addition of some thousand carcasses in our exportation of barreled beef, the propagation of swine's flesh, and improvement in the art of making good bacon, so much wanted among us by the great destruction of pigs, too frequent at our table, which are no way comparable in taste or magnificence to a well-grown, fat, yearling child, which roasted whole will make a considerable figure at a lord mayor's feast or any other public entertainment. But this and many others I omit, being studious of brevity.

Supposing that 1,000 families in this city would be constant customers for infants' flesh, besides others who might have it at merry-meetings, particularly at weddings and christenings, I compute that Dublin would take off annually about 20,000 carcasses; and the rest of the kingdom (where probably they will be sold somewhat cheaper) the remaining 80,000.

I can think of no one objection that will possibly be raised against this proposal, unless it should be urged that the number of people will be thereby much lessened in the kingdom. This I freely own, and it was indeed one principal design in offering it to the world. I desire the reader will observe, that I calculate my remedy for this one individual kingdom of Ireland and for no other that ever was, is, or I think ever can be upon earth. Therefore let no man talk to me of other expedients: of taxing our absentees at 5s. a pound: of using neither clothes nor household furniture except what is of our own growth and manufacture: of utterly rejecting the materials and instruments that promote foreign luxury: of curing the expensiveness of pride, vanity, idleness, and gaming in our own women: of introducing a vein of parsimony, prudence, and temperance: of learning to love our country, in the want of which we differ even from Laplanders and the inhabitants of Topinamboo: of quitting our animosities and factions, nor acting any longer like the Jews, who were murdering one another at the very moment their city was taken: of being a little cautious not to sell our country and conscience for nothing: of teaching landlords to have at least one degree of mercy toward their tenants: lastly, of putting a spirit of honesty, industry, and skill into our shopkeepers; who, if a resolution could now be taken to buy only our native goods, would immediately unite to cheat and exact upon us in the price, the measure, and the goodness, nor could ever yet be brought to make one fair proposal of just dealing, though often and earnestly invited to it.

30   Therefore I repeat, let no man talk to me of these and the like expedients, till he has at least some glimpse of hope that there will be ever some hearty and sincere attempt to put them in practice.

But as to myself, having been wearied out for many years with offering vain, idle, visionary thoughts, and at length utterly despairing of success, I fortunately fell upon this proposal; which, as it is wholly new, so it has something solid and real, of no expense and little trouble, full in our own power, and whereby we can incur no danger in disobliging England. For this kind of commodity will not bear exportation, the flesh being of too tender a consistence to admit a long continuance in salt, although perhaps I could name a country which would be glad to eat up our whole nation without it.

After all, I am not so violently bent upon my own opinion as to reject any offer proposed by wise men, which shall be found equally innocent, cheap, easy, and effectual. But before something of that kind shall be advanced in contradiction to my scheme, and offering a better, I desire the author or authors will be pleased maturely to consider two points. First, as things now stand, how they will be able to find food and raiment for 100,000 useless mouths and backs. And secondly, there being a round million of creatures in human figure throughout this kingdom, whose subsistence put into a common stock would leave them in debt 2,000,000£. sterling, adding those who are beggars by profession to the bulk of farmers, cottagers, and laborers, with the wives and children who are beggars in effect; I desire those politicians who dislike my overture, and may perhaps be so bold as to attempt an answer, that they will first ask the parents of these mortals, whether they would not at this day think it a great happiness to have been sold for food at a year old in the manner I prescribe, and thereby have avoided such a perpetual scene of misfortunes as they have since gone through by the oppression of landlords, the impossibility of paying rent without money or trade, the want of common sustenance, with neither house nor clothes to cover them from the inclemencies of the weather, and the most inevitable prospect of entailing the like or greater miseries upon their breed for ever.

I profess, in the sincerity of my heart, that I have not the least personal interest in endeavoring to promote this necessary work, having no other motive than the public good of my country, by advancing our trade, providing for infants, relieving the poor, and giving some pleasure to the rich. I have no children by which I can propose to get a single penny; the youngest being nine years old, and my wife past child-bearing.

📝 TOPICS FOR CRITICAL THINKING AND WRITING

1. In the fourth paragraph Swift speaks of proposals set forth by "projectors," that is, by advocates of other projects or proposals. Characterize the pamphleteer (not Swift but his persona, the invented "projector") who offers his "modest proposal." What sort of man does he think he is? What sort of man do we regard him as? Support your assertions with evidence.

2. In the first paragraph the speaker says that the sight of mothers begging is "melancholy." In this paragraph what assumption does the speaker make about women that in part gives rise to this melancholy? Now that you are familiar with the entire essay, explain Swift's strategy.

3. How might you argue that although this satire is primarily ferocious, it also contains some playful touches? What specific passages might support your argument?

4. Write your own "Modest Proposal," using some of Swift's strategies, exposing a topic of your own choice. Choose a serious topic (for instance,

racism, anti-Semitism, environmental pollution, unemployment), and offer a solution that is outrageous but that is developed with relentless logic. Your essay should be about 750 words.

5. Swift's proposal is, in large measure, built on taking a metaphor literally: landlords devour the Irish poor. Take a metaphor (for example, "Certain people should be put in their place," or "It's a dog-eat-dog world") and set forth a modest proposal (250 words) in which you take the metaphor literally.

 ### HENRY DAVID THOREAU

Henry David Thoreau (1817-62) was born in Concord, Massachusetts, where he spent most of his life ("I have traveled a good deal in Concord"). He taught and lectured, but chiefly he observed, thought, and wrote. From July 4, 1845, to September 8, 1847, he lived near Concord in a cabin at Walden Pond, an experience recorded in Walden *(1854).*

"Room for Your Thoughts" (editors' title) is from Walden, *Chapter 6.*

Room for Your Thoughts

I had three chairs in my house; one for solitude, two for friendship, three for society. When visitors came in larger and unexpected numbers there was but the third chair for them all, but they generally economized the room by standing up. It is surprising how many great men and women a small house will contain. I have had twenty-five or thirty souls, with their bodies, at once under my roof, and yet we often parted without being aware that we had come very near to one another. Many of our houses, both public and private, with their almost innumerable apartments, their huge halls and their cellars for the storage of wines and other munitions of peace, appear to me extravagantly large for their inhabitants. They are so vast and magnificent that the latter seem to be only vermin which infest them. I am surprised when the herald blows his summons before some Tremont or Astor or Middlesex House, to see come creeping out over the piazza for all inhabitants a ridiculous mouse, which soon again slinks into some hole in the pavement.

One inconvenience I sometimes experienced in so small a house, the difficulty of getting to a sufficient distance from my guest when we began to utter the big thoughts in big words. You want room for your thoughts to get into sailing trim and run a course or two before they make their port. The bullet of your thought must have overcome its lateral and ricochet motion and fallen into its last and steady course before it reaches the ear of the hearer, else it may plough out again through the side of his head. Also, our sentences wanted room to unfold and form their columns in the interval. Individuals, like nations, must have suitable broad and natural boundaries, even a considerable neutral ground, between them. I have found it a singular luxury to talk across the pond to a companion on the opposite side. In my house we were so near that we could not begin to hear—we could not speak low enough to be heard; as when you throw two stones into calm

water so near that they break each other's undulations. If we are merely loquacious and loud talkers, then we can afford to stand very near together,
cheek by jowl, and feel each other's breath; but if we speak reservedly and
thoughtfully, we want to be farther apart, that all animal heat and moisture
may have a chance to evaporate. If we would enjoy the most intimate society with that in each of us which is without, or above, being spoken to, we
must not only be silent, but commonly so far apart bodily that we cannot
possibly hear each other's voice in any case. Referred to this standard,
speech is for the convenience of those who are hard of hearing; but there
are many fine things which we cannot say if we have to shout. As the conversation began to assume a loftier and grander tone, we gradually shoved
our chairs farther apart till they touched the wall in opposite corners, and
then commonly there was not room enough.

[1854]

 TOPICS FOR CRITICAL THINKING AND WRITING

1. What does Thoreau mean when he says, in his first paragraph, that
   twenty-five or thirty people have been under his roof, "yet we often
   parted without being aware that we had come very near to one
   another"?
2. Explain Thoreau's metaphor, in the second paragraph, of thought as a
   bullet. And explain the paradox "we could not speak low enough to be
   heard."

 VIRGINIA WOOLF

*Virginia Woolf (1882–1941) is known chiefly as a novelist, but she
was also the author of short stories and essays, and in recent years
the range of her power has been increasingly recognized.*

*Woolf was self-educated in the library of her father, Leslie
Stephen, a distinguished man of letters. After her father's death she
moved to Bloomsbury, an unfashionable part of London where she
was part of a brilliant circle of friends—the Bloomsbury group—that
included Clive Bell and Roger Fry (art critics), J. M. Keynes (an economist), Lytton Strachey (a biographer), and E. M. Forster (novelist
and essayist). In 1907 she married Leonard Woolf, with whom ten
years later she established the Hogarth Press, which published some
of the most interesting literature of the period, including her own
novels. Woolf experienced several mental breakdowns, and in 1941,
fearing yet another, she drowned herself.*

The Death of the Moth

Moths that fly by day are not properly to be called moths; they do not excite
that pleasant sense of dark autumn nights and ivy-blossom which the commonest yellow-underwing asleep in the shadow of the curtain never fails to
rouse in us. They are hybrid creatures, neither gay like butterflies nor

somber like their own species. Nevertheless the present specimen, with his narrow hay-colored wings, fringed with a tassel of the same color, seemed to be content with life. It was a pleasant morning, mid-September, mild, benignant, yet with a keener breath than that of the summer months. The plow was already scoring the field opposite the window, and where the share had been, the earth was pressed flat and gleamed with moisture. Such vigor came rolling in from the fields and the down beyond that it was difficult to keep the eyes strictly turned upon the book. The rooks too were keeping one of their annual festivities; soaring round the tree tops until it looked as if a vast net with thousands of black knots in it had been cast up into the air; which, after a few moments, sank slowly down upon the trees until every twig seemed to have a knot at the end of it. Then, suddenly, the net would be thrown into the air again in a wider circle this time, with the utmost clamor and vociferation, as though to be thrown into the air and settle slowly down upon the tree tops were a tremendously exciting experience.

The same energy which inspired the rooks, the ploughmen, the horses, and even, it seemed, the lean bare-backed downs, sent the moth fluttering from side to side of his square of the windowpane. One could not help watching him. One was, indeed, conscious of a queer feeling of pity for him. The possibilities of pleasure seemed that morning so enormous and so various that to have only a moth's part in life, and a day moth's at that, appeared a hard fate, and his zest in enjoying his meager opportunities to the full, pathetic. He flew vigorously to one corner of his compartment, and, after waiting there a second, flew across to the other. What remained for him but to fly to a third corner and then to a fourth? That was all he could do, in spite of the size of the downs, the width of the sky, the far-off smoke of houses, and the romantic voice, now and then, of a steamer out at sea. What he could do he did. Watching him, it seemed as if a fiber, very thin but pure, of the enormous energy of the world had been thrust into his frail and diminutive body. As often as he crossed the pane, I could fancy that a thread of vital light became visible. He was little or nothing but life.

Yet, because he was so small, and so simple a form of the energy that was rolling in at the open window and driving its way through so many narrow and intricate corridors in my own brain and in those of other human beings, there was something marvelous as well as pathetic about him. It was as if someone had taken a tiny bead of pure life and decking it as lightly as possible with down and feathers, had set it dancing and zigzagging to show us the true nature of life. Thus displayed one could not get over the strangeness of it. One is apt to forget all about life, seeing it humped and bossed and garnished and cumbered so that it has to move with the greatest circumspection and dignity. Again, the thought of all that life might have been had he been born in any other shape caused one to view his simple activities with a kind of pity.

After a time, tired by his dancing apparently, he settled on the window ledge in the sun, and, the queer spectacle being at an end, I forgot about him. Then, looking up, my eye was caught by him. He was trying to resume his dancing, but seemed either so stiff or so awkward that he could only flutter to the bottom of the window-pane; and when he tried to fly across it he failed. Being intent on other matters I watched these futile attempts for a time without thinking, unconsciously waiting for him to resume his flight, as one waits for a machine, that has stopped momentarily, to start again without considering the reason of its failure. After perhaps a seventh attempt he slipped from the wooden ledge and fell, fluttering his wings, on to his back on the window sill. The helplessness of his attitude roused me. It flashed upon me that he was in difficulties; he could no longer raise himself; his legs struggled vainly. But, as I stretched out a pencil, meaning to help him to right himself, it came over me that the failure and awkwardness were the approach of death. I laid the pencil down again.

5   The legs agitated themselves once more. I looked as if for the enemy against which he struggled. I looked out of doors. What had happened there? Presumably it was midday, and work in the fields had stopped. Stillness and quiet had replaced the previous animation. The birds had taken themselves off to feed in the brooks. The horses stood still. Yet the power was there all the same, massed outside, indifferent, impersonal, not attending to anything in particular. Somehow it was opposed to the little hay-colored moth. It was useless to try to do anything. One could only watch the extraordinary efforts made by those tiny legs against an oncoming doom which could, had it chosen, have submerged an entire city, not merely a city, but masses of human beings; nothing, I knew, had any chance against death. Nevertheless after a pause of exhaustion the legs fluttered again. It was superb, this last protest, and so frantic that he succeeded at last in righting himself. One's sympathies, of course, were all on the side of life. Also, when there was nobody to care or to know, this gigantic effort on the part of an insignificant little moth, against a power of such magnitude, to retain what no one else valued or desired to keep, moved one strangely. Again, somehow, one saw life, a pure bead. I lifted the pencil again, useless though I knew it to be. But even as I did so, the unmistakable tokens of death showed themselves. The body relaxed, and instantly grew stiff. The struggle was over. The insignificant little creature now knew death. As I looked at the dead moth, this minute wayside triumph of so great a force over so mean an antagonist filled me with wonder. Just as life had been strange a few minutes before, so death was now as strange. The moth having righted himself now lay most decently and uncomplainingly composed. O yes, he seemed to say, death is stronger than I am.

[1941]

 # TOPICS FOR CRITICAL THINKING AND WRITING

1. On the basis of the first paragraph, how would you describe Woolf's voice, or persona, in this essay? By what means does she try to engage our attention and interest?

2. Does the essay have a thesis sentence? If not, in a sentence or two of your own, try to state the essay's main point.

3. What is the season and the time span covered? How are these relevant to the thesis of the essay?

4. Reread the second paragraph, taking note as you do of the variety in sentence lengths. What sentences strike you as particularly effective? What makes them effective?

5. In paragraph 3 Woolf says, "One is apt to forget all about life, seeing it humped and bossed and garnished and cumbered so that it has to move

with the greatest circumspection and dignity." What does she mean? Try to restate the idea in your own words.

6. Write an essay on an encounter with death or birth.

 ## LANGSTON HUGHES

Langston Hughes (1902-67) was born in Joplin, Mississippi. He lived part of his youth in Mexico, spent a year at Columbia University, served as a merchant seaman, and worked in a Paris nightclub, where he showed some of his poems to Dr. Alain Locke, a strong advocate of African-American literature. After returning to the United States, Hughes went on to publish poetry, fiction, plays, essays, and biographies.

Salvation

I was saved from sin when I was going on thirteen. But not really saved. It happened like this. There was a big revival at my Auntie Reed's church. Every night for weeks there had been much preaching, singing, praying, and shouting, and some very hardened sinners had been brought to Christ, and the membership of the church had grown by leaps and bounds. Then just before the revival ended, they held a special meeting for children, "to bring the young lambs to the fold." My aunt spoke of it for days ahead. That night I was escorted to the front row and placed on the mourners' bench with all the other young sinners, who had not yet been brought to Jesus.

My aunt told me that when you were saved you saw a light, and something happened to you inside! And Jesus came into your life! And God was with you from then on! She said you could see and hear and feel Jesus in your soul. I believed her. I had heard a great many old people say the same thing and it seemed to me they ought to know. So I sat there calmly in the hot, crowded church, waiting for Jesus to come to me.

The preacher preached a wonderful rhythmical sermon, all moans and shouts and lonely cries and dire pictures of hell, and then he sang a song about the ninety and nine safe in the fold, but one little lamb was left out in the cold. Then he said: "Won't you come? Won't you come to Jesus? Young lambs, won't you come?" And he held out his arms to all us young sinners there on the mourners' bench. And the little girls cried. And some of them jumped up and went to Jesus right away. But most of us just sat there.

A great many old people came and knelt around us and prayed, old women with jet-black faces and braided hair, old men with work-gnarled hands. And the church sang a song about the lower lights are burning, some poor sinners to be saved. And the whole building rocked with prayer and song.

5   Still I kept waiting to *see* Jesus.

Finally all the young people had gone to the altar and were saved, but one boy and me. He was a rounder's son named Westley. Westley and I were surrounded by sisters and deacons praying. It was very hot in the church, and getting late now. Finally Westley said to me in a whisper: "God damn! I'm tired o' sitting here. Let's get up and be saved." So he got up and was saved.

Then I was left all alone on the mourners' bench. My aunt came and knelt at my knees and cried, while prayers and songs swirled all around me in the little church. The whole congregation prayed for me alone, in a mighty wail of moans and voices. And I kept waiting serenely for Jesus, waiting, waiting—but he didn't come. I wanted to see him, but nothing happened to me. Nothing! I wanted something to happen to me, but nothing happened.

I heard the songs and the minister saying: "Why don't you come? My dear child, why don't you come to Jesus? Jesus is waiting for you. He wants you. Why don't you come? Sister Reed, what is this child's name?"

"Langston," my aunt sobbed.

10   "Langston, why don't you come? Why don't you come and be saved? Oh, Lamb of God! Why don't you come?"

Now it was really getting late. I began to be ashamed of myself, holding everything up so long. I began to wonder what God thought about Westley, who certainly hadn't seen Jesus either, but who was now sitting proudly on the platform, swinging his knickerbockered legs and grinning down at me, surrounded by deacons and old women on their knees praying. God had not struck Westley dead for taking his name in vain or for lying in the temple. So I decided that maybe to save further trouble, I'd better lie, too, and say that Jesus had come, and get up and be saved.

So I got up.

Suddenly the whole room broke into a sea of shouting, as they saw me rise. Waves of rejoicing swept the place. Women leaped in the air. My aunt threw her arms around me. The minister took me by the hand and led me to the platform.

When things quieted down, in a hushed silence, punctuated by a few ecstatic "Amens," all the new young lambs were blessed in the name of God. Then joyous singing filled the room.

15   That night, for the last time in my life but one—for I was a big boy twelve years old—I cried. I cried, in bed alone, and couldn't stop. I buried my head under the quilts, but my aunt heard me. She woke up and told my uncle I was crying because the Holy Ghost had come into my life, and because I had seen Jesus. But I was really crying because I couldn't bear to tell her that I had lied, that I had deceived everybody in the church, and I hadn't seen Jesus, and that now I didn't believe there was a Jesus any more, since he didn't come to help me.

[1940]

✏ TOPICS FOR CRITICAL THINKING AND WRITING

1. Do you find the piece amusing, or serious, or both? Explain.
2. How would you characterize the style or voice of the first three sentences? Childlike, or sophisticated, or what? How would you characterize the final sentence? How can you explain the change in style or tone?
3. Why does Hughes bother to tell us, in paragraph 11, that Westley was "swinging his knickerbockered legs and grinning"? Do you think that Westley too may have cried that night? Give your reasons.
4. Is the episode told from the point of view of someone "going on thirteen," or from the point of view of a mature man? Cite evidence to support your position.

5. One of the Golden Rules of narrative writing is "Show, don't tell." In about 500 words, report an experience—for instance, a death in the family, or a severe (perhaps unjust) punishment, or the first day in a new school—that produced strong feelings. Like Hughes, you may want to draw on an experience in which you were subjected to group pressure. Do not explicitly state what the feelings were; rather, let the reader understand the feelings chiefly through concretely detailed actions. But, like Hughes, you might state your thesis or basic position in your first paragraph and then indicate when and where the experience took place.

 MAY SARTON

May Sarton (1912–1995), was born in Belgium and was brought to the United States in 1916; in 1924 she became a citizen. A teacher of writing and a distinguished writer herself, she received numerous awards for her fiction, poetry, and essays.

The Rewards of Living a Solitary Life

The other day an acquaintance of mine, a gregarious and charming man, told me he had found himself unexpectedly alone in New York for an hour or two between appointments. He went to the Whitney and spent the "empty" time looking at things in solitary bliss. For him it proved to be a shock nearly as great as falling in love to discover that he could enjoy himself so much alone.

What had he been afraid of, I asked myself? That, suddenly alone, he would discover that he bored himself, or that there was, quite simply, no self there to meet? But having taken the plunge, he is now on the brink of adventure; he is about to be launched into his own inner space, space as immense, unexplored, and sometimes frightening as outer space to the astronaut. His every perception will come to him with a new freshness and, for a time, seem startlingly original. For anyone who can see things for himself with a naked eye becomes, for a moment or two, something of a genius. With another human being present vision becomes double vision, inevitably. We are busy wondering, what does my companion see or think of this, and what do I think of it? The original impact gets lost, or diffused.

"Music I heard with you was more than music." Exactly. And therefore music *itself* can only be heard alone. Solitude is the salt of personhood. It brings out the authentic flavor of every experience.

"Alone one is never lonely: the spirit adventures, walking / In a quiet garden, in a cool house, abiding single there."

5   Loneliness is most acutely felt with other people, for with others, even with a lover sometimes, we suffer from our differences of taste, temperament, mood. Human intercourse often demands that we soften the edge of perception, or withdraw at the very instant of personal truth for fear of hurting, or of being inappropriately present, which is to say naked, in a social sit-

uation. Alone we can afford to be wholly whatever we are, and to feel whatever we feel absolutely. That is a great luxury!

For me the most interesting thing about a solitary life, and mine has been that for the last twenty years, is that it becomes increasingly rewarding. When I can wake up and watch the sun rise over the ocean, as I do most days, and know that I have an entire day ahead, uninterrupted, in which to write a few pages, take a walk with my dog, lie down in the afternoon for a long think (why does one think better in a horizontal position?), read and listen to music, I am flooded with happiness.

I am lonely only when I am overtired, when I have worked too long without a break, when for the time being I feel empty and need filling up. And I am lonely sometimes when I come back home after a lecture trip, when I have seen a lot of people and talked a lot, and am full to the brim with experience that needs to be sorted out.

Then for a little while the house feels huge and empty, and I wonder where my self is hiding. It has to be recaptured slowly by watering the plants, perhaps, and looking again at each one as though it were a person, by feeding the two cats, by cooking a meal.

It takes a while, as I watch the surf blowing up in fountains at the end of the field, but the moment comes when the world falls away, and the self emerges again from the deep unconscious, bringing back all I have recently experienced to be explored and slowly understood, when I can converse again with my hidden powers, and so grow, and so be renewed, till death do us part.

[1974]

 TOPICS FOR CRITICAL THINKING AND WRITING

1. What does Sarton mean when she says "Anyone who can see things for himself with a naked eye becomes, for a moment or two, something of a genius"? Does your own experience confirm her comment? Explain.
2. What phrase in the last paragraph connects the ending with the first paragraph?
3. Drawing on Sarton's essay, explain in 500 words the distinction between being "alone" and being "lonely."

 GARRISON KEILLOR

This short essay, which we have titled "Something from the Sixties," comes from "The Talk of the Town," a heading used over several short, anonymous essays published weekly in The New Yorker. *The essay purports to be a letter from a friend, except for the first line ("A friend writes"), but one may conjecture that the piece was composed by Garrison Keillor, who, following a convention used in "The Talk of the Town," does not use the first person singular pronoun. Keillor is the author of several books, including* Lake Wobegon Days, *and was the host of a popular radio show, "A Prairie Home Companion."*

Something from the Sixties

A friend writes:

About five o'clock last Sunday evening, my son burst into the kitchen and said, "I didn't know it was so late!" He was due at a party immediately—a sixties party, he said—and he needed something from the sixties to wear. My son is almost fifteen years old, the size of a grown man, and when he bursts into a room glassware rattles and the cat on your lap grabs on to your knees and leaps from the starting block. I used to think the phrase "burst into the room" was only for detective fiction, until my son got his growth. He can burst in a way that, done by an older fellow, would mean that angels had descended into the front yard and were eating apples off the tree, and he does it whenever he's late—as being my son, he often is. I have so little sense of time that when he said he needed something from the sixties it took me a moment to place that decade. It's the one he was born toward the end of.

I asked, "What sort of stuff you want to wear?"

He said, "I don't know. Whatever they wore then."

5   We went up to the attic, into a long, low room under the eaves where I've squirrelled away some boxes of old stuff; I dug into one box, and the first thing I hauled out was the very thing he wanted. A thigh-length leather vest covered with fringe and studded with silver, it dates from around 1967, a fanciful time in college-boy fashions. Like many boys, I grew up in nice clothes my mother bought, but was meanwhile admiring Roy Rogers, Sergeant Rock, the Cisco Kid, and other sharp dressers, so when I left home I was ready to step out and be somebody. Military Surplus was the basic style then—olive drab, and navy-blue pea jackets—with a touch of Common Man in the work boots and blue work shirts, but if you showed up in Riverboat Gambler or Spanish Peasant or Rodeo King nobody blinked, nobody laughed. I haven't worn the vest in ten years, but a few weeks ago, seeing a picture of Michael Jackson wearing a fancy band jacket like the ones the Beatles wore on the cover of "Sgt. Pepper," I missed the fun I used to have getting dressed in the morning. Pull on the jeans, a shirt with brilliant-red roses, a pair of Red Wing boots. A denim jacket. Rose-tinted glasses. A cowboy hat. Or an engineer's cap. Or, instead of jeans, bib overalls. Or white trousers with blue stripes. Take off the denim jacket, take off the rose shirt, try the neon-green bowling shirt with "Moose" stitched on the pocket, the black dinner jacket. Now the dark-green Chinese Army cap. And an orange tie with hula dancers and palm trees.

Then—presto!—I pulled the rose shirt out. He put it on, and the vest, which weighs about fifteen pounds, and by then I had found him a hat—a broad-brimmed panama that ought to make you think of a cotton planter enjoying a Sazerac[1] on a veranda in New Orleans. I followed him down to his bedroom, where he admired himself in a full-length mirror.

"Who wore this?" he asked.

I said that I did.

"Did you really? This? You?"

---

[1]**Sazerac** A bourbon cocktail flavored with a bitter liqueur

10   Yes, I really did. After he was born, in 1969, I wore it less and less, finally settling down with what I think of as the Dad look, and now I would
no sooner wear my old fringed vest in public than walk around in a taffeta
tutu. I loved the fact that it fitted him so well, though, and his pleasure at the
heft and extravagance of the thing, the poses he struck in front of the mirror. Later, when he got home and reported that his costume was a big hit
and that all his friends had tried on the vest, it made me happy again. You
squirrel away old stuff on the principle of its being useful and interesting
someday; it's wonderful when the day finally arrives. That vest was waiting
for a boy to come along—a boy who has a flair for the dramatic, who bursts
into rooms—and to jump right into the part. I'm happy to be the audience.

[1984]

 TOPICS FOR CRITICAL THINKING AND WRITING

1. In the second line of this essay we are told that the action begins "About
   five o'clock last Sunday evening." Does it matter that we know what
   time it was, or what day of the week? Explain.

2. Much of paragraph 1 is used to describe the way the son enters the
   room. How does the description characterize the son? How does it relate to the point of the narrative?

3. Toward the end of paragraph 5 Keillor writes a string of fragments. Try
   to describe the effect of this rhetorical device.

4. In the next-to-last paragraph, what feelings toward his father does the
   son communicate in "Did you really? This? You?" What feelings does
   the father have for his son, and how do you know?

5. In the last paragraph Keillor says he settled down with "what I think of
   as the Dad look." When you read that, what picture of him comes to
   mind? Try to describe the clothes, the body stance, the expression of a
   man wearing "the Dad look." Be as specific as you can.

6. The conclusion to the piece is: "I'm happy to be the audience." What
   details in the account make the word "audience" especially fitting? And
   what other details persuade you that "happy" is the precise word to
   summarize the tone of the essay?

7. In the last paragraph the writer says, "You squirrel away old stuff on the
   principle of its being useful and interesting someday." What do you (or
   members of your family) "squirrel away"? Why? Explain, in two or three
   paragraphs.

CHAPTER 6

Thinking Critically about Essays

A Casebook on Francis Bacon's "Of Parents and Children"

In this chapter we give the text of a short essay by Francis Bacon (Bacon is customarily regarded as the first writer of essays in English). We include the following critiques:

1. An essay by a teacher, Juanita Miranda, indicating why she finds the essay to be of interest
2. An essay by a student, Anne Rosenberg, indicating why she does not find the essay to be of interest
3. A brief comment by C. S. Lewis, author of a standard history of literature of the period, in which Lewis explains why he thinks Bacon's essays appeal chiefly to adolescents

 FRANCIS BACON

Francis Bacon (1561–1626) was born into a well-connected Elizabethan family. A shrewd politician, he rose steadily, becoming Lord Chancellor of England in 1618, but in 1621 he was accused of taking bribes, and his last five years were spent in retirement. He did not write Shakespeare's plays, but he did write essays (we print one here) and longer philosophical treatises.

As we mention on page 101, Bacon introduced the word essay *(from the French* essayer, *"to try") into the English language in 1597, when he used the word for the title of a book of ten short pieces that were not much more than jottings from a notebook. The idea was that these writings were "attempts," "testings," not thoroughly revised and carefully thought out final versions. In 1612 Bacon published an amplified version, with 38 essays, and in 1625 he published the last version, with 58 essays.*

Of Parents and Children

The joys of parents are secret, and so are their griefs and fears; they cannot utter the one, nor they will not utter the other. Children sweeten labors, but they make misfortunes more bitter; they increase the cares of life, but they mitigate the remembrance of death. The perpetuity by generation[1] is common to beasts; but memory, merit, and noble works, are proper to[2] men: and surely a man shall see the noblest works and foundations have proceeded from childless men, which have sought to express the images of their minds where those of their bodies have failed; so the care of posterity is most in them that have no posterity. They that are the first raisers of their houses[3] are most indulgent towards their children, beholding them as the continuance, not only of their kind, but of their work; and so both children and creatures.[4]

The difference in affection of parents towards their several children is many times unequal, and sometimes unworthy, especially in the mother; as Solomon saith, "A wise son rejoiceth the father, but an ungracious son shames the mother." A man shall see, where there is a house full of children, one or two of the eldest respected,[5] and the youngest made wantons;[6] but in the midst some that are as it were forgotten, who, many times, nevertheless, prove the best. The illiberality of parents, in allowance towards their children, is an harmful error, makes them base, acquaints them with shifts, makes them sort[7] with mean company, and makes them surfeit more when they come to plenty: and, therefore, the proof is best[8] when men keep their authority towards their children, but not their purse. Men have a foolish manner (both parents, and schoolmasters, and servants) in creating and breeding an emulation between brothers during childhood, which many times sorteth to[9] discord when they are men, and disturbeth families. The Italians make little difference between children and nephews, or near kinsfolks; but so they be of the lump, they care not, though they pass not through their own body; and, to say truth, in nature it is much a like matter; insomuch that we see a nephew sometimes resembleth an uncle or a kinsman more than his own parent, as the blood happens.

Let parents choose betimes[10] the vocations and courses they mean their children should take, for then they are most flexible, and let them not too

---

[1]**generation** copulation   [2]**proper to** distinctive of   [3]**the first raisers of their houses** the first to make their families prosperous   [4]**creatures** creations, works   [5]**respected** given attention   [6]**made wantons** spoiled   [7]**sort** consort, associate with   [8]**the proof is best** experience proves it is best   [9]**sorteth to** turns into   [10]**betimes** early

much apply themselves to[11] the disposition of their children, as thinking they will take best to that which they have most mind to. It is true that if the affection or aptness of the children be extraordinary, then it is good not to cross it; but generally the precept is good, *Optimum elige, suave et facile illud faciet consuetudo.*[12]

Younger brothers are commonly fortunate, but seldom or never where the elder are disinherited.

TOPICS FOR CRITICAL THINKING AND WRITING

1. Paraphrase (that is, rewrite in your own words) Bacon's first paragraph. (An example of a paraphrase of the first sentence: Parents communicate to others neither the pleasures nor the difficulties and anxieties of parenthood, because they find no words adequate to express their pleasures, and they don't want to talk about their troubles.)

2. Bacon's sentences are often built on contrasts, and formulated to emphasize them. List six pairs of contrasting words and phrases in the first paragraph. Your list might begin with these contrasts in the first sentence:

    joys/griefs and fears
    cannot utter/will not utter

   How effective do you find this device? Do the contrasts help clarify his ideas, or do they obscure them?

3. Why, according to Bacon, should parents give generous allowances to their children? What arguments might support the opposing view, that parents, regardless of their wealth and for the children's own good, should allow children little or no money to spend?

4. What role, according to Bacon, should parents have in their children's choice of occupations and careers?

5. Try imitating Bacon's style. You might take one of his sentences as your opening sentence and write a paragraph developing the idea. You can borrow Bacon's ideas and you should try to use his syntax, but invent your own examples. Or you might write a paragraph drawing on Bacon's ideas and syntax but arguing the opposite view. The first sentence of your paragraph might be, "Let parents not choose the vocations and courses their children should take. . . ."

JUANITA MIRANDA

Juanita Miranda was born in Havana in 1953, but she was brought up in Florida. She has written, under a pseudonym, two books of science fiction and, under another pseudonym, several essays on the Bible. We reprint a brief essay that served as an introduction to a selection of Bacon's essays.

---

[11]**apply themselves to** consider   [12]***Optimum . . . consuetudo*** Choose the best; habit will make it pleasant and easy (Latin)

The Pleasure of Tasting Bacon

Perhaps the best way to get yourself into a frame of mind to enjoy Bacon's essays is to forget everything you may have heard about Bacon being an amazingly shrewd observer and the father of modern science—you will *not* learn from Bacon about the ways in which our world operates—and start reading the essays in something of the spirit that you might read a book of nursery rhymes or riddles. That is, read (at least at first) for the fun offered by the language.

Reading for fun may seem like an outdated or unworthy idea, but please be assured that respectable people have done it, and respected authors have recommended it. For instance, Virginia Woolf, in "The Modern Essay," argued that the chief job of a good essay is to offer pleasure:

> The principle which controls it is simply that it should give us pleasure; the desire which impels us when we take it from the shelf is simply to receive pleasure. Everything in an essay must be subdued to that end. (293)

It happens that, as she continues, Woolf specifically mentions Bacon, and the wisdom for which he is renowned. An essay, she says,

> should lay us under a spell with its first word, and we should only wake, refreshed, with its last. In the interval we may pass through the most various experiences of amusement, surprise, interest, indignation; we may soar to the heights of fantasy with [Charles] Lamb or plunge to the depths of wisdom with Bacon, but we must never be roused. The essay must lap us about and draw its curtain across the world. (293-94)

These words, written in England early in the twentieth century, reflect the privileged society into which Woolf was born, a society concerned more with books and works of art and a savoring of one's own pleasant experiences than with earning a living. Even in her novels Woolf often seems less concerned with carefully depicting the world around her—which is the traditional material of the novelist—than with the mind's exquisite responses—the famous "stream of consciousness." On the other hand, no one can say that Woolf was unaware of the realities around her. Her writings, especially the essays collected in *A Room of One's Own* (1929), are now regarded as among the most important feminist writings of our century. But in her writings *about* writings, she emphasizes not what those writings are about—the highly specific worlds that they depict—but the feel (so to speak) of the words on the page. And that is why her highest praise for a book is not that it teaches us about life but that it gives us pleasure.

What did Bacon himself say about his aims? We can get a clue in the Dedication to his collection of essays, where he apologizes for their brevity and says, "My hope is they may be as grains of salt that will rather give you an appetite than offend you with satiety." The imagery of food—"grains of salt"—suggests that Bacon hoped his essays would afford an immediate and almost sensuous pleasure.

Let's look, in our quest for pleasure, at some of the opening lines in Bacon's essays. He begins "Of Gardens" by saying,

> God Almighty first planted a garden. And indeed it is
> the purest of pleasures.

I imagine that even a reader who is not committed to the literal truth of the Hebrew Bible will take delight in this line, with its evocation of the very beginning of the world. Perhaps it is all a myth, we shrug, but what a lovely myth. And take the second line. Bacon, great advocate of the inductive method that is supposed to lie at the heart of scientific study, *ought* to be careful about generalizing, but here we are hardly concerned with whether or not it is true that creating a garden is "the purest of pleasures." Doubtless many of us can nominate purer pleasures—solving a mathematical problem, playing golf, sleeping late, or whatever. But somehow, at least for the moment, we are brought into Bacon's world, and—again, for the moment—we believe him. On putting the essay down we do not say to ourselves, "Yes, I must plant a garden, for it is the purest of pleasures," but we do feel that we have just experienced a great pleasure in reading the essay, whether its assertions are true or not.

Speaking of truth, let's look at the famous beginning of another essay, "Of Truth":

> "What is truth?" said jesting Pilate; and would not stay
> for an answer.

Bacon here is following the Gospel According to St. John (18.37), where Jesus says, " 'My task is to bear witness to the truth.'. . . Pilate said, 'What is truth?' With those words he went out again. . . ." Whether the Biblical Pilate was indeed "jesting" does not matter; Bacon's interpretation is, so to speak, more real—and more delightful to the mind—than whatever reality the Biblical scholars show us.

Let's look briefly at one essay, "Of Parents and Children," to see what it offers. Certainly one thing that it does *not* offer is a firm organization. It begins with an opening comment on the joys and griefs of parents and children (two sentences) and then drifts into a comment to the effect that childless men produce "the noblest works." The essay then moves to almost random observations about how parents should treat their children, and it concludes with an irrelevant comment about the fortunes of younger brothers.

A second thing that the essay does not offer is indisputable truth. For instance, the dubious assertion that "the noblest works . . . have proceeded from childless men" is supported by the dubious explanation that these men "have sought to express the images of their minds where those of their bodies have failed." Perhaps a reader momentarily pauses from reading the essay, and starts thinking about which men produced "the noblest works." How far can we go? How many of us know whether Plato, Mozart, Jefferson, Einstein—and, for that matter, Bacon and Virginia Woolf—did or did not have children? And how many of us are likely to bother to find out? True, we may briefly think of some people we know, and we may say that this or that person compensates for the lack of children by working hard, but that is not quite what Bacon is saying.

Does Bacon perhaps offer us a different sort of truth, truth not about what is what in the world, but how we should behave? Certainly the essays are filled with advice, much of it probably sound—at least some of the time. For instance he says that "The illiberality [i.e., miserliness] of parents, in allowance towards their children, is an harmful error, makes them base, acquaints them with shifts [i.e., deceits]. . . . " Possibly we nod our head in agreement, but possibly we say, if we come out from under the "spell" that the essay has cast (Virginia Woolf's word), "Nonsense." But it is best not to let the spell break; it is best (if we wish for pleasure) to remain within the essay. To quote Virginia Woolf once again, "The essay must lap us about and draw its curtain across the world." And now we can add that Woolf, at the end of her essay, returns to this image of the curtain. She says that an essay must have an *idea;* that is, the author of a successful essay convinces us that he or she is in earnest. Such an author has

> an obstinate conviction which lifts ephemeral sounds through the misty sphere of anybody's language to the land where there is a perpetual marriage, a perpetual union. Vague as all definitions are, a good essay must draw its curtain round us, but it must be a curtain that shuts us in, not out. (307)

It must be evident to all readers that if much that Bacon says is not true, or is no longer true—for instance his advice that parents should make early decisions about the careers of their children—he nevertheless makes compelling reading, probably for the very reason that Virginia Woolf suggests: Throughout his essays we see a strong attachment to ideas, and this energetic concern to get it right, to see clearly (even if he doesn't always see clearly) and to sharply formulate what he has seen, has enabled him to find words that draw us into his world. There is nothing wishy-washy about the writing, and we willingly allow the curtain to shut us within the essay.

[1994]

Work Cited

Woolf, Virginia. *The Common Reader: First and Second Series.* New York: Harcourt, 1948.

 ## TOPICS FOR CRITICAL THINKING AND WRITING

1. What is the author's thesis?
2. Do you think Miranda adequately supports her thesis? Explain.
3. Putting aside the question of whether you agree with the thesis, what suggestions can you offer that would strengthen the essay?

 ## ANNE ROSENBERG

Anne Rosenberg wrote this essay while an undergraduate at Tufts University.

Some Limitations of Bacon's Essays

Bacon's essays doubtless deserve a place in the history of literature, but they are badly dated and, to tell the truth, are rather boring. Let's begin with the second point.

Although his subjects are varied—ranging from ambition, architecture, gardens, parents and children, to the nature of truth—his style is pretty much the same. This would not in itself be a fault (most writers have a limited repertoire), but this style is a rather annoying one. It consists chiefly of two devices: (1) parallelism, often with a contrast in the ideas, and (2) quotation of authorities, sometimes from the Bible and sometimes from classical authors. Thus, to take the first point, "Of Parents and Children" begins this way:

> The joys of parents are secret, and so are their griefs
> and fears; they cannot utter the one, nor they will not utter
> the other.

This is interesting, but Bacon follows the formula so relentlessly that a reader tires of it. One comes to realize that if we read "The joys" we will in a moment hear about "griefs": if we read about "the one," we will in a moment hear about "the other." If we hear that something is sweet, we will in a moment hear that something else is bitter. Even the quotations that Bacon sprinkles in his essays, in an effort to add authority and to vary the voice, tend to use the same pattern. In "Of Parents and Children," for instance, he quotes from Proverbs, in the Hebrew Bible:

> As Solomon saith, "A wise son rejoiceth the father, but an
> ungracious son shames the mother."

And this quotation brings me to my other point, that the essays are badly dated. In particular, I want to point out that Bacon's world was a world in which men held almost all of the power. True, one woman, Queen Elizabeth, held immense power, but for the most part Bacon's world was a world of men, and women seem barely to exist. Apparently they exist chiefly as a means of bringing more men into the world. Thus, "Of Parents and Children" says nothing about women. Granted, "men" can include women, as when we say "All men are created equal," but in Bacon's essay it is pretty clear that when he says "men" he means males. The only reference to a female is in the line already quoted from the Bible (Proverbs 10.1), and in Bacon's introductory comment to that line. And exactly what does this line say? It says that a father takes joy in a wise son, and a mother is shamed by "an ungracious son." The implication is that if the son is "ungracious," it is the mother's fault, and she should be ashamed. Why should not the father be equally ashamed? Bacon doesn't tell us; he tells us only that the father is busy taking joy in his wise son. Apparently a mother can take no joy, and presumably no credit, for a wise son.

Bacon's lack of concern for women is, for me, the chief sign that his writing is irrelevant to the modern world, but of course many passages that have nothing to do with women can also be pointed to. For instance, Bacon says that parents should choose careers for their children early (naturally, he is thinking only of their sons), and he gives a most unpleasant reason: The children "are most flexible" when young, that is, they can easily be bent to their parents' will. Surely today we have better ideas about child-rearing.

Does this mean that we should not read Bacon? No. We can read him if we want to get an idea of what life was like in England and Europe in the late sixteenth century. He very clearly reveals to us—much more than Shakespeare, because Bacon was so a man of his age, without deep insight into human nature—what life was like in the period. He gave his readers worldly advice about how to get on in the world—how to repress those who were weaker than themselves, and how to fawn on those who were stronger. This is not surprising. Bacon was a political animal who came from a powerful family and who did not hesitate to adapt himself to those who were more powerful. As a judge, he took bribes; as a courtier, he betrayed his friend Essex when he got the signal that Queen Elizabeth wanted to get rid of Essex. The essays do not of course reveal these outrageous faults, but they do reveal a man who looks on life without feeling, and who tells his readers how to manipulate the world. One of his most famous lines is "Knowledge is power." Bacon seems concerned chiefly with power, and by now we know—or perhaps women especially know—that although power is immensely important it is not the whole of life. In fact, the Baconian lust for power has helped to lower the quality of life.

In "How Should One Read a Book?" Virginia Woolf offers some advice:

> Do not dictate to your author; try to become him. Be his fel-
> low-worker and accomplice. If you hang back, and reserve
> and criticize at first, you are preventing yourself from get-
> ting the fullest possible value from what you read. (282)

This seems to me to be very good advice, especially (as Woolf says) when one reads an author "at first." But the words "at first" imply that on a second or third or tenth reading, after one has done one's best "to become" the author's "fellow-worker and accomplice," there comes a time to step back and think for oneself, think critically about what one is doing (in this case, reading). And one may then say, if one is reading Bacon's *Essays,* "No, this is not interesting, and it is not true—at least for me." And at this point, after having patiently tried to join Bacon in his coldhearted view of human relationships, one closes the book.

Work Cited

Woolf, Virginia. *The Common Reader: First and Second Series.* New York: Harcourt, 1948.

 ## TOPICS FOR CRITICAL THINKING AND WRITING

1. What is the author's thesis?
2. Do you think Rosenberg adequately supports her thesis? Explain.
3. Putting aside the question of whether you agree with the thesis, what suggestions can you offer that would strengthen the essay?
4. Miranda and Rosenberg both quote from Virginia Woolf, but they quote different passages. What is the *purpose* of each writer in quoting from Woolf?

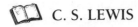 C. S. LEWIS

C[live] S[taples] Lewis (1898–1963) taught medieval and Renaissance literature at Oxford and later at Cambridge. In addition to writing about literature, he wrote fiction (including The Chronicles of Narnia*), poetry, and numerous essays and books on moral and religious topics.*

The following passage comes from Lewis's highly readable book on early Renaissance England, English Literature in the Sixteenth Century *(1954). We have given our own title to this extract from Lewis's discussion of Bacon's* Essays.

A Book for Adolescents

Even the completed *Essays* of 1625 is a book whose reputation curiously outweighs any real pleasure or profit that most people have found in it. . . . The truth is, it is a book for adolescents. It is they who underline (as I see from the copy before me) sentences like 'There is little friendshipe in the world, and least of all between equals': a man of 40 either disbelieves it or takes it for granted. No one, even if he wished, could really learn 'policie' from Bacon, for cunning, even more than virtue, lives in minute particulars. What makes young readers think they are learning is Bacon's manner; the dry, apophthegmatic sentences, in appearance so unrhetorical, so little concerned to produce an effect, fall on the ear like oracles and are thus in fact a most potent rhetoric. In that sense the *Essays* are a triumph of style, even of stylistic illusion. For the same reason they are better to quote than to reread.

[1954]

 TOPICS FOR CRITICAL THINKING AND WRITING

1. What are "apophthegmatic sentences"? Which sentences, if any, in "Of Parents and Children" are examples?
2. Do you agree that some of Bacon's sentences "fall on the ear like oracles"? If you do agree, explain why they have this effect.

STORIES TRUE AND FALSE

The word *story* comes from *history;* the stories that historians, biographers, and journalists narrate are supposed to be true accounts of what happened. The stories of novelists and short-story writers, however, are admittedly untrue; they are "fiction," things made up, imagined, manufactured. As readers, we come to a supposedly true story with expectations different from those we bring to fiction.

Consider the difference between reading a narrative in a newspaper and one in a book of short stories. If, while reading a newspaper, we come across a story of, say, a subway accident, we assume that the account is true, and we read it for the information about a relatively unusual event. Anyone hurt? What sort of people? In our neighborhood? Whose fault? When we read a book of fiction, however, we do not expect to encounter literal truths; we read novels and short stories not for facts but for pleasure and for some insight or for a sense of what an aspect of life means to the writer. Consider the following short story by Grace Paley.

 ## GRACE PALEY

Born in New York City, Grace Paley attended Hunter College and New York University but left without a degree. (She now teaches at Sarah Lawrence College.) While raising two children she wrote poetry and then, in the 1950s, turned to writing fiction.

Paley's chief subject is the life of little people struggling in the Big City. Of life she has said, "How daily life is lived is a mystery to me. You write about what's mysterious to you. What is it like? Why do people do this?" Of the short story she has said, *"It can be just telling a little tale, or writing a complicated philosophical story. It can be a song, almost."*

Samuel

Some boys are very tough. They're afraid of nothing. They are the ones who climb a wall and take a bow at the top. Not only are they brave on the roof, but they make a lot of noise in the darkest part of the cellar where even the super hates to go. They also jiggle and hop on the platform between the locked doors of the subway cars.

Four boys are jiggling on the swaying platform. Their names are Alfred, Calvin, Samuel, and Tom. The men and the women in the cars on either side watch them. They don't like them to jiggle or jump but don't want to interfere. Of course some of the men in the cars were once brave boys like these. One of them had ridden the tail of a speeding truck from New York to Rockaway Beach without getting off, without his sore fingers losing hold. Nothing happened to him then or later. He had made a compact with other boys who preferred to watch: Starting at Eighth Avenue and Fifteenth Street, he would get to some specified place, maybe Twenty-third and the river, by hopping the tops of the moving trucks. This was hard to do when one truck turned a corner in the wrong direction and the nearest truck was a couple of feet too high. He made three or four starts before succeeding. He had gotten his idea from a film at school called *The Romance of Logging*. He had finished high school, married a good friend, was in a responsible job and going to night school.

These two men and others looked at the four boys jumping and jiggling on the platform and thought, It must be fun to ride that way, especially now the weather is nice and we're out of the tunnel and way high over the Bronx. Then they thought, These kids do seem to be acting sort of stupid. They *are* little. Then they thought of some of the brave things they had done when they were boys and jiggling didn't seem so risky.

The ladies in the car became very angry when they looked at the four boys. Most of them brought their brows together and hoped the boys could see their extreme disapproval. One of the ladies wanted to get up and say, Be careful you dumb kids, get off that platform or I'll call a cop. But three of the boys were Negroes and the fourth was something else she couldn't tell for sure. She was afraid they'd be fresh and laugh at her and embarrass her. She wasn't afraid they'd hit her, but she was afraid of embarrassment. Another lady thought, Their mothers never know where they are. It wasn't true in this particular case. Their mothers all knew that they had gone to see the missile exhibit on Fourteenth Street.

5   Out on the platform, whenever the train accelerated, the boys would raise their hands and point them up to the sky to act like rockets going off, then they rat-tat-tatted the shatterproof glass pane like machine guns, although no machine guns had been exhibited.

For some reason known only to the motorman, the train began a sudden slowdown. The lady who was afraid of embarrassment saw the boys jerk forward and backward and grab the swinging guard chains. She had her own boy at home. She stood up with determination and went to the door. She slid it open and said, "You boys will be hurt. You'll be killed. I'm going to call the conductor if you don't just go into the next car and sit down and be quiet."

Two of the boys said, "Yes'm," and acted as though they were about to go. Two of them blinked their eyes a couple of times and pressed their lips together. The train resumed its speed. The door slid shut, parting the lady and the boys. She leaned against the side door because she had to get off at the next stop.

The boys opened their eyes wide at each other and laughed. The lady blushed. The boys looked at her and laughed harder. They began to pound each other's back. Samuel laughed the hardest and pounded Alfred's back until Alfred coughed and the tears came. Alfred held tight to the chain hook. Samuel pounded him even harder when he saw the tears. He said, "Why you bawling? You a baby, huh?" and laughed. One of the men whose boyhood had been more watchful than brave became angry. He stood up straight and looked at the boys for a couple of seconds. Then he walked in a citizenly way to the end of the car, where he pulled the emergency cord. Almost at once, with a terrible hiss, the pressure of air abandoned the brakes and the wheels were caught and held.

People standing in the most secure places fell forward, then backward. Samuel had let go of his hold on the chain so he could pound Tom as well as Alfred. All the passengers in the cars whipped back and forth, but he pitched only forward and fell head first to be crushed and killed between the cars.

10   The train had stopped hard, halfway into the station, and the conductor called at once for the trainmen who knew about this kind of death and how to take the body from the wheels and brakes. There was silence except for passengers from other cars who asked, What happened! What happened! The ladies waited around wondering if he might be an only child. The men recalled other afternoons with very bad endings. The little boys stayed close to each other, leaning and touching shoulders and arms and legs.

When the policeman knocked at the door and told her about it, Samuel's mother began to scream. She screamed all day and moaned all night, though the doctors tried to quiet her with pills.

Oh, oh, she hopelessly cried. She did not know how she could ever find another boy like that one. However, she was a young woman and she became pregnant. Then for a few months she was hopeful. The child born to her was a boy. They brought him to be seen and nursed. She smiled. But immediately she saw that this baby wasn't Samuel. She and her husband together have had other children, but never again will a boy exactly like Samuel be known.

[1968]

You might think about the ways in which "Samuel" differs from a newspaper story of an accident in a subway. (You might even want to write a newspaper version of the happening.) In some ways, of course, Paley's story faintly resembles an account that might appear in a newspaper. Journalists are taught to give information about who, what, when, where, and why, and Paley does provide this. Thus, the *characters* (Samuel and others) are the journalist's Who; the *plot* (the boys were jiggling on the platform, and when a man pulled the emergency cord one of them was killed) is the What; the *setting* (the subway, presumably in modern times) is the When and the Where; the *motivation* (the irritation of the man who pulls the emergency cord) is the Why.

To write about fiction you would think about these elements of fiction, asking yourself questions about each, both separately and how they work together. Much of the rest of this chapter will be devoted to examining such words as *character* and *plot,* but before you read those pages notice the following questions we've posed about "Samuel" and try responding to them. Your responses will teach you a good deal about what fiction is, and some of the ways in which it works.

 ## TOPICS FOR CRITICAL THINKING AND WRITING

1. Paley wrote the story, but an unspecified person *tells* it. Describe the voice of this narrator in the first paragraph. Is the voice neutral and objective, or do you hear some sort of attitude, a point of view? If you do hear an attitude, what words or phrases in the story indicate it?

2. What do you know about the setting—the locale—of "Samuel"? What can you infer about the neighborhood?

3. In the fourth paragraph we are told that "three of the boys were Negroes and the fourth was something else." Is race important in this story? Is Samuel "Negro" or "something else"? Does it matter?

4. Exactly *why* did a man walk "in a citizenly way to the end of the car, where he pulled the emergency cord"? Do you think the author blames him? What evidence can you offer to support your view? Do *you* blame him? Or do you blame the boys? Or anyone? Explain.

5. The story is called "Samuel," and it is, surely, about him. But what happens after Samuel dies? (You might want to list the events.) What else is the story about? (You might want to comment on why you believe the items in your list are important.)

6. Can you generalize about what the men think of the jigglers and about what the women think? Is Paley saying something about the sexes? About the attitudes of onlookers in a big city?

Plot and Character

In some stories, such as adventure stories, the emphasis is on physical action—wanderings and strange encounters. In Paley's "Samuel," however, although there is a violent death in the subway, the emphasis is less on an unusual happening than on other things: for instance, the contrast between some of the adults, the contrast between uptight adults and energetic children, and the impact of the death on Samuel's mother.

The novelist E. M. Forster, in a short critical study entitled *Aspects of the Novel* (1927), introduced a distinction between **flat characters** and **round characters.** A *flat character* is relatively simple and usually has only one trait: loving wife (or jealous wife), tyrannical husband (or meek husband), braggart, pedant, hypocrite, or whatever. Thus, in "Samuel" we are told about a man "whose boyhood had been more watchful than brave." This man walks "in a citizenly way" to the end of the subway car, where he pulls the emergency cord. He is, so to speak, the conventional solid citizen. He is flat, or uncomplicated, but that is probably part of what the author is getting at. A *round character,* on the other hand, embodies several or even many traits that cohere to form a complex personality. Of course in a story as short as "Samuel" we can hardly expect to find fully rounded characters, but we can say that, at least by comparison with the "citizenly" man, the man who had once been a wild kid, had gone to night school, and now holds a "responsible job" is relatively round. Paley's story asserts rather than shows the development of the character, but much fiction does show such a development. Whereas a flat character is usually *static* (at the end of the story the character is pretty much what he or she was at the start), a round character is likely to be *dynamic,* changing considerably as the story progresses.

A frequent assignment in writing courses is to set forth a character sketch, describing some person in the story or novel. In preparing such a sketch, take these points into consideration:

1. What the character says (but consider that what he or she says need not be taken at face value; the character may be hypocritical, or self-deceived, or biased—you will have to detect this from the context).
2. What the character does.
3. What other characters say about the character.
4. What others *do.* (A character who serves as a contrast to another character is called a *foil.*)

A character sketch can be complex and demanding, but usually you will want to do more than write a character sketch. You will probably discuss the character's function, or trace the development of his or her personality, or contrast the character with another. (One of the most difficult topics, the narrator's personality, will be discussed later in this chapter under the heading "Narrative Point of View.") In writing on one of these topics you will probably still want to keep in mind the four suggestions for getting at a character, but you will also want to go further, relating your findings to additional matters that we discuss later.

Most discussions of fiction are concerned with happenings and with *why* they happen. Why does Samuel die? Because (to put it too simply) his youthful high spirits clash with the values of a "citizenly" adult. Paley never explicitly says anything like this, but a reader of the story tries to make sense out of the details, filling in the gaps.

Things happen, in most good fiction, at least partly because the people have certain personalities or character traits (moral, intellectual, and emotional qualities) and, given their natures, because they respond plausibly to other personalities. What their names are and what they look like may help you to understand them, but probably the best guide to characters is what they do and what they say. As we get to know more about their drives and goals—and especially about the choices they make—we enjoy seeing the writer complete the portraits, finally presenting us with a coherent and credible picture of people in action. In this view, plot and character are inseparable. Plot is not simply a series of happenings, but happenings that come out of character, that reveal character, and that influence character. Henry James puts it thus: "What is character but the determination of incident? What is incident but the illustration of character?" James goes on: "It is an incident for a woman to stand up with her hand resting on a table and look out at you in a certain way."

Foreshadowing

Although some stories depend heavily on a plot with a surprise ending, other stories prepare the reader for the outcome, at least to some degree. The

foreshadowing that would eliminate surprise, or greatly reduce it, and thus destroy a story that has nothing else to offer, is a powerful tool in the hands of a writer of serious fiction. In "Samuel," the reader perhaps senses even in the first paragraph that these "tough" boys who "jiggle and hop on the platform" may be vulnerable, may come to an unfortunate end. When a woman says, "You'll be killed," the reader doesn't yet know if she is right, but a seed has been planted.

Even in such a story as Faulkner's "A Rose for Emily" (p. 177), where we are surprised to learn near the end that Miss Emily has slept beside the decaying corpse of her dead lover, from the outset we expect something strange; that is, we are not surprised by the surprise, only by its precise nature. The first sentence of the story tell us that after Miss Emily's funeral (the narrator begins at the end) the townspeople cross her threshold "out of curiosity to see the inside of her house, which no one save an old manservant . . . had seen in at least ten years." As the story progresses, we see Miss Emily prohibiting people from entering the house, we hear that after a certain point no one ever sees Homer Barron again, that "the front door remained closed," and (a few paragraphs before the end of the story) that the townspeople "knew that there was one room in that region above the stairs which no one had seen in forty years." The paragraph preceding the revelation that "the man himself lay in the bed" is devoted to a description of Homer's dust-covered clothing and toilet articles. In short, however much we are unprepared for the precise revelation, we are prepared for some strange thing in the house; and, given Miss Emily's purchase of poison and Homer's disappearance, we have some idea of what will be revealed.

James Joyce's "Araby" (p. 586) is another example of a story in which the beginning is a preparation for all that follows. Consider the first two paragraphs (a "blind" street is a dead-end street):

> North Richmond Street, being blind, was a quiet street except at the hour when the Christian Brothers' school set the boys free. An uninhabited house of two storeys stood at the blind end, detached from its neighbours in a square ground. The other houses of the street, conscious of decent lives within them, gazed at one another with brown imperturbable faces.
>
> The former tenant of our house, a priest, had died in the back drawing-room. Air, musty from having been long enclosed, hung in all the rooms, and the waste room behind the kitchen was littered with old useless papers. Among these I found a few paper-covered books, the pages of which were curled and damp: *The Abbot*, by Walter Scott, *The Devout Communicant* and *The Memoirs of Vidocq*. I liked the last best because its leaves were yellow. The wild garden behind the house contained a central apple-tree and a few straggling bushes under one of which I found the late tenant's rusty bicycle pump. He had been a very charitable priest; in his will he had left all his money to institutions and the furniture of his house to his sister.

Of course the full meaning of the passage will not become apparent until you have read the entire story. In a sense, a story has at least three lives:

- When we read the story sentence by sentence, trying to turn the sequence of sentences into a consistent whole
- When we have finished reading the story and we think back on it as a whole, even if we think no more than "That was a waste of time"

• When we reread a story, knowing already even as we read the first line how it will turn out at the end

Let's assume that you have not at some earlier time read the whole of "Araby." On the basis only of a reading of the first two paragraphs, what might you highlight or underline? Here are the words that one student marked:

blind	musty
quiet	kitchen was littered
set the boys free	leaves were yellow
brown imperturbable faces	wild garden . . . apple-tree
priest	charitable priest

No two readers will come up with exactly the same list (if you live on North Richmond Street, you will probably underline it and put an exclamation mark in the margin; and if you attended a parochial school, you'll probably underline "Christian Brothers' school"), but perhaps most readers—despite their varied experience—would agree that Joyce is giving us a picture of what he elsewhere called the "paralysis" of Ireland. How the story will turn out is, of course, unknown to a first-time reader. Perhaps the paralysis will increase, or perhaps it will be broken. Joyce goes on adding sentence to sentence, trying to shape the reader's response, and the reader goes on reading, making meaning out of the sentences.

Setting and Atmosphere

Foreshadowing normally makes use of **setting.** The setting or environment in the first two paragraphs of Joyce's "Araby" is not mere geography, not mere locale: it provides an **atmosphere,** an air that the characters breathe, a world in which they move. Narrowly speaking, the setting is the physical surroundings— the furniture, the architecture, the landscape, the climate—and these often are highly appropriate to the characters who are associated with them. Thus, in Emily Brontë's *Wuthering Heights* the passionate Earnshaw family is associated with Wuthering Heights, the storm-exposed moorland, whereas the mild Linton family is associated with Thrushcross Grange in the sheltered valley below.

Broadly speaking, setting includes not only the physical surroundings but also a point (or several points) in time. The background against which we see the characters and the happenings may be specified as morning or evening, spring or fall. In a good story, this temporal setting will probably be highly relevant; it will probably be part of the story's meaning, perhaps providing an ironic contrast to or exerting an influence on the characters.

Symbolism

Writers draw on experience, but an experience is not a happening through which the author necessarily passed; rather, it may be a thought, an emotion, or a vision that is meaningful and is embodied in the piece of fiction for all to read. Inevitably the writer uses **symbols.** Symbols are neither puzzles nor colorful details but are among the concrete embodiments that give the story whatever accuracy and meaning it has. Joyce's dead-end street, dead priest, apple tree, and rusty bicycle pump all help to define very precisely the condition of a thoroughly believable Dublin. In Hemingway's *A Farewell to Arms* the river in which Frederic Henry swims when he deserts the army is a river as material as the guns he flees from.

On the other hand, Joyce's dead-end street, dead priest, and "central apple-tree," along with many other details, may suggest Eden after the Fall, a decaying world, and (for some readers) a failed religion. Frederic Henry's swim in the river may suggest that Henry is cleansing himself from the war. The "tender" leaves mentioned at the outset of Chopin's "Ripe Figs" (p. 3) may suggest Babette's immaturity; the ripening figs may suggest a stage in her maturity; and the chrysanthemums, mentioned at the end of the story, may suggest the two older women, Maman and Frosine, enjoying an autumnal blossoming, a "second bloom," so to speak. If so, we can say that these things are symbolic; they are themselves, but they also stand for something more than themselves.

Narrative Point Of View

An author must choose a **point of view** (or sometimes, several points of view) from which he or she will narrate the story. The choice will contribute to the total effect that the story will have.

Narrative points of view can be divided into two sorts: **participant** (or **first-person**) and **nonparticipant** (or **third-person**). That is, the narrator may or may not be a character who participates in the story. Each of these two divisions can be subdivided:

    I. Participant (first-person narrative)
       A. Narrator as a major character
       B. Narrator as a minor character
   II. Nonparticipant (third-person narrative)
       A. Omniscient
       B. Selective omniscient
       C. Objective

Participant Points of View   In Frank O'Connor's "Guests of the Nation" (p. 590), the narrator is a major character. He, and not O'Connor, tells the story, and the story is chiefly about him; hence one can say that O'Connor uses a first-person (or participant) point of view. O'Connor has invented an Irishman who has fought against the English, and this narrator tells of the impact a happening had on him: "And anything that happened to me afterwards, I never felt the same about again."

But sometimes a first-person narrator tells a story that focuses on someone other than the narrator; he or she is a minor character, a peripheral witness, for example, to a story about Sally Jones, and we get the story of Sally filtered through, say, the eyes of her friend or brother or cat.

Nonparticipant Points of View   In a nonparticipant (third-person) point of view, the teller of the tale does not introduce himself or herself as a character. If the point of view is **omniscient,** the narrator relates what he or she wants to relate about the thoughts as well as the deeds of all the characters. The omniscient teller can enter the mind of any character; whereas the first-person narrator can only say, "I was angry" or "Jack seemed angry," the omniscient teller can say, "Jack was inwardly angry but gave no sign; Jill continued chatting, but she sensed his anger." Thus, in Paley's "Samuel," the narrator tells us that Samuel's mother was "hopeful," but when the new baby was born "immediately she saw that this baby wasn't Samuel."

Furthermore, a distinction can be made between **neutral omniscience** (the narrator recounts deeds and thoughts but does not judge) and **editorial omniscience** (the narrator not only recounts but also judges). An editorially omniscient narrator knows what goes on in the minds of all the characters and might comment approvingly or disapprovingly: "He closed the book, having finished the story, but, poor fellow, he had missed the meaning."

Because a short story can scarcely hope to develop a picture of several minds effectively, authors may prefer to limit their omniscience to the minds of a few of their characters, or even to that of only one of the characters; that is, they may use **selective omniscience** as the point of view. Selective omniscience provides a focus, especially if it is limited to a single character. When thus limited, the author sees one character from outside and from inside, but sees the other characters only from the outside and from the impact they have on the mind of this selected receptor. When selective omniscience attempts to record mental activity ranging from consciousness to the unconscious, from clear perceptions to confused longings, it is sometimes labeled the **stream-of-consciousness** point of view. The following example is from Katherine Anne Porter's "The Jilting of Granny Weatherall" (p. 1163):

> Her eyelids wavered and let in streamers of blue-gray light like tissue paper over her eyes. She must get up and pull the shades down or she'd never sleep. She was in bed again and the shades were not down. How could that happen? Better turn over, hide from the light, sleeping in the light gave you nightmares. "Mother, how do you feel now?" and a stinging wetness on her forehead. But I don't like having my face washed in cold water!

Finally, sometimes a third-person narrator does not enter even a single mind but records only what crosses an apparently dispassionate eye and ear. Such a point of view is **objective** (sometimes called the **camera** or **fly-on-the-wall** point of view). The absence of editorializing and of dissection of the mind often produces the effect of a play; we see and hear the characters in action. Much of Hemingway's "A Clean, Well-Lighted Place" (p. 1169) is objective, consisting of bits of dialogue that make the story look like a play:

> "Last week he tried to commit suicide," one waiter said.
> "Why?"
> "He was in despair."
> "What about?"
> "Nothing."
> "How do you know it was nothing?"
> "He has plenty of money."
> They sat together at a table that was close against the wall near the door of the café and looked at the terrace where the tables were all empty except where the old man sat in the shadow of the leaves of the tree that moved slightly in the wind. A girl and a soldier went by in the street. The street light shone on the brass number on his collar. The girl wore no head covering and hurried beside him.
> "The guard will pick him up," one waiter said.
> "What does it matter if he gets what he's after?"

Style and Point of View   If you reread the preceding quotation from Hemingway's "A Clean, Well-Lighted Place," you will notice that except for one long sentence (immediately after the dialogue), it consists chiefly of short (and for the most part simple) sentences. The dialogue is almost abrupt, but even the other material strikes a reader as—well, not so much as "objective" as something else, though we may find it hard to give a name to what we hear. Let's begin by looking at the long sentence:

> They sat together at a table that was close against the wall near the door of the café and looked at the terrace where the tables were all empty except where the old man sat in the shadow of the leaves of the tree that moved slightly in the wind.

A sentence of 50 words is unusual, but what besides its length gives this sentence its distinctive sound? Suppose we rewrite it, keeping the essential information and even keeping it as one sentence:

> Sitting together at a table close against the wall near the door of the café, they looked at the terrace, whose tables were empty except one where the old man sat in the shadow of the leaves of a tree moved slightly by the wind.

The chief changes are these: Instead of Hemingway's "they sat . . . and looked," we have used subordination ("Sitting. . . , they looked"), and we have eliminated the flatness or bleakness of Hemingway's "that . . . where . . . where . . . that." Our sentence is almost as long as Hemingway's, but the impression it makes on a reader is different. (How might you describe the difference?) It contains the same information, but—on the highest level, so to speak—it says something different because its *style* is different, just as in daily life "Hi" says something a little different from "How do you do?" And a difference in style is a difference in meaning.

Just as we rewrote Hemingway's long sentence, we can rewrite his short sentences, this time combining three sentences into one. First, here is Hemingway's version:

> A girl and a soldier went by in the street. The street light shone on the brass number on his collar. The girl wore no head covering and hurried beside him.

Now our revision, into one sentence:

> A bare-headed girl and a soldier passed by, the girl hurrying to keep up with the man, whose brass number on his collar glittered under the street light.

The information again is roughly the same, but again the effect is different. Because the choppiness is gone, the bleakness is gone, or at least it is much less evident. We are, so to speak, in a subtly different world. Why? Because the *style* is different. Hemingway's short, almost disconnected sentences, then, do not really give an objective view of something "out there"; rather, Hemingway's choice of certain words and certain grammatical constructions *creates* what is allegedly "out there."

Obviously a story told by a first-person narrator will have a distinctive style—let's say the voice of an adolescent boy, or an elderly widow, or a madman. The voice of a third-person narrator—especially the voice of a supposedly objective narrator—will be much less distinctive, but if, especially on rereading, you listen carefully, you will probably hear a distinctive tone. (Look, for instance, at the first paragraph of Grace Paley's "Samuel.") Put it this way: Even a supposedly objective point of view is not purely objective, since it represents the writer's choice of a style, a way of reporting material with an apparently dispassionate voice.

After reading a story, you may want to think at least briefly about what the story might be like if told from a different point of view. You may find it instructive, for instance, to rewrite "Samuel" from the "citizenly" man's point of view, or "Ripe Figs" from Babette's.

Determining and Discussing the Theme

First, we can distinguish between story (or plot) and theme in fiction. *Story* is concerned with "How does it turn out? What happens?" But **theme** is concerned with "What is it about? What does it add up to? What motif holds the happenings together? What does it make of life, and, perhaps, what wisdom does it offer?" In a good work of fiction, the details add up, or, to use Flannery O'Connor's words, they are "controlled by some overall purpose." In F. Scott Fitzgerald's *The Great Gatsby,* for example, there are many references to popular music, especially to jazz. These references contribute to our sense of the reality of Fitzgerald's depiction of America in the 1920s, but they do more: They help to comment on the shallowness of the white middle-class characters and they sometimes (very gently) remind us of an alternative culture. One might study Fitzgerald's references to music with an eye toward getting a deeper understanding of what the novel is about.

Suppose we think for a moment about the theme of Paley's "Samuel." Do we sense an "overall purpose" that holds the story together? Different readers inevitably will come up with different readings, that is, with different views of what the story is about. Here is one student's version:

    Whites cannot understand the feelings of blacks.

This statement gets at an important element in the story—the conflict between the sober-minded adults and the jiggling boys—but it apparently assumes that all of the adults are white, an inference that cannot be supported by pointing to evidence in the story. Further, we cannot be certain that Samuel is black. And, finally, even if Samuel and his mother are black, surely white readers *do understand his youthful enthusiasm and his mother's inconsolable grief.*

Here is a second statement:

    One should not interfere with the actions of others.

Does the story really offer such specific advice? This version of the theme seems to us to reduce the story to a too-simple code of action, a heartless rule of behavior, a rule that seems at odds with the writer's awareness of the mother's enduring grief.

A third version:

    Middle-class adults, acting from what seem to them to
    be the best of motives, may cause irreparable harm
    and grief.

This last statement seems to us to be one that can be fully supported by checking it against the story, but other equally valid statements can probably be made. How would you put it?

✔ A Checklist: Getting Ideas for Writing about Fiction

Here are some questions that may help to stimulate ideas about stories. Not every question is, of course, relevant to every story, but if after reading a story and thinking about it, you then run your eye over these questions, you will probably find some questions that will help you to think further about the story—in short, that will help you to get ideas.

As we have said in earlier chapters, it's best to do your thinking with a pen or pencil in hand. If some of the following questions seem to you to be especially relevant to the story you will be writing about, jot down—freely, without worrying about spelling—your initial responses, interrupting your writing only to glance again at the story when you feel the need to check the evidence.

Plot

1. Does the plot grow out of the characters, or does it depend on chance or coincidence? Did something at first strike you as irrelevant that later you perceived as relevant? Do some parts continue to strike you as irrelevant?
2. Does surprise play an important role, or does foreshadowing? If surprise is very important, can the story be read a second time with any interest? If so, what gives it this further interest?
3. What conflicts does the story include? Conflicts of one character against another? Of one character against the setting, or against society? Conflicts within a single character?
4. Are certain episodes narrated out of chronological order? If so, were you puzzled? Annoyed? On reflection, does the arrangement of episodes seem effective? Why, or why not? Are certain situations repeated? If so, what do you make out of the repetitions?

Character

1. Which character chiefly engages your interest? Why?
2. What purposes do minor characters serve? Do you find some who by their similarities and differences help to define each other or help to define the major character? How else is a particular character defined—by his or her words, actions (including thoughts and emotions), dress, setting, narrative point of view? Do certain characters act differently in the same, or in a similar, situation?
3. How does the author reveal character? By explicit authorial (editorial) comment, for instance, or, on the other hand, by revelation through dialogue? Through depicted action? Through the actions of other

characters? How are the author's methods especially suited to the whole of the story?

4. Is the behavior plausible—that is, are the characters well motivated?
5. If a character changes, why and how does he or she change? (You may want to jot down each event that influences a change.) Or did you change your attitude toward a character not because the character changes but because you came to know the character better?
6. Are the characters round or flat? Are they complex, or, on the other hand, highly typical (for instance, one-dimensional representatives of a social class or age)? Are you chiefly interested in a character's psychology, or does the character strike you as standing for something, such as honesty or the arrogance of power?
7. How has the author caused you to sympathize with certain characters? How does your response—your sympathy or lack of sympathy—contribute to your judgment of the conflict?

Point of View

1. Who tells the story? How much does the narrator know? Does the narrator strike you as reliable? What effect is gained by using this narrator?
2. How does the point of view help shape the theme? After all, the basic story of "Little Red Riding Hood"—what happens—remains unchanged whether told from the wolf's point of view or the girl's, but (to simplify grossly) if we hear the story from the wolf's point of view, we may feel that the story is about terrifying yet pathetic compulsive behavior; if from the girl's point of view, about terrified innocence.
3. It is sometimes said that the best writers are subversive, forcing readers to see something they do not want to see—something that is true but that violates their comfortable conventional ideas. Does this story oppose comfortable conventional views?
4. Does the narrator's language help you to construct a picture of the narrator's character, class, attitude, strengths, and limitations? (Jot down some evidence, such as colloquial or—on the other hand—formal expressions, ironic comments, figures of speech.) How far can you trust the narrator? Why?

Setting

1. Do you have a strong sense of the time and place? Is the story very much about, say, New England Puritanism, or race relations in the South in the late nineteenth century, or midwestern urban versus small-town life? If time and place are important, how and at what points in the story has the author conveyed this sense? If you do not strongly feel the setting, do you think the author should have made it more evident?
2. What is the relation of the setting to the plot and the characters? (For instance, do houses or rooms or their furnishings say something about their residents?) Would anything be lost if the descriptions of the setting were deleted from the story or the setting were changed?

Symbolism

1. Do certain characters seem to you to stand for something in addition to themselves? Does the setting—whether a house, a farm, a landscape, a town, a period—have an extra dimension?)

2. If you do believe that the story has symbolic elements, do you think they are adequately integrated within the story, or do they strike you as being too obviously stuck in?

Style

1. How has the point of view shaped or determined the style?

2. How would you characterize the style? Simple? Understated? Figurative? Or what, and why?

3. Do you think that the style is consistent? If it isn't—for instance, if there are shifts from simple sentences to highly complex ones—what do you make of the shifts?

Theme

1. Is the title informative? What does it mean or suggest? Did the meaning seem to change after you read the story? Does the title help you to formulate a theme? If you had written the story, what title would you use?

2. Do certain passages—dialogue or description—seem to you to point especially toward the theme? Do you find certain repetitions of words or pairs of incidents highly suggestive and helpful in directing your thoughts toward stating a theme? Flannery O'Connor, in *Mystery and Manners,* says, "In good fiction, certain of the details will tend to accumulate meaning from the action of the story itself, and when that happens, they become symbolic in the way they work." Does this story work that way?

3. Is the meaning of the story embodied in the whole story, or does it seem stuck in, for example in certain passages of editorializing?

4. Suppose someone asked you to state the point—the theme—of the story. Could you? And if you could, would you say that the theme of a particular story reinforces values you hold, or does it to some degree challenge them? Or is the concept of a theme irrelevant to this story?

FOUR SHORT STORIES

EDGAR ALLAN POE

Edgar Allan Poe (1809-49) was the son of traveling actors. His father abandoned the family almost immediately, and his mother died when Poe was two. The child was adopted—though never legally—by a prosperous merchant and his wife in Richmond, Virginia. The tensions were great, aggravated by Poe's drinking and heavy gambling, and in 1827 Poe left Richmond for Boston. He wrote, served briefly in the army, attended West Point but left within a year, and became an editor for the remaining eighteen years of his life. It was during these years, too, that he wrote the poems, essays, and fiction—especially detective stories and horror stories—that have made him famous.

The Cask of Amontillado

The thousand injuries of Fortunato I had borne as I best could, but when he ventured upon insult, I vowed revenge. You, who so well know the nature of my soul, will not suppose, however, that I gave utterance to a threat. At *length* I would be avenged; this was a point definitely settled—but the very definitiveness with which it was resolved precluded the idea of risk. I must not only punish, but punish with impunity. A wrong is unredressed when retribution overtakes its redresser. It is equally unredressed when the avenger fails to make himself felt as such to him who has done the wrong.

It must be understood that neither by word nor deed had I given Fortunato cause to doubt my good will. I continued, as was my wont, to smile in his face, and he did not perceive that my smile *now* was at the thought of his immolation.

He had a weak point—this Fortunato—although in other regards he was a man to be respected and even feared. He prided himself on his connoisseurship in wine. Few Italians have the true virtuoso spirit. For the most part their enthusiasm is adopted to suit the time and opportunity to practice imposture upon the British and Austrian *millionaires*. In painting and gemmary Fortunato, like his countrymen, was a quack, but in the matter of old wines he was sincere. In this respect I did not differ from him materially;—I was skillful in the Italian vintages myself, and bought largely whenever I could.

It was about dusk, one evening during the supreme madness of the carnival season, that I encountered my friend. He accosted me with excessive warmth, for he had been drinking much. The man wore motley. He had on a tight-fitting parti-striped dress, and his head was surmounted by the conical cap and bells. I was so pleased to see him, that I thought I should never have done wringing his hand.

5   I said to him—"My dear Fortunato, you are luckily met. How remarkably well you are looking to-day! But I have received a pipe[1] of what passes for Amontillado, and I have my doubts."

"How?" said he, "Amontillado? A pipe? Impossible! And in the middle of the carnival?"

"I have my doubts," I replied; "and I was silly enough to pay the full Amontillado price without consulting you in the matter. You were not to be found, and I was fearful of losing a bargain."

"Amontillado!"

"I have my doubts."

10   "Amontillado!"

"And I must satisfy them."

---

[1]**pipe** wine cask

"Amontillado!"

"As you are engaged, I am on my way to Luchesi. If any one has a critical turn, it is he. He will tell me—"

"Luchesi cannot tell Amontillado from Sherry."

15   "And yet some fools will have it that his taste is a match for your own."

"Come, let us go."

"Whither?"

"To your vaults."

"My friend, no; I will not impose upon your good nature. I perceive you have an engagement. Luchesi—"

20   "I have no engagement; come."

"My friend, no. It is not the engagement, but the severe cold with which I perceive you are afflicted. The vaults are insufferably damp. They are encrusted with nitre."

"Let us go, nevertheless. The cold is merely nothing. Amontillado! You have been imposed upon; and as for Luchesi, he cannot distinguish Sherry from Amontillado."

Thus speaking, Fortunato possessed himself of my arm. Putting on a mask of black silk, and drawing a *roquelaure*[2] closely about my person, I suffered him to hurry me to my palazzo.

There were no attendants at home; they had absconded to make merry in honor of the time. I had told them that I should not return until the morning, and had given them explicit orders not to stir from the house. These orders were sufficient, I well knew, to insure their immediate disappearance, one and all, as soon as my back was turned.

25   I took from their sconces two flambeaux, and giving one to Fortunato, bowed him through several suites of rooms to the archway that led into the vaults. I passed down a long and winding staircase, requesting him to be cautious as he followed. We came at length to the foot of the descent, and stood together on the damp ground of the catacombs of the Montresors.

The gait of my friend was unsteady, and the bells upon his cap jingled as he strode.

"The pipe," said he.

"It is farther on," said I; "but observe the white web-work which gleams from these cavern walls."

He turned towards me, and looked into my eyes with two filmy orbs that distilled the rheum of intoxication.

30   "Nitre?" he asked, at length.

"Nitre," I replied, "How long have you had that cough?"

"Ugh! ugh! ugh!—ugh! ugh! ugh!—ugh! ugh! ugh!—ugh! ugh! ugh!— ugh! ugh! ugh!"

My poor friend found it impossible to reply for many minutes.

"It is nothing," he said, at last.

35   "Come," I said, with decision, "we will go back; your health is precious. You are rich, respected, admired, beloved; you are happy, as once I was. You are a man to be missed. For me it is no matter. We will go back; you will be ill, and I cannot be responsible. Besides, there is Luchesi—"

"Enough," he said; "the cough is a mere nothing: it will not kill me. I shall not die of a cough."

---

[2]*roquelaure* short cloak

"True—true," I replied; "and, indeed, I had no intention of alarming you unnecessarily—but you should use all proper caution. A draught of this Medoc will defend us from the damps."

Here I knocked off the neck of a bottle which I drew from a long row of its fellows that lay upon the mould.

"Drink," I said, presenting him the wine.

40   He raised it to his lips with a leer. He paused and nodded to me familiarly, while his bells jingled.

"I drink," he said, "to the buried that repose around us."

"And I to your long life."

He again took my arm, and we proceeded.

"These vaults," he said, "are extensive."

45   "The Montresors," I replied, "were a great and numerous family."

"I forget your arms."

"A huge human foot d'or, in a field azure; the foot crushes a serpent rampant whose fangs are imbedded in the heel."

"And the motto?"

"Nemo me impune lacessit."[3]

50   "Good!" he said.

The wine sparkled in his eyes and the bells jingled. My own fancy grew warm with the Medoc. We had passed through walls of piled bones, with casks and puncheons intermingling, into the inmost recesses of the catacombs. I paused again, and this time I made bold to seize Fortunato by an arm above the elbow.

"The nitre!" I said; "see, it increases. It hangs like moss upon the vaults. We are below the river's bed. The drops of moisture tickle among the bones. Come, we will go back ere it is too late. Your cough—"

"It is nothing," he said; "let us go on. But first, another draught of the Medoc."

I broke and reached him a flagon of De Grâve. He emptied it at a breath. His eyes flashed with a fierce light. He laughed and threw the bottle upwards with a gesticulation I did not understand.

55   I looked at him in surprise. He repeated the movement—a grotesque one.

"You do not comprehend?" he said.

"Not I," I replied.

"Then you are not of the brotherhood."

"How?"

60   "You are not of the masons."[4]

"Yes, yes," I said, "yes, yes."

"You? Impossible! A mason?"

"A mason," I replied.

"A sign," he said.

65   "It is this," I answered, producing a trowel from beneath the folds of my *roquelaure.*

"You jest," he exclaimed, recoiling a few paces. "But let us proceed to the Amontillado."

[3]***Nemo me impune lacessit*** No one dare attack me with impunity (the motto of Scotland)   [4]**of the masons** i.e., a member of the Freemasons, an international secret fraternity

"Be it so," I said, replacing the tool beneath the cloak, and again offering him my arm. He leaned upon it heavily. We continued our route in search of the Amontillado. We passed through a range of low arches, descended, passed on, and descending again, arrived at a deep crypt, in which the foulness of the air caused our flambeaux rather to glow than flame.

At the most remote end of the crypt there appeared another less spacious. Its walls had been lined with human remains piled to the vault overhead, in the fashion of the great catacombs of Paris. Three sides of this interior crypt were still ornamented in this manner. From the fourth the bones had been thrown down, and lay promiscuously upon the earth, forming at one point a mound of some size. Within the wall thus exposed by the displacing of the bones, we perceived a still interior recess, in depth about four feet, in width three, in height six or seven. It seemed to have been constructed for no especial use within itself, but formed merely the interval between two of the colossal supports of the roof of the catacombs, and was backed by one of their circumscribing walls of solid granite.

It was in vain that Fortunato, uplifting his dull torch, endeavored to pry into the depths of the recess. Its termination the feeble light did not enable us to see.

70   "Proceed," I said; "herein is the Amontillado. As for Luchesi—"

"He is an ignoramus," interrupted my friend, as he stepped unsteadily forward, while I followed immediately at his heels. In an instant he had reached the extremity of the niche, and finding his progress arrested by the rock, stood stupidly bewildered. A moment more and I had fettered him to the granite. In its surface were two iron staples, distant from each other about two feet, horizontally. From one of these depended a short chain, from the other a padlock. Throwing the links about his waist, it was but the work of a few seconds to secure it. He was too much astounded to resist. Withdrawing the key I stepped back from the recess.

"Pass your hand," I said, "over the wall; you cannot help feeling the nitre. Indeed it is *very* damp. Once more let me *implore* you to return. No? Then I must positively leave you. But I must first render you all the little attentions in my power."

"The Amontillado!" ejaculated my friend, not yet recovered from his astonishment.

"True," I replied; "the Amontillado."

75   As I said these words I busied myself among the pile of bones of which I have before spoken. Throwing them aside, I soon uncovered a quantity of building-stone and mortar. With these materials and with the aid of my trowel, I began vigorously to wall up the entrance of the niche.

I had scarcely laid the first tier of masonry when I discovered that the intoxication of Fortunato had in a great measure worn off. The earliest indication I had of this was a low moaning cry from the depth of the recess. It was *not* the cry of a drunken man. There was then a long and obstinate silence. I laid the second tier, and the third, and the fourth; and then I heard the furious vibrations of the chain. The noise lasted for several minutes, during which, that I might hearken to it with the more satisfaction, I ceased my labors and sat down upon the bones. When at last the clanking subsided, I resumed the trowel, and finished without interruption the fifth, the sixth, and the seventh tier. The wall was now nearly upon a level with my breast. I again paused, and holding the flambeaux over the masonwork, threw a few feeble rays upon the figure within.

A succession of loud and shrill screams, bursting suddenly from the throat of the chained form, seemed to thrust me violently back. For a brief moment I hesitated—I trembled. Unsheathing my rapier, I began to grope with it about the recess; but the thought of an instant reassured me. I placed my hand upon the solid fabric of the catacombs, and felt satisfied. I reapproached the wall. I replied to the yells of him who clamored. I re-echoed—I aided—I surpassed them in volume and in strength. I did this, and the clamorer grew still.

It was now midnight, and my task was drawing to a close. I had completed the eight, the ninth, and the tenth tier. I had finished a portion of the last and the eleventh; there remained but a single stone to be fitted and plastered in. I struggled with its weight; I placed it partially in its destined position. But now there came from out the niche a low laugh that erected the hairs upon my head. It was succeeded by a sad voice, which I had difficulty in recognizing as that of the noble Fortunato. The voice said—

"Ha! ha! ha!—he! he! he!—a very good joke indeed—an excellent jest. We will have many a rich laugh about it at the palazzo—he! he! he!—over our wine—he! he! he!"

80   "The Amontillado!" I said.

"He! he! he!—he! he! he!—yes, the Amontillado. But is it not getting late? Will not they be awaiting us at the palazzo, the Lady Fortunato and the rest? Let us be gone."

"Yes," I said, "let us be gone."

"For the love of God, Montresor!"

85   "Yes," I said, "for the love of God!"

But to these words I hearkened in vain for a reply. I grew impatient. I called aloud;

"Fortunato!"

No answer. I called again;

"Fortunato!"

No answer still, I thrust a torch through the remaining aperture and let it fall within. There came forth in return only a jingling of the bells. My heart grew sick—on account of the dampness of the catacombs. I hastened to make an end of my labor. I forced the last stone into its position; I plastered it up. Against the new masonry I reerected the old rampart of bones. For the half of a century no mortal has disturbed them. *In pace requiescat!*[5]

[1846]

TOPICS FOR CRITICAL THINKING AND WRITING

1. To whom does Montresor tell his story? The story he tells happened fifty years earlier. Do we have any clues as to why he tells it now?

2. At the end of the story we learn that the murder occurred fifty years ago. Would the story be equally effective if Poe had had Montresor reveal that fact at the outset? Why, or why not?

3. Poe sets Montresor's story at dusk, "during the supreme madness of the carnival season." What is the "carnival season"? (If you are uncertain as to the meaning of "carnival," consult a dictionary.) What details of the story derive from the setting?

[5]In pace requiescat! May he rest in peace!

4. In the justifiably famous first line Montresor declares, "The thousand injuries of Fortunato I had borne as I best could, but when he ventured upon insult, I vowed revenge." Do we ever learn what those injuries and that insult were? What do we learn about Montresor from this declaration?

5. How does Montresor characterize Fortunato? What details of his portrait unwittingly enlist our sympathy for Fortunato? Does Montresor betray any sympathy for his victim?

6. "The Cask of Amontillado" is sometimes referred to as a "horror tale." Do you think it has anything in common with horror movies? If so, what? (You might begin by making a list of the characteristics of horror movies.) Why do people take pleasure in horror movies? Does this story offer any of the same sorts of pleasure? In any case, why might a reader take pleasure in this story?

7. Construct a definition of madness (you may want to do a little research, but if you make use of your findings, be sure to give credit to your sources) and write an essay of 500–750 words arguing whether or not Montresor is mad. (*Note:* You may want to distinguish between Montresor at the time of the killing and Montresor at the present.)

 EUDORA WELTY

Eudora Welty was born in 1909 in Jackson, Mississippi. Although she earned a bachelor's degree at the University of Wisconsin, and she spent a year studying advertising in New York City at the Columbia University Graduate School of Business, she has lived almost all of her life in Jackson.

In the preface to her Collected Stories *she says:*

> *I have been told, both in approval and in accusation, that I seem to love all my characters. What I do in writing of any character is to try to enter into the mind, heart and skin of a human being who is not myself. Whether this happens to be a man or a woman, old or young, with skin black or white, the primary challenge lies in making the jump itself. It is the act of a writer's imagination that I set most high.*

In addition to writing stories and novels, Welty has written a book about fiction, The Eye of the Story *(1977), and a memoir,* One Writer's Beginnings *(1984).*

A Worn Path

It was December—a bright frozen day in the early morning. Far out in the country there was an old Negro woman with her head tied in a red rag, coming along a path through the pinewoods. Her name was Phoenix Jackson. She was very old and small and she walked slowly in the dark pine shadows, moving a little from side to side in her steps, with the balanced heaviness and lightness of a pendulum in a grandfather clock. She carried a thin, small cane made from an umbrella, and with this she kept tapping the frozen earth in front of her. This made a grave and persistent noise in the still air, that seemed meditative like the chirping of a solitary little bird.

She wore a dark striped dress reaching down to her shoe tops, and an equally long apron of bleached sugar sacks, with a full pocket: all neat and tidy, but every time she took a step she might have fallen over her shoe-laces, which dragged from her unlaced shoes. She looked straight ahead. Her eyes were blue with age. Her skin had a pattern all its own of number-less branching wrinkles and as though a whole little tree stood in the middle of her forehead, but a golden color ran underneath, and the two knobs of her cheeks were illuminated by a yellow burning under the dark. Under the red rag her hair came down on her neck in the frailest of ringlets, still black, and with an odor like copper.

Now and then there was a quivering in the thicket. Old Phoenix said, "Out of my way, all you foxes, owls, beetles, jack rabbits, coons, and wild animals! . . . Keep out from under these feet, little bob-whites. . . . Keep the big wild hogs out of my path. Don't let none of those come running my di-rection. I got a long way." Under her small black-freckled hand her cane, limber as a buggy whip, would switch at the brush as if to rouse up any hid-ing things.

On she went. The woods were deep and still. The sun made the pine needles almost too bright to look at, up where the wind rocked. The cones dropped as light as feathers. Down in the hollow was the mourning dove—it was not too late for him.

5   The path ran up a hill. "Seem like there is chains about my feet, time I get this far," she said, in the voice of argument old people keep to use with themselves. "Something always take a hold of me on this hill—pleads I should stay."

After she got to the top she turned and gave a full, severe look behind her where she had come. "Up through pines," she said at length. "Now down through oaks."

Her eyes opened their widest, and she started down gently. But before she got to the bottom of the hill a bush caught her dress.

Her fingers were busy and intent, but her skirts were full and long, so that before she could pull them free in one place they were caught in an-other. It was not possible to allow the dress to tear. "I in the thorny bush," she said. "Thorns, you doing your appointed work. Never want to let folks pass—no sir. Old eyes thought you was a pretty little *green* bush."

Finally, trembling all over, she stood free, and after a moment dared to stoop for her cane.

10   "Sun so high!" she cried, leaning back and looking, while the thick tears went over her eyes. "The time getting all gone here."

At the foot of this hill was a place where a log was laid across the creek.

"Now comes the trial," said Phoenix.

Putting her right foot out, she mounted the log and shut her eyes. Lift-ing her skirt, levelling her cane fiercely before her, like a festival figure in some parade, she began to march across. Then she opened her eyes and she was safe on the other side.

"I wasn't as old as I thought," she said.

15   But she sat down to rest. She spread her skirts on the bank around her and folded her hands over her knees. Up above her was a tree in a pearly cloud of mistletoe. She did not dare to close her eyes, and when a little boy

brought her a little plate with a slice of marble-cake on it she spoke to him. "That would be acceptable," she said. But when she went to take it there was just her own hand in the air.

So she left that tree, and had to go through a barbed-wire fence. There she had to creep and crawl, spreading her knees and stretching her fingers like a baby trying to climb the steps. But she talked loudly to herself: she could not let her dress be torn now, so late in the day, and she could not pay for having her arm or leg sawed off if she got caught fast where she was.

At last she was safe through the fence and risen up out in the clearing. Big dead trees, like black men with one arm, were standing in the purple stalks of the withered cotton field. There sat a buzzard.

"Who you watching?"

In the furrow she made her way along.

20   "Glad this not the season for bulls," she said, looking sideways, "and the good Lord made his snakes to curl up and sleep in the winter. A pleasure I don't see no two-headed snake coming around that tree, where it come once. It took a while to get by him, back in the summer."

She passed through the old cotton and went into a field of dead corn. It whispered and shook and was taller than her head. "Through the maze now," she said, for there was no path.

Then there was something tall, black, and skinny there, moving before her.

At first she took it for a man. It could have been a man dancing in the field. But she stood still and listened, and it did not make a sound. It was as silent as a ghost.

"Ghost," she said sharply, "who be you the ghost of? For I have heard of nary death close by."

25   But there was no answer—only the ragged dancing in the wind.

She shut her eyes, reached out her hand, and touched a sleeve. She found a coat and inside that an emptiness, cold as ice.

"You scarecrow," she said. Her face lighted. "I ought to be shut up for good," she said with laughter. "My senses is gone, I too old. I the oldest people I ever know. Dance, old scarecrow," she said, "while I dancing with you."

She kicked her foot over the furrow, and with mouth drawn down, shook her head once or twice in a little strutting way. Some husks blew down and whirled in streamers about her skirts.

Then she went on, parting her way from side to side with the cane, through the whispering field. At last she came to the end, to a wagon track where the silver grass blew between the red ruts. The quail were walking around like pullets, seeming all dainty and unseen.

30   "Walk pretty," she said. "This the easy place. This the easy going."

She followed the track, swaying through the quiet bare fields, through the little strings of trees silver in their dead leaves, past cabins silver from weather, with the doors and windows boarded shut, all like old women under a spell sitting there. "I walking in their sleep," she said, nodding her head vigorously.

In a ravine she went where a spring was silently flowing through a hollow log. Old Phoenix bent and drank. "Sweet-gum makes the water sweet," she said, and drank more. "Nobody know who made this well, for it was here when I was born."

The track crossed a swampy part where the moss hung as white as lace from every limb. "Sleep on, alligators, and blow your bubbles." Then the track went into the road.

Deep, deep the road went down between the high green-colored banks. Overhead the live-oaks met, and it was as dark as a cave.

35   A black dog with a lolling tongue came up out of the weeds by the ditch. She was meditating, and not ready, and when he came at her she only hit him a little with her cane. Over she went in the ditch, like a little puff of milk-weed.

Down there, her senses drifted away. A dream visited her, and she reached her hand up, but nothing reached down and gave her a pull. So she lay there and presently went to talking. "Old woman," she said to herself, "that black dog come up out of the weeds to stall you off, and now there he sitting on his fine tail, smiling at you."

A white man finally came along and found her—a hunter, a young man, with his dog on a chain.

"Well, Granny!" he laughed. "what are you doing there?"

"Lying on my back like a June-bug waiting to be turned over, mister," she said, reaching up her hand.

40   He lifted her up, gave her a swing in the air, and set her down. "Anything broken, Granny?"

"No sir, them old dead weeds is springy enough," said Phoenix, when she had got her breath. "I thank you for your trouble."

"Where do you live, Granny?" he asked, while the two dogs were growling at each other.

"Away back yonder, sir, behind the ridge. You can't even see it from here."

"On your way home?"

45   "No, sir, I going to town."

"Why, that's too far! That's as far as I walk when I come out myself, and I get something for my trouble." He patted the stuffed bag he carried, and there hung down a little closed claw. It was one of the bob-whites, with its beak hooked bitterly to show it was dead. "Now you go on home, Granny!"

"I bound to go to town, mister," said Phoenix. "The time come around."

He gave another laugh, filling the whole landscape. "I know you old colored people! Wouldn't miss going to town to see Santa Claus!"

But something held Old Phoenix very still. The deep lines in her face went into a fierce and different radiation. Without warning, she had seen with her own eyes a flashing nickel fall out of the man's pocket onto the ground.

50   "How old are you, Granny?" he was saying.

"There is no telling, mister," she said, "no telling."

Then she gave a little cry and clapped her hands and said, "Git on away from here, dog! Look! Look at that dog!" She laughed as if in admiration. "He ain't scared of nobody. He a big black dog." She whispered, "Sic him!"

"Watch me get rid of that cur," said the man. "Sic him, Pete! Sic him!"

Phoenix heard the dogs fighting, and heard the man running and throwing sticks. She even heard a gunshot. But she was slowly bending forward by that time, further and further forward, the lids stretched down over her eyes, as if she were doing this in her sleep. Her chin was lowered almost to her knees. The yellow palm of her hand came out from the fold of her apron. Her fingers slid down and along the ground under the piece of money with the grace and care they would have in lifting an egg from under a sitting hen. Then she slowly straightened up, she stood erect, and the nickel was in her apron pocket. A bird flew by. Her lips moved. "God watching me the whole time. I come to stealing."

55   The man came back, and his own dog panted about them. "Well, I scared him off that time," he said, and then he laughed and lifted his gun and pointed it at Phoenix.

She stood straight and faced him.

"Doesn't the gun scare you?" he said, still pointing it.

"No, sir, I seen plenty go off closer by, in my day, and for less than what I done," she said, holding utterly still.

He smiled, and shouldered the gun. "Well, Granny," he said, "you must be a hundred years old, and scared of nothing. I'd give you a dime if I had any money with me. But you take my advice and stay home, and nothing will happen to you."

60   "I bound to go on my way, mister," said Phoenix. She inclined her head in the red rag. Then they went in different directions, but she could hear the gun shooting again and again over the hill.

She walked on. The shadows hung from the oak trees to the road like curtains. Then she smelled wood-smoke, and smelled the river, and she saw a steeple and the cabins on their steep steps. Dozens of little black children whirled around her. There ahead was Natchez shining. Bells were ringing. She walked on.

In the paved city it was Christmas time. There were red and green electric lights strung and crisscrossed everywhere, and all turned on in the daytime. Old Phoenix would have been lost if she had not distrusted her eyesight and depended on her feet to know where to take her.

She paused quietly on the sidewalk where people were passing by. A lady came along in the crowd, carrying an armful of red-, green-, and silver-wrapped presents; she gave off perfume like the red roses in hot summer, and Phoenix stopped her.

"Please, missy, will you lace up my shoe?" She held up her foot.

65   "What do you want, Grandma?"

"See my shoe," said Phoenix. "Do all right for out in the country, but wouldn't look right to go in a big building."

"Stand still then, Grandma," said the lady. She put her packages down on the sidewalk beside her and laced and tied both shoes tightly.

"Can't lace 'em with a cane," said Phoenix. "Thank you, missy. I doesn't mind asking a nice lady to tie up my shoe, when I gets out on the street."

Moving slowly and from side to side, she went into the big building and into a tower of steps, where she walked up and around and around until her feet knew to stop.

70   She entered a door, and there she saw nailed up on the wall the document that had been stamped with the gold seal and framed in the gold frame, which matched the dream that was hung up in her head.

"Here I be," she said. There was a fixed and ceremonial stiffness over her body.

"A charity case, I suppose," said an attendant who sat at the desk before her.

But Phoenix only looked above her head. There was sweat on her face, the wrinkles in her skin shone like a bright net.

"Speak up, Grandma," the woman said. "What's your name? We must have your history, you know. Have you been here before? What seems to be the trouble with you?"

75   Old Phoenix only gave a twitch to her face as if a fly were bothering her.

"Are you deaf?" cried the attendant.

But then the nurse came in.

"Oh, that's just old Aunt Phoenix," she said. "She doesn't come for her-self—she has a little grandson. She makes these trips just as regular as clock-work. She lives away back off the old Natchez Trace." She bent down. "Well, Aunt Phoenix, why don't you just take a seat? We won't keep you standing after your long trip." She pointed.

The old woman sat down, bolt upright in the chair.

80   "Now, how is the boy?" asked the nurse.

Old Phoenix did not speak.

"I said, how is the boy?"

But Phoenix only waited and stared straight ahead, her face very solemn and withdrawn into rigidity.

"Is his throat any better?" asked the nurse. "Aunt Phoenix, don't you hear me? Is your grandson's throat any better since the last time you came for the medicine?"

85   With her hands on her knees, the old woman waited, silent, erect and motionless, just as if she were in armor.

"You mustn't take up our time this way, Aunt Phoenix," the nurse said. "Tell us quickly about your grandson, and get it over. He isn't dead, is he?"

At last there came a flicker and then a flame of comprehension across her face, and she spoke.

"My grandson. It was my memory had left me. There I sat and forgot why I made my long trip."

"Forgot?" The nurse frowned. "After you came so far?"

90   Then Phoenix was like an old woman begging a dignified forgiveness for waking up frightened in the night. "I never did go to school, I was too old at the Surrender," she said in a soft voice. "I'm an old woman without an education. It was my memory fail me. My little grandson, he is just the same, and I forgot it in the coming."

"Throat never heals, does it?" said the nurse, speaking in a loud, sure voice to Old Phoenix. By now she had a card with something written on it, a little list. "Yes. Swallowed lye. When was it—January—two-three years ago—"

Phoenix spoke unasked now. "No, missy, he not dead, he just the same. Every little while his throat begin to close up again, and he not able to swal-low. He not get his breath. He not able to help himself. So the time come around, and I go on another trip for the soothing medicine."

"All right. The doctor said as long as you came to get it, you could have it," said the nurse. "But it's an obstinate case."

"My little grandson, he sit up there in the house all wrapped up, waiting by himself," Phoenix went on. "We is the only two left in the world. He suffer and it don't seem to put him back at all. He got a sweet look. He going to last. He wear a little patch quilt and peep out holding his mouth open like a little bird. I remembers so plain now. I not going to forget him again, no, the whole enduring time. I could tell him from all the others in creation."

95   "All right." The nurse was trying to hush her now. She brought her a bottle of medicine. "Charity," she said, making a check mark in a book.

Old Phoenix held the bottle close to her eyes and then carefully put it into her pocket.

"I thank you," she said.

"It's Christmas time, Grandma," said the attendant. "Could I give you a few pennies out of my purse?"

"Five pennies is a nickel," said Phoenix stiffly.

100   "Here's a nickel," said the attendant.

Phoenix rose carefully and held out her hand. She received the nickel and then fished the other nickel out of her pocket and laid it beside the new one. She stared at her palm closely, with her head on one side.

Then she gave a tap with her cane on the floor.

"This is what come to me to do," she said. "I going to the store and buy my child a little windmill they sells, made out of paper. He going to find it hard to believe there such a thing in the world. I'll march myself back where he waiting, holding it straight up in his hand."

She lifted her free hand, gave a little nod, turned round, and walked out of the doctor's office. Then her slow step began on the stairs, going down.

[1941]

 ## TOPICS FOR CRITICAL THINKING AND WRITING

1. If you do not know the legend of the phoenix, look it up in a dictionary or, better, in an encyclopedia. Then carefully reread the story, to learn whether the story in any way connects with the legend.
2. What do you think of the hunter?
3. What would be lost if the episode (with all of its dialogue) of Phoenix falling into the ditch and being helped out of it by the hunter were omitted?
4. Is Christmas a particularly appropriate time in which to set the story? Why or why not?
5. What do you make of the title?

 ## TOBIAS WOLFF

Tobias Wolff was born in Alabama in 1945, but he grew up in the state of Washington. He left high school before graduating, served as an apprentice seaman and as a weight-guesser in a carnival, and then joined the army, where he served four years as a paratrooper. After his discharge from the army, he hired private tutors to enable him to pass the entrance degree to Oxford University. At Oxford he did spectacularly well, graduating with First Class Honors in English.

Wolff has written stories, novels, and an autobiography (This Boy's Life); *he now teaches writing at Syracuse University.*

Powder

Just before Christmas my father took me skiing at Mount Baker. He'd had to fight for the privilege of my company, because my mother was still angry with him for sneaking me into a nightclub during his last visit, to see Thelonius Monk.

He wouldn't give up. He promised, hand on heart, to take good care of me and have me home for dinner on Christmas Eve, and she relented. But as we were checking out of the lodge that morning it began to snow, and in this snow he observed some quality that made it necessary for us to get in one last run. We got in several last runs. He was indifferent to my fretting. Snow whirled around us in bitter, blinding squalls, hissing like sand, and still we skied. As the lift bore us to the peak yet again, my father looked at his watch and said: "Criminey. This'll have to be a fast one."

By now I couldn't see the trail. There was no point in trying. I stuck to him like white on rice and did what he did and somehow made it to the bottom without sailing off a cliff. We returned our skis and my father put chains on the Austin-Healy while I swayed from foot to foot, clapping my mittens and wishing I were home. I could see everything. The green tablecloth, the plates with the holly pattern, the red candles waiting to be lit.

We passed a diner on our way out. "You want some soup?" my father asked. I shook my head. "Buck up," he said. "I'll get you there. Right, doctor?"

5   I was supposed to say, "Right, doctor," but I didn't say anything.

A state trooper waved us down outside the resort. A pair of sawhorses were blocking the road. The trooper came up to our car and bent down to my father's window. His face was bleached by the cold. Snowflakes clung to his eyebrows and to the fur trim of his jacket and cap.

"Don't tell me," my father said.

The trooper told him. The road was closed. It might get cleared, it might not. Storm took everyone by surprise. So much, so fast. Hard to get people moving. Christmas Eve. What can you do?

My father said: "Look. We're talking about four, five inches. I've taken this car through worse than that."

10   The trooper straightened up, boots creaking. His face was out of sight but I could hear him. "The road is closed."

My father sat with both hands on the wheel, rubbing the wood with his thumbs. He looked at the barricade for a long time. He seemed to be trying to master the idea of it. Then he thanked the trooper, and with a weird, old-maidy show of caution turned the car around. "Your mother will never forgive me for this," he said.

"We should have left before," I said. "Doctor."

He didn't speak to me again until we were both in a booth at the dinner, waiting for our burgers. "She won't forgive me," he said. "Do you understand? Never."

"I guess," I said, but no guesswork was required; she wouldn't forgive him.

15   "I can't let that happen." He bent toward me. "I'll tell you what I want. I want us to be all together again. Is that what you want?"

"Yes, sir."

He bumped my chin with his knuckles. "That's all I needed to hear."

When we finished eating he went to the pay phone in the back of the dinner, then joined me in the booth again. I figured he'd called my mother, but he didn't give a report. He sipped at his coffee and stared out the window at the empty road. "Come on, come on," he said. A little while later he said, "Come on!" When the trooper's car went past, lights flashing, he got up and dropped some money on the check. "O.K. Vámanos."

The wind had died. The snow was falling straight down, less of it now; lighter. We drove away from the resort, right up to the barricade. "Move it," my father told me. When I looked at him he said, "What are you waiting for?" I got out and dragged one of the sawhorses aside, then put it back after he drove through. He pushed the door open for me. "Now you're an accomplice," he said. "We go down together." He put the car into gear and gave me a look. "Joke, doctor."

20   "Funny, doctor."

Down the first long stretch I watched the road behind us, to see if the trooper was on our tail. The barricade vanished. Then there was nothing but snow: snow on the road, snow kicking up from the chains, snow on the trees, snow in the sky; and our trail in the snow. I faced around and had a shock. The lie of the road behind us had been marked by our own tracks, but there were no tracks ahead of us. My father was breaking virgin snow between a line of tall trees. He was humming "Stars Fell on Alabama." I felt snow brush along the floorboards under my feet. To keep my hands from shaking, I clamped them between my knees.

My father grunted in a thoughtful way and said, "Don't ever try this yourself."

"I won't."

"That's what you say now, but someday you'll get your license and then you'll think you can do anything. Only you won't be able to do this. You need, I don't know—a certain instinct."

25   "Maybe I have it."

"You don't. You have your strong points, but not . . . this. I only mention it, because I don't want you to get the idea this is something just anybody can do. I'm a great driver. That's not a virtue, O.K.? It's just a fact, and one you should be aware of. Of course you have to give the old heap some credit, too—there aren't many cars I'd try this with. Listen!"

I listened. I heard the slap of the chains, the stiff, jerky rasps of the wipers, the purr of the engine. It really did purr. The car was almost new. My father couldn't afford it, and kept promising to sell it, but here it was.

I said, "Where do you think that policeman went to?"

"Are you warm enough?" He reached over and cranked up the blower. Then he turned off the wipers. We didn't need them. The clouds had brightened. A few sparse, feathery flakes drifted into our slipstream and were swept away. We left the trees and entered a broad field of snow that ran level for a while and then tilted sharply downward. Orange stakes had been planted at intervals in two parallel lines and my father steered a course between them, though they were far enough apart to leave considerable doubt in my mind as to where exactly the road lay. He was humming again, doing little scat riffs around the melody.

30   "O.K. then. What are my strong points?"

"Don't get me started," he said. "It'd take all day."

"Oh, right. Name one."

"Easy. You always think ahead."

True. I always thought ahead. I was a boy who kept his clothes on numbered hangers to insure proper rotation. I bothered my teachers for homework assignments far ahead of their due dates so I could make up schedules. I thought ahead, and that was why I knew that there would be other troopers waiting for us at the end of our ride, if we got there. What I did not know was that my father would wheedle and plead his way past them—he didn't sing "O Tannenbaum" but just about—and get me home for dinner, buying a little more time before my mother decided to make the split final. I knew we'd get caught; I was resigned to it. And maybe for this reason I stopped moping and began to enjoy myself.

35   Why not? This was one for the books. Like being in a speedboat, but better. You can't go downhill in a boat. And it was all ours. And it kept coming, the laden trees, the unbroken surface of snow, the sudden white vistas. Here and there I saw hints of the road, ditches, fences, stakes, but not so many that I could have found my way. But then I didn't have to. My father was driving. My father in his 48th year, rumpled, kind, bankrupt of honor, flushed with certainty. He was a great driver. All persuasion, no coercion. Such subtlety at the wheel, such tactful pedalwork. I actually trusted him. And the best was yet to come—the switchbacks and hairpins. Impossible to describe. Except maybe to say this: If you haven't driven fresh powder, you haven't driven.

[1992]

 TOPICS FOR CRITICAL THINKING AND WRITING

1. How would you characterize the father?
2. How does the boy feel about his father?

 SANDRA CISNEROS

Sandra Cisneros, daughter of a Mexican father and a Mexican-American mother, was born in Chicago in 1954. A graduate of the Iowa Writers Workshop and a National Endowment for the Arts Fellow, she has taught creative writing at several universities and also in Chicago at an alternative high school for dropouts.

Cisneros has published two collections of stories ("Woman Hollering Creek" is the title story in her second collection, published in 1991) and two books of poetry.

Woman Hollering Creek

The day Don Serafin gave Juan Pedro Martínez Sánchez permission to take Cleófilas Enriqueta DeLeón Hernández as his bride, across her father's threshold, over several miles of dirt road and several miles of paved, over one border and beyond to a town *en el otro lado*—on the other side—already did he divine the morning his daughter would raise her hand over her eyes, look south, and dream of returning to the chores that never ended, six good-for-nothing brothers, and one old man's complaints.

He had said, after all, in the hubbub of parting: I am your father, I will never abandon you. He *had* said that, hadn't he, when he hugged and then let her go. But at the moment Cleófilas was busy looking for Chela, her maid of honor, to fulfill their bouquet conspiracy. She would not remember her father's parting words until later. *I am your father, I will never abandon you.*

Only now as a mother did she remember. Now, when she and Juan Pedrito sat by the creek's edge. How when a man and a woman love each other, sometimes that love sours. But a parent's love for a child, a child's for its parents, is another thing entirely.

This is what Cleófilas thought evenings when Juan Pedro did not come home, and she lay on her side of the bed listening to the hollow roar of the interstate, a distant dog barking, the pecan trees rustling like ladies in stiff petticoats—*shh-shh-shh, shh-shh-shh*—soothing her to sleep.

5   In the town where she grew up, there isn't very much to do except accompany the aunts and godmothers to the house of one or the other to play cards. Or walk to the cinema to see this week's film again, speckled and with one hair quivering annoyingly on the screen. Or to the center of town to order a milk shake that will appear in a day and a half as a pimple on her backside. Or to the girlfriend's house to watch the latest *telenovela* episode and try to copy the way the women comb their hair, wear their makeup.

But what Cleófilas has been waiting for, has been whispering and sighing and giggling for, has been anticipating since she was old enough to lean against the window displays of gauze and butterflies and lace, is passion. Not the kind on the cover of the *¡Alarma!* magazines, mind you, where the lover is photographed with the bloody fork she used to salvage her good name. But passion in its purest crystalline essence. The kind the books and songs and *telenovelas* describe when one finds, finally, the great love of one's life, and does whatever one can, must do, at whatever the cost.

Tú o Nadie. "You or No One." The title of the current favorite *telenovela.* The beautiful Lucía Méndez having to put up with all kinds of hardships of the heart, separation and betrayal, and loving, always loving no matter what, because *that* is the most important thing, and did you see Lucía Méndez on the Bayer aspirin commercials—wasn't she lovely? Does she dye her hair do you think? Cleófilas is going to go to the *farmacía* and buy a hair rinse; her girlfriend Chela will apply it—it's not that difficult at all.

Because you didn't watch last night's episode when Lucía confessed she loved him more than anyone in her life. In her life! And she sings the song "You or No One" in the beginning and end of the show. *Tú o Nadie.* Somehow one ought to live one's life like that, don't you think? You or no one. Because to suffer for love is good. The pain all sweet somehow. In the end.

Seguín. She had liked the sound of it. Far away and lovely. Not like *Monclova. Coahuia.* Ugly.

10   *Seguín, Tejas.* A nice sterling ring to it. The tinkle of money. She would
get to wear outfits like the women on the *tele,* like Lucía Méndez. And have
a lovely house, and wouldn't Chela be jealous.

And yes, they will drive all the way to Laredo to get her wedding dress.
That's what they say. Because Juan Pedro wants to get married right away,
without a long engagement since he can't take off too much time from
work. He has a very important position in Seguin with, with . . . a beer company, I think. Or was it tires? Yes, he has to be back. So they will get married
in the spring when he can take off work, and then they will drive off in his
new pickup—did you see it?—to their new home in Seguin. Well, not exactly new, but they're going to repaint the house. You know newlyweds.
New paint and new furniture. Why not? He can afford it. And later on add
maybe a room or two for the children. May they be blessed with many.

Well, you'll see. Cleófilas has always been so good with her sewing machine. A little *rrr, rrr, rrr* of the machine and *¡zas!* Miracles. She's always
been so clever, that girl. Poor thing. And without even a mama to advise her
on things like her wedding night. Well, may God help her. What with a father with a head like a burro, and those six clumsy brothers. Well, what do
you think! Yes, I'm going to the wedding. Of course! The dress I want to
wear just needs to be altered a teensy bit to bring it up to date. See, I saw a
new style last night that I thought would suit me. Did you watch last night's
episode of *The Rich Also Cry?* Well, did you notice the dress the mother was
wearing?

La Gritona.[1] Such a funny name for such a lovely *arroyo.* But that's
what they called the creek that ran behind the house. Though no one could
say whether the woman had hollered from anger or pain. The natives only
knew the *arroyo* one crossed on the way to San Antonio, and then once
again on the way back, was called Woman Hollering, a name no one from
these parts questioned, little less understood. *Pues, allá de los indios, quién
sabe[2]*—who knows, the townspeople shrugged, because it was of no concern to their lives how this trickle of water received its curious name.

"What do you want to know for?" Trini the laundromat attendant asked
in the same gruff Spanish she always used whenever she gave Cleófilas
change or yelled at her for something. First for putting too much soap in the
machines. Later, for sitting on a washer. And still later, after Juan Pedrito
was born, for not understanding that in this country you cannot let your
baby walk around with no diaper and his pee-pee hanging out, it wasn't
nice, *¿entiendes? Pues.[3]*

15   How could Cleófilas explain to a woman like this why the name
Woman Hollering fascinated her. Well, there was no sense talking to Trini.

On the other hand there were the neighbor ladies, one on either side of
the house they rented near the *arroyo.* The woman Soledad on the left, the
woman Dolores on the right.

The neighbor lady Soledad liked to call herself a widow, though how
she came to be one was a mystery. Her husband had either died, or run

---

[1]**La Gritona** the hollering woman; folklore includes many stories of rivers haunted
by female nature spirits or by women who lived tragic lives   [2]***Pues . . . sabe?*** Well,
with the Indians, who knows?   [3]***¿entiendes? Pues*** Do you understand? Well

away with an ice-house floozie, or simply gone out for cigarettes one after-noon and never came back. It was hard to say which since Soledad, as a rule, didn't mention him.

In the other house lived *la señora* Dolores, kind and very sweet, but her house smelled too much of incense and candles from the altars that burned continuously in memory of two sons who had died in the last war and one husband who had died shortly after from grief. The neighbor lady Dolores divided her time between the memory of these men and her gar-den, famous for its sunflowers—so tall they had to be supported with broom handles and old boards; red red cockscombs, fringed and bleeding a thick menstrual color; and, especially, roses whose sad scent reminded Cleófilas of the dead. Each Sunday *la señora* Dolores clipped the most beau-tiful of these flowers and arranged them on three modest headstones at the Seguin cemetery.

The neighbor ladies, Soledad, Dolores, they might've known once the name of the *arroyo* before it turned English but they did not know now. They were too busy remembering the men who had left through either choice or circumstance and would never come back.

20   Pain or rage, Cleófilas wondered when she drove over the bridge the first time as a newlywed and Juan Pedro had pointed it out. *La Gritona,* he had said, and she had laughed. Such a funny name for a creek so pretty and full of happily ever after.

The first time she had been so surprised she didn't cry out or try to de-fend herself. She had always said she would strike back if a man, any man, were to strike her.

But when the moment came, and he slapped her once, and then again, and again, until the lip split and bled an orchid of blood, she didn't fight back, she didn't break into tears, she didn't run away as she imagined she might when she saw such things in the *telenovelas.*

In her own home her parents had never raised a hand to each other or to their children. Although she admitted she may have been brought up a lit-tle leniently as an only daughter—*la consentida,* the princess—there were some things she would never tolerate. Ever.

Instead, when it happened the first time, when they were barely man and wife, she had been so stunned, it left her speechless, motionless, numb. She had done nothing but reach up to the heat on her mouth and stare at the blood on her hand as if even then she didn't understand.

25   She could think of nothing to say, said nothing. Just stroked the dark curls of the man who wept and would weep like a child, his tears of repen-tance and shame, this time and each.

The men at the ice house. From what she can tell, from the times during her first year when still a newlywed she is invited and accompanies her hus-band, sits mute beside their conversation, waits and sips a beer until it grows warm, twists a paper napkin into a knot, then another into a fan, one into a rose, nods her head, smiles, yawns, politely grins, laughs at the appro-priate moments, leans against her husband's sleeve, tugs at his elbow, and fi-nally becomes good at predicting where the talk will lead, from this Cleófi-las concludes each is nightly trying to find the truth lying at the bottom of the bottle like a gold doubloon on the sea floor.

They want to tell each other what they want to tell themselves. But what is bumping like a helium balloon at the ceiling of the brain never finds its way out. It bubbles and rises, it gurgles in the throat, it rolls across the surface of the tongue, and erupts from the lips—a belch.

If they are lucky, there are tears at the end of the long night. At any given moment, the fists try to speak. They are dogs chasing their own tails before lying down to sleep, trying to find a way, a route, an out, and—finally—get some peace.

In the morning sometimes before he opens his eyes. Or after they have finished loving. Or at times when he is simply across from her at the table putting pieces of food into his mouth and chewing. Cleófilas thinks, This is the man I have waited my whole life for.

30   Not that he isn't a good man. She has to remind herself why she loves him when she changes the baby's Pampers, or when she mops the bathroom floor, or tries to make the curtains for the doorways without doors, or whiten the linen. Or wonder a little when he kicks the refrigerator and says he hates this shitty house and is going out where he won't be bothered with the baby's howling and her suspicious questions, and her requests to fix this and this and this because if she had any brains in her head she'd realize he's been up before the rooster earning his living to pay for the food in her belly and the roof over her head and would have to wake up again early the next day so why can't you just leave me in peace, woman.

He is not very tall, no, and he doesn't look like the men on the *telenovelas.* His face still scarred from acne. And he has a bit of a belly from all the beer he drinks. Well, he's always been husky.

This man who farts and belches and snores as well as laughs and kisses and holds her. Somehow this husband whose whiskers she finds each morning in the sink, whose shoes she must air each evening on the porch, this husband who cuts his fingernails in public, laughs loudly, curses like a man, and demands each course of dinner be served on a separate plate like at his mother's, as soon as he gets home, on time or late, and who doesn't care at all for music or *telenovelas* or romance or roses or the moon floating pearly over the *arroyo,* or through the bedroom window for that matter, shut the blinds and go back to sleep, this man, this father, this rival, this keeper, this lord, this master, this husband till kingdom come.

A doubt. Slender as a hair. A washed cup set back on the shelf wrong-side-up. Her lipstick, and body talc, and hairbrush all arranged in the bathroom a different way.

No. Her imagination. The house the same as always. Nothing.

35   Coming home from the hospital with her new son, her husband. Something comforting in discovering her house slippers beneath the bed, the faded housecoat where she left it on the bathroom hook. Her pillow. Their bed.

Sweet sweet homecoming. Sweet as the scent of face powder in the air, jasmine, sticky liquor.

Smudged fingerprint on the door. Crushed cigarette in a glass. Wrinkle in the brain crumpling to a crease.

Sometimes she thinks of her father's house. But how could she go back there? What a disgrace. What would the neighbors say? Coming home like that with one baby on her hip and one in the oven. Where's your husband?

The town of gossips. The town of dust and despair. Which she has traded for this town of gossips. This town of dust, despair. Houses farther apart perhaps, though no more privacy because of it. No leafy *zócalo*[4] in the center of the town, though the murmur of talk is clear enough all the same. No huddled whispering on the church steps each Sunday. Because here the whispering begins at sunset at the ice house instead.

40   This town with its silly pride for a bronze pecan the size of a baby carriage in front of the city hall. TV repair shop, drugstore, hardware, dry cleaner's, chiropractor's, liquor store, bail bonds, empty storefront, and nothing, nothing, nothing of interest. Nothing one could walk to, at any rate. Because the towns here are built so that you have to depend on husbands. Or you stay home. Or you drive. If you're rich enough to own, allowed to drive, your own car.

There is no place to go. Unless one counts the neighbor ladies. Soledad on one side, Dolores on the other. Or the creek.

Don't go out there after dark, *mi'jita*.[5] Stay near the house. *No es bueno para la salud. Mala suerte.*[6] Bad luck. *Mal aire.* You'll get sick and the baby too. You'll catch a fright wandering about in the dark, and then you'll see how right we were.

The stream sometimes only a muddy puddle in the summer, though now in the springtime, because of the rains, a good-size alive thing, a thing with a voice all its own, all day and all night calling in its high, silver voice. Is it La Llorona, the weeping woman? La Llorona, who drowned her own children. Perhaps La Llorona is the one they named the creek after, she thinks, remembering all the stories she learned as a child.

La Llorona calling to her. She is sure of it. Cleófilas sets the baby's Donald Duck blanket on the grass. Listens. The day sky turning to night. The baby pulling up fistfuls of grass and laughing. La Llorona. Wonders if something as quiet as this drives a woman to the darkness under the trees.

45   What she needs is . . . and made a gesture as if to yank a woman's buttocks to his groin. Maximiliano, the foul-smelling fool from across the road, said this and set the men laughing, but Cleófilas just muttered. *Grosera,* and went on washing dishes.

She knew he said it not because it was true, but more because it was he who needed to sleep with a woman, instead of drinking each night at the ice house and stumbling home alone.

Maximiliano who was said to have killed his wife in an ice-house brawl when she came at him with a mop. I had to shoot, he had said—she was armed.

Their laughter outside the kitchen window. Her husband's, his friends'. Manolo, Beto, Efraín, el Perico. Maximiliano.

Was Cleófilas just exaggerating as her husband always said? It seemed the newspapers were full of such stories. This woman found on the side of the interstate. This one pushed from a moving car. This one's cadaver, this one unconscious, this one beaten blue. Her ex-husband, her husband, her lover, her father, her brother, her uncle, her friend, her co-worker. Always. The same grisly news in the pages of the dailies. She dunked a glass under the soapy water for a moment—shivered.

50   He had thrown a book. Hers. From across the room. A hot welt across the cheek. She could forgive that. But what stung more was the fact it was

---

[4]*zócalo* public square   [5]*mi'jita* daughter   [6]*No es . . . suerte* It's not healthy. Bad luck

her book, a love story by Corín Tellado, what she loved most now that she lived in the U.S., without a television set, without the *telenovelas.*

Except now and again when her husband was away and she could manage it, the few episodes glimpsed at the neighbor lady Soledad's house because Dolores didn't care for that sort of thing, though Soledad was often kind enough to retell what had happened on what episode of *María de Nadie,* the poor Argentine country girl who had the ill fortune of falling in love with the beautiful son of the Arrocha family, the very family she worked for, whose roof she slept under and whose floors she vacuumed, while in that same house, with the dust brooms and floor cleaners as witnesses, the square-jawed Juan Carlos Arrocha had uttered words of love, I love you, María, listen to me, *mi querida*[7] but it was she who had to say No, no, we are not of the same class, and remind him it was not his place nor hers to fall in love, while all the while her heart was breaking, can you imagine.

Cleófilas thought her life would have to be like that, like a *telenovela,* only now the episodes got sadder and sadder. And there were no commercials in between for comic relief. And no happy ending in sight. She thought this when she sat with the baby out by the creek behind the house. Cleófilas de . . . ? But somehow she would have to change her name to Topazio, or Yesenia, Cristal, Adriana, Stefania, Andrea, something more poetic than Cleófilas. Everything happened to women with names like jewels. But what happened to a Cleófilas? Nothing. But a crack in the face.

Because the doctor has said so. She has to go. To make sure the new baby is all right, so there won't be any problems when he's born, and the appointment card says next Tuesday. Could he please take her. And that's all.

No, she won't mention it. She promises. If the doctor asks she can say she fell down the front steps or slipped when she was out in the backyard, slipped out back, she could tell him that. She has to go back next Tuesday, Juan Pedro, please, for the new baby. For their child.

55   She could write to her father and ask maybe for money, just a loan, for the new baby's medical expenses. Well then if he'd rather she didn't. All right, she won't. Please don't anymore. Please don't. She knows it's difficult saving money with all the bills they have, but how else are they going to get out of debt with the truck payments? And after the rent and the food and the electricity and the gas and the water and the who-knows-what, well, there's hardly anything left. But please, at least for the doctor visit. She won't ask for anything else. She has to. Why is she so anxious? Because.

Because she is going to make sure the baby is not turned around backward this time to split her down the center. Yes. Next Tuesday at five-thirty. I'll have Juan Pedrito dressed and ready. But those are the only shoes he has. I'll polish them, and we'll be ready. As soon as you come from work. We won't make you ashamed.

Felice? It's me, Graciela.

No, I can't talk louder. I'm at work.

Look, I need kind of a favor. There's a patient, a lady here who's got a problem.

60   Well, wait a minute. Are you listening to me or what?

[7]*mi querida* my dearest

I can't talk real loud 'cause her husband's in the next room.

Well, would you just listen?

I was going to do this sonogram on her—she's pregnant, right?—and she just starts crying on me. *Híjole,* Felice! This poor lady's got black-and-blue marks all over. I'm not kidding.

From her husband. Who else? Another one of those brides from across the border. And her family's all in Mexico.

65   Shit. You think they're going to help her? Give me a break. This lady doesn't even speak English. She hasn't been allowed to call home or write or nothing. That's why I'm calling you.

She needs a ride.

Not to Mexico, you goof. Just to the Greyhound. In San Anto.

No, just a ride. She's got her own money. All you'd have to do is drop her off in San Antonio on your way home. Come on, Felice. Please? If we don't help her, who will? I'd drive her myself, but she needs to be on that bus before her husband gets home from work. What do you say?

I don't know. Wait.

70   Right away, tomorrow even.

Well, if tomorrow's no good for you . . .

It's a date, Felice. Thursday. At the Cash N Carry off I-10. Noon. She'll be ready.

Oh, and her name's Cleófilas.

I don't know. One of those Mexican saints, I guess. A martyr or something.

75   Cleófilas. C-L-E-O-F-I-L-A-S. Cle. O. Fi. Las. Write it down.

Thanks, Felice. When her kid's born she'll have to name her after us, right?

Yeah, you got it. A regular soap opera sometimes. *Qué vida, comadre. Bueno*[8] bye.

78   All morning that flutter of half-fear, half-doubt. At any moment Juan Pedro might appear in the doorway. On the street. At the Cash N Carry. Like in the dreams she dreamed.

There was that to think about, yes, until the woman in the pickup drove up. Then there wasn't time to think about anything but the pickup pointed toward San Antonio. Put your bags in the back and get in.

80   But when they drove across the *arroyo,* the driver opened her mouth and let out a yell as loud as any mariachi. Which startled not only Cleófilas, but Juan Pedrito as well.

Pues, look how cute. I scared you two, right? Sorry. Should've warned you. Every time I cross that bridge I do that. Because of the name, you know. Woman Hollering. *Pues,* I holler. She said this in a Spanish pocked with English and laughed. Did you ever notice, Felice continued, how nothing around here is named after a woman? Really. Unless she's the Virgin. I guess you're only famous if you're a virgin. She was laughing again.

That's why I like the name of that *arroyo.* Makes you want to holler like Tarzan, right?

Everything about this woman, this Felice, amazed Cleófilas. The fact that she drove a pickup. A pickup, mind you, but when Cleófilas asked if it

---

[8]*Qué . . . Bueno* What a life, pal. OK

was her husband's, she said she didn't have a husband. The pickup was hers. She herself had chosen it. She herself was paying for it.

I used to have a Pontiac Sunbird. But those cars are for *viejas.*[9] Pussy cars. Now this here is a *real* car.

85   What kind of talk was that coming from a woman? Cleófilas thought. But then again, Felice was like no woman she'd ever met. Can you imagine, when we crossed the *arroyo* she just started yelling like a crazy, she would say later to her father and brothers. Just like that. Who would've thought?

Who would've? Pain or rage, perhaps, but not a hoot like the one Felice had just let go. Makes you want to holler like Tarzan, Felice had said.

Then Felice began laughing again, but it wasn't Felice laughing. It was gurgling out of her own throat, a long ribbon of laughter, like water.

[1991]

 TOPICS FOR CRITICAL THINKING AND WRITING

1. In a sentence or two summarize the plot—the gist of what happens. Would you say that the plot is what is chiefly of interest in this story? If not, what *is* of interest?

2. Why do you suppose Cisneros included Soledad and Dolores in the story? What (if anything) do they contribute?

3. What is Cleófilas's view of marriage? What is the reality that she experiences? Do you blame her for leaving her husband? She *does* leave him, but do you think that her character changes? Explain.

---

[9]*viejas* old woman

CHAPTER 8

Thinking Critically about a Short Story

A Casebook on William Faulkner's "A Rose for Emily"

In this chapter we print Faulkner's story "A Rose for Emily," followed by pre-publication material, comments by Faulkner, and critical interpretations by three critics. More precisely, the supplementary material is as follows:

1. The first of five surviving pages of the manuscript, now in the Alderman Library at the University of Virginia. All of these surviving pages are damaged in the upper right corner. They are very close to the published version, but they differ in some significant ways. On the first page, for instance, in the second paragraph the date of the remission of taxes is given as 1904, whereas in the published version the date is 1894. Notice, too, that on the manuscript Faulkner has changed the name from Emily Wyatt to Emily Grierson.

2. The University of Virginia also possesses a 17-page typescript of the complete story. This version, too, is very close to the published story, but it includes an extended scene between Emily and Tobe, the black servant. We reprint this portion of the manuscript. We also reproduce the typescript version of the end of the story, which reveals that between the time Faulkner wrote the typescript and the time he published the story he slightly revised the ending.

3. Comments Faulkner made when he spoke about the story to students.

4. A very brief interpretation by Cleanth Brooks.

5. An interpretation by Hal Blythe.

6. An extract from a feminist interpretation by Judith Fetterley.

WILLIAM FAULKNER

William Faulkner (1897–1962) was brought up in Oxford, Missis-
sippi. His great-grandfather had been a Civil War hero, and his father
was treasurer of the University of Mississippi in Oxford; the family
was no longer rich, but it was still respected. In 1918 he enrolled in
the Royal Canadian Air Force, though he never saw overseas service.
After the war he returned to Mississippi and went to the university
for two years. He then moved to New Orleans, where he became
friendly with Sherwood Anderson, who was already an established
writer. In New Orleans Faulkner worked for the Times-Picayune; *still*
later, even after he had established himself as a major novelist with
The Sound and the Fury *(1929), he had to do some work in Holly-*
wood in order to make ends meet. In 1950 he was awarded the Nobel
Prize in Literature.

Almost all of Faulkner's writing is concerned with the people of
Yoknapatawpha, an imaginary county in Mississippi. "I discovered,"
he said, "that my own little postage stamp of native soil was worth
writing about and that I would never live long enough to exhaust it."
Though he lived for brief periods in Canada, New Orleans, New York,
Hollywood, and Virginia (where he died), he spent most of his life in
his native Mississippi.

A Rose for Emily

I

When Miss Emily Grierson died, our whole town went to her funeral: the
men through a sort of respectful affection for a fallen monument, the
women mostly out of curiosity to see the inside of her house, which no one
save an old manservant—a combined gardener and cook—had seen in at
least ten years.

It was a big, squarish frame house that had once been white, decorated
with cupolas and spires and scrolled balconies in the heavily lightsome style
of the seventies, set on what had once been our most select street. But
garages and cotton gins had encroached the obliterated even the august
names of that neighborhood; only Miss Emily's house was left, lifting its
stubborn and coquettish decay above the cotton wagons and the gasoline
pumps—an eyesore among eyesores. And now Miss Emily had gone to join
the representatives of those august names where they lay in the cedar-
bemused cemetery among the ranked and anonymous graves of Union and
Confederate soldiers who fell at the battle of Jefferson.

Alive, Miss Emily had been a tradition, a duty, and a care; a sort of hereditary obligation upon the town, dating from that day in 1894 when Colonel
Sartoris, the mayor—he who fathered the edict that no Negro woman
should appear on the streets without an apron—remitted her taxes, the dispensation dating from the death of her father on into perpetuity. Not that
Miss Emily would have accepted charity. Colonel Sartoris invented an involved tale to the effect that Miss Emily's father had loaned money to the
town, which the town, as a matter of business, preferred this way of

repaying. Only a man of Colonel Sartoris' generation and thought could have invented it, and only a woman could have believed it.

When the next generation, with its more modern ideas, became mayors and aldermen, this arrangement created some little dissatisfaction. On the first of the year they mailed her a tax notice. February came, and there was no reply. They wrote her a formal letter, asking her to call at the sheriff's office at her convenience. A week later the mayor wrote her himself, offering to call or to send his car for her, and received in reply a note on paper of an archaic shape, in a thin, flowing calligraphy in faded ink, to the effect that she no longer went out at all. The tax notice was also enclosed, without comment.

5   They called a special meeting of the Board of Aldermen. A deputation waited upon her, knocked at the door through which no visitor had passed since she ceased giving china-painting lessons eight or ten years earlier. They were admitted by the old Negro into a dim hall from which a staircase mounted into still more shadow. It smelled of dust and disuse—a close, dank smell. The Negro led them into the parlor. It was furnished in heavy, leather-covered furniture. When the Negro opened the blinds of one window they could see that the leather was cracked; and when they sat down, a faint dust rose sluggishly about their thighs, spinning with slow motes in the single sunray. On a tarnished gilt easel before the fireplace stood a crayon portrait of Miss Emily's father.

They rose when she entered—a small, fat woman in black, with a thin gold chain descending to her waist and vanishing into her belt, leaning on an ebony cane with a tarnished gold head. Her skeleton was small and spare; perhaps that was why what would have been merely plumpness in another was obesity in her. She looked bloated, like a body long submerged in motionless water, and of that pallid hue. Her eyes, lost in the fatty ridges of her face, looked like two small pieces of coal pressed into a lump of dough as they moved from one face to another while the visitors stated their errand.

She did not ask them to sit. She just stood in the door and listened quietly until the spokesman came to a stumbling halt. Then they could hear the invisible watch ticking at the end of the gold chain.

Her voice was dry and cold. "I have no taxes in Jefferson. Colonel Sartoris explained it to me. Perhaps one of you can gain access to the city records and satisfy yourselves."

"But we have. We are the city authorities, Miss Emily. Didn't you get a notice from the sheriff, signed by him?"

10   "I received a paper, yes," Miss Emily said. "Perhaps he considers himself the sheriff. . . . I have no taxes in Jefferson."

"But there is nothing on the books to show that, you see. We must go by the—"

"See Colonel Sartoris. I have no taxes in Jefferson."

"But, Miss Emily—"

"See Colonel Sartoris." (Colonel Sartoris had been dead almost ten years.) "I have no taxes in Jefferson. Tobe!" The Negro appeared. "Show these gentlemen out."

II

15   So she vanquished them, horse and foot, just as she had vanquished their fathers thirty years before about the smell. That was two years after her fa-

ther's death and a short time after her sweetheart—the one we believed would marry her—had deserted her. After her father's death she went out very little; after her sweetheart went away, people hardly saw her at all. A few of the ladies had the temerity to call, but were not received, and the only sign of life about the place was the Negro man—a young man then—going in and out with a market basket.

"Just as if a man—any man—could keep a kitchen properly," the ladies said; so they were not surprised when the smell developed. It was another link between the gross, teeming world and the high and mighty Griersons.

A neighbor, a woman, complained to the mayor, Judge Stevens, eighty years old.

"But what will you have me do about it, madam?" he said.

"Why, send her word to stop it," the woman said. "Isn't there a law?"

20   "I'm sure that won't be necessary," Judge Stevens said. "It's probably just a snake or a rat that nigger of hers killed in the yard. I'll speak to him about it."

The next day he received two more complaints, one from a man who came in diffident deprecation. "We really must do something about it, Judge. I'd be the last one in the world to bother Miss Emily, but we've got to do something." That night the Board of Aldermen met—three gray-beards and one younger man, a member of the rising generation.

"It's simple enough," he said. "Send her word to have her place cleaned up. Give her a certain time to do it in, and if she don't . . . "

"Dammit, sir," Judge Stevens said, "will you accuse a lady to her face of smelling bad?"

So the next night, after midnight, four men crossed Miss Emily's lawn and slunk about the house like burglars, sniffing along the base of the brick-work and at the cellar openings while one of them performed a regular sow-ing motion with his hand out of a sack slung from his shoulder. They broke open the cellar door and sprinkled lime there, and in all the out-buildings. As they recrossed the lawn, a window that had been dark was lighted and Miss Emily sat in it, the light behind her, and her upright torso motionless as that of an idol. They crept quietly across the lawn and into the shadow of the lo-custs that lined the street. After a week or two the smell went away.

25   That was when people had begun to feel really sorry for her. People in our town remembering how old lady Wyatt, her great-aunt, had gone com-pletely crazy at last, believed that the Griersons held themselves a little too high for what they really were. None of the young men were quite good enough for Miss Emily and such. We had long thought of them as a tableau; Miss Emily a slender figure in white in the background, her father a sprad-dled silhouette in the foreground, his back to her and clutching a horse-whip, the two of them framed by the back-flung front door. So when she got to be thirty and was still single, we were not pleased exactly, but vindicated; even with insanity in the family she wouldn't have turned down all of her chances if they had really materialized.

When her father died, it got about that the house was all that was left to her; and in a way, people were glad. At last they could pity Miss Emily. Being left alone, and a pauper, she had become humanized. Now she too would know the old thrill and the old despair of a penny more or less.

The day after his death all the ladies prepared to call at the house and offer condolence and aid, as is our custom. Miss Emily met them at the door, dressed as usual and with no trace of grief on her face. She told them that her father was not dead. She did that for three days, with the ministers calling on her, and the doctors, trying to persuade her to let them dispose of the body. Just as they were about to resort to law and force, she broke down, and they buried her father quickly.

We did not say she was crazy then. We believed she had to do that. We remembered all the young men her father had driven away, and we knew that with nothing left, she would have to cling to that which had robbed her, as people will.

III

She was sick for a long time. When we saw her again, her hair was cut short, making her look like a girl, with a vague resemblance to those angels in colored church windows—sort of tragic and serene.

30   The town had just let the contracts for paving the sidewalks, and in the summer after her father's death they began to work. The construction company came with niggers and mules and machinery, and a foreman named Homer Barron, a Yankee—a big, dark, ready man, with a big voice and eyes lighter than his face. The little boys would follow in groups to hear him cuss the niggers, and the niggers singing in time to the rise and fall of picks. Pretty soon he knew everybody in town. Whenever you heard a lot of laughing anywhere about the square, Homer Barron would be in the center of the group. Presently we began to see him and Miss Emily on Sunday afternoons driving in the yellow-wheeled buggy and the matched team of bays from the livery stable.

At first we were glad that Miss Emily would have an interest, because the ladies all said, "Of course a Grierson would not think seriously of a Northerner, a day laborer." But there were still others, older people, who said that even grief could not cause a real lady to forget *noblesse oblige*—without calling it *noblesse oblige*. They just said, "Poor Emily. Her kinsfolk should come to her." She had some kin in Alabama; but years ago her father had fallen out with them over the estate of old lady Wyatt, the crazy woman, and there was no communication between the two families. They had not even been represented at the funeral.

And as soon as the old people said, "Poor Emily," the whispering began. "Do you suppose it's really so?" they said to one another. "Of course it is. . . ." This behind their hands; rustling of craned silk and satin behind jalousies closed upon the sun of Sunday afternoon as the thin, swift clop-clop-clop of the matched team passed: "Poor Emily."

She carried her head high enough—even when we believed that she was fallen. It was as if she demanded more than ever the recognition of her dignity as the last Grierson; as if it had wanted that touch of earthiness to reaffirm her imperviousness. Like when she bought the rat poison, the arsenic. That was over a year after they had begun to say "Poor Emily," and while the two female cousins were visiting her.

"I want some poison," she said to the druggist. She was over thirty then, still a slight woman, though thinner than usual, with cold, haughty black eyes in a face the flesh of which was strained across the temples and about the eyesockets as you imagine a lighthouse-keeper's face ought to look. "I want some poison," she said.

35   "Yes, Miss Emily. What kind? For rats and such? I'd recom—"

"I want the best you have. I don't care what kind."

The druggist named several. "They'll kill anything up to an elephant. But what you want is—"

"Arsenic," Miss Emily said. "Is that a good one?"

"Is . . . arsenic? Yes ma'am. But what you want—"

40   "I want arsenic."

The druggist looked down at her. She looked back at him, erect, her face like a strained flag. "Why, of course," the druggist said. "If that's what you want. But the law requires you to tell what you are going to use it for."

Miss Emily just stared at him, her head tilted back in order to look him eye for eye, until he looked away and went and got the arsenic and wrapped it up. The Negro delivery boy brought her the package; the druggist didn't come back. When she opened the package at home there was written on the box, under the skull and bones: "For rats."

IV

So the next day we all said, "She will kill herself"; and we said it would be the best thing. When she had first begun to be seen with Homer Barron, we had said, "She will marry him." Then we said, "She will persuade him yet," because Homer himself had remarked—he liked men, and it was known that he drank with the younger men in the Elks' Club—that he was not a marrying man. Later we said, "Poor Emily," behind the jalousies as they passed on Sunday afternoon in the glittering buggy, Miss Emily with her head high and Homer Barron with his hat cocked and a cigar in his teeth, reins and whip in a yellow glove.

Then some of the ladies began to say that it was a disgrace to the town and a bad example to the young people. The men did not want to interfere, but at last the ladies forced the Baptist minister—Miss Emily's people were Episcopal—to call upon her. He would never divulge what happened during that interview, but he refused to go back again. The next Sunday they again drove about the streets, and the following day the minister's wife wrote to Miss Emily's relations in Alabama.

45   So she had blood-kin under her roof again and we sat back to watch developments. At first nothing happened. Then we were sure that they were to be married. We learned that Miss Emily had been to the jeweler's and ordered a man's toilet set in silver, with the letter H.B. on each piece. Two days later we learned that she had bought a complete outfit of men's clothing, including a nightshirt, and we said, "They are married." We were really glad. We were glad because the two female cousins were even more Grierson than Miss Emily had ever been.

So we were surprised when Homer Barron—the streets had been finished some time since—was gone. We were a little disappointed that there was not a public blowing-off but we believed that he had gone on to prepare for Miss Emily's coming, or to give a chance to get rid of the cousins. (By that time it was a cabal, and we were all Miss Emily's allies to help circumvent the cousins.) Sure enough, after another week they departed. And, as we had expected all along, within three days Homer Barron was back in town. A neighbor saw the Negro man admit him at the kitchen door at dusk one evening.

And that was the last we saw of Homer Barron. And of Miss Emily for some time. The Negro man went in and out with the market basket, but the front door remained closed. Now and then we would see her at a window for a moment, as the men did that night when they sprinkled the lime, but for almost six months she did not appear on the streets. Then we knew that this was to be expected too; as if that quality of her father which had thwarted her woman's life so many times had been too virulent and too furious to die.

When we next saw Miss Emily, she had grown fat and her hair was turning gray. During the next few years it grew grayer and grayer until it attained an even pepper-and-salt iron-gray, when it ceased turning. Up to the day of her death at seventy-four it was still that vigorous iron-gray, like the hair of an active man.

From that time on her front door remained closed, save for a period of six or seven years, when she was about forty, during which she gave lessons in china-painting. She fitted up a studio in one of the downstairs rooms, where the daughters and granddaughters of Colonel Sartoris' contemporaries were sent to her with the same regularity and in the same spirit that they were sent on Sundays with a twenty-five cent piece for the collection plate. Meanwhile her taxes had been remitted.

50   Then the newer generation became the backbone and the spirit of the town, and the painting pupils grew up and fell away and did not send their children to her with boxes of color and tedious brushes and pictures cut from the ladies' magazines. The front door closed upon the last one and remained closed for good. When the town got free postal delivery Miss Emily alone refused to let them fasten the metal numbers above her door and attach a mailbox to it. She would not listen to them.

Daily, monthly, yearly we watched the Negro grow grayer and more stooped, going in and out with the market basket. Each December we sent her a tax notice, which would be returned by the post office a week later, unclaimed. Now and then we could see her in one of the downstairs windows—she had evidently shut up the top floor of the house—like the carven torso of an idol in a niche, looking or not looking at us, we could never tell which. Thus she passed from generation to generation—dear, inescapable, impervious, tranquil, and perverse.

And so she died. Fell ill in the house filled with dust and shadows, with only a doddering Negro man to wait on her. We did not even know she was sick; we had long since given up trying to get any information from the Negro. He talked to no one, probably not even to her, for his voice had grown harsh and rusty, as if from disuse.

She died in one of the downstairs rooms, in a heavy walnut bed with a curtain, her gray head propped on a pillow yellow and moldy with age and lack of sunlight.

V

The Negro met the first of the ladies at the front door and let them in, with their hushed, sibilant voices and their quick, curious glances, and then he disappeared. He walked right through the house and out the back and was not seen again.

55   The two female cousins came at once. They held the funeral on the second day, with the town coming to look at Miss Emily beneath a mass of bought flowers, with the crayon face of her father musing profoundly above the bier and the ladies sibilant and macabre; and the very old men—some in their brushed Confederate uniforms—on the porch and the lawn, talking of

Miss Emily as if she had been a contemporary of theirs, believing that they had danced with her and courted her perhaps, confusing time with its mathematical progression, as the old do, to whom all the past is not a diminishing road, but, instead, a huge meadow which no winter ever quite touches, divided from them now by the narrow bottleneck of the most recent decade of years.

Already we knew that there was one room in that region above stairs which no one had seen in forty years, and which would have to be forced. They waited until Miss Emily was decently in the ground before they opened it.

The violence of breaking down the door seemed to fill this room with pervading dust. A thin, acrid pall as of the tomb seemed to lie everywhere upon this room decked and furnished as for a bridal: upon the valance curtains of faded rose color, upon the rose-shaded lights, upon the dressing table, upon the delicate array of crystal and the man's toilet things backed with tarnished silver, silver so tarnished that the monogram was obscured. Among them lay a collar and tie, as if they had just been removed, which, lifted, left upon the surface a pale crescent in the dust. Upon a chair hung the suit, carefully folded; beneath it the two mute shoes and the discarded socks.

The man himself lay in the bed.

For a long while we just stood there, looking down at the profound and fleshless grin. The body had apparently once lain in the attitude of an embrace, but now the long sleep that outlasts love, that conquers even the grimace of love, had cuckolded him. What was left of him, rotted beneath what was left of the nightshirt, had become inextricable from the bed in which he lay; and upon him and upon the pillow beside him lay that even coating of the patient and biding dust.

60   Then we noticed that in the second pillow was the indentation of a head. One of us lifted something from it, and leaning forward, that faint and invisible dust dry and acrid in the nostrils, we saw a long strand of iron-gray hair.

[1930]

✍ TOPICS FOR CRITICAL THINKING AND WRITING

1. Why does the narrator begin with what is almost the end of the story—the death of Miss Emily—rather than save this information for later? What devices does Faulkner use to hold the reader's interest throughout?

2. In a paragraph, offer a conjecture about Miss Emily's attitudes toward Homer Barron after he was last seen alive.

3. In a paragraph or two, characterize Miss Emily, calling attention not only to her eccentricities or even craziness, but also to what you conjecture to be her moral values.

4. In paragraph 44 we are told that the Baptist minister "would never divulge what happened" during the interview with Miss Emily. Why do you suppose Faulkner does not narrate or describe the interview? Let's assume that in his first draft of the story he *did* give a paragraph of narration or a short dramatic scene. Write such an episode.

(Continued on p. 189)

The first page of Faulkner's handwritten manuscript for "A Rose for Emily." (Photos pp. 184–188 from the William Faulkner Collection, Special Collections Department, Manuscripts Division, University of Virginia Library.)

dust and shadows, with only a dodder~~i~~ng negro man to wait on
her. We did not even know she was sick; we had long since given up
trying to get any inform~~a~~tion from the negro. He talked to no
one, probably not even to her, for his voice had grown ~~fuzzy~~
harsh and ~~dry~~ rusty, as though with disuse; the sparse words
which he did speak sounded as though he had learned them that
morning by rote---just enough of them to carry him through
the day.

She died in one of the downstairs rooms, in a heavy
walnut bed with a curtain, her gray head propped on a pillow
yellow and moldy with age and lack of sunlight, her voice
cold and strong to the last.

"But not till I'm gone," she said. "Dont you let a
soul in until I'm gone, do you hear?" Standing beside the bed,
his head in the dim light nimbused by a faint halo of napped,
perfectly white hair, the negro made a brief gesture with his
hand. Miss Emily lay with her eyes open, gazing into the opposite shadows of the room. Upon the coverlet her hands lay on
her breast, gnarled, blue with age, motionless. "Hah," she said.
"Then they can. Let 'em go up there and see what's in that
room. ~~And/you/wont/be/the/last/one,/either~~ Fools. ~~And~~ Let
'em. ~~And/you/wont/be/the/last/one~~ Satisfy their minds that
I am crazy. Do you think I am?" The negro made no reply, no
movement. He stood above the bed, ~~stooped/motionless/a/bit/of/the~~
~~sky/~~ motionless, musing: a secret and unfathomable soul behind
the death-mask of an ape and haloed like an angel. "Let 'em
go up there and open that door. And you wont be the last one,

13.

The printed version of Faulkner's "A Rose for Emily" omitted several passages of dialogue, shown
here in the typed manuscript on pages 13 to 15, between Miss Emily and her longtime manservant.

either. Will you?"

"I wont have to," the negro said. "I know what's in that room. I dont have to see."

"Hah," Miss Emily said. "You do, do you. How long have you known?" Again he made that brief sign with his hand. Miss Emily had not turned her head. She stared into the shadows where the high ceiling was lost. "You should be glad. Now you can go to Chicago, like you've been talking about for thirty years. And with what you'll get for the house and furniture.... Colonel Sartoris has the will. He'll see they dont rob you."

"I dont want any house," the negro said.

"You cant help yourself. It's signed and sealed thirty-five years ago. Wasn't that our agreement when I found I couldn't pay you any wages? that you were to have everything that was left if you outlived me, and I was to bury you with in a coffin with your name on a gold plate if I outlived you?" He said nothing. "Wasn't it?" Miss Emily said.

"I was young then. Wanted to be rich. But now I dont want any house."

"Not when you have wanted to go to Chicago for thirty years?" Their breathing was alike: each that harsh, rasping breath of the old, the short inhalations that do not reach the bottom of the lungs: tireless, precarious, on the verge of cessation for all time, as if anything might suffice: a word, a look. "What are you going to do, then?"

"Going to the poorhouse."

"The poorhouse? When I'm trying to fix you so you'll

14.

186

have neither to worry nor lift your hand as long as you live?

"I dont want nothing," the negro said. "I'm going to the poorhouse. I already told them."

"Well," Miss Emily said. She had not moved her head, not moved at all. "Do you mind telling me why you want to go to the poorhouse?"

Again he mused. The room was still save for their breathing: it was as though they had both quitted all living and all dying; all the travail of mortality and of breath. "So I can set on that hill in the sun all day and watch them trains pass. See them at night too, with the engine puffing and lights in all the windows.

"Oh," Miss Emily said. Motionless, her knotted hands lying on the yellowed coverlet beneath her chin and her chin resting upon her breast, she appeared to muse intently, as though she were listening to dissolution setting up within her. "Hah," she said.

Then she died, and the negro met the first of the ladies at the front door and let them in, with their hushed sibilant voices and their quick curious glances, and he went on to the back and disappeared. He walked right through the house and out the back and was not seen again.

The two female cousins came at once. They held the funeral on the second day, with the town coming to look at Miss Emily beneath a mass of bought flowers, with the crayon face of her father musing profoundly above the bier and the la-

15.

grin cemented into what had once been a pillow by a substance like hardened sealing-wax. One side of the covers was flung back, as though he were preparing to rise; we lifted the covers completely away, liberating still another sluggish cloud of infinitesimal dust, invisible and tainted. The body had apparently once lain in the attitude of an embrace, but now the long sleep that outlasts love, that conquers even the grimace of love, had cuckolded him: what was left of him lay beneath what was left of the nightshirt, become inextricable with the bed in which he lay, and upon him and upon the pillow beside him lay that even coating of the patient and biding dust. /¢/ Then we noticed that in the second pillow was the indentation of a head; one of us lifted something from it, and leaning forward, that faint and invisible dust lean and acrid in the nostrils, we saw a long strand of iron-gray hair.

The final paragraph of the typed manuscript was reworded and made into two paragraphs in the published version.

5. Suppose that Homer Barron's remains had been discovered before Miss Emily died, and that she was arrested and charged with murder. You are the prosecutor and you are running for a statewide political office. In 500 words, set forth your argument that—despite the fact that she is a public monument—she should be convicted. Or: You are the defense attorney, also running for office. In 500 words, set forth your defense.

6. Assume that Miss Emily kept a journal—perhaps even from her days as a young girl. Write some entries for the journal, giving her thoughts about some of the episodes reported in Faulkner's story.

 WILLIAM FAULKNER

Faulkner was writer-in-residence at the University of Virginia in 1957 and 1958. His talks and conversations with students were recorded and then published in Faulkner in the University, *edited by Frederick L. Gwynn and Joseph L. Blotner (1959), from which the following material is reprinted.*

Comments on "A Rose for Emily"

Q. Sir, it has been argued that "A Rose for Emily" is a criticism of the North, and others have argued saying that it is a criticism of the South. Now, could this story, shall we say, be more properly classified as a criticism of the times?

A. Now that I don't know, because I was simply trying to write about people. The writer uses environment—what he knows—and if there's a symbolism in which the lover represented the North and the woman who murdered him represents the South, I don't say that's not valid and not there, but it was no intention of the writer to say, Now let's see, I'm going to write a piece in which I will use a symbolism for the North and another symbol for the South, that he was simply writing about people, a story which he thought was tragic and true, because it came out of the human heart, the human aspiration, the human—the conflict of conscience with glands, with the Old Adam. It was a conflict not between the North and the South so much as between, well you might say, God and Satan.

Q. Sir, just a little more on that thing. You say it's a conflict between God and Satan. Well, I don't quite understand what you mean. Who is—did one represent the—

A. The conflict was in Miss Emily, that she knew that you do not murder people. She had been trained that you do not take a lover. You marry, you don't take a lover. She had broken all the laws of her tradition, her background, and she had finally broken the law of God too, which says you do not take human life. And she knew she was doing wrong, and that's why her own life was wrecked. Instead of murdering one lover, and then to go on and take another and when she used him up to murder him, she was expiating her crime.

5   *Q.* . . . She did do all the things that she had been taught not to do, and being a sensitive sort of a woman, it was sure to have told on her, but do you think it's fair to feel pity for her, because in a way she made her adjustment, and it seems to have wound up in a happy sort of way—certainly tragic, but maybe it suited her just fine.

A. Yes, it may have, but then I don't think that one should withhold pity simply because the subject of the pity, object of pity, is pleased and satisfied. I think the pity is in the human striving against its own nature, against its own conscience. That's what deserves the pity. It's not the state of the individual, it's man in conflict with his heart, or with his fellows, or with his environment—that's what deserves the pity. It's not that the man suffered, or that he fell off the house, or was run over by the train. It's that he was—that man is trying to do the best he can with his desires and impulses against his own moral conscience, and the conscience of, the social conscience of his time and his place—the little town he must live in, the family he's a part of.

. . .

Q. What is the meaning of the title "A Rose for Emily"?

A. Oh, it's simply the poor woman had had no life at all. Her father had kept her more or less locked up and then she had a lover who was about to quit her, she had to murder him. It was just "A Rose for Emily"—that's all

. . .

Q. I was wondering, one of your short stories, "A Rose for Emily," what ever inspired you to write this story . . . ?

10 *A.* That to me was another sad and tragic manifestation of man's condition in which he dreams and hopes, in which he is in conflict with himself or with his environment or with others. In this case there was the young girl with a young girl's normal aspirations to find love and then a husband and a family, who was brow-beaten and kept down by her father, a selfish man who didn't want her to leave home because he wanted a housekeeper, and it was a natural instinct of—repressed which—you can't repress it—you can mash it down but it comes up somewhere else and very likely in a tragic form, and that was simply another manifestation of man's injustice to man, of the poor tragic human being struggling with its own heart, with others, with its environment, for the simple things which all human beings want. In that case it was a young girl that just wanted to be loved and to love and to have a husband and a family.

Q. And that purely came from your imagination?

A. Well, the story did but the condition is there. It exists. I didn't invent that condition, I didn't invent the fact that young girls dream of someone to love and children and a home, but the story of what her own particular tragedy was was invented, yes. . . .

[1957–58]

 CLEANTH BROOKS

Cleanth Brooks (1906–94), a leading formalist critic (on formalist criticism see p. 432), is especially associated with critical essays on poetry, but he also wrote on drama and fiction. The following short comment is from an introductory book on Faulkner.

On "A Rose for Emily"

[An] important problem about this story has to do with whether it has a meaning for humanity in general. Does this account of Emily Grierson amount to anything more than a clinical case history? Or, to put it in another way, since a person who is insane cannot be held accountable for her actions, can her actions have any significance for all of us?

Miss Emily's mania is a manifestation—warped though it be—of her pride, her independence, her iron will. She has not crumpled up under the pressures exerted upon her. She has not given in. She has insisted on choosing a lover in spite of the criticism of the town. She has refused to be jilted. She will not be either held up to scorn or pitied. She demands that the situation be settled on her own terms.

What she does in order to get her own way is, of course, terrible. But there is an element of the heroic about it too, and the town evidently recognizes it as such. Can an act be both monstrous and heroic? For a person who can hold two contradictory notions in his head at the same time, the answer will be yes. We can give Miss Emily her due without condoning her crime and, in an age in which social conformity and respectability are the order of the day, her willingness to flout public opinion may even seem exhilarating. Faulkner, by the way, never shows any regard for respectability: in his fiction respectability is the first temptation to which every cowardly soul succumbs. Miss Emily is crazy, but she is no coward. She is the true aristocrat: let others strive to keep up with the Joneses, if they will. She will not. She is the "Jones" with whom others will do well to keep up.

I have said that the narrator never spells out what Miss Emily's story meant to him or to the town, but he has provided a very illuminating simile. He tells us that Miss Emily with her "cold, haughty black eyes" and her flesh "strained across the temples" looked "as you imagine a lighthouse-keeper's face ought to look."

A lighthouse provides a beacon for other people, not for the keeper of the light. He looks out into darkness. He serves others but lives in sheer isolation himself. His job is to warn others from being wrecked on the dangerous rocks on which his lighthouse is built. The simile really answers to Miss Emily's condition very well. For readers who demand a moral, this will have to serve. Miss Emily's story constitutes a warning against the sin of pride: heroic isolation pushed too far ends in homicidal madness.

[1983]

 ## TOPICS FOR CRITICAL THINKING AND WRITING

1. Brooks argues (paragraph 2) that "there is an element of the heroic" in Emily's behavior. Does he convince you? Why, or why not?
2. Brooks suggests that the simile of the lighthouse provides a sort of moral, and he formulates the moral thus: "Heroic isolation pushed too far ends in homicidal murder." Do you think this formulation is appropriate? If not, how might you formulate the moral? Or do you think that it is inappropriate to try to find a moral for this story? Explain.

 ## HAL BLYTHE

The following essay comes from a journal called Explicator, *which customarily gives as the title of the essay only the name of the work discussed.*

Faulkner's "A Rose for Emily"

Perhaps the most provocative aspect of Faulkner's "A Rose for Emily" is not the final revelation of the "long strand of iron-gray hair" (183) on Miss Emily's pillow, but her motive in killing Homer Barron. Conjecture has run from Ray West's theory of her attempt to stop time (205–11) to Jack Scherting's assertion of an unresolved Oedipal complex (397–405). A closer examination of Miss Emily's "lover," Homer Barron, reveals, however, another possible motive for Emily Grierson. Simply put, Faulkner hints that Miss Emily's "beau" ideal is homosexual and that she poisons him to save face, thus suggesting the chivalric courtship ritual, so subscribed to by the Old South, was in reality a sterile vision.

Faulkner's major clue to Homer Barron's sexual preference is the name chosen for Miss Emily's swain. Initially, Homer, calling to mind the poet of antiquity, evokes images of larger-than-life epic heroes for the reader. The surname, Barron, suggests the aristocratic and the chivalric nature of the courtly lover, who suddenly appears in Jefferson like a knight-errant from afar: "a big, dark ready man, with a big voice and eyes lighter than his face" (180). When this leader of men begins to court the town's lady, he seems to fulfill the chivalric ideal.

Faulkner, however, undercuts this romanticized vision. John Jacobs has previously noted that Homer Barron is a "day laborer, a Yankee, and perhaps a part Negro," concluding, "Although 'Barron' suggests nobility, this suitor is far from chivalric: he is neither serious about Miss Emily, nor careful to avoid town scandal" (77). But Jacobs overlooks significant evidence that Barron is not all he appears to be, evidence that leads to a different conclusion. When Barron is first introduced, the narrator observes, "The little boys would follow [him] in groups" (180) and later paraphrases Barron as saying "he liked men, and it was known that he drank with the younger men in the Elks' Club—that he was not a marrying man" (181). Because of the emphasis on Barron's surrounding himself with men, especially younger men, the given name that Faulkner chose for the "lover" takes on another meaning. Homer also conjures up images of Classical Greek society. In his *Sexual Life in Ancient Greece*, Hans Licht points out that "the Homeric epos also abounds in undoubted traces of ephebophilia [a man's love for a young man who has passed puberty], and that no one in the ancient times of Greece ever supposed otherwise" (449–50). Subtly, then, Faulkner has painted a picture of a modern pederast that helps the audience penetrate the chivalric illusion and see that Miss Emily's beau is gay.

Appropriately, the imagery surrounding Homer Barron is that of sterility. When he first appears, Barron is associated with "mules and machinery" (180), things that can never bear fruit. Jacobs comments that Barron's "last name refers to the fruitless, or barren, union with Miss Emily" (79). Moreover, even in death Barron and the bedroom are covered with "patient and biding dust" (183), Faulkner's traditional image of sterility.

5   So, while she may be killing Homer Barron to stop time and/or to try to resolve her Oedipal complex, the "high and mighty" Miss Emily could be poisoning her beau to save face. Discovering Homer Barron's true nature and how he had been using her to keep the good people of Jefferson from seeing his pedophilic deviation, she feels humiliated by his pseudo-

courtship. Consequently, she exacts a measure of revenge. Just as she finally manifested control of her dominating father with a crayon portrait, so the artist in her forever fashions Homer Barron in the shape of what she first thought him to be, a courtly lover. She knows that when the ever-curious townspeople inevitably uncover the macabre scene in the rose-colored bedroom, and because she had openly bought the "man's toilet set in silver" and "a complete outfit of men's clothing, including a nightshirt" (181), they will indeed conclude Homer Barron was her lover. She even positions the body in an embrace, an unlikely natural position for one having died in the throes of arsenic, to help the intruders believe the reality of her false ideal.

Faulkner's choice of the "lover's" name, the imagery, and the details surrounding Homer Barron's activities in Jefferson, then, provide a gap between the appearance and reality of the courtship ritual. Once again Faulkner has used sexual deviation to indicate the decay of an Old South tradition. The dramatic irony of having the swain a homosexual undercuts the Southern chivalric ideal and offers a logical motive for one of the most intriguing murders in literature.

[1989]

Works Cited

Faulkner, William. "A Rose for Emily." *Collected Stories of William Faulkner.* New York: Random House, 1950. 119–30. [Editors' note: We have altered the page references in the essay so that they now refer to pages in our textbook.]

Jacobs, John. "Ironic Allusions in 'A Rose for Emily'." *Notes on Mississippi Writers,* 14.2 (1982): 77–79.

Licht, Hans. *Sexual Life in Ancient Greece.* New York: Barnes & Noble, Inc., 1963.

Scherting, Jack. "Emily Grierson's Oedipus Complex: Motif, Motive, and Meaning in Faulkner's 'A Rose for Emily'." *Studies in Short Fiction,* 17 (1980): 397–405.

West, Ray. "Atmosphere and Theme in Faulkner's 'A Rose for Emily'." *The Writer in the Room: Selected Essays.* East Lansing: Michigan State UP, 1968. 205–11.

 ## TOPICS FOR CRITICAL THINKING AND DISCUSSION

1. Exactly what evidence does Blythe introduce in order to establish his thesis?
2. How convincing is the evidence? Explain.

 ## JUDITH FETTERLEY

Judith Fetterley, a professor at the State University of New York, Albany, is the author of an important book of feminist criticism, The Resisting Reader: A Feminist Approach to American Fiction *(1978).*

(On feminist criticism, see p. 444) We reprint part of her discussion of Faulkner.

A Rose for "A Rose for Emily"

. . . What is true for Emily in relation to her father is equally true for her in relation to Jefferson: her status as a lady is a cage from which she cannot escape. To them she is always *Miss* Emily; she is never referred to and never thought of as otherwise. In omitting her title from his, Faulkner emphasizes the point that the real violence done to Emily is in making her a "Miss"; the omission is one of his roses for her. Because she is *Miss* Emily *Grierson,* Emily's father dresses her in white, places her in the background, and drives away her suitors. Because she is Miss Emily Grierson, the town invests her with that communal significance which makes her the object of their obsession and the subject of their incessant scrutiny. And because she is a lady, the town is able to impose a particular code of behavior on her ("But there were still others, older people, who said that even grief could not cause a real lady to forget *noblesse oblige*") and to see in her failure to live up to that code an excuse for interfering in her life. As a lady, Emily is venerated, but veneration results in the more telling emotions of envy and spite: "It was another link between the gross, teeming world and the high and mighty Griersons"; "People . . . believed that the Griersons held themselves a little too high for what they really were." The violence implicit in the desire to see the monument fall and reveal itself for clay suggests the violence inherent in the original impulse to venerate.

The violence behind veneration is emphasized through another telling emblem in the story. Emily's position as an hereditary obligation upon the town dates from "that day in 1894 when Colonel Sartoris, the mayor—he who fathered the edict that no Negro woman should appear on the streets without an apron—remitted her taxes, the dispensation dating from the death of her father on into perpetuity." The conjunction of these two actions in the same syntactic unit is crucial, for it insists on their essential similarity. It indicates that the impulse to exempt is analogous to the desire to restrict, and that what appears to be a kindness or an act of veneration is in fact an insult. Sartoris' remission of Emily's taxes is a public declaration of the fact that a lady is not considered to be, and hence not allowed or enabled to be, economically independent (consider, in this connection, Emily's lessons in china painting; they are a latter-day version of Sartoris' "charity" and a brilliant image of Emily's economic uselessness). His act is a public statement of the fact that a lady, if she is to survive, must have either husband or father, and that, because Emily has neither, the town must assume responsibility for her. The remission of taxes that defines Emily's status dates from the death of her father, and she is handed over from one patron to the next, the town instead of husband taking on the role of father. Indeed, the use of the word "fathered" in describing Sartoris' behavior as mayor underlines the fact that his chivalric attitude toward Emily is simply a subtler and more dishonest version of her father's horsewhip.

The narrator is the last of the patriarchs who take upon themselves the burden of defining Emily's life, and his violence toward her is the most subtle of all. His tone of incantatory reminiscence and nostalgic veneration seems free of the taint of horsewhip and edict. Yet a thoroughgoing contempt for the "ladies" who spy and pry and gossip out of their petty jealousy and curiosity is one of the clearest strands in the narrator's consciousness. Emily is exempted from the general indictment because she is a *real* lady— that is, eccentric, slightly crazy, obsolete, a "stubborn and coquettish decay," absurd but indulged; "dear, inescapable, impervious, tranquil, and perverse"; indeed, anything and everything but human.

Not only does "A Rose for Emily" expose the violence done to a woman by making her a lady; it also explores the particular form of power the victim gains from this position and can use on those who enact this violence. "A Rose for Emily" is concerned with the consequences of violence for both the violated and the violators. One of the most striking aspects of the story is the disparity between Miss Emily Grierson and the Emily to whom Faulkner gives his rose in ironic imitation of the chivalric behavior the story exposes. The form of Faulkner's title establishes a camaraderie between author and protagonist and signals that a distinction must be made between the story Faulkner is telling and the story the narrator is telling. This distinction is of major importance because it suggests, of course, that the narrator, looking through a patriarchal lens, does not see Emily at all but rather a figment of his own imagination created in conjunction with the cumulative imagination of the town. Like Ellison's invisible man, nobody sees *Emily.* And because nobody sees *her,* she can literally get away with murder. Emily is characterized by her ability to understand and utilize the power that accrues to her from the fact that men do not see her but rather their concept of her: "'I have no taxes in Jefferson. Colonel Sartoris explained it to me. . . . Tobe! . . . Show these gentlemen out.'" Relying on the conventional assumptions about ladies who are expected to be neither reasonable nor in touch with reality, Emily presents an impregnable front that vanquishes the men "horse and foot, just as she had vanquished their fathers thirty years before." In spite of their "modern" ideas, this new generation, when faced with Miss Emily, are as much bound by the code of gentlemanly behavior as their fathers were ("They rose when she entered"). This code gives Emily a power that renders the gentlemen unable to function in a situation in which a lady neither sits down herself nor asks them to. They are brought to a "stumbling halt" and can do nothing when confronted with her refusal to engage in rational discourse. Their only recourse in the face of such eccentricity is to engage in behavior unbecoming to gentlemen, and Emily can count on their continuing to see themselves as gentlemen and her as a lady and on their returning a verdict of helpless noninterference.

5   It is in relation to Emily's disposal of Homer Barron, however, that Faulkner demonstrates most clearly the power of conventional assumptions about the nature of ladies to blind the town to what is going on and to allow Emily to murder with impunity. When Emily buys the poison, it never occurs to anyone that she intends to use it on Homer, so strong is the presumption that ladies when jilted commit suicide, not murder. And when her house begins to smell, the women blame it on the eccentricity of having a man servant rather than a woman, "as if a man—any man—could keep a kitchen properly." And then they hint that her eccentricity may have shaded over into madness, "remembering how old lady Wyatt, her great aunt, had

gone completely crazy at last." The presumption of madness, that preeminently female response to bereavement, can be used to explain away much in the behavior of ladies whose activities seem a bit odd. . . .

Not only is "A Rose for Emily" a supreme analysis of what men do to women by making them ladies; it is also an exposure of how this act in turn defines and recoils upon men. This is the significance of the dynamic that Faulkner establishes between Emily and Jefferson. And it is equally the point of the dynamic implied between the tableau of Emily and her father and the tableau which greets the men who break down the door of that room in the region above the stairs. When the would-be "suitors" finally get into her father's house, they discover the consequences of his oppression of her, for the violence contained in the rotted corpse of Homer Barron is the mirror image of the violence represented in the tableau, the back-flung front door flung back with a vengeance. Having been consumed by her father, Emily in turn feeds off Homer Barron, becoming, after his death, suspiciously fat. Or, to put it another way, it is as if, after her father's death, she has reversed his act of incorporating her by incorporating and becoming him, metamorphosed from the slender figure in white to the obese figure in black whose hair is "a vigorous iron-gray, like the hair of an active man." She has taken into herself the violence in him which thwarted her and has reenacted it upon Homer Barron.

[1978]

 ## TOPICS FOR CRITICAL THINKING AND DISCUSSION

1. Exactly what is Fetterley's view of the narrator? What is your view of the narrator? If there is a discrepancy between the two views, explain why you find her view unacceptable, and argue on behalf of your own.
2. If you have also read the selections by Cleanth Brooks (p. 190) and Hal Blythe (p. 191), in an essay of 500 words indicate which of the three writers seems to you to be the best reader of the story, and why.

CHAPTER 9

Reading (and Writing about) Drama

The college essays you write about plays will be similar in many respects to analytic essays about fiction. Unless you are writing a review of a performance, you probably won't try to write about all aspects of a play. Rather, you'll choose one significant aspect as your topic. For instance, if you are writing about Tennessee Williams's *The Glass Menagerie,* you might compare the aspirations of Jim Connor and Tom Wingfield, or you might compare Tom's illusions with those of his sister, Laura, and his mother, Amanda. Or you might examine the symbolism, perhaps limiting your essay topic to the glass animals but perhaps extending it to include other symbols, such as the fire escape, the lighting, and the Victrola. Similarly, if you are writing an analysis, you might decide to study the construction of one scene of a play or (if the play does not have a great many scenes) even the construction of the entire play.

The checklist on page 214 may help you to find a topic for the particular play you choose to write about.

A SAMPLE ESSAY

The following essay discusses the structure of *The Glass Menagerie.* It mentions various characters, but since its concern is with the arrangement of scenes, it does not (for instance) examine any of the characters in detail. Of course an essay might well be devoted to examining (for example) Williams's assertion that "There is much to admire in Amanda, and as much to love and pity as there is to laugh at," but an essay on the structure of the play is probably not the place to talk about Williams's characterization of Amanda.

Preliminary Notes

After deciding to write on the structure of the play, with an eye toward seeing the overall pattern that the parts form, the student reread *The Glass Menagerie* (page ■■■), jotted down some notes briefly summarizing each of the seven scenes, with an occasional comment, and then typed them. On rereading the typed notes, he added a few observations in handwriting.

nagging

1. begins with Tom talking to audience;
   ~~says he is a magician~~
   America, in 1930s
     "shouting and confusion"
   Father deserted
   Amanda nagging; ~~is she a bit cracked?~~
   Tom: bored, angry
   Laura: embarrassed, depressed

2. Laura: quit business school; sad, but
     Jim's name is mentioned, so,
     lighter tone introduced

out-and-out ──3. Tom and Amanda argue
battle   Tom almost destroys glass menagerie
               Rage: Can things get any worse?

4. T and A reconciled
     T to try to get a "gentleman caller"

reconciliation,
and
false hopes— 5. T tells A that Jim will visit
then final   things are looking up
collapse   6. Jim arrives; L terrified
                 still, A thinks things can work out

7. Lights go out (foreshadowing dark ending?)
     Jim a jerk, clumsy; breaks unicorn, but
     L doesn't seem to mind. Maybe he _is_ the
     right guy to draw her into normal world.
     Jim reveals he is engaged:
       "Desolation."

   Tom escapes into merchant marine, but
   can't escape memories. Speaks to
   audience. L. blows out candles (does
   this mean he forgets her? No, because
   he is remembering her right now. I don't
   get it, if the candles are supposed to
   be symbolic.)

These notes enabled the student to prepare a rough draft, which he then submitted to some classmates for peer review. (On peer review, see pages 24–25.)

Notice that the final version of the essay, printed below, is *not* merely a summary (a brief retelling of the plot). Although it does indeed include summary, it chiefly is devoted to showing *how* the scenes are related.

Title is focused; it announces topic and thesis

The Solid Structure of <u>The Glass Menagerie</u>

In the "Production Notes" Tennessee Williams calls <u>The Glass Menagerie</u> a "memory play," a term that the narrator in the play also uses. Memories often consist of fragments of episodes that are so loosely connected that they seem chaotic, and therefore we might think that <u>The Glass Menagerie</u> will consist of very loosely related episodes. However, the play covers only one episode, and though it gives the illusion of random talk, it really has a firm structure and moves steadily toward a foregone conclusion.

Opening paragraph closes in on thesis

Reasonable organization; the paragraph touches on the beginning and the end

Tennessee Williams divides the play into seven scenes. The first scene begins with a sort of prologue, and the last scene concludes with a sort of epilogue that is related to the prologue. In the prologue Tom addresses the audience and comments on the 1930s as a time when America was "blind" and was a place of "shouting and confusion." Tom also mentions that our lives consist of expectations, and though he does not say that our expectations are unfulfilled, near the end of the prologue he quotes a postcard that his father wrote to the family he deserted: "Hello-- Goodbye!" In the epilogue Tom tells us that he followed his "father's footsteps," deserting the family. And just before the

Brief but effective quotations

epilogue, near the end of Scene VII, we see what can be considered another desertion: Jim explains to Tom's sister Laura that he is engaged and therefore cannot visit

Useful generalization based on earlier details

Laura again. Thus the end is closely related to the beginning, and the play is the steady development of the initial implications.

Chronological organization is reasonable. Opening topic sentence lets readers know where they are going

The first three scenes show things going from bad to worse. Amanda is a nagging mother who finds her only relief in talking about the past to her crippled daughter Laura and her frustrated son Tom. When she was young she was beautiful and was eagerly courted by rich young men, but now the family is poor and this harping on the past can only bore or infuriate Tom and embarrass or depress Laura, who have no happy past to look back to, who see no happy future, and who can only be upset by Amanda's insistence that they should behave as she behaved long ago. The second scene

Brief plot summary supports thesis

deepens the despair: Amanda learns that the timorous Laura has not been attending a business school but has retreated in terror from this confrontation with the contemporary world. Laura's helplessness is made clear to the audience, and so is Amanda's lack of understanding. Near the end of the second scene, however, Jim's name is introduced; he is a boy Laura had a

crush on in high school, and so the
audience gets a glimpse of a happier Laura
and a sense that possibly Laura's world is
wider than the stifling tenement in which
she and her mother and brother live. But in
the third scene things get worse, when Tom
and Amanda have so violent an argument that
they are no longer on speaking terms. Tom
is so angry with his mother that he almost
by accident destroys his sister's treasured
collection of glass animals, the fragile,
lifeless world that is her refuge. The
apartment is literally full of the
"shouting and confusion" that Tom spoke of
in his prologue.

Useful summary
and transition

The first three scenes have revealed
a progressive worsening of relations; the
next three scenes reveal a progressive
improvement in relations. In Scene IV
Tom and his mother are reconciled, and
Tom reluctantly--apparently in an effort
to make up with his mother--agrees to
try to get a friend to come to dinner so
that Laura will have "a gentleman caller."
In Scene V Tom tells his mother that
Jim will come to dinner on the next night,
and Amanda brightens, because she sees
a possibility of security for Laura at
last. In Scene VI Jim arrives, and
despite Laura's initial terror, there
seems, at least in Amanda's mind, to

be the possibility that things will go
well.

The seventh scene, by far the longest,
at first seems to be fulfilling Amanda's
hopes. Despite the ominous fact that the
lights go out because Tom has not paid the
electric bill, Jim is at ease. He is an
insensitive oaf, but that doesn't seem to
bother Amanda, and almost miraculously he
manages to draw Laura somewhat out of her
sheltered world. Even when Jim in his
clumsiness breaks the horn off Laura's
treasured glass unicorn, she is not upset.
In fact, she is almost relieved because the
loss of the horn makes the animal less
"freakish" and he "will feel more at home
with the other horses." In a way, of
course, the unicorn symbolizes the crippled
Laura, who at least for the moment feels
less freakish and isolated now that she is
somewhat reunited with society through Jim.
But this is a play about life in a blind
and confused world, and though in a
previous age the father escaped, there can
be no escape now. Jim reveals that he is
engaged, Laura relapses into "desolation,"
Amanda relapses into rage and bitterness,
and Tom relapses into dreams of escape. In
a limited sense Tom does escape. He leaves
the family and joins the merchant marine,
but his last speech or epilogue tells us

that he cannot escape the memory of his sister: "Oh, Laura, Laura, I tried to leave you behind me, but I am more faithful than I intended to be!" And so the end of the

The essayist is thinking and commenting, not merely summarizing the plot

last scene brings us back again to the beginning of the first scene: we are still in a world of "the blind" and of "confusion." But now at the end of the play the darkness is deeper, the characters are lost forever in their unhappiness as Laura "blows the candles out," the darkness being literal but also symbolic of their extinguished hopes.

Numerous devices, such as repeated references to the absent father, to Amanda's youth, to Laura's Victrola, and of course to Laura's glass menagerie help to

Useful, thoughtful summary of thesis

tie the scenes together into a unified play. But beneath these threads of imagery and recurring motifs is a fundamental pattern that involves the movement from nagging (Scenes I and II) to open hostilities (Scene III) to temporary reconciliation (Scene IV) to false hopes (Scenes V and VI) to an impossible heightening of false hopes and then, in a swift descent, to an inevitable collapse (Scene VII). Tennessee Williams has constructed his play carefully. G. B. Tennyson says that a "playwright must 'build' his speeches, as the theatrical

*Effective
quotation from
an outside source*

expression has it" (13). But a playwright
must do more; the playwright must also
build the play out of scenes. Like Ibsen,
if Williams had been introduced to an
architect he might have said, "Architecture
is my business too."

Works Cited

Tennyson, G. B. An Introduction to Drama.

Documentation

New York: Holt, 1967.

Williams, Tennessee. The Glass Menagerie.
Literature for Composition. Ed. Sylvan
Barnet et al. 4th ed. New York:
HarperCollins, 1996. 511-554.

TYPES OF PLAYS

Most of the world's great plays written before the twentieth century may be regarded as one of two kinds: **tragedy** or **comedy.** Roughly speaking, tragedy dramatizes the conflict between the vitality of the individual life and the laws or limits of life. The tragic hero reaches a height, going beyond the experience of
others but at the cost of his or her life. Comedy, on the other hand, dramatizes
the vitality of the laws of social life. In comedy, the good life is seen to reside in
the shedding of an individualism that isolates, in favor of a union with a genial
and enlightened society. These points must be amplified a bit before we go on to
the further point that, of course, any important play does much more than can
be put into such crude formulas.

Tragedy

Tragic heroes usually go beyond the standards to which reasonable people ad-
here; they do some fearful deed which ultimately destroys them. This deed is
often said to be an act of **hubris,** a Greek word meaning something like "overweening pride." It may involve, for instance, violating a taboo, such as that
against taking life. But if the hubristic act ultimately destroys the man or woman
who performs it, it also shows that person (paradoxically) to be in some way
more fully a living being—a person who has experienced life more fully,
whether by heroic action or by capacity for enduring suffering—than the other
characters in the play. (If the tragic hero does not die, he or she is usually left in
some deathlike state, as is the blind Oedipus in *Oedipus Rex.*) In tragedy we see
humanity pushed to an extreme; the hero enters a world unknown to most and
reveals magnificence. After the hero's departure from the stage, we are left in a
world of littler people.

What has just been said may (or may not) be true of most tragedies, but it certainly is not true of all. If you are writing about a tragedy, you might consider whether the points just made are illustrated in your play. Is the hero guilty of hubris? Does the hero seem a greater person than the others in the play? An essay examining such questions probably requires not only a character sketch but also some comparison with other characters.

Tragedy commonly involves **irony** of two sorts: unconsciously ironic deeds and unconsciously ironic speeches. **Ironic deeds** have some consequence more or less the reverse of what the doer intends. Macbeth thinks that by killing Duncan he will gain happiness, but he finds that his deed brings him sleepless nights. Brutus thinks that by killing Caesar he will bring liberty to Rome, but he brings tyranny. In an **unconsciously ironic speech,** the words mean one thing to the speaker but something more significant to the audience, as when King Duncan, baffled by Cawdor's treason, says:

> There's no art
> To find the mind's construction in the face:
> He was a gentleman on whom I built
> An absolute trust.

At this moment Macbeth, whom we have already heard meditating the murder of Duncan, enters. Duncan's words are true, but he does not apply them to Macbeth, as the audience does. A few moments later Duncan praises Macbeth as "a peerless kinsman." Soon Macbeth will indeed become peerless, when he kills Duncan and ascends to the throne.[1] Sophocles' use of ironic deeds and speeches is so pervasive, especially in *Oedipus Rex,* that **Sophoclean irony** has become a critical term.

When the deed backfires or has a reverse effect, such as Macbeth's effort to gain happiness has, we have what Aristotle (the first—and still the greatest—drama critic) called a **peripeteia,** or a **reversal.** A character who comes to perceive what has happened (Macbeth's "I have lived long enough: my way of life / Is fall'n into the sere, the yellow leaf") experiences (in Aristotle's language) an **anagnorisis,** or **recognition.** Strictly speaking, for Aristotle the recognition was a matter of literal identification—for example, the recognition that Oedipus was the son of a man he killed. In *Macbeth,* the recognition in this sense is that Macduff, "from his mother's womb / Untimely ripped," is the man who fits the prophecy that Macbeth can be conquered only by someone not "of woman born."

In his analysis of drama, Aristotle says that the tragic hero comes to grief through his **hamartia,** a term sometimes translated as **tragic flaw** but perhaps better translated as **tragic error,** since *flaw* implies a moral fault. Thus it is a great error for Oedipus (however apparently justifiable his action) to kill a man old enough to be his father, and to marry a woman old enough to be his mother.

---

[1] **Dramatic irony** (ironic deeds, or happenings, and unconsciously ironic speeches) must be distinguished from **verbal irony,** which is produced when the speaker is *conscious* that his words mean something different from what they say. In *Macbeth* Lennox says. "The gracious Duncan / Was pitied of Macbeth. Marry, he was dead! / And the right valiant Banquo walked too late. /. . . / Men must not walk too late." He *says* nothing about Macbeth having killed Duncan and Banquo, but he *means* that Macbeth has killed them.

If we hold to the translation *flaw,* we begin to hunt for a fault in the tragic hero's character; and we say, for instance, that Oedipus is rash, or some such thing. In doing this, we may diminish or even overlook the hero's grandeur.

Comedy

Although in tragedy the hero usually seems to embody certain values that are superior to those of the surrounding society, in comedy the fullest life is seen to reside *within* enlightened social norms: At the beginning of a comedy we find banished dukes, unhappy lovers, crabby parents, jealous husbands, and harsh laws; but at the end we usually have a unified and genial society, often symbolized by a marriage feast to which everyone, or almost everyone, is invited. Early in *A Midsummer Night's Dream,* for instance, we meet quarreling young lovers and a father who demands that his daughter either marry a man she does not love or enter a convent. Such is the Athenian law. At the end of the play the lovers are properly matched, to everyone's satisfaction.

Speaking broadly, most comedies fall into one of two classes: **satiric comedy** or **romantic comedy.** In satiric comedy, the emphasis is on the obstructionists—the irate fathers, hardheaded businessmen, and other members of the establishment who at the beginning of the play seem to hold all of the cards, preventing joy from reigning. They are held up to ridicule because they are repressive monomaniacs enslaved to themselves, acting mechanistically (always irate, always hardheaded) instead of responding genially to the ups and downs of life. The outwitting of these obstructionists, usually by the younger generation, often provides the resolution of the plot. Ben Jonson, Molière, and George Bernard Shaw are in this tradition; their comedy, according to an ancient Roman formula, "chastens morals with ridicule"—that is, it reforms folly or vice by laughing at it. On the other hand, in romantic comedy (one thinks of Shakespeare's *A Midsummer Night's Dream, As You Like It,* and *Twelfth Night*) the emphasis is on a pair or pairs of delightful people who engage our sympathies as they run their obstacle race to the altar. There are obstructionists here too, but the emphasis is on festivity.

In writing about comedy you may, of course, be concerned with the function of one scene or character, but whatever your topic, you may find it helpful to begin by trying to decide whether the play is primarily romantic or primarily satiric (or something else). One way of getting at this is to ask yourself to what degree you sympathize with the characters. Do you laugh *with* them, sympathetically, or on the other hand do you laugh *at* them, regarding them as at least somewhat contemptible?

ELEMENTS OF DRAMA

Theme

If we have read or seen a drama thoughtfully, we ought to be able to formulate its **theme,** its underlying idea, and perhaps we can even go so far as to say its moral attitudes, its view of life, its wisdom. Some critics, it is true, have argued that the concept of theme is meaningless. They hold that *Macbeth,* for example, gives us only an extremely detailed history of one imaginary man. In this view, *Macbeth* says nothing to you or me; it only says what happened to some imaginary man. Even *Julius Caesar* says nothing about the historical Julius Caesar or about the nature of Roman politics. Here we can agree; no one would offer Shakespeare's play as evidence of what the historical Caesar said or did. But surely the view that the concept of theme is meaningless, and that a work tells us only about imaginary creatures, is a desperate one. We *can* say that we see in *Julius Caesar* the fall of power, or (if we are thinking of Brutus) the vulnerability of idealism, or some such thing.

To the reply that these are mere truisms, we can counter: Yes, but the truisms are presented in such a way that they take on life and become a part of us rather than remaining things of which we say, "I've heard it said, and I guess it's so." The play offers instruction, in a pleasant and persuasive way. And surely we are in no danger of equating the play with the theme that we sense underlies it. We recognize that the play presents the theme with such detail that our statement is only a wedge to help us enter into the play, so we can appropriate it more fully.

Some critics (influenced by Aristotle's statement that a drama is an imitation of an action) use **action** in a sense equivalent to theme. In this sense, the action is the underlying happening—the inner happening—for example, "the enlightenment of a character," or "the coming of unhappiness to a character," or "the finding of the self by self-surrender." One might say that the theme of *Macbeth*, for example, is embodied in some words that Macbeth himself utters: "Blood will have blood." Of course this is not to say that these words and no other words embody the theme or the action; it is only to say that these words seem to the writer (and, if the essay is effective, to the reader) to bring us close to the center of the play.

Plot

Plot is variously defined, sometimes as equivalent to *story* (in this sense a synopsis of *Julius Caesar* has the same plot as *Julius Caesar*), but more often, and more usefully, as the dramatist's particular *arrangement of the story*. Thus, because Shakespeare's *Julius Caesar* begins with a scene dramatizing an encounter between plebeians and tribunes, its plot is different from that of a play on Julius Caesar in which such a scene (not necessary to the story) is omitted.

Handbooks on drama often suggest that a plot (arrangement of happenings) should have a **rising action,** a **climax,** and a **falling action.** This sort of plot can be diagramed as a pyramid: The tension rises through complications or **crises** to a climax, at which point the climax is the apex, and the tension allegedly slackens as we witness the **dénouement** (literally, *unknotting*). Shakespeare sometimes used a pyramidal structure, placing his climax neatly in the middle of what seems to us to be the third of five acts. In *Hamlet,* the protagonist proves to his own satisfaction Claudius's guilt in 3.2, with the play within the play; but almost immediately he begins to worsen his position, by failing to kill Claudius when he is an easy target (3.3) and by contaminating himself with the murder of Polonius (3.4). In *Romeo and Juliet,* the first half shows Romeo winning Juliet, but when in 3.1 he kills her cousin Tybalt, Romeo sets in motion the second half of the play, the losing of Juliet and of his own life.

Of course, no law demands such a structure, and a hunt for the pyramid usually causes the hunter to overlook all the crises but the middle one. William Butler Yeats once suggestively diagramed a good plot not as a pyramid but as a line moving diagonally upward, punctuated by several crises. Perhaps it is sufficient to say that a good plot has its moments of tension, but the location of these will vary with the play. They are the product of **conflict,** but it should be noted that not all conflict produces tension; there is conflict but little tension in a ball game when the home team is ahead 10–0 and the visiting pitcher comes to bat in the ninth inning with two out and none on base.

Regardless of how a plot is diagramed, the **exposition** is that part that tells the audience what it has to know about the past, the **antecedent action.** Two gossiping servants who tell each other that after a year away in Paris the young master is coming home tomorrow with a new wife are giving the audience the exposition. But the exposition may also extend far into the play, being given in small, explosive revelations.

Exposition has been discussed as though it consists simply of informing the audience about events, but exposition can do much more. It can give us an understanding of the characters who themselves are talking about other characters, it can evoke a mood, and it can generate tension. When we summarize the opening act, and treat it as "mere exposition," we are probably losing what is dramatic in it.

In fact, exposition usually includes *foreshadowing.* Details given in the exposition, which we may at first take as mere background, often turn out to be highly relevant to later developments. For instance, in the very short first scene of *Macbeth* the witches introduce the name of Macbeth, but in such words as "Fair is foul" and "when the battle's lost and won" they also give glimpses of what will happen: Macbeth will become foul, and though he will seem to win (he becomes king) he will lose the most important battle. Similarly, during the exposition in the second scene we learn that Macbeth has loyally defeated Cawdor, who betrayed King Duncan, and Macbeth has been given Cawdor's title. Later we will find that, like Cawdor, Macbeth betrays Duncan. That is, in giving us the background about Cawdor, the exposition is also telling us (though we don't know it, when we first see or read the play) something about what will happen to Macbeth.

In writing about an aspect of plot, you may want to consider one of the following topics:

1. Is the plot improbable? If so, is the play therefore weak?
2. Does a scene that might at first glance seem unimportant or even irrelevant serve an important function?
3. If certain actions that could be shown onstage take place offstage, is there a reason? In *Macbeth,* for instance, why do you suppose the murder of Duncan takes place offstage, whereas Banquo and Macduff's family are murdered onstage? Why, then, might Shakespeare have preferred not to show us the murder of Duncan? What has he gained? (A good way to approach this sort of question is to think of what your own reaction would be if the action were shown on the stage.)
4. If there are several conflicts—for example, between pairs of lovers or between parents and their children and also between the parents them-

selves—how are these conflicts related? Are they parallel? Or contrasting?

5. Does the arrangement of scenes have a structure? For instance, do the scenes depict a rise and then a fall?

6. Does the plot seem satisfactorily concluded? Are there loose threads? If so, is the apparent lack of a complete resolution a weakness in the play? Or does it serve a function?

Gestures

The language of a play, broadly conceived, includes the **gestures** that the characters make and the settings in which they make them. As Ezra Pound says, "The medium of drama is not words, but persons moving about on a stage using words." Because plays are meant to be seen, make every effort to visualize the action when you read a play. Ibsen is getting at something important when he tells us in a stage direction that Nora "walks cautiously over to the door to the study and listens." Her silent actions tell us as much about her as many of her speeches do.

Gesture can be interpreted even more broadly: The mere fact that a character enters, leaves, or does not enter may be highly significant. John Russell Brown comments on the actions and the absence of certain words that in *Hamlet* convey the growing separation between King Claudius and his wife, Gertrude:

> Their first appearance together with a public celebration of marriage is a large and simple visual effect, and Gertrude's close concern for her son suggests a simple, and perhaps unremarkable modification. . . . But Claudius enters without Gertrude for his "Prayer Scene" (3.2) and, for the first time, Gertrude enters without him for the Closet Scene (3.4) and is left alone, again for the first time, when Polonius hides behind the arras. Thereafter earlier accord is revalued by an increasing separation, often poignantly silent and unexpected. When Claudius calls Gertrude to leave with him after Hamlet has dragged off Polonius' body, she makes no reply; twice more he urges her and she is still silent. But he does not remonstrate or question; rather he speaks of his own immediate concerns and, far from supporting her with assurances, becomes more aware of his own fears:
>
>
>
> O, come away!
> My soul is full of discord and dismay. (4.1.44-45)
>
>
>
> Emotion has been so heightened that it is remarkable that they leave together without further words. The audience has been aware of a new distance between Gertrude and Claudius, of her immobility and silence, and of his self-concern, haste, and insistence.[2]

---

[2]*Shakespeare's Plays in Performance* (New York: St. Martin's, 1967), p. 139.

Setting

Drama of the nineteenth and early twentieth centuries (for example, the plays of Henrik Ibsen, Anton Chekhov, and George Bernard Shaw) is often thought to be "realistic," but even a realistic playwright or stage designer selects from among many available materials. A **realistic setting** (indication of the **locale**), then, can say a great deal, and can even serve as a symbol. Over and over again in Ibsen we find the realistic setting of a nineteenth-century drawing room, with its heavy draperies and its bulky furniture, helping to convey his vision of a bourgeois world that oppresses the individual who struggles to affirm other values.

Twentieth-century dramatists are often explicit about the symbolic qualities of the setting. Here is an example from Eugene O'Neill's *Desire Under the Elms;* only a part of the initial stage direction is given:

> The house is in good condition but in need of paint. Its walls are a sickly grayish, the green of the shutters faded. Two enormous elms are on each side of the house. They bend their trailing branches down over the roof. They appear to protect and at the same time subdue. There is a sinister maternity in their aspect, a crushing, jealous absorption. . . . They are like exhausted women resting their sagging breasts and hands and hair on its roof. . . .

Not surprisingly, the action in the play includes deeds of "sinister maternity" (a mother kills her infant) and "jealous absorption."

In *The Glass Menagerie* Tennessee Williams tells us that

> the apartment faces an alley and is entered by a fire-escape, a structure whose name is a touch of accidental poetic truth, for all of these huge buildings are always burning with the slow and implacable fires of human desperation.

Characterization and Motivation

Characterization, or personality, is defined, as in fiction (see p. 143), by what the characters do (a stage direction tells us that "Nora dances more and more wildly"), by what they say (she asks her husband to play the piano), by what others say about them, and by the setting in which they move. The characters are also defined in part by other characters whom they in some degree resemble or from whom they in some degree differ. Hamlet, Laertes, and Fortinbras have each lost their fathers, but Hamlet spares the praying King Claudius, whereas Laertes, seeking vengeance on Hamlet for murdering Laertes's father, says he would cut Hamlet's throat in church; Hamlet meditates about the nature of action, but Fortinbras leads the Norwegians in a military campaign and ultimately acquires Denmark.

Other plays, of course, also provide examples of such **foils,** or characters who set one another off. Macbeth and Banquo both hear prophecies, but they act and react differently; Brutus is one kind of assassin, Cassius another, and Casca still another. Any analysis of a character, then, will probably have to take into account, in some degree, the other characters who help to show what he or she is, and who thus help to set forth his or her **motivation** (grounds for action, inner drives, goals).

ORGANIZING AN ANALYSIS OF A CHARACTER

As you read and reread, you'll annotate the text and will jot down (in whatever order they come to you) your thoughts about the character you are studying. Reading, with a view toward writing, you'll want to

1. Jot down traits as they come to mind ("kind," "forgetful," "enthusiastic").
2. Look back at the text, searching for supporting evidence (characteristic actions, brief supporting quotations); and of course you will also look for counterevidence so that you may modify your earlier impressions.

Brainstorming leads to an evaluation of your ideas and to a shaping of them. Evaluating and shaping lead to a tentative outline, and a tentative outline leads to the search for supporting evidence—the material that will constitute the body of your essay.

When you set out to write a first draft, review your annotations and notes and see if you can summarize your view of the character in one or two sentences:

X is . . . ,

or

Although X is . . . , she is also . . . .

That is, try to formulate a thesis sentence or a thesis paragraph, a proposition that you will go on to support.

You want to let your reader know early, probably in your first sentence—and almost certainly by the end of your first paragraph—which character you are writing about and what your overall thesis is.

First Draft

Here is the first draft of an opening paragraph that identifies the character and sets forth a thesis:

Romeo is a very interesting character, I think. In the beginning of the play Romeo is very adolescent. Romeo is smitten with puppy love for a woman named Rosaline. He desires to show all of his friends that he knows how a lover is supposed to act. When he sees Juliet he experiences true love. From the point when he sees Juliet he experiences true love, and from this point he steadily matures in Romeo and Juliet. He moves from a self-centered man to a man who lives not for himself but only for Juliet.

Later the student edited the draft. We reprint the original, with the additional editing in handwriting:

Romeo ~~is a very interesting character, I think.~~
~~In the beginning of the~~ *begins as an* ~~play Romeo is very~~ adolescent/~~Romeo is~~ smitten with puppy love for ~~a woman~~ ~~named~~ Rosaline/ *and a desire* ~~He desires~~ to show all of his friends that he knows how a lover is supposed to act. When he sees Juliet,∧ *however,* he experiences true love/∧ *and,* ~~From~~ *this* ~~the~~ point ~~when he sees Juliet he experiences true~~ ~~love, and from this point~~ he steadily matures, in ~~Romeo and Juliet.~~ ~~He moves~~ *moving* from a self-centered ~~man~~ *adolescen-* to a man who lives ~~not for himself but~~ only for Juliet.

Here is a revised version of another effective opening paragraph, effective partly because it identifies the character and offers a thesis:

In the last speech of Macbeth, Malcolm characterizes Lady Macbeth as "fiend-like," and indeed she invokes evil spirits and prompts her husband to commit murder. But despite her bold pose, her role in the murder, and her belief that she will be untroubled by guilt, she has a conscience that torments her and that finally drives her to suicide. She is not a mere heartless villain; she is a human being who is less strong--and more moral--than she thinks she is.

Notice that the paragraph quotes a word ("fiend-like") from the text. It happens that the writer goes on to argue that this word is *not* a totally accurate description, but the quotation nevertheless helps to bring the reader into close contact with the subject of the essay.

Notice also that in writing about literature we do not ordinarily introduce the thesis formally. We do not, that is, say "In this paper it is my intention to prove that . . . ." Such a sentence may be perfectly appropriate in a paper in political science, but in a paper on literature it is out of place.

The body of your essay will be devoted, of course, to supporting your thesis. If you have asserted that although Lady Macbeth is cruel and domineering she nevertheless is endowed with a conscience, you will go on in your essay to support those assertions with references to passages that demonstrate them. This does *not* mean that you tell the plot of the whole work; an essay on a character is by no means the same as a summary of the plot. But since you must support your generalizations, you will have to make brief references to specific episodes that reveal her personality, and almost surely you will quote an occasional word or passage.

There are many possible ways to organize an essay on a character. Much will depend, of course, on your purpose and thesis. For instance, you may want to show how the character develops—gains knowledge, or matures, or disintegrates. Or, again, you may want to show what the character contributes to the story or play as a whole. Or, to give yet another example, you may want to show that the character is unbelievable. Still, although no single organization is always right, two methods are common and effective. One is to let the organization of your essay follow closely the sequence of the literary work; that is, you might devote a paragraph to Lady Macbeth as we perceive her in the first act, and then in subsequent paragraphs go on to show that her character is later seen to be more complex than it at first appears. Such an essay may trace your changing responses. This does not mean that you need to write five paragraphs, one on her character in each of the five acts. But it does mean that you might begin with Lady Macbeth as you perceive her in, say, the first act, and then go on to the additional revelations of the rest of the play.

A second effective way of organizing an essay on a character is to set forth, early in the essay, the character's chief traits—let's say the chief strengths and two or three weaknesses—and then go on to study each trait you have listed. Here the organization would (in order to maintain the reader's interest) probably begin with the most obvious points and then move on to the less obvious, subtler points. The body of your essay, in any case, is devoted to offering evidence that supports your generalizations about the character.

What about a concluding paragraph? The concluding paragraph ought *not* to begin with the obviousness of "Thus we see," or "In conclusion," or "I recommend this play because. . . ." In fact, after you have given what you consider a sound sketch of the character, it may be appropriate simply to quit. Especially if your essay has moved from the obvious traits to the more subtle and more important traits, and if your essay is fairly short (say, fewer than 500 words), a reader may not need a conclusion. Further, there probably is no reason to blunt what you have just said by adding an unnecessary and merely repetitive summary. But if you do feel that a conclusion is necessary, you may find it effective to write a summary of the character, somewhat as you did in your opening. For the conclusion, relate the character's character to the entire drama—that is, try to give the reader a sense of the role that the character plays.

✔ A Checklist: Getting Ideas for Writing about Drama

The following questions may help you to formulate ideas for an essay on a play.

Plot and Conflict

1. Does the exposition introduce elements that will be ironically fulfilled? During the exposition do you perceive things differently from the way the characters perceive them?
2. Are certain happenings or situations recurrent? If so, what significance do you attach to them?
3. If there is more than one plot, do the plots seem to you to be related? Is one plot clearly the main plot and another plot a sort of subplot, a minor variation on the theme?
4. Do any scenes strike you as irrelevant?
5. Are certain scenes so strongly foreshadowed that you anticipated them? If so, did the happenings in these scenes merely fulfill your expectations, or did they also surprise you?
6. What kinds of conflict are there? One character against another, one group against another, one part of a personality against another part in the same person?
7. How is the conflict resolved? By an unambiguous triumph of one side or by a triumph that is also in some degree a loss for the triumphant side? Do you find the resolution satisfying, or unsettling, or what? Why?

Character

1. A dramatic character is not likely to be thoroughly realistic, a copy of someone we might know. Still, we can ask if the character is consistent and coherent. We can also ask if the character is complex or is, on the other hand, a rather simple representative of some human type.
2. How is the character defined? Consider what the character says and does and what others say about him or her and do to him or her. Also consider other characters who more or less resemble the character in question, because the similarities—and the differences—may be significant.
3. How trustworthy are the characters when they characterize themselves? When they characterize others?
4. Do characters change as the play goes on, or do we simply know them better at the end?

5. What do you make of the minor characters? Are they merely necessary to the plot, or are they foils to other characters? Or do they serve some other functions?

6. If a character is tragic, does the tragedy seem to you to proceed from a moral flaw, from an intellectual error, from the malice of others, from sheer chance, or from some combination of these?

7. What are the character's goals? To what degree do you sympathize with them? If a character is comic, do you laugh *with* or *at* the character?

8. Do you think the characters are adequately motivated?

9. Is a given character so meditative that you feel he or she is engaged less in a dialogue with others than in a dialogue with the self? If so, do you feel that this character is in large degree a spokesperson for the author, commenting not only on the world of the play but also on the outside world?

Nonverbal Language

1. If the playwright does not provide full stage directions, try to imagine for at least one scene what gestures and tones might accompany each speech. (The first scene is usually a good one to try your hand at.)

2. What do you make of the setting? Does it help to reveal character? Do changes of scene strike you as symbolic? If so, symbolic of what?

The Play on Film

1. If the play has been turned into a film, what has been added? What has been omitted? Why?

2. Has the film medium been used to advantage—for example, in focusing attention through close-ups or reaction shots (shots showing not the speaker but a person reacting to the speaker)? Or do some of the inventions, such as outdoor scenes that were not possible in the play, seem mere busywork, distracting from the urgency or the conflict or the unity of the play?

THREE SHORT PLAYS

 SUSAN GLASPELL

Susan Glaspell (1882–1948) was born in Davenport, Iowa, and educated at Drake University in Des Moines. In 1903 she married George Cram Cook and, with Cook and other writers, actors, and artists, in 1915 founded the Provincetown Players, a group that remained vital until 1929. Glaspell wrote Trifles *(1916) for the Provincetown Players, but she also wrote stories, novels, and a biography of her husband. In 1931 she won a Pulitzer Prize for* Alison's House, *a play*

Marjorie Vonnegut, Elinor M. Cox, John King, Arthur F. Hole, and T. W. Gibson in a scene from *Trifles,* as published in Theatre Magazine, January 1917. (Photograph courtesy of The Billy Rose Theatre Collection/New York Public Library)

about the family of a deceased poet who in some ways resembles Emily Dickinson.

Trifles

SCENE: *The kitchen in the now abandoned farmhouse of* JOHN WRIGHT, *a gloomy kitchen, and left without having been put in order—unwashed pans under the sink, a loaf of bread outside the breadbox, a dish towel on the table—other signs of incompleted work. At the rear the outer door opens, and the* SHERIFF *comes in, followed by the* COUNTY ATTORNEY *and* HALE. *The* SHERIFF *and* HALE *are men in middle life, the* COUNTY ATTORNEY *is a young man; all are much bundled up and go at once to the stove. They are followed by the two women—the* SHERIFF'S WIFE *first; she is a slight wiry woman, a thin nervous face.* MRS. HALE *is larger and would ordinarily be called more comfortable looking, but she is disturbed now and looks fearfully about as she enters. The women have come in slowly and stand close together near the door.*

COUNTY ATTORNEY *[rubbing his hands].* This feels good. Come up to the fire, ladies.

MRS. PETERS *[after taking a step forward].* I'm not—cold.

SHERIFF *[unbuttoning his overcoat and stepping away from the stove as if to the beginning of official business].* Now, Mr. Hale, before we move things about, you explain to Mr. Henderson just what you saw when you came here yesterday morning.

COUNTY ATTORNEY. By the way, has anything been moved? Are things just as you left them yesterday?

SHERIFF *[looking about].* It's just the same. When it dropped below zero last night, I thought I'd better send Frank out this morning to make a fire for us—no use getting pneumonia with a big case on; but I told him not to touch anything except the stove—and you know Frank.

COUNTY ATTORNEY. Somebody should have been left here yesterday.

SHERIFF. Oh—yesterday. When I had to send Frank to Morris Center for that man who went crazy—I want you to know I had my hands full yesterday. I knew you could get back from Omaha by today, and as long as I went over everything here myself—

COUNTY ATTORNEY. Well, Mr. Hale, tell just what happened when you came here yesterday morning.

HALE. Harry and I had started to town with a load of potatoes. We came along the road from my place; and as I got here, I said, "I'm going to see if I can't get John Wright to go in with me on a party telephone." I spoke to Wright about it once before, and he put me off, saying folks talked too much anyway, and all he asked was peace and quiet—I guess you know about how much he talked himself; but I thought maybe if I went to the house and talked about it before his wife, though I said to Harry that I didn't know as what his wife wanted made much difference to John—

COUNTY ATTORNEY. Let's talk about that later, Mr. Hale. I do want to talk about that, but tell now just what happened when you got to the house.

HALE. I didn't hear or see anything; I knocked at the door, and still it was all quiet inside. I knew they must be up, it was past eight o'clock. So I knocked again, and I thought I heard somebody say, "Come in." I wasn't sure, I'm not sure yet, but I opened the door—this door *[indicating the door by which the two women are still standing]*, and there in that rocker—*[pointing to it]* sat Mrs. Wright. *[They all look at the rocker.]*

COUNTY ATTORNEY. What—was she doing?

HALE. She was rockin' back and forth. She had her apron in her hand and was kind of—pleating it.

COUNTY ATTORNEY. And how did she—look?

HALE. Well, she looked queer.

COUNTY ATTORNEY. How do you mean—queer?

HALE. Well, as if she didn't know what she was going to do next. And kind of done up.

COUNTY ATTORNEY. How did she seem to feel about your coming?

HALE. Why, I don't think she minded—one way or other. She didn't pay much attention. I said, "How do, Mrs. Wright, it's cold, ain't it?" And she said, "Is it?"—and went on kind of pleating at her apron. Well, I was surprised; she didn't ask me to come up to the stove, or to set down, but just sat there, not even looking at me, so I said, "I want to see John." And then she—laughed. I guess you would call it a laugh. I thought of Harry and the team outside, so I said a little sharp: "Can't I see John?" "No," she says, kind o' dull like. "Ain't he home?" says I. "Yes," says she, "he's home." "Then why can't I see him?" I asked her, out of patience. " 'Cause he's dead," says she. "*Dead?*" says I. She just nodded her head, not getting a bit excited, but rockin' back and forth. "Why—where is he?" says I, not knowing what to say. She just pointed upstairs—like that *[himself pointing to the room above]*. I got up, with the idea of going up there. I walked from there to here—then I says, "Why, what did he die of?" "He died of a rope around his neck," says she, and just went on pleatin' at her apron. Well, I went out and called Harry. I thought I might—need help. We went upstairs, and there he was lyin'—

COUNTY ATTORNEY. I think I'd rather have you go into that upstairs, where you can point it all out. Just go on now with the rest of the story.

HALE. Well, my first thought was to get that rope off. I looked . . . *[Stops, his face twitches.]* . . . but Harry, he went up to him, and he said, "No, he's dead all right, and we'd better not touch anything." So we went back downstairs. She was still sitting that same way. "Has anybody been notified?" I asked. "No," says she, unconcerned. "Who did this, Mrs. Wright?" said Harry. He said it businesslike—and she stopped pleatin' of her apron. "I don't know," she says. "You don't *know?*" says Harry. "No," says she, "Weren't you sleepin' in the bed with him?" says Harry. "Yes," says she, "but I was on the inside." "Somebody slipped a rope round his neck and strangled him, and you didn't wake up?" says Harry. "I didn't wake up," she said after him. We must 'a looked as if we didn't see how that could be, for after a minute she said, "I sleep sound." Harry was going to ask her more questions, but I said maybe we ought to let her tell her story first to the coroner, or the sheriff, so Harry went fast as he could to Rivers' place, where there's a telephone.

COUNTY ATTORNEY. And what did Mrs. Wright do when she knew that you had gone for the coroner?

HALE. She moved from that chair to this over here . . . *[Pointing to a small chair in the corner.]* . . . and just sat there with her hands held together and looking down. I got a feeling that I ought to make some conversation, so I said I had come in to see if John wanted to put in a telephone, and at that she started to laugh, and then she stopped and looked at me—scared. *[The* COUNTY ATTORNEY, *who has had his notebook out, makes a note.]* I dunno, maybe it wasn't scared. I wouldn't like to say it was. Soon Harry got back, and then Dr. Lloyd came, and you, Mr. Peters, and so I guess that's all I know that you don't.

COUNTY ATTORNEY *[looking around].* I guess we'll go upstairs first—and then out to the barn and around there. *[To the* SHERIFF.*]* You're convinced that there was nothing important here—nothing that would point to any motive?

SHERIFF. Nothing here but kitchen things.

[The COUNTY ATTORNEY, *after again looking around the kitchen, opens the door of a cupboard closet. He gets up on a chair and looks on a shelf. Pulls his hand away, sticky.]*

COUNTY ATTORNEY. Here's a nice mess.

[The women draw nearer.]

MRS. PETERS *[to the other woman].* Oh, her fruit; it did freeze. *[To the* LAWYER.*]* She worried about that when it turned so cold. She said the fir'd go out and her jars would break.

SHERIFF. Well, can you beat the women! Held for murder and worryin' about her preserves.

COUNTY ATTORNEY. I guess before we're through she may have something more serious than preserves to worry about.

HALE. Well, women are used to worrying over trifles.

[The two women move a little closer together.]

COUNTY ATTORNEY *[with the gallantry of a young politician].* And yet, for all their worries, what would we do without the ladies? *[The women do not unbend. He goes to the sink, takes a dipperful of water from the pail and, pouring it into a basin, washes his hands. Starts to wipe*

them on the roller towel, turns it for a cleaner place.] Dirty towels!
[Kicks his foot against the pans under the sink.] Not much of a housekeeper, would you say, ladies?

MRS. HALE *[stiffly]*. There's a great deal of work to be done on a farm.

COUNTY ATTORNEY. To be sure. And yet . . . *[With a little bow to her.]* . . . I
know there are some Dickson county farmhouses which do not have
such roller towels. *[He gives it a pull to expose its full length again.]*

MRS. HALE. Those towels get dirty awful quick. Men's hands aren't always as
clean as they might be.

COUNTY ATTORNEY. Ah, loyal to your sex, I see. But you and Mrs. Wright were
neighbors. I suppose you were friends, too.

MRS. HALE *[shaking her head]*. I've not seen much of her of late years. I've
not been in this house—it's more than a year.

COUNTY ATTORNEY. And why was that? You didn't like her?

MRS. HALE. I liked her all well enough. Farmers' wives have their hands full,
Mr. Henderson. And then—

COUNTY ATTORNEY. Yes—?

MRS. HALE *[looking about]*. It never seemed a very cheerful place.

COUNTY ATTORNEY. No—it's not cheerful. I shouldn't say she had the home-
making instinct.

MRS. HALE. Well, I don't know as Wright had, either.

COUNTY ATTORNEY. You mean that they didn't get on very well?

MRS. HALE. No, I don't mean anything. But I don't think a place'd be any
cheerfuler for John Wright's being in it.

COUNTY ATTORNEY. I'd like to talk more of that a little later. I want to get the
lay of things upstairs now. *[He goes to the left, where three steps lead to
a stair door.]*

SHERIFF. I suppose anything Mrs. Peters does'll be all right. She was to take in
some clothes for her, you know, and a few little things. We left in such
a hurry yesterday.

COUNTY ATTORNEY. Yes, but I would like to see what you take, Mrs. Peters,
and keep an eye out for anything that might be of use to us.

MRS. PETERS. Yes, Mr. Henderson.

*[The women listen to the men's steps on the stairs, then look about
the kitchen.]*

MRS. HALE. I'd hate to have men coming into my kitchen, snooping around
and criticizing. *[She arranges the pans under sink which the LAWYER
had shoved out of place.]*

MRS. PETERS. Of course it's no more than their duty.

MRS. HALE. Duty's all right, but I guess that deputy sheriff that came out to
make the fire might have got a little of this on. *[Gives the roller towel a
pull.]* Wish I'd thought of that sooner. Seems mean to talk about her for
not having things slicked up when she had to come away in such a
hurry.

MRS. PETERS *[who has gone to a small table in the left rear corner of the
room, and lifted one end of a towel that covers a pan]*. She had bread
set. *[Stands still.]*

MRS. HALE *[eyes fixed on a loaf of bread beside the breadbox, which is on a
low shelf at the other side of the room. Moves slowly toward it]*. She
was going to put this in there. *[Picks up loaf, then abruptly drops it. In
a manner of returning to familiar things.]* It's a shame about her fruit.

I wonder if it's all gone. *[Gets up on the chair and looks.]* I think there's some here that's all right, Mrs. Peters. Yes—here; *[Holding it toward the window.]* this is cherries, too. *[Looking again.]* I declare I believe that's the only one. *[Gets down, bottle in her hand. Goes to the sink and wipes it off on the outside.]* She'll feel awful bad after all her hard work in the hot weather. I remember the afternoon I put up my cherries last summer. *[She puts the bottle on the big kitchen table, center of the room, front table. With a sigh, is about to sit down in the rocking chair. Before she is seated realizes what chair it is; with a slow look at it, steps back. The chair, which she has touched, rocks back and forth.]*

MRS. PETERS. Well, I must get those things from the front room closet. *[She goes to the door at the right, but after looking into the other room steps back.]* You coming with me, Mrs. Hale? You could help me carry them. *[They go into the other room; reappear,* MRS. PETERS *carrying a dress and skirt,* MRS. HALE *following with a pair of shoes.]*

MRS. PETERS. My, it's cold in there. *[She puts the cloth on the big table, and hurries to the stove.]*

MRS. HALE *[examining the skirt]*. Wright was close. I think maybe that's why she kept so much to herself. She didn't even belong to the Ladies' Aid. I suppose she felt she couldn't do her part, and then you don't enjoy things when you feel shabby. She used to wear pretty clothes and be lively, when she was Minnie Foster, one of the town girls singing in the choir. But that—oh, that was thirty years ago. This all you was to take in?

MRS. PETERS. She said she wanted an apron. Funny thing to want, for there isn't much to get you dirty in jail, goodness knows. But I suppose just to make her feel more natural. She said they was in the top drawer in this cupboard. Yes, here. And then her little shawl that always hung behind the door. *[Opens stair door and looks.]* Yes, here it is. *[Quickly shuts door leading upstairs.]*

MRS. HALE *[abruptly moving toward her]*. Mrs. Peters?

MRS. PETERS. Yes, Mrs. Hale?

MRS. HALE. Do you think she did it?

MRS. PETERS *[in a frightened voice]*. Oh, I don't know.

MRS. HALE. Well, I don't think she did. Asking for an apron and her little shawl. Worrying about her fruit.

MRS. PETERS *[starts to speak, glances up, where footsteps are heard in the room above. In a low voice]*. Mr. Peters says it looks bad for her. Mr. Henderson is awful sarcastic in speech, and he'll make fun of her sayin' she didn't wake up.

MRS. HALE. Well, I guess John Wright didn't wake when they was slipping that rope under his neck.

MRS. PETERS. No, it's strange. It must have been done awful crafty and still. They say it was such a—funny way to kill a man, rigging it all up like that.

MRS. HALE. That's just what Mr. Hale said. There was a gun in the house. He says that's what he can't understand.

MRS. PETERS. Mr. Henderson said coming out that what was needed for the case was a motive; something to show anger, or—sudden feeling.

MRS. HALE *[who is standing by the table].* Well, I don't see any signs of anger around here. *[She puts her hand on the dish towel which lies on the table, stands looking down at the table, one half of which is clean, the other half messy.]* It's wiped here. *[Makes a move as if to finish work, then turns and looks at loaf of bread outside the breadbox. Drops towel. In that voice of coming back to familiar things.]* Wonder how they are finding things upstairs? I hope she had it a little more red-up there. You know, it seems kind of *sneaking*. Locking her up in town and then coming out here and trying to get her own house to turn against her!

MRS. PETERS. But, Mrs. Hale, the law is the law.

MRS. HALE. I s'pose 'tis. *[Unbuttoning her coat.]* Better loosen up your things, Mrs. Peters. You won't feel them when you go out.

[MRS. PETERS takes off her fur tippet, goes to hang it on hook at the back of room, stands looking at the under part of the small corner table.]

MRS. PETERS. She was piecing a quilt. *[She brings the large sewing basket, and they look at the bright pieces.]*

MRS. HALE. It's log cabin pattern. Pretty, isn't it? I wonder if she was goin' to quilt it or just knot it?

[Footsteps have been heard coming down the stairs. The SHERIFF enters, followed by HALE and the COUNTY ATTORNEY.]

SHERIFF. They wonder if she was going to quilt it or just knot it. *[The men laugh, the women look abashed.]*

COUNTY ATTORNEY *[rubbing his hands over the stove].* Frank's fire didn't do much up there, did it? Well, let's go out to the barn and get that cleared up.

[The men go outside.]

MRS. HALE *[resentfully].* I don't know as there's anything so strange, our takin' up our time with little things while we're waiting for them to get the evidence. *[She sits down at the big table, smoothing out a block with decision.]* I don't see as it's anything to laugh about.

MRS. PETERS *[apologetically].* Of course they've got awful important things on their minds. *[Pulls up a chair and joins MRS. HALE at the table.]*

MRS. HALE *[examining another block].* Mrs. Peters, look at this one. Here, this is the one she was working on, and look at the sewing! All the rest of it has been so nice and even. And look at this! It's all over the place! Why, it looks as if she didn't know what she was about! *[After she has said this, they look at each other, then started to glance back at the door. After an instant MRS. HALE has pulled at a knot and ripped the sewing.]*

MRS. PETERS. Oh, what are you doing, Mrs. Hale?

MRS. HALE *[mildly].* Just pulling out a stitch or two that's not sewed very good. *[Threading a needle.]* Bad sewing always made me fidgety.

MRS. PETERS *[nervously].* I don't think we ought to touch things.

MRS. HALE. I'll just finish up this end. *[Suddenly stopping and leaning forward.]* Mrs. Peters?

MRS. PETERS. Yes, Mrs. Hale?

MRS. HALE. What do you suppose she was so nervous about?

MRS. PETERS. Oh—I don't know. I don't know as she was nervous. I sometimes sew awful queer when I'm just tired. *[MRS. HALE starts to say some-*

thing, looks at MRS. PETERS, *then goes on sewing.]* Well, I must get these things wrapped up. They may be through sooner than we think. *[Putting apron and other things together.]* I wonder where I can find a piece of paper, and string.

MRS. HALE. In that cupboard, maybe.

MRS. PETERS *[looking in cupboard]*. Why, here's a birdcage. *[Holds it up.]* Did she have a bird, Mrs. Hale?

MRS. HALE. Why, I don't know whether she did or not—I've not been here for so long. There was a man around last year selling canaries cheap, but I don't know as she took one; maybe she did. She used to sing real pretty herself.

MRS. PETERS *[glancing around]*. Seems funny to think of a bird here. But she must have had one, or why should she have a cage? I wonder what happened to it?

MRS. HALE. I s'pose maybe the cat got it.

MRS. PETERS. No, she didn't have a cat. She's got that feeling some people have about cats—being afraid of them. My cat got in her room, and she was real upset and asked me to take it out.

MRS. HALE. My sister Bessie was like that. Queer, ain't it?

MRS. PETERS *[examining the cage]*. Why, look at this door. It's broke. One hinge is pulled apart.

MRS. HALE *[looking, too]*. Looks as if someone must have been rough with it.

MRS. PETERS. Why, yes. *[She brings the cage forward and puts it on the table.]*

MRS. HALE. I wish if they're going to find any evidence they'd be about it. I don't like this place.

MRS. PETERS. But I'm awful glad you came with me, Mrs. Hale. It would be lonesome for me sitting here alone.

MRS. HALE. It would, wouldn't it? *[Dropping her sewing.]* But I tell you what I do wish, Mrs. Peters. I wish I had come over sometimes when *she* was here. I—*[Looking around the room.]*—wish I had.

MRS. PETERS. But of course you were awful busy, Mrs. Hale—your house and your children.

MRS. HALE. I could've come. I stayed away because it weren't cheerful—and that's why I ought to have come. I—I've never liked this place. Maybe because it's down in a hollow, and you don't see the road. I dunno what it is, but it's a lonesome place and always was. I wish I had come over to see Minnie Foster sometimes. I can see now—*[Shakes her head.]*

MRS. PETERS. Well, you mustn't reproach yourself, Mrs. Hale. Somehow we just don't see how it is with other folks until—something comes up.

MRS. HALE. Not having children makes less work—but it makes a quiet house, and Wright out to work all day, and no company when he did come in. Did you know John Wright, Mrs. Peters?

MRS. PETERS. Not to know him; I've seen him in town. They say he was a good man.

MRS. HALE. Yes—good; he didn't drink, and kept his word as well as most, I guess, and paid his debts. But he was a hard man, Mrs. Peters. Just to pass the time of day with him. *[Shivers.]* Like a raw wind that gets to the bone. *[Pauses, her eye falling on the cage.]* I should think she would 'a wanted a bird. But what do you suppose went with it?

MRS. PETERS. I don't know, unless it got sick and died. *[She reaches over and swings the broken door, swings it again; both women watch it.]*

MRS. HALE. You weren't raised round here, were you? *[MRS. PETERS shakes her head.]* You didn't know—her?

MRS. PETERS. Not till they brought her yesterday.

MRS. HALE. She—come to think of it, she was kind of like a bird herself—real sweet and pretty, but kind of timid and—fluttery. How—she—did—change. *[Silence; then as if struck by a happy thought and relieved to get back to everyday things.]* Tell you what, Mrs. Peters, why don't you take the quilt in with you? It might take up her mind.

MRS. PETERS. Why, I think that's a real nice idea, Mrs. Hale. There couldn't possibly be any objection to it, could there? Now, just what would I take? I wonder if her patches are in here—and her things. *[They look in the sewing basket.]*

MRS. HALE. Here's some red. I expect this has got sewing things in it *[Brings out a fancy box.]* What a pretty box. Looks like something somebody would give you. Maybe her scissors are in here. *[Opens box. Suddenly puts her hand to her nose.]* Why—*[MRS. PETERS bends nearer, then turns her face away.]* There's something wrapped up in this piece of silk.

MRS. PETERS. Why, this isn't her scissors.

MRS. HALE *[lifting the silk]*. Oh, Mrs. Peters—it's—*[MRS. PETERS bends closer.]*

MRS. PETERS. It's the bird.

MRS. HALE *[jumping up]*. But, Mrs. Peters—look at it. Its neck! Look at its neck! It's all—other side *to.*

MRS. PETERS. Somebody—wrung—its neck.

[Their eyes meet. A look of growing comprehension of horror. Steps are heard outside. MRS. HALE slips box under quilt pieces, and sinks into her chair. Enter SHERIFF and COUNTY ATTORNEY. MRS. PETERS rises.]

COUNTY ATTORNEY *[as one turning from serious things to little pleasantries]*. Well, ladies, have you decided whether she was going to quilt it or knot it?

MRS. PETERS. We think she was going to—knot it.

COUNTY ATTORNEY. Well, that's interesting, I'm sure. *[Seeing the birdcage.]* Has the bird flown?

MRS. HALE *[putting more quilt pieces over the box]*. We think the—cat got it.

COUNTY ATTORNEY *[preoccupied]*. Is there a cat?

[MRS. HALE glances in a quick covert way at MRS. PETERS.]

MRS. PETERS. Well, not now. They're superstitious, you know. They leave.

COUNTY ATTORNEY *[to SHERIFF PETERS, continuing an interrupted conversation]*. No sign at all of anyone having come from the outside. Their own rope. Now let's go up again and go over it piece by piece. *[They start upstairs.]* It would have to have been someone who knew just the—

[MRS. PETERS sits down. The two women sit there not looking at one another, but as if peering into something and at the same time holding back. When they talk now, it is the manner of feeling their way over strange ground, as if afraid of what they are saying, but as if they cannot help saying it.]

MRS. HALE. She liked the bird. She was going to bury it in that pretty box.

MRS. PETERS [*in a whisper*]. When I was a girl—my kitten—there was a boy took a hatchet, and before my eyes—and before I could get there—[*Covers her face an instant.*] If they hadn't held me back, I would have—[*Catches herself, looks upstairs where steps are heard, falters weakly.*]—hurt him.

MRS. HALE [*with a slow look around her*]. I wonder how it would seem never to have had any children around. [*Pause.*] No, Wright wouldn't like the bird—a thing that sang. She used to sing. He killed that, too.

MRS. PETERS [*moving uneasily*]. We don't know who killed the bird.

MRS. HALE. I knew John Wright.

MRS. PETERS. It was an awful thing was done in this house that night, Mrs. Hale. Killing a man while he slept, slipping a rope around his neck that choked the life out of him.

MRS. HALE. His neck. Choked the life out of him.

[*Her hand goes out and rests on the birdcage.*]

MRS. PETERS [*with a rising voice*]. We don't know who killed him. We don't *know.*

MRS. HALE [*her own feeling not interrupted*]. If there'd been years and years of nothing, then a bird to sing to you, it would be awful—still, after the bird was still.

MRS. PETERS [*something within her speaking*]. I know what stillness is. When we homesteaded in Dakota, and my first baby died—after he was two years old, and me with no other then—

MRS. HALE [*moving*]. How soon do you suppose they'll be through, looking for evidence?

MRS. PETERS. I know what stillness is. [*Pulling herself back.*] The law has got to punish crime, Mrs. Hale.

MRS. HALE [*not as if answering that*]. I wish you'd seen Minnie Foster when she wore a white dress with blue ribbons and stood up there in the choir and sang. [*A look around the room.*] Oh, I *wish* I'd come over here once in a while! That was a crime! That was a crime! Who's going to punish that?

MRS. PETERS [*looking upstairs*]. We mustn't—take on.

MRS. HALE. I might have known she needed help! I know how things can be—for women. I tell you, it's queer, Mrs. Peters. We live close together and we live far apart. We all go through the same things—it's all just a different kind of the same thing. [*Brushes her eyes, noticing the bottle of fruit, reaches out for it.*] If I was you, I wouldn't tell her her fruit was gone. Tell her it *ain't.* Tell her it's all right. Take this in to prove it to her. She—she may never know whether it was broke or not.

MRS. PETERS [*takes the bottle, looks about for something to wrap it in; takes petticoat from the clothes brought from the other room, very nervously begins winding this around the bottle. In a false voice*]. My, it's a good thing the men couldn't hear us. Wouldn't they just laugh! Getting all stirred up over a little thing like a—dead canary. As if that could have anything to do with—with—wouldn't they *laugh!*

[*The men are heard coming downstairs.*]

MRS. HALE [*under her breath*]. Maybe they would—maybe they wouldn't.

COUNTY ATTORNEY. No, Peters, it's all perfectly clear except a reason for doing it. But you know juries when it comes to women. If there was some definite thing. Something to show—something to make a story about—a thing that would connect up with this strange way of doing it.

[The women's eyes meet for an instant. Enter HALE *from outer door.]*

HALE. Well, I've got the team around. Pretty cold out there.

COUNTY ATTORNEY. I'm going to stay here awhile by myself. *[To the* SHERIFF.*]* You can send Frank out for me, can't you? I want to go over everything. I'm not satisfied that we can't do better.

SHERIFF. Do you want to see what Mrs. Peters is going to take in?

[The LAWYER *goes to the table, picks up the apron, laughs.]*

COUNTY ATTORNEY. Oh I guess they're not very dangerous things the ladies have picked up. *[Moves a few things about, disturbing the quilt pieces which cover the box. Steps back.]* No, Mrs. Peters doesn't need supervising. For that matter, a sheriff's wife is married to the law. Ever think of it that way, Mrs. Peters?

MRS. PETERS. Not—just that way.

SHERIFF *[chuckling]*. Married to the law. *[Moves toward the other room.]* I just want you to come in here a minute, George. We ought to take a look at these windows.

COUNTY ATTORNEY *[scoffingly]*. Oh, windows!

SHERIFF. We'll be right out, Mr. Hale.

*[HALE *goes outside. The* SHERIFF *follows the* COUNTY ATTORNEY *into the other room. Then* MRS. HALE *rises, hands tight together, looking intensely at* MRS. PETERS, *whose eyes take a slow turn, finally meeting,* MRS. HALE'S. *A moment* MRS. HALE *holds her, then her own eyes point the way to where the box is concealed. Suddenly* MRS. PETERS *throws back quilt pieces and tries to put the box in the bag she is wearing. It is too big. She opens box, starts to take the bird out, cannot touch it, goes to pieces, stands there helpless. Sound of a knob turning in the other room.* MRS. HALE *snatches the box and puts it in the pocket of her big coat. Enter* COUNTY ATTORNEY *and* SHERIFF.]*

COUNTY ATTORNEY *[facetiously]*. Well, Henry, at least we found out that she was not going to quilt it. She was going to—what is it you call it, ladies?

MRS. HALE *[her hand against her pocket]*. We call it—knot it, Mr. Henderson.

CURTAIN

[1916]

✐ TOPICS FOR CRITICAL THINKING AND WRITING

1. Briefly describe the setting, indicating what it "says" and what atmosphere it evokes.
2. Even before the first word of dialogue is spoken, what do you think the play tells us (in the entrance of the characters) about the distinction between the men and the women?
3. How would you characterize Mr. Henderson, the county attorney?
4. In what way or ways are Mrs. Peters and Mrs. Hale different from each other?
5. Several times the men "laugh" or "chuckle." In their contexts, what do these expressions of amusement convey?
6. On page 225, "*the women's eyes meet for an instant.*" What do you think this bit of action "says"? What do you understand by the exchange of glances?

7. On page 224, when Mrs. Peters tells of the boy who killed her cat, she says, "If they hadn't held me back, I would have—(*Catches herself, looks upstairs where steps are heard, falters weakly.*)—hurt him." What do you think she was about to say before she faltered? Why do you suppose Glaspell included this speech about Mrs. Peters's girlhood?

8. On page 221, Mrs. Hale, looking at a quilt, wonders whether Mrs. Wright "was going to quilt it or just knot it." The men are amused by the women's concern with this topic, and the last line of the play returns to the issue. What do you make of this emphasis on the matter?

9. We never see Mrs. Wright on stage. Nevertheless, by the end of *Trifles* we know a great deal about her. In an essay of 500–750 words explain both what we know about her—physical characteristics, habits, interests, personality, life before her marriage and after—and *how* we know these things.

10. The title of the play is ironic—the "trifles" are important. What other ironies do you find in the play? (On irony, see Glossary.)

11. Do you think the play is immoral? Explain.

12. Assume that the canary has been found, thereby revealing a possible motive, and that Minnie Wright is indicted for murder. You are the defense attorney. In 500 words set forth your defense. (Take any position you wish. For instance, you may want to argue that she committed justifiable homicide or that—on the basis of her behavior as reported by Mr. Hale—she is innocent by reason of insanity.)

13. Assume that the canary had been found and Minnie Wright convicted. Compose the speech you think she might have delivered before the sentence was given.

 ## WENDY WASSERSTEIN

*Wendy Wasserstein was born in Brooklyn, New York, in 1950, the daughter of immigrants from central Europe. After graduating from Mt. Holyoke College, she took creative writing courses at the City College of New York and then completed a degree program at the Yale School of Drama. Wasserstein has had a highly successful career as a playwright (*The Heidi Chronicles *won a Pulitzer Prize in 1989), and she has also achieved recognition for her television screenplays and a book of essays.*

*The Man in a Case *is based on a short story by Anton Chekhov, one of her favorite writers.*

The Man in a Case

LIST OF CHARACTERS
BYELINKOV
VARINKA

SCENE: *A small garden in the village of Mironitski. 1898.*
*[*BYELINKOV *is pacing. Enter* VARINKA *out of breath.]*
BYELINKOV. You are ten minutes late.

The Man in a Case. The Acting Company, Champaign-Urbana, Illinois, 1985. (Photo by Diane Gorodnitzki.)

VARINKA. The most amazing thing happened on my way over here. You know the woman who runs the grocery store down the road. She wears a black wig during the week, and a blond wig on Saturday nights. And she has the daughter who married an engineer in Moscow who is doing very well thank you and is living, God bless them, in a three-room apartment. But he really is the most boring man in the world. All he talks about is his future and his station in life. Well, she heard we were to be married and she gave me this basket of apricots to give to you.

BYELINKOV. That is a most amazing thing!

VARINKA. She said to me, Varinka, you are marrying the most honorable man in the entire village. In this village he is the only man fit to speak with my son-in-law.

BYELINKOV. I don't care for apricots. They give me hives.

VARINKA. I can return them. I'm sure if I told her they give you hives she would give me a basket of raisins or a cake.

BYELINKOV. I don't know this woman or her pompous son-in-law. Why would she give me her cakes?

VARINKA. She adores you!

BYELINKOV. She is emotionally loose.

VARINKA. She adores you by reputation. Everyone adores you by reputation. I tell everyone I am to marry Byelinkov, the finest teacher in the country.

BYELINKOV. You tell them this?

VARINKA. If they don't tell me first.

BYELINKOV. Pride can be an imperfect value.

VARINKA. It isn't pride. It is the truth. You are a great man!

BYELINKOV. I am the master of Greek and Latin at a local school at the end of the village of Mironitski.

[VARINKA *kisses him.*]

VARINKA. And I am to be the master of Greek and Latin's wife!

BYELINKOV. Being married requires a great deal of responsibility. I hope I am able to provide you with all that a married man must properly provide a wife.

VARINKA. We will be very happy.

BYELINKOV. Happiness is for children. We are entering into a social contract, an amicable agreement to provide us with a secure and satisfying future.

VARINKA. You are so sweet! You are the sweetest man in the world!

BYELINKOV. I'm a man set in his ways who saw a chance to provide himself with a small challenge.

VARINKA. Look at you! Look at you! Your sweet round spectacles, your dear collar always starched, always raised, your perfectly pressed pants always creasing at right angles perpendicular to the floor, and my most favorite part, the sweet little galoshes, rain or shine, just in case. My Byelinkov, never taken by surprise. Except by me.

BYELINKOV. You speak about me as if I were your pet.

VARINKA. You are my pet! My little school mouse.

BYELINKOV. A mouse?

VARINKA. My sweetest dancing bear with galoshes, my little stale babka.[1]

BYELINKOV. A stale babka?

VARINKA. I am not Pushkin.[2]

BYELINKOV [*laughs*]. That depends what you think of Pushkin.

VARINKA. You're smiling. I knew I could make you smile today.

BYELINKOV. I am a responsible man. Every day I have for breakfast black bread, fruit, hot tea, and every day I smile three times. I am halfway into my translation of the *Aeneid*[3] from classical Greek hexameter into Russian alexandrines. In twenty years I have never been late to school. I am a responsible man, but no dancing bear.

VARINKA. Dance with me.

BYELINKOV. Now? It is nearly four weeks before the wedding!

VARINKA. It's a beautiful afternoon. We are in your garden. The roses are in full bloom.

BYELINKOV. The roses have beetles.

VARINKA. Dance with me!

BYELINKOV. You are a demanding woman.

VARINKA. You chose me. And right. And left. And turn. And right. And left.

BYELINKOV. And turn. Give me your hand. You dance like a school mouse. It's a beautiful afternoon! We are in my garden. The roses are in full bloom! And turn. And turn. [*Twirls* VARINKA *around.*]

VARINKA. I am the luckiest woman!

[BYELINKOV *stops dancing.*]

Why are you stopping?

BYELNKOV. To place a lilac in your hair. Every year on this day I will place a lilac in your hair.

---

[1]**babka** cake with almonds and raisins   [2]**Pushkin** Alexander Pushkin (1799–1837), Russian poet   [3]***Aeneid*** Latin epic poem by the Roman poet Virgil (70–19 B.C.)

VARINKA. Will you remember?

BYELINKOV. I will write it down. *[Takes a notebook from his pocket.]* Dear Byelinkov, don't forget the day a young lady, your bride, entered your garden, your peace, and danced on the roses. On that day every year you are to place a lilac in her hair.

VARINKA. I love you.

BYELINKOV. It is convenient we met.

VARINKA. I love you.

BYELINKOV. You are a girl.

VARINKA. I am thirty.

BYELINKOV. But you think like a girl. That is an attractive attribute.

VARINKA. Do you love me?

BYELINKOV. We've never spoken about housekeeping.

VARINKA. I am an excellent housekeeper. I kept house for my family on the farm in Gadyatchsky. I can make a beetroot soup with tomatoes and aubergines which is so nice. Awfully awfully nice.

BYELINKOV. You are fond of expletives.

VARINKA. My beet soup, sir, is excellent!

BYELINKOV. Please don't be cross. I too am an excellent housekeeper. I have a place for everything in the house. A shelf for each pot, a cubby for every spoon, a folder for favorite recipes. I have cooked for myself for twenty years. Though my beet soup is not outstanding, it is sufficient.

VARINKA. I'm sure it's very good.

BYELINKOV. No. It is awfully, awfully not. What I am outstanding in, however, what gives me greatest pleasure, is preserving those things which are left over. I wrap each tomato slice I haven't used in a wet cloth and place it in the coolest corner of the house. I have had my shoes for seven years because I wrap them in the galoshes you are so fond of. And every night before I go to sleep I wrap my bed in quilts and curtains so I never catch a draft.

VARINKA. You sleep with curtains on your bed?

BYELINKOV. I like to keep warm.

VARINKA. I will make you a new quilt.

BYELINKOV. No. No new quilt. That would be hazardous.

VARINKA. It is hazardous to sleep under curtains.

BYELINKOV. Varinka, I don't like change very much. If one works out the arithmetic the final fraction of improvement is at best less than an eighth of value over the total damage caused by disruption. I never thought of marrying till I saw your eyes dancing among the familiar faces at the headmaster's tea. I assumed I would grow old preserved like those which are left over, wrapped suitably in my case of curtains and quilts.

VARINKA. Byelinkov, I want us to have dinners with friends and summer country visits. I want people to say, "Have you spent time with Varinka and Byelinkov? He is so happy now that they are married. She is just what he needed."

BYELINKOV. You have already brought me some happiness. But I never was a sad man. Don't ever think I thought I was a sad man.

VARINKA. My sweetest darling, you can be whatever you want! If you are sad, they'll say she talks all the time, and he is softspoken and kind.

BYELINKOV. And if I am difficult?

VARINKA. Oh, they'll say he is difficult because he is highly intelligent. All great men are difficult. Look at Lermontov, Tchaikovsky, Peter the Great.

BYELINKOV. Ivan the Terrible.[4]

VARINKA. Yes, him too.

BYELINKOV. Why are you marrying me? I am none of these things.

VARINKA. To me you are.

BYELINKOV. You have imagined this. You have constructed an elaborate romance for yourself. Perhaps you are the great one. You are the one with the great imagination.

VARINKA. Byelinkov, I am a pretty girl of thirty. You're right, I am not a woman. I have not made myself into a woman because I do not deserve that honor. Until I came to this town to visit my brother I lived on my family's farm. As the years passed I became younger and younger in fear that I would never marry. And it wasn't that I wasn't pretty enough or sweet enough, it was just that no man ever looked at me and saw a wife. I was not the woman who would be there when he came home. Until I met you I thought I would lie all my life and say I never married because I never met a man I loved. I will love you, Byelinkov. And I will help you to love me. We deserve the life everyone else has. We deserve not to be different.

BYELINKOV. Yes. We are the same as everyone else.

VARINKA. Tell me you love me.

BYELINKOV. I love you.

VARINKA *[takes his hands].* We will be very happy. I am very strong. *[Pauses.]* It is time for tea.

BYELINKOV. It is too early for tea. Tea is at half past the hour.

VARINKA. Do you have heavy cream? It will be awfully nice with apricots.

BYELINKOV. Heavy cream is too rich for teatime.

VARINKA. But today is special. Today you placed a lilac in my hair. Write in your note pad. Every year we will celebrate with apricots and heavy cream. I will go to my brother's house and get some.

BYELINKOV. But your brother's house is a mile from here.

VARINKA. Today it is much shorter. Today my brother gave me his bicycle to ride. I will be back very soon.

BYELINKOV. You rode to my house by bicycle! Did anyone see you!

VARINKA. Of course. I had such fun. I told you I saw the grocery store lady with the son-in-law who is doing very well thank you in Moscow, and the headmaster's wife.

BYELINKOV. You saw the headmaster's wife!

VARINKA. She smiled at me.

BYELINKOV. Did she laugh or smile?

VARINKA. She laughed a little. She said, "My dear, you are very progressive to ride a bicycle." She said you and your fiancé Byelinkov must ride together sometime. I wonder if he'll take off his galoshes when he rides a bicycle.

---

[4]**Lermontov . . . Ivan the Terrible** Mikhail Lermontov (1814–41), poet and novelist; Peter Ilich Tchaikovsky (1840–93), composer; Peter the Great (1672–1725) and Ivan the Terrible (1530–84), czars credited with making Russia a great European power

BYELINKOV. She said that?

VARINKA. She adores you. We had a good giggle.

BYELINKOV. A woman can be arrested for riding a bicycle. That is not progressive, it is a premeditated revolutionary act. Your brother must be awfully, awfully careful on behalf of your behavior. He has been careless—oh so careless—in giving you the bicycle.

VARINKA. Dearest Byelinkov, you are wrapping yourself under curtains and quilts! I made friends on the bicycle.

BYELINKOV. You saw more than the headmaster's wife and the idiot grocery woman.

VARINKA. She is not an idiot.

BYELINKOV. She is a potato-vending, sausage-armed fool!

VARINKA. Shhhh! My school mouse. Shhh!

BYELINKOV. What other friends did you make on this bicycle?

VARINKA. I saw students from my brother's classes. They waved and shouted, "Anthropos in love! Anthropos in love!!"

BYELINKOV. Where is that bicycle?

VARINKA. I left it outside the gate. Where are you going?

BYELINKOV *[muttering as he exits]*. Anthropos in love, anthropos in love.

VARINKA. They were cheering me on. Careful, you'll trample the roses.

BYELINKOV *[returning with the bicycle]*. Anthropos is the Greek singular for man. Anthropos in love translates as the Greek and Latin master in love. Of course they cheered you. Their instructor, who teaches them the discipline and contained beauty of the classics, is in love with a sprite on a bicycle. It is a good giggle, isn't it? A very good giggle! I am returning this bicycle to your brother.

VARINKA. But it is teatime.

BYELINKOV. Today we will not have tea.

VARINKA. But you will have to walk back a mile.

BYELINKOV. I have my galoshes on. *[Gets on the bicycle.]* Varinka, we deserve not to be different. *[Begins to pedal. The bicycle doesn't move.]*

VARINKA. Put the kickstand up.

BYELINKOV. I beg your pardon.

VARINKA *[giggling]*. Byelinkov, to make the bicycle move, you must put the kickstand up.

*[*BYELINKOV *puts it up and awkwardly falls off the bicycle as it moves.]*
[Laughing.] Ha ha ha. My little school mouse. You look so funny! You are the sweetest dearest man in the world. Ha ha ha!
[Pause.]

BYELINKOV. Please help me up. I'm afraid my galosh is caught.

VARINKA *[trying not to laugh]*. Your galosh is caught! *[Explodes in laughter again.]* Oh, you are so funny! I do love you so. *[Helps* BYELINKOV *up.]* You were right, my pet, as always. We don't need heavy cream for tea. The fraction of improvement isn't worth the damage caused by the disruption.

BYELINKOV. Varinka, it is still too early for tea. I must complete two stanzas of my translation before late afternoon. That is my regular schedule.

VARINKA. Then I will watch while you work.

BYELINKOV. No. You had a good giggle. That is enough.

VARINKA. Then while you work I will work too. I will make lists of guests for our wedding.

BYELINKOV. I can concentrate only when I am alone in my house. Please take
    your bicycle home to your brother.

VARINKA. But I don't want to leave you. You look so sad.

BYELINKOV. I never was a sad man. Don't ever think I was a sad man.

VARINKA. Byelinkov, it's a beautiful day, we are in your garden. The roses are
    in bloom.

BYELINKOV. Allow me to help you on to your bicycle. *[Takes* VARINKA*'s hand
    as she gets on the bike.]*

VARINKA. You are such a gentleman. We will be very happy.

BYELINKOV. You are very strong. Good day, Varinka.

> *[*VARINKA *pedals off.* BYELINKOV, *alone in the garden, takes out his pad
> and rips up the note about the lilac, strews it over the garden, then
> carefully picks up each piece of paper and places them all in a small
> envelope as lights fade to black.]*

[1986]

TOPICS FOR CRITICAL THINKING AND WRITING

1. You will probably agree that the scene where Byelinkov gets on the bicycle and pedals but goes nowhere is funny. But *why* is it funny? Can
you formulate some sort of theory of comedy based on this episode?

2. At the end of the play Byelinkov tears up the note but then collects the
pieces. What do you interpret these actions to mean?

HARVEY FIERSTEIN

*Harvey Fierstein was born in Brooklyn, New York, the son of parents
who had emigrated from Eastern Europe. While studying painting at
Pratt Institute he acted in plays and revues, and one of his plays was
produced in 1973, but he did not achieve fame until his* Torch Song
Trilogy *(1976-79) moved from Off Broadway to Broadway in 1982.*
Torch Song Trilogy *won the Theatre World Award, the Tony Award,
and the Drama Desk Award. In addition, Fierstein won the Best
Actor Tony Award and the Best Actor Drama Desk Award. He later
received a third Tony Award for the book for the musical version of*
La Cage aux Folles *(1983).*

On Tidy Endings

*The curtain rises on a deserted, modern Upper West Side apartment.
In the bright daylight that pours in through the windows we can see
the living room of the apartment. Far Stage Right is the galley
kitchen, next to it the multilocked front door with intercom. Stage
Left reveals a hallway that leads to the two bedrooms and baths.*

*Though the room is still fully furnished (couch, coffee table, etc.),
there are boxes stacked against the wall and several photographs*

On Tidy Endings (Photo: Peter Cunningham)

and paintings are on the floor leaving shadows on the wall where they once hung. Obviously someone is moving out. From the way the boxes are neatly labeled and stacked, we know that this is an organized person.

From the hallway just outside the door we hear the rattling of keys and two arguing voices:

JIM *[offstage].* I've got to be home by four. I've got practice.

MARION *[offstage].* I'll get you to practice, don't worry.

JIM *[offstage].* I don't want to go in there.

MARION *[offstage].* Jimmy, don't make Mommy crazy, alright? We'll go inside, I'll call Aunt Helen and see if you can go down and play with Robbie.

[The door opens. MARION *is a handsome woman of forty. Dressed in a business suit, her hair conservatively combed, she appears to be going to a business meeting.* JIM *is a boy of eleven. His playclothes are typical, but someone has obviously just combed his hair.* MARION *recovers the key from the lock.]*

JIM. Why can't I just go down and ring the bell?

MARION. Because I said so.

[As MARION *steps into the room she is struck by some unexpected emotion. She freezes in her path and stares at the empty apartment.* JIM *lingers by the door.]*

JIM. I'm going downstairs.

MARION. Jimmy, please.

JIM. This place gives me the creeps.

MARION. This was your father's apartment. There's nothing creepy about it.

JIM. Says you.

MARION. You want to close the door, please?

[JIM *reluctantly obeys.*]

MARION. Now, why don't you go check your room and make sure you didn't leave anything.

JIM. It's empty.

MARION. Go look.

JIM. I looked last time.

MARION [*trying to be patient*]. Honey, we sold the apartment. You're never going to be here again. Go make sure you have everything you want.

JIM. But Uncle Arthur packed everything.

MARION [*less patiently*]. Go make sure.

JIM. There's nothing in there.

MARION [*exploding*]. I said make sure!

[JIM *jumps, then realizing that she's not kidding, obeys.*]

MARION. Everything's an argument with that one. [*She looks around the room and breathes deeply. There is sadness here. Under her breath:*] I can still smell you. [*Suddenly not wanting to be alone.*] Jimmy? Are you okay?

JIM [*returning*]. Nothing. Told you so.

MARION. Uncle Arthur must have worked very hard. Make sure you thank him.

JIM. What for? Robbie says, [*fey mannerisms*] "They love to clean up things!"

MARION. Sometimes you can be a real joy.

JIM. Did you call Aunt Helen?

MARION. Do I get a break here? [*Approaching the boy understandingly.*] Wouldn't you like to say good-bye?

JIM. To who?

MARION. To the apartment. You and your daddy spent a lot of time here together. Don't you want to take one last look around?

JIM. Ma, get a real life.

MARION. "Get a real life." [*Going for the phone.*] Nice. Very nice.

JIM. Could you call already?

MARION [*dialing*]. Jimmy, what does this look like I'm doing?

[JIM *kicks at the floor impatiently. Someone answers the phone at the other end.*]

MARION [*into the phone*]. Helen? Hi, we're upstairs. . . . No, we just walked in the door. Jimmy wants to know if he can come down. . . . Oh, thanks.

[*Hearing that,* JIM *breaks for the door.*]

MARION [*yelling after him*]. Don't run in the halls! And don't play with the elevator buttons!

[*The door slams shut behind him.*]

MARION [*back to the phone*]. Hi. . . . No, I'm okay. It's a little weird being here. . . . No. Not since the funeral, and then there were so many people. Jimmy told me to get "a real life." I don't think I could handle anything realer. . . . No, please. Stay where you are. I'm fine. The doorman said Arthur would be right back and my lawyer should have been here already. . . . Well, we've got the papers to sign and a few other odds and ends to clean up. Shouldn't take long.

[The intercom buzzer rings.]

MARION. Hang on, that must be her. *[MARION goes to the intercom and speaks]* Yes? . . . Thank you. *[Back to the phone.]* Helen? Yeah, it's the lawyer. I'd better go. . . . Well, I could use a stiff drink, but I drove down. Listen, I'll stop by on my way out. Okay? Okay. 'Bye.

[She hangs up the phone, looks around the room. That uncomfortable feeling returns to her quickly. She gets up and goes to the front door, opens it and looks out. No one there yet. She closes the door, shakes her head knowing that she's being silly and starts back into the room. She looks around, can't make it and retreats to the door. She opens it, looks out, closes it, but stays right there, her hand on the doorknob. The bell rings. She throws open the door.]

MARION. That was quick.

[JUNE LOWELL still has her finger on the bell. Her arms are loaded with contracts. MARION's contemporary, JUNE is less formal in appearance and more hyper in her manner.]

JUNE. *That* was quicker. What, were you waiting by the door?

MARION *[embarrassed]*. No. I was just passing it. Come on in.

JUNE. Have you got your notary seal?

MARION. I think so.

JUNE. Great. Then you can witness. I left mine at the office and thanks to gentrification I'm double-parked downstairs. *[Looking for a place to dump her load.]* Where?

MARION *[definitely pointing to the coffee table]*. Anywhere. You mean you're not staying?

JUNE. If you really think you need me I can go down and find a parking lot. I think there's one over on Columbus. So, I can go down, park the car in the lot and take a cab back if you really think you need me.

MARION. Well . . . ?

JUNE. But you shouldn't have any problems. The papers are about as straightforward as papers get. Arthur is giving you power of attorney to sell the apartment and you're giving him a check for half the purchase price. Everything else is just signing papers that state that you know that you signed the other papers. Anyway, he knows the deal, his lawyers have been over it all with him, it's just a matter of signatures.

MARION *[not fine]*. Oh, fine.

JUNE. Unless you just don't want to be alone with him . . . ?

MARION. With Arthur? Don't be silly.

JUNE *[laying out the papers]*. Then you'll handle it solo? Great. My car thanks you, the parking lot thanks you, and the cab driver that wouldn't have gotten a tip thanks you. Come have a quick look-see.

MARION *[joining her on the couch]*. There are a lot of papers here.

JUNE. Copies. Not to worry. Start here.

[MARION starts to read.]

JUNE. I ran into Jimmy playing Elevator Operator.

[MARION jumps.]

JUNE. I got him off at the sixth floor. Read on.

MARION. This is definitely not my day for dealing with him.

[JUNE *gets up and has a look around.*]

JUNE. I don't believe what's happening to this neighborhood. You made quite an investment when you bought this place.

MARION. Collin was always very good at figuring out those things.

JUNE. Well, he sure figured this place right. What, have you tripled your money in ten years?

MARION. More.

JUNE. It's a shame to let it go.

MARION. We're not ready to be a two-dwelling family.

JUNE. So, sublet it again.

MARION. Arthur needs the money from the sale.

JUNE. Arthur got plenty already. I'm not crying for Arthur.

MARION. I don't hear you starting in again, do I?

JUNE. Your interests and your wishes are my only concern.

MARION. Fine.

JUNE. I still say we should contest Collin's will.

MARION. June . . . !

JUNE. You've got a child to support.

MARION. And a great job, and a husband with a great job. Tell me what Arthur's got.

JUNE. To my thinking, half of everything that should have gone to you. And more. All of Collin's personal effects, his record collection . . .

MARION. And I suppose their three years together meant nothing.

JUNE. When you compare them to your sixteen-year marriage? Not nothing, but not half of everything.

MARION *[trying to change the subject].* June, who gets which copies?

JUNE. Two of each to Arthur. One you keep. The originals and anything else come back to me. *[Looking around.]* I still say you should've sublet the apartment for a year and then sold it. You would've gotten an even better price. Who wants to buy an apartment when they know someone died in it. No one. And certainly no one wants to buy an apartment when they know the person died of AIDS.

MARION *[snapping].* June. Enough!

JUNE *[catching herself].* Sorry. That was out of line. Sometimes my mouth does that to me. Hey, that's why I'm a lawyer. If my brain worked as fast as my mouth I would have gotten a real job.

MARION *[holding out a stray paper].* What's this?

JUNE. I forgot. Arthur's lawyer sent that over yesterday. He found it in Collin's safety-deposit box. It's an insurance policy that came along with some consulting job he did in Japan. He either forgot about it when he made out his will or else he wanted you to get the full payment. Either way, it's yours.

MARION. Are you sure we don't split this?

JUNE. Positive.

MARION. But everything else . . . ?

JUNE. Hey, Arthur found it, his lawyer sent it to me. Relax, it's all yours. Minus my commission, of course. Go out and buy yourself something. Anything else before I have to use my cut to pay the towing bill?

MARION. I guess not.

JUNE *[starting to leave]*. Great. Call me when you get home. *[Stopping at the door and looking back.]* Look, I know that I'm attacking this a little coldly. I am aware that someone you loved has just died. But there's a time and place for everything. This is about tidying up loose ends, not holding hands. I hope you'll remember that when Arthur gets here. Call me.

[And she's gone.]

*[*MARION *looks ill at ease to be alone again. She nervously straightens the papers into neat little piles, looks at them and then remembers:]*

MARION. Pens. We're going to need pens.

[At last a chore to be done. She looks in her purse and finds only one. She goes to the kitchen and opens a drawer where SHE *finds two more. She starts back to the table with them but suddenly remembers something else. She returns to the kitchen and begins going through the cabinets until she finds what she's looking for: a blue Art Deco teapot. Excited to find it, she takes it back to the couch. Guilt strikes. She stops, considers putting it back, wavers, then:]*

MARION *[to herself]*. Oh, he won't care. One less thing to pack.

[She takes the teapot and places it on the couch next to her purse. She is happier. Now she searches the room with her eyes for any other treasures she may have overlooked. Nothing here. She wanders off into the bedroom. We hear keys outside the front door. ARTHUR *lets himself into the apartment carrying a load of empty cartons and a large shopping bag.* ARTHUR *is in his mid-thirties, pleasant looking though sloppily dressed in work clothes and slightly overweight.* ARTHUR *enters the apartment just as* MARION *comes out of the bedroom carrying a framed watercolor painting. They jump at the sight of each other.]*

MARION. Oh, hi, Arthur. I didn't hear the door.

ARTHUR *[staring at the painting]*. Well hello, Marion.

MARION *[guiltily]*. I was going to ask you if you were thinking of taking this painting because if you're not going to then I'll take it. Unless, of course, you want it.

ARTHUR. No. You can have it.

MARION. I never really liked it, actually. I hate cats. I didn't even like the show. I needed something for my college dorm room. I was never the rock star poster type. I kept it in the back of a closet for years until Collin moved in here and took it. He said he liked it.

ARTHUR. I do too.

MARION. Well, then you keep it.

ARTHUR. No. Take it.

MARION. We've really got no room for it. You keep it.

ARTHUR. I don't want it.

MARION. Well, if you're sure.

ARTHUR *[seeing the teapot]*. You want the teapot?

MARION. If you don't mind.

ARTHUR. One less thing to pack.

MARION. Funny, but that's exactly what I thought. One less thing to pack. You know, my mother gave it to Collin and me when we moved in to our first apartment. Silly sentimental piece of junk, but you know.

ARTHUR. That's not the one.

MARION. Sure it is. Hall used to make them for Westinghouse back in the thirties. I see them all the time at antiques shows and I always wanted to buy another, but they ask such a fortune for them.

ARTHUR. We broke the one your mother gave you a couple of years ago. That's a reproduction. You can get them almost anywhere in the Village for eighteen bucks.

MARION. Really? I'll have to pick one up.

ARTHUR. Take this one. I'll get another.

MARION. No, it's yours. You bought it.

ARTHUR. One less thing to pack.

MARION. Don't be silly. I didn't come here to raid the place.

ARTHUR. Well, was there anything else of Collin's that you thought you might like to have?

MARION. Now I feel so stupid, but actually I made a list. Not for me. But I started thinking about different people; friends, relatives, you know, that might want to have something of Collin's to remember him by. I wasn't sure just what you were taking and what you were throwing out. Anyway, I brought the list. *[Gets it from her purse.]* Of course these are only suggestions. You probably thought of a few of these people yourself. But I figured it couldn't hurt to write it all down. Like I said, I don't know what you are planning on keeping.

ARTHUR *[taking the list].* I was planning on keeping it all.

MARION. Oh, I know. But most of these things are silly. Like his high school yearbooks. What would you want with them?

ARTHUR. Sure. I'm only interested in his Gay period.

MARION. I didn't mean it that way. Anyway, you look it over. They're only suggestions. Whatever you decide to do is fine with me.

ARTHUR *[folding the list].* It would have to be, wouldn't it. I mean, it's all mine now. He did leave this all to me.

*[*MARION *is becoming increasingly nervous, but tries to keep a light approach as she takes a small bundle of papers from her bag.]*

MARION. While we're on the subject of what's yours. I brought a batch of condolence cards that were sent to you care of me. Relatives mostly.

ARTHUR *[taking them].* More cards? I'm going to have to have another printing of thank-you notes done.

MARION. I answered these last week, so you don't have to bother. Unless you want to.

ARTHUR. Forge my signature?

MARION. Of course not. They were addressed to both of us and they're mostly distant relatives or friends we haven't seen in years. No one important.

ARTHUR. If they've got my name on them, then I'll answer them myself.

MARION. I wasn't telling you not to, I was only saying that you don't have to.

ARTHUR. I understand.

*[*MARION *picks up the teapot and brings it to the kitchen.]*

MARION. Let me put this back.

ARTHUR. I ran into Jimmy in the lobby.

MARION. Tell me you're joking.

ARTHUR. I got him to Helen's.

MARION. He's really racking up the points today.

ARTHUR. You know, he still can't look me in the face.

MARION. He's reacting to all of this in strange ways. Give him time. He'll come around. He's really very fond of you.

ARTHUR. I know. But he's at that awkward age: under thirty. I'm sure in twenty years we'll be the best of friends.

MARION. It's not what you think.

ARTHUR. What do you mean?

MARION. Well, you know.

ARTHUR. No I don't know. Tell me.

MARION. I thought that you were intimating something about his blaming you for Collin's illness and I was just letting you know that it's not true. *[Foot in mouth, she braves on.]* We discussed it a lot and ... uh ... he understands that his father was sick before you two ever met.

ARTHUR. I don't believe this.

MARION. I'm just trying to say that he doesn't blame you.

ARTHUR. First of all, who asked you? Second of all, that's between him and me. And third and most importantly, of course he blames me. Marion, he's eleven years old. You can discuss all you want, but the fact is that his father died of a "fag" disease and I'm the only fag around to finger.

MARION. My son doesn't use that kind of language.

ARTHUR. Forget the language. I'm talking about what he's been through. Can you imagine the kind of crap he's taken from his friends? That poor kid's been chased and chastised from one end of town to the other. He's got to have someone to blame just to survive. He can't blame you, you're all he's got. He can't blame his father; he's dead. So, Uncle Arthur gets the shaft. Fine, I can handle it.

MARION. You are so wrong, Arthur. I know my son and that is not the way his mind works.

ARTHUR. I don't know what you know. I only know what I know. And all I know is what I hear and see. The snide remarks, the little smirks. . . . And it's not just the illness. He's been looking for a scapegoat since the day you and Collin first split up. Finally he has one.

MARION *[getting very angry now]*. Wait. Are you saying that if he's going to blame someone it should be me?

ARTHUR. I think you should try to see things from his point of view.

MARION. Where do you get off thinking you're privy to my son's point of view?

ARTHUR. It's not that hard to imagine. Life's rolling right along, he's having a happy little childhood, when suddenly one day his father's moving out. No explanations, no reasons, none of the fights that usually accompany such things. Divorce is hard enough for a kid to understand when he's listened to years of battles, but yours?

MARION. So what should we have done? Faked a few months' worth of fights before Collin moved out?

ARTHUR. You could have told him the truth, plain and simple.

MARION. He was seven years old at the time. How the hell do you tell a seven-year-old that his father is leaving his mother to go sleep with other men?

ARTHUR. Well, not like that.

MARION. You know, Arthur, I'm going to say this as nicely as I can: Butt out. You're not his mother and you're not his father.

ARTHUR. Thank you. I wasn't acutely aware of that fact. I will certainly keep that in mind from now on.

MARION. There's only so much information a child that age can handle.

ARTHUR. So it's best that he reach his capacity on the street.

MARION. He knew about the two of you. We talked about it.

ARTHUR. Believe me, he knew before you talked about it. He's young, not stupid.

MARION. It's very easy for you to stand here and criticize, but there are aspects that you will just never be able to understand. You weren't there. You have no idea what it was like for me. You're talking to someone who thought that a girl went to college to meet a husband. I went to protest rallies because I liked the music. I bought a guitar because I thought it looked good on the bed! This lifestyle, this knowledge that you take for granted, was all a little out of left field for me.

ARTHUR. I can imagine.

MARION. No, I don't think you can. I met Collin in college, married him right after graduation and settled down for a nice quiet life of Kids and Careers. You think I had any idea about this? Talk about life's little surprises. You live with someone for sixteen years, you share your life, your bed, you have a child together, and then you wake up one day and he tells you that to him it's all been a lie. A lie. Try that on for size. Here you are the happiest couple you know, fulfilling your every life fantasy and he tells you he's living a lie.

ARTHUR. I'm sure he never said that.

MARION. Don't be so sure. There was a lot of new ground being broken back then and plenty of it was muddy.

ARTHUR. You know that he loved you.

MARION. What's that supposed to do, make things easier? It doesn't. I was brought up to believe, among other things, that if you had love that was enough. So what if I wasn't everything he wanted. Maybe he wasn't exactly everything I wanted either. So, you know what? You count your blessings and you settle.

ARTHUR. No one has to settle. Not him. Not you.

MARION. Of course not. You can say, "Up yours!" to everything and everyone who depends and needs you, and go off to make yourself happy.

ARTHUR. It's not that simple.

MARION. No. This is simpler. Death is simpler. *[Yelling out:]* Happy now? *[They stare at each other. MARION calms the rage and catches her breath. ARTHUR holds his emotions in check.]*

ARTHUR. How about a nice hot cup of coffee? Tea with lemon? Hot cocoa with a marshmallow floating in it?

MARION. *[laughs]*. I was wrong. You *are* a mother. *[ARTHUR goes into the kitchen and starts preparing things. MARION loafs by the doorway.]*

MARION. I lied before. He *was* everything I ever wanted. *[ARTHUR stops, looks at her, and then changes the subject as he goes on with his work.]*

ARTHUR. When I came into the building and saw Jimmy in the lobby I absolutely freaked for a second. It's amazing how much they look alike. It was like seeing a little miniature Collin standing there.

MARION. I know. He's like Collin's clone. There's nothing of me in him.

ARTHUR. I always kinda hoped that when he grew up he'd take after me. Not much chance, I guess.

MARION. Don't do anything fancy in there.

ARTHUR. Please. Anything we can consume is one less thing to pack.

MARION. So you've said.

ARTHUR. So *we've* said.

MARION. I want to keep seeing you and I want you to see Jim. You're still part of this family. No one's looking to cut you out.

ARTHUR. Ah, who'd want a kid to grow up looking like me anyway. I had enough trouble looking like this. Why pass on the misery?

MARION. You're adorable.

ARTHUR. Is that like saying I have a good personality?

MARION. I think you are one of the most naturally handsome men I know.

ARTHUR. Natural is right, and the bloom is fading.

MARION. All you need is a few good nights' sleep to kill those rings under your eyes.

ARTHUR. Forget the rings under my eyes, *[grabbing his middle]* . . . how about the rings around my moon?

MARION. I like you like this.

ARTHUR. From the time that Collin started using the wheelchair until he died, about six months, I lost twenty-three pounds. No gym, no diet. In the last seven weeks I've gained close to fifty.

MARION. You're exaggerating.

ARTHUR. I'd prove it on the bathroom scale, but I sold it in working order.

MARION. You'd never know.

ARTHUR. Marion, *you'd* never know, but ask my belt. Ask my pants. Ask my underwear. Even my stretch socks have stretch marks. I called the ambulance at five A.M., he was gone at nine and by nine-thirty, I was on a firstname basis with Sara Lee. I can quote the business hours of every ice-cream parlor, pizzeria and bakery on the island of Manhattan. I know the location of every twenty-four-hour grocery in the greater New York area, and I have memorized the phone numbers of every Mandarin, Szechuan and Hunan restaurant with free delivery.

MARION. At least you haven't wasted your time on useless hobbies.

ARTHUR. Are you kidding? I'm opening my own Overeater's Hotline. We'll have to start small, but expansion is guaranteed.

MARION. You're the best, you know that? If I couldn't be everything that Collin wanted then I'm grateful that he found someone like you.

ARTHUR *[turning on her without missing a beat]*. Keep your goddamned gratitude to yourself. I didn't go through any of this for you. So your thanks are out of line. And he didn't find "someone like" me. It was me.

MARION *[frightened]*. I didn't mean . . .

ARTHUR. And I wish you'd remember one thing more: He died in my arms, not yours.

[MARION is totally caught off guard. She stares disbelieving, openmouthed. ARTHUR walks past her as he leaves the kitchen with place mats. He puts them on the coffee table. As he arranges the papers and place mats he speaks, never looking at her.]

ARTHUR. Look, I know you were trying to say something supportive. Don't waste your breath. There's nothing you can say that will make any of this easier for me. There's no way for you to help me get through this. And that's your fault. After three years you still have no idea or understanding of who I am. Or maybe you do know but refuse to accept it. I don't know and I don't care. But at least understand, from my point of view, who you are: You are my husband's *ex*-wife. If you like, the mother of *my* stepson. Don't flatter yourself into thinking you're any more than that. And whatever you are, you're certainly not my friend. *[He stops, looks up at her, then passes her again as he goes back to the kitchen.* MARION *is shaken, working hard to control herself. She moves toward the couch.]*

MARION. Why don't we just sign these papers and I'll be out of your way.

ARTHUR. Shouldn't you say *I'll* be out of *your* way? After all, I'm not just sign-ing papers. I'm signing away my home.

MARION *[resolved not to fight, she gets her purse].* I'll leave the papers here. Please have them notarized and returned to my lawyer.

ARTHUR. Don't forget my painting.

MARION. *[exploding].* What do you want from me, Arthur?

ARTHUR. *[yelling back].* I want you the hell out of my apartment! I want you out of my life! And I want you to leave Collin alone!

MARION. The man's dead. I don't know how much more alone I can leave him.

*[*ARTHUR *laughs at the irony, but behind the laughter is something much more desperate.]*

ARTHUR. Lots more, Marion. You've got to let him go.

MARION. For the life of me, I don't know what I did or what you think I did, for you to treat me like this. But you're not going to get away with it. You will not take your anger out on me. I will not stand here and be badgered and insulted by you. I know you've been hurt and I know you're hurting but you're not the only one who lost someone here.

ARTHUR *[topping her].* Yes I am! You didn't just lose him. I did! You lost him five years ago when he divorced you. This is not your moment of grief and loss, it's mine! *[Picking up the bundle of cards and throwing it to-ward her.]* These condolences do not belong to you, they're mine. *[Tossing her list back to her.]* His things are not yours to give away, they're mine! This death does not belong to you, it's mine! Bought and paid for outright. I suffered for it, I bled for it.

I was the one who cooked his meals. I was the one who spoon-fed them. I pushed his wheelchair. I carried and bathed him. I wiped his backside and changed his diapers. I breathed life into and wrestled fear out of his heart. I kept him alive for two years longer than any doctor thought possible and when it was time I was the one who prepared him for death.

I paid in full for my place in his life and I will *not* share it with you. We are not the two widows of Collin Redding. Your life was not here. Your husband didn't just die. You've got a son and a life somewhere else. Your husband's sitting, waiting for you at home, wondering, as I am, what the hell you're doing here and why you can't let go.

*[*MARION *leans back against the couch. She's blown away.* ARTHUR *stands staring at her.]*

ARTHUR *[quietly].* Let him go, Marion. He's mine. Dead or alive; mine.

[The teakettle whistles. ARTHUR *leaves the room, goes to the kitchen and pours the water as* MARION *pulls herself together.* ARTHUR *carries the loaded tray back into the living room and sets it down on the cof-fee table. He sits and pours a cup.]*

ARTHUR. One marshmallow or two?

[MARION stares, unsure as to whether the attack is really over or not.]

ARTHUR *[placing them in her cup]*. Take three, they're small.

[MARION smiles and takes the offered cup.]

ARTHUR *[campily]*. Now let me tell you how I *really* feel.

[MARION jumps slightly, then they share a small laugh. Silence as they each gather themselves and sip their refreshments]

MARION *[calmly]*. Do you think that I sold the apartment just to throw you out?

ARTHUR. I don't care about the apartment . . .

MARION. . . . Because I really didn't. Believe me.

ARTHUR. I know.

MARION. I knew the expenses here were too much for you, and I knew you couldn't afford to buy out my half . . . I figured if we sold it, that you'd at least have a nice chunk of money to start over with.

ARTHUR. You could've given me a little more time.

MARION. Maybe. But I thought the sooner you were out of here, the sooner you could go on with your life.

ARTHUR. Or the sooner you could go on with yours.

MARION. Maybe. *[Pauses to gather her thoughts.]* Anyway, I'm not going to tell you that I have no idea what you're talking about. I'd have to be worse than deaf and blind not to have seen the way you've been treated. Or mistreated. When I read Collin's obituary in the newspaper and saw my name and Jimmy's name and no mention of you. . . . *[Shakes her head, not knowing what to say.]* You know that his secretary was the one who wrote that up and sent it in. Not me. But I should have done something about it and I didn't. I know.

ARTHUR. Wouldn't have made a difference. I wrote my own obituary for him and sent it to the smaller papers. They edited me out.

MARION. I'm sorry. I remember, at the funeral, I was surrounded by all of Collin's family and business associates while you were left with your friends. I knew it was wrong. I knew I should have said something but it felt good to have them around me and you looked like you were holding up. . . . Wrong. But saying that it's all my fault for not letting go. . . ? There were other people involved.

ARTHUR. Who took their cue from you.

MARION. Arthur, you don't understand. Most people that we knew as a couple had no idea that Collin was Gay right up to his death. And even those that did know only found out when he got sick and the word leaked out that it was AIDS. I don't think I have to tell you how stupid and ill-informed most people are about homosexuality. And AIDS. . . ? The kinds of insane behavior that word inspires . . . ?

Those people at the funeral, how many times did they call to see how he was doing over these years? How many of them ever went to see him in the hospital? Did any of them even come here? So, why would you expect them to act any differently after his death?

So, maybe that helps to explain their behavior, but what about mine, right? Well, maybe there is no explanation. Only excuses. And excuse number one is that you're right, I have never really let go of him. And I am jealous of you. Hell, I was jealous of anyone that Collin ever talked to, let alone slept with . . . let alone loved.

The first year, after he moved out, we talked all the time about the different men he was seeing. And I always listened and advised. It was kind of fun. It kept us close. It kept me a part of his intimate life. And the bottom line was always that he wasn't happy with the men he was meeting. So, I was always allowed to hang on to the hope that one day he'd give it all up and come home. Then he got sick.

He called me, told me he was in the hospital and asked if I'd come see him. I ran. When I got to his door there was a sign, INSTRUCTIONS FOR VISITORS OF AN AIDS PATIENT. I nearly died.

ARTHUR. He hadn't told you?

MARION. No. And believe me, a sign is not the way to find these things out. I was so angry. . . . And he was so sick . . . I was sure that he'd die right then. If not from the illness then from the hospital staff's neglect. No one wanted to go near him and I didn't bother fighting with them because I understood that they were scared. I was scared. That whole month in the hospital I didn't let Jimmy visit him once.

You learn.

Well, as you know, he didn't die. And he asked if he could come stay with me until he was well. And I said yes. Of course, yes. Now, here's something I never thought I'd ever admit to anyone: had he asked to stay with me for a few weeks I would have said no. But he asked to stay with me until he was well and knowing there was no cure I said yes. In my craziness I said yes because to me that meant forever. That he was coming back to me forever. Not that I wanted him to die, but I assumed from everything I'd read. . . . And we'd be back together for whatever time he had left. Can you understand that?

[ARTHUR *nods.*]

MARION [*gathers her thoughts again*]. Two weeks later he left. He moved in here. Into this apartment that we had bought as an investment. Never to live in. Certainly never to live apart in. Next thing I knew, the name Arthur starts appearing in every phone call, every dinner conversation.

"Did you see the doctor?"

"Yes. Arthur made sure I kept the appointment."

"Are you going to your folks for Thanksgiving?"

"No. Arthur and I are having some friends over."

I don't know which one of us was more of a coward, he for not telling or me for not asking about you. But eventually you became a given. Then, of course, we met and became what I had always thought of as friends.

[ARTHUR *winces in guilt.*]

MARION. I don't care what you say, how could we not be friends with someone so great in common: love for one of the most special human beings there ever was. And don't try and tell me there weren't times when you enjoyed me being around as an ally. I can think of a dozen occasions when we ganged up on him, teasing him with our intimate knowledge of his personal habits.

[ARTHUR *has to laugh.*]

MARION. Blanket stealing? Snoring? Excess gas, no less? [*Takes a moment to enjoy this truce.*] I don't think that my loving him threatened your relationship. Maybe I'm not being truthful with myself. But I don't. I never tried to step between you. Not that I ever had the opportunity. Talk about being joined at the hip! And that's not to say I wasn't jealous. I was. Terribly. Hatefully. But always lovingly. I was happy for Collin because there was no way to deny that he was happy. With everything he was facing, he was happy. Love did that. You did that.

He lit up with you. He came to life. I envied that and all the time you spent together, but more, I watched you care for him (sometimes *overcare* for him), and I was in awe. I could never have done what you did. I never would have survived. I really don't know how you did.

ARTHUR. Who said I survived?

MARION. Don't tease. You did an absolutely incredible thing. It's not as if you met him before he got sick. You entered a relationship that you knew in all probability would end this way and you never wavered.

ARTHUR. Of course I did. Don't have me sainted, Marion. But sometimes you have no choice. Believe me, if I could've gotten away from him I would've. But I was a prisoner of love.

[He makes a campy gesture and pose.]

MARION. Stop.

ARTHUR. And there were lots of pluses. I got to quit a job I hated, stay home all day and watch game shows. I met a lot of doctors and learned a lot of big words. *[ARTHUR jumps up and goes to the pile of boxes where he extracts one and brings it back to the couch.]*

And then there was all the exciting traveling I got to do. This box has a souvenir from each one of our trips. Wanna see? *[MARION nods. He opens the box and pulls things out one by one. Holding up an old bottle.]*

This is from the house we rented in Reno when we went to clear out his lungs. *[Holding handmade potholders.]*

This is from the hospital in Reno. Collin made them. They had a great arts and crafts program. *[Copper bracelets.]*

These are from a faith healer in Philly. They don't do much for a fever, but they look great with a green sweater. *[Glass ashtrays.]*

These are from our first visit to the clinic in France. Such lovely people. *[A Bible.]*

This is from our second visit to the clinic in France. *[A bead necklace.]*

A Voodoo doctor in New Orleans. Next time we'll have to get there earlier in the year. I think he sold all the pretty ones at Mardi Gras. *[A tiny piñata.]*

Then there was Mexico. Black market drugs and empty wallets. *[Now pulling things out at random.]*

L.A., San Francisco, Houston, Boston. . . . We traveled everywhere they offered hope for sale and came home with souvenirs. *[ARTHUR quietly pulls a few more things out and then begins to put them all back into the box slowly. Softly as he works:]* Marion, I would have done anything, traveled anywhere to avoid . . . or delay. . . . Not just because I loved him so desperately, but when you've lived the way we did for three years . . . the battle becomes your life. *[He looks at her and then away.]* His last few hours were beyond any scenario I had imagined. He hadn't walked in nearly six months. He was totally incontinent. If he spoke two words in a week I was thankful. Days went by without his eyes ever focusing on me. He just stared out at I don't know what. Not the meals as I fed him. Not the TV I played constantly for company. Just out. Or maybe in.

It was the middle of the night when I heard his breathing become labored. His lungs were filling with fluid again. I knew the sound. I'd heard it a hundred times before. So, I called the ambulance and got him to the hospital.

They hooked him up to the machines, the oxygen, shot him with morphine and told me that they would do what they could to keep him alive.

But, Marion, it wasn't the machines that kept him breathing. He did it himself. It was that incredible will and strength inside him. Whether it came from his love of life or fear of death, who knows. But he'd been counted out a hundred times and a hundred times he fought his way back.

I got a magazine to read him, pulled a chair up to the side of his bed and holding his hand, I wondered whether I should call Helen to let the cleaning lady in or if he'd fall asleep and I could sneak home for an hour. I looked up from the page and he was looking at me. Really looking right into my eyes. I patted his cheek and said, "Don't worry, honey, you're going to be fine."

But there was something else in his eyes. He wasn't satisfied with that. And I don't know why, I have no idea where it came from, I just heard the words coming out of my mouth, "Collin, do you want to die?"

His eyes filled and closed, he nodded his head.

I can't tell you what I was thinking, I'm not sure I was. I slipped off my shoes, lifted his blanket and climbed into bed next to him. I helped him to put his arms around me, and mine around him, and whispered as gently as I could into his ear, "It's alright to let go now. It's time to go on." And he did.

Marion, you've got your life and your son. All I have is an intangible place in a man's history. Leave me that. Respect that.

MARION. I understand.

[ARTHUR suddenly comes to life, running to get the shopping bag that he'd left at the front door.]

ARTHUR. Jeez! With all the screamin' and sad storytelling I forgot something. *[He extracts a bouquet of flowers from the bag.]* I brung you flowers and everything.

MARION. You brought *me* flowers?

ARTHUR. Well, I knew you'd never think to bring me flowers and I felt that on an occasion such as this somebody oughta get flowers from somebody.

MARION. You know, Arthur, you're really making me feel like a worthless piece of garbage.

ARTHUR. So what else is new? *[He presents the flowers.]* Just promise me one thing: Don't press one in a book. Just stick them in a vase and when they fade just toss them out. No more memorabilia.

MARION. Arthur, I want to do something for you and I don't know what. Tell me what you want.

ARTHUR. I want little things. Not much. I want to be remembered. If you get a Christmas card from Collin's mother make sure she sent me one too.

If his friends call to see how you are, ask if they've called me. Have me to dinner so I can see Jimmy. Let me take him out now and then. Invite me to his wedding. *[They both laugh.]*

MARION. You've got it.

ARTHUR *[clearing the table].* Let me get all this cold cocoa out of the way. We still have the deed to do.

MARION *[checking her watch].* And I've got to get Jimmy home in time for practice.

ARTHUR. Band practice?

MARION. Baseball. *[Picking her list off the floor.]* About this list, you do what you want.

ARTHUR. Believe me, I will. But I promise to consider your suggestions. Just don't rush me. I'm not ready to give it all away. *[ARTHUR is off to the kitchen with his tray and the phone rings. He answers in the kitchen.]* "Hello? . . . Just a minute. *[Calling out.]* It's your eager Little Leaguer. *[MARION picks up the living room extension and ARTHUR hangs his up]*

MARION *[into phone].* Hello, honey. . . . I'll be down in five minutes. No. You know what? You come up here and get me. . . . No, I said you should come up here. . . . I said I want you to come up here. . . . Because I said so. . . . Thank you. *[She hangs the receiver.]*

ARTHUR *[rushing to the papers].* Alright, where do we start on these?

MARION *[getting out her seal].* I guess you should just start signing everything and I'll stamp along with you. Keep one of everything on the side for yourself.

ARTHUR. Now I feel so rushed. What am I signing?

MARIOM. You want to do this another time?

ARTHUR. No. Let's get it over with. I wouldn't survive another session like this.

[He starts to sign and she starts her job.]

MARION. I keep meaning to ask you; how are you?

ARTHUR *[at first puzzled and then:]* Oh, you mean my health? Fine. No. I'm fine. I've been tested, and nothing. We were very careful. We took many precautions. Collin used to make jokes about how we should invest in rubber futures.

MARION. I'll bet.

ARTHUR *[Stops what he's doing].* It never occurred to me until now. How about you?

MARION *[not stopping].* Well, we never had sex after he got sick.

ARTHUR. But before?

MARION *[stopping but not looking up].* I have the antibodies in my blood. No signs that it will ever develop into anything else. And it's been five years so my chances are pretty good that I'm just a carrier.

ARTHUR. I'm so sorry. Collin never told me.

MARION. He didn't know. In fact, other than my husband and the doctors, you're the only one I've told.

ARTHUR. You and your husband . . . ?

MARION. Have invested in rubber futures. There'd only be a problem if we wanted to have a child. Which we do. But we'll wait. Miracles happen every day.

ARTHUR. I don't know what to say.

MARION. Tell me you'll be be there if I ever need you.

[ARTHUR gets up, goes to her and puts his arm around her. They hold each other. He gently pushes her away to make a joke.]

ARTHUR. Sure! Take something else that should have been mine.

MARION. Don't even joke about things like that.

[The doorbell rings. They pull themselves together.]

ARTHUR. You know we'll never get these done today.

MARION. So, tomorrow.

[ARTHUR goes to open the door as MARION gathers her things. He opens the doors and JIMMY is standing in the hall.]

JIM. C'mon, Ma. I'm gonna be late.

ARTHUR. Would you like to come inside?

JIM. We've gotta go.

MARION. Jimmy, come on.

JIM. Ma!

[She glares. He comes in. ARTHUR closes the door.]

MARION *[holding out the flowers]*. Take these for Mommy.

JIM *[taking them]*. Can we go?

MARION *[picking up the painting]*. Say good-bye to your Uncle Arthur.

JIM. 'Bye, Arthur. Come on.

MARION. Give him a kiss.

ARTHUR. Marion, don't.

MARION. Give your uncle a kiss good-bye.

JIM. He's not my uncle.

MARION. No. He's a hell of a lot more than your uncle.

ARTHUR *[offering his hand]*. A handshake will do.

MARION. Tell Uncle Arthur what your daddy told you.

JIM. About what?

MARION. Stop playing dumb. You know.

ARTHUR. Don't embarrass him.

MARION. Jimmy, please.

JIM *[He regards his MOTHER's softer tone and then speaks]*. He said that after me and Mommy he loved you the most.

MARION *[standing behind him]*. Go on.

JIM. And that I should love you too. And make sure that you're not lonely or very sad.

ARTHUR. Thank you.

[ARTHUR reaches down to the boy and they hug. JIM gives him a little peck on the cheek and then breaks away.]

MARION *[going to open the door]*. Alright, kid, you done good. Now let's blow this joint before you muck it up.

[JIM rushes out the door. MARION turns to ARTHUR.]

MARION. A child's kiss is magic. Why else would they be so stingy with them. I'll call you.

[ARTHUR nods understanding. MARION pulls the door closed behind her. ARTHUR stands quietly as the lights fade to black.]

THE END

NOTE: *If being performed on film, the final image should be of ARTHUR leaning his back against the closed door on the inside of the apart-*

ment and MARION *leaning on the outside of the door. A moment of thought and then they both move on.*

[1987]

☞ TOPICS FOR CRITICAL THINKING AND WRITING

1. We first hear about AIDS on page 236. Were you completely surprised, or did you think the play might introduce the subject? That is, did the author in any way prepare you for the subject? If so, how?

2. So far as the basic story goes, June (the lawyer) is not necessary. Marion could have brought the papers with her. Why do you suppose Fierstein introduces June? What function(s) does she serve? How would you characterize her?

3. On page 237 Marion says of the teapot, "One less thing to pack." Arthur says the same words a moment later, and then he repeats them yet again. A little later, while drinking cocoa, he repeats the words, and Marion says, "So you've said," to which Arthur replies, "So *we've* said." Exactly what tone do you think should be used when Marion first says these words? When Arthur says them? And what significance, if any, do you attach to the fact that both characters speak these words?

4. A reviewer of the play said that Arthur is "bitchy" in many of his responses to Marion. What do you suppose the reviewer meant by this? Does the term imply that Fierstein presents a stereotype of the homosexual? If so, what is this stereotype? If you think that the term applies (even though you might not use such a word yourself), do you think that Fierstein's portrayal of Arthur is stereotypical? If it is stereotypical, is this a weakness in the play?

5. Arthur says that Jimmy blames him for Collin's death, but Marion denies it. Who do you think is right? Can a reader be sure? Why, or why not?

6. When Arthur tells Marion that she should have told Jimmy why Collin left her, Marion says, "How the hell do you tell a seven-year-old that his father is leaving his mother to go sleep with other men?" Arthur replies, "Well, not like that." What does Arthur mean? How *might* Marion have told Jimmy? Do you think she should have told Jimmy?

7. Do you agree with a reader who found Marion an unconvincing character because she is "so passive and unquestioningly loving in her regard for her ex-husband"? If you disagree, how would you argue your case?

8. During the course of the play, what (if anything) does Marion learn? What (if anything) does Arthur learn? What (if anything) does Jimmy learn? What (if anything) does the reader or viewer learn from the play?

9. One reader characterized the play as "propaganda." Do you agree? Why, or why not? And if you think *On Tidy Endings* is propaganda, are you implying that it is therefore deficient as a work of art?

A Casebook on William Shakespeare's The Tempest

In this chapter we give Shakespeare's play *The Tempest,* preceded by "A Note on the Elizabethan Theater." Other material follows:

1. An extract from a probable source, Montaigne's essay entitled "Of the Cannibals"
2. Part of an essay of 1906 by Lytton Strachey, taking issue with a common Victorian biographical view of the play
3. An essay by Jane Lee, arguing that although the play is rooted in its own age it nevertheless speaks to us
4. An essay by Stephen Greenblatt, perhaps the most eminent critic of the New Historicist school, emphasizing the need to face the "cruelty, injustice, and pain" that is part of our civilization
5. Part of a discussion between a scholar, Ralph Berry, and a director of the play, Jonathan Miller
6. Part of an essay on possible racist implications in the roles of Caliban and Ariel
7. An essay by Linda Bamber on "the traffic in women"

A NOTE ON THE ELIZABETHAN THEATER

Shakespeare's theater was wooden, round or polygonal (the Chorus in *Henry V* calls it a "wooden O"). About eight hundred spectators could stand in the yard in front of—and perhaps along the two sides of—the stage that jutted from the rear

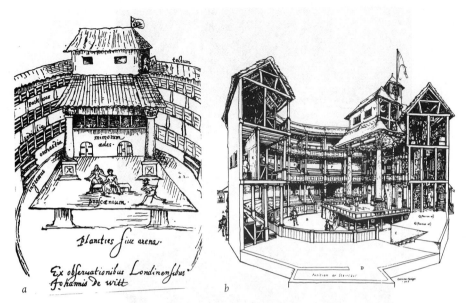

a. Johannes de Witt, a Continental visitor to London, made a drawing of the Swan Theater in about the year 1596. The original drawing is lost; this is Arend van Buchel's copy of it. (Copyright the British Museum.)   *b.* C. Walter Hodges's drawing (1965) of an Elizabethan playhouse. (Courtesy C. Walter Hodges)

wall, and another fifteen hundred or so spectators could sit in the three roofed galleries that ringed the stage.

That portion of the galleries that was above the rear of the stage was sometimes used by actors. For instance, in *The Tempest,* 3.3, a stage direction following line 17 mentions "Prospero on the top, invisible," that is, he is imagined to be invisible to the characters in the play.

Entry to the stage was normally gained by doors at the rear, but apparently on rare occasions use was made of a curtained alcove—or perhaps a booth—between the doors, which allowed characters to be "discovered" (revealed) as in the modern proscenium theater, which normally employs a curtain. Such "discovery" scenes are rare, but in all probability we have one at 5.1.172, where the stage direction says, "Here Prospero discovers Ferdinand and Miranda, playing at chess."

Although the theater as a whole was unroofed, the stage was protected by a roof, supported by two pillars. These could serve (by an act of imagination) as trees behind which actors might pretend to conceal themselves.

A performance was probably uninterrupted by intermissions or by long pauses for the changing of scenery; a group of characters leaves the stage, another enters, and if the locale has changed the new characters somehow tell us. (Modern editors customarily add indications of locales to help a reader, but it should be remembered that the action on the Elizabethan stage was continuous.)

WILLIAM SHAKESPEARE

Shakespeare (1564–1616) was born into a middle-class family in Stratford-upon-Avon. Although we have a fair number of records about his life—documents concerning marriage, the birth of chil-

Morris Carnovsky as Prospero. (Martha Swope)

*dren, the purchase of property, and so forth—it is not known exactly
why and when he turned to the theater. What we do know, however,
is important: He was an actor and a shareholder in a playhouse, and
he did write the plays that are attributed to him. The dates of some of
the plays can be set precisely, but the dates of some others can be set
only roughly. It is known that* The Tempest *was performed before the
King on 1 November 1611, and all scholars assume that the play was
written in the months immediately preceding this production.*

The Tempest[*]

NAMES OF THE ACTORS
ALONSO, *King of Naples*
SEBASTIAN, *his brother*
PROSPERO, *the right Duke of Milan*
ANTONIO, *his brother, the usurping Duke of Milan*
FERDINAND, *son to the King of Naples*
ADRIAN *and* ⎫
FRANCISCO,   ⎬ *lords*
CALIBAN, *a savage and deformed slave*

---

[*] Edited by David Bevington. Words or phrases followed by a degree symbol are explained at the foot of the page.

TRINCULO, *a jester*
STEPHANO, *a drunken butler*
MASTER *of a ship*
BOATSWAIN
MARINERS

MIRANDA, *daughter to Prospero*

ARIEL, *an airy spirit*
IRIS,
CERES,
JUNO,   *[presented by] spirits*
NYMPHS,
REAPERS,

[Other Spirits attending on PROSPERO*]*

THE SCENE: *An uninhabited island*

> ***1.1***   *A Tempestuous Noise of Thunder and Lightning Heard. Enter a*
> *Shipmaster and a Boatswain.*

MASTER. Boatswain!
BOATSWAIN. Here, Master. What cheer?
MASTER. Good,° speak to the mariners. Fall to 't yarely,° or we run our-
selves aground. Bestir, bestir!   *Exit.*
Enter Mariners.
BOATSWAIN. Heigh, my hearts! Cheerly, cheerly, my hearts! Yare, yare!   5
Take in the topsail. Tend° to the Master's whistle.—Blow° till thou
burst thy wind, if room enough!°
Enter ALONSO, SEBASTIAN, ANTONIO, FERDINAND, GONZALO, *and others.*
ALONSO. Good Boatswain, have care. Where's the Master? Play the
men.°
BOATSWAIN. I pray now, keep below.   10
ANTONIO. Where is the Master, Boatswain?
BOATSWAIN. Do you not hear him? You mar our labor. Keep° your cab-
ins! You do assist the storm.
GONZALO. Nay, good,° be patient.
BOATSWAIN. When the sea is. Hence! What cares these roarers° for the   15
name of king? To cabin! Silence! Trouble us not.
GONZALO. Good, yet remember whom thou hast aboard.
BOATSWAIN. None that I more love than myself. You are a councillor; if
you can command these elements to silence and work the peace of
the present,° we will not hand° a rope more. Use your authority. If   20

1.1 Location: On board ship, off the island's coast. 3 Good i.e., it's good
you've come, or, my good fellow.   **yarely** nimbly   **6 Tend** attend   **Blow** (Addressed to the wind.)   **7 if room enough** as long as we have sea room enough
8–9 Play the men act like men (?) ply, urge the men to exert themselves (?)
12 Keep remain in   **14 good** good fellow   **15 roarers** waves or winds, or both;
spoken to as though they were "bullies" or "blusterers"   **19–20 work . . . present**
bring calm to our present circumstances   **20 hand** handle

you cannot, give thanks you have lived so long and make yourself ready in your cabin for the mischance of the hour, if it so hap.° — Cheerly, good hearts!—Out of our way, I say.   *Exit.*

GONZALO. I have great comfort from this fellow. Methinks he hath no drowning mark upon him; his complexion is perfect gallows.°   25
Stand fast, good Fate, to his hanging! Make the rope of his destiny our cable, for our own doth little advantage.° If he be not born to be hanged, our case is miserable.°   *Exeunt [courtiers].*
Enter BOATSWAIN.

BOATSWAIN. Down with the topmast! Yare! Lower, lower! Bring her to try wi' the main course.° (*A cry within.*) A plague upon this howl-   30
ing! They are louder than the weather or our office.°
Enter SEBASTIAN, ANTONIO, *and* GONZALO.
Yet again? What do you here? Shall we give o'er° and drown? Have you a mind to sink?

SEBASTIAN. A pox o' your throat, you bawling, blasphemous, incharitable dog!   35

BOATSWAIN. Work you, then.

ANTONIO. Hang, cur! Hang, you whoreson, insolent noisemaker! We are less afraid to be drowned than thou art.

GONZALO. I'll warrant him for drowning,° though the ship were no stronger than a nutshell and as leaky as an unstanched° wench.   40

BOATSWAIN. Lay her ahold, ahold!° Set her two courses.° Off to sea again! Lay her off!
Enter MARINERS, *wet.*

MARINERS. All lost! To prayers, to prayers! All lost!
[*The* MARINERS *run about in confusion, exiting at random.*]

BOATSWAIN. What, must our mouths be cold?°

GONZALO. The King and Prince at prayers! Let's assist them, for our case   45
is as theirs.

SEBASTIAN. I am out of patience.

ANTONIO. We are merely° cheated of our lives by drunkards. This wide-chapped° rascal! Would thou mightst lie drowning the washing of ten tides!°   50

GONZALO. He'll be hanged yet, though every drop of water swear against it and gape at wid'st° to glut° him. (*A confused noise within:*)

---

22 hap happen   **25 complexion . . . gallows** appearance shows he was born to be hanged (and therefore, according to the proverb, in no danger of drowning) **27 our . . . advantage** our own cable is of little benefit   **28 case is miserable** circumstances are desperate   **29–30 Bring . . . course** sail her close to the wind by means of the mainsail   **31 our office** i.e., the noise we make at our work   **32 give o'er** give up   **39 warrant him for drowning** guarantee that he will never be drowned   **40 unstanched** insatiable, loose, unrestrained (suggesting also "incontinent" and "menstrual")   **41 ahold** ahull, close to the wind   **courses** sails, i.e., foresail as well as mainsail, set in an attempt to get the ship back out into open water   **44 must . . . cold** i.e., must we drown in the cold sea, or, let us heat up our mouths with liquor   **48 merely** utterly   **48–49 wide-chapped** with mouth wide open   **49–50 lie . . . tides** (Pirates were hanged on the shore and left until three tides had come in.)   **52 at wid'st** wide open   **glut** swallow

"Mercy on us!"—"We split,° we split!"—"Farewell my wife and
children!"—"Farewell, brother!"—"We split, we split, we split!"

[Exit BOATSWAIN.*]*

ANTONIO. Let's all sink wi' the King.   55
SEBASTIAN. Let's take leave of him.

Exit [with ANTONIO*].*

GONZALO. Now would I give a thousand furlongs of sea for an acre of
barren ground: long heath,° brown furze,° anything. The wills
above be done! But I would fain° die a dry death.   *Exit.*

1.2   *Enter* PROSPERO *[in his magic cloak] and* MIRANDA.

MIRANDA. If by your art,° my dearest father, you have
    Put the wild waters in this roar, allay° them.
    The sky, it seems, would pour down stinking pitch,
    But that the sea, mounting to th' welkin's cheek,°
    Dashes the fire out. O, I have suffered   5
    With those that I saw suffer! A brave° vessel,
    Who had, no doubt, some noble creature in her,
    Dashed all to pieces. O, the cry did knock
    Against my very heart! Poor souls, they perished.
    Had I been any god of power, I would   10
    Have sunk the sea within the earth or ere°
    It should the good ship so have swallowed and
    The freighting° souls within her.
PROSPERO.   Be collected.°
    No more amazement.° Tell your piteous° heart
    There's no harm done.
MIRANDA.   O, woe the day!
PROSPERO.   No harm.   15
    I have done nothing but° in care of thee,
    Of thee, my dear one, thee, my daughter, who
    Art ignorant of what thou art, naught knowing
    Of whence I am, nor that I am more better°
    Than Prospero, master of a full° poor cell,   20
    And thy no greater father.
MIRANDA.   More to know
    Did never meddle° with my thoughts.
PROSPERO.   'Tis time
    I should inform thee farther. Lend thy hand

---

53 split break apart   **58 heath** heather.   **furze** gorse, a weed growing on waste-
land   **59 fain** rather   **1.2 Location: The island, near Prospero's cell.** On the
Elizabethan stage, this cell is implicitly at hand throughout the play, although in
some scenes the convention of flexible distance allows us to imagine characters in
other parts of the island.   **1 art** magic   **2 allay** pacify   **4 welkin's cheek** sky's
face   **6 brave** gallant, splendid   **11 or ere** before   **13 freighting** forming the
cargo.   **collected** calm, composed   **14 amazement** consternation.   **piteous**
pitying   **16 but** except   **19 more better** of higher rank   **20 full** very   **22 med-
dle** mingle

And pluck my magic garment from me. So,
[laying down his magic cloak and staff]
Lie there, my art.—Wipe thou thine eyes. Have comfort.   25
The direful spectacle of the wreck,° which touched
The very virtue° of compassion in thee,
I have with such provision° in mine art
So safely ordered that there is no soul—
No, not so much perdition° as an hair   30
Betid° to any creature in the vessel
Which° thou heard'st cry, which thou saw'st sink. Sit down,
For thou must now know farther.

MIRANDA *[sitting]*.   You have often
Begun to tell me what I am, but stopped
And left me to a bootless inquisition,°   35
Concluding, "Stay, not yet."

PROSPERO.   The hour's now come;
The very minute bids thee ope thine ear.
Obey, and be attentive. Canst thou remember
A time before we came unto this cell?
I do not think thou canst, for then thou wast not   40
Out° three years old.

MIRANDA.   Certainly, sir, I can.

PROSPERO. By what? By any other house or person?
Of anything the image, tell me, that
Hath kept with thy remembrance.

MIRANDA.   'Tis far off,
And rather like a dream than an assurance   45
That my remembrance warrants.° Had I not
Four or five women once that tended me?

PROSPERO. Thou hadst, and more, Miranda. But how is it
That this lives in thy mind? What seest thou else
In the dark backward and abysm of time?°   50
If thou rememberest aught° ere thou cam'st here,
How thou cam'st here thou mayst.

MIRANDA.   But that I do not.

PROSPERO. Twelve year since, Miranda, twelve year since,
Thy father was the Duke of Milan and
A prince of power.

MIRANDA.   Sir, are not you my father?   55

PROSPERO. Thy mother was a piece° of virtue, and
She said thou wast my daughter; and thy father
Was Duke of Milan, and his only heir
And princess no worse issued.°

MIRANDA.   O the heavens!

---

26 wreck shipwreck   **27 virtue** essence   **28 provision** foresight   **30 perdition**
loss   **31 Betid** happened   **32 Which** whom   **35 bootless inquisition** profitless
inquiry   **41 Out** fully   **45–46 assurance . . . warrants** certainty that my memory
guarantees   **50 backward . . . time** abyss of the past   **51 aught** anything
56 piece masterpiece, exemplar   **59 no worse issued** no less nobly born,
descended

What foul play had we, that we came from thence?   60
Or blessèd was 't we did?

PROSPERO.   Both, both, my girl.
By foul play, as thou sayst, were we heaved thence,
But blessedly holp° hither.

MIRANDA.   O, my heart bleeds
To think o' the teen that I have turned you to,°
Which is from° my remembrance! Please you, farther.   65

PROSPERO. My brother and thy uncle, called Antonio—
I pray thee mark me—that a brother should
Be so perfidious!—he whom next° thyself
Of all the world I loved, and to him put
The manage° of my state, as at that time   70
Through all the seigniories° it was the first,
And Prospero the prime° duke, being so reputed
In dignity, and for the liberal arts
Without a parallel; those being all my study,
The government I cast upon my brother   75
And to my state grew stranger,° being transported°
And rapt in secret studies. Thy false uncle—
Dost thou attend me?

MIRANDA.   Sir, most heedfully.

PROSPERO. Being once perfected° how to grant suits,
How to deny them, who t' advance and who   80
To trash° for overtopping,° new created
The creatures° that were mine, I say, or changed 'em,
Or else new formed 'em;° having both the key°
Of officer and office, set all hearts i' the state
To what tune pleased his ear, that° now he was   85
The ivy which had hid my princely trunk
And sucked my verdure° out on 't.° Thou attend'st not.

MIRANDA. O, good sir, I do.

PROSPERO.   I pray thee, mark me.
I, thus neglecting worldly ends, all dedicated
To closeness° and the bettering of my mind   90
With that which, but by being so retired,
O'erprized all popular rate,° in my false brother

---

63 holp helped   **64 teen . . . to** trouble I've caused you to remember or put you to
65 from out of   **68 next** next to   **70 manage** management, administration
71 seigniories i.e., city-states of northern Italy   **72 prime** first in rank and importance   **76 to . . . stranger** i.e., withdrew from my responsibilities as duke. **trans-
ported** carried away   **79 perfected** grown skillful   **81 trash** check a hound by
tying a cord or weight to its neck. **overtopping** running too far ahead of the pack;
surmounting, exceeding one's authority   **82 creatures** dependents   **82–83 or
changed . . . formed 'em** i.e., either changed their loyalties and duties or else created new ones   **83 key** (1) key for unlocking (2) tool for tuning stringed instruments   **85 that** so that   **87 verdure** vitality. **on 't** of it   **90 closeness** retirement,
seclusion   **91–92 but . . . rate** i.e., were it not that its private nature caused me to
neglect my public responsibilities, had a value far beyond what public opinion
could appreciate, or, simply because it was done in such seclusion, had a value not
appreciated by popular opinion

Awaked an evil nature; and my trust,
Like a good parent,° did beget of° him
A falsehood in its contrary as great   95
As my trust was, which had indeed no limit,
A confidence sans° bound. He being thus lorded°
Not only with what my revenue yielded
But what my power might else° exact, like one
Who, having into° truth by telling of it,   100
Made such a sinner of his memory
To° credit his own lie,° he did believe
He was indeed the Duke, out o'° the substitution
And executing th' outward face of royalty°
With all prerogative. Hence his ambition growing—   105
Dost thou hear?
MIRANDA.   Your tale, sir, would cure deafness.
PROSPERO. To have no screen between this part he played
And him he played it for,° he needs will be°
Absolute Milan.° Me, poor man, my library
Was dukedom large enough. Of temporal royalties°   110
He thinks me now incapable; confederates°—
So dry° he was for sway°—wi' the King of Naples
To give him annual tribute, do him° homage,
Subject his coronet to his° crown, and bend°
The dukedom yet° unbowed—alas, poor Milan!—   115
To most ignoble stooping.
MIRANDA.   O the heavens!
PROSPERO. Mark his condition° and th' event,° then tell me
If this might be a brother.
MIRANDA.   I should sin
To think but° nobly of my grandmother.
Good wombs have borne bad sons.
PROSPERO.   Now the condition.   120
This King of Naples, being an enemy
To me inveterate, hearkens° my brother's suit,
Which was that he,° in lieu o' the premises°
Of homage and I know not how much tribute,

---

94 good parent (Alludes to the proverb that good parents often bear bad children;
see also line 120.)   **of** in   **97 sans** without.   **lorded** raised to lordship, with
power and wealth   **99 else** otherwise, additionally   **100 into** unto, against.
102 To so as to   **100–102 Who . . . lie** i.e., who, by repeatedly telling the lie (that
he was indeed Duke of Milan), made his memory such a confirmed sinner against
truth that he began to believe his own lie.   **103 out o'** as a result of   **104 And . . .
royalty** and (as a result of) his carrying out all the visible functions of royalty
107–108 To have . . . it for to have no separation or barrier between his role and
himself. (Antonio wanted to act in his own person, not as substitute.)   **108 needs
will be** insisted on becoming   **109 Absolute Milan** unconditional Duke of Milan
110 temporal royalties practical prerogatives and responsibilities of a sovereign
111 confederates conspires, allies himself   **112 dry** thirsty.   **sway** power
113 him i.e., the King of Naples   **114 his . . . his** Antonio's . . . the King of
Naples'   **bend** make bow down   **115 yet** hitherto   **117 condition** pact.
event outcome   **119 but** other than   **122 hearkens** listens to   **123 he** the King
of Naples   **in . . . premises** in return for the stipulation

Should presently extirpate° me and mine   125
Out of the dukedom and confer fair Milan,
With all the honors, on my brother. Whereon,
A treacherous army levied, one midnight
Fated to th' purpose did Antonio open
The gates of Milan, and, i' the dead of darkness,   130
The ministers for the purpose° hurried thence°
Me and thy crying self.

MIRANDA.   Alack, for pity!
I, not remembering how I cried out then,
Will cry it o'er again. It is a hint°
That wrings° mine eyes to 't.

PROSPERO.   Hear a little further,   135
And then I'll bring thee to the present business
Which now's upon 's, without the which this story
Were most impertinent.°

MIRANDA.   Wherefore° did they not
That hour destroy us?

PROSPERO.   Well demanded,° wench.°
My tale provokes that question. Dear, they durst not,   140
So dear the love my people bore me, nor set
A mark so bloody° on the business, but
With colors fairer° painted their foul ends.
In few,° they hurried us aboard a bark,°
Bore us some leagues to sea, where they prepared   145
A rotten carcass of a butt,° not rigged,
Nor tackle,° sail, nor mast; the very rats
Instinctively have quit° it. There they hoist us,
To cry to th' sea that roared to us, to sigh
To th' winds whose pity, sighing back again,   150
Did us but loving wrong.°

MIRANDA.   Alack, what trouble
Was I then to you!

PROSPERO.   O, a cherubin
Thou wast that did preserve me. Thou didst smile,
Infusèd with a fortitude from heaven,
When I have decked° the sea with drops full salt,   155
Under my burden groaned, which° raised in me
An undergoing stomach,° to bear up
Against what should ensue.

---

125 presently extirpate at once remove   **131 ministers ... purpose** agents employed to do this.   **thence** from there   **134 hint** occasion   **135 wrings** (1) con-
strains (2) wrings tears from   **138 impertinent** irrelevant.   **Wherefore** why
139 demanded asked.   **wench** (Here a term of endearment.)   **141–142 set ...
bloody** i.e., make obvious their murderous intent. (From the practice of marking
with the blood of the prey those who have participated in a successful hunt.)
143 fairer apparently more attractive   **144 few** few words.   **bark** ship
146 butt cask, tub   **147 Nor tackle** neither rigging   **148 quit** abandoned
151 Did ... wrong (i.e., the winds pitied Prospero and Miranda, though of necessity they blew them from shore)   **155 decked** covered (with salt tears); adorned
156 which i.e., the smile   **157 undergoing stomach** courage to go on

MIRANDA. How came we ashore?

PROSPERO. By Providence divine.   160
    Some food we had, and some fresh water, that
    A noble Neapolitan, Gonzalo,
    Out of his charity, who being then appointed
    Master of this design, did give us, with
    Rich garments, linens, stuffs,° and necessaries,   165
    Which since have steaded much.° So, of° his gentleness,
    Knowing I loved my books, he furnished me
    From mine own library with volumes that
    I prize above my dukedom.

MIRANDA.   Would° I might
    But ever° see that man!

PROSPERO.   Now I arise.   170
    [He puts on his magic cloak.]
    Sit still, and hear the last of our sea sorrow.°
    Here in this island we arrived; and here
    Have I, thy schoolmaster, made thee more profit°
    Than other princess'° can, that have more time
    For vainer° hours and tutors not so careful.   175

MIRANDA. Heavens thank you for 't! And now, I pray you, sir—
    For still 'tis beating in my mind—your reason
    For raising this sea storm?

PROSPERO.   Know thus far forth:
    By accident most strange, bountiful Fortune,
    Now my dear lady,° hath mine enemies   180
    Brought to this shore; and by my prescience
    I find my zenith° doth depend upon
    A most auspicious star, whose influence°
    If now I court not, but omit,° my fortunes
    Will ever after droop. Here cease more questions.   185
    Thou art inclined to sleep. 'Tis a good dullness,°
    And give it way.° I know thou canst not choose.
    [MIRANDA sleeps.]
    Come away,° servant, come! I am ready now.
    Approach, my Ariel, come.
    Enter ARIEL.

ARIEL. All hail, great master, grave sir, hail! I come   190
    To answer thy best pleasure; be 't to fly,
    To swim, to dive into the fire, to ride
    On the curled clouds, to thy strong bidding task°

---

165 stuffs supplies   **166 steaded much** been of much use.   **So, of** similarly, out
of   **169 Would** I wish   **170 But ever** i.e., someday   **171 sea sorrow** sorrowful
adventure at sea   **173 more profit** profit more   **174 princess'** princesses. (Or
the word may be *princes,* referring to royal children both male and female.)
175 vainer more foolishly spent   **180 my dear lady** (Refers to Fortune, not
Miranda.)   **182 zenith** height of fortune. (Astrological term.)   **183 influence**
astrological power   **184 omit** ignore   **186 dullness** drowsiness   **187 give it way**
let it happen (i.e., don't fight it)   **188 Come away** come   **193 task** make
demands upon

Ariel and all his quality.°
PROSPERO.   Hast thou, spirit,
Performed to point° the tempest that I bade thee?   195
ARIEL. To every article.
I boarded the King's ship. Now on the beak,°
Now in the waist,° the deck,° in every cabin,
I flamed amazement.° Sometimes I'd divide
And burn in many places; on the topmast,   200
The yards, and bowsprit would I flame distinctly,°
Then meet and join. Jove's lightning, the precursors
O' the dreadful thunderclaps, more momentary
And sight-outrunning° were not.° The fire and cracks
Of sulfurous roaring the most mighty Neptune°   205
Seem to besiege and make his bold waves tremble,
Yea, his dread trident shake.
PROSPERO.   My brave spirit!
Who was so firm, so constant, that this coil°
Would not infect his reason?
ARIEL.   Not a soul
But felt a fever of the mad° and played   210
Some tricks of desperation. All but mariners
Plunged in the foaming brine and quit the vessel,
Then all afire with me. The King's son, Ferdinand,
With hair up-staring° —then like reeds, not hair—
Was the first man that leapt; cried, "Hell is empty,   215
And all the devils are here!"
PROSPERO.   Why, that's my spirit!
But was not this nigh shore?
ARIEL.   Close by, my master.
PROSPERO. But are they, Ariel, safe?
ARIEL.   Not a hair perished.
On their sustaining garments° not a blemish,
But fresher than before; and, as thou bad'st° me,   220
In troops° I have dispersed them 'bout the isle.
The King's son have I landed by himself,
Whom I left cooling° of the air with sighs
In an odd angle° of the isle, and sitting,
His arms in this sad knot.° *[He folds his arms.]*
PROSPERO.   Of the King's ship,   225
The mariners, say how thou hast disposed,

---

194 quality (1) fellow spirits (2) abilities   **195 to point** to the smallest detail
197 beak prow   **198 waist** midships.   **deck** poop deck at the stern
199 flamed amazement struck terror in the guise of fire, i.e., Saint Elmo's fire
201 distinctly in different places   **204 sight-outrunning** swifter than sight.
were not could not have been   **205 Neptune** Roman god for the sea   **208 coil**
tumult   **210 of the mad** i.e., such as madmen feel   **214 up-staring** standing on
end   **219 sustaining garments** garments that buoyed them up in the sea
220 bad'st ordered   **221 troops** groups   **223 cooling of** cooling   **224 angle**
corner   **225 sad knot** (Folded arms are indicative of melancholy)

And all the rest o' the fleet.

ARIEL.   Safely in harbor
Is the King's ship; in the deep nook,° where once
Thou called'st me up at midnight to fetch dew°
From the still-vexed Bermudas,° there she's hid;   230
The mariners all under hatches stowed,
Who, with a charm joined to their suffered labor,°
I have left asleep. And for the rest o' the fleet,
Which I dispersed, they all have met again
And are upon the Mediterranean float°   235
Bound sadly home for Naples,
Supposing that they saw the King's ship wrecked
And his great person perish.

PROSPERO.   Ariel, thy charge
Exactly is performed. But there's more work.
What is the time o' the day?

ARIEL.   Past the mid season.°   240

PROSPERO. At least two glasses.° The time twixt six and now
Must by us both be spent most preciously.

ARIEL. Is there more toil? Since thou dost give me pains,°
Let me remember° thee what thou hast promised,
Which is not yet performed me.

PROSPERO.   How now? Moody?   245
What is 't thou canst demand?

ARIEL.   My liberty.

PROSPERO. Before the time be out? No more!

ARIEL.   I prithee,
Remember I have done thee worthy service,
Told thee no lies, made thee no mistakings, served
Without or grudge or grumblings. Thou did promise   250
To bate° me a full year.

PROSPERO.   Dost thou forget
From what a torment I did free thee?

ARIEL.   No.

PROSPERO. Thou dost, and think'st it much to tread the ooze
Of the salt deep,
To run upon the sharp wind of the north,   255
To do me° business in the veins° o' the earth
When it is baked° with frost.

ARIEL.   I do not, sir.

PROSPERO. Thou liest, malignant thing! Hast thou forgot

---

228 **nook** bay   229 **dew** (Collected at midnight for magical purposes; compare
with line 324.)   230 **still-vexed Bermudas** ever stormy Bermudas. (Perhaps refers
to the then recent Bermuda shipwreck; see play Introduction. The Folio text reads
"Bermoothes.")   232 **with . . . labor** by means of a spell added to all the labor they
have undergone   235 **float** sea   240 **mid season** noon   241 **glasses** hourglasses
243 **pains** labors   244 **remember** remind   251 **bate** remit, deduct   256 **do me**
do for me.   **veins** veins of minerals, or, underground streams, thought to be analogous to the veins of the human body   257 **baked** hardened

The foul witch Sycorax, who with age and envy°
Was grown into a hoop?° Hast thou forgot her?   260
ARIEL. No, sir.
PROSPERO. Thou hast. Where was she born? Speak. Tell me.
ARIEL. Sir, in Argier.°
PROSPERO.   O, was she so? I must
Once in a month recount what thou hast been,
Which thou forgett'st. This damned witch Sycorax,   265
For mischiefs manifold and sorceries terrible
To enter human hearing, from Argier,
Thou know'st, was banished. For one thing she did°
They would not take her life. Is not this true?
ARIEL. Ay, sir.   270
PROSPERO. This blue-eyed° hag was hither brought with child°
And here was left by the sailors. Thou, my slave,
As thou report'st thyself, was then her servant;
And, for° thou wast a spirit too delicate
To act her earthy and abhorred commands,   275
Refusing her grand hests,° she did confine thee,
By help of her more potent ministers
And in her most unmitigable rage,
Into a cloven pine, within which rift
Imprisoned thou didst painfully remain   280
A dozen years; within which space she died
And left thee there, where thou didst vent thy groans
As fast as mill wheels strike.° Then was this island—
Save° for the son that she did litter° here,
A freckled whelp,° hag-born°—not honored with   285
A human shape.
ARIEL.   Yes, Caliban her son.°
PROSPERO. Dull thing, I say so:° he, that Caliban
Whom now I keep in service. Thou best know'st
What torment I did find thee in. Thy groans
Did make wolves howl, and penetrate the breasts   290
Of ever-angry bears. It was a torment
To lay upon the damned, which Sycorax
Could not again undo. It was mine art,
When I arrived and heard thee, that made gape°
The pine and let thee out.
ARIEL.   I thank thee, master.   295

---

259 envy malice   **260 grown into a hoop** i.e., so bent over with age as to resemble a hoop   **263 Argier** Algiers   **268 one . . . did** (Perhaps a reference to her
pregnancy, for which her life would be spared.)   **271 blue-eyed** with dark circles
under the eyes or with blue eyelids, implying pregnancy.   **with child** pregnant
274 for because   **276 hests** commands   **283 as mill wheels strike** as the blades
of a mill wheel strike the water   **284 Save** except.   **litter** gave birth to
285 whelp offspring. (Used of animals.)   **hag-born** born of a female demon
286 Yes . . . son (Ariel is probably concurring with Prospero's comments about a
"freckled whelp," not contradicting the point about "A human shape.")   **287 Dull
. . . so** i.e., exactly, that's what I said, you dullard   **294 gape** open wide

PROSPERO. If thou more murmur'st, I will rend an oak
          And peg thee in his° knotty entrails till
          Thou hast howled away twelve winters.
ARIEL.   Pardon, master.
          I will be correspondent° to command
          And do my spriting° gently.°   300
PROSPERO. Do so, and after two days
          I will discharge thee.
ARIEL.   That's my noble master!
          What shall I do? Say what? What shall I do?
PROSPERO. Go make thyself like a nymph o' the sea. Be subject
          To no sight but thine and mine, invisible   305
          To every eyeball else. Go take this shape
          And hither come in 't. Go, hence with diligence!   *Exit [*ARIEL*].*
          Awake, dear heart, awake! Thou hast slept well.
          Awake!
MIRANDA.   The strangeness of your story put
          Heaviness° in me.
PROSPERO.   Shake it off. Come on,   310
          We'll visit Caliban, my slave, who never
          Yields us kind answer.
MIRANDA.   'Tis a villain, sir,
          I do not love to look on.
PROSPERO.   But, as 'tis,
          We cannot miss° him. He does make our fire,
          Fetch in our wood, and serves in offices°   315
          That profit us.—What ho! Slave! Caliban!
          Thou earth, thou! Speak.
CALIBAN (*within*).   There's wood enough within.
PROSPERO. Come forth, I say! There's other business for thee.
          Come, thou tortoise! When?°
          Enter ARIEL *like a water nymph.*
          Fine apparition! My quaint° Ariel,   320
          Hark in thine ear.   *[He whispers.]*
ARIEL.   My lord, it shall be done.   *Exit.*
PROSPERO. Thou poisonous slave, got° by the devil himself
          Upon thy wicked dam,° come forth!
          Enter CALIBAN.
CALIBAN. As wicked° dew as e'er my mother brushed
          With raven's feather from unwholesome fen°   325
          Drop on you both! A southwest° blow on ye
          And blister you all o'er!
PROSPERO. For this, be sure, tonight thou shalt have cramps,
          Side-stitches that shall pen thy breath up. Urchins°

297 his its   **299 correspondent** responsive, submissive   **300 spiriting** duties as
a spirit.   **gently** willingly, ungrudgingly   **310 Heaviness** drowsiness   **314 miss**
do without   **315 offices** functions, duties   **319 When** (An exclamation of impatience.)   **320 quaint** ingenious   **322 got** begotten, sired   **323 dam** mother.
(Used of animals.)   **324 wicked** mischievous, harmful   **325 fen** marsh, bog
326 southwest i.e., wind thought to bring disease   **329 Urchins** hedgehogs; here,
suggesting goblins in the guise of hedgehogs

Shall forth at vast° of night that they may work   330
All exercise on thee. Thou shalt be pinched
As thick as honeycomb,° each pinch more stinging
Than bees that made 'em.°

CALIBAN.   I must eat my dinner.
This island's mine, by Sycorax my mother,
Which thou tak'st from me. When thou cam'st first,   335
Thou strok'st me and made much of me, wouldst give me
Water with berries in 't, and teach me how
To name the bigger light, and how the less,°
That burn by day and night. And then I loved thee
And showed thee all the qualities o' th' isle,   340
The fresh springs, brine pits, barren place and fertile.
Cursed be I that did so! All the charms°
Of Sycorax, toads, beetles, bats, light on you!
For I am all the subjects that you have,
Which first was mine own king; and here you sty° me   345
In this hard rock, whiles you do keep from me
The rest o' th' island.

PROSPERO.   Thou most lying slave,
Whom stripes° may move, not kindness! I have used thee,
Filth as thou art, with humane° care, and lodged thee
In mine own cell, till thou didst seek to violate   350
The honor of my child.

CALIBAN. Oho, Oho! Would 't had been done!
Thou didst prevent me; I had peopled else°
This isle with Calibans.

MIRANDA.   Abhorrèd slave,
Which any print° of goodness wilt not take,   355
Being capable of all ill! I pitied thee,
Took pains to make thee speak, taught thee each hour
One thing or other. When thou didst not, savage,
Know thine own meaning, but wouldst gabble like
A thing most brutish, I endowed thy purposes°   360
With words that made them known. But thy vile race,°
Though thou didst learn, had that in 't which good natures
Could not abide to be with; therefore wast thou
Deservedly confined into this rock,
Who hadst deserved more than a prison.°   365

CALIBAN. You taught me language, and my profit on 't

---

330 **vast** lengthy, desolate time. (Malignant spirits were thought to be restricted to the hours of darkness.)   332 **As thick as honeycomb** i.e., all over, with as many pinches as a honeycomb has cells   333 **'em** i.e., the honeycomb   338 **the bigger ... less** i.e., the sun and the moon. (See Genesis 1:16: "God then made two great lights: the greater light to rule the day, and the less light to rule the night.") 342 **charms** spells   345 **sty** confine as in a sty   348 **stripes** lashes   349 **humane** (Not distinguished as a word from *human*.)   353 **peopled else** otherwise populated   354–365 **Abhorrèd ... prison** (Sometimes assigned by editors to Prospero.)   355 **print** imprint, impression   360 **purposes** meanings, desires 361 **race** natural disposition; species, nature

Is I know how to curse. The red plague° rid° you
For learning° me your language!

PROSPERO.   Hagseed,° hence!
Fetch us in fuel, and be quick, thou'rt best,°
To answer other business.° Shrugg'st thou, malice?   370
If thou neglect'st or dost unwillingly
What I command, I'll rack thee with old° cramps,
Fill all thy bones with aches,° make thee roar
That beasts shall tremble at thy din.

CALIBAN.   No, pray thee.
[Aside.] I must obey. His art is of such power   375
It would control my dam's god, Setebos,°
And make a vassal of him.

PROSPERO.   So, slave, hence!   *Exit* CALIBAN.
Enter FERDINAND; *and* ARIEL, *invisible,° playing and singing.* [FERDI-
NAND *does not see* PROSPERO *and* MIRANDA.]

ARIEL'*s Song.*

ARIEL. Come unto these yellow sands,
            And then take hands;
    Curtsied when you have,° and kissed   380
        The wild waves whist;°
Foot it featly° here and there,
        And, sweet sprites,° bear
    The burden.° Hark, hark!
        Burden, dispersedly° [within]. Bow-wow.   385
    The watchdogs bark.
        [Burden, dispersedly within.] Bow-wow.
Hark, hark! I hear
The strain of strutting chanticleer
        Cry Cock-a-diddle-dow.   390

FERDINAND. Where should this music be? I' th' air or th' earth?
    It sounds no more; and sure it waits upon°
    Some god o' th' island. Sitting on a bank,°
    Weeping again the King my father's wreck,
    This music crept by me upon the waters,   395
    Allaying both their fury and my passion°
    With its sweet air. Thence° I have followed it,
    Or it hath drawn me rather. But 'tis gone.

---

367 red plague plague characterized by red sores and evacuation of blood.
rid destroy   **368 learning** teaching.   **Hagseed** offspring of a female demon
369 thou'rt best you'd be well advised   **370 answer other business** perform
other tasks   **372 old** such as old people suffer, or, plenty of   **373 aches** (Pronounced "aitches.")   **376 Setebos** (A god of the Patagonians, named in Robert
Eden's *History of Travel*, 1577.)   **377 s.d. Ariel, invisible** (Ariel wears a garment
that by convention indicates he is invisible to the other characters.)   **380 Curtsied
. . . have** when you have curtsied   **380–381 kissed . . . whist** kissed the waves
into silence, or, kissed while the waves are being hushed   **382 Foot it featly** dance
nimbly   **383 sprites** spirits   **384 burden** refrain, undersong   **385 s.d. dispers-
edly** i.e., from all directions, not in unison   **392 waits upon** serves, attends
393 bank sandbank   **396 passion** grief   **397 Thence** i.e., from the bank on
which I sat

No, it begins again.

ARIEL's Song.

ARIEL. Full fathom five thy father lies.   400
    Of his bones are coral made.
    Those are pearls that were his eyes.
    Nothing of him that doth fade
    But doth suffer a sea change
    Into something rich and strange.   405
    Sea nymphs hourly ring his knell.°
    Burden [within]. Ding dong.
    Hark, now I hear them, ding dong bell.

FERDINAND. The ditty does remember° my drowned father.
  This is no mortal business, nor no sound   410
  That the earth owes.° I hear it now above me.

PROSPERO <i>[to</i> MIRANDA<i>].</i> The fringèd curtains of thine eye advance°
  And say what thou seest yond.

MIRANDA.   What is 't? A spirit?
  Lord, how it looks about! Believe me, sir,
  It carries a brave° form. But 'tis a spirit.   415

PROSPERO. No, wench, it eats and sleeps and hath such senses
  As we have, such. This gallant which thou seest
  Was in the wreck; and, but° he's something stained°
  With grief, that's beauty's canker,° thou mightst call him
  A goodly person. He hath lost his fellows   420
  And strays about to find 'em.

MIRANDA.   I might call him
  A thing divine, for nothing natural
  I ever saw so noble.

PROSPERO <i>[aside].</i>   It goes on,° I see,
  As my soul prompts it.—Spirit, fine spirit, I'll free thee
  Within two days for this.

FERDINAND <i>[seeing</i> MIRANDA<i>].</i> Most sure, the goddess   425
  On whom these airs° attend!—Vouchsafe° my prayer
  May know° if you remain° upon this island,
  And that you will some good instruction give
  How I may bear me° here. My prime° request,
  Which I do last pronounce, is—O you wonder!°—   430
  If you be maid or no?°

MIRANDA.   No wonder, sir,
  But certainly a maid.

FERDINAND.   My language? Heavens!

---

406 knell announcement of a death by the tolling of a bell   **409 remember** commemorate   **411 owes** owns   **412 advance** raise   **415 brave** excellent   **418 but** except that.   **something stained** somewhat disfigured   **419 canker** cankerworm (feeding on buds and leaves)   **423 It goes on** i.e., my plan works   **426 airs** songs. **Vouchsafe** grant   **427 May know** i.e., that I may know.   **remain** dwell   **429 bear me** conduct myself.   **prime** chief   **430 wonder** (Miranda's name means "to be wondered at.")   **431 maid or no** i.e., a human maiden as opposed to a goddess or married woman

I am the best° of them that speak this speech,
Were I but where 'tis spoken.

PROSPERO *[coming forward].*   How? The best?
What wert thou if the King of Naples heard thee?   435

FERDINAND.   A single° thing, as I am now, that wonders
To hear thee speak of Naples.° He does hear me,°
And that he does I weep.° Myself am Naples,
Who with mine eyes, never since at ebb,° beheld
The King my father wrecked.

MIRANDA.   Alack, for mercy!   440

FERDINAND.   Yes, faith, and all his lords, the Duke of Milan
And his brave son° being twain.

PROSPERO *[aside].*   The Duke of Milan
And his more braver° daughter could control° thee,
If now 'twere fit to do 't. At the first sight
They have changed eyes.° —Delicate Ariel,   445
I'll set thee free for this. *[To* FERDINAND.*]* A word, good sir.
I fear you have done yourself some wrong.° A word!

MIRANDA *[aside].*   Why speaks my father so ungently? This
Is the third man that e'er I saw, the first
That e'er I sighed for. Pity move my father   450
To be inclined my way!

FERDINAND.   O, if a virgin,
And your affection not gone forth, I'll make you
The Queen of Naples.

PROSPERO.   Soft, sir! One word more.
[Aside.] They are both in either's° pow'rs; but this swift business
I must uneasy° make, lest too light winning   455
Make the prize light.° *[To* FERDINAND.*]* One word more: I charge
    thee
That thou attend° me. Thou dost here usurp
The name thou ow'st° not, and hast put thyself
Upon this island as a spy, to win it
From me, the lord on 't.°

FERDINAND.   No, as I am a man.   460

MIRANDA.   There's nothing ill can dwell in such a temple.
If the ill spirit have so fair a house,
Good things will strive to dwell with 't.°

PROSPERO.   Follow me.—

---

433 best i.e., in birth   **436 single** (1) solitary, being at once King of Naples and
myself (2) feeble   **437, 438 Naples** the King of Naples   **437 He does hear me**
i.e., the King of Naples does hear my words, for I am King of Naples   **438 And . . .
weep** i.e., and I weep at this reminder that my father is seemingly dead, leaving me
heir   **439 at ebb** i.e., dry, not weeping   **442 son** (The only reference in the play
to a son of Antonio.)   **443 more braver** more splendid.   **control** refute
445 changed eyes exchanged amorous glances   **447 done . . . wrong** i.e., spoken falsely   **454 both in either's** each in the other's   **455 uneasy** difficult
455–456 light . . . light easy . . . cheap   **457 attend** follow, obey   **458 ow'st**
ownest   **460 on 't** of it   **463 strive . . . with 't** i.e., expel the evil and occupy the
temple, the body

Speak not you for him; he's a traitor.—Come,
I'll manacle thy neck and feet together.   465
Seawater shalt thou drink; thy food shall be
The fresh-brook mussels, withered roots, and husks
Wherein the acorn cradled. Follow.
FERDINAND.   No!
I will resist such entertainment° till
Mine enemy has more power.   470
He draws, and is charmed° from moving.
MIRANDA.   O dear father,
Make not too rash° a trial of him, for
He's gentle,° and not fearful.°
PROSPERO.   What, I say,
My foot° my tutor?—Put thy sword up, traitor,
Who mak'st a show but dar'st not strike, thy conscience
Is so possessed with guilt. Come, from thy ward,°   475
For I can here disarm thee with this stick
And make thy weapon drop. *[He brandishes his staff.]*
MIRANDA *[trying to hinder him].* Beseech you, father!
PROSPERO. Hence! Hang not on my garments.
MIRANDA.   Sir, have pity!
I'll be his surety.°
PROSPERO.   Silence! One word more
Shall make me chide thee, if not hate thee. What,   480
An advocate for an impostor? Hush!
Thou think'st there is no more such shapes as he,
Having seen but him and Caliban. Foolish wench,
To° the most of men this is a Caliban,
And they to him are angels.
MIRANDA.   My affections   485
Are then most humble; I have no ambition
To see a goodlier man.
PROSPERO *[to FERDINAND].* Come on, obey.
Thy nerves° are in their infancy again
And have no vigor in them.
FERDINAND.   So they are.
My spirits,° as in a dream, are all bound up.   490
My father's loss, the weakness which I feel,
The wreck of all my friends, nor this man's threats
To whom I am subdued, are but light° to me,
Might I but through my prison once a day
Behold this maid. All corners else° o' th' earth   495
Let liberty make use of; space enough
Have I in such a prison.

---

469 entertainment treatment   **470 s.d. charmed** magically prevented
471 rash harsh   **472 gentle** wellborn.   **fearful** frightening, dangerous, or perhaps, cowardly   **473 foot** subordinate. (Miranda, the foot, presumes to instruct
Prospero, the head.)   **475 ward** defensive posture (in fencing)   **479 surety** guarantee   **484 To** compared to   **488 nerves** sinews   **490 spirits** vital powers
493 light unimportant   **495 corners else** other corners, regions

PROSPERO *[aside]*. It works. *[To* FERDINAND.*]* Come on.—
    Thou hast done well, fine Ariel! *[To* FERDINAND.*]* Follow me.
    [To ARIEL.*]* Hark what thou else shalt do me.°
MIRANDA *[to* FERDINAND*]*   Be of comfort.
    My father's of a better nature, sir,   500
    Than he appears by speech. This is unwonted°
    Which now came from him.
PROSPERO *[to* ARIEL*]*.   Thou shalt be as free
    As mountain winds; but then° exactly do
    All points of my command.
ARIEL.   To th' syllable.
PROSPERO *[to* FERDINAND*]*. Come, follow. *[To* MIRANDA.*]* Speak not for
    him.   505

                                            Exeunt.

    2.1   *Enter* ALONSO, SEBASTIAN, ANTONIO, GONZALO, ADRIAN, FRANCISCO,
                      and others.

GONZALO *[to* ALONSO*]*. Beseech you, sir, be merry. You have cause,
    So have we all, of joy, for our escape
    Is much beyond our loss. Our hint° of woe
    Is common; every day some sailor's wife,
    The masters of some merchant, and the merchant,°   5
    Have just our theme of woe. But for the miracle,
    I mean our preservation, few in millions
    Can speak like us. Then wisely, good sir, weigh
    Our sorrow with° our comfort.
ALONSO.   Prithee, peace.
SEBASTIAN *[aside to* ANTONIO*]*. He receives comfort like cold porridge.°   10
ANTONIO *[aside to* SEBASTIAN*]*. The visitor° will not give him o'er° so.
SEBASTIAN. Look, he's winding up the watch of his wit; by and by it will
    strike.
GONZALO *[to* ALONSO*]*. Sir—
SEBASTIAN *[aside to* ANTONIO*]*. One. Tell.°   15
GONZALO. When every grief is entertained that's offered, comes to th'
    entertainer°—
SEBASTIAN. A dollar.°
GONZALO. Dolor comes to him, indeed. You have spoken truer than you
    purposed.   20
SEBASTIAN. You have taken it wiselier than I meant you should.

---

499 me for me   **501 unwonted** unusual   **503 then** until then, or, if that is to be
so **2.1 Location: Another part of the island.**   **3 hint** occasion   **5 masters . . .
the merchant** officers of some merchant vessel and the merchant himself, the
owner   **9 with** against   **10 porridge** (punningly suggested by *peace,* i.e., "peas"
or "pease," a common ingredient of porridge)   **11 visitor** one taking nourishment
and comfort to the sick, as Gonzalo is doing   **11 give him o'er** abandon him
15 Tell keep count   **16–17 When . . . entertainer** when every sorrow that presents itself is accepted without resistance, there comes to the recipient   **18 dollar**
widely circulated coin, the German thaler and the Spanish piece of eight (Sebastian
puns on *entertainer* in the sense of innkeeper; to Gonzalo, *dollar* suggests "dolor,"
grief)

GONZALO *[to* ALONSO*].* Therefore, my lord—
ANTONIO. Fie, what a spendthrift is he of his tongue!
ALONSO *[to* GONZALO*].* I prithee, spare.°
GONZALO. Well, I have done. But yet—   25
SEBASTIAN *[aside to* ANTONIO*].* He will be talking.
ANTONIO *[aside to* SEBASTIAN*].* Which, of he or Adrian, for a good wager,
    first begins to crow?°
SEBASTIAN. The old cock.°
ANTONIO. The cockerel.°   30
SEBASTIAN. Done. The wager?
ANTONIO. A laughter.°
SEBASTIAN. A match!°
ADRIAN. Though this island seem to be desert°—
ANTONIO. Ha, ha, ha!   35
SEBASTIAN. So, you're paid.°
ADRIAN. Uninhabitable and almost inaccessible—
SEBASTIAN. Yet—
ADRIAN. Yet—
ANTONIO. He could not miss 't.°   40
ADRIAN. It must needs be° of subtle, tender, and delicate temperance.°
ANTONIO. Temperance° was a delicate° wench.
SEBASTIAN. Ay, and a subtle,° as he most learnedly delivered.°
ADRIAN. The air breathes upon us here most sweetly.
SEBASTIAN. As if it had lungs, and rotten ones.   45
ANTONIO. Or as 'twere perfumed by a fen.
GONZALO. Here is everything advantageous to life.
ANTONIO. True, save° means to live.
SEBASTIAN. Of that there's none, or little.
GONZALO. How lush and lusty° the grass looks! How green!   50
ANTONIO. The ground indeed is tawny.°
SEBASTIAN. With an eye° of green in 't.

---

24 spare forbear, cease   **27–28 Which . . . crow** which of the two, Gonzalo or
Adrian, do you bet will speak (crow) first?   **29 old cock** i.e., Gonzalo   **30 cock-
erel** i.e., Adrian   **32 laughter** (1) burst of laughter (2) sitting of eggs. (When
Adrian, the *cockerel,* begins to speak two lines later, Sebastian loses the bet. The
Folio speech prefixes in lines 35–36 are here reversed so that Antonio enjoys his
laugh as the prize for winning, as in the proverb "He who laughs last laughs best" or
"He laughs that wins." The Folio assignment can work in the theater, however, if Sebastian pays for losing with a sardonic laugh of concession.)   **33 A match** a bargain; agreed   **34 desert** uninhabited   **36 you're paid** i.e., you've had your laugh
40 miss 't (1) avoid saying "Yet" (2) miss the island   **41 must needs be** has to be
temperance mildness of climate   **42 Temperance** a girl's name.   **delicate** (Here
it means "given to pleasure, voluptuous"; in line 44, "pleasant." Antonio is evidently
suggesting that *tender, and delicate temperance* sounds like a Puritan phrase,
which Antonio then mocks by applying the words to a woman rather than an island.
He began this bawdy comparison with a double entendre on *inaccessible,* line 37.)
43 subtle (Here it means "tricky, sexually crafty"; in line 41, "delicate.")   **delivered** uttered. (Sebastian joins Antonio in baiting the Puritans with his use of the
pious cant phrase *learnedly delivered.*)   **48 save** except   **50 lusty** healthy
51 tawny dull brown, yellowish   **52 eye** tinge, or spot (perhaps with reference to
Gonzalo's eye or judgment)

ANTONIO. He misses not much.

SEBASTIAN. No. He doth but° mistake the truth totally.

GONZALO. But the rarity of it is—which is indeed almost beyond   55
credit—

SEBASTIAN. As many vouched rarities° are.

GONZALO. That our garments, being, as they were, drenched in the sea,
hold notwithstanding their freshness and glosses, being rather
new-dyed than stained with salt water.   60

ANTONIO. If but one of his pockets° could speak, would it not say he
lies?

SEBASTIAN. Ay, or very falsely pocket up° his report.°

GONZALO. Methinks our garments are now as fresh as when we put
them on first in Afric, at the marriage of the King's fair daughter   65
Claribel to the King of Tunis.

SEBASTIAN. 'Twas a sweet marriage, and we prosper well in our return.

ADRIAN. Tunis was never graced before with such a paragon to° their
queen.

GONZALO. Not since widow Dido's° time.   70

ANTONIO *[aside to* SEBASTIAN*]*. Widow? A pox o' that! How came that
"widow" in? Widow Dido!

SEBASTIAN. What if he had said "widower Aeneas" too? Good Lord, how
you take° it!

ADRIAN *[to* GONZALO*]*. "Widow Dido" said you? You make me study of°   75
that. She was of Carthage, not of Tunis.

GONZALO. This Tunis, sir, was Carthage.

ADRIAN. Carthage?

GONZALO. I assure you, Carthage.

ANTONIO. His word is more than the miraculous harp.°   80

SEBASTIAN. He hath raised the wall, and houses too.

ANTONIO. What impossible matter will he make easy next?

SEBASTIAN. I think he will carry this island home in his pocket and give it
his son for an apple.

ANTONIO. And, sowing the kernels° of it in the sea, bring forth more   85
islands.

GONZALO. Ay.°

---

54 but merely   **57 vouched rarities** allegedly real though strange sights
61 pockets i.e., because they are muddy   **63 pocket up** i.e., conceal, suppress;
often used in the sense of "receive unprotestingly, fail to respond to a challenge."
his report (Sebastian's jest is that the evidence of Gonzalo's soggy and sea-stained
pockets would confute Gonzalo's speech and his reputation for truth telling.)
68 to for   **70 widow Dido** Queen of Carthage, deserted by Aeneas. (She was, in
fact, a widow when Aeneas, a widower, met her, but Antonio may be amused at
Gonzalo's prudish use of the term "widow" to describe a woman deserted by her
lover.)   **74 take** understand, respond to, interpret   **75 study of** think about
80 miraculous harp (Alludes to Amphion's harp, with which he raised the walls of
Thebes; Gonzalo has exceeded that deed by recreating ancient Carthage—*wall and
houses*—mistakenly on the site of modern-day Tunis. Some Renaissance commentators believed, like Gonzalo, that the two sites were near each other.)   **85 kernels**
seeds   **87 Ay** (Gonzalo may be reasserting his point about Carthage, or he may be
responding ironically to Antonio, who, in turn, answers sarcastically)

ANTONIO. Why, in good time.°

GONZALO *[to* ALONSO*]*. Sir, we were talking° that our garments seem now
    as fresh as when we were at Tunis at the marriage of your daugh-   90
    ter, who is now queen.

ANTONIO. And the rarest° that e'er came there.

SEBASTIAN. Bate,° I beseech you, widow Dido.

ANTONIO. O, widow Dido? Ay, widow Dido.

GONZALO. Is not, sir, my doublet° as fresh as the first day I wore it? I   95
    mean, in a sort.°

ANTONIO. That "sort"° was well fished for.

GONZALO. When I wore it at your daughter's marriage.

ALONSO. You cram these words into mine ears against
    The stomach of my sense.° Would I had never   100
    Married° my daughter there! For, coming thence,
    My son is lost and, in my rate,° she too,
    Who is so far from Italy removed
    I ne'er again shall see her. O thou mine heir
    Of Naples and of Milan, what strange fish   105
    Hath made his meal on thee?

FRANCISCO.   Sir, he may live.
    I saw him beat the surges° under him
    And ride upon their backs. He trod the water,
    Whose enmity he flung aside, and breasted
    The surge most swoll'n that met him. His bold head   110
    'Bove the contentious waves he kept, and oared
    Himself with his good arms in lusty° stroke
    To th' shore, that o'er his° wave-worn basis bowed,°
    As° stooping to relieve him. I not doubt
    He came alive to land.

ALONSO.   No, no, he's gone.   115

SEBASTIAN *[to* ALONSO*]*. Sir, you may thank yourself for this great loss,
    That° would not bless our Europe with your daughter,
    But rather° loose° her to an African,
    Where she at least is banished from your eye,°
    Who hath cause to wet the grief on 't.°

ALONSO.   Prithee, peace.   120

---

88 in good time (An expression of ironical acquiescence or amazement, i.e., "sure,
right away.")   **89 talking** saying   **92 rarest** most remarkable, beautiful   **93 Bate**
abate, except, leave out. (Sebastian says sardonically, surely you should allow
widow Dido to be an exception.)   **95 doublet** close-fitting jacket   **96 in a sort** in
a way   **97 sort** (Antonio plays on the idea of drawing lots and on "fishing" for
something to say.)   **100 The stomach . . . sense** my appetite for hearing them
101 Married given in marriage   **102 rate** estimation, opinion   **107 surges** waves
112 lusty vigorous   **113 his** its   **that . . . bowed** i.e., that projected out over the
base of the cliff that had been eroded by the surf, thus seeming to bend down
toward the sea.   **114 As** as if   **117 That** you who   **118 rather** would rather.
loose (1) release, let loose (2) lose   **119 is banished from your eye** is not constantly before your eye to serve as a reproachful reminder of what you have done
120 Who . . . on 't i.e., your eye, which has good reason to weep because of this,
or, Claribel, who has good reason to weep for it

SEBASTIAN. You were kneeled to and importuned° otherwise
    By all of us, and the fair soul herself
    Weighed between loathness and obedience at
    Which end o' the beam should bow.° We have lost your son,
    I fear, forever. Milan and Naples have   125
    More widows in them of this business' making°
    Than we bring men to comfort them.
    The fault's your own.
ALONSO. So is the dear'st° o' the loss.
GONZALO. My lord Sebastian,   130
    The truth you speak doth lack some gentleness
    And time° to speak it in. You rub the sore
    When you should bring the plaster.°
SEBASTIAN.   Very well.
ANTONIO. And most chirurgeonly.°
GONZALO *[to ALONSO]*. It is foul weather in us all, good sir,   135
    When you are cloudy.
SEBASTIAN *[to ANTONIO]*. Fowl° weather?
ANTONIO *[to SEBASTIAN]*.   Very foul.
GONZALO. Had I plantation° of this isle, my lord—
ANTONIO *[to SEBASTIAN]*. He'd sow 't with nettle seed.
SEBASTIAN.   Or docks, or mallows.°
GONZALO. And were the king on 't, what would I do?
SEBASTIAN. Scape° being drunk for want° of wine.   140
GONZALO. I' the commonwealth I would by contraries°
    Execute all things; for no kind of traffic°
    Would I admit; no name of magistrate;
    Letters° should not be known; riches, poverty,
    And use of service,° none; contract, succession,°   145
    Bourn, bound of land, tilth,° vineyard, none;
    No use of metal, corn,° or wine, or oil;
    No occupation; all men idle, all,
    And women too, but innocent and pure;
    No sovereignty—
SEBASTIAN.   Yet he would be king on 't.   150

---

121 importuned urged, implored   **122–124 the fair . . . bow** Claribel herself was
poised uncertainly between unwillingness to marry and obedience to her father as
to which end of the scales should sink, which should prevail   **126 of . . . making**
on account of this marriage and subsequent shipwreck   **129 dear'st** heaviest, most
costly   **132 time** appropriate time   **133 plaster** (A medical application.)
134 chirurgeonly like a skilled surgeon. (Antonio mocks Gonzalo's medical analogy of a *plaster* applied curatively to a wound.)   **136 Fowl** (with a pun on *foul,* returning to the imagery of lines 135–36)   **137 plantation** colonization (with subsequent wordplay on the literal meaning, "planting")   **138 docks, mallows** (Weeds
used as antidotes for nettle stings.)   **140 Scape** escape.   **want** lack. (Sebastian
jokes sarcastically that this hypothetical ruler would be saved from dissipation only
by the barrenness of the island.)   **141 by contraries** by what is directly opposite
to usual custom   **142 traffic** trade   **144 Letters** learning   **145 use of service**
custom of employing servants.   **succession** holding of property by right of inheritance   **146 Bourn . . . tilth** boundaries, property limits, tillage of soil   **147 corn**
grain

ANTONIO. The latter end of his commonwealth forgets the beginning.
GONZALO. All things in common nature should produce
　　Without sweat or endeavor. Treason, felony,
　　Sword, pike,° knife, gun, or need of any engine°
　　Would I not have; but nature should bring forth,   155
　　Of its own kind, all foison,° all abundance,
　　To feed my innocent people.
SEBASTIAN. No marrying 'mong his subjects?
ANTONIO. None, man, all idle—whores and knaves.
GONZALO. I would with such perfection govern, sir,   160
　　T' excel the Golden Age.°
SEBASTIAN.   'Save° His Majesty!
ANTONIO. Long live Gonzalo!
GONZALO.   And—do you mark me, sir?
ALONSO. Prithee, no more. Thou dost talk nothing to me.
GONZALO. I do well believe Your Highness, and did it to minister occa-
　　sion° to these gentlemen, who are of such sensible° and nimble   165
　　lungs that they always use° to laugh at nothing.
ANTONIO. 'Twas you we laughed at.
GONZALO. Who in this kind of merry fooling am nothing to you; so you
　　may continue, and laugh at nothing still.
ANTONIO. What a blow was there given!   170
SEBASTIAN. An° it had not fallen flat-long.°
GONZALO. You are gentlemen of brave mettle;° you would lift the moon
　　out of her sphere° if she would continue in it five weeks without
　　changing.
　　Enter ARIEL *[invisible] playing solemn music.*
SEBASTIAN. We would so, and then go a-batfowling.°   175
ANTONIO. Nay, good my lord, be not angry.
GONZALO. No, I warrant you, I will not adventure my discretion so
　　weakly.° Will you laugh me asleep? For I am very heavy.°
ANTONIO. Go sleep, and hear us.°
　　[All sleep except ALONSO, SEBASTIAN, *and* ANTONIO.*]*
ALONSO. What, all so soon asleep? I wish mine eyes   180
　　Would, with themselves, shut up my thoughts.° I find

---

154 pike lance.　**engine** instrument of warfare　**156 foison** plenty　**161 the
Golden Age** the age, according to Hesiod, when Cronus, or Saturn, ruled the world;
an age of innocence and abundance. **'Save** God save　**164–165 minister occasion** furnish opportunity　**sensible** sensitive.　**166 use** are accustomed　**171 An**
if.　**flat-long** with the flat of the sword, i.e., ineffectually. (Compare with "fallen
flat.")　**172 mettle** temperament, courage. (The sense of *metal,* indistinguishable
as a form from *mettle,* continues the metaphor of the sword.)　**173 sphere** orbit.
(Literally, one of the concentric zones occupied by planets in Ptolemaic astronomy.)
175 a-batfowling hunting birds at night with lantern and *bat,* or "stick"; also,
gulling a simpleton. (Gonzalo is the simpleton, or fowl, and Sebastian will use the
moon as his lantern.)　**177–178 adventure . . . weakly** risk my reputation for discretion for so trivial a cause (by getting angry at these sarcastic fellows)
178 heavy sleepy　**179 Go . . . us** i.e., get ready for sleep, and we'll do our part by
laughing　**181 Would . . . thoughts** would shut off my melancholy brooding when
they close themselves in sleep

They are inclined to do so.

SEBASTIAN.   Please you, sir,
Do not omit° the heavy° offer of it.
It seldom visits sorrow; when it doth,
It is a comforter.

ANTONIO.   We two, my lord,   185
Will guard your person while you take your rest,
And watch your safety.

ALONSO.   Thank you. Wondrous heavy.

                              [ALONSO sleeps. Exit ARIEL.]

SEBASTIAN. What a strange drowsiness possesses them!

ANTONIO. It is the quality o' the climate.

SEBASTIAN.   Why
Doth it not then our eyelids sink? I find not   190
Myself disposed to sleep.

ANTONIO.   Nor I. My spirits are nimble.
They° fell together all, as by consent;°
They dropped, as by a thunderstroke. What might,
Worthy Sebastian, O, what might—? No more.
And yet methinks I see it in thy face,   195
What thou shouldst be. Th' occasion speaks thee,° and
My strong imagination sees a crown
Dropping upon thy head.

SEBASTIAN.   What, art thou waking?

ANTONIO. Do you not hear me speak?

SEBASTIAN.   I do, and surely
It is a sleepy° language, and thou speak'st   200
Out of thy sleep. What is it thou didst say?
This is a strange repose, to be asleep
With eyes wide open—standing, speaking, moving—
And yet so fast asleep.

ANTONIO.   Noble Sebastian,
Thou lett'st thy fortune sleep—die, rather; wink'st°   205
Whiles thou art waking.

SEBASTIAN.   Thou dost snore distinctly;°
There's meaning in thy snores.

ANTONIO. I am more serious than my custom. You
Must be so too if heed° me, which to do
Trebles thee o'er.°

SEBASTIAN.   Well, I am standing water.°   210

ANTONIO. I'll teach you how to flow.

SEBASTIAN.   Do so. To ebb°

---

183 omit neglect. **heavy** drowsy **192 They** the sleepers. **consent** common
agreement   **197 occasion speaks thee** opportunity of the moment calls upon
you, i.e., proclaims you usurper of Alonso's crown   **200 sleepy** dreamlike, fantastic **205 wink'st** (you) shut your eyes **206 distinctly** articulately **209 if heed** if
you heed **210 Trebles thee o'er** makes you three times as great and rich.
standing water water that neither ebbs nor flows, at a standstill **211 ebb** recede,
decline

Hereditary sloth° instructs me.
ANTONIO.   O,
If you but knew how you the purpose cherish
Whiles thus you mock it!° How, in stripping it,
You more invest° it!° Ebbing men, indeed,   215
Most often do so near the bottom° run
By their own fear or sloth.
SEBASTIAN.   Prithee, say on.
The setting° of thine eye and cheek proclaim
A matter° from thee, and a birth indeed
Which throes° thee much to yield.°
ANTONIO.   Thus, sir: 220
Although this lord° of weak remembrance,° this
Who shall be of as little memory
When he is earthed,° hath here almost persuaded—
For he's a spirit of persuasion, only
Professes to persuade°—the King his son's alive,   225
'Tis as impossible that he's undrowned
As he that sleeps here swims.
SEBASTIAN.   I have no hope
That he's undrowned.
ANTONIO.   O, out of that "no hope"
What great hope have you! No hope that way° is
Another way so high a hope that even   230
Ambition cannot pierce a wink° beyond,
But doubt discovery there.° Will you grant with me
That Ferdinand is drowned?
SEBASTIAN.   He's gone.
ANTONIO.   Then tell me,
Who's the next heir of Naples?
SEBASTIAN.   Claribel.
ANTONIO. She that is Queen of Tunis; she that dwells   235
Ten leagues beyond man's life;° she that from Naples

212 **Hereditary sloth** natural laziness and the position of younger brother, one who cannot inherit   214 **If . . . mock it** if you only knew how much you really enhance the value of ambition even while your words mock your purpose   215 **invest** clothe. (Antonio's paradox is that, by skeptically stripping away illusions, Sebastian can see the essence of a situation and the opportunity it presents or that, by disclaiming and deriding his purpose, Sebastian shows how valuable it really is.) 214–215 **How . . . invest it** i.e., how the more you speak flippantly of ambition, the more you, in effect, affirm it.   216 **the bottom** i.e., on which unadventurous men may go aground and miss the tide of fortune   218 **setting** set expression (of earnestness)   219 **matter** matter of importance   220 **throes** causes pain, as in giving birth.   **yield** give forth, speak about   221 **this lord** i.e., Gonzalo. **remembrance** (1) power of remembering (2) being remembered after his death 223 **earthed** buried   224–225 **only . . . persuade** whose whole function (as a privy councillor) is to persuade   229 **that way** i.e., in regard to Ferdinand's being saved   231 **wink** glimpse   231–232 **Ambition . . . there** i.e., ambition itself cannot see any further than that hope (of the crown), is unsure of finding anything to achieve beyond it or even there.   236 **Ten . . . life** i.e., further than the journey of a lifetime

Can have no note,° unless the sun were post°—
The Man i' the Moon's too slow—till newborn chins
Be rough and razorable;° she that from° whom
We all were sea-swallowed, though some cast° again,   240
And by that destiny to perform an act
Whereof what's past is prologue, what to come
In yours and my discharge.°

SEBASTIAN. What stuff is this? How say you?
    'Tis true my brother's daughter's Queen of Tunis,   245
    So is she heir of Naples, twixt which regions
    There is some space.

ANTONIO.   A space whose every cubit°
    Seems to cry out, "How shall that Claribel
    Measure us° back to Naples? Keep° in Tunis,
    And let Sebastian wake."° Say this were death   250
    That now hath seized them, why, they were no worse
    Than now they are. There be° that can rule Naples
    As well as he that sleeps, lords that can prate°
    As amply and unnecessarily
    As this Gonzalo. I myself could make   255
    A chough of as deep chat.° O, that you bore
    The mind that I do! What a sleep were this
    For your advancement! Do you understand me?

SEBASTIAN. Methinks I do.

ANTONIO.   And how does your content°
    Tender° your own good fortune?

SEBASTIAN.   I remember   260
    You did supplant your brother Prospero.

ANTONIO.   True.
    And look how well my garments sit upon me,
    Much feater° than before. My brother's servants
    Were then my fellows. Now they are my men.

SEBASTIAN. But, for your conscience?   265

ANTONIO. Ay, sir, where lies that? If 'twere a kibe,°
    'Twould put me to° my slipper; but I feel not
    This deity in my bosom. Twenty consciences
    That stand twixt me and Milan,° candied° be they°
    And melt ere they molest!° Here lies your brother,   270
    No better than the earth he lies upon,

---

237 note news, intimation.   **post** messenger   **239 razorable** ready for shaving.
from on our voyage from   **240 cast** were disgorged (with a pun on *casting* of
parts for a play)   **243 discharge** performance   **247 cubit** ancient measure of
length of about twenty inches   **249 Measure us** i.e., traverse the cubits, find her
way.   **Keep** stay. (Addressed to Claribel.)   **250 wake** i.e., to his good fortune
252 There be there are those   **253 prate** speak foolishly   **255–256 I . . . chat** I
could teach a jackdaw to talk as wisely, or, be such a garrulous talker myself
259 content desire, inclination   **260 Tender** regard, look after   **263 feater** more
becomingly, fittingly   **266 kibe** chilblain, here a sore on the heel   **267 put me to**
oblige me to wear   **269 Milan** the dukedom of Milan.   **candied** frozen, con-
gealed in crystalline form   **be they** may they be   **270 molest** interfere

If he were that which now he's like—that's dead,
Whom I, with this obedient steel, three inches of it,
Can lay to bed forever; whiles you, doing thus,°
To the perpetual wink° for aye° might put   275
This ancient morsel, this Sir Prudence, who
Should not° upbraid our course. For all the rest,
They'll take suggestion° as a cat laps milk
They'll tell the clock° to any business that
We say befits the hour.

SEBASTIAN.   Thy case, dear friend,   280
Shall be my precedent. As thou gott'st Milan,
I'll come by Naples. Draw thy sword. One stroke
Shall free thee from the tribute° which thou payest,
And I the king shall love thee.

ANTONIO.   Draw together;
And when I rear my hand, do you the like   285
To fall it° on Gonzalo.   *[They draw.]*

SEBASTIAN.   O, but one word.
                                               [They talk apart.]

Enter ARIEL *[invisible], with music and song.*

ARIEL *[to* GONZALO*]*. My master through his art foresees the danger
That you, his friend, are in, and sends me forth—
For else his project dies—to keep them living.
                                   Sings in GONZALO's *ear.*
        While you here do snoring lie,   290
        Open-eyed conspiracy
              His time° doth take.
        If of life you keep a care,
        Shake off slumber, and beware.
              Awake, awake!   295

ANTONIO. Then let us both be sudden.°

GONZALO *[waking]*. Now, good angels preserve the King!
                                   [The others wake.]

ALONSO. Why, how now, ho, awake? Why are you drawn?
    Wherefore this ghastly looking?

GONZALO.   What's the matter?

SEBASTIAN. Whiles we stood here securing° your repose,   300
    Even now, we heard a hollow burst of bellowing
    Like bulls, or rather lions. Did 't not wake you?
    It struck mine ear most terribly.

ALONSO.   I heard nothing.

ANTONIO. O, 'twas a din to fright a monster's ear,
    To make an earthquake! Sure it was the roar   305
    Of a whole herd of lions.

---

274 thus similarly. (The actor makes a stabbing gesture.)   **275 wink** sleep, closing
of eyes   **aye** ever   **277 Should not** would not then be able to   **278 take**
suggestion respond to prompting   **279 tell the clock** i.e., agree, answer
appropriately, chime   **283 tribute** (See 1.2.113–124.)   **286 fall it** let it fall
292 time opportunity   **296 sudden** quick   **300 securing** standing guard over

ALONSO. Heard you this, Gonzalo?
GONZALO. Upon mine honor, sir, I heard a humming,
    And that a strange one too, which did awake me.
    I shaked you, sir, and cried.° As mine eyes opened,   310
    I saw their weapons drawn. There was a noise,
    That's verily.° 'Tis best we stand upon our guard,
    Or that we quit this place. Let's draw our weapons.
ALONSO. Lead off this ground, and let's make further search
    For my poor son.
GONZALO.   Heavens keep him from these beasts!   315
    For he is, sure, i' th' island.
ALONSO.   Lead away.
ARIEL *[aside]*. Prospero my lord shall know what I have done.
    So, King, go safely on to seek thy son.

                                        Exeunt [separately].

2.2 *Enter* CALIBAN *With a Burden of Wood. A Noise of Thunder Heard.*

CALIBAN. All the infections that the sun sucks up
    From bogs, fens, flats,° on Prosper fall, and make him
    By inchmeal° a disease! His spirits hear me,
    And yet I needs must° curse. But they'll nor° pinch,
    Fright me with urchin shows,° pitch me i' the mire,   5
    Nor lead me, like a firebrand,° in the dark
    Out of my way, unless he bid 'em. But
    For every trifle are they set upon me,
    Sometimes like apes, that mow° and chatter at me
    And after bite me; then like hedgehogs, which   10
    Lie tumbling in my barefoot way and mount
    Their pricks at my footfall. Sometimes am I
    All wound with° adders, who with cloven tongues
    Do hiss me into madness.
    Enter TRINCULO.
                        Lo, now, lo!
    Here comes a spirit of his, and to torment me   15
    For bringing wood in slowly. I'll fall flat.
    Perchance he will not mind° me.   *[He lies down.]*
TRINCULO. Here's neither bush nor shrub to bear off° any weather at all.
    And another storm brewing; I hear it sing i' the wind. Yond same
    black cloud, yond huge one, looks like a foul bombard° that would   20
    shed his° liquor. If it should thunder as it did before, I know not
    where to hide my head. Yond same cloud cannot choose but fall by
    pailfuls. *[Seeing* CALIBAN.*]* What have we here, a man or a fish? Dead
    or alive? A fish, he smells like a fish; a very ancient and fishlike

---

310 **cried** called out   312 **verily** true   **2.2 Location: Another part of the island.**   2 **flats** swamps   3 **By inchmeal** inch by inch   4 **needs must** have to.
nor neither   5 **urchin shows** elvish apparitions shaped like hedgehogs   6 **like a
firebrand** they in the guise of a will-o'-the-wisp   9 **mow** make faces   13 **wound
with** entwined by   17 **mind** notice   18 **bear off** keep off   20 **foul bombard**
dirty leather jug.   21 **his** its

smell; a kind of not-of-the-newest Poor John.° A strange fish! Were   25
I in England now, as once I was, and had but this fish painted,° not
a holiday fool there but would give a piece of silver. There would
this monster make a man. Any strange beast there makes a man.°
When they will not give a doit° to relieve a lame beggar, they will
lay out ten to see a dead Indian. Legged like a man, and his fins like   30
arms! Warm, o' my troth!° I do now let loose my opinion, hold it°
no longer: this is no fish, but an islander, that hath lately suffered°
by a thunderbolt. *[Thunder.]* Alas, the storm is come again! My best
way is to creep under his gaberdine.° There is no other shelter
hereabout. Misery acquaints a man with strange bedfellows. I will   35
here shroud° till the dregs° of the storm be past.

                       [He creeps under CALIBAN'*s garment.]*
Enter STEPHANO, *singing, [a bottle in his hand].*

STEPHANO.
"I shall no more to sea, to sea,
Here shall I die ashore—"
This is a very scurvy tune to sing at a man's funeral.
Well, here's my comfort.   *Drinks.*   40
(Sings.)
"The master, the swabber,° the boatswain, and I,
    The gunner and his mate,
Loved Mall, Meg, and Marian, and Margery,
    But none of us cared for Kate.
    For she had a tongue with a tang,°   45
    Would cry to a sailor, 'Go hang!'
She loved not the savor of tar nor of pitch,
Yet a tailor might scratch her where'er she did itch.°
    Then to sea, boys, and let her go hang!"
This is a scurvy tune too. But here's my comfort.   50
                              Drinks.

CALIBAN. Do not torment me!° O!
STEPHANO. What's the matter?° Have we devils here? Do you put tricks
    upon 's° with savages and men of Ind,° ha? I have not scaped
    drowning to be afeard now of your four legs. For it hath been said,
    "As proper° a man as ever went on four legs° cannot make him   55
    give ground"; and it shall be said so again while Stephano breathes
    at'° nostrils.

25 Poor John salted fish, type of poor fare   **26 painted** i.e., painted on a sign set
up outside a booth or tent at a fair   **28 make a man** (1) make one's fortune (2) be
indistinguishable from an Englishman   **29 doit** small coin   **31 o' my troth** by my
faith   **hold it** hold it in   **32 suffered** i.e., died   **34 garberdine** cloak, loose
upper garment   **36 shroud** take shelter   **dregs** i.e., last remains (as in a *bombard*
or jug, line 20)   **41 swabber** crew member whose job is to wash the decks
45 tang sting   **48 tailor . . . itch** (A dig at tailors for their supposed effeminacy
and a bawdy suggestion of satisfying a sexual craving.)   **51 Do . . . me** (Caliban assumes that one of Prospero's spirits has come to punish him.)   **52 What's the
matter** What's going on here?   **53 put tricks upon 's** trick us with conjuring
shows.   **Ind** India   **55 proper** handsome   **four legs** (The conventional phrase
would supply *two legs,* but the creature Stephano thinks he sees has four.)   **57 at'**
at the

CALIBAN. I'll kiss thy foot. I'll swear myself thy subject.   130
STEPHANO. Come on then. Down, and swear.
> [CALIBAN *kneels.*]

TRINCULO. I shall laugh myself to death at this puppy-headed monster. A
> most scurvy monster! I could find in my heart to beat him—

STEPHANO. Come, kiss.
TRINCULO. But that the poor monster's in drink.° An abominable   135
> monster!

CALIBAN. I'll show thee the best springs. I'll pluck thee berries.
> I'll fish for thee and get thee wood enough.
> A plague upon the tyrant that I serve!
> I'll bear him no more sticks, but follow thee,   140
> Thou wondrous man.

TRINCULO. A most ridiculous monster, to make a wonder of a poor
> drunkard!

CALIBAN. I prithee, let me bring thee where crabs° grow,
> And I with my long nails will dig thee pignuts,°   145
> Show thee a jay's nest, and instruct thee how
> To snare the nimble marmoset.° I'll bring thee
> To clustering filberts, and sometimes I'll get thee
> Young scamels° from the rock. Wilt thou go with me?

STEPHANO. I prithee now, lead the way without any more talking.—Trin-   150
> culo, the King and all our company else° being drowned, we will
> inherit° here.—Here, bear my bottle.—Fellow Trinculo, we'll fill
> him by and by again.

CALIBAN (*sings drunkenly*). Farewell, master, farewell, farewell!
TRINCULO. A howling monster; a drunken monster!   155
CALIBAN.
> No more dams I'll make for fish,
> > Nor fetch in firing°
> > At requiring,
> Nor scrape trenchering,° nor wash dish.
> > 'Ban, 'Ban, Ca-Caliban   160
> > Has a new master. Get a new man!°
> Freedom, high-day!° High-day, freedom! Freedom, high-day, free-
> dom!

STEPHANO. O brave monster! Lead the way.

Exeunt.

---

135 in drink drunk   **144 crabs** crab apples, or perhaps crabs   **145 pignuts**
earthnuts, edible tuberous roots   **147 marmoset** small monkey   **149 scamels**
(Possibly *seamews,* mentioned in a contemporary account, or shellfish, or perhaps
from *squamelle,* "furnished with little scales." Contemporary French and Italian
travel accounts report that the natives of Patagonia in South America ate small fish
described as *fort scameux* and *squame.*)   **151 else** in addition, besides ourselves.
152 inherit take possession   **157 firing** firewood   **159 trenchering** trenchers,
wooden plates   **161 Get a new man** (Addressed to Prospero.)   **162 high-day**
holiday

3.1   *Enter* FERDINAND, *bearing a log.*

FERDINAND. **There be some sports are painful, and their labor**
     Delight in them sets off.° Some kinds of baseness°
     Are nobly undergone,° and most poor° matters
     Point to rich ends. This my mean° task
     Would be as heavy to me as odious, but°   5
     The mistress which I serve quickens° what's dead
     And makes my labors pleasures. O, she is
     Ten times more gentle than her father's crabbed,
     And he's composed of harshness. I must remove
     Some thousands of these logs and pile them up,   10
     Upon a sore injunction.° My sweet mistress
     Weeps when she sees me work and says such baseness
     Had never like executor.° I forget;°
     But these sweet thoughts do even refresh my labors,
     Most busy lest when I do it.°
        Enter MIRANDA; *and* PROSPERO *[at a distance, unseen].*
MIRANDA.   Alas now, pray you,   15
     Work not so hard. I would the lightning had
     Burnt up those logs that you are enjoined° to pile!
     Pray, set it down and rest you. When this° burns,
     'Twill weep° for having wearied you. My father
     Is hard at study. Pray now, rest yourself.   20
     He's safe for these° three hours.
FERDINAND.   O most dear mistress,
     The sun will set before I shall discharge°
     What I must strive to do.
MIRANDA.   If you'll sit down,
     I'll bear your logs the while. Pray, give me that.
     I'll carry it to the pile.
FERDINAND.   No, precious creature,   25
     I had rather crack my sinews, break my back,
     Than you should such dishonor undergo
     While I sit lazy by.
MIRANDA.   It would become me
     As well as it does you; and I should do it
     With much more ease, for my good will is to it,   30

3.1. Location: Before Prospero's cell.   **1–2 There . . . sets off** some pastimes
are laborious, but the pleasure we get from them compensates for the effort. (Pleasure is *set off* by labor as a jewel is set off by its foil.)   **2 baseness** menial activity
3 undergone undertaken.   **most poor** poorest   **4 mean** lowly   **5 but** were it
not that   **6 quickens** gives life to   **11 sore injunction** severe command
13 Had . . . executor i.e., was never before undertaken by so noble a being.
I forget i.e., I forget that I'm supposed to be working, or, I forget my happiness, oppressed by my labor   **15 Most . . . it** i.e., busy at my labor but with my mind on
other things (?) (The line may be in need of emendation.)   **17 enjoined** commanded   **18 this** i.e., the log   **19 weep** i.e., exude resin   **21 these** the next
22 discharge complete

And yours it is against.
PROSPERO *[aside].*   Poor worm, thou art infected!
    This visitation° shows it.
MIRANDA.   You look wearily.
FERDINAND. No, noble mistress, 'tis fresh morning with me
    When you are by° at night. I do beseech you—
    Chiefly that I might set it in my prayers—   35
    What is your name?
MIRANDA.   Miranda.—O my father,
    I have broke your hest° to say so.
FERDINAND.   Admired Miranda!°
    Indeed the top of admiration, worth
    What's dearest° to the world! Full many a lady
    I have eyed with best regard,° and many a time   40
    The harmony of their tongues hath into bondage
    Brought my too diligent° ear. For several° virtues
    Have I liked several women, never any
    With so full soul but some defect in her
    Did quarrel with the noblest grace she owed°   45
    And put it to the foil.° But you, O you,
    So perfect and so peerless, are created
    Of° every creature's best!
MIRANDA.   I do not know
    One of my sex; no woman's face remember,
    Save, from my glass, mine own. Nor have I seen   50
    More that I may call men than you, good friend,
    And my dear father. How features are abroad°
    I am skilless° of; but, by my modesty,°
    The jewel in my dower, I would not wish
    Any companion in the world but you;   55
    Nor can imagination form a shape,
    Besides yourself, to like of.° But I prattle
    Something° too wildly, and my father's precepts
    I therein do forget.
FERDINAND.   I am in my condition°
    A prince, Miranda; I do think, a king—   60
    I would,° not so!—and would no more endure
    This wooden slavery° than to suffer
    The flesh-fly° blow° my mouth. Hear my soul speak:

32 visitation (1) Miranda's visit to Ferdinand (2) visitation of the plague, i.e., infec-
tion of love   **34 by** nearby   **37 hest** command.   **Admired Miranda** (Her name
means "to be admired or wondered at.")   **39 dearest** most treasured   **40 best regard** thoughtful and approving attention   **42 diligent** attentive.   **several** various
(also in line 43)   **45 owed** owned   **46 put . . . foil** (1) overthrew it (as in
wrestling) (2) served as a *foil,* or "contrast," to set it off   **48 Of** out of   **52 How
. . . abroad** what people look like in other places   **53 skilless** ignorant. **modesty**
virginity   **57 like of** be pleased with, be fond of   **58 Something** somewhat
59 condition rank   **61 would** wish (it were)   **62 wooden slavery** being compelled to carry wood   **63 flesh-fly** insect that deposits its eggs in dead flesh.
blow befoul with fly eggs

The very instant that I saw you did
My heart fly to your service, there resides   65
To make me slave to it, and for your sake
Am I this patient log-man.
MIRANDA.   Do you love me?
FERDINAND. O heaven, O earth, bear witness to this sound,
And crown what I profess with kind event°
If I speak true! If hollowly,° invert°   70
What best is boded° me to mischief!° I
Beyond all limit of what° else i' the world
Do love, prize, honor you.
MIRANDA [weeping].   I am a fool
To weep at what I am glad of.
PROSPERO [aside].   Fair encounter
Of two most rare affections! Heavens rain grace   75
On that which breeds between 'em!
FERDINAND.   Wherefore weep you?
MIRANDA. At mine unworthiness, that dare not offer
What I desire to give, and much less take
What I shall die° to want.° But this is trifling,
And all the more it seeks to hide itself   80
The bigger bulk it shows. Hence, bashful cunning,°
And prompt me, plain and holy innocence!
I am your wife, if you will marry me;
If not, I'll die your maid.° To be your fellow°
You may deny me, but I'll be your servant   85
Whether you will° or no.
FERDINAND.   My mistress,° dearest,
And I thus humble ever.
MIRANDA. My husband, then?
FERDINAND. Ay, with a heart as willing°
As bondage e'er of freedom. Here's my hand.   90
MIRANDA [clasping his hand]. And mine, with my heart in 't. And now
   farewell
Till half an hour hence.
FERDINAND.   A thousand thousand!°
                         Exeunt [FERDINAND and MIRANDA, separately].
PROSPERO. So glad of this as they I cannot be,
Who are surprised with all;° but my rejoicing
At nothing can be more. I'll to my book,   95
For yet ere suppertime must I perform
Much business appertaining.°
                                                              Exit.

---

69 kind event favorable outcome   **70 hollowly** insincerely, falsely.   **invert** turn
71 boded in store for.   **mischief** harm   **72 what** whatever   **79 die** (Probably
with an unconscious sexual meaning that underlies all of lines 77–81.)   **to want**
through lacking   **81 bashful cunning** coyness   **84 maid** handmaiden, servant.
fellow mate, equal   **86 will** desire it.   **My mistress** i.e., the woman I adore and
serve (not an illicit sexual partner)   **89 willing** desirous   **92 A thousand thousand** i.e., a thousand thousand farewells   **94 with all** by everything that has happened, or, *withal,* "with it"   **97 appertaining** related to this

3.2   *Enter* CALIBAN, STEPHANO, *and* TRINCULO.

STEPHANO. Tell not me. When the butt is out,° we will drink water, not a
    drop before. Therefore bear up and board 'em.° Servant monster,
    drink to me.

TRINCULO. Servant monster? The folly of° this island! They say there's
    but five upon this isle. We are three of them; if th' other two be   5
    brained° like us, the state totters.

STEPHANO. Drink, servant monster, when I bid thee. Thy eyes are almost
    set° in thy head.   *[Giving a drink.]*

TRINCULO. Where should they be set° else? He were a brave° monster in-
    deed if they were set in his tail.   10

STEPHANO. My man-monster hath drowned his tongue in sack. For my
    part, the sea cannot drown me. I swam, ere I could recover° the
    shore, five and thirty leagues° off and on.° By this light,° thou shalt
    be my lieutenant, monster, or my standard.°

TRINCULO. Your lieutenant, if you list;° he's no standard.°   15

STEPHANO. We'll not run,° Monsieur Monster.

TRINCULO. Nor go° neither, but you'll lie° like dogs and yet say nothing
    neither.

STEPHANO. Mooncalf, speak once in thy life, if thou beest a good moon-
    calf.   20

CALIBAN. How does thy honor? Let me lick they shoe.
    I'll not serve him. He is not valiant.

TRINCULO. Thou liest, most ignorant monster, I am in case to jostle a
    constable.° Why, thou debauched° fish, thou, was there ever man
    a coward that hath drunk so much sack° as I today? Wilt thou tell a   25
    monstrous lie, being but half a fish and half a monster?

CALIBAN. Lo, how he mocks me! Wilt thou let him, my lord?

TRINCULO. "Lord," quoth he? That a monster should be such a natural!°

CALIBAN. Lo, lo, again! Bite him to death, I prithee.

STEPHANO. Trinculo, keep a good tongue in your head. If you prove a   30
    mutineer—the next tree!° The poor monster's my subject, and he
    shall not suffer indignity.

CALIBAN. I thank my noble lord. Wilt thou be pleased
    To hearken once again to the suit I made to thee?

3.2. Location: Another part of the island.   1 out empty   **2 bear . . . 'em**
(Stephano uses the terminology of maneuvering at sea and boarding a vessel under
attack as a way of urging an assault on the liquor supply.)   **4 folly of** i.e., stupidity
found on   **6 be brained** are endowed with intelligence   **8 set** fixed in a drunken
stare, or, sunk, like the sun   **9 set** placed   **brave** fine, splendid   **12 recover** gain,
reach   **13 leagues** units of distance, each equaling about three miles.   **off and
on** intermittently.   **By this light** (An oath: by the light of the sun.)   **14 standard**
standard-bearer, ensign (as distinguished from *lieutenant*, lines 14–15)   **15 list** prefer.   **no standard** i.e., not able to stand up   **16 run** (1) retreat (2) urinate (taking
Trinculo's *standard*, line 15, in the old sense of "conduit")   **17 go** walk.   **lie** (1)
tell lies (2) lie prostrate (3) excrete   **23–24 in case . . . constable** i.e., in fit condition, made valiant by drink, to taunt or challenge the police   **24 debauched** (1) seduced away from proper service and allegiance (2) depraved   **25 sack** Spanish
white wine   **28 natural** (1) idiot (2) natural as opposed to unnatural, monsterlike
31 the next tree i.e., you'll hang

STEPHANO. Marry,° will I. Kneel and repeat it. I will stand, and so shall   35
    Trinculo.   *[CALIBAN kneels.]*
    Enter ARIEL, *invisible.*°
CALIBAN. As I told thee before, I am subject to a tyrant,
    A sorcerer, that by his cunning hath
    Cheated me of the island.
ARIEL *[mimicking* TRINCULO*]*. Thou liest.   40
CALIBAN. Thou liest, thou jesting monkey, thou!
    I would my valiant master would destroy thee.
    I do not lie.
STEPHANO. Trinculo, if you trouble him any more in 's tale, by this hand,
    I will supplant° some of your teeth.   45
TRINCULO. Why, I said nothing.
STEPHANO. Mum, then, and no more.—Proceed.
CALIBAN. I say by sorcery he got this isle;
    From me he got it. If thy greatness will
    Revenge it on him—for I know thou dar'st,   50
    But this thing° dare not—
STEPHANO. That's most certain.
CALIBAN. Thou shalt be lord of it, and I'll serve thee.
STEPHANO. How now shall this be compassed?° Canst thou bring me to
    the party?   55
CALIBAN. Yea, yea, my lord. I'll yield him thee asleep,
    Where thou mayst knock a nail into his head.
ARIEL. Thou liest; thou canst not.
CALIBAN. What a pied ninny's° this! Thou scurvy patch!—
    I do beseech thy greatness, give him blows   60
    And take his bottle from him. When that's gone
    He shall drink naught but brine, for I'll not show him
    Where the quick freshes° are.
STEPHANO. Trinculo, run into no further danger. Interrupt the monster
    one word further° and, by this hand, I'll turn my mercy out o'   65
    doors° and make a stockfish° of thee.
TRINCULO. Why, what did I? I did nothing. I'll go farther off.°
STEPHANO. Didst thou not say he lied?
ARIEL. Thou liest.
STEPHANO. Do I so? Take thou that. *[He beats* TRINCULO.*]*   70
    As you like this, give me the lie° another time.
TRINCULO. I did not give the lie. Out o' your wits and hearing too? A pox
    o' your bottle! This can sack and drinking do. A murrain° on your
    monster, and the devil take your fingers!
CALIBAN. Ha, ha, ha!   75

---

35 Marry i.e., indeed. (Originally an oath, "by the Virgin Mary.")   **36 s.d. invisible**
i.e., wearing a garment to connote invisibility, as at 1.2.377   **45 supplant** uproot,
displace   **51 this thing** i.e., Trinculo   **54 compassed** achieved   **59 pied ninny**
fool in motley.   **patch** fool   **63 quick freshes** running springs   **65 one word
further** i.e., one more time   **65–66 turn . . . doors** i.e., forget about being merciful.   **66 stockfish** dried cod beaten before cooking   **67 off** away   **71 give me
the lie** call me a liar to my face   **73 murrain** plague (Literally, a cattle disease)

STEPHANO. Now, forward with your tale. *[To* TRINCULO.*]*
    Prithee, stand further off.
CALIBAN. Beat him enough. After a little time
    I'll beat him too.
STEPHANO. Stand farther.—Come, proceed.   80
CALIBAN. Why, as I told thee, 'tis a custom with him
    I' th' afternoon to sleep. There thou mayst brain him,
    Having first seized his books; or with a log
    Batter his skull, or paunch° him with a stake,
    Or cut his weasand° with thy knife. Remember   85
    First to possess his books, for without them
    He's but a sot,° as I am, nor hath not
    One spirit to command. They all do hate him
    As rootedly as I. Burn but his books.
    He has brave utensils°—for so he calls them—   90
    Which, when he has a house, he'll deck withal.°
    And that most deeply to consider is
    The beauty of his daughter. He himself
    Calls her a nonpareil. I never saw a woman
    But only Sycorax my dam and she;   95
    But she as far surpasseth Sycorax
    As great'st does least.
STEPHANO. Is it so brave° a lass?
CALIBAN. Ay, lord. She will become° thy bed, I warrant,
    And bring thee forth brave brood.   100
STEPHANO. Monster, I will kill this man. His daughter and I will be king
    and queen—save Our Graces!—and Trinculo and thyself shall be
    viceroys. Dost thou like the plot, Trinculo?
TRINCULO. Excellent.
STEPHANO. Give me thy hand. I am sorry I beat thee; but, while thou   105
    liv'st, keep a good tongue in thy head.
CALIBAN. Within this half hour will he be asleep.
    Wilt thou destroy him then?
STEPHANO. Ay, on mine honor.
ARIEL *[aside]*. This will I tell my master.   110
CALIBAN. Thou mak'st me merry; I am full of pleasure.
    Let us be jocund.° Will you troll the catch°
    You taught me but whilere?°
STEPHANO. At thy request, monster, I will do reason, any reason.°—
    Come on, Trinculo, let us sing.   *Sings.* 115
    "Flout° 'em and scout 'em
    And scout 'em and flout 'em!
        Thought is free."
CALIBAN. That's not the tune.
    ARIEL *plays the tune on a tabor° and pipe.*

---

84 paunch stab in the belly   **85 weasand** windpipe   **87 sot** fool   **90 brave
utensils** fine furnishings   **91 deck withal** furnish it with   **98 brave** splendid,
attractive   **99 become** suit (sexually)   **112 jocund** jovial, merry.   **troll the catch**
sing the round   **113 but whilere** only a short time ago   **114 reason, any reason**
anything reasonable   **116 Flout** scoff at.   **scout** deride   **119 s.d. tabor** small
drum

STEPHANO. What is this same?   120

TRINCULO. This is the tune of our catch, played by the picture of
   Nobody.°

STEPHANO. If thou beest a man, show thyself in thy likeness. If thou
   beest a devil, take 't as thou list.°

TRINCULO. O, forgive me my sins!   125

STEPHANO. He that dies pays all debts.° I defy thee. Mercy upon us!

CALIBAN. Art thou afeard?

STEPHANO. No, monster, not I.

CALIBAN. Be not afeard. The isle is full of noises,
   Sounds, and sweet airs, that give delight and hurt not.   130
   Sometimes a thousand twangling instruments
   Will hum about mine ears, and sometimes voices
   That, if I then had waked after long sleep,
   Will make me sleep again; and then, in dreaming,
   The clouds methought would open and show riches   135
   Ready to drop upon me, that when I waked
   I cried to dream° again.

STEPHANO. This will prove a brave kingdom to me, where I shall have my
   music for nothing.

CALIBAN. When Prospero is destroyed.   140

STEPHANO. That shall be by and by.° I remember the story.

TRINCULO. The sound is going away. Let's follow it, and after do our
   work.

STEPHANO. Lead, monster; we'll follow. I would I could see this taborer!
   He lays it on.°   145

TRINCULO. Wilt come? I'll follow, Stephano.

                              Exeunt [following ARIEL's *music].*

3.3   *Enter* ALONSO, SEBASTIAN, ANTONIO, GONZALO, ADRIAN, FRANCISCO, *etc.*

GONZALO. By 'r lakin,° I can go no further, sir.
   My old bones aches. Here's a maze trod indeed
   Through forthrights and meanders!° By your patience,
   I needs must° rest me.

ALONSO.   Old lord, I cannot blame thee,
   Who am myself attached° with weariness,   5
   To th' dulling of my spirits.° Sit down and rest.
   Even here I will put off my hope, and keep it
   No longer for° my flatterer. He is drowned
   Whom thus we stray to find, and the sea mocks
   Our frustrate° search on land. Well, let him go.   10
   [ALONSO and GONZALO *sit.]*

121–122 picture of Nobody (Refers to a familiar figure with head, arms, and legs
but no trunk.)   **124 take 't . . . list** i.e., take my defiance as you please, as best you
can   **126 He . . . debts** i.e., if I have to die, at least that will be the end of all my
woes and obligations   **137 to dream** desirous of dreaming   **141 by and by** very
soon   **145 lays it on** i.e., plays the drum vigorously   **3.3. Location: Another
part of the island.   1 By 'r lakin** by our Ladykin, by our Lady   **3 forthrights
and meanders** paths straight and crooked   **4 needs must** have to   **5 attached**
seized   **6 To . . . spirits** to the point of being dull-spirited   **8 for** as   **10 frustrate**
frustrated

ANTONIO *[aside to* SEBASTIAN*]*. I am right° glad that he's so out of hope.
　Do not, for° one repulse, forgo the purpose
　That you resolved t' effect.
SEBASTIAN *[to* ANTONIO*]*.　　　　　　The next advantage
　Will we take thoroughly.°
ANTONIO*[to* SEBASTIAN*]*.　　　　　Let it be tonight,
　For, now° they are oppressed with travel,° they　　　　　　　　　15
　Will not, nor cannot, use° such vigilance
　As when they are fresh.
SEBASTIAN *[to* ANTONIO*]*.　　　　I say tonight. No more.
　Solemn and strange music; and PROSPERO *on the top,° invisible.*
ALONSO. What harmony is this? My good friends, hark!
GONZALO. Marvelous sweet music!
　Enter several strange shapes, bringing in a banquet, and dance
　about it with gentle actions of salutations; and, inviting the
　King, etc., to eat, they depart.
ALONSO. Give us kind keepers,° heavens! What were these?　　　　20
SEBASTIAN. A living° drollery.° Now I will believe
　That there are unicorns; that in Arabia
　There is one tree, the phoenix'° throne, one phoenix
　At this hour reigning there.
ANTONIO.　　　　　　　　　　I'll believe both;
　And what does else want credit,° come to me　　　　　　　　　25
　And I'll be sworn 'tis true. Travelers ne'er did lie,
　Though fools at home condemn 'em.
GONZALO.　　　　　　　　　　　If in Naples
　I should report this now, would they believe me
　If I should say I saw such islanders?
　For, certes,° these are people of the island,　　　　　　　　　30
　Who, though they are of monstrous° shape, yet note,
　Their manners are more gentle, kind, than of
　Our human generation you shall find
　Many, nay, almost any.
PROSPERO *[aside]*.　　　　　　Honest lord,
　Thou hast said well, for some of you there present　　　　　　35
　Are worse than devils.
ALONSO.　　　　　　　　I cannot too much muse°
　Such shapes, such gesture, and such sound, expressing—
　Although they want° the use of tongue—a kind
　Of excellent dumb discourse.
PROSPERO *[aside]*. - -　　　　　　Praise in departing.°

---

11 right very　**12 for** because of　**14 throughly** thoroughly　**15 now** now that.
travel (Spelled *trauaile* in the Folio and carrying the sense of labor as well as traveling.)　**16 use** apply　**17 s.d. on the top** at some high point of the tiring-house or
the theater, on a third level above the gallery　**20 kind keepers** guardian angels
21 living with live actors.　**drollery** comic entertainment, caricature, puppet
show　**23 phoenix** mythical bird consumed to ashes every five hundred to six
hundred years, only to be renewed into another cycle　**25 want credit** lack cre-
dence　**30 certes** certainly　**31 monstrous** unnatural　**36 muse** wonder at
38 want lack　**39 Praise in departing** i.e., save your praise until the end of the
performance (Proverbial)

FRANCISCO. They vanished strangely.

SEBASTIAN.   No matter, since   40
    They have left their viands° behind, for we have stomachs.°
    Will 't please you taste of what is here?

ALONSO.   Not I.

GONZALO. Faith, sir, you need not fear. When we were boys,
    Who would believe that there were mountaineers°
    Dewlapped° like bulls, whose throats had hanging at 'em   45
    Wallets° of flesh? Or that there were such men
    Whose heads stood in their breasts?° Which now we find
    Each putter-out of five for one° will bring us
    Good warrant° of.

ALONSO. I will stand to° and feed,
    Although my last°—no matter, since I feel   50
    The best° is past. Brother, my lord the Duke,
    Stand to, and do as we.   *[They approach the table.]*
    Thunder and lightning. Enter ARIEL, *like a harpy,° claps his wings*
    upon the table, and with a quaint device° the banquet vanishes.°

ARIEL. You are three men of sin, whom Destiny—
    That hath to instrument this lower world
    And what is in 't—the never-surfeited sea   55
    Hath caused to belch up you,° and on this island
    Where man doth not inhabit, you 'mongst men
    Being most unfit to live. I have made you mad;
    And even with suchlike valor° men hang and drown
    Their proper° selves.
             [ALONSO, SEBASTIAN, and ANTONIO draw their swords.]
                 You fools! I and my fellows   60
    Are ministers of Fate. The elements
    Of whom° your swords are tempered° may as well
    Wound the loud winds, or with bemocked-at° stabs
    Kill the still-closing° waters, as diminish
    One dowl° that's in my plume. My fellow ministers   65
    Are like° invulnerable. If° you could hurt,

---

41 viands provisions.   **stomachs** appetites   **44 mountaineers** mountain dwellers   **45 Dewlapped** having a dewlap, or fold of skin hanging from the neck, like cattle   **46 Wallets** pendent folds of skin, wattles   **47 in their breasts** (i.e., like the Anthropophagi described in *Othello*, 1.3.146)   **48 putter-out . . . one** one who invests money or gambles on the risks of travel on the condition that the traveler who returns safely is to receive five times the amount deposited; hence, any traveler   **49 Good warrant** assurance.   **stand to** fall to; take the risk   **50 Although my last** even if this were to be my last meal   **51 best** best part of life   **52 s.d. harpy** a fabulous monster with a woman's face and breasts and a vulture's body, supposed to be a minister of divine vengeance.   **quaint device** ingenious stage contrivance.   **the banquet vanishes** i.e., the food vanishes; the table remains until line 82   **53–56 whom . . . up you** you whom Destiny, controller of the sublunary world as its instrument, has caused the ever hungry sea to belch up   **59 suchlike valor** i.e., the reckless valor derived from madness   **60 proper** own   **62 whom** which.   **tempered** composed and hardened   **63 bemocked-at** scorned   **64 still-closing** always closing again when parted   **65 dowl** soft, fine feather   **66 like** likewise, similarly.   **If** even if

Your swords are now too massy° for your strengths
And will not be uplifted. But remember—
For that's my business to you—that you three
From Milan did supplant good Prospero;   70
Exposed unto the sea, which hath requit° it,
Him and his innocent child; for which foul deed
The powers, delaying, not forgetting, have
Incensed the seas and shores, yea, all the creatures,
Against your peace. Thee of thy son, Alonso,   75
They have bereft; and do pronounce by me
Ling'ring perdition,° worse than any death
Can be at once, shall step by step attend
You and your ways; whose° wraths to guard you from—
Which here, in this most desolate isle, else° falls   80
Upon your heads—is nothing° but heart's sorrow
And a clear° life ensuing.

*He vanishes in thunder; then, to soft music, enter the shapes
again, and dance, with mocks and mows,° and carrying out the
table.*

PROSPERO. Bravely° the figure of this harpy hast thou
Performed, my Ariel; a grace it had devouring.°
Of my instruction hast thou nothing bated°   85
In what thou hadst to say. So,° with good life°
And observation strange,° my meaner° ministers
Their several kinds° have done. My high charms work,
And these mine enemies are all knit up
In their distractions.° They now are in my power;   90
And in these fits I leave them, while I visit
Young Ferdinand, whom they suppose is drowned,
And his and mine loved darling.

                                                        [Exit above.]

GONZALO. I' the name of something holy, sir, why° stand you
In this strange stare?
ALONSO.   O, it° is monstrous, monstrous!   95
Methought the billows° spoke and told me of it;
The winds did sing it to me, and the thunder,
That deep and dreadful organ pipe, pronounced

---

67 massy heavy   **71 requit** requited, avenged   **77 perdition** ruin, destruction
79 whose (Refers to the heavenly powers.)   **80 else** otherwise   **81 is nothing**
there is no way   **82 clear** unspotted, innocent.   **s.d. mocks and mows** mocking
gestures and grimaces   **83 Bravely** finely, dashingly   **84 a grace . . . devouring**
i.e., you gracefully caused the banquet to disappear as if you had consumed it (with
puns on grace, meaning "gracefulness" and "a blessing on the meal," and on *devouring,* meaning "a literal eating" and "an all-consuming or ravishing grace")   **85 bated**
abated, omitted   **86 So** in the same fashion.   **good life** faithful reproduction
87 observation strange exceptional attention to detail.   **meaner** i.e., subordinate
to Ariel   **88 several kinds** individual parts   **90 distractions** trancelike state
94 why (Gonzalo was not addressed in Ariel's speech to the *three men of sin,* line
53, and is not, as they are, in a maddened state; see lines 105–107.)   **95 it** i.e., my
sin (also in line 96)   **96 billows** waves

The name of Prosper; it did bass my trespass.°
Therefor° my son i' th' ooze is bedded; and   100
I'll seek him deeper than e'er plummet° sounded,°
And with him there lie mudded.

                                                        Exit.

SEBASTIAN. But one fiend at a time,
   I'll fight their legions o'er.°
ANTONIO.   I'll be thy second.
                                *Exeunt [*SEBASTIAN *and* ANTONIO*].*
GONZALO. All three of them are desperate.° Their great guilt,   105
   Like poison given to work a great time after,
   Now 'gins to bite the spirits.° I do beseech you,
   That are of suppler joints, follow them swiftly
   And hinder them from what this ecstasy°
   May now provoke them to.
ADRIAN.   Follow, I pray you.   110
                                        Exeunt omnes.

      4.1 *Enter* PROSPERO, FERDINAND, *and* MIRANDA.

PROSPERO. If I have too austerely punished you,
   Your compensation makes amends, for I
   Have given you here a third° of mine own life,
   Or that for which I live; who once again
   I tender° to thy hand. All thy vexations   5
   Were but my trials of thy love, and thou
   Hast strangely° stood the test. Here, afore heaven,
   I ratify this my rich gift. O Ferdinand,
   Do not smile at me that I boast her off,°
   For thou shalt find she will outstrip all praise   10
   And make it halt° behind her.
FERDINAND.   I do believe it
   Against an oracle.°
PROSPERO. Then, as my gift and thine own acquisition
   Worthily purchased, take my daughter. But
   If thou dost break her virgin-knot before   15
   All sanctimonious° ceremonies may
   With full and holy rite be ministered,
   No sweet aspersion° shall the heavens let fall

99 bass my trespass proclaim my trespass like a bass note in music   **100 Therefor** in consequence of that   **101 plummet** a lead weight attached to a line for testing depth.   **sounded** probed, tested the depth of   **104 o'er** one after another **105 desperate** despairing and reckless   **107 bite the spirits** sap their vital powers through anguish   **109 ecstasy** mad frenzy   **4.1 Location: Before Prospero's cell.**   **3 a third** i.e., Miranda, into whose education Prospero has put a third of his life (?) or who represents a large part of what he cares about, along with his dukedom and his learned study (?)   **5 tender** offer   **7 strangely** extraordinarily **9 boast her off** i.e., praise her so, or, perhaps an error for "boast of her"; the Folio reads "boast her of"   **11 halt** limp   **12 Against an oracle** even if an oracle should declare otherwise   **16 sanctimonious** sacred   **18 aspersion** dew, shower

To make this contract grow; but barren hate,
Sour-eyed disdain, and discord shall bestrew   20
The union of your bed with weeds° so loathly
That you shall hate it both. Therefore take heed,
As Hymen's lamps shall light you.°

FERDINAND.   As I hope
For quiet days, fair issue,° and long life,
With such love as 'tis now, the murkiest den,   25
The most opportune place, the strong'st suggestion°
Our worser genius° can,° shall never melt
Mine honor into lust, to° take away
The edge° of that day's celebration
When I shall think or° Phoebus' steeds are foundered°   30
Or Night kept chained below.

PROSPERO.   Fairly spoke.
Sit then and talk with her. She is thine own.
[FERDINAND and MIRANDA sit and talk together.]
What,° Ariel! My industrious servant, Ariel!
Enter ARIEL.

ARIEL. What would my potent master? Here I am.

PROSPERO. Thou and thy meaner fellows° your last service   35
Did worthily perform, and I must use you
In such another trick.° Go bring the rabble,°
O'er whom I give thee power, here to this place.
Incite them to quick motion, for I must
Bestow upon the eyes of this young couple   40
Some vanity° of mine art. It is my promise,
And they expect it from me.

ARIEL.   Presently?°

PROSPERO. Ay, with a twink.°

ARIEL. Before you can say "Come" and "Go,"
And breathe twice, and cry "So, so,"   45
Each one, tripping on his toe,
Will be here with mop and mow.°
Do you love me, master? No?

PROSPERO. Dearly, my delicate Ariel. Do not approach
Till thou dost hear me call.

ARIEL.   Well; I conceive.°   *Exit.* 50

---

21 weeds (in place of the flowers customarily strewn on the marriage bed)   **23 As
. . . you** i.e., as you long for happiness and concord in your marriage. (Hymen was
the Greek and Roman god of marriage; his symbolic torches, the wedding torches,
were supposed to burn brightly for a happy marriage and smokily for a troubled
one.)   **24 issue** offspring   **26 suggestion** temptation   **27 worser genius** evil genius, or, evil attendant spirit.   **can** is capable of   **28 to** so as to   **29 edge** keen enjoyment, sexual ardor   **30 or** either.   **foundered** broken down, made lame. (Ferdinand will wait impatiently for the bridal night.)   **33 What** now then
35 meaner fellows subordinates   **37 trick** device.   **rabble** band, i.e., the
meaner fellows of line 35   **41 vanity** (1) illusion (2) trifle (3) desire for admiration,
conceit   **42 Presently** immediately   **43 with a twink** in the twinkling of an eye
47 mop and mow gestures and grimaces   **50 conceive** understand

PROSPERO. Look thou be true;° do not give dalliance
　　　Too much the rein. The strongest oaths are straw
　　　To the fire i' the blood. Be more abstemious,
　　　Or else good night° your vow!
FERDINAND.　　　　　　　　　　　　I warrant° you, sir,
　　　The white cold virgin snow upon my heart°　　　　　　　　55
　　　Abates the ardor of my liver.°
PROSPERO.　　　　　　　　　　Well.
　　　Now come, my Ariel! Bring a corollary,°
　　　Rather than want° a spirit. Appear, and pertly!° —
　　　No tongue!° All eyes! Be silent.　　　　　*Soft music.*
　　　Enter IRIS.°
IRIS. Ceres,° most bounteous lady, thy rich leas°　　　　　　60
　　　Of wheat, rye, barley, vetches,° oats, and peas;
　　　Thy turfy mountains, where live nibbling sheep,
　　　And flat meads° thatched with stover,° them to keep;
　　　Thy banks with pionèd and twillèd° brims,
　　　Which spongy° April at thy hest° betrims　　　　　　　65
　　　To make cold nymphs chaste crowns; and thy broom groves,°
　　　Whose shadow the dismissèd bachelor° loves,
　　　Being lass-lorn; thy poll-clipped° vineyard;
　　　And thy sea marge,° sterile and rocky hard,
　　　Where thou thyself dost air:° the queen o' the sky,°　　　70
　　　Whose watery arch° and messenger am I,
　　　Bids thee leave these, and with her sovereign grace,
　　　　　　　　　　JUNO *descends*° *[slowly in her car].*
　　　Here on this grass plot, in this very place,
　　　To come and sport. Her peacocks° fly amain.°
　　　Approach, rich Ceres, her to entertain.°　　　　　　　75
　　　Enter CERES.
CERES. Hail, many-colored messenger, that ne'er
　　　Dost disobey the wife of Jupiter,
　　　Who with thy saffron° wings upon my flowers
　　　Diffusest honeydrops, refreshing showers,

---

51 true true to your promise　**54 good night** i.e., say good-bye to.　**warrant** guarantee　**55 The white . . . heart** i.e., the ideal of chastity and consciousness of Miranda's chaste innocence enshrined in my heart　**56 liver** (as the presumed seat of the passions)　**57 corollary** surplus, extra supply　**58 want** lack.　**pertly** briskly　**59 No tongue** all the beholders are to be silent (lest the spirits vanish).　**s.d. Iris** goddess of the rainbow and Juno's messenger　**60 Ceres** goddess of the generative power of nature.　**leas** meadows　**61 vetches** plants for forage, fodder　**63 meads** meadows.　**stover** winter fodder for cattle　**64 pionèd and twillèd** undercut by the swift current and protected by roots and branches that tangle to form a barricade　**65 spongy** wet.　**hest** command　**66 broom groves** clumps of broom, gorse, yellow-flowered shrub　**67 dismissèd bachelor** rejected male lover　**68 poll-clipped** pruned, lopped at the top, or *pole-clipped,* "hedged in with poles"　**69 sea marge** shore　**70 thou . . . air** you take the air, go for walks.　**queen o' the sky** i.e., Juno　**71 watery arch** rainbow　**72 s.d. Juno descends** i.e., starts her descent from the "heavens" above the stage (?)　**74 peacocks** birds sacred to Juno and used to pull her chariot.　**amain** with full speed　**75 entertain** receive　**78 saffron** yellow

And with each end of thy blue bow° dost crown   80
My bosky° acres and my unshrubbed down,°
Rich scarf° to my proud earth. Why hath thy queen
Summoned me hither to this short-grassed green?

IRIS. A contract of true love to celebrate,
And some donation freely to estate°   85
On the blest lovers.

CERES.   Tell me, heavenly bow,
If Venus or her son,° as° thou dost know,
Do now attend the Queen? Since they did plot
The means that° dusky° Dis my daughter got,°
Her and her° blind boy's scandaled° company   90
I have forsworn.

IRIS. Of her society°
Be not afraid. I met her deity°
Cutting the clouds towards Paphos,° and her son
Dove-drawn° with her. Here thought they to have done°
Some wanton charm° upon this man and maid,   95
Whose vows are that no bed-right shall be paid
Till Hymen's torch be lighted; but in vain.
Mars's hot minion° is returned° again;
Her waspish-headed° son has broke his arrows,
Swears he will shoot no more, but play with sparrows°   100
And be a boy right out.°

[JUNO *alights.*]

CERES.   Highest Queen of state,°
Great Juno, comes; I know her by her gait.°

JUNO. How does my bounteous sister?° Go with me
To bless this twain, that they may prosperous be,
And honored in their issue.°   *They sing:* 105

JUNO. Honor, riches, marriage blessing,
Long continuance, and increasing,
Hourly joys be still° upon you!
Juno sings her blessings on you.

CERES. Earth's increase, foison plenty,°   110
Barns and garners° never empty,
Vines with clustering bunches growing,
Plants with goodly burden bowing;

---

80 bow i.e., rainbow   **81 bosky** wooded.   **unshrubbed down** open upland
82 scarf (The rainbow is like a colored silk band adorning the earth.)   **85 estate**
bestow   **87 son** i.e., Cupid.   **as** as far as   **89 that** whereby.   **dusky** dark.   **Dis
. . . got** (Pluto, or *Dis,* god of the infernal regions, carried off Proserpina, daughter
of Ceres, to be his bride in Hades.)   **90 her** i.e., Venus'.   **scandaled** scandalous
91 society company   **92 her deity** i.e., Her Highness   **93 Paphos** place on the island of Cyprus, sacred to Venus   **94 Dove-drawn** (Venus's chariot was drawn by
doves.)   **done** placed   **95 wanton charm** lustful spell   **98 Mars's hot minion**
i.e., Venus, the beloved of Mars.   **returned** i.e., returned to Paphos   **99 waspish-
headed** hotheaded, peevish   **100 sparrows** (Supposed lustful, and sacred to
Venus.)   **101 right out** outright.   **Highest . . . state** most majestic Queen
102 gait i.e., majestic bearing   **103 sister** i.e., fellow goddess (?)   **105 issue** offspring   **108 still** always   **110 foison plenty** plentiful harvest   **111 garners**
granaries

Spring come to you at the farthest
In the very end of harvest!°   115
Scarcity and want shall shun you;
Ceres' blessing so is on you.
FERDINAND. This is a most majestic vision, and
Harmonious charmingly.° May I be bold
To think these spirits?
PROSPERO.   Spirits, which by mine art   120
I have from their confines called to enact
My present fancies.
FERDINAND.   Let me live here ever!
So rare a wondered° father and a wife
Makes this place Paradise.
JUNO and CERES whisper, and send IRIS on employment.
PROSPERO.   Sweet now, silence!
Juno and Ceres whisper seriously;   125
There's something else to do. Hush and be mute,
Or else our spell is marred.
IRIS *[calling offstage].* You nymphs, called naiads,° of the windring°
    brooks,
With your sedged° crowns and ever-harmless° looks,
Leave your crisp° channels, and on this green land   130
Answer your summons; Juno does command.
Come, temperate° nymphs, and help to celebrate
A contract of true love. Be not too late.
                                        Enter certain nymphs.
You sunburned sicklemen,° of August weary,°
Come hither from the furrow° and be merry.   135
Make holiday; your rye-straw hats put on,
And these fresh nymphs encounter° every one
In country footing.°
*Enter certain reapers, properly° habited. They join with the
nymphs in a graceful dance, towards the end whereof PROSPERO
starts suddenly, and speaks; after which, to a strange, hollow,
and confused noise, they heavily° vanish.*
PROSPERO *[aside].* I had forgot that foul conspiracy
Of the beast Caliban and his confederates   140
Against my life. The minute of their plot
Is almost come. *[To the SPIRITS.]* Well done! Avoid;° no more!
FERDINAND *[to MIRANDA].* This is strange. Your father's in some passion
That works° him strongly.

---

115 In . . . harvest i.e., with no winter in between   **119 charmingly** enchanti-
ngly   **123 wondered** wonder-performing, wondrous   **128 naiads** nymphs of
springs, rivers, or lakes.   **windring** wandering, winding (?)   **129 sedged** made of
reeds.   **ever-harmless** ever innocent   **130 crisp** curled, rippled   **132 temper-**
ate chaste   **134 sicklemen** harvesters, field workers who cut down grain and
grass.   **of August weary** i.e., weary of the hard work of the harvest   **135 furrow**
i.e., plowed fields   **137 encounter** join   **138 country footing** country dancing.
s.d. properly suitably.   **heavily** slowly, dejectedly   **142 Avoid** withdraw
144 works affects, agitates

STEPHANO. I will fetch off my bottle, though I be o'er ears° for my labor.

CALIBAN. Prithee, my king, be quiet. Seest thou here,
This is the mouth o' the cell. No noise, and enter.
Do that good mischief which may make this island   215
Thine own forever, and I thy Caliban
For aye thy footlicker.

STEPHANO. Give me thy hand. I do begin to have bloody thoughts.

TRINCULO *[seeing the finery].* O King Stephano! O peer!°
O worthy Stephano! Look what a wardrobe here is for thee!   220

CALIBAN. Let it alone, thou fool, it is but trash.

TRINCULO. Oho, monster! We know what belongs to a frippery.° O King
Stephano!   *[He puts on a gown.]*

STEPHANO. Put off° that gown, Trinculo. By this hand, I'll have that
gown.   225

TRINCULO. Thy Grace shall have it.

CALIBAN. The dropsy° drown this fool! What do you mean
To dote thus on such luggage?° Let 't alone
And do the murder first. If he awake,
From toe to crown° he'll fill our skins with pinches,   230
Make us strange stuff.

STEPHANO. Be you quiet, monster.—Mistress line,° is not this my jerkin?°
[He takes it down.] Now is the jerkin under the line.° Now, jerkin,
you are like° to lose your hair and prove a bald° jerkin.

TRINCULO. Do, do!° We steal by line and level,° an 't like° Your Grace.   235

STEPHANO. I thank thee for that jest. Here's a garment for 't. *[He gives a
garment.]* Wit shall not go unrewarded while I am king of this
country. "Steal by line and level" is an excellent pass of pate.°
There's another garment for 't.

TRINCULO. Monster, come, put some lime° upon your fingers, and away   240
with the rest.

CALIBAN. I will have none on 't. We shall lose our time,

---

212 o'er ears i.e., totally submerged and perhaps drowned   **219 King . . . peer**
(Alludes to the old ballad beginning, "King Stephen was a worthy peer.")
222 frippery place where cast-off clothes are sold   **224 Put off** put down, or, take
off   **227 dropsy** disease characterized by the accumulation of fluid in the connective tissue of the body   **228 luggage** cumbersome trash   **230 crown** head
232 Mistress line (Addressed to the linden or lime tree upon which, at line 193,
Ariel hung the *glistering apparel.*)   **jerkin** jacket made of leather   **233 under the
line** under the lime tree (with punning sense of being south of the equinoctial line
or equator; sailors on long voyages to the southern regions were popularly supposed to lose their hair from scurvy or other diseases. Stephano also quibbles
bawdily on losing hair through syphilis, and in *Mistress* and *jerkin.*)   **234 like**
likely   **bald** (1) hairless, napless (2) meager   **235 Do, do** i.e., bravo. (Said in response to the jesting or to the taking of the jerkin, or both.)   **by line and level**
i.e., by means of plumb line and carpenter's level, methodically (with pun on *line,*
"lime tree," line 233, and *steal,* pronounced like *stale,* i.e., prostitute, continuing
Stephano's bawdy quibble).   **an 't like** if it please   **238 pass of pate** sally of wit.
(The metaphor is from fencing.)   **240 lime** birdlime, sticky substance (to give Caliban sticky fingers)

And all be turned to barnacles,° or to apes
With foreheads villainous° low.
STEPHANO. Monster, lay to° your fingers. Help to bear this° away where 245
    my hogshead° of wine is, or I'll turn you out of my kingdom. Go
    to,° carry this.
TRINCULO. And this.
STEPHANO. Ay, and this.
    [They load CALIBAN *with more and more garments.]*
    A noise of hunters heard. Enter divers spirits, in shape of dogs
    and hounds, hunting them about, PROSPERO *and* ARIEL *setting them*
    on.
PROSPERO. Hey, Mountain, hey!   250
ARIEL. Silver! There it goes, Silver!
PROSPERO. Fury, Fury! There, Tyrant, there! Hark! Hark!
    *[*CALIBAN, STEPHANO, *and* TRINCULO *are driven out.]*
    Go, charge my goblins that they grind their joints
    With dry° convulsions,° shorten up their sinews
    With agèd° cramps, and more pinch-spotted make them   255
    Than pard° or cat o' mountain.°
ARIEL.   Hark, they roar!
PROSPERO. Let them be hunted soundly.° At this hour
    Lies at my mercy all mine enemies.
    Shortly shall all my labors end, and thou
    Shalt have the air at freedom. For a little°   260
    Follow, and do me service.
                          Exeunt.

    5.1 *Enter* PROSPERO *in His Magic Robes, [With His Staff,] and* ARIEL.

PROSPERO. Now does my project gather to a head.
    My charms crack° not, my spirits obey, and Time
    Goes upright with his carriage.° How's the day?
ARIEL. On° the sixth hour, at which time, my lord,
    You said our work should cease.
PROSPERO.   I did say so,   5
    When first I raised the tempest. Say, my spirit,
    How fares the King and 's followers?
ARIEL.   Confined together
    In the same fashion as you gave in charge,
    Just as you left them; all prisoners, sir,

243 barnacles barnacle geese, formerly supposed to be hatched from barnacles attached to trees or to rotting timber; here, evidently used, like *apes,* as types of simpletons   **244 villainous** miserably   **245 lay to** start using   **this** i.e., the *glistering apparel.*   **246 hogshead** large cask   **246–247 Go to** (An expression of exhortation or remonstrance.)   **254 dry** associated with age, arthritic (?) **convulsions** cramps   **255 agèd** characteristic of old age   **256 pard** panther or leopard.   **cat o' mountain** wildcat   **257 soundly** thoroughly (and suggesting the sounds of the hunt)   **260 little** little while longer   5.1. **Location: Before Prospero's cell.**   **2 crack** collapse, fail. (The metaphor is probably alchemical, as in *project* and *gather to a head,* line 1.)   **3 his carriage** its burden. (Time is no longer heavily burdened and so can go *upright,* "standing straight and unimpeded.") **4 On** approaching

In the line grove° which weather-fends° your cell.   10
They cannot budge till your release.° The King,
His brother, and yours abide all three distracted,°
And the remainder mourning over them,
Brim full of sorrow and dismay; but chiefly
Him that you termed, sir, the good old lord, Gonzalo.   15
His tears runs down his beard like winter's drops
From eaves of reeds.° Your charm so strongly works 'em
That if you now beheld them your affections°
Would become tender.

PROSPERO.   Dost thou think so, spirit?
ARIEL. Mine would, sir, were I human.°
PROSPERO.   And mine shall.   20
Hast thou, which art but air, a touch,° a feeling
Of their afflictions, and shall not myself,
One of their kind, that relish all as sharply
Passion as they,° be kindlier° moved than thou art?
Though with their high wrongs I am struck to the quick,   25
Yet with my nobler reason 'gainst my fury
Do I take part. The rarer° action is
In virtue than in vengeance. They being penitent,
The sole drift of my purpose doth extend
Not a frown further. Go release them, Ariel.   30
My charms I'll break, their senses I'll restore,
And they shall be themselves.

ARIEL.   I'll fetch them, sir.

                                                        Exit.

*[*PROSPERO *traces a charmed circle with his staff.]*
PROSPERO. Ye elves of hills, brooks, standing lakes, and groves,
And ye that on the sands with printless foot
Do chase the ebbing Neptune, and do fly him   35
When he comes back; you demi-puppets° that
By moonshine do the green sour ringlets° make,
Whereof the ewe not bites; and you whose pastime
Is to make midnight mushrooms,° that rejoice
To hear the solemn curfew;° by whose aid,   40
Weak masters° though ye be, I have bedimmed
The noontide sun, called forth the mutinous winds,
And twixt the green sea and the azured vault°

10 line grove grove of lime trees.   **weather-fends** protects from the weather
11 your release you release them   **12 distracted** out of their wits   **17 eaves of
reeds** thatched roofs   **18 affections** disposition, feelings   **20 human** (Spelled *humane* in the Folio and encompassing both senses.)   **21 touch** sense, apprehension
23–24 that . . . they I who experience human passions as acutely as they
24 kindlier (1) more sympathetically (2) more naturally, humanly   **27 rarer** nobler   **36 demi-puppets** puppets of half size, i.e., elves and fairies   **37 green sour
ringlets** fairy rings, circles in grass (actually produced by mushrooms)   **39 midnight mushrooms** mushrooms appearing overnight   **40 curfew** evening bell,
usually rung at nine o'clock, ushering in the time when spirits are abroad
41 Weak masters i.e., subordinate spirits, as in 4.1.35 (?)   **43 the azured vault**
i.e., the sky

Set roaring war; to the dread rattling thunder
Have I given fire,° and rifted° Jove's stout oak°   45
With his own bolt;° the strong-based promontory
Have I made shake, and by the spurs° plucked up
The pine and cedar; graves at my command
Have waked their sleepers, oped, and let 'em forth
By my so potent art.° But this rough° magic   50
I here abjure, and when I have required°
Some heavenly music—which even now I do—
To work mine end upon their senses that°
This airy charm° is for, I'll break my staff,
Bury it certain fathoms in the earth,   55
And deeper than did ever plummet sound
I'll drown my book.   *Solemn music.*
Here enters ARIEL *before; then* ALONSO, *with a frantic gesture, at-
tended by* GONZALO; SEBASTIAN *and* ANTONIO *in like manner, at-
tended by* ADRIAN *and* FRANCISCO. *They all enter the circle which*
PROSPERO *had made, and there stand charmed; which* PROSPERO *ob-
serving, speaks:*
[To ALONSO.] A solemn air,° and° the best comforter
To an unsettled fancy,° cure thy brains,
Now useless, boiled° within thy skull! *[To* SEBASTIAN *and* ANTONIO.]
   There stand,   60
For you are spell-stopped.—
Holy Gonzalo, honorable man,
Mine eyes, e'en sociable° to the show° of thine,
Fall° fellowly drops. *[Aside.]* The charm dissolves apace,
And as the morning steals upon the night,   65
Melting the darkness, so their rising senses
Begin to chase the ignorant fumes° that mantle°
Their clearer° reason.—O good Gonzalo,
My true preserver, and a loyal sir
To him thou follow'st! I will pay thy graces°   70
Home° both in word and deed.—Most cruelly
Didst thou, Alonso, use me and my daughter.
Thy brother was a furtherer° in the act.—
Thou art pinched° for 't now, Sebastian. *[To* ANTONIO.] Flesh and
   blood,
You, brother mine, that entertained ambition,   75

44–45 to . . . fire I have discharged the dread rattling thunderbolt   **45 rifted**
riven, split.   **oak** a tree that was sacred to Jove   **46 bolt** lightning bolt   **47 spurs**
roots   **33–50 Ye . . . art** (This famous passage is an embellished paraphrase of
Golding's translation of Ovid's *Metamorphoses,* 7.197–219.)   **50 rough** violent
51 required requested   **53 their senses that** the senses of those whom   **54 airy
charm** i.e., music   **58 air** song.   **and** i.e., which is   **59 fancy** imagination
60 boiled i.e., extremely agitated   **63 sociable** sympathetic.   **show** appearance
64 Fall let fall   **67 ignorant fumes** fumes that render them incapable of comprehension.   **mantle** envelop   **68 clearer** growing clearer   **70 pay thy graces**
requite your favors and virtues   **71 Home** fully   **73 furtherer** accomplice
74 pinched punished, afflicted

Expelled remorse° and nature,° whom,° with Sebastian,
Whose inward pinches therefore are most strong,
Would here have killed your king, I do forgive thee,
Unnatural though thou art.—Their understanding
Begins to swell, and the approaching tide   80
Will shortly fill the reasonable shore°
That now lies foul and muddy. Not one of them
That yet looks on me, or would know me.—Ariel,
Fetch me the hat and rapier in my cell.

          *[*ARIEL *goes to the cell and returns immediately.]*

I will discase° me and myself present   85
As I was sometime Milan.° Quickly, spirit!
Thou shalt ere long be free.

            ARIEL *sings and helps to attire him.*

ARIEL.

    Where the bee sucks, there suck I.
    In a cowslip's bell I lie;
    There I couch° when owls do cry.   90
    On the bat's back I do fly
    After° summer merrily.
  Merrily, merrily shall I live now
  Under the blossom that hangs on the bough.

PROSPERO. Why, that's my dainty Ariel! I shall miss thee,   95
But yet thou shalt have freedom. So, so, so.°
To the King's ship, invisible as thou art!
There shalt thou find the mariners asleep
Under the hatches. The Master and the Boatswain
Being awake, enforce them to this place,   100
And presently,° I prithee.

ARIEL. I drink the air before me and return
Or ere° your pulse twice beat.

                       Exit.

GONZALO. All torment, trouble, wonder, and amazement
Inhabits here. Some heavenly power guide us   105
Out of this fearful° country!

PROSPERO.   Behold, sir King,
The wrongèd Duke of Milan, Prospero.
For more assurance that a living prince
Does now speak to thee, I embrace thy body;
And to thee and thy company I bid   110
A hearty welcome.   *[Embracing him.]*

ALONSO.   Whe'er thou be'st he or no,
Or some enchanted trifle° to abuse° me,
As late° I have been, I not know. Thy pulse
Beats as of flesh and blood; and, since I saw thee,

---

76 remorse pity.   **nature** natural feeling.   **whom** i.e., who   **81 reasonable
shore** shores of reason, i.e., minds. (Their reason returns, like the incoming tide.)
85 discase disrobe   **86 As . . . Milan** in my former appearance as Duke of Milan
90 couch lie   **92 After** i.e., pursuing   **96 So, so, so** (Expresses approval of Ariel's
help as valet.)   **101 presently** immediately   **103 Or ere** before   **106 fearful**
frightening   **112 trifle** trick of magic.   **abuse** deceive   **113 late** lately

Th' affliction of my mind amends, with which   115
I fear a madness held me. This must crave° —
An if this be at all° —a most strange story.°
Thy dukedom I resign,° and do entreat
Thou pardon me my wrongs.° But how should Prospero
Be living, and be here?

PROSPERO *[to* GONZALO*].* First, noble friend,   120
Let me embrace thine age,° whose honor cannot
Be measured or confined.   *[Embracing him.]*

GONZALO.   Whether this be
Or be not, I'll not swear.

PROSPERO.   You do yet taste
Some subtleties° o' th' isle, that will not let you
Believe things certain. Welcome, my friends all!   125
[Aside to SEBASTIAN *and* ANTONIO*.]* But you, my brace° of lords,
   were I so minded,
I here could pluck His Highness' frown upon you
And justify you° traitors. At this time
I will tell no tales.

SEBASTIAN.   The devil speaks in him.

PROSPERO.   No.
[To ANTONIO*.]* For you, most wicked sir, whom to call brother   130
Would even infect my mouth, I do forgive
Thy rankest fault—all of them; and require
My dukedom of thee, which perforce° I know
Thou must restore.

ALONSO.   If thou be'st Prospero,
Give us particulars of thy preservation,
How thou hast met us here, whom° three hours since   135
Were wrecked upon this shore; where I have lost—
How sharp the point of this remembrance is!—
My dear son Ferdinand.

PROSPERO.   I am woe° for 't, sir.

ALONSO. Irreparable is the loss, and Patience   140
Says it is past her cure.

PROSPERO.   I rather think
You have not sought her help, of whose soft grace°
For the like loss I have her sovereign° aid
And rest myself content.

ALONSO.   You the like loss?

PROSPERO. As great to me as late,° and supportable   145
To make the dear loss, have I° means much weaker

---

116 crave require   **117 An . . . all** if this is actually happening.   **story** i.e., explanation   **118 Thy . . . resign** (Alonso made arrangement with Antonio at the time of
Prospero's banishment for Milan to pay tribute to Naples; see 1.2.113–127.)
119 wrongs wrongdoings   **121 thine age** your venerable self   **124 subtleties** illusions, magical powers (playing on the idea of "pastries, concoctions")
126 brace pair   **128 justify you** prove you to be   **133 perforce** necessarily
135 whom i.e., who   **139 woe** sorry   **142 of . . . grace** by whose mercy
143 sovereign efficacious   **145 late** recent   **145–146 supportable . . . have I** to
make the deeply felt loss bearable, I have

Than you may call to comfort you; for I
Have lost my daughter.
ALONSO. A daughter?
    O heavens, that they were living both in Naples,   150
The king and queen there! That° they were, I wish
Myself were mudded° in that oozy bed
Where my son lies. When did you lose your daughter?
PROSPERO. In this last tempest. I perceive these lords
At this encounter do so much admire°   155
That they devour their reason° and scarce think
Their eyes do offices of truth, their words
Are natural breath.° But, howsoever you have
Been jostled from your senses, know for certain
That I am Prospero and that very duke   160
Which was thrust forth of° Milan, who most strangely
Upon this shore, where you were wrecked, was landed
To be the lord on 't. No more yet of this,
For 'tis a chronicle of day by day,°
Not a relation for a breakfast nor   165
Befitting this first meeting. Welcome, sir.
This cell's my court. Here have I few attendants,
And subjects none abroad.° Pray you, look in.
My dukedom since you have given me again,
I will requite° you with as good a thing,   170
At least bring forth a wonder to content ye
As much as me my dukedom.
    Here PROSPERO *discovers*° FERDINAND *and* MIRANDA, *playing at chess.*
MIRANDA. Sweet lord, you play me false.°
FERDINAND. No, my dearest love,
I would not for the world.   175
MIRANDA. Yes, for a score of kingdoms you should wrangle,
And I would call it fair play.°
ALONSO.   If this prove
A vision° of the island, one dear son
Shall I twice lose.
SEBASTIAN.   A most high miracle!
FERDINAND *[approaching his father].* Though the seas threaten, they   180
    are merciful;

---

151 That so that   **152 mudded** buried in the mud   **155 admire** wonder
156 devour their reason i.e., are openmouthed, dumbfounded   **156–158 scarce
. . . breath** scarcely believe that their eyes inform them accurately as to what they
see or that their words are naturally spoken   **161 of** from   **164 of day by day** requiring days to tell   **168 abroad** away from here, anywhere else   **170 requite**
repay   **172 s.d. discovers** i.e., by opening a curtain, presumably rearstage
173 play me false i.e., press your advantage   **176–177 Yes . . . play** i.e., yes,
even if we were playing for twenty kingdoms, something less than the whole world,
you would still press your advantage against me, and I would lovingly let you do it
as though it were fair play, or, if you were to play not just for stakes but literally for
kingdoms, my complaint would be out of order in that your "wrangling" would be
proper   **178 vision** illusion

    I have cursed them without cause.   *[He kneels.]*
ALONSO.   Now all the blessings
    Of a glad father compass° thee about!
    Arise, and say how thou cam'st here.   *[*FERDINAND *rises.]*
MIRANDA.   O, wonder!
    How many goodly creatures are there here!
    How beauteous mankind is! O brave° new world   185
    That has such people in 't!
PROSPERO.   'Tis new to thee.
ALONSO. What is this maid with whom thou wast at play?
    Your eld'st° acquaintance cannot be three hours.
    Is she the goddess that hath severed us,
    And brought us thus together?
FERDINAND.   Sir, she is mortal;   190
    But by immortal Providence she's mine.
    I chose her when I could not ask my father
    For his advice, nor thought I had one. She
    Is daughter to this famous Duke of Milan,
    Of whom so often I have heard renown,   195
    But never saw before; of whom I have
    Received a second life; and second father
    This lady makes him to me.
ALONSO.   I am hers.
    But O, how oddly will it sound that I
    Must ask my child forgiveness!
PROSPERO.   There, sir, stop.   200
    Let us not burden our remembrances with
    A heaviness° that's gone.
GONZALO.   I have inly° wept,
    Or should have spoke ere this. Look down, you gods,
    And on this couple drop a blessèd crown!
    For it is you that have chalked forth the way°   205
    Which brought us hither.
ALONSO.   I say amen, Gonzalo!
GONZALO. Was Milan° thrust from Milan, that his issue
    Should become kings of Naples? O, rejoice
    Beyond a common joy, and set it down
    With gold on lasting pillars: In one voyage   210
    Did Claribel her husband find at Tunis,
    And Ferdinand, her brother, found a wife
    Where he himself was lost; Prospero his dukedom
    In a poor isle; and all of us ourselves
    When no man was his own.°
ALONSO *[to* FERDINAND *and* MIRANDA*]*. Give me your hands.   215
    Let grief and sorrow still° embrace his° heart

---

182 compass encompass, embrace   **185 brave** splendid, gorgeously appareled,
handsome   **188 eld'st** longest   **202 heaviness** sadness.   **inly** inwardly
205 chalked . . . way marked as with a piece of chalk the pathway   **207 Was
Milan** was the Duke of Milan   **214–215 all . . . own** all of us have found ourselves
and our sanity when we all had lost our senses   **216 still** always. **his** that
person's

That° doth not wish you joy!

GONZALO.   Be it so! Amen!

Enter ARIEL, *with the* MASTER *and* BOATSWAIN *amazedly following.*

O, look, sir, look, sir! Here is more of us.
I prophesied, if a gallows were on land,
This fellow could not drown.—Now, blasphemy,°   220
That swear'st grace o'erboard,° not an oath° on shore?
Hast thou no mouth by land? What is the news?

BOATSWAIN. The best news is that we have safely found
Our King and company; the next, our ship—
Which, but three glasses° since, we gave out° split—   225
Is tight and yare° and bravely° rigged as when
We first put out to sea.

ARIEL *[aside to* PROSPERO*].* Sir, all this service
Have I done since I went.

PROSPERO *[aside to* ARIEL*].* My tricksy° spirit!

ALONSO. These are not natural events; they strengthen°
From strange to stranger. Say, how came you hither?   230

BOATSWAIN. If I did think, sir, I were well awake,
I'd strive to tell you. We were dead of sleep,°
And—how we know not—all clapped under hatches,
Where but even now, with strange and several° noises
Of roaring, shrieking, howling, jingling chains,   235
And more diversity of sounds, all horrible,
We were awaked; straightway at liberty;
Where we, in all her trim, freshly beheld
Our royal, good, and gallant ship, our Master
Cap'ring to eye° her. On a trice,° so please you,   240
Even in a dream, were we divided from them°
And were brought moping° hither.

ARIEL *[aside to* PROSPERO*].*   Was 't well done?

PROSPERO *[aside to* ARIEL*].* Bravely, my diligence. Thou shalt be free.

ALONSO. This is as strange a maze as e'er men trod,
And there is in this business more than nature   245
Was ever conduct° of. Some oracle
Must rectify our knowledge.

PROSPERO.   Sir, my liege,
Do not infest° your mind with beating on°
The strangeness of this business. At picked° leisure,
Which shall be shortly, single° I'll resolve° you,   250

---

217 That who   **220 blasphemy** i.e., blasphemer   **221 That swear'st grace o'erboard** i.e., you who banish heavenly grace from the ship by your blasphemies.
not an oath aren't you going to swear an oath   **225 glasses** i.e., hours.   **gave out**
reported, professed to be   **226 yare** ready.   **bravely** splendidly   **228 tricksy** ingenious, sportive   **229 strengthen** increase   **232 dead of sleep** deep in sleep
234 several diverse   **240 Cap'ring to eye** dancing for joy to see.   **On a trice** in
an instant   **241 them** i.e., the other crew members   **242 moping** in a daze
246 conduct guide   **248 infest** harass, disturb.   **beating on** worrying about
249 picked chosen, convenient   **250 single** privately, by my own human powers.
resolve satisfy, explain to

Which to you shall seem probable,° of every
These° happened accidents;° till when, be cheerful
And think of each thing well.° *[Aside to* ARIEL.*]* Come hither, spirit.
Set Caliban and his companions free.
Untie the spell. *[Exit* ARIEL.*]* How fares my gracious sir?   255
There are yet missing of your company
Some few odd° lads that you remember not.

Enter ARIEL, *driving in* CALIBAN, STEPHANO, *and* TRINCULO, *in their stolen apparel.*

STEPHANO. Every man shift° for all the rest,° and let no man take care for
    himself; for all is but fortune. Coragio,° bully monster,° coragio!

TRINCULO. If these be true spies° which I wear in my head, here's a   260
    goodly sight.

CALIBAN. O Setebos, these be brave° spirits indeed!
    How fine° my master is! I am afraid
    He will chastise me.

SEBASTIAN. Ha, ha!   265
    What things are these, my lord Antonio?
    Will money buy 'em?

ANTONIO.   Very like. One of them
    Is a plain fish, and no doubt marketable.

PROSPERO. Mark but the badges° of these men, my lords,
    Then say if they be true.° This misshapen knave,   270
    His mother was a witch, and one so strong
    That could control the moon, make flows and ebbs,
    And deal in her command without her power.°
    These three have robbed me, and this demidevil—
    For he's a bastard° one—had plotted with them   275
    To take my life. Two of these fellows you
    Must know and own.° This thing of darkness I
    Acknowledge mine.

CALIBAN.   I shall be pinched to death.

ALONSO. Is not this Stephano, my drunken butler?

SEBASTIAN. He is drunk now. Where had he wine?   280

ALONSO. And Trinculo is reeling ripe.° Where should they
    Find this grand liquor that hath gilded° 'em?
    [To TRINCULO.*]* How cam'st thou in this pickle?°

---

251 probable plausible   **251–252 of every These** about every one of these
252 accidents occurrences   **253 well** favorably   **257 odd** unaccounted for
258 shift provide.   **for all the rest** (Stephano drunkenly gets wrong the saying
"Every man for himself.")   **259 Coragio** courage   **bully monster** gallant monster.
(Ironical.)   **260 true spies** accurate observers (i.e., sharp eyes)   **262 brave** handsome   **263 fine** splendidly attired   **269 badges** emblems of cloth or silver worn
by retainers to indicate whom they serve. (Prospero refers here to the stolen clothes
as emblems of their villainy.)   **270 true** honest   **273 deal . . . power** wield the
moon's power, either without her authority or beyond her influence, or, even
though to do so was beyond Sycorax's own power   **275 bastard** counterfeit
277 own recognize, admit as belonging to you   **281 reeling ripe** stumblingly
drunk   **282 gilded** (1) flushed, made drunk (2) covered with gilt (suggesting the
horse urine)   **283 pickle** (1) fix, predicament (2) pickling brine (in this case, horse
urine)

TRINCULO. I have been in such a pickle since I saw you last that, I fear
      me, will never out of my bones. I shall not fear flyblowing.°   285
SEBASTIAN. Why, how now, Stephano?
STEPHANO. O, touch me not! I am not Stephano, but a cramp.
PROSPERO. You'd be king o' the isle, sirrah?°
STEPHANO. I should have been a sore° one, then.
ALONSO *[pointing to* CALIBAN*].* This is a strange thing as e'er I looked on. 290
PROSPERO. He is as disproportioned in his manners
      As in his shape.—Go, sirrah, to my cell.
      Take with you your companions. As you look
      To have my pardon, trim° it handsomely.
CALIBAN. Ay, that I will; and I'll be wise hereafter   295
      And seek for grace.° What a thrice-double ass
      Was I to take this drunkard for a god
      And worship this dull fool!
PROSPERO.   Go to. Away!
ALONSO. Hence, and bestow your luggage where you found it.
SEBASTIAN. Or stole it, rather.   300

                    [Exeunt CALIBAN, STEPHANO, *and* TRINCULO.*]*

PROSPERO. Sir, I invite Your Highness and your train
      To my poor cell, where you shall take your rest
      For this one night; which, part of it, I'll waste°
      With such discourse as, I not doubt, shall make it
      Go quick away: the story of my life,   305
      And the particular accidents° gone by
      Since I came to this isle. And in the morn
      I'll bring you to your ship, and so to Naples,
      Where I have hope to see the nuptial
      Of these our dear-belovèd solemnized;   310
      And thence retire me° to my Milan, where
      Every third thought shall be my grave.
ALONSO.   I long
      To hear the story of your life, which must
      Take° the ear strangely.
PROSPERO.   I'll deliver° all;
      And promise you calm seas, auspicious gales,   315
      And sail so expeditious that shall catch
      Your royal fleet far off.° *[Aside to* ARIEL.*]* My Ariel, chick,
      That is thy charge. Then to the elements
      Be free, and fare thou well!—Please you, draw near.°

                         Exeunt omnes [except PROSPERO*].*

---

285 flyblowing i.e., being fouled by fly eggs (from which he is saved by being
pickled) **288 sirrah** (Standard form of address to an inferior, here expressing rep-
rimand.) **289 sore** (1) tyrannical (2) sorry, inept (3) wracked by pain **294 trim**
prepare, decorate **296 grace** pardon, favor **303 waste** spend **306 accidents**
occurrences **311 retire me** return **314 Take** take effect upon, enchant.
deliver declare, relate **316–317 catch . . . far off** enable you to catch up with
the main part of your royal fleet, now afar off enroute to Naples (see 1.2.235–236)
319 draw near i.e., enter my cell

Epilogue *Spoken by* PROSPERO.

Now my charms are all o'erthrown,
And what strength I have 's mine own,
Which is most faint. Now, 'tis true,
I must be here confined by you
Or sent to Naples. Let me not,   5
Since I have my dukedom got
And pardoned the deceiver, dwell
In this bare island by your spell,
But release me from my bands°
With the help of your good hands.°   10
Gentle breath° of yours my sails
Must fill, or else my project fails,
Which was to please. Now I want°
Spirits to enforce,° art to enchant,
And my ending is despair,   15
Unless I be relieved by prayer,°
Which pierces so that it assaults°
Mercy itself, and frees° all faults.
As you from crimes° would pardoned be,
Let your indulgence° set me free.   20

                                                    Exit.

 TOPICS FOR CRITICAL THINKING AND WRITING

Act 1

1. Some directors of stage productions of *The Tempest* show, at the very beginning of the play, Ariel or Prospero presiding over the storm. What do you think of this idea, and why?

2. How would you characterize the Boatswain? And how would you characterize (on the basis of 1.1 only) Antonio? Sebastian? Gonzalo?

3. In 1.2, obviously Prospero's speeches from line 23 to line 185 are Shakespeare's attempt to provide necessary exposition. Some readers and spectators find the speeches tedious, and they find unsuccessful Shakespeare's attempts to make them dramatic by means of Miranda's brief comments). Your opinion? If you agree with these critics, try (for the sake of argument) to make a case on the other side. You might, for instance, take any one speech and show that it contains interestingly varied tones of voice—variations that, in effect, *are* dramatic action.

4. Some producers distribute parts of 1.1 throughout 1.2 in an effort to enliven 1.2. What do you think of this idea? If you think it has some merit,

---

Epilogue.   9 bands bonds   **10 hands** i.e., applause (the noise of which would break the spell of silence)   **11 Gentle breath** favorable breeze (produced by hands clapping or favorable comment)   **13 want** lack   **14 enforce** control   **16 prayer** i.e., Prospero's petition to the audience   **17 assaults** rightfully gains the attention of   **18 frees** obtains forgiveness for   **19 crimes** sins   **20 indulgence** (1) humoring, lenient approval (2) remission of punishment for sin exactly how would you divide 1.1, and exactly where in 1.2 would you put the pieces?

5. In 1.2. 89-90 Prospero speaks of himself as "neglecting worldly ends." To what degree do you think Prospero is responsible for what his enemies did to him?

6. How would you characterize Prospero's response to Ariel in 1.2.241–95? Are his speeches appropriate, or are they those of a tyrant? Or what?

7. In your opinion, how valid is Caliban's claim to the island in 1.2.334?

Act 2

1. In 2.1, Gonzalo gives his version of an ideal society (derived in part from an essay by Montaigne, printed on p. 316). How does Gonzalo's society compare with the society governed by Prospero?

2. In 2.1, Antonio presumably has nothing to gain by urging Sebastian to kill Alonso. Why do you suppose Shakespeare decided to have Sebastian make this suggestion?

3. In 2.2.25–30, Stephano says that he hopes he can get Caliban back to Naples, where he will make money from him. Do you think Shakespeare is implying that Prospero exploits Caliban in a more or less similar way? Or is Shakespeare implying a contrast? Or both?

4. In his song at the end of 2.2, Caliban thinks he has achieved freedom. How free is he?

Act 3

1. In the first scene of this act, why does Prospero assign hard labor to Ferdinand?

2. Read aloud, two or three times, Alonso's last speech in this scene. How does Alonso's mental condition compare with Sebastian's and Antonio's? Exactly how do you think each line in Alonso's speech should be spoken?

Act 4

1. Some directors of the play find Prospero's theatrical production (of Iris, and others) tedious, and they present it as comic. What do you think of this approach?

2. Look closely at Prospero's speech beginning "Our revels now are ended" (148). Many directors move this speech to the end of the play, thereby making it a sort of epilogue. If you were directing the play, would you make this change? Explain.

3. In 4.1.166, Prospero says, "We must prepare to meet with Caliban." Assuming that we tend to see some or all of the characters in the play at least somewhat symbolically (for instance, symbolic of power, or of goodness, or of stupidity), what might Caliban seem to stand for at this point in the play? Or is this a thoroughly wrong way of thinking about the characters?

Act 5

1. In 5.1.18-19, Ariel says that if Prospero saw the enchanted men he would pity them ("your affections / Would become tender"). What episodes do you find in the play where a character pities another character?
2. Do you think Prospero's punishment of Caliban is cruel, just, or merciful—or what? And why?
3. Prospero gives up his magic ("this rough magic / I here abjure" /5.1.50-51/). Shakespeare never tells us exactly *why* Prospero gives up his magic. What do you make of this action?
4. Many readers and spectators find Prospero still—despite his talk of forgiveness—very bitter in the last scene. What do you take his mental state to be? Do you think it is appropriate? Dramatically effective?
5. What *can* Prospero accomplish? What *has* he accomplished?

Additional Topics

1. *The Tempest* is Shakespeare's last play. Prospero's talk of retirement, and his putting away of magic, is sometimes seen as suggesting that Shakespeare is bidding farewell to the theater, the world of enchanting but insubstantial characters and stories. Do you think a biographical interpretation along these lines is useful? Explain.
2. A *foil* in drama is a character who contrasts with (and thereby helps to define) another character. Thus, Ariel and Caliban are often said to be foils, the one airy and light, the other earthy and clumsy. Take another pair of characters and show how they make an interesting contrast.
3. What, if anything, do Trinculo and Stephano contribute to the play?
4. Prospero has been seen as a racist-colonist. Do you agree? Support your argument with evidence.
5. *The Times Literary Supplement*, 2 September 1994, carried a favorable review of a production of *The Tempest*. The reviewer praised the company for performing the play

> as though it actually meant what it says, namely, that Prospero is wise and good; that his authority is educational; that self-restraint is both a virtue and the precondition of any meaningful freedom; that maturity, understanding and fulfillment are accessible only to innocence, which thus demands our protection; in short, that if only we go the right way about living them, our lives will prove to be self-justified, full of meaning and their own joyous reward. Such intuitions are, of course, not fashionable. One can see why a recent production had to have Ariel spit in Prospero's face on receiving his freedom. But why not just spit on Shakespeare, the play and on life while you're about it, and have done with the lot?

There's a great deal here to think about. Take some or all of it and offer your response.

MICHEL EYQUEM DE MONTAIGNE

No source is known for the plot of The Tempest, *but various bits in the play can be traced. For instance, Robert Eden's* History of Travail *(1577) mentions that the Patagonians worship a "great devil Setebos," and several writings concerning an English expedition that found its way from the Caribbean to Virginia in 1609 provided details about a shipwreck and about encounters with Indians.*

Gonzalo's description of an ideal commonwealth (2.1.141ff) probably is indebted to an essay by the French writer Montaigne (1533–92), first published in French in 1588 and translated into English by John Florio in 1603. Montaigne's essay concerns a topic that was much debated at the time: What is the nature of the "natural man"? Did the Indians before the encounter with Europeans live lives of "natural" virtue, or were they savages who were elevated by the religion and the civilization that the whites brought to them? To take a simple instance: Was their nudity a sign of their innocent and natural purity, or was it a sign of their ignorance, sexual corruption, and need for civilization? Which is superior, nature or nurture? *(The view that nature is in need of nurture of course provided a moral justification for colonization, and it was widely invoked later, especially during the Victorian period.)*

We print part of Montaigne's essay, in which he suggests that civilized people are prone to call barbaric any customs other than their own. Further, what civilized people call "wild" may be more properly regarded as "natural," whereas their own products of civilization may be regarded as un*natural, or as bastard. Elsewhere in the essay he suggests that although the natives of the New World had the habit of eating human flesh, they were very decent folk, superior to Europeans who tortured their own people and of course did not hesitate to torture the natives of the New World. (Shakespeare's Caliban is not said to eat human flesh, but his name probably is an anagram of* cannibals, *a word derived from* Caribales, *the name of a people Columbus encountered in the Caribbean.)*

Of the Cannibals

. . . I find (as far as I have been informed) there is nothing in that /Native American/ nation that is either barbarous or savage, unless men call that barbarism which is not common to them. As indeed, we have no other aim of truth and reason than the example and idea of the opinions and customs of the country we live in. There is ever perfect religion, perfect policy, perfect and complete use of all things. They are even savage, as we call those fruits wild which nature of herself and of her ordinary progress hath produced; whereas indeed, they are those which ourselves have altered by our artificial devices, and diverted from their common order, we should rather term savage. In those are the true and most profitable virtues and natural properties most lively and vigorous, which in these we have bastardized, applying them to the pleasure of our corrupted taste. And if notwithstanding, in divers fruits of those countries that were never tilled, we shall find that, in respect of ours, they are most excellent and as delicate unto our taste, there is no reason art should gain the point of honor of our great and puissant mother Nature. We have so much by our inventions surcharged the beauties and riches of her works that we have altogether overchoked her; yet wherever her purity shineth, she makes our vain and frivolous enterprises wonderfully ashamed. . . .

It is a nation . . . that hath no kind of traffic, no knowledge of letters, no intelligence of numbers, no name of magistrate, nor of politic superiority; no use of service, of riches, or of poverty; no contracts, no successions, no partitions, no occupation but idle; no respect of kindred but common, no apparel but natural, no manuring of lands, no use of wine, corn, or metal. The very words that import lying, falsehood, treason, dissimulations, covetousness, envy, detraction, and pardon, were never heard of amongst them. How dissonant would he find his imaginary commonwealth from this perfection?. . .

Furthermore, they live in a country of so exceeding pleasant and temperate situation that, as my testimonies have told me, it is very rare to see a sick body amongst them; and they have further assured me they never saw any man there either shaking with the palsy, toothless, with eyes dropping, or crooked and stooping through age.

 TOPICS FOR CRITICAL THINKING AND WRITING

1. Reread Montaigne's first sentence. Do you think that people have a tendency to slip into calling customs barbaric that are "not common to them"? What might be some examples? Is it clear to you that, for instance, corporal punishment (practiced in many parts of the world) is barbaric whereas imprisonment is humane?
2. What does Montaigne mean when he says that cultivated fruits are "bastardized"? Would you agree that at least some fruits and other products of civilization (or nurture) are inferior to those produced by nature? What do you think of extending the argument, saying that some tribes or races (or cultures?) are good by *nature* and are spoiled by *nurture* (codes of civilization)?
3. Some critics have suggested that in Gonzalo's description of an ideal community (2.1.141ff) Shakespeare is satirizing Montaigne. Your view? Your reasons?

 JANE LEE

Jane Lee, formerly of Tufts University, contributed this short essay to the playbill for a local production of The Tempest.

The Tempest *in Its Age and in Our Time*

"He was not of an age, but for all time." Thus Ben Jonson on Shakespeare, in a memorial poem published in 1623, seven years after Shakespeare's death.

Jonson may or may not have been sincere, but as a professional poet he knew what was expected of him, and he obliged with the expected sentiment—which happens to be true.

Let's begin with Shakespeare and his own age. No writer, not even the greatest, can wholly escape from his age, and Shakespeare can be profitably examined in his Elizabethan and Jacobean context. When we think of the Renaissance we think of the great voyages of discovery and of the widespread interest in what for Europe was the New World. Although Shakespeare displays only the slightest interest in the New World (he mentions America only once), and although for him a sea journey is of interest chiefly because it can lead to a shipwreck and thus get a comedy started, *The Tempest* indeed is influenced by Elizabethan literature of voyages. Shakespeare had been reading, or had heard of, accounts of *The Sea-Venture,* a ship that sailed from Plymouth for Virginia in 1609, carrying the new governor of the Virginia colony. *The Sea-Venture* was caught in a storm off the Bermudas and was thought to have been destroyed, but it was (miraculously, so it seemed) preserved. Numerous connections can be made between Shakespeare's play and the pamphlets describing the voyage to Bermuda and thence to Virginia, but one connection, very much of its time, is especially interesting. After recording that the governor tried to deal peaceably with the Indians but came to learn, when the Indians killed one of his men, "how little a fair and noble entreaty works upon a barbarous disposition," the writer wonders, "Can a leopard change his spots? Can a savage remaining savage be civil?" Such a reflection as this, of course, is relevant to Caliban, the "savage" of *The Tempest,* and to Prospero, who first sought to educate Caliban with "kindness" but who came to find kindness less effective than "stripes," i.e., lashes.

The Tempest, then, although set on an island in the Mediterranean, owes much to English and European thinking about the nature of the inhabitants of the New World, that is, to thinking about the nature of the "natural" man. Was the Indian a sort of unfallen man, a noble savage in an unfallen Eden, or was he even lower than the sinful European, who had been brought to some degree of civility by Christ's teachings and also by the stern discipline of governors?

And so the play can be seen as an early document in the history of English colonialism. Prospero, having enslaved the brutish Caliban and having seized his island, is now dependent on the slave: "We cannot miss /i.e. do without/ him. He does make our fire, / Fetch in our wood, and serves in offices / That profit us." Caliban has the qualities that the imperialistic white man customarily attributes to what Kipling almost three hundred years later called "the lesser breeds without the Law": he is lazy, smelly, and drunken, he worships devils, and he is lecherous and treacherous. The loyal courtier Gonzalo, unaware of Caliban, finds the air of the island sweet, the grass lush, a place fit for a utopian society in which there would be no crime and no need for hard labor, but Prospero finds that he must govern severely so long as Caliban and most of the shipwrecked people are on the island. All of this is to say, again, that *The Tempest* is of its own age, for it toys with the idea of Utopia—a word (meaning "no place" in Greek) invented by Sir Thomas More early in the English Renaissance. More gives the name to an imaginary society supposedly discovered during one of Amerigo Vespucci's voyages to the New World. His book, entitled *Utopia,* was widely read and discussed in Europe and in England.

5   Much can be said about *The Tempest* as a work of its age, but space is short and we must turn to the play as a work for all time. If *The Tempest* can be seen as a document in the history of colonialism, or in the history of Renaissance utopian thought, it can—and should—also be seen as a play that has very little to do with colonialism and very little to do with utopian thought, if by utopian thought we mean naive proposals for systems of government that will bring happiness to all citizens. In this, paradoxically, *The Tempest* resembles More's *Utopia,* for despite More's description of the admirable government of his imaginary people. More is not, at bottom, setting forth a proposal for a new kind of government that will convert European savages into moral people. Rather, More seems chiefly to be telling us not what government must do but what *individuals* must do if life is to be decent. What is needed is not an ideal government, but wise or enlightened *self*-government of the individual.

Let's look at one of Prospero's speeches. Prospero has at his mercy his treacherous brother, who had usurped the throne and set Prospero and Prospero's infant daughter adrift in a flimsy boat without a sail. Also under Prospero's magic spell are several other "men of sin." Prospero says:

> Though with their high wrongs I am struck to th' quick,
> Yet with my nobler reason 'gainst my fury
> Do I take part. The rarer action is
> In virtue than in vengeance. They being penitent,
> The sole drift of my purpose doth extend
> Not a frown further. Go, release them, Ariel.
> My Charms I'll break, their senses I'll restore,
> And they shall be themselves.

"The rarer action is / In virtue than in vengeance." "Virtue," here contrasted with "vengeance," obviously includes mercy; earlier in the play Prospero spoke of "The virtue of compassion." To put it a little differently, Prospero has conquered not only his wicked foes but his own quite understandable desire for vengeance, substituting forgiveness for it. This self-conquest, his greatest achievement, can be contrasted to the explosive passion of Caliban, who sought to rape Prospero's daughter, and to the murderous assertiveness of Prospero's brother and his allies. When, near the end of the play, Prospero says, "This thing of darkness I acknowledge mine," he is explicitly speaking of Caliban, but we can sense that he is also glancing at an enemy more dangerous than the savage islander; he is glancing at the dark impulse in himself, over which, however, he has triumphed.

And so, if Shakespeare was "of an age," he is also "for all time," just as, for example, More's *Utopia* is also both a Renaissance comment on the New World and (more important) a vision of how the individual—even in the corrupt Old World—should and can govern himself or herself. *The Tempest,* despite Gonzalo's utopian speech, like *Utopia* and like Plato's *Republic,* is not a treatise on government but on self-government. The connection with *The Republic* can be pursued for a moment. *The Republic* is a myth whose subject is the mind, for Plato's philosopher-kings are symbols of reason ruling over the passions of the enlightened man. When in *The Republic,* Glaucon (who doesn't quite get the point) doubts that Socrates' ideal state exists anywhere on earth, the reply is, "In heaven there is laid up a pattern of it, which he who desires may behold, and beholding, may set his own house in order."

The Tempest, like all good drama, gives us heightened images of our life, not merely life as it was lived at some remote historical period but life as we know it and feel it. To take a simple example, we feel the truth of even the loutish Trinculo's bitter observation that in England men will not give a coin "to relieve a lame beggar, /but/ will lay out ten to see a dead Indian." But *The Tempest* goes further than giving us a vivid image of life as we know it; like all other great drama, it gives us a memorable image of life *to live up to,* and thus perhaps it can, at least so far as any work of art can, help us to set our house in order. If Shakespeare was a colonialist, he was one in the sense that any great artist is: he explored the remote territory of the self, brought back his discoveries, and put them at our service.

[1993]

TOPICS FOR CRITICAL THINKING AND WRITING

1. In her second paragraph Lee says that Prospero "first sought to educate Caliban with 'kindness' but . . . came to find kindness less effective than 'stripes,' i.e. lashes." Examine Prospero's treatment of Caliban, from beginning to end. Does Prospero always rely on physical punishment? Is he sometimes—or always or often or never—cruel?
2. Does it make sense to say that *The Tempest* is (or may be) "for all time"? Explain.

STEPHEN GREENBLATT

Stephen Greenblatt, a professor of English at the University of California, Berkeley, is a specialist in the literature of the Renaissance. He is especially associated with a school of thought that he called the New Historicism, an approach discussed on page 440-41.

This essay originally appeared in 1991, in Chronicle of Higher Education, *a publication aimed chiefly at college and university teachers and administrators.*

The Best Way to Kill Our Literary Inheritance Is to Turn It Into a Decorous Celebration of the New World Order

The columnist George F. Will recently declared that Lynne V. Cheney, the chairman of the National Endowment for the Humanities, is "secretary of domestic defense."

"The foreign adversaries her husband, Dick, must keep at bay," Mr. Will wrote, "are less dangerous, in the long run, than the domestic forces with which she must deal." Who are these homegrown enemies, more dangerous even than Saddam Hussein with his arsenal of chemical weapons? The answer: professors of literature. You know, the kind of people who belong to that noted terrorist organization, the Modern Language Association.

Mr. Will, who made these allegations in *Newsweek* (April 22), doesn't name names—I suppose the brandishing of a list of the insidious fifth column's members is yet to come—but he does mention, as typical of the disease afflicting Western civilization, the professor who suggests that Shakespeare's *Tempest* is somehow about imperialism.

This is a curious example—since it is very difficult to argue that *The Tempest* is *not* about imperialism. (It is, of course, about many other things, as well, including the magical power of the theater.) The play—set on a mysterious island over whose inhabitants a European prince has assumed absolute control—is full of conspicuous allusions to contemporary debates over the project of colonization: The Virginia Company's official report on the state of its New World colony and the account by William Strachey, secretary of the settlement at Jamestown, of a violent storm and shipwreck off the coast of Bermuda, are examples.

5   Colonialism was not simply a given of the period. The great Spanish Dominican, Bartolomé de Las Casas argued that his countrymen should leave the New World, since they were bringing only exploitation and violence. Spanish jurists like Francisco de Vitoria presented cases against the enslavement of the Indians and against the claim to imperial possession of the Americas. The most searing attack on colonialism in the 16th century was written by the French essayist Montaigne, who in "Of Cannibals" wrote admiringly of the Indians and in "Of Coaches" lamented the whole European enterprise: "So many cities razed, so many nations exterminated, so many millions of people put to the sword, and the richest and most beautiful part of the world turned upside down, for the traffic in pearls and pepper!" We know that Shakespeare read Montaigne; one of the characters in *The Tempest* quotes from "Of Cannibals."

Shakespeare's imagination was clearly gripped by the conflict between the prince and the "savage" Caliban (is it too obvious to note the anagrammatic play on "cannibal"?). Caliban, enslaved by Prospero, bitterly challenges the European's right to sovereignty. The island was his birthright, he claims, and was unjustly taken from him. Caliban's claim is not upheld in *The Tempest,* but neither is it simply dismissed, and at the enigmatic close of the play all of the Europeans—every one of them—leave the island.

These are among the issues that literary scholars investigate and encourage their students to consider, and I would think that the columnists who currently profess an ardent interest in our cultural heritage would approve.

But for some of them such an investigation is an instance of what is intolerable—a wicked plot by renegade professors bent on sabotaging Western civilization by delegitimizing its founding texts and ideas. Such critics want a tame and orderly canon. The painful, messy struggles over rights and values, the political and sexual and ethical dilemmas that great art has taken upon itself to articulate and to grapple with, have no place in their curriculum. For them, what is at stake is the staunch reaffirmation of a shared and stable culture that is, as Mr. Will puts it, "the nation's social cement." Also at stake is the transmission of that culture to passive students.

But art, the art that matters, is not cement. It is mobile, complex, elusive, disturbing. A love of literature may help to forge community, but it is a community founded on imaginative freedom, the play of language, and scholarly honesty, not on flag waving, boosterism, and conformity.

10   The best way to kill our literary inheritance is to turn it into a decorous liturgical celebration of the new world order. Poets cannot soar when their feet are stuck in social cement.

The student of Shakespeare who asks about racism, misogyny, or anti-Semitism is not on the slippery slope toward what George Will calls "collective amnesia and deculturation." He or she is on the way to understanding something about *Othello, The Taming of the Shrew,* and *The Merchant of Venice.* It is, I believe, all but impossible to understand these plays without grappling with the dark energies upon which Shakespeare's art so powerfully draws.

And it is similarly difficult to come to terms with what *The Tempest* has to teach us about forgiveness, wisdom, and social atonement if we do not also come to terms with its relations to colonialism.

If we allow ourselves to think about the extent to which our magnificent cultural tradition—like that of every civilization we know of—is intertwined with cruelty, injustice, and pain, do we not, in fact, run the risk of "deculturation"? Not if our culture includes a regard for truth. Does this truth mean that we should despise or abandon great art?

Of course not.

15   Like most teachers, I am deeply committed to passing on the precious heritage of our language, and I take seriously the risk of collective amnesia. Yet there seems to me a far greater risk if professors of literature, frightened by intemperate attacks upon them in the press, refuse to ask the most difficult questions about the past—the risk that we might turn our artistic inheritance into a simple, reassuring, soporific lie.

[1991]

TOPICS FOR CRITICAL THINKING AND WRITING

1. In paragraph 3 Greenblatt says that in *Newsweek* (22 April 1991) George Will mentions, "as typical of the disease afflicting Western civilization, the professor who suggests that Shakespeare's *Tempest* is somehow about imperialism." Will's exact words are that some professors say "Shakespeare's *Tempest* reflects the imperialist rape of the Third World." Has Greenblatt reported Will's view fairly? Explain.

2. There is no doubt that Shakespeare derived some details of *The Tempest* from reports of the New World. Does this in itself mean that the play must in some degree be about the New World? Do *you* think it is about the New World? Entirely? In part? A little? Not at all? Explain.

3. In paragraph 12 Greenblatt says that *The Tempest* can "teach us about forgiveness, wisdom, and social atonement." Do you agree? If so, *what* can it teach us about these things?

RALPH BERRY AND JONATHAN MILLER

Ralph Berry is the author of several books on Shakespeare. Jonathan Miller, a physician by training, is a noted director of plays. We print part of an interview in which Berry questions Miller about his 1970 production of The Tempest.

A Production of The Tempest

JM. It's in disease that one understands health and I think that we can actually now by hindsight understand a great deal more of the relationship of white Europe to the black world. Knowing what we now know about the emergence of the black world and its revolt against the world of white Europe, I just don't think that we would have had the conceptual apparatus, the cognitive skills to visualise that until it began to break down. Now this is not because I wish to seize *The Tempest* or to hijack *The Tempest* and to fly it to a modern airport and make it do the work of anti-colonial radicalism, that would be I think a very crude and brutal thing to do. It is just that by bringing out that particular theme in *The Tempest* something rather rich happens which wouldn't occur if one simply played the rather romantic version of *The Tempest* where both Caliban and Ariel are impalpable spirits or gross clods. I mean I think that there is something very interesting also in seeing the trio of Prospero, Caliban and Ariel in the light of some metaphysical idea of the division of the human soul and the tripartite nature of the mind.

RB. How did your approach to *The Tempest* come into being?

JM. Well, it came into being in two ways. Very often I find that, although I spoke previously about not being exposed to theatrical clichés I've been exposed to a certain number of them and certainly some of my moves in the theatre have been prompted by a revulsion against certain well-established clichés, which are so glaring that hardly anyone who is aware of simply being at school could fail to notice them. Now the one which stuck in my gorge was the sequin-spangled, pointed-eared, flitting figure of Ariel on wires, his hands held stiffly behind him as he flew *à la* Peter Pan on and off the stage. This seemed to me to be sentimental and diminishing and similarly the scaly, web-footed monster of Caliban just didn't tell me anything about anyone, it wasn't a monster which meant anything in my imagination and it actually clotted my imagination and stopped it from thinking. But I had been reading some years before a book by an anthropologist called Mannoni, who had written a book on the revolt in Madagascar in 1947, and he had used as a metaphor in order to explain the relationships of the very protagonists of the revolt the image of *The Tempest* and he saw Caliban and Ariel as different forms of black response to white paternalism. In Caliban he saw the demoralised, detribalised, dispossessed shuffling field hand and in Ariel a rather deft accomplished black who actually absorbs all the techniques and skills of the white master; the house servant, who is then in a position to assume political power when the white master goes back home. And of course we had this situation only a few years ago in Nigeria, with the skilled civil servant Ibos and the unskilled tribal Hausas. Now once again I wasn't using *The Tempest* as a political cartoon to illustrate the Nigerian dilemma nor as it were to castigate modern colonialism or to expose the wickedness of Rhodesia, but to use the images of Rhodesia, Nigeria, and indeed the whole colonial theme as knowledge which the audience brought to bear on Shakespeare's play. They could scarcely avoid thinking of that situation when the two characters were represented as blacks. Now by doing it in this way I hoped to bring them into a closer relationship with the whole notion of subordination and mastery which I think is one of the things which Shakespeare is talking about with great eloquence in that play. And I think he is also talking about, in a sense, infantilism and about the way in which maturity is only arrived at by surrendering one's claim to control the whole of nature. A child after all arrives at maturity by appreciating the reality principle, and after all what is the reality principle? The reality principle is simply the understanding that there are certain things over which one has control, and there are most things over which one has no control.

RB. I think that the reality principle is certainly one of the immutable touchstones of Shakespeare's whole work.

5   *JM.* I think that this in a sense comes out very clearly in this play, particularly if you slant it in this manner. After all one of the most important aspects of the reality principle is that there is a limited control over other people's destinies, not just over the physical world, but over the moral world, and that certain infantile personalities flourish in the colonial situation because they meet people whose power to resist their will is diminished by their lack of skills and so you often get rather immature personalities flourishing in the colonial situation because the colonial situation has in it people who cannot resist the superior technology of advanced society, and Prospero achieves his maturity in surrendering his power over his slaves, in leaving the island and returning to the world in which he must actually face his peers and equals, in a society where everyone has access to the same skills.

RB. And indeed he looks forward to surrendering his power to his children.

JM. He surrenders three things: he surrenders the power over his own children, he surrenders the power over subordinates, or at least over helpless subordinates, and he surrenders this impractical desire for power over the forces of nature. By breaking his staff he is doing what the child really does after the age of five, of realising that his rage will not call down the tempest but only contempt.

[1977]

✍ TOPICS FOR CRITICAL THINKING AND WRITING

1. In his first paragraph Miller suggests that today we can see *The Tempest* in interesting ways that were unavailable to earlier ages. If you find this approach attractive, apply it to some literary work other than *The Tempest*. For instance, can we now see meanings in *Huckleberry Finn* that were unavailable to Mark Twain and his contemporary readers?

2. In paragraph 3 Miller summarizes an interpretation of Caliban and Ariel. Do you think this interpretation makes sense? Explain.

3. If you were producing *The Tempest* might you (like Miller) present Caliban and Ariel as black? Why? (You may want to take into account the next essay, by Errol G. Hill, in this book.)

4. Miller says (paragraph 3) that *The Tempest* is partly about "the whole notion of subordination and mastery." But *what* does it say about these notions?

5. Summarize Miller's view of "infantilism" (paragraphs 3–7) and its relation to Prospero. Next, indicate the degree to which you think this view of infantilism helps you to understand the play.

 ERROL G. HILL

Errol G. Hill, a theater historian, is the author of many studies, including Shakespeare in Sable: A History of Black Shakespearean Actors. *We reprint part of an essay that originally appeared in* Theatre History Studies.

Caliban and Ariel:
A Study in Black and White

When the establishment theatre slowly began to overcome its opposition to interracial casting in Shakespeare, Caliban was one of the first nonblack roles offered to black actors. The occasion was the 1944 production by Margaret Webster which opened at the Alvin Theatre in New York on January 25, 1945, after short tryout runs in Philadelphia and Boston. In the cast were Arnold Moss as Prospero, Canada Lee as Caliban, and the ballerina Vera Zorina as Ariel. Webster had, a few years earlier, created a breakthrough of sorts by casting Paul Robeson as Othello in the record-breaking Theatre Guild production of that play and now she was building on that success. The February 1945 issue of *Theatre Arts* defended her choice of Canada Lee for the role of Caliban:

> In picking the Negro actor for the role, Miss Webster made it clear that she meant to exploit his particular intensity, his power to come to grips with character, and not the pigmentation of his skin. "I do not intend," she insists, "to make Caliban a parable of the current state of the American Negro." Yet her willing eyes discover a ready parallel.

Webster may not have intended it, but she was setting a dangerous precedent. In his first night review of the production, one of the major New York critics observed that "Caliban is a perfect role for a Negro." The production ran for one hundred performances at the Alvin Theatre and was revived later that year at City Center, New York, for a further three weeks.

Now it is true that to the medieval and Elizabethan mind, blackness was associated with evil and hence with the devil who is "the prince of darkness" and personifies evil. Caliban, we are told in the play, was fathered by the devil and is referred to by Prospero as "a devil, a born devil" and "a thing of darkness." It can therefore be argued that he ought originally to have been played black. However, to my knowledge, there is no tradition of playing the role in blackface or of using a black actor prior to Webster's production, and certainly from a modern viewpoint there is no logical justification for casting a black actor as Caliban when the counterpart role of Ariel is given to a sylphlike white actor or, quite often, actress. If anything, the reverse is more appropriate.

Caliban's mother, we recall, was a foul blue-eyed witch called Sycorax who, pregnant with him, had been banished from Algiers to the island. She was either European or Mediterannean in origin and her misshapen son who, Shakespeare tells us, is freckled, must have shared his mother's ethnic pedigree. The delicate Ariel, on the other hand, was found on the island by Sycorax and imprisoned in a pine tree until freed by Prospero who promptly enslaved him as his personal genie. Though unhuman and free of the elements, Ariel inhabited the island prior to the arrival of foreigners and is presumably indigenous to the Caribbean—in any case hardly European. These considerations have been generally ignored in filling the roles. Instead Ariel, the creature of air and native to the Caribbean, is white. Caliban, the savage monster and would-be rapist from the Mediterranean, is black. It is beauty and the beast all over again, with white equating beauty and black bestiality.

[1984]

TOPICS FOR CRITICAL THINKING AND WRITING

1. Do you think that a director should or should not cast an African-American in the role of Caliban? Or is the matter of casting irrelevant?
2. Browse through the issues constituting the last two or three years of *Shakespeare Quarterly,* or the last two or three issues of *Shakespeare Survey* (an annual publication), taking special note of the comments on Caliban and Ariel in various productions. Summarize these, and then indicate which interpretations seem to you to be especially interesting and fruitful.

 LINDA BAMBER

Linda Bamber, author of Comic Women, Tragic Men: A Study of Gender and Genre in Shakespeare, *teaches English literature at Tufts University.*

The following essay, concerned with matters of gender, was written for this book.

The Tempest *and The* Traffic in Women

The Tempest, as many readers have noticed, recapitulates several themes from Shakespeare's earlier plays. Sometimes it seems to be doing so "consciously," if a play can be said to be conscious of its own procedures. First of all, in a series of swift and virtuosic variations, it recapitulates the theme of the masculine struggle for power against other men. Antonio and Sebastian conspire to kill Alonso for his crown; Caliban, Trinculo, and Stephano plot to kill Prospero for his power on the island; Ferdinand is accused of being a usuper of Prospero's power and is temporarily enslaved as punishment; and, of course, Antonio has conspired with Alonso to usurp Prospero's power in Milan and "extirpate"* Prospero himself. Behind this array of murderous

*All references are to the Signet Classic editions of Shakespeare's plays, Sylvan Barnet, gen. ed. (New York: NAL, 1987). 1.2.125.

conspiracies lie the history plays and the tragedies, in which men fight and kill each other for political power and revenge.

The mating of Miranda is another theme with a long history behind it. We may think of all the fathers in Shakespeare who have battled their daughters for the power to choose the daughter's sexual partner; more broadly, we may think of all the men—fathers, husbands and lovers—who have suffered and made others suffer when they lose control of "their" women's sexuality. Capulet, Brabantio, Egeus, and Lear fall into the first category; Othello, Leontes, Antony, and perhaps Hamlet fall into the second. In *The Tempest,* of course, the father and daughter do not struggle against each other. They are in perfect agreement as to the choice of Miranda's mate. And yet the play strips to its essentials—and thus makes legible—the father-daughter issue as well as the male power issue. Moreover, it is the play in which the fundamental connection between the two themes is most clearly spelled out.

In a brilliant essay called "The Traffic in Women: Notes on the 'Political Economy' of Sex,"[1] Gayle Rubin has appropriated for feminist purposes the insights of Claude Levi-Strauss's *The Elementary Structures of Kinship* in ways that may be pertinent to a reading of *The Tempest.* Levi-Strauss, as Rubin puts it, "sees the essence of kinship systems to lie in an exchange of women between men" (171). To give a woman to another family or tribe creates reciprocal obligations on the one hand and "affines" or allies on the other. It can make allies, in fact, out of enemies, and expand the scope and power of the man who gives the woman as a gift. This description of primitive social structure applies neatly to the action of *The Tempest,* in which Prospero's gift of Miranda to Alonso's family creates a kinship alliance with a former enemy and supersedes the bond between Alonso and Antonio. Miranda is Prospero's ticket home; or rather Prospero's ownership in her newly acquired sexuality is his ticket home. It may be objected that this is too harsh a description of Prospero's relationship to his daughter. He does, after all, negotiate quite delicately with her over her feelings for Ferdinand when Ferdinand first appears, and he seems to behave as if the marriage could not take place without her desire for it. But Levi-Strauss makes clear that the woman remains an "object in the exchange, not . . . one of the partners . . . even when the girl's feelings are taken into consideration, as, moreover, is usually the case." The partners are not "a man and a woman, . . . but two groups of men," and "in acquiescing to the proposed union, /the woman only/ precipitates or allows the exchange to take place, she cannot alter its nature."[2]

Fragments of the picture drawn by Rubin and Levi-Strauss appear in earlier plays, where they often seem somewhat inexplicable. For instance, in *A Midsummer Night's Dream* Egeus's will to control his daughter's choice of a husband seems utterly irrational, since Lysander and Demetrius are clearly meant to be indistinguishable from one another. But if we understand Egeus to be asserting his ownership in Hermia's sexuality, then his control is valuable for its own sake, not for its influence over Hermia's choice. "/Demetrius/ hath my love," declares Egeus,

> And what is mine my love shall render him.
> And she is mine, and all my right of her
> I do estate unto Demetrius. (1.1.95–98)

The actual husband is irrelevant. What matters are Egeus's rights of possession in his daughter, without which he has nothing to trade with other men.

5   Another puzzling moment that clears up in the light of the idea of the exchange of women is the one in which Othello responds to the news that Desdemona has been unfaithful to him. "Farewell content!" he cries, which is understandable enough; but then he goes on,

> Farewell the plumed troops, and the big wars
> That makes ambition virtue! O, farewell!
> Farewell . . . all quality,
> Pride, pomp, and circumstance of glorious war!
>   . . .
> Farewell! Othello's occupation's gone! (3.3.345–48, 350–51, 354)

There is no logical reason why Othello should not continue to perform his duties as a Venetian general even if his wife has been unfaithful. And yet Othello assumes that his relations with other men—the men who confer and acknowledge his power—have been catastrophically damaged by this event. Having lost his ownership in this daughter of Venice, Othello loses his connection to Venice itself and thus his "occupation." Prospero, by contrast, loses his occupation first but regains it when the woman *he* "owns" becomes marriageable.

Is the exchange of women part of the ideology of *The Tempest* or not? Does *The Tempest* simply reveal the mechanisms of the traffic in women (thus making it available for criticism) or is it committed to the system it depends on for its plot? The answer, as usual in Shakespeare, is "Both." Think, for instance, of *The Merchant of Venice,* which is both an anti-Semitic play and a play about anti-Semitism. And certainly when dealing with patriarchal structures of all kinds Shakespeare goes back and forth between endorsing and criticizing what he describes. I will begin, then, with some evidence of Shakespeare's commitment to the traffic in women and proceed to his uneasiness with it.

The journey that brings Alonso and his group to Prospero's island was originally a wedding journey, undertaken to deliver Alonso's daughter Claribel to the King of Tunis. In giving his daughter to a foreigner Alonso seems to be serving the "social aim of exogamy and alliance"[3] so important to the formation of kinship systems. But apparently Alonso has gone too far. Tunis is *too* far outside the immediate family, *too* "exo." After the shipwreck, Sebastian refuses to console Alonso for the presumed death of Ferdinand, berating him instead for his behavior toward Claribel:

> Sir, you may thank yourself for this great loss,
> That would not bless our Europe with your daughter,
> But rather loose her to an African.
>   . . .
> You were kneeled to and importuned otherwise
> By all of us; and the fair soul herself
> Weighed, between loathness and obedience, at
> Which end o' th' beam should bow. (2.1.128–30; 133–36.)

Not only has Prospero given to an African what he should have given to a European, but he has also failed to find an accommodation with his daughter's own desire. Clearly Alonso has played his hand badly. Sebastian tells him he will never see Claribel again, and neither, presumably, will he profit from his alliance with the King of Tunis.

The contrast with Prospero is obvious. While Alonso imposes his will on his daughter crudely, Prospero is full of subtlety and technique. While Alonso makes a useless alliance, Prospero makes a useful one. Like a conduct book or an instruction manual, the play teaches by negative as well as positive examples: *don't* do it that way, *do* do it this way. But like a conduct book or an instruction manual, the play never doubts that "it" should be done. The presence of the negative example is evidence of the play's committment to the traffic in women. Because Alonso does it wrong, Prospero seems to do it right. It is Alonso's failures that invite us to approve of Prospero's liberal, benevolent use of his patriarchal powers, to notice the effort he puts into their exercise, and to applaud his ultimate success. The reader's judgment is deflected onto Alonso, and the system itself is protected from criticism.

10   But the play does register a price for the traffic in women, and that price is the incest taboo. Levi-Strauss argues that the incest taboo "should best be understood as a mechanism to insure that ... exchanges [of women] take place between families and between groups" (Rubin 173). He quotes an informant as follows:

> What, would you like to marry your sister? What is the matter with you? Don't you want a brother-in-law? Don't you realize that if you marry another man's sister and another man marries your sister, you will have at least two brothers-in-law, while if you marry your own sister you will have none? With whom will you hunt, with whom will you garden, whom will you go visit? (Levi-Strauss 485)

This quotation makes it clear that there is something to be given up as well as something to be gained in the exchange of women. In *Civilization and Its Discontents* Freud argues that what we value about organized society is purchased at the price of the repression or sublimation of our instinctual life, and *The Tempest* can be read as a kind of gloss on that argument. By obeying the rules of exogamy Prospero creates a kinship alliance with Alonso; and "kinship," as Rubin says, "is organization, and organization gives power" (174). The power that Prospero gains, however, requires the renunciation of his own sexual gratification. The drama of that renunciation is played out in his relations with Caliban.

Caliban is most often read as the native "other" degraded by the European imagination and enslaved by European power. But he may also be read as *self*-difference, the otherness we reject within ourselves and specifically as the otherness of the body. "This thing of darkness," Prospero says at the end of the play, "I / Acknowledge mine" (5.1.275-6). Caliban has far more of a body than anyone else in the play; only Ferdinand offers any competition at all. Caliban is a suffering body, first of all, pinched and stung and cramped by Prospero's punishments. Then he is an alcoholic body, drunk and rowdy; a humiliated body, dunked in a cess-pool; and, most relevant to my discussion, a sexual body with desire for Miranda. It must be admitted that even Caliban's desire for Miranda is mixed with a "civilized" desire for kinship, power, and alliances with men. Reminded of the attempted rape, an unrepentant Caliban says,

> O ho, O ho! Would't had been done!
> Thou didst prevent me; I had peopled else
> This isle with Calibans. (1.2.349-51)

And Caliban "offers" Miranda to Stephano to lure him into the conspiracy against Prospero:

> And that most deeply to consider is
> The beauty of his daughter.
>   . . .
> She will become thy bed, I warrant,
> And bring thee forth brave brood. (3.2.102-3; 108-9)

But although Caliban is at one level a player in the male power game, at another level he is that which Prospero must control in order to succeed at the game, that is, his own instinctual life. Only Caliban has the power to elicit an intense emotional reaction from Prospero; the reaction is rage, and it interrupts the wedding masque that Prospero produces to celebrate Miranda's engagement to Ferdinand. As I argue elsewhere,[4] this rage may be related to the wedding masque itself, which marks the moment when Prospero gives up his sexual rights to his daughter. The rape that Caliban attempted and Prospero prevented can be seen as the site or symbol of Prospero's struggle with himself. It is worth noting in this context that Prospero has lived in involuntary celibacy during his entire stay on the island and that the return to Milan is in no way imagined as a return to a sexual partner.

Prospero's control of Caliban hurts. For one thing, Caliban's claim to have been himself usurped by Prospero is never answered, so it calls into question Prospero's own legitimacy and perhaps legitimacy per se. More significantly for my purposes, Caliban is a demonstration that we cannot actually separate repression of the body from something even closer to home, something like the repression of desire itself. Caliban's great speech about the music on the island concludes,

> . . . and then, in dreaming,
> The clouds methought would open and show riches
> Ready to drop upon me, that when I waked
> I cried to dream again. (3.3.145-48)

The enslavement of the grotesque, incestuous body is also, in *The Tempest,* the enslavement of the delicate soul. So much is given up, the play suggests, for the sake of social organization—for the sake of *having* a woman to exchange—that the whole system must be understood as problematic. Thus *The Tempest* questions its own ideology.

Does the play have any "consciousness" of the cost to *women* of the system it both supports and questions, or is it only the man who pays the price? Claribel, the violated woman, is remembered only by Gonzalo in his cheerful summing-up speech at the end of the play:

> . . . In one voyage
> Did Claribel her husband find at Tunis,
> And Ferdinand, her brother, found a wife
> Where he himself was lost. (5.1.208-11)

At first glance this appears to be a complete erasure of Claribel's experience. Her situation is exactly what it has always been, and yet now it is described as a joyful affair, and the description is allowed to stand. But of course it is Gonzalo who is speaking, and the play invites skepticism toward

Gonzalo. The ending of the play is much more somber than Gonzalo real-izes—perhaps even a little bitter. Is Gonzalo's fleeting mention of Claribel the opposite of what it seems, a reminder of a difficulty rather than a dismissal of it? Perhaps. But even if we grant that it is, this moment seems a most minimal acknowledgment of the price that is paid by women for kinship, for exogamy, for the traffic in women. The play accepts as inevitable the "distinction," as Rubin puts it, "between gift and giver" (174) and does not concern itself unduly with the tragedy for a woman of *being* the gift.

[1995]

Notes

[1]Gayle Rubin, "The Traffic in Women: Notes on the 'Political Economy' of Sex," in Rayna R. Reiter, ed., *Toward an Anthropology of Women* (New York: Monthly Review, 1975).

[2]Claude Levi-Strauss, *The Elementary Structures of Kinship* (Boston: Beacon, 1969), p. 115.

[3]Rubin, p. 173.

[4]Linda Bamber, *Comic Women, Tragic Men: Gender and Genre in Shakespeare* (Palo Alto: Stanford UP, 1982), p. 177.

TOPICS FOR CRITICAL THINKING AND WRITING

1. In paragraphs 3 and 4 Bamber points to scenes in *A Midsummer Night's Dream* and *Othello* that are clarified by the idea of "the traffic in women." If you are familiar with any other scenes in Shakespeare that are thus clarified, specify them and briefly explain how they fit into the pattern.

2. Bamber suggests that "the rape that Caliban attempted and Prospero prevented can be seen as the site or symbol of Prospero's struggle with himself." How might you support this assertion?

3. Bamber ends by saying that the play "does not concern itself unduly with the tragedy for a woman *being* the gift." Assuming the truth of her observation, do you think the play is therefore at fault? Explain.

CHAPTER 11

Reading (and Writing about) Poetry

THE SPEAKER AND THE POET

The **speaker,** or **voice,** or **mask,** or **persona** (Latin for *mask*) that speaks a poem is not usually identical with the poet who writes it. The author assumes a role, or counterfeits the speech of a person in a particular situation. The nineteenth-century English poet Robert Browning, for instance, in "My Last Duchess" invented a Renaissance Italian duke who, in his palace, talks about his first wife and his art collection with an emissary from a count who is negotiating to offer his daughter in marriage to the duke.

In reading a poem, then, the first and most important question to ask yourself is this: Who is speaking? If an audience and a setting are suggested, keep them in mind too, although these are not always indicated in a poem. Consider, for example, the following poem.

 EMILY DICKINSON (1830–1886)

I'm Nobody! Who are you?
Are you—Nobody—too?
Then there's a pair of us!
Don't tell! they'd banish us—you know!   4

How dreary—to be—Somebody!
How public—like a Frog—
To tell your name—the livelong June—
To an admiring Bog!   8

[1861?]

We can't quite say that the speaker is Emily Dickinson, though if we have read a fair number of her poems we can say that the voice in this poem is familiar, and perhaps here we *can* talk of Dickinson rather than of "the speaker of the poem," since this speaker (unlike Browning's Renaissance duke) clearly is not a figure utterly remote from the poet.

Let's consider the sort of person we hear in "I'm Nobody! Who are you?" (Read it aloud, to see if you agree with what we say. In fact, you should test each of our assertions by reading the poem aloud.) The voice in the first line is rather like that of a child playing a game with a friend. In the second and third lines the speaker sees the reader as a fellow spirit ("Are you—Nobody—too?") and invites the reader to join her ("Then there's a pair of us!"), to form a sort of conspiracy of silence against outsiders ("Don't tell!").

In "they'd banish us," however, we hear a word that a child would not be likely to use, and we probably feel that the speaker is a shy but (with the right companion) playful adult, who here is speaking to an intimate friend, the reader. By means of "banish," a word that brings to mind images of a king's court, the speaker almost comically inflates and thereby makes fun of the "they" who are opposed to "us." In the second stanza, or we might better say in the space between the two stanzas, the speaker puts aside the childlike manner. In "How dreary," the first words of the second stanza, we hear a sophisticated voice, one might even say a world-weary voice or a voice perhaps with more than a touch of condescension. But since by now we are paired with the speaker in a conspiracy against outsiders, we enjoy the contrast that the speaker makes between the Nobodies and the Somebodies. Who are these Somebodies, these people who would imperiously "banish" the speaker and the friend? What are the Somebodies like?

> How dreary—to be—Somebody!
> How public—like a Frog—
> To tell your name—the livelong June—
> To an admiring Bog!

The last two lines do at least two things: They amusingly explain to the speaker's new friend (the reader) in what way a Somebody is public (it proclaims its presence all day), and they indicate the absurdity of the Somebody-Frog's behavior (the audience is "an admiring Bog"). By the end of the poem we are quite convinced that it is better to be a Nobody (like Dickinson and the reader?) than a Somebody (a loudmouth).

But Dickinson did not, of course, always speak in this persona. In "Wild Nights," probably written in the same year as "I'm Nobody! Who are you?", Dickinson speaks as an impassioned lover, but we need not assume that the beloved is actually in the presence of the lover. In fact, since the second line says, "Were I with thee," the reader must assume that the person addressed is *not* present. The poem apparently represents a state of mind—a sort of talking to oneself—rather than an address to another person.

 Wild Nights—Wild Nights,
Were I with Thee
Wild Nights should be
Our luxury   4

Futile—the Winds
To a Heart in port—

Done with the Compass—
Done with the Chart!   8

Rowing in Eden—
Ah, the Sea!
Might I but moor—Tonight—
In Thee.   12

[c. 1861]

Clearly the speaker is someone passionately in love. The following questions invite you to look more closely at how the speaker of "Wild Nights" is characterized.

QUESTIONS FOR CRITICAL THINKING AND WRITING

1. How does this poem communicate the speaker's state of mind? For example, in the first stanza (lines 1–4), what—beyond the meaning of the words—is communicated by the repetition of "Wild Nights"? In the last stanza (lines 9–12), what is the tone of "Ah, the Sea!"? ("Tone" means something like emotional coloring, as for instance when one speaks of a "businesslike tone," a "bitter tone," or an "eager tone.")

2. Paraphrase (that is, put into your own words) the second stanza. What does this stanza communicate about the speaker's love for the beloved? Compare your paraphrase and the original. What does the form of the original sentences (the *omission,* for instance, of the verbs of lines 5 and 6 and of the subject in lines 7 and 8) communicate?

3. Paraphrase the last stanza. How does "Ah, the Sea!" fit into your paraphrase? If you had trouble fitting it in, do you think the poem would be better off without it? If not, why not?

The voice speaking a poem may, of course, have the ring of the author's own voice, and to make a distinction between speaker and author may at times seem perverse. In fact, some poetry (especially contemporary American poetry) is highly autobiographical. Still, even in autobiographical poems it may be convenient to distinguish between author and speaker. The speaker of a given poem is, let's say, Sylvia Plath in her role as parent, or Sylvia Plath in her role as daughter, not simply Sylvia Plath the poet.

THE LANGUAGE OF POETRY: DICTION AND TONE

How is a voice or mask or persona created? From the whole of language, the author consciously or unconsciously selects certain words and grammatical constructions; this selection constitutes the persona's diction. It is, then, partly by the diction that we come to know the speaker of a poem. Just as in life there is a difference between people who speak of a "belly button," a "navel," or an "umbilicus," so in poetry there is a difference between speakers who use one word rather than another. Of course it is also possible that all three of these words are part of a given speaker's vocabulary, and the speaker's choice among the three would depend on the situation. That is, in addressing a child, the speaker would probably use the word "belly button"; in addressing an adult other than a family member or close friend, the speaker might be more likely to use "navel"; and if the speaker is a physician addressing an audience of physicians, he or she might be most likely to use "umbilicus." But this is only to say, again, that the dramatic situation in which one finds oneself helps to define oneself, helps to establish the particular role that one is playing.

Of course some words are used in virtually all poems: *I, see, and,* and the like. Still, the grammatical constructions in which they appear may help to define the speaker. In Dickinson's "Wild Nights," for instance, expressions such as "Were I with Thee" and "Might I" indicate a speaker of an earlier century than ours, and probably an educated speaker.

Speakers have attitudes toward themselves, their subjects, and their audiences, and, consciously or unconsciously, they choose their words, pitch, and modulation accordingly; all these add up to their tone. In written literature, tone must be detected without the aid of the ear, although it's a good idea to read poetry aloud, trying to find the appropriate tone of voice. That is, the reader must understand by the selection and sequence of words the way the words are meant to sound—playful, angry, confidential, or ironic, for example. The reader must catch what Frost calls "the speaking tone of voice somehow entangled in the words and fastened to the page for the ear of the imagination."

Writing about the Speaker

Robert Frost once said that "everything written is as good as it is dramatic. . . . [A poem is] heard as sung or spoken by a person in a scene—in a character, in a setting. By whom, where and when is the question. By the dreamer of a better world out in a storm in autumn; by a lover under a window at night." Suppose, in reading a poem Frost published in 1916, we try to establish "by whom, where and when" it is spoken. We may not be able to answer all three questions in great detail, but let's see what the poem suggests. As you read it, you'll notice—alerted by the quotation marks—that there are *two* speakers; the poem is a tiny drama. Thus, the closing quotation marks at the end of line 9 signal to us that the first speech is finished.

 ROBERT FROST

The Telephone

"When I was just as far as I could walk
From here today
There was an hour
All still
When leaning with my head against a flower   5
I heard you talk.
Don't say I didn't, for I heard you say—
You spoke from that flower on the window sill—
Do you remember what it was you said?"

"First tell me what it was you thought you heard."   10

"Having found the flower and driven a bee away,
I leaned my head,
And holding by the stalk,
I listened and I thought I caught the word—
What was it? Did you call me by my name?   15
Or did you say—
Someone said 'Come'—I heard it as I bowed."

"I may have thought as much, but not aloud."

"Well, so I came."

                                                            [1916]

Suppose we ask: Who are these two speakers? What is their relationship? What's going on between them? Where are they? We don't think that these questions can be answered with absolute certainty, but we do think some answers are more probable than others. For instance, line 8 ("You spoke from that flower on the window sill") tells us that the speakers are in a room, probably of a home—rather than, say, in a railroad station—but we can't say whether the home is a farmhouse, or a house in a village, town, or city, or an apartment.

Let's put the questions (even if they may turn out to be unanswerable) into a more specific form.

▢ QUESTIONS FOR CRITICAL THINKING AND WRITING

1. One speaker speaks lines 1-9, 11-17, and 19. The other speaks lines 10 and 18. Do you think you can tell the gender of each speaker? For sure, probably, or not at all? On what do you base your answer?
2. Try to visualize this miniature drama. In line 7 the first speaker says, "Don't say I didn't, . . . " What happens—what do you see in your mind's eye—after line 6 that causes the speaker to say this?
3. Why do you suppose the speaker of lines 10 and 18 says so little? How would you characterize the tone of these two lines? What sort of relationship do you think exists between the two speakers?
4. How would you characterize the tone of lines 11-17? Of the last line of the poem?

If you haven't jotted down your responses, we suggest that you do so before reading what follows.

Journal Entries

Given questions somewhat like the preceding ones, students were asked to try to identify the speakers by sex, to speculate on their relationship, and then to add whatever they wished to say. One student recorded the following thoughts:

```
    These two people care about each other--maybe
husband and wife, or lovers--and a man is doing most
of the talking, though I can't prove it. He has
walked as far as possible--that is, as far as
possible and still get back on the same day--and he
```

seemed to hear the other person call him. He claims
that she spoke to him "from that flower on the window
sill," and that's why I think the second person is a
woman. She's at home, near the window. Somehow I
even imagine she was at the window near the kitchen
sink, maybe working while he was out on this long
walk.

Then she speaks one line; she won't say if she
did or didn't speak. She is very cautious, or
suspicious: "First tell me what it was you thought
you heard." Maybe she doesn't want to say something
and then have her husband embarrass her by saying,
"No, that's not what I thought." Or maybe she just
doesn't feel like talking. Then he claims that he
heard her speaking through a flower, as though the
flower was a telephone, just as though it was hooked
up to the flower on the window sill. But at first he
won't say what he supposedly heard, or "thought" he
heard. Instead, he says that maybe it was someone
else: "Someone said 'Come'." Is he teasing her?
Pretending that she may have a rival?

Then she speaks--again just one line, saying, "I
may have thought as much, but not aloud." She won't
admit that she did think this thought. And then the
man says, "Well, so I came." Just like that; short
and sweet. No more fancy talk about flowers as
telephones. He somehow (through telepathy?) got the
message, and so here he is. He seems like a sensitive
guy, playful (the stuff about the flowers as
telephones), but also he knows when to stop kidding
around.

Another student also identified the couple as a man and woman and thought
that this dialogue occurs after a quarrel:

As the poem goes on, we learn that the man wants
to be with the woman, but it starts by telling us
that he walked as far away from her as he could. He
doesn't say why, but I think from the way the woman
speaks later in the poem, they had a fight and he
walked out. Then, when he stopped to rest, he thought
he heard her voice. He really means that he was
thinking of her and he was hoping she was thinking of
him. So he returns, and he tells her he heard her
calling him, but he pretends he heard her call him
through a flower on their window sill. He can't admit
that he was thinking about her. This seems very
realistic to me; when someone feels a bit ashamed,
it's sometimes hard to admit that you were wrong, and
you want the other person to tell you that things are
OK anyhow. And judging from line 7, when he says
"Don't say I didn't," it seems that she is going to

interrupt him by denying it. She is still angry, or
maybe she doesn't want to make up too quickly. But he
wants to pretend that <u>she</u> called him back. So when he
says, "Do you remember what it was you said?" she
won't admit that she <u>was</u> thinking of him, and she
says, "First tell me what it was you thought you
heard." She's testing him a little. So he goes on,
with the business about flowers as telephones, and he
says "someone" called him. He understands that she
doesn't want to be pushed into forgiving him, so he
backs off. Then she is willing to admit that she did
think about him, but still she doesn't quite admit
it. She is too proud to say openly that she wants him
back but she does say, "I <u>may</u> have thought as
much,. . ." And then, since they both have preserved
their dignity, and also both have admitted that they
care about the other, he can say, "Well, so I came."

TOPICS FOR WRITING

1. In a paragraph or two or three, *evaluate* one of these two entries
   recorded by students. Do you think the comments are weak, plausible,
   or convincing, and *why* do you think so? Can you offer additional supporting evidence or, on the other hand, counterevidence? You may
   want to set forth your own scenario.

2. Two small questions: In a sentence or two, offer a suggestion as to why
   in line 11 Frost wrote, "and driven a bee away." After all, the bee plays
   no role in the poem. Second, in line 17 Frost has the speaker say, "I
   heard it as I bowed." Of course "bowed" rhymes with "aloud," but let's
   assume that the need for a rhyme did not dictate the choice of this
   word. Do you think "I heard it as I bowed" is better than, say, "I heard
   it as I waited," or "I heard it as I listened"? Why?

3. Write an essay of 500 words either about an uncanny experience of
   your own or about a quarrel or disagreement that was resolved in a way
   you had not expected.

FIGURATIVE LANGUAGE

Robert Frost has said, "Poetry provides the one permissible way of saying one
thing and meaning another." This, of course, is an exaggeration, but it shrewdly
suggests the importance of figurative language—saying one thing in terms of
something else. Words have their literal meanings, but they can also be used so
that something other than the literal meaning is implied. "My love is a rose" is, literally, nonsense, for a person is not a five-petaled, many-stamened plant with a
spiny stem. But the suggestions of *rose* (at least for Robert Burns, who compared
his beloved to a rose in the line "My love is like a red, red rose"), include "delicate beauty," "soft," and "perfumed," and thus the word *rose* can be meaningfully applied—figuratively rather than literally—to "my love." The girl is fragrant;

her skin is perhaps like a rose in texture and (in some measure) color; she will not keep her beauty long. The poet, that is, has communicated his perception very precisely.

People who write about poetry have found it convenient to name the various kinds of figurative language. Just as the student of geology employs such special terms as *kames* and *eskers,* the student of literature employs special terms to name things as accurately as possible. The following paragraphs discuss the most common terms.

In a **simile,** items from different classes are explicitly compared by a connective such as *like, as,* or *than,* or by a verb such as *appears* or *seems.* (If the objects compared are from the same class, for example, "Tokyo is like Los Angeles," no simile is present.)

Float like a butterfly, sting like a bee.

—*Muhammad Ali*

It is a beauteous evening, calm and free.
The holy time is quiet as a Nun,
Breathless with adoration.

—*William Wordsworth*

All of our thoughts will be fairer than doves.

—*Elizabeth Bishop*

Seems he a dove? His feathers are but borrowed.

—*Shakespeare*

A **metaphor** asserts the identity, without a connective such as *like* or a verb such as *appears,* of terms that are literally incompatible.

Umbrellas clothe the beach in every hue.

—*Elizabeth Bishop*

                                          The
whirlwind fife-and-drum of the storm bends the salt
marsh grass

—*Marianne Moore*

Two common types of metaphor have Greek names. In **synecdoche** the whole is replaced by the part, or the part by the whole. For example, *bread* in "Give us this day our daily bread" replaces all sorts of food. In **metonymy** something is named that replaces something closely related to it. For example, James Shirley names certain objects, using them to replace social classes (royalty and the peasantry) to which they are related:

Scepter and crown must tumble down
And in the dust be equal made
With the poor crooked scythe and spade.

The attribution of human feelings or characteristics or abstractions to inanimate objects is called **personification.**

          Memory,
    that exquisite blunderer.

—*Amy Clampitt*

There's Wrath who has learnt every trick of guerilla warfare,
The shamming dead, the night-raid, the feinted retreat.

—W. H. Auden

Hope, thou bold taster of delight.

—Richard Crashaw

Crashaw's personification, "Hope, thou bold taster of delight," is also an example of the figure called **apostrophe,** an address to a person or thing not literally listening. Wordsworth begins a sonnet by apostrophizing Milton:

Milton, thou shouldst be living at this hour.

What conclusions can we draw about figurative language? First, figurative language, with its literally incompatible terms, forces the reader to attend to the **connotations** (suggestions, associations) rather than to the **denotations** (dictionary definitions) of one of the terms. Second, although figurative language is said to differ from ordinary speech, it is found in ordinary speech as well as in poetry and other literary forms. "It rained cats and dogs," "War is hell," "Don't be a pig," "Mr. Know-it-all," and other tired figures are part of our daily utterances. But through repeated use, these, and most of the figures we use, have lost whatever impact they once had and are only a shade removed from expressions which, though once figurative, have become literal: the *eye* of a needle, a *branch* office, the *face* of a clock. Third, good figurative language is usually concrete, condensed, and interesting.

We should mention, too, that figurative language is not limited to literary writers; it is used by scientists and social scientists—by almost everyone who is concerned with effective expression. Take, for instance, R. H. Tawney's *Religion and the Rise of Capitalism* (1926), a classic of economics. Among the titles of Tawney's chapters are "The Economic Revolution," "The Puritan Movement," and "The New Medicine for Poverty," all of which include metaphors. (To take only the last: Poverty is seen as a sick person or a disease.) Or take this sentence from Tawney (almost any sentence will serve equally well to reveal his bent for metaphor): "By the end of the sixteenth century the divorce between religious theory and economic realities had long been evident." Figures are not a fancy way of speaking. Quite the opposite: Writers use figures because they are forceful and exact. Literal language would not only be less interesting, it would also be less precise.

IMAGERY AND SYMBOLISM

When we read *rose* we may more or less call to mind a picture of a rose, or perhaps we are reminded of the odor or texture of a rose. Whatever in a poem appeals to any of our senses (including sensations of heat as well as of sight, smell, taste, touch, sound) is an image. In short, images are the sensory content of a work, whether literal or figurative. When a poet says "My rose" and is speaking about a rose, we have no figure of speech—though we still have an image. If, however, "My rose" is a shortened form of "My love is a rose," some would say that the poet is using a metaphor; but others would say that because the first term is omitted ("My love is"), the rose is a symbol. A poem about the transience of a rose might compel the reader to feel that the transience of female beauty is the larger theme even though it is never explicitly stated.

Some symbols are **conventional symbols**—people have agreed to accept them as standing for something other than their literal meanings: A poem about the cross would probably be about Christianity; similarly, the rose has long been a symbol for love. In Virginia Woolf's novel *Mrs. Dalloway,* the husband communicates his love by proffering this conventional symbol: "He was holding out flowers—roses, red and white roses. (But he could not bring himself to say he loved her; not in so many words.)" Objects that are not conventional symbols, however, may also give rise to rich, multiple, indefinable associations. The following poem uses the traditional symbol of the rose, but uses it in a nontraditional way:

 WILLIAM BLAKE

The Sick Rose

O rose, thou art sick!
The invisible worm
That flies in the night,
In the howling storm,   4

Has found out thy bed
Of crimson joy,
And his dark secret love
Does thy life destroy.   8

[1794]

A reader might perhaps argue that the worm is invisible (line 2) merely because it is hidden within the rose, but an "invisible worm / That flies in the night" is more than a long, slender, soft-bodied, creeping animal; and a rose that has, or is, a "bed / Of crimson joy" is more than a gardener's rose. Blake's worm and rose suggest things beyond themselves—a stranger, more vibrant world than the world we are usually aware of. They are, in short, symbolic, though readers will doubtless differ in their interpretations. Perhaps we find ourselves half thinking, for example, that the worm is male, the rose female, and that the poem is about the violation of virginity. Or that the poem is about the destruction of beauty: Woman's beauty, rooted in joy, is destroyed by a power that feeds on her. But these interpretations are not fully satisfying: The poem presents a worm and a rose, and yet it is not merely about a worm and a rose. These objects resonate, stimulating our thoughts toward something else, but the something else is elusive. This is not to say, however, that symbols mean whatever any reader says they mean. A reader could scarcely support, we imagine, an interpretation arguing that the poem is about the need to love all aspects of nature. All interpretations are not equally valid; it's the writer's job to offer a reasonably persuasive interpretation.

A symbol, then, is an image so loaded with significance that it is not simply literal, and it does not simply stand for something else; it is both itself *and* something else that it richly suggests, a kind of manifestation of something too complex or too elusive to be otherwise revealed. Blake's poem is about a blighted rose and at the same time about much more. In a symbol, as Thomas Carlyle wrote, "the Infinite is made to blend with the Finite, to stand visible, and as it were, attainable there."

VERBAL IRONY AND PARADOX

Among the most common devices in poems is **verbal irony.** The speaker's words mean more or less the opposite of what they seem to say. Sometimes verbal irony takes the form of **overstatement,** or **hyperbole,** as when Lady Macbeth says, while sleepwalking, "All the perfumes of Arabia will not sweeten this little hand." Sometimes it takes the form of **understatement,** as when Andrew Marvell's speaker in "To His Coy Mistress" (p. 820) remarks with cautious wryness, "The grave's a fine and private place, / But none, I think, do there embrace," or when Sylvia Plath sees an intended suicide as "the big strip tease." Speaking broadly, intensely emotional contemporary poems like those of Plath often use irony to undercut—and thus make acceptable—the emotion presented.

Another common device in poems is **paradox:** the assertion of an apparent contradiction, as in Marvell's "am'rous birds of prey" in "To His Coy Mistress." Normally we think of amorous birds as gentle—doves, for example—and not as birds of prey, such as hawks. Another example of an apparent contradiction: In "Auld Lang Syne" there is the paradox that the remembrance of joy evokes a kind of sadness.

STRUCTURE

The arrangement of the parts, the organization of the entire poem, is its **structure.** Sometimes the poem is divided into blocks of, say, four lines each, but even if the poem is printed as a solid block it probably has some principle of organization. It may move, for example, from sorrow in the first two lines to joy in the next two or from a question in the first three lines to an answer in the last line.

Consider this short poem by an English poet of the seventeenth century.

 ROBERT HERRICK (1591–1674)

Upon Julia's Clothes

Whenas in silk my Julia goes,
Then, then (methinks) how sweetly flows
That liquefaction of her clothes.

Next, when I cast mine eyes, and see
That brave° vibration, each way free   5
O, how that glittering taketh me.

[1648]

⁵**brave** splendid

Student Essay: "Herrick's Julia, Julia's Herrick"

One student, Stan Wylie, began thinking about this poem by copying it, double-spaced, and by making the following notes on his copy:

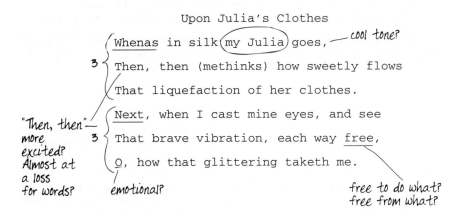

Upon Julia's Clothes

Whenas in silk my Julia goes, — *cool tone?*

Then, then (methinks) how sweetly flows

That liquefaction of her clothes.

Next, when I cast mine eyes, and see

That brave vibration, each way free,

O, how that glittering taketh me.

3

3

*"Then, then"—
more
excited?
Almost at
a loss
for words?*

emotional?

*free to do what?
free from what?*

The student got some further ideas by thinking about several of the questions that, in the checklist on page 356, we suggest you ask yourself while rereading a poem. Among the questions are these:

> Does the poem proceed in a straightforward way, or at some point or points
> does the speaker reverse course, altering his or her tone or perception?
> What is the effect on you of the form?

With such questions in mind, the student was stimulated to see if there is some sort of reversal or change in Herrick's poem, and if there is, how it is related to the structure. After rereading the poem several times, thinking about it in the light of these questions and perhaps others that came to mind, he produced the following notes:

```
Two stanzas, each of three lines, with the same
     structure
Basic structure of 1st stanza: When X (one line),
     then Y (two lines)
Basic structure of second stanza: Next (one line),
     then Z (two lines)
```

When he marked the text, after reading the poem a few times, he noticed that the last line—an exclamation of delight ("O, how that glittering taketh me")—is much more personal than the rest of the poem. A little further thought enabled him to refine this last perception:

```
Although the pattern of stanzas is repeated, the
somewhat analytic, detached tone of the beginning
("Whenas," "Then," "Next") changes to an open,
enthusiastic confession of delight in what the poet
sees.
```

Further thinking led to this:

> Although the title is "Upon Julia's Clothes," and the
> first five lines describe Julia's silken dress, the
> poem finally is not only about Julia's clothing but
> about the effect of Julia (moving in silk that
> liquefies or seems to become a liquid) on the poet.

This is a nice observation, but when the student looked again at the poem
the next day, and started to write about it, he found that he was able to refine his
observation.

> Even at the beginning, the speaker is not entirely
> detached, for he speaks of "my Julia."

In writing about Herrick's "Upon Julia's Clothes," the student tell us, the
thoughts did not come quickly or neatly. After two or three thoughts, he started
to write. Only after drafting a paragraph, and rereading the poem, did he notice
that the personal element appears not only in the last line ("taketh *me*") but even
in the first line ("*my* Julia"). In short, for almost all of us, the only way to get to a
good final essay is to read, to think, to jot down ideas, to write a draft, and to revise and revise again. Having gone through such processes, the student came up
with the following excellent essay.

By the way, the student did not hit on the final version of his title ("Herrick's
Julia, Julia's Herrick") until shortly before he typed his final version. His preliminary title was

Structure and Personality in
Herrick's "Upon Julia's Clothing"

That's a bit heavy-handed but at least it is focused, as opposed to such an unin-
formative title as "On a Poem." He soon revised his tentative title to

Julia, Julia's Clothing, and Julia's Poet

That's quite a good title: It is neat, and it is appropriate, since it moves (as the
poem and the essay do) from Julia and her clothing to the poet. Of course it
doesn't tell the reader exactly what the essay will be about, but it does stimulate
the reader's interest. The essayist's final title, however, is even better:

Herrick's Julia, Julia's Herrick

Again, it is neat (the balanced structure, and structure is part of the student's
topic), and it moves (as the poem itself moves) from Julia to the poet.

Herrick's Julia, Julia's Herrick

Robert Herrick's "Upon Julia's Clothes" begins

as a description of Julia's clothing and ends as an

expression of the poet's response not just to Julia's

clothing but to Julia herself. Despite the apparently

objective or detached tone of the first stanza and

the first two lines of the second stanza, the poem

finally conveys a strong sense of the speaker's excitement.

The first stanza seems to say, "Whenas" X (one line), "Then" Y (two lines). The second stanza repeats this basic structure of one line of assertion and two lines describing the consequence: "Next" (one line), "then" (two lines). But the logic or coolness of "Whenas," "Then," and "Next," and of such rather scientific language as "liquefaction" (a more technical-sounding word than "melting") and "vibration," is undercut by the breathlessness or excitement of "Then, then" (that is very different from a simple "Then"). It is also worth mentioning that although there is a personal rather than a fully detached note even in the first line, in "my Julia," this expression scarcely reveals much feeling. In fact, it reveals a touch of male chauvinism, a suggestion that the woman is a possession of the speaker's. Not until the last line does the speaker reveal that, far from Julia being his possession, he is possessed by Julia: "O, how that glittering taketh me." If he begins coolly, objectively, and somewhat complacently, and uses a structure that suggests a somewhat detached mind, in the exclamatory "O" he nevertheless at last confesses (to our delight) that he is enraptured by Julia.

Other things, of course, might be said about this poem. For instance, the writer says nothing about the changes in the basic iambic meter and their contributions to the poem. We have in mind not so much the trochees (a trochee is a metrical foot with a stressed syllable followed by an unstressed one) at the beginning of some lines, which is a fairly routine variation, but the spondees (two consecutive stresses) in "Then, then" and "O, how" and the almost-spondees in "Next, when," "each way free," and "that glittering." Also of interest are the two run-on lines (line 2 runs into 3, and 4 runs into 5) introducing related expressions, "That liquefaction" and "that brave vibration."

He also doesn't comment on the *s* and *z* sounds (*Whenas, silk, goes, thinks, sweetly flows*), which presumably imitate the sound of a silk gown in motion, a sound which can be said to resemble the sound of liquid, hence *liquefaction*—though the dress in motion also visually resembles flowing liquid. But the present essay seems excellent to us, and the neglected topics—sound effects in the poem—might be material for another essay.

 CHRISTINA ROSSETTI

In an Artist's Studio

One face looks out from all his canvases,
   One selfsame figure sits or walks or leans:
   We found her hidden just behind those screens,
That mirror gave back all her loveliness.
A queen in opal or in ruby dress,
   A nameless girl in freshest summer-greens
   A saint, an angel—every canvas means
The same one meaning, neither more nor less.   8
He feeds upon her face by day and night,
   And she with true kind eyes looks back on him,
Fair as the moon and joyful as the light:
   Not wan with waiting, not with sorrow dim;   12
Not as she is, but was when hope shone bright;
   Not as she is, but as she fills his dream.

[1856]

This poem is a sonnet. We discuss the form later, on page 355, but if you study the rhymes here you will notice that the first eight lines are united by rhymes, and the next six by different rhymes. A reader might, for a start at least, think about whether what is said has any relation to these units. The first eight lines are about the model, but are the next six equally about her or about someone else?

 TOPICS FOR CRITICAL THINKING

1. What do we know about the model in the first eight lines? What do we know about her in the last two lines?
2. How are the contrasts (between then and now, between model and painter) communicated by the repetition of "Not as she is," in lines 13 and 14?

EXPLICATION

A line-by-line commentary on what is going on in a text is an explication (literally, unfolding, or spreading out). Although your explication will for the most part move steadily from the beginning to the end of the selection, try to avoid writing along these lines (or, one might say, along this one line): "In the first line.... In the second line.... In the third line...." That is, don't hesitate to write such things as

```
The poem begins. . . . In the next line. . . . The
speaker immediately adds. . . . He then introduces. . . .
The next stanza begins by saying. . . .
```

And of course you can discuss the second line before the first if that seems the best way of handling the passage.

An explication is not concerned with the writer's life or times, and it is not a paraphrase (a rewording)—though it may include paraphrase if a passage in the original seems unclear, perhaps because of an unusual word or an unfamiliar expression. On the whole, however, an explication goes beyond paraphrase, seeking to make explicit what the reader perceives as implicit in the work. To this end it calls attention, as it proceeds, to the implications of words (for instance, to their tone), the function of rhymes (for instance, how they may connect ideas, as in *throne* and *alone*), the development of contrasts, and any other contributions to the meaning.

A Sample Explication

Take this short poem (published in 1917) by the Irish poet William Butler Yeats (1865-1939). The "balloon" in the poem is a dirigible, a blimp.

WILLIAM BUTLER YEATS

The Balloon of the Mind

Hands, do what you're bid:
Bring the balloon of the mind
That bellies and drags in the wind
Into its narrow shed.

[1917]

A student, Tina Washington, began thinking about the poem by copying it, double-spaced. Then she jotted down her first thoughts:

sounds abrupt
/
Hands, do what you're bid: —*balloon imagined by*
                                                    the mind? Or a mind
Bring the balloon of the mind   *like a balloon?*

That bellies and drags in the wind   *no real rhymes?*

Into its narrow shed.   *line seems to drag—*
                                                    it's so long!

Later she wrote some notes in a journal:

I'm still puzzled about the meaning of the words "The balloon of the mind." Does "balloon of the mind" mean a balloon that belongs to the mind, sort of like "a disease of the heart"? If so, it means a balloon that the mind <u>has</u>, a balloon that the mind possesses, I guess by imagining it. Or does it mean that the mind is <u>like</u> a balloon, as when you say "he's a pig of a man," meaning he is like a pig, he is a pig? Can it mean both? What's a balloon that the mind imagines? Something like dreams of fame, wealth? Castles in Spain.

Is Yeats saying that the "hands" have to work hard to make dreams a reality? Maybe. But maybe the idea really is that the mind is <u>like</u> a balloon--hard to keep under control, floating around. Very hard to keep the mind on the job. If the mind is like a balloon, it's hard to get it into the hangar (shed).

"Bellies." Is there such a verb? In this poem it seems to mean something like "puffs out" or "flops around in the wind." Just checked <u>The American Heritage Dictionary</u>, and it says "belly" can be a verb, "to swell out," "to bulge." Well, you learn something every day.

A later entry:

OK; I think the poem is about a writer trying to keep his balloon-like mind from floating around, trying to keep the mind under control, trying to keep it working at the job of writing something, maybe writing something with the "clarity, unity, and coherence" I keep hearing about in this course.

Here is the student's final version of the explication:

Yeats's "Balloon of the Mind" is about writing poetry, specifically about the difficulty of getting one's floating thoughts down in lines on the page. The first line, a short, stern, heavily stressed command to the speaker's hands, perhaps implies by its severe or impatient tone that these hands will be disobedient or inept or careless if not watched closely: the poor bumbling body so often fails to achieve the goals of the mind. The bluntness of the command in the first line is emphasized by the fact that all the subsequent lines have more syllables. Furthermore, the first line is a grammatically complete sentence, whereas the thought of line 2 spills over into the next lines, implying the difficulty of fitting ideas into confining spaces, that is, of getting one's thoughts into order, especially into a coherent poem.

Lines 2 and 3 amplify the metaphor already stated in the title (the product of the mind is an airy but unwieldy balloon), and they also contain a second command, "Bring." Alliteration ties this command, "Bring," to the earlier "bid"; it also ties both of these verbs to their object, "balloon," and to the verb that most effectively describes the balloon, "bellies." In comparison with the abrupt first line of the poem, lines 2 and 3 themselves seem almost swollen, bellying and dragging, an effect aided by using adjacent unstressed syllables ("of the," "[bell]ies and," "in the") and by using an eye rhyme ("mind" and "wind") rather than an exact rhyme. And then comes the short last line: almost before we could expect it, the cumbersome balloon—here, the idea that is to be packed into the stanza—is successfully lodged in its "narrow shed." Aside from the relatively colorless "into," the only words of more than one syllable in the poem are "balloon," "bellies," and "narrow," and all three emphasize the difficulty of the task. But after "narrow"—the word itself almost looks long and narrow, in this context like a hangar—we get the simplicity of the mono-syllable "shed." The difficult job is done, the thought

```
is safely packed away, the poem is completed--but again
with an off-rhyme ("bid" and "shed"), for neatness can
go only so far when hands and mind and a balloon are
involved.
```

Note: The reader of an explication needs to see the text, and because the explicated text is usually short, it is advisable to quote it all. (Remember, your imagined audience probably consists of your classmates; even if they have already read the work you are explicating, they have not memorized it, and so you helpfully remind them of the work by quoting it.) You can quote the entire text at the outset, or you can quote the first unit (for example, a stanza), then explicate that unit, and then quote the next unit, and so on. And if the poem or passage of prose is longer than, say, six lines, it is advisable to number each line at the right for easy reference.

RHYTHM AND VERSIFICATION: A GLOSSARY FOR REFERENCE

Rhythm (most simply, in English poetry, stresses at regular intervals) has a power of its own. A highly pronounced rhythm is common in such forms of poetry as charms, college yells, and lullabies; all of them are aimed at inducing a special effect magically. It is not surprising that *carmen,* the Latin word for poem or song, is also the Latin word for *charm* and the word from which our word *charm* is derived.''

In much poetry, rhythm is only half heard, but its presence is suggested by the way poetry is printed. Prose (from Latin *prorsus,* "forward," "straight on") keeps running across the paper until the right-hand margin is reached; then, merely because the paper has given out, the writer or printer starts again at the left, with a small letter. But verse (Latin *versus,* "a turning") often ends well short of the right-hand margin. The next line begins at the left—usually with a capital—not because paper has run out but because the rhythmic pattern begins again. Lines of poetry are continually reminding us that they have a pattern.

Note that a mechanical, unvarying rhythm may be good to put the baby to sleep, but it can be deadly to readers who want to stay awake. Poets vary their rhythm according to their purposes; they ought not to be so regular that they are (in W. H. Auden's words) "accentual pests." In competent hands, rhythm contributes to meaning; it says something. Ezra Pound has a relevant comment: "Rhythm *must* have meaning. It can't be merely a careless dash off, with no grip and no real hold to the words and sense, a tumty tum tumty tum tum ta."

Consider this description of Hell from *Paradise Lost* (stressed syllables are marked by ´, unstressed syllables by ˘):

Rócks, cáves, lákes, féns, bógs, déns, and shádes ŏf déath.

The normal line in *Paradise Lost* is written in iambic feet—alternate unstressed and stressed syllables—but in this line Milton immediately follows one heavy stress with another, helping to communicate the "meaning"—the oppressive monotony of Hell. As a second example, consider the function of the rhythm in two lines by Alexander Pope:

When Ajax strives some rock's vast weight to throw,
The line too labors, and the words move slow.

The stressed syllables do not merely alternate with the unstressed ones; rather the great weight of the rock is suggested by three consecutive stressed words, "rock's vast weight," and the great effort involved in moving it is suggested by another three consecutive stresses, "line too labors," and by yet another three, "words move slow." Note also the abundant pauses within the lines. In the first line, for example, unless one's speech is slovenly, one must pause at least slightly after "Ajax," "strives," "rock's," "vast," "weight," and "throw." The grating sounds in "Ajax" and "rock's" do their work, too, and so do the explosive *t's*.

When Pope wishes to suggest lightness, he reverses his procedure, and he groups *un*stressed syllables:

Not so, when swift Camilla scours the plain,
Flies o'er th' unbending corn, and skims along the main.

This last line has twelve syllables and is thus longer than the line about Ajax, but the addition of *along* helps to communicate lightness and swiftness because in this line (it can be argued) neither syllable of *along* is strongly stressed. If *along* is omitted, the line still makes grammatical sense and becomes more "regular," but it also becomes less imitative of lightness.

The very regularity of a line may be meaningful too. Shakespeare begins a sonnet thus:

When I do count the clock that tells the time.

This line about a mechanism runs with appropriate regularity. (It is worth noting, too, that "count the clock" and "tells the time" emphasize the regularity by the repetition of sounds and syntax.) But notice what Shakespeare does in the middle of the next line:

And see the brave day sunk in hideous night.

The technical vocabulary of **prosody** (the study of the principles of verse structure, including meter, rhyme and other sould effects, and stanzaic patterns) is large. An understanding of these terms will not turn anyone into a poet, but it will enable you to write about some aspects of poetry more efficiently. The following are the chief terms of prosody.

Meter

Most poetry written in English has a pattern of stressed (accented) sounds, and this pattern is the **meter** (from the Greek word for "measure"). Strictly speaking, we really should not talk of "unstressed" or "unaccented" syllables, since to utter a syllable—however lightly—is to give it some stress. It is really a matter of *relative* stress, but the fact is that "unstressed" or "unaccented" are parts of the established terminology of versification.

In a line of poetry, the **foot** is the basic unit of measurement. It is on rare occasions a single stressed syllable; but generally a foot consists of two or three syllables, one of which is stressed. The repetition of feet, then, produces a pattern of stresses throughout the poem.

Two cautions:

1. A poem will seldom contain only one kind of foot throughout; significant variations usually occur, but one kind of foot is dominant.

2. In reading a poem, one chiefly pays attention to the sense, not to pre-supposed metrical pattern. By paying attention to the sense, one often finds (reading aloud is a great help) that the stress falls on a word that according to the metrical pattern would be unstressed. Or a word that according to the pattern would be stressed may be seen to be unstressed. Furthermore, by reading for sense one finds that not all stresses are equally heavy; some are almost as light as unstressed syllables, and sometimes there is a **hovering stress**—that is, the stress is equally distributed over two adjacent syllables. To repeat: One reads for sense, allowing the syntax to help indicate the stresses.

Metrical Feet. The most common feet in English poetry are the six listed below.

Iamb (adjective: **iambic**): one unstressed syllable followed by one stressed syllable. The iamb, said to be the most common pattern in English speech, is surely the most common in English poetry. The following example has four iambic feet:

My héart is líke a síng-ing bírd.

> —*Christina Rossetti*

Trochee (trochaic): one stressed syllable followed by one unstressed.

Wé were véry tíred, wé were véry mérry

> —*Edna St. Vincent Millay*

Anapest (anapestic): two unstressed syllables followed by one stressed.

There are mán -y who sáy that a dóg has his dáy.

> —*Dylan Thomas*

Dactyl (dactylic): one stressed syllable followed by two unstressed. This trisyllabic foot, like the anapest, is common in light verse or verse suggesting joy, but its use is not limited to such material, as Longfellow's *Evangeline* shows. Thomas Hood's sentimental "The Bridge of Sighs" begins

Táke her up ténderly.

Spondee (spondaic): two stressed syllables; most often used as a substitute for an iamb or trochee.

Smárt lád, to slíp betímes awáy.

> —*A. E. Housman*

Pyrrhic: two unstressed syllables; it is often not considered a legitimate foot in English.

Metrical Lines. A metrical line consists of one or more feet and is named for the number of feet in it. The following names are used:

monometer: one foot	**pentameter:** five feet
dimeter: two feet	**hexameter:** six feet
trimeter: three feet	**heptameter:** seven feet
tetrameter: four feet	

A line is scanned for the kind and number of feet in it, and the **scansion** tells you if it is, say, anapestic trimeter (three anapests):

˘ ˘ ´   ˘ ˘ ´   ˘ ˘ ´
As I came to the edge of the woods.

—*Robert Frost*

Or, in another example, iambic pentameter:

˘ ´   ˘ ˘ ´ ˘ ˘ ´ ˘ ´ ˘ ´
The sum -mer thun-der, like a wood-en bell

—*Louise Bogan*

A line ending with a stress has a **masculine ending;** a line ending with an extra unstressed syllable has a **feminine ending.** The **caesura** (usually indicated by the symbol / /) is a slight pause within the line. It need not be indicated by punctuation (notice the fourth and fifth lines in the following quotation), and it does not affect the metrical count:

> Awake, my St. John! / / leave all meaner things
> To low ambition, / / and the pride of kings.
> Let us / / (since Life can little more supply
> Than just to look about us / / and to die)
> Expatiate free / / o'er all this scene of Man;
> A mighty maze! / / but not without a plan;
> A wild, / / where weeds and flowers promiscuous shoot;
> Or garden, / / tempting with forbidden fruit.

—*Alexander Pope*

The varying position of the caesura helps to give Pope's lines an informality that plays against the formality of the pairs of rhyming lines.

An **end-stopped line** concludes with a distinct syntactical pause, but a **run-on line** has its sense carried over into the next line without syntactical pause. (The running-on of a line is called **enjambment.**) In the following passage, only the first is a run-on line:

> Yet if we look more closely we shall find
> Most have the seeds of judgment in their mind:
> Nature affords at least a glimmering light;
> The lines, though touched but faintly, are drawn right.

—*Alexander Pope*

Meter produces **rhythm,** recurrences at equal intervals, but rhythm (from a Greek word meaning "flow") is usually applied to larger units than feet. Often it depends most obviously on pauses. Thus, a poem with run-on lines will have a different rhythm from a poem with end-stopped lines, even though both are in the same meter. And prose, though it is unmetrical, can have rhythm, too.

In addition to being affected by syntactical pause, rhythm is affected by pauses attributable to consonant clusters and to the length of words. Polysyllabic words establish a different rhythm from monosyllabic words, even in metrically identical lines. One can say, then, that rhythm is altered by shifts in meter, syntax, and the length and ease of pronunciation. But even with no such shift, even if a line is repeated verbatim, a reader may sense a change in rhythm. The rhythm of the final line of a poem, for example, may well differ from that of the line before, even though in all other respects the lines are identical, as in Frost's

"Stopping by Woods on a Snowy Evening" (p. 410), which concludes by repeating "And miles to go before I sleep." One may simply sense that this final line ought to be spoken, say, more slowly and with more stress on "miles."

Patterns of Sound

Though rhythm is basic to poetry, **rhyme**—the repetition of identical or similar stressed sound or sounds—is not. Rhyme is, presumably, pleasant in itself; it suggests order; and it also may be related to meaning, for it brings two words sharply together, often implying a relationship, as in the now trite *dove* and *love,* or in the more imaginative *throne* and *alone.*

Perfect, or **exact,** **rhyme:** Differing consonant sounds are followed by identical stressed vowel sounds, and the following sounds, if any, are identical (*foe—toe; meet—fleet; buffer—rougher*). Notice that perfect rhyme involves identity of sound, not of spelling. *Fix* and *sticks,* like *buffer* and *rougher,* are perfect rhymes.

Half-rhyme (or **off-rhyme**): Only the final consonant sounds of the words are identical; the stressed vowel sounds as well as the initial consonant sounds, if any, differ (*soul—oil; mirth—forth; trolley—bully*).

Eye rhyme: The sounds do not in fact rhyme, but the words look as though they would rhyme (*cough—bough*).

Masculine rhyme: The final syllables are stressed and, after their differing initial consonant sounds, are identical in sound (*stark—mark; support—retort*).

Feminine rhyme (or **double rhyme**): Stressed rhyming syllables are followed by identical unstressed syllables (*revival—arrival; flatter—batter*). **Triple rhyme** is a kind of feminine rhyme in which identical stressed vowel sounds are followed by two identical unstressed syllables (*machinery—scenery; tenderly—slenderly*).

End rhyme (or **terminal rhyme**): The rhyming words occur at the ends of the lines.

Internal rhyme: At least one of the rhyming words occurs within the line (Oscar Wilde's "Each narrow *cell* in which we *dwell*").

Alliteration: sometimes defined as the repetition of initial sounds ("All the *a*wful *a*uguries," or "*B*ring me my *b*ow of *b*urning gold"), and sometimes as the prominent repetition of a consonant ("*a*fter li*f*e's *f*it*f*ul *f*ever").

Assonance: the repetition, in words of proximity, of identical vowel sounds preceded and followed by differing consonant sounds. Whereas *tide* and *hide* are rhymes, *tide* and *mine* are assonantal.

Consonance: the repetition of identical consonant sounds and differing vowel sounds in words in proximity (*fail—feel; rough—roof; pitter—patter*). Sometimes consonance is more loosely defined merely as the repetition of a consonant (*fail—peel*).

Onomatopoeia: the use of words that imitate sounds, such as *hiss* and *buzz.* There is a mistaken tendency to see onomatopoeia everywhere—for example, in *thunder* and *horror.* Many words sometimes thought to be onomatopoeic are not clearly imitative of the thing they refer to; they merely contain some sounds that, when we know what the word means, seem to have some resemblance to the thing they denote. Tennyson's lines from "Come down, O maid" are usually cited as an example of onomatopoeia:

The moan of doves in immemorial elms
And murmuring of innumerable bees.

Stanzaic Patterns

Lines of poetry are commonly arranged in a rhythmical unit called a stanza (from an Italian word meaning "room" or "stopping-place"). Usually all the stanzas in a poem have the same rhyme pattern. A stanza is sometimes called a **verse,** though *verse* may also mean a single line of poetry. (In discussing stanzas, rhymes are indicated by identical letters. Thus, *abab* indicates that the first and third lines rhyme with each other, while the second and fourth lines are linked by a different rhyme. An unrhymed line is denoted by *x*.) Common stanzaic forms in English poetry are the following:

Couplet: a stanza of two lines, usually, but not necessarily, with end-rhymes. *Couplet* is also used for a pair of rhyming lines. The **octosyllabic couplet** is iambic or trochaic tetrameter:

Had we but world enough, and time,
This coyness, lady, were no crime.

—Andrew Marvell

Heroic couplet: a rhyming couplet of iambic pentameter, often "closed," that is, containing a complete thought, with a fairly heavy pause at the end of the first line and a still heavier one at the end of the second. Commonly, there is a parallel or an *antithesis* (contrast) within a line or between the two lines. It is called heroic because in England, especially in the eighteenth century, it was much used for heroic (epic) poems.

Some foreign writers, some our own despise;
The ancients only, or the moderns, prize.

—Alexander Pope

Triplet (or **tercet**): a three-line stanza, usually with one rhyme:

Whenas in silks my Julia goes
Then, then (methinks) how sweetly flows
That liquefaction of her clothes.

—Robert Herrick

Quatrain: a four-line stanza, rhymed or unrhymed. The **heroic** (or **elegiac**) **quatrain** is iambic pentameter, rhyming *abab*. That is, the first and third lines rhyme (so they are designated *a*), and the second and fourth lines rhyme (so they are designated *b*).

Sonnet: a fourteen-line poem, predominantly in iambic pentameter. The rhyme is usually according to one of two schemes. The **Italian** (or **Petrarchan**[1]) **sonnet** has two divisions: The first eight lines (rhyming *abba abba* are the **octave,** and the last six (rhyming *cd cd cd,* or a variant) are the **sestet.** The second kind of sonnet, the **English** (or **Shakespearean**) **sonnet,** is usually arranged into three quatrains and a couplet, rhyming *abab cdcd efef gg.* (For examples see pages 813–814.) In many sonnets there is a marked correspondence

---

[1] So called after Francesco Petrarch (1304–74), the Italian poet who perfected and popularized the form

between the rhyme scheme and the development of the thought. Thus an Italian sonnet may state a generalization in the octave and a specific example in the sestet. Or an English sonnet may give three examples—one in each quatrain—and draw a conclusion in the couplet.

Blank Verse and Free Verse

A good deal of English poetry is unrhymed, much of it in **blank verse,** that is, unrhymed iambic pentameter. Introduced into English poetry by Henry Howard, Earl of Surrey, in the middle of the sixteenth century, late in the century it became the standard medium (especially in the hands of Christopher Marlow and Shakespeare) of English drama. In the seventeenth century, Milton used it for *Paradise Lost,* and it has continued to be used in both dramatic and nondramatic literature. For an example, see the first scene of *Hamlet* (page 629), until the Ghost appears.

The second kind of unrhymed poetry fairly common in English, especially in the twentieth century, is **free verse** (or **vers libre**): rhythmical lines varying in length, adhering to no fixed metrical pattern and usually unrhymed. The pattern is often largely based on repetition and parallel grammatical structure. For an example, see T. S. Eliot's "The Love Song of J. Alfred Prufrock" (page 1020).

✔ A Checklist: Getting Ideas for Writing about Poetry

If you are going to write about a fairly short poem (say, under thirty lines), it's not a bad idea to copy out the poem, writing or typing it double-spaced. By writing it out you will be forced to notice details, down to the punctuation. After you have copied the poem, proofread it carefully against the original. Catching an error—even the addition or omission of a comma—may help you to notice a detail in the original that you might otherwise have overlooked. And of course, now that you have the poem with ample space between the lines, you have a worksheet with room for jottings.

A good essay is based on a genuine response to a poem; a response may be stimulated in part by first reading the poem aloud and then considering the following questions.

First Response

1. What was your response to the poem on first reading? Did some parts especially please or displease you, or puzzle you? After some study— perhaps checking the meanings of some of the words in a dictionary and reading the poem several times—did you modify your initial response to the parts and to the whole?

Speaker and Tone

1. Who is the speaker? (Consider age, sex, personality, frame of mind, and tone of voice.) Is the speaker defined fairly precisely (for instance, an older woman speaking to a child), or is the speaker simply a voice

meditating? (Jot down your first impressions, then reread the poem and make further jottings, if necessary.)

2. Do you think the speaker is fully aware of what he or she is saying, or does the speaker unconsciously reveal his or her personality and values? What is your attitude toward this speaker?

3. Is the speaker narrating or reflecting on an earlier experience or attitude? If so, does he or she convey a sense of new awareness, such as of regret for innocence lost?

Audience

1. To whom is the speaker speaking? What is the situation (including time and place)? (In some poems, a listener is strongly implied, but in others, especially those in which the speaker is meditating, there may be no audience other than the reader, who "overhears" the speaker.)

Structure and Form

1. Does the poem proceed in a straightforward way, or at some point or points does the speaker reverse course, altering his or her tone or perception? If there is a shift, what do you make of it?

2. Is the poem organized into sections? If so, what are these sections—stanzas, for instance—and how does each section (characterized, perhaps, by a certain tone of voice, or a group of rhymes) grow out of what precedes it?

3. What is the effect on you of the form—say, quatrains (stanzas of four lines) or blank verse (unrhymed lines of ten syllables)? If the sense overflows the form, running without pause from (for example) one quatrain into the next, what effect is created?

Center of Interest and Theme

1. What is the poem about? Is the interest chiefly in a distinctive character, or in meditation? That is, is the poem chiefly psychological or chiefly philosophical?

2. Is the theme stated explicitly (directly) or implicitly? How might you state the theme in a sentence?

Diction

1. Do certain words have rich and relevant associations that relate to other words and help to define the speaker or the theme or both?

2. What is the role of figurative language, if any? Does it help to define the speaker or the theme?

3. What do you think is to be taken figuratively or symbolically, and what literally?

Sound Effects

1. What is the role of sound effects, including repetitions of sound (for instance, alliteration) and of entire words, and shifts in versification?

2. If there are off-rhymes (for instance "dizzy" and "easy," or "home" and "come"), what effect do they have on you? Do they, for instance, add a note of tentativeness or uncertainty?

3. If there are unexpected stresses or pauses, what do they communicate about the speaker's experience? How do they affect you?

FIFTEEN POEMS ABOUT PEOPLE, PLACES, AND THINGS

People

 ROBERT BROWNING

Born in a suburb of London into a middle-class family, Browning (1812-89) was educated primarily at home, where he read widely. For a while he wrote for the stage, and in 1846 he married Elizabeth Barrett—herself a poet—and lived with her in Italy until her death in 1861. He then returned to England and settled in London with their son. Regarded as one of the most distinguished poets of the Victorian period, he is buried in Westminster Abbey.

My Last Duchess

Ferrara*

That's my last Duchess painted on the wall,
Looking as if she were alive. I call
That piece a wonder, now; Frà Pandolf's° hands
Worked busily a day, and there she stands.
Will't please you sit and look at her? I said   5
"Frà Pandolf" by design, for never read
Strangers like you that pictured countenance,
The depth and passion of its earnest glance,
But to myself they turned (since none puts by
The curtain I have drawn for you, but I)   10
And seemed as they would ask me, if they durst,
How such a glance came there; so, not the first
Are you to turn and ask thus. Sir, 'twas not
Her husband's presence only, called that spot
Of joy into the Duchess' cheek; perhaps   15
Frà Pandolf chanced to say "Her mantle laps
Over my lady's wrist too much," or, "Paint
Must never hope to reproduce the faint
Half-flush that dies along her throat." Such stuff
Was courtesy, she thought, and cause enough   20
For calling up that spot of joy. She had
A heart—how shall I say?—too soon made glad,
Too easily impressed; she liked whate'er

° **Ferrara** town in Italy   3 **Frà Pandolf** a fictitious painter

She looked on, and her looks went everywhere.
Sir, 'twas all one! My favor at her breast,   25
The dropping of the daylight in the west,
The bough of cherries some officious fool
Broke in the orchard for her, the white mule
She rode with round the terrace—all and each
Would draw from her alike the approving speech,   30
Or blush, at least. She thanked men—good! but thanked
Somehow—I know not how—as if she ranked
My gift of a nine-hundred-years-old name
With anybody's gift. Who'd stoop to blame
This sort of trifling? Even had you skill   35
In speech—(which I have not)—to make your will
Quite clear to such an one, and say, "Just this
Or that in you disgusts me; here you miss,
Or there exceed the mark"—and if she let
Herself be lessoned so, nor plainly set   40
Her wits to yours, forsooth, and made excuse,
—E'en then would be some stooping; and I choose
Never to stoop. Oh, Sir, she smiled, no doubt,
Whene'er I passed her; but who passed without
Much the same smile? This grew; I gave commands;   45
Then all smiles stopped together. There she stands
As if alive. Will't please you rise? We'll meet
The company below, then. I repeat,
The Count your master's known munificence
Is ample warrant that no just pretense   50
Of mine for dowry will be disallowed;
Though his fair daughter's self, as I avowed
At starting, is my object. Nay, we'll go
Together down, Sir. Notice Neptune, though,
Taming a sea-horse, thought a rarity,   55
Which Claus of Innsbruck° cast in bronze for me!

[1842]

 TOPICS FOR CRITICAL THINKING AND WRITING

1. Who is speaking to whom? On what occasion?
2. What words or lines especially convey the speaker's arrogance? What is our attitude toward the speaker? Loathing? Fascination? Respect? Explain.
3. The time and place are Renaissance Italy; how do they affect our attitude toward the duke? What would be the effect if the poem were set in the twentieth century?
4. Years after writing this poem, Browning explained that the duke's "commands" (line 45) were "that she should be put to death, or he might have had her shut up in a convent." Should the poem have been more explicit? Does Browning's later uncertainty indicate that the

56**Claus of Innsbruck** a fictitious sculptor

poem is badly thought out? Suppose we did not have Browning's comment on line 45; could the line then mean only that he commanded her to stop smiling and that she obeyed? Explain.

5. Elizabeth Barrett (not yet Mrs. Browning) wrote to Robert Browning that it was not "by the dramatic medium that poets teach most impressively. . . . It is too difficult for the common reader to analyze, and to discern between the vivid and the earnest." She went on, urging him to teach "in the directest and most impressive way, the mask thrown off." What teaching, if any, is in this poem? If there is any teaching here, would it be more impressive if Browning had not used the mask of a Renaissance duke? Explain.

6. You are the envoy, writing to the Count, your master, a 500-word report of your interview with the duke. What do you write?

7. You are the envoy, writing to the count, advising—as diplomatically as possible—for or against this marriage. Notice that this exercise, unlike #6, which calls for a *report,* calls for an *argument.*

  EDWIN ARLINGTON ROBINSON

Edwin Arlington Robinson (1869–1935) grew up in Gardiner, Maine, spent two years at Harvard, and then returned to Maine, where he published his first book of poetry in 1896. Though he received encouragement from neighbors, his finances were precarious, even after President Theodore Roosevelt, having been made aware of the book, secured for him an appointment as customs inspector in New York from 1905 to 1909. Additional books won fame for Robinson, and in 1922 he was awarded the first of the three Pulitzer Prizes for poetry that he would win.

Richard Cory

Whenever Richard Cory went down town,
We people on the pavement looked at him:
He was a gentleman from sole to crown,
Clean favored, and imperially slim.   4

And he was always quietly arrayed,
And he was always human when he talked;
But still he fluttered pulses when he said,
"Good-morning," and he glittered when he walked.   8

And he was rich—yes, richer than a king—
And admirably schooled in every grace:
In fine,° we thought that he was everything
To make us wish that we were in his place.   12

So on we worked, and waited for the light,
And went without the meat, and cursed the bread;
And Richard Cory, one calm summer night,
Went home and put a bullet through his head.   16

[1896]

---

10 **In fine** in short

 TOPICS FOR CRITICAL THINKING AND WRITING

1. Consult the entry on irony in the glossary. Then read the pages referred to in the entry. Finally, write an essay of 500 words on irony in "Richard Cory."
2. What do you think were Richard Cory's thoughts shortly before he "put a bullet through his head"? In 500 words, set forth his thoughts and actions (what he sees and does). If you wish, you can write in the first person, from Cory's point of view. Further, if you wish, your essay can be in the form of a suicide note.

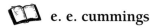 e. e. cummings

e. e. cummings was the pen name of Edwin Estlin Cummings (1894–1962), who grew up in Cambridge, Massachusetts, and was graduated from Harvard, where he became interested in modern literature and art, especially in the movements called cubism and futurism. His father, a conservative clergyman and a professor at Harvard, seems to have been baffled by the youth's interests, but Cummings's mother encouraged his artistic activities, including his use of unconventional punctuation and capitalization.

Politically liberal in his youth, Cummings became more conservative after a visit to Russia in 1931, but early and late his work emphasizes individuality and freedom of expression.

anyone lived in a pretty how town

anyone lived in a pretty how town
(with up so floating many bells down)
spring summer autumn winter
he sang his didn't he danced his did.   4

Women and men (both little and small)
cared for anyone not at all
they sowed their isn't they reaped their same
sun moon stars rain   8

children guessed (but only a few
and down they forgot as up they grew
autumn winter spring summer)
that noone loved him more by more   12

when by now and tree by leaf
she laughed his joy she cried his grief
bird by snow and stir by still
anyone's any was all to her   16

someones married their everyones
laughed their cryings and did their dance
(sleep wake hope and then) they
said their nevers they slept their dream   20

stars rain sun moon
(and only the snow can begin to explain
how children are apt to forget to remember
with up so floating many bells down)   24

one day anyone died i guess
(and noone stopped to kiss his face)
busy folk buried them side by side
little by little and was by was   28

all by all and deep by deep
and more by more they dream their sleep
noone and anyone earth by april
wish by spirit and if by yes.   32

Women and men (both dong and ding)
summer autumn winter spring
reaped their sowing and went their came
sun moon stars rain   36
                                                                  [1940]

 TOPICS FOR CRITICAL THINKING AND WRITING

1. Put into normal order (as far as possible) the words of the first two stanzas and then compare your version with cummings's. What does cummings gain—or lose?
2. Characterize the "anyone" who "sang his didn't" and "danced his did." In your opinion, how does he differ from the people who "sowed their isn't they reaped their same"?
3. Some readers interpret "anyone died" (line 25) to mean that the child matured and became as dead as the other adults. How might you support or refute this interpretation?

 LOUISE ERDRICH

Louise Erdrich was born in North Dakota in 1954; her father (born in Germany) and her mother (a Chippewa) both worked for the Bureau of Indian Affairs. After graduating from Dartmouth College in 1976, she returned to North Dakota to teach in the Poetry in the Schools Program. In 1979 she received a master's degree in creative writing from Johns Hopkins University. She now lives in New Hampshire with her husband and collaborator, Michael Dorris, a professor of Native American Studies at Dartmouth, and their five children. Although Erdrich is most widely known as a novelist, she has also won a reputation as a poet.

Indian Boarding School: The Runaways

Home's the place we head for in our sleep.
Boxcars stumbling north in dreams

don't wait for us. We catch them on the run.
The rails, old lacerations that we love,
shoot parallel across the face and break   5
just under Turtle Mountains.° Riding scars
you can't get lost. Home is the place they cross.
The lame guard strikes a match and makes the dark
less tolerant. We watch through cracks in boards
as the land starts rolling, rolling till it hurts   10
to be here, cold in regulation clothes.
We know the sheriff's waiting at midrun
to take us back. His car is dumb and warm.
The highway doesn't rock, it only hums
like a wing of long insults. The worn-down welts   15
of ancient punishment lead back and forth.

All runaways wear dresses, long green ones,
the color you would think shame was. We scrub
the sidewalks down because it's shameful work.
Our brushes cut the stone in watered arcs   20
and in the soak frail outlines shiver clear
a moment, things us kids pressed on the dark
face before it hardened, pale, remembering
delicate old injuries, the spines of names and leaves.

                                                      [1984]

⁶**Turtle Mountains** mountains in North Dakota and Manitoba

 TOPICS FOR CRITICAL THINKING AND WRITING

1. In line 4 the railroad tracks are called "old lacerations." What is the connection between the two?
2. What other imagery of injury do you find in the poem? In lines 20-24, what—literally—is "the dark / face" that "hardened, pale"?

RITA DOVE

Rita Dove was born in 1952 in Akron, Ohio. After graduating summa cum laude from Miami University (Ohio) she earned an M.F.A. at the Iowa Writers' Workshop. She has been awarded fellowships from the Guggenheim Foundation and the National Endowment for the Arts, and she now teaches at the University of Virginia. In 1993 she was appointed poet laureate for 1993-94. Dove is currently writing a book about the experiences of an African-American volunteer regiment in France during World War I.

Daystar

She wanted a little room for thinking:
but she saw diapers steaming on the line,

a doll slumped behind the door.
So she lugged a chair behind the garage
to sit out the children's naps.   5

Sometimes there were things to watch—
the pinched armor of a vanished cricket,
a floating maple leaf. Other days
she stared until she was assured
when she closed her eyes   10
she'd see only her own vivid blood.

She had an hour, at best, before Liza appeared
pouting from the top of the stairs.
And just *what* was mother doing
out back with the field mice? Why,   15

building a palace. Later
that night when Thomas rolled over and
lurched into her, she would open her eyes
and think of the place that was hers
for an hour—where   20
she was nothing,
pure nothing, in the middle of the day.

[1986]

TOPICS FOR CRITICAL THINKING AND WRITING

1. How would you characterize the woman who is the subject of the poem?
2. What do you make of the title?

Places
 BASHO

If the name of any Japanese poet is known in the United States, it is probably Matsuo Basho (1644-94). He lived most of his life in Edo (now called Tokyo), but he enjoyed traveling on foot in Japan and writing about his experiences. His most famous work, The Narrow Road to the Deep North *(1694), is a poetic diary recording one of his extended journeys. (It is available in several English translations.)*

We give here, however, a short poem in the form known as **haiku.** *A haiku has 17 syllables, arranged in 3 lines of 5, 7, and 5 syllables. Japanese poetry is unrhymed, but English versions—which may or may not follow the Japanese syllabic pattern—sometimes rhyme the first and third lines, as in the following translation of one of Basho's haiku:*

> *On the withered bough*
> *A crow alone is perching;*
> *Autumn evening now.*

The American poet Langston Hughes (1902-67) wrote a number of poems grouped under the title "Hokku" (a variant of haiku), one of which goes thus:

> *Keep straight down this block*
> *Then turn right where you will find*
> *A peach tree blooming.*

The subject matter of a haiku can be high or low—the Milky Way or the screech of automobile brakes—but usually it is connected with the seasons, and it is described objectively and sharply. Here is Basho's most famous haiku. (The translation does not preserve the syllabic count of the original.)

An Old Pond

An old pond;
A frog jumps in—
The sound of the water.

✏️ TOPIC FOR WRITING

Write at least one haiku. You need not use the 5-7-5 system if you don't want to; on the other hand, you may use rhyme if you wish. Some tips:

1. For a start, take some ordinary experience—tying your shoelaces, or seeing a cat at the foot of the stairs, or glancing out a window and seeing unexpected snowflakes, or hearing the alarm clock—and present it interestingly.
2. One way to make the experience interesting is to construct the poem in two parts—the first line balanced against the next two lines, or the first two lines balanced against the last line. If you construct a poem on this principle, the two sections should be related to each other, but they should also in some degree make a contrast with each other. Here is an example: "This handsome rooster / Struts before the clucking hens; / Inside, the pot is boiling." A second example, this one offering a contrast between pleasant sociability (the first two lines) and loneliness: "Look, O look, there go / Fireflies," I would like to say— / But I am alone."

📖 WILLIAM BLAKE

William Blake (1757-1827) was born in London and at fourteen was apprenticed for seven years to an engraver. A Christian visionary poet, he made his living by giving drawing lessons and by illustrating books, including his own Songs of Innocence (1789) and Songs of Experience (1794). These two books represent, he said, "two contrary states of the human soul." "London" comes from Experience.) In 1809 Blake exhibited his art, but the show was a failure.

Not until he was in his sixties, when he stopped writing poetry, did he achieve any public recognition—and then it was as a painter.

London

I wander through each chartered street,
Near where the chartered Thames does flow,
And mark in every face I meet
Marks of weakness, marks of woe.   4

In every cry of every man,
In every Infant's cry of fear,
In every voice, in every ban,
The mind-forged manacles I hear.   8

How the Chimney-sweeper's cry
Every black'ning Church appalls;
And the hapless Soldier's sigh
Runs in blood down Palace walls.   12

But most through midnight streets I hear
How the youthful Harlot's curse
Blasts the new-born Infant's tear,
And blights with plagues the Marriage hearse.   16

[1794]

 TOPICS FOR CRITICAL THINKING AND WRITING

1. What do you think Blake means by "mind-forged manacles" (line 8)? What might be some modern examples?
2. Paraphrase the second stanza.
3. Read the poem aloud, several times. How would you characterize the *tone*—sad, angry, or what? Of course the tone may vary from line to line, but what is the prevailing tone, if any?
4. An earlier version of the last stanza ran thus:

   But most the midnight harlots's curse
   From every dismal street I hear,
   Weaves around the marriage hearse
   And blasts the new-born infant's tear.

   Compare the two versions closely. Then consider which you think is more effective, and explain why.
5. Write a poem or a paragraph setting forth your response to a city or town that you know well.

 ALLEN GINSBERG

Allen Ginsberg, born in Newark, New Jersey, in 1926, graduated from Columbia University in 1948. After eight months in Columbia Psychiatric Institute—Ginsberg had pleaded insanity to avoid prose-

cution when the police discovered that a friend stored stolen goods in Ginsberg's apartment—he worked at odd jobs and finally left the nine-to-five world for a freer life in San Francisco. In the 1950s he established a reputation as an uninhibited declamatory poet whose chief theme was a celebration of those who were alienated from a repressive America. Ginsberg has received many awards and, though he now lives on a farm in New Jersey, often reads at college campuses throughout the country.

A Supermarket in California

What thoughts I have of you tonight, Walt Whitman, for I walked down the sidestreets under the trees with a headache self-conscious looking at the full moon.

In my hungry fatigue, and shopping for images, I went into the neon fruit supermarket, dreaming of your enumerations!

What peaches and what penumbras! Whole families shopping at night! Aisles full of husbands! Wives in the avocados, babies in the tomatoes!— and you, García Lorca,° what were you doing down by the watermelons?

I saw you, Walt Whitman, childless, lonely old grubber, poking among the meats in the refrigerator and eyeing the grocery boys.

I heard you asking questions of each: Who killed the pork chops? What price bananas? Are you my Angel?   5

I wandered in and out of the brilliant stacks of cans following you, and followed in my imagination by the store detective.

We strode down the open corridors together in our solitary fancy tasting artichokes, possessing every frozen delicacy, and never passing the cashier.

Where are we going, Walt Whitman? The doors close in an hour. Which way does your beard point tonight?

(I touch your book and dream of our odyssey in the supermarket and feel absurd.)

Will we walk all night through solitary streets? The trees add shade to shade, lights out in the houses, we'll both be lonely.   10

Will we stroll dreaming of the lost America of love past blue automobiles in driveways, home to our silent cottage?

Ah, dear father, graybeard, lonely old courage-teacher, what America did you have when Charon° quit poling his ferry and you got out on a smoking bank and stood watching the boat disappear on the black water of Lethe?

[1956]

¹**García Lorca** Federico García Lorca (1899–1936), Spanish poet (and, like Whitman and Ginsberg, a homosexual)   ¹²**Charon** in classical mythology, Charon ferried the souls of the dead across the river Styx, to Hades, where, after drinking from the river Lethe, they forgot the life they had lived

TOPICS FOR CRITICAL THINKING AND WRITING

1. Ginsberg calls his poem "A Supermarket in California." Need the market be in California, or can it be anywhere?
2. In the second line, Ginsberg explains why he went into the supermarket. Is the explanation clear, or puzzling, or some of each? Explain.
3. In the third section ("What peaches and what penumbras!"), what *is* a penumbra? Are the aisles full of them?
4. In line 8 ("Where are we going, Walt Whitman? The doors close in an hour. Which way does your beard point tonight?"), is Ginsberg hopeful or not about where he and Walt Whitman will stroll?
5. Read two or three Whitman poems (reprinted elsewhere in this book, pages 831–833). In what ways does Ginsberg's poem resemble Whitman's poems? In what ways is "A Supermarket" pure Ginsberg?

 ELIZABETH BISHOP

Elizabeth Bishop (1911–79) was born in Worcester, Massachusetts. Because her father died when she was eight months old and her mother was confined to a sanitarium four years later, Bishop was raised by relatives in New England and Nova Scotia. After graduating from Vassar College in 1934, where she was co-editor of the student literary magazine, she lived (on a small private income) for a while in Key West, France, and Mexico, and then for much of her adult life in Brazil, before returning to the United States to teach at Harvard. Her financial independence enabled her to write without worrying about the sales of her books and without having to devote energy to distracting jobs.

Filling Station

Oh, but it is dirty!
—this little filling station,
oil-soaked, oil-permeated
to a disturbing, over-all
black translucency.   5
Be careful with that match!

Father wears a dirty,
oil-soaked monkey suit
that cuts him under the arms,
and several quick and saucy   10
and greasy sons assist him
(it's a family filling station),
all quite thoroughly dirty.

Do they live in the station?
It has a cement porch   15
behind the pumps, and on it
a set of crushed and grease-

impregnated wickerwork;
on the wicker sofa
a dirty dog, quite comfy.   20

Some comic books provide
the only note of color—
of certain color. They lie
upon a big dim doily
draping a taboret   25
(part of the set), beside
a big hirsute begonia.

Why the extraneous plant?
Why the taboret?
Why, oh why, the doily?   30
(Embroidered in daisy stitch
with marguerites, I think,
and heavy with gray crochet.)

Somebody embroidered the doily.
Somebody waters the plant,   35
or oils it, maybe. Somebody
arranges the rows of cans
so that they softly say:
ESSO°—SO—SO—SO
to high-strung automobiles.   40
Somebody loves us all.

                                                            [1965]

 TOPICS FOR CRITICAL THINKING AND WRITING

1. Taking into account only the first 14 lines, how would you characterize
   the speaker?
2. Robert Lowell, a poet and a friend of Elizabeth Bishop, said of her
   poems that they have "a tone of . . . grave tenderness and sorrowing
   amusement." Do you agree? If so, illustrate his comment by calling attention to specific passages in "Filling Station." If you disagree, how
   would you describe the tone?
3. In lines 21–30, what evidence suggests that the speaker feels that her
   taste is superior to the taste of the family? Does she change her mind by
   the end of the poem, or not?
4. "High-strung" in the last stanza *is* a rather odd way to characterize automobiles. What else strikes you as odd in the last stanza?
5. In two or three paragraphs, characterize a store, or stand, or territory
   that you know. Focus on an aspect of it (as Bishop focuses on the dirt
   and oil) so that readers can see what you find odd, or interesting, or
   striking about it.

39**ESSO** a brand of gasoline, now Exxon

 X. J. KENNEDY

X. J. Kennedy was born in New Jersey in 1929. He has taught at Tufts University and is the author of several books of poems, books for children, and college textbooks.

Nothing in Heaven Functions as It Ought

Nothing in Heaven functions as it ought:
Peter's° bifocals, blindly sat on, crack;
His gates lurch wide with the cackle of a cock,
Not turn with a hush of gold as Milton° had thought;   4
Gangs of the slaughtered innocents keep huffing
The nimbus off the Venerable Bede°
Like that of an old dandelion gone to seed;
And the beatific choir keep breaking up, coughing.   8

But Hell, sleek Hell hath no freewheeling part:
None takes his own sweet time, none quickens pace.
Ask anyone, How come you here, poor heart?—
And he will slot a quarter through his face,   12
You'll hear an instant click, a tear will start
Imprinted with an abstract of his case.

[1965]

²**Peter** St. Peter, said to hold "the keys to the kingdom of Heaven" (Matt. 16.19)
⁴**Milton** John Milton (1608–74), author of *Paradise Lost,* an epic poem that includes a description of heaven   ⁶**the Venerable Bede** English church historian (d. 735)

 TOPICS FOR CRITICAL THINKING

1. Roughly speaking, how does Kennedy characterize Heaven? Does his characterization strike you as disrespectful? Why, or why not?
2. In the octave (the first eight lines of the sonnet) Kennedy uses off-rhymes (*crack, cock; huffing, coughing*), but in the sestet (the last six lines) all the rhymes are exact. How do the rhymes help to convey the meaning?
3. "Nothing in Heaven" is a sonnet. How does the form of the poem help to convey the meaning?

Things

 EMILY DICKINSON

Emily Dickinson (1830–86) was born into a proper New England family in Amherst, Massachusetts. Although she spent her seventeenth year a few miles away, at Mount Holyoke Seminary (now

Mount Holyoke College), in the next twenty years she left Amherst only five or six times, and in her last twenty years she may never have left her house. Her brother was probably right when he said that having seen something of the rest of the world—she had visited Washington with her father, when he was a member of Congress— "she could not resist the feeling that it was painfully hollow. It was to her so thin and unsatisfying in the face of the Great Realities of Life." Nevertheless, the following poem shows a keen interest in some things of the world.

I like to see it lap the Miles

I like to see it lap the Miles—
And lick the Valleys up—
And stop to feed itself at Tanks—
And then—prodigious step   4

Around a Pile of Mountains—
And supercilious peer
In Shanties—by the sides of Roads—
And then a Quarry pare   8

To fit its Ribs
And crawl between
Complaining all the while
In horrid—hooting stanza—   12
Then chase itself down Hill—

And neigh like Boanerges°—
Then—punctual as a Star
Stop—docile and omnipotent   16
At its own stable door—

[1862]

¹³**Boanerges** a name said (in Mark 3.17) to mean "Sons of Thunder"

 TOPICS FOR CRITICAL THINKING AND WRITING

1. What is Dickinson describing?
2. Suppose someone argued that this poem is about literature, especially about poetry, which draws on the experiences of the mind ("stop to feed itself at Tanks"), threatens to go out of control ("prodigious step," "horrid—hooting stanza," "chase itself down Hill"), but for the most part carefully orders its material ("pare," "crawl," "Stop—docile and omnipotent"). To what extent do you agree? Explain your position.

 JOHN KEATS

John Keats (1795–1821), son of a London stable keeper, was taken out of school when he was fifteen and was apprenticed to a surgeon

*and apothecary. In 1816 he was licensed to practice as an apothe-
cary-surgeon, but he almost immediately abandoned medicine and
decided to make a career as a poet. His progress was amazing; he
published books of poems—to mixed reviews—in 1817, 1818, and
1820, before dying of tuberculosis at the age of twenty-five. Today he
is esteemed as one of England's greatest poets.*

Ode to a Nightingale

My heart aches, and a drowsy numbness pains
   My sense, as though of hemlock° I had drunk,
Or emptied some dull opiate to the drains
   One minute past, and Lethe-wards° had sunk:
'Tis not through envy of thy happy lot,   5
   But being too happy in thine happiness—
      That thou, light-wingéd Dryad° of the trees,
         In some melodious plot
Of beechen green, and shadows numberless,
      Singest of summer in full-throated ease.   10

O, for a draught of vintage! that hath been
   Cooled a long age in the deep-delvéd earth,
Tasting of Flora° and the country green,
   Dance, and Provençal song,° and sunburnt mirth!
O for a beaker full of the warm South,   15
   Full of the true, the blushful Hippocrene,°
      With beaded bubbles winking at the brim,
         And purple-stainéd mouth;
That I might drink, and leave the world unseen,
      And with thee fade away into the forest dim: 20

Fade far away, dissolve, and quite forget
   What thou among the leaves hast never known,
The weariness, the fever, and the fret
   Here, where men sit and hear each other groan;
Where palsy shakes a few, sad, last gray hairs,   25
   Where youth grows pale, and specter-thin, and dies,
      Where but to think is to be full of sorrow
         And leaden-eyed despairs,
Where Beauty cannot keep her lustrous eyes,
      Or new Love pine at them beyond tomorrow.   30

²**hemlock** an opiate ⁴**Lethe-wards** toward Lethe, an underworld river whose
waters cause the dead to forget ⁷**Dryad** wood nymph ¹³**Flora** Roman goddess of
springtime and flowers ¹⁴**Provençal song** songs of late-medieval troubadours in
southern France ¹⁶**Hippocrene** the fountain of the Muses (goddesses of the arts),
whose water induced inspiration

Away! away! for I will fly to thee,
  Not charioted by Bacchus and his pards,°
But on the viewless° wings of Poesy,
  Though the dull brain perplexes and retards:
Already with thee! tender is the night,   35
  And haply the Queen-Moon is on her throne.
    Clustered around by all her starry Fays;°
      But here there is no light,
  Save what from heaven is with the breezes blown
    Through verdurous glooms and winding mossy ways.   40

I cannot see what flowers are at my feet,
  Nor what soft incense hangs upon the boughs,
But, in embalméd° darkness, guess each sweet
  Wherewith the seasonable month endows
The grass, the thicket, and the fruit tree wild;   45
  White hawthorn, and the pastoral eglantine;
    Fast fading violets covered up in leaves;
      And mid-May's eldest child,
    The coming musk-rose, full of dewy wine,
      The murmurous haunt of flies on summer eves.   50

Darkling° I listen; and for many a time
  I have been half in love with easeful Death,
Called him soft names in many a muséd rhyme,
  To take into the air my quiet breath;
Now more than ever seems it rich to die,   55
  To cease upon the midnight with no pain,
    While thou art pouring forth thy soul abroad
      In such an ecstasy!
  Still wouldst thou sing, and I have ears in vain—
    To thy high requiem become a sod.   60

Thou wast not born for death, immortal Bird!
  No hungry generations tread thee down;
The voice I hear this passing night was heard
  In ancient days by emperor and clown:
Perhaps the selfsame song that found a path   65
  Through the sad heart of Ruth,° when, sick for home,
    She stood in tears amid the alien corn;
      The same that ofttimes hath
  Charmed magic casements, opening on the foam
    Of perilous seas, in faery lands forlorn.   70

Forlorn! the very word is like a bell
  To toll me back from thee to my sole self!

---

³²**Bacchus and his pards** Bacchus, god of wine, rode in a chariot drawn by leopards (*pards*) ³³**viewless** invisible ³⁷**Fays** fairies ⁴³**embalméd** perfumed ⁵¹**Darkling** in darkness ⁶⁶**Ruth** an allusion to the Book of Ruth (see p. 957)

Adieu! the fancy cannot cheat so well
　　As she is famed to do, deceiving elf.
Adieu! adieu! thy plaintive anthem fades   75
　　Past the near meadows, over the still stream,
　　　　Up the hill side; and now 'tis buried deep
　　　　　In the next valley-glades:
　　Was it a vision, or a waking dream?
　　　Fled is that music:—Do I wake or sleep?   80

                                                                    [1819]

TOPICS FOR CRITICAL THINKING AND WRITING

1. Many readers report that they find the third stanza the least interesting in the poem. Do you share this view? In any case, why might this be so?
2. It is literally nonsense to say that the bird has lived forever (lines 61–67). What possible sense can we make out of the passage?
3. The song of the bird "fades" (line 75) and is "buried deep" (line 77). Is Keats thereby saying something about what the bird may symbolize?
4. At the end of the poem has the poet learned anything? If so, what?

 ## WALLACE STEVENS

Wallace Stevens (1879–1955), educated at Harvard and at New York Law School, earned his living as a lawyer and an insurance executive; at his death he was a vice president of the Hartford Accident and Indemnity Company. While pursuing this career, however, he also achieved distinction as a poet, and today he is widely regarded as among the most important American poets of the twentieth century.

Anecdote of the Jar

I placed a jar in Tennessee,
And round it was, upon a hill.
It made the slovenly wilderness
Surround that hill.   4

The wilderness rose up to it,
And sprawled around, no longer wild.
The jar was round upon the ground
And tall and of a port in air.   8

It took dominion everywhere.
The jar was gray and bare.
It did not give of bird or bush,
Like nothing else in Tennessee.   12

                                                                    [1923]

Stevens, asked for an interpretation of another poem, said (in *The Explicator,* November 1948): "Things that have their origin in the imagination or in the emotions (poems) . . . very often take on a form that is ambiguous or uncertain. It is not possible to attach a single, rational meaning to such things without destroying the imaginative or emotional ambiguity or uncertainty that is inherent in them and that is why poets do not like to explain. That the meanings given by others are sometimes meanings not intended by the poet or that were never present in his mind does not impair them as meanings."

TOPICS FOR CRITICAL THINKING AND WRITING

1. What is the meaning of line 8? Check "port" in a dictionary.
2. Do you think the poem suggests that the jar organizes slovenly nature, or that the jar impoverishes abundant nature? Or both, or neither? What do you think of the view that the jar is a symbol of the imagination, or of the arts, or of material progress?

ELIZABETH BISHOP

Elizabeth Bishop (1911–79) was born in Worcester, Massachusetts. Because her father died when she was eight months old and her mother was confined to a sanitarium four years later, Bishop was raised by relatives in New England and Nova Scotia. After graduating from Vassar College in 1934, where she was co-editor of the student literary magazine, she lived (on a small private income) for a while in Key West, France, and Mexico, and then for much of her adult life in Brazil, before returning to the United States to teach at Harvard. Her financial independence enabled her to write without worrying about the sales of her books and without having to devote energy to distracting jobs.

The Fish

I caught a tremendous fish
and held him beside the boat
half out of water, with my hook
fast in a corner of his mouth.
He didn't fight.   5
He hadn't fought at all.
He hung a grunting weight,
battered and venerable
and homely. Here and there
his brown skin hung in strips   10
like ancient wall-paper,
and its pattern of darker brown
was like wall-paper:
shapes like full-blown roses
stained and lost through age.   15
He was speckled with barnacles,
fine rosettes of lime,

and infested
with tiny white sea-lice,
and underneath two or three   20
rags of green weed hung down.
While his gills were breathing in
the terrible oxygen
—the frightening gills,
fresh and crisp with blood,   25
that can cut so badly—
I thought of the coarse white flesh
packed in like feathers,
the big bones and the little bones,
the dramatic reds and blacks   30
of his shiny entrails,
and the pink swim-bladder
like a big peony.
I looked into his eyes
which were far larger than mine   35
but shallower, and yellowed,
the irises backed and packed
with tarnished tinfoil
seen through the lenses
of old scratched isinglass.   40
They shifted a little, but not
to return my stare.
—It was more like the tipping
of an object toward the light.
I admired his sullen face,   45
the mechanism of his jaw,
and then I saw
that from his lower lip
—if you could call it a lip—
grim, wet, and weapon-like,   50
hung five old pieces of fish-line,
or four and a wire leader
with the swivel still attached,
with all their five big hooks
grown firmly in his mouth.   55
A green line, frayed at the end
where he broke it, two heavier lines,
and a fine black thread
still crimped from the strain and snap
when it broke and he got away.   60
Like medals with their ribbons
frayed and wavering,
a five-haired beard of wisdom
trailing from his aching jaw.
I stared and stared   65
and victory filled up
the little rented boat,
from the pool of bilge

where oil had spread a rainbow
around the rusted engine   70
to the bailer rusted orange,
the sun-cracked thwarts,
the oarlocks on their strings,
the gunnels—until everything
was rainbow, rainbow, rainbow!   75
And I let the fish go.

[1946]

 TOPICS FOR CRITICAL THINKING AND WRITING

1. In line 9 Bishop calls the fish "homely" and in succeeding lines compares him to a series of stained, scratched, and tarnished domestic objects. When (in line 44) she reports that she "admired his sullen face," did that take you by surprise, or had she prepared you for her admiration? Explain.
2. In lines 66–67 we're told that "victory filled up / the little rented boat." Whose victory was it? Or do you think the lines are deliberately ambiguous?
3. Why does the speaker pause in her story to describe the condition of the rented boat? Is a comparison between the boat and the fish implied?
4. What causes the "rainbow" in line 69? How do you understand "everything / was rainbow, rainbow, rainbow!" in lines 74–75?
5. Why does the speaker let the fish go? Is this ending a surprise, or has it been prepared for? Explain.

MARGE PIERCY

Marge Piercy, born in Detroit in 1936, was the first member of her family to attend college. After earning a bachelor's degree from the University of Michigan in 1957 and a master's degree from Northwestern University in 1958, she moved to Chicago. There she worked at odd jobs while writing novels (unpublished) and engaging in action on behalf of women and African-Americans and against the war in Vietnam. In 1970—the year she moved to Wellfleet, Massachusetts, where she still lives—she published her first book, a novel. Since then she has published other novels, short stories, poems, and essays.

Barbie Doll

This girlchild was born as usual
and presented dolls that did pee-pee
and miniature GE stoves and irons
and wee lipsticks the color of cherry candy.
Then in the magic of puberty, a classmate said: 5
You have a great big nose and fat legs.

She was healthy, tested intelligent,
possessed strong arms and back,
abundant sexual drive and manual dexterity.
She went to and fro apologizing.   10
Everyone saw a fat nose on thick legs.

She was advised to play coy,
exhorted to come on hearty,
exercise, diet, smile and wheedle.
Her good nature wore out   15
like a fan belt.
So she cut off her nose and her legs
and offered them up.

In the casket displayed on satin she lay
with the undertaker's cosmetics painted on,   20
a turned-up putty nose,
dressed in a pink and white nightie.
Doesn't she look pretty? everyone said.
Consummation at last.
To every woman a happy ending.   25

[1969]

 ## TOPICS FOR CRITICAL THINKING AND WRITING

1. The poem begins "This girlchild was born as usual" and ends with everyone admiring a woman in her casket. Overall, in a sentence, what has the poem been about?

2. In "the magic of puberty" (line 5), a classmate makes a remark. What was the remark? And how do you read the word "magic"? Does it describe supernatural effects? A quality that lends enchantment? Or what?

3. In stanza 2 we're given some "social science" facts (lines 7-9). In the same stanza we're also told what the girl does ("She went to and fro apologizing"). Why are we given these two rather different views of her?

4. Why is the poem called "Barbie Doll"?

5. In an essay of 500-750 words, explain what Piercy is saying about women in this poem. Does her view seem to you fair, slightly exaggerated, or greatly exaggerated?

6. Write a poem—or an essay of 500 words—about Ken, Barbie's companion doll. If you wish, closely imitate Marge Piercy's poem.

CHAPTER 12

Thinking Critically about Poetry

A Casebook on Emily Dickinson's "I heard a Fly buzz— when I died—"

In this chapter we give the text of Dickinson's poem, and we follow it with

1. A facsimile of Dickinson's manuscript
2. An interpretation by Gerhard Friedrich
3. An interpretation by John Ciardi, taking issue with Friedrich
4. A comment by Caroline Hogue, expressing support for Friedrich and disagreement with Ciardi
5. An interpretation by Eugene Hollahan, arguing that familiarity with the thought of Dickinson's period leads to an interpretation different from those previously offered
6. An interpretation by Karl Keller, arguing that the poem is both "macabre" and "funny"
7. An interpretation by Paula Bennett, arguing that "the poem is at the very least a grim joke"

 EMILY DICKINSON

Emily Dickinson (1830-86) was born into a proper New England family in Amherst, Massachusetts. Although she spent her seventeenth year a few miles away, at Mount Holyoke Seminary (now

Mount Holyoke College), in the next twenty years she left Amherst
only five or six times, and in her last twenty years she may never
have left her house. Her brother was probably right when he said that
having seen something of the rest of the world—she had visited
Washington with her father, when he was a member of Congress—
"she could not resist the feeling that it was painfully hollow. It was to
her so thin and unsatisfying in the face of the Great Realities of Life."
Dickinson lived with her parents (a somewhat reclusive mother and
an austere, remote father) and a younger sister; a married brother
lived in the house next door. She did, however, form some passionate
attachments, to women as well as men, but there is no evidence that
they found physical expression.

By the age of twelve Dickinson was writing witty letters, but she
apparently did not write more than an occasional poem before her
late twenties. At her death—she died in the house where she was
born—she left 1,775 poems, only a few of which had been published
(anonymously) during her lifetime.

I heard a Fly buzz—when I died—

I heard a Fly buzz—when I died—
The Stillness in the Room
Was like the Stillness in the Air—
Between the Heaves of Storm—

The Eyes around—had wrung them dry—   5
And Breaths were gathering firm
For the last Onset—when the King
Be witnessed—in the Room—

I willed my Keepsakes—Signed away
What portion of me be   10
Assignable—and then it was
There interposed a Fly—

With Blue—uncertain stumbling Buzz—
Between the light—and me—
And then the Windows failed—and then   15
I could not see to see—

[c. 1862]

I heard a Fly buzz - when
I died -
The Stillness in the Room
Was like the Stillness in the Air
Between the Heaves of Storm -

The Eyes around - had wrung them
dry -
And Breaths were gathering firm
For that last Onset - when the King
Be witnessed - in the Room -

I willed my Keepsakes - Signed away
What portion of me be
Assignable - and then it was
there interposed a Fly -

With Blue - uncertain stumbling Buzz -
Between the light - and me -
And then the Windows failed - and then
I could not see to see -

Manuscript of Emily Dickinson's "I heard a Fly buzz—when I died—" (Reprinted by permission of the publishers and the Trustees of Amherst College from *The Poems of Emily Dickinson,* Thomas H. Johnson, ed., Cambridge, Mass.: The Belknap Press of Harvard University Press, Copyright © 1951, 1955, 1979, 1983 by the President and Fellows of Harvard College.)

 GERHARD FRIEDRICH

Gerhard Friedrich was teaching at Haverford College when he published this interpretation in a journal called Explicator. *We follow Friedrich's interpretation with two others that comment on it, by John Ciardi and by Caroline Hogue.*

Dickinson's "I heard a Fly buzz—when I died—"

This poem seems to present two major problems to the interpreter. First, what is the significance of the buzzing fly in relation to the dying person, and second, what is the meaning of the double use of "see" in the last line? An analysis of the context helps to clear up these apparent obscurities, and a close parallel found in another Dickinson poem reinforces such interpretation.

In an atmosphere of outward quiet and inner calm, the dying person collectedly proceeds to bequeath his or her worldly possessions, and while engaged in this activity of "willing," finds his attention withdrawn by a fly's buzzing. The fly is introduced in intimate connection with "my keepsakes" and "what portion of me be assignable"; it follows—and is the culmination of—the dying person's preoccupation with cherished material things no longer of use to the departing owner. In the face of death, and even more of a possible spiritual life beyond death, one's concern with a few earthly belongings is but a triviality, and indeed a distraction from a momentous issue. The obtrusiveness of the inferior, physical aspects of existence, and the busybody activity associated with them, is poignantly illustrated by the intervening insect (cf. the line "Buzz the dull flies on the chamber window," in the poem beginning "How many times these low feet staggered"). Even so small a demonstrative, demonstrable creature is sufficient to separate the dying person from "the light," i.e. to blur the vision, to short-circuit mental concentration, so that spiritual awareness is lost. The last line of the poem may then be paraphrased to read: "Waylaid by irrelevant, tangible, finite objects of little importance, I was no longer capable of that deeper perception which would clearly reveal to me the infinite spiritual reality." As Emily Dickinson herself expressed it, in another, Second Series poem beginning "Their height in heaven comforts not":

I'm finite, I can't see.
        · · ·
This timid life of evidence
Keeps pleading, "I don't know."

The dying person does in fact not merely suffer an unwelcome external interruption of an otherwise resolute expectancy, but falls from a higher consciousness, from liberating insight, from faith, into an intensely skeptical mood. The fly's buzz is characterized as "blue, uncertain, stumbling," and emphasis on the finite physical reality goes hand in hand with a frustrating lack of absolute assurance. The only portion of a man not properly "assignable" may be that which dies and decomposes! To the dying person, the buzzing fly would thus become a timely, untimely reminder of man's final, cadaverous condition and putrefaction.

The sudden fall of the dying person into the captivity of an earth-heavy skepticism demonstrates of course the inadequacy of the earlier pseudo-stoicism. What seemed then like composure, was after all only a pause "between the heaves of storm"; the "firmness" of the second stanza proved to be less than veritable peace of mind and soul; and so we have a profoundly tragic human situation, namely the perennial conflict between two concepts of reality, most carefully delineated.

The poem should be compared with its illuminating counterpart of the Second Series, "Their height in heaven comforts not," and may be contrasted with "Death is a dialogue between," "I heard as if I had no ear," and the well-known "I never saw a moor."

 ## TOPICS FOR CRITICAL THINKING AND WRITING

1. Some readers of this short essay find that Friedrich's point—his interpretation of the poem—is not as clearly set forth as it should be. State, as concisely as possible, his interpretation. Then, if you had any difficulty with the essay, indicate where the difficulty lies. Finally, evaluate Friedrich's thesis in terms of the evidence that he presents or overlooks.

2. In his final paragraph Friedrich suggests that the poem "should be compared with" another poem and "may be contrasted with" three other poems. You may want to read these poems. But even without reading the poems, what do you think is implied in his argument? Do you agree that if someone compares poem A with another poem B by the same author, the implication probably is that B helps us to see, by resemblance, what A is? But why then would one *contrast* a poem with another poem by the same author? What can a contrast prove?

 ## JOHN CIARDI

John Ciardi (1916–86) was a teacher, critic, translator, and poet. In the following essay he replies to Gerhard Friedrich's interpretation.

Dickinson's "I heard a Fly buzz—when I died—"

I read Mr. Gerhard Friedrich's explication of Emily Dickinson's poem with great interest, but I find myself preferring a different explication.

Mr. Friedrich says of the fly: "Even so small a demonstrative, demonstrable creature is sufficient to separate the dying person from 'the light,' i.e. to blur the vision, to short-circuit mental concentration, so that spiritual awareness is lost. The last line of the poem may then be paraphrased to read: 'Waylaid by irrelevant, tangible, finite objects of little importance, I was no longer capable of that deeper perception which would clearly reveal to me the infinite spiritual reality.'"

Mr. Friedrich's argument is coherent and respectable, but I feel it tends to make Emily more purely mystical than I sense her to be. I understand that fly to be the last kiss of the world, the last buzz from life. Certainly Emily's tremendous attachment to the physical world, and her especial delight both in minute creatures for their own sake, and in minute actions for the sake of the dramatic implications that can be loaded into them, hardly needs to be documented. Any number of poems illustrate her delight in the special significance of tiny living things. "Elysium is as Far" will do as a single example of her delight in packing a total-life significance into the slightest actions:

> What fortitude the Soul contains,
> That it can so endure
> The accent of a coming Foot—
> The opening of a Door—

I find myself better persuaded, therefore, to think of the fly not as a distraction taking Emily's thoughts from glory and blocking the divine light (When did Emily ever think of living things as a distraction?), but as a last dear sound from the world as the light of consciousness sank from her, i.e. "the windows failed." And so I take the last line to mean simply: "And then there was no more of me, and nothing to see with."

TOPICS FOR CRITICAL THINKING AND WRITING

1. Ciardi suggests that other poems by Dickinson—he quotes one—help us to understand *this* poem. Putting aside whether or not you agree with his interpretation of "I heard a Fly buzz," do you think the example he quotes helps to support his argument? Explain.
2. Both Ciardi and Friedrich offer paraphrases of the last line of the poem. Which do you think is more accurate? How would *you* paraphrase the line?
3. How convincing do you find Ciardi's overall argument? Explain.

CAROLINE HOGUE

Caroline Hogue, writing (like Friedrich and Ciardi) in Explicator, *comments on the two earlier essays and adds her own further thoughts.*

Dickinson's "I heard a Fly buzz—when I died—"

Emily Dickinson's "I Heard A Fly Buzz When I Died" should be read, I think, with a particular setting in mind—a nineteenth-century deathbed scene. Before the age of powerful anodynes death was met in full consciousness, and the way of meeting it tended to be stereotype. It was affected with a public interest and concern, and was witnessed by family and friends. They crowded the death chamber to await expectantly a burst of dying energy to bring on the grand act of passing. Commonly it began with last-minute bequests, the wayward were called to repentance, the backslider to reform, gospel hymns were sung, and finally as climax the dying one gave witness in words to the Redeemer's presence in the room, how He hovered, transplendent in the upper air, with open arms outstretched to receive the departing soul. This was death's great moment. Variants there were, of course, in case of repentant and unrepentant sinners. Here in this poem the central figure of the drama is expected to make a glorious exit. The build-up is just right for it, but at the moment of climax "There interposed a fly." And what kind of a fly? A fly "with blue, uncertain stumbling buzz"—a blowfly.

How right is Mr. Gerhard Friedrich in his explication . . . to associate the fly with putrefaction and decay. And how wrong, I think, is Mr. John Ciardi . . . in calling the fly "the last kiss of the world," and speaking of it as one of the small creatures Emily Dickinson so delighted in. She could not possibly have entertained any such view of a blowfly. She was a practical housewife, and every housewife abhors a blowfly. It pollutes everything it touches. Its eggs are maggots. It is as carrion as a buzzard.

What we know of Emily Dickinson gives us assurance that just as she would abhor the blowfly she would abhor the deathbed scene. How devastatingly she disposes of the projected one in the poem. "They talk of hallowed things and embarrass my dog" she writes in 1862 in a letter to Mr. Higginson (*Letters*, 1958, II, 415).

 TOPIC FOR CRITICAL THINKING AND WRITING

What does Hogue contribute to the argument? How useful do you find her contribution? Explain.

 EUGENE HOLLAHAN

Eugene Hollahan teaches at Georgia State University, in Atlanta. Like the preceding interpretations, this one was published in Explicator, *but it takes an entirely different approach to the poem.*

Dickinson's "I heard a Fly buzz—when I died—"

Examining Emily Dickinson's poem which begins "I heard a fly buzz when I died" in the light of the theological tradition the author was nurtured in, the reader finds a new symbolic value for the intrusive fly which interacts with the setting, mood, thought, and texture of the poem. Assuming that the fly as an element in the poem takes on new meaning when seen as an example of Miss Dickinson's daring use of traditional Christian symbols for the purpose of dramatically rendering the experience of death and the afterlife, I herewith suggest that this dramatic lyric is spoken by a soul very possibly if not certainly burning for an eternity in Hell's darkness. In this reading of the poem, I see the fly as an agent or emissary of Satan, the Satan Puritans would expect to be present at the death of an individual possibly or certainly damned to Hell.

Certain facts and assumptions are necessary to this new reading of the poem. First, Miss Dickinson was deeply familiar with the Bible and hence would probably know the tradition that Beelzebub was the "Lord of the Insects"; by association, this designation of Beelzebub (sometimes identified with Satan himself) as "Lord of the Flies" links the poem to the Scriptural Hades. Next, the poet believed with other Puritans that the Elect would reveal at the moment of death some hopeful sign of their souls' eternal welfare. Moreover, we must remember the familiar popular tradition (still active) that at the moment of death both God *and* Satan are present, either in person or represented by an angel or emissary; in this tradition the soul decides by its moral or immoral actions which agent will carry away the immortal remains. Also, we must depend on the forcefulness of the traditional symbolic value of light, which in this poem is associated in a symbol-cluster (God-Light-Salvation); this light is ineluctably blocked from the dead soul by the interposition of the fly. Finally, we must remember that Miss Dickinson wrote many "death" poems in which she makes startling statements and brilliant dramatizations. Her famous remark, "That bareheaded life, under the grass, worries one like a wasp," is an epitome of many of her attitudes toward her subject.

Knowing then that the poet often dramatized in her poetry the drama-laden situation of the personality or soul after the death of the body, and keeping in mind the religious traditions she inherited, we may conclude that this "deathbed" poem, which is actually spoken by the soul some time after death, is in reality an organic development growing out of the theological background, dramatically using the idea of damnation. The poem then is seen to be an attempt to render a lyric monologue spoken by a soul presently in Hell. With this framework established, we can interpret the poem as follows.

The stunned soul speaks monotonously, remembering the moment of death. The first, most vivid detail is the buzzing fly, the *last* physical thing experienced. Next the hushed room is rendered. The "heaves of storm" suggest that this life has been stormy and the afterlife will be too. Subsequent experience will be violent. The watchers have wept their fill, and wait with bated breath to witness the "king" (will it be God or Death?). The "witness" would be the hoped-for sign, but if a sign of salvation is in the possible order of things then logically a sign of damnation would be possible, even if the watchers missed it. The speaker had assigned her worldly goods; however, a serious irony lies in the fact that the speaker did not realize the soul too was "assignable," and had in fact been assigned to its future destination by its actions. So at the moment of readiness, there arrives, probably unnoticed by the watchers, the sign of damnation, an "uncertain, stumbling" fly—uncertain, because until death redemption is possible. It "interposed" between the speaker and the light, the light "failed," and immediately the soul "could not see to see." The darkness this soul is plunged into is not mere physical darkness; it is darkness visible, the permanent darkness of Hell. The texture enforces this reading; "failed" has the echoic quality of a "fall"; the completeness of "could not see to see" clearly means more than physical death.

Emily Dickinson brooded about death and entertained the possibility of damnation as part of an honest confrontation of the inevitable experience. Here, an ordinary, homely detail from life shows rich symbolic resonance in an intensely dramatic lyric poem rising out of her troubled imagination.

TOPIC FOR CRITICAL THINKING AND WRITING

It is usually a good idea to think about the persona who speaks a poem. Hollahan suggests in his first paragraph that the speaker probably is "a soul very possibly if not certainly burning for an eternity in Hell's darkness." It is also usually a good idea to think of the dramatic circumstance of the poem, for instance, *where* the speaker is, and what other characters are present or are implied. Hollahan suggests that the fly is "an agent or emissary of Satan." What is his evidence? How convincing do you find this evidence?

KARL KELLER

Karl Keller, a professor of English and American literature, wrote a book about Emily Dickinson, from which we extract the following comment on "I heard a Fly buzz—when I died—." The title of the extract is our own.

A Playful Poem

The issue of play in Emily Dickinson's poetry reminds one that we have in her one of the major humorists in American literature. The cheer argues best a coherence to her entire ouvres, even as her play with setting, characterization, metaphor, and the organization of a poem reveals the clown in her.

Take her macabre poem beginning "I heard a Fly buzz—when I died." The point of view is deliberately funny: a woman sitting somewhere hereafter telling other dead how *she* died. There was, she remembers with her flip tale, really nothing to it. The scene of her dying, she *now* realizes, was too grand, and by contrast the moment of death was vulgar and funny. So, she shrugs, she could not really "see to see" what death was like. It was merely a harmless incident in her long existence, but it makes a good tale to tell.

> I heard a Fly buzz—when I died—
> The Stillness in the Room
> Was like the Stillness in the Air—
> Between the Heaves of Storm—

The Eyes around—had wrung them dry—
And Breaths were gathering firm
For that last Onset—when the King
Be witnessed—in the Room—

I willed my Keepsakes—Signed away
What portion of me be
Assignable—and then it was
There interposed a Fly—

With Blue—uncertain stumbling Buzz—
Between the light—and me—
And then the Windows failed—and then
I could not see to see—

The disciplined striving for meter and rhymes here, and the attractive failing, represent her pushing ahead with her story/idea, toying with hopeful approximations until they allude to poetic conventions without meeting them. The effect is not polyphonic orchestration so much as a convincing voice, a persona, a presence—the point of the poem anyway. Through "inadequacy" the poem achieves personality. The play personifies.

 ## TOPICS FOR CRITICAL THINKING AND WRITING

1. In his second paragraph Keller says that the poem is "macabre." Do you agree? Explain.
2. Keller argues, too, that "the point of view is deliberately funny." Your response?

 ## PAULA BENNETT

Paula Bennett, a university teacher, is the author of Emily Dickinson: Woman Poet *(1990), from which the following interpretation comes.*

Dickinson's "I heard a Fly buzz—when I died—"

Dickinson's rage against death, a rage that led her at times to hate both life and death, might have been alleviated, had she been able to gather hard evidence about an afterlife. But, of course, she could not. 'The *Bareheaded life*—under the grass—,' she wrote to Samuel Bowles in c. 1860, 'worries one like a Wasp' (*Letters*, 364). If death was the gate to a better life in 'the childhood of the kingdom of Heaven,' as the sentimentalists—and Christ—claimed, then, perhaps, there was compensation and healing for life's woes. In a poem such as 'I shall know why—when Time is over' (#193), Dickinson explores this possibility, deliberately adopting the 'naïve' childlike voice that faith in God's ultimate goodness and explicability requires, and ironi-

PART THREE

Standing Back:

Thinking Critically about Literature and Approaches to Literature

CHAPTER 13

What, Then, Is Literature?

If you have been reading this book more or less from the first chapter onward, by now you have read a fair number of works of literature. But these examples represent, of course, *our* idea of literature. Other editors might print very different kinds of things in their anthologies. True, no editor is likely to print the multiplication table or a page from the telephone book, but what about "Thirty days hath September" or the Pledge of Allegiance? Do these qualify as works of literature? If not, why not? This chapter will try to define *literature,* which is to say that we will argue on behalf of our view of what literature is. As you read it, test it not only against the works that you have read earlier in the book but also against your own ideas of what constitutes literature.

Perhaps the first thing to say is that it is impossible to define *literature* in a way that will satisfy everyone. And perhaps the second thing to say is that in the last twenty years or so, some serious thinkers have argued that it is impossible to set off certain verbal works from all others, and on some basis or other to designate them as *literature.* For one thing, it is argued, a work is just marks on paper or sounds in the air. The audience (reader or listener) turns these marks or sounds into something with meaning, and different audiences will construct different meanings out of what they read or hear. There are *texts* (birthday cards, sermons, political speeches, magazines, novels that sell by the millions and novels that don't sell at all, poems, popular songs, editorials, and so forth), but there is nothing that should be given the special title of *literature.* John M. Ellis, a literary critic, argues in *The Theory of Literary Criticism* (1974) that the word "literature" is something like the word "weed." A weed is just a plant that gardeners for one reason or another don't want in the garden; no plant has characteristics that clearly make it a weed and not merely a plant.

An important school of criticism known as *cultural materialism* argues that what is commonly called literature and is regarded with some awe as embodying eternal truths is in fact only a "cultural construct," like, say, the film industry. According to cultural materialism, the writers of "literature" are the products of their age, and they are producing a product for a market; the critic therefore ought to be chiefly concerned not with whether the text is beautiful or true—these ideas themselves are only social constructions—but, rather, with how writers are shaped by their times (for instance, how the physical conditions of the Elizabethan playhouse and how the attitudes of the Elizabethan playgoer influenced Shakespeare), and how writings work upon the readers and thus help to shape the times.

Although there is something to be said for the idea that *literature* is just an honorific word and not a body of work embodying eternal truths and eternal beauty, let's make the opposite assumption, at least for a start. Let's assume that certain verbal works are of a distinct sort—whether because the author shapes them, or because a reader perceives them a certain way—and that we can call these works *literature.* But what are these works like?

LITERATURE AND FORM

We all know why we value a newspaper (for instance) or a textbook or an atlas, but why do we value a verbal work that doesn't give us the latest news or important information about business cycles or the names of the capitals of nations? About a thousand years ago a Japanese woman, Shikibu Murasaki or Lady Murasaki (978?–1026), offered an answer in *The Tale of Genji,* a book often called the world's first novel. During a discussion about reading fiction, one of the characters offers an opinion as to why a writer tells a story:

> Again and again something in one's own life, or in the life around one, will seem so important that one cannot bear to let it pass into oblivion. There must never come a time, the writer feels, when people do not know about this.

Literature is about human experiences, but the experiences embodied in literature are not simply the shapeless experiences—the chaotic passing scene—captured by a mindless, unselective video camera. Poets, dramatists, and storytellers find or impose a shape on scenes (for instance, the history of two lovers), giving readers things to value—written or spoken accounts that are memorable not only for their content but also for their *form*—the shape of the speeches, of the scenes, of the plots. (In a little while we will see that form and content are inseparable, but for the moment, for textbook purposes, we can talk about them separately.)

Ezra Pound said that literature is "news that *stays* news." Now, "John loves Mary," written on a wall, or on the front page of a newspaper, is news, but it is not news that stays news. It may be of momentary interest to the friends of John and Mary, but it's not much more than simple information and there is no particular reason to value it. Literature is something else. The Johns and Marys in poems, plays, and stories—even though they usually are fairly ordinary individuals, and in many ways they often are rather like us—somehow become significant as we perceive them through the writer's eye and ear. The writer selects what is essential and makes us care about the characters. Their doings stay in our mind.

To say that their doings stay in our mind is *not* to deny that works of literature show signs of being the products of particular ages and environments. It is only to say that these works are not exclusively about those ages and environments; they speak to later readers. The love affairs that we read about in the newspaper are of no interest a day later, but the love of Romeo and Juliet, with its joys and sorrows, has interested people for four hundred years. Those who know the play may feel, with Lady Murasaki's spokesman, that there must never come a time when these things are not known. It should be mentioned, too, that readers find, on rereading a work, that the words are still of great interest but often for new reasons. That is, when as adolescents we read *Romeo and Juliet* we may value it for certain reasons, and when in maturity we reread it we may see it differently and we may value it for new reasons. It is news that remains news.

As the example of *Romeo and Juliet* indicates, literature need not be rooted in historical fact. Although guides in Verona find it profitable to point out Juliet's house, the play is not based on historical characters. Literature is about life, but it may be fictional, dealing with invented characters. In fact, almost all of the characters in literature are imaginary—though they *seem* real. In the words of Picasso,

> Art is not truth. Art is a lie that makes us realize truth. . . . The artist must know the manner whereby to convince others of the truthfulness of his lies.

We can put it this way: Literature shows *what happens* rather than what happened. It may indeed be accurate history, but the fact that it is factual is unimportant.

One reason literary works endure (whether they show us what we are or what we long for) is that their *form* makes their content memorable. In Picasso's terms, the artist knows how to shape lies (fictions, imagined happenings) into enduring forms. Because this discussion of literature is brief, we will illustrate the point by looking at one of the briefest literary forms, the proverb. (Our definition of literature is not limited to the grand forms of the novel, tragedy, and so on. It is wide enough, and democratic enough, to include brief, popular, spoken texts.) Consider this statement:

> A rolling stone gathers no moss.

Now let's compare it with a **paraphrase** (a restatement, a translation into other words), for instance "If a stone is always moving around, vegetation won't have a chance to grow on it." What makes the original version more powerful, more memorable? Surely much of the answer is that the original is more concrete and its form is more shapely. At the risk of being heavy-handed, we can analyze the shapeliness thus: *Stone* and *moss* (the two nouns in the sentence) each contain one syllable; *rolling* and *gathers* (the two words of motion) each contain two syllables, with the accent on the first syllable. Notice, too, the nice contrast between stone (hard) and moss (soft).

The reader probably *feels* this shapeliness unconsciously rather than perceives it consciously. That is, these connections become apparent when one starts to analyze, but the literary work can make its effect on a reader even before the reader analyzes. As T. S. Eliot said in his essay on Dante (1929), "Genuine poetry can communicate before it is understood." Indeed, our *first* reading of a work, when, so to speak, we are all eyes and ears (and the mind is highly receptive rather than sifting for evidence), is sometimes the most important reading. Experience proves that we can feel the effects of a work without yet understanding *how* the effects are achieved.

Probably most readers will agree that the words in the proverb are paired interestingly and meaningfully. And perhaps they will agree, too, that the sentence is not simply some information but is also (to quote one of Robert Frost's definitions of literature) "a performance in words." What the sentence *is,* we might say, is no less significant than what the sentence *says.* The sentence as a whole forms a memorable picture, a small but complete world, hard and soft, inorganic and organic, inert and moving. The idea set forth is simple—partly because it is highly focused and therefore it leaves out a lot—but it is also complex. By virtue of the contrasts, and, again, even by the pairing of monosyllabic nouns and of disyllabic words of motion, it is unified into a pleasing whole. For all of its specificity and its compactness—the proverb contains only six words—it expands our minds.

At this point it must be said that many contemporary critics, for one reason or another, deny that unity is a meaningful concept. For instance, they may insist that because each reader reads a text in his or her own way—in effect, each reader constructs or creates the text—it is absurd to talk about unity. Unity, it is said, is illusory. Or, on the other hand, if unity is real it is unwanted, a repressive cultural convention. We will discuss the point later, in Chapter 17, especially in conjunction with deconstruction and reader-response Theory, but here we will cite one example. Terry Eagleton, a Marxist critic, says in *Literary Theory* (1983), "There is absolutely no need to suppose that works of literature either do or should constitute harmonious wholes, and many suggestive frictions and collisions of meaning must be blandly 'processed' by literary criticism to induce them to do so" (81). Like other Marxists, Eagleton assumes that our society is riven with contradictions and that therefore the art it produces is also contradictory, fissured, fractured. The works are produced by a particular society and are consumed by that society, and therefore they are in effect propaganda for the present economic system, whether the authors know it or not. According to this view, critics who look for artistic unity falsify the works.

It should be mentioned, too, that some critics have no difficulty in finding contradictions. If contradictions are not evident, the critic may point out "absences" or "silences" or "omissions." That is, the critic may argue that certain material indeed is not in the text, but its absence shows that the author has sought to repress the contradiction. Thus, a poem, story, or play about heterosexual romantic love may be seen as embodying a contradiction because it does *not* include any reference to, say, gay or lesbian love, or to marriage as a patriarchal construction that oppresses women. If one operates this way, it is easy to deny that any work is unified.

On the other hand, it is entirely legitimate to think about the choices a writer makes, and to wonder why *this* is included in the work whereas *that* is not. Shakespeare chose, in his *King Lear,* to alter his source (*King Leir*) essentially; he dropped the happy ending (in the source, Leir is restored to the throne and his beloved daughter Cordelia does not die). An examination of the choices a writer makes is often far more useful than an examination aimed at chastising a writer for committing an ideological sin.

A Brief Exercise: Take a minute to think about some other proverb, for instance "Look before you leap," "Finders keepers," "Haste makes waste," or "Absence makes the heart grow fonder." Paraphrase it, and then ask yourself why the original is more interesting, more memorable, than your paraphrase.

LITERATURE AND MEANING

We have seen that the form of the proverb pleases the mind and the tongue, but what about **content** or **meaning?** We may enjoy the images and the sounds, but surely the words add up to something. After all, they are not just "tra la la." Probably most people would agree that the contents or the meaning of "A rolling stone gathers no moss" is something like this: "If you are always on the move— if, for instance, you don't stick to one thing but you keep switching schools, or jobs—you won't accomplish much."

Now, if this statement approximates the meaning of the proverb, we can say two things: (1) the proverb contains a good deal of truth, and (2) it certainly is not always true. Indeed this proverb is more or less contradicted by another proverb, "Nothing ventured, nothing gained." Many proverbs, in fact, contradict other proverbs. "Too many cooks spoil the broth," yes, but "Many hands make light work"; "Absence makes the heart grow fonder," yes, but "Out of sight, out of mind"; "He who hesitates is lost," yes, but "Look before you leap." The claim that literature offers insights, or illuminates experience, is not a claim that it offers irrefutable and unvarying truths, covering the whole of our experience. Of course literature does not give us *the* truth; rather it wakes us up, makes us see, helps us feel intensely some aspect of our experience, and perhaps to evaluate it. The novelist Franz Kafka said something to this effect, very strongly, in a letter of 1904:

> If the book we are reading does not wake us, as with a fist hammering on our skull, why then do we read it? . . . What we must have are those books which come upon us like ill-fortune, and distress us deeply, like the death of one we love better than ourselves. . . . A book must be an ice-axe to break the sea frozen inside us.

ARGUING ABOUT MEANING

Later we will discuss at length the question of whether one interpretation—one statement or formulation of the meaning of a work—is better than another, but a word should be said about it now. Suppose that while discussing "A rolling stone gathers no moss," someone said this to you:

> I don't think it means that if you are always on the move you won't accomplish anything. I think the meaning is something like the saying "There are no flies on him." First of all, what's so great about moss developing? Why do you say that the moss more or less represents worthwhile accomplishments? And why do you say that the implication is that someone should settle down? The way I see it is just the opposite: The proverb says that active people don't let stuff accumulate on them, don't get covered over. That is, active people, people who accomplish things (people who get somewhere) are always unencumbered, are people who don't stagnate.

What reply can be offered? Probably no reply will convince the person who interprets the proverb this way. Perhaps, then, we must conclude that (as the critic Northrop Frye said) reading is a picnic to which the writer brings the words and the reader brings the meanings. The remark is witty and is probably true. Certainly readers over the years have brought very different meanings to such works as the Bible and *Hamlet.*

Even if readers can never absolutely prove the truth of their interpretations, all readers have the obligation to make as convincing a case as possible. When you write about literature, you probably will begin (in your marginal jottings and in other notes) by setting down random expressions of feeling and even unsupported opinions, but later, when you are preparing to share your material with a reader, you will have to go further. You will have to try to show your reader *why* you hold the opinion you do. In short, as we have already said,

- You have to be aware of your assumptions.
- You have to offer plausible supporting evidence.
- You have to do so in a coherent and rhetorically effective essay.

That is, you'll have to make the reader in effect say, "Yes, I see exactly what you mean, and what you say makes a good deal of sense." You may not thoroughly convince your readers, but they will at least understand *why* you hold the views you do.

FORM AND MEANING

Let's turn now to a work not much longer than a proverb—a very short poem by Robert Frost (1874-1963).

The Span of Life

The old dog barks backward without getting up.
I can remember when he was a pup.

Read the poem aloud once or twice, physically experiencing Frost's "performance in words." Notice that the first line is harder to say than the second line, which more or less trips off the tongue. Why? Because in the first line we must pause between *old* and *dog,* between *backward* and *without,* and between *without* and *getting*—and in fact between *back* and *ward.* Further, when we read the poem aloud, or with the mind's ear, in the first line we hear four consecutive stresses in *old dog barks back,* a noticeable contrast to the rather jingling "when he was a pup" in the second line. No two readers will read the lines in exactly the same way, but it is probably safe to say that most readers will agree that in the first line they may stress fairly heavily as many as eight syllables, whereas in the second line they may stress only three or four:

The óld dóg bárks báckwàrd withòut gétting úp.
Í can remémber whén he wás a púp.

And so we can say that the form (a relatively effortful, hard-to-speak line followed by a bouncy line) shapes and indeed is part of the content (a description of a dog that no longer has the energy or the strength to leap up, followed by a memory of the dog as a puppy).

Thinking further about Frost's poem, we notice something else about the form. The first line is about a dog, but the second line is about a dog *and* a human being ("*I* can remember"). The speaker must be getting on, too. And although nothing is said about the dog as a *symbol* of human life, surely the reader, prompted by the title of the poem, makes a connection between the life span of a dog and that of a human being. Part of what makes the poem effective is that this point is *not* stated explicitly, not belabored. Readers have the pleasure of making the connection for themselves—under Frost's careful guidance.

Everyone knows that puppies are frisky and that old dogs are not—though perhaps not until we encountered this poem did we think twice about the fact that "the old dog barks backward without getting up." Or let's put it this way: Other people may have noticed this behavior, but perhaps only Frost thought (to use Lady Murasaki's words), "There must never come a time . . . when people do not know about this." And, fortunately for all of us, Frost had the ability to put his perception into memorable words. Part of what makes this performance in words especially memorable is, of course, the *relationship* between the two lines. Neither line in itself is anything very special, but because of the counterpoint the whole is more than the sum of the parts. Skill in handling language, obviously, is indispensable if the writer is to produce literature. A person may know a great deal about dogs and may be a great lover of dogs, but knowledge and love are not enough equipment to write even a two-line poem about a dog (or the span of life, or both). Poems, like other kinds of literature, are produced by people who know how to delight us with verbal performances.

Presumably Frost reported his observation about the dog not simply as a piece of dog lore, but because it concerns all of us. It is news that stays news. Once you have read or heard the poem, you can never again look at a puppy or an old dog in quite the way you used to—and probably the poem will keep coming to mind as you feel in your bones the effects of aging. If it at first seems odd to say that literature influences us, think of the debate concerning pornography. The chief reason for opposing pornography is that it exerts a bad influence on those who consume it. If indeed books and pictures can exert a bad influence, it seems reasonable to think that other books and pictures can exert a good influence. Fairness requires us to mention, however, that many thoughtful people disagree and argue that literature and art entertain us but do not really influence us in any significant way. In trying to solve this debate, perhaps one can rely only on one's own experience.

We can easily see that Robert Frost's "The Span of Life" is a work of literature—a work that uses language in a special way—if we contrast it with another short work in rhyme:

Thirty days hath September,
April, June, and November;
All the rest have thirty-one
Excepting February alone,
Which has twenty-eight in fine,
Till leap year gives it twenty-nine.

This information is important, but it is only information. The lines rhyme, giving the work some form, but there is nothing very interesting about it. (This is a matter of opinion; perhaps you will want to take issue.) It is true and therefore useful, but it is not of compelling interest. It is not news that stays news, probably because it only *tells* us facts rather than *shows* or *presents* human experience. We all remember the lines, but they do not hold our interest. "Thirty days" does not offer either the pleasure of an insight or the pleasure of an interesting tune. It has nothing of what the poet Thomas Gray said characterizes literature: "Thoughts that breathe, and words that burn."

As we will see, there are many ways of writing about literature, but one of the most interesting is to write not simply about the author's "thoughts" (or ideas) as abstractions but about the particular *ways* in which an author makes thoughts memorable, chiefly through the manipulation of words that at least glow if they don't "burn."

The poet W. H. Auden once defined literature as "a game of knowledge." His reference to a "game" reminds us of Frost's comment that literature is "a performance." Games have rules, forms, and conformity to the rules is part of the fun of playing a game. We don't want the basketball player to pick up the ball and run with it, or the tennis player to do away with the net. The fun in writing literature comes largely from performing effectively within the rules, or from introducing new rules and then working within them. For Auden, a work of art is "a verbal contraption," and in every work of art (as in a game), "Freedom and Law, System and Order are united in harmony" (*The Dyer's Hand* [1968], 50, 71).

We don't play (or watch) games because they teach us to be good citizens, or even because they will make us healthier; we play and watch them because they give us pleasure. But Auden's definition of literature is not simply "a game"; it is "a game of knowledge." When Auden speaks of knowledge he is speaking of the writer's understanding of human experience. We are back to Lady Murasaki's comment: "There must never come a time, the writer feels, when people do not know" about certain experiences. This knowledge that Lady Murasaki and Auden speak of is conveyed through words, arranged as in a performance or a game. The performance may be very brief, as in the highly structured proverb about a rolling stone or the equally structured pair of lines about the old dog, or it may be extended into a novel of a thousand pages. Many of the later pages in this book will be devoted to talking about structure in fiction, drama, and poetry.

THE LITERARY CANON

You may have heard people talk about the **canon** of literature, that is, talk about the recognized body of literature. *Canon* comes from a Greek word for a reed (it's the same as our word *cane*); a reed or cane was used as a measuringstick, and certain works were said to measure up to the idea of literature. Many plays by Shakespeare fit the measure and were accepted into the canon early (and they have stayed there), but many plays by his contemporaries never entered the canon—in their own day they were performed, maybe applauded, and some were published, but later generations have not valued them. In fact, some plays by Shakespeare, too, are almost never taught or performed, for instance, *Cymbeline* and *Timon of Athens.* And, conversely, some writers are known chiefly for a single work, although they wrote a great deal. The canon, in actuality, has always been highly varied. True, it chiefly contained the work of white males, but that was because in the Euro-American world until fairly recently white males were the people doing most of the writing, and white males controlled the publishing industry. (The reasons why women and persons of color were not doing much publishing are scarcely to the credit of white males, who controlled society, but that's not what we are talking about here.) Even in the traditional male-dominated canon, however, the range was great, including, for instance, ancient epic poems by Homer, tragedies and comedies by Shakespeare, brief lyrics by Emily Dickinson, and short stories and novels by James Joyce, Virginia Woolf, and Ralph Ellison.

Further, the canon—the group of works esteemed by a community of readers—keeps changing, partly because in different periods somewhat different measuring rods are used. For instance, Shakespeare's *Troilus and Cressida*—a play about war, in which heroism and worthy ideals are in short supply—for several hundred years was performed only rarely, but during the Vietnam War it became popular, doubtless because the play was seen as an image of that widely unpopular war. More important, however, than the shifting fortunes of individual works is the recent inclusion of material representing newly valued kinds of experiences. In our day we have increasingly become aware of the voices of women and of members of minority cultures, for instance, Native Americans, African-Americans, Latinos, lesbians, and gays. As a consequence, works by these people—giving voice to identities previously ignored by the larger society—are now taught in literature classes.

What is or is not literature, then, changes over the years; in the language of today's criticism, "literature" as a category of "verbal production and reception" is itself a "historical construction" rather than an unchanging reality. Insofar as a new generation finds certain verbal works pleasing, moving, powerful, memorable, compelling—beautiful and true, one might say—they become literature. Today a course in nineteenth-century American literature is likely to include works by Harriet Beecher Stowe and Frederick Douglass—but it probably also includes works by long-established favorites such as Emerson, Hawthorne and Whitman.

Some works have measured up for so long that they probably will always be valued, that is, they will always be part of the literary canon. But of course one cannot predict the staying power of new works. Doubtless some stories, novels, poems, and plays—as well, perhaps, as television scripts and popular songs—will endure. Most of the literature of *any* generation, however, measures up only briefly; later generations find it dated, uninteresting, unexciting. Lincoln's address at Gettysburg has endured as literature, but Kennedy's inaugural address—much praised in its day—now strikes many readers as thin, hollow, strained, even corny. (These adjectives of course imply value judgments; anyone who offers such judgments needs to support them, to argue them, not merely assert them. Elsewhere in this book we talk about arguing a thesis.) Even if Kennedy's inaugural address fades as literature, it will retain its historical importance. In this view, it belongs in a course in politics, but not in a course in literature.

LITERATURE, TEXTS, DISCOURSES, AND CULTURAL STUDIES

These pages have routinely spoken of *literature* and of literary *works,* terms recently often supplanted by *text.* Some say that *literature* is a word with elitist connotations. They may say, too, that a *work* is a crafted, finished thing, whereas a *text,* in modern usage, is something that in large measure is created (i.e., given meaning) by a reader. Further, the word *text* helps to erase the line between, on the one hand, what traditionally has been called literature—for instance, canonized material—and, on the other hand, popular verbal forms such as science fiction, westerns, sermons, political addresses, interviews, advertisements, comic strips, and bumper stickers (and, for that matter, nonverbal products such as sports events, architecture, fashion design, automobiles, and the offerings in a shopping mall). Texts or *discourses* of this sort (said to be parts of what is called a *discursive practice* or a *signifying practice*) in recent years have increasingly interested many people who used to teach literature ("great books") but who now teach *cultural studies.* In these courses the emphasis is not on objects inherently valuable and taught apart from the conditions of their production. Rather, the documents—whether plays by Shakespeare or comic books—are studied in their social and political contexts, especially in the light of the conditions of their production, distribution, and consumption. Thus, *Hamlet* would be related to the economic and political system of England around 1600, and *also* to the context today—the educational system, the theater industry, and so on—that produces the work. To study a work otherwise—to study a literary work as an esthetic object, something to be enjoyed and admired apart from its context—is, it is claimed, to "sacralize" it, to treat it as a sacred thing, and in effect to mummify it. (One might ask if it is really a bad thing to treat with respect—at least at the start—a work by, say, Shakespeare or George Eliot.)

IN BRIEF: A CONTEMPORARY AUTHOR SPEAKS ABOUT LITERATURE

Finally, in an effort to establish an idea of what literature is, let's listen to the words of John Updike, an author of stories, novels, and poems. Updike, as a highly successful writer, could of course be examined in the context of cultural studies: How are his novels promoted? To what extent do reviews of his books affect sales? To what extent do Updike's reviews of other people's books affect sales? What sorts of people (race, class, gender) read Updike? But Updike's own abundant comments about writing are almost entirely concerned with esthetic matters, as in the following passage. He is talking about stories, but we can apply his words to all sorts of literature:

> I want stories to startle and engage me within the first few sentences, and in their middle to widen or deepen or sharpen my knowledge of human activity, and to end by giving me a sensation of completed statement.

SUGGESTIONS FOR FURTHER READING

Subsequent chapters will cite a fair number of recent titles relevant to this chapter, but for a start a reader might first turn to an old but readable, humane, and still useful introduction, David Daiches, *A Study of Literature* (1948). Another book of the same generation, and still a useful introduction, is a businesslike survey of theories of literature by René Wellek and Austin Warren, *Theory of Literature,* 2nd ed. (1956). For a fairly recent, readable study, see Gerald Graff, *Professing Literature: An Institutional History* (1987).

Some basic reference works should be mentioned. C. Hugh Holman and

William Harmon have written an introductory dictionary of movements, critical terms, literary periods, and genres: *A Handbook to Literature,* 6th ed. (1992). For fuller discussions of critical terms, see Wendell V. Harris, *Dictionary of Concepts in Literary Criticism and Theory* (1992), which devotes several pages to each concept (for instance, "author," "context," "evaluation," "feminist literary criticism," "narrative") and gives a useful reading list for each entry.

Fairly similar to Harris's book are Irene Makaryk, ed., *Encyclopedia of Contemporary Literary Theory: Approaches, Scholars, Terms* (1993), and Michael Groden and Martin Kreiswirth, eds., *The Johns Hopkins Guide to Literary Theory and Criticism* (1994). *The Johns Hopkins Guide,* though it includes substantial entries on individual critics as well as on critical schools, is occasionally disappointing in the readability of some of its essays and especially in its coverage, since it does not include critical terms other than names of schools of criticism. Despite its title, it does not have entries for "theory" or for "criticism," nor does it have entries for such words as "canon" and "evaluation." In coverage (and also in the quality of many entries) it is inferior to an extremely valuable work with a misleadingly narrow title, *The New Princeton Encyclopedia of Poetry and Poetics,* eds. Alex Preminger and T. V. F. Brogan (1993). Although *The New Princeton Encyclopedia* of course does not include terms that are unique to, say, drama or fiction, it does include generous, lucid entries (with suggestions for further reading) on such terms as "allegory," "criticism," "canon," "irony," "sincerity," "theory," and "unity," and the long entries on "poetics," "poetry," and "poetry theories of" are in many respects entries on "literature."

For a collection of essays on the canon, see *Canons,* ed. Robert von Hallberg (1984); see also an essay by Robert Scholes, "Canonicity and Textuality," in *Introduction to Scholarship in Modern Languages and Literatures,* ed. Joseph Gibaldi, 2nd ed. (1992), 238-158. Gibaldi's collection includes essays on related topics, for instance literary theory (by Jonathan Culler) and cultural studies (by David Bathrick).

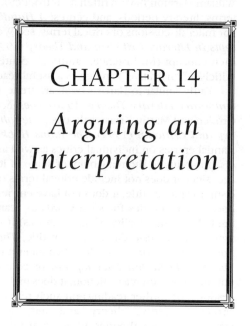

CHAPTER 14
Arguing an Interpretation

INTERPRETATION AND MEANING

We can define **interpretation** as a setting forth of the meaning, or, better, a setting forth of one or more of the meanings of a work of literature. This question of *meaning* versus *meanings* deserves a brief explanation. Although some critics believe that a work of literature has a single meaning, the meaning it had for the author, most critics hold that a work has several meanings, for instance the meaning it had for the author, the meaning(s) it had for its first readers (or viewers, if the work is a drama), the meaning(s) it had for later readers, and the meaning(s) it has for us today. Take *Hamlet* (1600–01), for example. Perhaps this play about a man who has lost his father had a very special meaning for Shakespeare, who had recently lost his own father. Further, Shakespeare had earlier lost a son named Hamnet, a variant spelling of Hamlet. The play, then, may have had important psychological meanings for Shakespeare—but the audience could not have shared (or even known) these meanings.

What *did* the play mean to Shakespeare's audience? Perhaps the original audience of *Hamlet*—people living in a monarchy, presided over by Queen Elizabeth I—were especially concerned with the issue (specifically raised in *Hamlet*) of whether a monarch's subjects ever have the right to overthrow the monarch. But obviously for twentieth-century Americans the interest in the play lies elsewhere, and the play must mean something else. If we are familiar with Freud, we may see in the play a young man who subconsciously lusts after his mother and seeks to kill his father (in the form of Claudius, Hamlet's uncle). Or we may see the play as largely about an alienated young man in a bourgeois society. Or—but the interpretations are countless.

IS THE AUTHOR'S INTENTION A GUIDE TO MEANING?

Shouldn't we be concerned, one might ask, with the *intentions* of the author? The question is reasonable, but there are difficulties, as the members of the Supreme Court find when they try to base their decisions on the original intent of the writers of the Constitution. First, for older works we almost never know what the intention is. Authors did not leave comments about their intentions. We have *Hamlet,* but we do not have any statement of Shakespeare's intention concerning this or any other play. One might argue that we can deduce Shakespeare's intention from the play itself, but to argue that we should study the play in the light of Shakespeare's intention, and that we can know his intention by studying the play, is to argue in a circle. We can say that Shakespeare must have intended to write a tragedy (if he intended to write a comedy he failed), but we can't go much further in talking about his intention.

Even if an author has gone on record expressing an intention, we may think twice before accepting the statement as decisive. The author may be speaking facetiously, deceptively, mistakenly, or (to be brief) unconvincingly. For instance, Thomas Mann said, probably sincerely and accurately, that he wrote one of his novels merely in order to entertain his family—but we may nevertheless take the book seriously and find it profound.

IS THE WORK THE AUTHOR'S OR THE READER'S?

A good deal of recent critical theory argues that the writer's views are by no means definitive, especially since writers—however independent they may think they are—largely reflect the ideas of their age. In current terminology, to accept the artist's statements about a work is "to privilege intentionalism." The idea that the person who seems to have created the work cannot comment definitively on it is especially associated with Roland Barthes (1915–80), author of a much-reprinted essay entitled "The Death of the Author," and Michel Foucault (1926–84), author of an equally famous essay entitled "What Is an Author?" (Barthes's essay appears in his *Image-Music-Text* [1977], Foucault's in *Foucault Reader* [1984].) Foucault, for example, assumes that the concept of the author is a repressive invention designed to impede the free circulation of ideas. In Foucault's view, the work belongs—or ought to belong—to the *perceiver,* not to the alleged maker.

Much can be said on behalf of this idea—and much can be said against it. On its behalf, one can again say that we can never entirely recapture the writer's intentions and sensations. Suppose, for instance, we are reading a work by Langston Hughes (1902–67), the African-American poet, essayist, and dramatist. None of us can exactly recover Hughes's attitudes; we cannot exactly recreate in our minds what it was like to be Langston Hughes in the 1930s and 1940s—an age that preceded the civil rights movement. We can read his texts, but we necessarily read them through our own eyes and in our own times, the 1990s.

Similarly, we can read or see a performance of an ancient Greek tragedy (let's say Sophocles's *King Oedipus*), but surely we cannot experience the play as did the Greeks, for whom it was part of an annual ritual. Further, a Greek spectator probably had seen earlier dramatic versions of the story. The Oedipus legend was, so to speak, part of the air that the Greeks breathed. Moreover we know (or think we know) things that the Greeks did not know. If we are familiar with Freud's view of the Oedipus complex—the idea that males wish to displace their fathers by sleeping with their mothers—we probably cannot experience Sophocles's *King Oedipus* without in some degree seeing it through Freud's eyes.

However, *against* the idea that works have no inherent core of meaning that all careful readers can perceive, one can argue that a competent writer shapes the work so that his or her meaning is largely evident to a competent reader—that is, to a reader familiar with the language and with the conventions of literature. (Writers of course do not mindlessly follow conventions; they can abide by, challenge, or even violate conventions, putting them to fresh purposes. But to deeply enjoy and understand a given work—say, an elegy—one needs some familiarity with other works of a similar kind.) Many people who write about literature assume a community of informed readers, and indeed this assumption seems to be supported by common sense.

WHAT CHARACTERIZES A GOOD INTERPRETATION?

Even the most vigorous advocates of the idea that meaning is indeterminate do not believe that all interpretations are equally significant. Rather, they believe that an interpretive essay is offered against a background of ideas, shared by essayist and reader, as to what constitutes a *persuasive argument.* Thus, an essay (even if it is characterized as "interpretive free play" or "creative engagement") will have to be coherent, plausible, and rhetorically effective. The *presentation* as well as the interpretation is significant. This means (to repeat a point made in Chapter 2) that the essayist cannot merely set down random expressions of feeling or unsupported opinions. The essayist must, on the contrary, convincingly *argue* a thesis—must point to evidence so that the reader will not only know what the essayist believes but will also understand why he or she believes it.

There are lots of ways of making sense (and even more ways of making nonsense), but one important way of helping readers to see things from your point of view is to do your best to face all of the complexities of the work. Put it this way: Some interpretations strike a reader as better than others because they are *more inclusive,* that is, because they *account for more of the details of the work.* The less satisfactory interpretations leave a reader pointing to some aspects of the work—to some parts of the whole—and saying, "Yes, but your explanation doesn't take account of. . . ." This does not mean, of course, that a reader must feel that a persuasive interpretation says the last word about the work. We always realize that the work—if we value it highly—is richer than the discussion, but, again, for us to value an interpretation we must find the interpretation plausible and inclusive.

Interpretation often depends not only on making connections among various elements of the work (for instance, among the characters in a story or among the images in a poem), and among the work and other works by the author, but also on making connections between the particular work and a **cultural context.** The cultural context usually includes other writers and specific works of literature, since a given literary work participates in a tradition. That is, if a work looks toward life, it also looks toward other works. A sonnet, for example, is about human experience, but it is also part of a tradition of sonnet writing. The more works of literature you are familiar with, the better equipped you are to interpret any particular work. Here is the way Robert Frost put it, in the preface to *Aforesaid:*

> A poem is best read in the light of all the other poems ever written. We read A the better to read B (we have to start somewhere; we may get very little out of A). We read B the better to read C, C the better to read D, D the better to go back and get something more out of A. Progress is not the aim, but circulation. The thing is to get among the poems where they hold each other apart in their places as the stars do.

Given the (debatable) views (1) that a work of literature may have several or even many meanings, (2) that some meanings may be unknowable to a modern spectator, and (3) that meaning is largely or even entirely determined by the viewer's particular circumstances, some students of literature prefer to say that they offer a "commentary" on the "significance" of a work rather than an "interpretation" of the "meaning."

AN EXAMPLE: INTERPRETING PAT MORA'S "IMMIGRANTS"

Let's think about interpreting a short poem by a contemporary poet, Pat Mora.

📖 Immigrants

wrap their babies in the American flag,
feed them mashed hot dogs and apple pie,
name them Bill and Daisy,
buy them blonde dolls that blink   5
blue eyes or a football and tiny cleats
before the baby can even walk,
speak to them in thick English,
    hallo, babee, hallo.
whisper in Spanish or Polish   10
when the babies sleep, whisper
in a dark parent bed, that dark
parent fear, "Will they like
our boy, our girl, our fine american
boy, our fine american girl?"   15

[1986]

Perhaps most readers will agree that the poem expresses or dramatizes a desire, attributed to "immigrants," that their child grow up in an Anglo mode.

(Mora is not saying that *all* immigrants have this desire; she has simply invented one speaker who says such-and-such. Of course *we* may say that Mora says all immigrants have this desire, but that is our interpretation.) For this reason the parents call their children Bill and Daisy (rather than, say, José and Juanita) and give them blonde dolls and a football (rather than dark-haired dolls and a soccer ball). Up to this point, the parents seem a bit silly in their mimicking of Anglo ways. But the second part of the poem gives the reader a more interior view of the parents, brings out the fear and hope and worried concern that lies behind the behavior: Some unspecified "they" may not "like / our boy, our girl." Who are "they"? Most readers probably will agree that "they" refers to native-born citizens, especially the blond, blue-eyed "all-American" Anglo types that until recently constituted the establishment in the United States.

One can raise further questions about the interpretation of the poem. Exactly what does the poet mean when she says that immigrants "wrap their babies in the American flag"? Are we to take this literally? If not, how are we to take it? And why in the last two lines is the word "american" not capitalized? Is Mora imitating the non-native speaker's uncertain grasp of English punctuation? (But if so, why does Mora capitalize "American" in the first line and "Spanish" and "Polish" later in the poem?) Or is she perhaps implying some mild reservation about becoming 100 percent American, some suggestion that in changing from Spanish or Polish to "american" there is some sort of loss?

A reader might seek Mora out and ask her why she didn't capitalize "american" in the last line, but Mora might not be willing to answer, or she might not give a straight answer, or she might say that she doesn't really know why—it just seemed right when she wrote the poem. Most authors do in fact take this last approach. When they are working as writers, they work by a kind of instinct, a kind of feel for the material. Later they can look critically at their writing, but that's another sort of experience.

To return to our basic question: What characterizes a good interpretation? The short answer is, Evidence, and especially evidence that seems to cover all relevant issues. In an essay it is not enough merely to assert an interpretation. Your readers don't expect you to make an airtight case, but because you are trying to help readers to understand a work—to see a work the way you do—you are obliged to

- Offer reasonable supporting evidence.
- Take account of what might be set forth as counterevidence to your thesis.

Of course your essay may originate in an intuition or an emotional response, a sense that the work is about such-and-such, but this intuition or emotion must then be examined, and it must stand a test of reasonableness. (It's usually a good idea to jot down in a journal your first responses to a work, and in later entries to reflect on them.) It is not enough in an essay merely to set forth your response. Your readers will expect you to *demonstrate* that the response is something that they can to a large degree share. They may not be convinced that the interpretation is right or true, but they must at least feel that the interpretation is plausible and in accord with the details of the work, rather than, say, highly eccentric and irreconcilable with some details.

This book includes five casebooks, each of which includes essays by critics advancing interpretations. When you read these interpretations, think about *why* you find some interpretations more convincing than others.

THINKING CRITICALLY ABOUT RESPONSES TO LITERATURE

Usually you will begin with a strong *response* to your reading—interest, boredom, bafflement, annoyance, shock, pleasure, or whatever. Fine. Then, if you are going to think critically about the work, you will go on to *examine* your response in order to understand it, or to deepen it, or to change it.

How can you change a response? Critical thinking involves seeing an issue from all sides, to as great a degree as possible. As you know, in ordinary language *to criticize* usually means to find fault, but in literary studies the term does not have a negative connotation. Rather, it means "to examine carefully." (The word *criticism* comes from a Greek verb meaning "to distinguish," "to decide," "to judge.") Nevertheless, in one sense the term *critical thinking* does approach the usual meaning, since critical thinking requires you to take a skeptical view of your response. You will, so to speak, argue with yourself, seeing if your response can stand up to doubts.

Let's say that you have found a story implausible. Question yourself:

- Exactly what is implausible in it?
- Is implausibility always a fault?
- If so, exactly why?

Your answers may deepen your response. Usually, in fact, you will find supporting evidence for your response, but in your effort to distinguish and to decide and to judge, try also (if only as an exercise) to find **counterevidence.** See what can be said against your position. (The best lawyers, it is said, prepare two cases—their own, and the other side's) As you consider the counterevidence you will sometimes find that it requires you to adjust your thesis. Fine. You may even find yourself developing an entirely different response. That's also fine, though of course the paper that you ultimately hand in should clearly argue a thesis.

Critical thinking, in short, means examining or exploring one's own responses, by questioning and testing them. Critical thinking is not so much a skill (though it does involve the ability to understand a text) as it is a *habit of mind,* or, rather, several habits, including

- Openmindedness
- Intellectual curiosity
- Willingness to work

It may involve, for instance, willingness to discuss the issues with others and to do research, a topic that will be treated separately in Appendix B, on writing a research paper.

THREE STUDENT INTERPRETATIONS OF ROBERT FROST'S "STOPPING BY WOODS ON A SNOWY EVENING"

Read Frost's "Stopping by Woods on a Snowy Evening," and then read the first interpretation, written by a first-year student. This interpretation is followed by a discussion that is devoted chiefly to two questions:

- What is the essayist's thesis?
- Does the essayist offer convincing evidence to support the thesis?

Two additional essays by first-year students, offering different interpretations of the poem, provide further material for you to analyze critically.

 ROBERT FROST (1874–1963)

Stopping by Woods on a Snowy Evening

Whose woods these are I think I know.
His house is in the village though;
He will not see me stopping here
To watch his woods fill up with snow.   4

My little horse must think it queer
To stop without a farmhouse near
Between the woods and frozen lake
The darkest evening of the year.   8

He gives his harness bells a shake
To ask if there is some mistake.
The only other sound's the sweep
Of easy wind and downy flake.   12

The woods are lovely, dark and deep.
But I have promises to keep,
And miles to go before I sleep,
And miles to go before I sleep.   16

[1923]

Darrel MacDonald

Stopping by Woods--and Going On

Robert Frost's "Stopping by Woods on a Snowy Evening" is about what the title says it is. It is also about something more than the title says.

When I say it is about what the title says, I mean that the poem really does give us the thoughts of a person who pauses (that is, a person who is "stopping") by woods on a snowy evening. (This person probably is a man, since Robert Frost wrote the poem and nothing in the poem clearly indicates that the speaker is not a man. But, and this point will be important, the speaker perhaps feels that he is not a very masculine man. As we will see, the word "queer" appears in the poem, and, also, the speaker uses the word "lovely," which sounds more like the word a woman would use than a man.) In line 3 the speaker says he is "stopping here," and it is clear that "here" is by woods, since "woods" is mentioned not only in the title but also in the first line of the poem, and again in the second stanza, and still again in the last stanza. It is equally clear that, as the title says, there is snow, and that the time is evening. The speaker mentions "snow" and "downy flake," and he says this is "The darkest evening of the year."

But in what sense is the poem about <u>more</u> than the title? The title does not tell us anything about the man who is "stopping by woods," but the poem—the man's meditation—tells us a lot about him. In the first stanza he reveals that he is uneasy at the thought that the owner of the woods may see him stopping by the woods. Maybe he is uneasy because he is trespassing, but the poem does not actually say that he has illegally entered someone else's property. More likely, he feels uneasy, almost ashamed, of watching the "woods fill up with snow." That is, he would not want anyone to see that he

actually is enjoying a beautiful aspect of nature and
is not hurrying about whatever his real business is
in thrifty Yankee style.

The second stanza gives more evidence that he
feels guilty about enjoying beauty. He feels so
guilty that he even thinks the horse thinks there is
something odd about him. In fact, he says that the
horse thinks he is "queer," which of course may just
mean odd, but also (as is shown by The American
Heritage Dictionary) it can mean "gay," "homosexual."
A real man, he sort of suggests, wouldn't spend time
looking at snow in the woods.

So far, then, the speaker in two ways has
indicated that he feels insecure, though perhaps he
does not realize that he has given himself away.
First, he expresses uneasiness that someone might see
him watching the woods fill up with snow. Second, he
expresses uneasiness when he suggests that even the
horse thinks he is strange, maybe even "queer" or
unmanly, or at least unbusinesslike. And so in the
last stanza, even though he finds the woods
beautiful, he decides not to stop and to see the
woods fill up with snow. And his description of the
woods as "lovely"--a woman's word--sounds as though
he may be something less than a he-man. He seems to
feel ashamed of himself for enjoying the sight of the
snowy woods and for seeing them as "lovely," and so
he tells himself that he has spent enough time
looking at the woods and that he must go on about his
business. In fact, he tells himself twice that he has
business to attend to. Why? Perhaps he is insisting

too much. Just as we saw that he was excessively nervous in the first stanza, afraid that someone might see him trespassing and enjoying the beautiful spectacle, now at the end he is again afraid that someone might see him loitering, and so he very firmly, using repetition as a form of emphasis, tries to reassure himself that he is not too much attracted by beauty and is a man of business who keeps his promises.

Frost gives us, then, a man who indeed is seen "stopping by woods on a snowy evening," but a man who, afraid of what society will think of him, is also afraid to "stop" long enough to fully enjoy the sight that attracts him, because he is driven by a sense that he may be seen to be trespassing and also may be thought to be unmanly. So after only a brief stop in the woods he forces himself to go on, a victim (though he probably doesn't know it) of the work ethic and of an over-simple idea of manliness.

Let's examine this essay briefly.

The title is interesting. It gives the reader a good idea of which literary work will be discussed ("Stopping by Woods") *and* it arouses interest, in this case by a sort of wordplay ("Stopping . . . Going On"). A title of this sort is preferable to a title that merely announces the topic, such as "An Analysis of Frost's 'Stopping by Woods' " or "On a Poem by Robert Frost."

The opening paragraph helpfully names the exact topic (Robert Frost's poem) and arouses interest by asserting that the poem is about something more than its title. The writer's thesis presumably will be a fairly specific assertion concerning what else the poem is "about."

The body of the essay, beginning with the second paragraph, begins to develop the thesis. (The **thesis** perhaps can be summarized thus: "The speaker, insecure of his masculinity, feels ashamed that he responds with pleasure to the sight of the snowy woods.") The writer's evidence in the second paragraph is that the word "queer" (a word sometimes used of homosexuals) appears, and that the word "lovely" is "more like the word a woman would use than a man." Readers of MacDonald's essay may at this point be unconvinced by this evidence, but probably they suspend judgement. In any case, he has offered what he considers to be evidence in support of his thesis.

The next paragraph dwells on what is said to be the speaker's uneasiness, and the following paragraph returns to the word "queer," which, MacDonald correctly says, can mean "gay, homosexual." The question of course is whether *here,* in this poem, the word has this meaning. Do we agree with MacDonald's assertion, in the last sentence of this paragraph, that Frost is suggesting that "A real man ... wouldn't spend time looking at snow in the woods"? Clearly this is the way MacDonald takes the poem—but is his response to these lines reasonable? After all, what Frost says is this: "The little horse must think it queer / To stop without a farmhouse near." Is it reasonable to see a reference to homosexuality (rather than merely to oddness) in *this* use of the word "queer"? Hasn't MacDonald offered a response that, so to speak, is private? It is *his* response—but are we likely to share it, to agree that we see it in Frost's poem?

The next paragraph, amplifying the point that the speaker is insecure, offers as evidence the argument that "lovely" is more often a woman's word than a man's. Probably most readers will agree on this point, though many or all might deny that only a gay man would use the word "lovely." And what do you think of MacDonald's assertions that the speaker of the poem "was excessively nervous in the first stanza" and is now "afraid that someone might see him loitering"? In your opinion, does the text lend much support to MacDonald's view?

The concluding paragraph effectively reasserts and clarifies MacDonald's thesis, saying that the speaker hesitates to stop and enjoy the woods because "he is driven by a sense that he may be seen to be trespassing and also may be thought to be unmanly."

The big question, then, is whether the thesis is argued *convincingly.* It certainly *is* argued, not merely asserted, but how convincing is the evidence? Does MacDonald offer enough to make you think that his response is one that you can share? Has he helped you to enjoy the poem by seeing things that you may not have noticed—or has he said things that, however interesting, seem to you not to be in close contact with the poem as you see it?

Here are two other interpretations of the same poem.

Sara Fong

"Stopping by Woods on a Snowy Evening"

as a Short Story

Robert Frost's "Stopping by Woods on a Snowy Evening" can be read as a poem about a man who pauses to observe the beauty of nature, and it can also be read as a poem about a man with a death wish, a man who seems to long to give himself up completely to nature and thus escape his responsibilities as a citizen. Much depends, apparently, on what a reader wants to emphasize. For instance, a reader can emphasize especially appealing lines about the beauty of nature: "The only other sound's the sweep / Of easy wind and downy flake," and "The woods are lovely, dark and deep." On the other hand, a reader can emphasize lines that show the speaker is fully aware of the responsibilities that most of us agree we have. For instance, at the very start of the poem he recognizes that the woods are not his but are owned by someone else, and at the end of the poem he recognizes that he has "promises to keep" and that before he sleeps (dies?) he must accomplish many things (go for "miles").

Does a reader have to choose between these two interpretations? I don't think so; to the contrary, I think it makes sense to read the poem as a kind of very short story, with a character whose developing thoughts make up a plot with four stages. In the first stage, the central figure is an ordinary person with rather ordinary thoughts. His very first thought is of the owner of the woods. He knows who the owner is, and since the owner lives in the village, the poet feels safe in trespassing, or at least in watching the woods "fill up with snow." Then, very subtly, the poet begins to tell us that although this seems to be an ordinary person thinking ordinary thoughts, he is a somewhat special person in a special situation. First of all, the horse thinks something is strange. He shakes his bells, wondering why the driver doesn't keep moving, as presumably ordinary drivers would. Second, we are told that this is "The darkest evening of the year." Frost could simply have said that the evening is dark, but he goes out of his way to make the evening a special evening.

We are now through with the first ten lines, and only six lines remain, yet in these six lines the story goes through two additional phases. The first three of these lines ("The only other sound's the sweep / Of easy wind and downy flake" and "The woods are lovely, dark and deep") are probably the most beautiful lines, in the sense that they are the ones that make us say, "I wish I were there," or "I'd love to experience this." We feel that the poet has moved from the ordinary thoughts of the first stanza, about such businesslike things as who owns the woods and where the owner's house is, to less materialistic thoughts, thoughts about the beauty of the nonhuman world of nature. And now, with the three final lines, we get the fourth stage of the story, the return to the ordinary world of people, the world of "promises." But this world that we get at the end is not exactly the same as the world we got at the beginning. The world at the beginning of the poem is a world of property (who owns the woods, and where the house is), but the world at the end of the poem is a world of unspecified and rather mysterious responsibilities ("promises to keep," "miles to go before I sleep"). It is almost as though the poet's experience of the beauty of nature--a beauty that for a moment made him forget the world of property--has in fact served to sharpen his sense that human beings have responsibilities. He clearly sees that "The woods are lovely, dark and deep," and then he says (I add the italics) "<u>But</u> I have promises to keep." The "but" would be logical if after saying that the woods

are lovely, dark and deep, he had said something like
"But in the daylight they look different," or "But
one can freeze to death in them." The logic of what
Frost says, however, is not at all clear: "The woods
are lovely, dark and deep, / But I have promises to
keep." What is the logical connection? We have to
supply one, something like "but, because we are human
beings we have responsibilities; we can refresh
ourselves by perceiving the beauties of nature, and
we can even for a moment get so caught up that we
seem to enter an enchanted forest ('the woods are
lovely, dark and deep'), but we cannot forget our
responsibilities."

My point is not that Frost ends with an
important moral, and it is also not that we have to
choose between saying it is a poem about nature or a
poem about a man with a death wish. Rather, my point
is that the poem takes us through several stages and
that, although the poem begins and ends with the
speaker in the woods, the speaker has undergone
mental experiences--has, we might say, gone through a
plot with a conflict (the appeal of the snowy woods
versus the call to return to the human world). It's
not a matter of good versus evil and of one side
winning. Frost in no way suggests that it is wrong to
feel the beauty of nature--even to the momentary
exclusion of all other thoughts. But the poem is
certainly not simply a praise of the beauty of
nature. Frost shows us, in this mini-story or
mini-drama, one character who sees the woods as
property, then sees them as a place of almost

overwhelming beauty, and then (maybe refreshed by this experience) rejoins the world of chores and responsibilities.

 ## TOPICS FOR CRITICAL THINKING AND WRITING

1. What is the thesis of the essay?
2. Does the essayist offer convincing evidence to support the thesis?
3. Do you consider the essay to be well written, poorly written, or something in between? On what evidence do you base your opinion?

Peter Franken

The Meaning of

"Stopping by Woods on a Snowy Evening"

Although on the surface there is nothing about religion in Robert Frost's "Stopping by Woods on a Snowy Evening," I think the poem is basically about a person's realization that he or she has a religious duty to help other people.

In Stanza One the poet tells us that he knows who owns the woods. The owner is God. Of course some individual may, during his lifetime, think that he owns the woods, but he is only the steward of the woods, a sort of caretaker. The true owner is God, whose "house is in the village," that is, who has a church in the village. At this stage in the poem, the poet is mistaken when he says that God will not see him, because God sees everything. So the poet's statement here is an example of unconscious irony.

In Stanzas Two and Three the poet tells us that God sent a sort of message to him, through the horse. The horse shakes his harness bells, telling the speaker that he (the speaker) is making a "mistake." It may also be that in the picture of a snowy night and a domestic animal Robert Frost is trying to subtly suggest that we remember the scene of the birth of Jesus, in a manger, with domestic animals. In any case, although the scene is very peaceful and quiet (except for the harness bells and the sound of the "easy wind"), God is watching over the speaker of this poem.

In Stanza Four, in the first line ("The woods are lovely, dark and deep") Robert Frost tells us of man's love of God's creation, and in the other lines of the stanza he says that proper love of the creation leads to an awareness of our responsibilities to other human beings. Robert Frost is very effective because he uses the device of understatement. He does not tell us exactly what these responsibilities are, so he leaves it to our imagination, but we can easily think of our many duties to our family and our fellow-citizens and our country.

 ## TOPICS FOR CRITICAL THINKING AND WRITING

1. What is the thesis of the essay?
2. Does the essayist offer convincing evidence to support the thesis?
3. Do you consider the essay to be well written, poorly written, or something in between? On what evidence do you base your opinion?

 ## SUGGESTIONS FOR FURTHER READING

The entries on "interpretation" in the reference works cited on page 403 ("What Is Literature?") provide a good starting point, as does Steven Mailloux's entry on "interpretation" in *Critical Terms for Literary Study*, eds. Frank Lentricchia and Thomas McLaughlin (1990). You may next want to turn to a short, readable, but highly thoughtful book by Monroe Beardsley, *The Possibility of Criticism* (1970). Also of interest are E. D. Hirsch, *Validity in Interpretation* (1967); Paul B. Armstrong, *Conflicting Readings: Variety and Validity in Interpretation* (1990); and Umberto Eco, with Richard Rorty, Jonathan Culler, and Christine Brooke-Rose, *Interpretation and Overinterpretation* (1992). This last title includes three essays by Eco, with responses by Rorty, Culler, and Brooke-Rose, and a final "Reply" by Eco.

CHAPTER 15

Arguing an Evaluation

CRITICISM AND EVALUATION

Although, as previously noted, in ordinary usage *criticism* implies finding fault, and therefore implies evaluation—"This story is weak"—in fact most literary criticism is *not* concerned with evaluation. Rather, it is chiefly concerned with *interpretation* (the setting forth of meaning) and with *analysis* (examination of relationships among the parts, or of causes and effects). For instance, an interpretation may argue that in *Death of a Salesman* Willy Loman is the victim of a cruel capitalistic economy, and an analysis may show how the symbolic setting of the play (a stage direction tells us that "towering, angular shapes" surround the salesman's house) contributes to the meaning. In our discussion of "What Is Literature?" we saw that an analysis of Robert Frost's "The Span of Life" (p. 398) called attention to the contrast between the meter of the first line (relatively uneven or irregular, with an exceptional number of heavy stresses) and the meter of the second (relatively even and jingling). The analysis also called attention to the contrast between the content of the first line (the old dog) and the second (the speaker's memory of a young dog):

> The old dog barks backward without getting up.
> I can remember when he was a pup.

In our discussion we did not worry about whether this poem deserves an A, B, or C, nor did we consider whether it was better or worse than some other poem by Frost, or by some other writer. And, to repeat, if one reads books and journals devoted to literary study, one finds chiefly discussions of meaning. For the most part, critics assume that the works they are writing about have value and are good enough to merit attention, so critics largely concern themselves with other matters.

Evaluative Language and the Canon

Still, some critical writing is indeed concerned with evaluation—with saying that works are good or bad, dated or classic, major or minor. (The language need not be as explicit as these words are; evaluation can also be conveyed through words like *moving, successful, effective, important,* or, on the other hand, *tedious, unsuccessful, weak,* and *trivial.*) In reviews of plays, books, movies, musical and dance performances, and films, professional critics usually devote much of their space to evaluating the work or the performance, or both. The reviewer seeks, finally, to tell readers whether to buy a book or a ticket—or to save their money and their time.

In short, although in our independent reading we read what we like, and we need not argue that one work is better than another, the issue of evaluation is evident all around us.

ARE THERE CRITICAL STANDARDS?

One approach to evaluating a work of literature, or, indeed, to evaluating anything at all, is to rely on personal taste. This approach is evident in a statement such as "I don't know anything about modern art, but I know what I like." The idea is old, at least as old as the Roman saying *De gustibus non est disputandum* ("There is no disputing tastes").

If we say "This is a good work" or "This book is greater than that book," are we saying anything beyond "I like this" and "I like this better than that"? Are all expressions of evaluation really nothing more than expressions of taste? Most people believe that if there are such things as works of art, or works of literature, there must be standards by which they can be evaluated, just as most other things are evaluated by standards. The standards for evaluating a scissors, for instance, are perfectly clear: it ought to cut cleanly, it ought not to need frequent sharpening, and it ought to feel comfortable in the hand. We may also want it to look nice (perhaps to be painted—or on the contrary to reveal its stainless steel), and to be inexpensive, rustproof, and so on, but in any case we can easily state our standards. Similarly, there are agreed-upon standards for evaluating figure skating, gymnastics, fluency in language, and so on.

But what are the standards for evaluating literature? In earlier pages we have implied one standard: In a good work of literature, all of the parts contribute to the whole, making a unified work. Some people would add that mere unity is not enough; a work of high quality needs not only to be unified but needs also to be complex. The writer offers a "performance in words" (Frost's words, again), and when we read, we can see if the writer has successfully kept all of the Indian clubs in the air. If, for instance, the stated content of the poem is mournful, yet the meter jingles, we can probably say that the performance is unsuccessful; at least one Indian club is clattering on the floor.

Here are some of the standards commonly set forth:

Personal taste
Truth, realism
Moral content
Esthetic qualities, for instance unity

Let's look at some of these in detail.

Morality and Truth as Standards

"It is always a writer's duty to make the world better." Thus wrote Dr. Samuel Johnson, in 1765, in his "Preface to Shakespeare." In this view, **morality** plays a large role; a story that sympathetically treated lesbian or gay love would, from a traditional Judeo-Christian perspective, be regarded as a bad story, or at least not as worthy as a story that celebrated heterosexual married love. On the other hand, a gay or lesbian critic, or anyone not committed to Judeo-Christian values, might regard the story highly because, in such a reader's view, it helps to educate readers and thereby does something "to make the world better."

But there are obvious problems. For one thing, a **gay** or lesbian story might strike even a reader with traditional values as a work that is effectively told, with believable and memorable characters, whereas a story of heterosexual married love might be unbelievable, awkwardly told, trite, sentimental, or whatever. (More about sentimentality in a moment.) How much value does one give to the ostensible content of the story, the obvious moral or morality, and how much value does one give to the artistry exhibited in telling the story?

People differ greatly about moral (and religious) issues. Edward Fitzgerald's 1859 translation of *The Rubáiyát of Omar Khayyám* (a twelfth-century Persian poem) suggests that God doesn't exist, or—perhaps worse—if He does exist, He doesn't care about us. That God does not exist is a view held by many moral people; it is also a view opposed by many moral people. The issue then may become a matter of **truth.** Does the value of the poem depend on which view is right? In fact, does a reader have to subscribe to Fitzgerald's view to enjoy (and to evaluate highly) the following stanza from the poem, in which Fitzgerald suggests that the pleasures of this world are the only paradise that we can experience?

A book of verses underneath the bough,
A jug of wine, a loaf of bread—and thou
　　Beside me singing in the wilderness—
Oh, wilderness were paradise enow!

Some critics can give high value to a literary work only if they share its beliefs, if they think that the work corresponds to reality. They measure the work against their vision of the truth.

Other readers can highly value a work of literature that expresses ideas they do not believe, arguing that literature does not require us to believe in its views. Rather, this theory claims, literature gives a reader a strong sense of *what it feels like* to hold certain views—even though the reader does not share those views. Take, for instance, a lyric poem in which Christina Rossetti (1830-94), a devout Anglican, expresses both spiritual numbness and spiritual hope. Here is one stanza from "A Better Resurrection":

My life is like a broken bowl,
   A broken bowl that cannot hold
One drop of water for my soul
   Or cordial in the searching cold;
Cast in the fire the perished thing;
   Melt and remould it, till it be
A royal cup for Him, my King:
   O Jesus, drink of me.

One need not be an Anglican suffering a crisis to find this poem of considerable interest. It offers insight into a state of mind, and the truth or falsity of religious belief is not at issue. Similarly, one can argue that although *The Divine Comedy* by Dante Alighieri (1265–1321) is deeply a Roman Catholic work, the non-Catholic reader can read it with interest and pleasure because of (for example) its rich portrayal of a wide range of characters, the most famous of whom perhaps are the pathetic lovers Paolo and Francesca. In Dante's view, they are eternally damned because they were unrepentant adulterers, but a reader need not share this belief.

Other Ways of Thinking about Truth and Realism

Other solutions to the problem of whether a reader must share a writer's beliefs have been offered. One extreme view says that beliefs are irrelevant, since literature has nothing to do with truth. In this view, a work of art does not correspond to anything "outside" itself, that is, to anything in the real world. If a work of art has any "truth," it is only in the sense of being internally consistent. Thus Shakespeare's *Macbeth*, like, say, "Rock-a-bye Baby," isn't making assertions about reality. *Macbeth* has nothing to do with the history of Scotland, just as (in this view) Shakespeare's *Julius Caesar* has nothing to do with the history of Rome, although Shakespeare borrowed some of his material from history books. These tragedies, like lullabies, are worlds in themselves—not to be judged against historical accounts of Scotland or Rome—and we are interested in the characters in the plays only as they exist *in the plays*. We may require, for instance, that the characters be consistent, believable, and engaging, but we cannot require that they correspond to historical figures. Literary works are neither true nor false; they are only (when successful) coherent and interesting. The poet William Butler Yeats perhaps had in mind something along these lines when he said that you can refute a philosopher, but you cannot refute the song of sixpence. And indeed "Sing a song of sixpence, / Pocket full of rye" has endured for a couple of centuries, perhaps partly because it has nothing to do with truth or falsity; it has created its own engaging world.

The view that we should not judge literature by how much it corresponds to our view of the world around us is held by many literary critics, and there probably is something (maybe a great deal) to it. For instance, some argue that there is no fixed, unchanging, "real" world around us; there is only what we perceive, what we ourselves "construct," and each generation, indeed each individual, constructs things differently.

And yet one can object, offering a commonsense response: Surely when we see a play, or read an engaging work of literature, whether it is old or new, we feel that somehow the work says something about the life around us, the real world. True, some of what we read—let's say, detective fiction—is chiefly fanciful; we read it to test our wits, or to escape, or to kill time. But most literature seems to be connected to life. This commonsense view, that literature is related to life, has an ancient history, and in fact almost everyone in the Western world believed it from the time of the ancient Greeks until the nineteenth century, and of course many people—including authors and highly skilled readers—still believe it today.

For instance, a concern for accuracy characterizes much writing. Many novelists do a great deal of research, especially into the settings where they will place their characters. And they are equally concerned with style—with the exactness of each word that they use. Flaubert is said to have spent a day writing a sentence and another day correcting it. The German author Rainer Maria Rilke has a delightful passage in *The Notebooks of Malte Laurids Brigge* (1910), in which he mentions someone who was dying in a hospital. The dying man heard a nurse mispronounce a word, and so (in Rilke's words) "he postponed dying." First he corrected the nurse's pronunciation, Rilke tells us, and "then he died. He was a poet and hated the approximate."

Certainly a good deal of literature, most notably the realistic short story and the novel, is devoted to giving a detailed picture that at least *looks like* the real world. One reason we read the fiction of Kate Chopin is to find out what "the real world" of Creole New Orleans in the late nineteenth century was like—as seen through Chopin's eyes, of course. (One need not be a Marxist to believe, with Karl Marx, that one learns more about industrial England from the novels of Dickens and Mrs. Gaskell than from economic treatises.) Writers of stories, novels, and plays are concerned to give plausible, indeed precise and insightful, images of the relationships between people. Writers of lyric poems presumably are specialists in presenting human feelings, the experience of love, for instance, or of the loss of faith. And presumably we are invited to compare the writer's created world to the world that we live in, perhaps to be reminded that our own lives can be richer than they are.

Even when a writer describes an earlier time, the implication is that the description is accurate, and especially that people *did* behave the way the writer says they did—and the way our own daily experience shows us that people do behave. Here is George Eliot at the beginning of her novel *Adam Bede* (1859):

> With a single drop of ink for a mirror, the Egyptian sorcerer undertook to reveal to any chance comer far-reaching visions of the past. This is what I undertake to do for you, reader. With this drop of ink at the end of my pen, I will show you the roomy workshop of Jonathan Burge, carpenter and builder in the village of Hayslope, as it appeared on the 18th of June, in the year of Our Lord, 1799.

Why do novelists like George Eliot give us detailed pictures, and cause us to become deeply involved in the lives of their characters? Another novelist, D. H. Lawrence, offers a relevant comment in the ninth chapter of *Lady Chatterley's Lover* (1928):

> It is the way our sympathy flows and recoils that really determines our lives. And here lies the vast importance of the novel, properly handled. It can inform and lead into new places the flow of our sympathetic consciousness, and it can lead our sympathy away in recoil from things gone dead. Therefore, the novel, properly handled, can reveal the most secret places of life.

In Lawrence's view, we can evaluate a novel in terms of its moral effect on the reader; the good novel, Lawrence claims, leads us into worlds—human relationships—that deserve our attention, and leads us away from "things gone dead," presumably relationships and values—whether political, moral, and religious—that no longer deserve to survive. To be blunt, Lawrence claims that good books improve us. His comment is similar to a more violent comment, quoted earlier, by Franz Kafka: "A book must be an ice-axe to break the frozen sea inside us."

Realism, of course, is not the writer's only tool. In *Gulliver's Travels* Swift gives us a world of Lilliputians, people about six inches tall. Is his book pure fancy, unrelated to life? Not at all. We perceive that the Lilliputians are (except for their size) pretty much like ourselves, and we realize that their tiny stature is an image of human pettiness, an *un*realistic device that helps us to see the real world more clearly.

The view that we have been talking about—that writers do connect us to the world—does not require realism, but it does assume that writers see, understand, and, through the medium of their writings, give us knowledge, deepen our understanding, and even perhaps improve our character. If, the argument goes, a work distorts reality—let's say because the author sees women superficially—the work is inferior. Some such assumption is found, for instance, in a comment by Elaine Savory Fido, who says that the work of Derek Walcott, a Caribbean poet and dramatist, is successful when Walcott deals with racism and with colonialism but is unsuccessful when he deals with women. "His treatment of women," Fido says in an essay in *Journal of Commonwealth Literature* (1986),

> is full of clichés, stereotypes and negativity. I shall seek to show how some of his worst writing is associated with these portraits of women, which sometimes lead him to the brink of losing verbal control, or give rise to a retreat into abstract, conventional terms which prevent any real treatment of the subject. (109)

We need not here be concerned with whether or not Fido's evaluations of Walcott's works about women and about colonialism are convincing; what concerns us is her assumption that works can be—should be—evaluated in terms of the keenness of the writer's perception of reality.

Although we *need* not be concerned with an evaluation, we may wish to be concerned with it, and, if so, we will probably find, perhaps to our surprise, that in the very process of arguing our evaluation (perhaps only to ourselves) we are also interpreting and reinterpreting. That is, we find ourselves observing passages closely, from a new point of view, and we may therefore find ourselves seeing them differently, finding new meanings in them.

IS SENTIMENTALITY A WEAKNESS— AND IF SO, WHY?

The presence of **sentimentality** is often regarded as a sign that a writer has failed to perceive accurately. Sentimentality is usually defined as excessive emotion, especially an excess of pity or sorrow. But when one thinks about it, who is to say when an emotion is "excessive"? Surely (to take an example) parents can be grief-stricken by the death of a child; and just as surely they may continue to be grief-stricken for the rest of their lives. Well, how about a child's grief for a dead pet, or an adult's grief for the death of an elderly person, a person who has lived a full life, for whom death might serve as a relief? Again, can any of us say how someone else ought to feel?

What each reader can say, however, is that the *expression* of grief in a particular literary work is or is not successful, convincing, engaging, moving. Though readers may not be able to say that the emotion is proper or improper, they can say that the literary expression of that emotion is successful or not. Consider the following poem by Eugene Field (1850-95).

📖 Little Boy Blue

The little toy dog is covered with dust,
    But sturdy and stanch he stands;
And the little toy soldier is red with rust,
    And his musket moulds in his hands.
Time was when the little toy dog was new,   5
    And the soldier was passing fair;
And that was the time when our Little Boy Blue
    Kissed them and put them there.

"Now, don't you go till I come," he said,
    "And don't you make any noise!"   10
So, toddling off to his trundle-bed,
    He dreamt of the pretty toys;
And, as he was dreaming, an angel song
    Awakened our Little Boy Blue—
Oh! the years are many, the years are long,   15
    But the little toy friends are true!

Ay, faithful to Little Boy Blue they stand,
    Each in the same old place—
Awaiting the touch of a little hand,
    The smile of a little face;   20
And they wonder, as waiting the long years through
    In the dust of that little chair,
What has become of our Little Boy Blue,
    Since he kissed them and put them there.

[1889]

Why do many readers find this poem sentimental, and of low quality? Surely not because it deals with the death of a child. Many other poems deal with this subject sympathetically, movingly, interestingly. Perhaps one sign of weak writing in "Little Boy Blue" is the insistence on the word *little*. The boy is little (five times, counting the title), the dog is little (twice), the toy soldier is little (once), the toys collectively are little (once), and Little Boy Blue has a little face, a little hand, and a little chair. Repetition is not an inherently bad thing, but perhaps here we feel that the poet is too insistently tugging at our sympathy, endlessly asserting the boy's charm yet not telling us anything interesting about the child other than that he was little and that he loved his "pretty toys." Real writers don't simply accept and repeat the Hallmark greeting card view of reality. Children are more interesting than "Little Boy Blue" reveals, and adults react to a child's death in a more complex way.

Further, the boy's death is in no way described or explained. A poet of course is not required to tell us that the child died of pneumonia, or in an automobile accident, but since Field did choose to give us information about the death we probably want something better than the assertion that when a child dies it is "awakened" by an "angel song." One might ask oneself if this is an interesting, plausible, healthy way of thinking of the death of a child. In talking about literature we want to be cautious about using the word *true,* for reasons already discussed, but can't we say that Field's picture of childhood and his explanation of death simply don't ring true? Don't we feel that he is talking nonsense? And finally, can't we be excused for simply not believing that the speaker of the poem, having left the arrangement of toys undisturbed for "many" years, thinks that therefore "the little toy friends are true," and that they "wonder" while "waiting the long years through." More nonsense. If we recall D. H. Lawrence's comment, we may feel that in this poem the poet has *not* properly directed "the flow of our sympathetic consciousness."

Let's look now at another poem on the death of a child, this one by X. J. Kennedy (b. 1929):

 ## Little Elegy

for a child who skipped rope

Here lies resting, out of breath,
Out of turns, Elizabeth
Whose quicksilver toes not quite
Cleared the whirring edge of night.   4

Earth whose circles round us skim
Till they catch the lightest limb,
Shelter now Elizabeth
And for her sake trip up Death.   8

[1961]

This is a "little" elegy—literally, since it is only eight lines long—for another child. We can't know for sure how the poet really felt, but will you agree that the work itself (presumably the expression of feeling) is both tenderhearted and restrained? It is also—we can use the word—true; the passing days (alluded to here in the reference to the ever-turning earth) really do finally catch everyone, even someone with "the lightest limb." Further, the poem is also witty: In the first stanza Elizabeth is said to be "Out of turns," a child's expression appropriately describing a child at play, but here also meaning that Elizabeth is no longer turning about in this world, and also that she died too early, before her expected time or turn. Notice, too, the fresh use of "out of breath," here meaning not only "breathless from exertion" (as a girl skipping rope would sometimes be) but also "unbreathing, dead."

In the second stanza the poet addresses the "Earth." Its revolutions (which resemble the circular motion of the skipping rope) catch all of us, but the earth will also "shelter" the dead girl, in a grave. The poem ends with a small, bitter joke about tripping up Death, thus continuing the imagery of skipping rope. The last line conveys (with great restraint) the unreconciled attitude most of us feel when hearing of the death of a child. No such note of resentment occurs in

Field's poem; one almost believes that Field thinks the death of Little Boy Blue is a very beautiful thing. His poem is all sweetness, uncomplicated by any perception of the pain that death causes.

Let's look at one more poem about death, although here the subject is not a child but several young men.

 ## GWENDOLYN BROOKS (b. 1917)

We Real Cool

The Pool Players.
Seven at the Golden Shovel

We real cool. We
Left school. We

Lurk late. We
Strike straight. We

Sing sin. We
Drink gin. We

Jazz June. We
Die soon.

[1960]

The subtitle pretty much tells us that the speakers are seven people who hang out at a pool hall called the Golden Shovel, and the last line tells us that they "Die soon," that is, while still young. The speaker uses Black English (one characteristic is the omission of the verb, as in "We real cool," instead of "We are real cool"), and he speaks for the group. The title and the first line of the poem each begin with the word "We," and the sense of group identity is emphasized by the fact that each line—except the last—ends with "We."

The death of these seven dropouts is communicated not only by what the poem explicitly says but also by what it does not say, or, rather, by what it shows. The "we" that occurs at the end of each of the first seven lines is missing from the eighth line; the group is no more. Beside the fact that they die—that we see them disappear—what can we say about them?

The young men have a strong sense of group identity but they have no connection with anyone else, except with June, a person who apparently exists only as a sexual object. There are no adults in the poem, and no whites. They live in an isolated world. We can say at least two other things about them: (1) They speak sentences of only three words, sentences of the utmost simplicity, and (2) the simplicity in fact is deceptive, because the language is vigorous, marked by strong rhythm and by interesting alliteration (repetition of initial sounds, as in "*L*urk *l*ate" and "*J*azz *J*une"). The speaker has something urgent to say, and he says it memorably. (Of course it is really Gwendolyn Brooks who is doing the talking, but Brooks has chosen to create this effective spokesperson, this character who holds our interest.) The poem, in short, communicates not only the group's severe limitations (behavior that will lead to early deaths) but also communicates the group's strengths (a sense of fellow feeling, a skill with language).

And can't we also say that the poem communicates the sadness of the waste of human lives, without tearfully tugging at our sleeve? Don't we feel that although the poet sympathizes with these seven young men (and all others who resemble them), she nevertheless does not try to sweeten the facts and take us into an unreal Little-Boy-Blue world where we can feel good about our response to death? She does not sentimentalize; she looks without flinching, and she tells it as it is. Perhaps we can even say that although the Golden Shovel and these seven young men may be inventions, the poem is a fiction that speaks the truth.

No one can tell you how you should feel about these three poems, but ask yourself if you agree with some or all of what has been said about them. Also ask yourself on what standards you base your own evaluation of them. Perhaps one way to begin is to ask yourself which of the first two poems ("Little Boy Blue" and "Little Elegy") you would prefer to read if you were so unfortunate as to have lost a child or a young sibling. Then explain *why* you answered as you did.

SUGGESTIONS FOR FURTHER READING

Most of the reference works cited at the end of the discussion of "What Is Literature" (p. 402) include entries on "evaluation." But for additional short discussions see chapter 18 ("Evaluation") in René Wellek and Austin Warren, *Theory of Literature,* 2nd ed. (1948); chapter 5 ("On Value-Judgments") in Northrop Frye, *The Stubborn Structure* (1970); and chapter 4 ("Evaluation") in John M. Ellis, *The Theory of Literary Criticism* (1974). For a longer discussion see chapters 10 and 11 ("Critical Evaluation" and "Aesthetic Value") in Monroe C. Beardsley, *Aesthetics* (1958). Also of interest is Joseph Strelka, ed., *Problems of Literary Evaluation* (1969). In Strelka's collection you may find it best to begin with the essays by George Boas, Northrop Frye, and David Daiches, and then to browse in the other essays.

CHAPTER 16

Writing about Literature: An Overview

THE NATURE OF CRITICAL WRITING

In everyday talk the commonest meaning of **criticism** is something like "finding fault." And to be critical is to be censorious. But a critic can see excellences as well as faults. Because we turn to criticism with the hope that the critic has seen something we have missed, the most valuable criticism is not that which shakes its finger at faults but that which calls our attention to interesting things going on in the work of art. Here is a statement by W. H. Auden (1907-73), suggesting that criticism is most useful when it calls our attention to things worth attending to:

> What is the function of a critic? So far as I am concerned, he can do me one or more of the following services:
>
> 1. Introduce me to authors or works of which I was hitherto unaware.
> 2. Convince me that I have undervalued an author or a work because I had not read them carefully enough.
> 3. Show me relations between works of different ages and cultures which I could never have seen for myself because I do not know enough and never shall.
> 4. Give a "reading" of a work which increases my understanding of it.
> 5. Throw light upon the process of artistic "Making."
> 6. Throw light upon the relation of art to life, science, economics, ethics, religion, etc.
>
> *The Dyer's Hand* (New York, 1963), pp. 8-9

Auden does not neglect the delight we get from literature, but he extends (especially in his sixth point) the range of criticism to include topics beyond the literary work itself. Notice too the emphasis on observing, showing, and illuminating, which suggests that the function of critical writing is not very different from the commonest view of the function of imaginative writing.

SOME CRITICAL APPROACHES

Formalist (or New) Criticism; Deconstruction; Reader-Response Criticism; Archetypal (or Myth) Criticism; Historical Scholarship; Marxist Criticism, The New Historicism; and Biographical Criticism; Psychological (or Psychoanalytic) Criticism; Gender (Feminist, and Lesbian and Gay) Criticism

Whenever we talk about a work of literature or of art, or, for that matter, even about a so-so movie or television show, what we say depends in large measure on certain conscious or unconscious assumptions that we make: "I liked it; the characters were very believable" (here the assumption is that characters ought to be believable); "I didn't like it; there was too much violence" (here the assumption is that violence ought not to be shown, or if it is shown it should be made abhorrent); "I didn't like it; it was awfully slow" (here the assumption probably is that there ought to be a fair amount of physical action, perhaps even changes of scene, rather than characters just talking); "I didn't like it; I don't think topics of this sort ought to be discussed publicly" (here the assumption is a moral one, that it is indecent to present certain topics); "I liked it partly because it was refreshing to hear such frankness" (here again the assumption is moral, and more or less the reverse of the previous one).

In short, whether we realize it or not, we judge the work from a particular viewpoint—its realism, its morality, or whatever.

Professional critics, too, work from assumptions, but their assumptions are usually highly conscious, and the critics may define their assumptions at length. They regard themselves as, for instance, Freudians or Marxists or gay critics. They read all texts through the lens of a particular theory, and their focus enables them to see things that otherwise might go unnoticed. It should be added, however, that if a lens or critical perspective or interpretive strategy helps us to see certain things, it also limits our vision. Many critics therefore regard their method not as an exclusive way of thinking but only as a useful tool.

What follows is a brief survey of the chief current approaches to literature. You may find, as you read these pages, that one or another approach sounds especially congenial, and you may therefore want to make use of it in your reading and writing. On the other hand, it's important to remember that works of literature are highly varied, and we read them for various purposes—to kill time, to enjoy fanciful visions, to be amused, to learn about alien ways of feeling, and to learn about ourselves. It may be best, therefore, to try to respond to each text in the way that the text seems to require rather than to read all texts according to a single formula. You'll find, of course, that some works will lead you to want to think about them from several angles. A play by Shakespeare may stimulate you to read a book about the Elizabethan playhouse, and another that offers a Marxist interpretation of the English Renaissance, and still another that offers a feminist analysis of Shakespeare's plays. All of these approaches, and others, may help to deepen your understanding of the literary works that you read.

Formalist Criticism (New Criticism)

Formalist criticism emphasizes the work as an independent creation, a self-contained unity, something to be studied in itself, not as part of some larger context, such as the author's life or a historical period. This kind of study is called formalist criticism because the emphasis is on the *form* of the work, the relationships between the parts—the construction of the plot, the contrasts between characters, the functions of rhymes, the point of view, and so on.

Cleanth Brooks, perhaps America's most distinguished formalist critic, in an essay in the *Kenyon Review* (Winter 1951), reprinted in *The Modern Critical Spectrum,* eds. Gerald Jay Goldberg and Nancy Marmer Goldberg (1962), set forth what he called his "articles of faith":

> That literary criticism is a description and an evaluation of its object.
>
> That the primary concern of criticism is with the problem of unity—the kind of whole which the literary work forms or fails to form, and the relation of the various parts to each other in building up this whole.
>
> That the formal relations in a work of literature may include, but certainly exceed, those of logic.
>
> That in a successful work, form and content cannot be separated.
>
> That form is meaning.

If you have read the earlier pages of this book you are already familiar with most of these ideas, but in the next few pages we will look into some of them in detail.

Formalist criticism is, in essence, *intrinsic* criticism, rather than extrinsic, for (at least in theory) it concentrates on the work itself, independent of its writer and the writer's background—that is, independent of biography, psychology, sociology, and history. The discussions of a proverb ("A rolling stone") and of a short poem by Frost ("The Span of Life") on pages 397–99 are brief examples. The gist is that a work of literature is complex, unified, and freestanding. In fact, of course, we usually bring outside knowledge to the work. For instance, a reader who is familiar with, say, *Hamlet* can hardly study some other tragedy by Shakespeare, let's say *Romeo and Juliet,* without bringing to the second play some conception of what Shakespearean tragedy is or can be. A reader of Alice Walker's *The Color Purple* inevitably brings unforgettable outside material (perhaps the experience of being an African-American, or at least some knowledge of the history of African-Americans) to the literary work. It is very hard to talk only about *Hamlet* or *The Color Purple* and not at the same time talk, or at least have in mind, aspects of human experience.

Formalist criticism of course begins with a personal response to the literary work, but it goes on to try to account for the response by closely examining the work. It assumes that the author shaped the poem, play, or story so fully that the work guides the reader's responses. The assumption that "meaning" is fully and completely presented within the text is not much in favor today, when many literary critics argue that the active or subjective reader (or even what Judith Fetterley, a feminist critic, has called "the resisting reader") and not the author of the text makes the "meaning." Still, even if one grants that the reader is active, not passive or coolly objective, one can hold with the formalists that the author is active too, constructing a text that in some measure controls the reader's responses. Of course, during the process of writing about our responses we may find that our responses change. A formalist critic would say that we see with increasing clarity what the work is really like, and what it really means. (Similarly, when authors write and revise a text they may change their understanding of what they are doing. A story that began as a lighthearted joke may turn into something far more serious than the writer imagined at the start, but, at least for the formalist critic, the final work contains a stable meaning that all competent readers can perceive.)

In practice, formalist criticism usually takes one of two forms, **explication** (the unfolding of meaning, line by line or even word by word) and **analysis** (the examination of the relations of parts). The essay on Yeats's "The Balloon of the Mind" (p. 348) is an explication, a setting forth of the implicit meanings of the words. The essays on Kate Chopin's "The Story of an Hour" (pp. 26 and 52) and on Tennessee Williams's *The Glass Menagerie* (p. 199) are analyses. The three essays on Frost's "Stopping by Woods on a Snowy Evening" (pp. 410-19) are chiefly analyses but with some passages of explication.

To repeat: Formalist criticism assumes that a work of art is stable. An artist constructs a coherent, comprehensible work, thus conveying to a reader an emotion or an idea. T. S. Eliot said that the writer can't just pour out emotions onto the page. Rather, Eliot said in an essay entitled "Hamlet and His Problems" (1919), "The only way of expressing emotion in the form of art is by finding an 'objective correlative'; in other words, a set of objects, a situation, a chain of events which shall be the formula of the *particular* emotion." With this in mind, consider again Robert Frost's "The Span of Life," a poem already discussed on page 398:

> The old dog barks backward without getting up.
> I can remember when he was a pup.

The image of an old dog barking backward, and the speaker's memory—apparently triggered by the old dog's bark—of the dog as a pup, presumably are the "objective correlative" of Frost's emotion or idea; Frost is "expressing emotion" through this "formula." And all of us, as competent readers, can grasp pretty accurately what Frost expressed. Frost's emotion, idea, meaning, or whatever is "objectively" embodied in the text. Formalist critics try to explain how and why literary works—*these* words, in *this* order—constitute unique, complex structures that embody or set forth meanings.

Formalist criticism, also called the **New Criticism** (to distinguish it from the historical and biographical writing that in earlier decades had dominated literary study), began to achieve prominence in the late 1920s and was the dominant form from the late 1930s until about 1970, and even today it is widely considered the best way for a student to begin to study a work of literature. For one thing, formal criticism empowers the student; that is, the student confronts the work immediately and is not told first to spend days or weeks or months in preparation—for instance reading Freud and his followers in order to write a psychoanalytic essay or reading Marx and Marxists in order to write a Marxist essay, or doing research on "necessary historical background" in order to write a historical essay.

Deconstruction

Deconstruction, or deconstructive or poststructural criticism, can almost be characterized as the opposite of everything that formalist criticism stands for. Deconstruction begins with the assumptions that the world is unknowable and that language is unstable, elusive, unfaithful. (Language is all of these things because meaning is largely generated by opposition: *hot* means something in opposition to *cold,* but a hot day may be 90 degrees whereas a hot oven is at least 400 degrees, and a "hot item" may be of any temperature.) Deconstructionists seek to show that a literary work (usually called "a text" or "a discourse") inevitably is self-contradictory. Unlike formalist critics—who hold that a competent author constructs a coherent work with a stable meaning, and that competent readers can perceive this meaning—deconstructionists (e.g., Barbara Johnson in *The Critical Difference* [1980]) hold that a work has no coherent meaning at the center. Jonathan Culler, in *On Deconstruction* (1982), says that "to deconstruct a discourse is to show how it undermines the philosophy it asserts" (86). (Johnson and Culler provide accessible introductions, but the major document is Jacques Derrida's seminal, difficult work, *Of Grammatology* [1967, trans. 1976].) This view holds that the text is only marks on paper, and therefore so far as a reader goes the author of a text is not the writer but the reader; texts are "indeterminate," "open," and "unstable."

Despite the emphasis on indeterminacy, one sometimes detects in deconstructionist interpretations a view associated with Marxism. This is the idea that authors are "socially constructed" from the "discourses of power" or "signifying practices" that surround them. Thus, although authors may think they are individuals with independent minds, their works usually reveal—unknown to the authors—the society's economic base. Deconstructionists "interrogate" a text, and they reveal what the authors were unaware of or had thought they had kept safely out of sight. That is, deconstructionists often find a rather specific meaning—though this meaning is one that might surprise the author.

Deconstruction is valuable insofar as—like the New Criticism—it encourages close, rigorous attention to the text. Furthermore, in its rejection of the claim that a work has a single stable meaning, Deconstruction has had a positive influence on the study of literature. The problem with Deconstruction, however, is that too often it is reductive, telling the same story about every text—that here, yet again, and again, we see how a text is incoherent and heterogeneous. There is, too, an irritating arrogance in some deconstructive criticism: "The author could not see how his/her text is fundamentally unstable and self-contradictory, but *I* can and now will interrogate the text and will issue my report." Readers should, of course, not prostrate themselves before texts, but there is something askew about an approach that often leads readers to conclude that they know a good deal more than the benighted author.

Aware that their emphasis on the instability of language implies that their own texts are unstable or even incoherent, some deconstructionists seem to aim at entertaining rather than at edifying. They probably would claim that they do not deconstruct meaning in the sense of destroying it; rather, they might say, they exuberantly multiply meanings, and to this end they may use such devices as puns, irony, and allusions, somewhat as a poet might, and just as though (one often feels) they think they are as creative as the writers they are commenting on. Indeed, for many deconstructionists, the traditional conception of "literature" is merely an elitist "construct." All "texts" or "discourses" (novels, scientific papers, a Kewpie doll on the mantel, watching TV, suing in court, walking the dog, and all other signs that human beings make) are of a piece; all are unstable systems of signifying, all are fictions, all are "literature." If literature (in the usual sense) occupies a special place in deconstruction it is because literature delights in its playfulness, its fictiveness, whereas other discourses nominally reject play-fulness and fictiveness.

Reader-Response Criticism

Probably all reading includes some sort of response—"This is terrific," "This is a bore," "I don't know what's going on here"—and probably almost all writing about literature begins with some such response, but specialists in literature dis-agree greatly about the role that response plays, or should play, in experiencing literature and in writing about it.

At one extreme are those who say that our response to a work of literature should be a purely aesthetic response—a response to a work of art—and not the response we would have to something comparable in real life. To take an obvi-ous point: If in real life we heard someone plotting a murder, we would inter-vene, perhaps by calling the police or by attempting to warn the victim. But when we hear Macbeth and Lady Macbeth plot to kill King Duncan, we watch with deep *interest;* we hear their words with *pleasure,* and maybe we even look forward to seeing the murder and to seeing what the characters then will say and what will happen to the murderers.

When you think about it, the vast majority of works of literature do not have a close, obvious resemblance to the reader's life. Most readers of *Macbeth* are not Scots, and no readers are Scottish kings or queens. (It's not just a matter of older literature; no readers of Toni Morrison's *Beloved* are nineteenth-century African-Americans.) The connections readers make between themselves and the lives in most of the books they read are not, on the whole, connections based on ethnic or professional identities, but, rather, connections with states of con-sciousness, for instance a young person's sense of isolation from the family, or a young person's sense of guilt for initial sexual experiences. Before we reject a work either because it seems too close to us ("I'm a man and I don't like the de-piction of this man"), or on the other hand too far from our experience ("I'm not a woman, so how can I enjoy reading about these women?"), we probably should try to follow the advice of Virginia Woolf, who said, "Do not dictate to your author; try to become him." Nevertheless, some literary works of the past may today seem intolerable, at least in part. There are passages in Mark Twain's *Huckleberry Finn* that deeply upset us today. We should, however, try to recon-struct the cultural assumptions of the age in which the work was written. If we do so, we may find that if in some ways it reflected its age, in other ways it chal-lenged that culture.

Still, some of our experiences, some of *what we are,* may make it virtually impossible for us to read a work sympathetically or "objectively," experiencing it only as a work of art and not as a part of life. Take so humble a form of literature as the joke. A few decades ago jokes about nagging wives and mothers-in-law were widely thought to be funny. Our fairly recent heightened awareness of sex-ism today makes those jokes unfunny. Twenty years ago the "meaning" of a joke about a nagging wife or about a mother-in-law was, in effect, "Here's a funny episode that shows what women typically are." Today the "meaning"—at least as the hearer conceives it—is "The unfunny story you have just told shows that you have stupid, stereotypical views of women." In short, the joke may "mean" one thing to the teller and a very different thing to the hearer.

Reader-response criticism, then, says that the "meaning" of a work is not merely something put into the work by the writer; rather, the "meaning" is an interpretation created or constructed or produced by the reader as well as the writer. Stanley Fish, an exponent of reader-response theory, in *Is There a Text in This Class?* (1980), puts it this way: "Interpretation is not the art of construing but of constructing. Interpreters do not decode poems; they make them" (327).

Let's now try to relate these ideas more specifically to comments about literature. If "meaning" is the production or creation not simply of the writer but also of the perceiver, does it follow that there is no such thing as a "correct" interpretation of the meaning of a work of literature? Answers to this question differ. At one extreme, the reader is said to construct or reconstruct the text under the firm guidance of the author. That is, the author so powerfully shapes or constructs the text—encodes an idea—that the reader is virtually compelled to perceive or reconstruct or decode it the way the author wants it to be perceived. (We can call this view *the objective view,* since it essentially holds that readers look objectively at the work and see what the author put into it.) At the other extreme, the reader constructs the meaning according to his or her own personality—that is, according to the reader's psychological identity. (We can call this view *the subjective view,* since it essentially holds that readers inevitably project their feelings into what they perceive.) An extreme version of the subjective view holds that there is no such thing as literature; there are only texts, some of which some readers regard in a particularly elitist way.

Against the objective view one can argue thus: No author can fully control a reader's response to every detail of the text. No matter how carefully constructed the text is, it leaves something—indeed, a great deal—to the reader's imagination. For instance, when Macbeth says that life "is a tale / Told by an idiot, full of sound and fury / Signifying nothing," are we getting a profound thought from Shakespeare or, on the contrary, are we getting a shallow thought from Macbeth, a man who does not see that his criminal deeds have been played out against a heaven that justly punishes his crimes? In short, the objective view neglects to take account of the fact that the author is not continually at our shoulder making sure that we interpret the work in a particular way.

It is probably true, as Flannery O'Connor says in *Mystery and Manners* (1957), that good writers select "every word, every detail, for a reason, every incident for a reason" (75), but there are always *gaps* or *indeterminacies,* to use the words of Wolfgang Iser, a reader-response critic. Readers always go beyond the text, drawing inferences, and evaluating the text in terms of their own experience. In the Hebrew Bible, for instance, in Genesis, the author tells us (chap. 22) that God commanded Abraham to sacrifice his son Isaac, and then says that "Abraham rose up early in the morning" and prepared to fulfill the command. We are not explicitly told *why* Abraham "rose up early in the morning," or how he spent the intervening night, but some readers take "early in the morning" to signify (reasonably?) that Abraham has had a sleepless night. Others take it to signify (reasonably?) that Abraham is prompt in obeying God's command. And of course some readers fill the gap with both explanations, or with neither. Doubtless much depends on the reader, but there is no doubt that readers "naturalize"—make natural, according to their own ideas—what they read.

In an extreme form the subjective view denies that authors can make us perceive the meanings that they try to put into their works. This position suggests that every reader has a different idea of what a work means, an idea that reflects the reader's own ideas. Every reader, then, is Narcissus, who looked into a pool of water and thought he saw a beautiful youth but really saw only a reflection of himself. But does every reader see his or her individual image in each literary work? Of course not. Even *Hamlet,* a play that has generated an enormous range of interpretation, is universally seen as a tragedy, a play that deals with painful realities. If someone were to tell us that *Hamlet* is a comedy, and that the end, with a pile of corpses, is especially funny, we would not say, "Oh, well, we all see things in our own way." Rather, we would make our exit as quickly as possible.

Many people who subscribe to one version or another of a reader-response theory would agree that they are concerned not with all readers but with what they call *informed readers* or *competent readers.* Thus, informed or competent readers are familiar with the conventions of literature. They understand, for instance, that in a play such as *Hamlet* the characters usually speak in verse. Such readers, then, do not express amazement that Hamlet often speaks metrically, and that he sometimes uses rhyme. These readers understand that verse is the normal language for most of the characters in the play, and therefore such readers do not characterize Hamlet as a poet. Informed, competent readers, in short, know the rules of the game. There will still, of course, be plenty of room for differences of interpretation. Some people will find Hamlet not at all blameworthy, others will find him somewhat blameworthy, and still others may find him highly blameworthy. In short, we can say that a writer works against a background that is *shared* by readers. As readers, we are familiar with various kinds of literature, and we read or see *Hamlet* as a particular kind of literary work, a tragedy, a play that evokes (in Shakespeare's words) "woe or wonder," sadness and astonishment. Knowing (in a large degree) how we ought to respond, our responses thus are not merely private.

Consider taking, as a guide to reading, a remark made by Mencius (372–289 BC), the Chinese Confucian philosopher. Speaking of reading *The Book of Odes,* the oldest Chinese anthology, Mencius said that "a reader must let his thought go to meet the intention as he would a guest." Of course we often cannot be sure about the author's intention (we don't know what Shakespeare intended to say in *Hamlet;* we have only the play itself), and even those relatively few authors who have explicitly stated their intentions may be untrustworthy for one reason or another. Still, there is something highly attractive in Mencius's suggestion that when we read we should—at least for a start—treat our author not with suspicion or hostility but with goodwill and with the expectation of pleasure.

What are the implications of reader-response theory for writing an essay on a work of literature? Even if we agree that we are talking only about competent readers, does this mean, then, that *almost* anything goes in setting forth one's responses in an essay? Most all advocates of any form of reader-response criticism agree on one thing: There are agreed-upon rules of *writing* if not of reading. This one point of agreement can be amplified to contain at least two aspects: (1) we all agree (at least more or less) as to what constitutes evidence, and (2) we all agree that a written response should be coherent. If you say that you find Hamlet to be less noble than his adversary, Claudius, you will be expected to provide evidence by pointing to specific passages, to specific things that Hamlet and Claudius say and do. And you will be expected to order the material into an effective, coherent sequence, so that the reader can move easily through your essay and will understand what you are getting at.

Archetypal Criticism (Myth Criticism)

Carl G. Jung, the Swiss psychiatrist, in *Contributions to Analytical Psychology* (1928) postulates the existence of a "collective unconscious," an inheritance in our brains consisting of "countless typical experiences [such as birth, escape from danger, selection of a mate] of our ancestors." Few people today believe in an inherited "collective unconscious," but many people agree that certain repeated experiences, such as going to sleep and hours later awakening, or the perception of the setting and of the rising sun, or of the annual death and rebirth of vegetation, manifest themselves in dreams, myths, and literature—in these instances, as stories of apparent death and rebirth. This archetypal plot of death and rebirth is said to be evident in Coleridge's *The Rime of the Ancient Mariner,* for example. The ship suffers a deathlike calm and then is miraculously restored to motion, and, in a sort of parallel rebirth, the mariner moves from spiritual death to renewed perception of the holiness of life. Another archetypal plot is the quest, which usually involves the testing and initiation of a hero, and thus essentially represents the movement from innocence to experience. In addition to archetypal plots there are archetypal characters, since an archetype is any recurring unit. Among archetypal characters are the scapegoat (as in Shirley Jackson's "The Lottery," p. 976), the hero (savior, deliverer), the terrible mother (witch, stepmother—even the wolf "grandmother" in the tale of Little Red Riding Hood), and the wise old man (father figure, magician).

Because, the theory holds, both writer and reader share unconscious memories, the tale an author tells (derived from the collective unconscious) may strangely move the reader, speaking to his or her collective unconscious. As Maud Bodkin puts it, in *Archetypal Patterns in Poetry* (1934), something within us "leaps in response to the effective presentation in poetry of an ancient theme" (4). But this emphasis on ancient (or repeated) themes has made archetypal criticism vulnerable to the charge that it is reductive. The critic looks for certain characters or patterns of action and values the work if the motifs are there, meanwhile overlooking what is unique, subtle, distinctive, and truly interesting about the work. That is, to put the matter crudely, a work is regarded as good if it is pretty much like other works, with the usual motifs and characters. A second weakness in some archetypal criticism is that in its search for the deepest meaning of a work the critic may crudely impose a pattern, seeing (for instance) the quest in every walk down the street. But perhaps to say this is to beg the question; it is the critic's job to write so persuasively that the reader at least tentatively accepts the critic's view. For a wide-ranging study of one particular motif, see Barbara Fass Leavy's *In Search of the Swan Maiden* (1994), a discussion of the legend of a swan maiden who is forced to marry a mortal because he possesses something of hers, usually a garment or an animal skin. Leavy analyzes several versions of the story, which she takes to be a representation not only of female rage against male repression but also a representation of male fear of female betrayal. Leavy ends her book by examining this motif in Ibsen's *A Doll's*

House. Her claim is that when Nora finds a lost object, the dance costume, she can flee from the tyrannical domestic world and thus regain her freedom.

If archetypal criticism sometimes seems farfetched, it is nevertheless true that one of its strengths is that it invites us to use comparisons, and comparing is often an excellent way to see not only what a work shares with other works but what is distinctive in the work. The most successful practitioner of archetypal criticism was the late Northrop Frye (1912-91), whose numerous books help readers to see fascinating connections between works. For Frye's explicit comments about archetypal criticism, as well as for examples of such criticism in action, see especially his *Anatomy of Criticism* (1957) and *The Educated Imagination* (1964). On archetypes see also chapter 16, "Archetypal Patterns," in Norman Friedman, *Form and Meaning in Fiction* (1975).

Historical Scholarship

Historical scholarship studies a work within its historical context. Thus, a student of *Julius Caesar, Hamlet,* or *Macbeth*—plays in which ghosts appear—may try to find out about Elizabethan attitudes toward ghosts. We may find, for instance, that the Elizabethans took ghosts more seriously than we do, or, on the other hand, we may find that ghosts were explained in various ways, for instance sometimes as figments of the imagination and sometimes as shapes taken by the devil in order to mislead the virtuous. Similarly, a historical essay concerned with *Othello* may be devoted to Elizabethan attitudes toward Moors, or to Elizabethan ideas of love, or, for that matter, to Elizabethan ideas of a daughter's obligations toward her father's wishes concerning her suitor. The historical critic assumes (and one can hardly dispute the assumption) that writers, however individualistic, are shaped by the particular social contexts in which they live. One can put it this way: The goal of **historical criticism** is to understand how people in the past thought and felt. It assumes that such understanding can enrich our understanding of a particular work. The assumption is, however, disputable, since one may argue that the artist—let's say Shakespeare—may *not* have shared the age's view on this or that. All of the half-dozen or so Moors in Elizabethan plays other than *Othello* are villainous or foolish, but this evidence, one can argue, does not prove that *therefore* Othello is villainous or foolish.

Marxist Criticism

One form of historical criticism is **Marxist criticism,** named for Karl Marx (1818-83). Actually, to say "one form" is misleading, since Marxist criticism today is varied, but essentially it sees history primarily as a struggle between socioeconomic classes, and it sees literature (and everything else, too) as the product of the economic forces of the period.

For Marxists, economics is the "base" or "infrastructure"; on this base rests a "superstructure" of ideology (law, politics, philosophy, religion, and the arts, including literature), reflecting the interests of the dominant class. Thus, literature is a material product, produced—like bread or battleships—in order to be consumed in a given society. Like every other product, literature is the product of work, and it *does* work. A bourgeois society, for example, will produce literature that in one way or another celebrates bourgeois values, for instance individualism. These works serve to assure the society that produces them that its values are solid, even universal. The enlightened Marxist writer or critic, on the other hand, exposes the fallacy of traditional values and replaces them with the truths found in Marxism. In the heyday of Marxism in the United States, during the depression of the 1930s, it was common for such Marxist critics as Granville Hicks to assert that the novel must show the class struggle.

Few critics of any sort would disagree that works of art in some measure reflect the age that produced them, but most contemporary Marxist critics go further. First, they assert—in a repudiation of what has been called "'vulgar' Marxist theory"—that the deepest historical meaning of a literary work is to be found in what it does *not* say, what its ideology does not permit it to express. Second, Marxists take seriously Marx's famous comment that "the philosophers have only *interpreted* the world in various ways; the point is to *change* it." The critic's job is to change the world, by revealing the economic basis of the arts. Not surprisingly, most Marxists are skeptical of such concepts as "genius" and "masterpiece." These concepts, they say, are part of the bourgeois myth that idealizes the individual and detaches art from its economic context. For an introduction to Marxist criticism, see Terry Eagleton, *Marxism and Literary Criticism* (1976).

New Historicism

A recent school of scholarship, called **New Historicism,** insists that there is no "history" in the sense of a narrative of indisputable past events. Rather, New Historicism holds that there is only our version—our narrative, our representation—of the past. In this view, each age projects its own preconceptions on the past; historians may think they are revealing the past, but they are revealing only their own historical situation and their personal preferences. Thus, in the nineteenth century and in the twentieth almost up to 1992, Columbus was represented as the heroic benefactor of humankind who discovered the New World. But even while plans were being made to celebrate the five-hundredth anniversary of his first voyage across the Atlantic, voices were raised in protest: Columbus did not "discover" a New World; after all, the indigenous people knew where they were, and it was Columbus who was lost, since he thought he was in India. In short, people who wrote history in, say, 1900 projected onto the past their current views (colonialism was a good thing), and people who wrote history in 1992 projected onto that same period a very different set of views (colonialism was a bad thing). Similarly, ancient Greece, once celebrated by historians as the source of democracy and rational thinking, is now more often regarded as a society that was built on slavery and on the oppression of women. And the Renaissance, once glorified as an age of enlightened thought, is now often seen as an age that tyrannized women, enslaved colonial people, and enslaved itself with its belief in witchcraft and astrology. Thinking about these changing views, one feels the truth of the witticism that the only thing more uncertain than the future is the past.

New Historicism is especially associated with Stephen Greenblatt, who popularized the term in 1982 in the preface to a collection of essays published in a journal called *Genre.* Greenblatt himself has said of New Historicism that "it's no doctrine at all" (*Learning to Curse* [1990]) but the term is nevertheless much used, and, as preceding remarks have suggested, it is especially associated with power, most especially with revealing the tyrannical practices of a society that others have glorified. New Historicism was in large measure shaped by the

1960s; the students who in that decade protested against the war in Vietnam by holding demonstrations were the full professors in the 1980s who protested against Ronald Reagan by writing articles exposing Renaissance colonialism. (In its most doctrinaire form, New Historicism assumes that a centralized authority creates cultural meanings.) Works of literature were used as a basis for a criticism of society. Academic writing of this sort was not dry, impartial, unimpassioned scholarship; rather, it connected the past with the present, and it offered value judgments. In Greenblatt's words,

> Writing that was not engaged, that withheld judgments, that failed to connect the present with the past seemed worthless. Such connection could be made either by analogy or causality; that is, a particular set of historical circumstances could be represented in such a way as to bring out homologies with aspects of the present or, alternatively, those circumstances could be analyzed as the generative forces that led to the modern condition. (*Learning to Curse* 167)

In *Literature for Composition* we include a short essay by Greenblatt (p. 320) in our casebook on Shakespeare's *The Tempest*.

For a collection of 15 essays exemplifying the New Historicism, see H. Aram Veeser, ed., *The New Historicism* (1989).

Biographical Criticism

One kind of historical research is the study of *biography,* which for our purposes includes not only biographies but also autobiographies, diaries, journals, letters, and so on. What experiences did (for example) Mark Twain undergo? Are some of the apparently sensational aspects of *Huckleberry Finn* in fact close to events that Twain experienced? If so, is he a "realist"? If not, is he writing in the tradition of the "tall tale"?

The really good biographies not only tell us about the life of the author—they enable us to return to the literary texts with a deeper understanding of how they came to be what they are. If, for example, you read Richard B. Sewall's biography of Emily Dickinson, you will find a wealth of material concerning her family and the world she moved in—for instance, the religious ideas that were part of her upbringing.

Biographical study may illuminate even the work of a living author. If you are writing about the poetry of Adrienne Rich, for example, you may want to consider what she has told us in many essays about her life, especially about her relations with her father and her husband.

See also, for biographical comment on a writer, Anne Rosenberg's essay (p. 135) in our casebook on Francis Bacon.

Psychological or Psychoanalytic Criticism

One form that biographical study may take is **psychological criticism** or *psychoanalytic criticism,* which usually examines the author and the author's writings in the framework of Freudian psychology. A central doctrine of Sigmund Freud (1856–1939) is the Oedipus complex, the view that all males (Freud seems not to have made his mind up about females) unconsciously wish to displace their fathers and to sleep with their mothers. According to Freud, hatred for the father and love of the mother, normally repressed, may appear disguised in dreams. Works of art, like dreams, are disguised versions of repressed wishes.

Consider, for instance, Edgar Allan Poe. An orphan before he was three years old, he was brought up in the family of John Allan, but he was never formally adopted. His relations with Allan were stormy, though he seems to have had better relations with Allan's wife and still better relations with an aunt, whose daughter he married. In the Freudian view, Poe's marriage to his cousin (the daughter of a mother figure) was a way of sleeping with his mother. Psychoanalytic critics allege that if we move from Poe's life to his work, we see this hatred for his father and love for his mother. Thus, the murderer in "The Cask of Amontillado" is said to voice Poe's hostility to his father, and the wine vault in which much of the story is set (an encompassing structure associated with fluids) is interpreted as symbolizing Poe's desire to return to his mother's womb. In Poe's other works, the longing for death is similarly taken to embody his desire to return to the womb.

Of course other psychoanalytic interpretations of Poe have been offered. For instance, Kenneth Silverman, author of a biography entitled *Edgar Allan Poe* (1991) and the editor of a collection entitled *New Essays on Poe's Major Tales* (1993), emphasizes the fact that Poe was orphaned before he was three and was separated from his brother and his infant sister. In *New Essays* Silverman relates this circumstance to the "many instances of engulfment" that he finds in Poe's work. Images of engulfment, he points out, "are part of a still larger network of images having to do with biting, devouring, and similar oral mutilation." Why are they common in Poe? Here is Silverman's answer:

> Current psychoanalytic thinking about childhood bereavement explains the fantasy of being swallowed up as representing a desire, mixed with dread, to merge with the dead; the wish to devour represents a primitive attempt at preserving loved ones, incorporating them so as not to lose them. (20)

Notice that psychoanalytic interpretations usually take us away from what the author consciously intended; they purport to tell us what the work reveals, whether or not the author was aware of this meaning. The "meaning" of the work is found not in the surface content of the work but in the author's psyche.

One additional example—and it is the most famous—of a psychoanalytic study of a work of literature may be useful. In *Hamlet and Oedipus* (1949) Ernest Jones, amplifying some comments by Freud, argued that Hamlet delays killing Claudius because Claudius (who has killed Hamlet's father and married Hamlet's mother) has done exactly what Hamlet himself wanted to do. For Hamlet to kill Claudius, then, would be to kill himself.

If this approach interests you, take a look at Norman N. Holland's *Psychoanalysis and Shakespeare* (1966) or Frederick Crew's study of Hawthorne, *The Sins of the Fathers* (1966). Crews, for instance, finds in Hawthorne's work evidence of unresolved Oedipal conflicts, and he accounts for the appeal of the fictions thus: The stories "rest on fantasy, but on the shared fantasy of mankind, and this makes for a more penetrating fiction than would any illusionistic slice of life" (263). For applications to other authors, look at Simon O. Lesser's *Fiction and the Unconscious* (1957), or at an anthology of criticism, *Literature and Psychoanalysis,* edited by Edith Kurzweil and William Phillips (1983).

Psychological criticism can also turn from the author and the work to the reader, seeking to explain why we, as readers, respond in certain ways. Why, for example, is *Hamlet* so widely popular? A Freudian answer is that it is universal because it deals with a universal (Oedipal) impulse. One can, however, ask whether it appeals as strongly to women as to men (again, Freud was unsure about the Oedipus complex in women) and, if so, why it appeals to them. Or, more generally, one can ask if males and females read in the same way.

In our casebook on *The Tempest* Jonathan Miller, in his interview with Ralph Berry, gets into psychoanalytic matters when he speaks of Prospero's infantilism. And one of the stories we reprint, Frank O'Connor's "My Oedipus Complex," deals with a Freudian matter in a comic way.

Gender Criticism (Feminist, and Lesbian and Gay Criticism)

This last question brings us to **gender criticism.** As we have seen, writing about literature usually seeks to answer questions. Historical scholarship, for instance, tries to answer such questions as "What did Shakespeare and his contemporaries believe about ghosts?" or "How did Victorian novelists and poets respond to Darwin's theory of evolution?" Gender criticism, too, asks questions. It is especially concerned with two issues, one about reading and one about writing: "Do men and women read in different ways?" and "Do they write in different ways?"

Feminist criticism can be traced back to the work of Virginia Woolf (1882–1941), but chiefly it grew out of the women's movement of the 1960s. The women's movement at first tended to hold that women are pretty much the same as men and therefore should be treated equally, but much recent feminist criticism has emphasized and explored the differences between women and men. Because the experiences of the sexes are different, the argument goes, their values and sensibilities are different, and their responses to literature are different. Further, literature written by women is different from literature written by men. Works written by women are seen by some feminist critics as embodying the experiences of a minority culture—a group marginalized by the dominant male culture. (If you have read Susan Glaspell's *Trifles* [page 216] you'll recall that this literary work itself is largely concerned about the differing ways that males and females perceive the world.) Of course, not all women are feminist critics, and not all feminist critics are women. Further, there are varieties of feminist criticism, but for a good introduction see *The New Feminist Criticism: Essays on Women, Literature, and Theory* (1985), edited by Elaine Showalter. For the role of men in feminist criticism, see *Engendering Men,* edited by Joseph A. Boone and Michael Cadden (1990). At this point it should also be said that some theorists, who hold that identity is socially constructed, strongly dispute the value of establishing "essentialist" categories such as *gay* and *lesbian*—a point that we will consider in a moment.

Feminist critics rightly point out that men have established the conventions of literature and that men have established the canon—that is, the body of literature that is said to be worth reading. Speaking a bit broadly, in this patriarchal or male-dominated body of literature, men are valued for being strong and active, whereas women are expected to be weak and passive. Thus, in the world of fairy tales, the admirable male is the energetic hero (Jack, the Giant-Killer) but the admirable female is the passive Sleeping Beauty. Active women such as the wicked stepmother or—a disguised form of the same thing—the witch are generally villainous. (There are of course exceptions, such as Gretel in "Hansel and Gretel.")

A woman hearing or reading the story of Sleeping Beauty or of Little Red Riding Hood (rescued by the powerful woodcutter), or any other work in which women seem to be trivialized, will respond differently than a man. For instance, a woman may be socially conditioned into admiring Sleeping Beauty, but only at great cost to her mental well-being. A more resistant female reader may recognize in herself no kinship with the beautiful, passive Sleeping Beauty and may respond to the story indignantly. Another way to put it is this: The male reader perceives a romantic story, but the resistant female reader perceives a story of oppression.

For discussions of the ways in which, it is argued, women *ought* to read, you may want to look at *Gender and Reading,* edited by Elizabeth A. Flynn and Patrocino Schweikart, and especially at Judith Fetterley's book *The Resisting Reader* (1978). Fetterley's point, briefly, is that women should resist the meanings (that is, the visions of how women ought to behave) that male authors—or female authors who have inherited patriarchal values—bury in their books. "To read the canon of what is currently considered classic American literature is perforce to identify as male," Fetterley says. "It insists on its universality in specifically male terms." Fetterley argues that a woman must read as a woman, "exorcising the male mind that has been implanted in women." In resisting the obvious meanings—for instance, the false claim that male values are universal values—women may discover more significant meanings. Fetterley argues that Faulkner's "A Rose for Emily"

> is a story not of a conflict between the South and the North or between the old order and the new; it is a story of the patriarchy North and South, new and old, and of the sexual conflict within it. As Faulkner himself has implied, it is a story of a woman victimized and betrayed by the system of sexual politics, who nevertheless has discovered, within the structures that victimize her, sources of power for herself. . . . "A Rose for Emily" is the story of how to murder your gentleman caller and get away with it. (34–35)

Fetterley goes on to argue that the society made Emily a "lady"—society dehumanized her by elevating her. For instance, Emily's father, seeking to shape her life, stood in the doorway of their house and drove away her suitors. So far as he was concerned, Emily was a nonperson, a creature whose own wishes were not to be regarded; he alone would shape her future. Because society (beginning with her father) made her a "lady"—a creature so elevated that she is not taken seriously as a passionate human being—she is able to kill Homer Barron and not be suspected. Here is Fetterley speaking of the passage in which the townspeople crowd into her house when her death becomes known:

> When the would-be "suitors" finally get into her father's house, they discover the consequences of his oppression of her, for the violence contained in the rotted corpse of Homer Barron is the mirror image of the violence represented in the tableau, the back-flung front door flung back with a vengeance. (42)

For additional material from Fetterley's essay on "A Rose for Emily," see our casebook on the story (p. 194).

Feminist criticism has been concerned not only with the depiction of women and men in a male-determined literary canon and with women's responses to these images but also with yet another topic: women's writing.

Women have had fewer opportunities than men to become writers of fiction, poetry, and drama—for one thing, they have been less well educated in the things that the male patriarchy valued—but even when they *have* managed to write, men sometimes have neglected their work simply because it was written by a woman. Feminists have further argued that certain forms of writing have been especially the province of women—for instance journals, diaries, and letters; and predictably, these forms have not been given adequate space in the traditional, male-oriented canon.

In 1972, in an essay entitled "When We Dead Awaken: Writing as Re-Vision," the poet and essayist Adrienne Rich effectively summed up the matter:

> A radical critique of literature, feminist in its impulse, would take the work first of all as a clue to how we live, how we have been living, how we have been led to imagine ourselves, how our language has trapped as well as liberated us; and how we can begin to see—and therefore live—afresh. . . . We need to know the writing of the past and know it differently than we have ever known it; not to pass on a tradition but to break its hold over us.

Much feminist criticism concerned with women writers has emphasized connections between the writer's biography and her life. Suzanne Juhasz, in her introduction to *Feminist Critics Read Emily Dickinson* (1983), puts it this way:

> The central assumption of feminist criticism is that gender informs the nature of art, the nature of biography, and the relation between them. Dickinson is a woman poet, and this fact is integral to her identity. Feminist criticism's sensitivity to the components of female experience in general and to Dickinson's identity as a woman generates essential insights about her. . . . Attention to the relationship between biography and art is a requisite of feminist criticism. To disregard it further strengthens those divisions continually created by traditional criticism, so that nothing about the woman writer can be seen whole. (1–5)

Feminist criticism has made many readers—men as well as women—increasingly aware of gender relationships within literary works. For an example, see the essay in this text (p. 326) by Linda Bamber, in our casebook on Shakespeare's *The Tempest.*

Lesbian criticism and **gay criticism** have their roots in feminist criticism; that is, feminist criticism introduced many of the questions that these other, newer developments are now exploring.

In 1979, in a book called *On Lies, Secrets, and Silence,* Adrienne Rich reprinted a 1975 essay on Emily Dickinson, "Vesuvius at Home." In her new preface to the reprinted essay she said that a lesbian-feminist reading of Dickinson would not have to prove that Dickinson slept with another woman. Rather, lesbian-feminist criticism "will ask questions hitherto passed over; it will not search obsessively for heterosexual romance as the key to a woman artist's life and work" (157–158). Obviously such a statement is also relevant to a male artist's life and work. It should be mentioned, too, that Rich's comments on lesbian reading and lesbianism as an image of creativity have been much discussed. For a brief survey, see Marilyn R. Farwell, "Toward a Definition of the Lesbian Literary Imagination," *Signs* 14 (1988): 100–18.

Before turning to some of the questions that lesbian and gay critics address it is necessary to say that lesbian criticism and gay criticism are not—to use a word now current in much criticism—symmetrical, chiefly because lesbian and gay relationships themselves are not symmetrical. For instance, straight society has traditionally been more tolerant of—or blinder to—lesbianism than to male homosexuality. Further, lesbian literary theory has tended to see its affinities more with feminist theory than with gay theory; that is, the emphasis has been on gender (male/female) rather than on sexuality (homosexuality/bisexuality/heterosexuality). On the other hand, some gays and lesbians have been writing what is now being called queer theory.

Now for some of the questions that this criticism addresses: (1) Do lesbians and gays read in ways that differ from the ways straight people read? (2) Do they write in ways that differ from those of straight people? (For instance, Gregory Woods argues in *Lesbian and Gay Writing: An Anthology of Critical Essays* [1990], edited by Mark Lilly, that "modern gay poets . . . use . . . paradox, as weapon and shield, against a world in which heterosexuality is taken for granted as being exclusively natural and healthy" [176]. Another critic, Jeffrey Meyers, writing in *Journal of English and Germanic Philology* 88 [1989]: 126–29, in an unsympathetic review of a book on gay writers contrasts gay writers of the past with those of the present. According to Meyers, closeted homosexuals in the past, writing out of guilt and pain, produced a distinctive literature that is more interesting than the productions of today's uncloseted writers.) (3) How have straight writers portrayed lesbians and gays, and how have lesbian and gay writers portrayed straight women and men? (4) What strategies did lesbian and gay writers use to make their work acceptable to a general public in an age when lesbian and gay behavior was unmentionable?

Questions such as these have stimulated critical writing especially about bisexual and lesbian and gay authors (for instance Virginia Woolf, Gertrude Stein, Elizabeth Bishop, Walt Whitman, Oscar Wilde, E. M. Forster, Hart Crane, Tennessee Williams), but they have also led to interesting writing on such a topic as Nathaniel Hawthorne's attitudes toward women. "An account of Hawthorne's misogyny that takes no account of his own and his culture's gender anxieties," Robert K. Martin says in Boone and Cadden's *Engendering Men,* "is necessarily inadequate" (122).

Shakespeare's work—and not only the sonnets, which praise a beautiful male friend—has stimulated a fair amount of gay criticism. Much of this criticism consists of "decoding" aspects of the plays. For instance, Seymour Kleinberg argues in *Essays on Gay Literature* (1985), ed. Stuart Kellogg, that Antonio in *The Merchant of Venice,* whose melancholy is not made clear by Shakespeare, is melancholy because (again, this is according to Kleinberg) Antonio's lover, Bassanio, is deserting him, and because Antonio is ashamed of his own sexuality:

> Antonio is a virulently anti-Semitic homosexual and is melancholic to the point of despair because his lover, Bassanio, wishes to marry an immensely rich aristocratic beauty, to leave the diversions of the Rialto to return to his own class and to sexual conventionality. Antonio is also in despair because he despises himself for his homosexuality, which is romantic, obsessive, and exclusive, and fills him with sexual shame. (113)

Several earlier critics had suggested that Antonio is a homosexual, hopelessly pining for Bassanio, but Kleinberg goes further and argues that Antonio and Bassanio are lovers, not just good friends, and that Antonio's hopeless and shameful (because socially unacceptable) passion for Bassanio becomes transformed into hatred for the Jew, Shylock. The play, according to Kleinberg, is partly about "a world where . . . sexual guilt is translated into ethnic hatred" (124).

Examination of matters of gender obviously can help to illuminate literary works, but it should be added, too, that some—perhaps most—critics write also as activists, reporting their findings not only to help us to understand and to enjoy the works of (say) Whitman, but also to change society's view of sexuality. Thus, in *Disseminating Whitman* (1991), Michael Moon is impatient with earlier critical rhapsodies about Whitman's universalism. It used to be said that Whitman's celebration of the male body was a sexless celebration of brotherly love in a democracy, but the gist of Moon's view is that we must neither whitewash Whitman's poems with such high-minded talk nor reject them as indecent; rather, we must see exactly what Whitman is saying about a kind of experience that society had shut its eyes to, and we must take Whitman's view seriously. Somewhat similarly, Gregory Woods in *Articulate Flesh* (1987) points out that until a few years ago discussions of Hart Crane regularly condemned his homosexuality, as is evident, for instance, in L. S. Dembo's characterization of Crane (quoted by Woods) as "uneducated, alcoholic, homosexual, paranoid, suicidal" (140). Gay and lesbian writers don't adopt this sort of manner. But it should also be pointed out that today there are straight critics who study lesbian or gay authors and write about them insightfully and without hostility.

One assumption in much lesbian and gay critical writing is that although gender greatly influences the ways in which we read, reading is a skill that can be learned, and therefore straight people—aided by lesbian and gay critics—can learn to read, with pleasure and profit, lesbian and gay writers. This assumption of course also underlies much feminist criticism, which often assumes that men must stop ignoring books by women and must learn (with the help of feminist critics) how to read them, and, in fact, how to read—with newly opened eyes— the sexist writings of men of the past and present.

In addition to the titles mentioned earlier concerning gay and lesbian criticism, consult Eve Kosofsky Sedgwick, *Between Men: English Literature and Male Homosocial Desire* (1985), and an essay by Sedgwick, "Gender Criticism," in *Redrawing the Boundaries,* ed. Stephen Greenblatt and Giles Gunn (1992).

While many in the field of lesbian and gay criticism have turned their energies toward examining the effects that an author's—or a character's—sexual identity may have upon the text, others have begun to question, instead, the concept of sexual identity itself.[1] Drawing upon the work of the French social historian Michel Foucault, critics such as David Halperin (*One Hundred Years of Homosexuality and Other Essays on Greek Love* [1990]) and Judith Butler (*Gender Trouble* [1989]) explore how various categories of identity, such as "heterosexual" and "homosexual," represent ways of defining human beings that are distinct to particular cultures and historical periods. These critics, affiliated with what is known as the social constructionist school of thought, argue that the way a given society (modern American, for instance, or ancient Greek) interprets sexuality will determine the particular categories within which individuals come to understand and to name their own desires. For such critics the goal of a lesbian or gay criticism is not to define the specificity of a lesbian or gay literature or mode of interpretations, but to show how the ideology, the normative understanding, of a given culture makes it seem natural to think about sexuality in terms of such identities as lesbian, gay, bisexual, or straight. By challenging

---

[1] This paragraph and the next two are by Lee Edelman of Tufts University.

the authority of those terms, or "denaturalizing" them, and by calling attention to moments in which literary (and nonliterary) representations make assumptions that reinforce the supposed inevitability of those distinctions, such critics attempt to redefine our understandings of the relations between sexuality and literature. They hope, in short, to make clear that sexuality is always, in a certain sense, "literary"; it is a representation of a fiction that society has constructed in order to make sense out of experience.

Because such critics have challenged the authority of the opposition between heterosexuality and homosexuality, and have read it as a historical construct rather than as a biological or psychological absolute, they have sometimes resisted the very terms *lesbian* and *gay*. Many now embrace what is called queer theory as an attempt to mark their resistance to the categories of identity they see our culture as imposing upon us.

Works written within this mode of criticism are often influenced by deconstructionist or psychoanalytic thought. They examine works by straight authors as frequently as they do works by writers who might be defined as lesbian or gay. Eve Kosofky Sedgwick's reading of *Billy Budd* in her book *Epistemology of the Closet* (1990) provides a good example of this sort of criticism. Reading Claggart as "the homosexual" in the text of Melville's novella, Sedgwick is not interested in defining his difference from other characters. Instead, she shows how the novella sets up a large number of oppositions—such as public and private, sincerity and sentimentality, health and illness—all of which have a relationship to the way in which a distinct "gay" identity was being produced by American society at the end of the nineteenth century. Other critics whose work in this field may be useful for students of literature are D. A. Miller, *The Novel and the Police* (1988); Diana Fuss, *Essentially Speaking* (1989) and *Identification Papers* (1995); Judith Butler, *Bodies that Matter* (1993); and Lee Edelman, *Homographesis: Essays in Gay Literary and Cultural Theory* (1993).

In this book, works that concern gay or lesbian experience include those by A. E. Housman, Gloria Naylor, Adrienne Rich, Walt Whitman, and Oscar Wilde.

This chapter began by making the obvious point that all readers, whether or not they consciously adopt a particular approach to literature, necessarily read through particular lenses. More precisely, a reader begins with a frame of interpretation—historical, psychological, sociological, or whatever—and from within the frame selects one of the several competing methodologies. Critics often make great—even grandiose—claims for their approaches. For example, Frederic Jameson, a Marxist, begins *The Political Unconscious: Narrative as a Socially Symbolic Act* (1981) thus:

> This book will argue the priority of the political interpretation of literary texts. It conceives of the political perspective not as some supplemental method, not as an optional auxiliary to other interpretive methods current today—the psychoanalytic or the myth-critical, the stylistic, the ethical, the structural—but rather as the absolute horizon of all reading and all interpretation. (7)

Readers who are chiefly interested in politics may be willing to assume "the priority of the political interpretation . . . as the absolute horizon of all reading and all interpretation," but other readers may respectfully decline to accept this assumption.

In talking about a critical approach, sometimes the point is made by saying that readers decode a text by applying a grid to it; the grid enables them to see certain things clearly. Good; but what is sometimes forgotten is that (since there is no such thing as a free lunch) a lens or a grid—an angle of vision or interpretive frame and a methodology—also prevents a reader from seeing certain other things. This is to be expected. What is important, then, is to remember this fact, and thus not to deceive ourselves by thinking that our keen tools enable us to see the whole. A psychoanalytic reading of, say, *Hamlet* may be helpful, but it does not reveal all that is in *Hamlet,* and it does not refute the perceptions of another approach, let's say a historical study. Each approach may illuminate aspects neglected by others.

It is too much to expect a reader to apply all useful methods (or even several) at once—that would be rather like looking through a telescope with one eye and through a microscope with the other—but it is not too much to expect readers to be aware of the limitations of their methods. If one reads much criticism, one finds two kinds of critics. There are, on the one hand, critics who methodically and mechanically peer through a lens or grid, and they of course find what one can easily predict they will find. On the other hand, there are critics who (despite what may be inevitable class and gender biases) are at least relatively open-minded in their approach—critics who, one might say, do not at the outset of their reading believe that their method assures them that (so to speak) they have got the text's number and that by means of this method they will expose the text for what it is. The philosopher Richard Rorty engagingly makes a distinction somewhat along these lines, in an essay he contributed to Umberto Eco's *Interpretation and Overinterpretation* (1992). There is a great difference, Rorty suggests,

> between knowing what you want to get out of a person or thing or text in advance and [on the other hand] hoping that the person or thing or text will help you want something different—that he or she or it will help you to change your purposes, and thus to change your life. This distinction, I think, helps us highlight the difference between methodical and inspired readings of texts. (106)

Rorty goes on to say he has seen an anthology of readings on Conrad's *Heart of Darkness,* containing a psychoanalytic reading, a reader-response reading, and so on. "None of the readers had, as far as I could see," Rorty says,

> been enraptured or destabilized by *Heart of Darkness.* I got no sense that the book had made a big difference to them, that they cared much about Kurtz or Marlow or the woman "with helmeted head and tawny cheeks" whom Marlow sees on the bank of the river. These people, and that book, had no more changed these readers' purposes than the specimen under the microscope changes the purpose of the histologist. (107)

The kind of criticism that Rorty prefers he calls "unmethodical" criticism and "inspired" criticism. It is, for Rorty, the result of an "encounter" with some aspect of a work of art "which has made a difference to the critic's conception of who she is, what she is good for, what she wants to do with herself . . ." (107). This is not a matter of "respect" for the text, Rorty insists. Rather, he says, "love" and "hate" are better words, "for a great love or a great loathing is the sort of thing that changes us by changing our purposes, changing the uses to which we shall put people and things and texts we encounter later" (107).

SUGGESTIONS FOR FURTHER READING

Because a massive list of titles may prove discouraging rather than helpful, it seems advisable here to give a short list of basic titles. (Titles already mentioned in this chapter—which are good places to begin—are *not* repeated in the following list.)

A good sampling of contemporary criticism (60 or so essays or chapters from books), representing all of the types discussed in this commentary except lesbian and gay criticism, can be found in *The Critical Tradition: Classic Texts and Contemporary Trends,* ed. David H. Richter (1989).

For a readable introduction to various approaches, written for students who are beginning the study of literary theory, see Steven Lynn, *Texts and Contexts* (1994). For a more advanced survey, that is, a work that assumes some familiarity with the material, see a short book by K. M. Newton, *Interpreting the Text: A Critical Introduction to the Theory and Practice of Literary Interpretation* (1990). A third survey, though considerably longer than the books by Lynn and Newton, is narrower because it confines itself to a study of critical writings about Shakespeare: Brian Vickers, *Appropriating Shakespeare: Contemporary Critical Quarrels* (1993), offers an astringent appraisal of deconstruction, New Historicism, psychoanalytic criticism, feminist criticism, and Marxist criticism. For a collection of essays on Shakespeare written from some of the points of view that Vickers deplores, see John Drakakis, ed., *Shakespearean Tragedy* (1992).

Sympathetic discussions (usually two or three pages long) of each approach, with fairly extensive bibliographic suggestions, are given in the appropriate articles in the four encyclopedic works by Harris, Makaryk, Groden and Kreiswirth, and Preminger and Brogan, listed on page 403, at the end of chapter 14, though only Groden and Kreiswirth (*Johns Hopkins Guide*) discuss lesbian and gay criticism (under "Gay Theory and Criticism"). For essays discussing feminist, gender, Marxist, psychoanalytic, deconstructive, New Historicist, and cultural criticism—as well as other topics not covered in this chapter—see Stephen Greenblatt and Giles Gunn, eds., *Redrawing the Boundaries: The Transformation of English and American Literary Studies* (1992).

FORMALIST CRITICISM (NEW CRITICISM)

Cleanth Brooks, *The Well Wrought Urn: Studies in the Structure of Poetry* (1947), especially chapters 1 and 11 ("The Language of Paradox" and "The Heresy of Paraphrase"); W. K. Wimsatt, *The Verbal Icon* (1954), especially "The Intentional Fallacy" and "The Affective Fallacy"; Murray Krieger, *The New Apologists for Poetry* (1956); and, for an accurate overview of a kind of criticism often misrepresented today, chapters 9-12 in volume 6 of René Wellek, *A History of Modern Criticism: 1750-1950.*

DECONSTRUCTION

Christopher Norris, *Deconstruction: Theory and Practice* (1982); Vincent B. Leitch, *Deconstructive Criticism: An Advanced Introduction and Survey* (1983); Christopher Norris, ed., *What Is Deconstruction?* (1988); Christopher Norris, *Deconstruction and the Interests of Theory* (1989).

READER-RESPONSE CRITICISM

Wolfgang Iser, *The Act of Reading: A Theory of Aesthetic Response* (1978); Wolfgang Iser, *Prospecting: From Reader Response to Literary Anthropology* (1993); Susan Sulleiman and Inge Crossman, eds., *The Reader in the Text* (1980); Jane P. Tompkins, ed., *Reader-Response Criticism* (1980); Norman N. Holland, *The Dynamics of Literary Response* (1973, 1989); Steven Mailloux, *Interpretive Conventions: The Reader in the Study of American Fiction* (1982).

ARCHETYPAL CRITICISM

G. Wilson Knight, *The Starlit Dome* (1941); Richard Chase, *Quest for Myth* (1949); Murray Krieger, ed., *Northrop Frye in Modern Criticism* (1966); Frank Lentricchia, *After the New Criticism* (1980).

HISTORICAL CRITICISM

For a brief survey of some historical criticism of the first half of this century, see René Wellek, *A History of Modern Criticism: 1750–1950,* volume 6, chapter 4 ("Academic Criticism"). E. M. W. Tillyard, *The Elizabethan World Picture* (1943), and Tillyard's *Shakespeare's History Plays* (1944), both of which relate Elizabethan literature to the beliefs of the age, are good examples of the historical approach.

MARXIST CRITICISM

Raymond Williams, *Marxism and Literature* (1977); Tony Bennett, *Formalism and Marxism* (1979); Lydia Sargent, ed., *Women and Revolution: A Discussion of the Unhappy Marriage of Marxism and Feminism* (1981); and for a brief survey of American Marxist writers of the 1930s and 1940s, see chapter 5 in volume 6 of René Wellek, *A History of Modern Criticism* (1986).

NEW HISTORICISM

Stephen Greenblatt, *Renaissance Self-Fashioning from More to Shakespeare* (1980), especially the first chapter; Brook Thomas, *The New Historicism: And Other Old-Fashioned Topics* (1991).

BIOGRAPHICAL CRITICISM

Leon Edel, *Literary Biography* (1957); Estelle C. Jellinek, ed., *Women's Autobiography: Essays in Criticism* (1980); James Olney, *Metaphors of Self: The Meaning of Autobiography* (1981). Among the most distinguished twentieth-century literary biographies is Richard Ellmann, *James Joyce* (1959, rev. ed. 1982).

PSYCHOLOGICAL OR PSYCHOANALYTIC CRITICISM

Edith Kurzeil and William Philips, eds., *Literature and Psychoanalysis* (1983); Maurice Charney and Joseph Reppen, eds., *Psychoanalytic Approaches to Literature and Film* (1987); Madelon Sprengnether, *The Spectral Mother: Freud, Feminism, and Psychoanalysis* (1990); Frederick Crews, *Out of My System* (1975).

GENDER CRITICISM (FEMINIST, AND LESBIAN AND GAY CRITICISM)

Gayle Greene and Coppélia Kahn, eds., *Making a Difference: Feminist Literary Criticism* (1985), including an essay by Bonnie Zimmerman on lesbian criticism; Catherine Belsey and Jane Moore, eds., *The Feminist Reader: Essays in Gender and the Politics of Literary Criticism* (1989); Toril Moi, ed., *French Feminist Thought* (1987); Elizabeth A. Flynn and Patrocinio P. Schweikart, eds., *Gender and Reading: Essays on Readers, Texts, and Contexts* (1986); Barbara Christian, *Black Feminist Criticism: Perspectives on Black Women Writers* (1985); Shoshana Felman, *What Does a Woman Want? Reading and Sexual Difference* (1993); Robert Martin, *The Homosexual Tradition in American Poetry* (1979); Henry Abelove et al., eds., *The Lesbian and Gay Studies Reader* (1993; although it has only a few essays concerning literature, it has an extensive bibliography on the topic).

A last word: If you want to read only a few pages about the nature and value of criticism, look at Helen Vendler's Introduction and The Function of Criticism in a collection of her essays, *The Music of What Happens* (1988). Vendler is aware that most criticism today is ideological—Marxist, Freudian, or whatever, and therefore concerned with the interpretation of meaning—but she is less concerned with ideology and meaning than with the causes of "the aesthetic power of the art work":

> It is natural that people under new cultural imperatives should be impelled to fasten new interpretations (from the reasonable to the fantastic) onto aesthetic objects from the past. But criticism cannot stop there. The critic may well begin, "Look at it this way for a change," but the sentence must continue, "and now don't you see it as more intelligibly beautiful and moving?" That is, if the interpretation does not reveal some hitherto occluded aspect of the aesthetic power of the art work, it is useless as art criticism (though it may be useful as cultural history or sociology or psychology or religion). (2)

PART FOUR

A Thematic
Anthology

CHAPTER 17

Parents and Children

Essays

 JOAN DIDION

Joan Didion was born in Sacramento in 1934, and she was educated at the University of California, Berkeley. She has written essays, stories, screenplays, and novels.

On Going Home

I am home for my daughter's first birthday. By "home" I do not mean the house in Los Angeles where my husband and I and the baby live, but the place where my family is, in the Central Valley of California. It is a vital although troublesome distinction. My husband likes my family but is uneasy in their house, because once there I fall into their ways, which are difficult, oblique, deliberately inarticulate, not my husband's ways. We live in dusty houses ("D-U-S-T," he once wrote with his finger on surfaces all over the house, but no one noticed it) filled with mementos quite without value to him (what could the Canton dessert plates mean to him? how could he have known about the assay scales, why should he care if he did know?), and we appear to talk exclusively about people we know who have been committed to mental hospitals, about people we know who have been booked on drunk-driving charges, and about property, particularly about property, land, price per acre and C-2 zoning and assessments and freeway access. My brother does not understand my husband's inability to perceive the advantage in the rather common real-estate transaction known as "sale-leaseback," and my husband in turn does not understand why so many of the people he hears about in my father's house have recently been committed to mental hospitals or booked on drunk-driving charges. Nor does he understand that when we talk about sale-leasebacks and right-of-way condemnations we are talking in code about the things we like best, the yellow fields and the cottonwoods and the rivers rising and falling and the mountain roads closing when the heavy snow comes in. We miss each other's points, have another drink and regard the fire. My brother refers to my husband, in his presence, as "Joan's husband." Marriage is the classic betrayal.

Or perhaps it is not any more. Sometimes I think that those of us who are now in our thirties were born into the last generation to carry the burden of "home," to find in family life the source of all tension and drama. I had by all objective accounts a "normal" and a "happy" family situation, and yet I was almost thirty years old before I could talk to my family on the telephone without crying after I had hung up. We did not fight. Nothing was wrong. And yet some nameless anxiety colored the emotional charges between me and the place that I came from. The question of whether or not you could go home again was a very real part of the sentimental and largely literary baggage with which we left home in the fifties; I suspect that it is irrelevant to the children born of the fragmentation after World War II. A few weeks ago in a San Francisco bar I saw a pretty young girl on crystal take off her clothes and dance for the cash prize in an "amateur-topless" contest. There was no particular sense of moment about this, none of the effect of romantic degradation, of "dark journey," for which my generation strives so assiduously. What sense could that girl possibly make of, say, *Long Day's Journey into Night?* Who is beside the point?

That I am trapped in this particular irrelevancy is never more apparent to me than when I am home. Paralyzed by the neurotic lassitude engendered by meeting one's past at every turn, around every corner, inside every cupboard, I go aimlessly from room to room. I decide to meet it head-on and clean out a drawer, and I spread the contents on the bed. A bathing suit I wore the summer I was seventeen. A letter of rejection from *The Nation,* an aerial photograph of the site for a shopping center my father did not build in 1954. Three teacups hand-painted with cabbage roses and signed "E. M.," my grandmother's initials. There is no final solution for letters of rejection from *The Nation* and teacups hand-painted in 1900. Nor is there any answer to snapshots of one's grandfather as a young man on skis, surveying around Donner Pass in the year 1910. I smooth out the snapshot and look into his face, and do and do not see my own. I close the drawer, and have another cup of coffee with my mother. We get along very well, veterans of a guerrilla war we never understood.

Days pass. I see no one. I come to dread my husband's evening call, not only because he is full of news of what by now seems to me our remote life in Los Angeles, people he has seen, letters which require attention, but because he asks what I have been doing, suggests uneasily that I get out, drive to San Francisco or Berkeley. Instead I drive across the river to a family graveyard. It has been vandalized since my last visit and the monuments are broken, overturned in the dry grass. Because I once saw a rattlesnake in the grass I stay in the car and listen to a country-and-Western station. Later I drive with my father to a ranch he has in the foothills. The man who runs his cattle on it asks us to the roundup, a week from Sunday, and although I know that I will be in Los Angeles I say, in the oblique way my family talks, that I will come. Once home I mention the broken monuments in the grave-yard. My mother shrugs.

5   I go to visit my great-aunts. A few of them think now that I am my cousin, or their daughter who died young. We recall an anecdote about a relative last seen in 1948, and they ask if I still like living in New York City. I have lived in Los Angeles for three years, but I say that I do. The baby is of-fered a horehound drop, and I am slipped a dollar bill "to buy a treat." Ques-tions trail off, answers are abandoned, the baby plays with the dust motes in a shaft of afternoon sun.

It is time for the baby's birthday party: a white cake, strawberry-marshmallow ice cream, a bottle of champagne saved from another party. In the evening, after she has gone to sleep, I kneel beside the crib and touch her face, where it is pressed against the slats, with mine. She is an open and trusting child, unprepared for and unaccustomed to the ambushes of family life, and perhaps it is just as well that I can offer her little of that life. I would like to give her more. I would like to promise her that she will grow up with a sense of her cousins and of rivers and of her great-grandmother's teacups, would like to pledge her a picnic on a river with fried chicken and her hair uncombed, would like to give her *home* for her birthday, but we live differ-ently now and I can promise her nothing like that. I give her a xylophone and a sundress from Madeira, and promise to tell her a funny story.

[1968]

 ## TOPICS FOR CRITICAL THINKING AND WRITING

1. Didion reveals that members of her family are difficult, inarticulate, poor housekeepers, and so forth. Do you find these revelations about her family distasteful? Would you mind seeing in print similarly unflat-tering things you had written about your own family? How might such revelations be justified? Are they justified in this essay?

2. Summarize the point of paragraph 2. Do you find Didion's speculations about the difference between her generation and succeeding genera-tions meaningful? Are they accurate for your generation?

3. Do you think that growing up necessarily involves estrangement from one's family? Explain.

 ## DAVID MASELLO

David Masello, an associate editor at Travel and Leisure, *lives in New York City.*

In My Father's House

Whenever I visit my father in Florida I surprise him. It means one less flight for him to worry about, and it also gives him a pure rush of joy that he rarely feels in days that can be filled with weather-channel reports, clipping coupons and driving to the convenience store for lottery tickets.

I am always near giddy with the anticipation of his surprise and often have to fight the impulse to let him know in advance that I am coming. This last trip I could hardly wait to drive up to the small town house he has shared for many years with his girlfriend (something of a ludicrous term, since they are both over 70) in a typical Florida development. I called him from the airport when I landed, having practiced my lines. As soon as he picked up the phone I asked, "So what do you want to do today—do we go to the beach or miniature golfing?"

"I hate to ask, but when do you have to leave?" my dad says within minutes of my arrival at his house, as he always does, and with a certain dread. His face registers a slight wince as he awaits my response. Already I could picture exactly how the final night of my stay would be. The three of us would be watching television, and at a certain point I would stand up to go back to the motel and pack for an early-morning flight. My dad would rise from his chair and retreat to the bathroom, where he would close the door and cry. His girlfriend would gently try to coax him out. As we walked to the car in the driveway he would slip me a $20 bill and begin to cry again, as would I. And so after days of constant activity and conversation, the final minutes of my visit would be in complete silence, neither of us able to compose ourselves sufficiently to utter any words.

Certain words, however, recited in a kind of litany, virtually always occur during each visit—the names of Civil War sites, with an occasional World War I battle thrown in. Since my dad's house is so small, I usually stay at a Howard Johnson motel on the beach. On the drive to the motel along a stretch of Florida gulf coast lined with vintage 1950's motels, the names spelled out in neon, I began the process of conversation that has become a routine with my father and me. Asking the rhetorical question, "You're still interested in the Civil War, right?" launches a topic he knows thoroughly and is eager to relate. "There's something about the names of the battle sites that haunts me," he says, as he has many times before. So we recite, in a kind of alternating joint mantra, the names—Shiloh, Chickamauga, Appomattox, the Wilderness, Gettysburg, Manassas. We say each name with a careful emphasis and clarity, even a poetic hush for full effect. In some ways it is our secret language, these battle site names.

5   From my motel balcony there was a view of a narrow, curving waterway that eventually led to the gulf and across which were small, appealing houses. Each was fitted with a tiny wooden dock at which a sailboat or a motorboat was moored. People could be seen hosing down their boats, sweeping patios or reclining in lawn chairs while reading newspapers. It was the kind of view that pleased my father. It was accessible, animated and reflected a certain rootedness that he has yet to feel in Florida; people lived in these houses, and collectively they became a neighborhood.

As I unpacked I put a Frank Sinatra tape into my Walkman and placed the earphones over my dad's ears. He moved a chair toward the view and began the newspaper crossword puzzle. For the first time in many months, I knew that my dad was content, that he wasn't worrying about the peculiar pain in his leg or about filling another blank day. On this visit especially, I realized how easy it was to give my father moments of real happiness.

It was also the first time in a long while that I, too, had come to Florida during a period of great happiness and change in my own life. I was beginning to fall in love with someone back in New York. It was a feeling that I must have had before. I had been in a relationship for eight years, but it had been unwinding for so long that it was difficult to recall the waves of affection and longing I now felt. A bouquet of flowers was on the dresser when I arrived in the motel room, sent by the person. So within minutes I managed to make my father exquisitely happy by simply being with him in the place where he lived. Realizing this, and knowing that I had secured love in New York where I lived, I, too, was happy.

My father has worried for years about my being alone. "Everybody gets rejected sometimes," he often says to me. He thinks that's the reason why at 35 I still don't have a girlfriend or a wife or ever talk about one. "You know I'm just kidding when I say it," my dad began what I knew how to finish, "but you'd make me the happiest man in the world if you found a nice Italian girl." I wanted to tell him so badly, right there in the motel room, with the dull clang of boat lines hitting their masts just beyond, squawking sea gulls and the occasional plop of big silver fish leaping in the waterway below, that I was in love and happy. But I couldn't, because it was another man that I loved.

I don't fault my dad for the fact that this news would trouble him deeply; there is no reason to try to radicalize him with this knowledge. The news, no matter how I presented it or whom I introduced as the man I love, would not be welcome. But I also won't lie and say that I am in love with a woman or that I'm sure I'll get married someday. I remain evasive only to the point of deceit. With the faintest strains of Sinatra's "Summer Wind" coming from the earphones my father has on and the quiet scrawl of his pencil filling in the crossword boxes, I read and reread the simple note of coded affection that came with the flowers. So much happiness was taking place in the motel room. As dusk approached, my dad and I remarked almost simultaneously on the oval-shaped silver fish that would fling themselves out of the water below, one eye, unlidded, wholly visible to us from our third-floor perch. I knew that detail would be a forever-memorable image that my dad and I would cite over and over again on each visit.

10   In the middle of my stay he overheard a phone conversation I was having in his kitchen and confronted me the next morning. Detecting a certain tenderness in my voice during the call, he asked with sudden rage, "What is there between you and that friend? Tell me, is he straight?" He began to form another question, but he was unable to complete the sentence.

In the trembling, awkward silence that followed, all had been asked and answered. My father's questions were, in fact, statements of his knowledge. We had played out our own peculiar battle and soon, while touring the sites we had mapped out that day, were back to reciting those of the Civil War.

[1994]

✏ TOPICS FOR CRITICAL THINKING AND WRITING

1. This piece appeared in *The New York Times Magazine,* where it was presented as an essay. But suppose you encountered it in a book of short stories. Would your response be different? That is, can it be (for instance) a good essay but a poor story, or vice versa?
2. What is the second question that the father is about to ask at the end of paragraph 10?

Fiction

 LUKE

Luke, the author of the third of the four Gospels, was a second-generation Christian, a fellow-worker with Paul. He probably was a Roman, though some early accounts refer to him as a Syrian; in any case, he wrote in Greek, probably composing the Gospel about A.D. *80–85. Jesus' Parable of the Prodigal Son (a parable is an extremely brief story from which a moral may be drawn) occurs only in this Gospel, in Chapter 15, verses 11–32.*

The Parable of The Prodigal Son

And he said, "A certain man had two sons: and the younger of them said to his father, 'Father, give me a portion of goods that falleth to me.' And he divided unto them his living. And not many days after, the younger son gathered all together, and took his journey into a far country, and there wasted his substance with riotous living.

"And when he had spent all, there arose a mighty famine in that land, and he began to be in want. And he went and joined himself to a citizen of that country, and he sent him into his fields to feed swine. And he would fain have filled his belly with the husks that the swine did eat: and no man gave unto him. And when he came to himself, he said, 'How many hired servants of my father's have bread enough and to spare, and I perish with hunger? I will arise and go to my father, and will say unto him, "Father, I have sinned against heaven, and before thee, and am no more worthy to be called thy son: make me as one of thy hired servants."'

"And he arose, and came to his father. But when he was yet a great way off, his father saw him, and had compassion, and ran, and fell on his neck, and kissed him. And the son said unto him, 'Father, I have sinned against heaven, and in thy sight, and am no more worthy to be called thy son.' But the father said to his servants, 'Bring forth the best robe, and put it on him, and put a ring on his hand, and shoes on his feet. And bring hither the fatted calf, and kill it, and let us eat, and be merry. For this my son was dead, and is alive again; he was lost, and is found.' And they began to be merry.

"Now his elder son was in the field, and as he came and drew nigh to the house, he heard music and dancing. And he called one of the servants, and asked what these things meant. And he said unto him 'Thy brother is come, and thy father hath killed the fatted calf, because he hath received him safe and sound.' And he was angry, and would not go in: therefore came his father out, and entreated him. And he answering said to his father 'Lo, these many years do I serve thee, neither transgressed I at any time thy commandment, and yet thou never gavest me a kid, that I might make merry with friends: but as soon as this thy son was come, which hath devoured thy living with harlots, thou hast killed for him the fatted calf.' And he said unto him, 'Son, thou art ever with me, and all that I have is thine. It was meet that we should make merry, and be glad: for this thy brother was dead, and is alive again: and was lost, and is found.'"

TOPICS FOR CRITICAL THINKING AND WRITING

1. What is the function of the older brother? Characterize him, and compare him with the younger brother.
2. Is the father foolish and sentimental? Do we approve or disapprove of his behavior at the end? Explain.

 KATE CHOPIN

Kate Chopin (1851–1904) was born into a prosperous family in St. Louis. In 1870 she married Oscar Chopin, a French-Creole businessman from Louisiana. They lived in New Orleans, where they had six children. Oscar died of malaria in 1882, and in 1884 Kate returned to St. Louis, where, living with her mother and children, she began to write fiction. She achieved a considerable reputation with her short stories, but her career as a publishing author pretty much came to an end after she published The Awakening *(1899), a novel whose sympathetic depiction of a woman who leaves her husband was much criticized.*

We reprint other stories by Chopin on pages 7, 12, and 32.

Regret

Mamzelle Aurélie possessed a good strong figure, ruddy cheeks, hair that was changing from brown to gray, and a determined eye. She wore a man's hat about the farm, and an old blue army overcoat when it was cold, and sometimes topboots.

Mamzelle Aurélie had never thought of marrying. She had never been in love. At the age of twenty she had received a proposal, which she had promptly declined, and at the age of fifty she had not yet lived to regret it.

So she was quite alone in the world, except for her dog Ponto, and the negroes who lived in her cabins and worked her crops, and the fowls, a few cows, a couple of mules, her gun (with which she shot chicken-hawks), and her religion.

One morning Mamzelle Aurélie stood upon her gallery,[1] contemplating, with arms akimbo, a small band of very small children who, to all intents and purposes, might have fallen from the clouds, so unexpected and bewildering was their coming, and so unwelcome. They were the children of her nearest neighbor, Odile, who was not such a near neighbor, after all.

5   The young woman had appeared but five minutes before, accompanied by these four children. In her arms she carried little Elodie; she dragged Ti Nomme by an unwilling hand; while Marcéline and Marcélette followed with irresolute steps.

Her face was red and disfigured from tears and excitement. She had been summoned to a neighboring parish by the dangerous illness of her mother; her husband was away in Texas—it seemed to her a million miles away; and Valsin was waiting with the mule-cart to drive her to the station.

[1]porch

"It's no question, Mamzelle Aurélie; you jus' got to keep those young-sters fo' me tell I come back. Dieu sait, I would n' botha you with 'em if it was any otha way to do! Make 'em mine you, Mamzelle Aurélie; don' spare 'em. Me, there, I'm half crazy between the chil'ren, an' Léon not home, an' maybe not even to fine po' maman alive encore!"[2]—a harrowing possibility which drove Odile to take a final hasty and convulsive leave of her discon-solate family.

She left them crowded into the narrow strip of shade on the porch of the long, low house; the white sunlight was beating in on the white old boards; some chickens were scratching in the grass at the foot of the steps, and one had boldly mounted, and was stepping heavily, solemnly, and aim-lessly across the gallery. There was a pleasant odor of pinks in the air, and the sound of negroes' laughter was coming across the flowering cotton-field.

Mamzelle Aurélie stood contemplating the children. She looked with a critical eye upon Marcéline, who had been left staggering beneath the weight of the chubby Elodie. She surveyed with the same calculating air Marcélette mingling her silent tears with the audible grief and rebellion of Ti Nomme. During those few contemplative moments she was collecting her-self, determining upon a line of action which should be identical with a line of duty. She began by feeding them.

10   If Mamzelle Aurélie's responsibilities might have begun and ended there, they could easily have been dismissed; for her larder was amply pro-vided against an emergency of this nature. But little children are not little pigs; they require and demand attentions which were wholly unexpected by Mamzelle Aurélie, and which she was ill prepared to give.

She was, indeed, very inapt in her management of Odile's children dur-ing the first few days. How could she know that Marcélette always wept when spoken to in a loud and commanding tone of voice? It was a peculiar-ity of Marcélette's. She became acquainted with Ti Nomme's passion for flowers only when he had plucked all the choicest gardenias and pinks for the apparent purpose of critically studying their botanical construction.

" 'Tain't enough to tell 'im, Mamzelle Aurélie," Marcéline instructed her; "you got to tie 'im in a chair. It's w'at maman all time do w'en he's bad: she tie 'im in a chair." The chair in which Mamzelle Aurélie tied Ti Nomme was roomy and comfortable, and he seized the opportunity to take a nap in it, the afternoon being warm.

At night, when she ordered them one and all to bed as she would have shooed the chickens into the hen-house, they stayed uncomprehending be-fore her. What about the little white nightgowns that had to be taken from the pillow-slip in which they were brought over, and shaken by some strong hand till they snapped like ox-whips? What about the tub of water which had to be brought and set in the middle of the floor, in which the little tired, dusty, sunbrowned feet had every one to be washed sweet and clean? And it made Marcéline and Marcélette laugh merrily—the idea that Mamzelle Aurélie should for a moment have believed that Ti Nomme could fall asleep without being told the story of *Croquemitaine* or *Loup-garou,* or both; or that Elodie could fall asleep at all without being rocked and sung to.

[2]again

"I tell you, Aunt Ruby," Mamzelle Aurélie informed her cook in confidence; "me, I'd rather manage a dozen plantation' than fo' chil'ren. It's terrassent! Bonté![3] Don't talk to me about chil'ren!"

15   " 'Tain' ispected sich as you would know airy thing 'bout 'em, Mamzelle Aurélie. I see dat plainly yistiddy w'en I spy dat li'le chile playin' wid yo' baskit o' keys. You don' know dat makes chillun grow up hard-headed, to play wid keys? Des like it make 'em teeth hard to look in a lookin'-glass. Them's the things you got to know in the raisin' an' manigement o' chillun."

Mamzelle Aurélie certainly did not pretend or aspire to such subtle and far-reaching knowledge on the subject as Aunt Ruby possessed, who had "raised five an' bared (buried) six" in her day. She was glad enough to learn a few little mother-tricks to serve the moment's need.

Ti Nomme's sticky fingers compelled her to unearth white aprons that she had not worn for years, and she had to accustom herself to his moist kisses—the expressions of an affectionate and exuberant nature. She got down her sewing-basket, which she seldom used, from the top shelf of the armoire, and placed it within the ready and easy reach which torn slips and buttonless waists demanded. It took her some days to become accustomed to the laughing, the crying, the chattering that echoed through the house and around it all day long. And it was not the first or the second night that she could sleep comfortably with little Elodie's hot, plump body pressed close against her, and the little one's warm breath beating her cheek like the fanning of a bird's wing.

But at the end of two weeks Mamzelle Aurélie had grown quite used to these things, and she no longer complained.

It was also at the end of two weeks that Mamzelle Aurélie, one evening, looking away toward the crib where the cattle were being fed, saw Valsin's blue cart turning the bend of the road. Odile sat beside the mulatto, upright and alert. As they drew near, the young woman's beaming face indicated that her homecoming was a happy one.

20   But this coming, unannounced and unexpected, threw Mamzelle Aurélie into a flutter that was almost agitation. The children had to be gathered. Where was Ti Nomme? Yonder in the shed, putting an edge on his knife at the grindstone. And Marcéline and Marcélette? Cutting and fashioning doll-rags in the corner of the gallery. As for Elodie, she was safe enough in Mamzelle Aurélie's arms; and she had screamed with delight at sight of the familiar blue cart which was bringing her mother back to her.

The excitement was all over, and they were gone. How still it was when they were gone! Mamzelle Aurélie stood upon the gallery, looking and listening. She could no longer see the cart; the red sunset and the blue-gray twilight had together flung a purple mist across the fields and road that hid it from her view. She could no longer hear the wheezing and creaking of its wheels. But she could still faintly hear the shrill, glad voices of the children.

She turned into the house. There was much work awaiting her, for the children had left a sad disorder behind them; but she did not at once set about the task of righting it. Mamzelle Aurélie seated herself beside the table. She gave one slow glance through the room, into which the evening shadows were creeping and deepening around her solitary figure. She let

[3]It's terrifying. Well!

her head fall down upon her bended arm, and began to cry. Oh, but she cried! Not softly, as women often do. She cried like a man, with sobs that seemed to tear her very soul. She did not notice Ponto licking her hand.

[1894]

TOPICS FOR CRITICAL THINKING AND WRITING

1. What does Mamzelle Aurélie look like? How does she dress? What attitude does Chopin have toward Mamzelle Aurélie's appearance?
2. What do we know of the setting? When does the story begin, and when does it end? In what ways does Chopin use the setting to present her story?
3. Mamzelle Aurélie's cook and, of course, the children's mother react to the children. Compare the ways they react with Mamzelle Aurélie's reaction.
4. How does Mamzelle Aurélie treat the children at the start of the story? Look, for example, at paragraph 9. What words seem to you to be the most prominent? What other paragraphs strike you as evidence as the story moves through its middle and conclusion?
5. At the end of the story, Mamzelle Aurélie sits at her table and weeps. What does she weep for? Do you think that she regrets not having married? In a paragraph tell us what you believe Chopin wants us to understand.

 FRANK O'CONNOR

"Frank O'Connor" was the pen name of Michael O'Donovan (1903-66), who was born in Cork, Ireland. Poverty compelled his family to take him out of school after the fourth grade. He worked at odd jobs and then, during "the troubles"—the armed conflict of 1918-21 that led to the establishment (1922) of the Irish Free State—he served in the Irish Republican Army, fighting the British, until he was captured. After his release from prison he worked as a librarian and as a director (1935-39) of the Abbey Theatre in Dublin. Still later, in the 1950s, he lived in the United States, teaching at Northwestern University and Harvard University.

Among his books—stories, novels, autobiographies, plays, translations of Gaelic poetry, and criticism—is The Lonely Voice, *a study of the short story.*

My Oedipus Complex

Father was in the army all through the war—the first war, I mean—so, up to the age of five, I never saw much of him, and what I saw did not worry me. Sometimes I woke and there was a big figure in khaki peering down at me in the candlelight. Sometimes in the early morning I heard the slamming of the front door and the clatter of nailed boots down the cobbles of the lane. These were Father's entrances and exits. Like Santa Claus he came and went mysteriously.

In fact, I rather liked his visits, though it was an uncomfortable squeeze between Mother and him when I got into the big bed in the early morning. He smoked, which gave him a pleasant musty smell, and shaved, an operation of astounding interest. Each time he left a trail of souvenirs—model tanks and Gurkha knives with handles made of bullet cases, and German helmets and cap badges and button-sticks, and all sorts of military equipment—carefully stowed away in a long box on top of the wardrobe, in case they ever came in handy. There was a bit of the magpie about Father; he expected everything to come in handy. When his back was turned, Mother let me get a chair and rummage through his treasures. She didn't seem to think so highly of them as he did.

The war was the most peaceful period of my life. The window of my attic faced southeast. My mother had curtained it, but that had small effect. I always woke with the first light and, with all the responsibilities of the previous day melted, feeling myself rather like the sun, ready to illumine and rejoice. Life never seemed so simple and clear and full of responsibilities as then. I put my feet out from under the clothes—I called them Mrs. Left and Mrs. Right—and invented dramatic situations for them in which they discussed the problems of the day. At least Mrs. Right did; she was very demonstrative, but I hadn't the same control of Mrs. Left, so she mostly contented herself with nodding agreement.

They discussed what Mother and I should do during the day, what Santa Claus should give a fellow for Christmas, and what steps should be taken to brighten the home. There was that little matter of the baby, for instance. Mother and I could never agree about that. Ours was the only house in the terrace without a new baby, and Mother said we couldn't afford one till Father came back from the war because they cost seventeen and six. That showed how simple she was. The Geneys up the road had a baby, and everyone knew they couldn't afford seventeen and six. It was probably a cheap baby, and Mother wanted something really good, but I felt she was too exclusive. The Geneys' baby would have done us fine.

5   Having settled my plans for the day, I got up, put a chair under the attic window, and lifted the frame high enough to stick out my head. The window overlooked the front gardens of the terrace behind ours, and beyond these it looked over a deep valley to the tall, red-brick houses terraced up the opposite hillside, which were all still in shadow, while those at our side of the valley were all lit up, though with long strange shadows that made them seem unfamiliar; rigid and painted.

After that I went into Mother's room and climbed into the big bed. She woke and I began to tell her of my schemes. By this time, though I never seem to have noticed it, I was petrified in my nightshirt, and I thawed as I talked until, the last frost melted, I fell asleep beside her and woke again only when I heard her below in the kitchen, making the breakfast.

After breakfast we went into town, heard Mass at St. Augustine's and said a prayer for Father, and did the shopping. If the afternoon was fine we either went for a walk in the country or a visit to Mother's great friend in the convent, Mother St. Dominic. Mother had them all praying for Father, and every night, going to bed, I asked God to send him back safe from the war to us. Little, indeed, did I know what I was praying for!

One morning, I got into the big bed, and there, sure enough, was Father in his usual Santa Claus manner, but later, instead of uniform, he put on his best blue suit, and Mother was as pleased as anything. I saw nothing to be pleased about, because, out of uniform, Father was altogether less interesting, but she only beamed, and explained that our prayers had been answered, and off we went to Mass to thank God for having brought Father safely home.

The irony of it! That very day when he came in to dinner he took off his boots and put on his slippers, donned the dirty old cap he wore about the house to save him from colds, crossed his legs, and began to talk gravely to Mother, who looked anxious. Naturally, I disliked her looking anxious, because it destroyed her good looks, so I interrupted him.

10   "Just a moment, Larry!" she said gently.

This was only what she said when we had boring visitors, so I attached no importance to it and went on talking.

"Do be quiet, Larry!" she said impatiently. "Don't you hear me talking to Daddy?"

This was the first time I had heard those ominous words, "talking to Daddy," and I couldn't help feeling that if this was how God answered prayers, he couldn't listen to them very attentively.

"Why are you talking to Daddy?" I asked with as great a show of indifference as I could muster.

15   "Because Daddy and I have business to discuss. Now, don't interrupt again!"

In the afternoon, at Mother's request, Father took me for a walk. This time we went into town instead of out to the country, and I thought at first, in my usual optimistic way, that it might be an improvement. It was nothing of the sort. Father and I had quite different notions of a walk in town. He had no proper interest in trams, ships, and horses, and the only thing that seemed to divert him was talking to fellows as old as himself. When I wanted to stop he simply went on, dragging me behind him by the hand; when he wanted to stop I had no alternative but to do the same. I noticed that it seemed to be a sign that he wanted to stop for a long time whenever he leaned against a wall. The second time I saw him do it I got wild. He seemed to be settling himself forever. I pulled him by the coat and trousers, but, unlike Mother who, if you were too persistent, got into a wax and said: "Larry, if you don't behave yourself, I'll give you a good slap," Father had an extraordinary capacity for amiable inattention. I sized him up and wondered would I cry, but he seemed to be too remote to be annoyed even by that. Really, it was like going for a walk with a mountain! He either ignored the wrenching and pummeling entirely, or else glanced down with a grin of amusement from his peak. I had never met anyone so absorbed in himself as he seemed.

At teatime, "talking to Daddy" began again, complicated this time by the fact that he had an evening paper, and every few minutes he put it down and told Mother something new out of it. I felt this was foul play. Man for man, I was prepared to compete with him any time for Mother's attention, but when he had it all made up for him by other people it left me no chance. Several times I tried to change the subject without success.

"You must be quiet while Daddy is reading, Larry," Mother said impatiently.

It was clear that she either genuinely liked talking to Father better than talking to me, or else that he had some terrible hold on her which made her afraid to admit the truth.

20   "Mummy," I said that night when she was tucking me up, "do you think if I prayed hard God would send Daddy back to the war?"

She seemed to think about that for a moment.

"No, dear," she said with a smile. "I don't think he would."

"Why wouldn't he, Mummy?"

"Because there isn't a war any longer, dear."

25   "But, Mummy, couldn't God make another war, if he liked?"

"He wouldn't like to, dear. It's not God who makes wars, but bad people."

"Oh!" I said.

I was disappointed about that. I began to think that God wasn't quite what he was cracked up to be.

Next morning I woke at my usual hour, feeling like a bottle of champagne. I put out my feet and invented a long conversation in which Mrs. Right talked of the trouble she had with her own father till she put him in the Home. I didn't quite know what the Home was but it sounded the right place for Father. Then I got my chair and stuck my head out of the attic window. Dawn was just breaking, with a guilty air that made me feel I had caught it in the act. My head bursting with stories and schemes, I stumbled in next door, and in the half-darkness scrambled into the big bed. There was no room at Mother's side so I had to get between her and Father. For the time being I had forgotten about him, and for several minutes I sat bolt upright, racking my brains to know what I could do with him. He was taking up more than his fair share of the bed, and I couldn't get comfortable, so I gave him several kicks that made him grunt and stretch. He made room all right, though. Mother waked and felt for me. I settled back comfortably in the warmth of the bed with my thumb in my mouth.

30   "Mummy!" I hummed, loudly and contentedly.

"Sssh! dear," she whispered. "Don't wake Daddy!"

This was a new development, which threatened to be even more serious than "talking to Daddy." Life without my early-morning conferences was unthinkable.

"Why?" I asked severely.

"Because poor Daddy is tired."

35   This seemed to me a quite inadequate reason, and I was sickened by the sentimentality of her "poor Daddy." I never liked that sort of gush; it always struck me as insincere.

"Oh!" I said lightly. Then in my most winning tone: "Do you know where I want to go with you today, Mummy?"

"No, dear," she sighed.

"I want to go down the Glen and fish for thornybacks with my new net, and then I want to go out to the Fox and Hounds, and—"

"Don't-wake-Daddy!" she hissed angrily, clapping her hand across my mouth.

40   But it was too late. He was awake, or nearly so. He grunted and reached for the matches. Then he stared incredulously at his watch.

"Like a cup of tea, dear?" asked Mother in a meek, hushed voice I had never heard her use before. It sounded almost as though she were afraid.

"Tea?" he exclaimed indignantly. "Do you know what the time is?"

"And after that I want to go up the Rathcooney Road," I said loudly, afraid I'd forget something in all those interruptions.

"Go to sleep at once, Larry!" she said sharply.

45   I began to snivel. I couldn't concentrate, the way that pair went on, and smothering my early-morning schemes was like burying a family from the cradle.

Father said nothing, but lit his pipe and sucked it, looking out into the shadows without minding Mother or me. I knew he was mad. Every time I made a remark Mother hushed me irritably. I was mortified. I felt it wasn't fair; there was even something sinister in it. Every time I had pointed out to her the waste of making two beds when we could both sleep in one, she had told me it was healthier like that, and now here was this man, this stranger, sleeping with her without the least regard for her health!

He got up early and made tea, but though he brought Mother a cup he brought none for me.

"Mummy," I shouted, "I want a cup of tea, too."

"Yes, dear," she said patiently. "You can drink from Mummy's saucer."

50   That settled it. Either Father or I would have to leave the house. I didn't want to drink from Mother's saucer; I wanted to be treated as an equal in my own home, so, just to spite her, I drank it all and left none for her. She took that quietly, too.

But that night when she was putting me to bed she said gently:

"Larry, I want you to promise me something."

"What is it?" I asked.

"Not to come in and disturb poor Daddy in the morning. Promise?"

55   "Poor Daddy" again! I was becoming suspicious of everything involving that quite impossible man.

"Why?" I asked.

"Because poor Daddy is worried and tired and he doesn't sleep well."

"Why doesn't he, Mummy?"

"Well, you know, don't you, that while he was at the war Mummy got the pennies from the Post Office?"

60   "From Miss MacCarthy?"

"That's right. But now, you see, Miss MacCarthy hasn't any more pennies, so Daddy must go out and find us some. You know what would happen if he couldn't?"

"No," I said, "tell us."

"Well, I think we might have to go out and beg for them like the poor old woman on Fridays. We wouldn't like that, would we?"

"No," I agreed. "We wouldn't."

65   "So you'll promise not to come in and wake him?"

"Promise."

Mind you, I meant that. I knew pennies were a serious matter, and I was all against having to go out and beg like the old woman on Fridays. Mother laid out all my toys in a complete ring round the bed so that, whatever way I got out, I was bound to fall over one of them.

When I woke I remembered my promise all right. I got up and sat on the floor and played—for hours, it seemed to me. Then I got my chair and looked out the attic window for more hours. I wished it was time for Father to wake; I wished someone would make me a cup of tea. I didn't feel in the least like the sun; instead, I was bored and so very, very cold! I simply longed for the warmth and depth of the big featherbed.

At last I could stand it no longer. I went into the next room. As there was still no room at Mother's side I climbed over her and she woke with a start.

70   "Larry," she whispered, gripping my arm very tightly, "what did you promise?"

"But I did, Mummy," I wailed, caught in the very act. "I was quiet for ever so long."

"Oh, dear, and you're perished!" she said sadly, feeling me all over. "Now, if I let you stay will you promise not to talk?"

"But I want to talk, Mummy," I wailed.

"That has nothing to do with it," she said with a firmness that was new to me. "Daddy wants to sleep. Now, do you understand that?"

75   I understood it only too well. I wanted to talk, he wanted to sleep—whose house was it, anyway?

"Mummy," I said with equal firmness, "I think it would be healthier for Daddy to sleep in his own bed."

That seemed to stagger her, because she said nothing for a while.

"Now, once for all," she went on, "you're to be perfectly quiet or go back to your own bed. Which is it to be?"

The injustice of it got me down. I had convicted her out of her own mouth of inconsistency and unreasonableness, and she hadn't even attempted to reply. Full of spite, I gave Father a kick, which she didn't notice but which made him grunt and open his eyes in alarm.

80   "What time is it?" he asked in a panic-stricken voice, not looking at Mother but the door, as if he saw someone there.

"It's early yet," she replied soothingly. "It's only the child. Go to sleep again. . . . Now, Larry," she added, getting out of bed, "you've wakened Daddy and you must go back."

This time, for all her quiet air, I knew she meant it, and knew that my principal rights and privileges were as good as lost unless I asserted them at once. As she lifted me, I gave a screech, enough to wake the dead, not to mind Father. He groaned.

"That damn child! Doesn't he ever sleep?"

"It's only a habit, dear," she said quietly, though I could see she was vexed.

85   "Well, it's time he got out of it," shouted Father, beginning to heave in the bed. He suddenly gathered all the bedclothes about him, turned to the wall, and then looked back over his shoulder with nothing showing only two small, spiteful, dark eyes. The man looked very wicked.

To open the bedroom door, Mother had to let me down, and I broke free and dashed for the farthest corner, screeching. Father sat bolt upright in bed.

"Shut up, you little puppy!" he said in a choking voice.

I was so astonished that I stopped screeching. Never, never had anyone spoken to me in that tone before. I looked at him incredulously and saw his face convulsed with rage. It was only then that I fully realized how God had codded me, listening to my prayers for the safe return of this monster.

"Shut up, you!" I bawled, beside myself.

90   "What's that you said?" shouted Father, making a wild leap out of bed.

"Mick, Mick!" cried Mother. "Don't you see the child isn't used to you?"

"I see he's better fed than taught," snarled Father, waving his arms wildly. "He wants his bottom smacked."

All his previous shouting was as nothing to these obscene words referring to my person. They really made my blood boil.

"Smack your own!" I screamed hysterically. "Smack your own! Shut up! Shut up!"

95   At this he lost his patience and let fly at me. He did it with the lack of conviction you'd expect of a man under Mother's horrified eyes, and it ended up as a mere tap, but the sheer indignity of being struck at all by a stranger, a total stranger who had cajoled his way back from the war into our big bed as a result of my innocent intercession, made me completely dotty. I shrieked and shrieked, and danced in my bare feet, and Father, looking awkward and hairy in nothing but a short gray army shirt, glared down at me like a mountain out for murder. I think it must have been then that I realized he was jealous too. And there stood Mother in her nightdress, looking as if her heart was broken between us. I hoped she felt as she looked. It seemed to me that she deserved it all.

From that morning out my life was a hell. Father and I were enemies, open and avowed. We conducted a series of skirmishes against one another, he trying to steal my time with Mother and I his. When she was sitting on my bed, telling me a story, he took to looking for some pair of old boots which he alleged he had left behind him at the beginning of the war. While he talked to Mother I played loudly with my toys to show my total lack of concern. He created a terrible scene one evening when he came in from work and found me at his box, playing with his regimental badges, Gurkha knives and button-sticks. Mother got up and took the box from me.

"You mustn't play with Daddy's toys unless he lets you, Larry," she said severely. "Daddy doesn't play with yours."

For some reason Father looked at her as if she had struck him and then turned away with a scowl.

"Those are not toys," he growled, taking down the box again to see had I lifted anything. "Some of those curios are very rare and valuable."

100   But as time went on I saw more and more how he managed to alienate Mother and me. What made it worse was that I couldn't grasp his method or see what attraction he had for Mother. In every possible way he was less winning than I. He had a common accent and made noises at his tea. I thought for a while that it might be the newspapers she was interested in, so I made up bits of news of my own to read to her. Then I thought it might be the smoking, which I personally thought attractive, and took his pipes and went round the house dribbling into them till he caught me. I even made noises at my tea, but Mother only told me I was disgusting. It all seemed to hinge round that unhealthy habit of sleeping together, so I made a point of dropping into their bedroom and nosing round, talking to myself, so that they wouldn't know I was watching them, but they were never up to anything that I could see. In the end it beat me. It seemed to depend on being grown-up and giving people rings, and I realized I'd have to wait.

But at the same time I wanted him to see that I was only waiting, not giving up the fight. One evening when he was being particularly obnoxious, chattering away well above my head, I let him have it.

"Mummy," I said, "do you know what I'm going to do when I grow up?"

"No, dear," she replied. "What?"

"I'm going to marry you," I said quietly.

105   Father gave a great guffaw out of him, but he didn't take me in. I knew it must only be pretense. And Mother, in spite of everything, was pleased. I felt she was probably relieved to know that one day Father's hold on her would be broken.

"Won't that be nice?" she said with a smile.

"It'll be very nice," I said confidently. "Because we're going to have lots and lots of babies."

"That's right, dear," she said placidly. "I think we'll have one soon, and then you'll have plenty of company."

I was no end pleased about that because it showed that in spite of the way she gave in to Father she still considered my wishes. Besides, it would put the Geneys in their place.

110   It didn't turn out like that, though. To begin with, she was very preoc-cupied—I supposed about where she would get the seventeen and six—and though Father took to staying out late in the evenings it did me no particular good. She stopped taking me for walks, became as touchy as blazes, and smacked me for nothing at all. Sometimes I wished I'd never mentioned the confounded baby—I seemed to have a genius for bringing calamity on my-self.

And calamity it was! Sonny arrived in the most appalling hullabaloo—even that much he couldn't do without a fuss—and from the first moment I disliked him. He was a difficult child—so far as I was concerned he was al-ways difficult—and demanded far too much attention. Mother was simply silly about him, and couldn't see when he was only showing off. As com-pany he was worse than useless. He slept all day, and I had to go round the house on tiptoe to avoid waking him. It wasn't any longer a question of not waking Father. The slogan now was "Don't-wake-Sonny!" I couldn't under-stand why the child wouldn't sleep at the proper time, so whenever Mother's back was turned I woke him. Sometimes to keep him awake I pinched him as well. Mother caught me at it one day and gave me a most un-merciful flaking.

One evening, when Father was coming in from work, I was playing trains in the front garden. I let on not to notice him; instead, I pretended to be talking to myself, and said in a loud voice: "If another bloody baby comes into this house, I'm going out."

Father stopped dead and looked at me over his shoulder.

"What's that you said?" he asked sternly.

115   "I was only talking to myself," I replied, trying to conceal my panic. "It's private."

He turned and went in without a word. Mind you, I intended it as a solemn warning, but its effect was quite different. Father started being quite nice to me. I could understand that, of course. Mother was quite sickening about Sonny. Even at mealtimes she'd get up and gawk at him in the cradle with an idiotic smile, and tell Father to do the same. He was always polite about it, but he looked so puzzled you could see he didn't know what she was talking about. He complained of the way Sonny cried at night, but she only got cross and said that Sonny never cried except when there was some-thing up with him—which was a flaming lie, because Sonny never had any-thing up with him, and only cried for attention. It was really painful to see how simple-minded she was. Father wasn't attractive, but he had a fine in-telligence. He saw through Sonny, and now he knew that I saw through him as well.

One night I woke with a start. There was someone beside me in the bed. For one wild moment I felt sure it must be Mother, having come to her senses and left Father for good, but then I heard Sonny in convulsions in the next room, and Mother saying: "There! There! There!" and knew it wasn't she. It was Father. He was lying beside me, wide awake, breathing hard and apparently as mad as hell.

After a while it came to me what he was mad about. It was his turn now. After turning me out of the big bed, he had been turned out himself. Mother had no consideration now for anyone but that poisonous pup, Sonny. I couldn't help feeling sorry for Father. I had been through it all myself, and even at that age I was magnanimous. I began to stroke him down and say: "There! There!" He wasn't exactly responsive.

"Aren't you asleep either?" he snarled.

120   "Ah, come on and put your arm around us, can't you?" I said, and he did, in a sort of way. Gingerly, I suppose, is how you'd describe it. He was very bony but better than nothing.

At Christmas he went out of his way to buy me a really nice model railway.

[1946]

TOPICS FOR CRITICAL THINKING AND WRITING

1. The boy is immensely egotistical. Why do we not detest him?
2. Is "My Oedipus Complex" a story or only a character sketch? Explain.
3. At the end of the piece, is the narrator still possessed by an Oedipus complex, or is he released from it? Explain. (If you don't know what an Oedipus complex is, begin by checking a dictionary or an encyclopedia.)
4. Write a narrative of 500–750 words setting forth an episode in which, resenting an apparent lack of loving attention, you sought to divert interest from a parent or sibling toward yourself. Let the reader understand your behavior from the action, not from explicit comment.

 TONI CADE BAMBARA

Toni Cade Bambara (b. 1939), was born in New York City and grew up in black districts of the city. After studying at the University of Florence and at City College in New York, where she received a master's degree, she worked for a while as a case investigator for the New York State Welfare Department. Later she directed a recreation program for hospital patients. Now that her literary reputation is established, she spends most of her time writing, though she has also served as writer in residence at Spelman College, in Atlanta.

My Man Bovanne

Blind people got a hummin jones[1] if you notice. Which is understandable completely once you been around one and notice what no eyes will force

---

[1] a need to hum

you into to see people, and you get past the first time, which seems to come out of nowhere, and it's like you in church again with fat-chest ladies and ole gents gruntin a hum low in the throat to whatever the preacher be saying. Shakey Bee bottom lip all swole up with Sweet Peach[2] and me explainin how come the sweet-potato bread was a dollar-quarter this time stead of dollar regular and he say uh hunh he understand, then he break into this *thizzin* kind of hum which is quiet, but fiercesome just the same, if you ain't ready for it. Which I wasn't. But I got used to it and the onliest time I had to say somethin bout it was when he was playin checkers on the stoop one time and he commenst to hummin quite churchy seem to me. So I says, "Look here Shakey Bee, I can't beat you and Jesus too." He stop.

So that's how come I asked My Man Bovanne to dance. He ain't my man mind you, just a nice old gent from the block that we all know cause he fixes things and the kids like him. Or used to fore Black Power got hold their minds and mess em around till they can't be civil to ole folks. So we at this benefit for my niece's cousin who's runnin for somethin with this Black party somethin or other behind her. And I press up close to dance with Bovanne who blind and I'm hummin and he hummin, chest to chest like talkin. Not jammin my breasts into the man. Wasn't bout tits. Was bout vibrations. And he dug it and asked me what color dress I had on and how my hair was fixed and how I was doin without a man, not nosy but nice-like, and who was at this affair and was the canapés dainty-stingy or healthy enough to get hold of proper. Comfy and cheery is what I'm tryin to get across. Touch talkin like the heel of the hand on the tambourine or on a drum.

But right away Joe Lee come up on us and frown for dancin so close to the man. My own son who knows what kind of warm I am about; and don't grown men all call me long distance and in the middle of the night for a little Mama comfort? But he frown. Which ain't right since Bovanne can't see and defend himself. Just a nice old man who fixes toasters and busted irons and bicycles and things and changes the lock on my door when my men friends get messy. Nice man. Which is not why they invited him. Grass roots you see. Me and Sister Taylor and the woman who does heads[3] at Mamies and the man from the barber shop, we all there on account of we grass roots. And I ain't never been souther than Brooklyn Battery and no more country than the window box on my fire escape. And just yesterday my kids tellin me to take them countrified rags off my head and be cool. And now can't get Black enough to suit 'em. So everybody passin sayin My Man Bovanne. Big deal, keep steppin and don't even stop a minute to get the man a drink or one of them cute sandwiches or tell him what's goin on. And him standin there with a smile ready case someone do speak he want to be ready. So that's how come I pull him on the dance floor and we dance squeezin past the tables and chairs and all them coats and people standin round up in each other face talkin bout this and that but got no use for this blind man who mostly fixes skates and skooters for all these folks when they were just kids. So I'm pressed up close and we touch talkin with the hum. And here come my daughter cuttin her eye at me[4] like she do when she tell me about my "apolitical" self like I got hoof and mouf disease and there ain't no hope at all. And I don't pay her no mind and just look up in Bovanne shadow face and tell him his stomach like a drum and he laugh. Laugh real

---

[2]a brand of snuff   [3]fixes hair in a beauty parlor   [4]giving me a dirty look

loud. And here come my youngest, Task, with a tap on my elbow like he the third grade monitor and I'm cuttin up on the line to assembly.

"I was just talkin on the drums," I explained when they hauled me into the kitchen. I figured drums was my best defense. They can get ready for drums what with all this heritage business. And Bovanne stomach just like that drum Task give me when he come back from Africa. You just touch it and it hum thizzm, thizzm. So I stuck to the drum story. "Just drummin that's all."

5   "Mama, what are you talkin about?"

"She had too much to drink," say Elo to Task cause she don't hardly say nuthin to me direct no more since that ugly argument about my wigs.

"Look here Mama," say Task, the gentle one. "We just trying to pull your coat. You were makin a spectacle of yourself out there dancing like that."

"Dancin like what?"

Task run a hand over his left ear like his father for the world and his father before that.

10   "Like a bitch in heat," say Elo.

"Well, uhh, I was goin to say like one of them sex-starved ladies gettin on in years and not too discriminating. Know what I mean?"

I don't answer cause I'll cry. Terrible thing when your own children talk to you like that. Pullin me out the party and hustlin me into some stranger's kitchen in the back of a bar just like the damn police. And ain't like I'm old old. I can still wear me some sleeveless dresses without the meat hanging off my arm. And I keep up with some thangs through my kids. Who ain't kids no more. To hear them tell it. So I don't say nuthin.

"Dancin with that tom," say Elo to Joe Lee, who leanin on the folks' freezer. "His feet can smell a cracker a mile away and go into their shuffle number post haste. And them eyes. He could be a little considerate and put on some shades. Who wants to look into them blown-out fuses that—"

"Is this what they call the generation gap?" I say.

15   "Generation gap," spits Elo, like I suggested castor oil and fricassee possum in the milk-shakes or somethin. "That's a white concept for a white phenomenon. There's no generation gap among Black people. We are a col—"

"Yeh, well never mind," says Joe Lee. "The point is Mama . . . well, it's pride. You embarrass yourself and us too dancin like that."

"I wasn't shame." Then nobody say nuthin. Them standin there in they pretty clothes with drinks in they hands and gangin up on me, and me in the third-degree chair and nary a olive to my name. Felt just like the police got hold to me.

"First of all," Task say, holdin up his hand and tickin off the offenses, "the dress. Now that dress is too short, Mama, and too low-cut for a woman your age. And Tamu's going to make a speech tonight to kick off the campaign and will be introducin you and expecting you to organize the council of elders—"

"Me? Didn nobody ask me nuthin. You mean Nisi? She change her name?"

20   "Well, Norton was supposed to tell you about it. Nisi wants to introduce you and then encourage the older folks to form a Council of the Elders to act as an advisory—"

"And you going to be standing there with your boobs out and that wig on your head and that hem up to your ass. And people'll say, 'Ain't that the horny bitch that was grindin with the blind dude?'"

"Elo, be cool a minute," say Task, gettin to the next finger. "And then there's the drinkin. Mama, you know you can't drink cause next thing you know you be laughin loud and carryin on," and he grab another finger for the loudness. "And then there's the dancin. You been tattooed on the man for four records straight and slow draggin even on the fast numbers. How you think that look for a woman your age?"

"What's my age?"

"What?"

25   "I'm axin you all a simple question. You keep talkin bout what's proper for a woman my age. How old am I anyhow?" And Joe Lee slams his eyes shut and squinches up his face to figure. And Task run a hand over his ear and stare into his glass like the ice cubes goin calculate for him. And Elo just starin at the top of my head like she goin rip the wig off any minute now.

"Is your hair braided up under that thing? If so, why don't you take it off? You always did do a neat cornroll."[5]

"Uh huh," cause I'm thinkin how she couldn't undo her hair fast enough talking bout cornroll so countrified. None of which was the subject. "How old, I say?"

"Sixtee-one or—"

"You a damn lie Joe Lee Peoples."

30   "And that's another thing," say Task on the fingers.

"You know what you all can kiss," I say, gettin up and brushin the wrinkles out my lap.

"Oh, Mama," Elo say, puttin a hand on my shoulder like she hasn't done since she left home and the hand landin light and not sure it supposed to be there. Which hurt me to my heart. Cause this was the child in our happiness fore Mr. Peoples die. And I carried that child strapped to my chest till she was nearly two. We was close is what I'm tryin to tell you. Cause it was more me in the child than the others. And even after Task it was the girl-child I covered in the night and wept over for no reason at all less it was she was a chub-chub like me and not very pretty, but a warm child. And how did things get to this, that she can't put a sure hand on me and say Mama we love you and care about you and you entitled to enjoy yourself cause you a good woman?

"And then there's Reverend Trent," say Task, glancin from left to right like they hatchin a plot and just now lettin me in on it. "You were suppose to be talking with him tonight, Mama, about giving us his basement for campaign headquarters and—"

"Didn nobody tell me nuthin. If grass roots mean you kept in the dark I can't use it. I really can't. And Reven Trent a fool anyway the way he tore into the widow man up there on Edgecomb cause he wouldn't take in three of them foster children and the woman not even comfy in the ground yet and the man's mind messed up and—"

[5]a hairstyle in which hair is interwoven into small braids

35   "Look here," say Task. "What we need is a family conference so we can get all this stuff cleared up and laid out on the table. In the meantime I think we better get back into the other room and tend to business. And in the meantime, Mama, see if you can't get to Reverend Trent and—"

"You want me to belly rub with the Reven, that it?"

"Oh damn," Elo say and go through the swingin door.

"We'll talk about all this at dinner. How's tomorrow night, Joe Lee?" While Joe Lee being self-important I'm wonderin who's doin the cookin and how come no body ax me if I'm free and do I get a corsage and things like that. Then Joe nod that it's O.K. and he go through the swingin door and just a little hubbub come through from the other room. Then Task smile his smile, lookin just like his daddy, and he leave. And it just me and this stranger's kitchen, which was a mess I wouldn't never let my kitchen look like. Poison you just to look at the pots. Then the door swing the other way and it's My Man Bovanne standin there sayin Miss Hazel but lookin at the deep fry and then at the steam table, and most surprised when I come up on him from the other direction and take him on out of there. Pass the folks pushin up towards the stage where Nisi and some other people settin and ready to talk, and folks gettin to the last of the sandwiches and the booze fore they settle down in one spot and listen serious. And I'm thinkin bout tellin Bovanne what a lovely long dress Nisi got on and the earrings and her hair piled up in a cone and the people bout to hear how we all gettin screwed and gotta form our own party and everybody there listenin and lookin. But instead I just haul the man on out of there, and Joe Lee and his wife look at me like I'm terrible, but they ain't said boo to the man yet. Cause he blind and old and don't nobody there need him since they grown up and don't need they skates fixed no more.

"Where we goin, Miss Hazel?" Him knowin all the time.

40   "First we gonna buy you some dark sunglasses. Then you comin with me to the supermarket so I can pick up tomorrow's dinner, which is going to be a grand thing proper and you invited. Then we going to my house."

"That be fine. I surely would like to rest my feet." Bein cute, but you got to let men play out they little show, blind or not. So he chat on bout how tired he is and how he appreciate me takin him in hand this way. And I'm thinkin I'll have him change the lock on my door first thing. Then I'll give the man a nice warm bath with jasmine leaves in the water and a little Epsom salt on the sponge to do his back. And then a good rubdown with rose water and olive oil. Then a cup of lemon tea with a taste in it. And a little talcum, some of that fancy stuff Nisi mother sent over last Christmas. And then a massage, a good face massage round the forehead which is the worrying part. Cause you gots to take care of the older folks. And let them know they still needed to run the mimeo machine and keep the spark plugs clean and fix the mailboxes for folks who might help us get the breakfast program goin, and the school for the little kids and the campaign and all. Cause old folks is the nation. That what Nisi was sayin and I mean to do my part.

"I imagine you are a very pretty woman, Miss Hazel."

"I surely am," I say just like the hussy my daughter always say I was.

[1972]

TOPICS FOR CRITICAL THINKING AND WRITING

1. If Hazel were your mother, how would you feel? Do your imagined feelings correspond to those that you felt while reading the story? If not (they probably don't), how do you explain the difference?
2. Does the author make Hazel a sympathetic figure? If so, how? If not, again, how?
3. Nisi says, "Old folks is the nation." What does she mean? What is your response to her statement?

 MAX APPLE

Max Apple was born in 1941 in Grand Rapids, Michigan, in a traditional Jewish home—he knew Yiddish before he knew English. He received a B.A. and a Ph.D. in English from the University of Michigan and has taught literature and creative writing at Rice University.

"I admit to experimenting," he has said of his stories and novels, but he adds, "I hope I've never lost sight of the most powerful question in narrative: What happens next? . . . None of the experiments can work if you don't create a character whom you care about and whom your reader can care about."

Bridging

At the Astrodome, Nolan Ryan is shaving the corners. He's going through the Giants in order. The radio announcer is not even mentioning that by the sixth the Giants haven't had a hit. The K's mount[1] on the scoreboard. Tonight Nolan passes the Big Train[2] and is now the all-time strikeout king. He's almost as old as I am and he still throws nothing but smoke. His fastball is an aspirin; batters tear their tendons lunging for his curve. Jessica and I have season tickets, but tonight she's home listening and I'm in the basement of St. Anne's Church watching Kay Randall's fingertips. Kay is holding her hands out from her chest, her fingertips on each other. Her fingers move a little as she talks and I can hear her nails click when they meet. That's how close I'm sitting.

Kay is talking about "bridging"; that's what her arched fingers represent.

"Bridging," she says, "is the way Brownies become Girl Scouts. It's a slow steady process. It's not easy, but we allow a whole year for bridging."

Eleven girls in brown shirts with red bandannas at their neck are imitating Kay as she talks. They hold their stumpy chewed fingertips out and bridge them. So do I.

5   I brought the paste tonight and the stick-on gold stars and the thread for sewing buttonholes.

[1]*K* is the symbol for a strikeout   [2]Walter Johnson (1887–1946), pitcher for the Washington Senators

"I feel a little awkward," Kay Randall said on the phone, "asking a man to do these errands . . . but that's my problem, not yours. Just bring the supplies and try to be at the church meeting room a few minutes before seven."

I arrive a half hour early.

"You're off your rocker," Jessica says. She begs me to drop her at the Astrodome on my way to the Girl Scout meeting. "After the game, I'll meet you at the main souvenir stand on the first level. They stay open an hour after the game. I'll be all right. There are cops and ushers every five yards."

She can't believe that I am missing this game to perform my functions as an assistant Girl Scout leader. Our Girl Scout battle has been going on for two months.

10   "Girl Scouts is stupid," Jessica says. "Who wants to sell cookies and sew buttons and walk around wearing stupid old badges?"

When she agreed to go to the first meeting, I was so happy I volunteered to become an assistant leader. After the meeting, Jessica went directly to the car the way she does after school, after a birthday party, after a ball game, after anything. A straight line to the car. No jabbering with girlfriends, no smiles, no dallying, just right to the car. She slides into the back seat, belts in, and braces herself for destruction. It has already happened once.

I swoop past five thousand years of stereotypes and accept my assistant leader's packet and credentials.

"I'm sure there have been other men in the movement," Kay says, "we just haven't had any in our district. It will be good for the girls."

Not for my Jessica. She won't bridge, she won't budge.

15   "I know why you're doing this," she says. "You think that because I don't have a mother, Kay Randall and the Girl Scouts will help me. That's crazy. And I know that Sharon is supposed to be like a mother too. Why don't you just leave me alone."

Sharon is Jessica's therapist. Jessica sees her twice a week. Sharon and I have a meeting once a month.

"We have a lot of shy girls," Kay Randall tells me. "Scouting brings them out. Believe me, it's hard to stay shy when you're nine years old and you're sharing a tent with six other girls. You have to count on each other, you have to communicate."

I imagine Jessica zipping up in her sleeping bag, mumbling good night to anyone who first says it to her, then closing her eyes and hating me for sending her out among the happy.

"She likes all sports, especially baseball," I tell my leader.

20   "There's room for baseball in scouting," Kay says. "Once a year the whole district goes to a game. They mention us on the big scoreboard."

"Jessica and I go to all the home games. We're real fans."

Kay smiles.

"That's why I want her in Girl Scouts. You know, I want her to go to things with her girlfriends instead of always hanging around with me at ball games."

"I understand," Kay says. "It's part of bridging."

25   With Sharon the term is "separation anxiety." That's the fastball, "bridging" is the curve. Amid all their magic words I feel as if Jessica and I are standing at home plate blindfolded.

While I await Kay and the members of Troop 111, District 6, I eye St. Anne in her grotto and St. Gregory and St. Thomas. Their hands are folded as if they started out bridging, ended up praying.

In October the principal sent Jessica home from school because Mrs. Simmons caught her in spelling class listening to the World Series through an earphone.

"It's against the school policy," Mrs. Simmons said. "Jessica understands school policy. We confiscate radios and send the child home."

"I'm glad," Jessica said. "It was a cheap-o radio. Now I can watch the TV with you."

30   They sent her home in the middle of the sixth game. I let her stay home for the seventh too.

The Brewers are her favorite American League team. She likes Rollie Fingers, and especially Robin Yount.

"Does Yount go in the hole[3] better than Harvey Kuenn used to?"

"You bet," I tell her. "Kuenn was never a great fielder but he could hit three hundred with his eyes closed."

Kuenn is the Brewers' manager. He has an artificial leg and can barely make it up the dugout steps, but when I was Jessica's age and the Tigers were my team, Kuenn used to stand at the plate, tap the corners with his bat, spit some tobacco juice, and knock liners up the alley.

35   She took the Brewers' loss hard.

"If Fingers wasn't hurt they would have squashed the Cards, wouldn't they?"

I agreed.

"But I'm glad for Andujar."

We had Andujar's autograph. Once we met him at a McDonald's. He was a relief pitcher then, an erratic right-hander. In St. Louis he improved. I was happy to get his name on a napkin. Jessica shook his hand.

40   One night after I read her a story, she said, "Daddy, if we were rich could we go to the away games too? I mean, if you didn't have to be at work every day."

"Probably we could," I said, "but wouldn't it get boring? We'd have to stay at hotels and eat in restaurants. Even the players get sick of it."

"Are you kidding?" she said. "I'd never get sick of it."

"Jessica has fantasies of being with you forever, following baseball or whatever," Sharon says. "All she's trying to do is please you. Since she lost her mother she feels that you and she are alone in the world. She doesn't want to let anyone or anything else into that unit, the two of you. She's afraid of any more losses. And, of course, her greatest worry is about losing you."

"You know," I tell Sharon, "that's pretty much how I feel too."

45   "Of course it is," she says. "I'm glad to hear you say it."

Sharon is glad to hear me say almost anything. When I complain that her $100-a-week fee would buy a lot of peanut butter sandwiches, she says she is "glad to hear me expressing my anger."

[3]when a shortstop moves to the right and backhands the ball to first or second

"Sharon's not fooling me," Jessica says. "I know that she thinks drawing those pictures is supposed to make me feel better or something. You're just wasting your money. There's nothing wrong with me."

"It's a long, difficult, expensive process," Sharon says. "You and Jessica have lost a lot. Jessica is going to have to learn to trust the world again. It would help if you could do it too."

So I decide to trust Girl Scouts. First Girl Scouts, then the world. I make my stand at the meeting of Kay Randall's fingertips. While Nolan Ryan breaks Walter Johnson's strikeout record and pitches a two-hit shutout, I pass out paste and thread to nine-year-olds who are sticking and sewing their lives together in ways Jessica and I can't.

II

50   Scouting is not altogether new to me. I was a Cub Scout. I owned a blue beanie and I remember very well my den mother, Mrs. Clark. A den mother made perfect sense to me then and still does. Maybe that's why I don't feel uncomfortable being a Girl Scout assistant leader.

We had no den father. Mr. Clark was only a photograph on the living room wall, the tiny living room where we held our monthly meetings. Mr. Clark was killed in the Korean War. His son John was in the troop. John was stocky but Mrs. Clark was huge. She couldn't sit on a regular chair, only on a couch or a stool without sides. She was the cashier in the convenience store beneath their apartment. The story we heard was that Walt, the old man who owned the store, felt sorry for her and gave her the job. He was her landlord too. She sat on a swivel stool and rang up the purchases.

We met at the store and watched while she locked the door; then we followed her up the steep staircase to her three-room apartment. She carried two wet glass bottles of milk. Her body took up the entire width of the staircase. She passed the banisters the way semi trucks pass each other on a narrow highway.

We were ten years old, a time when everything is funny, especially fat people. But I don't remember anyone ever laughing about Mrs. Clark. She had great dignity and character. So did John. I didn't know what to call it then, but I knew John was someone you could always trust.

She passed out milk and cookies, then John collected the cups and washed them. They didn't even have a television set. The only decoration in the room that barely held all of us was Mr. Clark's picture on the wall. We saw him in his uniform and we knew he died in Korea defending his country. We were little boys in blue beanies drinking milk in the apartment of a hero. Through that aura I came to scouting. I wanted Kay Randall to have all of Mrs. Clark's dignity.

55   When she took a deep breath and then bridged, Kay Randall had noticeable armpits. Her wide shoulders slithered into a tiny rib cage. Her armpits were like bridges. She said "bridging" like a mantra,[4] holding her hands before her for about thirty seconds at the start of each meeting.

"A promise is a promise," I told Jessica. "I signed up to be a leader, and I'm going to do it with you or without you."

"But you didn't even ask me if I liked it. You just signed up without talking it over."

[4]Buddhist charm or magic formula

"That's true; that's why I'm not going to force you to go along. It was my choice."

"What can you like about it? I hate Melissa Randall. She always has a cold."

60   "Her mother is a good leader."

"How do you know?"

"She's my boss. I've got to like her, don't I?" I hugged Jessica. "C'mon, honey, give it a chance. What do you have to lose?"

"If you make me go I'll do it, but if I have a choice I won't."

Every other Tuesday, Karen, the fifteen-year-old Greek girl who lives on the corner, babysits Jessica while I go to the Scout meetings. We talk about field trips and how to earn merit badges. The girls giggle when Kay pins a promptness badge on me, my first.

65   Jessica thinks it's hilarious. She tells me to wear it to work.

Sometimes when I watch Jessica brush her hair and tie her ponytail and make up her lunch kit I start to think that maybe I should just relax and stop the therapy and the scouting and all my not-so-subtle attempts to get her to invite friends over. I start to think that, in spite of everything, she's a good student and she's got a sense of humor. She's barely nine years old. She'll grow up like everyone else does. John Clark did it without a father; she'll do it without a mother. I start to wonder if Jessica seems to the girls in her class the way John Clark seemed to me: dignified, serious, almost an adult even while we were playing. I admired him. Maybe the girls in her class admire her. But John had that hero on the wall, his father in a uniform, dead for reasons John and all the rest of us understood.

My Jessica had to explain a neurologic disease she couldn't even pronounce. "I hate it when people ask me about Mom," she says. "I just tell them she fell off the Empire State Building."

III

Before our first field trip I go to Kay's house for a planning session. We're going to collect wildflowers in East Texas. It's a one-day trip. I arranged to rent the school bus.

I told Jessica that she could go on the trip even though she wasn't a troop member, but she refused.

70   We sit on colonial furniture in Kay's den. She brings in coffee and we go over the supply list. Another troop is joining ours so there will be twenty-two girls, three women, and me, a busload among the bluebonnets.

"We have to be sure the girls understand that the bluebonnets they pick are on private land and that we have permission to pick them. Otherwise they might pick them along the roadside, which is against the law."

I imagine all twenty-two of them behind bars for picking bluebonnets and Jessica laughing while I scramble for bail money.

I keep noticing Kay's hands. I notice them as she pours coffee, as she checks off the items on the list, as she gestures. I keep expecting her to bridge. She has large, solid, confident hands. When she finishes bridging I sometimes feel like clapping the way people do after the national anthem.

"I admire you," she tells me. "I admire you for going ahead with Scouts even though your daughter rejects it. She'll get a lot out of it indirectly from you."

75   Kay Randall is thirty-three, divorced, and has a Bluebird too. Her older

daughter is one of the stubby-fingered girls, Melissa. Jessica is right; Melissa always has a cold.

Kay teaches fifth grade and has been divorced for three years. I am the first assistant she's ever had.

"My husband, Bill, never helped with Scouts," Kay says. "He was pretty much turned off to everything except his business and drinking. When we separated I can't honestly say I missed him; he'd never been there. I don't think the girls miss him either. He only sees them about once a month. He has girlfriends, and his business is doing very well. I guess he has what he wants."

"And you?"

She uses one of those wonderful hands to move the hair away from her eyes, a gesture that makes her seem very young.

80 "I guess I do too. I've got the girls and my job. I'm lonesome, though. It's not exactly what I wanted."

We both think about what might have been as we sit beside her glass coffeepot with our lists of sachet supplies. If she was Barbra Streisand and I Robert Redford and the music started playing in the background to give us a clue and there was a long close-up of our lips, we might just fade into middle age together. But Melissa called for Mom because her mosquito bite was bleeding where she scratched it. And I had an angry daughter waiting for me. And all Kay and I had in common was Girl Scouts. We were both smart enough to know it. When Kay looked at me before going to put alcohol on the mosquito bite, our mutual sadness dripped from us like the last drops of coffee through the grinds.

"You really missed something tonight," Jessica tells me. "The Astros did a double steal. I've never seen one before. In the fourth they sent Thon and Moreno together, and Moreno stole home."

She knows batting averages and won-lost percentages too, just like the older boys, only they go out to play. Jessica stays in and waits for me.

During the field trip, while the girls pick flowers to dry and then manufacture into sachets, I think about Jessica at home, probably beside the radio. Juana, our once-a-week cleaning lady, agreed to work on Saturday so she could stay with Jessica while I took the all-day field trip.

85 It was no small event. In the eight months since Vicki died I had not gone away for an entire day.

I made waffles in the waffle iron for her before I left, but she hardly ate.

"If you want anything, just ask Juana."

"Juana doesn't speak English."

"She understands, that's enough."

90 "Maybe for you it's enough."

"Honey, I told you, you can come; there's plenty of room on the bus. It's not too late for you to change your mind."

"It's not too late for you either. There's going to be plenty of other leaders there. You don't have to go. You're just doing this to be mean to me."

I'm ready for this. I spent an hour with Sharon steeling myself. "Before she can leave you," Sharon said, "you'll have to show her that you can leave. Nothing's going to happen to her. And don't let her be sick that day either."

Jessica is too smart to pull the "I don't feel good" routine. Instead she becomes more silent, more unhappy looking than usual. She stays in her pajamas while I wash the dishes and get ready to leave.

95   I didn't notice the sadness as it was coming upon Jessica. It must have happened gradually in the years of Vicki's decline, the years in which I paid so little attention to my daughter. There were times when Jessica seemed to recognize the truth more than I did.

As my Scouts picked their wildflowers, I remembered the last outing I had planned for us. It was going to be a Fourth of July picnic with some friends in Austin. I stopped at the bank and got $200 in cash for the long weekend. But when I came home Vicki was too sick to move and the air conditioner had broken. I called our friends to cancel the picnic; then I took Jessica to the mall with me to buy a fan. I bought the biggest one they had, a 58-inch oscillating model that sounded like a hurricane. It could cool 10,000 square feet, but it wasn't enough.

Vicki was home sitting blankly in front of the TV set. The fan could move eight tons of air an hour, but I wanted it to save my wife. I wanted a fan that would blow the whole earth out of its orbit.

I had $50 left. I gave it to Jessica and told her to buy anything she wanted.

"Whenever you're sad, Daddy, you want to buy me things." She put the money back in my pocket. "It won't help." She was seven years old, holding my hand tightly in the appliance department at J. C. Penney's.

100   I watched Melissa sniffle even more among the wildflowers, and I pointed out the names of various flowers to Carol and JoAnne and Sue and Linda and Rebecca, who were by now used to me and treated me pretty much as they treated Kay. I noticed that the Girl Scout flower book had very accurate photographs that made it easy to identify the bluebonnets and buttercups and poppies. There were also several varieties of wild grasses.

We were only 70 miles from home on some land a wealthy rancher long ago donated to the Girl Scouts. The girls bending among the flowers seemed to have been quickly transformed by the colorful meadow. The gigglers and monotonous singers on the bus were now, like the bees, sucking strength from the beauty around them. Kay was in the midst of them and so, I realized, was I, not watching and keeping score and admiring from the distance but a participant, a player.

JoAnne and Carol sneaked up from behind me and dropped some dandelions down my back. I chased them; then I helped the other leaders pour the Kool-Aid and distribute the Baggies and the name tags for each girl's flowers.

My daughter is home listening to a ball game, I thought, and I'm out here having fun with nine-year-olds. It's upside down.

When I came home with dandelion fragments still on my back, Juana had cleaned the house and I could smell the taco sauce in the kitchen. Jessica was in her room. I suspected that she had spent the day listless and tearful, although I had asked her to invite a friend over.

105   "I had a lot of fun, honey, but I missed you."

She hugged me and cried against my shoulder. I felt like holding her the way I used to when she was an infant, the way I rocked her to sleep. But she was a big girl now and needed not sleep but wakefulness.

"I heard on the news that the Rockets signed Ralph Sampson," she sobbed, "and you hardly ever take me to any pro basketball games."

"But if they have a new center things will be different. With Sampson we'll be contenders. Sure I'll take you."

"Promise?"

110   "Promise." I promise to take you everywhere, my lovely child, and then
to leave you. I'm learning to be a leader.

[1984]

 TOPICS FOR CRITICAL THINKING AND WRITING

1. Jessica refuses to go to the meetings of the Brownies. Why, then, in
   your opinion, does the narrator continue to work with the Brownies?
2. In the context of the story, what does "bridging" mean? What bridges
   are being made, or not made?
3. How would you characterize the narrator's tone? How does the tone in
   which he tells his story shape your sense of the meaning of the story?

 AMY HEMPEL

Amy Hempel was born in Chicago in 1951. She was educated in California and at Columbia University, and now lives in New York City, where she writes fiction and serves as a contributing editor at Vanity Fair.

Today Will Be a Quiet Day

"I think it's the other way around," the boy said. "I think if the quake hit
now the *bridge* would collapse and the *ramps* would be left."

He looked at his sister with satisfaction.

"You are just trying to scare your sister," the father said. "You know
that is not true."

"No, really," the boy insisted, "and I heard birds in the middle of the
night. Isn't that a warning?"

5   The girl gave her brother a toxic look and ate a handful of Raisinets. The
three of them were stalled in traffic on the Golden Gate Bridge.

That morning, before waking his children, the father had canceled their
music lessons and decided to make a day of it. He wanted to know how they
were, is all. Just—how were they. He thought his kids were as self-contained
as one of those dogs you sometimes see carrying home its own leash. But
you could read things wrong.

Could you ever.

The boy had a friend who jumped from a floor of Langley Porter. The
friend had been there for two weeks, mostly playing Ping-Pong. All the
friend said the day the boy visited and lost every game was never play Ping-
Pong with a mental patient because it's all we do and we'll kill you. That
night the friend had cut the red belt he wore in two and left the other half
on his bed. That was this time last year when the boy was twelve years old.

You think you're safe, the father thought, but it's thinking you're invisible because you closed your eyes.

10   This day they were headed for Petaluma—the chicken, egg, and arm-
wrestling capital of the nation—for lunch. The father had offered to take

them to the men's arm-wrestling semifinals. But it was said that arm
wrestling wasn't so interesting since the new safety precautions, that hardly
anyone broke an arm or a wrist anymore. The best anyone could hope to see
would be dislocation, so they said they would rather go to Pete's. Pete's was
a gas station turned into a place to eat. The hamburgers there were named
after cars, and the gas pumps in front still pumped gas.

"Can I have one?" the boy asked, meaning the Raisinets.

"No," his sister said.

"Can I have two?"

"Neither of you should be eating candy before lunch," the father said.
He said it with the good sport of a father who enjoys his kids and gets a kick
out of saying Dad things.

15   "You mean dinner," said the girl. "It will be dinner before we get to
Pete's."

Only the northbound lanes were stopped. Southbound traffic flashed
past at the normal speed.

"Check it out," the boy said from the back seat. "Did you see the
bumper sticker on that Porsche? 'If you don't like the way I drive, stay off
the sidewalk.' "

He spoke directly to his sister. "I've just solved my Christmas shopping."

"I got the highest score in my class in Driver's Ed," she said.

20   "I thought I would let your sister drive home today," the father said.

From the back seat came sirens, screams for help, and then a dirge.

The girl spoke to her father in a voice rich with complicity. "Don't people make you want to give up?"

"Don't the two of you know any jokes? I haven't laughed all day," the father said.

"Did I tell you the guillotine joke?" the girl said.

25   "He hasn't laughed all day, so you must've," her brother said.

The girl gave her brother a look you could iron clothes with. Then her
gaze dropped down. "Oh-oh," she said, "Johnny's out of jail."

Her brother zipped his pants back up. He said, "Tell the joke."

"Two Frenchmen and a Belgian were about to be beheaded," the girl
began. "The first Frenchman was led to the block and blindfolded. The executioner let the blade go. But it stopped a quarter inch above the Frenchman's neck. So he was allowed to go free, and ran off shouting, 'C'est un
miracle! C'est un miracle!' "

"It's a miracle," the father said.

30   "Then the second Frenchman was led to the block, and same thing—
the blade stopped just before cutting off his head. So *he* got to go free, and
ran off shouting, 'C'est un miracle!'

"Finally the Belgian was led to the block. But before they could blind-
fold him, he looked up, pointed to the top of the guillotine, and cried, 'Voilà
la difficulté!'"

She doubled over.

"Maybe *I* would be wetting *my* pants if I knew what that meant," the
boy said.

"You can't explain after the punch line," the girl said, "and have it still
be funny."

35   "There's the problem," said the father.

The waitress handed out menus to the party of three seated in the corner booth of what used to be the lube bay. She told them the specialty of the
day was Moroccan chicken.

"That's what I want," the boy said. "Morerotten chicken."

But he changed his order to a Studeburger and fries after his father and
sister had ordered.

"So," the father said, "who misses music lessons?"

40   "I'm serious about what I asked you last week," the girl said. "About
switching to piano? My teacher says a real flutist only breathes with the
stomach, and I can't."

"The real reason she wants to change," said the boy, "is her waist will
get two inches bigger when she learns to stomach-breathe. That's what *else*
her teacher said."

The boy buttered a piece of sourdough bread and flipped a chunk of
cold butter onto his sister's sleeve.

"Jeezo-beezo," the girl said, "why don't they skip the knife and fork and
just set his place with a slingshot!"

"Who will ever adopt you if you don't mind your manners?" the father
said. "Maybe we could try a little quiet today."

45   "You sound like your tombstone," the girl said. "Remember what you
wanted it to say?"

Her brother joined in with his mouth full: "Today will be a quiet day."

"Because it never is with us around," the boy said.

"You guys," said the father.

The waitress brought plates. The father passed sugar to the boy and salt
to the girl without being asked. He watched the girl shake out salt onto the
fries.

50   "If I had a sore throat, I would gargle with those," he said.

"Looks like she's trying to melt a driveway," the boy offered.

The father watched his children eat. They ate fast. They called it
Hoovering. He finished while they sucked at straws in empty drinks.

"Funny," he said thoughtfully, "I'm not hungry anymore."

Every meal ended this way. It was his benediction, one of the Dad
things they expected him to say.

55   "That reminds me," the girl said. "Did you feed Rocky before we left?"

"Uh-uh," her brother said. "I fed him yesterday."

"*I* fed him yesterday!" the girl said.

"Okay, we'll compromise," the boy said. "We won't feed the cat today."

"I'd say you are out of bounds on that one," the father said.

60   He meant you could not tease her about animals. Once, during dinner,
that cat ran into the dining room shot from guns. He ran around the table at
top speed, then spun out on the parquet floor into a leg of the table. He fell
over onto his side and made short coughing sounds. "Isn't he smart?" the
girl had crooned, kneeling beside him. "He knows he's hurt."

For years, her father had to say that the animals seen on shoulders of
roads were napping.

"He never would have not fed Homer," she said to her father.

"Homer was a dog," the boy said. "If I forgot to feed him, he could just
go into the hills and bite a deer."

"Or a Campfire Girl selling mints at the front door," their father reminded them.

65   "Homer," the girl sighed. "I hope he likes chasing sheep on that ranch in the mountains."

The boy looked at her, incredulous.

"You *believed* that? You actually *believed* that?"

In her head, a clumsy magician yanked the cloth and the dishes all crashed to the floor. She took air into her lungs until they filled, and then she filled her stomach, too.

"I thought she knew," the boy said.

70   The dog was five years ago.

"The girl's parents insisted," the father said. "It's the law in California."

"Then I hate California," she said. "I hate its guts."

The boy said he would wait for them in the car, and left the table.

"What would help?" the father asked.

75   "For Homer to be alive," she said.

"What would help?"

"Nothing."

"Help."

She pinched a trail of salt on her plate.

80   "A ride," she said. "I'll drive."

The girl started the car and screamed, "Goddammit."

With the power off, the boy had tuned in the Spanish station. Mariachis exploded on ignition.

"Dammit isn't God's last name," the boy said, quoting another bumper sticker.

"Don't people make you want to give up?" the father said.

85   "No talking," the girl said to the rearview mirror, and put the car in gear.

She drove for hours. Through groves of eucalyptus with their damp peeling bark, past acacia bushes with yellow flowers pulsing off their stems. She cut over to the coast route and the stony gray-green tones of Inverness.

"What you'd call scenic," the boy tried.

Otherwise they were quiet.

No one said anything else until the sky started to close, and then it was the boy again, asking shouldn't they be going home.

90   "No, no," the father said, and made a show of looking out the window, up at the sky and back at his watch. "No," he said, "keep driving—it's getting earlier."

But the sky spilled rain, and the girl headed south toward the bridge. She turned on the headlights and the dashboard lit up green. She read off the odometer on the way home: "Twenty-six thousand, three hundred eighty three and eight-tenths miles."

"Today?" the boy said.

The boy got to Rocky first. "Let's play the cat," he said, and carried the Siamese to the upright piano. He sat on the bench holding the cat in his lap and pressed its paws to the keys. Rocky played "Born Free." He tried to twist away.

"Come on, Rocky, ten more minutes and we'll break."

95   "Give him to me," the girl said.

She puckered up and gave the cat a five-lipper.

"Bring the Rock upstairs," the father called. "Bring sleeping bags, too."

Pretty soon three sleeping bags formed a triangle in the master bedroom. The father was the hypotenuse. The girl asked him to brush out her hair, which he did while the boy ate a tangerine, peeling it up close to his face, inhaling the mist. Then he held each segment to the light to find seeds. In his lap, cat paws fluttered like dreaming eyes.

"What are you thinking?" the father asked.

100   "Me?" the girl said. "Fifty-seven T-bird, white with red interior, convertible. I drive it to Texas and wear skirts with rick-rack. I'm changing my name to Ruby," she said, "or else Easy."

The father considered her dream of a checkered future.

"Early ripe, early rot," he warned.

A wet wind slammed the window in its warped sash, and the boy jumped.

"I hate rain," he said. "I hate its guts."

105   The father got up and closed the window tighter against the storm. "It's a real frog-choker," he said.

In darkness, lying still, it was no less camp-like than if they had been under the stars, singing to a stone-ringed fire burned down to embers.

They had already said good-night some minutes earlier when the boy and girl heard their father's voice in the dark.

"Kids, I just remembered—I have some good news and some bad news. Which do you want first?"

It was his daughter who spoke. "Let's get it over with," she said. "Let's get the bad news over with."

110   The father smiled. They are all right, he decided. My kids are as right as this rain. He smiled at the exact spots he knew their heads were turned to his, and doubted he would ever feel—not better, but *more* than he did now.

"I lied," he said. "There is no bad news."

[1986]

▢ TOPICS FOR CRITICAL THINKING AND WRITING

1. The story begins with characters in a car on a bridge, talking about the possibility of the bridge collapsing during an earthquake. A few lines later we read about a boy who committed suicide. Moreover, we are told that the father somehow fears that he may not really know his children. When you began reading the story, did these ominous touches seem to you to be foreshadowing? That is, did they suggest to you that the story might end unhappily? Or, on the contrary, did you somehow feel, despite these threats, that the story would not end unhappily? Explain.

2. At the beginning of the story, the father says that the boy is trying to "scare" the sister. How would you characterize the relationship between the two children?

3. The mother is never mentioned. Should we have been told if she is dead, or if she has abandoned the family, or whatever? Why do you hold the view that you hold?

4. We are told that the father "gets a kick out of saying Dad things" to his children. Try your hand at inventing some "Dad things" that he might have said in this story.

5. The point of the joke about the guillotine is that it doesn't pay to point out the source of difficulties. How does this joke help you to make sense of the story?

 JAMAICA KINCAID

Jamaica Kincaid (b. 1949) was born in St. John's, Antigua, in the West Indies. She was educated at the Princess Margaret School in Antigua, and, briefly, at Westchester Community College and Franconia College. Since 1974 she has been a contributor to The New Yorker.

Kincaid is the author of four books, At the Bottom of the River *(1983, a collection of short pieces, including "Girl"),* Annie John *(1985, a second book recording a girl's growth, including "Columbus in Chains"),* A Small Place *(1988, a passionate essay about the destructive effects of colonialism), and* Lucy *(1990, a short novel about a young black woman who comes to the United States from the West Indies).*

Girl

Wash the white clothes on Monday and put them on the stone heap; wash the color clothes on Tuesday and put them on the clothesline to dry; don't walk barehead in the hot sun; cook pumpkin fritters in very hot sweet oil; soak your little clothes right after you take them off; when buying cotton to make yourself a nice blouse, be sure that it doesn't have gum on it, because that way it won't hold up well after a wash; soak salt fish overnight before you cook it; is it true that you sing benna[1] in Sunday School?; always eat your food in such a way that it won't turn someone else's stomach; on Sundays try to walk like a lady and not like the slut you are so bent on becoming; don't sing benna in Sunday School; you mustn't speak to wharf-rat boys, not even to give directions; don't eat fruits on the street—flies will follow you; *but I don't sing benna on Sundays at all and never in Sunday school;* this is how to sew on a button; this is how to make a buttonhole for the button you have just sewed on; this is how to hem a dress when you see the hem coming down and so to prevent yourself from looking like the slut I know you are so bent on becoming; this is how you iron your father's khaki shirt so that it doesn't have a crease; this is how you iron your father's khaki pants so that they don't have a crease; this is how you grow okra—far from the house, because okra tree harbors red ants; when you are growing dasheen, make sure it gets plenty of water or else it makes your throat itch when you are eating it; this is how you sweep a corner; this is how you sweep a whole house; this is how you sweep a yard; this is how you smile to someone you don't like too much; this is how you set a table for dinner with an important guest; this is how you smile to someone you don't like at all;

[1]Calypso music

this is how you smile to someone you like completely; this is how you set a table for tea; this is how you set a table for dinner; this is how you set a table for lunch; this is how you set a table for breakfast; this is how to behave in the presence of men who don't know you very well, and this way they won't recognize immediately the slut I have warned you against becoming; be sure to wash every day, even if it is with your own spit; don't squat down to play marbles—you are not a boy, you know; don't pick people's flowers—you might catch something; don't throw stones at blackbirds, because it might not be a blackbird at all; this is how to make a bread pudding; this is how to make doukona;[2] this is how to make pepper pot; this is how to make a good medicine for a cold; this is how to make good medicine to throw away a child before it even becomes a child; this is how to catch a fish; this is how to throw back a fish you don't like, and that way something bad won't fall on you; this is how to bully a man; this is how a man bullies you; this is how to love a man, and if this doesn't work there are other ways, and if they don't work don't feel too bad about giving up; this is how to spit up in the air if you feel like it, and this is how to move quick so that it doesn't fall on you; this is how to make ends meet; always squeeze bread to make sure it's fresh; *but what if the baker won't let me feel the bread?;* you mean to say that after all you are really going to be the kind of woman who the baker won't let near the bread?

[1978]

[2]spicy pudding made of plantains

 ## TOPIC FOR CRITICAL THINKING AND WRITING.

In a paragraph, identify the two characters whose voices we hear in this story. Explain what we know about them (their circumstances and their relationship). Cite specific evidence from the text. For example, what is the effect of the frequent repetition of "this is how"? Are there other words or phrases frequently repeated?

 ## AMY TAN

Amy Tan was born in 1952 in Oakland, California, 2½ years after her parents had emigrated from China. She entered Linfield College in Oregon but then followed a boyfriend to California State University at San Jose, where she shifted her major from premedical studies to English. After earning a master's degree in linguistics from San Jose, Tan worked as a language consultant and then, under the name of May Brown, as a freelance business writer.

In 1985, having decided to try her hand at fiction, she joined the Squaw Valley Community of Writers, a fiction workshop. In 1987 she visited China with her mother; on her return to the United States she leaned that her agent had sold her first book. The Joy Luck Club, a collection of 16 interwoven stories (including "Two Kinds") about

*four Chinese mothers and their four American daughters. In 1991
she published a second book,* The Kitchen God's Wife.

Two Kinds

My mother believed you could be anything you wanted to be in America.
You could open a restaurant. You could work for the government and get
good retirement. You could buy a house with almost no money down. You
could become rich. You could become instantly famous.

"Of course, you can be prodigy, too," my mother told me when I was
nine. "You can be best anything. What does Auntie Lindo know? Her daughter, she is only best tricky."

America was where all my mother's hopes lay. She had come to San
Francisco in 1949 after losing everything in China: her mother and father,
her family home, her first husband, and two daughters, twin baby girls. But
she never looked back with regret. Things could get better in so many
ways.

We didn't immediately pick the right kind of prodigy. At first my
mother thought I could be a Chinese Shirley Temple. We'd watch Shirley's
old movies on TV as though they were training films. My mother would
poke my arm and say, "*Ni kan.* You watch." And I would see Shirley tapping
her feet, or singing a sailor song, or pursing her lips into a very round O
while saying "Oh, my goodness."

5   "*Ni kan,*" my mother said, as Shirley's eyes flooded with tears. "You already know how. Don't need talent for crying!"

Soon after my mother got this idea about Shirley Temple, she took me
to the beauty training school in the Mission District and put me in the
hands of a student who could barely hold the scissors without shaking. Instead of getting big fat curls, I emerged with an uneven mass of crinkly
black fuzz. My mother dragged me off to the bathroom and tried to wet
down my hair.

"You look like Negro Chinese," she lamented, as if I had done this on
purpose.

The instructor of the beauty training school had to lop off these soggy
clumps to make my hair even again. "Peter Pan is very popular these days,"
the instructor assured my mother. I now had hair the length of a boy's, with
curly bangs that hung at a slant two inches above my eyebrows. I liked the
haircut, and it made me actually look forward to my future fame.

In fact, in the beginning I was just as excited as my mother, maybe even
more so. I pictured this prodigy part of me as many different images, and I
tried each one on for size. I was a dainty ballerina girl standing by the curtain, waiting to hear the music that would send me floating on my tiptoes. I
was like the Christ child lifted out of the straw manger, crying with holy indignity. I was Cinderella stepping from her pumpkin carriage with sparkly
cartoon music filling the air.

10   In all of my imaginings I was filled with a sense that I would soon become perfect. My mother and father would adore me. I would be beyond reproach. I would never feel the need to sulk, or to clamor for anything.

But sometimes the prodigy in me became impatient. "If you don't hurry up and get me out of here, I'm disappearing for good," it warned. "And then you'll always be nothing."

Every night after dinner my mother and I would sit at the Formica-topped kitchen table. She would present new tests, taking her examples from stories of amazing children that she had read in *Ripley's Believe It or Not* or *Good Housekeeping, Reader's Digest,* or any of a dozen other magazines she kept in a pile in our bathroom. My mother got these magazines from people whose houses she cleaned. And since she cleaned many houses each week, we had a great assortment. She would look through them all, searching for stories about remarkable children.

The first night she brought out a story about a three-year-old boy who knew the capitals of all the states and even of most of the European countries. A teacher was quoted as saying that the little boy could also pronounce the names of the foreign cities correctly. "What's the capital of Finland?" my mother asked me, looking at the story.

All I knew was the capital of California, because Sacramento was the name of the street we lived on in Chinatown. "Nairobi!" I guessed, saying the most foreign word I could think of. She checked to see if that might be one way to pronounce *Helsinki* before showing me the answer.

15   The tests got harder—multiplying numbers in my head, finding the queen of hearts in a deck of cards, trying to stand on my head without using my hands, predicting the daily temperatures in Los Angeles, New York, and London. One night I had to look at a page from the Bible for three minutes and then report everything I could remember. "Now Jehoshaphat had riches and honor in abundance and . . . that's all I remember, Ma," I said.

And after seeing, once again, my mother's disappointed face, something inside me began to die. I hated the tests, the raised hopes and failed expectations. Before going to bed that night I looked in the mirror above the bathroom sink, and when I saw only my face staring back—and understood that it would always be this ordinary face—I began to cry. Such a sad, ugly girl! I made high-pitched noises like a crazed animal, trying to scratch out the face in the mirror.

And then I saw what seemed to be the prodigy side of me—a face I had never seen before. I looked at my reflection, blinking so that I could see more clearly. The girl staring back at me was angry, powerful. She and I were the same. I had new thoughts, willful thoughts—or, rather, thoughts filled with lots of won'ts. I won't let her change me, I promised myself. I won't be what I'm not.

So now when my mother presented her tests, I performed listlessly, my head propped on one arm. I pretended to be bored. And I was. I got so bored that I started counting the bellows of the foghorns out on the bay while my mother drilled me in other areas. The sound was comforting and reminded me of the cow jumping over the moon. And the next day I played a game with myself, seeing if my mother would give up on me before eight bellows. After a while I usually counted only one bellow, maybe two at most. At last she was beginning to give up hope.

Two or three months went by without any mention of my being a prodigy. And then one day my mother was watching the *Ed Sullivan Show* on TV. The TV was old and the sound kept shorting out. Every time my mother got halfway up from the sofa to adjust the set, the sound would come back on and Sullivan would be talking. As soon as she sat down, Sullivan would go silent again. She got up—the TV broke into loud piano music. She sat down—silence. Up and down, back and forth, quiet and loud. It was like a stiff, embraceless dance between her and the TV set. Finally, she stood by the set with her hand on the sound dial.

20   She seemed entranced by the music, a frenzied little piano piece with a mesmerizing quality, which alternated between quick, playful passages and teasing, lilting ones.

"*Ni kan,*" my mother said, calling me over with hurried hand gestures. "Look here."

I could see why my mother was fascinated by the music. It was being pounded out by a little Chinese girl, about nine years old, with a Peter Pan haircut. The girl had the sauciness of a Shirley Temple. She was proudly modest, like a proper Chinese child. And she also did a fancy sweep of a curtsy, so that the fluffy skirt of her white dress cascaded to the floor like the petals of a large carnation.

In spite of these warning signs, I wasn't worried. Our family had no piano and we couldn't afford to buy one, let alone reams of sheet music and piano lessons. So I could be generous in my comments when my mother badmouthed the little girl on TV.

"Play note right, but doesn't sound good!" my mother complained. "No singing sound."

25   "What are you picking on her for?" I said carelessly. "She's pretty good. Maybe she's not the best, but she's trying hard." I knew almost immediately that I would be sorry I had said that.

"Just like you," she said. "Not the best. Because you not trying." She gave a little huff as she let go of the sound dial and sat down on the sofa.

The little Chinese girl sat down also, to play an encore of "Anitra's Tanz," by Grieg.[1] I remember the song, because later on I had to learn how to play it.

Three days after watching the *Ed Sullivan Show* my mother told me what my schedule would be for piano lessons and piano practice. She had talked to Mr. Chong, who lived on the first floor of our apartment building. Mr. Chong was a retired piano teacher, and my mother had traded housecleaning services for weekly lessons and a piano for me to practice on every day, two hours a day, from four until six.

When my mother told me this, I felt as though I had been sent to hell. I whined, and then kicked my foot a little when I couldn't stand it anymore.

30   "Why don't you like me the way I am?" I cried. "I'm *not* a genius! I can't

[1]a section from the incidental music that Edward Grieg (1843–1907) wrote for *Peer Gynt,* a play by Henrik Ibsen

play the piano. And even if I could, I wouldn't go on TV if you paid me a million dollars!"

My mother slapped me. "Who ask you to be genius?" she shouted. "Only ask you be your best. For you sake. You think I want you to be genius? Hnnh! What for! Who ask you!"

"So ungrateful," I heard her mutter in Chinese. "If she had as much talent as she has temper, she'd be famous now."

Mr. Chong, whom I secretly nicknamed Old Chong, was very strange, always tapping his fingers to the silent music of an invisible orchestra. He looked ancient in my eyes. He had lost most of the hair on the top of his head, and he wore thick glasses and had eyes that always looked tired. But he must have been younger than I thought, since he lived with his mother and was not yet married.

I met Old Lady Chong once, and that was enough. She had a peculiar smell, like a baby that had done something in its pants, and her fingers felt like a dead person's, like an old peach I once found in the back of the refrigerator; its skin just slid off the flesh when I picked it up.

35   I soon found out why Old Chong had retired from teaching piano. He was deaf. "Like Beethoven!" he shouted to me. "We're both listening only in our head!" And he would start to conduct his frantic silent sonatas.

Our lessons went like this. He would open the book and point to different things, explaining their purpose: "Key! Treble! Bass! No sharps or flats! So this is C major! Listen now and play after me!"

And then he would play the C scale a few times, a simple chord, and then, as if inspired by an old unreachable itch, he would gradually add more notes and running trills and a pounding bass until the music was really something quite grand.

I would play after him, the simple scale, the simple chord, and then just play some nonsense that sounded like a cat running up and down on top of garbage cans. Old Chong would smile and applaud and say, "Very good! But now you must learn to keep time!"

So that's how I discovered that Old Chong's eyes were too slow to keep up with the wrong notes I was playing. He went through the motions in half time. To help me keep rhythm, he stood behind me and pushed down on my right shoulder for every beat. He balanced pennies on top of my wrists so that I would keep them still as I slowly played scales and arpeggios. He had me curve my hand around an apple and keep that shape when playing chords. He marched stiffly to show me how to make each finger dance up and down, staccato, like an obedient little soldier.

40   He taught me all these things, and that was how I also learned I could be lazy and get away with mistakes, lots of mistakes. If I hit the wrong notes because I hadn't practiced enough, I never corrected myself. I just kept playing in rhythm. And Old Chong kept conducting his own private reverie.

So maybe I never really gave myself a fair chance. I did pick up the basics pretty quickly, and I might have become a good pianist at that young age. But I was so determined not to try, not to be anybody different, that I learned to play only the most ear-splitting preludes, the most discordant hymns.

Over the next year I practiced like this, dutifully in my own way. And then one day I heard my mother and her friend Lindo Jong both talking in a loud, bragging tone of voice so that others could hear. It was after church, and I was leaning against a brick wall, wearing a dress with stiff white petti-coats. Auntie Lindo's daughter, Waverly, who was my age, was standing far-ther down the wall, about five feet away. We had grown up together and shared all the closeness of two sisters, squabbling over crayons and dolls. In other words, for the most part, we hated each other. I thought she was snotty. Waverly Jong had gained a certain amount of fame as "Chinatown's Littlest Chinese Chess Champion."

"She bring home too many trophy," Auntie Lindo lamented that Sunday. "All day she play chess. All day I have no time do nothing but dust off her winnings." She threw a scolding look at Waverly, who pretended not to see her.

"You lucky you don't have this problem," Auntie Lindo said with a sigh to my mother.

45   And my mother squared her shoulders and bragged: "Our problem worser than yours. If we ask Jing-mei wash dish, she hear nothing but music. It's like you can't stop this natural talent."

And right then I was determined to put a stop to her foolish pride.

A few weeks later Old Chong and my mother conspired to have me play in a talent show that was to be held in the church hall. By then my parents had saved up enough to buy me a secondhand piano, a black Wurlitzer spinet with a scarred bench. It was the showpiece of our living room.

For the talent show I was to play a piece called "Pleading Child," from Schumann's *Scenes From Childhood.*[2] It was a simple, moody piece that sounded more difficult than it was. I was supposed to memorize the whole thing. But I dawdled over it, playing a few bars and then cheating, looking up to see what notes followed. I never really listened to what I was playing. I daydreamed about being somewhere else, about being someone else.

The part I liked to practice best was the fancy curtsy: right foot out, touch the rose on the carpet with a pointed foot, sweep to the side, bend left leg, look up, and smile.

50   My parents invited all the couples from their social club to witness my debut. Auntie Lindo and Uncle Tin were there. Waverly and her two older brothers had also come. The first two rows were filled with children either younger or older than I was. The littlest ones got to go first. They recited simple nursery rhymes, squawked out tunes on miniature violins, and twirled hula hoops in pink ballet tutus, and when they bowed or curtsied, the audience would sigh in unison, "*Awww,*" and then clap enthusiastically.

When my turn came, I was very confident. I remember my childish ex-citement. It was as if I knew, without a doubt, that the prodigy side of me really did exist. I had no fear whatsoever, no nervousness. I remember thinking, This is it! This is it! I looked out over the audience, at my mother's blank face, my father's yawn, Auntie Lindo's stiff-lipped smile, Waverly's sulky expression. I had on a white dress, layered with sheets of lace, and a

[2]a piano work by Robert Schumann (1810–56) with twelve titled sections and an epilogue

pink bow in my Peter Pan haircut. As I sat down, I envisioned people jumping to their feet and Ed Sullivan rushing up to introduce me to everyone on TV.

And I started to play. Everything was so beautiful. I was so caught up in how lovely I looked that I wasn't worried about how I would sound. So I was surprised when I hit the first wrong note. And then I hit another, and another. A chill started at the top of my head and began to trickle down. Yet I couldn't stop playing, as though my hands were bewitched. I kept thinking my fingers would adjust themselves back, like a train switching to the right track. I played this strange jumble through to the end, the sour notes staying with me all the way.

When I stood up, I discovered my legs were shaking. Maybe I had just been nervous, and the audience, like Old Chong, had seen me go through the right motions and had not heard anything wrong at all. I swept my right foot out, went down on my knee, looked up, and smiled. The room was quiet, except for Old Chong, who was beaming and shouting, "Bravo! Bravo! Well done!" But then I saw my mother's face, her stricken face. The audience clapped weakly, and as I walked back to my chair, with my whole face quivering as I tried not to cry, I heard a little boy whisper loudly to his mother, "That was awful," and the mother whispered, "Well, she certainly tried."

And now I realized how many people were in the audience—the whole world, it seemed. I was aware of eyes burning into my back. I felt the shame of my mother and father as they sat stiffly through the rest of the show.

55   We could have escaped during intermission. Pride and some strange sense of honor must have anchored my parents to their chairs. And so we watched it all: The eighteen-year-old boy with a fake moustache who did a magic show and juggled flaming hoops while riding a unicycle. The breasted girl with white makeup who sang an aria from *Madame Butterfly* and got an honorable mention. And the eleven-year-old boy who won first prize playing a tricky violin song that sounded like a busy bee.

After the show the Hsus, the Jongs, and the St. Clairs, from the Joy Luck Club, came up to my mother and father.

"Lots of talented kids," Auntie Lindo said vaguely, smiling broadly.

"That was somethin' else," my father said, and I wondered if he was referring to me in a humorous way, or whether he even remembered what I had done.

Waverly looked at me and shrugged her shoulders. "You aren't a genius like me," she said matter-of-factly. And if I hadn't felt so bad, I would have pulled her braids and punched her stomach.

60   But my mother's expression was what devastated me: a quiet, blank look that said she had lost everything. I felt the same way, and everybody seemed now to be coming up, like gawkers at the scene of an accident, to see what parts were actually missing.

When we got on the bus to go home, my father was humming the busy-bee tune and my mother was silent. I kept thinking she wanted to wait until we got home before shouting at me. But when my father unlocked the door to our apartment, my mother walked in and went straight to the back, into the bedroom. No accusations. No blame. And in a way, I felt disappointed. I had been waiting for her to start shouting, so that I could shout back and cry and blame her for all my misery.

I had assumed that my talent-show fiasco meant that I would never have to play the piano again. But two days later, after school, my mother came out of the kitchen and saw me watching TV.

"Four clock," she reminded me, as if it were any other day. I was stunned, as though she were asking me to go through the talent-show torture again. I planted myself more squarely in front of the TV.

"Turn off TV," she called from the kitchen five minutes later.

65   I didn't budge. And then I decided. I didn't have to do what my mother said anymore. I wasn't her slave. This wasn't China. I had listened to her before, and look what happened. She was the stupid one.

She came out of the kitchen and stood in the arched entryway of the living room. "Four clock," she said once again, louder.

"I'm not going to play anymore," I said nonchalantly. "Why should I? I'm not a genius."

She stood in front of the TV. I saw that her chest was heaving up and down in an angry way.

"No!" I said, and I now felt stronger, as if my true self had finally emerged. So this was what had been inside me all along.

70   "No! I won't!" I screamed.

"She snapped off the TV, yanked me by the arm and pulled me off the floor. She was frighteningly strong, half pulling, half carrying me toward the piano as I kicked the throw rugs under my feet. She lifted me up and onto the hard bench. I was sobbing by now, looking at her bitterly. Her chest was heaving even more and her mouth was open, smiling crazily as if she were pleased that I was crying.

"You want me to be someone that I'm not!" I sobbed. "I'll never be the kind of daughter you want me to be!"

"Only two kinds of daughters," she shouted in Chinese. "Those who are obedient and those who follow their own mind! Only one kind of daughter can live in this house. Obedient daughter!"

"Then I wish I weren't your daughter. I wish you weren't my mother," I shouted. As I said these things I got scared. It felt like worms and toads and slimy things crawling out of my chest, but it also felt good, that this awful side of me had surfaced, at last.

75   "Too late change this," my mother said shrilly.

And I could sense her anger rising to its breaking point. I wanted to see it spill over. And that's when I remembered the babies she had lost in China, the ones we never talked about. "Then I wish I'd never been born!" I shouted. "I wish I were dead! Like them."

It was as if I had said magic words. Alakazam!—her face went blank, her mouth closed, her arms went slack, and she backed out of the room, stunned, as if she were blowing away like a small brown leaf, thin, brittle, lifeless.

It was not the only disappointment my mother felt in me. In the years that followed, I failed her many times, each time asserting my will, my right to fall short of expectations. I didn't get straight As. I didn't become class president. I didn't get into Stanford. I dropped out of college.

Unlike my mother, I did not believe I could be anything I wanted to be. I could only be me.

80   And for all those years we never talked about the disaster at the recital or my terrible declarations afterward at the piano bench. Neither of us talked about it again, as if it were a betrayal that was now unspeakable. So I never found a way to ask her why she had hoped for something so large that failure was inevitable.

And even worse, I never asked her about what frightened me the most: Why had she given up hope? For after our struggle at the piano, she never mentioned my playing again. The lessons stopped. The lid to the piano was closed, shutting out the dust, my misery, and her dreams.

So she surprised me. A few years ago she offered to give me the piano, for my thirtieth birthday. I had not played in all those years. I saw the offer as a sign of forgiveness, a tremendous burden removed.

"Are you sure?" I asked shyly. "I mean, won't you and Dad miss it?"

"No, this your piano," she said firmly. "Always your piano. You only one can play."

85   "Well, I probably can't play anymore," I said. "It's been years."

"You pick up fast," my mother said, as if she knew this was certain. "You have natural talent. You could be genius if you want to."

"No, I couldn't."

"You just not trying," my mother said. And she was neither angry nor sad. She said it as if announcing a fact that could never be disproved. "Take it," she said.

But I didn't at first. It was enough that she had offered it to me. And after that, every time I saw it in my parents' living room, standing in front of the bay window, it made me feel proud, as if it were a shiny trophy that I had won back.

90   Last week I sent a tuner over to my parents' apartment and had the piano reconditioned, for purely sentimental reasons. My mother had died a few months before, and I had been getting things in order for my father, a little bit at a time. I put the jewelry in special silk pouches. The sweaters she had knitted in yellow, pink, bright orange—all the colors I hated—I put in mothproof boxes. I found some old Chinese silk dresses, the kind with little slits up the sides. I rubbed the old silk against my skin, and then wrapped them in tissue and decided to take them home with me.

After I had the piano tuned, I opened the lid and touched the keys. It sounded even richer than I remembered. Really, it was a very good piano. Inside the bench were the same exercise notes with handwritten scales, the same secondhand music books with their covers held together with yellow tape.

I opened up the Schumann book to the dark little piece I had played at the recital. It was on the left-hand page, "Pleading Child." It looked more difficult than I remembered. I played a few bars, surprised at how easily the notes came back to me.

And for the first time, or so it seemed, I noticed the piece on the right-hand side. It was called "Perfectly Contented." I tried to play this one as well. It had a lighter melody but with the same flowing rhythm and turned out to be quite easy. "Pleading Child" was shorter but slower; "Perfectly

Contented" was longer but faster. And after I had played them both a few times, I realized they were two halves of the same song.

[1989]

TOPICS FOR CRITICAL THINKING AND WRITING

1. Try to recall your responses when you had finished reading the first three paragraphs. At that point, how did the mother strike you? Now that you have read the entire story, is your view of her different? If so, in what way(s)?
2. When the narrator looks in the mirror, she discovers "the prodigy side," a face she "had never seen before." What do you think she is discovering?
3. If you enjoyed the story, point out two or three passages that you found particularly engaging, and briefly explain why they appeal to you.
4. Do you think this story is interesting only because it may give a glimpse of life in a Chinese-American family? Or do you find it interesting for additional reasons? Explain.
5. Conceivably the story could have ended with the fourth paragraph from the end. What do the last three paragraphs contribute?

Poetry

 ROBERT HAYDEN

Robert Hayden (1913-80) was born in Detroit, Michigan. His parents divorced when he was a child, and he was brought up by a neighboring family, whose name he adopted. In 1942, at the age of 29, he graduated from Detroit City College (now Wayne State University), and he received a master's degree from the University of Michigan. He taught at Fisk University from 1946 to 1969 and after that, for the remainder of his life, at the University of Michigan. In 1979 he was appointed Consultant in Poetry to the Library of Congress, the first African-American to hold the post.

Those Winter Sundays

Sundays too my father got up early
and put his clothes on in the blueblack cold,
then with cracked hands that ached
from labor in the weekday weather made
banked fires blaze. No one ever thanked him.   5

I'd wake and hear the cold splintering, breaking.
When the rooms were warm, he'd call,
and slowly I would rise and dress,
fearing the chronic angers of that house,

Speaking indifferently to him,   10
who had driven out the cold
and polished my good shoes as well.
What did I know, what did I know
of love's austere and lonely offices?

[1962]

 ## TOPICS FOR CRITICAL THINKING AND WRITING

1. In line 1, what does the word "too" tell us about the father? What does it suggest about the speaker and the implied hearer of the poem?
2. How old do you believe the speaker was at the time he recalls in the second and third stanzas? What details suggest this age?
3. What is the meaning of "offices" in the last line? What does this word suggest that other words Hayden might have chosen do not?
4. What do you take to be the speaker's present attitude toward his father? What circumstances, do you imagine, prompted his memory of "Those Winter Sundays"?
5. In a page or two, try to get down the exact circumstances when you spoke "indifferently," or not at all, to someone who had deserved your gratitude.

 ## THEODORE ROETHKE

Theodore Roethke (1908-63) was born in Saginaw, Michigan, and educated at the University of Michigan and Harvard. From 1947 until his death he taught at the University of Washington in Seattle, where he exerted considerable influence on the next generation of poets. Many of Roethke's best poems are lyrical memories of his childhood.

My Papa's Waltz

The whiskey on your breath
Could make a small boy dizzy;
but I hung on like death:
Such waltzing was not easy.   4

We romped until the pans
Slid from the kitchen shelf;
My mother's countenance
Could not unfrown itself.   8

The hand that held my wrist
Was battered on one knuckle;
At every step you missed
My right ear scraped a buckle.   12

You beat time on my head
With a palm caked hard by dirt,
Then waltzed me off to bed
Still clinging to your shirt.   16

[1948]

TOPICS FOR CRITICAL THINKING AND WRITING

1. Do the syntactical pauses vary much from stanza to stanza? Be specific. Would you say that the rhythm suggests lightness? Why?
2. Does the rhythm parallel or ironically contrast with the episode described? Was the dance a graceful waltz? Explain.
3. What would you say is the function of the stresses in lines 13–14?

GWENDOLYN BROOKS

*Gwendolyn Brooks was born in Topeka, Kansas, in 1917 but was raised in Chicago's South Side, where she has spent most of her life. Brooks has taught in several colleges and universities and she has written a novel (*Maud Martha, *1953) and a memoir (*Report from Part One, *1972), but she is best known as a poet. In 1950, when she won the Pulitzer Prize for Poetry, she became the first African-American writer to win a Pulitzer Prize. In 1985 Brooks became Consultant in Poetry to the Library of Congress.*

The Mother

Abortions will not let you forget.
You remember the children you got that you did not get,
The damp small pulps with a little or with no hair,
The singers and workers that never handled the air.
You will never neglect or beat   5
Them, or silence or buy with a sweet.
You will never wind up the sucking-thumb
Or scuttle off ghosts that come.
You will never leave them, controlling your luscious sigh,
Return for a snack of them, with gobbling mother-eye.   10

I have heard in the voices of the wind the voices of my dim killed children.
I have contracted. I have eased
My dim dears at the breasts they could never suck.
I have said, Sweets, if I sinned, if I seized

Your luck   15
And your lives from your unfinished reach,
If I stole your births and your names,
Your straight baby tears and your games,
Your stilted or lovely loves, your tumults, your marriages, aches, and your
    deaths,
If I poisoned the beginnings of your breaths,   20
Believe that even in my deliberateness I was not deliberate.
Though why should I whine,
Whine that the crime was other than mine?—
Since anyhow you are dead.
Or rather, or instead,   25
You were never made.
But that too, I am afraid,
Is faulty: oh, what shall I say, how is the truth to be said?
You were born, you had body, you died.
It is just that you never giggled or planned or cried.   30

Believe me, I loved you all.
Believe me, I knew you, though faintly, and I loved, I loved you all.

[1987]

 ## TOPICS FOR CRITICAL THINKING AND WRITING

1. The first ten lines sound like a chant. What gives them that quality?
   What makes them nonetheless serious?
2. In lines 20–23 the mother attempts to deny the "crime" but cannot.
   What is her reasoning here?
3. Do you find the last lines convincing? Explain.

 ## SYLVIA PLATH

*Sylvia Plath (1932–63) was born in Boston, the daughter of German
immigrants. While still an undergraduate at Smith College, she published in* Seventeen *and* Mademoiselle, *but her years at college, like
her later years, were marked by manic-depressive periods. After graduating from college she went to England to study at Cambridge University, where she met the English poet Ted Hughes, whom she married in 1956. The marriage was unsuccessful, and they separated.
One day she committed suicide by turning on the kitchen gas.*

Daddy

You do not do, you do not do
Any more, black shoe
In which I have lived like a foot
For thirty years, poor and white,
Barely daring to breathe or Achoo.   5

Daddy, I have had to kill you.
You died before I had time—
Marble-heavy, a bag full of God,
Ghastly statue with one gray toe
Big as a Frisco seal   10

And a head in the freakish Atlantic
Where it pours bean green over blue
In the waters off beautiful Nauset.
I used to pray to recover you.
Ach, du.°   15

In the German tongue, in the Polish town
Scraped flat by the roller
Of wars, wars, wars.
But the name of the town is common.
My Polack friend   20

Says there are a dozen or two.
So I never could tell where you
Put your foot, your root,
I never could talk to you.
The tongue stuck in my jaw.   25

It stuck in a barb wire snare.
Ich, ich, ich, ich,°
I could hardly speak.
I thought every German was you.
And the language obscene   30

An engine, an engine
Chuffing me off like a Jew.
A Jew to Dachau, Auschwitz, Belsen.°
I began to talk like a Jew.
I think I may well be a Jew.   35

The snows of the Tyrol, the clear beer of Vienna
Are not very pure or true.
With my gypsy ancestress and my weird luck
And my Taroc pack and my Taroc pack
I may be a bit of a Jew.   40

I have always been scared of *you,*
With your Luftwaffe,° your gobbledygoo.
And your neat moustache
And your Aryan eye, bright blue,
Panzer-man,° panzer-man, O You—   45

---

¹⁵**Ach, du** O, you (German)   ²⁷**Ich, ich, ich, ich** I, I, I, I   ³³**Dachau, Auschwitz, Belsen** concentration camps   ⁴²**Luftwaffe** German airforce   ⁴⁵**Panzer-man** member of a tank crew

Not God but a swastika
So black no sky could squeak through.
Every woman adores a Fascist,
The boot in the face, the brute
Brute heart of a brute like you.   50

You stand at the blackboard, daddy,
In the picture I have of you,
A cleft in your chin instead of your foot
But no less a devil for that, no not
Any less the black man who   55

Bit my pretty red heart in two.
I was ten when they buried you.
At twenty I tried to die
And get back, back, back to you.
I thought even the bones would do.   60

But they pulled me out of the sack,
And they stuck me together with glue,
And then I knew what to do.
I made a model of you,
A man in black with a Meinkampf° look   65

And a love of the rack and the screw.
And I said I do, I do.
So daddy, I'm finally through.
The black telephone's off at the root,
The voices just can't worm through.   70

If I've killed one man, I've killed two—
The vampire who said he was you
And drank my blood for a year,
Seven years, if you want to know.
Daddy, you can lie back now.   75

There's a stake in your fat black heart
And the villagers never liked you.
They are dancing and stamping on you.
They always *knew* it was you.
Daddy, daddy, you bastard, I'm through.   80

[1965]

 # TOPICS FOR CRITICAL THINKING AND WRITING

1. Many readers find in this poem something that reminds them of nursery
   rhymes. If you are among these readers, specify the resemblance(s).
2. Some critics have called parts of the poem "surrealistic." Check a college dictionary, and then argue in a paragraph or two why the word is
   or is not appropriate.
3. Is this a poem whose experience a reader can share? Explain.

°65**Meinkampf** *My Struggle* (title of Hitler's autobiography)

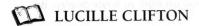 LUCILLE CLIFTON

Lucille Clifton (née Sayles) was born in New York State in 1936 and was educated at Howard University and Fredonia State Teachers College. In addition to publishing 7 books of poetry, she has written 15 children's books. Clifton has received numerous awards, including a grant from the National Endowment for the Arts. She teaches creative writing at the University of California, Santa Cruz.

wishes for sons

i wish them cramps.
i wish them a strange town
and the last tampon.
i wish them no 7-11.   4

i wish them one week early
and wearing a white skirt.
i wish them one week late.

later i wish them hot flashes   8
and clots like you
wouldn't believe. let the
flashes come when they
meet someone special.   12
let the clots come
when they want to.

let them think they have accepted
arrogance in the universe,   16
then bring them to gynecologists
not unlike themselves.

[1990]

 TOPICS FOR CRITICAL THINKING AND WRITING

1. How would you characterize Clifton's "wishes for sons"? Are the wishes sympathetic, hostile, or what?
2. How would you paraphrase or interpret the last two lines?
3. The poem, including the title, has no capital letters. But it does have periods. What other rhythms does it have?
4. Try freewriting a page or two of wishes: for someone you love, or don't love, or both; for someone in the news. Your wishes can be for more than one person; they can be practical, or not.

 RUTH WHITMAN

Ruth Whitman was born in New York City in 1922 and was educated at Radcliffe and Harvard. She has published several books of poetry and has also published translations from French, Greek, and

*Yiddish. She is also the author of a book on how to write poetry, Be-
coming a Poet (1982).*

Listening to grownups quarreling

standing in the hall against the
wall with my little brother, blown
like leaves against the wall by their   4
voices, my head like a pingpong ball
between the paddles of their anger:
I knew what it meant
to tremble like a leaf.   8

Cold with their wrath, I heard
the claws of the rain
pounce. Floods
poured through the city,   12
skies clapped over me,
and I was shaken, shaken
like a mouse
between their jaws.   16

[1968]

 ## TOPICS FOR CRITICAL THINKING AND WRITING

1. Whitman compares herself to a leaf in the first stanza, and her head is
   like a pingpong ball. What other comparisons does she use in stanza 2?
2. In a paragraph (or a journal entry), compare yourself to some nonhuman figure as you overhear grownups quarreling, or talking about an
   event that you were not intended to be part of.

 ## SHARON OLDS

*Sharon Olds was born in San Francisco in 1942 and was educated at
Stanford University and Columbia University. She has published several volumes of poetry and has received major awards.*

I Go Back to May 1937

I see them standing at the formal gates of their colleges,
I see my father strolling out
under the ochre sandstone arch, the
red tiles glinting like bent
plates of blood behind his head, I   5

see my mother with a few light books at her hip
standing at the pillar made of tiny bricks with the
wrought-iron gate still open behind her, its
sword-tips black in the May air,
they are about to graduate, they are about to get married, 10
they are kids, they are dumb, all they know is they are
innocent, they would never hurt anybody.
I want to go up to them and say Stop,
don't do it—she's the wrong woman,
he's the wrong man, you are going to do things 15
you cannot imagine you would ever do,
you are going to do bad things to children,
you are going to suffer in ways you never heard of,
you are going to want to die. I want to go
up to them there in the late May sunlight and say it, 20
her hungry pretty blank face turning to me,
her pitiful beautiful untouched body,
his arrogant handsome blind face turning to me,
his pitiful beautiful untouched body,
but I don't do it. I want to live. I 25
take them up like the male and female
paper dolls and bang them together
at the hips like chips of flint as if to
strike sparks from them, I say
Do what you are going to do, and I will tell about it. 30

[1987]

 TOPICS FOR CRITICAL THINKING AND WRITING

1. Having read the poem, how do you understand its title? How does Olds seem to define "I"? What does she mean by "Go Back to"? And why "May 1937"?

2. In the first line Olds says, "I see them." *How* does she see them? Actually? In imagination? In photographs? Or can't we know?

3. Consider the comparisons, such as the simile in lines 4–5 ("red tiles glinting like bent / plates of blood") and the metaphor in lines 8–9 (the uprights of the wrought-iron gate are "sword-tips"). What do they tell us about the speaker's view of things?

4. Observe where the sentences of the poem begin and end. Can you explain these sentence boundaries? What shifts of meaning or mood accompany the end of one sentence and the beginning of the next?

5. How are the mother and father characterized when young? Are these characterizations consistent or inconsistent with the violent emotions of lines 13–19?

6. How do you read the last line? Do you feel that the speaker is, for example, angry, or vengeful, or sympathetic, or resigned? How do you interpret "and I will tell about it."? To whom will she "tell about it," and how?

JUDITH ORTIZ COFER

Born in Puerto Rico in 1952 of a Puerto Rican mother and a United States mainland father who served in the Navy, Judith Ortiz Cofer was educated both in Puerto Rico and on the mainland. After earning a bachelor's and a master's degree in English, she did further graduate work at Oxford and then taught English in Florida. She has published seven volumes of poetry.

My Father in the Navy: A Childhood Memory

Stiff and immaculate
in the white cloth of his uniform
and a round cap on his head like a halo,
he was an apparition on leave from a shadow-world
and only flesh and blood when he rose from below   5
the waterline where he kept watch over the engines
and dials making sure the ship parted the waters
on a straight course.
Mother, brother and I kept vigil
on the nights and dawns of his arrivals,   10
watching the corner beyond the neon sign of a quasar
for the flash of white our father like an angel
heralding a new day.
His homecomings were the verses
we composed over the years making up   15
the siren's song that kept him coming back
from the bellies of iron whales
and into our nights
like the evening prayer.

[1987]

 TOPIC FOR CRITICAL THINKING

Some readers of the poem find the father dead and the poet rethinking her childhood memories. Others find the father alive and also find the poet rethinking her memories. What is your opinion?

 DAVID MURA

David Mura (b. 1952) is a sansei, *a third-generation Japanese-American. In addition to publishing a book of poems, he has published "A Male Grief" (an essay on pornography) and* Turning Japanese *(a memoir of his visit to Japan). Mura has received several*

awards, including a US/Japan Creative Artist Fellowship, and an
NEA Literature Fellowship.

An Argument: On 1942

For my mother

Near Rose's Chop Suey and Jinosuke's grocery,
the temple where incense hovered and inspired
dense evening chants (prayers for Buddha's mercy,
colorless and deep), that day he was fired . . .   4

—No, no, no, she tells me. Why bring it back?
The camps are over. (Also overly dramatic.)
Forget *shoyu*-stained *furoshiki,*° *mochi*° on a stick:
You're like a terrier, David, gnawing a bone, an old, old trick . . .   8

Mostly we were bored. Women cooked and sewed,
men played blackjack, dug gardens, a *benjo.*°
Who noticed barbed wire, guards in the towers?
We were children, hunting stones, birds, wild flowers.   12

Yes, Mother hid tins of *tsukemono*° and eel
beneath the bed. And when the last was peeled,
clamped tight her lips, growing thinner and thinner.
But cancer not the camps made her throat blacker   16

. . . And she didn't die then . . . after the war, in St. Paul,
you weren't even born. Oh I know, I know, it's all
part of your job, your way, but why can't you glean
how far we've come, how much I can't recall—   20

David, it was so long ago—how useless it seems . . .

[1989]

 TOPICS FOR CRITICAL THINKING AND WRITING

1. Mura's poem is called "An Argument: On 1942." What happened in
   1942 that the poem is about? Does the poem allow you to guess? What
   was the *argument* about?
2. What is the mother's position?
3. The mother says (last line): "David, it was so long ago—how useless it
   seems." Speaking of "An Argument," Mura has said, "As with much of
   my work, I think of this poem as a political poem." How might you justify his remark? How might he answer his mother's last line?
4. If the poem reminds you of an experience in your life, or your family's
   life, in a brief essay (about three typed pages) try to set down the central argument.

[7]**shoyo-stained** *furoshiki* a soy-sauce-stained scarf that is used to carry things
mochi rice cakes   [10]**benjo** toilet   [13]**tsukemono** Japanese pickles [Author's notes]

The original cast of *The Glass Menagerie*— Lorette Taylor, Julie Hayden, Eddie Dowling, and Anthony Ross. (New York Public Library, The Billy Rose Theater Collection)

Drama

 TENNESSEE WILLIAMS

Tennessee Williams (1914–83) was born Thomas Lanier Williams in Columbus, Mississippi. During his childhood his family moved to St. Louis, where his father had accepted a job as manager of a shoe company. Williams has written that neither he nor his sister Rose could adjust to the change from the South to the Midwest, but the children had already been deeply troubled. Nevertheless, at the age of 16 he achieved some distinction as a writer when his prize-winning essay in a nationwide contest was published. After high school he attended the University of Missouri but flunked ROTC and was therefore withdrawn from school by his father. He worked in a shoe factory for a while, then attended Washington University, where he wrote several plays. He finally graduated from the University of Iowa with a major in playwrighting. After graduation he continued to write, supporting himself with odd jobs such as waiting on tables and running elevators. His first commercial success was The Glass Menagerie *(produced in Chicago in 1944, and in New York in 1945); among his other plays are* A Streetcar Named Desire *(1947),* Cat on a Hot Tin Roof *(1955), and* Suddenly Last Summer *(1958).*

The Glass Menagerie

nobody, not even the rain, has such small hands.
                              —e. e. cummings

LIST OF CHARACTERS

AMANDA WINGFIELD, *the mother. A little woman of great but confused vitality clinging frantically to another time and place. Her characterization must be carefully created, not copied from type. She is not paranoiac, but her life is paranoia. There is much to admire in Amanda, and as much to love and pity as there is to laugh at. Certainly she has endurance and a kind of heroism, and though her foolishness makes her unwittingly cruel at times, there is tenderness in her slight person.*

LAURA WINGFIELD, *her daughter. Amanda, having failed to establish contact with reality, continues to live vitally in her illusions, but Laura's situation is even graver. A childhood illness has left her crippled, one leg slightly shorter than the other, and held in a brace. This defect need not be more than suggested on the stage. Stemming from this, Laura's separation increases till she is like a piece of her own glass collection, too exquisitely fragile to move from the shelf.*

TOM WINGFIELD, *her son. And the narrator of the play. A poet with a job in a warehouse. His nature is not remorseless, but to escape from a trap he has to act without pity.*

JIM O'CONNOR, *the gentleman caller. A nice, ordinary, young man.*

SCENE. *An alley in St. Louis.*

PART I. *Preparation for a Gentleman Caller.*

PART II. *The Gentleman Calls.*

TIME. *Now and the Past.*

Scene I

The Wingfield apartment is in the rear of the building, one of those vast hive-like conglomerations of cellular living-units that flower as warty growths in overcrowded urban centers of lower middle-class population and are symptomatic of the impulse of this largest and fundamentally enslaved section of American society to avoid fluidity and differentiation and to exist and function as one interfused mass of automatism.

The apartment faces an alley and is entered by a fire-escape, a structure whose name is a touch of accidental poetic truth, for all of these huge buildings are always burning with the slow and implacable fires of human desperation. The fire-escape is included in the set—that is, the landing of it and steps descending from it.

The scene is memory and is therefore nonrealistic. Memory takes a lot of poetic license. It omits some details; others are exaggerated, according to the emotional value of the articles it touches, for mem-

*ory is seated predominantly in the heart. The interior is therefore
rather dim and poetic.*

*At the rise of the curtain, the audience is faced with the dark,
grim rear wall of the Wingfield tenement. This building, which runs
parallel to the footlights, is flanked on both sides by dark, narrow alleys which run into murky canyons of tangled clotheslines, garbage
cans and the sinister latticework of neighboring fire-escapes. It is up
and down these side alleys that exterior entrances and exits are
made, during the play. At the end of* TOM's *opening commentary, the
dark tenement wall slowly reveals (by means of a transparency) the
interior of the ground floor Wingfield apartment.*

*Downstage is the living room, which also serves as a sleeping
room for* LAURA, *the sofa unfolding to make her bed. Upstage, center,
and divided by a wide arch or second proscenium with transparent
faded portieres (or second curtain), is the dining room. In an old-
fashioned what-not in the living room are seen scores of transparent
glass animals. A blown-up photograph of the father hangs on the wall
of the living room, facing the audience, to the left of the archway. It is
the face of a very handsome young man in a doughboy's First World
War cap. He is gallantly smiling, ineluctably smiling, as if to say, "I
will be smiling forever."*

*The audience hears and sees the opening scene in the dining
room through both the transparent fourth wall of the building and
the transparent gauze portieres of the dining-room arch. It is during
this revealing scene that the fourth wall slowly ascends, out of sight.*

*This transparent exterior wall is not brought down again until
the very end of the play, during* TOM's *final speech.*

*The narrator is an undisguised convention of the play. He takes
whatever license with dramatic convention as is convenient to his
purposes.*

TOM *enters dressed as a merchant sailor from alley, stage left, and
strolls across the front of the stage to the fire-escape. There he stops
and lights a cigarette. He addresses the audience.*

TOM. Yes, I have tricks in my pocket, I have things up my sleeve. But I am
the opposite of a stage magician. He gives you illusion that has the appearance of truth. I give you truth in the pleasant disguise of illusion. To
begin with, I turn back time. I reverse it to that quaint period, the thirties, when the huge middle class of America was matriculating in a
school for the blind. Their eyes had failed them, or they had failed their
eyes, and so they were having their fingers pressed forcibly down on
the fiery Braille alphabet of a dissolving economy. In Spain there was
revolution. Here there was only shouting and confusion. In Spain there
was Guernica. Here there were disturbances of labor, sometimes pretty
violent, in otherwise peaceful cities such as Chicago, Cleveland, Saint
Louis. . . . This is the social background of the play.
[Music.]

The play is memory. Being a memory play, it is dimly lighted, it is
sentimental, it is not realistic. In memory everything seems to happen
to music. That explains the fiddle in the wings. I am the narrator of the
play, and also a character in it. The other characters are my mother,
Amanda, my sister, Laura, and a gentleman caller who appears in the

final scenes. He is the most realistic character in the play, being an emissary from a world of reality that we were somehow set apart from. But since I have a poet's weakness for symbols, I am using this character also as a symbol; he is the long delayed but always expected something that we live for. There is a fifth character in the play who doesn't appear except in this larger-than-life photograph over the mantel. This is our father who left us a long time ago. He was a telephone man who fell in love with long distances; he gave up his job with the telephone company and skipped the light fantastic out of town. . . . The last we heard of him was a picture post-card from Mazatlan, on the Pacific coast of Mexico, containing a message of two words—"Hello—Goodbye!" and no address. I think the rest of the play will explain itself. . . .

AMANDA*'s voice becomes audible through the portieres.*

    [Legend on Screen: "Où Sont les Neiges?"]

    He divides the portieres and enters the upstage area.

    AMANDA *and* LAURA *are seated at a drop-leaf table. Eating is indicated by gestures without food or utensils.* AMANDA *faces the audience.* TOM *and* LAURA *are seated in profile.*

    The interior has lit up softly and through the scrim we see AMANDA *and* LAURA *seated at the table in the upstage area.*

AMANDA *[calling].* Tom?

TOM. Yes, Mother.

AMANDA. We can't say grace until you come to the table!

TOM. Coming, Mother. *[He bows slightly and withdraws, reappearing a few moments later in his place at the table.]*

AMANDA *[to her son].* Honey, don't *push* with your *fingers.* If you have to push with something, the thing to push with is a crust of bread. And chew—chew! Animals have sections in their stomachs which enable them to digest food without mastication, but human beings are supposed to chew their food before they swallow it down. Eat food leisurely, son, and really enjoy it. A well-cooked meal has lots of delicate flavors that have to be held in the mouth for appreciation. So chew your food and give your salivary glands a chance to function!

    TOM *deliberately lays his imaginary fork down and pushes his chair back from the table.*

TOM. I haven't enjoyed one bite of this dinner because of your constant directions on how to eat it. It's you that makes me rush through meals with your hawk-like attention to every bite I take. Sickening—spoils my appetite—all this discussion of animals' secretion—salivary glands—mastication!

AMANDA *[lightly].* Temperament like a Metropolitan star! *[He rises and crosses downstage.]* You're not excused from the table.

TOM. I am getting a cigarette.

AMANDA. You smoke too much.

    LAURA *rises.*

LAURA. I'll bring in the blanc mange.

    He remains standing with his cigarette by the portieres during the following.

AMANDA *[rising].* No, sister, no, sister—you be the lady this time and I'll be the darky.

LAURA. I'm already up.

AMANDA. Resume your seat, little sister—I want you to stay fresh and pretty—for gentlemen callers!

LAURA. I'm not expecting any gentlemen callers.

AMANDA [crossing out to kitchenette. Airily]. Sometimes they come when they are least expected! Why, I remember one Sunday afternoon in Blue Mountain—[Enters kitchenette.]

TOM. I know what's coming!

LAURA. Yes. But let her tell it.

TOM. Again?

LAURA. She loves to tell it.

AMANDA returns with bowl of dessert.

AMANDA. One Sunday afternoon in Blue Mountain—your mother received— seventeen!—gentlemen callers! Why, sometimes there weren't chairs enough to accommodate them all. We had to send the nigger over to bring in folding chairs from the parish house.

TOM [remaining at portieres]. How did you entertain those gentlemen callers?

AMANDA. I understood the art of conversation!

TOM. I bet you could talk.

AMANDA. Girls in those days knew how to talk, I can tell you.

TOM. Yes?

[Image: AMANDA as a Girl on a Porch Greeting Callers.]

AMANDA. They knew how to entertain their gentlemen callers. It wasn't enough for a girl to be possessed of a pretty face and a graceful figure— although I wasn't slighted in either respect. She also needed to have a nimble wit and a tongue to meet all occasions.

TOM. What did you talk about?

AMANDA. Things of importance going on in the world! Never anything coarse or common or vulgar. [She addresses TOM as though he were seated in the vacant chair at the table though he remains by portieres. He plays this scene as though he held the book.] My callers were gentlemen— all! Among my callers were some of the most prominent young planters of the Mississippi Delta—planters and sons of planters!

TOM motions for music and a spot of light on AMANDA.

Her eyes lift, her face glows, her voice becomes rich and elegiac.
[Screen Legend: "Où Sont les Neiges?"]

There was young Champ Laughlin who later became vice-president of the Delta Planters Bank. Hadley Stevenson who was drowned in Moon Lake and left his widow one hundred and fifty thousand in Government bonds. There were the Cutrere brothers, Wesley and Bates. Bates was one of my bright particular beaux! He got in a quarrel with that wild Wainright boy. They shot it out on the floor of Moon Lake Casino. Bates was shot through the stomach. Died in the ambulance on his way to Memphis. His widow was also well-provided for, came into eight or ten thousand acres, that's all. She married him on the rebound—never loved her—carried my picture on him the night he died! And there was that boy that every girl in Delta had set her cap for! That beautiful, brilliant young Fitzhugh boy from Green County!

TOM. What did he leave his widow?

AMANDA. He never married! Gracious, you talk as though all of my old admirers had turned up their toes to the daisies!

TOM. Isn't this the first you mentioned that still survives?

AMANDA. That Fitzhugh boy went North and made a fortune—came to be known as the Wolf of Wall Street! He had the Midas touch, whatever he touched turned to gold! And I could have been Mrs. Duncan J. Fitzhugh, mind you! But—I picked your *father!*

LAURA *[rising]*. Mother, let me clear the table.

AMANDA. No dear, you go in front and study your typewriter chart. Or practice your shorthand a little. Stay fresh and pretty!—It's almost time for our gentlemen callers to start arriving. *[She flounces girlishly toward the kitchenette.]* How many do you suppose we're going to entertain this afternoon?

TOM *throws down the paper and jumps up with a groan.*

LAURA *[alone in the dining room]*. I don't believe we're going to receive any, Mother.

AMANDA *[reappearing, airily]*. What? No one—not one? You must be joking! *[LAURA nervously echoes her laugh. She slips in a fugitive manner through the half-open portieres and draws them gently behind her. A shaft of very clear light is thrown on her face against the faded tapestry of the curtains.] [Music: "The Glass Menagerie" Under Faintly.] [Lightly.]* Not one gentleman caller? It can't be true! There must be a flood, there must have been a tornado!

LAURA. It isn't a flood, it's not a tornado, Mother. I'm just not popular like you were in Blue Mountain. . . . *[TOM utters another groan. LAURA glances at him with a faint, apologetic smile. Her voice catching a little.]* Mother's afraid I'm going to be an old maid.

[The Scene Dims Out with "Glass Menagerie" Music.]

Scene II

"Laura, Haven't You Ever Liked Some Boy?"

On the dark stage the screen is lighted with the image of blue roses. Gradually LAURA*'s figure becomes apparent and the screen goes out. The music subsides.*

LAURA *is seated in the delicate ivory chair at the small clawfoot table.*

She wears a dress of soft violet material for a kimono—her hair tied back from her forehead with a ribbon.

She is washing and polishing her collection of glass.

AMANDA *appears on the fire-escape steps. At the sound of her ascent,* LAURA *catches her breath, thrusts the bowl of ornaments away and seats herself stiffly before the diagram of the typewriter keyboard as though it held her spellbound. Something has happened to* AMANDA. *It is written in her face as she climbs to the landing: a look that is grim and hopeless and a little absurd.*

She has on one of those cheap or imitation velvety-looking cloth coats with imitation fur collar. Her hat is five or six years old, one of those dreadful cloche hats that were worn in the late twenties, and she is clasping an enormous black patent-leather pocketbook with nickel clasp and initials. This is her full-dress outfit, the one she usually wears to the D.A.R.

Before entering she looks through the door.

She purses her lips, opens her eyes wide, rolls them upward and shakes her head.

Then she slowly lets herself in the door. Seeing her mother's expression LAURA *touches her lips with a nervous gesture.*

LAURA. Hello, Mother, I was—[*She makes a nervous gesture toward the chart on the wall.* AMANDA *leans against the shut door and stares at* LAURA *with a martyred look.*]

AMANDA. Deception? Deception? [*She slowly removes her hat and gloves, continuing the swift suffering stare. She lets the hat and gloves fall on the floor—a bit of acting.*]

LAURA [*shakily*]. How was the D.A.R. meeting? [AMANDA *slowly opens her purse and removes a dainty white handkerchief which she shakes out delicately and delicately touches to her lips and nostrils.*] Didn't you go to the D.A.R. meeting, Mother?

AMANDA [*faintly, almost inaudibly*].—No.—No. [*Then more forcibly.*] I did not have the strength—to go to the D.A.R. In fact, I did not have the courage! I wanted to find a hole in the ground and hide myself in it forever! [*She crosses slowly to the wall and removes the diagram of the typewriter keyboard. She holds it in front of her for a second, staring at it sweetly and sorrowfully—then bites her lips and tears it in two pieces.*]

LAURA [*faintly*]. Why did you do that, Mother? [AMANDA *repeats the same procedure with the chart of the Gregg Alphabet.*] Why are you—

AMANDA. Why? Why? How old are you, Laura?

LAURA. Mother, you know my age.

AMANDA. I thought that you were an adult; it seems that I was mistaken.
[*She crosses slowly to the sofa and sinks down and stares at* LAURA.]

LAURA. Please don't stare at me, Mother.

AMANDA *closes her eyes and lowers her head. Count ten.*

AMANDA. What are we going to do, what is going to become of us, what is the future?

Count ten.

LAURA. Has something happened, Mother? [AMANDA *draws a long breath and takes out the handkerchief again. Dabbing process.*] Mother, has—something happened?

AMANDA. I'll be all right in a minute. I'm just bewildered—[*count five*]—by life. . . .

LAURA. Mother, I wish that you would tell me what's happened.

AMANDA. As you know, I was supposed to be inducted into my office at the D.A.R. this afternoon. [*Image: A Swarm of Typewriters.*] But I stopped off at Rubicam's Business College to speak to your teachers about your having a cold and ask them what progress they thought you were making down there.

LAURA. Oh. . . .

AMANDA. I went to the typing instructor and introduced myself as your mother. She didn't know who you were. Wingfield, she said. We don't have any such student enrolled at the school! I assured her she did, that you had been going to classes since early in January. "I wonder," she said, "if you could be talking about that terribly shy little girl who dropped out of school after only a few days' attendance?" "No," I said, "Laura, my daughter, has been going to school every day for the past six weeks!" "Excuse me," she said. She took the attendance book out and there was your name, unmistakably printed, and all the dates you were absent until they decided that you had dropped out of school. I still said, "No, there must have been some mistake! There must have been some mix-up in the records!" And she said, "No—I remember her perfectly now. Her hand shook so that she couldn't hit the right keys! The first time we gave a speed-test, she broke down completely—was sick at the stomach and almost had to be carried into the wash-room! After that morning she never showed up any more. We phoned the house but never got any answer"—while I was working at Famous and Barr, I suppose, demonstrating those—Oh! I felt so weak I could barely keep on my feet. I had to sit down while they got me a glass of water! Fifty dollars' tuition, all of our plans—my hopes and ambitions for you—just gone up the spout, just gone up the spout like that. *[LAURA draws a long breath and gets awkwardly to her feet. She crosses to the victrola and winds it up.]* What are you doing?

LAURA. Oh! *[She releases the handle and returns to her seat.]*

AMANDA. Laura, where have you been going when you've gone out pretending that you were going to business college?

LAURA. I've just been going out walking.

AMANDA. That's not true.

LAURA. It is. I just went walking.

AMANDA. Walking? Walking? In winter? Deliberately courting pneumonia in that light coat? Where did you walk to, Laura?

LAURA. It was the lesser of two evils, Mother. *[Image: Winter Scene in Park.]* I couldn't go back up. I—threw up—on the floor!

AMANDA. From half past seven till after five every day you mean to tell me you walked around in the park, because you wanted to make me think that you were still going to Rubicam's Business College?

LAURA. It wasn't as bad as it sounds. I went inside places to get warmed up.

AMANDA. Inside where?

LAURA. I went in the art museum and the bird-houses at the Zoo. I visited the penguins every day! Sometimes I did without lunch and went to the movies. Lately I've been spending most of my afternoons in the Jewelbox, that big glass house where they raise the tropical flowers.

AMANDA. You did all this to deceive me, just for the deception? *[LAURA looks down.]* Why?

LAURA. Mother, when you're disappointed, you get that awful suffering look on your face, like the picture of Jesus' mother in the museum!

AMANDA. Hush!

LAURA. I couldn't face it.

Pause. A whisper of strings.

[Legend: "The Crust of Humility."]

AMANDA *[hopelessly fingering the huge pocketbook]*. So what are we going to do the rest of our lives? Stay home and watch the parades go by? Amuse ourselves with the glass menagerie, darling? Eternally play those worn-out phonograph records your father left as a painful reminder of

him? We won't have a business career—we've given that up because it
gave us nervous indigestion! *[Laughs wearily.]* What is there left but de-
pendency all our lives? I know so well what becomes of unmarried
women who aren't prepared to occupy a position. I've seen such pitiful
cases in the South—barely tolerated spinsters living upon the grudging
patronage of sister's husband or brother's wife!—stuck away in some
little mousetrap of a room—encouraged by one in-law to visit another—
little birdlike women without any nest—eating the crust of humility all
their life! Is that the future that we've mapped out for ourselves? I swear
it's the only alternative I can think of! It isn't a very pleasant alternative,
is it? Of course—some girls *do marry.* *[Laura twists her hands nervously.]* Haven't you ever liked some boy?

LAURA. Yes. I liked one once. *[Rises.]* I came across his picture a while ago.

AMANDA *[with some interest]*. He gave you his picture?

LAURA. No, it's in the year-book.

AMANDA *[disappointed]*. Oh—a high-school boy.

[Screen Image: JIM as a High-School Hero Bearing a Silver Cup.]

LAURA. Yes. His name was Jim. *[LAURA lifts the heavy annual from the clawfoot table.]* Here he is in *The Pirates of Penzance.*

AMANDA *[absently]*. The what?

LAURA. The operetta the senior class put on. He had a wonderful voice and
we sat across the aisle from each other Mondays, Wednesdays and Fridays in the Aud. Here he is with the silver cup for debating! See his
grin?

AMANDA *[absently]*. He must have had a jolly disposition.

LAURA. He used to call me—Blue Roses.

[Image: Blue Roses.]

AMANDA. Why did he call you such a name as that?

LAURA. When I had that attack of pleurosis—he asked me what was the matter when I came back. I said pleurosis—he thought that I said Blue
Roses! So that's what he always called me after that. Whenever he saw
me, he'd holler, "Hello, Blue Roses!" I didn't care for the girl that he
went out with. Emily Meisenbach. Emily was the best-dressed girl at Soldan. She never struck me, though, as being sincere. . . . It says in the
Personal Section—they're engaged. That's—six years ago! They must
be married by now.

AMANDA. Girls that aren't cut out for business careers usually wind up married to some nice man. *[Gets up with a spark of revival.]* Sister, that's
what you'll do!

LAURA *utters a startled, doubtful laugh. She reaches quickly for a piece
of glass.*

LAURA. But, Mother—

AMANDA. Yes? *[Crossing to photograph.]*

LAURA *[in a tone of frightened apology]*. I'm—crippled!

[Image: Screen.]

AMANDA. Nonsense! Laura, I've told you never, never to use that word. Why,
you're not crippled, you just have a little defect—hardly noticeable,
even! When people have some slight disadvantage like that, they cultivate other things to make up for it—develop charm—and vivacity—
and—*charm!* That's all you have to do! *[She turns again to the photograph.]* One thing your father had *plenty of*—was *charm!*

TOM *motions to the fiddle in the wings.*
[The Scene Fades out with Music.]

Scene III

[Legend on the Screen: "After the Fiasco—"]
    TOM *speaks from the fire-escape landing.*
TOM. After the fiasco at Rubicam's Business College, the idea of getting a
gentleman caller for Laura began to play a more important part in
Mother's calculations. It became an obsession. Like some archetype of
the universal unconscious, the image of the gentleman caller haunted
our small apartment. . . . *[Image: Young Man at Door with Flowers.]*
An evening at home rarely passed without some allusion to this image,
this specter, this hope. . . . Even when he wasn't mentioned, his presence hung in Mother's preoccupied look and in my sister's frightened,
apologetic manner—hung like a sentence passed upon the Wingfields!
Mother was a woman of action as well as words. She began to take logical steps in the planned direction. Late that winter and in the early
spring—realizing that extra money would be needed to properly
feather the nest and plume the bird—she conducted a vigorous campaign on the telephone, roping in subscribers to one of those magazines for matrons called *The Home-maker's Companion,* the type of
journal features the serialized sublimations of ladies of letters who think
in terms of delicate cuplike breasts, slim, tapering waists, rich, creamy
thighs, eyes like wood-smoke in autumn, fingers that soothe and caress
like strains of music, bodies as powerful as Etruscan sculpture.
[Screen Image: Glamor Magazine Cover.]
    AMANDA *enters with phone on long extension cord. She is spotted
in the dim stage.*
AMANDA. Ida Scott? This is Amanda Wingfield! We *missed* you at the D.A.R.
last Monday! I said to myself: She's probably suffering with that sinus
condition! How is that sinus condition? Horrors! Heaven have mercy!—
You're a Christian martyr, yes, that's what you are, a Christian martyr!
Well, I just now happened to notice that your subscription to the *Com-
panion's* about to expire! Yes, it expires with the next issue, honey!—
just when that wonderful new serial by Bessie Mae Hopper is getting off
to such an exciting start. Oh, honey, it's something that you can't miss!
You remember how *Gone With the Wind* took everybody by storm?
You simply couldn't go out if you hadn't read it. All everybody *talked*
was Scarlett O'Hara. Well, this is a book that critics already compare to
Gone With the Wind. It's the *Gone With the Wind* of the post-World
War generation!—What?—Burning?—Oh, honey, don't let them burn,
go take a look in the oven and I'll hold the wire! Heavens—I think she's
hung up!
[Dim Out.]
    *[Legend on Screen: "You Think I'm in Love with Continental
Shoemakers?"]*
    Before the stage is lighted, the violent voices of TOM *and* AMANDA
*are heard. They are quarreling behind the portieres. In front of them
stands* LAURA *with clenched hands and panicky expression.*
    A clear pool of light on her figure throughout this scene.

TOM. What in Christ's name am I—

AMANDA *[shrilly]*. Don't you use that—

TOM. Supposed to do!

AMANDA. Expression! Not in my—

TOM. Ohhh!

AMANDA. Presence! Have you gone out of your senses?

TOM. I have, that's true, *driven* out!

AMANDA. What is the matter with you, you—big—big—IDIOT!

TOM. Look—I've got *no thing,* no single thing—

AMANDA. Lower your voice!

TOM. In my life here that I can call my OWN! Everything is—

AMANDA. Stop that shouting!

TOM. Yesterday you confiscated my books! You had the nerve to—

AMANDA. I took that horrible novel back to the library—yes! That hideous book by that insane Mr. Lawrence. *[*TOM *laughs wildly.]* I cannot control the output of diseased minds or people who cater to them—*[*TOM *laughs still more wildly.]* BUT I WON'T ALLOW SUCH FILTH BROUGHT INTO MY HOUSE! No, no, no, no, no!

TOM. House, house! Who pays rent on it, who makes a slave of himself to—

AMANDA *[fairly screeching]*. Don't you DARE to—

TOM. No, no, *I* musn't say things! *I've* got to just—

AMANDA. Let me tell you—

TOM. I don't want to hear any more! *[He tears the portieres open. The upstage area is lit with a turgid smoky red glow.]*

AMANDA*'s hair is in metal curlers and she wears a very old bathrobe, much too large for her slight figure, a relic of the faithless Mr. Wingfield.*

An upright typewriter and a wild disarray of manuscripts are on the dropleaf table. The quarrel was probably precipitated by AMANDA*'s interruption of his creative labor. A chair lying overthrown on the floor.*

Their gesticulating shadows are cast on the ceiling by the fiery glow.

AMANDA. You *will* hear more, you—

TOM. No, I won't hear more, I'm going out!

AMANDA. You come right back in—

TOM. Out, out, out! Because I'm—

AMANDA. Come back here, Tom Wingfield! I'm not through talking to you!

TOM. Oh, go—

LAURA *[desperately]*. Tom!

AMANDA. You're going to listen, and no more insolence from you! I'm at the end of my patience! *[He comes back toward her.]*

TOM. What do you think I'm at? Aren't I supposed to have any patience to reach the end of, Mother? I know, I know. It seems unimportant to you, what I'm *doing*—what I *want* to do—having a little *difference* between them! You don't think that—

AMANDA. I think you've been doing things that you're ashamed of. That's why you act like this. I don't believe that you go every night to the movies. Nobody goes to the movies night after night. Nobody in their right minds goes to the movies as often as you pretend to. People don't go to the movies at nearly midnight, and movies don't let out at two A.M. Come in stumbling. Muttering to yourself like a maniac! You get three hours' sleep and then go to work. Oh, I can picture the way you're doing down there. Moping, doping, because you're in no condition.

TOM *[wildly]*. No, I'm in no condition!

AMANDA. What right have you got to jeopardize your job? Jeopardize the security of us all? How do you think we'd manage if you were—

TOM. Listen! You think I'm crazy *about* the *warehouse? [He bends fiercely toward her slight figure.]* You think I'm in love with the Continental Shoemakers? You think I want to spend fifty-five *years* down there in that—*celotex interior!* with—*fluorescent—tubes!* Look! I'd rather somebody picked up a crowbar and battered out my brains—than go back mornings! *I go!* Every time you come in yelling that God damn *"Rise and Shine!" "Rise and Shine!"* I say to myself "How *lucky dead people are!"* But I get up. I *go!* For sixty-five dollars a month I give up all that I dream of doing and being *ever!* And you say self—*self's* all I ever think of. Why, listen, if self is what I thought of, Mother, I'd be where he is—GONE! *[Pointing to father's picture.]* As far as the system of transportation reaches! *[He starts past her. She grabs his arm.]* Don't grab at me, Mother!

AMANDA. Where are you going?

TOM. I'm going to the *movies!*

AMANDA. I don't believe that lie!

TOM *[crouching toward her, overtowering her tiny figure. She backs away, gasping]*. I'm going to opium dens! Yes, opium dens, dens of vice and criminals' hang-outs, Mother. I've joined the Hogan gang, I'm a hired assassin, I carry a tommy-gun in a violin case! I run a string of cat-houses in the Valley! They call me Killer, Killer Wingfield, I'm leading a double-life, a simple, honest warehouse worker by day, by night a dynamic *czar* of the *underworld, Mother.* I go to gambling casinos, I spin away fortunes on the roulette table! I wear a patch over one eye and a false mustache, sometimes I put on green whiskers. On those occasions they call me—*El Diablo!* Oh, I could tell you things to make you sleepless! My enemies plan to dynamite this place. They're going to blow us all sky-high some night! I'll be glad, very happy, and so will you! You'll go up, up on a broomstick, over Blue Mountain with seventeen gentlemen callers! You ugly—babbling old—*witch*.... *(He goes through a series of violent, clumsy movements, seizing his overcoat, lunging to the door, pulling it fiercely open. The women watch him, aghast. His arm catches in the sleeve of the coat as he struggles to pull it on. For a moment he is pinioned by the bulky garment. With an outraged groan he tears the coat off again, splitting the shoulders of it, and hurls it across the room. It strikes against the shelf of* LAURA's *glass collection, there is a tinkle of shattering glass.* LAURA *cries out as if wounded.]*

[Music Legend: "The Glass Menagerie."]

LAURA *[shrilly]*. My glass!—menagerie.... *[She covers her face and turns away.]*

But AMANDA *is still stunned and stupefied by the "ugly witch" so that she barely notices this occurrence. Now she recovers her speech.*

AMANDA *[in an awful voice]*. I won't speak to you—until you apologize!

[She crosses through portieres and draws them together behind her. TOM *is left with* LAURA. LAURA *clings weakly to the mantel with her face*

averted. TOM *stares at her stupidly for a moment. Then he crosses to shelf. Drops awkwardly to his knees to collect the fallen glass, glancing at* LAURA *as if he would speak but couldn't.)*
    "The Glass Menagerie" steals in as
    [The Scene Dims Out.]

Scene IV

The interior is dark. Faint light in the alley.
    A deep-voiced bell in a church is tolling the hour of five as the scene commences.
    TOM *appears at the top of the alley. After each solemn boom of the bell in the tower, he shakes a little noise-maker or rattle as if to express the tiny spasm of man in contrast to the sustained power and dignity of the Almighty. This and the unsteadiness of his advance make it evident that he has been drinking.*
    As he climbs the few steps to the fire-escape landing light steals up inside. LAURA *appears in night-dress, observing* TOM's *empty bed in the front room.*
    TOM *fishes in his pockets for the door-key, removing a motley assortment of articles in the search, including a perfect shower of movie-ticket stubs and an empty bottle. At last he finds the key, but just as he is about to insert it, it slips from his fingers. He strikes a match and crouches below the door.*

TOM *[bitterly].* One crack—and it falls through!
    LAURA *opens the door.*
LAURA. Tom! Tom, what are you doing?
TOM. Looking for a door-key.
LAURA. Where have you been all this time?
TOM. I have been to the movies.
LAURA. All this time at the movies?
TOM. There was a very long program. There was a Garbo picture and a Mickey Mouse and a travelogue and a newsreel and a preview of coming attractions. And there was an organ solo and a collection for the milk-fund—simultaneously—which ended up in a terrible fight between a fat lady and an usher!
LAURA *[innocently].* Did you have to stay through everything?
TOM. Of course! And, oh, I forgot! There was a big stage show! The headliner on this stage show was Malvolio the Magician. He performed wonderful tricks, many of them, such as pouring water back and forth between pitchers. First it turned to wine and then it turned to beer and then it turned to whiskey. I know it was whiskey it finally turned into because he needed somebody to come up out of the audience to help him, and I came up—both shows! It was Kentucky Straight Bourbon. A very generous fellow, he gave souvenirs. *[He pulls from his back pocket a shimmering rainbow-colored scarf.]* He gave me this. This is his magic scarf. You can have it, Laura. You wave it over a canary cage and you get a bowl of gold-fish. You wave it over the gold-fish bowl and they fly away canaries. . . . But the wonderfullest trick of all was the coffin trick. We nailed him into a coffin and he got out of the coffin without removing one nail. *[He has come inside.]* There is a trick that would

come in handy for me—get me out of this 2 by 4 situation! *[Flops onto bed and starts removing shoes.]*

LAURA. Tom—Shhh!

TOM. What you shushing me for?

LAURA. You'll wake up Mother.

TOM. Goody, goody! Pay 'er back for all those "Rise an' Shines." *[Lies down, groaning.]* You know it don't take much intelligence to get yourself into a nailed-up coffin, Laura. But who in hell ever got himself out of one without removing one nail?

As if in answer, the father's grinning photograph lights up.

> *[Scene Dims Out.]*

> *Immediately following: The church bell is heard striking six. At the sixth stroke the alarm clock goes off in* AMANDA*'s room, and after a few moments we hear her calling: "Rise and Shine! Rise and Shine!* LAURA, *go tell your brother to rise and shine!"*

TOM *[sitting up slowly]*. I'll rise—but I won't shine.

> *The light increases.*

AMANDA. Laura, tell your brother his coffee is ready.

> LAURA *slips into front room.*

LAURA. Tom! it's nearly seven. Don't make Mother nervous. *[He stares at her stupidly. Beseechingly.]* Tom, speak to Mother this morning. Make up with her, apologize, speak to her!

TOM. She won't to me. It's her that started not speaking.

LAURA. If you just say you're sorry she'll start speaking.

TOM. Her not speaking—is that such a tragedy?

LAURA. Please—please!

AMANDA *[calling from kitchenette]*. Laura, are you going to do what I asked you to do, or do I have to get dressed and go out myself?

LAURA. Going, going—soon as I get on my coat! *[She pulls on a shapeless felt hat with nervous, jerky movement, pleadingly glancing at* TOM. *Rushes awkwardly for coat. The coat is one of* AMANDA*'s, inaccurately made-over, the sleeves too short for* LAURA.*]* Butter and what else?

AMANDA *[entering upstage]*. Just butter. Tell them to charge it.

LAURA. Mother, they make such faces when I do that.

AMANDA. Sticks and stones may break my bones, but the expression on Mr. Garfinkel's face won't harm us! Tell your brother his coffee is getting cold.

LAURA *[at door]*. Do what I asked you, will you, will you, Tom?

> *He looks sullenly away.*

AMANDA. Laura, go now or just don't go at all!

LAURA *[rushing out]*. Going—going! *[A second later she cries out.* TOM *springs up and crosses to the door.* AMANDA *rushes anxiously in.* TOM *opens the door.]*

TOM. Laura?

LAURA. I'm all right. I slipped, but I'm all right.

AMANDA *[peering anxiously after her]*. If anyone breaks a leg on those fire-escape steps, the landlord ought to be sued for every cent he possesses! *[She shuts door. Remembers she isn't speaking and returns to other room.]*

> *As* TOM *enters listlessly for his coffee, she turns her back to him and stands rigidly facing the window on the gloomy gray vault of the*

areaway. Its light on her face with its aged but childish features is cruelly sharp, satirical as a Daumier print.

[Music Under: "Ave Maria."]

TOM *glances sheepishly but sullenly at her averted figure and slumps at the table. The coffee is scalding hot; he sips it and gasps and spits it back in the cup. At his gasp,* AMANDA *catches her breath and half turns. Then catches herself and turns back to window.*

TOM *blows on his coffee, glancing sidewise at his mother. She clears her throat.* TOM *clears his. He starts to rise. Sinks back down again, scratches his head, clears his throat again.* AMANDA *coughs.* TOM *raises his cup in both hands to blow on it, his eyes staring over the rim of it at his mother for several moments. Then he slowly sets the cup down and awkwardly and hesitantly rises from the chair.*

TOM *[hoarsely]*. Mother. I—I apologize. Mother. *[*AMANDA *draws a quick, shuddering breath. Her face works grotesquely. She breaks into child-like tears.]* I'm sorry for what I said, for everything that I said, I didn't mean it.

AMANDA *[sobbingly]*. My devotion has made me a witch and so I make myself hateful to my children!

TOM. No you *don't*.

AMANDA. I worry so much, don't sleep, it makes me nervous!

TOM *[gently]*. I understand that.

AMANDA. I've had to put up a solitary battle all these years. But you're my right-hand bower! Don't fall down, don't fail!

TOM *[gently]*. I try, Mother.

AMANDA *[with great enthusiasm]*. Try and you will SUCCEED! *[The notion makes her breathless.]* Why, you—you're just *full* of natural endowments! Both of my children—they're *unusual* children! Don't you think I know it? I'm so—*proud!* Happy and—feel I've—so much to be thankful for but—Promise me one thing, son!

TOM. What, Mother?

AMANDA. Promise, son, you'll—never be a drunkard!

TOM *[turns to her grinning]*. I will never be a drunkard, Mother.

AMANDA. That's what frightened me so, that you'd be drinking! Eat a bowl of Purina!

TOM. Just coffee, Mother.

AMANDA. Shredded wheat biscuit?

TOM. No. No, Mother, just coffee.

AMANDA. You can't put in a day's work on an empty stomach. You've got ten minutes—don't gulp! Drinking too-hot liquids makes cancer of the stomach. . . . Put cream in.

TOM. No, thank you.

AMANDA. To cool it.

TOM. No! No, thank you, I want it black.

AMANDA. I know, but it's not good for you. We have to do all that we can to build ourselves up. In these trying times we live in, all that we have to cling to is—each other. . . . That's why it's so important to—Tom, I—I sent out your sister so I could discuss something with you. If you hadn't spoken I would have spoken to you. *[Sits down.]*

TOM *[gently]*. What is it, Mother, that you want to discuss?

AMANDA. Laura!

TOM *puts his cup down slowly.*
    [Legend on Screen: "Laura."]
    [Music: "The Glass Menagerie."]

TOM. —Oh.—Laura . . .

AMANDA *[touching his sleeve].* You know how Laura is. So quiet but—still water runs deep! She notices things and I think she—broods about them. *[*TOM *looks up.]* A few days ago I came in and she was crying.

TOM. What about?

AMANDA. You.

TOM. Me?

AMANDA. She has an idea that you're not happy here.

TOM. What gave her that idea?

AMANDA. What gives her any idea? However, you do act strangely. I—I'm not criticizing, understand *that!* I know your ambitions do not lie in the warehouse, that like everybody in the whole wide world—you've had to—make sacrifices, but—Tom—Tom—life's not easy, it calls for—Spartan endurance! There's so many things in my heart that I cannot describe to you! I've never told you but I—*loved* your father. . . .

TOM *[gently].* I know that, Mother.

AMANDA. And you—when I see you taking after his ways! Staying out late—and—well, you *had* been drinking the night you were in that—terrifying condition! Laura says that you hate the apartment and that you go out nights to get away from it! Is that true, Tom?

TOM. No. You say there's so much in your heart that you can't describe to me. That's true of me, too. There's so much in my heart that I can't describe to *you!* So let's respect each other's—

AMANDA. But, why—*why,* Tom—are you always so *restless?* Where do you go to, nights?

TOM. I—go to the movies.

AMANDA. Why do you go to the movies so much, Tom?

TOM. I go to the movies because—I like adventure. Adventure is something I don't have much of at work, so I go to the movies.

AMANDA. But, Tom, you go to the movies *entirely too much!*

TOM. I like a lot of adventure.

    AMANDA *looks baffled, then hurt. As the familiar inquisition resumes he becomes hard and impatient again.* AMANDA *slips back into her querulous attitude toward him.*
    [Image on Screen: Sailing Vessel with Jolly Roger.]

AMANDA. Most young men find adventure in their careers.

TOM. Then most young men are not employed in a warehouse.

AMANDA. The world is full of young men employed in warehouses and offices and factories.

TOM. Do all of them find adventure in their careers?

AMANDA. They do or they do without it! Not everybody has a craze for adventure.

TOM. Man is by instinct a lover, a hunter, a fighter, and none of those instincts are given much play at the warehouse!

AMANDA. Man is by instinct! Don't quote instinct to me! Instinct is something that people have got away from! It belongs to animals! Christian adults don't want it!

TOM. What do Christian adults want, then, Mother?

AMANDA. Superior things! Things of the mind and the spirit! Only animals have to satisfy instincts! Surely your aims are somewhat higher than theirs! Than monkeys—pigs—

TOM. I reckon they're not.

AMANDA. You're joking. However, that isn't what I wanted to discuss.

TOM *[rising]*. I haven't much time.

AMANDA *[pushing his shoulders]*. Sit down.

TOM. You want me to punch in red at the warehouse, Mother?

AMANDA. You have five minutes. I want to talk about Laura.

[Legend: "Plans and Provisions."]

TOM. All right! What about Laura?

AMANDA. We have to be making plans and provisions for her. She's older than you, two years, and nothing has happened. She just drifts along doing nothing. It frightens me terribly how she just drifts along.

TOM. I guess she's the type that people call home girls.

AMANDA. There's no such type, and if there is, it's a pity! That is unless the home is hers, with a husband!

TOM. What?

AMANDA. Oh, I can see the handwriting on the wall as plain as I see the nose in the front of my face! It's terrifying! More and more you remind me of your father! He was out all hours without explanation—Then *left! Goodbye!* And me with the bag to hold. I saw that letter you got from the Merchant Marine. I know what you're dreaming of. I'm not standing here blindfolded. Very well, then. Then *do* it! But not till there's somebody to take your place.

TOM. What do you mean?

AMANDA. I mean that as soon as Laura has got somebody to take care of her, married, a home of her own, independent—why, then you'll be free to go wherever you please, on land, on sea, whichever way the wind blows! But until that time you've got to look out for your sister. I don't say me because I'm old and don't matter! I say for your sister because she's young and dependent. I put her in business college—a dismal failure! Frightened her so it made her sick to her stomach. I took her over to the Young People's League at the church. Another fiasco. She spoke to nobody, nobody spoke to her. Now all she does is fool with those pieces of glass and play those worn-out records. What kind of a life is that for a girl to lead!

TOM. What can I do about it?

AMANDA. Overcome selfishness! Self, self, self is all that you ever think of! *[*TOM *springs up and crosses to get his coat. It is ugly and bulky. He pulls on a cap with earmuffs.]* Where is your muffler? Put your wool muffler on! *[He snatches it angrily from the closet and tosses it around his neck and pulls both ends tight.]* Tom! I haven't said what I had in mind to ask you.

TOM. I'm too late to—

AMANDA *[catching his arms—very importunately. Then shyly]*. Down at the warehouse, aren't there some—nice young men?

TOM. No!

AMANDA. There *must* be—*some.*

TOM. Mother—

Gesture.

AMANDA. Find out one that's clean-living—doesn't drink and—ask him out for sister!

TOM. What?

AMANDA. For *sister!* To *meet!* Get *acquainted!*

TOM *[stamping to door].* Oh, my *go-osh!*

AMANDA. Will you? *[He opens door. Imploringly.]* Will you? *[He starts down.]* Will you? *Will* you dear?

TOM *[calling back].* YES!

> AMANDA *closes the door hesitantly and with a troubled but faintly hopeful expression.*
>
> *[Screen Image: Glamor Magazine Cover.]*
>
> Spot AMANDA *at phone.*

AMANDA. Ella Cartwright? This is Amanda Wingfield! How are you honey? How is that kidney condition? *[Count five.]* Horrors! *[Count five.]* You're a Christian martyr, yes, honey, that's what you are, a Christian martyr! Well, I just happened to notice in my little red book that your subscription to the *Companion* has just run out! I knew that you wouldn't want to miss out on the wonderful serial starting in this new issue. It's by Bessie Mae Hopper, the first thing she's written since *Honeymoon for Three.* Wasn't that a strange and interesting story? Well, this one is even lovelier, I believe. It has a sophisticated society background. It's all about the horsey set on Long Island!

[Fade Out.]

Scene V

[Legend on Screen: "Annunciation."] Fade with music.

> *It is early dusk of a spring evening. Supper has just been finished at the Wingfield apartment.* AMANDA *and* LAURA *in light colored dresses are removing dishes from the table, in the upstage area, which is shadowy, their movements formalized almost as a dance or ritual, their moving forms as pale and silent as moths.*
>
> TOM, *in white shirt and trousers, rises from the table and crosses toward the fire-escape.*

AMANDA *[as he passes her].* Son, will you do me a favor?

TOM. What?

AMANDA. Comb your hair! You look so pretty when your hair is combed! *[*TOM *slouches on sofa with evening paper. Enormous caption "Franco Triumphs."]* There is only one respect in which I would like you to emulate your father.

TOM. What respect is that?

AMANDA. The care he always took of his appearance. He never allowed himself to look untidy. *[He throws down the paper and crosses to fire-escape.]* Where are you going?

TOM. I'm going out to smoke.

AMANDA. You smoke too much. A pack a day at fifteen cents a pack. How much would that amount to in a month? Thirty times fifteen is how much, Tom? Figure it out and you will be astounded at what you could save. Enough to give you a night-school course in accounting at Washington U! Just think what a wonderful thing that would be for you, son!

TOM *is unmoved by the thought.*

TOM. I'd rather smoke. *[He steps out on landing, letting the screen door slam.]*

AMANDA *[sharply]*. I know! That's the tragedy of it. . . . *[Alone, she turns to look at her husband's picture.]*

[Dance Music: "All the World Is Waiting for the Sunrise!"]

TOM *[to the audience]*. Across the alley from us was the Paradise Dance Hall. On evenings in spring the windows and doors were open and the music came outdoors. Sometimes the lights were turned out except for a large glass sphere that hung from the ceiling. It would turn slowly about and filter the dusk with delicate rainbow colors. Then the orchestra played a waltz or a tango, something that had a slow and sensuous rhythm. Couples would come outside, to the relative privacy of the alley. You could see them kissing behind ashpits and telephone poles. This was the compensation for lives that passed like mine, without any change or adventure. Adventure and change were imminent in this year. They were waiting around the corner for all these kids. Suspended in the mist over Berchtesgaden, caught in the folds of Chamberlain's umbrella—In Spain there was Guernica! But here there was only hot swing music and liquor, dance halls, bars, and movies, and sex that hung in the gloom like a chandelier and flooded the world with brief, deceptive rainbows. . . . All the world was waiting for bombardments!

AMANDA *turns from the picture and comes outside.*

AMANDA *[sighing]*. A fire-escape landing's a poor excuse for a porch. *[She spreads a newspaper on a step and sits down, gracefully and demurely as if she were settling into a swing on a Mississippi veranda.]* What are you looking at?

TOM. The moon.

AMANDA. Is there a moon this evening?

TOM. It's rising over Garfinkel's Delicatessen.

AMANDA. So it is! A little silver slipper of a moon. Have you made a wish on it yet?

TOM. Um-hum.

AMANDA. What did you wish for?

TOM. That's a secret.

AMANDA. A secret, huh? Well, I won't tell mine either. I will be just as mysterious as you.

TOM. I bet I can guess what yours is.

AMANDA. Is my head so transparent?

TOM. You're not a sphinx.

AMANDA. No, I don't have secrets. I'll tell you what I wished for on the moon. Success and happiness for my precious children! I wish for that whenever there's a moon, and when there isn't a moon, I wish for it, too.

TOM. I thought perhaps you wished for a gentleman caller.

AMANDA. Why do you say that?

TOM. Don't you remember asking me to fetch one?

AMANDA. I remember suggesting that it would be nice for your sister if you brought some nice young man from the warehouse. I think I've made that suggestion more than once.

TOM. Yes, you have made it repeatedly.

AMANDA. Well?

TOM. We are going to have one.

AMANDA. *What?*

TOM. A gentleman caller!

[The Annunciation Is Celebrated with Music.]

AMANDA *rises.*

[Image on Screen: Caller with Bouquet.]

AMANDA. You mean you have asked some nice young man to come over?

TOM. Yep. I've asked him to dinner.

AMANDA. You really did?

TOM. I did!

AMANDA. You did, and did he—*accept?*

TOM. He did!

AMANDA. Well, well—well, well! That's—lovely!

TOM. I thought that you would be pleased.

AMANDA. It's definite, then?

TOM. Very definite.

AMANDA. Soon?

TOM. Very soon.

AMANDA. For heaven's sake, stop putting on and tell me some things, will you?

TOM. What things do you want me to tell you?

AMANDA. Naturally I would like to know when he's *coming!*

TOM. He's coming tomorrow.

AMANDA. *Tomorrow?*

TOM. Yep. Tomorrow.

AMANDA. But, Tom!

TOM. Yes, Mother?

AMANDA. Tomorrow gives me no time!

TOM. Time for what?

AMANDA. Preparations! Why didn't you phone me at once, as soon as you asked him, the minute that he accepted? Then, don't you see, I could have been getting ready!

TOM. You don't have to make any fuss.

AMANDA. Oh, Tom, Tom, Tom, of course I have to make a fuss! I want things nice, not sloppy! Not thrown together. I'll certainly have to do some fast thinking, won't I?

TOM. I don't see why you have to think at all.

AMANDA. You just don't know. We can't have a gentleman caller in a pigsty! All my wedding silver has to be polished, the monogrammed table linen ought to be laundered! The windows have to be washed and fresh curtains put up. And how about clothes? We have to *wear* something, don't we?

TOM. Mother, this boy is no one to make a fuss over!

AMANDA. Do you realize he's the first young man we've introduced to your sister? It's terrible, dreadful, disgraceful that poor little sister has never received a single gentleman caller! Tom, come inside! *[She opens the screen door.]*

TOM. What for?

AMANDA. I want to ask you some things.

TOM. If you're going to make such a fuss, I'll call it off, I'll tell him not to come.

AMANDA. You certainly won't do anything of the kind. Nothing offends people worse than broken engagements. It simply means I'll have to work like a Turk! We won't be brilliant, but we'll pass inspection. Come on inside. [TOM *follows, groaning.]* Sit down.

TOM. Any particular place you would like me to sit?

AMANDA. Thank heavens I've got that new sofa! I'm also making payments on a floor lamp I'll have sent out! And put the chintz covers on, they'll brighten things up! Of course I'd hoped to have these walls repapered. . . . What is the young man's name?

TOM. His name is O'Connor.

AMANDA. That, of course, means fish—tomorrow is Friday! I'll have that salmon loaf—with Durkee's dressing! What does he do? He works at the warehouse?

TOM. Of course! How else would I—

AMANDA. Tom, he—doesn't drink?

TOM. Why do you ask me that?

AMANDA. Your father *did!*

TOM. Don't get started on that!

AMANDA. He *does* drink, then?

TOM. Not that I know of!

AMANDA. Make sure, be certain! The last thing I want for my daughter's a boy who drinks!

TOM. Aren't you being a little premature? Mr. O'Connor has not yet appeared on the scene!

AMANDA. But will tomorrow. To meet your sister, and what do I know about his character? Nothing! Old maids are better off than wives of drunkards!

TOM. Oh, my God!

AMANDA. Be still!

TOM [*leaning forward to whisper]*. Lots of fellows meet girls whom they don't marry!

AMANDA. Oh, talk sensibly, Tom—and don't be sarcastic! [*She has gotten a hairbrush.]*

TOM. What are you doing?

AMANDA. I'm brushing that cow-lick down! What is this young man's position at the warehouse?

TOM [*submitting grimly to the brush and the interrogation]*. This young man's position is that of a shipping clerk, Mother.

AMANDA. Sounds to me like a fairly responsible job, the sort of a job *you* would be in if you just had more *get-up.* What is his salary? Have you got any idea?

TOM. I would judge it to be approximately eighty-five dollars a month.

AMANDA. Well—not princely, but—

TOM. Twenty more than I make.

AMANDA. Yes, how well I know! But for a family man, eighty-five dollars a month is not much more than you can just get by on. . . .

TOM. Yes, but Mr. O'Connor is not a family man.

AMANDA. He might be, mightn't he? Some time in the future?

TOM. I see. Plans and provisions.

AMANDA. You are the only man that I know of who ignores the fact that the future becomes the present, the present the past, and the past turns into everlasting regret if you don't plan for it!

TOM. I will think that over and see what I can make of it.

AMANDA. Don't be supercilious with your mother! Tell me some more about this—what do you call him?

TOM. James D. O'Connor. The D. is for Delaney.

AMANDA. Irish on *both* sides! *Gracious!* And doesn't drink?

TOM. Shall I call him up and ask him right this minute?

AMANDA. The only way to find out about those things is to make discreet inquiries at the proper moment. When I was a girl in Blue Mountain and it was suspected that a young man drank, the girl whose attentions he had been receiving, if any girl *was,* would sometimes speak to the minister of his church, or rather her father would if her father was living, and sort of feel him out on the young man's character. That is the way such things are discreetly handled to keep a young woman from making a tragic mistake!

TOM. Then how did you happen to make a tragic mistake?

AMANDA. That innocent look of your father's had everyone fooled! He *smiled*—the world was *enchanted!* No girl can do worse than put herself at the mercy of a handsome appearance! I hope that Mr. O'Connor is not too good-looking.

TOM. No, he's not too good-looking. He's covered with freckles and hasn't too much of a nose.

AMANDA. He's not right-down homely, though?

TOM. Not right-down homely. Just medium homely, I'd say.

AMANDA. Character's what to look for in a man.

TOM. That's what I've always said, Mother.

AMANDA. You've never said anything of the kind and I suspect you would never give it a thought.

TOM. Don't be suspicious of me.

AMANDA. At least I hope he's the type that's up and coming.

TOM. I think he really goes in for self-improvement.

AMANDA. What reason have you to think so?

TOM. He goes to night school.

AMANDA *[beaming]*. Splendid! What does he do, I mean study?

TOM. Radio engineering and public speaking!

AMANDA. Then he has visions of being advanced in the world! Any young man who studies public speaking is aiming to have an executive job some day! And radio engineering? A thing for the future! Both of these facts are very illuminating. Those are the sort of things that a mother should know concerning any young man who comes to call on her daughter. Seriously or—not.

TOM. One little warning. He doesn't know about Laura. I didn't let on that we had dark ulterior motives. I just said, why don't you come have dinner with us? He said okay and that was the whole conversation.

AMANDA. I bet it was! You're eloquent as an oyster. However, he'll know about Laura when he gets here. When he sees how lovely and sweet and pretty she is, he'll thank his lucky stars he was asked to dinner.

TOM. Mother, you mustn't expect too much of Laura.

AMANDA. What do you mean?

TOM. Laura seems all those things to you and me because she's ours and we love her. We don't even notice she's crippled any more.

AMANDA. Don't say crippled! You know that I never allow that word to be used!

TOM. But face facts, Mother. She is and—that's not all—

AMANDA. What do you mean "not all"?

TOM. Laura is very different from other girls.

AMANDA. I think the difference is all to her advantage.

TOM. Not quite all—in the eyes of others—strangers—she's terribly shy and lives in a world of her own and those things make her seem a little peculiar to people outside the house.

AMANDA. Don't say peculiar.

TOM. Face the facts. She is.

[The Dance-Hall Music Changes to a Tango that Has a Minor and Somewhat Ominous Tone.]

AMANDA. In what way is she peculiar—may I ask?

TOM *[gently]*. She lives in a world of her own—a world of—little glass ornaments, Mother. . . . *[Gets up.* AMANDA *remains holding brush, looking at him, troubled.]* She plays old phonograph records and—that's about all—*[He glances at himself in the mirror and crosses to door.]*

AMANDA *[sharply]*. Where are you going?

TOM. I'm going to the movies. *[Out screen door.]*

AMANDA. Not to the movies, every night to the movies! *[Follows quickly to screen door.]* I don't believe you always go to the movies! *[He is gone.* AMANDA *looks worriedly after him for a moment. Then vitality and optimism return and she turns from the door. Crossing to portieres.]* Laura! Laura! *[*LAURA *answers from kitchenette.]*

LAURA. Yes, Mother.

AMANDA. Let those dishes go and come in front! *[Laura appears with dish towel. Gaily.]* Laura, come here and make a wish on the moon!

LAURA *[entering]*. Moon—moon?

AMANDA. A little silver slipper of a moon. Look over your left shoulder, Laura, and make a wish! *[*LAURA *looks faintly puzzled as if called out of sleep.* AMANDA *seizes her shoulders and turns her at angle by the door.]* Now! Now, darling, *wish!*

LAURA. What shall I wish for, Mother?

AMANDA *[her voice trembling and her eyes suddenly filling with tears]*. Happiness! Good Fortune!

The violin rises and the stage dims out.

Scene VI

[Image: High School Hero.]

TOM. And so the following evening I brought Jim home to dinner. I had known Jim slightly in high school. In high school Jim was a hero. He had tremendous Irish good nature and vitality with the scrubbed and polished look of white chinaware. He seemed to move in a continual spotlight. He was a star in basketball, captain of the debating club, president of the senior class and the glee club and he sang the male lead in the annual light operas. He was always running or bounding, never just walking. He seemed always at the point of defeating the law of gravity. He was shooting with such velocity through his adolescence that you would logically expect him to arrive at nothing short of the White House by the time he was thirty. But Jim apparently ran into more interference after his graduation from Soldan. His speed had definitely slowed. Six years after he left high school he was holding a job that wasn't much better than mine.

[Image: Clerk.]

He was the only one at the warehouse with whom I was on friendly terms. I was valuable to him as someone who could remember his former glory, who had seen him win basketball games and the silver cup in debating. He knew of my secret practice of retiring to a cabinet of the washroom to work on poems when business was slack in the warehouse. He called me Shakespeare. And while the other boys in the warehouse regarded me with suspicious hostility, Jim took a humorous attitude toward me. Gradually his attitude affected the others, their hostility wore off and they also began to smile at me as people smile at an oddly fashioned dog who trots across their path at some distance.

I knew that Jim and Laura had known each other at Soldan, and I had heard Laura speak admiringly of his voice. I didn't know if Jim remembered her or not. In high school Laura had been as unobtrusive as Jim had been astonishing. If he did remember Laura, it was not as my sister, for when I asked him to dinner, he grinned and said, "You know, Shakespeare, I never thought of you as having folks!"

He was about to discover that I did. . . .

[Light up Stage.]

[Legend on Screen: "The Accent of a Coming Foot."]

Friday evening. It is about five o'clock of a late spring evening which comes "scattering poems in the sky."

A delicate lemony light is in the Wingfield apartment.

AMANDA *has worked like a Turk in preparation for the gentleman caller. The results are astonishing. The new floor lamp with its rose-silk shade is in place, a colored paper lantern conceals the broken light fixture in the ceiling, new billowing white curtains are at the windows, chintz covers are on chairs and sofa, a pair of new sofa pillows make their initial appearance.*

Open boxes and tissue paper are scattered on the floor.

LAURA *stands in the middle with lifted arms while* AMANDA *crouches before her, adjusting the hem of the new dress, devout and ritualistic. The dress is colored and designed by memory. The arrangement of* LAURA*'s hair is changed; it is softer and more becoming. A fragile, unearthly prettiness has come out in* LAURA: *she is like a piece of translucent glass touched by light, given a momentary radiance, not actual, not lasting.*

AMANDA *[impatiently].* Why are you trembling?

LAURA. Mother, you've made me so nervous!

AMANDA. How have I made you nervous?

LAURA. By all this fuss! You make it seem so important!

AMANDA. I don't understand you, Laura. You couldn't be satisfied with just sitting home, and yet whenever I try to arrange something for you, you seem to resist it. *[She gets up.]* Now take a look at yourself. No, wait! Wait just a moment—I have an idea!

LAURA. What is it now?

AMANDA *produces two powder puffs which she wraps in handkerchiefs and stuffs in* LAURA*'s bosom.*

LAURA. Mother, what are you doing?

AMANDA. They call them "Gay Deceivers"!

LAURA. I won't wear them!

AMANDA. You will!

LAURA. Why should I?

AMANDA. Because, to be painfully honest, your chest is flat.

LAURA. You make it seem like we were setting a trap.

AMANDA. All pretty girls are a trap, a pretty trap, and men expect them to be. *[Legend: "A Pretty Trap."]* Now look at yourself, young lady. This is the prettiest you will ever be! I've got to fix myself now! You're going to be surprised by your mother's appearance! *[She crosses through portieres, humming gaily.]*

LAURA *moves slowly to the long mirror and stares solemnly at herself.*

A wind blows the white curtains inward in a slow, graceful motion and with a faint, sorrowful sighing.

AMANDA *[off stage]*. It isn't dark enough yet. *[She turns slowly before the mirror with a troubled look.]*

[Legend on Screen: "This Is My Sister: Celebrate Her with Strings!" Music.]

AMANDA *[laughing, off]*. I'm going to show you something. I'm going to make a spectacular appearance!

LAURA. What is it, Mother?

AMANDA. Possess your soul in patience—you will see! Something I've resurrected from that old trunk! Styles haven't changed so terribly much after all.... *[She parts the portieres.]* Now just look at your mother! *[She wears a girlish frock of yellowed voile with a blue silk sash. She carries a bunch of jonquils—the legend of her youth is nearly revived. Feverishly.]* This is the dress in which I led the cotillion. Won the cakewalk twice at Sunset Hill, wore one spring to the Governor's ball in Jackson! See how I sashayed around the ballroom, Laura? *[She raises her skirt and does a mincing step around the room.]* I wore it on Sundays for my gentlemen callers! I had it on the day I met your father—I had malaria fever all that spring. The change of climate from East Tennessee to the Delta—weakened resistance—I had a little temperature all the time—not enough to be serious—just enough to make me restless and giddy! Invitations poured in—parties all over the Delta!—"Stay in bed," said Mother, "you have fever!"—but I just wouldn't.—I took quinine but kept on going, going!—Evenings, dances!—Afternoons, long, long rides! Picnics—lovely!—So lovely, that country in May.—All lacy with dogwood, literally flooded with jonquils!—That was the spring I had the craze for jonquils. Jonquils became an absolute obsession. Mother said, "Honey, there's no more room for jonquils." And still I kept bringing in more jonquils. Whenever, wherever I saw them, I'd say, "Stop! Stop! I see jonquils!" I made the young men help me gather the jonquils! It was a joke, Amanda and her jonquils! Finally there were no more vases to hold them, every available space was filled with jonquils. No vases to hold them? All right, I'll hold them myself! And then I—*[She stops in front of the picture.]* *[Music.]* met your father! Malaria fever and jonquils and then—this—boy.... *[She switches on the rose-colored lamp.]* I hope they get here before it starts to rain. *[She crosses upstage and places the jonquils in bowl on table.]* I gave your brother a little extra change so he and Mr. O'Connor could take the service car home.

LAURA [*with altered look*]. What did you say his name was?

AMANDA. O'Connor.

LAURA. What is his first name?

AMANDA. I don't remember. Oh, yes, I do. It was—Jim!

> LAURA *sways slightly and catches hold of a chair.*
>
> [*Legend on Screen: "Not Jim!"*]

LAURA [*faintly*]. Not—Jim!

AMANDA. Yes, that was it, it was Jim! I've never known a Jim that wasn't nice!

> [*Music: Ominous.*]

LAURA. Are you sure his name is Jim O'Connor?

AMANDA. Yes. Why?

LAURA. Is he the one that Tom used to know in high school?

AMANDA. He didn't say so. I think he just got to know him at the warehouse.

LAURA. There was a Jim O'Connor we both knew in high school—[*Then, with effort.*] If that is the one that Tom is bringing to dinner—you'll have to excuse me, I won't come to the table.

AMANDA. What sort of nonsense is this?

LAURA. You asked me once if I'd ever liked a boy. Don't you remember I showed you this boy's picture?

AMANDA. You mean the boy you showed me in the year book?

LAURA. Yes, that boy.

AMANDA. Laura, Laura, were you in love with that boy?

LAURA. I don't know, Mother. All I know is I couldn't sit at the table if it was him!

AMANDA. It won't be him! It isn't the least bit likely. But whether it is or not, you will come to the table. You will not be excused.

LAURA. I'll have to be, Mother.

AMANDA. I don't intend to humor your silliness, Laura. I've had too much from you and your brother, both! So just sit down and compose yourself till they come. Tom has forgotten his key so you'll have to let them in, when they arrive.

LAURA [*panicky*]. Oh, Mother—*you* answer the door!

AMANDA [*lightly*]. I'll be in the kitchen—busy!

LAURA. Oh, Mother, please answer the door, don't make me do it!

AMANDA [*crossing into kitchenette*]. I've got to fix the dressing for the salmon. Fuss, fuss—silliness!—over a gentleman caller!

> *Door swings shut.* LAURA *is left alone.*
>
> [*Legend: "Terror!"*]
>
> *She utters a low moan and turns off the lamp—sits stiffly on the edge of the sofa, knotting her fingers together.*
>
> [*Legend on Screen: "The Opening of a Door!"*]
>
> TOM *and* JIM *appear on the fire-escape steps and climb to landing. Hearing their approach,* LAURA *rises with a panicky gesture. She retreats to the portieres.*
>
> *The doorbell.* LAURA *catches her breath and touches her throat. Low drums.*

AMANDA [*calling*]. Laura, sweetheart! The door!

> LAURA *stares at it without moving.*

JIM. I think we just beat the rain.

TOM. Uh-huh. [*He rings again, nervously.* JIM *whistles and fishes for a cigarette.*]

AMANDA [*very, very gaily*]. Laura, that is your brother and Mr. O'Connor! Will you let them in, darling?

> LAURA *crosses toward kitchenette door.*

LAURA [*breathlessly*]. Mother—you go to the door!

> AMANDA *steps out of kitchenette and stares furiously at* LAURA. *She points imperiously at the door.*

LAURA. Please, please!

AMANDA [*in a fierce whisper*]. What is the matter with you, you silly thing?

LAURA [*desperately*]. Please, you answer it, *please!*

AMANDA. I told you I wasn't going to humor you, Laura. Why have you chosen this moment to lose your mind?

LAURA. Please, please, please, you go!

AMANDA. You'll have to go to the door because I can't!

LAURA [*despairingly*]. I can't either!

AMANDA. Why?

LAURA. I'm *sick!*

AMANDA. I'm sick, too—of your nonsense! Why can't you and your brother be normal people? Fantastic whims and behavior! [TOM *gives a long ring.*] Preposterous goings on! Can you give me one reason—[*Calls out lyrically.*] COMING! JUST ONE SECOND!—why should you be afraid to open a door? Now you answer it, Laura!

LAURA. Oh, oh, oh . . . [*She returns through the portieres. Darts to the victrola and winds it frantically and turns it on.*]

AMANDA. Laura Wingfield, you march right to that door!

LAURA. Yes—yes, Mother!

> A faraway, scratchy rendition of "Dardanella" softens the air and gives her strength to move through it. She slips to the door and draws it cautiously open.

> > TOM *enters with caller,* JIM O'CONNOR.

TOM. Laura, this is Jim. Jim, this is my sister, Laura.

JIM [*stepping inside*]. I didn't know that Shakespeare had a sister!

LAURA [*retreating stiff and trembling from the door*]. How—how do you do?

JIM [*heartily extending his hand*]. Okay!

> LAURA *touches it hesitantly with hers.*

JIM. Your hand's *cold*, Laura!

LAURA. Yes, well—I've been playing the victrola. . . .

JIM. Must have been playing classical music on it! You ought to play a little hot swing music to warm you up!

LAURA. Excuse me—I haven't finished playing the victrola. . . .

> She turns awkwardly and hurries into the front room. She pauses a second by the victrola. Then catches her breath and darts through the portieres like a frightened deer.

JIM [*grinning*]. What was the matter?

TOM. Oh—with Laura? Laura is—terribly shy.

JIM. Shy, huh? It's unusual to meet a shy girl nowadays. I don't believe you ever mentioned you had a sister.

TOM. Well, now you know. I have one. Here is the *Post Dispatch*. You want a piece of it?

JIM. Uh-huh.

TOM. What piece? The comics?

JIM. Sports! *[Glances at it.]* Ole Dizzy Dean is on his bad behavior.

TOM *[disinterest]*. Yeah? *[Lights cigarette and crosses back to fire-escape door.]*

JIM. Where are *you* going?

TOM. I'm going out on the terrace.

JIM *[goes after him]*. You know, Shakespeare—I'm going to sell you a bill of goods!

TOM. What goods?

JIM. A course I'm taking.

TOM. Huh?

JIM. In public speaking! You and me, we're not the warehouse type.

TOM. Thanks—that's good news. But what has public speaking got to do with it?

JIM. It fits you for—executive positions!

TOM. Awww.

JIM. I tell you it's done a helluva lot for me.

 [Image: Executive at Desk.]

TOM. In what respect?

JIM. In every! Ask yourself what is the difference between you an' me and men in the office down front? Brains?—No!—Ability?—No! Then what? Just one little thing—

TOM. What is that one little thing?

JIM. Primarily it amounts to—social poise! Being able to square up to people and hold your own on any social level!

AMANDA *[off stage]*. Tom?

TOM. Yes, Mother?

AMANDA. Is that you and Mr. O'Connor?

TOM. Yes, Mother.

AMANDA. Well, you just make yourselves comfortable in there.

TOM. Yes, Mother.

AMANDA. Ask Mr. O'Connor if he would like to wash his hands.

JIM. Aw—no—no—thank you—I took care of that at the warehouse. Tom—

TOM. Yes?

JIM. Mr. Mendoza was speaking to me about you.

TOM. Favorably?

JIM. What do you think?

TOM. Well—

JIM. You're going to be out of a job if you don't wake up.

TOM. I am waking up—

JIM. You show no signs.

TOM. The signs are interior.

 [Image on Screen: The Sailing Vessel with Jolly Roger Again.]

TOM. I'm planning to change. *[He leans over the rail speaking with quiet exhilaration. The incandescent marquees and signs of the first-run movie houses light his face from across the alley. He looks like a voyager.]* I'm right at the point of committing myself to a future that doesn't include the warehouse and Mr. Mendoza or even a night-school course in public speaking.

JIM. What are you gassing about?

TOM. I'm tired of the movies.

JIM. Movies!

TOM. Yes, movies! Look at them—*[a wave toward the marvels of Grand Avenue.]* All of those glamorous people—having adventures—hogging it all, gobbling the whole thing up! You know what happens? People go to the *movies* instead of *moving!* Hollywood characters are supposed to have all the adventures for everybody in America, while everybody in America sits in a dark room and watches them have them! Yes, until there's a war. That's when adventure becomes available to the masses! *Everyone's* dish, not only Gable's! Then the people in the dark room come out of the dark room to have some adventures themselves— Goody, goody—It's our turn now, to go to the South Sea Island—to make a safari—to be exotic, far-off—But I'm not patient. I don't want to wait till then. I'm tired of the *movies* and I am *about* to *move!*

JIM *[incredulously]*. Move?

TOM. Yes.

JIM. When?

TOM. Soon!

JIM. Where? Where?

[Theme Three: Music Seems to Answer the Question, while TOM *Thinks it Over. He Searches among his Pockets.]*

TOM. I'm starting to boil inside. I know I seem dreamy, but inside—well, I'm boiling! Whenever I pick up a shoe, I shudder a little thinking how short life is and what I am doing!—Whatever that means. I know it doesn't mean shoes—except as something to wear on a traveler's feet *[Finds paper.]* Look—

JIM. What?

TOM. I'm a member.

JIM *[reading]*. The Union of Merchant Seamen.

TOM. I paid my dues this month, instead of the light bill.

JIM. You will regret it when they turn the lights off.

TOM. I won't be here.

JIM. How about your mother?

TOM. I'm like my father. The bastard son of a bastard! See how he grins? And he's been absent going on sixteen years!

JIM. You're just talking, you drip. How does your mother feel about it?

TOM. Shhh—Here comes Mother! Mother is not acquainted with my plans!

AMANDA *[enters portieres]*. Where are you all?

TOM. On the terrace, Mother.

They start inside. She advances to them. TOM *is distinctly shocked at her appearance. Even* JIM *blinks a little. He is making his first contact with girlish Southern vivacity and in spite of the nightschool course in public speaking is somewhat thrown off the beam by the unexpected outlay of social charm.*

Certain responses are attempted by JIM *but are swept aside by* AMANDA*'s gay laughter and chatter.* TOM *is embarrassed but after the first shock* JIM *reacts very warmly. Grins and chuckles, is altogether won over.*

[Image: AMANDA *as a Girl.]*

AMANDA *[coyly smiling, shaking her girlish ringlets]*. Well, well, well, so this is Mr. O'Connor. Introductions entirely unnecessary. I've heard so much about you from my boy. I finally said to him, Tom—good gracious!—why don't you bring this paragon to supper? I'd like to meet this nice young man at the warehouse!—Instead of just hearing him sing your praises so much! I don't know why my son is so standoffish—that's not Southern behavior! Let's sit down and—I think we could stand a little more air in here! Tom, leave the door open. I felt a nice fresh breeze a moment ago. Where has it gone? Mmm, so warm already! And not quite summer, even. We're going to burn up when summer really gets started. However, we're having—we're having a very light supper. I think light things are better fo' this time of year. The same as light clothes are. Light clothes an' light food are what warm weather calls fo'. You know our blood gets so thick during th' winter—it takes a while fo' us to *adjust* ou'selves!—when the season changes. . . . It's come so quick this year. I wasn't prepared. All of a sudden—heavens! Already summer!—I ran to the trunk an' pulled out this light dress—Terribly old! Historical almost! But feels so good—so good an' co-ol, y'know. . . .

TOM. Mother—

AMANDA. Yes, honey?

TOM. How about—supper?

AMANDA. Honey, you go ask Sister if supper is ready! You know that Sister is in full charge of supper! Tell her you hungry boys are waiting for it. *[To JIM.]* Have you met Laura?

JIM. She—

AMANDA. Let you in? Oh, good, you've met already! It's rare for a girl as sweet an' pretty as Laura to be domestic! But Laura is, thank heavens, not only pretty but also very domestic. I'm not at all. I never was a bit. I never could make a thing but angel-food cake. Well, in the South we had so many servants. Gone, gone, gone. All vestiges of gracious living! Gone completely! I wasn't prepared for what the future brought me. All of my gentlemen callers were sons of planters and so of course I assumed that I would be married to one and raise my family on a large piece of land with plenty of servants. But man proposes—and woman accepts the proposal!—To vary that old, old saying a little bit—I married no planter! I married a man who worked for the telephone company!—that gallantly smiling gentleman over there! *[Points to the picture.]* A telephone man who—fell in love with long distance!—Now he travels and I don't even know where!—But what am I going on for about my—tribulations! Tell me yours—I hope you don't have any! Tom?

TOM *[returning]*. Yes, Mother?

AMANDA. Is supper nearly ready?

TOM. It looks to me like supper is on the table.

AMANDA. Let me look—*[She rises prettily and looks through portieres.]* Oh, lovely—But where is Sister?

TOM. Laura is not feeling well and she says that she thinks she'd better not come to the table.

AMANDA. What?—Nonsense!—Laura? Oh, Laura!

LAURA *[off stage, faintly]*. Yes, Mother.

AMANDA. You really must come to the table. We won't be seated until you come to the table! Come in, Mr. O'Connor. You sit over there and I'll—Laura? Laura Wingfield! You're keeping us waiting, honey! We can't say grace until you come to the table!

The back door is pushed weakly open and LAURA *comes in. She is obviously quite faint, her lips trembling, her eyes wide and staring. She moves unsteadily toward the table.*

[*Legend: "Terror!"*]

Outside a summer storm is coming abruptly. The white curtains billow inward at the windows and there is a sorrowful murmur and deep blue dusk.

LAURA *suddenly stumbles—She catches a chair with a faint moan.*

TOM. Laura!

AMANDA. Laura! *[There is a clap of thunder.]* [*Legend: "Ah!"*] *[Despairingly.]* Why, Laura, you *are* sick, darling! Tom, help your sister into the living room, dear! Sit in the living room, Laura—rest on the sofa. Well! *[To the gentleman caller.]* Standing over the hot stove made her ill!—I told her that it was just too warm this evening, but—*[*TOM *comes back in.* LAURA *is on the sofa.]* Is LAURA all right now?

TOM. Yes.

AMANDA. What is that? Rain? A nice cool rain has come up! *[She gives the gentleman caller a frightened look.]* I think we may—have grace—now . . . *[*TOM *looks at her stupidly.]* Tom, honey—you say grace!

TOM. Oh . . . "For these and all thy mercies—" *[They bow their heads,* AMANDA *stealing a nervous glance at* JIM. *In the living room* LAURA, *stretched on the sofa, clenches her hand to her lips, to hold back a shuddering sob.]* God's Holy Name be praised—
[The Scene Dims Out.]

Scene VII

A Souvenir

Half an hour later. Dinner is just being finished in the upstage area which is concealed by the drawn portieres.

As the curtain rises LAURA *is still huddled upon the sofa, her feet drawn under her, her head resting on a pale blue pillow, her eyes wide and mysteriously watchful. The new floor lamp with its shade of rose-colored silk gives a soft, becoming light to her face, bringing out the fragile, unearthly prettiness which usually escapes attention. There is a steady murmur of rain, but it is slackening and stops soon after the scene begins; the air outside becomes pale and luminous as the moon breaks out.*

A moment after the curtain rises, the lights in both rooms flicker and go out.

JIM. Hey, there, Mr. Light Bulb!

AMANDA *laughs nervously.*

[*Legend: "Suspension of a Public Service."*]

AMANDA. Where was Moses when the lights went out? Ha-ha. Do you know the answer to that one, Mr. O'Connor?

JIM. No, Ma'am, what's the answer?

AMANDA. In the dark! *[*JIM *laughs appreciatively.]* Everybody sit still. I'll light the candles. Isn't it lucky we have them on the table? Where's a match? Which of you gentlemen can provide a match?

JIM. Here.

AMANDA. Thank you, sir.

JIM. Not at all, Ma'am!

AMANDA. I guess the fuse has burnt out. Mr. O'Connor, can you tell a burnt-out fuse? I know I can't and Tom is a total loss when it comes to mechanics. *[Sound: Getting Up: Voices Recede a Little to Kitchenette.]* Oh, be careful you don't bump into something. We don't want our gentleman caller to break his neck. Now wouldn't that be a fine howdy-do?

JIM. Ha-ha! Where is the fuse-box?

AMANDA. Right here next to the stove. Can you see anything?

JIM. Just a minute.

AMANDA. Isn't electricity a mysterious thing? Wasn't it Benjamin Franklin who tied a key to a kite? We live in such a mysterious universe, don't we? Some people say that science clears up all the mysteries for us. In my opinion it only creates more! Have you found it yet?

JIM. No, Ma'am. All these fuses look okay to me.

AMANDA. Tom!

TOM. Yes, Mother?

AMANDA. That light bill I gave you several days ago. The one I told you we got the notices about?

TOM. Oh.—Yeah.

[Legend: "Ha!"]

AMANDA. You didn't neglect to pay it by any chance?

TOM. Why, I—

AMANDA. Didn't! I might have known it!

JIM. Shakespeare probably wrote a poem on that light bill, Mrs. Wingfield.

AMANDA. I might have known better than to trust him with it! There's such a high price for negligence in this world!

JIM. Maybe the poem will win a ten-dollar prize.

AMANDA. We'll just have to spend the remainder of the evening in the nineteenth century, before Mr. Edison made the Mazda lamp!

JIM. Candlelight is my favorite kind of light.

AMANDA. That shows you're romantic! But that's no excuse for Tom. Well, we got through dinner. Very considerate of them to let us get through dinner before they plunged us into everlasting darkness, wasn't it, Mr. O'Connor?

JIM. Ha-ha!

AMANDA. Tom, as a penalty for your carelessness you can help me with the dishes.

JIM. Let me give you a hand.

AMANDA. Indeed you will not!

JIM. I ought to be good for something.

AMANDA. Good for something? *[Her tone is rhapsodic.]* You? Why, Mr. O'Connor, nobody, *nobody's* given me this much entertainment in years—as you have!

JIM. Aw, now, Mrs. Wingfield!

AMANDA. I'm not exaggerating, not one bit! But Sister is all by her lonesome. You go keep her company in the parlor! I'll give you this lovely old candelabrum that used to be on the altar at the church of the Heavenly Rest. It was melted a little out of shape when the church burnt down. Lightning struck it one spring. Gypsy Jones was holding a revival at the time and he intimated that the church was destroyed because the Episcopalians gave card parties.

JIM. Ha-ha.

AMANDA. And how about coaxing Sister to drink a little wine? I think it would be good for her! Can you carry both at once?

JIM. Sure. I'm Superman!

AMANDA. Now, Thomas, get into this apron!

The door of kitchenette swings closed on AMANDA's *gay laughter; the flickering light approaches the portieres.*

LAURA *sits up nervously as he enters. Her speech at first is low and breathless from the almost intolerable strain of being alone with a stranger.*

[Legend: "I Don't Suppose You Remember Me at All!"]

In her first speeches in this scene, before JIM's *warmth overcomes her paralyzing shyness,* LAURA's *voice is thin and breathless as though she has run up a steep flight of stairs.*

JIM's *attitude is gently humorous. In playing this scene it should be stressed that while the incident is apparently unimportant, it is to* LAURA *the climax of her secret life.*

JIM. Hello, there, Laura.

LAURA *[faintly]*. Hello. *[She clears her throat.]*

JIM. How are you feeling now? Better?

LAURA. Yes. Yes, thank you.

JIM. This is for you. A little dandelion wine. *[He extends it toward her with extravagant gallantry.]*

LAURA. Thank you.

JIM. Drink it—but don't get drunk! *[He laughs heartily.* LAURA *takes the glass uncertainly; laughs shyly.]* Where shall I set the candles?

LAURA. Oh—oh, anywhere . . .

JIM. How about here on the floor? Any objections?

LAURA. No.

JIM. I'll spread a newspaper under to catch the drippings. I like to sit on the floor. Mind if I do?

LAURA. Oh, no.

JIM. Give me a pillow?

LAURA. What?

JIM. A pillow!

LAURA. Oh . . . *[Hands him one quickly.]*

JIM. How about you? Don't you like to sit on the floor?

LAURA. Oh—yes.

JIM. Why don't you, then?

LAURA. I—will.

JIM. Take a pillow! *[*LAURA *does. Sits on the other side of the candelabrum.* JIM *crosses his legs and smiles engagingly at her.]* I can't hardly see you sitting way over there.

LAURA. I can—see you.

JIM. I know, but that's not fair, I'm in the limelight. *[*LAURA *moves her pillow closer.]* Good! Now I can see you! Comfortable?

LAURA. Yes.

JIM. So am I. Comfortable as a cow. Will you have some gum?

LAURA. No, thank you.

JIM. I think that I will indulge, with your permission. *[Musingly unwraps it and holds it up.]* Think of the fortune made by the guy that invented the first piece of chewing gum. Amazing, huh? The Wrigley Building is one of the sights of Chicago.—I saw it summer before last when I went up to the Century of Progress. Did you take in the Century of Progress?

LAURA. No, I didn't.

JIM. Well, it was quite a wonderful exposition. What impressed me most was the Hall of Science. Gives you an idea of what the future will be in America, even more wonderful than the present time is! *[Pause. Smiling at her.]* Your brother tells me you're shy. Is that right, Laura?

LAURA. I—don't know.

JIM. I judge you to be an old-fashioned type of girl. Well, I think that's a pretty good type to be. Hope you don't think I'm being too personal—do you?

LAURA *[hastily, out of embarrassment]*. I believe I *will* take a piece of gum, if you—don't mind. *[Clearing her throat.]* Mr. O'Connor, have you—kept up with your singing?

JIM. Singing? Me?

LAURA. Yes. I remember what a beautiful voice you had.

JIM. When did you hear me sing?

[Voice Offstage in the Pause]
    Voice *[offstage].*

O blow, ye winds, heigh-ho.
A-roving I will go!
I'm off to my love
With a boxing glove—
Ten thousand miles away!

JIM. You say you've heard me sing?

LAURA. Oh, yes! Yes, very often . . . I—don't suppose you remember me—at all?

JIM *[smiling doubtfully]*. You know I have an idea I've seen you before. I had that idea soon as you opened the door. It seemed almost like I was about to remember your name. But the name that I started to call you—wasn't a name! And so I stopped myself before I said it.

LAURA. Wasn't it—Blue Roses?

JIM *[springs up, grinning]*. Blue Roses! My gosh, yes—Blue Roses! That's what I had on my tongue when you opened the door! Isn't it funny what tricks your memory plays? I didn't connect you with the high school somehow or other. But that's where it was; it was high school. I didn't even know you were Shakespeare's sister! Gosh, I'm sorry.

LAURA. I didn't expect you to. You—barely knew me!

JIM. But we did have a speaking acquaintance, huh?

LAURA. Yes, we—spoke to each other.

JIM. When did you recognize me?

LAURA. Oh, right away!

JIM. Soon as I came in the door?

LAURA. When I heard your name I thought it was probably you. I knew that Tom used to know you a little in high school. So when you came in the door—Well, then I was—sure.

JIM. Why didn't you *say* something, then?

LAURA *[breathlessly]*. I didn't know what to say, I was—too surprised!

JIM. For goodness' sakes! You know, this sure is funny!

LAURA. Yes! Yes, isn't it, though. . . .

JIM. Didn't we have a class in something together?

LAURA. Yes, we did.

JIM. What class was that?

LAURA. It was—singing—Chorus!

JIM. Aw!

LAURA. I sat across the aisle from you in the Aud.

JIM. Aw.

LAURA. Mondays, Wednesdays and Fridays.

JIM. Now I remember—you always came in late.

LAURA. Yes, it was so hard for me, getting upstairs. I had a brace on my leg—it clumped so loud!

JIM. I never heard any clumping.

LAURA *[wincing at the recollection]*. To me it sounded like—thunder!

JIM. Well, well, well. I never even noticed.

LAURA. And everybody was seated before I came in. I had to walk in front of all those people. My seat was in the back row. I had to go clumping all the way up the aisle with everyone watching!

JIM. You shouldn't have been self-conscious.

LAURA. I know, but I was. It was always such a relief when the singing started.

JIM. Aw, yes, I've placed you now! I used to call you Blue Roses. How was it that I got started calling you that?

LAURA. I was out of school a little while with pleurosis. When I came back you asked me what was the matter. I said I had pleurosis—you thought I said Blue Roses. That's what you always called me after that!

JIM. I hope you didn't mind.

LAURA. Oh, no—I liked it. You see, I wasn't acquainted with many—people. . . .

JIM. As I remember you sort of stuck by yourself.

LAURA. I—I—never had much luck at—making friends.

JIM. I don't see why you wouldn't.

LAURA. Well, I—started out badly.

JIM. You mean being—

LAURA. Yes, it sort of—stood between me—

JIM. You shouldn't have let it!

LAURA. I know, but it did, and—

JIM. You were shy with people!

LAURA. I tried not to be but never could—

JIM. Overcome it?

LAURA. No, I—I never could!

JIM. I guess being shy is something you have to work out of kind of gradually.

LAURA *[sorrowfully]*. Yes—I guess it—

JIM. Takes time!

LAURA. Yes—

JIM. People are not so dreadful when you know them. That's what you have to remember! And everybody has problems, not just you, but practically everybody has got some problems. You think of yourself as having the only problems, as being the only one who is disappointed. But just look around you and you will see lots of people as disappointed as you are. For instance, I hoped when I was going to high school that I would be further along at this time, six years after, than I am now—You remember that wonderful write-up I had in *The Torch?*

LAURA. Yes! *[She rises and crosses to table.]*

JIM. It said I was bound to succeed in anything I went into! *[LAURA returns with the annual.]* Holy Jeez! *The Torch!* [He accepts it reverently. They smile across it with mutual wonder. Laura crouches beside him and they begin to turn through it. LAURA's shyness is dissolving in his warmth.]*

LAURA. Here you are in *Pirates of Penzance!*

JIM *[wistfully]*. I sang the baritone lead in that operetta.

LAURA *[rapidly]*. So—*beautifully!*

JIM *[protesting]*. Aw—

LAURA. Yes, yes—beautifully—beautifully!

JIM. You heard me?

LAURA. All three times!

JIM. No!

LAURA. Yes!

JIM. All three performances?

LAURA *[looking down]*. Yes.

JIM. Why?

LAURA. I—wanted to ask you to—autograph my program.

JIM. Why didn't you ask me to?

LAURA. You were always surrounded by your own friends so much that I never had a chance to.

JIM. You should have just—

LAURA. Well, I—thought you might think I was—

JIM. Thought I might think you was—what?

LAURA. Oh—

JIM *[with reflective relish]*. I was beleaguered by females in those days.

LAURA. You were terribly popular!

JIM. Yeah—

LAURA. You had such a—friendly way—

JIM. I was spoiled in high school.

LAURA. Everybody—liked you!

JIM. Including you?

LAURA. I—yes, I—I did, too—*[She gently closes the book in her lap.]*

JIM. Well, well, well!—Give me that program, Laura. *[She hands it to him. He signs it with a flourish.]* There you are—better late than never!

LAURA. Oh, I—what a—surprise!

JIM. My signature isn't worth very much right now. But some day—maybe— it will increase in value! Being disappointed is one thing and being discouraged is something else. I am disappointed but I'm not discouraged. I'm twenty-three years old. How old are you?

LAURA. I'll be twenty-four in June.

JIM. That's not old age!

LAURA. No, but—

JIM. You finished high school?

LAURA *[with difficulty]*. I didn't go back.

JIM. You mean you dropped out?

LAURA. I made bad grades in my final examinations. *[She rises and replaces the book and the program. Her voice strained.]* How is—Emily Meisenbach getting along?

JIM. Oh, that kraut-head!

LAURA. Why do you call her that?

JIM. That's what she was.

LAURA. You're not still—going with her?

JIM. I never see her.

LAURA. It said in the Personal Section that you were—engaged!

JIM. I know, but I wasn't impressed by that—propaganda!

LAURA. It wasn't—the truth?

JIM. Only in Emily's optimistic opinion!

LAURA. Oh—

> *[Legend: "What Have You Done since High School?"]*
>
> JIM *lights a cigarette and leans indolently back on his elbows smiling at* LAURA *with a warmth and charm which light her inwardly with altar candles. She remains by the table and turns in her hands a piece of glass to cover her tumult.*

JIM *[after several reflective puffs on a cigarette]*. What have you done since high school? *[She seems not to hear him.]* Huh? *[*LAURA *looks up.]* I said what have you done since high school, Laura?

LAURA. Nothing much.

JIM. You must have been doing something these six long years.

LAURA. Yes.

JIM. Well, then, such as what?

LAURA. I took a business course at business college—

JIM. How did that work out?

LAURA. Well, not very—well—I had to drop out, it gave me—indigestion—
JIM *laughs gently.*

JIM. What are you doing now?

LAURA. I don't do anything—much. Oh, please don't think I sit around doing nothing! My glass collection takes up a good deal of my time. Glass is something you have to take good care of.

JIM. What did you say—about glass?

LAURA. Collection I said—I have one—*[She clears her throat and turns away again, acutely shy.]*

JIM *[abruptly]*. You know what I judge to be the trouble with you? Inferiority complex! Know what that is? That's what they call it when someone low-rates himself! I understand it because I had it, too. Although my case was not so aggravated as yours seems to be. I had it until I took up public speaking, developed my voice, and learned that I had an aptitude for science. Before that time I never thought of myself as being outstanding in any way whatsoever! Now I've never made a regular study of it, but I have a friend who says I can analyze people better than doctors that make a profession of it. I don't claim that to be necessarily true, but I can sure guess a person's psychology, Laura! *[Takes out his gum.]* Excuse me, Laura. I always take it out when the flavor is gone. I'll use this scrap of paper to wrap it in. I know how it is to get it stuck on a shoe. Yep—that's what I judge to be your principal trouble. A lack of confidence in yourself as a person. You don't have the proper amount of faith in yourself. I'm basing that fact on a number of your remarks and also on certain observations I've made. For instance that clumping you thought was so awful in high school. You say that you even dreaded to walk into class. You see what you did? You dropped out of school, you gave up an education because of a clump, which as far as I know was practically nonexistent! A little physical defect is what you have. Hardly noticeable even! Magnified thousands of times by imagination! You know what my strong advice to you is? Think of yourself as *superior* in some way!

LAURA. In what way would I think?

JIM. Why, man alive, Laura! Just look about you a little. What do you see? A world full of common people! All of 'em born and all of 'em going to die! Which of them has one-tenth of your good points! Or mine! Or anyone else's, as far as that goes—Gosh! Everybody excels in some one thing. Some in many! *[Unconsciously glances at himself in the mirror.]* All you've got to do is discover in *what!* Take me, for instance. *[He adjusts his tie at the mirror.]* My interest happens to lie in electrodynamics. I'm taking a course in radio engineering at night school, Laura, on top of a fairly responsible job at the warehouse. I'm taking that course and studying public speaking.

LAURA. Ohhhh.

JIM. Because I believe in the future of television! *[Turning back to her.]* I wish to be ready to go up right along with it. Therefore I'm planning to get in on the ground floor. In fact, I've already made the right connections and all that remains is for the industry itself to get under way! Full steam—*[His eyes are starry.]* Knowledge—Zzzzzp! *Money*—Zzzzzp!— *Power!* That's the cycle democracy is built on! *[His attitude is convincingly dynamic.* LAURA *stares at him, even her shyness eclipsed in her absolute wonder. He suddenly grins.]* I guess you think I think a lot of myself!

LAURA. No—o-o-o, I—

JIM. Now how about you? Isn't there something you take more interest in than anything else?

LAURA. Well, I do—as I said—have my—glass collection—
A peal of girlish laughter from the kitchen.

JIM. I'm not right sure I know what you're talking about. What kind of glass is it?

LAURA. Little articles of it, they're ornaments mostly! Most of them are little animals made out of glass, the tiniest little animals in the world. Mother calls them a glass menagerie! Here's an example of one, if you'd like to see it! This one is one of the oldest. It's nearly thirteen. *[He stretches out his hand.]* *[Music: "The Glass Menagerie."]* Oh, be careful—if you breathe, it breaks!

JIM. I'd better not take it. I'm pretty clumsy with things.

LAURA. Go on, I trust you with him! *[Places it in his palm.]* There now— you're holding him gently! Hold him over the light, he loves the light! You see how the light shines through him?

JIM. It sure does shine!

LAURA. I shouldn't be partial, but he is my favorite one.

JIM. What kind of a thing is this one supposed to be?

LAURA. Haven't you noticed the single horn on his forehead?

JIM. A unicorn, huh?

LAURA. Mmm-hmmm!

JIM. Unicorns, aren't they extinct in the modern world?

LAURA. I know!

JIM. Poor little fellow, he must feel sort of lonesome.

LAURA [smiling]. Well, if he does he doesn't complain about it. He stays on a shelf with some horses that don't have horns and all of them seem to get along nicely together.

JIM. How do you know?

LAURA [lightly]. I haven't heard any arguments among them!

JIM [grinning]. No arguments, huh? Well, that's a pretty good sign! Where shall I set him?

LAURA. Put him on the table. They all like a change of scenery once in a while!

JIM [stretching]. Well, well, well, well—Look how big my shadow is when I stretch!

LAURA. Oh, oh, yes—it stretches across the ceiling!

JIM [crossing to door]. I think it's stopped raining. [Opens fire-escape door.] Where does the music come from?

LAURA. From the Paradise Dance Hall across the alley.

JIM. How about cutting the rug a little, Miss Wingfield?

LAURA. Oh, I—

JIM. Or is your program filled up? Let me have a look at it. [Grasps imaginary card.] Why, every dance is taken! I'll just have to scratch some out. [Waltz Music: "La Golondrina."] Ahhh, a waltz! [He executes some sweeping turns by himself then holds his arms toward LAURA.]

LAURA [breathlessly]. I—can't dance!

JIM. There you go, that inferiority stuff!

LAURA. I've never danced in my life!

JIM. Come on, try!

LAURA. Oh, but I'd step on you!

JIM. I'm not made out of glass.

LAURA. How—how—how do we start?

JIM. Just leave it to me. You hold your arms out a little.

LAURA. Like this?

JIM. A little bit higher. Right. Now don't tighten up, that's the main thing about it—relax.

LAURA [laughing breathlessly]. It's hard not to.

JIM. Okay.

LAURA. I'm afraid you can't budge me.

JIM. What do you bet I can't? [He swings her into motion.]

LAURA. Goodness, yes, you can!

LAURA. Let yourself go, now, Laura, just let yourself go.

LAURA. I'm—

JIM. Come on!

LAURA. Trying!

JIM. Not so stiff—Easy does it!

LAURA. I know but I'm—

JIM. Loosen th' backbone! There now, that's a lot better.

LAURA. Am I?

JIM. Lots, lots better! *[He moves her about the room in a clumsy waltz.]*

LAURA. Oh, my!

JIM. Ha-ha!

LAURA. Goodness, yes you can!

JIM. Ha-ha-ha! *[They suddenly bump into the table.* JIM *stops.]* What did we hit on?

LAURA. Table.

JIM. Did something fall off it? I think—

LAURA. Yes.

JIM. I hope that it wasn't the little glass horse with the horn!

LAURA. Yes.

JIM. Aw, aw, aw. Is it broken?

LAURA. Now it is just like all the other horses.

JIM. It's lost its—

LAURA. Horn! It doesn't matter. Maybe it's a blessing in disguise.

JIM. You'll never forgive me. I bet that that was your favorite piece of glass.

LAURA. I don't have favorites much. It's no tragedy, Freckles. Glass breaks so easily. No matter how careful you are. The traffic jars the shelves and things fall off them.

JIM. Still I'm awfully sorry that I was the cause.

LAURA *[smiling]*. I'll just imagine he had an operation. The horn was removed to make him feel less—freakish! *[They both laugh.]* Now he will feel more at home with the other horses, the ones that don't have horns . . .

JIM. Ha-ha, that's very funny! *[Suddenly serious.]* I'm glad to see that you have a sense of humor. You know—you're—well—very different! Surprisingly different from anyone else I know! *[His voice becomes soft and hesitant with a genuine feeling.]* Do you mind me telling you that? *[*LAURA *is abashed beyond speech.]* You make me feel sort of—I don't know how to put it! I'm usually pretty good at expressing things, but— This is something that I don't know how to say! *[*LAURA *touches her throat and clears it—turns the broken unicorn in her hands.]* *[Even softer.]* Has anyone ever told you that you were pretty? *[Pause: Music.]* *[*LAURA *looks up slowly, with wonder, and shakes her head.]* Well, you are! In a very different way from anyone else. And all the nicer because of the difference, too. *[His voice becomes low and husky.* LAURA *turns away, nearly faint with the novelty of her emotions.]* I wish that you were my sister. I'd teach you to have some confidence in yourself. The difference people are not like other people, but being different is nothing to be ashamed of. Because other people are not such wonderful people. They're one hundred times one thousand. You're one times one! They walk all over the earth. You just stay here. They're common as—weeds, but—you—well, you're *Blue Roses!*

[Image on Screen: Blue Roses.]

[Music Changes.]

LAURA. But blue is wrong for—roses . . .

JIM. It's right for you—You're—pretty!

LAURA. In what respect am I pretty?

JIM. In all respects—believe me! Your eyes—your hair—are pretty! Your hands are pretty! *[He catches hold of her hand.]* You think I'm making this up because I'm invited to dinner and have to be nice. Oh, I could do that! I could put on an act for you, Laura, and say lots of things without being very sincere. But this time I am. I'm talking to you sincerely. I happened to notice you had this inferiority complex that keeps you from feeling comfortable with people. Somebody needs to build your confidence up and make you proud instead of shy and turning away and—blushing—Somebody ought to—ought to—*kiss* you. Laura! *[His hand slips slowly up her arm to her shoulder.] [Music Swells Tumultuously.] [He suddenly turns her about and kisses her on the lips. When he releases her* LAURA *sinks on the sofa with a bright, dazed look.* JIM *backs away and fishes in his pocket for a cigarette.] [Legend on Screen: "Souvenir."]* Stumble-john! *[He lights the cigarette, avoiding her look. There is a peal of girlish laughter from* AMANDA *in the kitchen.* LAURA *slowly raises and opens her hand. It still contains the little broken glass animal. She looks at it with a tender, bewildered expression.]* Stumble-john! I shouldn't have done that—That was way off the beam. You don't smoke, do you? *[She looks up, smiling, not hearing the question. He sits beside her a little gingerly. She looks at him speechlessly—waiting. He coughs decorously and moves a little farther aside as he considers the situation and senses her feelings, dimly, with perturbation. Gently.]* Would you—care for a—mint? *[She doesn't seem to hear him but her look grows brighter even.]* Peppermint—Life Saver? My pocket's a regular drug store—wherever I go . . . *[He pops a mint in his mouth. Then gulps and decides to make a clean breast of it. He speaks slowly and gingerly.]* Laura, you know, if I had a sister like you, I'd do the same thing as Tom. I'd bring out fellows—introduce her to them. The right type of boys of a type to—appreciate her. Only—well—he made a mistake about me. Maybe I've got no call to be saying this. That may not have been the idea in having me over. But what if it was? There's nothing wrong about that. The only trouble is that in my case—I'm not in a situation to—do the right thing. I can't take down your number and say I'll phone. I can't call up next week and—ask for a date. I thought I had better explain the situation in case you misunderstood it and—hurt your feelings. . . . *[Pause. Slowly, very slowly,* LAURA*'s look changes, her eyes returning slowly from his to the ornament in her palm.]*

AMANDA *utters another gay laugh in the kitchen.*

LAURA *[faintly].* You—won't—call again?

JIM. No, Laura, I can't. *[He rises from the sofa.]* As I was just explaining, I've—got strings on me, Laura, I've—been going steady! I go out all the time with a girl named Betty. She's a home-girl like you, and Catholic, and Irish, and in a great many ways we—get along fine. I met her last summer on a moonlight boat trip up the river to Alton, on the *Majestic.* Well—right away from the start it was—love! *[Legend: Love!] [*LAURA *sways slightly forward and grips the arm of the sofa. He fails to notice, now enrapt in his own comfortable being.]* Being in love has made a new man of me! *[Leaning stiffly forward, clutching the arm of the sofa,* LAURA *struggles visibly with her storm. But* JIM *is oblivious, she is a long way off.]* The power of love is really pretty tremendous! Love is something that—changes the whole world, Laura! *[The storm abates a little and* LAURA *leans back. He notices her again.]* It happened that Betty's aunt took sick, she got a wire and had to go to Centralia. So Tom—when he asked me to dinner—I naturally just accepted the invitation, not knowing that you—that he—that I—*[He stops awkwardly.]* Huh—I'm a stumble-john! *[He flops back on the sofa. The holy candles in the altar of* LAURA*'s face have been snuffed out! There is a look of almost infinite desolation.* JIM *glances at her uneasily.]* I wish that you would—say something. *[She bites her lip which was trembling and then bravely smiles. She opens her hand again on the broken glass ornament. Then she gently takes his hand and raises it level with her own. She carefully places the unicorn in the palm of his hand, then pushes his fingers closed upon it.]* What are you—doing that for? You want me to have him?—Laura? *[She nods.]* What for?

LAURA. A—souvenir . . .

> *She rises unsteadily and crouches beside the victrola to wind it up.*
>> *[Legend on Screen: "Things Have a Way of Turning Out So Badly."]*
>> *[Or Image: "Gentleman Caller Waving Good-Bye!—Gaily."]*
>> *At this moment* AMANDA *rushes brightly back in the front room. She bears a pitcher of fruit punch in an old-fashioned cut-glass pitcher and a plate of macaroons. The plate has a gold border and poppies painted on it.*

AMANDA. Well, well, well! Isn't the air delightful after the shower? I've made you children a little liquid refreshment. *[Turns gaily to the gentleman caller.]* Jim, do you know that song about lemonade?

> "Lemonade, lemonade
> Made in the shade and stirred with a spade—
> Good enough for any old maid!"

JIM *[uneasily].* Ha-ha! No—I never heard it.

AMANDA. Why, Laura! You look so serious!

JIM. We were having a serious conversation.

AMANDA. Good! Now you're better acquainted!

JIM *[uncertainly].* Ha-ha! Yes.

AMANDA. You modern young people are much more serious-minded than my generation. I was so gay as a girl!

JIM. You haven't changed, Mrs. Wingfield.

AMANDA. Tonight I'm rejuvenated! The gaiety of the occasion, Mr. O'Connor! *[She tosses her head with a peal of laughter. Spills lemonade.]* Oooo! I'm baptizing myself!

JIM. Here—let me—

AMANDA *[setting the pitcher down].* There now. I discovered we had some maraschino cherries. I dumped them in, juice and all!

JIM. You shouldn't have gone to that trouble, Mrs. Wingfield.

AMANDA. Trouble, trouble? Why it was loads of fun! Didn't you hear me cutting up in the kitchen? I bet your ears were burning! I told Tom how outdone with him I was for keeping you to himself so long a time! He should have brought you over much, much sooner! Well, now that you've found your way, I want you to be a very frequent caller! Not just occasional but all the time. Oh, we're going to have a lot of gay times together! I see them coming! Mmm, just breathe that air! So fresh, and the moon's so pretty! I'll skip back out—I know where my place is when young folks are having a—serious conversation!

JIM. Oh, don't go out, Mrs. Wingfield. The fact of the matter is I've got to be going.

AMANDA. Going, now? You're joking! Why, it's only the shank of the evening, Mr. O'Connor!

JIM. Well, you know how it is.

AMANDA. You mean you're a young workingman and have to keep working-men's hours. We'll let you off early tonight. But only on the condition that next time you stay later. What's the best night for you? Isn't Satur-day night the best night for you workingmen?

JIM. I have a couple of time-clocks to punch, Mrs. Wingfield. One at morn-ing, another one at night!

AMANDA. My, but you *are* ambitious! You work at night, too?

JIM. No, Ma'am, not work but—Betty! *[He crosses deliberately to pick up his hat. The band at the Paradise Dance Hall goes into a tender waltz.]*

AMANDA. Betty? Betty? Who's—Betty! *[There is an ominous cracking sound in the sky.]*

JIM. Oh, just a girl. The girl I go steady with! *[He smiles charmingly. The sky falls.]*

[Legend: "The Sky Falls."]

AMANDA *[a long-drawn exhalation]*. Ohhh . . . Is it a serious romance, Mr. O'Connor?

JIM. We're going to be married the second Sunday in June.

AMANDA. Ohhhh—how nice! Tom didn't mention that you were engaged to be married.

JIM. The cat's not out of the bag at the warehouse yet. You know how they are. They call you Romeo and stuff like that. *[He stops at the oval mir-ror to put on his hat. He carefully shapes the brim and the crown to give a discreetly dashing effect.]* It's been a wonderful evening, Mrs. Wingfield. I guess this is what they mean by Southern hospitality.

AMANDA. It really wasn't anything at all.

JIM. I hope it don't seem like I'm rushing off. But I promised Betty I'd pick her up at the Wabash depot, an' by the time I get my jalopy down there her train'll be in. Some women are pretty upset if you keep 'em waiting.

AMANDA. Yes, I know—The tyranny of women! *[Extends her hand.]* Good-bye, Mr. O'Connor. I wish you luck—and happiness—and success! All three of them, and so does Laura!—Don't you, Laura?

LAURA. Yes!

JIM *[taking her hand]*. Goodbye, Laura. I'm certainly going to treasure that souvenir. And don't you forget the good advice I gave you. *[Raises his voice to a cheery shout.]* So long, Shakespeare! Thanks again, ladies—good night!

He grins and ducks jauntily out.

Still bravely grimacing, AMANDA *closes the door on the gentleman caller. Then she turns back to the room with a puzzled expression. She and* LAURA *don't dare to face each other.* LAURA *crouches beside the victrola to wind it.*

AMANDA *[faintly]*. Things have a way of turning out so badly. I don't believe that I would play the victrola. Well, well—well—Our gentleman caller was engaged to be married! Tom!

TOM [*from back*]. Yes, Mother?

AMANDA. Come in here a minute. I want to tell you something awfully funny.

TOM [*enters with macaroon and a glass of the lemonade*]. Has the gentleman caller gotten away already?

AMANDA. The gentleman caller has made an early departure. What a wonderful joke you played on us!

TOM. How do you mean?

AMANDA. You didn't mention that he was engaged to be married.

TOM. Jim? Engaged?

AMANDA. That's what he just informed us.

TOM. I'll be jiggered! I didn't know about that.

AMANDA. That seems very peculiar.

TOM. What's peculiar about it?

AMANDA. Didn't you call him your best friend down at the warehouse?

TOM. He is, but how did I know?

AMANDA. It seems extremely peculiar that you wouldn't know your best friend was going to be married!

TOM. The warehouse is where I work, not where I know things about people!

AMANDA. You don't know things anywhere! You live in a dream; you manufacture illusions! [*He crosses to door.*] Where are you going?

TOM. I'm going to the movies.

AMANDA. That's right, now that you've had us make such fools of ourselves. The effort, the preparations, all the expense! The new floor lamp, the rug, the clothes for Laura! All for what? To entertain some other girl's fiancé! Go to the movies, go! Don't think about us, a mother deserted, an unmarried sister who's crippled and has no job! Don't let anything interfere with your selfish pleasure! Just go, go, go—to the movies!

TOM. All right, I will! The more you shout about my selfishness to me the quicker I'll go, and I won't go to the movies!

AMANDA. Go, then! Then go to the moon—you selfish dreamer!

TOM *smashes his glass on the floor. He plunges out on the fire-escape, slamming the door.* LAURA *screams—cut by door.*

Dance-hall music up. TOM *goes to the rail and grips it desperately, lifting his face in the chill white moonlight penetrating the narrow abyss of the alley.*

[*Legend on Screen: "And So Good-Bye . . . "*]

TOM*'s closing speech is timed with the interior pantomime. The interior scene is played as though viewed through sound-proof glass.* AMANDA *appears to be making a comforting speech to* LAURA *who is huddled upon the sofa. Now that we cannot hear the mother's speech, her silliness is gone and she has dignity and tragic beauty.* LAURA*'s dark hair hides her face until at the end of the speech she lifts it to smile at her mother.* AMANDA*'s gestures are slow and graceful, almost dancelike, as she comforts the daughter. At the end of her speech she glances a moment at the father's picture—then withdraws through the portieres. At close of* TOM*'s speech,* LAURA *blows out the candles, ending the play.*

TOM. I didn't go to the moon, I went much further—for time is the longest distance between two places—Not long after that I was fired for writing

a poem on the lid of a shoe-box. I left Saint Louis. I descended the steps of this fire-escape for a last time and followed, from then on, in my father's footsteps, attempting to find in motion what was lost in space—I traveled around a great deal. The cities swept about me like dead leaves, leaves that were brightly colored but torn away from the branches. I would have stopped, but I was pursued by something. It always came upon me unawares, taking me altogether by surprise. Perhaps it was a familiar bit of music. Perhaps it was only a piece of transparent glass—Perhaps I am walking along a street at night, in some strange city, before I have found companions. I pass the lighted window of a shop where perfume is sold. The window is filled with pieces of colored glass, tiny transparent bottles in delicate colors, like bits of a shattered rainbow. Then all at once my sister touches my shoulder. I turn around and look into her eyes . . . Oh, Laura, Laura, I tried to leave you behind me, but I am more faithful than I intended to be! I reach for a cigarette, I cross the street, I run into the movies or a bar, I buy a drink, I speak to the nearest stranger—anything that can blow your candles out! [LAURA *bends over the candles.*]—for nowadays the world is lit by lightning! Blow out your candles, Laura—and so goodbye . . .
She blows the candles out.
[The Scene Dissolves.]

[1944]

Production Notes

Being a "memory play," *The Glass Menagerie* can be presented with unusual freedom of convention. Because of its considerably delicate or tenuous material, atmospheric touches and subtleties of direction play a particularly important part. Expressionism and all other unconventional techniques in drama have only one valid aim, and that is a closer approach to truth. When a play employs unconventional techniques, it is not, or certainly shouldn't be, trying to escape its responsibility of dealing with reality, or interpreting experience, but is actually or should be attempting to find a closer approach, a more penetrating and vivid expression of things as they are. The straight realistic play with its genuine frigidaire and authentic ice cubes, its characters that speak exactly as its audience speaks, corresponds to the academic landscape and has the same virtue of a photographic likeness. Everyone should know nowadays the unimportance of the photographic in art: that truth, life, or reality is an organic thing which the poetic imagination can represent or suggest, in essence, only through transformation, through changing into other forms than those which were merely present in appearance.

These remarks are not meant as comments only on this particular play. They have to do with a conception of a new, plastic theater which must take the place of the exhausted theater of realistic conventions if the theater is to resume vitality as a part of our culture.

The Screen Device

There is *only one important difference between the original and acting version of the play* and that is the *omission* in the latter of the device which I tentatively included in my *original* script. This device was the use of a screen on which were projected magic-lantern slides bearing images or titles. I do not regret the omission of this device from the . . . Broadway production. The extraordinary power of Miss Taylor's performance made it suitable to have the utmost simplicity in the physical production. But I think it may be interesting to some readers to see how this device was conceived. So I am putting it into the published manuscript. These images and legends, projected from behind, were cast on a section of wall between the front-room and dining-room areas, which should be indistinguishable from the rest when not in use.

The purpose of this will probably be apparent. It is to give accent to certain values in each scene. Each scene contains a particular point (or several) which is structurally the most important. In an episodic play, such as this, the basic structure or narrative line may be obscured from the audience; the effect may seem fragmentary rather than architectural. This may not be the fault of the play so much as a lack of attention in the audience. The legend or image upon the screen will strengthen the effect of what is merely allusion in the writing and allow the primary point to be made more simply and lightly than if the entire responsibility were on the spoken lines. Aside from this structural value, I think the screen will have a definite emotional appeal, less definable but just as important. An imaginative producer or director may invent many other uses for this device than those indicated in the present script. In fact the possibilities of the device seem much larger to me than the instance of this play can possibly utilize.

The Music

Another extra-literary accent in this play is provided by the use of music. A single recurring tune, "The Glass Menagerie," is used to give emotional emphasis to suitable passages. This tune is like circus music, not when you are on the grounds or in the immediate vicinity of the parade, but when you are at some distance and very likely thinking of something else. It seems under those circumstances to continue almost interminably and it weaves in and out of your preoccupied consciousness; then it is the lightest, most delicate music in the world and perhaps the saddest. It expresses the surface vivacity of life with the underlying strain of immutable and inexpressible sorrow. When you look at a piece of delicately spun glass you think of two things: how beautiful it is and how easily it can be broken. Both of those ideas should be woven into the recurring tune, which dips in and out of the play as if it were carried on a wind that changes. It serves as a thread of connection and allusion between the narrator with his separate point in time and space and the subject of his story. Between each episode it returns as reference to the emotion, nostalgia, which is the first condition of the play. It is primarily Laura's music and therefore comes out most clearly when the play focuses upon her and the lovely fragility of glass which is her image.

The Lighting

The lighting in the play is not realistic. In keeping with the atmosphere of memory, the stage is dim. Shafts of light are focused on selected areas or actors, sometimes in contradistinction to what is the apparent center. For instance, in the quarrel scene between Tom and Amanda, in which Laura has no active part, the clearest pool of light is on her figure. This is also true of the supper scene. The light upon Laura should be distinct from the others, having a peculiar pristine clarity such as light used in early religious portraits of female saints or madonnas. A certain correspondence to light in religious paintings, such as El Greco's, where the figures are radiant in atmosphere that is relatively dusky, could be effectively used throughout the play. (It will also permit a more effective use of the screen.) A free, imaginative use of light can be of enormous value in giving a mobile, plastic quality to plays of a more or less static nature.

✒ TOPICS FOR CRITICAL THINKING AND WRITING

1. When produced in New York, the magic-lantern slides were omitted. Is the device an extraneous gimmick? Might it even interfere with the play, by oversimplifying and thus in a way belittling the actions?

2. What does the victrola offer to Laura? Why is the typewriter a better symbol (for the purposes of the play) than, say, a piano? After all, Laura could have been taking piano lessons. Explain the symbolism of the unicorn, and the loss of its horn. What is Laura saying to Jim in the gesture of giving him the unicorn?

3. Laura escapes to her glass menagerie. To what do Amanda and Tom escape? How complete is Tom's escape at the end of the play?

4. What is meant at the end when Laura blows out the candles? Is she blowing out illusions? Or life? Or both?

5. Did Williams make a slip in having Amanda say Laura is "crippled" on page 553?

6. There is an implication that had Jim not been going steady he might have rescued Laura, but Jim also seems to represent (for example, in his lines about money and power) the corrupt outside world that no longer values humanity. Is this a slip on Williams's part, or is it an interesting complexity?

7. On page 553 Williams says, in a stage direction, "Now that we cannot hear the mother's speech, her silliness is gone and she has dignity and tragic beauty." Is Williams simply dragging in the word "tragic" because of its prestige, or is it legitimate? "Tragedy" is often distinguished from "pathos": in the tragic, the suffering is experienced by persons who act and are in some measure responsible for their suffering; in the pathetic, the suffering is experienced by the passive and the innocent. For example, in discussing Aeschylus's *The Suppliants* (in *Greek Tragedy*), H. D. F. Kitto says, "The Suppliants are not only pathetic, as the victims of outrage, but also tragic, as the victims of their own misconceptions." Given this distinction, to what extent are Amanda and Laura tragic? Pathetic?

EDWARD ALBEE

Edward Albee (b. 1928) in infancy was adopted by the multimillionaires who owned the chain of Albee theaters. Though surrounded by material comfort, he was an unhappy child who disliked his adoptive parents. The only member of his family with whom he seems to have

The 1962 Cherry Lane Theater production of *The Sandbox* starred John C. Becker and Jane Hoffman. (Photograph © 1962 Alix Jeffrey/Harvard Theatre Collection.)

had an affectionate relationship was his grandmother. His work at school and in college was poor, but he wrote a good deal even as an adolescent; when in 1960 he achieved sudden fame with Zoo Story *(written in 1958), he had already written plays for more than a decade. Among his other plays are* The Death of Bessie Smith *(1960),* The Sandbox *(1960),* The American Dream *(1961),* Who's Afraid of Virginia Woolf *(1962),* A Delicate Balance *(1966), and* The Man Who Had Three Arms *(1983).*

The Sandbox

THE PLAYERS
THE YOUNG MAN, *25, a good looking, well-built boy in a bathing suit*
MOMMY, *55, a well-dressed, imposing woman*
DADDY, *60, a small man; gray, thin*
GRANDMA, *86, a tiny, wizened woman with bright eyes*
THE MUSICIAN, *no particular age, but young would be nice*

NOTE: *When, in the course of the play,* MOMMY *and* DADDY *call each other by these names, there should be no suggestion of regionalism. These names are of empty affection and point up the pre-senility and vacuity of their characters.*

THE SCENE: *A bare stage, with only the following: Near the footlights, far stage-right, two simple chairs set side by side, facing the audience; near the footlights, far stage-left, a chair facing stage-right with a music stand before it; farther back, and stage-center, slightly elevated and raked, a large child's sandbox with a toy pail and shovel; the background is the sky, which alters from brightest day to deepest night.*

At the beginning, it is brightest day, the YOUNG MAN *is alone on stage, to the rear of the sandbox, and to one side. He is doing calisthenics; he does calisthenics until quite at the very end of the play. These calisthenics, employing the arms only, should suggest the beating and fluttering of wings. The* YOUNG MAN *is, after all, the Angel of Death.*

> MOMMY *and* DADDY *enter from the stage-left,* MOMMY *first.*

MOMMY *[motioning to* DADDY*].* Well, here we are; this is the beach.

DADDY *[whining].* I'm cold.

MOMMY *[dismissing him with a little laugh].* Don't be silly; it's as warm as toast. Look at that nice young man over there: *he* doesn't think it's cold. *[Waves to the* YOUNG MAN.*]* Hello.

YOUNG MAN *[with an endearing smile].* Hi!

MOMMY *[looking about].* This will do perfectly ... don't you think so, Daddy? There's sand there ... and the water beyond. What do you think, Daddy?

DADDY *[vaguely].* Whatever you say, Mommy.

MOMMY *[with the same little laugh].* Well, of course ... whatever I say. Then, it's settled, is it?

DADDY *[shrugs].* She's *your* mother, not mine.

MOMMY. *I* know she's my mother. What do you take me for? *[A pause.]* All right, now; let's get on with it. *[She shouts into the wings, stage-left.]* You! Out there! You can come in now.

> *The* MUSICIAN *enters, seats himself in the chair, stage-left, places music on the music stand, is ready to play.* MOMMY *nods approvingly.*

MOMMY. Very nice; very nice. Are you ready, Daddy? Let's go get Grandma.

DADDY. Whatever you say, Mommy.

MOMMY *[Leading the way out, stage-left].* Of course, whatever I say. *[To the* MUSICIAN.*]* You can begin now.

> *The* MUSICIAN *begins playing;* MOMMY *and* DADDY *exit; the* MUSICIAN, *all the while playing nods to the* YOUNG MAN.

YOUNG MAN *[with the same endearing smile].* Hi!

> *After a moment,* MOMMY *and* DADDY *re-enter, carrying* GRANDMA. *She is borne in by their hands under her armpits; she is quite rigid; her legs are drawn up; her feet do not touch the ground; the expression on her ancient face is that of puzzlement and fear.*

DADDY. Where do we put her?

MOMMY *[the same little laugh].* Wherever I say, of course. Let me see ... well ... all right, over there ... in the sandbox. *[Pause.]* Well, what are you waiting for Daddy? ... The sandbox!

> *Together they carry* GRANDMA *over to the sandbox and more or less dump her in.*

GRANDMA *[righting herself to a sitting position; her voice a cross between a baby's laugh and cry].* Ahhhhhh! Graaaaa!

DADDY *[dusting himself].* What do we do now?

MOMMY *[to the* MUSICIAN*].* You can stop now. *[The* MUSICIAN *stops.]* *[Back to* DADDY.*]* What do you mean, what do we do now? We go over there and sit down, of course. *[To the* YOUNG MAN.*]* Hello there.

YOUNG MAN *[again smiling].* Hi!

> MOMMY *and* DADDY *move to the chairs, stage-right, and sit down. A pause.*

GRANDMA *[same as before].* Ahhhhhh! Ahhaaaaaa! Graaaaaa!

DADDY. Do you think . . . do you think she's . . . comfortable?

MOMMY *[impatiently]*. How would I know?

DADDY *[pause]*. What do we do now?

MOMMY *[as if remembering]*. We . . . wait. We . . . sit here . . . and we wait . . . that's what we do.

DADDY *[after a pause]*. Shall we talk to each other?

MOMMY *[with that little laugh; picking something off her dress]*. Well, *you* can talk, if you want to . . . if you can think of anything to *say* . . . if you can think of anything *new*.

DADDY *[thinks]*. No . . . I suppose not.

MOMMY *[with a triumphant laugh]*. Of course not!

GRANDMA *[banging the toy shovel against the pail]*. Haaaaaa! Ah-haaaaaa!

MOMMY *[out over the audience]*. Be quiet, Grandma . . . just be quiet, and wait.

    GRANDMA *throws a shovelful of sand at* MOMMY.

MOMMY *[still out over the audience]*. She's throwing sand at me! You stop that, Grandma; you stop throwing sand at Mommy! *[To* DADDY.*]* She's throwing sand at me.

    DADDY *looks around at* GRANDMA, *who screams at him.*

GRANDMA. GRAAAAA!

MOMMY. Don't look at her. Just . . . sit here . . . be very still . . . and wait. *[To the* MUSICIAN.*]* You . . . uh . . . you go ahead and do whatever it is you do.

    The MUSICIAN *plays.*

       MOMMY *and* DADDY *are fixed, staring out beyond the audience.*

       GRANDMA *looks at them, looks at the* MUSICIAN, *looks at the sandbox, throws down the shovel.*

GRANDMA. Ah-haaaaaa! Graaaaaa! *[Looks for reaction; gets none. Now . . . directly to the audience.]* Honestly! What a way to treat an old woman! Drag her out of the house . . . stick her in a car . . . bring her out here from the city . . . dump her in a pile of sand . . . and leave her here to set. I'm eighty-six years old! I was married when I was seventeen. To a farmer. He died when I was thirty. *[To the* MUSICIAN.*]* Will you stop that, please?

    The MUSICIAN *stops playing.*

I'm a feeble old woman . . . how do you expect anybody to hear me over that peep! peep! peep! *[To herself.]* There's no respect around here. *[To the* YOUNG MAN.*]* There's no respect around here!

YOUNG MAN *[same smile]*. Hi!

GRANDMA *[after a pause, a mild double-take, continues, to the audience]*. My husband died when I was thirty *[indicates* MOMMY*]*, and I had to raise that big cow over there all by my lonesome. You can imagine what *that* was like. Lordy! *[To the* YOUNG MAN.*]* Where'd they get *you?*

YOUNG MAN. Oh . . . I've been around for a while.

GRANDMA. I'll bet you have! Heh, heh, heh. Will you look at you!

YOUNG MAN *[flexing his muscles]*. Isn't that something? *[Continues his calisthenics.]*

GRANDMA. Boy, oh boy; I'll say. Pretty good.

YOUNG MAN *[sweetly]*. I'll say.

GRANDMA. Where ya from?

YOUNG MAN. Southern California.

GRANDMA *[nodding].* Figgers, figgers. What's your name, honey?

YOUNG MAN. I don't know. . . .

GRANDMA *[to the audience].* Bright, too!

YOUNG MAN. I mean . . . I mean, they haven't given me one yet . . . the studio . . .

GRANDMA *[giving him the once-over].* You don't say . . . you don't say. Well . . . uh, I've got to talk some more . . . don't you go 'way.

YOUNG MAN. Oh, no.

GRANDMA *[turning her attention back to the audience].* Fine; fine. *[Then, once more, back to the* YOUNG MAN.*]* You're . . . you're an actor, hunh?

YOUNG MAN *[beaming].* Yes. I am.

GRANDMA *[to the audience again; shrugs].* I'm smart that way. *Anyhow,* I had to raise . . . *that* over there all by my lonesome; and what's next to her there . . . that's what she married. Rich? I tell you . . . money, money, money. They took me off the *farm* . . . which was real decent of them . . . and they moved me into the big town house with *them* . . . fixed a nice place for me under the stove . . . gave me an army blanket . . . and my own dish . . . my very own dish! So, what have I got to complain about? Nothing, of course. I'm not complaining. *[She looks up at the sky, shouts to someone offstage.]* Shouldn't it be getting dark now, dear?

The lights dim; night comes on. The MUSICIAN *begins to play; it becomes deepest night. There are spots on all the players, including the* YOUNG MAN, *who is, of course, continuing his calisthenics.*

DADDY *[stirring].* It's nighttime.

MOMMY. Shhhh. Be still . . . wait.

DADDY *[whining].* It's so hot.

MOMMY. Shhhhhh. Be still . . . wait.

GRANDMA *[to herself].* That's better. Night. *[To the* MUSICIAN.*]* Honey, do you play all through this part?

The MUSICIAN *nods.*

Well, keep it nice and soft; that's a good boy.

The MUSICIAN *nods again; plays softly.*

That's nice.

There is an off-stage rumble.

DADDY *[starting].* What was that?

MOMMY *[beginning to weep].* It was nothing.

DADDY. It was . . . it was . . . thunder . . . or a wave breaking . . . or something.

MOMMY *[whispering, through her tears].* It was an off-stage rumble . . . and you know what *that* means. . . .

DADDY. I forget. . . .

MOMMY *[barely able to talk].* It means the time has come for poor Grandma . . . and I can't bear it!

DADDY *[vacantly].* I . . . I suppose you've got to be brave.

GRANDMA *[mocking].* That's right, kid; be brave. You'll bear up; you'll get over it.

[Another off-stage rumble . . . louder.]

MOMMY. Ohhhhhhhhhh . . . poor Grandma . . . poor Grandma. . . .

GRANDMA *[to* MOMMY*].* I'm fine! I'm all right! It hasn't happened yet!

A violent off-stage rumble. All the lights go out, save the spot on the
YOUNG MAN; *the* MUSICIAN *stops playing.*

MOMMY. Ohhhhhhhhhh. . . . Ohhhhhhhhhh. . . .

Silence.

GRANDMA. Don't put the lights up yet . . . I'm not ready; I'm not quite ready.
[Silence.] All right, dear . . . I'm about done.

The lights come up again, to brightest day; the MUSICIAN *begins to play.*
GRANDMA *is discovered, still in the sandbox, lying on her side, propped*
up on an elbow, half covered, busily shoveling sand over herself.

GRANDMA. *[muttering].* I don't know how I'm supposed to do anything with
this goddam toy shovel. . . .

DADDY. Mommy! It's daylight!

MOMMY *[brightly].* So it is! Well! Our long night is over. We must put away
our tears, take off our mourning . . . and face the future. It's our duty.

GRANDMA *[still shoveling; mimicking].* . . . take off our mourning . . . face
the future. . . . Lordy!

MOMMY *and* DADDY *rise, stretch.* MOMMY *waves to the young man.*

YOUNG MAN *[with that smile].* Hi!

GRANDMA *plays dead. (!)* MOMMY *and* DADDY *go over to look at her; she is*
a little more than half buried in the sand; the toy shovel is in her
hands, which are crossed on her breast.

MOMMY *[before the sandbox; shaking her head].* Lovely! It's . . . it's hard to
be sad . . . she looks . . . so happy. *[With pride and conviction.]* It pays
to do things well. *[To the* MUSICIAN.*]* All right, you can stop now, if you
want to. I mean, stay around for a swim, or something; it's all right with
us. *[She sighs heavily.]* Well, Daddy . . . off we go.

DADDY. Brave Mommy!

MOMMY. Brave Daddy!

They exit, stage-left.

GRANDMA *[after they leave; lying quite still].* It pays to do things well. . . .
Boy, oh boy! *[She tries to sit up]* . . . well, kids . . . *[but she finds she*
can't] . . . I . . . I can't get up, I . . . I can't move. . . .

The YOUNG MAN *stops his calisthenics, nods to the* MUSICIAN, *walks over*
to GRANDMA, *kneels down by the sandbox.*

GRANDMA. I . . . can't move. . . .

YOUNG MAN. Shhhhh . . . be very still. . . .

GRANDMA. I . . . I can't move. . . .

YOUNG MAN. Uh . . . ma'am; I . . . I have a line here.

GRANDMA. Oh, I'm sorry, sweetie; you go right ahead.

YOUNG MAN. I am . . . uh . . .

GRANDMA. Take your time, dear.

YOUNG MAN *[prepares; delivers the line like a real amateur].* I am the Angel
of Death. I am . . . uh . . . I am come for you.

GRANDMA. What . . . wha . . . *[Then, with resignation.]* . . . ohhhh . . .
ohhhh, I see.

The YOUNG MAN *bends over, kisses* GRANDMA *gently on the forehead.*

GRANDMA *[her eyes closed, her hands folded on her breast again, the shovel*
between her hands, a sweet smile on her face]. Well . . . that was very
nice, dear . . .

YOUNG MAN *[still kneeling].* Shhhhhh . . . be still. . . .

GRANDMA. What I mean was . . . you did that very well, dear. . . .

YOUNG MAN *[blushing].* . . . oh . . .

GRANDMA. No; I mean it. You've got that . . . you've got a quality.

YOUNG MAN *[with his endearing smile].* Oh . . . thank you; thank you very much . . . ma'am.

GRANDMA *[slowly; softly—as the* YOUNG MAN *puts his hands on top of* GRANDMA's*].* You're . . . you're welcome . . . dear.
Tableau. The MUSICIAN *continues to play as the curtain slowly comes down.*

CURTAIN

[1960]

 # TOPICS FOR CRITICAL THINKING AND WRITING

1. In a sentence characterize Mommy, and in another sentence characterize Daddy.
2. Of the four characters in the play, which is the most sympathetic? Set forth your answer, with supporting evidence, in two paragraphs, devoting the first to the three less sympathetic characters, the second to the most sympathetic character.
3. In a longer play, *The American Dream,* Albee uses the same four characters that he uses in *The Sandbox.* Of *The American Dream,* he wrote:

   > The play is . . . a condemnation of complacency, cruelty, emasculation and vacuity; it is a stand against the fiction that everything in this slipping land of ours is peachy-keen.

   To what extent does this statement help you to understand (and to enjoy) *The Sandbox?*
4. In *The New York Times Magazine,* 25 February 1962, Albee protested against the view that his plays, and others of the so-called Theater of the Absurd, are depressing. He includes a quotation from Martin Esslin's book, *The Theatre of the Absurd:*

   > Ultimately . . . the Theatre of the Absurd does not reflect despair or a return to dark irrational forces but expresses modern man's endeavor to come to terms with the world in which he lives. It attempts to make him face up to the human condition as it really is, to free him from illusions that are bound to cause constant maladjustment and disappointment. . . . For the dignity of man lies in his ability to face reality in all its senselessness; to accept it freely, without fear, without illusions—and to laugh at it.

   In what ways is this statement helpful? In what ways is it not helpful? Explain.

CHAPTER 18

Innocence and Experience

Essays

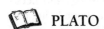 PLATO

*Plato (427–347 B.C.), born in Athens, the son of an aristocratic fam-
ily, wrote thirty dialogues in which Socrates is the chief speaker.
Socrates, about twenty-five years older than Plato, was a philosopher
who called himself a gadfly to Athenians. For his efforts at stinging
them into thought, the Athenians executed him in 399 B.C. "The Myth
of the Cave" is the beginning of Book VII of Plato's dialogue entitled*
The Republic. *Socrates is talking with Glaucon.*

*For Plato, true knowledge is philosophic insight or awareness of
the Good, not mere opinion or the knack of getting along in this
world by remembering how things have usually worked in the past.
To illustrate his idea that awareness of the Good is different from the
ability to recognize the things of this shabby world, Plato (through
his spokesman Socrates) resorts to an allegory: Men imprisoned in a
cave see on a wall in front of them the shadows or images of objects
that are really behind them, and they hear echoes, not real voices.
(The shadows are caused by the light from a fire behind the objects,
and the echoes by the cave's acoustical properties.) The prisoners, unable to perceive the real objects and the real voices, mistakenly think
that the shadows and the echoes are real, and some of them grow
highly adept at dealing with this illusory world. Were Plato writing
today, he might have made the cave a movie theater: We see on the
screen in front of us images caused by an object (film, passing in
front of light) that is behind us. Moreover, the film itself is an illusory*

image, for it bears only the traces of a yet more real world—the world that was photographed—outside of the movie theater. And when we leave the theater to go into the real world, our eyes have become so accustomed to the illusory world that we at first blink with discomfort—just as Plato's freed prisoners do when they move out of the cave—at the real world of bright day, and we long for the familiar darkness. So too, Plato suggests, dwellers in ignorance may prefer the familiar shadows of their unenlightened world ("the world of becoming") to the bright world of the eternal Good ("the world of being") that education reveals.

We have just used the word "education." You will notice that the first sentence in the translation (by Benjamin Jowett) says that the myth will show "how far our nature is enlightened or unenlightened." In the original Greek the words here translated "enlightened" and "unenlightened" are paideia *and* apaideusia. *No translation can fully catch the exact meanings of these elusive words. Depending on the context,* paideia *may be translated as "enlightenment," education," "civilization," "culture," "knowledge of the good."*

The Myth of the Cave

And now, I said, let me show in a figure how far our nature is enlightened or unenlightened—Behold! human beings living in an underground den, which has a mouth open toward the light and reaching all along the den; here they have been from their childhood, and have their legs and necks chained so that they cannot move, and can only see before them, being prevented by the chains from turning round their heads. Above and behind them a fire is blazing at a distance, and between the fire and the prisoners there is a raised way; and you will see, if you look, a low wall built along the way, like the screen which marionette players have in front of them, over which they show the puppets.

I see.

And do you see, I said, men passing along the wall carrying all sorts of vessels, and statues and figures of animals made of wood and stone and various materials, which appear over the wall? Some of them are talking, others silent.

You have shown me a strange image, and they are strange prisoners.

5   Like ourselves, I replied; and they see only their own shadows, or the shadows of one another, which the fire throws on the opposite wall of the cave?

True, he said; how could they see anything but the shadows if they were never allowed to move their heads?

And of the objects which are being carried in like manner they would only see the shadows?

Yes, he said.

And if they were able to converse with one another, would they not suppose that they were naming what was actually before them?

10   Very true.

And suppose further that the prison had an echo which came from the other side, would they not be sure when one of the passersby spoke that the voice which they heard came from the passing shadow?

No question, he replied.

To them, I said, the truth would be literally nothing but the shadows of the images.

That is certain.

15   And now look again, and see what will naturally follow if the prisoners are released and disabused of their error. At first, when any of them is liberated and compelled suddenly to stand up and turn his neck round and walk and look toward the light, he will suffer sharp pains; the glare will distress him, and he will be unable to see the realities of which in his former state he had seen the shadows; and then conceive some one saying to him, that what he saw before was an illusion, but that now, when he is approaching nearer to being and his eye is turned toward more real existence, he has a clearer vision—what will be his reply? And you may further imagine that his instructor is pointing to the objects as they pass and requiring him to name them—will he not be perplexed? Will he not fancy that the shadows which he formerly saw are truer than the objects which are now shown to him?

Far truer.

And if he is compelled to look straight at the light, will he not have a pain in his eyes which will make him turn away to take refuge in the objects of vision which he can see, and which he will conceive to be in reality clearer than the things which are now being shown to him?

True, he said.

And suppose once more, that he is reluctantly dragged up a steep and rugged ascent, and held fast until he is forced into the presence of the sun himself, is he not likely to be pained and irritated? When he approaches the light his eyes will be dazzled, and he will not be able to see anything at all of what are now called realities.

20   Not all in a moment, he said.

He will require to grow accustomed to the sight of the upper world. And first he will see the shadows best, next the reflections of men and other objects in the water, and then the objects themselves; then he will gaze upon the light of the moon and the stars and the spangled heaven; and he will see the sky and the stars by night better than the sun or the light of the sun by day?

Certainly.

Last of all he will be able to see the sun, and not mere reflections of him in the water, but he will see him in his own proper place, and not in another; and he will contemplate him as he is.

Certainly.

25   He will then proceed to argue that this is he who gives the season and the years, and is the guardian of all that is in the visible world, and in a certain way the cause of all things which he and his fellows have been accustomed to behold?

Clearly, he said, he would first see the sun and then reason about him.

And when he remembered his old habitation, and the wisdom of the den and his fellow-prisoners, do you not suppose that he would felicitate himself on the change, and pity them?

Certainly, he would.

And if they were in the habit of conferring honors among themselves on those who were quickest to observe the passing shadows and to remark which of them went before, and which followed after, and which were together, and who were therefore best able to draw conclusions as to the future, do you think that he would care for such honors and glories, or envy the possessors of them? Would he not say with Homer,

Better to be the poor servant of a poor master,

and to endure anything, rather than think as they do and live after their manner?

30   Yes, he said, I think that he would rather suffer anything than entertain these false notions and live in this miserable manner.

Imagine once more, I said, such an one coming suddenly out of the sun to be replaced in his old situation; would he not be certain to have his eyes full of darkness?

To be sure, he said.

And if there were a contest, and he had to compete in measuring the shadows with the prisoners who had never moved out of the den, while his sight was still weak, and before his eyes had become steady (and the time which would be needed to acquire this new habit of sight might be very considerable), would he not be ridiculous? Men would say of him that up he went and down he came without his eyes; and that it was better not even to think of ascending; and if any one tried to loose another and lead him up to the light, let them only catch the offender, and they would put him to death.

No question, he said.

35   This entire allegory, I said, you may now append, dear Glaucon, to the previous argument; the prison-house is the world of sight, the light of the fire is the sun, and you will not misapprehend me if you interpret the journey upwards to be the ascent of the soul into the intellectual world according to my poor belief, which, at your desire, I have expressed—whether rightly or wrongly God knows. But, whether true or false, my opinion is that in the world of knowledge the idea of good appears last of all, and is seen only with an effort; and, when seen, is also inferred to be the universal author of all things beautiful and right, parent of light and of the lord of light in this visible world, and the immediate source of reason and truth in the intellectual; and that this is the power upon which he would act rationally either in public or private life must have his eye fixed.

I agree, he said, as far as I am able to understand you.

Moreover, I said, you must not wonder that those who attain to this beatific vision are unwilling to descend to human affairs; for their souls are ever hastening into the upper world where they desire to dwell; which desire of theirs is very natural, if our allegory may be trusted.

Yes, very natural.

And is there anything surprising in one who passes from divine contemplations to the evil state of man, misbehaving himself in a ridiculous manner; if, while his eyes are blinking and before he has become accustomed to the surrounding darkness, he is compelled to fight in courts of law, or in other places, about the images or the shadows of images of justice, and is endeavoring to meet the conceptions of those who have never yet seen absolute justice?

40   Anything but surprising, he replied.

Any one who has common sense will remember that the bewilderments of the eyes are of two kinds, and arise from two causes, either from coming out of the light or from going into the light, which is true of the mind's eye, quite as much as of the bodily eye; and he who remembers this when he sees any one whose vision is perplexed and weak, will not be too ready to laugh; he will first ask whether that soul of man has come out of the brighter life, and is unable to see because unaccustomed to the dark, or having turned from darkness to the day is dazzled by excess of light. And he will count the one happy in his condition and state of being, and he will pity the other; or, if he have a mind to laugh at the soul which comes from below into the light, there will be more reason in this than in the laugh which greets him who returns from above out of the light into the den.

That, he said, is very just distinction.

But then, if I am right, certain professors of education must be wrong when they say that they can put a knowledge into the soul which was not there before, like sight into blind eyes.

They undoubtedly say this, he replied.

45   Whereas, our argument shows that the power and capacity of learning exists in the soul already; and that just as the eye was unable to turn from darkness to light without the whole body, so too the instrument of knowledge can only by the movement of the whole soul be turned from the world of becoming into that of being, and learn by degrees to endure the sight of being, and of the brightest and best of being, or in other words, of the good.

Very true.

And must there not be some art which will effect conversion in the easiest and quickest manner; not implanting the faculty of sight, for that exists already, but has been turned in the wrong direction, and is looking away from the truth?

Yes, he said, such an art may be presumed.

And whereas the other so-called virtues of the soul seem to be akin to bodily qualities, for even when they are not originally innate they can be implanted later by habit and exercise, the virtue of wisdom more than anything else contains a divine element which always remains, and by this conversion is rendered useful and profitable; or, on the other hand, hurtful and useless. Did you never observe the narrow intelligence flashing from the keen eye of a clever rogue—how eager he is, how clearly his paltry soul sees the way to his end; he is the reverse of blind, but his keen eyesight is forced into the service of evil, and he is mischievous in proportion to his cleverness?

50   Very true, he said.

But what if there had been a circumcision of such natures in the days of their youth; and they had been severed from those sensual pleasures, such as eating and drinking, which, like leaden weights, were attached to them at their birth, and which drag them down and turn the vision of their souls upon the things that are below—if, I say, they had been released from these impediments and turned in the opposite direction, the very same faculty in them would have seen the truth as keenly as they see what their eyes are turned to now.

Very likely.

Yes, I said; and there is another thing which is likely, or rather a necessary inference from what has preceded, that neither the uneducated and uninformed of the truth, nor yet those who never make an end of their education, will be able ministers of State; not the former, because they have no single aim of duty which is the rule of all their actions, private as well as public; nor the latter, because they will not act at all except upon compulsion, fancying that they are already dwelling apart in the islands of the blest.

Very true, he replied.

55   Then, I said, the business of us who are the founders of the State will be to compel the best minds to attain that knowledge which we have already shown to be the greatest of all—they must continue to ascend until they arrive at the good; but when they have ascended and seen enough we must not allow them to do as they do now.

What do you mean?

I mean that they remain in the upper world: but this must not be allowed; they must be made to descend again among the prisoners in the den, and partake of their labors and honors, whether they are worth having or not.

But is not this unjust? he said; ought we to give them a worse life, when they might have a better?

You have again forgotten, my friend, I said, the intention of the legislator, who did not aim at making any one class in the State happy above the rest; the happiness was to be in the whole State, and he held the citizens together by persuasion and necessity, making them benefactors of the State, and therefore benefactors of one another; to this end he created them, not to please themselves, but to be his instruments in binding up the State.

60   True, he said, I had forgotten.

Observe, Glaucon, that there will be no justice in compelling our philosophers to have a care and providence of others; we shall explain to them that in other States, men of their class are not obliged to share in the toils of politics: and this is reasonable, for they grow up at their own sweet will, and the government would rather not have them. Being self-taught, they cannot be expected to show any gratitude for a culture which they have never received. But we have brought you into the world to be rulers of the hive, kings of yourselves and of the other citizens, and have educated you far better and more perfectly than they have been educated, and you are better able to share in the double duty. Wherefore each of you, when his turn comes, must go down to the general underground abode, and get the habit of seeing in the dark. When you have acquired the habit, you will see ten thousand times better than the inhabitants of the den, and you will know what the several images are, and what they represent, because you have seen the beautiful and just and good in their truth. And thus our State which is also yours will be a reality, and not a dream only, and will be administered in a spirit unlike that of other States, in which men fight with one another about shadows only and are distracted in the struggle for power, which in their eyes is a great good. Whereas the truth is that the State in which the rulers are most reluctant to govern is always the best and most quietly governed, and the State in which they are most eager, the worst.

Quite true, he replied.

And will our pupils, when they hear this, refuse to take their turn at the toils of State, when they are allowed to spend the greater part of their time with one another in the heavenly light?

Impossible, he answered; for they are just men, and the commands which we impose upon them are just; there can be no doubt that every one

of them will take office as a stern necessity, and not after the fashion of our
present rulers of State.

65   Yes, my friend, I said; and there lies the point. You must contrive for
your future rulers another and a better life than that of a ruler, and then you
may have a well-ordered State; for only in the State which offers this, will
they rule who are truly rich, not in silver and gold, but in virtue and wisdom,
which are the true blessings of life. Whereas if they go to the administration
of public affairs, poor and hungering after their own private advantage,
thinking that hence they are to snatch the chief good, order there can never
be; for they will be fighting about office, and the civil and domestic broils
which thus arise will be the ruin of the rulers themselves and of the whole
State.

Most true, he replied.

And the only life which looks down upon the life of political ambition is
that of true philosophy. Do you know of any other?

Indeed, I do not, he said.

And those who govern ought not to be lovers of the task? For, if they
are, there will be rival lovers, and they will fight.

70   No question.

Who then are those whom we shall compel to be guardians? Surely they
will be the men who are wisest about affairs of State, and by whom the State
is best administered, and who at the same time have other honors and another and a better life than that of politics?

They are the men, and I will choose them, he replied.

And now shall we consider in what way such guardians will be produced, and how they are to be brought from darkness to light—as some are
said to have ascended from the world below to the gods?

By all means, he replied.

75   The process, I said, is not the turning over of an oyster-shell,[1] but the
turning round of a soul passing from a day which is little better than night to
the true day of being, that is, the ascent from below which we affirm to be
true philosophy?

Quite so.

✒ TOPICS FOR CRITICAL THINKING AND WRITING

1. Plato is not merely reporting one of Socrates' conversations; he is teaching. What advantages does a dialogue have over a narrative or an essay
   as a way of teaching philosophy? How is the form of a dialogue especially suited to solving a problem?
2. If you don't know the etymology of the word *conversion,* look it up in
   a dictionary. How is the etymology appropriate to Plato's idea about
   education?
3. In paragraph 19, describing the prisoner as "reluctantly dragged" upward and "forced" to look at the sun, Socrates asks: "Is he not likely to

[1]**turning . . . an oyster-shell** an allusion to a game in which two parties fled or
pursued according as an oyster shell which was thrown into the air fell with the
dark or light side uppermost.

be pained and irritated?" Can you recall experiencing pain and irritation while learning something you later were glad to have learned? Can you recall learning something new *without* experiencing pain and irritation?

4. "The State in which rulers are most reluctant to govern is always the best and most quietly governed, and the State in which they are most eager, the worst" (paragraph 61). What does Socrates mean? Using examples from contemporary politics, defend this proposition, or argue against it.

5. Can you account for the power of this myth or fable? In our introductory comment (page 563) we tried to clarify the message by saying that a movie theater might serve as well as a cave, but in fact if the story were recast using a movie theater, would the emotional power be the same? Why or why not?

6. The metaphors of education as conversion and ascent are linked by the metaphor of light. Consider such expressions as "I see" (meaning "I understand") and "Let me give an illustration" (from the Latin *in* = in, *lustrare* = to make bright). What other expressions about light are used metaphorically to describe intellectual comprehension?

7. Write an allegory of your own, for instance using a sport, college, business activity, or a family in order to explain some aspect of reality.

 MAYA ANGELOU

Maya Angelou, born Marguerita Johnson in 1928 in St. Louis, spent her early years in California and Arkansas. She has worked as a cook, a streetcar conductor, a television screenwriter, and an actress, and she has written poems and five autobiographical books. The following selection comes from her first autobiography, I Know Why the Caged Bird Sings *(1970).*

Graduation

The children in Stamps trembled visibly with anticipation. Some adults were excited too, but to be certain the whole young population had come down with graduation epidemic. Large classes were graduating from both the grammar school and the high school. Even those who were years removed from their own day of glorious release were anxious to help with preparations as a kind of dry run. The junior students who were moving into the vacating classes' chairs were tradition-bound to show their talents for leadership and management. They strutted through the school and around the campus exerting pressure on the lower grades. Their authority was so new that occasionally if they pressed a little too hard it had to be overlooked. After all, next term was coming, and it never hurt a sixth grader to have a play sister in the eighth grade, or a tenth-year student to be able to call a twelfth grader Bubba. So all was endured in a spirit of shared understanding. But the graduating classes themselves were the nobility. Like travelers with exotic destinations on their minds, the graduates were remarkably forgetful. They came to school without their books, or tablets or even pencils. Volunteers fell over themselves to secure replacements for the missing equipment. When accepted, the willing workers might or might not be thanked, and it was of no importance to the pregraduation rites. Even teachers were respectful of the now quiet and aging seniors, and tended to speak to them, if not as equals, as beings only slightly lower than themselves. After tests were returned and grades given, the student body, which acted like an extended family, knew who did well, who excelled, and what piteous ones had failed.

Unlike the white high school, Lafayette County Training School distinguished itself by having neither lawn, nor hedges, nor tennis court, nor climbing ivy. Its two buildings (main classrooms, the grade school and home economics) were set on a dirt hill with no fence to limit either its boundaries or those of bordering farms. There was a large expanse to the left of the school which was used alternately as a baseball diamond or a basketball court. Rusty hoops on the swaying poles represented the permanent recreational equipment, although bats and balls could be borrowed from the P.E. teacher if the borrower was qualified and if the diamond wasn't occupied.

Over this rocky area relieved by a few shady tall persimmon trees the graduating class walked. The girls often held hands and no longer bothered to speak to the lower students. There was a sadness about them, as if this old world was not their home and they were bound for higher ground. The boys, on the other hand, had become more friendly, more outgoing. A decided change from the closed attitude they projected while studying for finals. Now they seemed not ready to give up the old school, the familiar paths and classrooms. Only a small percentage would be continuing on to college—one of the South's A & M (agricultural and mechanical) schools, which trained Negro youths to be carpenters, farmers, handymen, masons, maids, cooks and baby nurses. Their future rode heavily on their shoulders, and blinded them to the collective joy that had pervaded the lives of the boys and girls in the grammar school graduating class.

Parents who could afford it had ordered new shoes and ready-made clothes for themselves from Sears and Roebuck or Montgomery Ward. They also engaged the best seamstresses to make the floating graduating dresses and to cut down secondhand pants which would be pressed to a military slickness for the important event.

5   Oh, it was important, all right. Whitefolks would attend the ceremony, and two or three would speak of God and home, and the Southern way of life, and Mrs. Parsons, the principal's wife, would play the graduation march while the lower-grade graduates paraded down the aisles and took their seats below the platform. The high school seniors would wait in empty classrooms to make their dramatic entrance.

In the Store I was the person of the moment. The birthday girl. The center. Bailey had graduated the year before, although to do so he had had to forfeit all pleasures to make up for his time lost in Baton Rouge.

My class was wearing butter-yellow piqué dresses, and Momma launched out on mine. She smocked the yoke into tiny crisscrossing puckers, then shirred the rest of the bodice. Her dark fingers ducked in and out of the lemony cloth as she embroidered raised daisies around the hem. Before she considered herself finished she had added a crocheted cuff on the puff sleeves, and a pointy crocheted collar.

I was going to be lovely. A walking model of all the various styles of fine hand sewing and it didn't worry me that I was only twelve years old and merely graduating from the eighth grade. Besides, many teachers in Arkansas Negro schools had only that diploma and were licensed to impart wisdom.

The days had become longer and more noticeable. The faded beige of former times had been replaced with strong and sure colors. I began to see my classmates' clothes, their skin tones, and the dust that waved off pussy willows. Clouds that lazed across the sky were objects of great concern to me. Their shiftier shapes might have held a message that in my new happiness and with a little bit of time I'd soon decipher. During that period I looked at the arch of heaven so religiously my neck kept a steady ache. I had taken to smiling more often, and my jaws hurt from the unaccustomed activity. Between the two physical sore spots, I suppose I could have been uncomfortable, but that was not the case. As a member of the winning team (the graduating class of 1940) I had outdistanced unpleasant sensations by miles. I was headed for the freedom of open fields.

10   Youth and social approval allied themselves with me and we trammeled memories of slights and insults. The wind of our swift passage remodeled my features. Lost tears were pounded to mud and then to dust. Years of withdrawal were brushed aside and left behind, as hanging ropes of parasitic moss.

My work alone had awarded me a top place and I was going to be one of the first called in the graduating ceremonies. On the classroom blackboard, as well as on the bulletin board in the auditorium, there were blue stars and white stars and red stars. No absences, no tardinesses, and my academic work was among the best of the year. I could say the preamble to the Constitution even faster than Bailey. We timed ourselves often: "We the people of the United States in order to form a more perfect union . . ." I had memorized the Presidents of the United States from Washington to Roosevelt in chronological as well as alphabetical order.

My hair pleased me too. Gradually the black mass had lengthened and thickened, so that it kept at last to its braided pattern, and I didn't have to yank my scalp off when I tried to comb it.

Louise and I had rehearsed the exercises until we tired out ourselves. Henry Reed was class valedictorian. He was a small, very black boy with hooded eyes, a long, broad nose and an oddly shaped head. I had admired him for years because each term he and I vied for the best grades in our class. Most often he bested me, but instead of being disappointed I was pleased that we shared top places between us. Like many Southern Black children, he lived with his grandmother, who was as strict as Momma and as kind as she knew how to be. He was courteous, respectful and soft-spoken to elders, but on the playground he chose to play the roughest games. I admired him. Anyone, I reckoned, sufficiently afraid or sufficiently dull could be polite. But to be able to operate at a top level with both adults and children was admirable.

His valedictory speech was entitled "To Be or Not To Be." The rigid tenth-grade teacher had helped him to write it. He'd been working on the dramatic stresses for months.

15   The weeks until graduation were filled with heady activities. A group of small children were to be presented in a play about buttercups and daisies and bunny rabbits. They could be heard throughout the building practicing

their hops and their little songs that sounded like silver bells. The older girls (non-graduates, of course) were assigned the task of making refreshments for the night's festivities. A tangy scent of ginger, cinnamon, nutmeg and chocolate wafted around the home economics building as the budding cooks made samples for themselves and their teachers.

In every corner of the workshop, axes and saws split fresh timber as the woodshop boys made sets and stage scenery. Only the graduates were left out of the general bustle. We were free to sit in the library at the back of the building or look in quite detachedly, naturally, on the measures being taken for our event.

Even the minister preached on graduation the Sunday before. His subject was, "Let your light so shine that men will see your good works and praise your Father, Who is in Heaven." Although the sermon was purported to be addressed to us, he used the occasion to speak to backsliders, gamblers, and general ne'er-do-wells. But since he had called our names at the beginning of the service we were mollified.

Among Negroes the tradition was to give presents to children going only from one grade to another. How much more important this was when the person was graduating at the top of the class. Uncle Willie and Momma had sent away for a Mickey Mouse watch like Bailey's. Louise gave me four embroidered handkerchiefs. (I gave her three crocheted doilies.) Mrs. Sneed, the minister's wife, made me an underskirt to wear for graduation, and nearly every customer gave me a nickel or maybe even a dime with the instruction "Keep on moving to high ground," or some such encouragement.

Amazingly the great day finally dawned and I was out of bed before I knew it. I threw open the back door to see it more clearly, but Momma said, "Sister, come away from that door and put your robe on."

20   I hoped the memory of that morning would never leave me. Sunlight was itself still young, and the day had none of the insistence maturity would bring it in a few hours. In my robe and barefoot in the backyard, under cover of going to see about my new beans, I gave myself up to the gentle warmth and thanked God that no matter what evil I had done in my life He had allowed me to live to see this day. Somewhere in my fatalism I had expected to die, accidentally, and never have the chance to walk up the stairs in the auditorium and gracefully receive my hard-earned diploma. Out of God's merciful bosom I had won reprieve.

Bailey came out in his robe and gave me a box wrapped in Christmas paper. He said he had saved his money for months to pay for it. It felt like a box of chocolates, but I knew Bailey wouldn't save money to buy candy when we had all we could want under our noses.

He was as proud of the gift as I. It was a soft-leather-bound copy of a collection of poems by Edgar Allan Poe, or, as Bailey and I called him, "Eap." I turned to "Annabel Lee" and we walked up and down the garden rows, the cool dirt between our toes, reciting the beautifully sad lines.

Momma made a Sunday breakfast although it was only Friday. After we finished the blessing, I opened my eyes to find the watch on my plate. It was a dream of a day. Everything went smoothly and to my credit, I didn't have to be reminded or scolded for anything. Near evening I was too jittery to attend to chores, so Bailey volunteered to do all before his bath.

Days before, we had made a sign for the Store and as we turned out

the lights Momma hung the cardboard over the doorknob. It read clearly:
CLOSED. GRADUATION.

25   My dress fitted perfectly and everyone said that I looked like a sunbeam
in it. On the hill, going toward the school, Bailey walked behind with Uncle
Willie, who muttered, "Go on, Ju." He wanted him to walk ahead with us because it embarrassed him to have to walk so slowly. Bailey said he'd let the
ladies walk together, and the men would bring up the rear. We all laughed,
nicely.

Little children dashed by out of the dark like fireflies. Their crepe-paper
dresses and butterfly wings were not made for running and we heard more
than one rip, dryly, and the regretful "uh uh" that followed.

The school blazed without gaiety. The windows seemed cold and unfriendly from the lower hill. A sense of ill-fated timing crept over me, and if
Momma hadn't reached for my hand I would have drifted back to Bailey and
Uncle Willie, and possibly beyond. She made a few slow jokes about my feet
getting cold, and tugged me along to the now-strange building.

Around the front steps, assurance came back. There were my fellow
"greats," the graduating class. Hair brushed back, legs oiled, new dresses
and pressed pleats, fresh pocket handkerchiefs and little handbags, all
homesewn. Oh, we were up to snuff, all right. I joined my comrades and
didn't even see my family go in to find seats in the crowded auditorium.

The school band struck up a march and all classes filed in as had been
rehearsed. We stood in front of our seats, as assigned, and on a signal from
the choir director, we sat. No sooner had this been accomplished than the
band started to play the national anthem. We rose again and sang the song,
after which we recited the pledge of allegiance. We remained standing for a
brief minute before the choir director and the principal signaled to us,
rather desperately I thought, to take our seats. The command was so unusual that our carefully rehearsed and smooth-running machine was thrown
off. For a full minute we fumbled for our chairs and bumped into each other
awkwardly. Habits change or solidify under pressure, so in our state of nervous tension we had been ready to follow our usual assembly pattern: the
American National Anthem, then the pledge of allegiance, then the song
every Black person I knew called the Negro National Anthem. All done in
the same key, with the same passion and most often standing on the same
foot.

30   Finding my seat at last, I was overcome with a presentiment of worse
things to come. Something unrehearsed, unplanned, was going to happen,
and we were going to be made to look bad. I distinctly remember being explicit in the choice of pronoun. It was "we," the graduating class, the unit,
that concerned me then.

The principal welcomed "parents and friends" and asked the Baptist
minister to lead us in prayer. His invocation was brief and punchy, and for a
second I thought we were getting back on the high road to right action.
When the principal came back to the dais, however, his voice had changed.
Sounds always affected me profoundly and the principal's voice was one of
my favorites. During assembly it melted and lowed weakly into the audience. It had not been in my plan to listen to him, but my curiosity was
piqued and I straightened up to give him my attention.

He was talking about Booker T. Washington, our "late great leader," who said we can be as close as the fingers on the hand, etc. . . . Then he said a few vague things about friendship and the friendship of kindly people to those less fortunate than themselves. With that his voice nearly faded, thin, away. Like a river diminishing to a stream and then to a trickle. But he cleared his throat and said, "Our speaker tonight, who is also our friend, came from Texarkana to deliver the commencement address, but due to the irregularity of the train schedule, he's going to, as they say, 'speak and run.'" He said that we understood and wanted the man to know that we were most grateful for the time he was able to give us and then something about how we were willing always to adjust to another's program, and without more ado—"I give you Mr. Edward Donleavy."

Not one but two white men came through the door offstage. The shorter one walked to the speaker's platform, and the tall one moved over to the center seat and sat down. But that was our principal's seat, and already occupied. The dislodged gentleman bounced around for a long breath or two before the Baptist minister gave him his chair, then with more dignity than the situation deserved, the minister walked off the stage.

Donleavy looked at the audience once (on reflection, I'm sure that he wanted only to reassure himself that we were really there), adjusted his glasses and began to read from a sheaf of papers.

35   He was glad "to be here and to see the work going on just as it was in the other schools."

At the first "Amen" from the audience I willed the offender to immediate death by choking on the word. But Amen's and Yes, sir's began to fall around the room like rain through a ragged umbrella.

He told us of the wonderful changes we children in Stamps had in store. The Central School (naturally, the white school was Central) had already been granted improvements that would be in use in the fall. A well-known artist was coming from Little Rock to teach art to them. They were going to have the newest microscopes and chemistry equipment for their laboratory. Mr. Donleavy didn't leave us long in the dark over who made these improvements available to Central High. Nor were we to be ignored in the general betterment scheme he had in mind.

He said that he had pointed out to people at a very high level that one of the first-line football tacklers at Arkansas Agricultural and Mechanical College had graduated from good old Lafayette County Training School. Here fewer Amen's were heard. Those few that did break through lay dully in the air with the heaviness of habit.

He went on to praise us. He went on to say how he had bragged that "one of the best basketball players at Fisk sank his first ball right here at Lafayette County Training School."

40   The white kids were going to have a chance to become Galileos and Madame Curies and Edisons and Gauguins, and our boys (the girls weren't even in on it) would try to be Jesse Owenses and Joe Louises.

Owens and the Brown Bomber were great heroes in our world, but what school official in the white-goddom of Little Rock had the right to decide that those two men must be our only heroes? Who decided that for Henry Reed to become a scientist he had to work like George Washington Carver, as a bootblack, to buy a lousy microscope? Bailey was obviously always going to be too small to be an athlete, so which concrete angel glued to what country seat had decided that if my brother wanted to become a lawyer he had to first pay penance for his skin by picking cotton and hoeing corn and studying correspondence books at night for twenty years?

The man's dead words fell like bricks around the auditorium and too many settled in my belly. Constrained by hard-learned manners I couldn't look behind me, but to my left and right the proud graduating class of 1940 had dropped their heads. Every girl in my row had found something new to do with her handkerchief. Some folded the tiny squares into love knots, some into triangles, but most were wadding them, then pressing them flat on their yellow laps.

On the dais, the ancient tragedy was being replayed. Professor Parsons sat, a sculptor's reject, rigid. His large, heavy body seemed devoid of will or willingness, and his eyes said he was no longer with us. The other teachers examined the flag (which was draped stage right) or their notes, or the windows which opened on our now-famous playing diamond.

Graduation, the hush-hush magic time of frills and gifts and congratulations and diplomas, was finished for me before my name was called. The accomplishment was nothing. The meticulous maps, drawn in three colors of ink, learning and spelling decasyllabic words, memorizing the whole of *The Rape of Lucrece*—it was nothing. Donleavy had exposed us.

45   We were maids and farmers, handymen and washerwomen, and anything higher that we aspired to was farcical and presumptuous. Then I wished that Gabriel Prosser and Nat Turner had killed all whitefolks in their beds and that Abraham Lincoln had been assassinated before the signing of the Emancipation Proclamation, and that Harriet Tubman had been killed by that blow on her head and Christopher Columbus had drowned in the *Santa Maria.*

It was awful to be Negro and have no control over my life. It was brutal to be young and already trained to sit quietly and listen to charges brought against my color and no chance of defense. We should all be dead. I thought I should like to see us all dead, one on top of the other. A pyramid of flesh with the whitefolks on the bottom, as the broad base, then the Indians with their silly tomahawks and teepees and wigwams and treaties, the Negroes with their mops and recipes and cotton sacks and spirituals sticking out of their mouths. The Dutch children should all stumble in their wooden shoes and break their necks. The French should choke to death on the Louisiana Purchase (1803) while silkworms ate all the Chinese with their stupid pigtails. As a species, we were an abomination. All of us.

Donleavy was running for election, and assured our parents that if he won we could count on having the only colored paved playing field in that part of Arkansas. Also—he never looked up to acknowledge the grunts of acceptance—also, we were bound to get some new equipment for the home economics building and the workshop.

He finished, and since there was no need to give any more than the most perfunctory thank-you's, he nodded to the men on the stage, and the tall white man who was never introduced joined him at the door. They left with the attitude that now they were off to something really important. (The graduation ceremonies at Lafayette County Training school had been a mere preliminary.)

The ugliness they left was palpable. An uninvited guest who wouldn't leave. The choir was summoned and sang a modern arrangement of "Onward, Christian Soldiers," with new words pertaining to graduates seeking their place in the world. But it didn't work. Elouise, the daughter of the Baptist minister, recited "Invictus," and I could have cried at the impertinence of "I am the master of my fate, I am the captain of my soul."

50   My name had lost its ring of familiarity and I had to be nudged to go and receive my diploma. All my preparations had fled. I neither marched up to the stage like a conquering Amazon, nor did I look in the audience for Bailey's nod of approval. Marguerite Johnson, I heard the name again, my honors were read, there were noises in the audience of appreciation, and I took my place on the stage as rehearsed.

I thought about colors I hated: ecru, puce, lavender, beige and black.

There was shuffling and rustling around me, then Henry Reed was giving his valedictory address, "To Be or Not to Be." Hadn't he heard the white-folks? We couldn't *be,* so the question was a waste of time. Henry's voice came out clear and strong. I feared to look at him. Hadn't he got the message? There was no "nobler in the mind" for Negroes because the world didn't think we had minds, and they let us know it. "Outrageous fortune"? Now, that was a joke. When the ceremony was over I had to tell Henry Reed some things. That is, if I still cared. Not "rub," Henry, "erase." "Ah, there's the erase." Us.

Henry had been a good student in elocution. His voice rose on tides of promise and fell on waves of warnings. The English teacher had helped him to create a sermon winging through Hamlet's soliloquy. To be a man, a doer, a builder, a leader, or to be a tool, an unfunny joke, a crusher of funky toad-stools. I marveled that Henry could go through with the speech as if we had a choice.

I had been listening and silently rebutting each sentence with my eyes closed; then there was a hush, which in an audience warns that something unplanned is happening. I looked up and saw Henry Reed, the conservative, the proper, the A student, turn his back to the audience and turn to us (the proud graduating class of 1940) and sing, nearly speaking,

> Lift ev'ry voice and sing
> Till earth and heaven ring
> Ring with the harmonies of Liberty . . .

It was the poem written by James Weldon Johnson. It was the music composed by J. Rosamond Johnson. It was the Negro National Anthem. Out of habit we were singing it.

55   Our mothers and fathers stood in the dark hall and joined the hymn of encouragement. A kindergarten teacher led the small children onto the stage and the buttercups and daisies and bunny rabbits marked time and tried to follow:

> Stony the road we trod
> Bitter the chastening rod
> Felt in the days when hope, unborn, had died.
> Yet with a steady beat
> Have not our weary feet
> Come to the place for which our fathers sighed?

Every child I knew had learned that song with his ABC's and along with "Jesus Loves Me This I Know." But I personally had never heard it before. Never heard the words, despite the thousands of times I had sung them. Never thought they had anything to do with me.

On the other hand, the words of Patrick Henry had made such an impression on me that I had been able to stretch myself tall and trembling and say, "I know not what course others may take, but as for me, give me liberty or give me death."

And now I heard, really for the first time:

We have come over a way that with tears has been watered,
We have come, treading our path through the blood of the slaughtered.

While echoes of the song shivered in the air, Henry Reed bowed his head, said "Thank you," and returned to his place in the line. The tears that slipped down many faces were not wiped away in shame.

60   We were on top again. As always, again. We survived. The depths had been icy and dark, but now a bright sun spoke to our souls. I was no longer simply a member of the proud graduating class of 1940; I was a proud member of the wonderful, beautiful Negro race.

Oh, Black known and unknown poets, how often have your auctioned pains sustained us? Who will compute the lonely nights made less lonely by your songs, or the empty pots made less tragic by your tales?

If we were a people much given to revealing secrets, we might raise monuments and sacrifice to the memories of our poets, but slavery cured us of that weakness. It may be enough, however, to have it said that we survive in exact relationship to the dedication of our poets (include preachers, musicians and blues singers).

[1969]

 ## TOPICS FOR CRITICAL THINKING AND WRITING

1. In the first paragraph notice such overstatements as "glorious release," "the graduating classes themselves were the nobility," and "exotic destinations." Find further examples in the next few pages. What is the function of this diction?

2. How would you define "poets" as Angelou uses the word in the last sentence?

3. Characterize the writer as you perceive her up to the middle of paragraph 29. Support your characterizations with references to specific passages. Next, characterize her in the paragraph beginning "It was awful to be Negro" (paragraph 46). Next, characterize her on the basis of the entire essay. Finally, in a sentence, try to describe the change, telling the main attitudes or moods that she goes through.

Fiction

 ## NATHANIEL HAWTHORNE

Nathaniel Hawthorne (1804–64) was born in Salem, Massachusetts, the son of a sea captain. Two of his ancestors were judges; one had

persecuted Quakers, another had served at the Salem witch trials. After graduating from Bowdoin College in Maine he went back to Salem in order to write in relative seclusion. In 1831 he published "My Kinsman, Major Molineux"; in 1835 he published "Young Goodman Brown" and "The Maypole of Merry Mount"; and in 1837 he published "Dr. Heidegger's Experiment."

From 1839 to 1841 Hawthorne worked in the Boston Customs House and then spent a few months as a member of a communal society, Brook Farm. In 1842 he married. From 1846 to 1849 he was a surveyor at the Salem Customs House; from 1849 to 1850 he wrote The Scarlet Letter, *the book that made him famous. From 1853 to 1857 he served as American consul in Liverpool, England, a plum awarded him in exchange for writing a campaign biography of a former college classmate, President Franklin Pierce. In 1860, after living in England and Italy, he returned to the United States, settling in Concord, Massachusetts.*

In his stories and novels Hawthorne keeps returning to the Puritan past, studying guilt, sin, and isolation.

Dr. Heidegger's Experiment

That very singular man, old Dr. Heidegger, once invited four venerable friends to meet him in his study. There were three white-bearded gentlemen, Mr. Medbourne, Colonel Killigrew, and Mr. Gascoigne, and a withered gentlewoman, whose name was the Widow Wycherly. They were all melancholy old creatures, who had been unfortunate in life, and whose greatest misfortune it was that they were not long ago in their graves. Mr. Medbourne, in the vigor of his age, had been a prosperous merchant, but had lost his all by a frantic speculation, and was now little better than a mendicant. Colonel Killigrew had wasted his best years, and his health and substance, in the pursuit of sinful pleasures which had given birth to a brood of pains, such as the gout, and divers other torments of soul and body. Mr. Gascoigne was a ruined politician, a man of evil fame, or at least had been so, till time had buried him from the knowledge of the present generation, and made him obscure instead of infamous. As for the Widow Wycherly, tradition tells us that she was a great beauty in her day; but, for a long while past, she had lived in deep seclusion, on account of certain scandalous stories which had prejudiced the gentry of the town against her. It is a circumstance worth mentioning, that each of these three old gentlemen, Mr. Medbourne, Colonel Killigrew, and Mr. Gascoigne, were early lovers of the Widow Wycherly, and had once been on the point of cutting each other's throats for her sake. And before proceeding farther, I will merely hint that Dr. Heidegger and all his four guests were sometimes thought to be a little beside themselves; as is not unfrequently the case with old people, when worried either by present troubles or woeful recollections.

"My dear old friends," said Dr. Heidegger, motioning them to be seated, "I am desirous of your assistance in one of those little experiments with which I amuse myself here in my study."

If all stories were true, Dr. Heidegger's study must have been a very curious place. It was a dim, old-fashioned chamber, festooned with cobwebs, and besprinkled with antique dust. Around the walls stood several oaken bookcases, the lower shelves of which were filled with rows of gigantic folios and black-letter quartos, and the upper with little parchment-covered duodecimos. Over the central bookcase was a bronze bust of Hippocrates,[1] with which, according to some authorities, Dr. Heidegger was accustomed to hold consultations in all difficult cases of his practice. In the obscurest corner of the room stood a tall and narrow oaken closet, with its door ajar, within which doubtfully appeared a skeleton. Between two of the bookcases hung a looking glass, presenting its high and dusty plate within a tarnished gilt frame. Among many wonderful stories related of this mirror, it was fabled that the spirits of all the doctor's deceased patients dwelt within its verge, and would stare him in the face whenever he looked thitherward. The opposite side of the chamber was ornamented with the full-length portrait of a young lady, arrayed in the faded magnificence of silk, satin, and brocade, and with a visage as faded as her dress. Above half a century ago, Dr. Heidegger had been on the point of marriage with this young lady; but, being affected with some slight disorder, she had swallowed one of her lover's prescriptions, and died on the bridal evening. The greatest curiosity of the study remains to be mentioned; it was a ponderous folio volume, bound in black leather, with massive silver clasps. There were no letters on the back, and nobody could tell the title of the book. But it was well known to be a book of magic; and once, when a chambermaid had lifted it, merely to brush away the dust, the skeleton had rattled in its closet, the picture of the young lady had stepped one foot upon the floor, and several ghastly faces had peeped forth from the mirror; while the brazen head of Hippocrates frowned, and said—"Forbear!"

Such was Dr. Heidegger's study. On the summer afternoon of our tale, a small round table, as black as ebony, stood in the center of the room, sustaining a cut-glass vase of beautiful form and elaborate workmanship. The sunshine came through the window, between the heavy festoons of two faded damask curtains, and fell directly across this vase; so that a mild splendor was reflected from it on the ashen visages of the five old people who sat around. Four champagne glasses were also on the table.

5   "My dear old friends," repeated Dr. Heidegger, "may I reckon on your aid in performing an exceedingly curious experiment?"

Now Dr. Heidegger was a very strange old gentleman, whose eccentricity had become the nucleus for a thousand fantastic stories. Some of these fables, to my shame be it spoken, might possibly be traced back to mine own veracious self; and if any passages of the present tale should startle the reader's faith, I must be content to bear the stigma of a fictionmonger.

When the doctor's four guests heard him talk of his proposed experiment, they anticipated nothing more wonderful than the murder of a mouse in an air pump, or the examination of a cobweb by the microscope, or some similar nonsense, with which he was constantly in the habit of pestering his intimates. But without waiting for a reply, Dr. Heidegger hobbled across the chamber, and returned with the same ponderous folio, bound in black leather, which common report affirmed to be a book of magic. Undoing the silver clasps, he opened the volume, and took from among its black-letter pages a rose, or what was once a rose, though now the green leaves and crimson petals had assumed one brownish hue, and the ancient flower seemed ready to crumble to dust in the doctor's hands.

[1]Greek physician (460?–377? B.C.), considered the father of medicine

"This rose," said Dr. Heidegger, with a sigh, "this same withered and crumbling flower, blossomed five-and-fifty years ago. It was given me by Sylvia Ward, whose portrait hangs yonder; and I meant to wear it in my bosom at our wedding. Five-and-fifty years it has been treasured between the leaves of this old volume. Now, would you deem it possible that this rose of half a century could ever bloom again?"

"Nonsense!" said the Widow Wycherly, with a peevish toss of her head. "You might as well ask whether an old woman's wrinkled face could ever bloom again."

10   "See!" answered Dr. Heidegger.

He uncovered the vase, and threw the faded rose into the water which it contained. At first it lay lightly on the surface of the fluid, appearing to imbibe none of its moisture. Soon, however, a singular change began to be visible. The crushed and dried petals stirred, and assumed a deepening tinge of crimson, as if the flower were reviving from a deathlike slumber; the slender stalk and twigs of foliage became green; and there was the rose of half a century, looking as fresh as when Sylvia Ward had first given it to her lover. It was scarcely full blown; for some of its delicate red leaves curled modestly around its moist bosom, within which two or three dewdrops were sparkling.

"That is certainly a very pretty deception," said the doctor's friends; carelessly, however, for they had witnessed greater miracles at a conjurer's show; "pray how was it effected?"

"Did you never hear of the 'Fountain of Youth'?" asked Dr. Heidegger, "which Ponce de Leon, the Spanish adventurer, went in search of, two or three centuries ago?"

"But did Ponce de Leon ever find it?" said the Widow Wycherly.

15   "No," answered Dr. Heidegger, "for he never sought it in the right place. The famous Fountain of Youth, if I am rightly informed, is situated in the southern part of the Floridian peninsula, not far from Lake Macaco. Its source is overshadowed by several gigantic magnolias, which, though numberless centuries old, have been kept as fresh as violets by the virtues of this wonderful water. An acquaintance of mine, knowing my curiosity in such matters, had sent me what you see in the vase."

"Ahem!" said Colonel Killigrew, who believed not a word of the doctor's story; "and what may be the effect of this fluid on the human frame?"

"You shall judge for yourself, my dear colonel," replied Dr. Heidegger; "and all of you, my respected friends, are welcome to so much of this admirable fluid as may restore to you the bloom of youth. For my own part, having had much trouble in growing old, I am in no hurry to grow young again. With your permission, therefore, I will merely watch the progress of the experiment."

While he spoke, Dr. Heidegger had been filling the four champagne glasses with the water of the Fountain of Youth. It was apparently impregnated with an effervescent gas, for little bubbles were continually ascending from the depths of the glasses, and bursting in silvery spray at the surface. As the liquor diffused a pleasant perfume, the old people doubted not that it possessed cordial and comfortable properties; and, though utter skeptics as to its rejuvenescent power, they were inclined to swallow it at once. But Dr. Heidegger besought them to stay a moment.

"Before you drink, my respectable old friends," said he, "it would be well that, with the experience of a lifetime to direct you, you should draw up a few general rules for your guidance, in passing a second time through the perils of youth. Think what a sin and a shame it would be, if with your peculiar advantages, you should not become patterns of virtue and wisdom to all the young people of the age!"

20   The doctor's four venerable friends made him no answer, except by a feeble and tremulous laugh; so very ridiculous was the idea, that, knowing how closely repentance treads behind the steps of error, they should ever go astray again.

"Drink then," said the doctor, bowing; "I rejoice that I have so well selected the subjects of my experiment."

With palsied hands they raised the glasses to their lips. The liquor, if it really possessed such virtues as Dr. Heidegger imputed to it, could not have been bestowed on four human beings who needed it more woefully. They looked as if they had never known what youth or pleasure was, but had been the offspring of Nature's dotage, and always the gray, decrepit, sapless, miserable creatures, who now sat stooping round the doctor's table, without life enough in their souls or bodies to be animated even by the prospect of growing young again. They drank off the water, and replaced their glasses on the table.

Assuredly, there was an almost immediate improvement in the aspect of the party, not unlike what might have been produced by a glass of generous wine, together with a sudden glow of cheerful sunshine, brightening over all their visages at once. There was a healthful suffusion on their cheeks, instead of the ashen hue that had made them look so corpselike. They gazed at one another, and fancied that some magic power had really begun to smooth away the deep and sad inscription which Father Time had been so long engraving on their brows. The Widow Wycherly adjusted her cap, for she felt almost like a woman again.

"Give us more of this wondrous water!" cried they eagerly. "We are younger—but we are still too old! Quick—give us more!"

25   "Patience, patience!" quoth Dr. Heidegger, who sat watching the experiment with philosophic coolness. "You have been a long time growing old. Surely you might be content to grow young in half an hour! But the water is at your service."

Again he filled the glasses with the liquor of youth, enough of which still remained in the vase to turn half the old people in the city to the age of their own grandchildren. While the bubbles were yet sparkling on the brim, the doctor's four guests snatched their glasses from the table, and swallowed the contents of a single gulp. Was it delusion? Even while the draught was passing down their throats, it seemed to have wrought a change on their whole systems. Their eyes grew clear and bright; a dark shade deepened among their silvery locks; they sat around the table, three gentlemen of middle age, and a woman hardly beyond her buxom prime.

"My dear widow, you are charming!" cried Colonel Killigrew, whose eyes had been fixed upon her face, while the shadows of age were flitting from it like darkness from the crimson daybreak.

The fair widow knew, of old, that Colonel Killigrew's compliments were not always measured by sober truth; so she started up and ran to the mirror, still dreading that the ugly visage of an old woman would meet her gaze. Meanwhile, the three gentlemen behaved in such a manner as proved that the water of the Fountain of Youth possessed some intoxicating qualities; unless, indeed, their exhilaration of spirits were merely a lightsome dizziness, caused by the sudden removal of the weight of years. Mr. Gascoigne's mind seemed to run on political topics, but whether relating to the past, present, or future, could not easily be determined, since the same ideas and phrases have been in vogue these fifty years. Now he rattled forth full-throated sentences about patriotism, national glory, and the people's rights; now he muttered some perilous stuff or other, in a sly and doubtful whisper, so cautiously that even his own conscience could scarcely catch the secret; and now again he spoke in measured accents, and a deeply deferential tone, as if a royal ear were listening to his well-turned periods. Colonel Killigrew all this time had been trolling forth a jolly bottle song, and ringing his glass in symphony with the chorus, while his eyes wandered towards the buxom figure of the Widow Wycherly. On the other side of the table, Mr. Medbourne was involved in a calculation of dollars and cents, with which was strangely intermingled a project for supplying the East Indies with ice, by harnessing a team of whales to the polar icebergs.

As for the Widow Wycherly, she stood before the mirror curtsying and simpering to her own image, and greeting it as the friend whom she loved better than all the world beside. She thrust her face close to the glass, to see whether some long-remembered wrinkle or crow's-foot had indeed vanished. She examined whether the snow had so entirely melted from her hair, that the venerable cap could be safely thrown aside. At last, turning briskly away, she came with a sort of dancing step to the table.

30   "My dear old doctor," cried she, "pray favor me with another glass!"

"Certainly, my dear madam, certainly!" replied the complaisant doctor; "see! I have already filled the glasses."

There, in fact, stood the four glasses, brimful of this wonderful water, the delicate spray of which, as it effervesced from the surface, resembled the tremulous glitter of diamonds. It was now so nearly sunset that the chamber had grown duskier than ever; but a mild and moonlike splendor gleamed from within the vase, and rested alike on the four guests, and on the doctor's venerable figure. He sat in a high-backed, elaborately carved, oaken armchair, with a gray dignity of aspect that might have well befitted that very Father Time whose power had never been disputed save by this fortunate company. Even while quaffing the third draught of the Fountain of Youth, they were almost awed by the expression of his mysterious visage.

But, the next moment, the exhilarating gush of young life shot through their veins. They were now in the happy prime of youth. Age, with its miserable train of cares, and sorrows, and diseases, was remembered only as the trouble of a dream from which they had joyously awoke. The fresh gloss of the soul, so early lost, and without which the world's successive scenes had been but a gallery of faded pictures, again threw its enchantment over all their prospects. They felt like new-created beings, in a new-created universe.

"We are young! We are young!" they cried, exultingly.

35   Youth, like the extremity of age, had effaced the strongly marked characteristics of middle life, and mutually assimilated them all. They were a group of merry youngsters, almost maddened with the exuberant frolicsomeness of their years. The most singular effect of their gaiety was an impulse to mock the infirmity and decrepitude of which they had so lately been the victims. They laughed loudly at their old-fashioned attire, the wide-skirted coats and flapped waistcoats of the young men, and the ancient cap and gown of the blooming girl. One limped across the floor, like a gouty

grandfather; one set a pair of spectacles astride of his nose, and pretended to pore over the black-letter pages of the book of magic; a third seated himself in an armchair, and strove to imitate the venerable dignity of Dr. Heidegger. Then all shouted mirthfully, and leaped about the room. The Widow Wycherly—if so fresh a damsel could be called a widow—tripped up to the doctor's chair, with a mischievous merriment in her rosy face.

"Doctor, you dear old soul," cried she, "get up and dance with me!" And then the four young people laughed louder than ever, to think what a queer figure the poor old doctor would cut.

"Pray excuse me," answered the doctor quietly. "I am old and rheumatic, and my dancing days were over long ago. But either of these gay young gentlemen will be glad of so pretty a partner."

"Dance with me, Clara!" cried Colonel Killigrew.

"No, no, I will be her partner!" shouted Mr. Gascoigne.

40   "She promised me her hand, fifty years ago!" exclaimed Mr. Medbourne.

They all gathered round her. One caught both her hands in his passionate grasp—another threw his arm about her waist—the third buried his hand among the glossy curls that clustered beneath the widow's cap. Blushing, panting, struggling, chiding, laughing, her warm breath fanning each of their faces by turns, she strove to disengage herself, yet still remained in their triple embrace. Never was there a livelier picture of youthful rivalship, with bewitching beauty for the prize. Yet, by a strange deception, owing to the duskiness of the chamber, and the antique dresses which they still wore, the tall mirror is said to have reflected the figures of the three old, gray, withered grandsires, ridiculously contending for the skinny ugliness of a shriveled grandam.

But they were young: their burning passions proved them so. Inflamed to madness by the coquetry of the girl-widow, who neither granted nor quite withheld her favors, the three rivals began to interchange threatening glances. Still keeping hold of the fair prize, they grappled fiercely at one another's throats. As they struggled to and fro, the table was overturned, and the vase dashed into a thousand fragments. The precious Water of Youth flowed in a bright stream across the floor, moistening the wings of a butterfly, which, grown old in the decline of summer, had alighted there to die. The insect fluttered lightly through the chamber, and settled on the snowy head of Dr. Heidegger.

"Come, come, gentlemen!—come, Madam Wycherly," exclaimed the doctor, "I really must protest against this riot."

They stood still, and shivered; for it seemed as if gray Time were calling them back from their sunny youth, far down into the chill and darksome vale of years. They looked at old Dr. Heidegger, who sat in his carved armchair, holding the rose of half a century, which he had rescued from among the fragments of the shattered vase. At the motion of his hand, the four rioters resumed their seats; the more readily, because their violent exertions had wearied them, youthful though they were.

45   "My poor Sylvia's rose!" ejaculated Dr. Heidegger, holding it in the light of the sunset clouds; "it appears to be fading again."

And so it was. Even while the party were looking at it, the flower continued to shrivel up, till it became as dry and fragile as when the doctor had first thrown it into the vase. He shook off the few drops of moisture which clung to its petals.

"I love it as well thus as in its dewy freshness," observed he, pressing the withered rose to his withered lips. While he spoke, the butterfly fluttered down from the doctor's snowy head, and fell upon the floor.

His guests shivered again. A strange chillness, whether of the body or spirit they could not tell, was creeping gradually over them all. They gazed at one another, and fancied that each fleeting moment snatched away a charm, and left a deepening furrow where none had been before. Was it an illusion? Had the changes of a lifetime been crowded into so brief a space, and were they now four aged people, sitting with their old friend, Dr. Heidegger?

"Are we grown old again, so soon?" cried they dolefully.

50   In truth, they had. The Water of Youth possessed merely a virtue more transient than that of wine. The delirium which it created had effervesced away. Yes! they were old again. With a shuddering impulse that showed her a woman still, the widow clasped her skinny hands before her face, and wished that the coffin lid were over it, since it could be no longer beautiful.

"Yes, friends, ye are old again," said Dr. Heidegger; "and lo! the Water of Youth is all lavished on the ground. Well—I bemoan it not; for if the fountain gushed at my very doorstep, I would not stoop to bathe my lips in it— no, though its delirium were for years instead of moments. Such is the lesson ye have taught me!"

But the doctor's four friends had taught no such lesson to themselves. They resolved forthwith to make a pilgrimage to Florida, and quaff at morning, noon, and night, from the Fountain of Youth.

[1837]

✐ TOPICS FOR CRITICAL THINKING AND WRITING

1. Characterize the narrator, paying special attention to his tone.
2. Briefly describe, as objectively as possible, the furnishings of Dr. Heidegger's study. Then consider whether *as the narrator describes it* it is a frightening place, the dwelling of the mad scientist of horror fiction and film.
3. Characterize Dr. Heidegger.
4. Evaluate the assertion that "Dr. Heidegger's Experiment" is a cynical story. In thinking about the topic, consider not only the plot of the story but the tone with which it is narrated.

JAMES JOYCE

James Joyce (1882–1941) was born into a middle-class family in Dublin, Ireland. His father drank and became increasingly irresponsible and unemployable, and the family sank in the social order. Still, Joyce received a strong classical education at excellent Jesuit schools and at University College, Dublin, where he studied modern languages. In 1902, at the age of 20, he left Ireland so that he might spend the rest of his life writing about life in Ireland. ("The shortest way to Tara," he said, "is via Holyhead," i.e., the shortest way to the heart of Ireland is to take ship away.) In Trieste, Zurich, and Paris he supported his family in a variety of ways, sometimes teaching English in a Berlitz school of language. His fifteen stories, collected under the title of Dubliners, *were written between 1904 and 1907, but he could not get them published until 1914. Next came a highly autobiographical novel,* Portrait of the Artist as a Young Man *(1916).* Ulysses *(1922), a large novel covering eighteen hours in Dublin, was for some years banned by the United States Post Office, though few if any readers today find it offensive. He spent most of the rest of his life working on* Finnegans Wake *(1939).*

Araby

North Richmond Street, being blind, was a quiet street except at the hour when the Christian Brothers' School set the boys free. An uninhabited house of two stories stood at the blind end, detached from its neighbors in a square ground. The other houses of the street, conscious of decent lives within them, gazed at one another with brown imperturbable faces.

The former tenant of our house, a priest, had died in the back drawingroom. Air, musty from having been long enclosed, hung in all the rooms, and the waste room behind the kitchen was littered with old useless papers. Among these I found a few paper-covered books, the pages of which were curled and damp: *The Abbot,* by Walter Scott, *The Devout Communicant* and *The Memoirs of Vidocq.* I liked the last best because its leaves were yellow. The wild garden behind the house contained a central apple-tree and a few straggling bushes under one of which I found the late tenant's rusty bicycle-pump. He had been a very charitable priest; in his will he had left all his money to institutions and the furniture of his house to his sister.

When the short days of winter came dusk fell before we had well eaten our dinners. When we met in the street the houses had grown somber. The space of sky above us was the color of ever-changing violet and towards it the lamps of the street lifted their feeble lanterns. The cold air stung us and we played till our bodies glowed. Our shouts echoed in the silent street. The career of our play brought us through the dark muddy lanes behind the houses where we ran the gantlet of the rough tribes from the cottages, to the back doors of the dark dripping gardens where odors arose from the ashpits, to the dark odorous stables where a coachman smoothed and combed the horse or shook music from the buckled harness. When we returned to the street light from the kitchen windows had filled the areas. If my uncle was seen turning the corner we hid in the shadow until we had seen him safely housed. Or if Mangan's sister came out on the doorstep to call her brother in to his tea we watched her from our shadow peer up and down the street. We waited to see whether she would remain or go in and, if she remained, we left our shadow and walked up to Mangan's steps resignedly. She was waiting for us, her figure defined by the light from the half-opened door. Her brother always teased her before he obeyed and I stood by the railings looking at her. Her dress swung as she moved her body and the soft rope of her hair tossed from side to side.

Every morning I lay on the floor in the front parlor watching her door. The blind was pulled down to within an inch of the sash so that I could not be seen. When she came out on the doorstep my heart leaped. I ran to the hall, seized my books and followed her. I kept her brown figure always in my eye and, when we came near the point at which our ways diverged, I quickened my pace and passed her. This happened morning after morning. I had never spoken to her, except for a few casual words, and yet her name was like a summons to all my foolish blood.

5   Her image accompanied me even in places the most hostile to romance. On Saturday evenings when my aunt went marketing I had to go to carry some of the parcels. We walked through the flaring streets, jostled by drunken men and bargaining women, amid the curses of laborers, the shrill litanies of shop-boys who stood on guard by the barrels of pigs' cheeks, the nasal chanting of street-singers, who sang a *come-all-you* about O'Donovan Rossa, or a ballad about the troubles in our native land. These noises converged in a single sensation of life for me: I imagined that I bore my chalice safely through a throng of foes. Her name sprang to my lips at moments in strange prayers and praises which I myself did not understand. My eyes were often full of tears (I could not tell why) and at times a flood from my heart seemed to pour itself out into my bosom. I thought little of the future. I did not know whether I would ever speak to her or not or, if I spoke to her, how I could tell her of my confused adoration. But my body was like a harp and her words and gestures were like fingers running upon the wires.

One evening I went into the back drawing-room in which the priest had died. It was a dark rainy evening and there was no sound in the house. Through one of the broken panes I heard the rain impinge upon the earth, the fine incessant needles of water playing in the sodden beds. Some distant lamp or lighted window gleamed below me. I was thankful that I could see so little. All my senses seemed to desire to veil themselves and, feeling that I was about to slip from them, I pressed the palms of my hands together until they trembled, murmuring: *O love! O love!* many times.

At last she spoke to me. When she addressed the first words to me I was so confused that I did not know what to answer. She asked me was I going to *Araby.* I forget whether I answered yes or no. It would be a splendid bazaar, she said; she would love to go.

—And why can't you? I asked.

While she spoke she turned a silver bracelet round and round her wrist. She could not go, she said, because there would be a retreat that week in her convent. Her brother and two other boys were fighting for their caps and I was alone at the railings. She held one of the spikes, bowing her head towards me. The light from the lamp opposite our door caught the white curve of a neck, lit up her hair that rested there and, falling, lit up the hand upon the railing. It fell over one side of her dress and caught the white border of a petticoat, just visible as she stood at ease.

10   —It's well for you, she said.

—If I go, I said, I will bring you something.

What innumerable follies laid waste my waking and sleeping thoughts after that evening! I wished to annihilate the tedious intervening days. I chafed against the work of school. At night in my bedroom and by day in the classroom her image came between me and the page I strove to read. The syllables of the word *Araby* were called to me through the silence in which my soul luxuriated and cast an Eastern enchantment over me. I asked for leave to go to the bazaar on Saturday night. My aunt was surprised and hoped it was not some Freemason affair. I answered few questions in class, I watched my master's face pass from amiability to sternness; he hoped I was not beginning to idle. I could not call my wandering thoughts together. I had hardly any patience with the serious work of life which, now that it stood between me and my desire, seemed to me child's play, ugly monotonous child's play.

On Saturday morning I reminded my uncle that I wished to go to the bazaar in the evening. He was fussing at the hall-stand, looking for the hat-brush, and answered me curtly:

—Yes, boy, I know.

15   As he was in the hall I could not go into the front parlor and lie at the window. I left the house in bad humor and walked slowly towards the school. The air was pitilessly raw and already my heart misgave me.

When I came home to dinner my uncle had not yet been home. Still it was early. I sat staring at the clock for some time and, when its ticking began to irritate me, I left the room. I mounted the staircase and gained the upper part of the house. The high cold empty gloomy rooms liberated me and I went from room to room singing. From the front window I saw my companions playing below in the street. Their cries reached me weakened and indistinct and, leaning my forehead against the cool glass, I looked over at the dark house where she lived. I may have stood there for an hour, seeing nothing but the brown-clad figure cast by my imagination, touched discreetly by the lamplight at the curved neck, at the hand upon the railings and at the border below the dress.

When I came downstairs again I found Mrs. Mercer sitting at the fire. She was an old garrulous woman, a pawnbroker's widow, who collected used stamps for some pious purpose. I had to endure the gossip of the tea-table. The meal was prolonged beyond an hour and still my uncle did not come. Mrs. Mercer stood up to go: she was sorry she couldn't wait any longer, but it was after eight o'clock and she did not like to be out late, as the night air was bad for her. When she had gone I began to walk up and down the room, clenching my fists. My aunt said:

—I'm afraid you may put off your bazaar for this night of Our Lord.

At nine o'clock I heard my uncle's latchkey in the halldoor. I heard him talking to himself and heard the hall-stand rocking when it had received the weight of his overcoat. I could interpret these signs. When he was midway through his dinner I asked him to give me the money to go to the bazaar. He had forgotten.

20   —The people are in bed and after their first sleep now, he said.

I did not smile. My aunt said to him energetically:

—Can't you give him the money and let him go? You've kept him late enough as it is.

My uncle said he was very sorry he had forgotten. He said he believed in the old saying: *All work and no play makes Jack a dull boy.* He asked me where I was going and, when I had told him a second time he asked me did I know *The Arab's Farewell to His Steed.* When I left the kitchen he was about to recite the opening lines of the piece to my aunt.

I held a florin tightly in my hand as I strode down Buckingham Street towards the station. The sight of the streets thronged with buyers and glaring with gas recalled to me the purpose of my journey. I took my seat in a third-class carriage of a deserted train. After an intolerable delay the train moved out of the station slowly. It crept onward among ruinous houses and over the twinkling river. At Westland Row Station a crowd of people pressed to the carriage doors; but the porters moved them back, saying that it was a special train for the bazaar. I remained alone in the bare carriage. In a few minutes the train drew up beside an improvised wooden platform. I passed out on to the road and saw by the lighted dial of a clock that it was ten minutes to ten. In front of me was a large building which displayed the magical name.

25   I could not find any sixpenny entrance and, fearing that the bazaar would be closed, I passed in quickly through a turnstile, handing a shilling to a weary-looking man. I found myself in a big hall girdled at half its height by a gallery. Nearly all the stalls were closed and the greater part of the hall was in darkness. I recognized a silence like that which pervades a church after a service. I walked into the center of the bazaar timidly. A few people were gathered about the stalls which were still open. Before a curtain, over which the words *Café Chantant* were written in colored lamps, two men were counting money on a salver. I listened to the fall of the coins.

Remembering with difficulty why I had come I went over to one of the stalls and examined porcelain vases and flowered tea-sets. At the door of the stall a young lady was talking and laughing with two young gentlemen. I remarked their English accents and listened vaguely to their conversation.

—O, I never said such a thing!

—O, but you did!

—O, but I didn't!

30   —Didn't she say that?

—Yes. I heard her.

—O, there's a . . . fib!

Observing me the young lady came over and asked me did I wish to buy anything. The tone of her voice was not encouraging; she seemed to have spoken to me out of a sense of duty. I looked humbly at the great jars that stood like eastern guards at either side of the dark entrance to the stall and murmured:

—No, thank you.

35   The young lady changed the position of one of the vases and went back to the two young men. They began to talk of the same subject. Once or twice the young lady glanced at me over her shoulder.

I lingered before her stall, though I knew my stay was useless, to make my interest in her wares seem the more real. Then I turned away slowly and walked down the middle of the bazaar. I allowed the two pennies to fall against the sixpence in my pocket. I heard a voice call from one end of the gallery that the light was out. The upper part of the hall was now completely dark.

Gazing up into the darkness I saw myself as a creature driven and derided by vanity; and my eyes burned with anguish and anger.

[1905]

TOPICS FOR CRITICAL THINKING AND WRITING

1. Joyce wrote a novel called *A Portrait of the Artist as a Young Man.* Write an essay of about 500 words on "Araby" as a portrait of the artist as a boy.

2. In an essay of about 500 words, consider the role of images of darkness and blindness and what they reveal to us about "Araby" as a story of the fall from innocence into painful awareness.

3. How old, approximately, is the narrator of "Araby" at the time of the experience he describes? How old is he at the time he tells his story? On what evidence do you base your estimates?

4. The boy, apparently an only child, lives with an uncle and aunt, rather than with parents. Why do you suppose Joyce put him in this family setting rather than some other?

5. The story is rich in images of religion. This in itself is not surprising, for the story is set in Roman Catholic Ireland, but the religious images are not simply references to religious persons or objects. In an essay of 500 to 750 words, discuss how these images reveal the narrator's state of mind.

 FRANK O'CONNOR

"Frank O'Connor" was the pen name of Michael O'Donovan (1903-66), who was born in Cork, Ireland. Poverty compelled his family to take him out of school after the fourth grade. He worked at odd jobs and then, during "the troubles"—the armed conflict of 1918-21 that led to the establishment (1922) of the Irish Free State— he served in the Irish Republican Army, fighting the British until he was captured. After his release from prison he worked as a librarian and as a director (1935-39) of the Abbey Theatre in Dublin. Still later, in the 1950s, he lived in the United States, teaching at North-western University and Harvard University.

Among his books—stories, novels, autobiographies, plays, translations of Gaelic poetry, and criticism—is The Lonely Voice, *a study of the short story.*

Guests of the Nation

I

At dusk the big Englishman, Belcher, would shift his long legs out of the ashes and say "Well, chums, what about it?" and Noble or me would say "All right, chum" (for we had picked up some of their curious expressions), and the little Englishman, Hawkins, would light the lamp and bring out the cards. Sometimes Jeremiah Donovan would come up and supervise the game and get excited over Hawkins's cards, which he always played badly, and shout at him as if he was one of our own "Ah, you divil, you, why didn't you play the tray?"

But ordinarily Jeremiah was a sober and contented poor devil like the big Englishman, Belcher, and was looked up to only because he was a fair hand at documents, though he was slow enough even with them. He wore a small cloth hat and big gaiters over his long pants, and you seldom saw him with his hands out of his pockets. He reddened when you talked to him, tilting from toe to heel and back, and looking down all the time at his big farmer's feet. Noble and me used to make fun of his broad accent, because we were from the town.

I couldn't at the time see the point of me and Noble guarding Belcher and Hawkins at all, for it was my belief that you could have planted that pair down anywhere from this to Claregalway and they'd have taken root there like a native weed. I never in my short experience seen two men to take to the country as they did.

They were handed on to us by the Second Battalion when the search for them became too hot, and Noble and myself, being young, took over with a natural feeling of responsibility, but Hawkins made us look like fools when he showed that he knew the country better than we did.

5   "You're the bloke they calls Bonaparte," he says to me. "Mary Brigid O'Connell told me to ask you what you done with the pair of her brother's socks you borrowed."

For it seemed, as they explained it, that the Second used to have little evenings, and some of the girls of the neighborhood turned in, and, seeing they were such decent chaps, our fellows couldn't leave the two Englishmen out of them. Hawkins learned to dance "The Walls of Limerick," "The Siege of Ennis," and "The Waves of Tory" as well as any of them, though, naturally, we couldn't return the compliment, because our lads at that time did not dance foreign dances on principle.

So whatever privileges Belcher and Hawkins had with the Second they just naturally took with us, and after the first day or two we gave up all pretense of keeping a close eye on them. Not that they could have got far, for they had accents you could cut with a knife and wore khaki tunics and overcoats with civilian pants and boots. But it's my belief that they never had any idea of escaping and were quite content to be where they were.

It was a treat to see how Belcher got off with the old woman of the house where we were staying. She was a great warrant to scold, and cranky even with us, but before ever she had a chance of giving our guests, as I may call them, a lick of her tongue, Belcher had made her his friend for life. She was breaking sticks, and Belcher, who hadn't been more than ten minutes in the house, jumped up from his seat and went over to her.

"Allow me, madam," he says, smiling his queer little smile, "please allow me"; and he takes the bloody hatchet. She was struck too paralytic to speak, and after that, Belcher would be at her heels, carrying a bucket, a basket, or a load of turf, as the case might be. As Noble said, he got into looking before she leapt, and hot water, or any little thing she wanted, Belcher would have it ready for her. For such a huge man (and though I am five foot ten myself I had to look up at him) he had an uncommon shortness—or should I say lack?—of speech. It took us some time to get used to him, walking in and out, like a ghost, without a word. Especially because Hawkins talked enough for a platoon, it was strange to hear big Belcher with his toes in the ashes come out with a solitary "Excuse me, chum," or "That's right, chum." His one and only passion was cards, and I will say for him that he was a good cardplayer. He could have fleeced myself and Noble, but whatever we lost to him Hawkins lost to us, and Hawkins played with the money Belcher gave him.

10   Hawkins lost to us because he had too much old gab, and we probably lost to Belcher for the same reason. Hawkins and Noble would spit at one another about religion into the early hours of the morning, and Hawkins worried the soul out of Noble, whose brother was a priest, with a string of questions that would puzzle a cardinal. To make it worse, even in treating of holy subjects, Hawkins had a deplorable tongue. I never in all my career met a man who could mix such a variety of cursing and bad language into an argument. He was a terrible man, and a fright to argue. He never did a stroke of work, and when he had no one else to talk to, he got stuck in the old woman.

He met his match in her, for one day when he tried to get her to complain profanely of the drought, she gave him a great comedown by blaming it entirely on Jupiter Pluvius (a deity neither Hawkins nor I had ever heard of, though Noble said that among the pagans it was believed that he had something to do with the rain). Another day he was swearing at the capitalists for starting the German war when the old lady laid down her iron, puckered up her little crab's mouth, and said: "Mr. Hawkins, you can say what you like about the war, and think you'll deceive me because I'm only a simple poor countrywoman, but I know what started the war. It was the Italian Count that stole the heathen divinity out of the temple in Japan. Believe me, Mr. Hawkins, nothing but sorrow and want can follow the people that disturb the hidden powers."

A queer old girl, all right.

II

We had our tea one evening, and Hawkins lit the lamp and we all sat into cards. Jeremiah Donovan came in too, and sat down and watched us for a while, and it suddenly struck me that he had no great love for the two Englishmen. It came as a great surprise to me, because I hadn't noticed anything about him before.

Late in the evening a really terrible argument blew up between Hawkins and Noble, about capitalists and priests and love of your country.

15   "The capitalists," says Hawkins with an angry gulp, "pays the priests to tell you about the next world so as you won't notice what the bastards are up to in this."

"Nonsense, man!" says Noble, losing his temper. "Before ever a capitalist was thought of, people believed in the next world."

Hawkins stood up as though he was preaching a sermon.

"Oh, they did, did they?" he says with a sneer. "They believed all the things you believe, isn't that what you mean? And you believe that God created Adam, and Adam created Shem, and Shem created Jehoshaphat. You believe all that silly old fairytale about Eve and Eden and the apple. Well, listen to me, chum. If you're entitled to hold a silly belief like that, I'm entitled to hold my silly belief—which is that the first thing your God created was a bleeding capitalist, with morality and Rolls-Royce complete. Am I right, chum?" he says to Belcher.

"You're right, chum," says Belcher with his amused smile, and got up from the table to stretch his long legs into the fire and stroke his moustache. So, seeing that Jeremiah Donovan was going, and that there was no knowing when the argument about religion would be over, I went out with him. We strolled down to the village together, and then he stopped and started blushing and mumbling and saying I ought to be behind, keeping guard on the prisoners. I didn't like the tone he took with me, and anyway I was bored with life in the cottage, so I replied by asking him what the hell he wanted guarding them at all for. I told him I'd talked it over with Noble, and that we'd both rather be out with a fighting column.

20   "What use are those fellows to us?" says I.

He looked at me in surprise and said: "I thought you knew we were keeping them as hostages."

"Hostages?" I said.

"The enemy have prisoners belonging to us," he says, "and now they're talking of shooting them. If they shoot our prisoners, we'll shoot theirs."

"Shoot them?" I said.

25   "What else did you think we were keeping them for?" he says.

"Wasn't it very unforeseen of you not to warn Noble and myself of that in the beginning?" I said.

"How was it?" says he. "You might have known it."

"We couldn't know it, Jeremiah Donovan," says I. "How could we when they were on our hands so long?"

"The enemy have our prisoners as long and longer," says he.

30   "That's not the same thing at all," says I.

"What difference is there?" says he.

I couldn't tell him, because I knew he wouldn't understand. If it was only an old dog that was going to the vet's, you'd try and not get too fond of him, but Jeremiah Donovan wasn't a man that would ever be in danger of that.

"And when is this thing going to be decided?" says I.

"We might hear tonight," he says. "Or tomorrow or the next day at latest. So if it's only hanging round here that's a trouble to you, you'll be free soon enough."

35   It wasn't the hanging round that was a trouble to me at all by this time. I had worse things to worry about. When I got back to the cottage the argument was still on. Hawkins was holding forth in his best style, maintaining that there was no next world, and Noble was maintaining that there was; but I could see that Hawkins had had the best of it.

"Do you know what, chum?" he was saying with a saucy smile. "I think you're just as big a bleeding unbeliever as I am. You say you believe in the next world, as you know just as much about the next world as I do, which is sweet damn-all. What's heaven? You don't know. Where's heaven? You don't know. You know sweet damn-all! I ask you again, do they wear wings?"

"Very well, then," says Noble, "they do. Is that enough for you? They do wear wings."

"Where do they get them, then? Who makes them? Have they a factory for wings? Have they a sort of store where you hands in your chit and takes your bleeding wings?"

"You're an impossible man to argue with," says Noble. "Now, listen to me—" And they were off again.

40   It was long after midnight when we locked up and went to bed. As I

blew out the candle I told Noble what Jeremiah Donovan was after telling me. Noble took it very quietly. When we'd been in bed about an hour he asked me did I think we ought to tell the Englishmen. I didn't think we should, because it was more than likely that the English wouldn't shoot our men, and even if they did, the brigade officers, who were always up and down with the Second Battalion and knew the Englishmen well, wouldn't be likely to want them plugged. "I think so too," says Noble. "It would be great cruelty to put the wind up them now."

"It was very unforeseen of Jeremiah Donovan anyhow," says I.

It was next morning that we found it so hard to face Belcher and Hawkins. We went about the house all day scarcely saying a word. Belcher didn't seem to notice; he was stretched into the ashes as usual, with his usual look of waiting in quietness for something unforeseen to happen, but Hawkins noticed and put it down to Noble's being beaten in the argument of the night before.

"Why can't you take a discussion in the proper spirit?" he says severely. "You and your Adam and Eve! I'm a Communist, that's what I am. Communist or anarchist, it all comes to much the same thing." And for hours he went round the house, muttering when the fit took him. "Adam and Eve! Adam and Eve! Nothing better to do with their time than picking bleeding apples!"

III

I don't know how we got through that day, but I was very glad when it was over, the tea things were cleared away, and Belcher said in his peaceable way: "Well, chums, what about it?" We sat round the table and Hawkins took out the cards, and just then I heard Jeremiah Donovan's footstep on the path and a dark presentiment crossed my mind. I rose from the table and caught him before he reached the door.

45   "What do you want?" I asked.

"I want those two soldier friends of yours," he says, getting red.

"Is that the way, Jeremiah Donovan?" I asked.

"That's the way. There were four of our lads shot this morning, one of them a boy of sixteen."

"That's bad," I said.

50   At that moment Noble followed me out, and the three of us walked down the patch together, talking in whispers. Feeney, the local intelligence officer, was standing by the gate.

"What are you going to do about it?" I asked Jeremiah Donovan.

"I want you and Noble to get them out; tell them they're being shifted again; that'll be the quietest way."

"Leave me out of that," says Noble under his breath.

Jeremiah Donovan looks at him hard.

55   "All right," he says. "You and Feeney get a few tools from the shed and dig a hole by the far end of the bog. Bonaparte and myself will be after you. Don't let anyone see you with the tools. I wouldn't like it to go beyond ourselves."

We saw Feeney and Noble go round to the shed and went in ourselves. I left Jeremiah Donovan to do the explanations. He told them that he had orders to send them back to the Second Battalion. Hawkins let out a mouthful of curses, and you could see that though Belcher didn't say anything, he was a bit upset too. The old woman was for having them stay in spite of us, and she didn't stop advising them until Jeremiah Donovan lost his temper and turned on her. He had a nasty temper, I noticed. It was pitch-dark in the cottage by this time, but no one thought of lighting the lamp, and in the darkness the two Englishmen fetched their topcoats and said good-bye to the old woman.

"Just as a man makes a home of a bleeding place, some bastard at headquarters thinks you're too cushy and shunts you off," says Hawkins, shaking her hand.

"A thousand thanks, madam," says Belcher. "A thousand thanks for everything"—as though he'd made it up.

We went round to the back of the house and down towards the bog, it was only then that Jeremiah Donovan told them. He was shaking with excitement.

60   "There were four of our fellows shot in Cork this morning and now you're to be shot as a reprisal."

"What are you talking about?" snaps Hawkins. "It's bad enough being mucked about as we are without having to put up with your funny jokes."

"It isn't a joke," says Donovan. "I'm sorry, Hawkins, but it's true," and begins on the usual rigmarole about duty and how unpleasant it is.

I never noticed that people who talk a lot about duty find it much of a trouble to them.

"Oh, cut it out!" says Hawkins.

65   "Ask Bonaparte," says Donovan, seeing that Hawkins isn't taking him seriously. "Isn't it true, Bonaparte?"

"It is," I say, and Hawkins stops.

"Ah, for Christ's sake, chum."

"I mean it, chum," I say.

"You don't sound as if you meant it."

70   "If he doesn't mean it, I do," says Donovan, working himself up.

"What have you against me, Jeremiah Donovan?"

"I never said I had anything against you. But why did your people take out four of our prisoners and shoot them in cold blood?"

He took Hawkins by the arm and dragged him on, but it was impossible to make him understand that we were in earnest. I had the Smith and Wesson in my pocket and I kept fingering it and wondering what I'd do if they put up a fight for it or ran, and wishing to God they'd do one or the other. I knew if they did run for it, that I'd never fire on them. Hawkins wanted to know was Noble in it, and when we said yes, he asked us why Noble wanted to plug him. Why did any of us want to plug him? What had he done to us? Weren't we all chums? Didn't we understand him and didn't he understand us? Did we imagine for an instant that he'd shoot us for all the so-and-so officers in the so-and-so British Army?

By this time we'd reached the bog, and I was so sick I couldn't even answer him. We walked along the edge of it in the darkness, and every now and then Hawkins would call a halt and begin all over again, as if he was wound up, about our being chums, and I knew that nothing but the sight of the grave would convince him that we had to do it. And all the time I was hoping that something would happen; that they'd run for it or that Noble would take over the responsibility from me. I had the feeling that it was worse on Noble than on me.

IV

75   At last we saw the lantern in the distance and made towards it. Noble was carrying it, and Feeney was standing somewhere in the darkness behind him, and the picture of them so still and silent in the bogland brought it home to me that we were in earnest, and banished the last bit of hope I had.

Belcher, on recognizing Noble, said: "Hallo, chum," in his quiet way, but Hawkins flew at him at once, and the argument began all over again, only this time Noble had nothing to say for himself and stood with his head down, holding the lantern between his legs.

It was Jeremiah Donovan who did the answering. For the twentieth time, as though it was haunting his mind, Hawkins asked if anybody thought he'd shoot Noble.

"Yes, you would," says Jeremiah Donovan.

"No, I wouldn't, damn you!"

80   "You would, because you'd know you'd be shot for not doing it."

"I wouldn't, not if I was to be shot twenty times over. I wouldn't shoot a pal. And Belcher wouldn't—isn't that right, Belcher?"

"That's right chum," Belcher said, but more by way of answering the question than of joining in the argument. Belcher sounded as though whatever unforeseen thing he'd always been waiting for had come at last.

"Anyway, who says Noble would be shot if I wasn't? What do you think I'd do if I was in his place, out in the middle of a blasted bog?"

"What would you do?" asks Donovan.

85   "I'd go with him wherever he was going, of course. Share my last bob with him and stick by him through thick and thin. No one can ever say of me that I let down a pal."

"We had enough of this," says Jeremiah Donovan, cocking his revolver. "Is there any message you want to send?"

"No, there isn't."

"Do you want to say your prayers?"

Hawkins came out with a cold-blooded remark that even shocked me and turned on Noble again.

90   "Listen to me, Noble," he says. "You and me are chums. You can't come over to my side, so I'll come over to your side. That show you I mean what I say? Give me a rifle and I'll go along with you and the other lads."

Nobody answered him. We knew that was no way out.

"Hear what I'm saying?" he says. "I'm through with it. I'm a deserter or anything else you like. I don't believe in your stuff, but it's no worse than mine. That satisfy you?"

Noble raised his head, but Donovan began to speak and he lowered it again without replying.

"For the last time, have you any message to send?" says Donovan in a cold, excited sort of voice.

95   "Shut up, Donovan! You don't understand me, but these lads do. They're not the sort to make a pal and kill a pal. They're not the tools of any capitalist."

I alone of the crowd saw Donovan raise his Webley to the back of Hawkins's neck, and as he did so I shut my eyes and tried to pray. Hawkins had begun to say something else when Donovan fired, and as I opened my eyes at the bang, I saw Hawkins stagger at the knees and lie out flat at

Noble's feet, slowly and as quiet as a kid falling asleep, with the lantern-light on his lean legs and bright farmer's boots. We all stood very still, watching him settle out in the last agony.

Then Belcher took out a handkerchief and began to tie it about his own eyes (in our excitement we'd forgotten to do the same for Hawkins), and, seeing it wasn't big enough, turned and asked for the loan of mine. I gave it to him and he knotted the two together and pointed with his foot at Hawkins.

"He's not quite dead," he says. "Better give him another."

Sure enough, Hawkins's left knee is beginning to rise. I bend down and put my gun to his head; then, recollecting myself, I get up again. Belcher understands what's in my mind.

100   "Give him his first," he says. "I don't mind. Poor bastard, we don't know what's happening to him now."

I knelt and fired. By this time I didn't seem to know what I was doing. Belcher, who was fumbling a bit awkwardly with the handkerchiefs, came out with a laugh as he heard the shot. It was the first time I heard him laugh and it sent a shudder down my back; it sounded so unnatural.

"Poor bugger!" he said quietly. "And last night he was so curious about it all. It's very queer, chums, I always think. Now he knows as much about it as they'll ever let him know, and last night he was all in the dark."

Donovan helped him to tie the handkerchiefs about his eyes. "Thanks, chum," he said. Donovan asked if there were any messages he wanted sent.

"No, chum," he says. "Not for me. If any of you would like to write to Hawkins's mother, you'll find a letter from her in his pocket. He and his mother were great chums. But my missus left me eight years ago. Went away with another fellow and took the kid with her. I like the feeling of a home, as you may have noticed, but I couldn't start again after that."

105   It was an extraordinary thing, but in those few minutes Belcher said more than in all the weeks before. It was just as if the sound of the shot had started a flood of talk in him and he could go on the whole night like that, quite happily, talking about himself. We stood round like fools now that he couldn't see us any longer. Donovan looked at Noble, and Noble shook his head. Then Donovan raised his Webley, and at that moment Belcher gives his queer laugh again. He may have thought we were talking about him, or perhaps he noticed the same thing I'd noticed and couldn't understand it.

"Excuse me, chums," he says. "I feel I'm talking the hell of a lot, and so silly, about my being so handy about a house and things like that. But this thing came on me suddenly. You'll forgive me, I'm sure."

"You don't want to say a prayer?" asked Donovan.

"No, chum," he says. "I don't think it would help. I'm ready, and you boys want to get it over."

"You understand that we're only doing our duty?" says Donovan.

110   Belcher's head was raised like a blind man's, so that you could only see his chin and the tip of his nose in the lantern-light.

"I never could make out what duty was myself," he said. "I think you're all good lads, if that's what you mean. I'm not complaining."

Noble, just as if he couldn't bear any more of it, raised his fist at Donovan, and in a flash Donovan raised his gun and fired. The big man went over like a sack of meal, and this time there was no need of a second shot.

I don't remember much about the burying, but that it was worse than all the rest because we had to carry them to the grave. It was all mad lonely with nothing but a patch of lantern-light between ourselves and the dark, and birds hooting and screeching all round, disturbed by the guns. Noble went through Hawkins's belongings to find the letter from his mother, and then joined his hands together. He did the same with Belcher. Then, when we'd filled in the grave, we separated from Jeremiah Donovan and Feeney and took our tools back to the shed. All the way we didn't speak a word. The kitchen was dark and cold as we'd left it, and the old woman was sitting over the hearth, saying her beads. We walked past her into the room, and Noble struck a match to light the lamp. She rose quietly and came to the doorway with all her cantankerousness gone.

"What did ye do with them?" she asked in a whisper, and Noble started so that the match went out in his hand.

115   "What's that?" he asked without turning round.

"I heard ye," she said.

"What did you hear?" asked Noble.

"I heard ye. Do ye think I didn't hear ye, putting the spade back in the houseen?"

Noble struck another match and this time the lamp lit for him.

120   "Was that what ye did to them?" she asked.

Then, by God, in the very doorway, she fell on her knees and began praying, and after looking at her for a minute or two Noble did the same by the fireplace. I pushed my way out past her and left them at it. I stood at the door, watching the stars and listening to the shrieking of the birds dying out over the bogs. It is so strange what you feel at times like that you can't describe it. Noble says he saw everything ten times the size, as though there were nothing in the whole world but that little patch of bog with the two Englishmen stiffening into it, but with me it was as if the patch of bog where the Englishmen were was a million miles away, and even Noble and the old woman, mumbling behind me, and the birds and the bloody stars were all far away, and I was somehow very small and very lost and lonely like a child astray in the snow. And anything that happened to me afterwards, I never felt the same about again.

[1931]

TOPICS FOR CRITICAL THINKING AND WRITING

1. Although the narrator, Noble, and Donovan are all patriotic Irishmen, Donovan's attitude toward the English prisoners is quite different from that of the other two. How does that difference in attitude help point up the story's theme?

2. How does the constant bickering between Noble and Hawkins help to prepare us for the conclusion of the story? How does it contribute to the theme?

3. When he hears he is about to be shot, Hawkins, to save his life, volunteers to join the Irish cause. Is his turnabout simply evidence of his cowardice and hypocrisy? Explain.

4. Throughout most of the story Belcher is shy and speaks little; just before his execution, however, he suddenly becomes loquacious. Is he

trying to stall for time? Would it have been more in character for Belcher to have remained stoically taciturn to the end, or do the narrator's remarks about Belcher's change make it plausible?

5. Does the old woman's presence in the story merely furnish local color or picturesqueness? If so, is it necessary or desirable? Or does her presence further contribute to the story's meaning? If so, how?

6. The following is the last paragraph of an earlier version. Which is the more effective conclusion? Why?

> So then, by God, she fell on her two knees by the door, and began telling her beads, and after a minute or two Noble went on his knees by the fireplace, so I pushed my way past her, and stood at the door, watching the stars and listening to the damned shrieking of the birds. It is so strange what you feel at such moments, and not to be written afterwards. Noble says he felt he seen everything ten times as big, perceiving nothing around him but the little patch of black bog with the two Englishmen stiffening into it; but with me it was the other way, as though the patch of bog where the two Englishmen were was a thousand miles away from me, and even Noble mumbling just behind me and the old woman and the birds and the bloody stars were all far away, and I was somehow very small and very lonely. And nothing that ever happened to me after I never felt the same about again.

7. How does the point of view (see pages 146–47) help to emphasize the narrator's development from innocence to awareness? If the story had been told in the third person, how would it have affected the story's impact?

HISAYE YAMAMOTO

Hisaye Yamamoto was born in 1921 in Redondo Beach, California. Before the Second World War she contributed to the Japan-California Daily News, *but when the United States entered the war she and her family were interned, along with more than a hundred thousand other persons of Japanese ancestry. She was sent to the Colorado River Relocation Center in Poston, Arizona, where she wrote for the camp's newspaper.*

Yamamoto writes chiefly of rural Japanese-Americans, usually setting her stories in the depression or in the 1940s. "Yoneko's Earthquake" appeared in Best American Short Stories of 1952. *Five of her stories have been collected in a volume called* Seventeen Syllables *(1985). We reprint the title story on page 890.*

Yoneko's Earthquake

Yoneko Hosoume became a free-thinker on the night of March 10, 1933, only a few months after her first actual recognition of God. Ten years old at the time, of course she had heard rumors about God all along, long before

Marpo came. Her cousins who lived in the city were all Christians, living as they did right next door to a Baptist church exclusively for Japanese people. These city cousins, of whom there were several, had been baptized en masse, and were very proud of their condition. Yoneko was impressed when she heard of this and thereafter was given to referring to them as "my cousins, the Christians." She, too, yearned at times after Christianity, but she realized the absurdity of her whim, seeing that there was no Baptist church for Japanese in the rural community she lived in. Such a church would have been impractical, moreover, since Yoneko, her father, her mother, and her little brother Seigo were the only Japanese thereabouts. They were the only ones, too, whose agriculture was so diverse as to include blackberries, cabbages, rhubarb, potatoes, cucumbers, onions, and cantaloupes. The rest of the countryside there was like one vast orange grove.

Yoneko had entered her cousins' church once, but she could not recall the sacred occasion without mortification. It had been one day when the cousins had taken her and Seigo along with them to Sunday school. The church was a narrow, wooden building mysterious-looking because of its unusual bluish-gray paint and its steeple, but the basement schoolroom inside had been disappointingly ordinary, with desks, a blackboard, and erasers. They had all sung "Let Us Gather at the River" in Japanese. This goes:

Mamonaku kanata no
Nagare no soba de
Tanoshiku ai-masho
Mata tomodachi to

Mamonaku ai-masho
Kirei-na, kirei-na kawa de
Tanoshiku ai-masho
Mata tomodachi to.

Yoneko had not known the words at all, but always clever in such situations, she had opened her mouth and grimaced nonchalantly to the rhythm. What with everyone else singing at the top of his lungs, no one had noticed that she was not making a peep. Then everyone had sat down again and the man had suggested, "Let us pray." Her cousins and the rest had promptly curled their arms on the desks to make nests for their heads, and Yoneko had done the same. But not Seigo. Because when the room had become so still that one was aware of the breathing, the creaking, and the chittering in the trees outside, Seigo, sitting with her, had suddenly flung his arm around her neck and said with concern, "Sis, what are you crying for? Don't cry." Even the man had laughed and Yoneko had been terribly ashamed that Seigo should thus disclose them to be interlopers. She had pinched him fiercely and he had begun to cry, so she had had to drag him outside, which was a fortunate move, because he had immediately wet his pants. But he had been only three then, so it was not very fair to expect dignity of him.

So it remained for Marpo to bring the word of God to Yoneko, Marpo with the face like brown leather, the thin mustache like Edmund Lowe's,[1] and the rare, breathtaking smile like white gold. Marpo, who was twenty-

[1] a movie actor popular in the 1930s

seven years old, was a Filipino and his last name was lovely, something like Humming Wing, but no one ever ascertained the spelling of it. He ate principally rice, just as though he were Japanese, but he never sat down to the Hosoume table, because he lived in the bunkhouse out by the barn and cooked on his own kerosene stove. Once Yoneko read somewhere that Filipinos trapped wild dogs, starved them for a time, then, feeding them mountains of rice, killed them at the peak of their bloatedness, thus insuring themselves meat ready to roast, stuffing and all, without further ado. This, the book said, was considered a delicacy. Unable to hide her disgust and her fascination, Yoneko went straightway to Marpo and asked, "Marpo, is it true that you eat dogs?" and he, flashing that smile, answered, "Don't be funny, honey!" This caused her no end of amusement, because it was a poem, and she completely forgot about the wild dogs.

Well, there seemed to be nothing Marpo could not do. Mr. Hosoume said Marpo was the best hired man he had ever had, and he said this often, because it was an irrefutable fact among Japanese in general that Filipinos in general were an indolent lot. Mr. Hosoume ascribed Marpo's industry to his having grown up in Hawaii, where there is known to be considerable Japanese influence. Marpo had gone to a missionary school there and he owned a Bible given him by one of his teachers. This had black leather covers that gave as easily as cloth, golden edges, and a slim purple ribbon for a marker. He always kept it on the little table by his bunk, which was not a bed with springs but a low, three-plank shelf with a mattress only. On the first page of the book, which was stiff and black, his teacher had written in large swirls of white ink, "As we draw near to God, He will draw near to us."

5   What, for instance, could Marpo do? Why, it would take an entire, leisurely evening to go into his accomplishments adequately, because there was not only Marpo the Christian and Marpo the best hired man, but Marpo the athlete, Marpo the musician (both instrumental and vocal), Marpo the artist, and Marpo the radio technician:

(1) As an athlete, Marpo owned a special pair of black shoes, equipped with sharp nails on the soles, which he kept in shape with the regular application of neatsfoot oil. Putting these on, he would dash down the dirt road to the highway, a distance of perhaps half a mile, and back again. When he first came to work for the Hosoumes, he undertook this sprint every evening before he went to get his supper but, as time went on, he referred to these shoes less and less and, in the end, when he left, he had not touched them for months. He also owned a muscle-builder sent him by Charles Atlas which, despite his unassuming size, he could stretch the length of his outspread arms; his teeth gritted then and his whole body became temporarily victim to a jerky vibration. (2) As an artist, Marpo painted larger-than-life water colors of his favorite movie stars, all of whom were women and all of whom were blonde, like Ann Harding and Jean Harlow, and tacked them up on his walls. He also made for Yoneko a folding contraption of wood holding two pencils, one with lead and one without, with which she, too, could obtain double-sized likenesses of any picture she wished. It was a fragile instrument, however, and Seigo splintered it to pieces one day when Yoneko was away at school. He claimed he was only trying to copy Boob McNutt from the funny paper when it failed. (3) As a musician, Marpo owned a violin for which he had paid over one hundred dollars. He kept this in a case whose lining was red velvet, first wrapping it

gently in a brilliant red silk scarf. This scarf, which weighed nothing, he tucked under his chin when he played, gathering it up delicately by the center and flicking it once to unfurl it—a gesture Yoneko prized. In addition to this, Marpo was a singer, with a soft tenor which came out in professional quavers and rolled r's when he applied a slight pressure to his Adam's apple with thumb and forefinger. His violin and vocal repertoire consisted of the same numbers, mostly hymns and Irish folk airs. He was especially addicted to "The Rose of Tralee" and the "Londonderry Air." (4) Finally, as a radio technician who had spent two previous winters at a specialists' school in the city, Marpo had put together a bulky table-size radio which brought in equal proportions of static and entertainment. He never got around to building a cabinet to house it and its innards of metal and glass remained public throughout its lifetime. This was just as well, for not a week passed without Marpo's deciding to solder one bit or another. Yoneko and Seigo became a part of the great listening audience with such fidelity that Mr. Hosoume began remarking the fact that they dwelt more with Marpo than with their own parents. He eventually took a serious view of the matter and bought the naked radio from Marpo, who thereupon put away his radio manuals and his soldering iron in the bottom of his steamer trunk and divided more time among his other interests.

However, Marpo's versatility was not revealed, as it is here, in a lump. Yoneko uncovered it fragment by fragment every day, by dint of unabashed questions, explorations among his possessions, and even silent observation, although this last was rare. In fact, she and Seigo visited with Marpo at least once a day and both of them regularly came away amazed with their findings. The most surprising thing was that Marpo was, after all this, a rather shy young man meek to the point of speechlessness in the presence of Mr. and Mrs. Hosoume. With Yoneko and Seigo, he was somewhat more self-confident and at ease.

It is not remembered now just how Yoneko and Marpo came to open their protracted discussion on religion. It is sufficient here to note that Yoneko was an ideal apostle, adoring Jesus, desiring Heaven, and fearing Hell. Once Marpo had enlightened her on these basics, Yoneko never questioned their truth. The questions she put up to him, therefore, sought neither proof of her exegeses nor balm for her doubts, but simply additional color to round out her mental images. For example, who did Marpo suppose was God's favorite movie star? Or, what sound did Jesus' laughter have (it must be like music, she added, nodding sagely, answering herself to her own satisfaction), and did Marpo suppose that God's sense of humor would have appreciated the delicious chant she had learned from friends at school today:

> There ain't no bugs on us,
> There ain't no bugs on us,
> There may be bugs on the rest of you mugs,
> But there ain't no bugs on us!

Or, did Marpo believe Jesus to have been exempt from stinging eyes when he shampooed that long, naturally wavy hair of his?

To shake such faith, there would have been required a most monstrous upheaval of some sort, and it might be said that this is just what happened. For early on the evening of March 10, 1933, a little after five o'clock this was, as Mrs. Hosoume was getting supper, as Marpo was finishing up in the fields alone because Mr. Hosoume had gone to order some chicken fertilizer, and as Yoneko and Seigo were listening to Skippy, a tremendous roar came out of nowhere and the Hosoume house began shuddering violently as though some giant had seized it in his two hands and was giving it a good shaking. Mrs. Hosoume, who remembered similar, although milder experiences, from her childhood in Japan, screamed, *"Jishin, jishin!"* [2] before she ran and grabbed Yoneko and Seigo each by a hand and dragged them outside with her. She took them as far as the middle of the rhubarb patch near the house, and there they all crouched, pressed together, watching the world about them rock and sway. In a few minutes, Marpo, stumbling in from the fields, joined them, saying, "Earthquake, earthquake!" and he gathered them all in his arms, as much to protect them as to support himself.

10   Mr. Hosoume came home later that evening in a stranger's car, with another stranger driving the family Reo. Pallid, trembling, his eyes wildly staring, he could have been mistaken for a drunkard, except that he was famous as a teetotaler. It seemed that he had been on the way home when the first jolt came, that the old green Reo had been kissed by a broken live wire dangling from a suddenly leaning pole. Mr. Hosoume, knowing that the end had come by electrocution, had begun to writhe and kick and this had been his salvation. His hands had flown from the wheel, the car had swerved into a ditch, freeing itself from the sputtering wire. Later, it was found that he was left permanently inhibited about driving automobiles and permanently incapable of considering electricity with calmness. He spent the larger part of his later life weakly, wandering about the house or fields and lying down frequently to rest because of splitting headaches and sudden dizzy spells.

So it was Marpo who went back into the house as Yoneko screamed, "No, Marpo, no!" and brought out the Hosoumes' kerosene stove, the food, the blankets, while Mr. Hosoume huddled on the ground near his family.

The earth trembled for days afterwards. The Hosoumes and Marpo Humming Wing lived during that time on a natural patch of Bermuda grass between the house and the rhubarb patch remembering to take three meals a day and retire at night. Marpo ventured inside the house many times despite Yoneko's protests and reported the damage slight: a few dishes had been broken; a gallon jug of mayonnaise had fallen from the top pantry shelf and spattered the kitchen floor with yellow blobs and pieces of glass.

Yoneko was in constant terror during this experience. Immediately on learning what all the commotion was about, she began praying to God to end this violence. She entreated God, flattered Him, wheedled Him, commanded Him, but He did not listen to her at all—inexorably, the earth went on rumbling. After three solid hours of silent, desperate prayer, without any results whatsoever, Yoneko began to suspect that God was either powerless, callous, downright cruel, or nonexistent. In the murky night, under a strange moon wearing a pale ring of light, she decided upon the last as the most plausible theory. "Ha," was one of the things she said tremulously to Marpo, when she was not begging him to stay out of the house, "you and your God!"

The others soon oriented themselves to the catastrophe with philosophy, saying how fortunate they were to live in the country where the peril

[2] earthquake (Japanese)

was less than in the city and going so far as to regard the period as a sort of vacation from work, with their enforced alfresco existence a sort of camping trip. They tried to bring Yoneko to partake of this pleasant outlook, but she, shivering with each new quiver, looked on them as dreamers who refused to see things as they really were. Indeed, Yoneko's reaction was so notable that the Hosoume household thereafter spoke of the event as "Yoneko's earthquake."

15   After the earth subsided and the mayonnaise was mopped off the kitchen floor, life returned to normal, except that Mr. Hosoume stayed at home most of the time. Sometimes, if he had a relatively painless day, he would have supper on the stove when Mrs. Hosoume came in from the fields. Mrs. Hosoume and Marpo did all the field labor now, except on certain overwhelming days when several Mexicans were hired to assist them. Marpo did most of the driving, too, and it was now he and Mrs. Hosoume who went into town on the weekly trip for groceries. In fact, Marpo became indispensable and both Mr. and Mrs. Hosoume often told each other how grateful they were for Marpo.

When summer vacation began and Yoneko stayed at home, too, she found the new arrangement rather inconvenient. Her father's presence cramped her style: for instance, once when her friends came over and it was decided to make fudge, he would not permit them, saying fudge used too much sugar and that sugar was not a plaything; once when they were playing paper dolls, he came along and stuck his finger up his nose and pretended he was going to rub some snot off onto the dolls. Things like that. So, on some days, she was very much annoyed with her father.

Therefore when her mother came home breathless from the fields one day and pushed a ring at her, a gold-colored ring with a tiny glasslike stone in it, saying, "Look, Yoneko, I'm going to give you this ring. If your father asks where you got it, say you found it on the street." Yoneko was perplexed but delighted both by the unexpected gift and the chance to have some secret revenge on her father, and she said, certainly, she was willing to comply with her mother's request. Her mother went back to the fields then and Yoneko put the pretty ring on her middle finger, taking up the loose space with a bit of newspaper. It was similar to the rings found occasionally in boxes of Crackerjack, except that it appeared a bit more substantial.

Mr. Hosoume never asked about the ring; in fact, he never noticed she was wearing one. Yoneko thought he was about to, once, but he only reproved her for the flamingo nail polish she was wearing, which she had applied from a vial brought over by Yvonne Fournier, the French girl two orange groves away. "You look like a Filipino," Mr. Hosoume said sternly, for it was another irrefutable fact among Japanese in general that Filipinos in general were a gaudy lot. Mrs. Hosoume immediately came to her defense, saying that in Japan, if she remembered correctly, young girls did the same thing. In fact, she remembered having gone to elaborate lengths to tint her fingernails: she used to gather, she said, the petals of the red *tsubobana* or the purple *kogane* (which grows on the underside of stones), grind them well, mix them with some alum powder, then cook the mixture and leave it to stand overnight in an envelope of either persimmon or sugar potato leaves (both very strong leaves). The second night, just before going to bed, she used to obtain threads by ripping a palm leaf (because real thread was dear) and tightly bind the paste to her fingernails under shields of persimmon or sugar potato leaves. She would be helpless for the night, the finger-tips bound so well that they were alternately numb or aching, but she would grit her teeth and tell herself that the discomfort indicated the success of the operation. In the morning, finally releasing her fingers, she would find the nails shining with a translucent red-orange color.

Yoneko was fascinated, because she usually thought of her parents as having been adults all their lives. She thought that her mother must have been a beautiful child, with or without bright fingernails, because, though surely past thirty, she was even yet a beautiful person. When she herself was younger, she remembered, she had at times been so struck with her mother's appearance that she had dropped to her knees and mutely clasped her mother's legs in her arms. She had left off this habit as she learned to control her emotions, because at such times her mother had usually walked away, saying, "My, what a clinging child you are. You've got to learn to be a little more independent." She also remembered she had once heard some-one comparing her mother to "a dewy, half-opened rosebud."

20   Mr. Hosoume, however, was irritated. "That's no excuse for Yoneko to begin using paint on her fingernails," he said. "She's only ten."

"Her Japanese age is eleven,[3] and we weren't much older," Mrs. Hosoume said.

"Look," Mr. Hosoume said, "if you're going to contradict every piece of advice I give the children, they'll end up disobeying us both and doing what they very well please. Just because I'm ill just now is no reason for them to start being disrespectful."

"When have I ever contradicted you before?" Mrs. Hosoume said.

"Countless times," Mr. Hosoume said.

25   "Name one instance," Mrs. Hosoume said.

Certainly there had been times, but Mr. Hosoume could not happen to mention the one requested instance on the spot and he became quite angry. "That's quite enough of your insolence," he said. Since he was speaking in Japanese, his exact accusation was that she was *nama-iki,* which is a shade more revolting than being merely insolent.

"*Nama-iki, nama-iki?*" said Mrs. Hosoume. "How dare you? I'll not have anyone calling me *nama-iki!*"

"At that, Mr. Hosoume went up to where his wife was ironing and slapped her smartly on the face. It was the first time he had ever laid hands on her. Mrs. Hosoume was immobile for an instant, but she resumed her ironing as though nothing had happened, although she glanced over at Marpo, who happened to be in the room reading a newspaper. Yoneko and Seigo forgot they were listening to the radio and stared at their parents, thunderstruck.

"Hit me again," said Mrs. Hosoume quietly, as she ironed. "Hit me all you wish."

30   Mr. Hosoume was apparently about to, but Marpo stepped up and put his hand on Mr. Hosoume's shoulder. "The children are here," said Marpo, "the children."

"Mind your own business," said Mr. Hosoume in broken English. "Get out of here!"

[3]By Japanese reckoning a child becomes one year old on the first New Year's Day following his or her birth.

Marpo left, and that was about all. Mrs. Hosoume went on ironing, Yoneko and Seigo turned back to the radio, and Mr. Hosoume muttered that Marpo was beginning to forget his place. Now that he thought of it, he said, Marpo had been increasingly impudent towards him since his illness. He said just because he was temporarily an invalid was no reason for Marpo to start being disrespectful. He added that Marpo had better watch his step or that he might find himself jobless one of these fine days.

And something of the sort must have happened. Marpo was here one day and gone the next, without even saying good-bye to Yoneko and Seigo. That was also the day the Hosoume family went to the city on a weekday afternoon, which was most unusual. Mr. Hosoume, who now avoided driving as much as possible, handled the cumbersome Reo as though it were a nervous stallion, sitting on the edge of the seat and hugging the steering wheel. He drove very fast and about halfway to the city struck a beautiful collie which had dashed out barking from someone's yard. The car jerked with the impact, but Mr. Hosoume drove right on and Yoneko, wanting suddenly to vomit, looked back and saw the collie lying very still at the side of the road.

When they arrived at the Japanese hospital, which was their destination, Mr. Hosoume cautioned Yoneko and Seigo to be exemplary children and wait patiently in the car. It seemed hours before he and Mrs. Hosoume returned, she walking with very small, slow steps and he assisting her. When Mrs. Hosoume got in the car, she leaned back and closed her eyes. Yoneko inquired as to the source of her distress, for she was obviously in pain, but she only answered that she was feeling a little under the weather and that the doctor had administered some necessarily astringent treatment. At that, Mr. Hosoume turned around and advised Yoneko and Seigo that they must tell no one of coming to the city on a weekday afternoon, absolutely no one, and Yoneko and Seigo readily assented. On the way home, they passed the place of the encounter with the collie, and Yoneko looked up and down the stretch of road but the dog was nowhere to be seen.

35   Not long after that, the Hosoumes got a new hired hand, an old Japanese man who wore his gray hair in a military cut and who, unlike Marpo, had no particular interests outside working, eating, sleeping, and playing an occasional game of *goh*[4] with Mr. Hosoume. Before he came Yoneko and Seigo played sometimes in the empty bunkhouse and recalled Marpo's various charms together. Privately, Yoneko was wounded more than she would admit even to herself that Marpo should have subjected her to such an abrupt desertion. Whenever her indignation became too great to endure gracefully, she would console herself by telling Seigo that, after all, Marpo was a mere Filipino, an eater of wild dogs.

Seigo never knew about the disappointing new hired man, because he suddenly died in the night. He and Yoneko had spent the hot morning in the nearest orange grove, she driving him to distraction by repeating certain words he could not bear to hear: she had called him Serge, a name she had read somewhere, instead of Seigo; and she had chanted off the name of the tires they were rolling around like hoops as Goodrich Silver-TO-town, Goodrich Silver-TO-town, instead of Goodrich Silvertown. This had enraged him, and he had chased her around the trees most of the morning. Finally she had taunted him from several trees away by singing "You're a Yellow-streaked Coward," which was one of several small songs she had composed.

[4]a Japanese game for two, played with pebblelike counters on a board

Seigo had suddenly grinned and shouted, "Sure!" and walked off, leaving her, as he intended, with a sense of emptiness. In the afternoon, they had perspired and followed the potato-digging machine and the Mexican workers, both hired for the day, around the field, delighting in unearthing marble-sized, smooth-skinned potatoes that both the machine and the men had missed. Then, in the middle of the night, Seigo began crying, complaining of a stomach ache. Mrs. Hosoume felt his head and sent her husband for the doctor, who smiled and said Seigo would be fine in the morning. He said it was doubtless the combination of green oranges, raw potatoes, and the July heat. But as soon as the doctor left, Seigo fell into a coma and a drop of red blood stood out on his underlip, where he had evidently bit it. Mr. Hosoume again fetched the doctor, who was this time very grave and wagged his head, saying several times, "It looks very bad." So Seigo died at the age of five.

Mrs. Hosoume was inconsolable and had swollen eyes in the morning for weeks afterwards. She now insisted on visiting the city relatives each Sunday, so that she could attend church services with them. One Sunday, she stood up and accepted Christ. It was through accompanying her mother to many of these services that Yoneko finally learned the Japanese words to "Let Us Gather at the River." Mrs. Hosoume also did not seem interested in discussing anything but God and Seigo. She was especially fond of reminding visitors how adorable Seigo had been as an infant, how she had been unable to refrain from dressing him as a little girl and fixing his hair in bangs until he was two. Mr. Hosoume was very gentle with her and when Yoneko accidently caused her to giggle once, he nodded and said, "Yes, that's right, Yoneko, we must make your mother laugh and forget about Seigo." Yoneko herself did not think about Seigo at all. Whenever the thought of Seigo crossed her mind, she instantly began composing a new song, and this worked very well.

One evening, when the new hired man had been with them a while, Yoneko was helping her mother with the dishes when she found herself being examined with such peculiarly intent eyes that, with a start of guilt, she began searching in her mind for a possible crime she had lately committed. But Mrs. Hosoume only said, "Never kill a person, Yoneko, because if you do, God will take from you someone you love."

"Oh, that," said Yoneko quickly, "I don't believe in that, I don't believe in God." And her words tumbling pell-mell over one another, she went on eagerly to explain a few of her reasons why. If she neglected to mention the test she had given God during the earthquake, it was probably because she was a little upset. She had believed for a moment that her mother was going to ask about the ring (which, alas, she had lost already, somewhere in the flumes[5] along the cantaloupe patch).

[1951]

 # TOPICS FOR CRITICAL THINKING AND WRITING

1. Why does Mrs. Hosoume tell Yoneko not to tell Mr. Hosoume where the ring came from?
2. Why does Mr. Hosoume strike his wife?

[5]irrigation channels

3. Why does Marpo disappear on the same day that Mrs. Hosoume goes to the hospital?

4. Why does Mrs. Hosoume say—out of the blue, so far as Yoneko is concerned—"Never kill a person, Yoneko"?

 JOHN UPDIKE

John Updike (b. 1932) grew up in Shillington, Pennsylvania, where his father was a teacher and his mother was a writer. After receiving a B.A. degree from Harvard he studied drawing at Oxford for a year, but an offer from The New Yorker *magazine brought him back to the United States. He at first served as a reporter for the magazine, but soon began contributing poetry, essays, and fiction. Today he is one of America's most prolific and well-known writers.*

A & P

In walks these three girls in nothing but bathing suits. I'm in the third check-out slot, with my back to the door, so I don't see them until they're over by the bread. The one that caught my eye first was the one in the plaid green two-piece. She was a chunky kid, with a good tan and a sweet broad soft-looking can with those two crescents of white just under it, where the sun never seems to hit, at the top of the backs of her legs. I stood there with my hand on a box of HiHo crackers trying to remember if I rang it up or not. I ring it up again and the customer starts giving me hell. She's one of these cash-register-watchers, a witch about fifty with rouge on her cheekbones and no eyebrows, and I know it made her day to trip me up. She'd been watching cash registers for fifty years and probably never seen a mistake before.

By the time I got her feathers smoothed and her goodies into a bag— she gives me a little snort in passing, if she'd been born at the right time they would have burned her over in Salem—by the time I get her on her way the girls had circled around the bread and were coming back, without a push-cart, back my way along the counters, in the aisle between the checkouts and the Special bins. They didn't even have shoes on. There was this chunky one, with the two-piece—it was bright green and the seams on the bra were still sharp and her belly was still pretty pale so I guessed she just got it (the suit)—there was this one, with one of those chubby berry-faces, the lips all bunched together under her nose, this one, and a tall one, with black hair that hadn't quite frizzed right, and one of these sunburns right across under the eyes, and a chin that was too long—you know, the kind of girl other girls think is very "striking" and "attractive" but never quite makes it, as they very well know, which is why they like her so much—and then the third one, that wasn't quite so tall. She was the queen. She kind of led them, the other two peeking around and making their shoulders round. She didn't look around, not this queen, she just walked straight on slowly, on these long white prima-donna legs. She came down a little hard on her heels, as if she didn't walk in her bare feet that much, putting down her heels and then letting the weight move along to her toes as if she was testing the floor with every step, putting a little deliberate extra action into it. You never know for sure how girls' minds work (do they really think it's a mind in there or just a little buzz like a bee in a glass jar?) but you got the idea she had talked the other two into coming in here with her, and now she was showing them how to do it, walk slow and hold yourself straight.

She had on a kind of dirty pink—beige maybe, I don't know—bathing suit with a little nubble all over it and, what got me, the straps were down. They were off her shoulders looped loose around the cool tops of her arms, and I guess as a result the suit had slipped on her, so all around the top of the cloth there was this shining rim. If it hadn't been there you wouldn't have known there could have been anything whiter than those shoulders. With the straps pushed off, there was nothing between the top of the suit and the top of her head except just *her,* this clean bare plane of the top of her chest down from the shoulder bones like a dented sheet of metal tilted in the light. I mean, it was more than pretty.

She had sort of oaky hair that the sun and salt had bleached, done up in a bun that was unravelling, and a kind of prim face. Walking into the A & P with your straps down, I suppose it's the only kind of face you *can* have. She held her head so high her neck, coming up out of those white shoulders, looked kind of stretched, but I didn't mind. The longer her neck was, the more of her there was.

5   She must have felt in the corner of her eye me and over my shoulder Stokesie in the second slot watching, but she didn't tip. Not this queen. She kept her eyes moving across the racks, and stopped, and turned so slow it made my stomach rub the inside of my apron, and buzzed to the other two, who kind of huddled against her for relief, and then they all three of them went up the cat and dog food-breakfast cereal-macaroni-rice-raisins-seasonings-spreads-spaghetti-soft drinks-crackers-and-cookies aisle. From the third slot I look straight up this aisle to the meat counter, and I watched them all the way. The fat one with the tan sort of fumbled with the cookies, but on second thought she put the package back. The sheep pushing their carts down the aisle—the girls were walking against the usual traffic (not that we have one-way signs or anything)—were pretty hilarious. You could see them, when Queenie's white shoulders dawned on them, kind of jerk, or hop, or hiccup, but their eyes snapped back to their own baskets and on they pushed. I bet you could set off dynamite in the A & P and the people would by and large keep reaching and checking oatmeal off their lists and muttering "Let me see, there was a third thing, began with A, asparagus, no, ah, yes, applesauce!" or whatever it is they do mutter. But there was no doubt, this jiggled them. A few house slaves in pin curlers even look around after pushing their carts past to make sure what they had seen was correct.

You know, it's one thing to have a girl in a bathing suit down on the beach, where what with the glare nobody can look at each other much anyway, and another thing in the cool of the A & P, under the fluorescent lights, against all those stacked packages, with her feet paddling along naked over our checker-board green-and-cream rubber-tile floor.

"Oh, Daddy," Stokesie said beside me. "I feel so faint."

"Darling," I said. "Hold me tight." Stokesie's married, with two babies chalked up on his fuselage already, but as far as I can tell that's the only difference. He's twenty-two, and I was nineteen this April.

"Is it done?" he asks, the responsible married man finding his voice. I forgot to say he thinks he's going to be a manager some sunny day, maybe in 1990 when it's called the Great Alexandrov and Petrooshki Tea Company or something.

10   What he meant was, our town is five miles from a beach, with a big summer colony out on the Point, but we're right in the middle of town, and the women generally put on a shirt or shorts or something before they get out of the car into the street. And anyway these are usually women with six children and varicose veins mapping their legs and nobody, including them, could care less. As I say, we're right in the middle of town, and if you stand at our front doors you can see two banks and the Congregational church and the newspaper store and three real estate offices and about twenty-seven old freeloaders tearing up Central Street because the sewer broke again. It's not as if we're on the Cape; we're north of Boston and there's people in this town haven't seen the ocean for twenty years.

The girls had reached the meat counter and were asking McMahon something. He pointed, they pointed, and they shuffled out of sight behind a pyramid of Diet Delight peaches. All that was left for us to see was old McMahon patting his mouth and looking after them sizing up their joints. Poor kids, I began to feel sorry for them, they couldn't help it.

Now here comes the sad part of the story, at least my family says it's sad, but I don't think it's so sad myself. The store's pretty empty, it being Thursday afternoon, so there was nothing much to do except lean on the register and wait for the girls to show up again. The whole store was like a pinball machine and I didn't know which tunnel they'd come out of. After a while they come around out of the far aisle, around the light bulbs, records at discount of the Caribbean Six or Tony Martin Sings or some such gunk you wonder they waste the wax on, sixpacks of candy bars, and plastic toys done up in cellophane that fall apart when a kid looks at them anyway. Around they come, Queenie still leading the way, and holding a little gray jar in her hand. Slots Three through Seven are unmanned and I could see her wondering between Stokes and me, but Stokesie with his usual luck draws an old party in baggy gray pants who stumbles up with four giant cans of pineapple juice (what do these bums *do* with all that pineapple juice? I've often asked myself) so the girls come to me. Queenie puts down the jar and I take it into my fingers icy cold. Kingfish Fancy Herring Snacks in Pure Sour Cream: 49¢. Now her hands are empty, not a ring or a bracelet, bare as God made them, and I wonder where the money's coming from. Still with the prim look she lifts a folded dollar bill out of the hollow at the center of her nubbled pink top. The jar went heavy in my hand. Really, I thought that was so cute.

Then everybody's luck begins to run out. Lengel comes in from haggling with a truck full of cabbages on the lot and is about to scuttle into the door marked MANAGER behind which he hides all day when the girls touch his eye. Lengel's pretty dreary, teaches Sunday school and the rest, but he doesn't miss that much. He comes over and says, "Girls, this isn't the beach."

Queenie blushes, though maybe it's just a brush of sunburn I was noticing for the first time, now that she was so close. "My mother asked me to pick up a jar of herring snacks." Her voice kind of startled me, the way voices do when you see the people first, coming out so flat and dumb yet kind of tony, too, the way it ticked over "pick up" and "snacks." All of a sudden I slid right down her voice into her living room. Her father and the other men were standing around in ice-cream coats and bow ties and the women were in sandals picking up herring snacks on toothpicks off a big glass plate and they were all holding drinks the color of water with olives and sprigs of mint in them. When my parents have somebody over they get lemonade and if it's a real racy affair Schlitz in tall glasses with "They'll Do It Every Time" cartoons stencilled on.

15   "That's all right," Lengel said. "But this isn't the beach." His repeating this struck me as funny, as if it had just occurred to him, and he had been thinking all these years the A & P was a great big dune and he was the head lifeguard. He didn't like my smiling—as I say he doesn't miss much—but he concentrates on giving the girls that sad Sunday-school-superintendent stare.

Queenie's blush was no sunburn now, and the plump one in plaid, that I liked better from the back—a really sweet can—pipes up, "We weren't doing any shopping. We just came in for the one thing."

"That makes no difference," Lengel tells her, and I could see from the way his eyes went that he hadn't noticed she was wearing a two-piece before. "We want you decently dressed when you come in here."

"We *are* decent," Queenie says suddenly, her lower lip pushing, getting sore now that she remembers her place, a place from which the crowd that runs the A & P must look pretty crummy. Fancy Herring Snacks flashed in her very blue eyes.

"Girls, I don't want to argue with you. After this come in here with your shoulders covered. It's our policy." He turns his back. That's policy for you. Policy is what the kingpins want. What the others want is juvenile delinquency.

20   All this while, the customers had been showing up with their carts but, you know, sheep, seeing a scene, they had all bunched up on Stokesie, who shook open a paper bag as gently as peeling a peach, not wanting to miss a word. I could feel in the silence everybody getting nervous, most of all Lengel, who asks me, "Sammy, have you rung up this purchase?"

I thought and said "No" but it wasn't about that I was thinking. I go through the punches, 4, 9, GROC, TOT—it's more complicated than you think and after you do it often enough, it begins to make a little song, that you hear words to, in my case "Hello (*bing*) there, you (*gung*) hap-py peepul (*splat*)!"—the *splat* being the drawer flying out. I uncrease the bill, tenderly as you may imagine, it just having come from between the two smoothest scoops of vanilla I had ever known were there, and pass a half and a penny into her narrow pink palm and nestle the herrings in a bag and twist its neck and hand it over, all the time thinking.

The girls, and who'd blame them, are in a hurry to get out, so I say "I quit" to Lengel quick enough for them to hear, hoping they'll stop and watch me, their unsuspected hero. They keep right on going, into the electric eye; the door flies open and they flicker across the lot to their car, Queenie and Plaid and Big Tall Goony-Goony (not that as raw material she was so bad), leaving me with Lengel and a kink in his eyebrow.

"Did you say something, Sammy?"

"I said I quit."

25   "I thought you did."

"You didn't have to embarrass them."

"It was they who were embarrassing us."

I started to say something that came out "Fiddle-de-doo." It's a saying of my grandmother's, and I know she would have been pleased.

"I don't think you know what you're saying," Lengel said.

30   "I know you don't," I said. "But I do." I pull the bow at the back of my apron and start shrugging it off my shoulders. A couple customers that had been heading for my slot begin to knock against each other, like scared pigs in a chute.

Lengel sighs and begins to look very patient and old and gray. He's been a friend of my parents for years. "Sammy, you don't want to do this to your Mom and Dad," he tells me. It's true, I don't. But it seems to me that once you begin a gesture it's fatal not to go through with it. I fold the apron, "Sammy" stitched in red on the pocket, and put it on the counter, and drop the bow tie on top of it. The bow tie is theirs, if you've ever wondered. "You'll feel this for the rest of your life," Lengel says, and I know that's true, too, but remembering how he made that pretty girl blush makes me so scrunchy inside I punch the No Sale tab and the machine whirs "pee-pul" and the drawer splats out. One advantage to this scene taking place in summer, I can follow this up with a clean exit, there's no fumbling around getting your coat and galoshes, I just saunter into the electric eye in my white shirt that my mother ironed the night before, and the door heaves itself open, and outside the sunshine is skating round on the asphalt.

I look around for my girls, but they're gone, of course. There wasn't anybody but some young married screaming with her children about some candy they didn't get by the door of a powder-blue Falcon station wagon. Looking back in the big windows, over the bags of peat moss and aluminum lawn furniture stacked on the pavement, I could see Lengel in my place in the slot, checking the sheep through. His face was dark gray and his back stiff, as if he'd just had an injection of iron, and my stomach kind of fell as I felt how hard the world was going to be to me hereafter.

[1962]

 TOPICS FOR CRITICAL THINKING AND WRITING

1. In what sort of community is this A & P located? To what extent does this community resemble yours?

2. Do you think Sammy is a male chauvinist pig? Why, or why not? And if you think he is, do you find the story offensive? Again, why or why not?

3. In the last line of the story Sammy says, "I felt how hard the world was going to be to me hereafter." Do you think the world is going to be hard to Sammy? Why, or why not? And if it is hard to him, is this because of a virtue or a weakness in Sammy?

4. Write Lengel's version of the story (500–1000 words) as he might narrate it to his wife during dinner. Or write the story from Queenie's point of view.

5. Speaking of contemporary fiction Updike said:

> I want stories to startle and engage me within the first few sentences, and in their middle to widen or deepen or sharpen my knowledge of human activity, and to end by giving me a sensation of completed statement.

Let's assume that you share Updike's view of what a story should do. To what extent do you think "A & P" fulfills these demands? (You may want to put your response in the form of a letter to Updike.)

 ## LILIANA HEKER

Liliana Heker, born in Argentina in 1943, achieved fame in 1966 with the publication of her first book. She has continued to write fiction, and she has also been influential in her role as the editor of a literary magazine. "The Stolen Party," first published in Spanish in 1982, was translated and printed in Other Fires: Short Fiction by Latin American Women *(1985), edited and translated by Alberto Manguel.*

The Stolen Party

As soon as she arrived she went straight to the kitchen to see if the monkey was there. It was: what a relief! She wouldn't have liked to admit that her mother had been right. *Monkeys at a birthday?* her mother had sneered. *Get away with you, believing any nonsense you're told!* She was cross, but not because of the monkey, the girl thought; it's just because of the party.

"I don't like you going," she told her. "It's a rich people's party."

"Rich people go to Heaven too," said the girl, who studied religion at school.

"Get away with Heaven," said the mother. "The problem with you, young lady, is that you like to fart higher than your ass."

5   The girl didn't approve of the way her mother spoke. She was barely nine, and one of the best in her class.

"I'm going because I've been invited," she said. "And I've been invited because Luciana is my friend. So there."

"Ah yes, your friend," her mother grumbled. She paused. "Listen, Rosaura," she said at last. "That one's not your friend. You know what you are to them? The maid's daughter, that's what."

Rosaura blinked hard: she wasn't going to cry. Then she yelled: "Shut up! You know nothing about being friends!"

Every afternoon she used to go to Luciana's house and they would both finish their homework while Rosaura's mother did the cleaning. They had their tea in the kitchen and they told each other secrets. Rosaura loved everything in the big house, and she also loved the people who lived there.

10   "I'm going because it will be the most lovely party in the whole world, Luciana told me it would. There will be a magician, and he will bring a monkey and everything."

The mother swung around to take a good look at her child, and pompously put her hands on her hips.

"Monkeys at a birthday?" she said. "Get away with you, believing any nonsense you're told!"

Rosaura was deeply offended. She thought it unfair of her mother to accuse other people of being liars simply because they were rich. Rosaura too wanted to be rich, of course. If one day she managed to live in a beautiful

palace, would her mother stop loving her? She felt very sad. She wanted to
go to that party more than anything else in the world.

"I'll die if I don't go," she whispered, almost without moving her lips.

15   And she wasn't sure whether she had been heard, but on the morning
of the party she discovered that her mother had starched her Christmas
dress. And in the afternoon, after washing her hair, her mother rinsed it in
apple vinegar so that it would be all nice and shiny. Before going out,
Rosaura admired herself in the mirror, with her white dress and glossy hair,
and thought she looked terribly pretty.

Señora Ines also seemed to notice. As soon as she saw her, she said:

"How lovely you look today, Rosaura."

Rosaura gave her starched skirt a slight toss with her hands and walked
into the party with a firm step. She said hello to Luciana and asked about the
monkey. Luciana put on a secretive look and whispered into Rosaura's ear:
"He's in the kitchen. But don't tell anyone, because it's a surprise."

Rosaura wanted to make sure. Carefully she entered the kitchen and
there she saw it: deep in thought, inside its cage. It looked so funny that the
girl stood there for a while, watching it, and later, every so often, she would
slip out of the party unseen and go and admire it. Rosaura was the only one
allowed into the kitchen. Señora Ines had said: "You yes, but not the others,
they're much too boisterous, they might break something." Rosaura had
never broken anything. She even managed the jug of orange juice, carrying
it from the kitchen into the dining room. She held it carefully and didn't spill
a single drop. And Señora Ines had said: "Are you sure you can manage a jug
as big as that?" Of course she could manage. She wasn't a butterfingers, like
the others. Like that blonde girl with the bow in her hair. As soon as she saw
Rosaura, the girl with the bow had said:

20   "And you? Who are you?"

"I'm a friend of Luciana," said Rosaura.

"No," said the girl with the bow, "you are not a friend of Luciana because I'm her cousin and I know all her friends. And I don't know you."

"So what," said Rosaura. "I come here every afternoon with my mother
and we do our homework together."

"You and your mother do your homework together?" asked the girl,
laughing.

25   "I and Luciana do our homework together," said Rosaura, very seriously.

The girl with the bow shrugged her shoulders.

"That's not being friends," she said. "Do you go to school together?"

"No."

"So where do you know her from?" said the girl, getting impatient.

30   Rosaura remembered her mother's words perfectly. She took a deep
breath.

"I'm the daughter of the employee," she said.

Her mother had said very clearly: "If someone asks, you say you're the
daughter of the employee; that's all." She also told her to add: "And proud of
it." But Rosaura thought that never in her life would she dare say something
of the sort.

"What employee?" said the girl with the bow. "Employee in a shop?"

"No," said Rosaura angrily. "My mother doesn't sell anything in any
shop, so there."

35   "So how come she's an employee?" said the girl with the bow.

Just then Señora Ines arrived saying *shh shh,* and asked Rosaura if she wouldn't mind helping serve out the hotdogs, as she knew the house so much better than the others.

"See?" said Rosaura to the girl with the bow, and when no one was looking she kicked her in the shin.

Apart from the girl with the bow, all the others were delightful. The one she liked best was Luciana, with her golden birthday crown; and then the boys. Rosaura won the sack race, and nobody managed to catch her when they played tag. When they split into two teams to play charades, all the boys wanted her for their side. Rosaura felt she had never been so happy in all her life.

But the best was still to come. The best came after Luciana blew out the candles. First the cake. Señora Ines had asked her to help pass the cake around, and Rosaura had enjoyed the task immensely, because everyone called out to her, shouting "Me, me!" Rosaura remembered a story in which there was a queen who had the power of life or death over her subjects. She had always loved that, having the power of life or death. To Luciana and the boys she gave the largest pieces, and to the girl with the bow she gave a slice so thin one could see through it.

40   After the cake came the magician, tall and bony, with a fine red cape. A true magician: he could untie handkerchiefs by blowing on them and make a chain with links that had no openings. He could guess what cards were pulled out from a pack, and the monkey was his assistant. He called the monkey "partner." "Let's see here, partner," he would say, "turn over a card." And, "Don't run away, partner: time to work now."

The final trick was wonderful. One of the children had to hold the monkey in his arms and the magician said he would make him disappear.

"What, the boy?" they all shouted.

"No, the monkey!" shouted back the magician.

Rosaura thought that this was truly the most amusing party in the whole world.

45   The magician asked a small fat boy to come and help, but the small fat boy got frightened almost at once and dropped the monkey on the floor. The magician picked him up carefully, whispered something in his ear, and the monkey nodded almost as if he understood.

"You mustn't be so unmanly, my friend," the magician said to the fat boy.

"What's unmanly?" said the fat boy.

The magician turned around as if to look for spies.

"A sissy," said the magician. "Go sit down."

50   Then he stared at all the faces, one by one. Rosaura felt her heart tremble.

"You, with the Spanish eyes," said the magician. And everyone saw that he was pointing at her.

She wasn't afraid. Neither holding the monkey, nor when the magician made him vanish; not even when, at the end, the magician flung his red cape over Rosaura's head and uttered a few magic words . . . and the monkey reappeared, chattering happily, in her arms. The children clapped furiously. And before Rosaura returned to her seat, the magician said:

"Thank you very much, my little countess."

She was so pleased with the compliment that a while later, when her mother came to fetch her, that was the first thing she told her.

55   "I helped the magician and he said to me, 'Thank you very much, my little countess.' "

It was strange because up to then Rosaura had thought that she was angry with her mother. All along Rosaura had imagined that she would say to her: "See that the monkey wasn't a lie?" But instead she was so thrilled that she told her mother all about the wonderful magician.

Her mother tapped her on the head and said: "So now we're a countess!"

But one could see that she was beaming.

And now they both stood in the entrance, because a moment ago Señora Ines, smiling, had said: "Please wait here a second."

60   Her mother suddenly seemed worried.

"What is it?" she asked Rosaura.

"What is what?" said Rosaura. "It's nothing; she just wants to get the presents for those who are leaving, see?"

She pointed at the fat boy and at a girl with pigtails who were also waiting there, next to their mothers. And she explained about the presents. She knew, because she had been watching those who left before her. When one of the girls was about to leave, Señora Ines would give her a bracelet. When a boy left, Señora Ines gave him a yo-yo. Rosaura preferred the yo-yo because it sparkled, but she didn't mention that to her mother. Her mother might have said: "So why don't you ask for one, you blockhead?" That's what her mother was like. Rosaura didn't feel like explaining that she'd be horribly ashamed to be the odd one out. Instead she said:

"I was the best-behaved at the party."

65   And she said no more because Señora Ines came out into the hall with two bags, one pink and one blue.

First she went up to the fat boy, gave him a yo-yo out of the blue bag, and the fat boy left with his mother. Then she went up to the girl and gave her a bracelet out of the pink bag, and the girl with the pigtails left as well.

Finally she came up to Rosaura and her mother. She had a big smile on her face and Rosaura liked that. Señora Ines looked down at her, then looked up at her mother, and then said something that made Rosaura proud:

"What a marvelous daughter you have, Herminia."

For an instant, Rosaura thought that she'd give her two presents: the bracelet and the yo-yo. Señora Ines bent down as if about to look for something. Rosaura also leaned forward, stretching out her arm. But she never completed the movement.

70   Señora Ines didn't look in the pink bag. Nor did she look in the blue bag. Instead she rummaged in her purse. In her hand appeared two bills.

"You really and truly earned this," she said handing them over. "Thank you for all your help, my pet."

Rosaura felt her arms stiffen, stick close to her body, and then she noticed her mother's hand on her shoulder. Instinctively she pressed herself against her mother's body. That was all. Except her eyes. Rosaura's eyes had a cold, clear look that fixed itself on Señora Ines's face.

Señora Ines, motionless, stood there with her hand outstretched. As if she didn't dare draw it back. As if the slightest change might shatter an infinitely delicate balance.

[1982]

TOPICS FOR CRITICAL THINKING AND WRITING

1. The first paragraph tells us, correctly, that Rosaura's mother is wrong about the monkey. By the time the story is over, is the mother right about anything? If so, what?

2. Characterize Señora Ines. Why does she offer Rosaura money instead of a yo-yo or a bracelet? By the way, do you assume she is speaking deceptively when she tells Rosaura that she bars other children from the kitchen on the grounds that "they might break something"? On what do you base your view?

3. What do you make of the last paragraph? Why does Señora Ines stand with her hand outstretched, "as if she didn't dare draw it back"? What "infinitely delicate balance" might be shattered?

 PATRICIA GRACE

Patricia Grace was born in Wellington, New Zealand, in 1937, of Ngati Raukawa, Ngati Toa, and Te Ati Awa descent. In 1974 she received the first grant awarded to a Maori writer, and in 1975 she became the first Maori woman to publish a book of stories. She is the author of five novels, a play, a book of poems, and several volumes of short stories.

Butterflies

The grandmother plaited her granddaughter's hair and then she said, "Get your lunch. Put it in your bag. Get your apple. You come straight back after school, straight home here. Listen to the teacher," she said. "Do what she say."

Her grandfather was out on the step. He walked down the path with her and out onto the footpath. He said to a neighbor, "Our granddaughter goes to school. She lives with us now."

"She's fine," the neighbor said. "She's terrific with her two plaits in her hair."

"And clever," the grandfather said. "Writes every day in her book."

5   "She's fine," the neighbor said.

The grandfather waited with his granddaughter by the crossing and then he said, "Go to school. Listen to the teacher. Do what she say."

When the granddaughter came home from school her grandfather was hoeing around the cabbages. Her grandmother was picking beans. They stopped their work.

"You bring your book home?" the grandmother asked.

"Yes."

10   "You write your story?"

"Yes."

"What's your story?"

"About the butterflies."

"Get your book then. Read your story."

15   The granddaughter took her book from her schoolbag and opened it.

"I killed all the butterflies," she read. "This is me and this is all the butterflies."

"And your teacher like your story, did she?"

"I don't know."

"What your teacher say?"

20   "She said butterflies are beautiful creatures. They hatch out and fly in the sun. The butterflies visit all the pretty flowers, she said. They lay their eggs and then they die. You don't kill butterflies, that's what she said."

The grandmother and the grandfather were quiet for a long time, and their granddaughter, holding the book, stood quite still in the warm garden.

"Because you see," the grandfather said, "your teacher, she buy all her cabbages from the supermarket and that's why."

[1988]

TOPICS FOR CRITICAL THINKING AND WRITING

1. On the basis of the first six paragraphs, how would you characterize the grandparents? How would you characterize the grandfather at the end of the story?

2. Why do you suppose Grace makes the relationship between a girl and her grandparents rather than between the girl and her parents? Or, for that matter, why not a boy and his parents? Would the story have a different feel? Explain.

3. The story is told from an objective point of view. Suppose Grace had told it from the grandfather's point of view. Rewrite the final paragraph, using his point of view, and compare your version with Grace's. Which do you prefer? Why?

4. You are a teacher. You have just read this story and you recognize yourself in it. Record your response in your journal (i.e., record the teacher's response).

Poetry

 WILLIAM BLAKE

William Blake (1757–1827) was born in London and at fourteen was apprenticed for seven years to an engraver. A Christian visionary poet, he made his living by giving drawing lessons and by illustrating books, including his own Songs of Innocence *(1789) and* Songs of Experience *(1794). These two books represent, he said, "two contrary states of the human soul." ("Infant Joy" comes from* Innocence, *"Infant Sorrow" and "The Echoing Green" come from* Experience.) *In 1809 Blake exhibited his art, but the show was a failure. Not until he was in his sixties, when he stopped writing poetry, did he achieve any public recognition—and then it was as a painter.*

"Infant Joy" by William Blake, from *Songs of Innocence*. (By permission of the Provost and Fellows of King's College, Cambridge)

Infant Joy

"I have no name,
I am but two days old."
What shall I call thee?
"I happy am,
Joy is my name."   5
Sweet joy befall thee!

Pretty joy!
Sweet joy but two days old,
Sweet joy I call thee;
Thou dost smile,   10
I sing the while—
Sweet joy befall thee.

[1789]

"Infant Sorrow" by William Blake, from *Songs of Experience*. By permission of the Provost and Fellows of King's College, Cambridge)

Infant Sorrow

My mother groand! my father wept.
Into the dangerous world I leapt,
Helpless, naked, piping loud;
Like a fiend hid in a cloud.   4

Struggling in my father's hands,
Striving against my swadling bands;
Bound and weary I thought best
To sulk upon my mother's breast.   8

[1794]

TOPICS FOR CRITICAL THINKING AND WRITING

1. "Infant Joy" begins "I have no name," but by line 5 the infant says "Joy is my name." What does the mother reply? Does she know the infant's name?
2. In line 9 the mother says, "Sweet joy I call thee." Does the line suggest how the mother has learned the name? What is the child's response?
3. In "Infant Sorrow," why is the infant sorrowful? What does the baby struggle against? Does "Like a fiend" suggest that it is inherently wicked and therefore should be repressed? Or does the adult world wickedly repress energy?
4. Why does the mother groan? Why does the father weep? Is the world "dangerous" to the infant in other than an obviously physical sense? To what degree are its parents its enemies? To what degree does the infant yield to them? In the last line, one might expect a newborn baby to nurse. What does this infant do?
5. Compare "Infant Joy" with "Infant Sorrow." What differences in sound do you hear? In "Infant Sorrow," for instance, look at lines 3, 5, 6, and 7. What repeated sounds do you hear?

The Echoing Green

The Sun does arise,
And make happy the skies;
The merry bells ring
To welcome the Spring;
The skylark and thrush,   5
The birds of the bush,
Sing louder around
To the bells' cheerful sound,
While our sports shall be seen
On the Echoing Green.   10

Old John, with white hair,
Does laugh away 'care,
Sitting under the oak,
Among the old folk.
They laugh at our play,   15
And soon they all say:
"Such, such were the joys
When we all, girls and boys,
In our youth time were seen
On the Echoing Green."   20

Till the little ones, weary,
No more can be merry;
The sun does descend,
And our sports have an end.
Round the laps of their mothers   25
Many sisters and brothers,
Like birds in their nest,
Are ready for rest,

And sport no more seen
On the darkening Green.   30

[1789]

TOPICS FOR CRITICAL THINKING AND WRITING

1. Who speaks the poem? (Go through the poem, picking up the clues
   that identify the speaker.)
2. When does the poem begin? And when does it end?
3. What is a "green," and why in this poem does it "echo?"
4. Try writing a piece entitled "Such, such were the joys . . ." You may
   need to affect a few years to write it, but try to get down what really
   were the joys of your childhood.

GERARD MANLEY HOPKINS

*Gerard Manley Hopkins (1844–89) was born near London and was
educated at Oxford, where he studied the classics. A convert from
Anglicanism to Roman Catholicism, he was ordained a Jesuit priest
in 1877. After serving as a parish priest and teacher, he was appointed Professor of Greek at the Catholic University in Dublin.*

*Hopkins published only a few poems during his lifetime, partly
because he believed that the pursuit of literary fame was incompatible with his vocation as a priest, and partly because he was aware
that his highly individual style might puzzle readers.*

Spring and Fall

To a Young Child

Márgarét áre you griéving
Over Goldengrove unleaving?
Leáves, like the thíngs of mán, you
With your fresh thoughts care for, can you?
Ah! ás the héart grows older   5
It will come to such sights colder
By and by, nor spare a sigh
Though worlds of wanwood leafmeal lie;
And yet you will weep and know why.
Now no matter, child, the name: 10
Sórrow's spríngs áre the same.
Nor mouth had, no nor mind, expressed
What héart heárd of, ghost° guéssed:
It iś the blíght mán was bórn for,
It is Margaret you mourn for.   15

[1880]

---

[13] **ghost** spirit

TOPICS FOR CRITICAL THINKING AND WRITING

1. What is the speaker's age? His tone? What is the relevance of the title to Margaret? What meanings are in "Fall"? Is there more than one meaning to "spring"? (Notice especially the title and line 11.)
2. What is meant by Margaret's "fresh thoughts" (line 4)? Paraphrase lines 3–4 and lines 12–13.
3. "Wanwood" and "leafmeal" are words coined by Hopkins. What are their suggestions?
4. What does "blight" mean in line 14?
5. Why is it not contradictory for the speaker to say that Margaret weeps for herself (line 15) after saying that she weeps for "Goldengrove unleaving" (line 2)?

 A. E. HOUSMAN

Alfred Edward Housman (1859–1936) was born in rural Shropshire, England, and educated in classics and philosophy at Oxford University. Although he was a brilliant student, his final examination was unexpectedly weak—in fact, he failed—and he did not receive the academic appointment that he had anticipated. He began working as a civil servant at the British Patent Office, but in his spare time he wrote scholarly articles on Latin literature, and these writings in 1892 won him an appointment as Professor of Latin at the University of London. In 1911 he was appointed to Cambridge. During his lifetime he published (in addition to his scholarly writings) only two thin books of poetry, A Shropshire Lad *(1898) and* Last Poems *(1922), and a highly readable lecture called* The Name and Nature of Poetry *(1933). After his death a third book of poems,* More Poems *(1936), was published.*

When I Was One-and-Twenty

When I was one-and-twenty
  I heard a wise man say,
"Give crowns and pounds and guineas
  But not your heart away;
Give pearls away and rubies   5
  But keep your fancy free."
But I was one-and-twenty,
  No use to talk to me.

When I was one-and-twenty
  I heard him say again,   10
"The heart out of the bosom
  Was never given in vain;
'Tis paid with sighs a plenty
  And sold for endless rue."
And I am two-and-twenty,   15
  And oh, 'tis true, 'tis true.

[1896]

TOPICS FOR CRITICAL THINKING AND WRITING

1. In line 6, what does "fancy" mean?
2. In your own words, what is the advice of the "wise man"?
3. In a paragraph, indicate what you think the speaker's attitude is toward himself. In a second paragraph, indicate what *our* attitude toward him is.

 e. e. cummings

Edwin Estlin Cummings (1894–1962), who used the pen name e. e. cummings, grew up in Cambridge, Massachusetts, and was graduated from Harvard, where he became interested in modern literature and art, especially in the movements called Cubism and Futurism. His father, a conservative clergyman and a professor at Harvard, seems to have been baffled by the youth's interests, but Cummings's mother encouraged his artistic activities, including unconventional punctuation.

Politically liberal in his youth, Cummings became more conservative after a visit to Russia in 1931, but early and late his work emphasizes individuality and freedom of expression.

in Just-

in Just-
spring　　when the world is mud-
luscious the little
lame balloonman

whistles　far　and wee 　　　　　　　　　　　5

and eddieandbill come
running from marbles and
piracies and it's
spring

when the world is puddle-wonderful 　　　　　　10

the queer
old balloonman whistles
far　and　wee
and bettyandisbel come dancing

from hop-scotch and jump-rope and 　　　　　　15

it's
spring
and
　the
　　goat-footed 　　　　　　　　　　　　　　20

balloonMan　whistles
far
and
wee

[1920]

TOPICS FOR CRITICAL THINKING AND WRITING

1. Why "eddieandbill" and "bettyandisbel" rather than "eddie and bill" and "betty and isabel"? And why not "eddie and betty," and "bill and isabel"?
2. What are some of the effects that Cummings may be getting at by his unusual arrangement of words on the page? Compare, for instance, the physical appearance of "Whistles far and wee" in line 5 with the appearance of the same words in lines 12–13 and 21–24.
3. Because the balloonman is "lame" (line 4) or "goat-footed" (line 20), many readers find an allusion to the Greek god Pan, the goat-footed god of woods, fields, and flocks, and the inventor of a primitive wind instrument consisting of a series of reeds, "Pan's pipes." (If you are unfamiliar with Pan, consult an encyclopedia or a guide to mythology.) Do you agree that Cummings is alluding to Pan? If so, what is the point of the allusion?

 LOUISE GLÜCK

Louise Glück (b. 1943) was born in New York City and attended Sarah Lawrence College and Columbia University. She has taught at Goddard College in Vermont and at Warren Wilson College in North Carolina. Her volume of poems, The Triumph of Achilles *(1985), won the National Book Critics Circle Award for poetry.*

The School Children

The children go forward with their little satchels.
And all morning the mothers have labored
to gather the late apples, red and gold,
like words of another language.

And on the other shore   5
are those who wait behind great desks
to receive these offerings.

How orderly they are—the nails
on which the children hang
their overcoats of blue or yellow wool.   10

And the teachers shall instruct them in silence
and the mothers shall scour the orchards for a way out,
drawing to themselves the gray limbs of the fruit trees
bearing so little ammunition.

[1975]

 TOPICS FOR CRITICAL THINKING AND WRITING

1. Which words in the poem present a cute picture-postcard view of small children going to school?
2. Which words undercut this happy scene?
3. In the last stanza we read that "the teachers shall instruct" and "the mothers shall scour." What, if anything, is changed if we substitute "will" for "shall"?

Gretel in Darkness

This is the world we wanted. All who would have seen us dead
Are dead. I hear the witch's cry
Break in the moonlight through a sheet of sugar: God rewards.
Her tongue shrivels into gas. . . .

                             Now, far from women's arms   5
And memory of women, in our father's hut
We sleep, are never hungry.
Why do I not forget?
My father bars the door, bars harm
From this house, and it is years.   10

No one remembers. Even you, my brother,
Summer afternoons you look at me as though you meant
To leave, as though it never happened. But I killed for you.
I see armed firs, the spires of that gleaming kiln come back, come back—

Nights I turn to you to hold me but you are not there.   15
Am I alone? Spies
Hiss in the stillness, Hansel we are there still, and it is real, real,
That black forest, and the fire in earnest.

[1975]

 TOPICS FOR CRITICAL THINKING AND WRITING

1. How, as the poem develops, is the first sentence of the poem modified?
   Is this the world "we" wanted? What does Gretel believe that Hansel
   wants?
2. In stanza 3 Gretel says

                          But I killed for you.
   I see . . . the spires of that gleaming kiln come back, come back—

   Whether you know the story or not from *Grimm's Fairy Tales,* how do
   you understand Gretel's plight?
3. Why is the poem called "Gretel in Darkness"? What does the poem
   seem to tell us about how men and women face danger?

Drama

A NOTE ON THE ELIZABETHAN THEATER

Shakespeare's theater was wooden, round or polygonal (the Chorus in *Henry V*
calls it a "wooden O"). About eight hundred spectators could stand in the yard in
front of—and perhaps along the two sides of—the stage that jutted from the rear
wall, and another fifteen hundred or so spectators could sit in the three roofed

galleries that ringed the stage. That portion of the galleries that was above the rear of the stage was sometimes used by actors. Entry to the stage was normally gained by doors at the rear but some use was made of a curtained alcove—or perhaps a booth—between the doors, which allowed characters to be "discovered" (revealed) as in the modern proscenium theater, which normally employs a curtain. A performance was probably uninterrupted by intermissions or by long pauses for the changing of scenery; a group of characters leaves the stage, another enters, and if the locale was changed, the new characters somehow tell us. (Modern editors customarily add indications of locales to help a reader, but it should be understood that the action on the Elizabethan stage was continuous.)

A NOTE ON THE TEXT OF *HAMLET*

Shakespeare's *Hamlet* comes to us in three versions. The first, known as the First Quarto (Q1), was published in 1603. It is an illegitimate garbled version, perhaps derived from the memory of the actor who played Marcellus (this part is conspicuously more accurate than the rest of the play) in a short version of the play. The second printed version (Q2), which appeared in 1604, is almost twice as long as Q1; all in all, it is the best text we have, doubtless published (as Q1 was not) with the permission of Shakespeare's theatrical company. The third printed version, in the First Folio (the collected edition of Shakespeare's plays, published in 1623), is also legitimate, but it seems to be an acting version, for it lacks some two hundred lines of Q2. On the other hand, the Folio text includes some ninety lines not found in Q2. Because Q2 is the longest version, giving us more than the play as Shakespeare conceived it than either of the other texts, it serves as the basic version for this text. Unfortunately, the printers of it often worked carelessly: Words and phrases are omitted, there are plain misreadings of what must have been in Shakespeare's manuscript, and speeches are sometimes wrongly assigned. It was therefore necessary to turn to the First Folio for many readings. It has been found useful, also, to divide the play into acts and scenes; these divisions, not found in Q2 (and only a few are found in the Folio), are purely editorial additions, and they are therefore enclosed in square brackets.

We use the text edited by David Bevington.

 ## WILLIAM SHAKESPEARE

William Shakespeare (1564–1616) was born in Stratford, England, of middle-class parents. Nothing of interest is known about his early years, but by 1590 he was acting and writing plays in London. By the end of the following decade he had worked in all three Elizabethan dramatic genres—tragedy, comedy, and history. Romeo and Juliet, *for example, was written about 1595, the year of* Richard II, *and in the following year he wrote* A Midsummer Night's Dream. Julius Caesar *(1599) probably preceded* As You Like It *by one year, and* Hamlet *probably followed* As You Like It *by less than a year. Among the plays that followed* King Lear *(1605–06) were* Macbeth *(1605–06) and several "romances"—plays that have happy endings but that seem more meditative and closer to tragedy than such comedies as* A Midsummer Night's Dream, As You Like It, *and* Twelfth Night.

Kevin Kline as Hamlet. (New York Shakespeare Festival)

Hamlet, Prince of Denmark

[DRAMATIS PERSONAE

GHOST *of Hamlet, the former King of Denmark*
CLAUDIUS, *King of Denmark, the former King's brother*
GERTRUDE, *Queen of Denmark, widow of the former King and now wife of Claudius*
HAMLET, *Prince of Denmark, son of the late King and of Gertrude*

POLONIUS, *councillor to the King*
LAERTES, *his son*
OPHELIA, *his daughter*
REYNALDO, *his servant*

HORATIO, *Hamlet's friend and fellow student*

VOLTIMAND,
CORNELIUS,
ROSENCRANTZ,
GUILDENSTERN, } *members of the Danish court*
OSRIC,
A GENTLEMAN,
A LORD,

BERNARDO,
FRANCISCO, } *officers and soldiers on watch*
MARCELLUS,

FORTINBRAS, *Prince of Norway*
CAPTAIN *in his army*

Three or Four PLAYERS, *taking the roles of* PROLOGUE, PLAYER KING, PLAYER
   QUEEN, *and* LUCIANUS
Two MESSENGERS
FIRST SAILOR
Two CLOWNS, *a gravedigger and his companion*
PRIEST
FIRST AMBASSADOR *from England*

*Lords, Soldiers, Attendants, Guards, other Players, Followers of Laertes,
   other Sailors, another Ambassador or Ambassadors from England*

SCENE: *DENMARK*]

   1.1   *Enter* BERNARDO *and* FRANCISCO, *two sentinels [meeting].*

BERNARDO. Who's there?
FRANCISCO. Nay, answer me.° Stand and unfold yourself.°
BERNARDO. Long live the King!
FRANCISCO. Bernardo?
BERNARDO. He.   5
FRANCISCO. You come most carefully upon your hour.
BERNARDO. 'Tis now struck twelve. Get thee to bed, Francisco.
FRANCISCO. For this relief much thanks. 'Tis bitter cold,
   And I am sick at heart.
BERNARDO. Have you had quiet guard?   10
FRANCISCO. Not a mouse stirring.
BERNARDO. Well, good night.
   If you do meet Horatio and Marcellus,
   The rivals° of my watch, bid them make haste.
   Enter HORATIO *and* MARCELLUS.
FRANCISCO. I think I hear them.—Stand, ho! Who is there?   15
HORATIO. Friends to this ground.°
MARCELLUS. And liegemen to the Dane.°
FRANCISCO. Give° you good night.
MARCELLUS. O, farewell, honest soldier. Who hath relieved you?
FRANCISCO. Bernardo hath my place. Give you good night.   20
                                       Exit FRANCISCO.

MARCELLUS. Holla! Bernardo!
BERNARDO. Say, what, is Horatio there?
HORATIO. A piece of him.
BERNARDO. Welcome, Horatio. Welcome, good Marcellus.
HORATIO. What, has this thing appeared again tonight?   25
BERNARDO. I have seen nothing.
MARCELLUS. Horatio says 'tis but our fantasy,°
   And will not let belief take hold of him
   Touching this dreaded sight twice seen of us.
   Therefore I have entreated him along°   30
   With us to watch° the minutes of this night,

1.1 Location: Elsinore castle. A guard platform. 2 me (Francisco emphasizes
that *he* is the sentry currently on watch.)   **unfold yourself** reveal your identity
14 rivals partners   **16 ground** country, land   **17 liegemen to the Dane** men
sworn to serve the Danish king   **18 Give** i.e., may God give   **27 fantasy**
imagination   **30 along** to come along   **31 watch** keep watch during

That if again this apparition come
He may approve° our eyes and speak to it.

HORATIO. Tush, tush, 'twill not appear.

BERNARDO.   Sit down awhile,
And let us once again assail your ears,   35
That are so fortified against our story,
What° we have two nights seen.

HORATIO.   Well, sit we down,
And let us hear Bernardo speak of this.

BERNARDO. Last night of all,°
When yond same star that's westward from the pole°   40
Had made his° course t' illume° that part of heaven
Where now it burns, Marcellus and myself,
The bell then beating one—

Enter GHOST.

MARCELLUS. Peace, break thee off! Look where it comes again!

BERNARDO. In the same figure like the King that's dead.   45

MARCELLUS. Thou art a scholar.° Speak to it, Horatio.

BERNARDO. Looks 'a° not like the King? Mark it, Horatio.

HORATIO. Most like. It harrows me with fear and wonder.

BERNARDO. It would be spoke to.°

MARCELLUS.   Speak to it, Horatio.

HORATIO. What art thou that usurp'st° this time of night,   50
Together with that fair and warlike form
In which the majesty of buried Denmark°
Did sometime° march? By heaven, I charge thee, speak!

MARCELLUS. It is offended.

BERNARDO.   See, it stalks away.

HORATIO. Stay! Speak, speak! I charge thee, speak!   55

                                        Exit GHOST.

MARCELLUS. 'Tis gone and will not answer.

BERNARDO. How now, Horatio? You tremble and look pale.
Is not this something more than fantasy?
What think you on 't?°

HORATIO. Before my God, I might not this believe   60
Without the sensible° and true avouch°
Of mine own eyes.

MARCELLUS.   Is it not like the King?

HORATIO. As thou art to thyself.
Such was the very armor he had on
When he the ambitious Norway° combated.   65
So frowned he once when, in an angry parle,°

---

33 **approve** corroborate   37 **What** with what   39 **Last . . . all** i.e., this *very* last
night. (Emphatic.)   40 **pole** polestar, north star   41 **his** its.   **illume** illuminate
46 **scholar** one learned enough to know how to question a ghost properly   47 **'a**
he   49 **It . . . to** (It was commonly believed that a ghost could not speak until spoken to.)   50 **usurp'st** wrongfully takes over   52 **buried Denmark** the buried
King of Denmark   53 **sometime** formerly   59 **on 't** of it   61 **sensible** confirmed
by the senses.   **avouch** warrant, evidence   65 **Norway** King of Norway
66 **parle** parley

He smote the sledded° Polacks° on the ice.
'Tis strange.

MARCELLUS. Thus twice before, and jump° at this dead hour,
With martial stalk° hath he gone by our watch.   70

HORATIO. In what particular thought to work° I know not,
But in the gross and scope° of mine opinion
This bodes some strange eruption to our state.

MARCELLUS. Good now,° sit down, and tell me, he that knows,
Why this same strict and most observant watch   75
So nightly toils° the subject° of the land,
And why such daily cast° of brazen cannon
And foreign mart° for implements of war,
Why such impress° of shipwrights, whose sore task
Does not divide the Sunday from the week.   80
What might be toward,° that this sweaty haste
Doth make the night joint-laborer with the day?
Who is 't that can inform me?

HORATIO.   That can I;
At least, the whisper goes so. Our last king,
Whose image even but now appeared to us,   85
Was, as you know, by Fortinbras of Norway,
Thereto pricked on° by a most emulate° pride,°
Dared to the combat; in which our valiant Hamlet—
For so this side of our known world° esteemed him—
Did slay this Fortinbras; who by a sealed° compact   90
Well ratified by law and heraldry
Did forfeit, with his life, all those his lands
Which he stood seized° of, to the conqueror;
Against the° which a moiety competent°
Was gagèd° by our king, which had returned°   95
To the inheritance° of Fortinbras
Had he been vanquisher, as, by the same cov'nant°
And carriage of the article designed,°
His fell to Hamlet. Now, sir, young Fortinbras,
Of unimprovèd mettle° hot and full,   100
Hath in the skirts° of Norway here and there
Sharked up° a list° of lawless resolutes°

---

67 sledded traveling on sleds. **Polacks** Poles **69 jump** exactly **70 stalk** stride
71 to work i.e., to collect my thoughts and try to understand this **72 gross and
scope** general drift **74 Good now** (An expression denoting entreaty or expostula-
tion.) **76 toils** causes to toil. **subject** subjects **77 cast** casting **78 mart** buying and selling **79 impress** impressment, conscription **81 toward** in preparation **87 pricked on** incited. **emulate** emulous, ambitious. **Thereto . . . pride**
(Refers to old Fortinbras, not the Danish King.) **89 this . . . world** i.e., all Europe,
the Western world **90 sealed** certified, confirmed **93 seized** possessed
94 Against the in return for. **moiety competent** corresponding portion
95 gagèd engaged, pledged. **had returned** would have passed **96 inheritance**
possession **97 cov'nant** i.e., the *sealed compact* of line 90 **98 carriage . . .
designed** carrying out of the article or clause drawn up to cover the point
100 unimprovèd mettle untried, undisciplined spirits **101 skirts** outlying regions, outskirts **102 Sharked up** gathered up, as a shark takes fish. **list** i.e.,
troop. **resolutes** desperadoes

For food and diet° to some enterprise
That hath a stomach° in 't, which is no other—
As it doth well appear unto our state—   105
But to recover of us, by strong hand
And terms compulsatory, those foresaid lands
So by his father lost. And this, I take it,
Is the main motive of our preparations,
The source of this our watch, and the chief head°   110
Of this posthaste and rummage° in the land.
BERNARDO. I think it be no other but e'en so.
Well may it sort° that this portentous figure
Comes armèd through our watch so like the King
That was and is the question° of these wars.   115
HORATIO. A mote° it is to trouble the mind's eye.
In the most high and palmy° state of Rome,
A little ere the mightiest Julius fell,
The graves stood tenantless, and the sheeted° dead
Did squeak and gibber in the Roman streets;   120
As° stars with trains° of fire and dews of blood,
Disasters° in the sun; and the moist star°
Upon whose influence Neptune's° empire stands°
Was sick almost to doomsday° with eclipse.
And even the like precurse° of feared events,   125
As harbingers° preceding still° the fates
And prologue to the omen° coming on,
Have heaven and earth together demonstrated
Unto our climatures° and countrymen.
Enter GHOST.
But soft,° behold! Lo, where it comes again!   130
I'll cross° it, though it blast° me. *[It spreads his° arms.]*
   Stay, *illusion!*
If thou hast any sound or use of voice,
Speak to me!
If there be any good thing to be done
That may to thee do ease and grace to me,   135
Speak to me!
If thou art privy to° thy country's fate,

---

103 For food and diet i.e., they are to serve as *food,* or "means," *to some enterprise;* also they serve in return for the rations they get   **104 stomach** (1) a spirit of daring (2) an appetite that is fed by the *lawless resolutes*   **110 head** source   **111 rummage** bustle, commotion   **113 sort** suit   **115 question** focus of contention   **116 mote** speck of dust   **117 palmy** flourishing   **119 sheeted** shrouded   **121 As** (This abrupt transition suggests that matter is possibly omitted between lines 120 and 121.)   **trains** trails   **122 Disasters** unfavorable signs or aspects.   **moist star** i.e., moon, governing tides   **123 Neptune** god of the sea.   **stands** depends   **124 sick ... doomsday** (See Matthew 24:29 and Revelation 6:12.)   **125 precurse** heralding, foreshadowing   **126 harbingers** forerunners.   **still** continually   **127 omen** calamitous event   **129 climatures** regions   **130 soft** i.e., enough, break off   **131 cross** stand in its path, confront.   **blast** wither, strike with a curse.   **s.d. his** its   **137 privy to** in on the secret of

Which, happily,° foreknowing may avoid,
O, speak!
Or if thou hast uphoarded in thy life   140
Extorted treasure in the womb of earth,
For which, they say, you spirits oft walk in death,
Speak of it! *[The cock crows.]* Stay and speak!—Stop it, Marcellus.

MARCELLUS. Shall I strike at it with my partisan?°

HORATIO. Do, if it will not stand.   *[They strike at it.]* 145

BERNARDO. 'Tis here!

HORATIO. 'Tis here!   *[Exit* GHOST.*]*

MARCELLUS. 'Tis gone.
We do it wrong, being so majestical,
To offer it the show of violence,   150
For it is as the air invulnerable,
And our vain blows malicious mockery.

BERNARDO. It was about to speak when the cock crew.

HORATIO. And then it started like a guilty thing
Upon a fearful summons. I have heard   155
The cock, that is the trumpet° to the morn,
Doth with his lofty and shrill-sounding throat
Awake the god of day, and at his warning,
Whether in sea or fire, in earth or air,
Th' extravagant and erring° spirit hies°   160
To his confine; and of the truth herein
This present object made probation.°

MARCELLUS. It faded on the crowing of the cock.
Some say that ever 'gainst° that season comes
Wherein our Savior's birth is celebrated,   165
This bird of dawning singeth all night long,
And then, they say, no spirit dare stir abroad;
The nights are wholesome, then no planets strike,°
No fairy takes,° nor witch hath power to charm,
So hallowed and so gracious° is that time.   170

HORATIO. So have I heard and do in part believe it.
But, look, the morn in russet mantle clad
Walks o'er the dew of yon high eastward hill.
Break we our watch up, and by my advice
Let us impart what we have seen tonight   175
Unto young Hamlet; for upon my life,
This spirit, dumb to us, will speak to him.
Do you consent we shall acquaint him with it,
As needful in our loves, fitting our duty?

MARCELLUS. Let's do 't, I pray, and I this morning know   180
Where we shall find him most conveniently.

                                                    Exeunt.

---

138 happily haply, perchance   **144 partisan** long-handled spear   **156 trumpet**
trumpeter   **160 extravagant and erring** wandering beyond bounds. (The words
have similar meaning.)   **hies** hastens   **162 probation** proof   **164 'gainst** just before   **168 strike** destroy by evil influence   **169 takes** bewitches   **170 gracious**
full of grace

1.2 *Flourish. Enter* CLAUDIUS, *King of Denmark,* GERTRUDE *the Queen, [the]
Council, as*° POLONIUS *and his son* LAERTES, HAMLET, *cum aliis*° *[including*
VOLTIMAND *and* CORNELIUS].

KING. Though yet of Hamlet our° dear brother's death
    The memory be green, and that it us befitted
    To bear our hearts in grief and our whole kingdom
    To be contracted in one brow of woe,
    Yet so far hath discretion fought with nature   5
    That we with wisest sorrow think on him
    Together with remembrance of ourselves.
    Therefore our sometime° sister, now our queen,
    Th' imperial jointress° to this warlike state,
    Have we, as 'twere with a defeated joy—   10
    With an auspicious and a dropping eye,°
    With mirth in funeral and with dirge in marriage,
    In equal scale weighing delight and dole°—
    Taken to wife. Nor have we herein barred
    Your better wisdoms, which have freely gone   15
    With this affair along. For all, our thanks.
    Now follows that you know° young Fortinbras,
    Holding a weak supposal° of our worth,
    Or thinking by our late dear brother's death
    Our state to be disjoint and out of frame,   20
    Co-leaguèd with° this dream of his advantage,°
    He hath not failed to pester us with message
    Importing° the surrender of those lands
    Lost by his father, with all bonds° of law,
    To our most valiant brother. So much for him.   25
    Now for ourself and for this time of meeting.
    Thus much the business is: we have here writ
    To Norway, uncle of young Fortinbras—
    Who, impotent° and bed-rid, scarcely hears
    Of this his nephew's purpose—to suppress   30
    His° further gait° herein, in that the levies,
    The lists, and full proportions are all made
    Out of his subject;° and we here dispatch
    You, good Cornelius, and you, Voltimand,
    For bearers of this greeting to old Norway,   35
    Giving to you no further personal power
    To business with the King more than the scope

1.2. Location: The castle.   s.d. as i.e., such as, including.   **cum aliis** with others
1 our my. (The royal "we"; also in the following lines.)   **8 sometime** former
9 jointress woman possessing property with her husband   **11 With . . . eye** with
one eye smiling and the other weeping   **13 dole** grief   **17 that you know** what
you know already, that; or, that you be informed as follows   **18 weak supposal**
low estimate   **21 Co-leaguèd with** joined to, allied with.   **dream . . . advantage**
illusory hope of having the advantage. (His only ally is this hope.)   **23 Importing**
pertaining to   **24 bonds** contracts   **29 impotent** helpless   **31 His** i.e., Fortinbras'.   **gait** proceeding   **31–33 in that . . . subject** since the levying of troops and
supplies is drawn entirely from the King of Norway's own subjects

Of these dilated° articles allow.   *[He gives a paper.]*
Farewell, and let your haste commend your duty.°
CORNELIUS, VOLTIMAND. In that, and all things, will we show our duty.   40
KING. We doubt it nothing.° Heartily farewell.
                                    [Exeunt VOLTIMAND *and* CORNELIUS.*]*
And now, Laertes, what's the news with you?
You told us of some suit; what is 't, Laertes?
You cannot speak of reason to the Dane°
And lose your voice.° What wouldst thou beg, Laertes,   45
That shall not be my offer, not thy asking?
The head is not more native° to the heart,
The hand more instrumental° to the mouth,
Than is the throne of Denmark to thy father.
What wouldst thou have, Laertes?
LAERTES.   My dread lord,   50
Your leave and favor° to return to France,
From whence though willingly I came to Denmark
To show my duty in your coronation,
Yet now I must confess, that duty done,
My thoughts and wishes bend again toward France   55
And bow them to your gracious leave and pardon.°
KING. Have you your father's leave? What says Polonius?
POLONIUS. H'ath,° my lord, wrung from me my slow leave
By laborsome petition, and at last
Upon his will I sealed° my hard° consent.   60
I do beseech you, give him leave to go.
KING. Take thy fair hour,° Laertes. Time be thine,
And thy best graces spend it at thy will!°
But now, my cousin° Hamlet, and my son—
HAMLET. A little more than kin, and less than kind.°   65
KING. How is it that the clouds still hang on you?
HAMLET. Not so, my lord. I am too much in the sun.°
QUEEN. Good Hamlet, cast thy nighted color° off,
And let thine eye look like a friend on Denmark.°
Do not forever with thy vailèd lids°   70

---

38 dilated set out at length   **39 let . . . duty** let your swift obeying of orders,
rather than mere words, express your dutifulness   **41 nothing** not at all   **44 the
Dane** the Danish king   **45 lose your voice** waste your speech   **47 native** closely
connected, related   **48 instrumental** serviceable   **51 leave and favor** kind permission   **56 bow . . . pardon** entreatingly make a deep bow, asking your permission to depart   **58 H'ath** he has   **60 sealed** (as if sealing a legal document).
hard reluctant   **62 Take thy fair hour** enjoy your time of youth   **63 And . . .
will** and may your finest qualities guide the way you choose to spend your time
64 cousin any kin not of the immediate family   **65 A little . . . kind** i.e., closer
than an ordinary nephew (since I am stepson), and yet more separated in natural
feeling (with pun on *kind* meaning "affectionate" and "natural," "lawful." This line
is often read as an aside, but it need not be. The King chooses perhaps not to respond to Hamlet's cryptic and bitter remark.)   **67 the sun** i.e., the sunshine of the
King's royal favor (with pun on *son*)   **68 nighted color** (1) mourning garments of
black (2) dark melancholy   **69 Denmark** the King of Denmark   **70 vailèd lids**
lowered eyes

Seek for thy noble father in the dust.
Thou know'st 'tis common,° all that lives must die,
Passing through nature to eternity.
HAMLET. Ay, madam, it is common.
QUEEN.   If it be,
Why seems it so particular° with thee?   75
HAMLET. Seems, madam? Nay, it is. I know not "seems."
'Tis not alone my inky cloak, good Mother,
Nor customary° suits of solemn black,
Nor windy suspiration° of forced breath,
No, nor the fruitful° river in the eye,   80
Nor the dejected havior° of the visage,
Together with all forms, moods,° shapes of grief,
That can denote me truly. These indeed seem,
For they are actions that a man might play.
But I have that within which passes show;   85
These but the trappings and the suits of woe.
KING. 'Tis sweet and commendable in your nature, Hamlet,
To give these mourning duties to your father.
But you must know your father lost a father,
That father lost, lost his, and the survivor bound   90
In filial obligation for some term
To do obsequious° sorrow. But to persever°
In obstinate condolement° is a course
Of impious stubbornness. 'Tis unmanly grief.
It shows a will most incorrect to heaven,   95
A heart unfortified,° a mind impatient,
An understanding simple° and unschooled.
For what we know must be and is as common
As any the most vulgar thing to sense,°
Why should we in our peevish opposition   100
Take it to heart? Fie, 'tis a fault to heaven,
A fault against the dead, a fault to nature,
To reason most absurd, whose common theme
Is death of fathers, and who still° hath cried,
From the first corpse° till he that died today,   105
"This must be so." We pray you, throw to earth
This unprevailing° woe and think of us
As of a father; for let the world take note,
You are the most immediate° to our throne,
And with no less nobility of love   110
Than that which dearest father bears his son

72 **common** of universal occurrence. (But Hamlet plays on the sense of "vulgar" in
line 74.)   **75 particular** personal   **78 customary** (1) socially conventional (2) habitual with me   **79 suspiration** sighing   **80 fruitful** abundant   **81 havior** expression   **82 moods** outward expression of feeling   **92 obsequious** suited to obsequies or funerals.   **persever** persevere   **93 condolement** sorrowing
96 unfortified i.e., against adversity   **97 simple** ignorant   **99 As . . . sense** as the
most ordinary experience   **104 still** always   **105 the first corpse** (Abel's)
107 unprevailing unavailing, useless   **109 most immediate** next in succession

Do I impart toward° you. For° your intent
In going back to school° in Wittenberg,°
It is most retrograde° to our desire,
And we beseech you bend you° to remain   115
Here in the cheer and comfort of our eye,
Our chiefest courtier, cousin, and our son.

QUEEN. Let not thy mother lose her prayers, Hamlet.
I pray thee, stay with us, go not to Wittenberg.

HAMLET. I shall in all my best° obey you, madam.   120

KING. Why, 'tis a loving and a fair reply.
Be as ourself in Denmark. Madam, come.
This gentle and unforced accord of Hamlet
Sits smiling to° my heart, in grace° whereof
No jocund° health that Denmark drinks today   125
But the great cannon to the clouds shall tell,
And the King's rouse° the heaven shall bruit again,°
Respeaking earthly thunder.° Come away.

Flourish. Exeunt all but HAMLET.

HAMLET. O, that this too too sullied° flesh would melt,
Thaw, and resolve itself into a dew!   130
Or that the Everlasting had not fixed
His canon° 'gainst self-slaughter! O God, God,
How weary, stale, flat, and unprofitable
Seem to me all the uses° of this world!
Fie on 't, ah fie! 'Tis an unweeded garden   135
That grows to seed. Things rank and gross in nature
Possess it merely.° That it should come to this!
But two months dead—nay, not so much, not two.
So excellent a king, that was to° this
Hyperion° to a satyr,° so loving to my mother   140
That he might not beteem° the winds of heaven
Visit her face too roughly. Heaven and earth,
Must I remember? Why, she would hang on him
As if increase of appetite had grown
By what it fed on, and yet within a month—   145
Let me not think on 't; frailty, thy name is woman!—
A little month, or ere° those shoes were old
With which she followed my poor father's body,

112 impart toward i.e., bestow my affection on.   **For** as for   **113 to school** i.e.,
to your studies.   **Wittenberg** famous German university founded in 1502
114 retrograde contrary   **115 bend you** incline yourself   **120 in all my best** to
the best of my ability   **124 to** i.e., at.   **grace** thanksgiving   **125 jocund** merry
127 rouse drinking of a draft of liquor.   **bruit again** loudly echo   **128 thunder**
i.e., of trumpet and kettledrum, sounded when the King drinks; see 1.4.8–12
129 sullied defiled. (The early quartos read *sallied;* the Folio, *solid.*)   **132 canon**
law   **134 all the uses** the whole routine   **137 merely** completely   **139 to** in
comparison to   **140 Hyperion** Titan sun-god, father of Helios.   **satyr** a lecherous
creature of classical mythology, half-human but with a goat's legs, tail, ears, and
horns   **141 beteem** allow   **147 or ere** even before

Like Niobe,° all tears, why she, even she—
O God, a beast, that wants discourse of reason,°   150
Would have mourned longer—married with my uncle,
My father's brother, but no more like my father
Than I to Hercules. Within a month,
Ere yet the salt of most unrighteous tears
Had left the flushing in her gallèd° eyes,   155
She married. O, most wicked speed, to post°
With such dexterity to incestuous° sheets!
It is not, nor it cannot come to good.
But break, my heart, for I must hold my tongue.
        Enter HORATIO, MARCELLUS, *and* BERNARDO.
HORATIO. Hail to your lordship!
HAMLET.   I am glad to see you well.   160
    Horatio!—or I do forget myself.
HORATIO. The same, my lord, and your poor servant ever.
HAMLET. Sir, my good friend; I'll change that name° with you.
    And what make you from° Wittenberg, Horatio?
    Marcellus.   165
MARCELLUS. My good lord.
HAMLET. I am very glad to see you. *[To* BERNARDO.*]* Good even, sir.—
    But what in faith make you from Wittenberg?
HORATIO. A truant disposition, good my lord.
HAMLET. I would not hear your enemy say so,   170
    Nor shall you do my ear that violence
    To make it truster of your own report
    Against yourself. I know you are no truant.
    But what is your affair in Elsinore?
    We'll teach you to drink deep ere you depart.   175
HORATIO. My lord, I came to see your father's funeral.
HAMLET. I prithee, do not mock me, fellow student;
    I think it was to see my mother's wedding.
HORATIO. Indeed, my lord, it followed hard° upon.
HAMLET. Thrift, thrift, Horatio! The funeral baked meats°   180
    Did coldly° furnish forth the marriage tables.
    Would I had met my dearest° foe in heaven
    Or ever° I had seen that day, Horatio!
    My father!—Methinks I see my father.

---

149 Niobe Tantalus' daughter, Queen of Thebes, who boasted that she had more
sons and daughters than Leto; for this, Apollo and Artemis, children of Leto, slew
her fourteen children. She was turned by Zeus into a stone that continually dropped
tears.   **150 wants . . . reason** lacks the faculty of reason   **155 gallèd** irritated, inflamed   **156 post** hasten   **157 incestuous** (In Shakespeare's day, the marriage of
a man like Claudius to his deceased brother's wife was considered incestuous.)
163 change that name i.e., give and receive reciprocally the name of "friend"
(rather than talk of "servant")   **164 make you from** are you doing away from
179 hard close   **180 baked meats** meat pies   **181 coldly** i.e., as cold leftovers
182 dearest closest (and therefore deadliest)   **183 Or ever** before

HORATIO. Where, my lord?

HAMLET.   In my mind's eye, Horatio.   185

HORATIO. I saw him once. 'A° was a goodly king.

HAMLET. 'A was a man. Take him for all in all,
    I shall not look upon his like again.

HORATIO. My lord, I think I saw him yesternight.

HAMLET. Saw? Who?   190

HORATIO. My lord, the King your father.

HAMLET. The King my father?

HORATIO. Season your admiration° for a while
    With an attent° ear till I may deliver,
    Upon the witness of these gentlemen,   195
    This marvel to you.

HAMLET.   For God's love, let me hear!

HORATIO. Two nights together had these gentlemen,
    Marcellus and Bernardo, on their watch,
    In the dead waste° and middle of the night,
    Been thus encountered. A figure like your father,   200
    Armèd at point° exactly, cap-à-pie,°
    Appears before them, and with solemn march
    Goes slow and stately by them. Thrice he walked
    By their oppressed and fear-surprisèd eyes
    Within his truncheon's° length, whilst they, distilled°   205
    Almost to jelly with the act° of fear,
    Stand dumb and speak not to him. This to me
    In dreadful° secrecy impart they did,
    And I with them the third night kept the watch,
    Where, as they had delivered, both in time,   210
    Form of the thing, each word made true and good,
    The apparition comes. I knew your father;
    These hands are not more like.

HAMLET.   But where was this?

MARCELLUS. My lord, upon the platform where we watch.

HAMLET. Did you not speak to it?

HORATIO.   My lord, I did,   215
    But answer made it none. Yet once methought
    It lifted up its head and did address
    Itself to motion, like as it would speak;°
    But even then° the morning cock crew loud,
    And at the sound it shrunk in haste away   220
    And vanished from our sight.

HAMLET.   'Tis very strange.

HORATIO. As I do live, my honored lord, 'tis true,

---

186 'A he   **193 Season your admiration** restrain your astonishment   **194 attent**
attentive   **199 dead waste** desolate stillness   **201 at point** correctly in every detail.   **cap-à-pie** from head to foot   **205 truncheon** officer's staff.   **distilled** dissolved   **206 act** action, operation   **208 dreadful** full of dread   **217–218 did . . .
speak** began to move as though it were about to speak   **219 even then** at that
very instant

      And we did think it writ down in our duty
      To let you know of it.
HAMLET. Indeed, indeed, sirs. But this troubles me.   225
      Hold you the watch tonight?
ALL.   We do, my lord.
HAMLET. Armed, say you?
ALL. Armed, my lord.
HAMLET. From top to toe?
ALL. My lord, from head to foot.   230
HAMLET. Then saw you not his face?
HORATIO. O, yes, my lord, he wore his beaver° up.
HAMLET. What° looked he, frowningly?
HORATIO. A countenance more in sorrow than in anger.
HAMLET. Pale or red?   235
HORATIO. Nay, very pale.
HAMLET. And fixed his eyes upon you?
HORATIO. Most constantly.
HAMLET. I would I had been there.
HORATIO. It would have much amazed you.   240
HAMLET. Very like, very like. Stayed it long?
HORATIO. While one with moderate haste might tell° a hundred.
MARCELLUS, BERNARDO. Longer, longer.
HORATIO. Not when I saw 't.
HAMLET. His beard was grizzled°—no?   245
HORATIO. It was, as I have seen it in his life,
      A sable silvered.°
HAMLET.   I will watch tonight.
      Perchance 'twill walk again.
HORATIO.   I warrant° it will.
HAMLET. If it assume my noble father's person,
      I'll speak to it though hell itself should gape   250
      And bid me hold my peace. I pray you all,
      If you have hitherto concealed this sight,
      Let it be tenable° in your silence still,
      And whatsoever else shall hap tonight,
      Give it an understanding but no tongue.   255
      I will requite your loves. So, fare you well.
      Upon the platform twixt eleven and twelve
      I'll visit you.
ALL.   Our duty to your honor.
HAMLET. Your loves, as mine to you. Farewell.

                           Exeunt [all but HAMLET*].*   260

      My father's spirit in arms! All is not well.
      I doubt° some foul play. Would the night were come!
      Till then sit still, my soul. Foul deeds will rise,
      Though all the earth o'erwhelm them, to men's eyes.

                                  Exit.

232 **beaver** visor on the helmet   233 **What** how   242 **tell** count   245 **grizzled**
gray   247 **sable silvered** black mixed with white   248 **warrant** assure you
253 **tenable** held   261 **doubt** suspect

1.3   *Enter* LAERTES *and* OPHELIA, *his sister.*

LAERTES. My necessaries are embarked. Farewell.
　　And, sister, as the winds give benefit
　　And convoy is assistant,° do not sleep
　　But let me hear from you.
OPHELIA.　　　　　　　　　Do you doubt that?
LAERTES. For Hamlet, and the trifling of his favor,　　　　　5
　　Hold it a fashion and a toy in blood,°
　　A violet in the youth of primy° nature,
　　Forward,° not permanent, sweet, not lasting,
　　The perfume and suppliance° of a minute—
　　No more.
OPHELIA.　　　No more but so?
LAERTES.　　　　　　　　　　Think it no more.　　　　10
　　For nature crescent° does not grow alone
　　In thews° and bulk, but as this temple° waxes
　　The inward service of the mind and soul
　　Grows wide withal.° Perhaps he loves you now,
　　And now no soil° nor cautel° doth besmirch　　　　15
　　The virtue of his will;° but you must fear,
　　His greatness weighed,° his will is not his own.
　　For he himself is subject to his birth.
　　He may not, as unvalued persons do,
　　Carve° for himself, for on his choice depends　　　　20
　　The safety and health of this whole state,
　　And therefore must his choice be circumscribed
　　Unto the voice and yielding° of that body
　　Whereof he is the head. Then if he says he loves you,
　　It fits your wisdom so far to believe it　　　　　　25
　　As he in his particular act and place°
　　May give his saying deed, which is no further
　　Than the main voice° of Denmark goes withal.°
　　Then weigh what loss your honor may sustain
　　If with too credent° ear you list° his songs,　　　　30
　　Or lose your heart, or your chaste treasure open
　　To his unmastered importunity.
　　Fear it, Ophelia, fear it, my dear sister,
　　And keep you in the rear of your affection,°
　　Out of the shot and danger of desire.　　　　　　35

1.3. Location: Polonius' chambers.   3 convoy is assistant means of conveyance are available   **6 toy in blood** passing amorous fancy   **7 primy** in its
prime, springtime   **8 Forward** precocious   **9 suppliance** supply, filler   **11 crescent** growing, waxing   **12 thews** bodily strength.   **temple** i.e., body   **14 Grows
wide withal** grows along with it   **15 soil** blemish.   **cautel** deceit   **16 will** desire
17 His greatness weighed if you take into account his high position   **20 Carve**
i.e., choose   **23 voice and yielding** assent, approval   **26 in . . . place** in his particular restricted circumstances   **28 main voice** general assent.   **withal** along
with   **30 credent** credulous.   **list** listen to   **34 keep . . . affection** don't advance
as far as your affection might lead you. (A military metaphor.)

The chariest° maid is prodigal enough
If she unmask° her beauty to the moon.°
Virtue itself scapes not calumnious strokes.
The canker galls° the infants of the spring
Too oft before their buttons° be disclosed,°   40
And in the morn and liquid dew° of youth
Contagious blastments° are most imminent.
Be wary then; best safety lies in fear.
Youth to itself rebels,° though none else near.

OPHELIA. I shall the effect of this good lesson keep   45
As watchman to my heart. But, good my brother,
Do not, as some ungracious° pastors do,
Show me the steep and thorny way to heaven,
Whiles like a puffed° and reckless libertine
Himself the primrose path of dalliance treads,   50
And recks° not his own rede.°

Enter POLONIUS.

LAERTES.   O, fear me not.°
I stay too long. But here my father comes.
A double° blessing is a double grace;
Occasion smiles upon a second leave.°

POLONIUS. Yet here, Laertes? Aboard, aboard, for shame!   55
The wind sits in the shoulder of your sail,
And you are stayed for. There—my blessing with thee!
And these few precepts in thy memory
Look° thou character.° Give thy thoughts no tongue,
Nor any unproportioned° thought his° act.   60
Be thou familiar,° but by no means vulgar.°
Those friends thou hast, and their adoption tried,°
Grapple them unto thy soul with hoops of steel,
But do not dull thy palm° with entertainment
Of each new-hatched, unfledged courage.° Beware   65
Of entrance to a quarrel, but being in,
Bear 't that° th' opposèd may beware of thee.
Give every man thy ear, but few thy voice;

---

36 chariest most scrupulously modest   **37 If she unmask** if she does no more than show her beauty.   **moon** (Symbol of chastity.)   **39 canker galls** cankerworm destroys   **40 buttons** buds.   **disclosed** opened   **41 liquid dew** i.e., time when dew is fresh and bright   **42 blastments** blights   **44 Youth . . . rebels** youth is inherently rebellious   **47 ungracious** ungodly   **49 puffed** bloated, or swollen with pride   **51 recks** heeds.   **rede** counsel.   **fear me not** don't worry on my account   **53 double** (Laertes has already bid his father good-bye.)   **54 Occasion . . . leave** happy is the circumstance that provides a second leave-taking. (The goddess Occasion, or Opportunity, smiles.)   **59 Look** be sure that.   **character** inscribe   **60 unproportioned** badly calculated, intemperate.   **his** its   **61 familiar** sociable.   **vulgar** common   **62 and their adoption tried** and also their suitability for adoption as friends having been tested   **64 dull thy palm** i.e., shake hands so often as to make the gesture meaningless   **65 courage** young man of spirit   **67 Bear 't that** manage it so that

Take each man's censure,° but reserve thy judgment.
Costly thy habit° as thy purse can buy,   70
But not expressed in fancy;° rich, not gaudy,
For the apparel oft proclaims the man,
And they in France of the best rank and station
Are of a most select and generous chief in that.°
Neither a borrower nor a lender be,   75
For loan oft loses both itself and friend,
And borrowing dulleth edge of husbandry.°
This above all: to thine own self be true,
And it must follow, as the night the day,
Thou canst not then be false to any man.   80
Farewell. My blessing season° this in thee!
LAERTES. Most humbly do I take my leave, my lord.
POLONIUS. The time invests° you. Go, your servants tend.°
LAERTES. Farewell, Ophelia, and remember well
What I have said to you.   85
OPHELIA. 'Tis in my memory locked,
And you yourself shall keep the key of it.
LAERTES. Farewell.

Exit LAERTES.

POLONIUS. What is 't, Ophelia, he hath said to you?
OPHELIA. So please you, something touching the Lord Hamlet.   90
POLONIUS. Marry,° well bethought.
'Tis told me he hath very oft of late
Given private time to you, and you yourself
Have of your audience been most free and bounteous.
If it be so—as so 'tis put on° me,   95
And that in way of caution—I must tell you
You do not understand yourself so clearly
As it behooves° my daughter and your honor.
What is between you? Give me up the truth.
OPHELIA. He hath, my lord, of late made many tenders°   100
Of his affection to me.
POLONIUS. Affection? Pooh! You speak like a green girl,
Unsifted° in such perilous circumstance.
Do you believe his tenders, as you call them?
OPHELIA. I do not know, my lord, what I should think.   105
POLONIUS. Marry, I will teach you. Think yourself a baby
That you have ta'en these tenders for true pay
Which are not sterling.° Tender° yourself more dearly,
Or—not to crack the wind° of the poor phrase,

69 censure opinion, judgment   **70 habit** clothing   **71 fancy** excessive ornament, decadent fashion   **74 Are . . . that** are of a most refined and well-bred preeminence in choosing what to wear   **77 husbandry** thrift   **81 season** mature
83 invests besieges, presses upon.   **tend** attend, wait   **91 Marry** i.e., by the Virgin Mary. (A mild oath.)   **95 put on** impressed on, told to   **98 behooves** befits
100 tenders offers   **103 Unsifted** i.e., untried   **108 sterling** legal currency.
Tender hold, look after, offer   **109 crack the wind** i.e., run it until it is broken-winded

Running it thus—you'll tender me a fool.° 110

OPHELIA. My lord, he hath importuned me with love
In honorable fashion.

POLONIUS. Ay, fashion° you may call it. Go to,° go to.

OPHELIA. And hath given countenance° to his speech, my lord,
With almost all the holy vows of heaven. 115

POLONIUS. Ay, springes° to catch woodcocks.° I do know,
When the blood burns, how prodigal° the soul
Lends the tongue vows. These blazes, daughter,
Giving more light than heat, extinct in both
Even in their promise as it° is a-making, 120
You must not take for fire. From this time
Be something° scanter of your maiden presence.
Set your entreatments° at a higher rate
Than a command to parle.° For Lord Hamlet,
Believe so much in him° that he is young, 125
And with a larger tether may he walk
Than may be given you. In few,° Ophelia,
Do not believe his vows, for they are brokers,°
Not of that dye° which their investments° show,
But mere implorators° of unholy suits, 130
Breathing° like sanctified and pious bawds,
The better to beguile. This is for all:°
I would not, in plain terms, from this time forth
Have you so slander° any moment° leisure
As to give words or talk with the Lord Hamlet. 135
Look to 't, I charge you. Come your ways.°

OPHELIA. I shall obey, my lord.

Exeunt.

1.4   *Enter* HAMLET, HORATIO, *and* MARCELLUS.

HAMLET. The air bites shrewdly;° it is very cold.

HORATIO. It is a nipping and an eager° air.

HAMLET. What hour now?

HORATIO.   I think it lacks of° twelve.

---

110 tender me a fool (1) show yourself to me as a fool (2) show me up as a fool
(3) present me with a grandchild. (*Fool* was a term of endearment for a child.)
113 fashion mere form, pretense.   **Go to** (An expression of impatience.)
114 countenance credit, confirmation   **116 springes** snares.   **woodcocks** birds
easily caught; here used to connote gullibility   **117 prodigal** prodigally   **120 it**
i.e., the promise   **122 something** somewhat   **123 entreatments** negotiations for
surrender. (A military term.)   **124 parle** discuss terms with the enemy. (Polonius
urges his daughter, in the metaphor of military language, not to meet with Hamlet
and consider giving in to him merely because he requests an interview.)   **125 so
. . . him** this much concerning him   **127 In few** briefly   **128 brokers** go-
betweens, procurers   **129 dye** color or sort.   **investments** clothes. (The vows
are not what they seem.)   **130 mere implorators** out and out solicitors
131 Breathing speaking   **132 for all** once for all, in sum   **134 slander** abuse,
misuse.   **moment** moment's   **136 Come your ways** come along
1.4. Location: The guard platform.   1 shrewdly keenly, sharply
2 eager biting   **3 lacks of** is just short of

MARCELLUS. No, it is struck.

HORATIO.   Indeed? I heard it not.
It then draws near the season°   5
Wherein the spirit held his wont° to walk.
     A flourish of trumpets, and two pieces° go off [within].
What does this mean, my lord?

HAMLET. The King doth wake° tonight and takes his rouse,°
Keeps wassail,° and the swaggering upspring° reels;°
And as he drains his drafts of Rhenish° down,   10
The kettledrum and trumpet thus bray out
The triumph of his pledge.°

HORATIO.   It is a custom?

HAMLET. Ay, marry, is 't,
But to my mind, though I am native here
And to the manner° born, it is a custom   15
More honored in the breach than the observance.°
This heavy-headed revel east and west°
Makes us traduced and taxed of° other nations.
They clepe° us drunkards, and with swinish phrase°
Soil our addition;° and indeed it takes   20
From our achievements, though performed at height,°
The pith and marrow of our attribute.°
So, oft it chances in particular men,
That for° some vicious mole of nature° in them,
As in their birth—wherein they are not guilty,   25
Since nature cannot choose his° origin—
By their o'ergrowth of some complexion,°
Oft breaking down the pales° and forts of reason,
Or by some habit that too much o'erleavens°
The form of plausive° manners, that these men,   30
Carrying, I say, the stamp of one defect,
Being nature's livery° or fortune's star,°
His virtues else,° be they as pure as grace,
As infinite as man may undergo,°

---

5 season time   **6 held his wont** was accustomed.   **s.d. pieces** i.e., of ordnance,
cannon   **8 wake** stay awake and hold revel.   **takes his rouse** carouses   **9 wassail** carousal.   **upspring** wild German dance.   **reels** dances   **10 Rhenish** Rhine
wine   **12 The triumph ... pledge** i.e., his feat in draining the wine in a single
draft   **15 manner** custom (of drinking)   **16 More ... observance** better neglected than followed   **17 east and west** i.e., everywhere   **18 taxed of** censured
by   **19 clepe** call.   **with swinish phrase** i.e., by calling us swine   **20 addition**
reputation   **21 at height** outstandingly   **22 The pith ... attribute** the essence of
the reputation that others attribute to us   **24 for** on account of.   **mole of nature**
natural blemish in one's constitution   **26 his** its   **27 their o'ergrowth ...
complexion** the excessive growth in individuals of some natural trait   **28 pales**
palings, fences (as of a fortification)   **29 o'erleavens** induces a change throughout
(as yeast works in dough)   **30 plausive** pleasing   **32 nature's livery** sign of one's
servitude to nature.   **fortune's star** the destiny that chance brings   **33 His
virtues else** i.e., the other qualities of *these men* (line 30)   **34 may undergo** can
sustain

Shall in the general censure° take corruption   35
From that particular fault. The dram of evil
Doth all the noble substance often dout
To his own scandal.°
    Enter GHOST.
HORATIO.   Look, my lord, it comes!
HAMLET. Angels and ministers° of grace defend us!
Be thou° a spirit of health° or goblin damned,   40
Bring° with thee airs from heaven or blasts from hell,
Be thy intents° wicked or charitable,
Thou com'st in such a questionable° shape
That I will speak to thee. I'll call thee Hamlet,
King, father, royal Dane. O, answer me!   45
Let me not burst in ignorance, but tell
Why thy canonized° bones, hearsèd° in death,
Have burst their cerements;° why the sepulcher
Wherein we saw thee quietly inurned°
Hath oped his ponderous and marble jaws   50
To cast thee up again. What may this mean,
That thou, dead corpse, again in complete steel,°
Revisits thus the glimpses of the moon,°
Making night hideous, and we fools of nature°
So horridly to shake our disposition°   55
With thoughts beyond the reaches of our souls?
Say, why is this? Wherefore? What should we do?
    [The GHOST*] beckons [*HAMLET*]*.
HORATIO. It beckons you to go away with it,
As if it some impartment° did desire
To you alone.
MARCELLUS.   Look with what courteous action   60
It wafts you to a more removèd ground.
But do not go with it.
HORATIO.   No, by no means.
HAMLET. It will not speak. Then I will follow it.
HORATIO. Do not, my lord!
HAMLET.   Why, what should be the fear?
I do not set my life at a pin's fee,°   65
And for my soul, what can it do to that,

---

35 general censure general opinion that people have of him   **36–38 The dram
... scandal** i.e., the small drop of evil blots out or works against the noble substance of the whole and brings it into disrepute. To *dout* is to blot out. (A famous
crux.)   **39 ministers of grace** messengers of God   **40 Be thou** whether you are.
spirit of health good angel   **41 Bring** whether you bring   **42 Be thy intents**
whether your intentions are   **43 questionable** inviting question   **47 canonized**
buried according to the canons of the church.   **hearsèd** coffined   **48 cerements**
grave clothes   **49 inurned** entombed   **52 complete steel** full armor
53 glimpses of the moon pale and uncertain moonlight   **54 fools of nature**
mere men, limited to natural knowledge and subject to nature   **55 So ... disposition** to distress our mental composure so violently   **59 impartment** communication   **65 fee** value

Being a thing immortal as itself?
It waves me forth again. I'll follow it.

HORATIO. What if it tempt you toward the flood,° my lord,
 Or to the dreadful summit of the cliff   70
 That beetles o'er° his° base into the sea,
 And there assume some other horrible form
 Which might deprive your sovereignty of reason°
 And draw you into madness? Think of it.
 The very place puts toys of desperation,°   75
 Without more motive, into every brain
 That looks so many fathoms to the sea
 And hears it roar beneath.

HAMLET. It wafts me still.—Go on, I'll follow thee.

MARCELLUS. You shall not go, my lord.   *[They try to stop him.]*

HAMLET.   Hold off your hands!   80

HORATIO. Be ruled. You shall not go.

HAMLET.   My fate cries out,°
 And makes each petty° artery° in this body
 As hardy as the Nemean lion's° nerve.°
 Still am I called. Unhand me, gentlemen.
 By heaven, I'll make a ghost of him that lets° me!   85
 I say, away!—Go on, I'll follow thee.

            Exeunt GHOST *and* HAMLET.

HORATIO. He waxes desperate with imagination.

MARCELLUS. Let's follow. 'Tis not fit thus to obey him.

HORATIO. Have after.° To what issue° will this come?

MARCELLUS. Something is rotten in the state of Denmark.   90

HORATIO. Heaven will direct it.°

MARCELLUS.   Nay, let's follow him.

                Exeunt.

1.5 *Enter* GHOST *and* HAMLET.

HAMLET. Whither wilt thou lead me? Speak. I'll go no further.

GHOST. Mark me.

HAMLET.   I will.

GHOST.   My hour is almost come,
 When I to sulfurous and tormenting flames
 Must render up myself.

HAMLET.   Alas, poor ghost!

GHOST. Pity me not, but lend thy serious hearing   5
 To what I shall unfold.

---

69 flood sea **71 beetles o'er** overhangs threateningly (like bushy eyebrows).
his its **73 deprive . . . reason** take away the rule of reason over your mind
75 toys of desperation fancies of desperate acts, i.e., suicide **81 My fate cries
out** my destiny summons me **82 petty** weak. **artery** (through which the vital
spirits were thought to have been conveyed) **83 Nemean lion** one of the monsters slain by Hercules in his twelve labors. **nerve** sinew **85 lets** hinders
89 Have after let's go after him. **issue** outcome **91 it** i.e., the outcome
1.5. Location: The battlements of the castle.

HAMLET. Speak. I am bound° to hear.

GHOST. So art thou to revenge, when thou shalt hear.

HAMLET. What?

GHOST. I am thy father's spirit,   10
  Doomed for a certain term to walk the night,
  And for the day confined to fast° in fires,
  Till the foul crimes° done in my days of nature°
  Are burnt and purged away. But that° I am forbid
  To tell the secrets of my prison house,   15
  I could a tale unfold whose lightest word
  Would harrow up° thy soul, freeze thy young blood,
  Make thy two eyes like stars start from their spheres,°
  Thy knotted and combinèd locks° to part,
  And each particular hair to stand on end   20
  Like quills upon the fretful porcupine.
  But this eternal blazon° must not be
  To ears of flesh and blood. List, list, O, list!
  If thou didst ever thy dear father love—

HAMLET. O God!   25

GHOST. Revenge his foul and most unnatural murder.

HAMLET. Murder?

GHOST. Murder most foul, as in the best° it is,
  But this most foul, strange, and unnatural.

HAMLET. Haste me to know 't, that I, with wings as swift   30
  As meditation or the thoughts of love,
  May sweep to my revenge.

GHOST.   I find thee apt;
  And duller shouldst thou be° than the fat° weed
  That roots itself in ease on Lethe° wharf,
  Wouldst thou not stir in this. Now, Hamlet, hear.   35
  'Tis given out that, sleeping in my orchard,°
  A serpent stung me. So the whole ear of Denmark
  Is by a forgèd process° of my death
  Rankly abused.° But know, thou noble youth,
  The serpent that did sting thy father's life   40
  Now wears his crown.

HAMLET. O, my prophetic soul! My uncle!

GHOST. Ay, that incestuous, that adulterate° beast,
  With witchcraft of his wit, with traitorous gifts°—
  O wicked wit and gifts, that have the power   45

---

7 bound (1) ready (2) obligated by duty and fate. (The Ghost, in line 8, answers in
the second sense.)   **12 fast** do penance by fasting   **13 crimes** sins.   **of nature** as
a mortal   **14 But that** were it not that   **17 harrow up** lacerate, tear   **18 spheres**
i.e., eye-sockets, here compared to the orbits or transparent revolving spheres in
which, according to Ptolemaic astronomy, the heavenly bodies were fixed
19 knotted . . . locks hair neatly arranged and confined   **22 eternal blazon** revelation of the secrets of eternity   **28 in the best** even at best   **33 shouldst thou
be** you would have to be.   **fat** torpid, lethargic   **34 Lethe** the river of forgetfulness
in Hades   **36 orchard** garden   **38 forgèd process** falsified account   **39 abused**
deceived   **43 adulterate** adulterous   **44 gifts** (1) talents (2) presents

So to seduce!—won to his shameful lust
The will of my most seeming-virtuous queen.
O Hamlet, what a falling off was there!
From me, whose love was of that dignity
That it went hand in hand even with the vow°   50
I made to her in marriage, and to decline
Upon a wretch whose natural gifts were poor
To° those of mine!
But virtue,° as it° never will be moved,
Though lewdness court it in a shape of heaven,°   55
So lust, though to a radiant angel linked,
Will sate itself in a celestial bed°
And prey on garbage.
But soft, methinks I scent the morning air.
Brief let me be. Sleeping within my orchard,   60
My custom always of the afternoon,
Upon my secure° hour thy uncle stole,
With juice of cursèd hebona° in a vial,
And in the porches of my ears° did pour
The leprous distillment,° whose effect   65
Holds such an enmity with blood of man
That swift as quicksilver it courses through
The natural gates and alleys of the body,
And with a sudden vigor it doth posset°
And curd, like eager° droppings into milk,   70
The thin and wholesome blood. So did it mine,
And a most instant tetter° barked° about,
Most lazar-like,° with vile and loathsome crust,
All my smooth body.
Thus was I, sleeping, by a brother's hand   75
Of life, of crown, of queen at once dispatched,°
Cut off even in the blossoms of my sin,
Unhouseled,° disappointed,° unaneled,°
No reckoning° made, but sent to my account
With all my imperfections on my head.   80
O, horrible! O, horrible, most horrible!
If thou hast nature° in thee, bear it not.

50 even with the vow with the very vow   **53 To** compared to   **54 virtue, as it** as virtue   **55 shape of heaven** heavenly form   **57 sate . . . bed** cease to find sexual pleasure in a virtuously lawful marriage   **62 secure** confident, unsuspicious   **63 hebona** a poison. (The word seems to be a form of *ebony*, though it is thought perhaps to be related to *henbane*, a poison, or to *ebenus*, "yew.")   **64 porches of my ears** ears as a porch or entrance of the body   **65 leprous distillment** distillation causing leprosylike disfigurement   **69 posset** coagulate, curdle   **70 eager** sour, acid   **72 tetter** eruption of scabs.   **barked** recovered with a rough covering, like bark on a tree   **73 lazar-like** leperlike   **76 dispatched** suddenly deprived   **78 Uphouseled** without having received the Sacrament.   **disappointment** unready (spiritually) for the last journey.   **unaneled** without having received extreme unction   **79 reckoning** settling of accounts   **82 nature** i.e., the promptings of a son

Let not the royal bed of Denmark be
A couch for luxury° and damnèd incest.
But, howsoever thou pursues this act,   85
Taint not thy mind nor let thy soul contrive
Against thy mother aught. Leave her to heaven
And to those thorns that in her bosom lodge,
To prick and sting her. Fare thee well at once.
The glowworm shows the matin° to be near,   90
And 'gins to pale his° uneffectual fire.
Adieu, adieu, adieu! Remember me.

                                                    [Exit.]

HAMLET. O all you host of heaven! O earth! What else?
    And shall I couple° hell? O, fie! Hold,° hold, my heart,
    And you, my sinews, grow not instant° old,   95
    But bear me stiffly up. Remember thee?
    Ay, thou poor ghost, whiles memory holds a seat
    In this distracted globe.° Remember thee?
    Yea, from the table° of my memory
    I'll wipe away all trivial fond° records,   100
    All saws° of books, all forms,° all pressures° past
    That youth and observation copied there,
    And thy commandment all alone shall live
    Within the book and volume of my brain,
    Unmixed with baser matter. Yes, by heaven!   105
    O most pernicious woman!
    O villain, villain, smiling, damnèd villain!
    My tables°—meet it is° I set it down
    That one may smile, and smile, and be a villain.
    At least I am sure it may be so in Denmark.   110

                                                    [Writing.]

    So uncle, there you are.° Now to my word:
    It is "Adieu, adieu! Remember me."
    I have sworn't.
        Enter HORATIO *and* MARCELLUS.
HORATIO. My lord, my lord!
MARCELLUS. Lord Hamlet!   115
HORATIO. Heavens secure him!°
HAMLET. So be it.
MARCELLUS. Hilo, ho, ho, my lord!
HAMLET. Hillo, ho, ho, boy! Come, bird, come.°
MARCELLUS. How is 't, my noble lord?   120
HORATIO. What news, my lord?

84 luxury lechery   **90 matin** morning   **91 his** its   **94 couple** add.   **Hold** hold together   **95 instant** instantly   **98 globe** (1) head (2) world   **99 table** tablet, slate   **100 fond** foolish   **101 saws** wise sayings.   **forms** shapes or images copied onto the slate; general ideas.   **pressures** impressions stamped   **108 tables** writing tablets.   **meet it is** it is fitting   **111 there you are** i.e., there, I've written that down against you   **116 secure him** keep him safe   **119 Hilo . . . come** (A falconer's call to a hawk in air. Hamlet mocks the hallooing as though it were a part of hawking.)

HAMLET. O, wonderful!

HORATIO. Good my lord, tell it.

HAMLET. No, you will reveal it.

HORATIO. Not I, my lord, by heaven.　　　　　　　　　　　125

MARCELLUS. Nor I, my lord.

HAMLET. How say you, then, would heart of man once° think it?
　　But you'll be secret?

HORATIO, MARCELLUS.　　　　Ay, by heaven, my lord.

HAMLET. There's never a villain dwelling in all Denmark
　　But he's an arrant° knave.　　　　　　　　　　　　130

HORATIO. There needs no ghost, my lord, come from the grave
　　To tell us this.

HAMLET.　　　　　　Why, right, you are in the right.
　　And so, without more circumstance° at all,
　　I hold it fit that we shake hands and part,
　　You as your business and desire shall point you—　　135
　　For every man hath business and desire,
　　Such as it is—and for my own poor part,
　　Look you, I'll go pray.

HORATIO. These are but wild and whirling words, my lord.

HAMLET. I am sorry they offend you, heartily;　　　　　140
　　Yes, faith, heartily.

HORATIO.　　　　　　　　There's no offense, my lord.

HAMLET. Yes, but Saint Patrick,° but there is, Horatio,
　　And much offense° too. Touching this vision here,
　　It is an honest ghost,° that let me tell you.
　　For your desire to know what is between us,　　　　145
　　O'ermaster 't as you may. And now, good friends,
　　As you are friends, scholars, and soldiers,
　　Give me one poor request.

HORATIO. What is 't, my lord? We will.

HAMLET. Never make known what you have seen tonight.　　150

HORATIO, MARCELLUS. My lord, we will not.

HAMLET. Nay, but swear 't.

HORATIO. In faith, my lord, not I.°

MARCELLUS. Nor I, my lord, in faith.

HAMLET. Upon my sword.°　　　　　　　*[He holds out his sword.]*　155

MARCELLUS. We have sworn, my lord, already.°

HAMLET. Indeed, upon my sword, indeed.

GHOST *[cries under the stage].* Swear.

HAMLET. Ha, ha, boy, sayst thou so? Art thou there, truepenny?°
　　Come on, you hear this fellow in the cellarage.　　　160

---

127 once ever　**130 arrant** thoroughgoing　**133 circumstance** ceremony,
elaboration　**142 Saint Patrick** The keeper of Purgatory and patron saint of all
blunders and confusion.)　**143 offense** (Hamlet deliberately changes Horatio's "no
offense taken" to "an offense against all decency.")　**144 an honest ghost** i.e., a
real ghost and not an evil spirit　**153 In faith . . . I** i.e., I swear not to tell what I
have seen. (Horatio is not refusing to swear.)　**155 sword** i.e., the hilt in the form
of a cross　**156 We . . . already** i.e., we swore in *faith*　**159 truepenny** honest
old fellow

Consent to swear.

HORATIO.   Propose the oath, my lord.

HAMLET. Never to speak of this that you have seen,
     Swear by my sword.

GHOST *[beneath]*. Swear.   *[They swear.°]*

HAMLET. *Hic et ubique?°* Then we'll shift our ground.   165

[He moves to another spot.]

Come hither, gentlemen,
And lay your hands again upon my sword.
Swear by my sword
Never to speak of this that you have heard.

GHOST *[beneath]*. Swear by his sword.   *[They swear.]* 170

HAMLET. Well said, old mole. Canst work i' th' earth so fast?
     A worthy pioneer!° —Once more removed, good friends.

[He moves again.]

HORATIO. O day and night, but this is wondrous strange!

HAMLET. And therefore as a stranger° give it welcome.
     There are more things in heaven and earth, Horatio,   175
     Than are dreamt of in your philosophy.°
     But come;
     Here, as before, never, so help you mercy,°
     How strange or odd soe'er I bear myself—
     As I perchance hereafter shall think meet   180
     To put an antic° disposition on—
     That you, at such times seeing me, never shall,
     With arms encumbered° thus, or this headshake,
     Or by pronouncing of some doubtful phrase
     As "Well, we know," or "We could, an if° we would,"   185
     Or "If we list° to speak," or "There be, an if they might,"
     Or such ambiguous giving out,° to note°
     That you know aught° of me—this do swear,
     So grace and mercy at your most need help you.

GHOST *[beneath]*. Swear.   *[They swear.]* 190

HAMLET. Rest, rest, perturbèd spirit! So, gentlemen,
     With all my love I do commend me to you;°
     And what so poor a man as Hamlet is
     May do t' express his love and friending° to you,
     God willing, shall not lack.° Let us go in together,   195

And still° your fingers on your lips, I pray.
The time° is out of joint. O cursèd spite°
That ever I was born to set it right!

[They wait for him to leave first.]

Nay, come, let's go together.°

Exeunt.

2.1   *Enter old* POLONIUS *with his man [*REYNALDO*].*

POLONIUS. Give him this money and these notes, Reynaldo.

[He gives money and papers.]

REYNALDO. I will, my lord.
POLONIUS. You shall do marvelous° wisely, good Reynaldo,
  Before you visit him, to make inquire°
  Of his behavior.
REYNALDO.   My lord, I did intend it.   5
POLONIUS. Marry, well said, very well said. Look you, sir,
  Inquire me first what Danskers° are in Paris,
  And how, and who, what means,° and where they keep,°
  What company, at what expense; and finding
  By this encompassment° and drift° of question   10
  That they do know my son, come you more nearer
  Than your particular demands will touch it.°
  Take you,° as 'twere, some distant knowledge of him,
  As thus, "I know his father and his friends,
  And in part him." Do you mark this, Reynaldo?   15
REYNALDO. Ay, very well, my lord.
POLONIUS. "And in part him, but," you may say, "not well.
  But if 't be he I mean, he's very wild,
  Addicted so and so," and there put on° him
  What forgeries° you please—marry, none so rank°   20
  As may dishonor him, take heed of that,
  But, sir, such wanton,° wild, and usual slips
  As are companions noted and most known
  To youth and liberty.
REYNALDO. As gaming, my lord.   25
POLONIUS. Ay, or drinking, fencing, swearing,
  Quarreling, drabbing°—you may go so far.
REYNALDO. My lord, that would dishonor him.
POLONIUS. Faith, no, as you may season° it in the charge.
  You must not put another scandal on him   30

---

196 still always   **197 The time** the state of affairs.   **spite** i.e., the spite of Fortune
199 let's go together (Probably they wait for him to leave first, but he refuses this
ceremoniousness.)   **2.1 Location: Polonius' chambers.**   **3 marvelous** mar-
velously   **4 inquire** inquiry   **7 Danskers** Danes   **8 what means** what wealth
(they have).   **keep** dwell   **10 encompassment** roundabout talking.   **drift** gradual approach or course   **11–12 come . . . it** you will find out more this way than
by asking pointed questions (*particular demands*)   **13 Take you** assume, pretend
19 put on impute to   **20 forgeries** invented tales.   **rank** gross   **22 wanton**
sportive, unrestrained   **27 drabbing** whoring   **29 season** temper, soften

That he is open to incontinency;°
That's not my meaning. But breathe his faults so quaintly°
That they may seem the taints of liberty,°
The flash and outbreak of a fiery mind,
A savageness in unreclaimèd blood,   35
Of general assault.°

REYNALDO. But, my good lord—
POLONIUS. Wherefore should you do this?
REYNALDO. Ay, my lord, I would know that.
POLONIUS. Marry, sir, here's my drift,   40
And I believe it is a fetch of warrant.°
You laying these slight sullies on my son,
As 'twere a thing a little soiled wi' the working,°
Mark you,
Your party in converse,° him you would sound,°   45
Having ever° seen in the prenominate crimes°
The youth you breathe° of guilty, be assured
He closes with you in this consequence:°
"Good sir," or so, or "friend," or "gentleman,"
According to the phrase or the addition°   50
Of man and country.
REYNALDO.   Very good, my lord.
POLONIUS. And then, sir, does 'a this—'a does—what was I about
to say? By the Mass, I was about to say something. Where did
I leave?
REYNALDO. At "closes in the consequence."   55
POLONIUS. At "closes in the consequence," ay, marry.
He closes thus: "I know the gentleman,
I saw him yesterday," or "th' other day,"
Or then, or then, with such or such, "and as you say,
There was 'a gaming," "there o'ertook in 's rouse,"°   60
"There falling out° at tennis," or perchance
"I saw him enter such a house of sale,"
Videlicet° a brothel, or so forth. See you now,
Your bait of falsehood takes this carp° of truth;
And thus do we of wisdom and of reach,°   65
With windlasses° and with assays of bias,°
By indirections find directions° out.

31 incontinency habitual sexual excess   **32 quaintly** artfully, subtly   **33 taints
of liberty** faults resulting from free living   **35–36 A savageness . . . assault** a
wildness in untamed youth that assails all indiscriminately   **41 fetch of warrant**
legitimate trick   **43 soiled wi' the working** soiled by handling while it is being
made, i.e., by involvement in the ways of the world   **45 converse** conversation.
sound i.e., sound out   **46 Having ever** if he has ever.   **prenominate crimes**
before-mentioned offenses   **47 breathe** speak   **48 closes . . . consequence** takes
you into his confidence in some fashion, as follows   **50 addition** title   **60 o'ertook in 's rouse** overcome by drink   **61 falling out** quarreling   **63 Videlicet**
namely   **64 carp** a fish   **65 reach** capacity, ability   **66 windlasses** i.e., circuitous
paths. (Literally, circuits made to head off the game in hunting.)   **assays of bias** attempts through indirection (like the curving path of the bowling ball, which is
biased or weighted to one side)   **67 directions** i.e., the way things really are

So by my former lecture and advice
Shall you my son. You have° me, have you not?
REYNALDO. My lord, I have.
POLONIUS.   God b'wi'° ye; fare ye well.   70
REYNALDO. Good my lord.
POLONIUS. Observe his inclination in yourself.°
REYNALDO. I shall, my lord.
POLONIUS. And let him ply his music.
REYNALDO. Well, my lord.   75
POLONIUS. Farewell.

                                                    Exit REYNALDO.

     Enter OPHELIA.
                        How now, Ophelia, what's the matter?
OPHELIA. O my lord, my lord, I have been so affrighted!
POLONIUS. With what, i' the name of God?
OPHELIA. My lord, as I was sewing in my closet,°
     Lord Hamlet, with his doublet° all unbraced,°   80
     No hat upon his head, his stockings fouled,
     Ungartered, and down-gyvèd° to his ankle,
     Pale as his shirt, his knees knocking each other,
     And with a look so piteous in purport°
     As if he had been loosèd out of hell   85
     To speak of horrors—he comes before me.
POLONIUS. Mad for thy love?
OPHELIA.   My lord, I do not know,
     But truly I do fear it.
POLONIUS.   What said he?
OPHELIA. He took me by the wrist and held me hard.
     Then goes he to the length of all his arm,   90
     And, with his other hand thus o'er his brow
     He falls to such perusal of my face
     As° 'a would draw it. Long stayed he so.
     At last, a little shaking of mine arm
     And thrice his head thus waving up and down,   95
     He raised a sigh so piteous and profound
     As it did seem to shatter all his bulk°
     And end his being. That done, he lets me go,
     And with his head over his shoulder turned
     He seemed to find his way without his eyes,   100
     For out o' doors he went without their helps,
     And to the last bended their light on me.
POLONIUS. Come, go with me. I will go seek the King.
     This is the very ecstasy° of love,
     Whose violent property° fordoes° itself   105
     And leads the will to desperate undertakings

---

69 have understand   **70 b' wi'** be with   **72 in yourself** in your own person (as
well as by asking questions)   **79 closet** private chamber   **80 doublet** close-fitting
jacket.   **unbraced** unfastened   **82 down-gyvèd** fallen to the ankles (like gyves or
fetters)   **84 in purport** in what it expressed   **93 As** as if (also in line 97)
97 bulk body   **104 ecstasy** madness   **105 property** nature.   **fordoes** destroys

As oft as any passion under heaven
That does afflict our natures. I am sorry.
What, have you given him any hard words of late?
OPHELIA. No, my good lord, but as you did command   110
    I did repel his letters and denied
    His access to me.
POLONIUS.   That hath made him mad.
    I am sorry that with better heed and judgment
    I had not quoted° him. I feared he did but trifle
    And meant to wrack° thee. But beshrew my jealousy!°   115
    By heaven, it is as proper to our age°
    To cast beyond° ourselves in our opinions
    As it is common for the younger sort
    To lack discretion. Come, go we to the King.
    This must be known,° which, being kept close,° might move   120
    More grief to hide than hate to utter love.°
    Come.

                                                  Exeunt.

2.2   *Flourish. Enter* KING *and* QUEEN, ROSENCRANTZ,
            and GUILDENSTERN *[with others].*

KING. Welcome, dear Rosencrantz and Guildenstern.
    Moreover that° we much did long to see you,
    The need we have to use you did provoke
    Our hasty sending. Something have you heard
    Of Hamlet's transformation—so call it,   5
    Sith nor° th' exterior nor the inward man
    Resembles that° it was. What it should be,
    More than his father's death, that thus hath put him
    So much from th' understanding of himself,
    I cannot dream of. I entreat you both   10
    That, being of so young days° brought up with him,
    And sith so neighbored to° his youth and havior,°
    That you vouchsafe your rest° here in our court
    Some little time, so by your companies
    To draw him on to pleasures, and to gather   15
    So much as from occasion° you may glean,
    Whether aught to us unknown afflicts him thus
    That, opened,° lies within our remedy.

---

114 quoted observed   **115 wrack** ruin, seduce.   **beshrew my jealousy** a plague
upon my suspicious nature   **116 proper . . . age** characteristic of us (old) men
117 cast beyond overshoot, miscalculate. (A metaphor from hunting.)
120 known made known (to the King).   **close** secret   **120–121 might . . . love**
i.e., might cause more grief (because of what Hamlet might do) by hiding the
knowledge of Hamlet's strange behavior to Ophelia than unpleasantness by telling it
2.2. Location: The castle.   **2 Moreover that** besides the fact that   **6 Sith nor**
since neither   **7 that** what   **11 of . . . days** from such early youth   **12 And sith
so neighbored to** and since you are (or, and since that time you are) intimately acquainted with.   **havior** demeanor   **13 vouchsafe your rest** please to stay
16 occasion opportunity   **18 opened** being revealed

QUEEN. Good gentlemen, he hath much talked of you,
    And sure I am two men there is not living   20
    To whom he more adheres. If it will please you
    To show us so much gentry° and good will
    As to expend your time with us awhile
    For the supply and profit of our hope,°
    Your visitation shall receive such thanks   25
    As fits a king's remembrance.°
ROSENCRANTZ.   Both Your Majesties
    Might, by the sovereign power you have of° us,
    Put your dread° pleasures more into command
    Than to entreaty.
GUILDENSTERN.   But we both obey,
    And here give up ourselves in the full bent°   30
    To lay our service freely at your feet,
    To be commanded.
KING. Thanks, Rosencrantz and gentle Guildenstern.
QUEEN. Thanks, Guildenstern and gentle Rosencrantz.
    And I beseech you instantly to visit   35
    My too much changèd son. Go, some of you,
    And bring these gentlemen where Hamlet is.
GUILDENSTERN. Heavens make our presence and our practices°
    Pleasant and helpful to him!
QUEEN.   Ay, amen!
    Exeunt ROSENCRANTZ *and* GUILDENSTERN *[with some attendants].*
    Enter POLONIUS.
POLONIUS. Th' ambassadors from Norway, my good lord,   40
    Are joyfully returned.
KING. Thou still° hast been the father of good news.
POLONIUS. Have I, my lord? I assure my good liege
    I hold° my duty, as° I hold my soul,
    Both to my God and to my gracious king;   45
    And I do think, or else this brain of mine
    Hunts not the trail of policy° so sure
    As it hath used to do, that I have found
    The very cause of Hamlet's lunacy.
KING. O, speak of that! That do I long to hear.   50
POLONIUS. Give first admittance to th' ambassadors.
    My news shall be the fruit° to that great feast.
KING. Thyself do grace° to them and bring them in.
                                 [Exit POLONIUS.*]*
    He tells me, my dear Gertrude, he hath found
    The head and source of all your son's distemper.   55

---

22 gentry courtesy   **24 supply . . . hope** aid and furtherance of what we hope for   **26 As fits . . . remembrance** as would be a fitting gift of a king who rewards true service   **27 of** over   **28 dread** inspiring awe   **30 in . . . bent** to the utmost degree of our capacity. (An archery metaphor.)   **38 practices** doings   **42 still** always   **44 hold** maintain.   **as** as firmly as   **47 policy** sagacity   **52 fruit** dessert   **53 grace** honor (punning on *grace* said before a *feast,* line 52)

QUEEN. I doubt° it is no other but the main,°
    His father's death and our o'erhasty marriage.
    *Enter Ambassadors [*VOLTIMAND *and* CORNELIUS, *with* POLONIUS*].*
KING. Well, we shall sift him.°—Welcome, my good friends!
    Say, Voltimand, what from our brother° Norway?
VOLTIMAND. Most fair return of greetings and desires.°   60
    Upon our first,° he sent out to suppress
    His nephew's levies, which to him appeared
    To be a preparation 'gainst the Polack,
    But, better looked into, he truly found
    It was against Your Highness. Whereat grieved   65
    That so his sickness, age, and impotence°
    Was falsely borne in hand,° sends out arrests°
    On Fortinbras, which he, in brief, obeys,
    Receives rebuke from Norway, and in fine°
    Makes vow before his uncle never more   70
    To give th' assay° of arms against Your Majesty.
    Whereon old Norway, overcome with joy,
    Gives him three thousand crowns in annual fee
    And his commission to employ those soldiers,
    So levied as before, against the Polack,   75
    With an entreaty, herein further shown,   *[giving a paper]*
    That it might please you to give quiet pass
    Through your dominions for this enterprise
    On such regards of safety and allowance°
    As therein are set down.
KING.   It likes° us well,
    And at our more considered° time we'll read,   80
    Answer, and think upon this business.
    Meantime we thank you for your well-took labor.
    Go to your rest; at night we'll feast together.
    Most welcome home!
                            Exeunt Ambassadors.
POLONIUS.   This business is well ended.
    My liege, and madam, to expostulate°   85
    What majesty should be, what duty is,
    Why day is day, night night, and time is time,
    Were nothing but to waste night, day, and time.
    Therefore, since brevity is the soul of wit,°
    And tediousness the limbs and outward flourishes,   90
    I will be brief. Your noble son is mad.

---

56 doubt fear, suspect.   **main** chief point, principal concern   **58 sift him** question Polonius closely   **59 brother** fellow king   **60 desires** good wishes
61 Upon our first at our first words on the business   **66 impotence** helplessness
67 borne in hand deluded, taken advantage of.   **arrests** orders to desist   **69 in fine** in conclusion   **71 give th' assay** make trial of strength, challenge   **79 On . . . allowance** i.e., with such considerations for the safety of Denmark and permission for Fortinbras   **80 likes** pleases   **81 considered** suitable for deliberation   **86 expostulate** expound, inquire into   **90 wit** sense or judgment

Mad call I it, for, to define true madness,
What is 't but to be nothing else but mad?
But let that go.
QUEEN.   More matter, with less art.   95
POLONIUS. Madam, I swear I use no art at all.
That he's mad, 'tis true; 'tis true 'tis pity,
And pity 'tis 'tis true—a foolish figure,°
But farewell it, for I will use no art.
Mad let us grant him, then, and now remains   100
That we find out the cause of this effect,
Or rather say, the cause of this defect,
For this effect defective comes by cause.°
Thus it remains, and the remainder thus.
Perpend.°   105
I have a daughter—have while she is mine—
Who, in her duty and obedience, mark,
Hath given me this. Now gather and surmise.°
[He reads the letter.] "To the celestial and my soul's idol, the most
beautified Ophelia"—   110
That's an ill phrase, a vile phrase; "beautified" is a vile phrase. But
you shall hear. Thus: *[He reads.]*
"In her excellent white bosom,° these,° etc."
QUEEN. Came this from Hamlet to her?
POLONIUS. Good madam, stay° awhile, I will be faithful.°   *[He reads.]* 115

"Doubt thou the stars are fire,
        Doubt that the sun doth move,
    Doubt° truth to be a liar,
        But never doubt I love.
O dear Ophelia, I am ill at these numbers.° I have not art to 120
reckon° my groans. But that I love thee best, O most best, believe
it. Adieu.
        Thine evermore, most dear lady, whilst this machine° is to him,
                                                                Hamlet."

This in obedience hath my daughter shown me,   125
And, more above,° hath his solicitings,
As they fell out° by° time, by means, and place,
All given to mine ear.°
KING.   But how hath she
Received his love?
POLONIUS.   What do you think of me?

---

98 figure figure of speech   **103 For . . . cause** i.e., for this defective behavior, this
madness, has a cause   **105 Perpend** consider   **108 gather and surmise** draw
your own conclusions   **113 In . . . bosom** (The letter is poetically addressed to her
heart.)   **these** i.e., the letter   **115 stay** wait.   **faithful** i.e., in reading the letter
accurately   **118 Doubt** suspect   **120 ill . . . numbers** unskilled at writing verses
121 reckon (1) count (2) number metrically, scan   **123 machine** i.e., body
126 more above moreover   **127 fell out** occurred.   **by** according to   **128 given
. . . ear** i.e., told me about

KING. As of a man faithful and honorable.   130
POLONIUS. I would fain° prove so. But what might you think,
    When I had seen this hot love on the wing—
    As I perceived it, I must tell you that,
    Before my daughter told me—what might you,
    Or my dear Majesty your queen here, think,   135
    If I had played the desk or table book,°
    Or given my heart a winking,° mute and dumb,
    Or looked upon this love with idle sight?°
    What might you think? No, I went round° to work,
    And my young mistress thus I did bespeak:°   140
    "Lord Hamlet is a prince out of thy star;°
    This must not be." And then I prescripts° gave her,
    That she should lock herself from his resort,°
    Admit no messengers, receive no tokens.
    Which done, she took the fruits of my advice;   145
    And he, repellèd—a short tale to make—
    Fell into a sadness, then into a fast,
    Thence to a watch,° thence into a weakness,
    Thence to a lightness,° and by this declension°
    Into the madness wherein now he raves,   150
    And all we° mourn for.
KING *[to the* QUEEN*].*   Do you think 'tis this?
QUEEN. It may be, very like.
POLONIUS. Hath there been such a time—I would fain know that—
    That I have positively said "'Tis so,"
    When it proved otherwise?
KING.   Not that I know.   155
POLONIUS. Take this from this,° if this be otherwise.
    If circumstances lead me, I will find
    Where truth is hid, though it were hid indeed
    Within the center.°
KING.   How may we try° it further?
POLONIUS. You know sometimes he walks four hours together   160
    Here in the lobby.
QUEEN.   So he does indeed.
POLONIUS. At such a time I'll loose° my daughter to him.
    Be you and I behind an arras° then.

131 fain gladly   **136 played . . . table book** i.e., remained shut up, concealing the
information   **137 given . . . winking** closed the eyes of my heart to this
138 with idle sight complacently or incomprehendingly   **139 round** roundly,
plainly   **140 bespeak** address   **141 out of thy star** above your sphere, position
142 prescripts orders   **143 his resort** his visits   **148 watch** state of sleepless-
ness   **149 lightness** lightheadedness.   **declension** decline, deterioration (with a
pun on the grammatical sense)   **151 all we** all of us, or, into everything that we
156 Take this from this (The actor probably gestures, indicating that he means
his head from his shoulders, or his staff of office or chain from his hands or neck, or
something similar.)   **159 center** middle point of the earth (which is also the center
of the Ptolemaic universe).   **try** test, judge   **162 loose** (as one might release an animal that is being mated)   **163 arras** hanging, tapestry

Mark the encounter. If he love her not
And be not from his reason fall'n thereon,°   165
Let me be no assistant for a state,
But keep a farm and carters.°

KING.   We will try it.

Enter HAMLET *[reading on a book].*

QUEEN. But look where sadly° the poor wretch comes reading.

POLONIUS. Away, I do beseech you both, away.
I'll board° him presently.° O, give me leave.°   170

Exeunt KING *and* QUEEN *[with attendants].*

How does my good Lord Hamlet?

HAMLET. Well, God-a-mercy.°

POLONIUS. Do you know me, my lord?

HAMLET. Excellent well. You are a fishmonger.°

POLONIUS. Not I, my lord.   175

HAMLET. Then I would you were so honest a man.

POLONIUS. Honest, my lord?

HAMLET. Ay, sir. To be honest, as this world goes, is to be one man
picked out of ten thousand.

POLONIUS. That's very true, my lord.   180

HAMLET. For if the sun breed maggots in a dead dog, being a good kissing carrion°—Have you a daughter?

POLONIUS. I have, my lord.

HAMLET. Let her not walk i' the sun.° Conception° is a blessing, but as
your daughter may conceive, friend, look to 't.   185

POLONIUS *[aside].* How say you by that? Still harping on my daughter.
Yet he knew me not at first; 'a° said I was a fishmonger. 'A is far
gone. And truly in my youth I suffered much extremity for love,
very near this. I'll speak to him again.—What do you read, my lord?

HAMLET. Words, words, words.   190

POLONIUS. What is the matter,° my lord?

HAMLET. Between who?

POLONIUS. I mean, the matter that you read, my lord.

HAMLET. Slanders, sir; for the satirical rogue says here that old men have
gray beards, that their faces are wrinkled, their eyes purging° thick   195
amber° and plum-tree gum, and that they have a plentiful lack of
wit,° together with most weak hams. All which, sir, though I most
powerfully and potently believe, yet I hold it not honesty° to have
it thus set down, for yourself, sir, shall grow old° as I am, if like a
crab you could go backward.   200

---

165 thereon on that account   **167 carters** wagon drivers   **168 sadly** seriously
170 board accost.   **presently** at once.   **give me leave** i.e., excuse me, leave me
alone. (Said to those he hurries offstage, including the King and Queen.)   **172 God-
a-mercy** God have mercy, i.e., thank you   **174 fishmonger** fish merchant
181–182 a good kissing carrion i.e., a good piece of flesh for kissing, or for the
sun to kiss   **184 i' the sun** in public (with additional implication of the sunshine of
princely favors).   **Conception** (1) understanding (2) pregnancy   **187 'a** he
191 matter substance. (But Hamlet plays on the sense of "basis for a dispute.")
195 purging discharging.   **196 amber** i.e., resin, like the resinous *plum-tree gum*
197 wit understanding   **198 honesty** decency, decorum   **199 old** as old

POLONIUS *[aside]*. Though this be madness, yet there is method in 't.—
    Will you walk out of the air,° my lord?

HAMLET. Into my grave.

POLONIUS. Indeed, that's out of the air. *[Aside.]* How pregnant° some-
    times his replies are! A happiness° that often madness hits on,   205
    which reason and sanity could not so prosperously° be delivered
    of. I will leave him and suddenly° contrive the means of meeting
    between him and my daughter.—My honorable lord, I will most
    humbly take my leave of you.

HAMLET. You cannot, sir, take from me anything that I will more will-   210
    ingly part withal°—except my life, except my life, except my life.
        Enter GUILDENSTERN *and* ROSENCRANTZ.

POLONIUS. Fare you well, my lord.

HAMLET. These tedious old fools!°

POLONIUS. You go to seek the Lord Hamlet. There he is.

ROSENCRANTZ *[to* POLONIUS*]*. God save you, sir!   215

                                    [Exit POLONIUS.*]*

GUILDENSTERN. My honored lord!

ROSENCRANTZ. My most dear lord!

HAMLET. My excellent good friends! How dost thou, Guildenstern? Ah,
    Rosencrantz! Good lads, how do you both?

ROSENCRANTZ. As the indifferent° children of the earth.   220

GUILDENSTERN. Happy in that we are not overhappy.
    On Fortune's cap we are not the very button.

HAMLET. Nor the soles of her shoe?

ROSENCRANTZ. Neither, my lord.

HAMLET. Then you live about her waist, or in the middle of her favors?° 225

GUILDENSTERN. Faith, her privates we.°

HAMLET. In the secret parts of Fortune? O, most true, she is a strumpet.°
    What news?

ROSENCRANTZ. None, my lord, but the world's grown honest.

HAMLET. Then is doomsday near. But your news is not true. Let me ques- 230
    tion more in particular. What have you, my good friends, deserved
    at the hands of Fortune that she sends you to prison hither?

GUILDENSTERN. Prison, my lord?

HAMLET. Denmark's a prison.

ROSENCRANTZ. Then is the world one.   235

HAMLET. A goodly one, in which there are many confines,° wards,° and
    dungeons, Denmark being one o' the worst.

ROSENCRANTZ. We think not so, my lord.

HAMLET. Why then 'tis none to you, for there is nothing either good or
    bad but thinking makes it so. To me it is a prison.   240

---

202 out of the air (The open air was considered dangerous for sick people.)
204 pregnant quick-witted, full of meaning.   **205 happiness** felicity of expression   **206 prosperously** successfully   **207 suddenly** immediately   **211 withal**
with   **213 old fools** i.e., old men like Polonius   **220 indifferent** ordinary, at neither extreme of fortune or misfortune   **225 favors** i.e., sexual favors   **226 her
privates we** i.e., (1) we are sexually intimate with Fortune, the fickle goddess who
bestows her favors indiscriminately (2) we are her private citizens   **227 strumpet**
prostitute. (A common epithet for indiscriminate Fortune; see line 452.)   **236 confines** places of confinement.   **wards** cells

ROSENCRANTZ. Why then, your ambition makes it one. 'Tis too narrow for your mind.

HAMLET. O God, I could be bounded in a nutshell and count myself a king of infinite space, were it not that I have bad dreams.

GUILDENSTERN. Which dreams indeed are ambition, for the very sub- 245 stance of the ambitious° is merely the shadow of a dream.

HAMLET. A dream itself is but a shadow.

ROSENCRANTZ. Truly, and I hold ambition of so airy and light a quality that it is but a shadow's shadow.

HAMLET. Then are our beggars bodies,° and our monarchs and out- 250 stretched° heroes the beggars' shadows. Shall we to the court? For, by my fay,° I cannot reason.

ROSENCRANTZ, GUILDENSTERN. We'll wait upon° you.

HAMLET. No such matter. I will not sort° you with the rest of my ser- vants, for, to speak to you like an honest man, I am most dreadfully 255 attended.° But, in the beaten way° of friendship, what make° you at Elsinore?

ROSENCRANTZ. To visit you, my lord, no other occasion.

HAMLET. Beggar that I am, I am even poor in thanks; but I thank you, and sure, dear friends, my thanks are too dear a halfpenny.° Were you 260 not sent for? Is it your own inclining? Is it a free° visitation? Come, come, deal justly with me. Come, come. Nay, speak.

GUILDENSTERN. What should we say, my lord?

HAMLET. Anything but to the purpose.° You were sent for, and there is a kind of confession in your looks which your modesties° have not 265 craft enough to color.° I know the good King and Queen have sent for you.

ROSENCRANTZ. To what end, my lord?

HAMLET. That you must teach me. But let me conjure° you, by the rights of our fellowship, by the consonancy of our youth,° by the obliga- 270 tion of our ever-preserved love, and by what more dear a better° proposer could charge° you withal, be even° and direct with me whether you were sent for or no.

ROSENCRANTZ [aside to GUILDENSTERN]. What say you?

HAMLET [aside]. Nay, then, I have an eye of° you.—If you love me, hold 275 not off.°

245–246 the very . . . ambitious that seemingly very substantial thing that the am- bitious pursue   **250 bodies** i.e., solid substances rather than shadows (since beg- gars are not ambitious)   **250–251 outstretched** (1) far-reaching in their ambition (2) elongated as shadows   **252 fay** faith   **253 wait upon** accompany, attend. (But Hamlet uses the phrase in the sense of providing menial service.)   **254 sort** class, categorize   **255–256 dreadfully attended** waited upon in slovenly fashion **256 beaten way** familiar path, tried-and-true course.   **make** do   **260 too dear a halfpenny** (1) too expensive at even a halfpenny, i.e., of little worth (2) too expen- sive *by* a halfpenny in return for worthless kindness   **261 free** voluntary **264 Anything but to the purpose** anything except a straightforward answer. (Said ironically.)   **265 modesties** sense of shame.   **266 color** disguise   **269 con- jure** adjure, entreat   **270 the consonancy of our youth** our closeness in our younger days   **271 better** more skillful   **272 charge** urge.   **even** straight, honest **275 of** on   **276 hold not off** don't hold back

GUILDENSTERN. My lord, we were sent for.

HAMLET. I will tell you why; so shall my anticipation prevent your discovery,° and your secrecy to the King and Queen molt no feather.° I have of late—but wherefore I know not—lost all my mirth, forgone all custom of exercises; and indeed it goes so heavily with my disposition that this goodly frame, the earth, seems to me a sterile promontory; this most excellent canopy, the air, look you, this brave° o'erhanging firmament, this majestical roof fretted° with golden fire, why, it appeareth nothing to me but a foul and pestilent congregation° of vapors. What a piece of work° is a man! How noble in reason, how infinite in faculties, in form and moving how express° and admirable, in action how like an angel, in apprehension° how like a god! The beauty of the world, the paragon of animals! And yet, to me, what is this quintessence° of dust? Man delights not me—no, nor woman neither, though by your smiling you seem to say so.   280   285   290

ROSENCRANTZ. My lord, there was no such stuff in my thoughts.

HAMLET. Why did you laugh, then, when I said man delights not me?

ROSENCRANTZ. To think, my lord, if you delight not in man, what Lenten entertainment° the players shall receive from you. We coted° them on the way, and hither are they coming to offer you service.   295

HAMLET. He that plays the king shall be welcome; His Majesty shall have tribute° of° me. The adventurous knight shall use his foil and target,° the lover shall not sigh gratis,° the humorous man° shall end his part in peace,° the clown shall make those laugh whose lungs are tickle o' the sear,° and the lady shall say her mind freely, or the blank verse shall halt° for 't. What players are they?   300

ROSENCRANTZ. Even those you were wont to take such delight in, the tragedians° of the city.   305

HAMLET. How chances it they travel? Their residence,° both in reputation and profit, was better both ways.

ROSENCRANTZ. I think their inhibition° comes by the means of the late° innovation.°

278–279 so . . . discovery in that way my saying it first will spare you from revealing the truth   **279 molt no feather** i.e., not diminish in the least   **284 brave** splendid   **fretted** adorned (with fretwork, as in a vaulted ceiling)   **286 congregation** mass.   **piece of work** masterpiece   **288 express** well-framed, exact, expressive   **288–289 apprehension** power of comprehending   **290 quintessence** the fifth essence of ancient philosophy, beyond earth, water, air, and fire, supposed to be the substance of the heavenly bodies and to be latent in all things   **295–296 Lenten entertainment** meager reception (appropriate to Lent)   **296 coted** overtook and passed by   **299 tribute** (1) applause (2) homage paid in money.   **of** from   **299–300 foil and target** sword and shield   **300 gratis** for nothing.   **humorous man** eccentric character, dominated by one trait or "humor"   **301 in peace** i.e., with full license   **302 tickle o' the sear** easy on the trigger, ready to laugh easily. (A *sear* is part of a gunlock.)   **303 halt** limp   **305 tragedians** actors   **306 residence** remaining in their usual place, i.e., in the city   **308 inhibition** formal prohibition (from acting plays in the city)   **late** recent.   **309 innovation** i.e., the new fashion in satirical plays performed by boy actors in the "private" theaters; or possibly a political uprising; or the strict limitations set on the theaters in London in 1600

HAMLET. Do they hold the same estimation they did when I was in the   310
    city? Are they so followed?

ROSENCRANTZ. No, indeed are they not.

HAMLET. How comes it? Do they grow rusty?

ROSENCRANTZ. Nay, their endeavor keeps° in the wonted° pace. But
    there is, sir, an aerie° of children, little eyases,° that cry out on the   315
    top of question° and are most tyrannically° clapped for 't. These
    are now the fashion, and so berattle° the common stages°—so they
    call them—that many wearing rapiers° are afraid of goose quills°
    and dare scarce come thither.

HAMLET. What, are they children? Who maintains 'em? How are they es-   320
    coted?° Will they pursue the quality° no longer than they can
    sing?° Will they not say afterwards, if they should grow themselves
    to common° players—as it is most like,° if their means are no bet-
    ter°—their writers do them wrong to make them exclaim against
    their own succession?°   325

ROSENCRANTZ. Faith, there has been much to-do° on both sides, and the
    nation holds it no sin to tar° them to controversy. There was for a
    while no money bid for argument unless the poet and the player
    went to cuffs in the question.°

HAMLET. Is 't possible?   330

GUILDENSTERN. O, there has been much throwing about of brains.

HAMLET. Do the boys carry it away?°

ROSENCRANTZ. Ay, that they do, my lord—Hercules and his load° too.°

HAMLET. It is not very strange; for my uncle is King of Denmark, and
    those that would make mouths° at him while my father lived give   335
    twenty, forty, fifty, a hundred ducats° apiece for his picture in lit-
    tle.° 'Sblood,° there is something in this more than natural, if phi-
    losophy° could find it out.

                                   A flourish [of trumpets within].

GUILDENSTERN. There are the players.

---

314 keeps continues.   **wonted** usual   **315 aerie** nest.   **eyases** young hawks
315–316 cry . . . question speak shrilly, dominating the controversy (in decrying
the public theaters)   **316 tyrannically** outrageously   **317 berattle** berate, clamor
against.   **common stages** public theaters   **318 many wearing rapiers** i.e., many
men of fashion, afraid to patronize the common players for fear of being satirized by
the poets writing for the boy actors.   **goose quills** i.e., pens of satirists   **320–321
escoted** maintained.   **321 quality** (acting) profession   **321–322 no longer . . .
sing** i.e., only until their voices change   **323 common** regular, adult   **like** likely
323–324 if . . . better if they find no better way to support themselves   **325 succession** i.e., future careers   **326 to-do** ado   **327 tar** set on (as dogs)   **327–329
There . . . question** i.e., for a while, no money was offered by the acting companies to playwrights for the plot to a play unless the satirical poets who wrote for the
boys and the adult actors came to blows in the play itself   **332 carry it away** i.e.,
win the day   **333 Hercules . . . load** (Thought to be an allusion to the sign of the
Globe Theatre, which was Hercules bearing the world on his shoulders.)   **313–333
How . . . load too** (The passage, omitted from the early quartos, alludes to the so-
called War of the Theaters, 1599-1602, the rivalry between the children's companies and the adult actors.)   **335 mouths** faces   **336 ducats** gold coins.   **336–337
in little** in miniature.   **337 'Sblood** by God's (Christ's) blood   **338 philosophy**
i.e., scientific inquiry

HAMLET. Gentlemen, you are welcome to Elsinore. Your hands, come 340
  then. Th' appurtenance° of welcome is fashion and ceremony. Let
  me comply° with you in this garb,° lest my extent° to the players,
  which, I tell you, must show fairly outwards,° should more appear
  like entertainment° than yours. You are welcome. But my uncle-
  father and aunt-mother are deceived.   345
GUILDENSTERN. In what, my dear lord?
HAMLET. I am but mad north-north-west.° When the wind is southerly I
  know a hawk from a handsaw.°
  Enter POLONIUS.
POLONIUS. Well be with you, gentlemen!
HAMLET. Hark you, Guildenstern, and you too; at each ear a hearer. That 350
  great baby you see there is not yet out of his swaddling clouts.°
ROSENCRANTZ. Haply° he is the second time come to them, for they say
  an old man is twice a child.
HAMLET. I will prophesy he comes to tell me of the players. Mark it.—
  You say right, sir, o' Monday morning, 'twas then indeed.   355
POLONIUS. My lord, I have news to tell you.
HAMLET. My lord, I have news to tell you. When Roscius° was an actor in
  Rome—
POLONIUS. The actors are come hither, my lord.
HAMLET. Buzz,° buzz!   360
POLONIUS. Upon my honor—
HAMLET. Then came each actor on his ass.
POLONIUS. The best actors in the world, either for tragedy, comedy,
  history, pastoral, pastoral-comical, historical-pastoral, tragical-
  historical, tragical-comical-historical-pastoral, scene individable,° 365
  or poem unlimited.° Seneca° cannot be too heavy, nor Plautus° too
  light. For the law of writ and the liberty,° these° are the only men.
HAMLET. O Jephthah, judge of Israel,° what a treasure hadst thou!
POLONIUS. What a treasure had he, my lord?
HAMLET. Why,   370
  "One fair daughter, and no more,
  The which he lovèd passing° well."

341 appurtenance proper accompaniment   **342 comply** observe the formalities
of courtesy   **garb** i.e., manner.   **my extent** that which I extend, i.e., my polite behavior   **343 show fairly outwards** show every evidence of cordiality
344 entertainment a (warm) reception   **347 north-north-west** just off true
north, only partly   **348 hawk, handsaw** i.e., two very different things, though also
perhaps meaning a mattock (or *back*) and a carpenter's cutting tool, respectively;
also birds, with a play on *hernshaw*, or heron   **351 swaddling clouts** cloths in
which to wrap a newborn baby   **352 Haply** perhaps   **357 Roscius** a famous
Roman actor who died in 62 B.C.   **360 Buzz** (An interjection used to denote stale
news.)   **365 scene individable** a play observing the unity of place; or perhaps one
that is unclassifiable, or performed without intermission   **366 poem unlimited** a
play disregarding the unities of time and place; one that is all-inclusive.   **Seneca**
writer of Latin tragedies.   **Plautus** writer of Latin comedy   **367 law ... liberty**
dramatic composition both according to the rules and disregarding the rules.
these i.e., the actors   **368 Jephthah ... Israel** (Jephthah had to sacrifice his
daughter; see Judges 11. Hamlet goes on to quote from a ballad on the theme.)
372 passing surpassingly

POLONIUS *[aside]*. Still on my daughter.

HAMLET. Am I not i' the right, old Jephthah?

POLONIUS. If you call me Jephthah, my lord, I have a daughter that I love   375
    passing well.

HAMLET. Nay, that follows not.

POLONIUS. What follows then, my lord?

HAMLET. Why,

      "As by lot,° God wot,"°   380

and then, you know,

      "It came to pass, as most like° it was"—

the first row° of the pious chanson° will show you more, for look
where my abridgement° comes.

Enter the Players.

You are welcome, masters; welcome, all. I am glad to see thee well.   385
Welcome, good friends. O, old friend! Why, thy face is valanced°
since I saw thee last. Com'st thou to beard° me in Denmark? What,
my young lady° and mistress! By 'r Lady,° your ladyship is nearer to
heaven than when I saw you last, by the altitude of a chopine.°
Pray God your voice, like a piece of uncurrent° gold, be not   390
cracked within the ring.° Masters, you are all welcome. We'll e'en
to 't° like French falconers, fly at anything we see. We'll have a
speech straight.° Come, give us a taste of your quality.° Come, a
passionate speech.

FIRST PLAYER. What speech, my good lord?   395

HAMLET. I heard thee speak me a speech once, but it was never acted, or
if it was, not above once, for the play, I remember, pleased not the
million; 'twas caviar to the general.° But it was—as I received it,
and others, whose judgments in such matters cried in the top of°
mine—an excellent play, well digested° in the scenes, set down   400
with as much modesty° as cunning.° I remember one said there
were no sallets° in the lines to make the matter savory, nor no matter in the phrase that might indict° the author of affectation, but
called it an honest method, as wholesome as sweet, and by very
much more handsome° than fine.° One speech in 't I chiefly loved: 405
'twas Aeneas' tale to Dido, and thereabout of it especially when he

---

380 lot chance. **wot** knows **382 like** likely, probable **383 row** stanza.
chanson ballad, song **384 my abridgment** something that cuts short my conversation; also, a diversion **386 valanced** fringed (with a beard) **387 beard** confront, challenge (with obvious pun) **388 young lady** i.e., boy playing women's
parts **By 'r Lady** by Our Lady **389 chopine** thick-soled shoe of Italian fashion
390 uncurrent not passable as lawful coinage **391 cracked ... ring** i.e.,
changed from adolescent to male voice, no longer suitable for women's roles.
(Coins featured rings enclosing the sovereign's head; if the coin was cracked within
this ring, it was unfit for currency.) **391–392 e'en to 't** go at it **393 straight** at
once **quality** professional skill **398 caviar to the general** caviar to the multitude, i.e., a choice dish too elegant for coarse tastes **399 cried in the top of** i.e.,
spoke with greater authority than **400 digested** arranged, ordered **401 modesty**
moderation, restraint. **cunning** skill **402 sallets** i.e., something savory, spicy im-
proprieties **403 indict** convict **405 handsome** well-proportioned. **fine** elaborately ornamented, showy

speaks of Priam's slaughter.° If it live in your memory, begin at this
line: let me see, let me see—
    "The rugged Pyrrhus,° like th' Hyrcanian° beast"—
'Tis not so. It begins with Pyrrhus: 410
    "The rugged° Pyrrhus, he whose sable° arms,
    Black as his purpose, did the night resemble
    When he lay couchèd° in the ominous horse,°
    Hath now this dread and black complexion smeared
    With heraldry more dismal.° Head to foot   415
    Now is he total gules,° horridly tricked°
    With blood of fathers, mothers, daughters, sons,
    Baked and impasted° with the parching streets,°
    That lend a tyrannous° and a damnèd light
    To their lord's° murder. Roasted in wrath and fire,   420
    And thus o'ersizèd° with coagulate gore,
    With eyes like carbuncles,° the hellish Pyrrhus
    Old grandsire Priam seeks."
So proceed you.
POLONIUS. 'Fore God, my lord, well spoken, with good accent and good   425
    discretion.
FIRST PLAYER.   "Anon he finds him
    Striking too short at Greeks. His antique° sword,
    Rebellious to his arm, lies where it falls,
    Repugnant° to command. Unequal matched,   430
    Pyrrhus at Priam drives, in rage strikes wide,
    But with the whiff and wind of his fell° sword
    Th' unnervèd° father falls. Then senseless Ilium,°
    Seeming to feel this blow, with flaming top
    Stoops to his° base, and with a hideous crash   435
    Takes prisoner Pyrrhus' ear. For, lo! His sword,
    Which was declining° on the milky° head
    Of reverend Priam, seemed i' th' air to stick.
    So as a painted° tyrant Pyrrhus stood,

---

407 Priam's slaughter the slaying of the ruler of Troy, when the Greeks finally
took the city   **409 Pyrrhus** a Greek hero in the Trojan War, also known as Neop-
tolemus, son of Achilles—another avenging son.   **Hyrcanian beast** i.e., tiger. (On
the death of Priam, see Virgil, *Aeneid*, 2.506 ff.; compare the whole speech with
Marlowe's *Dido Queen of Carthage*, 2.1.214 ff. On the *Hyrcanian* tiger, see
Aeneid, 4.366–367. Hyrcania is on the Caspian Sea.)   **411 rugged** shaggy, savage.
sable black (for reasons of camouflage during the episode of the Trojan horse)
413 couchèd concealed.   **ominous horse** fateful Trojan horse, by which the
Greeks gained access to Troy   **415 dismal** ill-omened   **416 total gules** entirely
red. (A heraldic term.)   **tricked** spotted and smeared. (Heraldic.)   **418 impasted**
crusted, like a thick paste.   **with . . . streets** by the parching heat of the streets
(because of the fires everywhere)   **419 tyrannous** cruel   **420 their lord's** i.e.,
Priam's   **421 o'ersizèd** covered as with size or glue   **422 carbuncles** large fiery-
red precious stones thought to emit their own light   **428 antique** ancient, long-
used   **430 Repugnant** disobedient, resistant   **432 fell** cruel   **433 unnervèd**
strengthless.   **senseless Ilium** inanimate citadel of Troy   **435 his** its   **437 declining** descending.   **milky** white-haired   **439 painted** i.e., painted in a picture

And, like a neutral to his will and matter,°   440
Did nothing.
But as we often see against° some storm
A silence in the heavens, the rack° stand still,
The bold winds speechless, and the orb° below
As hush as death, anon the dreadful thunder   445
Doth rend the region,° so, after Pyrrhus' pause,
A rousèd vengeance sets him new a-work
And never did the Cyclops'° hammers fall
On Mars's armor forged for proof eterne°
With less remorse° than Pyrrhus' bleeding sword   450
Now falls on Priam.
Out, out, thou strumpet Fortune! All you gods
In general synod° take away her power!
Break all the spokes and fellies° from her wheel,
And bowl the round nave° down the hill of heaven°   455
As low as to the fiends!"

POLONIUS. This is too long.

HAMLET. It shall to the barber's with your beard.—Prithee, say on. He's
for a jig° or a tale of bawdry, or he sleeps. Say on; come to
Hecuba.°   460

FIRST PLAYER. "But who, ah woe! had° seen the moblèd° queen"—

HAMLET. "The moblèd queen?"

POLONIUS. That's good. "Moblèd queen" is good.

FIRST PLAYER. "Run barefoot up and down, threat'ning the flames°
With bisson rheum,° a clout° upon that head   465
Where late° the diadem stood, and, for a robe,
About her lank and all o'erteemèd° loins
A blanket, in the alarm of fear caught up—
Who this had seen, with tongue in venom steeped,
'Gainst Fortune's state° would treason have pronounced.°   470
But if the gods themselves did see her then
When she saw Pyrrhus make malicious sport
In mincing with his sword her husband's limbs,
The instant burst of clamor that she made,
Unless things mortal move them not at all,   475
Would have made milch° the burning eyes of heaven,°
And passion° in the gods."

440 like ... matter i.e., as though suspended between his intention and its fulfillment   **442 against** just before   **443 rack** mass of clouds   **444 orb** globe, earth
446 region sky   **448 Cyclops** giant armor makers in the smithy of Vulcan
449 proof eterne eternal resistance to assault   **450 remorse** pity   **453 synod** assembly   **454 fellies** pieces of wood forming the rim of a wheel   **455 nave** hub.
hill of heaven Mount Olympus   **459 jig** comic song and dance often given at the
end of a play   **460 Hecuba** wife of Priam   **461 who ... had** anyone who had
(also in line 469).   **moblèd** muffled   **464 threat'ning the flames** i.e., weeping
hard enough to dampen the flames   **465 bisson rheum** blinding tears.   **clout**
cloth   **466 late** lately   **467 all o'erteemèd** utterly worn out with bearing children
470 state rule, managing.   **pronounced** proclaimed   **476 milch** milky, moist
with tears.   **burning eyes of heaven** i.e., heavenly bodies   **477 passion** overpowering emotion

POLONIUS. Look whe'er° he has not turned his color and has tears in 's
eyes. Prithee, no more.

HAMLET. 'Tis well; I'll have thee speak out the rest of this soon.—Good   480
my lord, will you see the players well bestowed?° Do you hear, let
them be well used, for they are the abstract° and brief chronicles of
the time. After your death you were better have a bad epitaph than
their ill report while you live.

POLONIUS. My lord, I will use them according to their desert.   485

HAMLET. God's bodikin,° man, much better. Use every man after his
desert, and who shall scape whipping? Use them after° your own
honor and dignity. The less they deserve, the more merit is in your
bounty. Take them in.

POLONIUS. Come, sirs.   490

[Exit.]

HAMLET. Follow him, friends. We'll hear a play tomorrow. *[As they start
to leave,* HAMLET *detains the* FIRST PLAYER.*]* Dost thou hear me, old
friend? Can you play *The Murder of Gonzago?*

FIRST PLAYER. Ay, my lord.

HAMLET. We'll ha 't° tomorrow night. You could, for a need, study° a   495
speech of some dozen or sixteen lines which I would set down and
insert in 't, could you not?

FIRST PLAYER. Ay, my lord.

HAMLET. Very well. Follow that lord, and look you mock him not. *(Exeunt Players.)* My good friends, I'll leave you till night. You are wel-   500
come to Elsinore.

ROSENCRANTZ. Good my lord!

*Exeunt [*ROSENCRANTZ *and* GUILDENSTERN*].*

HAMLET. Ay, so, goodbye to you.—Now I am alone.
O, what a rogue and peasant slave am I!
Is it not monstrous that this player here,   505
But° in a fiction, in a dream of passion,
Could force his soul so to his own conceit°
That from her working° all his visage wanned,°
Tears in his eyes, distraction in his aspect,°
A broken voice, and his whole function suiting   510
With forms to his conceit?° And all for nothing!
For Hecuba!
What's Hecuba to him, or he to Hecuba,
That he should weep for her? What would he do
Had he the motive and the cue for passion   515
That I have? He would drown the stage with tears
And cleave the general ear° with horrid° speech,

---

478 whe'er whether   **481 bestowed** lodged   **482 abstract** summary account
486 God's bodikin by God's (Christ's) little body, *bodykin.* (Not to be confused
with *bodkin,* "dagger.")   **487 after** according to   **495 ha 't** have it   **study** memorize   **506 But** merely   **507 force . . . conceit** bring his innermost being so entirely into accord with his conception (of the role)   **508 from her working** as a
result of, or in response to, his soul's activity.   **wanned** grew pale   **509 aspect**
look, glance   **510–511 his whole . . . conceit** all his bodily powers responding
with actions to suit his thought   **517 the general ear** everyone's ear.   **horrid**
horrible

Make mad the guilty and appall° the free,°
Confound the ignorant,° and amaze° indeed
The very faculties of eyes and ears. Yet I,   520
A dull and muddy-mettled° rascal, peak°
Like John-a-dreams,° unpregnant of° my cause,
And can say nothing—no, not for a king
Upon whose property° and most dear life
A damned defeat° was made. Am I a coward?   525
Who calls me villain? Breaks my pate° across?
Plucks off my beard and blows it in my face?
Tweaks me by the nose? Gives me the lie i' the throat°
As deep as to the lungs? Who does me this?
Ha, 'swounds,° I should take it; for it cannot be   530
But I am pigeon-livered° and lack gall
To make oppression bitter,° or ere this
I should ha' fatted all the region kites°
With this slave's offal.° Bloody, bawdy villain!
Remorseless,° treacherous, lecherous, kindless° villain!   535
O, vengeance!
Why, what an ass am I! This is most brave,°
That I, the son of a dear father murdered,
Prompted to my revenge by heaven and hell,
Must like a whore unpack my heart with words   540
And fall a-cursing, like a very drab,°
A scullion!° Fie upon 't, foh! About,° my brains!
Hum, I have heard
That guilty creatures sitting at a play
Have by the very cunning° of the scene°   545
Been struck so to the soul that presently°
They have proclaimed their malefactions;
For murder, though it have no tongue, will speak
With most miraculous organ. I'll have these players
Play something like the murder of my father   550
Before mine uncle. I'll observe his looks;
I'll tent° him to the quick.° If 'a do blench,°
I know my course. The spirit that I have seen

518 appall (literally, make pale.)   **free** innocent   **519 Confound the ignorant**
i.e., dumbfound those who know nothing of the crime that has been committed.
amaze stun   **521 muddy-mettled** dull-spirited.   **peak** mope, pine   **522 John-a-**
dreams a sleepy, dreaming idler.   **unpregnant of** not quickened by   **524 prop-**
erty i.e., the crown; also character, quality   **525 damned defeat** damnable act of
destruction   **526 pate** head   **528 Gives . . . throat** calls me an out-and-out liar
530 'swounds by his (Christ's) wounds   **531 pigeon-livered** (The pigeon or dove
was popularly supposed to be mild because it secreted no gall.)   **532 bitter** i.e.,
bitter to me   **533 region kites** kites (birds of prey) of the air   **534 offal** entrails
535 Remorseless pitiless.   **kindless** unnatural   **537 brave** fine, admirable. (Said
ironically.)   **541 drab** whore   **542 scullion** menial kitchen servant (apt to be foul-
mouthed).   **About** about it, to work   **545 cunning** art, skill.   **scene** dramatic
presentation   **546 presently** at once   **552 tent** probe.   **the quick** the tender
part of a wound, the core.   **blench** quail, flinch

May be the devil, and the devil hath power
T' assume a pleasing shape; yea, and perhaps,   555
Out of my weakness and my melancholy,
As he is very potent with such spirits,°
Abuses° me to damn me. I'll have grounds
More relative° than this. The play's the thing
Wherein I'll catch the conscience of the King.   560

Exit.

3.1   *Enter* KING, QUEEN, POLONIUS, OPHELIA, ROSENCRANTZ, GUILDERNSTERN, *lords.*

KING. And can you by no drift of conference°
    Get from him why he puts on this confusion,
    Grating so harshly all his days of quiet
    With turbulent and dangerous lunacy?
ROSENCRANTZ. He does confess he feels himself distracted,   5
    But from what cause 'a will by no means speak.
GUILDENSTERN. Nor do we find him forward° to be sounded,°
    But with a crafty madness keeps aloof
    When we would bring him on to some confession
    Of his true state.
QUEEN.   Did he receive you well?   10
ROSENCRANTZ. Most like a gentleman.
GUILDENSTERN. But with much forcing of his disposition.°
ROSENCRANTZ. Niggard° of question,° but of our demands
    Most free in his reply.
QUEEN.   Did you assay° him
    To any pastime?   15
ROSENCRANTZ. Madam, it so fell out that certain players
    We o'erraught° on the way. Of these we told him,
    And there did seem in him a kind of joy
    To hear of it. They are here about the court,
    And, as I think, they have already order   20
    This night to play before him.
POLONIUS.   'Tis most true,
    And he beseeched me to entreat Your Majesties
    To hear and see the matter.
KING. With all my heart, and it doth much content me
    To hear him so inclined.   25
    Good gentlemen, give him a further edge°
    And drive his purpose into these delights.
ROSENCRANTZ. We shall, my lord.

                        Exeunt ROSENCRANTZ *and* GUILDENSTERN.
KING.   Sweet Gertrude, leave us too,
    For we have closely° sent for Hamlet hither,

---

557 spirits humors (of melancholy)   **558 Abuses** deludes   **559 relative** cogent,
pertinent   **3.1. Location: The castle.**   **1 drift of conference** directing of conversation   **7 forward** willing.   **sounded** questioned   **12 disposition** inclination
13 Niggard stingy.   **question** conversation   **14 assay** try to win   **17 o'er-
raught** overtook   **26 edge** incitement   **29 closely** privately

That he, as 'twere by accident, may here   30
Affront° Ophelia.
Her father and myself, lawful espials,°
Will so bestow ourselves that seeing, unseen,
We may of their encounter frankly judge,
And gather by him, as he is behaved,   35
If 't be th' affliction of his love or no
That thus he suffers for.
QUEEN.   I shall obey you.
And for your part, Ophelia, I do wish
That your good beauties be the happy cause
Of Hamlet's wildness. So shall I hope your virtues   40
Will bring him to his wonted° way again,
To both your honors.
OPHELIA.   Madam, I wish it may.

[Exit QUEEN.*]*

POLONIUS. Ophelia, walk you here.—Gracious,° so please you,
We will bestow° ourselves. *[To* OPHELIA.*]* Read on this book,

[giving her a book]

That show of such an exercise° may color°   45
Your loneliness.° We are oft to blame in this—
'Tis too much proved°—that with devotion's visage
And pious action we do sugar o'er
The devil himself.
KING *[aside].* O, 'tis too true!   50
How smart a lash that speech doth give my conscience!
The harlot's cheek, beautied with plastering art,
Is not more ugly to° the thing° that helps it
Than is my deed to my most painted word.
O heavy burden!   55
POLONIUS. I hear him coming. Let's withdraw, my lord.

[The KING *and* POLONIUS *withdraw.°]*
Enter HAMLET. *[*OPHELIA *pretends to read a book.]*

HAMLET. To be, or not to be, that is the question:
Whether 'tis nobler in the mind to suffer
The slings° and arrows of outrageous fortune,
Or to take arms against a sea of troubles   60
And by opposing end them. To die, to sleep—
No more—and by a sleep to say we end
The heartache and the thousand natural shocks
That flesh is heir to. 'Tis a consummation
Devoutly to be wished. To die, to sleep;   65

---

31 Affront confront, meet   **32 espials** spies   **41 wonted** accustomed   **43 Gracious** Your Grace (i.e., the King)   **44 bestow** conceal   **45 exercise** religious exercise. (The book she reads is one of devotion.)   **color** give a plausible appearance
to **46 loneliness** being alone   **47 too much proved** too often shown to be true,
too often practiced   **53 to** compared to   **the thing** i.e., the cosmetic   **56 s.d.
withdraw** (The King and Polonius may retire behind an arras. The stage directions
specify that they "enter" again near the end of the scene.)   **59 slings** missiles

To sleep, perchance to dream. Ay, there's the rub,°
For in that sleep of death what dreams may come,
When we have shuffled° off this mortal coil,°
Must give us pause. There's the respect°
That makes calamity of so long life.°   70
For who would bear the whips and scorns of time,
Th' oppressor's wrong, the proud man's contumely,°
The pangs of disprized° love, the law's delay,
The insolence of office,° and the spurns°
That patient merit of th' unworthy takes,°   75
When he himself might his quietus° make
With a bare bodkin?° Who would fardels° bear,
To grunt and sweat under a weary life,
But that the dread of something after death,
The undiscovered country from whose bourn°   80
No traveler returns, puzzles the will,
And makes us rather bear those ills we have
Than fly to others that we know not of?
Thus conscience does make cowards of us all;
And thus the native hue° of resolution   85
Is sicklied o'er with the pale cast° of thought,
And enterprises of great pitch° and moment°
With this regard° their currents° turn awry
And lose the name of action.—Soft you° now,
The fair Ophelia. Nymph, in thy orisons°   90
Be all my sins remembered.
OPHELIA.   Good my lord,
How does your honor for this many a day?
HAMLET. I humbly thank you; well, well, well.
OPHELIA. My lord, I have remembrances of yours,
That I have longèd long to redeliver.   95
I pray you, now receive them.   *[She offers tokens.]*
HAMLET. No, not I, I never gave you aught.
OPHELIA. My honored lord, you know right well you did,
And with them words of so sweet breath composed
As made the things more rich. Their perfume lost,   100
Take these again, for to the noble mind
Rich gifts wax poor when givers prove unkind.
There, my lord.   *[She gives tokens.]*
HAMLET. Ha, ha! Are you honest?°

---

66 rub (Literally, an obstacle in the game of bowls.)   **68 shuffled** sloughed, cast
coil turmoil   **69 respect** consideration   **70 of . . . life** so long-lived, something
we willingly endure for so long (also suggesting that long life is itself a calamity)
72 contumely insolent abuse   **73 disprized** unvalued   **74 office** officialdom
spurns insults   **75 of . . . takes** receives from unworthy persons   **76 quietus** ac-
quitance; here, death   **77 a bare bodkin** a mere dagger, unsheathed   **fardels**
burdens   **80 bourn** frontier, boundary   **85 native hue** natural color, complexion   **86 cast** tinge, shade of color   **87 pitch** height (as of a falcon's flight)   **moment** importance   **88 regard** respect, consideration   **currents** courses   **89
Soft you** i.e., wait a minute, gently   **90 orisons** prayers   **104 honest** (1) truthful (2) chaste

OPHELIA. My lord?   105

HAMLET. Are you fair?°

OPHELIA. What means your lordship?

HAMLET. That if you be honest and fair, your honesty° should admit no discourse° to your beauty.

OPHELIA. Could beauty, my lord, have better commerce° than with hon- 110
esty?

HAMLET. Ay, truly, for the power of beauty will sooner transform honesty from what it is to a bawd than the force of honesty can translate beauty into his° likeness. This was sometime° a paradox,° but now the time° gives it proof. I did love you once. 115

OPHELIA. Indeed, my lord, you made me believe so.

HAMLET. You should not have believed me, for virtue cannot so inoculate° our old stock but we shall relish of it.° I loved you not.

OPHELIA. I was the more deceived.

HAMLET. Get thee to a nunnery.° Why wouldst thou be a breeder of sin- 120
ners? I am myself indifferent honest,° but yet I could accuse me of such things that it were better my mother had not borne me: I am very proud, revengeful, ambitious, with more offenses at my beck° than I have thoughts to put them in, imagination to give them shape, or time to act them in. What should such fellows as I do 125
crawling between earth and heaven? We are arrant knaves all; believe none of us. Go thy ways to a nunnery. Where's your father?

OPHELIA. At home, my lord.

HAMLET. Let the doors be shut upon him, that he may play the fool nowhere but in 's own house. Farewell. 130

OPHELIA. O, help him, you sweet heavens!

HAMLET. If thou dost marry, I'll give thee this plague for thy dowry: be thou as chaste as ice, as pure as snow, thou shalt not escape calumny. Get thee to a nunnery, farewell. Or, if thou wilt needs marry, marry a fool, for wise men know well enough what mon- 135
sters° you° make of them. To a nunnery, go, and quickly too. Farewell.

OPHELIA. Heavenly powers, restore him!

HAMLET. I have heard of your paintings too, well enough. God hath given you one face, and you make yourselves another. You jig,° 140
you amble,° and you lisp, you nickname God's creatures,° and make your wantonness your ignorance.° Go to, I'll no more on 't;° it hath made me mad. I say we will have no more marriage. Those

106 fair (1) beautiful (2) just, honorable   **108 your honesty** your chastity
109 discourse to familiar dealings with   **110 commerce** dealings, intercourse
114 his its   **sometime** formerly   **a paradox** a view opposite to commonly held
opinion.   **115 the time** the present age   **117–118 inoculate** graft, be engrafted
to   **118 but . . . it** that we do not still have about us a taste of the old stock, i.e., retain our sinfulness   **120 nunnery** convent (with possibly an awareness that the
word was also used derisively to denote a brothel)   **121 indifferent honest** reasonably virtuous   **123 beck** command   **135–136 monsters** (An illusion to the
horns of a cuckold.)   **you** i.e., you women   **140 jig** dance   **141 amble** move
coyly   **you nickname . . . creatures** i.e., you give trendy names to things in place
of their God-given names   **142 make . . . ignorance** i.e., excuse your affectation
on the grounds of pretended ignorance   **on 't** of it

that are married already—all but one—shall live. The rest shall
keep as they are. To a nunnery, go.   145

Exit.

OPHELIA. O, what a noble mind is here o'erthrown!
    The courtier's, soldier's, scholar's, eye, tongue, sword,
    Th' expectancy° and rose° of the fair state,
    The glass of fashion and the mold of form,°
    Th' observed of all observers,° quite, quite down!   150
    And I, of ladies most deject and wretched,
    That sucked the honey of his music° vows,
    Now see that noble and most sovereign reason
    Like sweet bells jangled out of tune and harsh,
    That unmatched form and feature of blown° youth   155
    Blasted° with ecstasy.° O, woe is me,
    T' have seen what I have seen, see what I see!
    Enter KING *and* POLONIUS.
KING. Love? His affections° do not that way tend;
    Nor what he spake, though it lacked form a little,
    Was not like madness. There's something in his soul   160
    O'er which his melancholy sits on brood,°
    And I do doubt° the hatch and the disclose°
    Will be some danger; which for to prevent,
    I have in quick determination
    Thus set it down:° he shall with speed to England   165
    For the demand of° our neglected tribute.
    Haply the seas and countries different
    With variable objects° shall expel
    This something-settled matter in his heart,°
    Whereon his brains still° beating puts him thus   170
    From fashion of himself.° What think you on 't?
POLONIUS. It shall do well. But yet do I believe
    The origin and commencement of his grief
    Sprung from neglected love.—How now, Ophelia?
    You need not tell us what Lord Hamlet said;   175
    We heard it all.—My lord, do as you please,
    But, if you hold it fit, after the play
    Let his queen-mother° all alone entreat him
    To show his grief. Let her be round° with him;
    And I'll be placed, so please you, in the ear   180

---

148 **expectancy** hope   **rose** ornament   149 **The glass . . . form** the mirror of
true fashioning and the pattern of courtly behavior   150 **Th' observed . . .
observers** i.e., the center of attention and honor in the court   152 **music** musical, sweetly uttered   155 **blown** blooming   156 **Blasted** withered   **ecstasy**
madness   158 **affections** emotions, feelings   161 **sits on brood** sits like a
bird on a nest, about to *hatch* mischief (line 169)   162 **doubt** fear   **disclose**
disclosure, hatching   165 **set it down** resolved   166 **For . . . of** to demand
168 **variable objects** various sights and surroundings to divert him   169 **This
something . . . heart** the strange matter settled in his heart   170 **still** continually
171 **From . . . himself** out of his natural manner   178 **queen-mother** queen and
mother   179 **round** blunt

Of all their conference. If she find him not,°
To England send him, or confine him where
Your wisdom best shall think.

KING.   It shall be so.
Madness in great ones must not unwatched go.

Exeunt.

3.2   *Enter* HAMLET *and three of the Players.*

HAMLET. Speak the speech, I pray you, as I pronounced it to you, trip-
pingly on the tongue. But if you mouth it, as many of our players°
do, I had as lief° the town crier spoke my lines. Nor do not saw the
air too much with your hand, thus, but use all gently; for in the very
torrent, tempest, and, as I may say, whirlwind of your passion, you   5
must acquire and beget a temperance that may give it smoothness.
O, it offends me to the soul to hear a robustious° periwig-pated°
fellow tear a passion to tatters, to very rags, to split the ears of the
groundlings,° who for the most part are capable of° nothing but inexplicable dumb shows° and noise. I would have such a fellow   10
whipped for o'erdoing Termagant.° It out-Herods Herod.° Pray
you, avoid it.

FIRST PLAYER. I warrant your honor.

HAMLET. Be not too tame neither, but let your own discretion be your
tutor. Suit the action to the word, the word to the action, with this   15
special observance, that you o'erstep not the modesty° of nature.
For anything so o'erdone is from° the purpose of playing, whose
end, both at the first and now, was and is to hold as 't were the mirror up to nature, to show virtue her feature, scorn° her own image,
and the very age and body of the time° his° form and pressure.°   20
Now this overdone or come tardy off,° though it makes the unskill-
ful° laugh, cannot but make the judicious grieve, the censure of the
which one° must in your allowance° o'erweigh a whole theater of
others. O, there be players that I have seen play, and heard others
praise, and that highly, not to speak it profanely,° that, neither hav-   25

181 find him not fails to discover what is troubling him   **3.2. Location: The
castle.   2 our players** players nowadays.   **3 I had as lief** I would just as soon
7 robustious violent, boisterous.   **periwig-pated** wearing a wig   **9 groundlings**
spectators who paid least and stood in the yard of the theater   **capable of** able to
understand   **10 dumb shows** mimed performances, often used before Shakespeare's time to precede a play or each act   **11 Termagant** a supposed deity of the
Mohammedans, not found in any English medieval play but elsewhere portrayed as
violent and blustering   **Herod** Herod of Jewry. (A character in *The Slaughter of
the Innocents* and other cycle plays. The part was played with great noise and fury.)
16 modesty restraint, moderation   **17 from** contrary to   **19 scorn** i.e., something foolish and deserving of scorn   **20 the very . . . time** i.e., the present state of
affairs   **his** its.   **pressure** stamp, impressed character   **21 come tardy off** inade-
quately done   **21–22 the unskillful** those lacking in judgment   **22–23 the censure . . . one** the judgment of even one of whom   **23 your allowance** your scale
of values   **25 not . . . profanely** (Hamlet anticipates his idea in lines 27–29 that
some men were not made by God at all.)

ing th' accent of Christians° nor the gait of Christian, pagan, nor
man,° have so strutted and bellowed that I have thought some of
nature's journeymen° had made men and not made them well, they
imitated humanity so abominably.°

FIRST PLAYER. I hope we have reformed that indifferently° with us, sir.   30

HAMLET. O, reform it altogether. And let those that play your clowns
speak no more than is set down for them; for there be of them°
that will themselves laugh, to set on some quantity of barren° spectators to laugh too, though in the meantime some necessary question of the play be then to be considered. That's villainous, and   35
shows a most pitiful ambition in the fool that uses it. Go make you
ready.

[Exeunt Players.]

Enter POLONIUS, GUILDENSTERN, *and* ROSENCRANTZ.

How now, my lord, will the King hear this piece of work?

POLONIUS. And the Queen too, and that presently.°

HAMLET. Bid the players make haste.   40

[Exit POLONIUS.*]*

Will you two help to hasten them?

ROSENCRANTZ. Ay, my lord.

Exeunt they two.

HAMLET.   What ho, Horatio!

Enter HORATIO.

HORATIO. Here, sweet lord, at your service.

HAMLET. Horatio, thou art e'en as just a man
As e'er my conversation coped withal.°   45

HORATIO. O, my dear lord—

HAMLET.   Nay, do not think I flatter,
For what advancement may I hope from thee
That no revenue hast but thy good spirits
To feed and clothe thee? Why should the poor be flattered?
No, let the candied° tongue lick absurd pomp,   50
And crook the pregnant° hinges of the knee
Where thrift° may follow fawning. Dost thou hear?
Since my dear soul was mistress of her choice
And could of men distinguish her election,°
Sh' hath sealed thee° for herself, for thou hast been   55
As one, in suffering all, that suffers nothing,
A man that Fortune's buffets and rewards
Hast ta'en with equal thanks; and blest are those
Whose blood° and judgment are so well commeddled°

26 Christians i.e., ordinary decent folk   **26–27 nor man** i.e., nor any human
being at all   **28 journeymen** laborers who are not yet masters in their trade
29 abominably (Shakespeare's usual spelling, *abbominably*, suggests a literal
though etymologically incorrect meaning, "removed from human nature.")   **30 indifferently** tolerably   **32 of them** some among them   **33 barren** i.e., of wit
39 presently at once   **45 my . . . withal** my dealings encountered   **50 candied**
sugared, flattering   **51 pregnant** compliant   **52 thrift** profit   **54 could . . . election** could make distinguishing choices among persons   **55 sealed thee** (Literally,
as one would seal a legal document to mark possession.)   **59 blood** passion.
commeddled commingled

That they are not a pipe for Fortune's finger   60
To sound what stop° she please. Give me that man
That is not passion's slave, and I will wear him
In my heart's core, ay, in my heart of heart,
As I do thee.—Something too much of this.—
There is a play tonight before the King.   65
One scene of it comes near the circumstance
Which I have told thee of my father's death.
I prithee, when thou seest that act afoot,
Even with the very comment of thy soul°
Observe my uncle. If his occulted° guilt   70
Do not itself unkennel° in one speech,
It is a damnèd° ghost that we have seen,
And my imaginations are as foul
As Vulcan's stithy.° Give him heedful note,
For I mine eyes will rivet to his face,   75
And after we will both our judgments join
In censure of his seeming.°
HORATIO.   Well, my lord.
    If 'a steal aught° the whilst this play is playing
    And scape detecting, I will pay the theft.
    [Flourish.] Enter trumpets and kettledrums, KING, QUEEN, POLONIUS,
    OPHELIA, *[*ROSENCRANTZ, GUILDENSTERN, *and other lords, with guards*
    carrying torches].
HAMLET. They are coming to the play. I must be idle.°   80
    Get you a place.   *[The* KING, QUEEN, *and courtiers sit.]*
KING. How fares our cousin° Hamlet?
HAMLET. Excellent, i' faith, of the chameleon's dish:° I eat the air,
    promise-crammed. You cannot feed capons° so.
KING. I have nothing with° this answer, Hamlet. These words are not   85
    mine.°
HAMLET. No, nor mine now.° *[To* POLONIUS.*]* My lord, you played once i'
    th' university, you say?
POLONIUS. That did I, my lord, and was accounted a good actor.
HAMLET. What did you enact?   90
POLONIUS. I did enact Julius Caesar. I was killed i' the Capitol; Brutus
    killed me.

---

61 stop hole in a wind instrument for controlling the sound   **69 very . . . soul**
your most penetrating observation and consideration   **70 occulted** hidden
71 unkennel (As one would say of a fox driven from its lair.)   **72 damnèd** in
league with Satan   **74 stithy** smithy, place of stiths (anvils)   **77 censure of his**
seeming judgment of his appearance or behavior   **78 If 'a steal aught** if he gets
away with anything   **80 idle** (1) unoccupied (2) mad   **82 cousin** i.e., close relative   **83 chameleon's dish** (Chameleons were supposed to feed on air. Hamlet deliberately misinterprets the King's *fares* as "feeds." By his phrase *eat the air* he also
plays on the idea of feeding himself with the promise of succession, of being the
heir.)   **84 capons** roosters castrated and *crammed* with feed to make them succu-
lent   **85 have . . . with** make nothing of, or gain nothing from   **86 are not mine**
do not respond to what I asked   **87 nor mine now** (Once spoken, words are
proverbially no longer the speaker's own—and hence should be uttered warily.)

HAMLET. It was a brute° part° of him to kill so capital a calf° there.—Be
    the players ready?

ROSENCRANTZ. Ay, my lord. They stay upon° your patience.   95

QUEEN. Come hither, my dear Hamlet, sit by me.

HAMLET. No, good Mother, here's metal° more attractive.

POLONIUS *[to the* KING*].* O, ho, do you mark that?

HAMLET. Lady, shall I lie in your lap?

                                          [Lying down at OPHELIA*'s feet.]*

OPHELIA. No, my lord.   100

HAMLET. I mean, my head upon your lap?

OPHELIA. Ay, my lord.

HAMLET. Do you think I meant country matters?°

OPHELIA. I think nothing, my lord.

HAMLET. That's a fair thought to lie between maids' legs.   105

OPHELIA. What is, my lord?

HAMLET. Nothing.°

OPHELIA. You are merry, my lord.

HAMLET. Who, I?

OPHELIA. Ay, my lord.   110

HAMLET. O God, your only jig maker.° What should a man do but be
    merry? For look you how cheerfully my mother looks, and my fa-
    ther died within 's° two hours.

OPHELIA. Nay, 'tis twice two months, my lord.

HAMLET. So long? Nay then, let the devil wear black, for I'll have a suit of 115
    sables.° O heavens! Die two months ago, and not forgotten yet?
    Then there's hope a great man's memory may outlive his life half a
    year. But, by 'r Lady, 'a must build churches, then, or else shall 'a
    suffer not thinking on,° with the hobbyhorse, whose epitaph is
    "For O, for O, the hobbyhorse is forgot."°   120

The trumpets sound. Dumb show follows.

    Enter a King and a Queen [very lovingly]; the Queen em-
bracing him, and he her. [She kneels, and makes show of protes-
tation unto him.] He takes her up, and declines his head upon
her neck. He lies him down upon a bank of flowers. She, seeing

---

93 brute (The Latin meaning of *brutus,* "stupid," was often used punningly with
the name Brutus.)   **part** (1) deed (2) role   **calf** fool   **95 stay upon** await
97 metal substance that is *attractive,* i.e., magnetic, but with suggestion also of
mettle, "disposition"   **103 country matters** sexual intercourse (making a bawdy
pun on the first syllable of *country*)   **107 Nothing** the figure zero or naught, suggesting the female sexual anatomy. (*Thing* not infrequently has a bawdy connotation of male or female anatomy, and the reference here could be male.)   **111 only**
jig maker very best composer of jigs, i.e., pointless merriment. (Hamlet replies sardonically to Ophelia's observation that he is merry by saying, "If you're looking for
someone who is really merry, you've come to the right person.")   **113 within 's**
within this (i.e., these)   **115–116 suit of sables** garments trimmed with the fur of
the sable and hence suited for a wealthy person, not a mourner (but with a pun on
sable, "black," ironically suggesting mourning once again)   **119 suffer . . . on** undergo oblivion   **120 For . . . forgot** (Verse of a song occurring also in *Love's*
Labor's Lost, 3.1.27–28. The hobbyhorse was a character made up to resemble a
horse and rider, appearing in the morris dance and such May-game sports. This song
laments the disappearance of such customs under pressure from the Puritans.)

him asleep, leaves him. Anon comes in another man, takes off
his crown, kisses it, pours poison in the sleeper's ears, and leaves
him. The Queen returns, finds the King dead, makes passionate
action. The Poisoner with some three or four come in again,
seem to condole with her. The dead body is carried away. The
Poisoner woos the Queen with gifts; she seems harsh awhile, but
in the end accepts love.

[Exeunt players.]

OPHELIA. What means this, my lord?

HAMLET. Marry, this' miching mallico;° it means mischief.

OPHELIA. Belike° this show imports the argument° of the play.

Enter Prologue.

HAMLET. We shall know by this fellow. The players cannot keep coun-
sel;° they'll tell all.					125

OPHELIA. Will 'a tell us what this show meant?

HAMLET. Ay, or any show that you will show him. Be not you° ashamed
to show, he'll not shame to tell you what it means.

OPHELIA. You are naught,° you are naught. I'll mark the play.

PROLOGUE. For us, and for our tragedy,					130
	Here stooping° to your clemency,
	We beg your hearing patiently.

[Exit.]

HAMLET. Is this a prologue, or the posy of a ring?°

OPHELIA. 'Tis brief, my lord.

HAMLET. As woman's love.					135

Enter [two Players as] King and Queen.

PLAYER KING. Full thirty times hath Phoebus' cart° gone round
	Neptune's salt wash° and Tellus'° orbèd ground,
	And thirty dozen moons with borrowed° sheen
	About the world have times twelve thirties been,
	Since love our hearts and Hymen° did our hands					140
	Unite commutual° in most sacred bands.°

PLAYER QUEEN. So many journeys may the sun and moon
	Make us again count o'er ere love be done!
	But, woe is me, you are so sick of late,
	So far from cheer and from your former state,					145
	That I distrust° you. Yet, though I distrust,
	Discomfort° you, my lord, it nothing° must.
	For women's fear and love hold quantity;°
	In neither aught, or in extremity.°

122 this' miching mallico this is sneaking mischief   **123 Belike** probably
argument plot   **124–125 counsel** secret   **127 Be not you** provided you are not
129 naught indecent. (Ophelia is reacting to Hamlet's pointed remarks about not
being ashamed to show all.)   **131 stooping** bowing   **133 posy . . . ring** brief
motto in verse inscribed in a ring   **136 Phoebus' cart** the sun-god's chariot, making its yearly cycle   **137 salt wash** the sea   **Tellus** goddess of the earth, of the
orbèd ground   **138 borrowed** i.e., reflected   **140 Hymen** god of matrimony
141 commutual mutually   **bands** bonds   **146 distrust** am anxious about
147 Discomfort distress   **nothing** not at all   **148 hold quantity** keep proportion with one another   **149 In . . . extremity** i.e., women fear and love either too
little or too much, but the two, fear and love, are equal in either case

Now, what my love is, proof° hath made you know,   150
And as my love is sized,° my fear is so.
Where love is great, the littlest doubts are fear;
Where little fears grow great, great love grows there.

PLAYER KING. Faith, I must leave thee, love, and shortly too;
My operant powers° their functions leave to do.°   155
And thou shalt live in this fair world behind,°
Honored, beloved; and haply one as kind
For husband shalt thou—

PLAYER QUEEN.   O, confound the rest!
Such love must needs be treason in my breast.
In second husband let me be accurst!   160
None° wed the second but who° killed the first.

HAMLET. Wormwood,° wormwood.

PLAYER QUEEN. The instances° that second marriage move°
Are base respects of thrift,° but none of love.
A second time I kill my husband dead   165
When second husband kisses me in bed.

PLAYER KING. I do believe you think what now you speak,
But what we do determine oft we break.
Purpose is but the slave to memory,°
Of violent birth, but poor validity,°   170
Which° now, like fruit unripe, sticks on the tree,
But fall unshaken when they mellow be.
Most necessary 'tis that we forget
To pay ourselves what to ourselves is debt.°
What to ourselves in passion we propose,   175
The passion ending, doth the purpose lose.
The violence of either grief or joy
Their own enactures° with themselves destroy.
Where joy most revels, grief doth most lament;
Grief joys, joy grieves, on slender accident.°   180
This world is not for aye,° nor 'tis not strange
That even our loves should with our fortunes change;
For 'tis a question left us yet to prove,
Whether love lead fortune, or else fortune love.
The great man down,° you mark his favorite flies;   185
The poor advanced makes friends of enemies.°

150 proof experience   **151 sized** in size   **155 operant powers** vital functions.
leave to do cease to perform   **156 behind** after I have gone   **161 None** i.e., let
no woman.   **but who** except the one who   **162 Wormwood** i.e., how bitter.
(Literally, a bitter-tasting plant.)   **163 instances** motives.   **move** motivate
164 base . . . thrift ignoble considerations of material prosperity   **169 Purpose
. . . memory** our good intentions are subject to forgetfulness   **170 validity**
strength, durability   **171 Which** i.e., purpose   **173–174 Most . . . debt** it's inevitable that in time we forget the obligations we have imposed on ourselves
178 enactures fulfillments   **179–180 Where . . . accident** the capacity for extreme joy and grief go together, and often one extreme is instantly changed into its
opposite on the slightest provocation   **181 aye** ever   **185 down** fallen in fortune
186 The poor . . . enemies when one of humble station is promoted, you see his
enemies suddenly becoming his friends

And hitherto° doth love on fortune tend;°
For who not needs° shall never lack a friend,
And who in want° a hollow friend doth try°
Directly seasons him° his enemy.   190
But, orderly to end where I begun,
Our wills and fates do so contrary run°
That our devices still° are overthrown;
Our thoughts are ours, their ends° none of our own.
So think thou wilt no second husband wed,   195
But die thy thoughts when thy first lord is dead.

PLAYER QUEEN. Nor° earth to me give food, nor heaven light,
Sport and repose lock from me day and night,°
To desperation turn my trust and hope,
An anchor's cheer° in prison be my scope!°   200
Each opposite that blanks° the face of joy
Meet what I would have well and it destroy!°
Both here and hence° pursue me lasting strife
If, once a widow, ever I be wife!

HAMLET. If she should break it now!   205

PLAYER KING. 'Tis deeply sworn. Sweet, leave me here awhile;
My spirits° grow dull, and fain I would beguile
The tedious day with sleep.

PLAYER QUEEN.   Sleep rock thy brain,
And never come mischance between us twain!

                              [He sleeps.] Exit [Player Queen].

HAMLET. Madam, how like you this play?   210

QUEEN. The lady doth protest too much,° methinks.

HAMLET. O, but she'll keep her word.

KING. Have you heard the argument?° Is there no offense in 't?

HAMLET. No, no, they do but jest,° poison in jest. No offense° i' the
world.   215

KING. What do you call the play?

HAMLET. *The Mousetrap.* Marry, how? Tropically.° This play is the image
of a murder done in Vienna. Gonzago is the Duke's° name, his
wife, Baptista. You shall see anon. 'Tis a knavish piece of work, but

---

187 hitherto up to this point in the argument, or, to this extent   **tend** attend
188 who not needs he who is not in need (of wealth)   **189 who in want** he
who, being in need   **try** test (his generosity)   **190 seasons him** ripens him into
192 Our . . . run what we want and what we get go so contrarily   **193 devices
still** intentions continually   **194 ends** results   **197 Nor** let neither   **198 Sport
. . . night** may day deny me its pastimes and night its repose   **200 anchor's
cheer** anchorite's or hermit's fare   **my scope** the extent of my happiness
201 blanks causes to blanch or grow pale   **201–202 Each . . . destroy** may
every adverse thing that causes the face of joy to turn pale meet and destroy everything that I desire to see prosper   **203 hence** in the life hereafter   **207 spirits**
vital spirits   **211 doth . . . much** makes too many promises and protestations
213 argument plot   **214 jest** make believe   **213–214 offense . . . offense** cause
for objection . . . actual injury, crime   **217 Tropically** figuratively. (The First
Quarto reading, *trapically,* suggests a pun on *trap* in *Mousetrap.*)   **218 Duke's** i.e.,
King's. (A slip that may be due to Shakespeare's possible source, the alleged murder
of the Duke of Urbino by Luigi Gonzaga in 1538.)

what of that? Your Majesty, and we that have free° souls, it touches   220
us not. Let the galled jade° wince, our withers° are unwrung.°
Enter Lucianus.
This is one Lucianus, nephew to the King.

OPHELIA. You are as good as a chorus,° my lord.

HAMLET. I could interpret° between you and your love, if I could see the
puppets dallying.°   225

OPHELIA. You are keen,° my lord, you are keen.

HAMLET. It would cost you a groaning to take off mine edge.

OPHELIA. Still better, and worse.°

HAMLET. So° you mis-take° your husbands. Begin, murder; leave thy
damnable faces and begin. Come, the croaking. raven doth bellow   230
for revenge.

LUCIANUS. Thoughts black, hands apt, drugs fit, and time agreeing,
Confederate season,° else° no creature seeing,°
Thou mixture rank, of midnight weeds collected,
With Hecate's ban° thrice blasted, thrice infected,   235
Thy natural magic and dire property°
On wholesome life usurp immediately.

[He pours the poison into the sleeper's ear.]

HAMLET. 'A poisons him i' the garden for his estate.° His° name's Gonzago. The story is extant, and written in very choice Italian.
You shall see anon how the murderer gets the love of Gonzago's   240
wife.

[CLAUDIUS rises.]

OPHELIA. The King rises.

HAMLET. What, frighted with false fire?°

QUEEN. How fares my lord?

POLONIUS. Give o'er the play.   245

KING. Give me some light. Away!

POLONIUS. Lights, lights, lights!

Exeunt all but HAMLET *and* HORATIO.

---

220 free guiltless   **221 galled jade** horse whose hide is rubbed by saddle or harness. **withers** the part between the horse's shoulder blades   **unwrung** not
rubbed sore   **223 chorus** (In many Elizabethan plays, the forthcoming action was
explained by an actor known as the "chorus"; at a puppet show, the actor who
spoke the dialogue was known as an "interpreter," as indicated by the lines following.)   **224 interpret** (1) ventriloquize the dialogue, as in puppet show (2) act as
pander   **225 puppets dallying** (With suggestion of sexual play, continued in
keen, "sexually aroused," *groaning,* "moaning in pregnancy," and *edge,* "sexual desire" or "impetuosity.")   **226 keen** sharp, bitter   **228 Still . . . worse** more keen,
always *bettering* what other people say with witty wordplay, but at the same time
more offensive   **229 So** even thus (in marriage)   **mis-take** take falseheartedly
and cheat on. (The marriage vows say "for better, for worse.")   **233 Confederate
season** the time and occasion conspiring (to assist the murderer)   **else** otherwise   **seeing** seeing me   **235 Hecate's ban** the curse of Hecate, the goddess
of witchcraft   **236 dire property** baleful quality   **238 estate** i.e., the kingship.
His i.e., the King's   **243 false fire** the blank discharge of a gun loaded with
powder but no shot

HAMLET. "Why, let the strucken deer go weep,
              The hart ungallèd° play.
        For some must watch,° while some must sleep;   250
              Thus runs the world away."°
        Would not this,° sir, and a forest of feathers°—if the rest of my for-
        tunes turn Turk with° me—with two Provincial roses° on my
        razed° shoes, get me a fellowship in a cry° of players?°
HORATIO. Half a share.   255
HAMLET. A whole one, I.
            "For thou dost know, O Damon° dear,
                This realm dismantled° was
            Of Jove himself, and now reigns here
                A very, very—pajock."°   260
HORATIO. You might have rhymed.
HAMLET. O good Horatio, I'll take the ghost's word for a thousand
        pound. Didst perceive?
HORATIO. Very well, my lord.
HAMLET. Upon the talk of the poisoning?   265
HORATIO. I did very well note him.
        Enter ROSENCRANTZ *and* GUILDENSTERN.
HAMLET. Aha! Come, some music! Come, the recorders.°
            "For if the King like not the comedy,
            Why then, belike, he likes it not, perdy."°
        Come, some music.   270
GUILDENSTERN. Good my lord, vouchsafe me a word with you.
HAMLET. Sir, a whole history.
GUILDENSTERN. The King, sir—
HAMLET. Ay, sir, what of him?
GUILDENSTERN. Is in his retirement° marvelous distempered.°   275
HAMLET. With drink, sir?
GUILDENSTERN. No, my lord, with choler.°
HAMLET. Your wisdom should show itself more richer to signify this to

---

248–251 Why . . . away (Probably from an old ballad, with allusion to the popular
belief that a wounded deer retires to weep and die; compare with *As You Like It*,
2.1.33-66.)   **249 ungallèd** unafflicted   **250 watch** remain awake   **251 Thus
. . . away** thus the world goes   **252 this** i.e., the play   **feathers** (Allusion to the
plumes that Elizabethan actors were fond of wearing.)   **253 turn Turk with** turn
renegade against, go back on   **Provincial roses** rosettes of ribbon, named for
roses grown in a part of France   **254 razed** with ornamental slashing   **cry** pack
(of hounds)   **fellowship . . . players** partnership in a theatrical company
257 Damon the friend of Pythias, as Horatio is friend of Hamlet; or, a traditional
pastoral name   **258 dismantled** stripped, divested   **258–260 This realm . . .
pajock** i.e., Jove, representing divine authority and justice, has abandoned this
realm to its own devices, leaving in his stead only a peacock or vain pretender to
virtue (though the rhyme-word expected in place of *pajock or* "peacock" suggests
that the realm is now ruled over by an "ass")   **267 recorders** wind instruments of
the flute kind   **269 perdy** (A corruption of the French *par dieu*, "by God.")
275 retirement withdrawal to his chambers   **distempered** out of humor. (But
Hamlet deliberately plays on the wider application to any illness of mind or body, as
in line 308, especially to drunkenness.)   **277 choler** anger. (But Hamlet takes the
word in its more basic humoral sense of "bilious disorder.")

the doctor, for for me to put him to his purgation° would perhaps
plunge him into more choler.   280

GUILDENSTERN. Good my lord, put your discourse into some frame° and
start° not so wildly from my affair.

HAMLET. I am tame, sir. Pronounce.

GUILDENSTERN. The Queen, your mother, in most great affliction of spirit,
hath sent me to you.   285

HAMLET. You are welcome.

GUILDENSTERN. Nay, good my lord, this courtesy is not of the right
breed.° If it shall please you to make me a wholesome answer, I
will do your mother's commandment; if not, your pardon° and my
return shall be the end of my business.   290

HAMLET. Sir, I cannot.

ROSENCRANTZ. What, my lord?

HAMLET. Make you a wholesome answer; my wit's diseased. But, sir,
such answer as I can make, you shall command, or rather, as you
say, my mother. Therefore no more, but to the matter. My mother,   295
you say—

ROSENCRANTZ. Then thus she says: your behavior hath struck her into
amazement and admiration.°

HAMLET. O wonderful son, that can so stonish a mother! But is there no
sequel at the heels of this mother's admiration? Impart.   300

ROSENCRANTZ. She desires to speak with you in her closet° ere you go to
bed.

HAMLET. We shall obey, were she ten times our mother. Have you any
further trade with us?

ROSENCRANTZ. My lord, you once did love me.   305

HAMLET. And do still, by these pickers and stealers.°

ROSENCRANTZ. Good my lord, what is your cause of distemper? You do
surely bar the door upon your own liberty° if you deny° your griefs
to your friend.

HAMLET. Sir, I lack advancement.   310

ROSENCRANTZ. How can that be, when you have the voice of the King
himself for your succession in Denmark?

HAMLET. Ay, sir, but "While the grass grows"°—the proverb is some-
thing° musty.

Enter the Players° with recorders.

O, the recorders. Let me see one. *[He takes a recorder.]*   315

---

279 purgation (Hamlet hints at something going beyond medical treatment to
bloodletting and the extraction of confession.)   **281 frame** order.   **282 start** shy
or jump away (like a horse; the opposite of *tame* in line 283)   **288 breed** (1) kind
(2) breeding, manners   **289 pardon** permission to depart   **298 admiration** bewilderment   **301 closet** private chamber   **306 pickers and stealers** i.e., hands.
(So called from the catechism, "to keep my hands from picking and stealing.")
308 liberty i.e., being freed from *distemper*, line 307; but perhaps with a veiled
threat as well.   **deny** refuse to share   **313 While . . . grows** (The rest of the
proverb is "the silly horse starves"; Hamlet may not live long enough to succeed to
the kingdom.)   **313–314 something** somewhat.   **s.d. Players** actors

To withdraw° with you: why do you go about to recover the wind°
of me, as if you would drive me into a toil?°

GUILDENSTERN. O, my lord, if my duty be too bold, my love is too unmannerly.°

HAMLET. I do not well understand that.° Will you play upon this pipe?   320

GUILDENSTERN. My lord, I cannot.

HAMLET. I pray you.

GUILDENSTERN. Believe me, I cannot.

HAMLET. I do beseech you.

GUILDENSTERN. I know no touch of it, my lord.   325

HAMLET. It is as easy as lying. Govern these ventages° with your fingers
and thumb, give it breath with your mouth, and it will discourse
most eloquent music. Look you, these are the stops.

GUILDENSTERN. But these cannot I command to any utterance of harmony. I have not the skill.   330

HAMLET. Why, look you now, how unworthy a thing you make of me!
You would play upon me, you would seem to know my stops, you
would pluck out the heart of my mystery, you would sound° me
from my lowest note to the top of my compass,° and there is much
music, excellent voice, in this little organ,° yet cannot you make it   335
speak. 'Sblood, do you think I am easier to be played on than a
pipe? Call me what instrument you will, though you can fret° me,
you cannot play upon me.

Enter POLONIUS.

God bless you, sir!

POLONIUS. My lord, the Queen would speak with you, and presently.°   340

HAMLET. Do you see yonder cloud that's almost in shape of a camel?

POLONIUS. By the Mass and 'tis, like a camel indeed.

HAMLET. Methinks it is like a weasel.

POLONIUS. It is backed like a weasel.

HAMLET. Or like a whale.   345

POLONIUS. Very like a whale.

HAMLET. Then I will come to my mother by and by.° *[Aside.]* They fool
me° to the top of my bent.° —I will come by and by.

POLONIUS. I will say so.

[Exit.]

HAMLET. "By and by" is easily said. Leave me, friends.   350

[Exeunt all but HAMLET.*]*

'Tis now the very witching time° of night,

---

316 withdraw speak privately   **recover the wind** get to the windward side
(thus driving the game into the *toil,* or "net")   **317 toil** snare   **318–319 if . . .
unmannerly** if I am using an unmannerly boldness, it is my love that occasion it
320 I . . . that i.e., I don't understand how genuine love can be unmannerly
326 ventages finger-holes or *stops* (line 328) of the recorder   **333 sound**
(1) fathom (2) produce sound in   **334 compass** range (of voice)   **335 organ**
musical instrument   **337 fret** irritate (with a quibble on *fret,* meaning the piece of
wood, gut, or metal that regulates the fingering on an instrument)   **340 presently**
at once   **347 by and by** quite soon   **347–348 fool me** trifle with me, humor my
fooling.   **348 top of my bent** limit of my ability or endurance. (Literally, the extent to which a bow may be bent.)   **351 witching time** time when spells are cast
and evil is abroad

When churchyards yawn and hell itself breathes out
Contagion to this world. Now could I drink hot blood
And do such bitter business as the day
Would quake to look on. Soft, now to my mother.   355
O heart, lose not thy nature!° Let not ever
The soul of Nero° enter this firm bosom.
Let me be cruel, not unnatural;
I will speak daggers to her, but use none.
My tongue and soul in this be hypocrites: 360
How in my words soever° she be shent,°
To give them seals° never my soul consent!

                                                              Exit.

3.3   *Enter* KING, ROSENCRANTZ, *and* GUILDENSTERN.

KING.   I like him° not, nor stands it safe with us
   To let his madness range. Therefore prepare you.
   I your commission will forthwith dispatch,°
   And he to England shall along with you.
   The terms of our estate° may not endure   5
   Hazard so near 's as doth hourly grow
   Out of his brows.°
GUILDENSTERN.   We will ourselves provide.
   Most holy and religious fear° it is
   To keep those many many bodies safe
   That live and feed upon Your Majesty.   10
ROSENCRANTZ.   The single and peculiar° life is bound
   With all the strength and armor of the mind
   To keep itself from noyance,° but much more
   That spirit upon whose weal depends and rests
   The lives of many. The cess° of majesty   15
   Dies not alone, but like a gulf° doth draw
   What's near it with it; or it is a massy° wheel
   Fixed on the summit of the highest mount,
   To whose huge spokes ten thousand lesser things
   Are mortised° and adjoined, which, when it falls,°   20
   Each small annexment, petty consequence,°
   Attends° the boisterous ruin. Never alone
   Did the King sigh, but with a general groan.

---

356 nature natural feeling   **357 Nero** murderer of his mother, Agrippina
361 How . . . soever however much by my words   **shent** rebuked   **362 give
them seals** i.e., confirm them with deeds   **3.3 Location: The castle.**   **1 him** i.e.,
his behavior   **3 dispatch** prepare, cause to be drawn up   **5 terms of our estate**
circumstances of my royal position   **7 Out of his brows** i.e., from his brain, in the
form of plots and threats   **8 religious fear** sacred concern   **11 single and
peculiar** individual and private   **13 noyance** harm   **15 cess** decease, cessation
16 gulf whirlpool   **17 massy** massive   **20 mortised** fastened (as with a fitted
joint).   **when it falls** i.e., when it descends, like the wheel of Fortune, bringing a
king down with it   **21 Each . . . consequence** i.e., every hanger-on and unimportant person or thing connected with the King   **22 Attends** participates in

KING. Arm° you, I pray you, to this speedy voyage,

    For we will fetters put about this fear,   25

    Which now goes too free-footed.

ROSENCRANTZ.   We will haste us.

        *Exeunt gentlemen [*ROSENCRANTZ *and* GUILDENSTERN*].*

  Enter POLONIUS.

POLONIUS. My lord, he's going to his mother's closet.

    Behind the arras° I'll convey myself

    To hear the process.° I'll warrant she'll tax him home,°

    And, as you said—and wisely was it said—   30

    'Tis meet° that some more audience than a mother,

    Since nature makes them partial, should o'erhear

    The speech, of vantage.° Fare you well, my liege.

    I'll call upon you ere you go to bed

    And tell you what I know.

KING.   Thanks, dear my lord.   35

                         *Exit [*POLONIUS*].*

    O, my offense is rank! It smells to heaven.

    It hath the primal eldest curse° upon 't,

    A brother's murder. Pray can I not,

    Though inclination be as sharp as will;°

    My stronger guilt defeats my strong intent,   40

    And like a man to double business bound°

    I stand in pause where I shall first begin,

    And both neglect. What if this cursèd hand

    Were thicker than itself with brother's blood,

    Is there not rain enough in the sweet heavens   45

    To wash it white as snow? Whereto serves mercy

    But to confront the visage of offense?°

    And what's in prayer but this twofold force,

    To be forestallèd° ere we come to fall,

    Or pardoned being down? Then I'll look up.   50

    My fault is past. But O, what form of prayer

    Can serve my turn? "Forgive me my foul murder"?

    That cannot be, since I am still possessed

    Of those effects for which I did the murder:

    My crown, mine own ambition, and my Queen.   55

    May one be pardoned and retain th' offense?°

    In the corrupted currents° of this world

---

24 Arm prepare   **28 arras** screen of tapestry placed around the walls of household apartments. (On the Elizabethan stage, the arras was presumably over a door or discovery space in the tiring-house facade.)   **29 process** proceedings   **tax him home** reprove him severely   **31 meet** fitting   **33 of vantage** from an advantageous place, or, in addition   **37 the primal eldest curse** the curse of Cain, the first murderer; he killed his brother Abel   **39 Though . . . will** though my desire is as strong as my determination   **41 bound** (1) destined (2) obliged. (The King wants to repent and still enjoy what he has gained.)   **46–47 Whereto . . . offense** what function does mercy serve other than to meet sin face to face?   **49 forestallèd** prevented (from sinning)   **56 th' offense** the thing for which one offended   **57 currents** courses

Offense's gilded hand° may shove by° justice,
And oft 'tis seen the wicked prize° itself
Buys out the law. But 'tis not so above.   60
There° is no shuffling,° there the action lies°
In his° true nature, and we ourselves compelled,
Even to the teeth and forehead° of our faults,
To give in° evidence. What then? What rests?°
Try what repentance can. What can it not?   65
Yet what can it, when one cannot repent?
O wretched state, O bosom black as death,
O limèd° soul that, struggling to be free,
Art more engaged!° Help, angels! Make assay.°
Bow, stubborn knees, and heart with strings of steel,   70
Be soft as sinews of the newborn babe!
All may be well.   *[He kneels.]*
Enter HAMLET.

HAMLET. Now might I do it pat,° now 'a is a-praying;
And now I'll do 't. *[He draws his sword.]* And so 'a goes to heaven,
And so am I revenged. That would be scanned:°   75
A villain kills my father, and for that,
I, his sole son, do this same villain send
To heaven.
Why, this is hire and salary, not revenge.
'A took my father grossly, full of bread,°   80
With all his crimes broad blown,° as flush° as May;
And how his audit° stands who knows save° heaven?
But in our circumstance and course of thought°
'Tis heavy with him. And am I then revenged,
To take him in the purging of his soul,   85
When he is fit and seasoned° for his passage?
No!
Up, sword, and know thou a more horrid hent.°
                                 [He puts up his sword.]
When he is drunk asleep, or in his rage,°
Or in th' incestuous pleasure of his bed,   90
At game,° a-swearing, or about some act

---

58 gilded hand hand offering gold as a bribe   **shove by** thrust aside   **59 wicked prize** prize won by wickedness   **61 There** i.e., in heaven   **shuffling** escape by trickery   **the action lies** the accusation is made manifest. (A legal metaphor.)
62 his its   **63 to the teeth and forehead** face to face, concealing nothing
64 give in provide.   **rests** remains   **68 limèd** caught as with birdlime, a sticky substance used to ensnare birds   **69 engaged** entangled   **assay** trial. (Said to himself.)   **73 pat** opportunely   **75 would be scanned** needs to be looked into, or, would be interpreted as follows   **80 grossly, full of bread** i.e., enjoying his worldly pleasures rather than fasting. (See Ezekiel 16:49.)   **81 crimes broad blown** sins in full bloom   **flush** vigorous   **82 audit** account.   **save** except for   **83 in . . . thought** as we see it from our mortal perspective   **86 seasoned** matured, readied   **88 know . . . hent** await to be grasped by me on a more horrid occasion   **hent** act of seizing   **89 drunk . . . rage** dead drunk, or in a fit of sexual passion   **91 game** gambling

That has no relish° of salvation in 't—
Then trip him, that his heels may kick at heaven,
And that his soul may be as damned and black
As hell, whereto it goes. My mother stays.°   95
This physic° but prolongs thy sickly days.

                                                                    Exit.

KING. My words fly up, my thoughts remain below.
Words without thoughts never to heaven go.

                                                                    Exit.

3.4   *Enter [*QUEEN*]* GERTRUDE *and* POLONIUS.

POLONIUS. 'A will come straight. Look you lay home° to him.
Tell him his pranks have been too broad° to bear with,
And that Your Grace hath screened and stood between
Much heat° and him. I'll shroud° me even here.
Pray you, be round° with him.   5
HAMLET *[within].* Mother, Mother, Mother!
QUEEN. I'll warrant you, fear me not.
Withdraw, I hear him coming.

                                    *[*POLONIUS *hides behind the arras.]*

    Enter HAMLET.

HAMLET. Now, Mother, what's the matter?
QUEEN. Hamlet, thou hast thy father° much offended.   10
HAMLET. Mother, you have my father much offended.
QUEEN. Come, come, you answer with an idle° tongue.
HAMLET. Go, go, you question with a wicked tongue.
QUEEN. Why, how now, Hamlet?
HAMLET.   What's the matter now?
QUEEN. Have you forgot me?°
HAMLET.   No, by the rood,° not so: 15
    You are the Queen your husband's brother's wife,
    And—would it were not so!—you are my mother.
QUEEN. Nay, then, I'll set those to you that can speak.°
HAMLET. Come, come, and sit you down; you shall not budge.
    You go not till I set you up a glass   20
    Where you may see the inmost part of you.
QUEEN. What wilt thou do? Thou wilt not murder me?
    Help, ho!
POLONIUS *[behind the arras].* What ho! Help!
HAMLET *[drawing].* How now? A rat? Dead for a ducat,° dead!   25

---

92 relish trace, savor   **95 stays** awaits (me)   **96 physic** purging (by prayer), or,
Hamlet's postponement of the killing   **3.4 Location: The Queen's private chamber   1 lay home** thrust to the heart, reprove him soundly   **2 broad** unrestrained
4 Much heat i.e., the King's anger   **shroud** conceal (with ironic fitness to Polonius' imminent death. The word is only in the First Quarto: the Second Quarto and
the Folio read "silence.")   **5 round** blunt   **10 thy father** i.e., your stepfather,
Claudius   **12 idle** foolish   **15 forgot me** i.e., forgotten that I am your mother
rood cross of Christ   **18 speak** i.e., to someone so rude   **25 Dead for a ducat**
i.e., I bet a ducat he's dead; or, a ducat is his life's fee

[He thrusts his rapier through the arras.]
POLONIUS *[behind the arras]*. O, I am slain!   *[He falls and dies.]*
QUEEN.   O me, what hast thou done?
HAMLET. Nay, I know not. Is it the King?
QUEEN. O, what a rash and bloody deed is this!
HAMLET. A bloody deed—almost as bad, good Mother,
    As kill a King, and marry with his brother.   30
QUEEN. As kill a King!
HAMLET.   Ay, lady, it was my word.
                    [He parts the arras and discovers POLONIUS.*]*
    Thou wretched, rash, intruding fool, farewell!
    I took thee for thy better. Take thy fortune.
    Thou find'st to be too busy° is some danger.—
    Leave wringing of your hands. Peace, sit you down,   35
    And let me wring your heart, for so I shall,
    If it be made of penetrable stuff,
    If damnèd custom° have not brazed° it so
    That it be proof° and bulwark against sense.°
QUEEN. What have I done, that thou dar'st wag thy tongue   40
    In noise so rude against me?
HAMLET.   Such an act
    That blurs the grace and blush of modesty,
    Calls virtue hypocrite, takes off the rose
    From the fair forehead of an innocent love
    And sets a blister° there, makes marriage vows   45
    As false as dicers' oaths. O, such a deed
    As from the body of contraction° plucks
    The very soul, and sweet religion makes°
    A rhapsody° of words. Heaven's face does glow
    O'er this solidity and compound mass   50
    With tristful visage, as against the doom,
    Is thought-sick at the act.°
QUEEN.   Ay me, what act,
    That roars so loud and thunders in the index?°
HAMLET *[showing her two likenesses]*. Look here upon this picture, and
        on this,
    The counterfeit presentment° of two brothers.   55
    See what a grace was seated on this brow:
    Hyperion's° curls, the front° of Jove himself,
    An eye like Mars° to threaten and command,
    A station° like the herald Mercury°

34 **busy** nosey   38 **damnèd custom** habitual wickedness   **brazed** brazened,
hardened   39 **proof** armor   **sense** feeling   45 **sets a blister** i.e., brands as a
harlot   47 **contraction** the marriage contract   48 **sweet religion makes** i.e.,
makes marriage vows   49 **rhapsody** senseless string   49–52 **Heaven's . . . act**
heaven's face blushes at this solid world compounded of the various elements, with
sorrowful face as though the day of doom were near, and is sick with horror at the
deed (i.e., Gertrude's marriage)   53 **index** table of contents, prelude or preface
55 **counterfeit presentment** portrayed representation   57 **Hyperion's** the sun-
god's   **front** brow   58 **Mars** god of war   59 **station** manner of standing
Mercury winged messenger of the gods

New-lighted° on a heaven-kissing hill—   60
A combination and a form indeed
Where every god did seem to set his seal°
To give the world assurance of a man.
This was your husband. Look you now what follows:
Here is your husband, like a mildewed ear,°   65
Blasting° his wholesome brother. Have you eyes?
Could you on this fair mountain leave° to feed
And batten° on this moor?° Ha, have you eyes?
You cannot call it love, for at your age
The heyday° in the blood° is tame, it's humble,   70
And waits upon the judgment, and what judgment
Would step from this to this? Sense,° sure, you have,
Else could you not have motion, but sure that sense
Is apoplexed,° for madness would not err,°
Nor sense to ecstasy was ne'er so thralled,   75
But° it reserved some quantity of choice
To serve in such a difference.° What devil was 't
That thus hath cozened° you at hoodman-blind?°
Eyes without feeling, feeling without sight,
Ears without hands or eyes, smelling sans° all,   80
Or but a sickly part of one true sense
Could not so mope.° O shame, where is thy blush?
Rebellious hell,
If thou canst mutine° in a matron's bones,
To flaming youth let virtue be as wax   85
And melt in her own fire.° Proclaim no shame
When the compulsive ardor gives the charge,
Since frost itself as actively doth burn,
And reason panders will.°
QUEEN. O Hamlet, speak no more!   90
　　Thou turn'st mine eyes into my very soul,
　　And there I see such black and grainèd° spots

---

60 New-lighted newly alighted　　**62 set his seal** i.e., affix his approval　　**65 ear** i.e., of grain　　**66 Blasting** blighting　　**67 leave** cease　　**68 batten** gorge　　**moor** barren or marshy ground (suggesting also "dark-skinned")　　**70 heyday** state of excitement　　**blood** passion　　**72 Sense** perception through the five senses (the functions of the middle or sensible soul)　　**74 apoplexed** paralyzed. (Hamlet goes on to explain that, without such a paralysis of will, mere madness would not so err, nor would the five senses so enthrall themselves to *ecstasy* or lunacy; even such deranged states of mind would be able to make the obvious choice between Hamlet Senior and Claudius.)　　**err** so err　　**76 But** but that　　**77 To . . . difference** to help in making a choice between two such men　　**78 cozened** cheated **hoodman-blind** blindman's buff. (In this game, says Hamlet, the devil must have pushed Claudius toward Gertrude while she was blindfolded.)　　**80 sans** without　　**82 mope** be dazed, act aimlessly　　**84 mutine** incite mutiny　　**85–86 be as wax . . . fire** melt like a candle or stick of sealing wax held over the candle flame **86–89 Proclaim . . . will** call it no shameful business when the compelling ardor of youth delivers the attack, i.e., commits lechery, since the *frost* of advanced age burns with as active a fire of lust and reason perverts itself by fomenting lust rather than restraining it　　**92 grainèd** dyed in grain, indelible

As will not leave their tinct.°
HAMLET.   Nay, but to live
  In the rank sweat of an enseamèd° bed,
  Stewed° in corruption, honeying and making love   95
  Over the nasty sty!
QUEEN. O, speak to me no more!
  These words like daggers enter in my ears.
  No more, sweet Hamlet!
HAMLET.   A murderer and a villain,
  A slave that is not twentieth part the tithe°   100
  Of your precedent lord,° a vice° of kings,
  A cutpurse of the empire and the rule,
  That from a shelf the precious diadem stole
  And put it in his pocket!
QUEEN. No more!   105
  Enter GHOST *[in his nightgown].*
HAMLET. A king of shreds and patches° —
  Save me, and hover o'er me with your wings,
  You heavenly guards! What would your gracious figure?
QUEEN. Alas, he's mad!
HAMLET. Do you not come your tardy son to chide,   110
  That, lapsed° in time and passion, lets go by
  Th' important° acting of your dread command?
  O, say!
GHOST. Do not forget. This visitation
  Is but to whet thy almost blunted purpose.   115
  But look, amazement° on thy mother sits.
  O, step between her and her fighting soul!
  Conceit° in weakest bodies strongest works.
  Speak to her, Hamlet.
HAMLET.   How is it with you, lady?
QUEEN. Alas, how is 't with you,   120
  That you do bend your eye on vacancy,
  And with th' incorporal° air do hold discourse?
  Forth at your eyes your spirits wildly peep,
  And, as the sleeping soldiers in th' alarm,°
  Your bedded° hair, like life in excrements,°   125
  Start up and stand on end. O gentle son,
  Upon the heat and flame of thy distemper°

---

93 leave their tinct surrender their color   **94 enseamèd** saturated in the grease
and filth of passionate lovemaking   **95 Stewed** soaked, bathed (with a suggestion of "stew," brothel)   **100 tithe** tenth part   **101 precedent lord** former
husband   **vice** buffoon. (A reference to the Vice of the morality plays.)
106 shreds and patches i.e., motley, the traditional costume of the clown or fool
111 lapsed delaying   **112 important** importunate, urgent   **116 amazement**
distraction   **118 Conceit** imagination   **122 incorporal** immaterial   **124 as . . .**
alarm like soldiers called out of sleep by an alarum   **125 bedded** laid flat   **like**
life in excrements i.e., as though hair, an outgrowth of the body, had a life of its
own. (Hair was thought to be lifeless because it lacks sensation, and so its standing
on end would be unnatural and ominous.)   **127 distemper** disorder

Sprinkle cool patience. Whereon do you look?
HAMLET. On him, on him! Look you how pale he glares!
    His form and cause conjoined,° preaching to stones,   130
    Would make them capable.°—Do not look upon me,
    Lest with this piteous action you convert
    My stern effects.° Then what I have to do
    Will want true color—tears perchance for blood.°
QUEEN. To whom do you speak this?   135
HAMLET. Do you see nothing there?
QUEEN. Nothing at all, yet all that is I see.
HAMLET. Nor did you nothing hear?
QUEEN. No, nothing but ourselves.
HAMLET. Why, look you there, look how it steals away!   140
    My father, in his habit° as° he lived!
    Look where he goes even now out at the portal!

                                       Exit GHOST.

QUEEN. This is the very° coinage of your brain.
    This bodiless creation ecstasy
    Is very cunning in.°   145
HAMLET. Ecstasy?
    My pulse as yours doth temperately keep time,
    And makes as healthful music. It is not madness
    That I have uttered. Bring me to the test,
    And I the matter will reword,° which madness   150
    Would gambol° from. Mother, for love of grace,
    Lay not that flattering unction° to your soul
    That not your trespass but my madness speaks.
    It will but skin° and film the ulcerous place,
    Whiles rank corruption, mining° all within,   155
    Infects unseen. Confess yourself to heaven,
    Repent what's past, avoid what is to come,
    And do not spread the compost° on the weeds
    To make them ranker. Forgive me this my virtue;°
    For in the fatness° of these pursy° times   160
    Virtue itself of vice must pardon beg,
    Yea, curb° and woo for leave° to do him good.
QUEEN. O Hamlet, thou hast cleft my heart in twain.
HAMLET. O, throw away the worser part of it,
    And live the purer with the other half.   165
    Good night. But go not to my uncle's bed;

---

130 His . . . conjoined his appearance joined to his cause for speaking   **131 capable** receptive   **132–133 convert . . . effects** divert me from my stern duty   **134 want . . . blood** lack plausibility so that (with a play on the normal sense of *color*) I shall shed colorless tears instead of blood   **141 habit** clothes   **as** as when   **143 very** mere   **144–145 This . . . in** madness is skillful in creating this kind of hallucination   **150 reword** repeat word for word   **151 gambol** skip away   **152 unction** ointment   **154 skin** grow a skin for   **155 mining** working under the surface   **158 compost** manure   **159 this my virtue** my virtuous talk in reproving you   **160 fatness** grossness   **pursy** flabby, out of shape   **162 curb** bow, bend the knee   **leave** permission

Assume a virtue, if you have it not.
That monster, custom, who all sense doth eat,°
Of habits devil,° is angel yet in this,
That to the use of actions fair and good   170
He likewise gives a frock or livery°
That aptly° is put on. Refrain tonight,
And that shall lend a kind of easiness
To the next abstinence; the next more easy;
For use° almost can change the stamp of nature,°   175
And either°. . . the devil, or throw him out
With wondrous potency. Once more, good night;
And when you are desirous to be blest,
I'll blessing beg of you.° For this same lord,

                                    [pointing to POLONIUS.*]*

I do repent; but heaven hath pleased it so   180
To punish me with this, and this with me,
That I must be their scourge and minister.°
I will bestow° him, and will answer° well
The death I gave him. So, again, good night.
I must be cruel only to be kind.   185
This° bad begins, and worse remains behind.°
One word more, good lady.

QUEEN.   What shall I do?

HAMLET. Not this by no means that I bid you do:
Let the bloat° King tempt you again to bed,
Pinch wanton° on your cheek, call you his mouse,   190
And let him, for a pair of reechy° kisses,
Or paddling° in your neck with his damned fingers,
Make you to ravel all this matter out°
That I essentially am not in madness,
But mad in craft.° 'Twere good° you let him know,   195
For who that's but a Queen, fair, sober, wise,
Would from a paddock,° from a bat, a gib,°
Such dear concernings° hide? Who would do so?

168 who . . . eat which consumes all proper or natural feeling, all sensibility
169 Of habits devil devil-like in prompting evil habits   **171 livery** an outer appearance, a customary garb (and hence a predisposition easily assumed in time of stress)   **172 aptly** readily   **175 use** habit.   **the stamp of nature** our inborn traits
176 And either (A defective line, usually emended by inserting the word *master* after *either,* following the Fourth Quarto and early editors.)   **178–179 when . . . you** i.e., when you are ready to be penitent and seek God's blessing, I will ask your blessing as a dutiful son should   **182 their scourge and minister** i.e., agent of heavenly retribution. (By *scourge,* Hamlet also suggests that he himself will eventually suffer punishment in the process of fulfilling heaven's will.)   **183 bestow** stow, dispose of   **answer** account or pay for   **186 This** i.e., the killing of Polonius.   **behind** to come   **189 bloat** bloated   **190 Pinch wanton** i.e., leave his love pinches on your cheeks, branding you as wanton   **191 reechy** dirty, filthy
192 paddling fingering amorously   **193 ravel . . . out** unravel, disclose   **195 in craft** by cunning.   **good** (Said sarcastically; also the following eight lines.)
197 paddock toad   **gib** tomcat   **198 dear concernings** important affairs

No, in despite of sense and secrecy,°
Unpeg the basket° on the house's top,   200
Let the birds fly, and like the famous ape,°
To try conclusions,° in the basket creep
And break your own neck down.°

QUEEN. Be thou assured, if words be made of breath,
And breath of life, I have no life to breathe   205
What thou hast said to me.

HAMLET. I must to England. You know that?

QUEEN.   Alack,
I had forgot. 'Tis so concluded on.

HAMLET. There's letters sealed, and my two schoolfellows,
Whom I will trust as I will adders fanged,   210
They bear the mandate; they must sweep my way
And marshal me to knavery.° Let it work.°
For 'tis the sport to have the enginer°
Hoist with° his own petard,° and 't shall go hard
But I will° delve one yard below their mines°   215
And blow them at the moon. O, 'tis most sweet
When in one line° two crafts° directly meet.
This man shall set me packing.°
I'll lug the guts into the neighbor room.
Mother, good night indeed. This counselor   220
Is now most still, most secret, and most grave,
Who was in life a foolish prating knave.—
Come, sir, to draw toward an end° with you.—
Good night, Mother.

Exeunt [separately, HAMLET *dragging in* POLONIUS].

4.1   *Enter* KING *and* QUEEN,° *with* ROSENCRANTZ *and* GUILDENSTERN.

KING. There's matter° in these sighs, these profound heaves.°
You must translate; 'tis fit we understand them.

199 sense and secrecy secrecy that common sense requires   **200 Unpeg the basket** open the cage, i.e., let out the secret   **201 famous ape** (In a story now lost.) **202 try conclusions** test the outcome (in which the ape apparently enters a cage from which birds have been released and then tries to fly out of the cage as they have done, falling to its death)   **203 down** in the fall; utterly   **211–212 sweep ... knavery** sweep a path before me and conduct me to some *knavery* or treachery prepared for me   **212 work** proceed   **213 enginer** maker of military contrivances **214 Hoist with** blown up by.   **petard** an explosive used to blow in a door or make a breach   **214–215 't shall ... will** unless luck is against me, I will   **215 mines** tunnels used in warfare to undermine the enemy's emplacements; Hamlet will countermine by going under their mines   **217 in one line** i.e., mines and countermines on a collision course, or the countermines directly below the mines   **crafts** acts of guile, plots   **218 set me packing** set me to making schemes, and set me to lugging (him), and, also, send me off in a hurry   **223 draw ... end** finish up (with a pun on *draw,* "pull")   **4.1 Location: The castle.   s.d. Enter ... Queen** (Some editors argue that Gertrude never exits in 3.4 and that the scene is continuous here, as suggested in the Folio, but the Second Quarto marks an entrance for her and at line 35 Claudius speaks of Gertrude's *closet* as though it were elsewhere. A short time has elapsed, during which the King has become aware of her highly wrought emotional state.)   **1 matter** significance.   **heaves** heavy sighs

    Where is your son?
QUEEN. Bestow this place on us a little while.

                  [Exeunt ROSENCRANTZ *and* GUILDENSTERN.*]*
    Ah, mine own lord, what have I seen tonight!   5
KING. What, Gertrude? How does Hamlet?
QUEEN. Mad as the sea and wind when both contend
    Which is the mightier. In his lawless fit,
    Behind the arras hearing something stir,
    Whips out his rapier, cries, "A rat, a rat!"   10
    And in this brainish apprehension° kills
    The unseen good old man.
KING.   O heavy° deed!
    It had been so with us,° had we been there.
    His liberty is full of threats to all—
    To you yourself, to us, to everyone.   15
    Alas, how shall this bloody deed be answered?°
    It will be laid to us, whose providence°
    Should have kept short,° restrained, and out of haunt°
    This mad young man. But so much was our love,
    We would not understand what was most fit,   20
    But, like the owner of a foul disease,
    To keep it from divulging,° let it feed
    Even on the pith of life. Where is he gone?
QUEEN. To draw apart the body he hath killed,
    O'er whom his very madness, like some ore°   25
    Among a mineral° of metals base,
    Shows itself pure: 'a weeps for what is done.
KING. O Gertrude, come away!
    The sun no sooner shall the mountains touch
    But we will ship him hence, and this vile deed   30
    We must with all our majesty and skill
    Both countenance° and excuse.—Ho, Guildenstern!
Enter ROSENCRANTZ *and* GUILDENSTERN.
    Friends both, go join you with some further aid.
    Hamlet in madness hath Polonius slain,
    And from his mother's closet hath he dragged him.   35
    Go seek him out, speak fair, and bring the body
    Into the chapel. I pray you, haste in this.
                  [Exeunt ROSENCRANTZ *and* GUILDENSTERN.*]*
    Come, Gertrude, we'll call up our wisest friends
    And let them know both what we mean to do
    And what's untimely done°.   40
    Whose whisper o'er the world's diameter,°

---

11 brainish apprehension headstrong conception   **12 heavy** grievous   **13 us**
i.e., me. (The royal "we"; also in line 15.)   **16 answered** explained   **17 providence** foresight   **18 short** i.e., on a short tether.   **out of haunt** secluded
22 divulging becoming evident   **25 ore** vein of gold   **26 mineral** mine
32 countenance put the best face on   **40 And . . . done** (A defective line; conjectures as to the missing words include *So, haply, slander* [Capell and others]; *For,
haply, slander* [Theobald and others]; and *So envious slander* [Jenkins].)
41 diameter extent from side to side

As level° as the cannon to his blank,°
Transports his poisoned shot, may miss our name
And hit the woundless° air. O, come away!
My soul is full of discord and dismay.   45

Exeunt.

4.2   *Enter* HAMLET.

HAMLET. Safely stowed.

ROSENCRANTZ, GUILDENSTERN *[within].* Hamlet! Lord Hamlet!

HAMLET. But soft, what noise? Who calls on Hamlet? O, here they come.
Enter ROSENCRANTZ *and* GUILDENSTERN.

ROSENCRANTZ. What have you done, my lord, with the dead body?

HAMLET. Compounded it with dust, whereto 'tis kin.   5

ROSENCRANTZ. Tell us where 'tis, that we may take it thence
And bear it to the chapel.

HAMLET. Do not believe it.

ROSENCRANTZ. Believe what?

HAMLET. That I can keep your counsel and not mine own.° Besides, to   10
be demanded of° a sponge, what replication° should be made by
the son of a king?

ROSENCRANTZ. Take you me for a sponge, my lord?

HAMLET. Ay, sir, that soaks up the King's countenance,° his rewards, his
authorities.° But such officers do the King best service in the end.   15
He keeps them, like an ape, an apple, in the corner of his jaw, first
mouthed to be last swallowed. When he needs what you have
gleaned, it is but squeezing you, and, sponge, you shall be dry
again.

ROSENCRANTZ. I understand you not, my lord.   20

HAMLET. I am glad of it. A knavish speech sleeps in° a foolish ear.

ROSENCRANTZ. My lord, you must tell us where the body is and go with
us to the King.

HAMLET. The body is with the King, but the King is not with the body.°
The King is a thing—   25

GUILDENSTERN. A thing, my lord?

HAMLET. Of nothing.° Bring me to him. Hide fox, and all after!°

Exeunt [running].

42 **As level** with as direct aim.   **his blank** its target at point-blank range
44 **woundless** invulnerable   **4.2. Location: The castle.**   **10 That . . . own** i.e.,
that I can follow your advice (by telling where the body is) and still keep my own
secret   **11 demanded of** questioned by   **replication** reply   **14 countenance**
favor   **15 authorities** delegated power, influence   **21 sleeps in** has no meaning
to   **24 The . . . body** (Perhaps alludes to the legal commonplace of "the king's two
bodies," which drew a distinction between the sacred office of kingship and the
particular mortal who possessed it at any given time. Hence, although Claudius'
body is necessarily a part of him, true kingship is not contained in it. Similarly,
Claudius will have Polonius' body when it is found, but there is no kingship in this
business either.)   **27 Of nothing** (1) of no account (2) lacking the essence of kingship, as in lines 24–25 and note   **Hide . . . after** (An old signal cry in the game of
hide-and-seek, suggesting that Hamlet now runs away from them.)

4.3   *Enter* KING, *and two or three.*

KING. I have sent to seek him, and to find the body.
How dangerous is it that this man goes loose!
Yet must not we put the strong law on him.
He's loved of° the distracted° multitude,
Who like not in their judgment, but their eyes,°   5
And where 'tis so, th' offender's scourge° is weighed,°
But never the offense. To bear all smooth and even,°
This sudden sending him away must seem
Deliberate pause.° Diseases desperate grown
By desperate appliance° are relieved,   10
Or not at all.

Enter ROSENCRANTZ, GUILDENSTERN, *and all the rest.*

                                   How now, what hath befall'n?
ROSENCRANTZ. Where the dead body is bestowed, my lord,
We cannot get from him.
KING.   But where is he?
ROSENCRANTZ. Without, my lord; guarded, to know your pleasure.
KING. Bring him before us.
ROSENCRANTZ.   Ho! Bring in the lord.   15
They enter [with HAMLET*].*
KING. Now, Hamlet, where's Polonius?
HAMLET. At supper.
KING. At supper? Where?
HAMLET. Not where he eats, but where 'a is eaten. A certain convocation
of politic worms° are e'en° at him. Your worm° is your only em-   20
peror for diet.° We fat all creatures else to fat us, and we fat our-
selves for maggots. Your fat king and your lean beggar is but vari-
able service°—two dishes, but to one table. That's the end.
KING. Alas, alas!
HAMLET. A man may fish with the worm that hath eat° of a king, and eat   25
of the fish that hath fed of that worm.
KING. What dost thou mean by this?
HAMLET. Nothing but to show you how a king may go a progress°
through the guts of a beggar.
KING. Where is Polonius?   30
HAMLET. In heaven. Send thither to see. If your messenger find him not
there, seek him i' th' other place yourself. But if indeed you find
him not within this month, you shall nose him as you go up the
stairs into the lobby.

4.3 Location: The castle.   4 of by.   **distracted** fickle, unstable   **5 Who . . .
eyes** who choose not by judgment but by appearance   **6 scourge** punishment.
(Literally, blow with a whip.)   **weighed** sympathetically considered   **7 To . . .
even** to manage the business in an unprovocative way   **9 Deliberate pause** carefully considered action   **10 appliance** remedies   **20 politic worms** crafty worms
(suited to a master spy like Polonius).   **e'en** even now   **Your worm** your average
worm. Compare *your fat king and your lean beggar* in line 22.)   **21 diet** food,
eating (with a punning reference to the Diet of Worms, a famous *convocation* held
in 1521)   **22–23 variable service** different courses of a single meal   **27 eat** eaten
(Pronounced *et.*)   **28 progress** royal journey of state

KING [*to some attendants*]. Go seek him there.   35

HAMLET. 'A will stay till you come.

[*Exeunt attendants.*]

KING. Hamlet, this deed, for thine especial safety—
    Which we do tender,° as we dearly° grieve
    For that which thou hast done—must send thee hence
    With fiery quickness. Therefore prepare thyself.   40
    The bark° is ready, and the wind at help,
    Th' associates tend,° and everything is bent°
    For England.

HAMLET. For England!

KING. Ay, Hamlet.   45

HAMLET. Good.

KING. So is it, if thou knew'st our purposes.

HAMLET. I see a cherub° that sees them. But come, for England!
    Farewell, dear mother.

KING. Thy loving father, Hamlet.   50

HAMLET. My mother. Father and mother is man and wife, man and wife
    is one flesh, and so, my mother. Come, for England!

Exit.

KING. Follow him at foot;° tempt him with speed aboard.
    Delay it not. I'll have him hence tonight.
    Away! For everything is sealed and done   55
    That else leans on° th' affair. Pray you, make haste.

[*Exeunt all but the* KING.]

    And, England,° if my love thou hold'st at aught°—
    As my great power thereof may give thee sense,°
    Since yet thy cicatrice° looks raw and red
    After the Danish sword, and thy free awe°   60
    Pays homage to us—thou mayst not coldly set°
    Our sovereign process,° which imports at full,°
    By letters congruing° to that effect,
    The present° death of Hamlet. Do it, England,
    For like the hectic° in my blood he rages,   65
    And thou must cure me. Till I know 'tis done,
    Howe'er my haps,° my joys were ne'er begun.

Exit.

4.4 *Enter* FORTINBRAS *with his army over the stage.*

FORTINBRAS. Go, Captain, from me greet the Danish king.
    Tell him that by his license° Fortinbras

---

38 tender regard, hold dear. **dearly** intensely **41 bark** sailing vessel **42 tend** wait. **bent** in readiness **48 cherub** (Cherubim are angels of knowledge. Hamlet hints that both he and heaven are onto Claudius' tricks.) **53 at foot** close behind, at heel **56 leans on** bears upon, is related to **57 England** i.e., King of England **at aught** at any value **58 As . . . sense** for so my great power may give you a just appreciation of the importance of valuing my love **59 cicatrice** scar **60 free awe** voluntary show of respect **61 coldly set** regard with indifference **62 process** command. **imports at full** conveys specific directions for **63 congruing** agreeing **64 present** immediate **65 hectic** persistent fever **67 haps** fortunes **4.4 Location: The coast of Denmark.** **2 license** permission

Craves the conveyance of° a promised march
Over his kingdom. You know the rendezvous.
If that His Majesty would aught with us,   5
We shall express our duty° in his eye;°
And let him know so.
CAPTAIN. I will do 't, my lord.
FORTINBRAS. Go softly° on.   *[Exeunt all but the* CAPTAIN.*]*
 Enter HAMLET, ROSENCRANTZ, *[*GUILDENSTERN,*] etc.*
HAMLET. Good sir, whose powers° are these?   10
CAPTAIN. They are of Norway, sir.
HAMLET. How purposed, sir, I pray you?
CAPTAIN. Against some part of Poland.
HAMLET. Who commands them, sir?
CAPTAIN. The nephew to old Norway, Fortinbras.   15
HAMLET. Goes it against the main° of Poland, sir,
Or for some frontier?
CAPTAIN. Truly to speak, and with no addition,°
We go to gain a little patch of ground
That hath in it no profit but the name.   20
To pay° five ducats, five, I would not farm it;°
Nor will it yield to Norway or the Pole
A ranker° rate, should it be sold in fee.°
HAMLET. Why, then the Polack never will defend it.
CAPTAIN. Yes, it is already garrisoned.   25
HAMLET. Two thousand souls and twenty thousand ducats
Will not debate the question of this straw.°
This is th' impostume° of much wealth and peace,
That inward breaks, and shows no cause without
Why the man dies. I humbly thank you, sir.   30
CAPTAIN. God b' wi' you, sir.

              [Exit.]
ROSENCRANTZ.   Will 't please you go, my lord?
HAMLET. I'll be with you straight. Go a little before.

           [Exeunt all except HAMLET.*]*
How all occasions do inform against° me
And spur my dull revenge! What is a man,
If his chief good and market of° his time   35
Be but to sleep and feed? A beast, no more.
Sure he that made us with such large discourse,°
Looking before and after,° gave us not
That capability and godlike reason
To fust° in us unused. Now, whether it be   40
Bestial oblivion,° or some craven° scruple

3 **the conveyance of** escort during   6 **duty** respect.   **eye** presence   **9 softly**
slowly, circumspectly   **10 powers** forces   **16 main** main part   **18 addition**
exaggeration   **21 To pay** i.e., for a yearly rental of.   **farm it** take a lease of it
23 ranker higher.   **in fee** fee simple, outright   **27 debate . . . straw** settle this trifling matter   **28 impostume** abscess   **33 inform against** denounce, betray; take
shape against   **35 market of** profit of, compensation for   **37 discourse** power of
reasoning   **38 Looking before and after** able to review past events and anticipate
the future   **40 fust** grow moldy   **41 oblivion** forgetfulness.   **craven** cowardly

Of thinking too precisely° on th' event° —
A thought which, quartered, hath but one part wisdom
And ever three parts coward—I do not know
Why yet I live to say "This thing's to do,"   45
Sith° I have cause, and will, and strength, and means
To do 't. Examples gross° as earth exhort me:
Witness this army of such mass and charge,°
Led by a delicate and tender° prince,
Whose spirit with divine ambition puffed   50
Makes mouths° at the invisible event,°
Exposing what is mortal and unsure
To all that fortune, death, and danger dare,°
Even for an eggshell. Rightly to be great
Is not to stir without great argument,   55
But greatly to find quarrel in a straw
When honor's at the stake.° How stand I, then,
That have a father killed, a mother stained,
Excitements of° my reason and my blood,
And let all sleep, while to my shame I see   60
The imminent death of twenty thousand men
That for a fantasy° and trick° of fame
Go to their graves like beds, fight for a plot°
Whereon the numbers cannot try the cause,°
Which is not tomb enough and continent°   65
To hide the slain? O, from this time forth
My thoughts be bloody or be nothing worth!

                                                       Exit.

  4.5   *Enter* HORATIO, *[*QUEEN*]* GERTRUDE, *and a* GENTLEMAN.

QUEEN. I will not speak with her.
GENTLEMAN.   She is importunate,
    Indeed distract.° Her mood will needs be pitied.
QUEEN. What would she have?
GENTLEMAN. She speaks much of her father, says she hears
    There's tricks° i' the world, and hems,° and beats her heart,°   5
    Spurns enviously at straws,° speaks things in doubt°
    That carry but half sense. Her speech is nothing,

42 precisely scrupulously. **event** outcome   **46 Sith** since   **47 gross** obvious
48 charge expense   **49 delicate and tender** of fine and youthful qualities
51 Makes mouths makes scornful faces.   **invisible event** unforeseeable outcome
53 dare could do (to him)   **54–57 Rightly . . . stake** true greatness does not normally consist of rushing into action over some trivial provocation; however, when
one's honor is involved, even a trifling insult requires that one respond greatly (?)
at the stake (A metaphor from gambling or bear-baiting.)   **59 Excitements of**
promptings by   **62 fantasy** fanciful caprice, illusion.   **trick** trifle, deceit   **63 plot**
plot of ground   **64 Whereon . . . cause** on which there is insufficient room for the
soldiers needed to engage in a military contest   **65 continent** receptacle; container   **4.5. Location: The castle.**   **2 distract** distracted   **5 tricks** deceptions.
hems makes "hmm" sounds.   **heart** i.e., breast   **6 Spurns . . . straws** kicks spite-
fully, takes offense at trifles.   **in doubt** obscurely

Yet the unshapèd use° of it doth move
The hearers to collection;° they yawn° at it,
And botch° the words up fit to their own thoughts,   10
Which,° as her winks and nods and gestures yield° them,
Indeed would make one think there might be thought,°
Though nothing sure, yet much unhappily.°
HORATIO. 'Twere good she were spoken with, for she may strew
Dangerous conjectures in ill-breeding° minds.   15
QUEEN. Let her come in.   *[Exit* GENTLEMAN.*]*
    [Aside.] To my sick soul, as sin's true nature is,
Each toy° seems prologue to some great amiss.°
So full of artless jealousy is guilt,
It spills itself in fearing to be spilt.°   20
    Enter OPHELIA ° *[distracted].*
OPHELIA. Where is the beauteous majesty of Denmark?
QUEEN. How now, Ophelia?
OPHELIA *[she sings].*
            "How should I your true love know
                From another one?
            By his cockle hat° and staff,   25
                And his sandal shoon."°
QUEEN. Alas, sweet lady, what imports this song?
OPHELIA. Say you? Nay, pray you, mark.
            "He is dead and gone, lady,   *[Song.]*
                He is dead and gone;   30
            At his head a grass-green turf,
                At his heels a stone."
        O, ho!
QUEEN. Nay, but Ophelia—
OPHELIA. Pray you, mark.   *[Sings.]*   35
            "White his shroud as the mountain snow"—
    Enter KING.
QUEEN. Alas, look here, my lord.
OPHELIA.
            "Larded° with sweet flowers;   *[Song.]*
            Which bewept to the ground did not go
                With true-love showers."°   40
KING. How do you, pretty lady?
OPHELIA. Well, God 'ild° you! They say the owl° was a baker's daughter.

---

8 unshapèd use incoherent manner   **9 collection** inference, a guess at some sort
of meaning.   **yawn** gape, wonder; grasp. (The Folio reading, *aim,* is possible.)
10 botch patch   **11 Which** which words.   **yield** deliver, represent   **12 thought**
intended   **13 unhappily** unpleasantly near the truth, shrewdly   **15 ill-breeding**
prone to suspect the worst and to make mischief   **18 toy** trifle.   **amiss** calamity
19–20 So . . . split guilt is so full of suspicion that it unskillfully betrays itself in fearing betrayal   **20 s.d. Enter Ophelia** (In the First Quarto, Ophelia enters, "playing
on a lute, and her hair down, singing.")   **25 cockle hat** hat with cockle-shell stuck
in it as a sign that the wearer had been a pilgrim to the shrine of Saint James of Com-
postela in Spain   **26 shoon** shoes   **38 Larded** decorated   **40 showers** i.e., tears
42 God 'ild God yield or reward.   **owl** (Refers to a legend about a baker's daughter
who was turned into an owl for being ungenerous when Jesus begged a loaf of
bread.)

Lord, we know what we are, but know not what we may be. God
be at your table!

KING. Conceit° upon her father.   45

OPHELIA. Pray let's have no words of this; but when they ask you what it
means, say you this:

> "Tomorrow is Saint Valentine's day,   *[Song.]*
> All in the morning betime,°
> And I a maid at your window,   50
> To be your Valentine.
> Then up he rose, and donned his clothes,
> And dupped° the chamber door,
> Let in the maid, that out a maid
> Never departed more."   55

KING. Pretty Ophelia—

OPHELIA. Indeed, la, without an oath, I'll make an end on 't: *[Sings.]*

> "By Gis° and by Saint Charity,
> Alack, and fie for shame!
> Young men will do 't, if they come to 't;   60
> By Cock,° they are to blame.
> Quoth she, 'Before you tumbled me,
> You promised me to wed.' "

He answers:

> " 'So would I ha' done, by yonder sun,   65
> An° thou hadst not come to my bed.' "

KING. How long hath she been thus?

OPHELIA. I hope all will be well. We must be patient, but I cannot
choose but weep to think they would lay him i' the cold ground.
My brother shall know of it. And so I thank you for your good coun-   70
sel. Come, my coach! Good night, ladies, good night, sweet ladies,
good night, good night.

[Exit.]

KING *[to* HORATIO*]*. Follow her close. Give her good watch, I pray you.

[Exit HORATIO.*]*

O, this is the poison of deep grief; it springs
All from her father's death—and now behold!   75
O Gertrude, Gertrude,
When sorrows come, they come not single spies,°
But in battalions. First, her father slain;
Next, your son gone, and he most violent author
Of his own just remove;° the people muddied,°   80
Thick and unwholesome in their thoughts and whispers
For good Polonius' death—and we have done but greenly,°
In hugger-mugger° to inter him; poor Ophelia
Divided from herself and her fair judgment,
Without the which we are pictures or mere beasts;   85

---

45 **Conceit** brooding   49 **betime** early   53 **dupped** did up, opened   58 **Gis**
Jesus   61 **Cock** (A perversion of "God" in oaths; here also with a quibble on the
slang word for penis.)   66 **An** if   77 **spies** scouts sent in advance of the main
force   80 **remove** removal.   **muddied** stirred up, confused   82 **greenly** in an in-
experienced way, foolishly   83 **hugger-mugger** secret haste

Last, and as much containing° as all these,
Her brother is in secret come from France,
Feeds on this wonder, keeps himself in clouds,°
And wants° not buzzers° to infect his ear
With pestilent speeches of his father's death,   90
Wherein necessity,° of matter beggared,°
Will nothing stick our person to arraign
In ear and ear.° O my dear Gertrude, this,
Like to a murdering piece,° in many places
Gives me superfluous death.°   *A noise within.*   95

QUEEN. Alack, what noise is this?

KING. Attend!°
Where is my Switzers?° Let them guard the door.
Enter a MESSENGER.
What is the matter?

MESSENGER.   Save yourself, my lord!
The ocean, overpeering of his list,°   100
Eats not the flats° with more impetuous° haste
Than young Laertes, in a riotous head,°
O'erbears your officers. The rabble call him lord,
And, as° the world were now but to begin,
Antiquity forgot, custom not known,   105
The ratifiers and props of every word,°
They cry, "Choose we! Laertes shall be king!"
Caps,° hands, and tongues applaud it to the clouds,
"Laertes shall be king, Laertes king!"

QUEEN. How cheerfully on the false trail they cry!   110
                                                A noise within.
O, this is counter,° you false Danish dogs!
Enter LAERTES *with others.*

KING. The doors are broke.

LAERTES. Where is this King?—Sirs, stand you all without.

ALL. No, let's come in.

LAERTES. I pray you, give me leave.   115

ALL. We will, we will.

LAERTES. I thank you. Keep the door. *[Exeunt followers.]* O thou vile king,
Give me my father!

86 as much containing as full of serious matter   **88 Feeds ... clouds** feeds his
resentment or shocked grievance, holds himself inscrutable and aloof amid all this
rumor   **89 wants** lacks.   **buzzers** gossipers, informers   **91 necessity** i.e., the need
to invent some plausible explanation.   **of matter beggared** unprovided with facts
92–93 Will ... ear will not hesitate to accuse my (royal) person in everybody's ears
94 murdering piece cannon loaded so as to scatter its shot   **95 Gives ... death**
kills me over and over   **97 Attend** i.e., guard me   **98 Switzers** Swiss guards, mer-
cenaries   **100 overpeering of his list** overflowing its shore, boundary   **101 flats**
i.e., flatlands near shore.   **impetuous** violent (perhaps also with the meaning
of *impiteous* [*impitious,* Q2], "pitiless")   **102 head** insurrection   **104 as** as if
106 The ratifiers ... word i.e., *antiquity* (or tradition) and *custom* ought to confirm (*ratify*) and underprop our every word or promise.   **108 Caps** (The caps are
thrown in the air.)   **111 counter** (A hunting term, meaning to follow the trail in a
direction opposite to that which the game has taken.)

QUEEN *[restraining him]*. Calmly, good Laertes.

LAERTES. That drop of blood that's calm proclaims me bastard,
 Cries cuckold to my father, brands the harlot   120
 Even here, between° the chaste unsmirchèd brow
 Of my true mother.

KING.   What is the cause, Laertes,
 That thy rebellion looks so giantlike?
 Let him go, Gertrude. Do not fear our° person.
 There's such divinity doth hedge° a king   125
 That treason can but peep to what it would,°
 Acts little of his will.° Tell me, Laertes,
 Why thou art thus incensed. Let him go, Gertrude.
 Speak, man.

LAERTES.   Where is my father?

KING.   Dead.

QUEEN. But not by him.

KING.   Let him demand his fill.   130

LAERTES. How came he dead? I'll not be juggled with.°
 To hell, allegiance! Vows, to the blackest devil!
 Conscience and grace, to the profoundest pit!
 I dare damnation. To this point I stand,°
 That both the worlds I give to negligence,°   135
 Let come what comes, only I'll be revenged
 Most throughly° for my father.

KING. Who shall stay you?

LAERTES. My will, not all the world's.°
 And for° my means, I'll husband them so well   140
 They shall go far with little.

KING.   Good Laertes,
 If you desire to know the certainty
 Of your dear father, is 't writ in your revenge
 That, swoopstake,° you will draw both friend and foe,
 Winner and loser?   145

LAERTES. None but his enemies.

KING. Will you know them, then?

LAERTES. To his good friends thus wide I'll ope my arms,
 And like the kind life-rendering pelican°
 Repast° them with my blood.

KING.   Why, now you speak   150

---

121 between in the middle of **124 fear our** fear for my **125 hedge** protect, as with a surrounding barrier **126 can . . . would** can only peep furtively, as through a barrier, at what it would intend **127 Acts . . . will** (but) performs little of what it intends **131 juggled with** cheated, deceived **134 To . . . stand** I am resolved in this **135 both . . . negligence** i.e., both this world and the next are of no consequence to me **137 throughly** thoroughly **139 My will . . . world's** I'll stop (*stay*) when my will is accomplished, not for anyone else's. **140 for** as for **144 swoopstake** i.e., indiscriminately. (Literally, taking all stakes on the gambling table at once. *Draw* is also a gambling term, meaning "take from.") **149 pelican** (Refers to the belief that the female pelican fed its young with its own blood.) **150 Repast** feed

Like a good child and a true gentleman.
That I am guiltless of your father's death,
And am most sensibly° in grief for it,
It shall as level° to your judgment 'pear
As day does to your eye.   *A noise within.* 155

LAERTES. How now, what noise is that?

Enter OPHELIA.

KING.   Let her come in.

LAERTES. O heat, dry up my brains! Tears seven times salt
Burn out the sense and virtue° of mine eye!
By heaven, thy madness shall be paid with weight°
Till our scale turn the beam.° O rose of May!   160
Dear maid, kind sister, sweet Ophelia!
O heavens, is 't possible a young maid's wits
Should be as mortal as an old man's life?
Nature is fine in° love, and where 'tis fine
It sends some precious instance° of itself   165
After the thing it loves.°

OPHELIA.   *[Song.]*
       "They bore him barefaced on the bier,
            Hey non nonny, nonny, hey nonny,
       And in his grave rained many a tear—"
Fare you well, my dove!   170

LAERTES. Hadst thou thy wits and didst persuade° revenge,
It could not move thus.

OPHELIA. You must sing "A-down a-down," and you "call him a-down-
a."° O, how the wheel° becomes it! It is the false steward° that
stole his master's daughter.   175

LAERTES. This nothing's more than matter.°

OPHELIA. There's rosemary,° that's for remembrance; pray you, love, remember. And there is pansies;° that's for thoughts.

LAERTES. A document° in madness, thoughts and remembrance fitted.

OPHELIA. There's fennel° for you, and columbines.° There's rue° for 180
you, and here's some for me; we may call it herb of grace o' Sundays. You must wear your rue with a difference.° There's a daisy.°

---

153 sensibly feelingly   **154 level** plain   **158 virtue** faculty, power   **159 paid
with weight** repaid, avenged equally or more   **160 beam** crossbar of a balance
164 fine in refined by   **165 instance** token   **166 After . . . loves** i.e., into the
grave, along with Polonius   **171 persuade** argue cogently for   **173–174 You . . .
a-down-a** (Ophelia assigns the singing of refrains, like her own "Hey non nonny,"
to others present.)   **174 wheel** spinning wheel as accompaniment to the song, or
refrain   **false steward** (The story is unknown.)   **176 This . . . matter** this seeming nonsense is more eloquent than sane utterance   **177 rosemary** (Used as a symbol of remembrance both at weddings and at funerals.)   **178 pansies** (Emblems of
love and courtship; perhaps from French *pensées,* "thoughts.")   **179 document** instruction, lesson   **180 fennel** (Emblem of flattery.)   **columbines** (Emblems of
unchastity or ingratitude.)   **rue** (Emblem of repentance—a signification that is evident in its popular name, *herb of grace.*)   **182 with a difference** (A device used
in heraldry to distinguish one family from another on the coat of arms, here suggesting that Ophelia and the others have different causes of sorrow and repentance;
perhaps with a play on *rue* in the sense of "ruth," "pity.")   **daisy** (Emblem of dissembling, faithlessness.)

I would give you some violets,° but they withered all when my fa-
ther died. They say 'a made a good end—
[Sings.] "For bonny sweet Robin is all my joy."   185
LAERTES. Thought° and affliction, passion,° hell itself,
    She turns to favor° and to prettiness.
OPHELIA.   *[Song.]*
        "And will 'a not come again?
        And will 'a not come again?
            No, no, he is dead.   190
            Go to thy deathbed,
        He never will come again.

        "His beard was as white as snow,
        All flaxen was his poll.°
            He is gone, he is gone,   195
            And we cast away moan.
        God ha' mercy on his soul!"
    And of all Christian souls, I pray God. God b' wi' you.
                        [Exit, followed by GERTRUDE.*]*
LAERTES. Do you see this, O God?
KING. Laertes, I must commune with your grief,   200
    Or you deny me right. Go but apart,
    Make choice of whom° your wisest friends you will,
    And they shall hear and judge twixt you and me.
    If by direct or by collateral hand°
    They find us touched,° we will our kingdom give,   205
    Our crown, our life, and all that we call ours
    To you in satisfaction; but if not,
    Be you content to lend your patience to us,
    And we shall jointly labor with your soul
    To give it due content.
LAERTES.   Let this be so.   210
    His means of death, his obscure funeral—
    No trophy,° sword, nor hatchment° o'er his bones,
    No noble rite, nor formal ostentation°—
    Cry to be heard, as 'twere from heaven to earth,
    That° I must call 't in question.°
KING.   So you shall,   215
    And where th' offense is, let the great ax fall.
    I pray you, go with me.
                        Exeunt.

       4.6   *Enter* HORATIO *and others.*

HORATIO. What are they that would speak with me?
GENTLEMAN. Seafaring men, sir. They say they have letters for you.
HORATIO. Let them come in.

183 violets (Emblems of faithfulness.)   **186 Thought** melancholy   **passion** suffering   **187 favor** grace, beauty   **194 poll** head   **202 whom** whichever of
204 collateral hand indirect agency   **205 us touched** me implicated   **213 trophy** memorial.   **hatchment** tablet displaying the armorial bearings of a deceased
person   **213 ostentation** ceremony   **215 That** so that.   **call 't in question** demand an explanation   **4.6. Location: The castle.**

[Exit GENTLEMAN.*]*

I do not know from what part of the world
I should be greeted, if not from Lord Hamlet.   5
Enter Sailors.

FIRST SAILOR. God bless you, sir.

HORATIO. Let him bless thee too.

FIRST SAILOR. 'A shall, sir, an 't° please him. There's a letter for you, sir—
it came from th' ambassador° that was bound for England—if your
name be Horatio, as I am let to know it is.   *[He gives a letter.]*   10

HORATIO *[reads].* "Horatio, when thou shalt have overlooked° this, give
these fellows some means° to the King; they have letters for him.
Ere we were two days old at sea, a pirate of very warlike appoint-
ment° gave us chase. Finding ourselves too slow of sail, we put on
a compelled valor, and in the grapple I boarded them. On the in-   15
stant they got clear of our ship, so I alone became their prisoner.
They have dealt with me like thieves of mercy,° but they knew
what they did: I am to do a good turn for them. Let the King have
the letters I have sent, and repair° thou to me with as much speed
as thou wouldest fly death. I have words to speak in thine ear will   20
make thee dumb, yet are they much too light for the bore° of the
matter. These good fellows will bring thee where I am. Rosencrantz and Guildenstern hold their course for England. Of them I
have much to tell thee. Farewell.

He that thou knowest thine, Hamlet."   25

Come, I will give you way° for these your letters,
And do 't the speedier that you may direct me
To him from whom you brought them.

Exeunt.

4.7 *Enter* KING *and* LAERTES.

KING. Now must your conscience my acquittance seal,°
And you must put me in your heart for friend,
Sith° you have heard, and with a knowing ear,
That he which hath your noble father slain
Pursued my life.

LAERTES.   It well appears. But tell me   5
Why you proceeded not against these feats°
So crimeful and so capital° in nature,
As by your safety, greatness, wisdom, all things else,
You mainly° were stirred up.

KING.   O, for two special reasons,   10
Which may to you perhaps seem much unsinewed,°
But yet to me they're strong. The Queen his mother
Lives almost by his looks, and for myself—

8 an 't if it   **9 th' ambassador** (Evidently Hamlet. The sailor is being circumspect.)
11 overlooked looked over   **12 means** means of access   **13–14 appointment**
equipage   **17 thieves of mercy** merciful thieves   **19 repair** come   **21 bore** cal-
iber, i.e., importance   **26 way** means of access   **4.7 Location: The castle.**   **1 my
acquittance seal** confirm or acknowledge my innocence   **3 Sith** since   **6 feats**
acts   **7 capital** punishable by death   **9 mainly** greatly   **11 unsinewed** weak

My virtue or my plague, be it either which—
She is so conjunctive° to my life and soul   15
That, as the star moves not but in his° sphere,°
I could not but by her. The other motive
Why to a public count° I might not go
Is the great love the general gender° bear him,
Who, dipping all his faults in their affection,   20
Work° like the spring° that turneth wood to stone,
Convert his gyves° to graces, so that my arrows,
Too slightly timbered° for so loud° a wind,
Would have reverted° to my bow again
But not where I had aimed them.   25

LAERTES. And so have I a noble father lost,
A sister driven into desperate terms,°
Whose worth, if praises may go back° again,
Stood challenger on mount° of all the age
For her perfections. But my revenge will come.   30

KING. Break not your sleeps for that. You must not think
That we are made of stuff so flat and dull
That we can let our beard be shook with danger
And think it pastime. You shortly shall hear more.
I loved your father, and we love ourself;   35
And that, I hope, will teach you to imagine—

Enter a MESSENGER *with letters.*

How now? What news?

MESSENGER. Letters, my lord, from Hamlet:
This to Your Majesty, this to the Queen.

                                          [He gives letters.]

KING. From Hamlet? Who brought them?   40

MESSENGER. Sailors, my lord, they say. I saw them not.
They were given me by Claudio. He received them
Of him that brought them.

KING.   Laertes, you shall hear them.—
Leave us.

                                          [Exit MESSENGER.*]*

[He reads.] "High and mighty, you shall know I am set naked° on   45
your kingdom. Tomorrow shall I beg leave to see your kingly eyes,
when I shall, first asking your pardon,° thereunto recount the occasion of my sudden and more strange return.   Hamlet."

What should this mean? Are all the rest come back?

---

15 conjunctive closely united. (An astronomical metaphor.) **16 his** its. **sphere**
one of the hollow spheres in which, according to Ptolemaic astronomy, the planets
were supposed to move **18 count** account, reckoning, indictment **19 general
gender** common people **21 Work** operate, act. **spring** i.e., a spring with such a
concentration of lime that it coats a piece of wood with limestone, in effect gilding
and petrifying it **22 gyves** fetters (which, gilded by the people's praise, would
look like badges of honor) **23 slightly timbered** light. **loud** (suggesting public
outcry on Hamlet's behalf) **24 reverted** returned **27 terms** state, condition
28 go back i.e., recall what she was **29 on mount** set up on high **45 naked**
destitute, unarmed, without following **47 pardon** permission

Or is it some abuse,° and no such thing?°   50
LAERTES. Know you the hand?
KING.   'Tis Hamlet's character.° "Naked!"
    And in a postscript here he says "alone."
    Can you devise° me?
LAERTES. I am lost in it, my lord. But let him come.
    It warms the very sickness in my heart   55
    That I shall live and tell him to his teeth,
    "Thus didst thou."°
KING.   If it be so, Laertes—
    As how should it be so? How otherwise?°—
    Will you be ruled by me?
LAERTES.   Ay, my lord,
    So° you will not o'errule me to a peace.   60
KING. To thine own peace. If he be now returned,
    As checking at° his voyage, and that° he means
    No more to undertake it, I will work him
    To an exploit, now ripe in my device,°
    Under the which he shall not choose but fall;   65
    And for his death no wind of blame shall breathe,
    But even his mother shall uncharge the practice°
    And call it accident.
LAERTES.   My lord, I will be ruled,
    The rather if you could devise it so
    That I might be the organ.°
KING.   It falls right.   70
    You have been talked of since your travel much,
    And that in Hamlet's hearing, for a quality
    Wherein they say you shine. Your sum of parts°
    Did not together pluck such envy from him
    As did that one, and that, in my regard,   75
    Of the unworthiest siege.°
LAERTES. What part is that, my lord?
KING. A very ribbon in the cap of youth,
    Yet needful too, for youth no less becomes°
    The light and careless livery that it wears   80
    Than settled age his sables° and his weeds°
    Importing health and graveness.° Two months since
    Here was a gentleman of Normandy.

---

50 abuse deceit.   **no such thing** not what it appears   **51 character** handwriting
53 devise explain to   **57 Thus didst thou** i.e., here's for what you did to my father   **58 As . . . otherwise** how can this (Hamlet's return) be true? Yet how otherwise than true (since we have the evidence of his letter)?   **60 So** provided that
62 checking at i.e., turning aside from (like a falcon leaving the quarry to fly at a
chance bird).   **that** if   **64 device** devising, invention   **67 uncharge the practice**
acquit the stratagem of being a plot   **70 organ** agent, instrument   **73 Your . . .
parts** i.e., all your other virtues   **76 unworthiest siege** least important rank
79 no less becomes is no less suited by   **81 his sables** its rich robes furred with
sable.   **weeds** garments   **82 Importing . . . graveness** signifying a concern for
health and dignified prosperity; also, giving an impression of comfortable prosperity

I have seen myself, and served against, the French,
And they can well° on horseback, but this gallant   85
Had witchcraft in 't; he grew unto his seat,
And to such wondrous doing brought his horse
As had he been incorpsed and demi-natured°
With the brave beast. So far he topped° my thought
That I in forgery° of shapes and tricks   90
Come short of what he did.

LAERTES.   A Norman was 't?

KING. A Norman.

LAERTES. Upon my life, Lamord.

KING.   The very same.

LAERTES. I know him well. He is the brooch° indeed
And gem of all the nation.   95

KING. He made confession° of you,
And gave you such a masterly report
For art and exercise in your defense,°
And for your rapier most especial,
That he cried out 'twould be a sight indeed   100
If one could match you. Th' escrimers° of their nation,
He swore, had neither motion, guard, nor eye
If you opposed them. Sir, this report of his
Did Hamlet so envenom with his envy
That he could nothing do but wish and beg   105
Your sudden° coming o'er, to play° with you.
Now, out of this—

LAERTES.   What out of this, my lord?

KING. Laertes, was your father dear to you?
Or are you like the painting of a sorrow,
A face without a heart?

LAERTES.   Why ask you this?   110

KING. Not that I think you did not love your father,
But that I know love is begun by time,°
And that I see, in passages of proof,°
Time qualifies° the spark and fire of it.
There lives within the very flame of love   115
A kind of wick or snuff° that will abate it,
And nothing is at a like goodness still,°
For goodness, growing to a pleurisy,°
Dies in his own too much.° That° we would do,

85 can well are skilled   **88 As ... demi-natured** as if he had been of one body and nearly of one nature (like the centaur)   **89 topped** surpassed   **90 forgery** imagining   **94 brooch** ornament   **96 confession** testimonial, admission of superiority   **98 For ... defense** with respect to your skill and practice with your weapon   **101 escrimers** fencers   **106 sudden** immediate. **play** fence   **112 begun by time** i.e., created by the right circumstance and hence subject to change **113 passages of proof** actual instances that prove it   **114 qualifies** weakens, moderates   **116 snuff** the charred part of a candlewick   **117 nothing ... still** nothing remains at a constant level of perfection   **118 pleurisy** excess, plethora. (Literally, a chest inflammation.)   **119 in ... much** of its own excess.   **That** that which

We should do when we would; for this "would" changes   120
And hath abatements° and delays as many
As there are tongues, are hands, are accidents,°
And then this "should" is like a spendthrift sigh,°
That hurts by easing.° But, to the quick o' th' ulcer:°
Hamlet comes back. What would you undertake   125
To show yourself in deed your father's son
More than in words?

LAERTES.   To cut his throat i' the church.

KING. No place, indeed, should murder sanctuarize;°
Revenge should have no bounds. But good Laertes,
Will you do this,° keep close within your chamber.   130
Hamlet returned shall know you are come home.
We'll put on those shall° praise your excellence
And set a double varnish on the fame
The Frenchman gave you, bring you in fine° together,
And wager on your heads. He, being remiss,°   135
Most generous,° and free from all contriving,
Will not peruse the foils, so that with ease,
Or with a little shuffling, you may choose
A sword unbated,° and in a pass of practice°
Requite him for your father.

LAERTES.   I will do 't,   140
And for that purpose I'll anoint my sword.
I bought an unction° of a mountebank°
So mortal that, but dip a knife in it,
Where it draws blood no cataplasm° so rare,
Collected from all simples° that have virtue°   145
Under the moon,° can save the thing from death
That is but scratched withal. I'll touch my point
With this contagion, that if I gall° him slightly,
It may be death.

KING.   Let's further think of this,
Weigh what convenience both of time and means   150
May fit us to our shape.° If this should fail,
And that our drift look through our bad performance,°

---

121 abatements diminutions   **122 As ... accidents** as there are tongues to dissuade, hands to prevent, and chance events to intervene   **123 spendthrift sigh** (An allusion to the belief that sighs draw blood from the heart.)   **124 hurts by easing** i.e., costs the heart blood and wastes precious opportunity even while it affords emotional relief.   **quick o' th' ulcer** i.e., heart of the matter   **128 sanctuarize** protect from punishment. (Alludes to the right of sanctuary with which certain religious places were invested.)   **130 Will you do this** if you wish to do this   **132 put on those shall** arrange for some to   **134 in fine** finally   **135 remiss** negligently unsuspicious   **136 generous** noble-minded   **139 unbated** not blunted, having no button.   **pass of practice** treacherous thrust   **142 unction** ointment.   **mountebank** quack doctor   **144 cataplasm** plaster or poultice   **145 simples** herbs.   **virtue** potency   **146 Under the moon** i.e., anywhere (with reference perhaps to the belief that herbs gathered at night had a special power)   **148 gall** graze, wound   **151 shape** part we propose to act   **152 drift ... performance** intention should be made visible by our bungling

'Twere better not assayed. Therefore this project
Should have a back or second, that might hold
If this did blast in proof.° Soft, let me see.   155
We'll make a solemn wager on your cunnings°—
I ha 't!
When in your motion you are hot and dry—
As° make your bouts more violent to that end—
And that he calls for drink, I'll have prepared him   160
A chalice for the nonce,° whereon but sipping,
If he by chance escape your venomed stuck,°
Our purpose may hold there. *[A cry within.]* But stay, what noise?
Enter QUEEN.
QUEEN. One woe doth tread upon another's heel,
So fast they follow. Your sister's drowned, Laertes.   165
LAERTES. Drowned! O, where?
QUEEN. There is a willow grows askant° the brook,
That shows his hoar leaves° in the glassy stream;
Therewith fantastic garlands did she make
Of crowflowers, nettles, daisies, and long purples,°   170
That liberal° shepherds give a grosser name,°
But our cold° maids do dead men's fingers call them.
There on the pendent° boughs her crownet° weeds
Clamb'ring to hang, an envious sliver° broke,
When down her weedy° trophies and herself   175
Fell in the weeping brook. Her clothes spread wide,
And mermaidlike awhile they bore her up,
Which time she chanted snatches of old lauds,°
As one incapable of° her own distress,
Or like a creature native and endued°   180
Unto that element. But long it could not be
Till that her garments, heavy with their drink,
Pulled the poor wretch from her melodious lay
To muddy death.
LAERTES.   Alas, then she is drowned?
QUEEN. Drowned, drowned.   185
LAERTES. Too much of water hast thou, poor Ophelia,
And therefore I forbid my tears. But yet
It is our trick;° nature her custom holds,

155 blast in proof burst in the test (like a cannon)   **156 cunnings** respective
skills   **159 As** i.e., and you should   **161 nonce** occasion   **162 stuck** thrust.
(From *stoccado,* a fencing term.)   **167 askant** aslant   **168 hoar leaves** white or
gray undersides of the leaves   **170 long purples** early purple orchids   **171 liberal** free-spoken.   **a grosser name** (The testicle-resembling tubers of the orchid,
which also in some cases resemble *dead men's fingers,* have earned various slang
names like "dogstones" and "cullions.")   **172 cold** chaste   **173 pendent** over-
hanging.   **crownet** made into a chaplet or coronet   **174 envious sliver** malicious
branch   **175 weedy** i.e., of plants   **178 lauds** hymns   **179 incapable of** lacking
capacity to apprehend   **180 endued** adapted by nature   **188 It is our trick** i.e.,
weeping is our natural way (when sad)

Let shame say what it will. *[He weeps.]* When these are gone,
The woman will be out.° Adieu, my lord.   190
I have a speech of fire that fain would blaze,
But that this folly douts° it.

Exit.

KING.   Let's follow, Gertrude.
How much I had to do to calm his rage!
Now fear I this will give it start again;
Therefore let's follow.   195

Exeunt.

5.1 *Enter two Clowns° [with spades and mattocks].*

FIRST CLOWN. Is she to be buried in Christian burial, when she willfully
        seeks her own salvation?°
SECOND CLOWN. I tell thee she is; therefore make her grave straight.° The
        crowner° hath sat on her,° and finds it° Christian burial.
FIRST CLOWN. How can that be, unless she drowned herself in her own   5
        defense?
SECOND CLOWN. Why, 'tis found so.°
FIRST CLOWN. It must be *se offendendo,*° it cannot be else. For here lies
        the point: if I drown myself wittingly, it argues an act, and an act
        hath three branches—it is to act, to do, and to perform. Argal,° she 10
        drowned herself wittingly.
SECOND CLOWN. Nay, but hear you, goodman° delver—
FIRST CLOWN. Give me leave. Here lies the water; good. Here stands the
        man; good. If the man go to this water and drown himself, it is, will
        he, nill he,° he goes, mark you that. But if the water come to him   15
        and drown him, he drowns not himself. Argal, he that is not guilty
        of his own death shortens not his own life.
SECOND CLOWN. But is this law?
FIRST CLOWN. Ay, marry, is 't—crowner's quest° law.
SECOND CLOWN. Will you ha' the truth on 't? If this had not been a gentle- 20
        woman, she should have been buried out o' Christian burial.
FIRST CLOWN. Why, there thou sayst.° And the more pity that great folk
        should have countenance° in this world to drown or hang them-
        selves, more than their even-Christian.° Come, my spade. There is

189–190 **When . . . out** when my tears are all shed, the woman in me will be expended, satisfied   192 **douts** extinguishes. (The Second Quarto reads "drowns.")
5.1. Location: A churchyard.   s.d. Clowns rustics   2 **salvation** (A blunder for
"damnation," or perhaps a suggestion that Ophelia was taking her own shortcut to
heaven.)   3 **straight** straightway, immediately. (But with a pun on *strait,* "narrow.")   4 **crowner** coroner.   **sat on her** conducted an inquest on her case
finds it gives his official verdict that her means of death was consistent with
7 **found so** determined so in the coroner's verdict   8 **se offendendo** (A comic
mistake for *se defendendo,* a term used in verdicts of justifiable homicide.)
10 **Argal** (Corruption of *ergo,* "therefore.")   12 **goodman** (An honorific title often
used with the name of a profession or craft.)   15 **will he, nill he** whether he will
or no, willy-nilly   19 **quest** inquest   22 **there thou sayst** i.e., that's right
23 **countenance** privilege   24 **even-Christian** fellow Christians

no ancient° gentlemen but gardeners, ditchers, and grave makers.   25
They hold up° Adam's profession.

SECOND CLOWN. Was he a gentleman?

FIRST CLOWN. 'A was the first that ever bore arms.°

SECOND CLOWN. Why, he had none.

FIRST CLOWN. What, art a heathen? How dost thou understand the Scrip-   30
ture? The Scripture says Adam digged. Could he dig without arms?°
I'll put another question to thee. If thou answerest me not to the
purpose, confess thyself° —

SECOND CLOWN. Go to.

FIRST CLOWN. What is he that builds stronger than either the mason, the   35
shipwright, or the carpenter?

SECOND CLOWN. The gallows maker, for that frame° outlives a thousand
tenants.

FIRST CLOWN. I like thy wit well, in good faith. The gallows does well.°
But how does it well? It does well to those that do ill. Now thou   40
dost ill to say the gallows is built stronger than the church. Argal,
the gallows may do well to thee. To 't again, come.

SECOND CLOWN. "Who builds stronger than a mason, a shipwright, or a
carpenter?"

FIRST CLOWN. Ay, tell me that, and unyoke.°   45

SECOND CLOWN. Marry, now I can tell.

FIRST CLOWN. To 't.

SECOND CLOWN. Mass,° I cannot tell.

Enter HAMLET *and* HORATIO *[at a distance].*

FIRST CLOWN. Cudgel thy brains no more about it, for your dull ass will
not mend his pace with beating; and when you are asked this ques-   50
tion next, say "a grave maker." The houses he makes lasts till
doomsday. Go get thee in and fetch me a stoup° of liquor.

[Exit SECOND CLOWN. FIRST CLOWN *digs.]*
Song.

"In youth, when I did love, did love,°
  Methought it was very sweet,
To contract—O—the time for—a—my behove,°   55
  O, methought there—a—was nothing—a—meet."°

HAMLET. Has this fellow no feeling of his business, 'a° sings in grave-
making?

HORATIO. Custom hath made it in him a property of easiness.°

---

25 ancient going back to ancient times   **26 hold up** maintain   **28 bore arms** (To
be entitled to bear a coat of arms would make Adam a gentleman, but as one who
bore a spade, our common ancestor was an ordinary delver in the earth.)   **31 arms**
i.e., the arms of the body   **33 confess thyself** (The saying continues, "and be
hanged.")   **37 frame** (1) gallows (2) structure   **39 does well** (1) is an apt answer
(2) does a good turn   **45 unyoke** i.e., after this great effort, you may unharness the
team of your wits   **48 Mass** by the Mass   **52 stoup** two-quart measure   **53 In . . .
love** (This and the two following stanzas, with nonsensical variations, are from a
poem attributed to Lord Vaux and printed in *Tottel's Miscellany*, 1557. The *O* and *a*
[for "ah"] seemingly are the grunts of the digger.)   **55 To contract . . . behove**
i.e., to shorten the time for my own advantage. (Perhaps he means to *prolong* it.)
56 meet suitable, i.e., more suitable   **57 'a** that he   **59 property of easiness**
something he can do easily and indifferently

HAMLET. 'Tis e'en so. The hand of little employment hath the daintier   60
sense.°

FIRST CLOWN.   *Song.*
        "But age with his stealing steps
                Hath clawed me in his clutch,
        And hath shipped me into the land,°
                As if I had never been such."   65
                                        [He throws up a skull.]

HAMLET. That skull had a tongue in it and could sing once. How the
knave jowls° it to the ground, as if 'twere Cain's jawbone, that did
the first murder! This might be the pate of a politician,° which this
ass now o'erreaches,° one that would circumvent God, might it
not?   70

HORATIO. It might, my lord.

HAMLET. Or of a courtier, which could say, "Good morrow, sweet lord!
How dost thou, sweet lord?" This might be my Lord Such-a-one,
that praised my Lord Such-a-one's horse when 'a meant to beg it,
might it not?   75

HORATIO. Ay, my lord.

HAMLET. Why, e'en so, and now my Lady Worm's, chapless,° and
knocked about the mazard° with a sexton's spade. Here's fine revolution,° an° we had the trick to see° 't. Did these bones cost no
more the breeding but° to play at loggets° with them? Mine ache to   80
think on 't.

FIRST CLOWN.   *Song.*
        "A pickax and a spade, a spade,
                For and° a shrouding sheet;
        O, a pit of clay for to be made
                For such a guest is meet."   85
                                    [He throws up another skull.]

HAMLET. There's another. Why may not that be the skull of a lawyer?
Where be his quiddities° now, his quillities,° his cases, his
tenures,° and his tricks? Why does he suffer this mad knave now to
knock him about the sconce° with a dirty shovel, and will not tell
him of his action of battery?° Hum, this fellow might be in 's time a   90
great buyer of land, with his statutes, his recognizances,° his fines,

---

60–61 daintier sense more delicate sense of feeling   **64 into the land** i.e., toward
my grave (?) (But note the lack of rhyme in *steps, land.*)   **67 jowls** dashes (with a
pun on *jowl,* "jawbone")   **68 politician** schemer, plotter   **69 o'erreaches** circum-
vents, gets the better of (with a quibble on the literal sense)   **77 chapless** having no
lower jaw.   **78 mazard** i.e., head. (Literally, a drinking vessel.)   **78–79 revolution**
turn of Fortune's wheel, change.   **79 an** if   **trick to see** knack of seeing
79–80 cost . . . but involve so little expense and care in upbringing that we may
80 loggets a game in which pieces of hard wood shaped like Indian clubs or bowling
pins are thrown to lie as near as possible to a stake   **83 For and** and moreover
87 quiddities subtleties, quibbles. (From Latin *quid,* "a thing.")   **quillities** verbal
niceties, subtle distinctions. (Variation of *quiddities.*)   **88 tenures** the holding of a
piece of property or office, or the conditions or period of such holding   **89 sconce**
head   **90 action of battery** lawsuit about physical assault   **91 statutes, recognizances** legal documents guaranteeing a debt by attaching land and property

his double° vouchers,° his recoveries.° Is this the fine of his fines
and the recovery of his recoveries, to have his fine pate full of fine
dirt?° Will his vouchers vouch him no more of his purchases, and
double ones too, than the length and breadth of a pair of inden-   95
tures?° The very conveyances° of his lands will scarcely lie in this
box,° and must th' inheritor° himself have no more, ha?

HORATIO. Not a jot more, my lord.

HAMLET. Is not parchment made of sheepskins?

HORATIO. Ay, my lord, and of calves' skins too.   100

HAMLET. They are sheep and calves which seek out assurance in that.° I
will speak to this fellow.—Whose grave's this, sirrah?°

FIRST CLOWN. Mine, sir.   *[Sings.]*

"O, pit of clay for to be made
    For such a guest is meet."   105

HAMLET. I think it be thine, indeed, for thou liest in 't.

FIRST CLOWN. You lie out on 't, sir, and therefore 'tis not yours. For my
part, I do not lie in 't, yet it is mine.

HAMLET. Thou dost lie in 't, to be in 't and say it is thine. 'Tis for the
dead, not for the quick;° therefore thou liest.   110

FIRST CLOWN. 'Tis a quick lie, sir; 'twill away again from me to you.

HAMLET. What man dost thou dig it for?

FIRST CLOWN. For no man, sir.

HAMLET. What woman, then?

FIRST CLOWN. For none, neither.   115

HAMLET. Who is to be buried in 't?

FIRST CLOWN. One that was a woman, sir, but, rest her soul, she's dead.

HAMLET. How absolute° the knave is! We must speak by the card,° or
equivocation° will undo us. By the Lord, Horatio, this three years I
have took° note of it: the age is grown so picked° that the toe of   120
the peasant comes so near the heel of the courtier, he galls his
kibe.°—How long hast thou been grave maker?

FIRST CLOWN. Of all the days i' the year, I came to 't that day that our last
king Hamlet overcame Fortinbras.

HAMLET. How long is that since?   125

FIRST CLOWN. Cannot you tell that? Every fool can tell that. It was that
very day that young Hamlet was born—he that is mad and sent into
England.

91–92 fines, recoveries ways of converting entailed estates into "fee simple" or
freehold   **92 double** signed by two signatories   **vouchers** guarantees of the legal-
ity of a title to real estate   **92–94 fine of his fines . . . fine pate . . . fine dirt** end
of his legal maneuvers . . . elegant head . . . minutely sifted dirt   **95–96 pair of in-
dentures** legal document drawn up in duplicate on a single sheet and then cut
apart on a zigzag line so that each pair was uniquely matched. (Hamlet may refer to
two rows of teeth or dentures.)   **96 conveyances** deeds   **97 box** (1) deed box
(2) coffin. ("Skull" has been suggested.)   **inheritor** possessor, owner   **101 assurance in that** safety in legal parchments   **102 sirrah** (A term of address to inferi-
ors.)   **110 quick** living   **118 absolute** strict, precise   **by the card** i.e., with pre-
cision. (Literally, by the mariner's compass-card, on which the points of
the compass were marked.)   **119 equivocation** ambiguity in the use of terms
120 took taken   **picked** refined, fastidious   **121–122 galls his kibe** chafes the
courtier's chilblain

HAMLET. Ay, marry, why was he sent into England?

FIRST CLOWN. Why, because 'a was mad. 'A shall recover his wits there,   130
or if 'a do not, 'tis no great matter there.

HAMLET. Why?

FIRST CLOWN. 'Twill not be seen in him there. There the men are as mad
as he.

HAMLET. How came he mad?   135

FIRST CLOWN. Very strangely, they say.

HAMLET. How strangely?

FIRST CLOWN. Faith, e'en with losing his wits.

HAMLET. Upon what ground?°

FIRST CLOWN. Why, here in Denmark. I have been sexton here, man and   140
boy, thirty years.

HAMLET. How long will a man lie i' th' earth ere he rot?

FIRST CLOWN. Faith, if 'a be not rotten before 'a die—as we have many
pocky° corpses nowadays, that will scarce hold the laying in°—'a
will last you° some eight year or nine year. A tanner will last you   145
nine year.

HAMLET. Why he more than another?

FIRST CLOWN. Why, sir, his hide is so tanned with his trade that 'a will
keep out water a great while, and your water is a sore° decayer of
your whoreson° dead body. *[He picks up a skull.]* Here's a skull   150
now hath lien you° i' th' earth three-and-twenty years.

HAMLET. Whose was it?

FIRST CLOWN. A whoreson mad fellow's it was. Whose do you think it
was?

HAMLET. Nay, I know not.   155

FIRST CLOWN. A pestilence on him for a mad rogue! 'A poured a flagon of
Rhenish° on my head once. This same skull, sir, was, sir, Yorick's
skull, the King's jester.

HAMLET. This?

FIRST CLOWN. E'en that.   160

HAMLET. Let me see. *[He takes the skull.]* Alas, poor Yorick! I knew him,
Horatio, a fellow of infinite jest, of most excellent fancy. He hath
bore° me on his back a thousand times, and now how abhorred in
my imagination it is! My gorge rises° at it. Here hung those lips that
I have kissed I know not how oft. Where be your gibes now? Your   165
gambols, your songs, your flashes of merriment that were wont° to
set the table on a roar? Not one now, to mock your own grinning?°
Quite chopfallen?° Now get you to my lady's chamber and tell her,

---

139 ground cause. (But, in the next line, the gravedigger takes the word in the
sense of "land," "country.")   **144 pocky** rotten, diseased. (Literally, with the pox,
or syphilis.)   **hold the laying in** hold together long enough to be interred
145 last you last. (*You* is used colloquially here and in the following lines.)
149 sore i.e., terrible, great   **150 whoreson** i.e., vile, scurvy   **151 lien you** lain.
(See the note at line 144.)   **157 Rhenish** Rhine wine   **163 bore** borne   **164 My
gorge rises** i.e., I feel nauseated   **166 were wont** used   **167 mock your own
grinning** mock at the way your skull seems to be grinning (just as you used to
mock at yourself and those who grinned at you)   **168 chopfallen** (1) lacking the
lower jaw (2) dejected

let her paint an inch thick, to this favor° she must come. Make her
laugh at that. Prithee, Horatio, tell me one thing.   170

HORATIO. What's that, my lord?

HAMLET. Dost thou think Alexander looked o' this fashion i' th' earth?

HORATIO. E'en so.

HAMLET. And smelt so? Pah! *[He throws down the skull.]*

HORATIO. E'en so, my lord.   175

HAMLET. To what base uses we may return, Horatio! Why may not imagination trace the noble dust of Alexander till 'a find it stopping a
bunghole?°

HORATIO. 'Twere to consider too curiously° to consider so.

HAMLET. No, faith, not a jot, but to follow him thither with modesty°   180
enough, and likelihood to lead it. As thus: Alexander died, Alexander was buried, Alexander returneth to dust, the dust is earth, of
earth we make loam,° and why of that loam whereto he was con-
verted might they not stop a beer barrel?
Imperious° Caesar, dead and turned to clay,   185
Might stop a hole to keep the wind away.
O, that that earth which kept the world in awe
Should patch a wall t' expel the winter's flaw!°
Enter KING, QUEEN, LAERTES, *and the corpse [of* OPHELIA, *in proces-
sion, with* PRIEST, *lords, etc.].*
But soft,° but soft awhile! Here comes the King,
The Queen, the courtiers. Who is this they follow?   190
And with such maimèd° rites? This doth betoken
The corpse they follow did with desperate hand
Fordo° its own life. 'Twas of some estate.°
Couch we° awhile and mark.
[He and HORATIO *conceal themselves.* OPHELIA'*s body is taken to the
grave.]*

LAERTES. What ceremony else?   195

HAMLET *[to* HORATIO*].* That is Laertes, a very noble youth. Mark.

LAERTES. What ceremony else?

PRIEST. Her obsequies have been as far enlarged
As we have warranty.° Her death was doubtful,
And but that great command o'ersways the order°   200
She should in ground unsanctified been lodged°
Till the last trumpet. For° charitable prayers,
Shards,° flints, and pebbles should be thrown on her.
Yet here she is allowed her virgin crants,°

---

169 favor aspect, appearance   **178 bunghole** hole for filling or emptying a cask
179 curiously minutely   **180 modesty** plausible moderation   **183 loam** mortar
consisting chiefly of moistened clay and straw   **185 Imperious** imperial
188 flaw gust of wind   **189 soft** i.e., wait, be careful   **191 maimèd** mutilated, incomplete   **193 Fordo** destroy.   **estate** rank   **194 Couch we** let's hide, lie low
199 warranty i.e., ecclesiastical authority   **200 great . . . order** orders from on
high overrule the prescribed procedures   **201 She should . . . lodged** she should
have been buried in unsanctified ground   **202 For** in place of   **203 Shards** broken bits of pottery   **204 crants** garlands betokening maidenhood

Her maiden strewments,° and the bringing home   205
Of bell and burial.°

LAERTES. Must there no more be done?

PRIEST.   No more be done.
We should profane the service of the dead
To sing a requiem and such rest° to her
As to peace-parted souls.°

LAERTES.   Lay her i' th' earth,   210
And from her fair and unpolluted flesh
May violets° spring! I tell thee, churlish priest,
A ministering angel shall my sister be
When thou liest howling.°

HAMLET *[to* HORATIO*]*.   What, the fair Ophelia!

QUEEN *[scattering flowers]*. Sweets to the sweet! Farewell.   215
I hoped thou shouldst have been my Hamlet's wife.
I thought thy bride-bed to have decked, sweet maid,
And not t' have strewed thy grave.

LAERTES.   O, treble woe
Fall ten times treble on that cursèd head
Whose wicked deed thy most ingenious sense°   220
Deprived thee of! Hold off the earth awhile,
Till I have caught her once more in mine arms.
[He leaps into the grave and embraces OPHELIA.*]*
Now pile your dust upon the quick and dead,
Till of this flat a mountain you have made
T' o'ertop old Pelion or the skyish head   225
Of blue Olympus.°

HAMLET *[coming forward]*. What is he whose grief
Bears such an emphasis,° whose phrase of sorrow
Conjures the wandering stars° and makes them stand
Like wonder-wounded° hearers? This is I,
Hamlet the Dane.°

LAERTES *[grappling with him°]*. The devil take thy soul!   230

HAMLET. Thou pray'st not well.
I prithee, take thy fingers from my throat,
For though I am not splenitive° and rash,

---

205 strewments flowers strewn on a coffin   **205–206 bringing . . . burial** laying
the body to rest, to the sound of the bell   **209 such rest** i.e., to pray for such rest
210 peace-parted souls those who have died at peace with God   **212 violets**
(See 4.5.183 and note)   **214 howling** i.e., in hell   **220 ingenious sense** a mind
that is quick, alert, of fine qualities   **225–226 Pelion, Olympus** sacred mountains
in the north of Thessaly; see also *Ossa*, below, at line 257   **227 emphasis** i.e.,
rhetorical and florid emphasis. (*Phrase* has a similar rhetorical connotation.)
228 wandering stars planets   **229 wonder-wounded** struck with amazement
230 the Dane (This title normally signifies the King; see 1.1.17 and note.)   **s.d.
grappling with him** The testimony of the First Quarto that "*Hamlet leaps in after
Laertes*" and the "Elegy on Burbage" ("Oft have I seen him leap into the grave")
seem to indicate one way in which this fight was staged; however, the difficulty of
fitting two contenders and Ophelia's body into a confined space (probably the trap-
door) suggests to many editors the alternative, that Laertes jumps out of the grave to
attack Hamlet.)   **233 splenitive** quick-tempered

Yet have I in me something dangerous,
   Which let thy wisdom fear. Hold off thy hand.   235
KING. Pluck them asunder.
QUEEN. Hamlet, Hamlet!
ALL. Gentlemen!
HORATIO. Good my lord, be quiet.
   [HAMLET and LAERTES are parted.]
HAMLET. Why, I will fight with him upon this theme   240
   Until my eyelids will no longer wag.°
QUEEN. O my son, what theme?
HAMLET. I loved Ophelia. Forty thousand brothers
   Could not with all their quantity of love
   Make up my sum. What wilt thou do for her?   245
KING. O, he is mad, Laertes.
QUEEN. For love of God, forbear him.°
HAMLET. 'Swounds,° show me what thou'lt do.
   Woo't° weep? Woo't fight? Woo't fast? Woo't tear thyself?
   Woo't drink up° eisel?° Eat a crocodile?°   250
   I'll do 't. Dost come here to whine?
   To outface me with leaping in her grave?
   Be buried quick° with her, and so will I.
   And if thou prate of mountains, let them throw
   Millions of acres on us, till our ground,   255
   Singeing his pate° against the burning zone,°
   Make Ossa° like a wart! Nay, an° thou'lt mouth,°
   I'll rant as well as thou.
QUEEN.   This is mere° madness,
   And thus awhile the fit will work on him;
   Anon, as patient as the female dove   260
   When that her golden couplets° are disclosed,°
   His silence will sit drooping.
HAMLET.   Hear you, sir,
   What is the reason that you use me thus?
   I loved you ever. But it is no matter.
   Let Hercules himself do what he may,   265
   The cat will mew, and dog will have his day.°

                                                      Exit HAMLET.

---

241 wag move. (A fluttering eyelid is a conventional sign that life has not yet gone.)
247 forbear him leave him alone   **248 'Swounds** by His (Christ's) wounds
249 Woo't wilt thou   **250 drink up** drink deeply.   **eisel** vinegar.   **crocodile**
(Crocodiles were tough and dangerous, and were supposed to shed hypocritical
tears.)   **253 quick** alive   **256 his pate** its head, i.e., top.   **burning zone** zone in
the celestial sphere containing the sun's orbit, between the tropics of Cancer and
Capricorn   **257 Ossa** another mountain in Thessaly. (In their war against the
Olympian gods, the giants attempted to heap Ossa on Pelion to scale Olympus.)
an if.   **mouth** i.e., rant   **258 mere** utter   **261 golden couplets** two baby pigeons, covered with yellow down.   **disclosed** hatched   **265–266 Let . . . day** i.e.,
(1) even Hercules couldn't stop Laertes' theatrical rant (2) I, too, will have my turn;
i.e., despite any blustering attempts at interference, every person will sooner or
later do what he or she must do

KING. I pray thee, good Horatio, wait upon him.

[Exit] HORATIO.

[To LAERTES.*]* Strengthen your patience in° our last night's speech;
We'll put the matter to the present push.° —
Good Gertrude, set some watch over your son.—   270
This grave shall have a living° monument.
An hour of quiet° shortly shall we see;
Till then, in patience our proceeding be.

Exeunt.

5.2   *Enter* HAMLET *and* HORATIO.

HAMLET. So much for this, sir; now shall you see the other.°
    You do remember all the circumstance?
HORATIO. Remember it, my lord!
HAMLET. Sir, in my heart there was a kind of fighting
    That would not let me sleep. Methought I lay   5
    Worse than the mutines° in the bilboes.° Rashly,°
    And praised be rashness for it—let us know°
    Our indiscretion° sometimes serves us well
    When our deep plots do pall,° and that should learn° us
    There's a divinity that shapes our ends,   10
    Rough-hew° them how we will—
HORATIO.   That is most certain.
HAMLET. Up from my cabin,
    My sea-gown° scarfed° about me, in the dark
    Groped I to find out them,° had my desire,
    Fingered° their packet, and in fine° withdrew   15
    To mine own room again, making so bold,
    My fears forgetting manners, to unseal
    Their grand commission; where I found, Horatio—
    Ah, royal knavery!—an exact command,
    Larded° with many several° sorts of reasons   20
    Importing° Denmark's health and England's too,
    With, ho! such bugs° and goblins in my life,°
    That on the supervise,° no leisure bated,°
    No, not to stay° the grinding of the ax,
    My head should be struck off.

268 in i.e., by recalling   **269 present push** immediate test   **271 living** lasting.
(For Laertes' private understanding, Claudius also hints that Hamlet's death will
serve as such a monument.)   **272 hour of quiet** time free of conflict
5.2. Location: The castle.   1 see the other hear the other news   **6 mutines**
mutineers.   **bilboes** shackles.   **Rashly** on impulse. (This adverb goes with lines
12 ff.)   **7 know** acknowledge   **8 indiscretion** lack of foresight and judgment
(not an indiscreet act)   **9 pall** fail, falter, go stale.   **learn** teach   **11 Rough-hew**
shape roughly   **13 sea-gown** seaman's coat.   **scarfed** loosely wrapped   **14 them**
i.e., Rosencrantz and Guildenstern   **15 Fingered** pilfered, pinched.   **in fine** finally, in conclusion   **20 Larded** garnished.   **several** different   **21 Importing** relating to   **22 bugs** bugbears, hobgoblins.   **in my life** i.e., to be feared if I were allowed to live   **23 supervise** reading.   **leisure bated** delay allowed   **24 stay**
await

HORATIO.   Is 't possible?   25

HAMLET *[giving a document]*.

> Here's the commission. Read it at more leisure.
> But wilt thou hear now how I did proceed?

HORATIO. I beseech you.

HAMLET. Being thus benetted round with villainies—

> Ere I could make a prologue to my brains,   30
> They had begun the play°—I sat me down,
> Devised a new commission, wrote it fair.°
> I once did hold it, as our statists° do,
> A baseness° to write fair, and labored much
> How to forget that learning, but, sir, now   35
> It did me yeoman's° service. Wilt thou know
> Th' effect° of what I wrote?

HORATIO.   Ay, good my lord.

HAMLET. An earnest conjuration° from the King,

> As England was his faithful tributary,
> As love between them like the palm° might flourish,   40
> As peace should still° her wheaten garland° wear
> And stand a comma° 'tween their amities,
> And many suchlike "as"es° of great charge,°
> That on the view and knowing of these contents,
> Without debatement further more or less,   45
> He should those bearers put to sudden death,
> Not shriving time° allowed.

HORATIO.   How was this sealed?

HAMLET. Why, even in that was heaven ordinant.°

> I had my father's signet° in my purse,
> Which was the model° of that Danish seal;   50
> Folded the writ° up in the form of th' other,
> Subscribed° it, gave 't th' impression,° placed it safely,
> The changeling° never known. Now, the next day
> Was our sea fight, and what to this was sequent°
> Thou knowest already.   55

HORATIO. So Guildenstern and Rosencrantz go to 't.

HAMLET. Why, man, they did make love to this employment.

> They are not near my conscience. Their defeat°
> Does by their own insinuation° grow.

30–31 Ere . . . play before I could consciously turn my brain to the matter, it had started working on a plan   **32 fair** in a clear hand   **33 statists** statesmen **34 baseness** i.e., lower-class trait   **36 yeoman's** i.e., substantial, faithful, loyal **37 effect** purport   **38 conjuration** entreaty   **40 palm** (An image of health; see Psalm 92:12)   **41 still** always.   **wheaten garland** (Symbolic of fruitful agriculture, of peace and plenty.)   **42 comma** (Indicating continuity, link.)   **43 "as"es** (1) the "whereases" of a formal document (2) asses.   **charge** (1) import (2) burden (appropriate to asses)   **47 shriving time** time for confession and absolution   **48 ordinant** directing   **49 signet** small seal   **50 model** replica   **51 writ** writing **52 Subscribed** signed (with forged signature).   **impression** i.e., with a wax seal **53 changeling** i.e., substituted letter (Literally, a fairy child substituted for a human one)   **54 was sequent** followed   **58 defeat** destruction   **59 insinuation** intrusive intervention, sticking their noses in my business

'Tis dangerous when the baser° nature comes   60
Between the pass° and fell° incensèd points
Of mighty opposites.°
HORATIO.   Why, what a king is this!
HAMLET. Does it not, think thee, stand me now upon°—
He that hath killed my king and whored my mother,
Popped in between th' election° and my hopes,   65
Thrown out his angle° for my proper° life,
And with such cozenage°—is 't not perfect conscience
To quit° him with this arm? And is 't not to be damned
To let this canker° of our nature come
In° further evil?   70
HORATIO. It must be shortly known to him from England
What is the issue of the business there.
HAMLET. It will be short. The interim is mine,
And a man's life's no more than to say "one."°
But I am very sorry, good Horatio,   75
That to Laertes I forgot myself,
For by the image of my cause I see
The portraiture of his. I'll court his favors.
But, sure, the bravery° of his grief did put me
Into a tow'ring passion.
HORATIO.   Peace, who comes here?   80
Enter a Courtier [OSRIC].
OSRIC. Your lordship is right welcome back to Denmark.
HAMLET. I humbly thank you, sir. *[To* HORATIO.*]* Dost know this water
fly?
HORATIO. No, my good lord.
HAMLET. Thy state is the more gracious, for 'tis a vice to know him. He   85
hath much land, and fertile. Let a beast be lord of beasts, and his
crib° shall stand at the King's mess.° 'Tis a chuff,° but, as I say, spa-
cious in the possession of dirt.
OSRIC. Sweet lord, if your lordship were at leisure, I should impart a
thing to you from His Majesty.   90
HAMLET. I will receive it, sir, with all diligence of spirit.
Put your bonnet° to his° right use; 'tis for the head.
OSRIC. I thank your lordship, it is very hot.
HAMLET. No, believe me, 'tis very cold. The wind is northerly.
OSRIC. It is indifferent° cold, my lord, indeed.   95

---

60 baser of lower social station   **61 pass** thrust.   **fell** fierce   **62 opposites** an-
tagonists   **63 stand me now upon** become incumbent on me now   **65 election**
(The Danish monarch was "elected" by a small number of high-ranking electors.)
66 angle fishhook.   **proper** very   **67 cozenage** trickery   **68 quit** requite, pay
back   **69 canker** ulcer   **69–70 come In** grow into   **74 a man's . . . "one"** one's
whole life occupies such a short time, only as long as it takes to count to 1
79 bravery bravado   **87 crib** manger   **86–87 Let . . . mess** i.e., if a man, no matter how beastlike, is as rich in livestock and possessions as Osric, he may eat at the
King's table   **87 chuff** boor, churl. (The Second Quarto spelling, *chough*, is a variant spelling that also suggests the meaning here of "chattering jackdaw.")   **92 bonnet** any kind of cap or hat.   **his** its   **95 indifferent** somewhat

HAMLET. But yet methinks it is very sultry and hot for my complexion.°

OSRIC. Exceedingly, my lord. It is very sultry, as 'twere—I cannot tell how. My lord, His Majesty bade me signify to you that 'a has laid a great wager on your head. Sir, this is the matter—

HAMLET. I beseech you, remember.   100

[HAMLET moves him to put on his hat.]

OSRIC. Nay, good my lord; for my ease,° in good faith. Sir, here is newly come to court Laertes—believe me, an absolute° gentleman, full of most excellent differences,° of very soft society° and great show-ing.° Indeed, to speak feelingly° of him, he is the card° or calen-dar° of gentry,° for you shall find in him the continent of what part   105 a gentleman would see.°

HAMLET. Sir, his definement° suffers no perdition° in you,° though I know to divide him inventorially° would dozy° th' arithmetic of memory, and yet but yaw° neither° in respect of° his quick sail. But, in the verity of extolment,° I take him to be a soul of great ar- 110 ticle,° and his infusion° of such dearth and rareness° as, to make true diction° of him, his semblable° is his mirror and who else would trace° him his umbrage,° nothing more.

OSRIC. Your lordship speaks most infallibly of him.

HAMLET. The concernancy,° sir? Why do we wrap the gentleman in our   115 more rawer breath?°

OSRIC. Sir?

HORATIO. Is 't not possible to understand in another tongue?° You will do 't,° sir, really.

HAMLET. What imports the nomination° of this gentleman?   120

OSRIC. Of Laertes?

HORATIO *[to HAMLET].* His purse is empty already; all 's golden words are spent.

96 complexion temperament   **101 for my ease** (A conventional reply declining the invitation to put his hat back on.)   **102 absolute** perfect   **103 differences** special qualities   **soft society** agreeable manners   **103–104 great showing** distin-guished appearance   **104 feelingly** with just perception   **card** chart, map. **104–105 calendar** guide   **gentry** good breeding   **105–106 the continent . . . see** one who contains in him all the qualities a gentleman would like to see. (A *con-tinent* is that which contains.)   **107 definement** definition (Hamlet proceeds to mock Osric by throwing his lofty diction back at him.)   **perdition** loss, diminution **you** your description   **108 divide him inventorially** enumerate his graces **dozy** dizzy.   **109 yaw** swing unsteadily off course. (Said of a ship.)   **neither** for all that   **in respect of** in comparison with   **110 in . . . extolment** in true praise (of him)   **110–111 of great article** one with many articles in his inventory **111 infusion** essence, character infused into him by nature.   **dearth and rareness** rarity   **111–112 make true diction** speak truly   **112 semblable** only true likeness   **112–113 who . . . trace** any other person who would wish to fol-low.   **113 umbrage** shadow   **115 concernancy** import, relevance   **116 rawer breath** unrefined speech that can only come short in praising him   **118 to under-stand . . . tongue** i.e., for you, Osric, to understand when someone else speaks your language. (Horatio twits Osric for not being able to understand the kind of flowery speech he himself uses, when Hamlet speaks in such a vein. Alternatively, all this could be said to Hamlet.)   **118–119 You will do 't** i.e., you can if you try, or, you may well have to try (to speak plainly)   **120 nomination** naming

HAMLET. Of him, sir.

OSRIC. I know you are not ignorant—   125

HAMLET. I would you did, sir. Yet in faith if you did, it would not much
approve° me. Well, sir?

OSRIC. You are not ignorant of what excellence Laertes is—

HAMLET. I dare not confess that, lest I should compare with him in excellence. But to know a man well were to know himself.°   130

OSRIC. I mean, sir, for° his weapon; but in the imputation laid on him by
them,° in his meed° he's unfellowed.°

HAMLET. What's his weapon?

OSRIC. Rapier and dagger.

HAMLET. That's two of his weapons—but well.°   135

OSRIC. The King, sir, hath wagered with him six Barbary horses, against
the which he° has impawned,° as I take it, six French rapiers and
poniards,° with their assigns,° as girdle, hangers,° and so.° Three
of the carriages,° in faith, are very dear to fancy,° very responsive°
to the hilts, most delicate° carriages, and of very liberal conceit.°   140

HAMLET. What call you the carriages?

HORATIO *[to* HAMLET*]*. I knew you must be edified by the margent° ere
you had done.

OSRIC. The carriages, sir, are the hangers.

HAMLET. The phrase would be more germane to the matter if we could 145
carry a cannon by our sides; I would it might be hangers till then.
But, on: six Barbary horses against six French swords, their assigns,
and three liberal-conceited carriages; that's the French bet against
the Danish. Why is this impawned, as you call it?

OSRIC. The King, sir, hath laid,° sir, that in a dozen passes° between 150
yourself and him, he shall not exceed you three hits. He hath laid
on twelve for nine, and it would come to immediate trial, if your
lordship would vouchsafe the answer.°

HAMLET. How if I answer no?

OSRIC. I mean, my lord, the opposition of your person in trial.   155

HAMLET. Sir, I will walk here in the hall. If it please His Majesty, it is the
breathing time° of day with me. Let° the foils be brought, the gen-

---

127 approve commend   **129–130 I dare . . . himself** I dare not boast of knowing
Laertes' excellence lest I seem to imply a comparable excellence in myself. Certainly, to know another person well, one must know oneself.   **131 for** i.e., with
131–132 imputation . . . them reputation given him by others   **132 meed** merit.
unfellowed unmatched   **135 but well** but never mind   **137 he** i.e., Laertes.
impawned staked, wagered   **138 poniards** daggers.   **assigns** appurtenances
hangers straps on the sword belt (*girdle*), from which the sword hung.   **and so**
and so on   **139 carriages** (An affected way of saying *hangers;* literally, gun carriages.)   **dear to fancy** delightful to the fancy.   **responsive** corresponding
closely, matching or well adjusted   **140 delicate** (i.e., in workmanship)   **liberal
conceit** elaborate design   **142 margent** margin of a book, place for explanatory
notes   **150 laid** wagered   **passes** bouts. (The odds of the betting are hard to explain. Possibly the King bets that Hamlet will win at least five out of twelve, at
which point Laertes raises the odds against himself by betting he will win nine.)
153 vouchsafe the answer be so good as to accept the challenge. (Hamlet deliberately takes the phrase in its literal sense of replying.)   **157 breathing time** exercise period.   **Let** i.e., if

tleman willing, and the King hold his purpose, I will win for him an
I can; if not, I will gain nothing but my shame and the odd hits.

OSRIC. Shall I deliver you° so?   160

HAMLET. To this effect, sir—after what flourish your nature will.

OSRIC. I commend° my duty to your lordship.

HAMLET. Yours, yours. *[Exit OSRIC.]* 'A does well to commend it himself;
there are no tongues else for 's turn.°

HORATIO. This lapwing° runs away with the shell on his head.   165

HAMLET. 'A did comply with his dug° before 'a sucked it. Thus has he—
and many more of the same breed that I know the drossy° age
dotes on—only got the tune° of the time and, out of an habit of encounter,° a kind of yeasty° collection,° which carries them
through and through the most fanned and winnowed opinions;°   170
and do° but blow them to their trial, the bubbles are out.°

Enter a LORD.

LORD. My lord, His Majesty commended him to you by young Osric,
who brings back to him that you attend him in the hall. He sends to
know if your pleasure hold to play with Laertes, or that° you will
take longer time.   175

HAMLET. I am constant to my purposes; they follow the King's pleasure.
If his fitness speaks, mine is ready;° now or whensoever, provided
I be so able as now.

LORD. The King and Queen and all are coming down.

HAMLET. In happy time.°   180

LORD. The Queen desires you to use some gentle entertainment° to
Laertes before you fall to play.

HAMLET. She well instructs me.   *[Exit LORD.]*

HORATIO. You will lose, my lord.

HAMLET. I do not think so. Since he went into France, I have been in   185
continual practice; I shall win at the odds. But thou wouldst not
think how ill all's here about my heart; but it is no matter.

HORATIO. Nay, good my lord—

---

160 deliver you report what you say   **162 commend** commit to your favor.
(A conventional salutation, but Hamlet wryly uses a more literal meaning, "recommend," "praise," in line 163.)   **164 for 's turn** for his purposes, i.e., to do it for
him   **165 lapwing** (A proverbial type of youthful forwardness. Also, a bird that
draws intruders away from its nest and was thought to run about with its head in
the shell when newly hatched; a seeming reference to Osric's hat.)   **166 comply
. . . dug** observe ceremonious formality toward his nurse's or mother's teat
167 drossy laden with scum and impurities, frivolous   **168 tune** temper, mood,
manner of speech   **168–169 an habit of encounter** a demeanor in conversing
(with courtiers of his own kind)   **169 yeasty** frothy.   **collection** i.e., of current
phrases   **169–170 carries . . . opinions** sustains them right through the scrutiny
of persons whose opinions are select and refined. (Literally, like grain separated
from its chaff. Osric is both the chaff and the bubbly froth on the surface of the
liquor that is soon blown away.)   **171 and do** yet do   **blow . . . out** test them by
merely blowing on them, and their bubbles burst   **174 that** if   **177 If . . . ready** if
he declares his readiness, my convenience waits on his   **180 In happy time** (A
phrase of courtesy indicating that the time is convenient.)   **181 entertainment**
greeting

HAMLET. It is but foolery, but it is such a kind of gaingiving° as would
    perhaps trouble a woman.   190
HORATIO. If your mind dislike anything, obey it. I will forestall their re-
    pair° hither and say you are not fit.
HAMLET. Not a whit, we defy augury. There is special providence in the
    fall of a sparrow. If it be now, 'tis not to come; if it be not to come,
    it will be now; if it be not now, yet it will come. The readiness is all.   195
    Since no man of aught he leaves knows, what is 't to leave betimes?
    Let be.°
    *A table prepared. [Enter] trumpets, drums, and officers with
    cushions;* KING, QUEEN, *[*OSRIC,*] and all the state; foils, daggers, [and
    wine borne in;] and* LAERTES.
KING. Come, Hamlet, come and take this hand from me.
    [The KING *puts* LAERTES' *hand into* HAMLET'*s.]*
HAMLET *[to* LAERTES*].* Give me your pardon, sir. I have done you wrong,
    But pardon 't as you are a gentleman.   200
    This presence° knows,
    And you must needs have heard, how I am punished°
    With a sore distraction. What I have done
    That might your nature, honor, and exception°
    Roughly awake, I here proclaim was madness.   205
    Was 't Hamlet wronged Laertes? Never Hamlet.
    If Hamlet from himself be ta'en away,
    And when he's not himself does wrong Laertes,
    Then Hamlet does it not, Hamlet denies it.
    Who does it, then? His madness. If 't be so,   210
    Hamlet is of the faction° that is wronged;
    His madness is poor Hamlet's enemy.
    Sir, in this audience
    Let my disclaiming from a purposed evil
    Free me so far in your most generous thoughts   215
    That I have° shot my arrow o'er the house
    And hurt my brother.
LAERTES.   I am satisfied in nature,°
    Whose motive° in this case should stir me most
    To my revenge. But in my terms of honor
    I stand aloof, and will no reconcilement   220
    Till by some elder masters of known honor
    I have a voice° and precedent of peace°
    To keep my name ungored.° But till that time
    I do receive your offered love like love,
    And will not wrong it.
HAMLET.   I embrace it freely,   225

---

189 **gaingiving** misgiving   191–192 **repair** coming   196–197 **Since . . . Let be**
since no one has knowledge of what he is leaving behind, what does an early death
matter after all? Enough; don't struggle against it.   201 **presence** royal assembly
202 **punished** afflicted   204 **exception** disapproval   211 **faction** party
216 **That I have** as if I had   217 **in nature** i.e., as to my personal feelings
218 **motive** prompting   222 **voice** authoritative pronouncement.   **of peace** for
reconciliation   223 **name ungored** reputation unwounded

And will this brothers' wager frankly° play.—
Give us the foils. Come on.

LAERTES.   Come, one for me.

HAMLET. I'll be your foil,° Laertes. In mine ignorance
Your skill shall, like a star i' the darkest night,
Stick fiery off° indeed.

LAERTES.   You mock me, sir.   230

HAMLET. No, by this hand.

KING. Give them the foils, young Osric. Cousin Hamlet,
You know the wager?

HAMLET.   Very well, my lord.
Your Grace has laid the odds o'° the weaker side.

KING. I do not fear it; I have seen you both.   235
But since he is bettered,° we have therefore odds.

LAERTES. This is too heavy. Let me see another.

[He exchanges his foil for another.]

HAMLET. This likes me° well. These foils have all a length?

[They prepare to play.]

OSRIC. Ay, my good lord.

KING. Set me the stoups of wine upon that table.   240
If Hamlet give the first or second hit,
Or quit in answer of the third exchange,°
Let all the battlements their ordnance fire.
The King shall drink to Hamlet's better breath,°
And in the cup an union° shall he throw   245
Richer than that which four successive kings
In Denmark's crown have worn. Give me the cups,
And let the kettle° to the trumpet speak,
The trumpet to the cannoneer without,
The cannons to the heavens, the heaven to earth,   250
"Now the King drinks to Hamlet." Come, begin.

Trumpets the while.

And you, the judges, bear a wary eye.

HAMLET. Come on, sir.

LAERTES. Come, my lord.   *[They play.* HAMLET *scores a hit.]*

HAMLET. One.   255

LAERTES. No.

HAMLET. Judgment.

OSRIC.   A hit, a very palpable hit.

Drum, trumpets, and shot. Flourish. A piece goes off.

LAERTES. Well, again.

KING. Stay, give me drink. Hamlet, this pearl is thine.

---

226 frankly without ill feeling or the burden of rancor   **228 foil** thin metal background which sets a jewel off (with pun on the blunted rapier for fencing)
230 Stick fiery off stand out brilliantly   **234 laid the odds o'** bet on, backed
236 is bettered has improved; is the odds-on favorite. (Laertes' handicap is the "three hits" specified in line 151.)   **238 likes me** pleases me   **242 Or . . . exchange** i.e., or requites Laertes in the third bout for having won the first two
244 better breath improved vigor   **245 union** pearl. (So called, according to Pliny's *Natural History,* 9, because pearls are *unique,* never identical.)   **248 kettle** kettledrum

[He drinks, and throws a pearl in HAMLET's *cup.]*
    Here's to thy health. Give him the cup.   260
HAMLET. I'll play this bout first. Set it by awhile.
    Come. *[They play.]* Another hit; what say you?
LAERTES. A touch, a touch, I do confess 't.
KING. Our son shall win.
QUEEN.   He's fat° and scant of breath.
    Here, Hamlet, take my napkin,° rub thy brows.   265
    The Queen carouses° to thy fortune, Hamlet.
HAMLET. Good, madam!
KING Gertrude, do not drink.
QUEEN. I will, my lord, I pray you pardon me.   *[She drinks.]*
KING *[aside]*. It is the poisoned cup. It is too late.   270
HAMLET. I dare not drink yet, madam; by and by.
QUEEN. Come, let me wipe thy face.
LAERTES *[to* KING*]*. My lord, I'll hit him now.
KING.   I do not think 't.
LAERTES *[aside]*. And yet it is almost against my conscience.
HAMLET. Come, for the third, Laertes. You do but dally.   275
    I pray you, pass° with your best violence;
    I am afeard you make a wanton of me.°
LAERTES. Say you so? Come on.   *[They play.]*
OSRIC. Nothing neither way.
LAERTES. Have at you now!
    *[*LAERTES *wounds* HAMLET; *then, in scuffling, they change rapiers,°*
    and HAMLET *wounds* LAERTES.*]*
KING.   Part them! They are incensed.   280
HAMLET. Nay, come, again.   *[The* QUEEN *falls.]*
OSRIC.   Look to the Queen there, ho!
HORATIO. They bleed on both sides. How is it, my lord?
OSRIC. How is 't, Laertes?
LAERTES. Why, as a woodcock° to mine own springe,° Osric;
    I am justly killed with mine own treachery.   285
HAMLET. How does the Queen?
KING.   She swoons to see them bleed.
QUEEN. No, no, the drink, the drink—O my dear Hamlet—
    The drink, the drink! I am poisoned.   *[She dies.]*
HAMLET. O villainy! Ho, let the door be locked!
    Treachery! Seek it out.   290
                     *[*LAERTES *falls. Exit* OSRIC.*]*
LAERTES. It is here, Hamlet. Hamlet, thou art slain.
    No med'cine in the world can do thee good;
    In thee there is not half an hour's life.

---

264 fat not physically fit, out of training   **265 napkin** handkerchief
266 carouses drinks a toast   **276 pass** thrust   **277 make . . . me** i.e., treat me
like a spoiled child, trifle with me   **280 s.d. in scuffling, they change rapiers**
(This stage direction occurs in the Folio. According to a widespread stage tradition,
Hamlet receives a scratch, realizes that Laertes' sword is unbated, and accordingly
forces an exchange.)   **284 woodcock** a bird, a type of stupidity or as a decoy.
springe trap, snare

The treacherous instrument is in thy hand,
Unbated° and envenomed. The foul practice°   295
Hath turned itself on me. Lo, here I lie,
Never to rise again. Thy mother's poisoned.
I can no more. The King, the King's to blame.
HAMLET. The point envenomed too? Then, venom, to thy work.

[He stabs the KING.*]*

ALL. Treason! Treason!   300
KING. O, yet defend me, friends! I am but hurt.
HAMLET *[forcing the* KING *to drink]*.

Here, thou incestuous, murderous, damnèd Dane,
Drink off this potion. Is thy union° here?
Follow my mother.   *[The* KING *dies.]*
LAERTES.   He is justly served.
It is a poison tempered° by himself.   305
Exchange forgiveness with me, noble Hamlet.
Mine and my father's death come not upon thee,
Nor thine on me!   *[He dies.]*
HAMLET. Heaven make thee free of it! I follow thee.
I am dead, Horatio. Wretched Queen, adieu!   310
You that look pale and tremble at this chance,°
That are but mutes° or audience to this act,
Had I but time—as this fell° sergeant,° Death,
Is strict° in his arrest°—O, I could tell you—
But let it be. Horatio, I am dead;   315
Thou livest. Report me and my cause aright
To the unsatisfied.
HORATIO.   Never believe it.
I am more an antique Roman° than a Dane.
Here's yet some liquor left.

[He attempts to drink from the poisoned cup.
HAMLET *prevents him.]*

HAMLET.   As thou'rt a man,
Give me the cup! Let go! By heaven, I'll ha 't.   320
O God, Horatio, what a wounded name,
Things standing thus unknown, shall I leave behind me!
If thou didst ever hold me in thy heart,
Absent thee from felicity awhile,
And in this harsh world draw thy breath in pain   325
To tell my story. *A march afar off [and a volley within].*
     What warlike noise is this?
Enter OSRIC.
OSRIC. Young Fortinbras, with conquest come from Poland,

---

295 Unbated not blunted with a button.   **practice** plot   **303 union** pearl. (See
line 245; with grim puns on the word's other meanings: marriage, shared death.)
305 tempered mixed   **311 chance** mischance   **312 mutes** silent observers.
(Literally, actors with nonspeaking parts.)   **313 fell** cruel.   **sergeant** sheriff's officer   **314 strict** (1) severely just (2) unavoidable.   **arrest** (1) taking into custody
(2) stopping my speech   **318 Roman** (Suicide was an honorable choice for many
Romans as an alternative to a dishonorable life.)

                      To th' ambassadors of England gives
                      This warlike volley.
HAMLET.   O, I die, Horatio!
    The potent poison quite o'ercrows° my spirit.   330
    I cannot live to hear the news from England,
    But I do prophesy th' election lights
    On Fortinbras. He has my dying voice.°
    So tell him, with th' occurents° more and less
    Which have solicited°—the rest is silence.   *[He dies.]* 335
HORATIO. Now cracks a noble heart. Good night, sweet prince,
    And flights of angels sing thee to thy rest!

                                              [March within.]
    Why does the drum come hither?

                  Enter FORTINBRAS, *with the [English] Ambassadors*
                          [with drum, colors, and attendants].

FORTINBRAS. Where is this sight?
HORATIO.   What is it you would see?
    If aught of woe or wonder, cease your search.   340
FORTINBRAS. This quarry° cries on havoc.° O proud Death,
    What feast° is toward° in thine eternal cell,
    That thou so many princes at a shot
    So bloodily hast struck?
FIRST AMBASSADOR.   The sight is dismal,
    And our affairs from England come too late.   345
    The ears are senseless that should give us hearing,
    To tell him his commandment is fulfilled,
    That Rosencrantz and Guildenstern are dead.
    Where should we have our thanks?
HORATIO.   Not from his° mouth,
    Had it th' ability of life to thank you.   350
    He never gave commandment for their death.
    But since, so jump° upon this bloody question,°
    You from the Polack wars, and you from England,
    And here arrived, give order that these bodies
    High on a stage° be placèd to the view,   355
    And let me speak to th' yet unknowing world
    How these things came about. So shall you hear
    Of carnal, bloody, and unnatural acts,
    Of accidental judgments,° casual° slaughters,
    Of deaths put on° by cunning and forced cause,°   360
    And, in this upshot, purposes mistook

---

330 o'ercrows triumphs over (like the winner in a cockfight)   **333 voice** vote
334 occurrents events, incidents   **335 solicited** moved, urged. (Hamlet doesn't
finish saying what the events have prompted—presumably, his acts of vengeance,
or his reporting of those events to Fortinbras.)   **341 quarry** heap of dead.   **cries
on havoc** proclaims a general slaughter   **342 feast** i.e., Death feasting on those
who have fallen.   **toward** in preparation   **349 his** i.e., Claudius'   **352 jump** precisely, immediately.   **question** dispute, affair   **355 stage** platform   **359 judgments** retributions.   **casual** occurring by chance   **360 put on** instigated.
forced cause contrivance

Fall'n on th' inventors' heads. All this can I
Truly deliver.

FORTINBRAS.   Let us haste to hear it,
And call the noblest to the audience.
For me, with sorrow I embrace my fortune.   365
I have some rights of memory° in this kingdom,
Which now to claim my vantage° doth invite me.

HORATIO. Of that I shall have also cause to speak,
And from his mouth whose voice will draw on more.°
But let this same be presently° performed,   370
Even while men's minds are wild, lest more mischance
On° plots and errors happen.

FORTINBRAS.   Let four captains
Bear Hamlet, like a soldier, to the stage,
For he was likely, had he been put on,°
To have proved most royal; and for his passage,°   375
The soldiers' music and the rite of war
Speak° loudly for him.
Take up the bodies. Such a sight as this
Becomes the field,° but here shows much amiss.
Go bid the soldiers shoot.   380

Exeunt [marching, bearing off the dead bodies;
a peal of ordnance is shot off].

▱ TOPICS FOR CRITICAL THINKING AND WRITING

Act 1

1. The first scene (like many other scenes in this play) is full of expressions of uncertainty. What are some are these uncertainties? The Ghost
   first appears at 1.1.42. Does his appearance surprise us, or have we
   been prepared for it? Or is there both preparation and surprise? Do the
   last four speeches of 1.1 help to introduce a note of hope? If so, how?

2. Does the King's opening speech in 1.2 reveal him to be an accomplished public speaker—or are lines 10-14 offensive? In his second
   speech (lines 41-49), what is the effect of naming Laertes four times?
   Claudius sometimes uses the royal pronouns ("we," "our"), sometimes
   the more intimate "I" and "my." Study his use of these in lines 1-4 and
   in 106-117. What do you think he is getting at?

3. Hamlet's first soliloquy (1.2.129-159) reveals that more than just his father's death distresses him. Be as specific as possible about the causes
   of Hamlet's anguish here. What traits does Hamlet reveal in his conversation with Horatio (1.2.160-258)?

4. What do you make of Polonius's advice to Laertes (1.3.55-81)? Is it
   sound? Sound advice, but here uttered by a fool? Ignoble advice? How

366 of memory traditional, remembered, unforgotten   **367 vantage** favorable
opportunity   **369 voice . . . more** vote will influence still others   **370 presently**
immediately   **372 On** on the basis of; on top of   **374 put on** i.e., invested in royal
office and so put to the test   **375 passage** i.e., from life to death   **377 Speak** (let
them) speak   **379 Becomes the field** suits the field of battle

would one follow the advice of line 78: "to thine own self be true"? In his words to Ophelia in 1.3.102-136, what does he reveal about himself?

5. Can 1.4.17-38 reasonably be taken as a speech on the "tragic flaw"? (On this idea, see page 205.) Or is the passage a much more limited discussion, a comment simply on Danish drinking habits?

6. Hamlet is convinced in 1.5.93-104 that the Ghost has told the truth, indeed, the only important truth. But do we detect in 105-112 a hint of a tone suggesting that Hamlet delights in hating villainy? If so, can it be said that later this delight grows, and that in some scenes (e.g., 3.3) we feel that Hamlet has almost become a diabolic revenger? Explain.

Act 2

1. Characterize Polonius on the basis of 2.1.1-76.

2. In light of what we have seen of Hamlet, is Ophelia's report of his strange behavior when he visits her understandable?

3. Why does 2.2.33-34 seem almost comic? How do these lines help us to form a view about Rosencrantz and Guildenstern?

4. Is "the hellish Pyrrhus" (2.2.422) Hamlet's version of Claudius? Or is he Hamlet, who soon will be responsible for the deaths of Polonius, Rosencrantz and Guildenstern, Claudius, Gertrude, Ophelia, and Laertes? Explain.

5. Is the player's speech (2.2.427ff) a huffing speech? If so, why? To distinguish it from the poetry of the play itself? To characterize the bloody deeds that Hamlet cannot descend to?

6. In 2.2.504-42 Hamlet rebukes himself for not acting. Why has he not acted? Because he is a coward (line 531)? Because he has a conscience? Because no action can restore his father and his mother's purity? Because he doubts the Ghost? What reason(s) can you offer?

Act 3

1. What do you make out of Hamlet's assertion to Ophelia: "I loved you not" (3.1.118)? Of his characterization of himself as full of "offenses" (3.1.121-27)? Why is Hamlet so harsh to Ophelia?

2. In 3.3.36-72 Claudius's conscience afflicts him. But is he repentant? What makes you say so?

3. Is Hamlet other than abhorrent in 3.3.73-96? Do we want him to kill Claudius at this moment, when Claudius (presumably with his back to Hamlet) is praying? Why?

4. The Ghost speaks of Hamlet's "almost blunted purpose" (3.4.115). Is the accusation fair? Explain.

5. How would you characterize the Hamlet who speaks in 3.4.209-24?

Act 4

1. Is Gertrude protecting Hamlet when she says he is mad (4.1.7), or does she believe that he is mad? If she believes he is mad, does it follow that she no longer feels ashamed and guilty? Explain.

2. Why should Hamlet hide Polonius's body (in 4.2)? Is he feigning madness? Is he on the edge of madness? Explain.

3. How can we explain Hamlet's willingness to go to England (4.3.52)?

4. Judging from 4.5, what has driven Ophelia mad? Is Laertes heroic, or somewhat foolish? Consider also the way Claudius treats him in 4.7.

Act 5

1. Would anything be lost if the grave-diggers in 5.1 were omitted?

2. To what extent do we judge Hamlet severely for sending Rosencrantz and Guildenstern to their deaths, as he reports in 5.2? On the whole, do we think of Hamlet as an intriguer? What other intrigues has he engendered? How successful were they?

3. Does 5.2.193–97 show a paralysis of the will, or a wise recognition that more is needed than mere human scheming? Explain.

4. Does 5.2.280 suggest that Laertes takes advantage of a momentary pause and unfairly stabs Hamlet? Is the exchange of weapons accidental, or does Hamlet (as in Olivier's film version), realizing that he has been betrayed, deliberately get possession of Laertes's deadly weapon?

5. Fortinbras is often cut from the play. How much is lost by the cut? Explain.

6. Fortinbras gives Hamlet a soldier's funeral. Is this ridiculous? Can it fairly be said that, in a sense, Hamlet has been at war? Explain.

General Questions

1. Hamlet in 5.2.10–11 speaks of a "divinity that shapes our ends." To what extent does "divinity" (or Fate or mysterious Chance) play a role in the happenings?

2. How do Laertes, Fortinbras, and Horatio help to define Hamlet for us?

3. T. S. Eliot says (in "Shakespeare and the Stoicism of Seneca") that Hamlet, having made a mess, "dies fairly well pleased with himself." Evaluate.

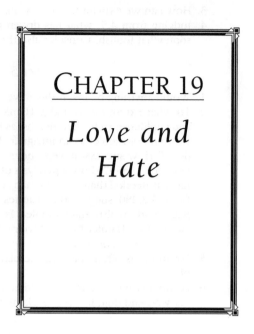

CHAPTER 19

Love and Hate

Essays

 SEI SHŌNAGON

Sei Shōnagon was a Japanese woman who, in the tenth century, served for some ten years as a lady-in-waiting to the empress in Kyoto. Her Pillow Book—*a marvellous collection of lists, eyewitness reports, and brief essays—established the Japanese tradition of* zui-hitsu, *"spontaneous writing" (literally, "to follow the brush").*

Not much is known about Sei Shōnagon. Her book tells us nothing of her early years, and the date and circumstances of her death are unknown. Scholars conjecture that she was born about 965 and that she became a lady-in-waiting during the early 990s. It is evident from her book that she was witty, snobbish, and well versed in the etiquette of love at court.

The passage that we here reprint appears in a list entitled "Hateful Things."

A Lover's Departure

A lover who is leaving at dawn announces that he has to find his fan and his paper. "I know I put them somewhere last night," he says. Since it is pitch dark, he gropes about the room, bumping into the furniture and muttering, "Strange! Where on earth can they be?" Finally he discovers the objects. He thrusts the paper into the breast of his robe with a great rustling sound; then he snaps open his fan and busily fans away with it. Only now is he ready to take his leave. What charmless behavior! "Hateful" is an understatement.

Equally disagreeable is the man who, when leaving in the middle of the night, takes care to fasten the cord of his headdress. This is quite unnecessary; he could perfectly well put it gently on his head without tying the cord. And why must he spend time adjusting his cloak or hunting costume? Does he really think someone may see him at this time of night and criticize him for not being impeccably dressed?

A good lover will behave as elegantly at dawn as at any other time. He drags himself out of bed with a look of dismay on his face. The lady urges him on: "Come, my friend, it's getting light. You don't want anyone to find you here." He gives a deep sigh, as if to say that the night has not been nearly long enough and that it is agony to leave. Once up, he does not instantly pull on his trousers. Instead he comes close to the lady and whispers whatever was left unsaid during the night. Even when he is dressed, he still lingers, vaguely pretending to be fastening his sash.

Presently he raises the lattice, and the two lovers stand together by the side door while he tells her how he dreads the coming day, which will keep them apart; then he slips away. The lady watches him go, and this moment of parting will remain among her most charming memories.

5   Indeed, one's attachment to a man depends largely on the elegance of his leave-taking. When he jumps out of bed, scurries about the room, tightly fastens his trouser-sash, rolls up the sleeves of his Court cloak, overrobe, or hunting costume, stuffs his belongings into the breast of his robe and then briskly secures the outer sash—one really begins to hate him.

 TOPICS FOR CRITICAL THINKING AND WRITING

1. What are your first responses to this passage? Later—even if only thirty minutes later—reread the passage and think about whether your responses change.
2. On the basis of this short extract, how would you characterize Sei Shōnagon? Can you imagine that you and she might become close friends or lovers?
3. Write a journal entry or two on the topic "Hateful Things."

 JUDITH ORTIZ COFER

Born in Puerto Rico in 1952 of a Puerto Rican mother and a United States mainland father who served in the Navy, Judith Ortiz Cofer was educated both in Puerto Rico and on the mainland. After earning a bachelor's and a master's degree in English, she did further graduate work at Oxford and then taught English in Florida. She has published seven volumes of poetry.

The following selection comes from an autobiography, Silent Dancing *(1990).*

I Fell in Love, Or My Hormones Awakened

I fell in love, or my hormones awakened from their long slumber in my body, and suddenly the goal of my days was focused on one thing: to catch a glimpse of my secret love. And it had to remain secret, because I had, of course, in the great tradition of tragic romance, chosen to love a boy who was totally out of my reach. He was not Puerto Rican; he was Italian and rich. He was also an older man. He was a senior at the high school when I came in as a freshman. I first saw him in the hall, leaning casually on a wall that was the border line between girlside and boyside for underclassmen. He looked extraordinarily like a young Marlon Brando—down to the ironic little smile. The total of what I knew about the boy who starred in every one of my awkward fantasies was this: that he was the nephew of the man who owned the supermarket on my block; that he often had parties at his parents' beautiful home in the suburbs which I would hear about; that this family had money (which came to our school in many ways)—and this fact made my knees weak: and that he worked at the store near my apartment building on weekends and in the summer.

My mother could not understand why I became so eager to be the one sent out on her endless errands. I pounced on every opportunity from Friday to late Saturday afternoon to go after eggs, cigarettes, milk (I tried to drink as much of it as possible, although I hated the stuff)—the staple items that she would order from the "American" store.

Week after week I wandered up and down the aisles, taking furtive glances at the stock room in the back, breathlessly hoping to see my prince. Not that I had a plan. I felt like a pilgrim waiting for a glimpse of Mecca. I did not expect him to notice me. It was sweet agony.

One day I did see him. Dressed in a white outfit like a surgeon: white pants and shirt, white cap, and (gross sight, but not to my love-glazed eyes) blood-smeared butcher's apron. He was helping to drag a side of beef into the freezer storage area of the store. I must have stood there like an idiot, because I remember that he did see me, he even spoke to me! I could have died. I think he said, "Excuse me," and smiled vaguely in my direction.

5   After that, I *willed* occasions to go to the supermarket. I watched my mother's pack of cigarettes empty ever so slowly. I wanted her to smoke them fast. I drank milk and forced it on my brother (although a second glass for him had to be bought with my share of Fig Newton cookies which we both liked, but we were restricted to one row each). I gave my cookies up for love, and watched my mother smoke her L&M's with so little enthusiasm that I thought (God, no!) that she might be cutting down on her smoking or maybe even giving up the habit. At this crucial time!

I thought I had kept my lonely romance a secret. Often I cried hot tears on my pillow for the things that kept us apart. In my mind there was no doubt that he would never notice me (and that is why I felt free to stare at him—I was invisible). He could not see me because I was a skinny Puerto Rican girl, a freshman who did not belong to any group he associated with.

At the end of the year I found out that I had not been invisible. I learned one little lesson about human nature—adulation leaves a scent, one that we are all equipped to recognize, and no matter how insignificant the source, we seek it.

In June the nuns at our school would always arrange for some cultural extravaganza. In my freshman year it was a Roman banquet. We had been studying Greek drama (as a prelude to church history—it was at a fast clip that we galloped through Sophocles and Euripedes toward the early Christian martyrs), and our young, energetic Sister Agnes was in the mood for spectacle. She ordered the entire student body (it was a small group of under 300 students) to have our mothers make us togas out of sheets. She handed out a pattern on mimeo pages fresh out of the machine. I remember the intense smell of the alcohol on the sheets of paper, and how almost everyone in the auditorium brought theirs to their noses and inhaled deeply—mimeographed handouts were the school-day buzz that the new Xerox generation of kids is missing out on. Then, as the last couple of weeks of school dragged on, the city of Paterson becoming a concrete oven, and us wilting in our uncomfortable uniforms, we labored like frantic Roman slaves to build a splendid banquet hall in our small auditorium. Sister Agnes wanted a raised dais where the host and hostess would be regally enthroned.

She had already chosen our Senator and Lady from among our ranks. The Lady was to be a beautiful new student named Sophia, a recent Polish immigrant, whose English was still practically unintelligible, but whose features, classically perfect without a trace of makeup, enthralled us. Everyone talked about her gold hair cascading past her waist, and her voice which could carry a note right up to heaven in choir. The nuns wanted her for God. They kept saying that she had vocation. We just looked at her in awe, and the boys seemed afraid of her. She just smiled and did as she was told. I don't know what she thought of it all. The main privilege of beauty is that others will do almost everything for you, including thinking.

10   Her partner was to be our best basketball player, a tall, red-haired senior whose family sent its many offspring to our school. Together, Sophia and her senator looked like the best combination of immigrant genes our community could produce. It did not occur to me to ask then whether anything but their physical beauty qualified them for the starring roles in our production. I had the highest average in the church history class, but I was given the part of one of many "Roman Citizens." I was to sit in front of the plastic fruit and recite a greeting in Latin along with the rest of the school when our hosts came into the hall and took their places on their throne.

On the night of our banquet, my father escorted me in my toga to the door of our school. I felt foolish in my awkwardly draped sheet (blouse and skirt required underneath). My mother had no great skill as a seamstress. The best she could do was hem a skirt or a pair of pants. That night I would have traded her for a peasant woman with a golden needle. I saw other Roman ladies emerging from their parents' cars looking authentic in sheets of material that folded over their bodies like the garments on a statue by Michaelangelo. How did they do it? How was it that I always got it just slightly wrong, and worse, I believed that other people were just too polite to mention it. "The poor little Puerto Rican girl," I could hear them thinking. But in reality, I must have been my worst critic, self-conscious as I was.

Soon, we were all sitting at our circle of tables joined together around the dais. Sophia glittered like a golden statue. Her smile was beatific: a perfect, silent Roman lady. Her "senator" looked uncomfortable, glancing around at his buddies, perhaps waiting for the ridicule that he would surely get in the locker room later. The nuns in their black habits stood in the background watching us. What were they supposed to be, the Fates? Nubian slaves? The dancing girls did their modest little dance to tinny music from their finger cymbals, then the speeches were made. Then the grape juice "wine" was raised in a toast to the Roman Empire we all knew would fall within the week—before finals anyway.

All during the program I had been in a state of controlled hysteria. My secret love sat across the room from me looking supremely bored. I watched his every move, taking him in gluttonously. I relished the shadow of his eyelashes on his ruddy cheeks, his pouty lips smirking sarcastically at the ridiculous sight of our little play. Once he slumped down on his chair, and our sergeant-at-arms nun came over and tapped him sharply on his shoulder. He drew himself up slowly, with disdain. I loved his rebellious spirit. I believed myself still invisible to him in my "nothing" status as I looked upon my beloved. But toward the end of the evening, as we stood chanting our farewells in Latin, he looked straight across the room and into my eyes! How did I survive the killing power of those dark pupils? I trembled in a new way. I was not cold—I was burning! Yet I shook from the inside out, feeling light-headed, dizzy.

The room began to empty and I headed for the girls' lavatory. I wanted to relish the miracle in silence. I did not think for a minute that anything more would follow. I was satisfied with the enormous favor of a look from my beloved. I took my time, knowing that my father would be waiting outside for me, impatient, perhaps glowing in the dark in his phosphorescent white Navy uniform. The others would ride home. I would walk home with my father, both of us in costume. I wanted as few witnesses as possible. When I could no longer hear the crowds in the hallway, I emerged from the bathroom, still under the spell of those mesmerizing eyes.

15   The lights had been turned off in the hallway and all I could see was the lighted stairwell, at the bottom of which a nun would be stationed. My father would be waiting just outside. I nearly screamed when I felt someone grab me by the waist. But my mouth was quickly covered by someone else's mouth. I was being kissed. My first kiss and I could not even tell who it was. I pulled away to see that face not two inches away from mine. It was he. He smiled down at me. Did I have a silly expression on my face? My glasses felt crooked on my nose. I was unable to move or to speak. More gently, he lifted my chin and touched his lips to mine. This time I did not forget to enjoy it. Then, like the phantom lover that he was, he walked away into the darkened corridor and disappeared.

I don't know how long I stood there. My body was changing right there in the hallway of a Catholic school. My cells were tuning up like musicians in an orchestra, and my heart was a chorus. It was an opera I was composing, and I wanted to stand very still and just listen. But, of course, I heard my father's voice talking to the nun. I was in trouble if he had had to ask about me. I hurried down the stairs making up a story on the way about feeling sick. That would explain my flushed face and it would buy me a little privacy when I got home.

The next day Father announced at the breakfast table that he was leaving on a six month tour of Europe with the Navy in a few weeks and that at the end of the school year my mother, my brother, and I would be sent to

Puerto Rico to stay for half a year at Mamá's (my mother's mother) house. I was devastated. This was the usual routine for us. We had always gone to Mamá's to stay when Father was away for long periods. But this year it was diffrent for me. I was in love, and . . . my heart knocked against my bony chest at this thought . . . he loved me too? I broke into sobs and left the table.

In the next week I discovered the inexorable truth about parents. They can actually carry on with their plans right through tears, threats, and the awful spectacle of a teenager's broken heart. My father left me to my mother who impassively packed while I explained over and over that I was at a crucial time in my studies and that if I left my entire life would be ruined. All she would say was, "You are an intelligent girl, you'll catch up." Her head was filled with visions of *casa*[1] and family reunions, long gossip sessions with her mamá and sisters. What did she care that I was losing my one chance at true love?

In the meantime I tried desperately to see him. I thought he would look for me too. But the few times I saw him in the hallway, he was always rushing away. It would be long weeks of confusion and pain before I realized that the kiss was nothing but a little trophy for his ego. He had no interest in me other than as his adorer. He was flattered by my silent worship of him, and he had *bestowed* a kiss on me to please himself, and to fan the flames. I learned a lesson about the battle of the sexes then that I have never forgotten: the object is not always to win, but most times simply to keep your opponent (synonymous at times with "the loved one") guessing.

20   But this is too cynical a view to sustain in the face of that overwhelming rush of emotion that is first love. And in thinking back about my own experience with it, I can be objective only to the point where I recall how sweet the anguish was, how caught up in the moment I felt, and how every nerve in my body was involved in this salute to life. Later, much later, after what seemed like an eternity of dragging the weight of unrequited love around with me, I learned to make myself visible and to relish the little battles required to win the greatest prize of all. And much later, I read and understood Camus'[2] statement about the subject that concerns both adolescent and philosopher alike: if love were easy, life would be too simple.

[1990]

▱ TOPICS FOR CRITICAL THINKING AND WRITING

1. If you agree with us that Cofer's essay is amusing, try to analyze the sources of its humor. *Why* are some passages funny?

2. In paragraph 9 Cofer says, "The main privilege of beauty is that others will do almost everything for you, including thinking." Do you agree that the beautiful are privileged? If so, draw on your experience (as one of the privileged or the unprivileged) to recount an example or two. By the way, Cofer seems to imply (paragraph 10) that the academically gifted should be privileged, or at least should be recognized as candidates for leading roles (e.g., that of "a perfect, silent Roman lady") in

[1]home   [2]Albert Camus (1913–1960), French novelist and philosopher

school productions. Is it any fairer to privilege brains than to privilege beauty? Explain.

3. In her final paragraph Cofer speaks of the experience as a "salute to life." What do you think she means by that?

4. Cofer is describing a state that is (or used to be) called "puppy love." If you have experienced anything like what Cofer experienced, write your own autobiographical essay. (You can of course amplify or censor as you wish.) If you have experienced a love that you think is more serious, more lasting, write about *that*.

 GARY SOTO

Gary Soto was born in Fresno, California, in 1952. While at Fresno State College he studied poetry with Philip Levine, and in his senior year he published his first poem, in the Iowa Review. *He has published several books of poetry since then, and he has won numerous prizes and grants. Since 1977 he has taught English and Chicano studies at the University of California, Berkeley.*

The following essay comes from Small Faces *(1986), a collection of autobiographical sketches.*

Like Mexicans

My grandmother gave me bad advice and good advice when I was in my early teens. For the bad advice, she said that I should become a barber because they made good money and listened to the radio all day. "Honey, they don't work como burros,"[1] she would say every time I visited her. She made the sound of donkeys braying. "Like that, honey!" For the good advice, she said that I should marry a Mexican girl. "No Okies, hijo"[2]—she would say— "Look, my son. He marry one and they fight every day about I don't know what and I don't know what." For her, everyone who wasn't Mexican, black, or Asian were Okies. The French were Okies, the Italians in suits were Okies. When I asked about Jews, whom I had read about, she asked for a picture. I rode home on my bicycle and returned with a calendar depicting the important races of the world. "Pues si, son Okies tambien!"[3] she said, nodding her head. She waved the calendar away and we went to the living room where she lectured me on the virtues of the Mexican girl: first, she could cook and, second, she acted like a woman, not a man, in her husband's home. She said she would tell me about a third when I got a little older.

I asked my mother about it—becoming a barber and marrying Mexican. She was in the kitchen. Steam curled from a pot of boiling beans, the radio was on, looking as squat as a loaf of bread. "Well, if you want to be a barber—they say they make good money." She slapped a round steak with a knife, her glasses slipping down with each strike. She stopped and looked up. "If you find a good Mexican girl, marry her of course." She returned to

---

[1]like burros   [2]son   [3]Well, yes, they're Okies too

slapping the meat and I went to the backyard where my brother and David King were sitting on the lawn feeling the inside of their cheeks.

"This is what girls feel like," my brother said, rubbing the inside of his cheek. David put three fingers inside his mouth and scratched. I ignored them and climbed the back fence to see my best friend, Scott, a second-generation Okie. I called him and his mother pointed to the side of the house where his bedroom was, a small aluminum trailer, the kind you gawk at when they're flipped over on the freeway, wheels spinning in the air. I went around to find Scott pitching horseshoes.

I picked up a set of rusty ones and joined him. While we played, we talked about school and friends and record albums. The horseshoes scuffed up dirt, sometimes ringing the iron that threw out a meager shadow like a sundial. After three argued-over games, we pulled two oranges apiece from his tree and started down the alley still talking school and friends and record albums. We pulled more oranges from the alley and talked about who we would marry. "No offense, Scott," I said with an orange slice in my mouth, "but I would never marry an Okie." We walked in step, almost touching, with a sled of shadows dragging behind us. "No offense, Gary," Scott said, "but I would *never* marry a Mexican." I looked at him: a fang of orange slice showed from his munching mouth. I didn't think anything of it. He had his girl and I had mine. But our seventh-grade vision was the same: to marry, get jobs, buy cars and maybe a house if we had money left over.

5   We talked about our future lives until, to our surprise, we were on the downtown mall, two miles from home. We bought a bag of popcorn at Penneys and sat on a bench near the fountain watching Mexican and Okie girls pass. "That one's mine," I pointed with my chin when a girl with eyebrows arched into black rainbows ambled by. "She's cute," Scott said about a girl with yellow hair and a mouthful of gum. We dreamed aloud, our chins busy pointing out girls. We agreed that we couldn't wait to become men and lift them onto our laps.

But the woman I married was not Mexican but Japanese. It was a surprise to me. For years, I went about wide-eyed in my search for the brown girl in a white dress at a dance. I searched the playground at the baseball diamond. When the girls raced for grounders, their hair bounced like something that couldn't be caught. When they sat together in the lunchroom, heads pressed together, I knew they were talking about us Mexican guys. I saw them and dreamed them. I threw my face into my pillow, making up sentences that were good as in the movies.

But when I was twenty, I fell in love with this other girl who worried my mother, who had my grandmother asking once again to see the calendar of the Important Races of the World. I told her I had thrown it away years before. I took a much-glanced-at snapshot from my wallet. We looked at it together, in silence. Then grandma reclined in her chair, lit a cigarette, and said, "Es pretty." She blew and asked with all her worry pushed up to her forehead: "Chinese?"

I was in love and there was no looking back. She was the one. I told my mother who was slapping hamburger into patties. "Well, sure if you want to marry her," she said. But the more I talked, the more concerned she became. Later I began to worry. Was it all a mistake? "Marry a Mexican girl," I heard my mother say in my mind. I heard it at breakfast. I heard it over math problems, between Western Civilization and cultural geography. But then one afternoon while I was hitchhiking home from school, it struck me like a baseball in the back: my mother wanted me to marry someone of my own social class—a poor girl. I considered my fiancee, Carolyn, and she didn't look poor, though I knew she came from a family of farm workers and pull-yourself-up-by-your-bootstraps ranchers. I asked my brother, who was marrying Mexican poor that fall, if I should marry a poor girl. He screamed "Yeah" above his terrible guitar playing in his bedroom. I considered my sister who had married Mexican. Cousins were dating Mexican. Uncles were remarrying poor women. I asked Scott, who was still my best friend, and he said, "She's too good for you, so you better not."

I worried about it until Carolyn took me home to meet her parents. We drove in her Plymouth until the houses gave way to farms and ranches and finally her house fifty feet from the highway. When we pulled into the drive, I panicked and begged Carolyn to make a U-turn and go back so we could talk about it over a soda. She pinched my cheek, calling me a "silly boy." I felt better, though, when I got out of the car and saw the house: the chipped paint, a cracked window, boards for a walk to the back door. There were rusting cars near the barn. A tractor with a net of spiderwebs under a mulberry. A field. A bale of barbed wire like children's scribbling leaning against an empty chicken coop. Carolyn took my hand and pulled me to my future mother-in-law who was coming out to greet us.

10   We had lunch: sandwiches, potato chips, and iced tea. Carolyn and her mother talked mostly about neighbors and the congregation at the Japanese Methodist Church in West Fresno. Her father, who was in khaki work clothes, excused himself with a wave that was almost a salute and went outside. I heard a truck start, a dog bark, and then the truck rattle away.

Carolyn's mother offered another sandwich, but I declined with a shake of my head and a smile. I looked around when I could, when I was not saying over and over that I was a college student, hinting that I could take care of her daughter. I shifted my chair. I saw newspapers piled in corners, dusty cereal boxes and vinegar bottles in corners. The wallpaper was bubbled from rain that had come in from a bad roof. Dust. Dust lay on lamp shades and window sills. These people are just like Mexicans, I thought. Poor people.

Carolyn's mother asked me through Carolyn if I would like a *sushi*. A plate of black and white things were held in front of me. I took one, wide-eyed, and turned it over like a foreign coin. I was biting into one when I saw a kitten crawl up the window screen over the sink. I chewed and the kitten opened its mouth of terror as she crawled higher, wanting in to paw the leftovers from our plates. I looked at Carolyn who said that the cat was just showing off. I looked up in time to see it fall. It crawled up, then fell again.

We talked for an hour and had apple pie and coffee, slowly. Finally, we got up with Carolyn taking my hand. Slightly embarrassed, I tried to pull away but her grip held me. I let her have her way as she led me down the hallway with her mother right behind me. When I opened the door, I was startled by a kitten clinging to the screen door, its mouth screaming "cat food, dog biscuits, *sushi*. . . . " I opened the door and the kitten, still holding on, whined in the language of hungry animals. When I got into Carolyn's car, I looked back: the cat was still clinging. I asked Carolyn if it were possibly hungry, but she said the cat was being silly. She started the car, waved to her mother, and bounced us over the rain-poked drive, patting my thigh for being her lover baby. Carolyn waved again. I looked back, waving, then gawking at a window screen where there were now three kittens clawing and screaming to get in. Like Mexicans, I thought. I remembered the Molinas and how the cats clung to their screens—cats they shot down with squirt guns. On the highway, I felt happy, pleased by it all. I patted Carolyn's thigh. Her people were like Mexicans, only different.

[1986]

 TOPICS FOR CRITICAL THINKING AND WRITING

1. Do you agree that Soto implies that the differences between his Mexican-American family and Carolyn's Japanese-American family are slight? Judging only from what he says in the essay, do their differences seem slight to you? Explain.

2. If you are familiar with a couple who are from different ethnic backgrounds, write an essay discussing the degree to which ethnicity is evident in their lives. For instance, do the two people enjoy the same foods, and do they share the same religious beliefs? If not, do the differences make for richness or for difficulty?

Fiction

 OSCAR WILDE

Oscar Wilde (1854-1900) was born in Dublin, Ireland. He studied at Trinity College, Dublin, and then at Oxford University, where he established himself as a distinguished student. After graduation he settled in London, where he achieved some notice as a poet and essayist, and fame as a playwright and a lecturer. His best play, The Importance of Being Earnest *(1895), still holds the stage. By 1895 he was known as the leading advocate of the aesthetic movement, also called the art for art's sake movement. Briefly, the idea is that beauty has nothing to do with truth or morality; beauty is its own excuse for being. In 1895, at the height of his career, Wilde was arrested on charges of homosexuality, convicted, and sentenced to two years at hard labor. (In 1891 Wilde—already married and the father of two children—had established a relationship with a young man, Lord Alfred Douglas; Douglas's father publicly denounced Wilde, and Wilde sued for libel, lost, and then found himself on trial.) After completing his prison sentence he was in disgrace. He left England and spent his three remaining years in France, living under an assumed name.*

The Happy Prince

High above the city, on a tall column, stood the statue of the Happy Prince. He was gilded all over with thin leaves of fine gold, for eyes he had two bright sapphires, and a large red ruby glowed on his sword-hilt.

He was very much admired indeed. "He is as beautiful as a weather-cock," remarked one of the town councillors who wished to gain a reputation for having artistic tastes; "only not quite so useful," he added, fearing lest people should think him unpractical, which he really was not.

"Why can't you be like the Happy Prince?" asked a sensible mother of her little boy who was crying for the moon. "The Happy Prince never dreams of crying for anything."

"I am glad there is some one in the world who is quite happy," muttered a disappointed man as he gazed at the wonderful statue.

5   "He looks just like an angel," said the charity children as they came out of the cathedral in their bright scarlet cloaks and their clean white pinafores.

"How do you know?" said the Mathematical Master, "you have never seen one."

"Ah! but we have, in our dreams," answered the children; and the Mathematical Master frowned and looked very severe, for he did not approve of children dreaming.

One night there flew over the city a little swallow. His friends had gone away to Egypt six weeks before, but he had stayed behind, for he was in love with the most beautiful reed. He had met her early in the spring as he was flying down the river after a big yellow moth, and had been so attracted by her slender waist that he had stopped to talk to her.

"Shall I love you?" said the swallow, who liked to come to the point at once, and the reed made him a low bow. So he flew round and round her, touching the water with his wings and making silver ripples. This was his courtship, and it lasted all through the summer.

10   "It is a ridiculous attachment," twittered the other swallows; "she has not money, and far too many relations"; and, indeed, the river was quite full of reeds. Then, when the autumn came, they all flew away.

After they had gone he felt lonely, and began to tire of his lady-love. "She has no conversation," he said, "and I am afraid that she is a coquette, for she is always flirting with the wind." And certainly, whenever the wind blew, the reed made the most graceful curtsies. "I admit that she is domestic," he continued, "but I love travelling, and my wife, consequently, should love travelling also."

"Will you come away with me?" he said finally to her; but the reed shook her head, she was so attached to her home.

"You have been trifling with me," he cried, "I am off to the pyramids. Good-bye!" and he flew away.

All day long he flew, and at night-time he arrived at the city. "Where shall I put up?" he said; "I hope the town has made preparations."

15   Then he saw the statue on the tall column. "I will put up there," he cried; "it is a fine position with plenty of fresh air." So he alighted just between the feet of the Happy Prince.

"I have a golden bedroom," he said softly to himself as he looked round, and he prepared to go to sleep; but just as he was putting his head under his wing, a large drop of water fell on him. "What a curious thing!" he cried. "There is not a single cloud in the sky, the stars are quite clear and bright, and yet it is raining. The climate in the north of Europe is really dreadful. The reed used to like the rain, but that was merely her selfishness."

Then another drop fell.

"What is the use of a statue if it cannot keep the rain off?" he said; "I must look for a good chimney-pot," and he determined to fly away.

But before he had opened his wings, a third drop fell, and he looked up and saw——ah! what did he see?

20   The eyes of the Happy Prince were filled with tears, and tears were running down his golden cheeks. His face was so beautiful in the moonlight that the little swallow was filled with pity.

"Who are you?" he said.

"I am the Happy Prince."

"Why are you weeping then?" asked the swallow; "you have quite drenched me."

"When I was alive and had a human heart," answered the statue, "I did not know what tears were, for I lived in the Palace of Sans-Souci,[1] where sorrow is not allowed to enter. In the day-time I played with my companions in the garden, and in the evening I led the dance in the Great Hall. Round the garden ran a very lofty wall, but I never cared to ask what lay beyond it, everything about me was so beautiful. My courtiers called me the Happy Prince, and happy indeed I was, if pleasure be happiness. So I lived, and so I died. And now that I am dead they have set me up here so high that I can see all the ugliness and all the misery of my city, and though my heart is made of lead, yet I cannot choose but weep."

25   "What, is he not solid gold?" said the swallow to himself. He was too polite to make any personal remarks out loud.

"Far away," continued the statue in a low musical voice, "far away in a little street, there is a poor house. One of the windows is open, and through it I can see a woman seated at a table. Her face is thin and worn, and she has coarse red hands, all pricked by the needle, for she is a seamstress. She is embroidering passion-flowers on a satin gown for the loveliest of the Queen's maids-of-honour to wear at the next Court-ball. In a bed in the corner of the room, her little boy is lying ill. He has a fever, and is asking for oranges. His mother has nothing to give him but river water, so he is crying. Swallow, Swallow, little Swallow, will you not bring her the ruby out of my sword-hilt? My feet are fastened to this pedestal and I cannot move."

"I am waited for in Egypt," said the Swallow. "My friends are flying up and down the Nile and talking to the large lotus-flowers. Soon they will go to sleep in the tomb of the great King. The King is there himself in his painted coffin. He is wrapped in yellow linen and embalmed with spices. Round his neck is a chain of pale green jade, and his hands are like withered leaves."

"Swallow, Swallow, little Swallow," said the Prince, "will you not stay with me for one night and be my messenger? The boy is so thirsty, and the mother so sad."

"I don't think I like boys," answered the swallow. "Last summer, when I was staying on the river, there were two rude boys, the miller's sons, who were always throwing stones at me. They never hit me, of course; we swallows fly far too well for that, and besides, I come of a family famous for its agility; but still, it was a mark of disrespect."

30   But the Happy Prince looked so sad that the little swallow was sorry. "It

[1]without care (French)

is very cold here," he said; "but I will stay with you for one night and be your messenger."

"Thank you, little Swallow," said the Prince.

So the swallow picked out the great ruby from the Prince's sword and flew away with it in his beak over the roofs of the town.

He passed by the cathedral tower, where the white marble angels were sculptured. He passed by the palace and heard the sound of dancing. A beautiful girl came out on the balcony with her lover. "How wonderful the stars are," he said to her, "and how wonderful is the power of love!" "I hope my dress will be ready in time for the State-ball," she answered; "I have ordered passion-flowers to be embroidered on it; but the seamstresses are so lazy."

He passed over the river and saw the lanterns hanging to the masts of the ships. He passed over the Ghetto and saw the old Jews bargaining with each other and weighing out money in copper scales. At last he came to the poor house and looked in. The boy was tossing feverishly on his bed, and the mother had fallen asleep, she was so tired. In he hopped, and laid the great ruby on the table beside the woman's thimble. Then he flew gently round the bed, fanning the boy's forehead with his wings. "How cool I feel," said the boy, "I must be getting better"; and he sank into a delicious slumber.

35   Then the swallow flew back to the Happy Prince and told him what he had done. "It is curious," he remarked, "but I feel quite warm now, although it is so cold."

"That is because you have done a good action," said the Prince. And the little swallow began to think, and then he fell asleep. Thinking always made him sleepy.

When day broke, he flew down to the river and had a bath. "What a remarkable phenomenon," said the professor of ornithology as he was passing over the bridge. "A swallow in winter!" And he wrote a long letter about it to the local newspaper. Every one quoted it, it was full of so many words that they could not understand.

"To-night I go to Egypt," said the swallow, and he was in high spirits at the prospect. He visited all the public monuments and sat a long time on top of the church steeple. Wherever he went the sparrows chirruped and said to each other, "What a distinguished stranger!" so he enjoyed himself very much.

When the moon rose, he flew back to the Happy Prince. "Have you any commissions for Egypt?" he cried; "I am just starting."

40   "Swallow, Swallow, little Swallow," said the Prince, "will you not stay with me one night longer?"

"I am waited for in Egypt," answered the swallow. "To-morrow my friends will fly up to the Second Cataract. The river-horse couches there among the bulrushes, and on a great granite throne sits the god Memnon. All night long he watches the stars, and when the morning star shines, he utters one cry of joy, and then he is silent. At noon the yellow lions come down to the water's edge to drink. They have eyes like green beryls, and their roar is louder than the roar of the cataract."

"Swallow, Swallow, little Swallow," said the Prince, "far away across the city I see a young man in a garret. He is leaning over a desk covered with papers, and in a tumbler by his side there is a bunch of withered violets. His hair is brown and crisp, and his lips are red as a pomegranate, and he has large and dreamy eyes. He is trying to finish a play for the director of the theatre, but he is too cold to write any more. There is no fire in the grate, and hunger has made him faint."

"I will wait with you one night longer," said the swallow, who really had a good heart. "Shall I take him another ruby?"

"Alas! I have no ruby now," said the Prince; "my eyes are all that I have left. They are made of rare sapphires, which were brought out of India a thousand years ago. Pluck out one of them and take it to him. He will sell it to the jeweller, and buy food and firewood, and finish his play."

45   "Dear Prince," said the swallow, "I cannot do that"; and he began to weep.

"Swallow, Swallow, little Swallow," said the Prince, "do as I command you."

So the swallow plucked out the Prince's eye and flew away to the student's garret. It was easy enough to get in, as there was a hole in the roof. Through this he darted, and came into the room. The young man had his head buried in his hands, so he did not hear the flutter of the bird's wings, and when he looked up, he found the beautiful sapphire lying on the withered violets.

"I am beginning to be appreciated," he cried; "this is from some great admirer. Now I can finish my play," and he looked quite happy.

The next day the swallow flew down to the harbour. He sat on the mast of a large vessel and watched the sailors hauling big chests out of the hold with ropes. "Heave a-hoy!" they shouted as each chest came up. "I am going to Egypt!" cried the swallow, but nobody minded, and when the moon rose, he flew back to the Happy Prince.

50   "I am come to bid you good-bye," he cried.

"Swallow, Swallow, little Swallow," said the Prince, "will you not stay with me one night longer?"

"It is winter," answered the swallow, "and the chill snow will soon be here. In Egypt the sun is warm on the green palm-trees, and the crocodiles lie in the mud and look lazily about them. My companions are building a nest in the Temple of Baalbec, and the pink and white doves are watching them and cooing to each other. Dear Prince, I must leave you, but I will never forget you, and next spring I will bring you back two beautiful jewels in place of those you have given away. The ruby shall be redder than a red rose, and the sapphire shall be as blue as the great sea."

"In the square below," said the Happy Prince, "there stands a little match-girl. She has let her matches fall in the gutter, and they are all spoiled. Her father will beat her if she does not bring home some money, and she is crying. She has no shoes or stockings, and her little head is bare. Pluck out my other eye, and give it to her, and her father will not beat her."

"I will stay with you one night longer," said the swallow, "but I cannot pluck out your eye. You would be quite blind then."

55   "Swallow, Swallow, little Swallow," said the Prince, "do as I command you."

So he plucked out the Prince's other eye and darted down with it. He swooped past the match-girl and slipped the jewel into the palm of her hand. "What a lovely bit of glass," cried the little girl; and she ran home, laughing.

Then the swallow came back to the Prince. "You are blind now," he said, "so I will stay with you always."

"No, little Swallow," said the poor Prince, "you must go away to Egypt."

"I will stay with you always," said the swallow, and he slept at the Prince's feet.

60　All the next day he sat on the Prince's shoulder and told him stories of what he had seen in strange lands. He told him of the red ibises, who stand in long rows on the banks of the Nile and catch gold fish in their beaks; of the Sphinx, who is as old as the world itself, and lives in the desert, and knows everything; of the merchants, who walk slowly by the side of their camels and carry amber beads in their hands; of the King of the Mountains of the Moon, who is as black as ebony and worships a large crystal; of the great green snake that sleeps in a palm-tree and has twenty priests to feed it with honey-cakes; and of the pygmies, who sail over a big lake on large flat leaves and are always at war with the butterflies.

"Dear little Swallow," said the Prince, "you tell me of marvellous things, but more marvellous than anything is the suffering of men and of women. There is no mystery so great as misery. Fly over my city, little Swallow, and tell me what you see there."

So the swallow flew over the great city and saw the rich making merry in their beautiful houses, while the beggars were sitting at the gates. He flew into dark lanes and saw the white faces of starving children looking out listlessly at the black streets. Under the archway of a bridge, two little boys were lying in one another's arms to try and keep themselves warm. "How hungry we are!" they said. "You must not lie here," shouted the watchman, and they wandered out into the rain.

Then he flew back and told the Prince what he had seen.

"I am covered with fine gold," said the Prince, "you must take it off, leaf by leaf, and give it to my poor; the living always think that gold can make them happy."

65　Leaf after leaf of the fine gold the Swallow picked off, till the Happy Prince looked quite dull and grey. Leaf after leaf of the fine gold he brought to the poor, and the children's faces grew rosier, and they laughed and played games in the street. "We have bread now!" they cried.

Then the snow came, and after the snow came the frost. The streets looked as if they were made of silver, they were so bright and glistening; long icicles like crystal daggers hung down from the eaves of the houses, everybody went about in furs; and the little boys wore scarlet caps and skated on the ice.

The poor little swallow grew colder and colder, but he would not leave the Prince, he loved him too well. He picked up crumbs outside the baker's door when the baker was not looking, and tried to keep himself warm by flapping his wings.

But at last he knew that he was going to die. He had just strength to fly up to the Prince's shoulder once more. "Good-bye, dear Prince!" he murmured, "will you let me kiss your hand?"

"I am glad that you are going to Egypt at last, little Swallow," said the Prince, "you have stayed too long here; but you must kiss me on the lips, for I love you."

70　"It is not to Egypt that I am going," said the swallow. "I am going to the house of death. Death is the brother of sleep, is he not?"

And he kissed the Happy Prince on the lips and fell down dead at his feet.

At that moment a curious crack sounded inside the statue, as if something had broken. The fact is that the leaden heart had snapped right in two. It certainly was a dreadfully hard frost.

Early the next morning the mayor was walking in the square below in company with the town councillors. As they passed the column, he looked up at the statue: "Dear me! how shabby the Happy Prince looks!" he said.

"How shabby indeed!" cried the town councillors, who always agreed with the mayor, and they went up to look at it.

75   "The ruby has fallen out of his sword, his eyes are gone, and he is golden no longer," said the mayor; "in fact, he is little better than a beggar!"

"Little better than a beggar," said the town councillors.

"And here is actually a dead bird at his feet!" continued the mayor. "We must really issue a proclamation that birds are not allowed to die here." And the town clerk made a note of the suggestion.

So they pulled down the statue of the Happy Prince. "As he is no longer beautiful, he is no longer useful," said the art professor at the university.

Then they melted the statue in a furnace, and the mayor held a meeting of the corporation to decide what was to be done with the metal. "We must have another statue, of course," he said, "and it shall be a statue of myself."

80   "Of myself," said each of the town councillors, and they quarrelled. When I last heard of them, they were quarrelling still.

"What a strange thing!" said the overseer of the workmen at the foundry. "This broken lead heart will not melt in the furnace. We must throw it away." So they threw it on a dust-heap where the dead swallow was also lying.

"Bring me the two most precious things in the city," said God to one of His Angels; and the Angel brought Him the leaden heart and the dead bird.

"You have rightly chosen," said God, "for in my garden of Paradise this little bird shall sing for evermore, and in my city of gold the Happy Prince shall praise me."

[1886]

TOPICS FOR CRITICAL THINKING AND WRITING

1. Do you think this story has a moral? If so, what is the moral?
2. Think of some fairy tale that you know rather well, perhaps *Cinderella* or *Sleeping Beauty* or *Rumpelstiltskin.* Does it have a moral? If so, what is the moral? If it has a moral, is the moral partly what makes it interesting? If it doesn't have a moral, what makes the story interesting?
3. As the brief biographical note indicates, Oscar Wilde was homosexual. Do you think that the story in any way(s) reveals his sexual orientation? Do you think that straights and gays read the story in pretty much the same way? Explain.

VIRGINIA WOOLF

Virginia Woolf (1882–1941) is known chiefly as a novelist, but she was also the author of short stories and essays, and in recent years the range of her power has been increasingly recognized.

Woolf was self-educated in the library of her father, Leslie Stephen, an important English scholar, literary critic, and biographer. In 1907 she married Leonard Woolf, with whom ten years later she established the Hogarth Press, which published some of the most interesting literature of the period, including her own novels. Woolf experienced several mental breakdowns, and in 1941, fearing yet another, she drowned herself.

Lappin and Lapinova*

They were married. The wedding march pealed out. The pigeons fluttered. Small boys in Eaton jackets threw rice: a fox terrier sauntered across the path; and Ernest Thorburn led his bride to the car through the small inquisitive crowd of complete strangers which always collects in London to enjoy other people's happiness or unhappiness. Certainly he looked handsome and she looked shy. More rice was thrown, and the car moved off.

That was on Tuesday. Now it was Saturday. Rosalind had still to get used to the fact that she was Mrs. Ernest Thorburn. Perhaps she never would get used to the fact that she was Mrs. Ernest Anybody, she thought, as she sat in the bow window of the hotel looking over the lake to the mountains, and waited for her husband to come down to breakfast. Ernest was a difficult name to get used to. It was not the name she would have chosen. She would have preferred Timothy, Antony, or Peter. He did not look like Ernest either. The name suggested the Albert Memorial,[1] mahogany sideboards, steel engravings of the Prince Consort with his family—her mother-in-law's dining-room in Porchester Terrace in short.

But here he was. Thank goodness he did not look like Ernest—no. But what did he look like? She glanced at him sideways. Well, when he was eating toast he looked like a rabbit. Not that anyone else would have seen a likeness to a creature so diminutive and timid in this spruce, muscular young man with the straight nose, the blue eyes, and the very firm mouth. But that made it all the more amusing. His nose twitched very slightly when he ate. So did her pet rabbit's. She kept watching his nose twitch; and then she had to explain, when he caught her looking at him, why she laughed.

"It's because you're like a rabbit, Ernest," she said. "Like a wild rabbit," she added, looking at him. "A hunting rabbit; a King Rabbit; a rabbit that makes laws for all the other rabbits."

5   Ernest had no objection to being that kind of rabbit, and since it amused her to see him twitch his nose—he had never known that his nose twitched—he twitched it on purpose. And she laughed and laughed; and he laughed too, so that the maiden ladies and the fishing man and the Swiss waiter in his greasy jacket all guessed right; they were very happy. But how long does such happiness last? they asked themselves; and each answered according to his own circumstances.

lapin is French for rabbit   [1]a memorial, in Hyde Park, London, dedicated in 1872 to Prince Albert (1819–61), consort of Queen Victoria. A bronze statue of the prince stands in a tabernacle which rests on a platform. The platform's corners are adorned with sculptural groups representing Industry, Commerce, Agriculture, and Science. The whole is a memorial to Victorian culture, which by Woolf's time was much ridiculed.

At lunch time, seated on a clump of heather beside the lake, "Lettuce, rabbit?" said Rosalind, holding out the lettuce that had been provided to eat with the hard-boiled eggs. "Come and take it out of my hand," she added, and he stretched out and nibbled the lettuce and twitched his nose.

"Good rabbit, nice rabbit," she said, patting him, as she used to pat her tame rabbit at home. But that was absurd. He was not a tame rabbit, whatever he was. She turned it into French. "Lapin," she called him. But whatever he was, he was not a French rabbit. He was simply and solely English— born at Porchester Terrace, educated at Rugby; now a clerk in His Majesty's Civil Service. So she tried "Bunny" next; but that was worse. "Bunny" was someone plump and soft and comic; he was thin and hard and serious. Still, his nose twitched. "Lappin," she exclaimed suddenly; and gave a little cry as if she had found the very word she looked for.

"Lappin, Lappin, King Lappin," she repeated. It seemed to suit him exactly; he was not Ernest, he was King Lappin. Why? She did not know.

When there was nothing new to talk about on their long solitary walks—and it rained, as everyone had warned them that it would rain; or when they were sitting over the fire in the evening, for it was cold, and the maiden ladies had gone and the fishing man, and the waiter only came if you rang the bell for him, she let her fancy play with the story of the Lappin tribe. Under her hands—she was sewing; he was reading—they became very real, very vivid, very amusing. Ernest put down the paper and helped her. There were the black rabbits and the red; there were the enemy rabbits and the friendly. There were the wood in which they lived and the outlying prairies and the swamp. Above all there was King Lappin, who, far from having only the one trick—that he twitched his nose—became as the days passed an animal of the greatest character; Rosalind was always finding new qualities in him. But above all he was a great hunter.

10   "And what," said Rosalind, on the last day of the honeymoon, "did the King do to-day?"

In fact they had been climbing all day; and she had worn a blister on her heel; but she did not mean that.

"To-day," said Ernest, twitching his nose as he bit the end off his cigar, "he chased a hare." He paused; struck a match, and twitched again.

"A woman hare," he added.

"A white hare!" Rosalind exclaimed, as if she had been expecting this. "Rather a small hare; silver grey; with big bright eyes?"

15   "Yes," said Ernest, looking at her as she had looked at him, "a smallish animal; with eyes popping out of her head, and two little front paws dangling." It was exactly how she sat, with her sewing dangling in her hands; and her eyes, that were so big and bright, were certainly a little prominent.

"Ah, Lapinova," Rosalind murmured.

"Is that what she's called?" said Ernest—"the real Rosalind?" He looked at her. He felt very much in love with her.

"Yes; that's what she's called," said Rosalind. "Lapinova." And before they went to bed that night it was all settled. He was King Lappin; she was Queen Lapinova. They were the opposite of each other; he was bold and determined; she wary and undependable. He ruled over the busy world of rabbits; her world was a desolate, mysterious place, which she ranged mostly by moonlight. All the same, their territories touched; they were King and Queen.

Thus when they came back from their honeymoon they possessed a private world, inhabited, save for the one white hare, entirely by rabbits. No one guessed that there was such a place, and that of course made it all the more amusing. It made them feel, more even than most young married couples, in league together against the rest of the world. Often they looked slyly at each other when people talked about rabbits and woods and traps and shooting. Or they winked furtively across the table when Aunt Mary said that she could never bear to see a hare in a dish—it looked so like a baby; or when John, Ernest's sporting brother, told them what price rabbits were fetching that autumn in Wiltshire, skins and all. Sometimes when they wanted a gamekeeper, or a poacher or a Lord of the Manor, they amused themselves by distributing the parts among their friends. Ernest's mother, Mrs. Reginald Thorburn, for example, fitted the part of the Squire to perfection. But it was all secret—that was the point of it; nobody save themselves knew that such a world existed.

20   Without that world, how, Rosalind wondered, that winter could she have lived at all? For instance, there was the golden-wedding party, when all the Thorburns assembled at Porchester Terrace to celebrate the fiftieth anniversary of that union which had been so blessed—had it not produced Ernest Thorburn? and so fruitful—had it not produced nine other sons and daughters into the bargain, many themselves married and also fruitful? She dreaded that party. But it was inevitable. As she walked upstairs she felt bitterly that she was an only child and an orphan at that; a mere drop among all those Thorburns assembled in the great drawing-room with the shiny satin wallpaper and the lustrous family portraits. The living Thorburns much resembled the painted; save that instead of painted lips they had real lips; out of which came jokes; jokes about schoolrooms, and how they had pulled the chair from under the governess; jokes about frogs and how they had put them between the virgin sheets of maiden ladies. As for herself, she had never even made an apple-pie bed. Holding her present in her hand she advanced toward her mother-in-law sumptuous in yellow satin; and toward her father-in-law decorated with a rich yellow carnation. All round them on tables and chairs there were golden tributes, some nestling in cotton wool; others branching resplendent—candlesticks; cigar boxes; chains; each stamped with the goldsmith's proof that it was solid gold, hallmarked, authentic. But her present was only a little pinchbeck[2] box pierced with holes; an old sand caster, an eighteenth-century relic, once used to sprinkle sand over wet ink. Rather a senseless present she felt—in an age of blotting paper; and as she proffered it, she saw in front of her the stubby black handwriting in which her mother-in-law when they were engaged had expressed the hope that "My son will make you happy." No, she was not happy. Not at all happy. She looked at Ernest, straight as a ramrod with a nose like all the noses in the family portraits; a nose that never twitched at all.

Then they went down to dinner. She was half hidden by the great chrysanthemums that curled their red and gold petals into large tight balls. Everything was gold. A gold-edged card with gold initials intertwined recited the list of all the dishes that would be set one after another before them. She dipped her spoon in a plate of clear golden fluid. The raw white

[2]imitation gold

fog outside had been turned by the lamps into a golden mesh that blurred the edges of the plates and gave the pineapples a rough golden skin. Only she herself in her white wedding dress peering ahead of her with her prominent eyes seemed insoluble as an icicle.

As the dinner wore on, however, the room grew steamy with heat. Beads of perspiration stood out on the men's foreheads. She felt that her icicle was being turned to water. She was being melted; dispersed; dissolved into nothingness; and would soon faint. Then through the surge in her head and the din in her ears she heard a woman's voice exclaim, "But they breed so!"

The Thorburns—yes; they breed so, she echoed; looking at all the round red faces that seemed doubled in the giddiness that overcame her; and magnified in the gold mist that enhaloed them. "They breed so." Then John bawled:

"Little devils! . . . Shoot'em! Jump on'em with big boots! That's the only way to deal with 'em . . . rabbits!"

25   At that word, that magic word, she revived. Peeping between the chrysanthemums she saw Ernest's nose twitch. It rippled, it ran with successive twitches. And at that a mysterious catastrophe befell the Thorburns. The golden table became a moor with the gorse in full bloom; the din of voices turned to one peal of lark's laughter ringing down from the sky. It was a blue sky—clouds passed slowly. And they had all been changed—the Thorburns. She looked at her father-in-law, a furtive little man with dyed moustaches. His foible was collecting things—seals, enamel boxes, trifles from eighteenth-century dressing tables which he hid in the drawers of his study from his wife. Now she saw him as he was—a poacher, stealing off with his coat bulging with pheasants and partridges to drop them stealthily into a three-legged pot in his smoky little cottage. That was her real father-in-law—a poacher. And Celia, the unmarried daughter, who always nosed out other people's secrets, the little things they wished to hide—she was a white ferret[3] with pink eyes, and a nose clotted with earth from her horrid underground nosings and pokings. Slung round men's shoulders, in a net, and thrust down a hole—it was a pitiable life—Celia's; it was none of her fault. So she saw Celia. And then she looked at her mother-in-law—whom they dubbed The Squire. Flushed, coarse, a bully—she was all that, as she stood returning thanks, but now that Rosalind—that is Lapinova—saw her, she saw behind her the decayed family mansion, the plaster peeling off the walls, and heard her, with a sob in her voice, giving thanks to her children (who hated her) for a world that had ceased to exist. There was a sudden silence. They all stood with their glasses raised; they all drank; then it was over.

"Oh, King Lappin!" she cried as they went home together in the fog, "if your nose hadn't twitched just at that moment, I should have been trapped!"

"But you're safe," said King Lappin, pressing her paw.

"Quite safe," she answered.

And they drove back through the Park, King and Queen of the marsh, of the mist, and of the gorse-scented moor.

---

[3]white ferrets—albino polecats—were often used to hunt rats and rabbits

30   Thus time passed; one year; two years of time. And on a winter's night, which happened by a coincidence to be the anniversary of the golden-wedding party—but Mrs. Reginald Thorburn was dead; the house was to let; and there was only a caretaker in residence—Ernest came home from the office. They had a nice little home; half a house above a saddler's shop in South Kensington, not far from the tube[4] station. It was cold, with fog in the air, and Rosalind was sitting over the fire, sewing.

"What d'you think happened to me to-day?" she began as soon as he had settled himself down with his legs stretched to the blaze. "I was crossing the stream when—"

"What stream?" Ernest interrupted her.

"The stream at the bottom, where our wood meets the black wood," she explained.

Ernest looked completely blank for a moment.

35   "What the deuce are you talking about?" he asked.

"My dear Ernest!" she cried in dismay, "King Lappin," she added, dangling her little front paws in the firelight. But his nose did not twitch. Her hands—they turned to hands—clutched the stuff she was holding; her eyes popped half out of her head. It took him five minutes at least to change from Ernest Thorburn to King Lappin; and while she waited she felt a load on the back of her neck, as if somebody were about to wring it. At last he changed to King Lappin; his nose twitched; and they spent the evening roaming the woods much as usual.

But she slept badly. In the middle of the night she woke, feeling as if something strange had happened to her. She was stiff and cold. At last she turned on the light and looked at Ernest lying beside her. He was sound asleep. He snored. But even though he snored, his nose remained perfectly still. It looked as if it had never twitched at all. Was it possible that he was really Ernest; and that she was really married to Ernest? A vision of her mother-in-law's dining-room came before her; and there they sat, she and Ernest, grown old, under the engravings, in front of the sideboard. . . . It was their golden-wedding day. She could not bear it.

"Lappin, King Lappin!" she whispered, and for a moment his nose seemed to twitch of its own accord. But he still slept. "Wake up, Lappin, wake up!" she cried.

Ernest woke; and seeing her sitting bolt upright beside him he asked:

40   "What's the matter?"

"I thought my rabbit was dead!" she whimpered. Ernest was angry.

"Don't talk such rubbish, Rosalind," he said. "Lie down and go to sleep."

He turned over. In another moment he was sound asleep and snoring.

But she could not sleep. She lay curled up on her side of the bed, like a hare in its form.[5] She had turned out the light, but the street lamp lit the ceiling faintly, and the trees outside made a lacy network over it as if there were a shadowy grove on the ceiling in which she wandered, turning, twisting, in and out, round and round, hunting, being hunted, hearing the bay of hounds and horns; flying, escaping . . . until the maid drew the blinds and brought their early tea.

45   Next day she could settle to nothing. She seemed to have lost something. She felt as if her body had shrunk; it had grown small, and black and

4subway   5the resting place of a hare

hard. Her joints seemed stiff too, and when she looked in the glass, which she did several times as she wandered about the flat, her eyes seemed to burst out of her head, like currants in a bun. The rooms also seemed to have shrunk. Large pieces of furniture jutted out at odd angles and she found herself knocking against them. At last she put on her hat and went out. She walked along the Cromwell Road; and every room she passed and peered into seemed to be a dining-room where people sat eating under steel engravings, with thick yellow lace curtains, and mahogany sideboards. At last she reached the Natural History Museum; she used to like it when she was a child. But the first thing she saw when she went in was a stuffed hare standing on sham snow with pink glass eyes. Somehow it made her shiver all over. Perhaps it would be better when dusk fell. She went home and sat over the fire, without a light, and tried to imagine that she was out alone on a moor; and there was a stream rushing; and beyond the stream a dark wood. But she could get no further than the stream. At last she squatted down on the bank on the wet grass, and sat crouched in her chair, with her hands dangling empty, and her eyes glazed, like glass eyes, in the firelight. Then there was the crack of a gun. . . . She started as if she had been shot. It was only Ernest, turning his key in the door. She waited, trembling. He came in and switched on the light. There he stood, tall, handsome, rubbing his hands that were red with cold.

"Sitting in the dark?" he said.

"Oh, Ernest, Ernest!" she cried, starting up in her chair.

"Well, what's up now?" he asked briskly, warming his hands at the fire.

"It's Lapinova . . ." she faltered, glancing wildly at him out of her great started eyes. "She's gone, Ernest. I've lost her!"

50   Ernest frowned. He pressed his lips tight together.

"Oh, that's what's up, is it?" he said, smiling rather grimly at his wife. For ten seconds he stood there, silent; and she waited, feeling hands tightening at the back of her neck.

"Yes," he said at length. "Poor Lapinova . . ." He straightened his tie at the looking-glass over the mantelpiece.

"Caught in a trap," he said, "killed," and sat down and read the newspaper.

So that was the end of that marriage.

[1938]

 # TOPICS FOR CRITICAL THINKING AND WRITING

1. What is the point of view and the tone of the first paragraph? Of the second?

2. We are told that Rosalind and Ernest—King Lappin and Queen Lapinova—"were the opposite of each other; he was bold and determined; she wary and undependable." Are these brief characterizations adequate, or are the characters more complex?

3. Why, at the golden-wedding party, does Rosalind feel that she is being "dissolved into nothingness"?

4. The story ends with this sentence: "So that was the end of that marriage." Why did the marriage end? And what, if anything, does this rather flat sentence add to the story?

5. Write a story, a narrative essay, or a journal entry about the end of a relationship. The relationship need not be between husband and wife, or
lovers, or friends. It might be between a teacher and a student, a coach
and an athlete, or siblings, for example.

 ZORA NEALE HURSTON

*Zora Neale Hurston (c. 1901–60) was brought up in Eatonville,
Florida, a town said to be the first all-black self-governing town in the
United States. Her mother died in 1904, and when Hurston's father
remarried, Hurston felt out of place. In 1914, then at about the age of
fourteen, she joined a traveling theatrical group as a maid, hoping to
save money for school. Later, by working at such jobs as manicurist
and waitress, she put herself through college, entering Howard University in 1923. After receiving a scholarship, she transferred in 1926
to Barnard College in New York, where she was the first black student in the college. After graduating from Barnard in 1928 she
taught drama, worked as an editor, and studied anthropology. But
when grant money ran out in 1932 she returned to Eatonville to edit
the folk material that she had collected during four years of field-
work, and to do some further writing. She steadily published from
1932 to 1938—stories, folklore, and two novels—but she gained very
little money. Further, although she played a large role in the Harlem
Renaissance in the 1930s, she was criticized by Richard Wright and
other influential black authors for portraying blacks as stereotypes
and for being politically conservative. To many in the 1950s her writing seemed reactionary, almost embarrassing in an age of black
protest, and she herself—working as a domestic, a librarian, and a
substitute teacher—was almost forgotten. She died in a county welfare home in Florida and is buried in an unmarked grave.*

Sweat

It was eleven o'clock of a Spring night in Florida. It was Sunday. Any other
night, Delia Jones would have been in bed for two hours by this time. But
she was a washwoman, and Monday morning meant a great deal to her. So
she collected the soiled clothes on Saturday when she returned the clean
things. Sunday night after church, she sorted them and put the white things
to soak. It saved her almost a half day's start. A great hamper in the bedroom
held the clothes that she brought home. It was so much neater than a number of bundles lying around.

She squatted in the kitchen floor beside the great pile of clothes, sorting
them into small heaps according to color, and humming a song in a mournful key, but wondering through it all where Sykes, her husband, had gone
with her horse and buckboard.[1]

Just then something long, round, limp and black fell upon her shoulders
and slithered to the floor beside her. A great terror took hold of her. It soft-

[1] an open wagon

ened her knees and dried her mouth so that it was a full minute before she could cry out or move. Then she saw that it was the big bull whip her husband like to carry when he drove.

She lifted her eyes to the door and saw him standing there bent over with laughter at her fright. She screamed at him.

5   "Sykes, what you throw dat whip on me like dat? You know it would skeer me—looks just like a snake, an' you knows how skeered Ah is of snakes."

"Course Ah knowed it! That's how come Ah done it." He slapped his leg with his hand and almost rolled on the ground in his mirth. "If you such a big fool dat you got to have a fit over a earth worm or a string, Ah don't keer how bad Ah skeer you."

"You aint go no business doing it. Gawd knows it's a sin. Some day Ah'm gointuh drop dead from some of yo' foolishness. 'Nother thing, where you been wid mah rig? Ah feeds dat pony. He aint fuh you to be drivin' wid no bull whip."

"Yo sho is one aggravatin' nigger woman!" he declared and stepped into the room. She resumed her work and did not answer him at once. "Ah done tole you time and again to keep them white folks' clothes outa dis house."

He picked up the whip and glared down at her. Delia went on with her work. She went out into the yard and returned with a galvanized tub and set it on the washbench. She saw that Sykes had kicked all of the clothes together again, and now stood in her way truculently, his whole manner hoping, *praying,* for an argument. But she walked calmly around him and commenced to re-sort the things.

10   "Next time, Ah'm gointer to kick 'em outdoors," he threatened as he struck a match along the leg of his corduroy breeches.

Delia never looked up from her work, and her thin, stooped shoulders sagged further.

"Ah aint for no fuss t'night Sykes. Ah just come from taking sacrament at the church house."

He snorted scornfully. "Yeah, you just come from de church house on a Sunday night, but heah you is gone to work on them clothes. You aint nothing but a hypocrite. One of them amen-corner Christians—sing, whoop, shout, then come home and wash white folks clothes on the Sabbath."

He stepped roughly upon the whitest pile of things, kicking them helter-skelter as he crossed the room. His wife gave a little scream of dismay, and quickly gathered them together again.

15   "Sykes, you quit grindin' dirt into these clothes! How can Ah git through by Sat'day if Ah don't start on Sunday?"

"Ah don't keer if you never git through. Anyhow, Ah done promised Gawd and a couple of other men, Ah aint gointer have it in mah house. Don't gimme no lip neither, else Ah'll throw 'em out and put mah fist up side yo' head to boot."

Delia's habitual meekness seemed to slip from her shoulders like a blown scarf. She was on her feet; her poor little body, her bare knuckly hands bravely defying the strapping hulk before her.

"Looka heah, Sykes, you done gone too fur. Ah been married to you fur fifteen years, and Ah been takin' in washin' for fifteen years. Sweat, sweat, sweat! Work and sweat, cry and sweat, pray and sweat!"

"What's that got to do with me?" he asked brutally.

20   "What's it got to do with you, Sykes? Mah tub of suds is filled yo' belly with vittles more times than yo' hands is filled it. Mah sweat is done paid for this house and Ah reckon Ah kin keep on sweatin' in it."

She seized the iron skillet from the stove and struck a defensive pose, which act surprised him greatly, coming from her. It cowed him and he did not strike her as he usually did.

"Naw you won't," she panted, "that ole snaggle-toothed black woman you runnin' with aint comin' heah to pile up on *mah* sweat and blood. You aint paid for nothin' on this place, and Ah'm gointer stay right heah till Ah'm toted out foot foremost."

"Well, you better quit gittin' me riled up, else they'll be totin' you out sooner than you expect. Ah'm so tired of you Ah don't know whut to do. Gawd! how Ah hates skinny wimmen!"

A little awed by this new Delia, he sidled out of the door and slammed the back gate after him. He did not say where he had gone, but she knew too well. She knew very well that he would not return until nearly daybreak also. Her work over, she went on to bed but not to sleep at once. Things had come to a pretty pass!

25   She lay awake, gazing upon the debris that cluttered their matrimonial trail. Not an image left standing along the way. Anything like flowers had long ago been drowned in the salty stream that had been pressed from her heart. Her tears, her sweat, her blood. She had brought love to the union and he had brought a longing for the flesh. Two months after the wedding, he had given her the first brutal beating. She had the memory of numerous trips to Orlando with all of his wages when he had returned to her penni-less, even before the first year had passed. She was young and soft then, but now she thought of her knotty, muscled limbs, her harsh knuckly hands, and drew herself up into an unhappy little ball in the middle of the big feather bed. Too late now to hope for love, even if it were not Bertha it would be someone else. This case differed from the others only in that she was bolder than the others. Too late for everything except her little home. She had built it for her old days, and planted one by one the trees and flow-ers there. It was lovely to her, lovely.

Somehow before sleep came, she found herself saying aloud: "Oh well, whatever goes over the Devil's back, is got to come under his belly. Some-time or ruther, Sykes, like everybody else, is gointer reap his sowing." After that she was able to build a spiritual earthworks against her husband. His shells could no longer reach her. *Amen.* She went to sleep and slept until he announced his presence in bed by kicking her feet and rudely snatching the cover away.

"Gimme some kivah heah, an' git yo' damn foots over on yo' own side! Ah oughter mash you in yo' mouf fuh drawing dat skillet on me."

Delia went clear to the rail without answering him. A triumphant indif-ference to all that he was or did.

The week was as full of work for Delia as all other weeks, and Saturday found her behind her little pony, collecting and delivering clothes.

30   It was a hot, hot day near the end of July. The village men on Joe Clarke's porch even chewed cane listlessly. They did not hurl the cane-knots as usual. They let them dribble over the edge of the porch. Even conversa-tion had collapsed under the heat.

"Heah comes Delia Jones," Jim Merchant said, as the shaggy pony came 'round the bend of the road toward them. The rusty buckboard was heaped with baskets of crisp, clean laundry.

"Yep," Joe Lindsay agreed. "Hot or col', rain or shine, jes ez reg'lar ez de weeks roll roun' Delia carries 'em an' fetches 'em on Sat'day."

"She better if she wanter eat," said Moss. "Syke Jones aint wuth de shot an' powder hit would tek tuh kill 'em. Not to *bub* he aint."

"He sho' aint," Walter Thomas chimed in. "It's too bad, too, cause she wuz a right pritty lil trick when he got huh. Ah'd uh mah'ied huh mahseff if he hadnter beat me to it."

35 Delia nodded briefly at the men as she drove past.

"Too much knockin' will ruin *any* 'oman. He done beat huh 'nough tuh kill three women, let 'lone change they looks," said Elijah Mosely. "How Syke kin stommuck dat big black greasy Mogul[2] he's layin' roun' wid, gits me. Ah swear dat eight-rock couldn't kiss a sardine can Ah done thowed out de back do' 'way las' yeah."

"Aw, she's fat, thass how come. He's allus been crazy 'bout fat women," put in Merchant. "He'd a' been tied up wid one long time ago if he could a' found one tuh have him. Did Ah tell yuh 'bout him come sidlin' roun' *mah* wife—bringin' her a basket uh pee-cans outa his yard fuh a present? Yes-sir, mah wife! She tol' him tuh take 'em right straight back home, cause Delia works so hard ovah dat washtub she reckon everything en de place taste lak sweat an' soapsuds. Ah jus' wisht Ah'd a' caught 'im 'roun' dere! Ah'd a' made his hips ketch on fiah down dat shell road."

"Ah know he done it, too. Ah sees 'im grinnin' at every 'oman dat passes," Walter Thomas said. "But even so, he useter eat some mighty big hunks uh humble pie tuh git dat lil' 'oman he got. She wuz ez pritty ez a speckled pup! Dat wuz fifteen yeahs ago. He useter be so skeered uh losin' huh, she could make him do some parts of a husband's duty. Dey never wuz de same in de mind."

"There oughter be a law about him," said Lindsay. "He aint fit tuh carry guts tuh a bear."

40 Clarke spoke for the first time. "Taint no law on earth dat kin make a man be decent if it aint in 'im. There's plenty men dat takes a wife lak dey do a joint uh sugar-cane. It's round, juicy an' sweet when dey gits it. But dey squeeze an' grind, squeeze an' grind an' wring tell dey wring every drop uh pleasure dat's in 'em out. When dey's satisfied dat dey is wring dry, dey treats 'em jes lak dey do a cane-chew. Dey thows 'em away. Dey knows whut dey is doin' while dey is at it, an' hates theirselves fuh it but they keeps on hangin' after huh tell she's empty. Den dey hates huh fuh bein' a cane-chew an' in de way."

"We oughter take Syke an' dat stray 'oman uh his'n down in Lake How-ell swamp an' lay on de rawhide till they cain't say 'Lawd a' mussy.' He allus wuz uh ovahbearin' niggah, but since dat white 'oman from up north done teached 'im how to run a automobile, he done got too biggety to live—an' we oughter kill 'im," Old Man Anderson advised.

A grunt of approval went around the porch. But the heat was melting their civic virtue and Elijah Moseley began to bait Joe Clarke.

---

[2]big person

"Come on, Joe, git a melon outa dere an' slice it up for yo' customers. We'se all sufferin' wid de heat. De bear's done got *me!*"

"Thass right, Joe, a watermelon is jes' whut Ah needs tuh cure de eppizudicks,"[3] Walter Thomas joined forces with Moseley. "Come on dere, Joe. We all is steady customers an' you aint set us up in a long time. Ah chooses dat long, bowlegged Floridy favorite."

"A god, an' be dough. You all gimme twenty cents and slice away," Clarke retorted. "Ah needs a col' slice m'self. Heah, everybody chip in. Ah'll lend y'll mah meat knife."

The money was quickly subscribed and the huge melon brought forth. At that moment, Sykes and Bertha arrived. A determined silence fell on the porch and the melon was put away again.

Merchant snapped down the blade of his jackknife and moved toward the store door.

"Come on in, Joe, an' gimme a slab uh sow belly an' uh pound uh coffee—almost fuhgot 'twas Sat'day. Got to git on home." Most of the men left also.

Just then Delia drove past on her way home, as Sykes was ordering magnificently for Bertha. It pleased him for Delia to see.

"Git whutsoever yo' heart desires, Honey. Wait a minute, Joe. Give huh two bottles uh strawberry soda-water, uh quart uh parched groundpeas, an' a block uh chewin' gum."

With all this they left the store, with Sykes reminding Bertha that this was his town and she could have it if she wanted it.

The men returned soon after they left, and held their watermelon feast. "Where did Syke Jones git dat 'oman from nohow?" Lindsay asked.

"Ovah Apopka. Guess dey musta been cleanin' out de town when she lef'. She don't look lak a thing but a hunk uh liver wid hair on it."

"Well, she sho' kin squall," Dave Carter contributed. "When she gits ready tuh laff, she jes' opens huh mouf an' latches it back tuh de las' notch. No ole grandpa alligator down in Lake Bell aint got nothin' on huh."

Bertha had been in town three months now. Sykes was still paying her room rent at Della Lewis'—the only house in town that would have taken her in. Sykes took her frequently to Winter Park to "stomps."[4] He still assured her that he was the swellest man in the state.

"Sho' you kin have dat lil' ole house soon's Ah kin git dat 'oman outa dere. Everything b'longs tuh me an' you sho' kin have it. Ah sho' 'bominates uh skinny 'oman. Lawdy, you sho' is got one portly shape on you! You kin git *anything* you wants. Dis is *mah* town an' you sho' kin have it.

Delia's work-worn knees crawled over the earth in Gethsemane and on the rocks of Calvary[5] many, many times during these months. She avoided the villagers and meeting places in her effort to be blind and deaf. But Bertha nullified this to a degree, by coming to Delia's house to call Sykes out to her at the gate.

Delia and Sykes fought all the time now with no peaceful interludes. They slept and ate in silence. Two or three times Delia had attempted a

3 i.e., epizootic, an epidemic among animals 4 dances 5 Gethsemane was the garden where Jesus prayed just before he was betrayed (Matthew 26:36–47); Calvary was the hill where he was crucified

timid friendliness, but she was repulsed each time. It was plain that the breaches must remain agape.

The sun had burned July to August. The heat streamed down like a million hot arrows, smiting all things living upon the earth. Grass withered, leaves browned, snakes went blind in shedding and men and dogs went mad. Dog days!

60   Delia came home one day and found Sykes there before her. She wondered, but started to go on into the house without speaking, even though he was standing in the kitchen door and she must either stoop under his arm or ask him to move. He made no room for her. She noticed a soap box beside the steps, but paid no particular attention to it, knowing that he must have brought it there. As she was stooping to pass under his outstretched arm, he suddenly pushed her backward, laughingly.

"Look in de box dere Delia, Ah done brung yuh somethin'!"

She nearly fell upon the box in her stumbling, and when she saw what it held, she all but fainted outright.

"Syke! Syke, mah Gawd! You take dat rattlesnake 'way from heah! You *gottuh*. Oh, Jesus, have mussy!"

"Ah aint gut tuh do nuthin' uh de kin'—fact is Ah aint got tuh do nothin' but die. Taint no use uh you puttin' on airs makin' out lak you sceered uh dat snake—he's gointer stay right heah tell he die. He wouldn't bite me cause Ah knows how tuh handle 'im. Nohow he wouldn't risk breakin' out his fangs 'gin *yo'* skinny laigs."

65   "Naw, now Syke, don't keep dat thing 'roun' heah tuh skeer me tuh death. You knows Ah'm even feared uh earth worms. Thass de biggest snake Ah evah did see. Kill 'im Syke, please."

"Doan ast me tuh do nothin' fuh yuh. Goin' 'roun' tryin' to be so damn asterperious. Naw, Ah aint gonna kill it. Ah think uh damn sight mo' uh him dan you! Dat's a nice snake an' anybody doan lak 'im kin jes' hit de grit."

The village soon heard that Sykes had the snake, and came to see and ask questions.

"How de hen-fire did you ketch dat six-foot rattler, Syke?" Thomas asked.

"He's full uh frogs so he caint hardly move, thass how Ah eased up on 'm. But Ah'm a snake charmer an' knows how tuh handle 'em. Shux, dat aint nothin'. Ah could ketch one eve'y day if Ah so wanted tuh."

70   "Whut he needs is a heavy hick'ry club leaned real heavy on his head. Dat's de bes 'way tuh charm a rattlesnake."

"Naw, Walt, y'll jes' don't understand dese diamon' backs lak Ah do," said Sykes in a superior tone of voice.

The village agreed with Walter, but the snake stayed on. His box remained by the kitchen door with its screen wire covering. Two or three days later it had digested its meal of frogs and literally came to life. It rattled at every movement in the kitchen or the yard. One day as Delia came down the kitchen steps she saw his chalky-white fangs curved like scimitars hung in the wire meshes. This time she did not run away with averted eyes as usual. She stood for a long time in the doorway in a red fury that grew bloodier for every second that she regarded the creature that was her torment.

That night she broached the subject as soon as Sykes sat down to the table.

"Syke, Ah wants you tuh take dat snake 'way fum heah. You done starved me an' Ah put up widcher, you done beat me an Ah took dat, but you done kilt all mah insides bringin' dat varmint heah."

75   Sykes poured out a saucer full of coffee and drank it deliberately before he answered her.

"A whole lot Ah keer 'bout how you feels inside uh out. Dat snake aint goin' no damn wheah till Ah gits ready fuh 'im tuh go. So fur as beatin' is concerned, yuh aint took near all dat you gointer take ef yuh stay 'roun' *me*."

Delia pushed back her plate and got up from the table. "Ah hates you, Sykes," she said calmly. "Ah hates you tuh de same degree dat Ah useter love yuh. Ah done took an' took till mah belly is full up tuh mah neck. Dat's de reason Ah got mah letter fum de church an' moved mah membership tuh Woodbridge—so Ah don't haftuh take no sacrament wid yuh. Ah don't wan-tuh see yuh, 'roun' me atall. Lay 'roun' wid dat 'oman all yuh wants tuh, but gwan 'way fum me an' mah house. Ah hates yuh lak uh suck-egg dog."

Sykes almost let the huge wad of corn bread and collard greens he was chewing fall out of his mouth in amazement. He had a hard time whipping himself to the proper fury to try to answer Delia.

"Well, Ah'm glad you does hate me. Ah'm sho' tiahed uh you hangin' ontuh me. Ah don't want yuh. Look at yuh stringey ole neck! Yo' raw-bony laigs an' arms is enough tuh cut uh man tuh death. You looks jes' lak de devvul's doll-baby tuh *me*. You cain't hate me no worse dan Ah hates you. Ah been hatin' *you* fuh years."

80   "Yo' ole black hide don't look lak nothin' tuh me, but uh passle uh wrinkled up rubber, wid yo' big ole yeahs flappin' on each side lak up paih uh buzzard wings. Don't think Ah'm gointuh be run 'way fum mah house neither. Ah'm goin' tuh de white folks about *you*, mah young man, de very nex' time you lay yo' han's on me. Mah cup is done run ovah." Delia said this with no signs of fear and Sykes departed from the house, threatening her, but made not the slightest move to carry out any of them.

That night he did not return at all, and the next day being Sunday, Delia was glad that she did not have to quarrel before she hitched up her pony and drove the four miles to Woodbridge.

She stayed to the night service—"love feast"—which was very warm and full of spirit. In the emotional winds her domestic trials were borne far and wide so that she sang as she drove homeward,

"Jurden water,[6] black an' col'
Chills de body, not de soul
An' Ah wantah cross Jurden in uh calm time."

She came from the barn to the kitchen door and stopped.

"Whut's de mattah, ol' satan, you aint kickin' up yo' racket?" She ad-dressed the snake's box. Complete silence. She went on into the house with a new hope in its birth struggles. Perhaps her threat to go to the white folks had frightened Sykes! Perhaps he was sorry! Fifteen years of misery and sup-pression had brought Delia to the place where she would hope *anything* that looked towards a way over or through her wall of inhibitions.

---

[6] the River Jordan, which the Jews had to cross in order to reach the promised land

85   She felt in the match safe behind the stove at once for a match. There was only one there.

"Dat niggah wouldn't fetch nothin heah tuh save his rotten neck, but he kin run thew whut Ah brings quick enough. Now he done toted off nigh on tuh haff uh box uh matches. He done had dat 'oman heah in mah house, too."

Nobody but a woman could tell how she knew this even before she struck the match. But she did and it put her into a new fury.

Presently she brought in the tubs to put the white things to soak. This time she decided she need not bring the hamper out of the bedroom; she would go in there and do the sorting. She picked up the pot-bellied lamp and went in. The room was small and the hamper stood hard by the foot of the white iron bed. She could sit and reach through the bedposts—resting as she worked.

"Ah wantah cross Jurden in uh calm time." She was singing again. The mood of the "love feast" had returned. She threw back the lid of the basket almost gaily. Then, moved by both horror and terror, she sprang back toward the door. *There lay the snake in the basket!* He moved sluggishly at first, but even as she turned round and round, jumped up and down in an insanity of fear, he began to stir vigorously. She saw him pouring his awful beauty from the basket upon the bed, then she seized the lamp and ran as fast as she could to the kitchen. The wind from the open door blew out the light and the darkness added to her terror. She sped to the darkness of the yard, slamming the door after her before she thought to set down the lamp. She did not feel safe even on the ground, so she climbed up in the hay barn.

90   There for an hour or more she lay sprawled upon the hay a gibbering wreck.

Finally she grew quiet, and after that, coherent thought. With this, stalked through her a cold, bloody rage. Hours of this. A period of introspection, a space of retrospection, then a mixture of both. Out of this an awful calm.

"Well, Ah done de bes' Ah could. If things aint right, Gawd knows taint mah fault."

She went to sleep—a twitchy sleep—and woke up to a faint gray sky. There was a loud hollow sound below. She peered out. Sykes was at the wood-pile, demolishing a wire-covered box.

He hurried to the kitchen door, but hung outside there some minutes before he entered, and stood some minutes more inside before he closed it after him.

95   The gray in the sky was spreading. Delia descended without fear now, and crouched beneath the low bedroom window. The drawn shade shut out the dawn, shut in the night. But the thin walls held back no sound.

"Dat ol' scratch is woke up now!" She mused at the tremendous whirr inside, which every woodsman knows, is one of the sound illusions. The rattler is a ventriloquist. His whirr sounds to the right, to the left, straight ahead, behind, close under foot—everywhere but where it is. Woe to him who guesses wrong unless he is prepared to hold up his end of the argument! Sometimes he strikes without rattling at all.

Inside, Sykes heard nothing until he knocked a pot lid off the stove while trying to reach the match safe in the dark. He had emptied his pockets at Bertha's.

The snake seemed to wake up under the stove and Sykes made a quick leap into the bedroom. In spite of the gin he had had, his head was clearing now.

"Mah Gawd!" he chattered, "ef Ah could on'y strack uh light!"

100   The rattling ceased for a moment as he stood paralyzed. He waited. It seemed that the snake waited also.

"Oh, fuh de light! Ah thought he'd be too sick"—Sykes was muttering to himself when the whirr began again, closer, right underfoot this time. Long before this, Sykes' ability to think had been flattened down to primitive instinct and he leaped—onto the bed.

Outside Delia heard a cry that might have come from a maddened chimpanzee, a stricken gorilla. All the terror, all the horror, all the rage that man possibly could express, without a recognizable human sound.

A tremendous stir inside there, another series of animal screams, the intermittent whirr of the reptile. The shade torn violently down from the window, letting in the red dawn, a huge brown hand seizing the window stick, great dull blows upon the wooden floor punctuating the gibberish of sound long after the rattle of the snake had abruptly subsided. All this Delia could see and hear from her place beneath the window, and it made her ill. She crept over to the four-o'clocks[7] and stretched herself on the cool earth to recover.

She lay there. "Delia, Delia!" She could hear Sykes calling in a most despairing tone as one who expected no answer. The sun crept on up, and he called. Delia could not move—her legs were gone flabby. She never moved, he called, and the sun kept rising.

105   "Mah Gawd!" She heard him moan, "Mah Gawd fum Heben!" She heard him stumbling about and got up from her flower-bed. The sun was growing warm. As she approached the door she heard him call out hopefully, "Delia, is dat you Ah heah?"

She saw him on his hands and knees as soon as she reached the door. He crept an inch or two toward her—all that he was able, and she saw his horribly swollen neck and his one open eye shining with hope. A surge of pity too strong to support bore her away from that eye that must, could not, fail to see the tubs. He would see the lamp. Orlando with its doctors was too far. She could scarcely reach the Chinaberry tree, where she waited in the growing heat while inside she knew the cold river was creeping up and up to extinguish that eye which must know by now that she knew.

[1926]

 ## TOPICS FOR CRITICAL THINKING AND WRITING

1. Summarize the relationship of Delia and Sykes before the time of the story.
2. How do the men on Joe Clark's porch further your understanding of Delia and Sykes and of the relationship between the two?
3. To what extent is Delia responsible for Sykes's death? To what extent is Sykes responsible? Do you think that Delia's action (or inaction) at the end of the story is immoral? Why, or why not?

[7]flowers that open in the late afternoon

4. To what extent does the relationship between African-Americans and whites play a role in the lives of the characters in "Sweat" and in the outcome of the story?

5. Are the African-Americans in "Sweat" portrayed stereotypically, as some of Hurston's critics charged? (See the biographical note, page 760.) How, on the evidence available in this story, might Hurston's fiction be defended from that charge?

 ALICE MUNRO

Alice Munro was born in 1931 in Wingham, Ontario, Canada, a relatively rural community and the sort of place in which she sets much of her fiction. She began publishing stories when she was an undergraduate at the University of Western Ontario. She left Western after two years and worked in a library and in a bookstore. She then married and moved to Victoria, British Columbia, where she founded a bookstore. She continued to write while raising three children. She divorced and remarried; much of her fiction concerns marriage or divorce, which is to say it concerns shifting relationships in a baffling world.

How I Met My Husband

We heard the plane come over at noon, roaring through the radio news, and we were sure it was going to hit the house, so we all ran out into the yard. We saw it come in over the treetops, all red and silver, the first closeup plane I ever saw. Mrs. Peebles screamed.

"Crash landing," their little boy said. Joey was his name.

"It's okay," said Dr. Peebles. "He knows what he's doing." Dr. Peebles was only an animal doctor, but had a calming way of talking, like any doctor.

This was my first job—working for Dr. and Mrs. Peebles, who had bought an old house out on the Fifth Line, about five miles out of town. It was just when the trend was starting of town people buying up old farms, not to work them but to live on them.

5   We watched the plane land across the road, where the fairgrounds used to be. It did make a good landing field, nice and level for the old race track, and the barns and display sheds torn down now for scrap lumber so there was nothing in the way. Even the old grandstand bays had burned.

"All right," said Mrs. Peebles, snappy as she always was when she got over her nerves. "Let's go back in the house. Let's not stand here gawking like a set of farmers."

She didn't say that to hurt my feelings. It never occurred to her.

I was just setting the dessert down when Loretta Bird arrived, out of breath, at the screen door.

"I thought it was going to crash into the house and kill youse all!"

10   She lived on the next place and the Peebleses thought she was a country-woman, they didn't know the difference. She and her husband didn't farm, he worked on the roads and had a bad name for drinking. They had seven children and couldn't get credit at the HiWay Grocery. The Peebleses

made her welcome, not knowing any better, as I say, and offered her dessert.

Dessert was never anything to write home about, at their place. A dish of Jello-O or sliced bananas or fruit out of a tin. "Have a house without a pie, be ashamed until you die," my mother used to say, but Mrs. Peebles operated differently.

Loretta Bird saw me getting the can of peaches.

"Oh, never mind," she said. "I haven't got the right kind of stomach to trust what comes out of those tins, I can only eat home canning."

I could have slapped her. I bet she never put down fruit in her life.

15   "I know what he's landed here for," she said. "He's got permission to use the fairgrounds and take people up for rides. It costs a dollar. It's the same fellow who was over at Palmerston[1] last week and was up the lakeshore before that. I wouldn't go up, if you paid me."

"I'd jump at the chance," Dr. Peebles said. "I'd like to see this neighborhood from the air."

Mrs. Peebles said she would just as soon see it from the ground. Joey said he wanted to go and Heather did, too. Joey was nine and Heather was seven.

"Would you, Edie?" Heather said.

I said I didn't know. I was scared, but I never admitted that, especially in front of children I was taking care of.

20   "People are going to be coming out here in their cars raising dust and trampling your property, if I was you I would complain," Loretta said. She hooked her legs around the chair rung and I knew we were in for a lengthy visit. After Dr. Peebles went back to his office or out on his next call and Mrs. Peebles went for her nap, she would hang around me while I was trying to do the dishes. She would pass remarks about the Peebleses in their own house.

"She wouldn't find time to lay down in the middle of the day, if she had seven kids like I got."

She asked me did they fight and did they keep things in the dresser drawer not to have babies with. She said it was a sin if they did. I pretended I didn't know what she was talking about.

I was fifteen and away from home for the first time. My parents had made the effort and sent me to high school for a year, but I didn't like it. I was shy of strangers and the work was hard, they didn't make it nice for you or explain the way they do now. At the end of the year the averages were published in the paper, and mine came out on the very bottom, 37 percent. My father said that's enough and I didn't blame him. The last thing I wanted, anyway, was to go on and end up teaching school. It happened the very day the paper came out with my disgrace in it, Dr. Peebles was staying at our place for dinner, having just helped one of our cows have twins, and he said I looked smart to him and his wife was looking for a girl to help. He said she felt tied down, with the two children, out in the country. I guess she would, my mother said, being polite, though I could tell from her face she was wondering what on earth it would be like to have only two children and no barn work, and then to be complaining.

[1] a town in Ontario, Canada

When I went home I would describe to them the work I had to do, and it made everybody laugh. Mrs. Peebles had an automatic washer and dryer, the first I ever saw. I have had those in my own home for such a long time now it's hard to remember how much of a miracle it was to me, not having to struggle with the wringer and hang up and haul down. Let alone not having to heat water. Then there was practically no baking. Mrs. Peebles said she couldn't make pie crust, the most amazing thing I ever heard a woman admit. I could, of course, and I could make light biscuits and a white cake and dark cake, but they didn't want it, she said they watched their figures. The only thing I didn't like about working there, in fact, was feeling half hungry a lot of the time. I used to bring back a box of doughnuts made out at home, and hide them under my bed. The children found out, and I didn't mind sharing, but I thought I better bind them to secrecy.

25   The day after the plane landed Mrs. Peebles put both children in the car and drove over to Chesley, to get their hair cut. There was a good woman then at Chesley for doing hair. She got hers done at the same place, Mrs. Peebles did, and that meant they would be gone a good while. She had to pick a day Dr. Peebles wasn't going out into the country, she didn't have her own car. Cars were still in short supply then, after the war.

I loved being left in the house alone, to do my work at leisure. The kitchen was all white and bright yellow, with fluorescent lights. That was before they ever thought of making the appliances all different colors and doing the cupboards like dark old wood and hiding the lighting. I loved light. I loved the double sink. So would anybody new-come from washing dishes in a dishpan with a rag-plugged hole on an oilcloth-covered table by light of a coal-oil lamp. I kept everything shining.

The bathroom too. I had a bath in there once a week. They wouldn't have minded if I took one oftener, but to me it seemed like asking too much, or maybe risking making it less wonderful. The basin and the tub and the toilet were all pink, and there were glass doors with flamingoes painted on them, to shut off the tub. The light had a rosy cast and the mat sank under your feet like snow, except that it was warm. The mirror was three-way. With the mirror all steamed up and the air like a perfume cloud, from things I was allowed to use, I stood up on the side of the tub and admired myself naked, from three directions. Sometimes I thought about the way we lived out at home and the way we lived here and how one way was so hard to imagine when you were living the other way. But I thought it was still a lot easier, living the way we lived at home, to picture something like this, the painted flamingoes and the warmth and the soft mat, than it was anybody knowing only things like this to picture how it was the other way. And why was that?

I was through my jobs in no time, and had the vegetables peeled for supper and sitting in cold water besides. Then I went into Mrs. Peebles' bedroom. I had been in there plenty of times, cleaning, and I always took a good look in her closet, at the clothes she had hanging there. I wouldn't have looked in her drawers, but a closet is open to anybody. That's a lie. I would have looked in drawers, but I would have felt worse doing it and been more scared she could tell.

Some clothes in her closet she wore all the time, I was quite familiar with them. Others she never put on, they were pushed to the back. I was disappointed to see no wedding dress. But there was one long dress I could just see the skirt of, and I was hungering to see the rest. Now I took note of where it hung and lifted it out. It was satin, a lovely weight on my arm, light bluish-green in color, almost silvery. It had a fitted, pointed waist and a full skirt and an off-the-shoulder fold hiding the little sleeves.

30   Next thing was easy. I got out of my own things and slipped it on. I was slimmer at fifteen than anybody would believe who knows me now and the fit was beautiful. I didn't, of course, have a strapless bra on, which was what it needed, I just had to slide my straps down my arms under the material. Then I tried pinning up my hair, to get the effect. One thing led to another. I put on rouge and lipstick and eyebrow pencil from her dresser. The heat of the day and the weight of the satin and all the excitement made me thirsty, and I went out to the kitchen, got-up as I was, to get a glass of ginger ale with ice cubes from the refrigerator. The Peebleses drank ginger ale, or fruit drinks, all day, like water, and I was getting so I did too. Also there was no limit on ice cubes which I was so fond of I would even put them in a glass of milk.

I turned from putting the ice tray back and saw a man watching me through the screen. It was the luckiest thing in the world I didn't spill the ginger ale down the front of me then and there.

"I never meant to scare you. I knocked but you were getting the ice out, you didn't hear me."

I couldn't see what he looked like, he was dark the way somebody is pressed up against a screen door with the bright daylight behind them. I only knew he wasn't from around here.

"I'm from the plane over there. My name is Chris Watters and what I was wondering was if I could use that pump."

35   There was a pump in the yard. That was the way the people used to get their water. Now I noticed he was carrying a pail.

"You're welcome," I said. "I can get it from the tap and save you pumping." I guess I wanted him to know we had piped water, didn't pump ourselves.

"I don't mind the exercise." He didn't move, though, and finally he said "Were you going to a dance?"

Seeing a stranger there had made me entirely forget how I was dressed.

"Or is that the way ladies around here generally get dressed up in the afternoon?"

40   I didn't know how to joke back then. I was too embarrassed.

"You live here? Are you the lady of the house?"

"I'm the hired girl."

Some people change when they find that out, their whole way of looking at you and speaking to you changes, but his didn't.

"Well, I just wanted to tell you you look very nice. I was so surprised when I looked in the door and saw you. Just because you looked so nice and beautiful."

45   I wasn't even old enough then to realize how out of the common it is, for a man to say something like that to a woman, or somebody he is treating like a woman. For a man to say a word like *beautiful.* I wasn't old enough to realize or to say anything back, or in fact to do anything but wish he would go away. Not that I didn't like him, but just that it upset me so, having him look at me, and me trying to think of something to say.

He must have understood. He said good-bye, and thanked me, and went and started filling his pail from the pump. I stood behind the Venetian blinds in the dining room, watching him. When he had gone, I went into the bedroom and took the dress off and put it back in the same place. I dressed in my own clothes and took my hair down and washed my face, wiping it on Kleenex, which I threw in the wastebasket.

The Peebleses asked me what kind of man he was. Young, middle-aged, short, tall? I couldn't say.

"Good-looking?" Dr. Peebles teased me.

I couldn't think a thing but that he would be coming to get his water again, he would be talking to Dr. or Mrs. Peebles, making friends with them, and he would mention seeing me that first afternoon, dressed up. Why not mention it? He would think it was funny. And no idea of the trouble it would get me into.

50   After supper the Peebleses drove into town to go to a movie. She wanted to go somewhere with her hair fresh done. I sat in my bright kitchen wondering what to do, knowing I would never sleep. Mrs. Peebles might not fire me, when she found out, but it would give her a different feeling about me altogether. This was the first place I ever worked but I already had picked up things about the way people feel when you are working for them. The like to think you aren't curious. Not just that you aren't dishonest, that isn't enough. They like to feel you don't notice things, that you don't think or wonder about anything but what they liked to eat and how they liked things ironed, and so on. I don't mean they weren't kind to me, because they were. They had me eat my meals with them (to tell the truth I expected to, I didn't know there were families who don't) and sometimes they took me along in the car. But all the same.

I went up and checked on the children being asleep and then I went out. I had to do it. I crossed the road and went in the old fairgrounds gate. The plane looked unnatural sitting there, and shining with the moon. Off at the far side of the fairgrounds, where the bush was taking over, I saw his tent.

He was sitting outside it smoking a cigarette. He saw me coming.

"Hello, were you looking for a plane ride? I don't start taking people up till tomorrow." Then he looked again and said, "Oh, it's you. I didn't know you without your long dress on."

My heart was knocking away, my tongue was dried up. I had to say something. But I couldn't. My throat was closed and I was like a deaf-and-dumb.

55   "Did you want a ride? Sit down. Have a cigarette."

I couldn't even shake my head to say no, so he gave me one.

"Put it in your mouth or I can't light it. It's a good thing I'm used to shy ladies."

I did. It wasn't the first time I had smoked a cigarette, actually. My girl-friend out home, Muriel Lowe, used to steal them from her brother.

"Look at your hand shaking. Did you just want to have a chat, or what?"

60   In one burst I said, "I wisht you wouldn't say anything about that dress."

"What dress? Oh, the long dress."

"It's Mrs. Peebles'."

"Whose? Oh, the lady you work for? Is that it? She wasn't home so you got dressed up in her dress, eh? You got dressed up and played queen. I don't blame you. You're not smoking the cigarette right. Don't just puff. Draw it in. Did anybody ever show you how to inhale? Are you scared I'll tell on you? Is that it?"

I was so ashamed at having to ask him to connive this way I couldn't nod. I just looked at him and he saw *yes.*

65   "Well I won't. I won't in the slightest way mention it or embarrass you. I give you my word of honor."

Then he changed the subject, to help me out, seeing I couldn't even thank him.

"What do you think of this sign?"

It was a board sign lying practically at my feet.

SEE THE WORLD FROM THE SKY. ADULTS $1.00, CHILDREN 50¢. QUALIFIED PILOT.

70   "My old sign was getting pretty beat up, I thought I'd make a new one. That's what I've been doing with my time today."

The lettering wasn't all that handsome, I thought. I could have done a better one in half an hour.

"I'm not an expert at sign making."

"It's very good," I said.

"I don't need it for publicity, word of mouth is usually enough. I turned away two carloads tonight. I felt like taking it easy. I didn't tell them ladies were dropping in to visit me."

75   Now I remembered the children and I was scared again, in case one of them had waked up and called me and I wasn't there.

"Do you have to go so soon?"

I remembered some manners. "Thank you for the cigarette."

"Don't forget. You have my word of honor."

I tore off across the fairgrounds, scared I'd see the car heading home from town. My sense of time was mixed up, I didn't know how long I'd been out of the house. But it was all right, it wasn't late, the children were asleep. I got in bed myself and lay thinking what a lucky end to the day, after all, and among things to be grateful for I could be grateful Loretta Bird hadn't been the one who caught me.

80   The yard and borders didn't get trampled, it wasn't as bad as that. All the same it seemed very public, around the house. The sign was on the fair-grounds gate. People came mostly after supper but a good many in the afternoon, too. The Bird children all came without fifty cents between them and hung on the gate. We got used to the excitement of the plane coming in and taking off, it wasn't excitement anymore. I never went over, after that one time, but would see him when he came to get his water. I would be out on the steps doing sitting-down work, like preparing vegetables, if I could.

"Why don't you come over? I'll take you up in my plane."

"I'm saving my money," I said, because I couldn't think of anything else.

"For what? For getting married?"

I shook my head.

85   "I'll take you up for free if you come sometime when it's slack. I thought you would come, and have another cigarette."

I made a face to hush him, because you never could tell when the children would be sneaking around the porch, or Mrs. Peebles herself listening in the house. Sometimes she came out and had a conversation with him. He told her things he hadn't bothered to tell me. But then I hadn't thought to ask. He told her he had been in the war, that was where he learned to fly a plane, and now he couldn't settle down to ordinary life, this was what he liked. She said she couldn't imagine anybody liking such a thing. Though sometimes, she said, she was almost bored enough to try anything herself, she wasn't brought up to living in the country. It's all my husband's idea, she said. This was news to me.

"Maybe you ought to give flying lessons," she said.

"Would you take them?"

She just laughed.

90   Sunday was a busy flying day in spite of it being preached against from two pulpits. We were all sitting out watching. Joey and Heather were over on the fence with the Bird kids. Their father had said they could go, after their mother saying all week they couldn't.

A car came down the road past the parked cars and pulled up right in the drive. It was Loretta Bird who got out, all importance, and on the driver's side another woman got out, more sedately. She was wearing sunglasses.

"This is a lady looking for the man that flies the plane," Loretta Bird said. "I heard her inquire in the hotel coffee shop where I was having a Coke and I brought her out."

"I'm sorry to bother you," the lady said. "I'm Alice Kelling, Mr. Waters' fiancée."

This Alice Kelling had on a pair of brown and white checked slacks and a yellow top. Her bust looked to me rather low and bumpy. She had a worried face. Her hair had had a permanent, but had grown out, and she wore a yellow band to keep it off her face. Nothing in the least pretty or even young-looking about her. But you could tell from how she talked she was from the city, or educated, or both.

95   Dr. Peebles stood up and introduced himself and his wife and me and asked her to be seated.

"He's up in the air right now, but you're welcome to sit and wait. He gets his water here and he hasn't been yet. He'll probably take his break about five."

"That is him, then?" said Alice Kelling, wrinkling and straining at the sky.

"He's not in the habit of running out on you, taking a different name?" Dr. Peebles laughed. He was the one, not his wife, to offer iced tea. Then she sent me into the kitchen to fix it. She smiled. She was wearing sunglasses too.

"He never mentioned his fiancée," she said.

100   I loved fixing iced tea with lots of ice and slices of lemon in tall glasses. I ought to have mentioned before, Dr. Peebles was an abstainer, at least around the house, or I wouldn't have been allowed to take the place. I had to fix a glass for Loretta Bird too, though it galled me, and when I went out she had settled in my lawn chair, leaving me the steps.

"I knew you was a nurse when I first heard you in that coffee shop."

"How would you know a thing like that?"

"I get my hunches about people. Was that how you met him, nursing?"

"Chris? Well yes. Yes, it was."

105   "Oh, were you overseas?" said Mrs. Peebles.

"No, it was before he went overseas. I nursed him when he was stationed at Centralia and had a ruptured appendix. We got engaged and then he went overseas. My, this is refreshing, after a long drive."

"He'll be glad to see you," Dr. Peebles said. "It's a rackety kind of life, isn't it, not staying one place long enough to really make friends."

"Youse've had a long engagement," Loretta Bird said.

Alice Kelling passed that over. "I was going to get a room at the hotel, but when I was offered directions I came on out. Do you think I could phone them?"

110   "No need," Dr. Peebles said. "You're five miles away from him if you stay at the hotel. Here, you're right across the road. Stay with us. We've got rooms on rooms, look at this big house."

Asking people to stay, just like that, is certainly a country thing, and maybe seemed natural to him now, but not to Mrs. Peebles, from the way she said, oh yes, we have plenty of room. Or to Alice Kelling, who kept protesting, but let herself be worn down. I got the feeling it was a temptation to her to be that close. I was trying for a look at her ring. Her nails were painted red, her fingers were freckled and wrinkled. It was a tiny stone. Muriel Lowe's cousin had one twice as big.

Chris came to get his water, late in the afternoon just as Dr. Peebles had predicted. He must have recognized the car from a way off. He came smiling.

"Here I am chasing after you to see what you're up to," called Alice Kelling. She got up and went to meet him and they kissed, just touched, in front of us.

"You're going to spend a lot on gas that way," Chris said.

115   Dr. Peebles invited Chris to stay for supper since he had already put up the sign that said: NO MORE RIDES TILL 7 P.M. Mrs. Peebles wanted it served in the yard, in spite of the bugs. One thing strange to anybody from the country is this eating outside. I had made a potato salad earlier and she had made a jellied salad, that was one thing she could do, so it was just a matter of getting those out, and some sliced meat and cucumbers and fresh leaf lettuce. Loretta Bird hung around for some time saying, "Oh, well, I guess I better get home to those yappers," and, "It's so nice just sitting here, I sure hate to get up," but nobody invited her, I was relieved to see, and finally she had to go.

That night after rides were finished Alice Kelling and Chris went off somewhere in her car. I lay awake till they got back. When I saw the car lights sweep my ceiling I got up to look down on them through the slats of my blind. I don't know what I thought I was going to see. Muriel Lowe and I used to sleep on her front veranda and watch her sister and her sister's boyfriend saying good night. Afterward we couldn't get to sleep, for longing for somebody to kiss us and rub up against us and we would talk about suppose you were out in a boat with a boy and he wouldn't bring you in to shore unless you did it, or what if somebody got you trapped in a barn, you would have to, wouldn't you, it wouldn't be your fault. Muriel said her two girl cousins used to try with a toilet paper roll that one of them was a boy. We wouldn't do anything like that; just lay and wondered.

All that happened was that Chris got out of the car on one side and she got out on the other and they walked off separately—him toward the fair-grounds and her toward the house. I got back in bed and imagined about me coming home with him, not like that.

Next morning Alice Kelling got up late and I fixed a grapefruit for her the way I had learned and Mrs. Peebles sat down with her to visit and have another cup of coffee. Mrs. Peebles seemed pleased enough now, having company. Alice Kelling said she guessed she better get used to putting in a day just watching Chris take off and come down, and Mrs. Peebles said she didn't know if she should suggest it because Alice Kelling was the one with the car, but the lake was only twenty-five miles away and what a good day for a picnic.

Alice Kelling took her up on the idea and by eleven o'clock they were in the car, with Joey and Heather and a sandwich lunch I had made. The only thing was that Chris hadn't come down, and she wanted to tell him where they were going.

120　"Edie'll go over and tell him," Mrs. Peebles said. "There's no problem."

Alice Kelling wrinkled her face and agreed.

"Be sure and tell him we'll be back by five!"

I didn't see that he would be concerned about knowing this right away, and I thought of him eating whatever he ate over there, alone, cooking on his camp stove, so I got to work and mixed up a crumb cake and baked it, in between the other work I had to do; then, when it was a bit cooled, wrapped it in a tea towel. I didn't do anything to myself but take off my apron and comb my hair. I would like to have put some makeup on, but I was too afraid it would remind him of the way he first saw me, and that would humiliate me all over again.

He had come and put another sign on the gate: NO RIDES THIS P.M. APOLO-GIES. I worried that he wasn't feeling well. No sign of him outside and the tent flap was down. I knocked on the pole.

125　"Come in," he said, in a voice that would just as soon have said *Stay out.*

I lifted the flap.

"Oh, it's you. I'm sorry. I didn't know it was you."

He had been just sitting on the side of the bed, smoking. Why not at least sit and smoke in the fresh air?

"I brought a cake and hope you're not sick," I said.

130　"Why would I be sick? Oh—that sign. That's all right. I'm just tired of talking to people. I don't mean you. Have a seat." He pinned back the tent flap. "Get some fresh air in here."

I sat on the edge of the bed, there was no place else. It was one of those fold-up cots, really: I remembered and gave him his fiancée's message.

He ate some of the cake. "Good."

"Put the rest away for when you're hungry later."

"I'll tell you a secret. I won't be around here much longer."

135　"Are you getting married?"

"Ha ha. What time did you say they'd be back?"

"Five o'clock."

"Well, by that time this place will have seen the last of me. A plane can get further than a car." He unwrapped the cake and ate another piece of it, absent-mindedly.

"Now you'll be thirsty."

140   "There's some water in the pail."

"It won't be very cold. I could bring some fresh. I could bring some ice from the refrigerator."

"No," he said. "I don't want you to go. I want a nice long time of saying good-bye to you."

He put the cake away carefully and sat beside me and started those little kisses, so soft, I can't ever let myself think about them, such kindness in his face and lovely kisses, all over my eyelids and neck and ears, all over, then me kissing back as well as I could (I had only kissed a boy on a dare before, and kissed my own arms for practice) and we lay back on the cot and pressed together, just gently, and he did some other things, not bad things or not in a bad way. It was lovely in the tent, that smell of grass and hot tent cloth with the sun beating down on it, and he said, "I wouldn't do you any harm for the world." Once, when he had rolled on top of me and we were sort of rocking together on the cot, he said softly, "Oh, no," and freed himself and jumped up and got the water pail. He splashed some of it on his neck and face, and the little bit left, on me lying there.

"That's to cool us off, miss."

145   When we said good-bye I wasn't at all sad, because he held my face and said, "I'm going to write you a letter. I'll tell you where I am and maybe you can come and see me. Would you like that? Okay then. You wait." I was really glad I think to get away from him, it was like he was piling presents on me I couldn't get the pleasure of till I considered them alone.

No consternation at first about the plane being gone. They thought he had taken somebody up, and I didn't enlighten them. Dr. Peebles had phoned he had to go to the country, so there was just us having supper, and then Loretta Bird thrusting her head in the door and saying, "I see he's took off."

"What?" said Alice Kelling, and pushed back her chair.

"The kids come and told me this afternoon he was taking down his tent. Did he think he'd run through all the business there was around here? He didn't take off without letting you know, did he?"

"He'll send me word," Alice Kelling said. "He'll probably phone tonight. He's terribly restless, since the war."

150   "Edie, he didn't mention to you, did he?" Mrs. Peebles said. "When you took over the message?"

"Yes," I said. So far so true.

"Well why didn't you say?" All of them were looking at me. "Did he say where he was going?"

"He said he might try Bayfield," I said. What made me tell such a lie? I didn't intend it.

"Bayfield, how far is that?" said Alice Kelling.

155   Mrs. Peebles said, "Thirty, thirty-five miles."

"That's not far. Oh, well, that's really not far at all. It's on the lake, isn't it?"

You'd think I'd be ashamed of myself, setting her on the wrong track. I did it to give him more time, whatever time he needed. I lied for him, and also, I have to admit, for me. Women should stick together and not do things like that. I see that now, but didn't then. I never thought of myself as being in any way like her, or coming to the same troubles, ever.

She hadn't taken her eyes off me. I thought she suspected my lie.

"When did he mention this to you?"

160   "Earlier."

"When you were over at the plane?"

"Yes."

"You must've stayed and had a chat." She smiled at me, not a nice smile. "You must've stayed and had a little visit with him."

"I took a cake," I said, thinking that telling some truth would spare me telling the rest.

165   "We didn't have a cake," said Mrs. Peebles rather sharply.

"I baked one."

Alice Kelling said, "That was very friendly of you."

"Did you get permission," said Loretta Bird. "You never know what these girls'll do next," she said. "It's not they mean harm so much, as they're ignorant."

"The cake is neither here nor there," Mrs. Peebles broke in. "Edie, I wasn't aware you knew Chris that well."

170   I didn't know what to say.

"I'm not surprised," Alice Kelling said in a high voice. "I knew by the look of her as soon as I saw her. We get them at the hospital all the time." She looked hard at me with a stretched smile. "Having their babies. We have to put them in a special ward because of their diseases. Little country tramps. Fourteen and fifteen years old. You should see the babies they have, too."

"There was a bad woman here in town had a baby that pus was running out of its eyes," Loretta Bird put in.

"Wait a minute," said Mrs. Peebles. "What is this talk? Edie. What about you and Mr. Watters? Were you intimate with him?"

"Yes," I said. I was thinking of us lying on the cot and kissing, wasn't that intimate? And I would never deny it.

175   They were all one minute quiet, even Loretta Bird.

"Well," said Mrs. Peebles. "I am surprised. I think I need a cigarette. This is the first of any such tendencies I've seen in her," she said, speaking to Alice Kelling, but Alice Kelling was looking at me.

"Loose little bitch." Tears ran down her face. "Loose little bitch, aren't you? I knew as soon as I saw you. Men despise girls like you. He just made use of you and went off, you know that, don't you? Girls like you are just nothing, they're just public conveniences, just filthy little rags!"

"Oh now," said Mrs. Peebles.

"Filthy," Alice Kelling sobbed. "Filthy little rags!"

180   "Don't get yourself upset," Loretta Bird said. She was swollen up with pleasure at being in on this scene. "Men are all the same."

"Edie, I'm very surprised," Mrs. Peebles said. "I thought your parents were so strict. You don't want to have a baby, do you?"

I'm still ashamed of what happened next. I lost control, just like a six-year-old, I started howling. "You don't get a baby from just doing that!"

"You see. Some of them are that ignorant," Loretta Bird said.

But Mrs. Peebles jumped up and caught my arms and shook me.

185   "Calm down. Don't get hysterical. Calm down. Stop crying. Listen to me. Listen. I'm wondering, if you know what being intimate means. Now tell me. What did you think it meant?"

"Kissing," I howled.

She let go. "Oh, Edie. Stop it. Don't be silly. It's all right. It's all a misunderstanding. Being intimate means a lot more than that. Oh I *wondered*."

"She's trying to cover up, now," said Alice Kelling. "Yes. She's not so stupid. She sees she got herself in trouble."

"I believe her," Mrs. Peebles said. "This is an awful scene."

190   "Well there is one way to find out," said Alice Kelling, getting up. "After all, I am a nurse."

Mrs. Peebles drew a breath and said, "No. No. Go to your room, Edie. And stop that noise. This is too disgusting."

I heard the car start in a little while. I tried to stop crying, pulling back each wave as it started over me. Finally I succeeded, and lay heaving on the bed.

Mrs. Peebles came and stood in the doorway.

"She's gone," she said. "That Bird woman too. Of course, you know you should never have gone near that man and that is the cause of all this trouble. I have a headache. As soon as you can, go and wash your face in cold water and get at the dishes and we will not say any more about this."

195   Nor we didn't. I didn't figure out till years later the extent of what I had been saved from. Mrs. Peebles was not very friendly to me afterward, but she was fair. Not very friendly is the wrong way of describing what she was. She had never been very friendly. It was just that now she had to see me all the time and it got on her nerves, a little.

As for me, I put it all out of my mind like a bad dream and concentrated on waiting for my letter. The mail came every day except Sunday, between one-thirty and two in the afternoon, a good time for me because Mrs. Peebles was always having her nap. I would get the kitchen all cleaned and then go up to the mailbox and sit in the grass, waiting. I was perfectly happy, waiting, I forgot all about Alice Kelling and her misery and awful talk and Mrs. Peebles and her chilliness and the embarrassment of whether she told Dr. Peebles and the face of Loretta Bird, getting her fill of other people's troubles. I was always smiling when the mailman got there, and continued smiling even after he gave me the mail and I saw today wasn't the day. The mailman was a Carmichael. I knew by his face because there are a lot of Carmichaels living out by us and so many of them have a sort of sticking-out top lip. So I asked his name (he was a young man, shy, but good-humored, anybody could ask him anything) and then I said, "I knew by your face!" He was pleased by that and always glad to see me and got a little less shy. "You've got the smile I've been waiting on all day!" he used to holler out the car window.

It never crossed my mind for a long time a letter might not come. I believed in it coming just like I believed the sun would rise in the morning. I just put off my hope from day to day, and there was the goldenrod out around the mailbox and the children gone back to school, and the leaves turning, and I was wearing a sweater when I went to wait. One day walking back with the hydro bill stuck in my hand, that was all, looking across at the fairgrounds with the full-blown milkweed and dark teasels, so much like fall, it just struck me: *No letter was ever going to come.* It was an impossible idea to get used to. No, not impossible. If I thought about Chris's face when he said he was going to write to me, it was impossible, but if I forgot that and thought about the actual tin mailbox, empty, it was plain and true. I kept on going to meet the mail, but my heart was heavy now like a lump of lead. I only smiled because I thought of the mailman counting on it, and he didn't have an easy life, with the winter driving ahead.

Till it came to me one day there were women doing this with their lives, all over. There were women just waiting and waiting by mailboxes for one letter or another. I imagined me making this journey day after day and year after year, and my hair starting to go gray, and I thought, I was never made to go on like that. So I stopped meeting the mail. If there were women all through life waiting, and women busy and not waiting, I knew which I had to be. Even though there might be things the second kind of women have to pass up and never know about, it still is better.

I was surprised when the mailman phoned the Peebleses' place in the evening and asked for me. He said he missed me. He asked if I would like to go to Goderich, where some well-known movie was on, I forget now what. So I said yes, and I went out with him for two years and he asked me to marry him, and we were engaged a year more while I got my things together, and then we did marry. He always tells the children the story of how I went after him by sitting by the mailbox every day, and naturally I laugh and let him, because I like for people to think what pleases them and makes them happy.

[1974]

TOPICS FOR CRITICAL THINKING AND WRITING

1. Since Edie tells the story, we know about the other characters only as much as she tells us. Do you think her view of Mrs. Peebles and of Loretta Bird is accurate? On what do you base your answer?
2. Edie offers explicit comments about Mrs. Peebles and Loretta Bird, but not about Alice Kelling, or at least not to the same degree. Why?
3. Characterize Edie.
4. What do you think of the title? Why?

RAYMOND CARVER

Raymond Carver (1938–88) was born in Clatskanie, a logging town in Oregon. In 1963 he graduated from Humboldt State College in northern California and then did further study at the University of Iowa.

His early years were not easy—he married while still in college, divorced a little later, and sometimes suffered from alcoholism. In his last years he found domestic happiness, but he died of cancer at the age of 50.

As a young man he wrote poetry while working at odd jobs (janitor, deliveryman, etc.); later he turned to fiction, though he continued to write poetry. Most of his fiction is of a sort called "minimalist," narrating in a spare, understated style stories about bewildered and sometimes exhausted men and women. His later work, by his own admission, was "larger."

Popular Mechanics

Early that day the weather turned and the snow was melting into dirty water. Streaks of it ran down from the little shoulder-high window that faced the backyard. Cars slushed by on the street outside, where it was getting dark. But it was getting dark on the inside too.

He was in the bedroom pushing clothes into a suitcase when she came to the door.

I'm glad you're leaving! I'm glad you're leaving! she said. Do you hear?

He kept on putting his things into the suitcase.

5   Son of a bitch! I'm so glad you're leaving! She began to cry. You can't even look me in the face, can you?

Then she noticed the baby's picture on the bed and picked it up.

He looked at her and she wiped her eyes and stared at him before turning and going back to the living room.

Bring that back, he said.

Just get your things and get out, she said.

10   He did not answer. He fastened the suitcase, put on his coat, looked around the bedroom before turning off the light. Then he went out to the living room.

She stood in the doorway of the little kitchen, holding the baby.

I want the baby, he said.

Are you crazy?

No, but I want the baby. I'll get someone to come by for his things.

15   You're not touching this baby, she said.

The baby had begun to cry and she uncovered the blanket from around his head.

Oh, oh, she said, looking at the baby.

He moved toward her.

For God's sake! she said. She took a step back into the kitchen.

20   I want the baby.

Get out of here!

She turned and tried to hold the baby over in a corner behind the stove.

But he came up. He reached across the stove and tightened his hands on the baby.

Let go of him, he said.

25   Get away, get away! she cried.

The baby was red-faced and screaming. In the scuffle they knocked down a flowerpot that hung behind the stove.

He crowded her into the wall then, trying to break her grip. He held on to the baby and pushed with all his weight.

Let go of him, he said.

Don't, she said. You're hurting the baby, she said.

30   I'm not hurting the baby, he said.

The kitchen window gave no light. In the near-dark he worked on her fisted fingers with one hand and with the other hand he gripped the screaming baby up under an arm near the shoulder.

She felt her fingers being forced open. She felt the baby going from her.

No! she screamed just as her hands came loose.

She would have it, this baby. She grabbed for the baby's other arm. She caught the baby around the wrist and leaned back.

35   But he would not let go. He felt the baby slipping out of his hands and he pulled back very hard.

In this manner, the issue was decided.

[1981]

 TOPICS FOR CRITICAL THINKING AND WRITING

1. Some readers object to "minimalist" writings (briefly defined in the biographical note on p. 781) on the grounds that the stories (1) lack ideas, (2) do not describe the characters in depth, and (3) are written in a drab style. Does Carver's story seem to you to suffer from these alleged weaknesses? Explain.

2. Here is the first paragraph of the story:

> Early that day the weather turned and the snow was melting into dirty water. Streaks of it ran down from the little shoulder-high window that faced the backyard. Cars slushed by on the street outside, where it was getting dark. But it was getting dark on the inside too.

When Carver first published the story, the paragraph was slightly different. Here is the earlier version:

> During the day the sun had come out and the snow melted into dirty water. Streaks of water ran down from the little, shoulder-high window that faced the back yard. Cars slushed by on the street outside. It was getting dark, outside and inside.

How would you account for the changes?

3. The last line—"In this manner, the issue was decided"—in the original version ran thus:

> In this manner they decided the issue.

Do you consider the small change an improvement? Why, or why not?

What We Talk About When We Talk About Love

My friend Mel McGinnis was talking. Mel McGinnis is a cardiologist, and sometimes that gives him the right.

The four of us were sitting around his kitchen table drinking gin. Sunlight filled the kitchen from the big windows behind the sink. There were Mel and me and his second wife, Teresa—Terri, we called her—and my wife, Laura. We lived in Albuquerque then. But we were all from somewhere else.

There was an ice bucket on the table. The gin and the tonic water kept going around, and we somehow got on the subject of love. Mel thought real love was nothing less than spiritual love. He said he'd spent five years in a seminary before quitting to go to medical school. He said he still looked back on those years in the seminary as the most important years in his life.

Terri said the man she lived with before she lived with Mel loved her so much he tried to kill her. Then Terri said, "He beat me up one night. He dragged me around the living room by my ankles. He kept saying, 'I love you, I love you, you bitch.' He went on dragging me around the living room. My head kept knocking on things." Terri looked around the table. "What do you do with love like that?"

5   She was a bone-thin woman with a pretty face, dark eyes, and brown hair that hung down her back. She liked necklaces made of turquoise, and long pendant earrings.

"My God, don't be silly. That's not love, and you know it," Mel said. "I don't know what you'd call it, but I sure know you wouldn't call it love."

"Say what you want to, but I know it was," Terri said. "It may sound crazy to you, but it's true just the same. People are different, Mel. Sure, sometimes he may have acted crazy. Okay. But he loved me. In his own way maybe, but he loved me. There was love there, Mel. Don't say there wasn't."

Mel let out his breath. He held his glass and turned to Laura and me. "The man threatened to kill me," Mel said. He finished his drink and reached for the gin bottle. "Terri's a romantic. Terri's of the kick-me-so-I'll-know-you-love-me school. Terri, hon, don't look that way." Mel reached across the table and touched Terri's cheek with his fingers. He grinned at her.

"Now he wants to make up," Terri said.

10   "Make up what?" Mel said. "What is there to make up? I know what I know. That's all."

"How'd we get started on this subject, anyway?" Terri said. She raised her glass and drank from it. "Mel always has love on his mind," she said. "Don't you, honey?" She smiled, and I thought that was the last of it.

"I just wouldn't call Ed's behavior love. That's all I'm saying, honey," Mel said. "What about you guys?" Mel said to Laura and me. "Does that sound like love to you?"

"I'm the wrong person to ask," I said. "I didn't even know the man. I've only heard his name mentioned in passing. I wouldn't know. You'd have to know the particulars. But I think what you're saying is that love is an absolute."

Mel said, "The kind of love I'm talking about is. The kind of love I'm talking about, you don't try to kill people."

15   Laura said, "I don't know anything about Ed, or anything about the situation. But who can judge anyone else's situation?"

I touched the back of Laura's hand. She gave me a quick smile. I picked up Laura's hand. It was warm, the nails polished, perfectly manicured. I encircled the broad wrist with my fingers, and I held her.

"When I left, he drank rat poison," Terri said. She clasped her arms with her hands. "They took him to the hospital in Santa Fe. That's where we lived then, about ten miles out. They saved his life. But his gums went crazy from it. I mean they pulled away from his teeth. After that, his teeth stood out like fangs. My God," Terri said. She waited a minute, then let go of her arms and picked up her glass.

"What people won't do!" Laura said.

"He's out of the action now," Mel said. "He's dead."

20   Mel handed me the saucer of limes. I took a section, squeezed it over my drink, and stirred the ice cubes with my finger.

"It gets worse," Terri said. "He shot himself in the mouth. But he bungled that too. Poor Ed," she said. Terri shook her head.

"Poor Ed nothing," Mel said. "He was dangerous."

Mel was forty-five years old. He was tall and rangy with curly soft hair. His face and arms were brown from the tennis he played. When he was sober, his gestures, all his movements, were precise, very careful.

"He did love me though, Mel. Grant me that," Terri said. "That's all I'm asking. He didn't love me the way you love me. I'm not saying that. But he loved me. You can grant me that, can't you?"

25   "What do you mean, he bungled it?" I said.

Laura leaned forward with her glass. She put her elbows on the table and held her glass in both hands. She glanced from Mel to Terri and waited with a look of bewilderment on her open face, as if amazed that such things happened to people you were friendly with.

"How'd he bungle it when he killed himself?" I said.

"I'll tell you what happened," Mel said. "He took this twenty-two pistol he'd bought to threaten Terri and me with. Oh, I'm serious, the man was always threatening. You should have seen the way we lived in those days. Like fugitives. I even bought a gun myself. Can you believe it? A guy like me? But I did. I bought one for self-defense and carried it in the glove compartment. Sometimes I'd have to leave the apartment in the middle of the night. To go to the hospital, you know? Terri and I weren't married then, and my first wife had the house and kids, the dog, everything, and Terri and I were living in this apartment here. Sometimes, as I say, I'd get a call in the middle of the night and have to go into the hospital at two or three in the morning. It'd be dark out there in the parking lot, and I'd break into a sweat before I could even get to my car. I never knew if he was going to come up out of the shrubbery or from behind a car and start shooting. I mean, the man was crazy. He was capable of wiring a bomb, anything. He used to call my service at all hours and say he needed to talk to the doctor, and when I'd return the call, he'd say, 'Son of a bitch, your days are numbered.' Little things like that. It was scary, I'm telling you."

"I still feel sorry for him," Terri said.

30   "It sounds like a nightmare," Laura said. "But what exactly happened after he shot himself?"

Laura is a legal secretary. We'd met in a professional capacity. Before we knew it, it was a courtship. She's thirty-five, three years younger than I am. In addition to being in love, we like each other and enjoy one another's company. She's easy to be with.

"What happened?" Laura said.

Mel said, "He shot himself in the mouth in his room. Someone heard the shot and told the manager. They came in with a passkey, saw what had happened, and called an ambulance. I happened to be there when they brought him in, alive but past recall. The man lived for three days. His head swelled up to twice the size of a normal head. I'd never seen anything like it, and I hope I never do again. Terri wanted to go in and sit with him when she found out about it. We had a fight over it. I didn't think she should see him like that. I didn't think she should see him like that. I didn't think she should see him, and I still don't."

"Who won the fight?" Laura said.

35   "I was in the room with him when he died," Terri said. "He never came up out of it. But I sat with him. He didn't have anyone else."

"He was dangerous," Mel said. "If you call that love, you can have it."

"It was love," Terri said. "Sure, it's abnormal in most people's eyes. But he was willing to die for it. He did die for it."

"I sure as hell wouldn't call it love," Mel said. "I mean, no one knows what he did it for. I've seen a lot of suicides, and I couldn't say anyone ever knew what they did it for."

Mel put his hands behind his neck and tilted his chair back. "I'm not interested in that kind of love," he said. "If that's love, you can have it."

40   Terri said, "We were afraid. Mel even made a will out and wrote to his brother in California who used to be a Green Beret. Mel told him who to look for if something happened to him."

Terri drank from her glass. She said, "But Mel's right—we lived like fugitives. We were afraid. Mel was, weren't you, honey? I even called the police at one point, but they were no help. They said they couldn't do anything until Ed actually did something. Isn't that a laugh?" Terri said.

She poured the last of the gin into her glass and waggled the bottle. Mel got up from the table and went to the cupboard. He took down another bottle.

"Well, Nick and I know what love is," Laura said. "For us, I mean," Laura said. She bumped my knee with her knee. "You're supposed to say something now," Laura said, and turned her smile on me.

For an answer, I took Laura's hand and raised it to my lips. I made a big production out of kissing her hand. Everyone was amused.

45   "We're lucky," I said.

"You guys," Terri said. "Stop that now. You're making me sick. You're still on the honeymoon, for God's sake. You're still gaga, for crying out loud. Just wait. How long have you been together now? How long has it been? A year? Longer than a year?"

"Going on a year and a half," Laura said, flushed and smiling.

"Oh, now," Terri said. "Wait awhile."

She held her drink and gazed at Laura.

50   "I'm only kidding," Terri said.

Mel opened the gin and went around the table with the bottle.

"Here, you guys," he said. "Let's have a toast. I want to propose a toast. A toast to love. To true love," Mel said.

We touched glasses.

"To love," we said.

55   Outside in the backyard, one of the dogs began to bark. The leaves of the aspen that leaned past the window ticked against the glass. The afternoon sun was like a presence in this room, the spacious light of ease and generosity. We could have been anywhere, somewhere enchanted. We raised our glasses again and grinned at each other like children who had agreed on something forbidden.

"I'll tell you what real love is," Mel said. "I mean, I'll give you a good example. And then you can draw your own conclusions." He poured more gin into his glass. He added an ice cube and a sliver of lime. We waited and sipped our drinks. Laura and I touched knees again. I put a hand on her warm thigh and left it there.

"What do any of us really know about love?" Mel said. "It seems to me we're just beginners at love. We say we love each other and we do, I don't doubt it. I love Terri and Terri loves me, and you guys love each other too. You know the kind of love I'm talking about now. Physical love, that impulse that drives you to someone special, as well as love of the other person's being, his or her essence, as it were. Carnal love and, well, call it sentimental love, the day-to-day caring about the other person. But sometimes I have a hard time accounting for the fact that I must have loved my first wife too. But I did, I know I did. So I suppose I am like Terri in that regard. Terri and Ed." He thought about it and then he went on. "There was a time when I thought I loved my first wife more than life itself. But now I hate her guts. I do. How do you explain that? What happened to that love? What happened to it, is what I'd like to know. I wish someone could tell me. Then there's Ed. Okay, we're back to Ed. He loves Terri so much he tries to kill her and he winds up killing himself." Mel stopped talking and swallowed from his glass. "You guys have been together eighteen months and you love each other. It shows all over you. You glow with it. But you both loved other people before you met each other. You've both been married before, just like us. And you probably loved other people before that too, even. Terri and I have been together five years, been married for four. And the terrible thing, the terrible thing is, but the good thing too, the saving grace, you might say, is that if something happened to one of us—excuse me for saying this—but if something happened to one of us tomorrow, I think the other one, the other person, would grieve for a while, you know, but then the surviving party would go out and love again, have someone else soon enough. All this, all of this love we're talking about, it would just be a memory. Maybe not even a memory. Am I wrong? Am I way off base? Because I want you to set me straight if you think I'm wrong. I want to know. I mean, I don't know anything, and I'm the first one to admit it."

"Mel, for God's sake," Terri said. She reached out and took hold of his wrist. "Are you getting drunk? Honey? Are you drunk?"

"Honey, I'm just talking," Mel said. "All right? I don't have to be drunk to say what I think. I mean, we're all just talking, right?" Mel said. He fixed his eyes on her.

60   "Sweetie, I'm not criticizing," Terri said.

She picked up her glass.

"I'm not on call today," Mel said. "Let me remind you of that. I am not on call," he said.

"Mel, we love you," Laura said.

Mel looked at Laura. He looked at her as if he could not place her, as if she was not the woman she was.

65   "Love you too, Laura," Mel said. "And you, Nick, love you too. You know something?" Mel said. "You guys are our pals," Mel said.

He picked up his glass.

Mel said, "I was going to tell you about something. I mean, I was going to prove a point. You see, this happened a few months ago, but it's still going on right now, and it ought to make us feel ashamed when we talk like we know what we're talking about when we talk about love."

"Come on now," Terri said. "Don't talk like you're drunk if you're not drunk."

"Just shut up for once in your life," Mel said very quietly. "Will you do me a favor and do that for a minute? So as I was saying, there's this old couple who had this car wreck out on the interstate. A kid hit them and they were all torn to shit and nobody was giving them much chance to pull through."

70   Terri looked at us and then back at Mel. She seemed anxious, or maybe that's too strong a word.

Mel was handing the bottle around the table.

"I was on call that night," Mel said. "It was May or maybe it was June. Terri and I had just sat down to dinner when the hospital called. There'd been this thing out on the interstate. Drunk kid, teenager, plowed his dad's pickup into this camper with this old couple in it. They were up in their mid-seventies, that couple. The kid—eighteen, nineteen, something—he was DOA. Taken the steering wheel through his sternum. The old couple, they were alive, you understand. I mean, just barely. But they had everything. Multiple fractures, internal injuries, hemorrhaging, contusions, lacerations, the works, and they each of them had themselves concussions. They were in a bad way, believe me. And, of course, their age was two strikes against them. I'd say she was worse off than he was. Ruptured spleen along with everything else. Both kneecaps broken. But they'd been wearing their seatbelts and, God knows, that's what saved them for the time being."

"Folks, this is an advertisement for the National Safety Council," Terri said. "This is your spokesman, Dr. Melvin R. McGinnis, talking." Terri laughed. "Mel," she said, "sometimes you're just too much. But I love you, hon," she said.

"Honey, I love you," Mel said.

75   He leaned across the table. Terri met him halfway. They kissed.

"Terri's right," Mel said as he settled himself again. "Get those seatbelts on. But seriously, they were in some shape, those oldsters. By the time I got down there, the kid was dead, as I said. He was off in a corner, laid out on a gurney. I took one look at the old couple and told the ER nurse to get me a neurologist and an orthopedic man and a couple of surgeons down there right away."

He drank from his glass. "I'll try to keep this short," he said. "So we took the two of them up to the OR and worked like fuck on them most of the night. They had these incredible reserves, those two. You see that once in a while. So we did everything that could be done, and toward morning we're giving them a fifty-fifty chance, maybe less than that for her. So here they are, still alive the next morning. So, okay, we move them into the ICU, which is where they both kept plugging away at it for two weeks, hitting it better and better on all the scopes. So we transfer them out to their own room."

Mel stopped talking. "Here," he said, "let's drink this cheapo gin the hell up. Then we're going to dinner, right? Terri and I know a new place. That's where we'll go, to this new place we know about. But we're not going until we finish up this cut-rate, lousy gin."

Terri said, "We haven't actually eaten there yet. But it looks good. From the outside, you know."

80   "I like food," Mel said. "If I had it to do all over again, I'd be a chef, you know? Right? Terri?" Mel said.

He laughed. He fingered the ice in his glass.

"Terri knows," he said. "Terri can tell you. But let me say this. If I could come back again in a different life, a different time and all, you know what? I'd like to come back as a knight. You were pretty safe wearing all that armor. It was all right being a knight until gunpowder and muskets and pistols came along."

"Mel would like to ride a horse and carry a lance," Terri said.

"Carry a woman's scarf with you everywhere," Laura said.

85   "Or just a woman," Mel said.

"Shame on you," Laura said.

Terri said, "Suppose you came back as a serf. The serfs didn't have it so good in those days," Terri said.

"The serfs never had it good," Mel said. "But I guess even the knights were vessels to someone. Isn't that the way it worked? But then everyone is always a vessel to someone. Isn't that right? Terri? But what I liked about knights, besides their ladies, was that they had that suit of armor, you know, and they couldn't get hurt very easy. No cars in those days, you know? No drunk teenagers to tear into your ass."

"Vassals," Terri said.

90   "What?" Mel said.

"Vassals," Terri said. "They were called vassals, not vessels."

"Vassals, vessels," Mel said, "what the fuck's the difference? You knew what I meant anyway. All right," Mel said. "So I'm not educated. I learned my stuff. I'm a heart surgeon, sure, but I'm just a mechanic. I go in and fuck around and fix things. Shit," Mel said.

"Modesty doesn't become you," Terri said.

"He's just a humble sawbones," I said. "But sometimes they suffocated in all that armor, Mel. They'd even have heart attacks if it got too hot and they were too tired and worn out. I read somewhere that they'd fall off their horses and not be able to get up because they were too tired to stand with all that armor on them. They got trampled by their own horses sometimes."

95   "That's terrible," Mel said. "That's a terrible thing, Nicky. I guess they'd just lay there and wait until somebody came along and made a shish kebab out of them."

"Some other vessel," Terri said.

"That's right," Mel said. "Some vassal would come along and spear the bastard in the name of love. Or whatever the fuck it was they fought over in those days."

"Same things we fight over these days," Terri said.

Laura said, "Nothing's changed."

100   The color was still high in Laura's cheeks. Her eyes were bright. She brought her glass to her lips.

Mel poured himself another drink. He looked at the label closely as if studying a long row of numbers. Then he slowly put the bottle down on the table and slowly reached for the tonic water.

"What about the old couple?" Laura said. "You didn't finish that story you started."

Laura was having a hard time lighting her cigarette. Her matches kept going out.

The sunshine inside the room was different now, changing, getting thinner. But the leaves outside the window were still shimmering, and I stared at the pattern they made on the panes and on the Formica counter. They weren't the same patterns, of course.

105   "What about the old couple?" I said.

"Older but wiser," Terri said.

Mel stared at her.

Terri said, "Go on with your story, hon. I was only kidding. Then what happened?"

"Terri, sometimes," Mel said.

110   "Please, Mel," Terri said. "Don't always be so serious, sweetie. Can't you take a joke?"

"Where's the joke?" Mel said.

He held his glass and gazed steadily at his wife.

"What happened?" Laura said.

Mel fastened his eyes on Laura. He said, "Laura, if I didn't have Terri and if I didn't love her so much, and if Nick wasn't my best friend, I'd fall in love with you. I'd carry you off, honey," he said.

115   "Tell your story," Terri said. "Then we'll go to that new place, okay?"

"Okay?" Mel said. "Where was I?" he said. He stared at the table and then he began again.

"I dropped in to see each of them every day, sometimes twice a day if I was up doing other calls anyway. Casts and bandages, head to foot, the both of them. You know, you've seen it in the movies. That's just the way they looked, just like in the movies. Little eye-holes and nose-holes and mouth-holes. And she had to have her legs slung up on top of it. Well, the husband was very depressed for the longest while. Even after he found out that his wife was going to pull through, he was still very depressed. Not about the accident, though. I mean, the accident was one thing, but it wasn't every-thing. I'd get up to his mouth-hole, you know, and he'd say no, it wasn't the accident exactly but it was because he couldn't see her through his eye-holes. He said that was what was making him feel so bad. Can you imagine? I'm telling you, the man's heart was breaking because he couldn't turn his goddamn head and *see* his goddamn wife."

Mel looked around the table and shook his head at what he was going to say.

"I mean, it was killing the old fart just because he couldn't *look* at the fucking woman."

120   We all looked at Mel.

"Do you see what I'm saying?" he said.

Maybe we were a little drunk by then. I know it was hard keeping things in focus. The light was draining out of the room, going back through the window where it had come from. Yet nobody made a move to get up from the table to turn on the overhead light.

"Listen," Mel said. "Let's finish this fucking gin. There's about enough left here for one shooter all around. Then let's go eat. Let's go to the new place."

"He's depressed," Terri said. "Mel, why don't you take a pill?"

125   Mel shook his head. "I've taken everything there is."

"We all need a pill now and then," I said.

"Some people are born needing them," Terri said.

She was using her finger to rub at something on the table. Then she stopped rubbing.

"I think I want to call my kids," Mel said. "Is that all right with everybody? I'll call my kids," he said.

130   "Terri said, "What if Marjorie answers the phone? You guys, you've heard us on the subject of Marjorie? Honey, you know you don't want to talk to Marjorie. It'll make you feel even worse."

"I don't want to talk to Marjorie," Mel said. "But I want to talk to my kids."

"There isn't a day goes by that Mel doesn't say he wishes she'd get married again. Or else die," Terri said. "For one thing," Terri said, "she's bankrupting us. Mel says it's just to spite him that she won't get married again. She has a boyfriend who lives with her and the kids, so Mel is supporting the boyfriend too."

"She's allergic to bees," Mel said. "If I'm not praying she'll get married again, I'm praying she'll get herself stung to death by a swarm of fucking bees."

"Shame on you," Laura said.

135   "Bzzzzzzz," Mel said, turning his fingers into bees and buzzing them at Terri's throat. Then he let his hands drop all the way to his sides.

"She's vicious," Mel said. "Sometimes I think I'll go up there dressed like a beekeeper. You know, that hat that's like a helmet with the plate that comes down over your face, the big gloves, and the padded coat? I'll knock on the door and let a loose hive of bees in the house. But first I'd make sure the kids were out, of course."

He crossed one leg over the other. It seemed to take him a lot of time to do it. Then he put both feet on the floor and leaned forward, elbows on the table, his chin cupped in his hands.

"Maybe I won't call the kids, after all. Maybe it isn't such a hot idea. Maybe we'll just go eat. How does that sound?"

"Sounds fine to me," I said. "Eat or not eat. Or keep drinking. I could head right on out into the sunset."

140   "What does that mean, honey?" Laura said.

"It just means what I said," I said. "It means I could just keep going. That's all it means."

"I could eat something myself," Laura said. "I don't think I've ever been so hungry in my life. Is there something to nibble on?"

"I'll put out some cheese and crackers," Terri said.

But Terri just sat there. She did not get up to get anything.

145   Mel turned his glass over. He spilled it out on the table.

"Gin's gone," Mel said.

Terri said, "Now what?"

I could hear my heart beating. I could hear everyone's heart. I could hear the human noise we sat there making, not one of us moving, not even when the room went dark.

[1981]

✄ TOPICS FOR CRITICAL THINKING AND WRITING

1. Terri believes Ed's dealings with her and (as well as his suicide) show that he loved her. How else might his actions be interpreted? And in your opinion, why does she interpret his actions the way that she does?

2. Mel says that if he could come back in a different life, he would come back as a knight. What does this tell us about Mel?

3. What *kinds* of love get discussed? Sexual attraction, of course, but what other kinds of love?

4. We usually expect something to *happen* in a story, an action to reach some sort of completion. What, if anything, happens in this story? For instance, can we say that such-and-such a character changes?

5. Mel asks his companions, "What do any of us really know about love?" What is *your* response?

 TOBIAS WOLFF

*Tobias Wolff was born in Alabama in 1945, but he grew up in the state of Washington. He left high school before graduating, served as an apprentice seaman and as a weight-guesser in a carnival, and then joined the army, where he served four years as a paratrooper. After his discharge from the army, he hired private tutors to enable him to pass the entrance degree to Oxford University. At Oxford he did spectacularly well, graduating with First Class Honors in English. Wolff has written stories, novels, and an autobiography (*This Boy's Life*); he now teaches writing at Syracuse University.*

Say Yes

They were doing the dishes, his wife washing while he dried. He'd washed the night before. Unlike most men he knew, he really pitched in on the housework. A few months earlier he'd overheard a friend of his wife's congratulate her on having such a considerate husband, and he thought, *I try.* Helping out with the dishes was a way he had of showing how considerate he was.

They talked about different things and somehow got on the subject of whether white people should marry black people. He said that all things considered, he thought it was a bad idea.

"Why?" she asked.

Sometimes his wife got this look where she pinched her brows together and bit her lower lip and stared down at something. When he saw her like this he knew he should keep his mouth shut, but he never did. Actually it made him talk more. She had that look now.

5   "Why?" she asked again, and stood there with her hand inside a bowl, not washing it but just holding it above the water.

"Listen," he said, "I went to school with blacks, and I've worked with blacks and lived on the same street with blacks, and we've always gotten along just fine. I don't need you coming along now and implying that I'm a racist."

"I didn't imply anything," she said, and began washing the bowl again, turning it around in her hand as though she were shaping it. "I just don't see what's wrong with a white person marrying a black person, that's all."

"They don't come from the same culture as we do. Listen to them sometime—they even have their own language. That's okay with me, I *like* hearing them talk"—he did; for some reason it always made him feel happy—

"but it's different. A person from their culture and a person from our culture could never really *know* each other."

"Like you know me?" his wife asked.

10   "Yes. Like I know you."

"But if they love each other," she said. She was washing faster now, not looking at him.

Oh boy, he thought. He said, "Don't take my word for it. Look at the statistics. Most of those marriages break up."

"Statistics." She was piling dishes on the drainboard at a terrific rate, just swiping at them with the cloth. Many of them were greasy, and there were flecks of food between the tines of the forks. "All right," she said, "what about foreigners? I suppose you think the same thing about two foreigners getting married."

"Yes," he said, "as a matter of fact I do. How can you understand someone who comes from a completely different background?"

15   "Different," said his wife. "Not the same, like us."

"Yes, different," he snapped, angry with her for resorting to this trick of repeating his words so that they sounded crass, or hypocritical. "These are dirty," he said, and dumped all the silverware back into the sink.

The water had gone flat and gray. She stared down at it, her lips pressed tight together, then plunged her hands under the surface. "Oh!" she cried, and jumped back. She took her right hand by the wrist and held it up. Her thumb was bleeding.

"Ann, don't move," he said. "Stay right there." He ran upstairs to the bathroom and rummaged in the medicine chest for alcohol, cotton, and a Band-Aid. When he came back down she was leaning against the refrigerator with her eyes closed, still holding her hand. He took the hand and dabbed at her thumb with the cotton. The bleeding had stopped. He squeezed it to see how deep the wound was and a single drop of blood welled up, trembling and bright, and fell to the floor. Over the thumb she stared at him accusingly. "It's shallow," he said. "Tomorrow you won't even know it's there." He hoped that she appreciated how quickly he had come to her aid. He'd acted out of concern for her, with no thought of getting anything in return, but now the thought occurred to him that it would be a nice gesture on her part not to start up that conversation again, as he was tired of it. "I'll finish up here," he said. "You go and relax."

"That's okay," she said. "I'll dry."

20   He began to wash the silverware again, giving a lot of attention to the forks.

"So," she said, "you wouldn't have married me if I'd been black."

"For Christ's sake, Ann!"

"Well, that's what you said, didn't you?"

"No, I did not. The whole question is ridiculous. If you had been black we probably wouldn't even have met. You would have had your friends and I would have had mine. The only black girl I ever really knew was my partner in the debating club, and I was already going out with you by then."

25   "But if we had met, and I'd been black?"

"Then you probably would have been going out with a black guy." He picked up the rinsing nozzle and sprayed the silverware. The water was so hot that the metal darkened to pale blue, then turned silver again.

"Let's say I wasn't," she said. "Let's say I am black and unattached and we meet and fall in love."

He glanced over at her. She was watching him and her eyes were bright. "Look," he said, taking a reasonable tone, "this is stupid. If you were black you wouldn't be you." As he said this he realized it was absolutely true. There was no possible way of arguing with the fact that she would not be herself if she were black. So he said it again: "If you were black you wouldn't be you."

"I know," she said, "but let's just say."

30   He took a deep breath. He had won the argument but he still felt cornered. "Say what?" he asked.

"That I'm black, but still me, and we fall in love. Will you marry me?"

He thought about it.

"Well?" she said, and stepped close to him. Her eyes were even brighter. "Will you marry me?"

"I'm thinking," he said.

35   "You won't, I can tell. You're going to say no."

"Let's not move too fast on this," he said. "There are lots of things to consider. We don't want to do something we would regret for the rest of our lives."

"No more considering. Yes or no."

"Since you put it that way—"

"Yes or no."

40   "Jesus, Ann. All right. No."

She said, "Thank you," and walked from the kitchen into the living room. A moment later he heard her turning the pages of a magazine. He knew that she was too angry to be actually reading it, but she didn't snap through the pages the way he would have done. She turned them slowly, as if she were studying every word. She was demonstrating her indifference to him, and it had the effect he knew she wanted it to have. It hurt him.

He had no choice but to demonstrate his indifference to her. Quietly, thoroughly, he washed the rest of the dishes. Then he dried them and put them away. He wiped the counters and the stove and scoured the linoleum where the drop of blood had fallen. While he was at it, he decided, he might as well mop the whole floor. When he was done the kitchen looked new, the way it looked when they were first shown the house, before they had ever lived here.

He picked up the garbage pail and went outside. The night was clear and he could see a few stars to the west, where the lights of the town didn't blur them out. On El Camino the traffic was steady and light, peaceful as a river. He felt ashamed that he had let his wife get him into a fight. In another thirty years or so they would both be dead. What would all that stuff matter then? He thought of the years they had spent together, and how close they were, and how well they knew each other, and his throat tightened so that he could hardly breathe. His face and neck began to tingle. Warmth flooded his chest. He stood there for a while, enjoying these sensations, then picked up the pail and went out the back gate.

The two mutts from down the street had pulled over the garbage can again. One of them was rolling around on his back and the other had something in her mouth. Growling, she tossed it into the air, leaped up and caught it, growled again and whipped her head from side to side. When they saw him coming they trotted away with short, mincing steps. Normally he would heave rocks at them, but this time he let them go.

45   The house was dark when he came back inside. She was in the bathroom. He stood outside the door and called her name. He heard bottles clinking, but she didn't answer him. "Ann, I'm really sorry," he said. "I'll make it up to you, I promise."

"How?" she said.

He wasn't expecting this. But from a sound in her voice, a level and definite note that was strange to him, he knew that he had to come up with the right answer. He leaned against the door. "I'll marry you," he whispered.

"We'll see," she said. "Go on to bed. I'll be out in a minute."

He undressed and got under the covers. Finally he heard the bathroom door open and close.

50   "Turn off the light," she said from the hallway.

"What?"

"Turn off the light."

He reached over and pulled the chain on the bedside lamp. The room went dark. "All right," he said. He lay there, but nothing happened. "All right," he said again. Then he heard a movement across the room. He sat up, but he couldn't see a thing. The room was silent. His heart pounded the way it had on their first night together, the way it still did when he woke at a noise in the darkness and waited to hear it again—the sound of someone moving through the house, a stranger.

[1985]

 TOPICS FOR CRITICAL THINKING AND WRITING

1. On the basis of the first paragraph, characterize the husband.
2. What is your attitude toward him during the discussion of interracial marriage? What is your attitude toward him at the end of the story?
3. Why, in your opinion, does Wolff include the bit about the two dogs?
4. What do you make of the final paragraph?

 GLORIA NAYLOR

Gloria Naylor (b. 1950), a native of New York City, holds a bachelor's degree from Brooklyn College and a master's degree in Afro-American Studies from Yale University. "The Two" comes from The Women of Brewster Place *(1982), a book that won the American Book Award for First Fiction. Naylor has subsequently published two novels and* Centennial *(1986), a work of nonfiction.*

The Two

At first they seemed like such nice girls. No one could remember exactly when they had moved into Brewster. It was earlier in the year before Ben[1]

---

[1]the custodian of Brewster Place

was killed—of course, it had to be before Ben's death. But no one remembered if it was in the winter or spring of that year that the two had come. People often came and went on Brewster Place like a restless night's dream, moving in and out in the dark to avoid eviction notices or neighborhood bulletins about the dilapidated condition of their furnishings. So it wasn't until the two were clocked leaving in the mornings and returning in the evenings at regular intervals that it was quietly absorbed that they now claimed Brewster as home. And Brewster waited, cautiously prepared to claim them, because you never knew about young women, and obviously single at that. But when no wild music or drunken friends careened out of the corner building on weekends, and especially, when no slightly eager husbands were encouraged to linger around that first-floor apartment and run errands for them, a suspended sigh of relief floated around the two when they dumped their garbage, did their shopping, and headed for the morning bus.

The women of Brewster had readily accepted the lighter, skinny one. There wasn't much threat in her timid mincing walk and the slightly protruding teeth she seemed so eager to show everyone in her bell-like good mornings and evenings. Breaths were held a little longer in the direction of the short dark one—too pretty, and too much behind. And she insisted on wearing those thin Qiana dresses that the summer breeze molded against the maddening rhythm of the twenty pounds of rounded flesh that she swung steadily down the street. Through slitted eyes, the women watched their men watching her pass, knowing the bastards were praying for a wind. But since she seemed oblivious to whether these supplications went answered, their sighs settled around her shoulders too. Nice girls.

And so no one even cared to remember exactly when they had moved into Brewster Place, until the rumor started. It had first spread through the block like a sour odor that's only faintly perceptible and easily ignored until it starts growing in strength from the dozen mouths it had been lying in, among clammy gums and scum-coated teeth. And then it was everywhere—lining the mouths and whitening the lips of everyone as they wrinkled up their noses at its pervading smell, unable to pinpoint the source or time of its initial arrival. Sophie could—she had been there.

It wasn't that the rumor had actually begun with Sophie. A rumor needs no true parent. It only needs a willing carrier, and it found one in Sophie. She had been there—on one of those August evenings when the sun's absence is a mockery because the heat leaves the air so heavy it presses the naked skin down on your body, to the point that a sheet becomes unbearable and sleep impossible. So most of Brewster was outside that night when the two had come in together, probably from one of those air-conditioned movies downtown, and had greeted the ones who were loitering around their building. And they had started up the steps when the skinny one tripped over a child's ball and the darker one had grabbed her by the arm and around the waist to break her fall. "Careful, don't wanna lose you now." And the two of them had laughed into each other's eyes and went into the building.

5   The smell had begun there. It outlined the image of the stumbling woman and the one who had broken her fall. Sophie and a few other women sniffed at the spot and then, perplexed, silently looked at each other. Where had they seen that before? They had often laughed and touched each other—held each other in joy or its dark twin—but where had

they seen *that* before? It came to them as the scent drifted down the steps and entered their nostrils on the way to their inner mouths. They had seen that—done that—with their men. That shared moment of invisible communion reserved for two and hidden from the rest of the world behind laughter or tears or a touch. In the days before babies, miscarriages, and other broken dreams, after stolen caresses in barn stalls and cotton houses, after intimate walks from church and secret kisses with boys who were now long forgotten or permanently fixed in their lives—that was where. They could almost feel the odor moving about in their mouths, and they slowly knitted themselves together and let it out into the air like a yellow mist that began to cling to the bricks on Brewster.

So it got around that the two in 312 were *that* way. And they had seemed like such nice girls. Their regular exits and entrances to the block were viewed with a jaundiced eye. The quiet that rested around their door on the weekends hinted of all sorts of secret rituals, and their friendly indifference to the men on the street was an insult to the women as a brazen flaunting of unnatural ways.

Since Sophie's apartment windows faced theirs from across the air shaft, she became the official watchman for the block, and her opinions were deferred to whenever the two came up in conversation. Sophie took her position seriously and was constantly alert for any telltale signs that might creep out around their drawn shades, across from which she kept a religious vigil. An entire week of drawn shades was evidence enough to send her flying around with reports that as soon as it got dark they pulled their shades down and put on the lights. Heads nodded in knowing unison—a definite sign. If doubt was voiced with a "But I pull my shades down at night too," a whispered "Yeah, but you're not *that* way" was argument enough to win them over.

Sophie watched the lighter one dumping their garbage, and she went outside and opened the lid. Her eyes darted over the crushed tin cans, vegetable peelings, and empty chocolate chip cookie boxes. What do they do with all them chocolate chip cookies? It was surely a sign, but it would take some time to figure that one out. She saw Ben go into their apartment, and she waited and blocked his path as he came out, carrying his toolbox.

"What ya see?" She grabbed his arm and whispered wetly in his face.

10   Ben stared at her squinted eyes and drooping lips and shook his head slowly. "Uh, uh, uh, it was terrible."

"Yeah?" She moved in a little closer.

"Worst busted faucet I seen in my whole life." He shook her hand off his arm and left her standing in the middle of the block.

"You old sop bucket," she muttered, as she went back up on her stoop. A broken faucet, huh? Why did they need to use so much water?

Sophie had plenty to report that day. Ben had said it was terrible in there. No, she didn't know exactly what he had seen, but you can imagine— and they did. Confronted with the difference that had been thrust into their predictable world, they reached into their imaginations and, using an ancient pattern, weaved themselves a reason for its existence. Out of necessity they stitched all of their secret fears and lingering childhood nightmares into this existence, because even though it was deceptive enough to try and look as they looked, talk as they talked, and do as they did, it had to have some hidden stain to invalidate it—it was impossible for them both to be right. So they leaned back, supported by the sheer weight of their numbers and comforted by the woven barrier that kept them protected from the yellow mist that enshrouded the two as they came and went on Brewster Place.

15   Lorraine was the first to notice the change in the people on Brewster Place. She was a shy but naturally friendly woman who got up early, and had read the morning paper and done fifty sit-ups before it was time to leave for work. She came out of her apartment eager to start her day by greeting any of her neighbors who were outside. But she noticed that some of the people who had spoken to her before made a point of having something else to do with their eyes when she passed, although she could almost feel them staring at her back as she moved on. The ones who still spoke only did so after an uncomfortable pause, in which they seemed to be peering through her before they begrudged her a good morning or evening. She wondered if it was all in her mind and she thought about mentioning it to Theresa, but she didn't want to be accused of being too sensitive again. And how would Tee even notice anything like that anyway? She had a lousy attitude and hardly ever spoke to people. She stayed in that bed until the last moment and rushed out of the house fogged-up and grumpy, and she was used to being stared at—by men at least—because of her body.

Lorraine thought about these things as she came up the block from work, carrying a large paper bag. The group of women on her stoop parted silently and let her pass.

"Good evening," she said, as she climbed the steps.

Sophie was standing on the top step and tried to peek into the bag. "You been shopping, huh? What ya buy?" It was almost an accusation.

"Groceries." Lorraine shielded the top of the bag from view and squeezed past her with a confused frown. She saw Sophie throw a knowing glance to the others at the bottom of the stoop. What was wrong with this old woman? Was she crazy or something?

20   Lorraine went into her apartment. Theresa was sitting by the window, reading a copy of *Mademoiselle*. She glanced up from her magazine. "Did you get my chocolate chip cookies?"

"Why good evening to you, too, Tee. And how was my day? Just wonderful." She sat the bag down on the couch. "The little Baxter boy brought in a puppy for show-and-tell, and the damn thing pissed all over the floor and then proceeded to chew the heel off my shoe, but, yes, I managed to hobble to the store and bring you your chocolate chip cookies."

Oh, Jesus, Theresa thought, she's got a bug up her ass tonight.

"Well, you should speak to Mrs. Baxter. She ought to train her kid better than that." She didn't wait for Lorraine to stop laughing before she tried to stretch her good mood. "Here, I'll put those things away. Want me to make dinner so you can rest? I only worked half a day, and the most tragic thing that went down was a broken fingernail and that got caught in my typewriter."

Lorraine followed Theresa into the kitchen. "No, I'm not really tired, and fair's fair, you cooked last night. I didn't mean to tick off like that; it's just that . . . well, Tee, have you noticed that people aren't as nice as they used to be?"

25   Theresa stiffened. Oh, God, here she goes again. "What people, Lorraine? Nice in what way?"

"Well, the people in this building and on the street. No one hardly speaks anymore. I mean, I'll come in and say good evening—and just silence. It wasn't like that when we first moved in. I don't know, it just makes you wonder; that's all. What are they thinking?"

"I personally don't give a shit what they're thinking. And their good evenings don't put any bread on my table."

"Yeah, but you didn't see the way that woman looked at me out there. They must feel something or know something. They probably—"

"They, they, they!" Theresa exploded. "You know, I'm not starting up with this again, Lorraine. Who in the hell are they? And where in the hell are we? Living in some dump of a building in this God-forsaken part of town around a bunch of ignorant niggers with the cotton still under their fingernails because of you and your theys. They knew something in Linden Hills, so I gave up an apartment for you that I'd been in for the last four years. And then they knew in Park Heights, and you made me so miserable there we had to leave. Now these mysterious theys are on Brewster Place. Well, look out that window, kid. There's a big wall down that block, and this is the end of the line for me. I'm not moving anymore, so if that's what you're working yourself up to—save it!"

30   When Theresa became angry she was like a lump of smoldering coal, and her fierce bursts of temper always unsettled Lorraine.

"You see, that's why I didn't want to mention it." Lorraine began to pull at her fingers nervously. "You're always flying up and jumping to conclusions—no one said anything about moving. And I didn't know your life has been so miserable since you met me. I'm sorry about that," she finished tearfully.

Theresa looked at Lorraine, standing in the kitchen door like a wilted leaf, and she wanted to throw something at her. Why didn't she ever fight back? The very softness that had first attracted her to Lorraine was now a frequent cause for irritation. Smoked honey. That's what Lorraine had reminded her of, sitting in her office clutching that application. Dry autumn days in Georgia woods, thick bloated smoke under a beehive, and the first glimpse of amber honey just faintly darkened about the edges by the burning twigs. She had flowed just that heavily into Theresa's mind and had stuck there with a persistent sweetness.

But Theresa hadn't known then that this softness filled Lorraine up to the very middle and that she would bend at the slightest pressure, would be constantly seeking to surround herself with the comfort of everyone's goodwill, and would shrivel up at the least touch of disapproval. It was becoming a drain to be continually called upon for this nurturing and support that she just didn't understand. She had supplied it at first out of love for Lorraine, hoping that she would harden eventually, even as honey does when exposed to the cold. Theresa was growing tired of being clung to—of being the one who was leaned on. She didn't want a child—she wanted someone who could stand toe to toe with her and be willing to slug it out at times. If they practiced that way with each other, then they could turn back to back and beat the hell out of the world for trying to invade their territory. But she had found no such sparring partner in Lorraine, and the strain of fighting alone was beginning to show on her.

"Well, if it was that miserable, I would have been gone a long time ago," she said, watching her words refresh Lorraine like a gentle shower.

35   "I guess you think I'm some sort of a sick paranoid, but I can't afford to have people calling my job or writing letters to my principal. You know I've already lost a position like that in Detroit. And teaching is my whole life, Tee."

"I know," she sighed, not really knowing at all. There was no danger of that ever happening on Brewster Place. Lorraine taught too far from this neighborhood for anyone here to recognize her in that school. No, it wasn't her job she feared losing this time, but their approval. She wanted to stand out there and chat and trade makeup secrets and cake recipes. She wanted to be secretary of their block association and be asked to mind their kids while they ran to the store. And none of that was going to happen if they couldn't even bring themselves to accept her good evenings.

Theresa silently finished unpacking the groceries. "Why did you buy cottage cheese? Who eats that stuff?"

"Well, I thought we should go on a diet."

"If *we* go on a diet, then you'll disappear. You've got nothing to lose but your hair."

40   "Oh, I don't know. I thought that we might want to try and reduce our hips or something." Lorraine shrugged playfully.

"No, thank you. We are very happy with our hips the way they are," Theresa said, as she shoved the cottage cheese to the back of the refrigerator. "And even when I lose weight, it never comes off there. My chest and arms just get smaller, and I start looking like a bottle of salad dressing."

The two women laughed, and Theresa sat down to watch Lorraine fix dinner. "You know, this behind has always been my downfall. When I was coming up in Georgia with my grandmother, the boys used to promise me penny candy if I would let them pat my behind. And I used to love those jawbreakers—you know, the kind that lasted all day and kept changing colors in your mouth. So I was glad to oblige them, because in one afternoon I could collect a whole week's worth of jawbreakers."

"Really. That's funny to you? Having some boy feeling all over you."

Theresa sucked her teeth. "We were only kids, Lorraine. You know, you remind me of my grandmother. That was one straight-laced old lady. She had a fit when my brother told her what I was doing. She called me into the smokehouse and told me in this real scary whisper that I could get pregnant from letting little boys pat my butt and that I'd end up like my cousin Willa. But Willa and I had been thick as fleas, and she had already given me a step-by-step summary of how she'd gotten into her predicament. But I sneaked around to her house that night just to double-check her story, since that old lady had seemed so earnest. 'Willa, are you sure?' I whispered through her bedroom window. 'I'm tellin' ya, Tee,' she said. 'Just keep both feet on the ground and you home free.' Much later I learned that advice wasn't too biologically sound, but it worked in Georgia because those country boys didn't have much imagination."

45   Theresa's laughter bounced off of Lorraine's silent, rigid back and died in her throat. She angrily tore open a pack of the chocolate chip cookies.

"Yeah," she said, staring at Lorraine's back and biting down hard into the cookie, "it wasn't until I came up north to college that I found out there's a whole lot of things that a dude with a little imagination can do to you even with both feet on the ground. You see, Willa forgot to tell me not to bend over or squat or—"

"Must you!" Lorraine turned around from the stove with her teeth clenched tightly together.

"Must I what, Lorraine? Must I talk about things that are as much a part of life as eating or breathing or growing old? Why are you always so uptight about sex or men?"

"I'm not uptight about anything. I just think its disgusting when you go on and on about—"

"There's nothing disgusting about it, Lorraine. You've never been with a man, but I've been with quite a few—some better than others. There were a couple who I still hope to this day will die a slow, painful death, but then there were some who were good to me—in and out of bed."

50   "If they were so great, then why are you with me?" Lorraine's lips were trembling.

"Because—" Theresa looked steadily into her eyes and then down at the cookie she was twirling on the table. "Because," she continued slowly, "you can take a chocolate chip cookie and put holes in it and attach it to your ears and call it an earring, or hang it around your neck on a silver chain and pre- tend it's a necklace—but it's still a cookie. See—you can toss it in the air and call it a Frisbee or even a flying saucer, if the mood hits you, and it's still just a cookie. Send it spinning on a table—like this—until it's a wonderful blur of amber and brown light that you can imagine to be a topaz or rusted gold or old crystal, but the law of gravity has got to come into play, sometime, and it's got to come to rest—sometime. Then all the spinning and pretending and hoopla is over with. And you know what you got?"

"A chocolate chip cookie," Lorraine said.

"Uh-huh." Theresa put the cookie in her mouth and winked. "A les- bian." She got up from the table. "Call me when dinner's ready, I'm going back to read." She stopped at the kitchen door. "Now, why are you putting gravy on that chicken, Lorraine? You know it's fattening."

[1982]

 TOPICS FOR CRITICAL THINKING AND WRITING

1. The first sentence says, "At first they seemed like such nice girls." What do we know about the person who says it? What does it tell us (and imply) about the "nice girls"?
2. What is Sophie's role in the story?
3. In the second part of the story, who is the narrator? Does she or he know Theresa's thoughts, or Lorraine's, or both?
4. How does the story end? What do you think will happen between Lor- raine and Theresa?
5. Try writing a page or less that is the *end* of a story about two people (men, women, children—but *people*) whose relationship is going to end soon, or is going to survive, because of, or despite, its difficulties.

📖 RITA DOVE

Rita Dove (b. 1952) is chiefly known as a poet, but she has also published short stories and, most recently, a novel. She was appointed the nation's poet laureate for 1993-94.

Second-Hand Man

Virginia couldn't stand it when someone tried to shorten her name—like *Ginny,* for example. But James Evans didn't. He set his twelve-string guitar down real slow.

"Miss Virginia," he said, "you're a fine piece of woman."

Seemed he'd been asking around. Knew everything about her. Knew she was bold and proud and didn't cotton to no silly niggers. Vir-gin-ee-a he said, nice and slow. Almost Russian, the way he said it. Right then and there she knew this man was for her.

He courted her just inside a year, came by nearly every day. First she wouldn't see him for more than half an hour at a time. She'd send him away; he knew better than to try to force her. Another fellow did that once—kept coming by when she said she had other things to do. She told him he do it once more, she'd be waiting at the door with a pot of scalding water to teach him some manners. Did, too. Fool didn't believe her—she had the pot waiting on the stove and when he came up those stairs, she was standing in the door. He took one look at her face and turned and ran. He was lucky those steps were so steep. She only got a little piece of his pant leg.

5   No, James knew his stuff. He'd come on time and stay till she told him he needed to go.

She'd met him out at Summit Beach one day. In the Twenties, that was the place to go on hot summer days! Clean yellow sand all around the lake, and an amusement park that ran from morning to midnight. She went there with a couple of girl friends. They were younger than her and a little silly. But they were sweet. Virginia was nineteen then. "High time," everyone used to say to her, but she'd just lift her head and go on about her business. She weren't going to marry just any old Negro. He had to be perfect.

There was a man who was chasing her around about that time, too. Tall dark Negro—Sterling Williams was his name. Pretty as a panther. Married, he was. Least that's what everyone said. Left a wife in Washington, D.C. A little crazy, the wife—poor Sterling was trying to get a divorce.

Well, Sterling was at Summit Beach that day, too. He followed Virginia around, trying to buy her root beer. Everybody loved root beer that summer. Root beer and vanilla ice cream—the Boston Cooler. But she wouldn't pay him no mind. People said she was crazy—Sterling was the best catch in Akron, they said.

"Not for me," Virginia said. "I don't want no second-hand man."

10   But Sterling wouldn't give up. He kept buying root beers and having to drink them himself.

Then she saw James. He'd just come up from Tennessee, working his way up on the riverboats. Folks said his best friend had been lynched down there and he turned his back on the town and said he was never coming back. Well, when she saw this cute little man in a straw hat and a twelve-string guitar under his arm, she got a little flustered. Her girlfriends whispered around to find out who he was, but she acted like she didn't even see him.

He was the hit of Summit Beach. Played that twelve-string guitar like a devil. They'd take off their shoes and sit on the beach toward evening. All the girls loved James. "Oh, Jimmy," they'd squeal, "play us a *loooove* song!" He'd laugh and pick out a tune:

> I'll give you a dollar if you'll come out tonight
> If you'll come out tonight,
> If you'll come out tonight.
> I'll give you a dollar if you'll come out tonight
> And dance by the light of the moon.

Then the girls would giggle. "Jimmy," they screamed, "you outta be 'shamed of yourself!" He'd sing the second verse then:

> I danced with a girl with a hole in her stockin',
> And her heel kep' a-rockin',
> And her heel kep' a-rockin';
> I danced with a girl with a hole in her stockin',
> And we danced by the light of the moon.

Then they'd all priss and preen their feathers and wonder which would be best—to be in fancy clothes and go on being courted by these dull factory fellows, or to have a hole in their stockings and dance with James.

15   Virginia never danced. She sat a bit off to one side and watched them make fools of themselves.

Then one night near season's end, they were all sitting down by the water, and everyone had on sweaters and was in a foul mood because the cold weather was coming and there wouldn't be no more parties. Someone said something about hating having the good times end, and James struck up a nice and easy tune, looking across the fire straight at Virginia:

> As I was lumb'ring down de street,
> Down de street, down de street,
> A han'some gal I chanced to meet,
> Oh, she was fair to view!

> I'd like to make dat gal my wife,
> Gal my wife, gal my wife.
> I'd be happy all my life
> If I had her by me.

She knew he was the man. She'd known it a long while, but she was just biding her time. He called on her the next day. She said she was busy canning peaches. He came back the day after. They sat on the porch and watched the people go by. He didn't talk much, except to say her name like that:

"Vir-gin-ee-a," he said, "you're a mighty fine woman."

She sent him home a little after that. He showed up again a week later. She was angry at him and told him she didn't have time for playing around. But he'd brought his twelve-string guitar, and he said he'd been practicing

all week just to play a couple of songs for her. She let him in then and made
him sit on the stool while she sat on the porch swing. He sang the first song.
It was a floor thumper.

> There is a gal in our town,
> She wears a yallow striped gown,
> And when she walks the streets aroun',
> The hollow of her foot makes a hole in the ground.
>
> Ol' folks, young folks, cl'ar the kitchen,
> Ol' folks, young folks, cl'ar the kitchen,
> Ol' Virginny never tire.

20   She got a little mad then, but she knew he was baiting her. Seeing how
much she would take. She knew he wasn't singing about her, and she'd already heard how he said her name. It was time to let the dog in out of the
rain, even if he shook his wet all over the floor. So she leaned back and put
her hands on her hips, real slow.

"I just *know* you ain't singing about me."

"Virginia," he replied, with a grin would've put Rudolph Valentino to
shame, "I'd *never* sing about you that way."

He pulled a yellow scarf out of his trouser pocket. Like melted butter it
was, with fringes.

"I saw it yesterday and thought how nice it would look against your
skin," he said.

25   That was the first present she ever accepted from a man. Then he sang
his other song:

> I'm coming, I'm coming!
> Virginia, I'm coming to stay.
> Don't hold it agin' me
> For running away.
>
> And if I can win ya,
> I'll never more roam,
> I'm coming Virginia,
> My dixie land home.

She was gone for him. Not like those girls on the beach: she had enough
sense left to crack a joke or two. "You saying I look like the state of Virginia?" she asked, and he laughed. But she was gone.

She didn't let him know it, though, not for a long while. Even when he
asked her to marry him, eight months later, he was trembling and thought
she just might refuse out of some woman's whim. No, he courted her
proper. Every day for a little while. They'd sit on the porch until it got too
cold and then they'd sit in the parlor with two or three bright lamps on. Her
mother and father were glad Virginia'd found a beau, but they weren't taking any chances. Everything had to be proper.

He got down, all trembly, on one knee and asked her to be his wife. She
said yes. There's a point when all this dignity and stuff get in the way of Destiny. He kept on trembling; he didn't believe her.

"What?" he said.

30   "I said yes," Virginia answered. She was starting to get angry. Then he
saw that she meant it, and he went into the other room to ask her father for
her hand in marriage.

But people are too curious for their own good, and there's some things they never need to know, but they're going to find them out one way or the other. James had come all the way up from Tennessee and that should have been far enough, but he couldn't hide that snake any more. It just crawled out from under the rock when it was good and ready.

The snake was Jeremiah Morgan. Some fellows from Akron had gone off for work on the riverboats, and some of these fellows had heard about James. That twelve-string guitar and straw hat of his had made him pretty popular. So, story got to town that James had a baby somewhere. And joined up to this baby—but long dead and buried—was a wife.

Virginia had been married six months when she found out from sweet-talking, side-stepping Jeremiah Morgan who never liked her no-how after she'd laid his soul to rest one night when he'd taken her home from a dance. (She always carried a brick in her purse—no man could get the best of her!)

Jeremiah must have been the happiest man in Akron the day he found out. He found it out later than most people—things like that have a way of circulating first among those who know how to keep it from spreading to the wrong folks—then when the gossip's gotten to everyone else, it's handed over to the one who knows what to do with it.

35   "Ask that husband of your'n what else he left in Tennessee besides his best friend," was all Jeremiah said at first.

No no-good Negro like Jeremiah Morgan could make Virginia beg for information. She wouldn't bite.

"I ain't got no need for asking my husband nothing," she said, and walked away. She was going to choir practice.

He stood where he was, yelled after her like any old common person. "Mrs. Evans always talking about being Number 1! It looks like she's Number 2 after all."

Her ears burned from the shame of it. She went on to choir practice and sang her prettiest; and straight when she was back home she asked:

40   "What's all this number two business?"

James broke down and told her the whole story—how he'd been married before, when he was seventeen, and his wife dying in childbirth and the child not quite right because of being blue when it was born. And how when his friend was strung up he saw no reason for staying. And how when he met Virginia, he found out pretty quick what she'd done to Sterling Williams and that she'd never have no second-hand man, and he had to have her, so he never said a word about his past.

She took off her coat and hung it in the front closet. She unpinned her hat and set it in its box on the shelf. She reached in the back of the closet and brought out his hunting rifle and the box of bullets. She didn't see no way out but to shoot him.

"Put that down!" he shouted. "I love you!"

"You were right not to tell me," she said, "because I sure as sin wouldn't have married you. I don't want you now."

45   "Virginia!" he said. He was real scared. "How can you shoot me down like this?"

No, she couldn't shoot him when he stood there looking at her with those sweet brown eyes, telling her how much he loved her.

"You have to sleep sometime," she said, and sat down to wait.

He didn't sleep for three nights. He knew she meant business. She sat up in their best chair with the rifle across her lap, but he wouldn't sleep. He sat at the table and told her over and over that he loved her and he hadn't known what else to do at the time.

"When I get through killing you," she told him, "I'm going to write to Tennessee and have them send that baby up here. It won't do, farming a child out to any relative with an extra plate."

50   She held onto that rifle. Not that he would have taken it from her—not that that would've saved him. No, the only thing would've saved him was running away. But he wouldn't run either.

Sitting there, Virginia had lots of time to think. He was afraid of what she might do, but he wouldn't leave her, either. Some of what he was saying began to sink in. He had lied, but that was the only way to get her—she could see the reasoning behind that. And except for that, he was perfect. It was hardly like having a wife before at all. And the baby—anyone could see the marriage wasn't meant to be anyway.

On the third day about midnight, she laid down the rifle.

"You will join the choir and settle down instead of plucking on that guitar anytime anyone drop a hat," she said. "And we will write to your aunt in Tennessee and have that child sent up here." Then she put the rifle back in the closet.

The child never made it up to Ohio—it had died a month before Jeremiah ever opened his mouth. That hit James hard. He thought it was his fault and all, but Virginia made him see the child was sick and was probably better off with its Maker than it would be living out half a life.

55   James made a good tenor in the choir. The next spring, Virginia had her first baby and they decided to name her Belle. That's French for beautiful. And she was, too.

[1985]

 TOPICS FOR CRITICAL THINKING AND WRITING

1. From what point of view is the story told? How would you characterize the narrator?
2. If you found some passages that amused you, or that especially amused you, specify two or three and explain *why* you found them amusing.

Poetry

 ANONYMOUS

Western Wind

Westron wind, when will thou blow?
The small rain down can rain.
Christ, that my love were in my arms,
And I in my bed again.

[c. 1500]

TOPICS FOR CRITICAL THINKING AND WRITING

1. In "Western Wind," what do you think is the tone of the speaker's voice in the first two lines? Angry? Impatient? Supplicating? Be as precise as possible. What is the tone in the next two lines?
2. In England, the west wind, warmed by the Gulf Stream, rises in the spring. What associations link the wind and rain of lines 1 and 2 with lines 3 and 4?
3. Ought we to have been told why the lovers are separated? Explain.

 ANONYMOUS

"Edward" is a folk ballad, or popular ballad—an anonymous story told in song. Popular ballads acquired their distinctive flavor by being passed down orally from generation to generation, each singer consciously or unconsciously modifying his or her inheritance. Most ballad singers probably were composers only by accident; they intended to transmit what they had heard, but their memories were sometimes faulty and their imaginations active.

The ballad—like other oral literature such as the nursery rhyme or the counting-out rhyme ("one potato, two potato")—is filled with repetion of words and phrases, and even of lines. Sometimes, in fact, the story is told by repeating lines with only a few significant variations. This incremental repetition (repetition with slight variations advancing the narrative) is the heart of "Edward."

Edward

"Why dois your brand° sae° drap wi' bluid,
    Edward, Edward?
Why dois your brand sae drap wi' bluid?
    And why sae sad gang° yee, O?"   4
"O, I hae killed my hauke sae guid,
    Mither, mither,
O, I hae killed my hauke sae guid,
    And I had nae mair bot hee, O."   8

"Your haukis bluid was nevir sae reid,
    Edward, Edward,
Your haukis bluid was nevir sae reid,
    My deir son I tell thee, O."   12
"O, I hae killed my reid-roan steid,
    Mither, mither,
O, I hae killed my reid-roan steid,
    That erst° was sae fair and frie,° O."   16

¹**brand** sword **sae** so ⁴**gang** go ¹⁶**erst** once **frie** spirited

"Your steid was auld, and ye hae gat mair,
 Edward, Edward,
Your steid was auld, and ye hae gat mair,
 Sum other dule° ye drie,° O."   20
"O, I hae killed my fadir deir,
 Mither, mither,
O, I hae killed my fadir deir,
 Alas, and wae is mee, O!"   24

"And whatten penance wul ye drie for that,
 Edward, Edward?
And whatten penance wul ye drie for that?
 My deir son, now tell me, O."   28
"Ile set my feit in yonder boat,
 Mither, mither,
Ile set my feit in yonder boat,
 And Ile fare ovir the sea, O."   32

"And what wul ye doe wi' your towirs and your ha',°
 Edward, Edward,
And what wul ye doe wi' your towirs and your ha',
 That were sae fair to see, O?"   36
"Ile let thame stand tul they doun fa',°
 Mither, mither,
Ile let thame stand tul they doun fa',
 For here nevir mair maun° I bee, O."   40

"And what wul ye leive to your bairns° and your wife,
 Edward, Edward?
And what wul ye leive to your bairns and your wife,
 When ye gang ovir the sea, O?"   44
"The warldis° room, late° them beg thrae° life,
 Mither, mither,
The warldis room, late them beg thrae life,
 For thame nevir mair wul I see, O."   48

"And what wul ye leive to your ain mither deir,
 Edward, Edward?
And what wul ye leive to your ain mither deir?
 My deir son, now tell me, O."   52
"The curse of hell frae me sall ye beir,
 Mither, mither,
The curse of hell frae me sall ye beir.
Sic° counseils ye gave to me, O."   56

 ## TOPICS FOR CRITICAL THINKING AND WRITING

1. How much do we know about Edward? His class? His motivation? His character? How much do we know about the mother? Why, do you suppose, the mother at the outset asks Edward about the blood?

---

[20]**dule** grief **drie** suffer [33]**ha'** hall [37]**fa'** fall [40]**maun** must [41]**bairns** children
[45]**warldis** world's **late** let **thrae** through [56]**Sic** such

2. The third and seventh lines of each stanza repeat the first and fifth lines. Read the poem (or at least two stanzas) aloud, omitting the third and seventh lines of the stanzas. How much difference does it make? Why?

 CHRISTOPHER MARLOWE

Christopher Marlowe (1564-93), English poet and playwright, was born in the same year as Shakespeare. An early death, in a tavern brawl, cut short what might have been a brilliant career.

Marlowe's "Come Live with Me" is a pastoral poem; that is, it de-picts shepherds and shepherdesses in an idyllic, timeless setting. This poem engendered many imitations and replies, two of which we reprint after Marlowe's.

Come Live with Me and Be My Love

Come live with me and be my love,
And we will all the pleasures prove,
That hills and valleys, dales and fields,
And all the craggy mountains yields.   4

There we will sit upon the rocks,
And see the shepherds feed their flocks,
By shallow rivers to whose falls
Melodious birds sing madrigals.   8

And I will make thee beds of roses
With a thousand fragrant posies,
A cap of flowers, and a kirtle
Embroidered all with leaves of myrtle;   12

A gown made of the finest wool
Which from our pretty lambs we pull;
Fair lined slippers for the cold,
With buckles of the purest gold;   16

A belt of straw and ivy buds,
With coral clasps and amber studs:
And if these pleasures may thee move,
Come live with me and be my love.   20

The shepherds' swains shall dance and sing
For thy delight each May morning:
If these delights thy mind may move,
Then live with me and be my love.   24

[1599-1600]

 TOPIC FOR CRITICAL THINKING AND WRITING

Read the poem two or three times, preferably aloud. Of course Marlowe's poem is not to be taken seriously as a picture of the pastoral (shepherd) life, but if you have enjoyed the poem, exactly what have you enjoyed?

SIR WALTER RALEIGH

Walter Raleigh (1552-1618) is known chiefly as a soldier and a colonizer—he was the founder of the settlement in Virginia, and he introduced tobacco into Europe—but in his own day he was known also as a poet.

The Nymph's Reply to the Shepherd

If all the world and love were young,
And truth in every shepherd's tongue,
These pretty pleasures might me move,
To live with thee, and be thy love.   4

Time drives the flocks from field to fold,
When rivers rage, and rocks grow cold,
And Philomel° becometh dumb,
The rest complains of cares to come.   8

The flowers do fade, and wanton fields,
To wayward winter reckoning yields,
A honey tongue, a heart of gall,
Is fancy's spring, but sorrow's fall.   12

Thy gowns, thy shoes, thy beds of roses,
Thy cap, thy kirtle, and thy posies,
Soon break, soon wither, soon forgotten:
In folly ripe, in reason rotten.   16

Thy belt of straw and ivy buds,
Thy coral clasps and amber studs,
All these in me no means can move,
To come to thee, and be thy love.   20

But could youth last, and love still breed,
Had joys no date, nor age no need,
Then these delights my mind might move,
To live with thee and be thy love.   24

                                                                [c. 1600]

 TOPICS FOR CRITICAL THINKING AND WRITING

1. What is the season in Marlowe's poem? What season(s) does Raleigh envision?
2. Some readers find puns in line 12, in "fancy's spring, but sorrow's fall." How do you paraphrase and interpret the line?
3. How would you describe the tone of the final stanza?

7**Philomel** in Greek mythology, Philomela was a beautiful woman who was raped and later transformed into a chattering sparrow, but in most Roman versions she is transformed into the nightingale, noted for its beautiful song

4. Now that you have read Raleigh's poem, reread Marlowe's. Do you now, in the context of Raleigh's poem, enjoy Marlowe's more than before, or less? Why?

JOHN DONNE

John Donne (1572–1631) wrote religious poetry as well as love poetry. In the following lyric, he alters Marlowe's pastoral setting to a setting involving people engaged in fishing. The poem thus belongs to a type called piscatory lyric (Latin piscis, *"fish").*

The Bait

Come live with me, and be my love,
And we will some new pleasures prove
Of golden sands, and crystal brooks,
With silken lines, and silver hooks.   4

There will the river whispering run
Warmed by thy eyes, more than the Sun.
And there th'enamored fish will stay,
Begging themselves they may betray.   8

When thou wilt swim in that live bath,
Each fish, which every channel hath,
Will amorously to thee swim,
Gladder to catch thee, than thou him.   12

If thou, to be so seen, beest loath,
By Sun, or Moon, thou darknest both,
And if my self have leave to see,
I need not their light, having thee.   16

Let others freeze with angling reeds,
And cut their legs, with shells and weeds,
Or treacherously poor fish beset,
With strangling snare, or windowy net: 20

Let coarse bold hands, from slimy nest
The bedded fish in banks out-wrest,
Or curious traitors, sleavesilk flies
Bewitch poor fishes' wandring eyes.   24

For thee, thou needst no such deceit,
For thou thy self art thine own bait;
That fish, that is not catched thereby,
Alas, is wiser far than I.   28

[1633]

TOPICS FOR CRITICAL THINKING AND WRITING

1. In Donne's first stanza, which words especially indicate that we are (as in Marlowe's poem) in an idealized world?
2. Which words later in Donne's poem indicate what (for Donne) the real world of fishing is?
3. Paraphrase the last stanza, making it as clear as possible.

 ## MICHAEL DRAYTON

Michael Drayton (1563–1631), born a year earlier than Shakespeare, like Shakespeare wrote sonnets as well as plays. We print one of his many sonnets.

Since There's No Help

Since there's no help, come let us kiss and part;
Nay, I have done, you get no more of me,
And I am glad, yea glad with all my heart
That thus so cleanly I myself can free;   4
Shake hands for ever, cancel all our vows,
And when we meet at any time again,
Be it not seen in either of our brows
That we one jot of former love retain.   8
Now at the last gasp of Love's latest breath,
When, his pulse failing, Passion speechless lies,
When Faith is kneeling by his bed of death,
And Innocence is closing up his eyes,   12
   Now if thou wouldst, when all have given him over,
   From death to life thou mightst him yet recover.

[1619]

 ## TOPICS FOR CRITICAL THINKING AND WRITING

1. What seems to be the background to the poem? That is, who is speaking to whom, and under what circumstances?
2. How would you describe the tone of the first line?
3. Why do you suppose the speaker says "Nay" in line 2? What might the speaker's audience have said or done during or at the end of the first line?
4. The third quatrain (lines 9–12) introduce several abstractions: Love, Passion, Faith, Innocence. What sort of scene is imagined here?
5. What is the speaker's gist in the final two lines? In the light of these lines, what do you make of the first four lines?

WILLIAM SHAKESPEARE

Shakespeare (1564–1616) was born into a middle-class family in Stratford-upon-Avon. Although we have a fair number of records about his life—documents concerning marriage, the birth of children, the purchase of property, and so forth—it is not known exactly why and when he turned to the theater. What we do know, however, is important: He was an actor and a shareholder in a playhouse, and he did write the plays that are attributed to him. The dates of some of the plays can be set precisely, but the dates of some others can be only roughly set. Hamlet was probably written between 1600 and 1601, and The Tempest was certainly written in 1611. Most of Shakespeare's 154 sonnets were probably written in the late 1590s, but they were not published until 1609.

Sonnet 29

When, in disgrace with Fortune and men's eyes,
I all alone beweep my outcast state,
And trouble deaf heaven with my bootless° cries,
And look upon myself and curse my fate,   4
Wishing me like to one more rich in hope,
Featured like him, like him° with friends possessed,
Desiring this man's art and that man's scope,
With what I most enjoy contented least;   8
Yet in these thoughts myself almost despising,
Haply° I think on thee, and then my state,
Like to the lark at break of day arising
From sullen earth, sings hymns at heaven's gate;   12
  For thy sweet love rememb'red such wealth brings,
  That then I scorn to change my state with kings.

[c. 1600]

 TOPICS FOR CRITICAL THINKING AND WRITING

1. Paraphrase the first eight lines. Then, in a sentence, summarize the speaker's state of mind to this point in the poem.
2. Summarize the speaker's state of mind in lines 9–12. What does "sullen earth" (line 12) suggest to you?
3. Notice that every line in the poem except line 11 ends with a comma or semicolon, indicating a pause. How does the lack of punctuation at the end of line 11 affect your reading of this line and your understanding of the speaker's emotion?

---

3 **bootless** unless   6 **like him, like him** like a second man, like a third man
10 **Haply** perchance

4. In the last two lines of a sonnet Shakespeare often summarizes the preceding lines. In this sonnet, how does the *structure* (the organization)
   of the summary differ from that of the statement in the first twelve
   lines? Why? (Try reading the last lines as if they were reversed. Thus:

   For then I scorn to change my state with kings,
   Since thy sweet love rememb'red such wealth brings.

   Which version do you like better? Why?
5. The "thee" of this poem is almost certainly a man, not a woman. Is the
   "love" of the poem erotic love, or can it be taken as something like
   brotherly love or even as loving-kindness?
6. Write a paragraph (or a sonnet) describing how thinking of someone
   you love—or hate—changes your mood.

Sonnet 116

Let me not to the marriage of true minds
Admit impediments; love is not love
Which alters when it alteration finds,
Or bends with the remover to remove.   4
O, no, it is an ever-fixèd mark°
That looks on tempests and is never shaken;
It is the star° to every wand'ring bark,
Whose worth's unknown, although his height be taken.   8
Love's not Time's fool,° though rosy lips and cheeks
Within his bending sickle's compass° come;
Love alters not with his° brief hours and weeks
But bears° it out even to the edge of doom.°   12
   If this be error and upon° me proved,
   I never writ, nor no man ever loved.

                                                              [c. 1600]

 TOPICS FOR CRITICAL THINKING AND WRITING

1. Paraphrase (that is, put into your own words) "Let me not to the marriage of true minds / Admit impediments." Is there more than one appropriate meaning of "Admit"?
2. Notice that the poem celebrates "the marriage of true minds," not bodies. In a sentence or two, using only your own words, summarize Shakespeare's idea of the nature of such love, both what it is and what it is
   not.
3. Paraphrase lines 13–14. What is the speaker's tone here? Would you say
   that the tone is different from the tone in the rest of the poem?
4. Write a paragraph or a poem defining either love or hate. Or see if you
   can find such a definition in a popular song. Bring the lyrics to class.

---

[5]**ever-fixèd mark** seamark, guide to mariners   [7]**the star** the North Star   [9]**fool**
plaything   [10]**compass** range, circle   [11]**his** Time's   [12]**bears** survives   **doom** Judgment Day   [13]**upon** against

 **JOHN DONNE**

John Donne (1572–1631) was born into a Roman Catholic family in England, but in the 1590s he abandoned that faith. In 1615 he became an Anglican priest and soon was known as a great preacher. A hundred and sixty of his sermons survive, including one with the famous line "No man is an island, entire of itself; every man is a piece of the continent, a part of the main; if a clod be washed away by the sea, Europe is the less . . . ; and therefore never send to know for whom the bell tolls; it tolls for thee." From 1621 until his death he was dean of St. Paul's Cathedral in London. His love poems (often bawdy and cynical) are said to be his early work, and his "Holy Sonnets" (among the greatest religious poems written in English) his later work.

A Valediction: Forbidding Mourning

As virtuous men pass mildly away,
    And whisper to their souls, to go,
Whilst some of their sad friends do say,
    "The breath goes now," and some say, "No":   4

So let us melt, and make no noise.
    No tear-floods, nor sigh-tempests move.
'Twere profanation of our joys
    To tell the laity our love.   8

Moving of the earth° brings harms and fears,
    Men reckon what it did and meant;
But trepidation of the spheres,
    Though greater far, is innocent.°   12

Dull sublunary° lovers' love
    (Whose soul is sense) cannot admit
Absence, because it doth remove
    Those things which elemented it.   16

But we, by a love so much refined
    That our selves know not what it is,
Inter-assurèd of the mind,
    Care less, eyes, lips, and hands to miss.   20

Our two souls therefore, which are one,
    Though I must go, endure not yet
A breach, but an expansion,
    Like gold to airy thinness beat.   24

---

⁹**Moving of the earth** an earthquake   ¹¹⁻¹²**But trepidation . . . innocent** But the movement of the heavenly spheres (in Ptolemaic astronomy), though far greater, is harmless   ¹³**sublunary** under the moon, i.e., earthly

If they be two, they are two so
    As stiff twin compasses° are two:
Thy soul, the fixed foot, makes no show
    To move, but doth, if the other do.   28

And though it in the center sit,
    Yet when the other far doth roam,
It leans, and hearkens after it,
    And grows erect, as that comes home.   32

Such wilt thou be to me, who must
    Like the other foot, obliquely run:
Thy firmness makes my circle just,
    And makes me end where I begun.   36
[1611]

☞ TOPICS FOR CRITICAL THINKING AND WRITING

1. The first stanza describes the death of "virtuous men." To what is their death compared in the second stanza?
2. Who is the speaker of this poem? To whom does he speak and what is the occasion? Explain the title.
3. What is the meaning of "laity" in line 8? What does it imply about the speaker and his beloved?
4. In the fourth stanza the speaker contrasts the love of "dull sublunary lovers" (i.e., ordinary mortals) with the love he and his beloved share. What is the difference?
5. In the figure of the carpenter's or draftsperson's compass (lines 25–36) the speaker offers reasons—some stated clearly, some not so clearly—why he will end where he began. In 250 words explain these reasons.
6. In line 35 Donne speaks of his voyage as a "circle." Explain in a paragraph why the circle is traditionally a symbol of perfection.
7. Write a farewell note—or poem—to someone you love (or hate).

The Canonization

For God's sake hold your tongue, and let me love,
    Or chide my palsy, or my gout,
My five grey hairs, or ruined fortune flout,
    With wealth your state, your mind with arts improve,
        Take you a course, get you a place,   5
        Observe his Honour, or his Grace,
Or the King's real, or his stamped face°
    Contemplate; what you will, approve,°
    So you will let me love.

---

²⁶**compasses** i.e., a carpenter's compass   ⁵⁻⁷**Take . . . face** Get yourself a career or an appointment at court; look at some lord ("his Honour"), or some bishop ("his Grace"), or look at the king or at his image stamped on coins   ⁸**approve** test, experience

Alas, alas, who's injured by my love?   10
    What merchant's ships have my sighs drowned?
Who says my tears have overflowed his ground?
    When did my colds a forward spring remove?
        When did the heats which my veins fill
        Add one more to the plaguy bill?°   15
Soldiers find wars, and lawyers find out still
    Litigious men, which quarrels move,
    Though she and I do love.

Call us what you will, we are made such by love;
    Call her one, me another fly,   20
We are tapers too, and at our own cost die,
    And we in us find the Eagle and the Dove.
        The Phoenix riddle° hath more wit
        By us; we two being one, are it.
So to one neutral thing both sexes fit,   25
    We die and rise° the same, and prove
    Mysterious by this love.

We can die by it, if not live by love,
    And if unfit for tombs and hearse
Our legend be, it will be fit for verse;   30
    And if no piece of chronicle° we prove,
        We'll build in sonnets pretty rooms;
        As well a well-wrought urn becomes
The greatest ashes, as half-acre tombs,
    And by these hymns, all shall approve°   35
    Us canonized for love:

And thus invoke us; 'You whom reverend love
    Made one another's hermitage;
You, to whom love was peace, that now is rage;
    Who did the whole world's soul contract, and drove   40
        Into the glasses of your eyes
        (So made such mirrors, and such spies,
That they did all to you epitomize),
    Countries, towns, courts: beg from above
    A pattern° of your love!'   45

[1633]

---

¹⁵**plaguy bill** lists (bills) of plague victims were posted weekly   ²³**The Phoenix riddle** a mythological bird said to burn itself up every thousand years and to rise reborn from the ashes; since there was only one phoenix, not two, the birth of a new phoenix was a "riddle"   ²⁶**die and rise** the words have a sexual implication; *to die* is to have an orgasm   ³¹**chronicle** history   ³⁵**approve** allow, grant
⁴⁵**pattern** model, i.e., earthly lovers beg the saints of love for a model so they will know how to behave like perfect lovers

TOPICS FOR CRITICAL THINKING AND WRITING

1. The first and last lines of each stanza end with the word "love." Do you think the display of ingenuity makes it difficult for a reader to take the poem very seriously? If not, why not?

2. What would you say is the speaker's attitude toward himself and toward love, in the first two stanzas? What are his attitudes by the end of the poem?

3. The poem treats profane love as though it were divine love. Do you think Donne is simply being clever? Or is he being blasphemous? Or can you take the poem as a serious treatment of sexual love and also of religion? Argue your case.

 ## ROBERT HERRICK

Robert Herrick (1591–1674) was born in London, the son of a gold-smith. After taking an M.A. at Cambridge, he was ordained in the Church of England, and later he was sent to the country parish of Dean Prior in Devonshire, where he wrote most of his poetry. A loyal supporter of the king, in 1647 he was expelled from his parish by the Puritans, though in 1662 he was restored to Dean Prior.

Corinna's Going A-Maying

Get up, get up, for shame; the blooming morn
Upon her wings presents the god unshorn.°
    See how Aurora throws her fair
    Fresh-quilted colors through the air.
    Get up, sweet slug-a-bed, and see   5
    The dew bespangling herb and tree.
Each flower has wept, and bowed toward the East,
Above an hour since; yet you not dressed,
    Nay! not so much as out of bed?
    When all the birds have matins said   10
    And sung their thankful hymns, 'tis sin,
    Nay, profanation to keep in,
Whenas a thousand virgins on this day
Spring, sooner than the lark, to fetch in May.

Rise! and put on your foliage, and be seen   15
To come forth, like the springtime, fresh and green,
    And sweet as Flora. Take no care
    For jewels for your gown, or hair;
    Fear not, the leaves will strew
    Gems in abundance upon you;   20
Besides, the childhood of the day has kept,
Against° you come, some orient pearls unwept;
    Come, and receive them while the light
    Hangs on the dewlocks of the night,

²**god unshorn** Apollo, the sun god, whose uncut locks are rays   ²²**against** until

And Titan° on the eastern hill   25
    Retires himself or else stands still
Till you come forth. Wash, dress, be brief in praying!
Few beads° are best, when once we go a-Maying.

Come, my Corinna, come; and, coming, mark
How each field turns a street, each street a park   30
    Made green and trimmed with trees. See how
    Devotion gives each house a bough
    Or branch; each porch, each door, ere this
    An ark, a tabernacle, is,
Made up of white-thorn, neatly interwove;   35
As if here were those cooler shades of love.
    Can such delights be in the street
    And open fields, and we not see't?
    Come, we'll abroad; and let's obey
    The proclamation made for May,   40
And sin no more, as we have done, by staying;
But, my Corinna, come, let's go a-Maying.

There's not a budding boy or girl this day
But is got up, and gone to bring in May.
    A deal of youth, ere this, is come   45
    Back, and with white-thorn laden home.
    Some have despatched their cakes and cream,
    Before that we have left to dream;
And some have wept and wooed and plighted troth,
And chose their priest, ere we can cast off sloth.   50
    Many a green-gown° has been given,
    Many a kiss, both odd and even;
    Many a glance, too, has been sent
    From out the eye, love's firmament;
Many a jest told of the keys' betraying   55
This night, and locks picked, yet we're not a-Maying.

Come, let us go while we are in our prime,
And take the harmless folly of the time.
    We shall grow old apace, and die
    Before we know our liberty.   60
    Our life is short, and our days run
    As fast away as does the sun;
And, as a vapor or a drop of rain,
Once lost, can ne'er be found again,
    So, when or you or I are made   65
    A fable, song, or fleeting shade,
    All love, all liking, all delight,
    Lies drowned with us in endless night.
Then while time serves, and we are but decaying,
Come, my Corinna, come, let's go a-Maying.   70

[1648]

---

²⁵**Titan** the sun   ²⁸**beads** rosary beads   ⁵¹**green-gown** grass-stained gown

TOPICS FOR CRITICAL THINKING AND WRITING

1. In line 41 the speaker tells Corinna to "sin no more." What is her sin? What other words in the poem, besides "sin," come from the world of religion? How would you characterize the religion of the poem?
2. If the last stanza were omitted, do you think the poem would be weakened or strengthened? Why?

ANDREW MARVELL

Born in 1621 near Hull in England, Marvell attended Trinity College, Cambridge, and graduated in 1638. During the Civil War he was tutor to the daughter of Sir Thomas Fairfax in Yorkshire at Nun Appleton House, where most of his best-known poems were written. In 1657 he was appointed assistant to John Milton, the Latin Secretary for the Commonwealth. After the Restoration of the monarchy in 1659 until his death, Marvell represented Hull as a member of parliament. Most of his poems were not published until after his death in 1678.

To His Coy Mistress

Had we but world enough, and time,
This coyness, lady, were no crime.
We would sit down, and think which way
To walk, and pass our long love's day.
Thou by the Indian Ganges' side   5
Should'st rubies find: I by the tide
Of Humber° would complain.° I would
Love you ten years before the Flood,
And you should, if you please, refuse
Till the conversion of the Jews.   10
My vegetable° love should grow
Vaster than empires, and more slow.
An hundred years should go to praise
Thine eyes, and on thy forehead gaze:
Two hundred to adore each breast: 15
But thirty thousand to the rest.
An age at least to every part,
And the last age should show your heart.
For, lady, you deserve this state,
Nor would I love at lower rate,   20
    But at my back I always hear
Time's winged chariot hurrying near;
And yonder all before us lie

⁷**Humber** river in England   **complain** write love poems   ¹¹**vegetable** slowly growing

Deserts of vast eternity.
Thy beauty shall no more be found,   25
Nor in thy marble vault shall sound
My echoing song; then worms shall try
That long preserved virginity,
And your quaint honor turn to dust,
And into ashes all my lust.   30
The grave's a fine and private place,
But none, I think, do there embrace.
    Now therefore, while the youthful hue
Sits on thy skin like morning dew,
And while thy willing soul transpires   35
At every pore with instant fires,
Now let us sport us while we may;
And now, like am'rous birds of prey,
Rather at once our time devour,
Than languish in his slow-chapt° power,   40
Let us roll all our strength, and all
Our sweetness, up into one ball;
And tear our pleasures with rough strife
Thorough° the iron gates of life.
Thus, though we cannot make our sun   45
Stand still, yet we will make him run.

[1641]

⁴⁰**slow-chapt** slowly devouring   ⁴⁴**thorough** through

TOPICS FOR CRITICAL THINKING AND WRITING

1. What does "coy" mean in the title, and "coyness" in line 2?
2. Do you think that the speaker's claims in lines 1–20 are so inflated that we detect behind them a playfully ironic tone? Explain. Why does the speaker say in line 8 that he would love "ten years before the Flood," rather than merely "since the Flood"?
3. What do you make of lines 21–24? Why is time behind the speaker, and eternity in front of him? Is this "eternity" the same as the period discussed in lines 1–20? Discuss the change in the speaker's tone after line 20.

 WILLIAM BLAKE

William Blake (1757–1827) was born in London and at fourteen was apprenticed for seven years to an engraver. A Christian vision-ary poet, he made his living by giving drawing lessons and by illus-trating books, including his own Songs of Innocence *(1789) and* Songs of Experience *(1794). These two books represent, he said, "two contrary states of the human soul." ("The Clod and the Pebble" comes from* Experience.) *In 1809 Blake exhibited his art, but the show was*

*a failure. Not until he was in his sixties, when he stopped writing po-
etry, did he achieve any public recognition—and then it was as a
painter.*

The Clod and the Pebble

"Love seeketh not Itself to please,
Nor for itself hath any care;
But for another gives its ease,
And builds a Heaven in Hell's despair."   4

    So sang a little Clod of Clay,
    Trodden with the cattle's feet;
    But a Pebble of the brook,
    Warbled out these meters meet: 8

"Love seeketh only Self to please,
To bind another to its delight;
Joys in another's loss of ease,
And builds a Hell in Heaven's despite."   12

[1794]

☑ TOPICS FOR CRITICAL THINKING AND WRITING

1. Can one reasonably argue that the clod is feminine, the pebble masculine? Can one reasonably argue that the clod needs the pebble and the
   pebble needs the clod? Explain.
2. The clod and the pebble each express an uncompromising view. Does
   Blake express a preference for one or for the other? Or does he imply
   that both points of view have merit? Explain.

The Garden of Love

I went to the Garden of Love,
And saw what I never had seen:
A Chapel was built in the midst,
Where I used to play on the green.   4

And the gates of this Chapel were shut,
And "Thou shalt not" writ over the door;
So I turn'd to the Garden of Love,
That so many sweet flowers bore,   8

And I saw it was filled with graves,
And tomb-stones where flowers should be;
And Priests in black gowns were walking their rounds,
And binding with briars my joys & desires.   12

[1794]

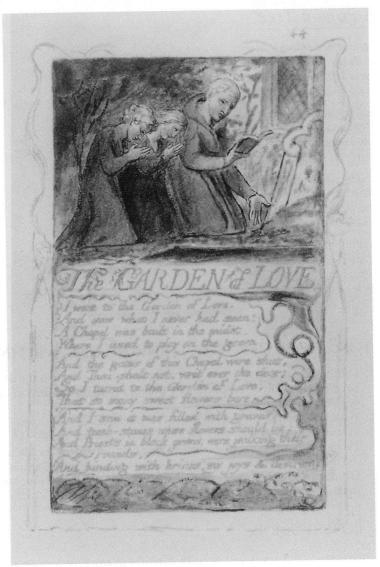

"The Garden of Love" by William Blake, from *Songs of Experience*. (By permission of the Provost and Fellows of King's College, Cambridge)

☐ TOPICS FOR CRITICAL THINKING AND WRITING

1. What is the speaker's mood as he surveys "the Garden of Love"? What does he report?
2. Does the form of the poem contribute to the speaker's mood? Try taking out the *ands* wherever you can, consistent with the meaning of the sentences. There is a change in effect, but can you say what it is?
3. In a brief essay (500 words) compare Blake's "The Echoing Green" (p. 621) with "The Garden of Love."

A Poison Tree

I was angry with my friend:
I told my wrath, my wrath did end.
I was angry with my foe:
I told it not, my wrath did grow.   4

And I watered it in fears,
Night and morning with my tears:
And I sunnèd it with smiles,
And with soft deceitful wiles.   8

And it grew both day and night,
Till it bore an apple bright.
And my foe beheld it shine,
And he knew that it was mine.   12

And into my garden stole
When the night had veiled the pole:
In the morning glad I see
My foe outstretched beneath the tree.   16

[1794]

 TOPICS FOR CRITICAL THINKING AND WRITING

1. In the first stanza, the speaker describes two actions. What is the difference between them? Does the poem indicate that we should choose one action over the other?
2. What reaction do you have to the speaker in stanza 2?
3. In stanzas 3 and 4, what does the "foe" do? Paraphrase line 14.
4. The poem ends, "In the morning glad I see / My foe outstretched beneath the tree." Does the reader share this gladness to any degree? Explain.
5. Like many of Blake's other poems, this one has a childlike tone. Does the tone enrich or does it impoverish the poem? Why?

 ROBERT BURNS

Robert Burns (1759-96) was born in Ayrshire in southwestern Scotland, the son of a farmer. Mostly self-educated, he began writing poetry at 15 and by 27 was acclaimed as Scotland's greatest poet. He became a tax inspector and lived with his family in Dumfries, where he began collecting and editing Scottish folk songs. Many of his best poems and songs were written in the Scots dialect, though he also wrote perfect English.

Mary Morison

O Mary, at thy window be,
    It is the wished, the trysted hour!
Those smiles and glances let me see,
    That make the miser's treasure poor: 4

How blithely wad I bide the stour,°
    A weary slave frae sun to sun,
Could I the rich reward secure,
    The lovely Mary Morison.   8

Yestreen when to the trembling string
    The dance gaed° through the lighted ha',
To thee my fancy took its wing,
    I sat, but neither heard nor saw: 12
Though this was fair, and that was braw,°
    And yon the toast of a' the town,
I sighed, and said amang them a',
    "Ye are na Mary Morison."   16

O Mary, canst thou wreck his peace,
    Wha for thy sake wad gladly die?
Or canst thou break that heart of his,
    Whase only faut° is loving thee?   20
If love for love thou wilt na gie,°
    At least be pity to me shown!
A thought ungentle canna be
    The thought o' Mary Morison.   24

[1788]

5bide the stour endure the struggle   **10gaed** went   **13braw** handsome   **20faut** fault   **21gie** give

John Anderson My Jo

John Anderson my jo,° John,
    When we were first acquent,
Your locks were like the raven,
    Your bonnie brow was brent;°   4
But now your brow is beld, John,
    Your locks are like the snaw,
But blessings on your frosty pow,°
    John Anderson my jo!   8

John Anderson my jo, John,
    We clamb the hill thegither,
And monie a cantie° day, John
    We've had wi' ane anither: 12
Now we maun° totter down, John,
    And hand in hand we'll go,
And sleep thegither at the foot,
    John Anderson my jo!   16

[1788]

☐ TOPICS FOR CRITICAL THINKING AND WRITING

1. In the first poem, do you think the speaker is really addressing Mary Morison?

1jo sweetheart   **4brent** smooth   **7pow** head   **11cantie** happy
13maun must

2. In "Mary Morison," how convincing are the assertions of the first stanza (that her smiles and glances are more valuable than great wealth, that he would willingly be a "weary slave" if only he could win her)? Does the third stanza somehow sound truer, more convincing? If so, why? The poem is excellent throughout, but many readers find the second stanza the best of the three. Do you?

3. In "John Anderson My Jo," the speaker cannot be identified with Burns, but do we feel that there is in the poem anything of the particular accent of an old lady? Why?

 EDGAR ALLAN POE

Edgar Allan Poe (1809–49) was the son of traveling actors. His father abandoned the family almost immediately, and his mother died when Poe was two. The child was adopted—though never legally—by a prosperous merchant and his wife in Richmond. The tensions were great, aggravated by Poe's drinking and heavy gambling, and in 1827 Poe left Richmond for Boston. He wrote, served briefly in the army, attended West Point but left within a year, and became an editor for the remaining eighteen years of his life. It was during these years, too, that he wrote the poems, essays, and fiction—especially detective stories and horror stories—that have made him famous.

To Helen*

Helen, thy beauty is to me
    Like those Nicean° barks of yore,
That gently, o'er a perfumed sea,
    The weary, way-worn wanderer bore
    To his own native shore.   5

On desperate seas long wont to roam,
    Thy hyacinth hair,° thy classic face,
Thy Naiad° airs have brought me home
    To the glory that was Greece
And the grandeur that was Rome.   10

Lo! in yon brilliant window-niche
    How statue-like I see thee stand!
    The agate lamp within thy hand,
Ah! Psyche,° from the regions which
    Are Holy Land!°   15

                                                            [1831–43]

---

*Helen Helen of Troy, considered the most beautiful woman of ancient times
²Nicean perhaps referring to Nicea, an ancient city associated with the god Dionysus, or perhaps meaning "victorious," from Nike, Greek goddess of Victory
⁷hyacinth hair naturally curling hair, like that of Hyacinthus, beautiful Greek youth beloved by Apollo   ⁸Naiad a nymph associated with lakes and streams   ¹⁴Psyche Greek for "soul"   ¹⁵Holy Land ancient Rome or Athens, i.e., a sacred realm of art

TOPICS FOR CRITICAL THINKING AND WRITING

1. In the first stanza, to what is Helen's beauty compared? To whom does the speaker apparently compare himself? What does "way-worn" in line 4 suggest to you? To what in the speaker's experience might the "native shore" in line 5 correspond?

2. What do you take "desperate seas" to mean in line 6, and who has been traveling them? To what are they contrasted in line 8? How does "home" seem to be defined in this stanza (stanza 2)?

3. What further light is shed on the speaker's home or destination in stanza 3?

4. Do you think that "To Helen" can be a love poem and also a poem about spiritual beauty or about the love of art? Explain.

 ROBERT BROWNING

Born in a suburb of London into a middle-class family, Browning (1812–89) was educated primarily at home, where he read widely. For a while he wrote for the English stage, but after marrying Elizabeth Barrett in 1846—she too was a poet—he lived with her in Italy until her death in 1861. He then returned to England and settled in London with their son. Regarded as one of the most distinguished poets of the Victorian period, he is buried in Westminster Abbey.

Porphyria's Lover

The rain set early in tonight,
    The sullen wind was soon awake,
It tore the elm-tops down for spite,
    And did its worst to vex the lake:
I listened with heart fit to break.   5
When glided in Porphyria; straight
    She shut the cold out and the storm,
And kneeled and made the cheerless grate
    Blaze up, and all the cottage warm;
Which done, she rose, and from her form   10
Withdrew the dripping cloak and shawl,
    And laid her soiled gloves by, untied
Her hat and let the damp hair fall,
    And, last, she sat down by my side
And called me. When no voice replied,   15
She put my arm about her waist,
    And made her smooth white shoulder bare
And all her yellow hair displaced,
    And stooping, made my cheek lie there,
And spread, o'er all, her yellow hair,   20
Murmuring how she loved me—she
    Too weak, for all her heart's endeavor,
To set its struggling passion free
    From pride, and vainer ties dissever,
And give herself to me forever.   25

But passion sometimes would prevail,
        Nor could tonight's gay feast restrain
A sudden thought of one so pale
        For love of her, and all in vain:
So, she was come through wind and rain.   30
Be sure I looked up at her eyes
        Happy and proud; at last I knew
Porphyria worshiped me; surprise
        Made my heart swell, and still it grew
While I debated what to do.   35
That moment she was mine, mine, fair,
        Perfectly pure and good: I found
A thing to do, and all her hair
        In one long yellow string I wound
Three times her little throat around,   40
And strangled her. No pain felt she;
        I am quite sure she felt no pain.
As a shut bud that holds a bee,
        I warily opened her lids: again
Laughed the blue eyes without a stain.   45
And I untightened next the tress
        About her neck; her cheek once more
Blushed bright beneath my burning kiss:
        I propped her head up as before,
Only, this time my shoulder bore   50
Her head, which droops upon it still:
        The smiling rosy little head,
So glad it has its utmost will,
        That all it scorned at once is fled,
And I, its love, am gained instead!   55
Porphyria's love: she guessed not how
Her darling one wish would be heard.
And thus we sit together now,
        And all night long we have not stirred,
And yet God has not said a word!   60

[1834]

✏ TOPICS FOR CRITICAL THINKING AND WRITING

1. Exactly why did the speaker murder Porphyria?
2. You are a lawyer assigned to defend the speaker against the charge of murder. In 500 to 750 words, write your defense.

Soliloquy of the Spanish Cloister

I

Gr-r-r—there go, my heart's abhorrence!
        Water your damned flower-pots, do!
If hate killed men, Brother Lawrence,
        God's blood, would not mine kill you!   4

What? your myrtle-bush wants trimming?
    Oh, that rose has prior claims—
Needs its leaden vase filled brimming?
    Hell dry you up with its flames!   8

II

At the meal we sit together:
    Salve tibi!° I must hear
Wise talk of the kind of weather,
    Sort of season, time of year: 12
Not a plenteous cork-crop: scarcely
    Dare we hope oak-galls,° I doubt:
What's the Latin name for "parsley"?
    What's the Greek name for Swine's Snout?   16

III

Whew! We'll have our platter burnished,
    Laid with care on our own shelf!
With a fire-new spoon we're furnished,
    And a goblet for ourself,   20
Rinsed like something sacrificial
    Ere 'tis fit to touch our chaps—
Marked with L for our initial!
    (He-he! There his lily snaps!)   24

IV

Saint, forsooth! While brown Dolores
    Squats outside the Convent bank
With Sanchicha, telling stories,
    Steeping tresses in the tank,   28
Blue-black, lustrous, thick like horsehairs,
    —Can't I see his dead eye glow,
Bright as 'twere a Barbary corsair's?°
    (That is, if he'd let it show!)   32

V

When he finishes refection,°
    Knife and fork he never lays
Cross-wise, to my recollection,
    As do I, in Jesu's praise.   36
I the Trinity illustrate,
    Drinking watered orange-pulp—
In three sips the Arian° frustrate;
    While he drains his at one gulp.   40

10*Salve tibi!* Hail to thee!   14**oak-galls** growths on oak leaves, used in making ink
31**Barbary corsair** Berber pirate   33**refection** dinner   39**Arian** Arius, a fourth-
century heretic, denied the doctrine of the Trinity

VI

Oh, those melons? If he's able
    We're to have a feast! so nice!
One goes to the Abbot's table,
    All of us get each a slice.   44
How go on your flowers? None double?
    Not one fruit-sort can you spy?
Strange! And I, too, at such trouble,
    Keep them close-nipped on the sly!   48

VII

There's a great text in Galatians,°
    Once you trip on it, entails
Twenty-nine distinct damnations,
    One sure, if another fails: 52
If I trip him just a-dying,
    Sure of heaven as sure can be,
Spin him around and send him flying
    Off to hell, a Manichee?°   56

VIII

Or, my scrofulous French novel
    On gray paper with blunt type!
Simply glance at it, you grovel
    Hand and foot in Belial's° gripe: 60
If I double down its pages
    At the woeful sixteenth print,°
When he gathers his greengages,°
    Ope a sieve and slip it in't?   64

IX

Or, there's Satan! One might venture
    Pledge one's soul to him, yet leave
Such a flaw in the indenture
    As he'd miss till, past retrieve,   68
Blasted lay that rose-acacia
    We're so proud of!° *Hy, Zy, Hine*° . . .
'St, there's Vespers! *Plena gratiâ*
    Ave, Virgo!° Gr-r-r—you swine!   72

[1839]

---

⁴⁹**Galatians** a book of the New Testament   ⁵⁶**Manichee** a kind of heretic   ⁶⁰**Belial** a devil   ⁶²**sixteenth print** presumably an obscene picture   ⁶³**greengages** yellowish-green plums   ⁶⁵⁻⁷⁰**Or, . . . proud of** The speaker apparently contemplates pledging his own soul to the devil (who in exchange will snare Lawrence) but leaving a loophole so that he can escape the pledge.   ⁷⁰**Hy, Zy, Hine** the sound of bells (?) an incantation (?)   ⁷¹⁻⁷²**Plena . . . Virgo!** "Hail, Virgin, full of grace!"

TOPICS FOR CRITICAL THINKING AND WRITING

1. In which lines does the speaker quote or parody Brother Lawrence?
2. In a paragraph or two, set forth your guesses about why the speaker hates Brother Lawrence.
3. In a paragraph, characterize Brother Lawrence.
4. In an essay of about 500 words, characterize the speaker.

 WALT WHITMAN

Walt Whitman (1819-92) was born in a farmhouse in rural Long Island, New York, but was brought up in Brooklyn, then an independent city in New York. He attended public school for a few years (1825-30), apprenticed as a printer in the 1830s, and then worked as a typesetter, journalist, and newspaper editor. In 1855 he published the first edition of a collection of his poems, Leaves of Grass, *a book that he revised and republished throughout the remainder of his life. During the Civil War, he served as a volunteer nurse for the Union army.*

In the third edition of Leaves of Grass *(1860) Whitman added two groups of poems, one called "Children of Adam" and the other (named for an aromatic grass that grows near ponds and swamps) called "Calamus." "Children of Adam" celebrates heterosexual relations, whereas "Calamus" celebrates what Whitman called "manly love." Although the "Calamus" poems seem clearly homosexual, perhaps the very fact that Whitman published them made them seem relatively innocent; in any case, those nineteenth-century critics who condemned Whitman for the sexuality of his writing concentrated on the poems in "Children of Adam."*

We give three poems from the "Calamus" section. All three were originally published in the third edition of Leaves of Grass *(1860), and all were revised into their final forms in the 1867 edition. We give them in the 1867 versions. We also give the manuscripts for two of the poems, showing them in their earliest extant versions.*

When I Heard at the Close of the Day

When I heard at the close of the day how my name had been
      receiv'd with plaudits in the capitol, still it was not a happy
      night for me that follow'd,
And else when I carous'd, or when my plans were accomplish'd,
      still I was not happy,
But the day when I rose at dawn from the bed of perfect health,
      refresh'd, singing, inhaling the ripe breath of autumn,
When I saw the full moon in the west grow pale and disappear in
      the morning light,
When I wander'd alone over the beach, and undressing bathed,   5
      laughing with the cool waters, and saw the sun rise,
And when I thought how my dear friend my lover was on his way
      coming, O then I was happy,

O then each breath tasted sweeter, and all that day my food
    nourish'd me more, and the beautiful day pass'd well,
And the next came with equal joy, and with the next at evening
    came my friend,
And that night while all was still I heard the waters roll slowly
    continually up the shores,
I heard the hissing rustle of the liquid and sands as directed to   10
    me whispering to congratulate me,
For the one I love most lay sleeping by me under the same cover
    in the cool night,
In the stillness in the autumn moonbeams his face was inclined
    toward me,
And his arm lay lightly around my breast—and that night I was
    happy.

[1867]

☑ TOPICS FOR CRITICAL THINKING AND WRITING

1. Let's assume that the word *plot*—the gist of what happens—can be applied not only to prose fiction and to plays but also to lyric poems. How
   would you summarize the plot of this poem?
2. If someone were to ask you why "When I Heard at the Close of the Day"
   is regarded as a poem rather than as prose arranged to look like a poem,
   what would you reply?

I Saw in Louisiana a Live-Oak Growing

I saw in Louisiana a live-oak growing,
All alone stood it and the moss hung down from the branches,
Without any companion it grew there uttering joyous leaves of
    dark green,
And its look, rude, unbending, lusty, made me think of myself,
But I wonder'd how it could utter joyous leaves standing alone
    there without its friend near, for I knew I could not,   5
And I broke off a twig with a certain number of leaves upon it,
    and twined around it a little moss,
And brought it away, and I have placed it in sight in my room,
It is not needed to remind me as of my own dear friends,
(For I believe lately I think of little else than of them,)
Yet it remains to me a curious token, it makes me think of manly
    love;   10
For all that, and though the live-oak glistens there in Louisiana
    solitary in a wide flat space,
Uttering joyous leaves all its life without a friend a lover near,
I know very well I could not.

[1867]

II

I saw in Louisiana a
live-oak growing,
All alone stood it, and the
moss hung down from the
branches,
Without any companion it grew
there, glistening out ~~with~~
joyous leaves of dark green,
And its look, rude, unbending,
lusty, made me think of
myself;
But I wondered how it could
utter joyous leaves, standing
alone there without its friend,
its lover - For I knew I could
not;
And I plucked a twig with
a certain number of leaves
upon it, and twined around
it a little moss, and brought
it away - And I have placed
it in sight in my room,

2

Walt Whitman, "I Saw in Louisiana a Live-Oak Growing," manuscript of 1860. On the first leaf, in line 3 Whitman deleted "with." On the second leaf, in the third line (line 8 of the printed text) he added, with a caret, "lately." In the sixth line on this leaf he deleted "I write

(continued)

It is not needed to remind
me as of my friends, (for I
believe *lately* think of little
else than of them,)
Yet it remains to me a
curious token — it makes
me think of manly love,
~~these pieces, and name
them after it~~ ;
For all that, and though the
live oak
~~tree~~ glistens there in Louisiana, solitary in a wide
flat space, uttering joyous
leaves all its life, without
a friend, a lover, near — I
know very well I could
not.

these pieces, and name them after it," replacing the deletion with "it makes me think of manly love." In the next line he deleted "tree" and inserted "live oak." When he reprinted the poem in the 1867 version of *Leaves of Grass,* he made further changes, as you will see if you compare the printed text with this manuscript version. (Walt Whitman Collection. Clifton Waller Barrett Library, Manuscripts Division, University of Virginia Library)

Razzia.

Up and down the roads
    going — North and South
    excursions making,
Power enjoying — elbow stretch-
    ing — fingers clutching,
Armed and fearless — eating,
    drinking, sleeping, loving,
No law less than myself
    owning — Sailing, soldiering,
    thieving, threatening,
Misers, menials, priests alarming —
    Air breathing, water drinking,
    on the turf or the sea-beach
    dancing,
With birds singing — with fishes
    swimming — with trees
    branching and leaving,
Cities wrenching, ease scorning,
    statutes mocking, feebleness
    chasing,
Fulfilling my foray. —

Walt Whitman, "Razzia," manuscript of 1860. The title is Italian for "Raid." For the 1867 edition of *Leaves of Grass,* Whitman revised and retitled the poem, calling it "We Two Boys Together Clinging." See page 836 for the revised version. (Walt Whitman Collection. Clifton Waller Barrett Library, Manuscripts Division, University of Virginia Library)

TOPIC FOR CRITICAL THINKING AND WRITING

Compare the final version (1867) of the poem with the manuscript version of 1860. Which version do you prefer? Why?

We Two Boys Together Clinging

We two boys together clinging,
One the other never leaving,
Up and down the roads going, North and South excursions
    making,
Power enjoying, elbows stretching, fingers clutching,
Arm'd and fearless, eating, drinking, sleeping, loving,   5
No law less than ourselves owning, sailing, soldiering, thieving,
    threatening,
Misers, menials, priests alarming, air breathing, water drinking, on
    the turf or the sea-beach dancing,
Cities wrenching, ease scorning, statutes mocking, feebleness chasing,
Fulfilling our foray.

[1867]

 TOPIC FOR CRITICAL THINKING AND WRITING

Compare the final version (1867) of the poem with the manuscript version (entitled "Razzia," p. 835) of 1860. Which version do you prefer? Why?

 MATTHEW ARNOLD

Matthew Arnold (1822–88) was the son of a famous educator, Dr. Thomas Arnold, the headmaster of Rugby School. After graduating from Oxford, he became an inspector of schools, a post he held until two years before his death. Besides writing poetry, Arnold wrote literary criticism and was appointed professor of poetry at Oxford from 1857 to 1867. He traveled widely on the Continent and gave several lectures in the United States.

Dover Beach

The sea is calm to-night.
The tide is full, the moon lies fair
Upon the straits;—on the French coast the light
Gleams and is gone; the cliffs of England stand,
Glimmering and vast, out in the tranquil bay.   5
Come to the window, sweet is the night-air!
Only, from the long line of spray

Where the sea meets the moon-blanch'd land,
Listen! you hear the grating roar
Of pebbles which the waves draw back, and fling,   10
At their return, up the high strand,
Begin, and cease, and then again begin,
With tremulous cadence slow, and bring
The eternal note of sadness in.

Sophocles long ago   15
Heard it on the Ægean, and it brought
Into his mind the turbid ebb and flow
Of human misery; we
Find also in the sound a thought,
Hearing it by this distant northern sea.   20

The Sea of Faith
Was once, too, at the full, and round earth's shore
Lay like the folds of a bright girdle furl'd.
But now I only hear
Its melancholy, long, withdrawing roar,   25
Retreating, to the breath
Of the night-wind, down the vast edges drear
And naked shingles° of the world.

Ah, love, let us be true
To one another! for the world, which seems   30
To lie before us like a land of dreams,
So various, so beautiful, so new,
Hath really neither joy, nor love, nor light,
Nor certitude, nor peace, nor help for pain;
And we are here as on a darkling plain   35
Swept with confused alarms of struggle and flight,
Where ignorant armies clash by night.

[c. 1851]

 TOPICS FOR CRITICAL THINKING AND WRITING

1. What do you make of the figure of the "Sea of Faith" (line 21)? Do you
   think the poem implies that the "Sea of Faith," now at the ebb, will (like
   the literal sea) again be at the full?
2. The last section (lines 29–37) makes no use of the sea metaphor, but it
   introduces the "darkling plain." Does this ending seem tacked on? Or
   do you think it is sufficiently related by references to darkness and to
   noises? Support your opinion.
3. Do you agree that the last lines of this Victorian poem (from line 29,
   "Ah, love") in effect say, "You are a woman, and are therefore more
   spiritual than I am, so console me"? Explain your position.

28**shingles** pebbled beaches

WILLIAM BUTLER YEATS

William Butler Yeats (1865–1939) was born in Dublin, Ireland. The early Yeats was much interested in highly lyrical, romantic poetry, often drawing on Irish mythology. The later poems, say from about 1910 (and especially after Yeats met Ezra Pound in 1911), are often more colloquial, more down-to-earth; these later poems often employ mythological references, too, but one feels that the poems are more hardheaded. He was awarded the Nobel Prize in Literature in 1923.

For Anne Gregory*

"Never shall a young man,
Thrown into despair
By those great honey-coloured
Ramparts at your ear
Love you for yourself alone   5
And not your yellow hair."

"But I can get a hair-dye
And set such colour there,
Brown, or black, or carrot,
That young men in despair   10
May love me for myself alone
And not my yellow hair."

"I heard an old religious man
But yesternight declare
That he had found a text to prove   15

That only God, my dear,
Could love you for yourself alone
And not your yellow hair."

                                                          [1930]

*Yeats was 65 when he wrote this poem for Anne Gregory, the 19-year-old grand-daughter of Lady Augusta Gregory, a woman whom Yeats had admired.

 TOPICS FOR CRITICAL THINKING AND WRITING

1. What does it mean to say that one wants to be loved "for oneself alone"?
2. How satisfactory is the answer given to the young woman?
3. Is the poem sexist? Explain.

 EZRA POUND

Ezra Pound (1885–1972), born in Hailey, Idaho, and raised in Philadelphia, was one of the most influential American poets of the twentieth century. He prepared to be a teacher of medieval and

renaissance Spanish, Italian, and French literature, but his career as an academician ended abruptly when he was fired from Wabash College for having a woman in his room overnight. Pound went to Venice, where he did odd jobs, and then to London, where he met T. S. Eliot and played a large role in editing Eliot's long poem The Waste Land. *Among the other poets whom he assisted was Robert Frost, who was then living in England. In 1924 Pound settled in Italy. He espoused Mussolini's cause, was arrested by the American forces in 1944, and (having been declared insane and therefore not fit to be tried for treason) was confined in a mental institution in Washington, D.C. Released in 1958, he spent the remainder of his life in Italy.*

"The River-Merchant's Wife" is based on an English translation of a Chinese poem by Li Po (700?–62).

The River-Merchant's Wife: A Letter*

While my hair was still cut straight across my forehead
I played about the front gate, pulling flowers.
You came by on bamboo stilts, playing horse,
You walked about my seat, playing with blue plums.
And we went on living in the village of Chokan:°   5
Two small people, without dislike or suspicion.
At fourteen I married My Lord you.
I never laughed, being bashful.
Lowering my head, I looked at the wall.
Called to, a thousand times, I never looked back.   10

At fifteen I stopped scowling,
I desired my dust to be mingled with yours
Forever and forever and forever.
Why should I climb the lookout?

At sixteen you departed,   15
You went into far Ku-to-yen,° by the river of swirling eddies,
And you have been gone five months.
The monkeys make sorrowful noise overhead.

You dragged your feet when you went out.
By the gate now, the moss is grown, the different mosses,   20
Too deep to clear them away!
The leaves fall early this autumn, in wind.
The paired butterflies are already yellow with August
Over the grass in the West garden;
They hurt me. I grow older.   25
If you are coming down through the narrows of the river Kiang,
Please let me know before hand,
And I will come out to meet you
    As far as Cho-fu-sa.°

[1915]

---

*The poem is a free translation of Li Po's "Two Letters from Chang-Kan." **5Chokan** Chang-kan, near Nanking   **16Ku-to-yen** an island several hundred miles up the river Kiang from Nanking   **30Cho-fu-sa** a beach near Ku-to-yen

TOPICS FOR CRITICAL THINKING AND WRITING

1. In line 7 the speaker addresses her husband with a formal title, "My Lord you." What was their relation in the first six lines?
2. How would you classify the images of the final stanza? And how would you characterize the speaker's tone in the final lines?
3. Ford Maddox Ford, reviewing the book in which this poem appeared, said in 1927: "The quality of great poetry is that without comment as without effort it presents you with images that stir your emotions; so you are made a better man; you are softened, rendered more supple of mind, more open to the vicissitudes and necessities of your fellow men. When you have read 'The River-Merchant's Wife' you are added to. You are a better man or woman than you were before." Do you believe it? If so, are we in this case "added to" because we see a model for behavior? But how, then, would "My Last Duchess" (p. 358) add to us?
4. The last sentence is the longest, and immediately follows two sentences so short that they both fit in a single line. What, then, is the effect of the last sentence?

 EDNA ST. VINCENT MILLAY

Edna St. Vincent Millay (1892–1950) was born in Rockland, Maine. Even as a child she wrote poetry, and by the time she graduated from Vassar College (1917) she had achieved some note as a poet. Millay settled for a while in Greenwich Village, a center of Bohemian activity in New York City, where she wrote, performed in plays, and engaged in feminist causes. In 1923, the year she married, she became the first woman to win the Pulitzer Prize for Poetry. Numerous other awards followed. Though she is best known as a lyric poet—especially as a writer of sonnets—she also wrote memorable political poetry and nature poetry as well as short stories, plays, and a libretto for an opera.

The Spring and the Fall

In the spring of the year, in the spring of the year,
I walked the road beside my dear.
The trees were black where the bark was wet.
I see them yet, in the spring of the year.
He broke me a bough of the blossoming peach   5
That was out of the way and hard to reach.

In the fall of the year, in the fall of the year,
I walked the road beside my dear.
The rooks went up with a raucous trill.
I hear them still, in the fall of the year.   10
He laughed at all I dared to praise,
And broke my heart, in little ways.

Year be springing or year be falling,
The bark will drip and the birds be calling.
There's much that's fine to see and hear   15
In the spring of a year, in the fall of a year.
'Tis not love's going hurts my days,
But that it went in little ways.

[1923]

 TOPICS FOR CRITICAL THINKING AND WRITING

1. The first stanza describes the generally happy beginning of a love story.
   Where do you find the first hint of an unhappy ending?
2. Describe the rhyme scheme of the first stanza, including internal rhymes.
   Do the second and third stanzas repeat the pattern, or are there some
   variations? What repetition of sounds other than rhyme do you note?
3. Paraphrase the last two lines. How do you react to them; that is, do you
   find the conclusion surprising, satisfying (or unsatisfying), recognizable
   from your own experience, anticlimactic, or what?
4. In two or three paragraphs explain how the imagery of the poem contributes to its meaning.

Love Is Not All: It Is Not Meat nor Drink

Love is not all: it is not meat nor drink
Nor slumber nor a roof against the rain;
Nor yet a floating spar to men that sink
And rise and sink and rise and sink again;   4
Love can not fill the thickened lung with breath,
Nor clean the blood, nor set the fractured bone;
Yet many a man is making friends with death
Even as I speak, for lack of love alone.   8

It well may be that in a difficult hour,
Pinned down by pain and moaning for release,
Or nagged by want past resolution's power,
I might be driven to sell your love for peace,   12
Or trade the memory of this night for food.
It well may be. I do not think I would.

[1931]

 TOPICS FOR CRITICAL THINKING AND WRITING

1. "Love Is Not All" is a sonnet. Using your own words, briefly summarize
   the argument of the octet (the first 8 lines). Next, paraphrase the sestet,
   line by line. On the whole, does the sestet repeat the idea of the octet,
   or does it add a new idea? Whom did you imagine to be speaking the

octet? What does the sestet add to your knowledge of the speaker and the occasion? (And how did you paraphrase line 11?)

2. The first and last lines of the poem consist of words of one syllable, and both lines have a distinct pause in the middle. Do you imagine the lines to be spoken in the same tone of voice? If not, can you describe the difference and account for it?

3. Lines 7 and 8 appear to mean that the absence of love can be a cause of death. To what degree do you believe that to be true?

4. Would you call "Love Is Not All" a love poem? Why or why not? Describe the kind of person who might include the poem in a love letter or valentine, or who would be happy to receive it. (One of our friends recited it at her wedding. What do you think of that idea?)

 ROBERT FROST

Robert Frost (1874–1963) was born in California. After his father's death in 1885, Frost's mother brought the family to New England, where she taught in high schools in Massachusetts and New Hampshire. Frost studied for part of one term at Dartmouth College in New Hampshire, then did odd jobs (including teaching), and from 1897 to 1899 was enrolled as a special student at Harvard. He later farmed in New Hampshire, published a few poems in local newspapers, left the farm and taught again, and in 1912 left for England, where he hoped to achieve more popular success as a writer. By 1915 he had won a considerable reputation, and he returned to the United States, settling on a farm in New Hampshire and cultivating the image of the country-wise farmer-poet. In fact he was well read in the classics, in the Bible, and in English and American literature.

Among Frost's many comments about literature, here are three: "Writing is unboring to the extent that it is dramatic"; "Every poem is . . . a figure of the will braving alien entanglements"; and, finally, a poem "begins in delight and ends in wisdom. . . . It runs a course of lucky events, and ends in a clarification of life—not necessarily a great clarification, such as sects and cults are founded on, but in a momentary stay against confusion."

The Silken Tent

She is as in a field a silken tent
At midday when a sunny summer breeze
Has dried the dew and all its ropes relent,
So that in guys it gently sways at ease,　　　　　　　　　　4
And its supporting central cedar pole,
That is its pinnacle to heavenward
And signifies the sureness of the soul,
Seems to owe naught to any single cord,　　　　　　　　　8
But strictly held by none, is loosely bound
By countless silken ties of love and thought

Page from Frost's notebooks, showing "*The Silken Tent*." (Printed with the permission of The Poetry/Rare Books Collection, University Libraries, State University of New York at Buffalo)

To everything on earth the compass round,
And only by one's going slightly taut   12
In the capriciousness of summer air
Is of the slightest bondage made aware.

[1943]

TOPICS FOR CRITICAL THINKING AND WRITING

1. The second line places the scene at "midday" in "summer." In addition to giving us the concreteness of a setting, do these words help to characterize the woman whom the speaker describes? If so, how?
2. The tent is supported by "guys" (not men, but the cords or "ties" of line 10) and by its "central cedar pole." What does Frost tell us about these ties? What does he tell us about the pole?
3. What do you make of lines 12–14?
4. In a sentence, a paragraph, or a poem, construct a simile that explains a relationship.

 ADRIENNE RICH

Adrienne Rich, born in 1929 in Baltimore, was educated at Radcliffe College. Her first book of poems, A Change of World, *published in 1951 when she was still an undergraduate, was selected by W. H. Auden for the Yale Series of Younger Poets. In 1953 she married an economist and had three sons, but as she indicates in several books, she felt confined by the full-time domestic role that she was expected to play, and the marriage did not last. Much of her poetry is concerned with issues of gender and power. When her ninth book,* Diving into the Wreck *(1973), won the National Book Award, Rich accepted the award not as an individual but on behalf of women everywhere.*

Diving into the Wreck

First having read the book of myths,
and loaded the camera,
and checked the edge of the knife-blade,
I put on
the body-armor of black rubber   5
the absurd flippers
the grave and awkward mask.
I am having to do this
not like Cousteau° with his
assiduous team   10
aboard the sun-flooded schooner
but here alone.

There is a ladder.
The ladder is always there
hanging innocently   15
close to the side of the schooner.
We know what it is for,
we who have used it.
Otherwise
it's a piece of maritime floss   20
some sundry equipment.

I go down.
Rung after rung and still
the oxygen immerses me
the blue light   25
the clear atoms

of our human air.
I go down.
My flippers cripple me,
I crawl like an insect down the ladder   30

---

⁹**Cousteau** Jacques Cousteau (b. 1910) French underwater explorer

and there is no one
to tell me when the ocean
will begin.

First the air is blue and then
it is bluer and then green and then   35
black I am blacking out and yet
my mask is powerful
it pumps my blood with power
the sea is another story
the sea is not a question of power   40
I have to learn alone
to turn my body without force
in the deep element.

And now: it is easy to forget
what I came for   45
among so many who have always
lived here
swaying their crenellated fans
between the reefs
and besides   50
you breathe differently down here.

I came to explore the wreck.
The words are purposes.
The words are maps.
I came to see the damage that was done   55
and the treasures that prevail.
I stroke the beam of my lamp
slowly along the flank
of something more permanent
than fish or weed   60

the thing I came for:
the wreck and not the story of the wreck
the thing itself and not the myth
the drowned face always staring
toward the sun   65
the evidence of damage

worn by salt and sway into this threadbare beauty
the ribs of the disaster
curving their assertion
among the tentative haunters.   70

This is the place.
And I am here, the mermaid whose dark hair
streams black, the merman in his armored body
We circle silently
about the wreck   75
we dive into the hold.
I am she: I am he

whose drowned face sleeps with open eyes
whose breasts still bear the stress
whose silver, copper, vermeil cargo lies   80
obscurely inside barrels
half-wedged and left to rot
we are the half-destroyed instruments
that once held to a course
the water-eaten log   85
the fouled compass

We are, I am, you are
by cowardice or courage
the one who find our way
back to this scene   90
carrying a knife, a camera
a book of myths
in which
our names do not appear.

                                                        [1973]

 ## TOPICS FOR CRITICAL THINKING AND WRITING

1. Do you think the "wreck" can be defined fairly precisely? In any case, what do you think the wreck is?
2. In lines 62–63 the speaker says that she came to explore "the wreck and not the story of the wreck / the thing itself and not the myth." Lines 1 and 92 speak of a "book of myths." What sort of "myths" do you think the poet is talking about?
3. In line 72 the speaker is a mermaid; in line 73, a merman; in lines 74 and 76, "we"; and in line 77, "I am she: I am he." What do you make of this?

Novella

Two people in a room, speaking harshly.
One gets up, goes out to walk.
(That is the man.)
The other goes out into the next room
and washes the dishes, cracking one.   5
(That is the woman.)
It gets dark outside.
The children quarrel in the attic.
She has no blood left in her heart.
The man comes back to a dark house.   10
The only light is in the attic.
He has forgotten his key.
He rings at his own door
and hears sobbing on the stairs.
The lights go on in the house.   15

The door closes behind him.
Outside, separate as minds,
the stars too come alight.

[1967]

TOPICS FOR CRITICAL THINKING AND WRITING

1. Rewrite the poem along these lines:

   My husband and I are in a room, speaking harshly.
   He gets up, goes out to walk.
   I go out into the next room
   and wash the dishes, cracking one.
   It gets dark outside.

   Has the poem been improved, or weakened, or simply changed? Explain.
2. What, if anything, do the last two lines contribute to the poem?
3. A *novella* is a long short story, or a short novel (usually about 50–100 pages). Why do you suppose Rich called this short poem "Novella"?
4. In one typed page, write your own "Novella." You may be a character in the plot, but keep your voice third person.

XI. *

Every peak is a crater. This is the law of volcanoes,
making them eternally and visibly female.
No height without depth, without a burning core,
though our straw soles shred on the hardened lava.
I want to travel with you to every sacred mountain   5
smoking within like the sibyl stooped over her tripod,
I want to reach for your hand as we scale the path,
to feel your arteries glowing in my clasp,
never failing to note the small, jewel-like flower
unfamiliar to us, nameless till we rename her,   10
that clings to the slowly altering rock—
that detail outside ourselves that brings us to ourselves,
was here before us, knew we would come, and sees beyond us.

[1978]

TOPICS FOR CRITICAL THINKING AND WRITING

1. What use does the speaker make of a volcano in the first four lines? Can you restate her point *without* using a volcano?
2. How can a "detail outside ourselves . . . bring us to ourselves" (12)?
3. Try to use a volcano or mountain to characterize a relationship.

*From *Twenty-One Love Poems*

ROBERT PACK

Robert Pack, born in New York city in 1929, was educated at Dartmouth College and at Columbia University. The author of several books of poems, he teaches at Middlebury College in Vermont.

The Frog Prince

(A Speculation on Grimm's Fairy Tale)

Imagine the princess' surprise!
Who would have thought a frog's cold frame
Could hold the sweet and gentle body
Of a prince? How can I name   4
The joy she must have felt to learn
His transformation was the wonder
Of her touch—that she too, in
Her way, had been transformed under   8
Those clean sheets? Such powers were
Like nothing she had ever read.
And in the morning when her mother
Came and saw them there in bed,   12
Heard how a frog became a prince;
What was it that her mother said?

[1980]

 TOPICS FOR CRITICAL THINKING AND WRITING

1. Fairy-tale characters seldom have characteristics that go beyond the legend they are in. What characteristics does Pack give to the princess? How do you understand "she too, in / Her way, had been transformed" (lines 7–8)?
2. And "What was it that her mother said?"
3. Transform a fairy tale that you know by giving one character or two some realistic traits. Retell the story, or one scene from it.

 ELLEN BRYANT VOIGHT

Ellen Bryant Voight was born in Virginia in 1943 and educated at Converse College and the University of Iowa. She is the author of several books of poems and has taught writing at Massachusetts Institute of Technology and at Warren Wilson College.

Quarrel

Since morning they have been quarreling—
the sun pouring its implacable white bath

over the birches, each one undressing
slyly, from the top down—and they hammer
at each other with their knives, nailfiles,   5
graters of complaint as the day unwinds,
the plush clouds lowering a gray matte°
for the red barn. Lunch, the soup
like batting in their mouths, last week,
last year, they're moving on to always   10
and never, their shrill pitiful children
crowd around but they see the top of this
particular mountain, its glacial headwall,
the pitch is terrific all through dinner,
and they are committed, the sun long gone,   15
the two of them back to back in the blank
constricting bed, like marbles on aluminum—
O this fierce love
that needs to reproduce in one another
wounds inflicted by the world.   20

[1983]

 ## TOPICS FOR CRITICAL THINKING AND WRITING

1. The quarrel has been going on "Since morning. . . ." What do we know
   about the people quarreling? When will the quarrel end? What do we
   know about why they quarrel?
2. The quarrel is set, in part, in a landscape. What does the speaker tell us
   about the landscape? Is the landscape set off from the quarrel or a part
   of it?
3. In line 18 did "love" surprise you? On rereading the poem, does the
   word make sense in the context of the whole? Explain.

---

⁷**matte** dull paint finish

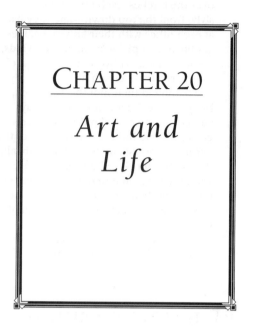

CHAPTER 20

Art and Life

A WORD ABOUT CONNECTIONS BETWEEN LITERATURE AND THE OTHER ARTS

Although the word *art* perhaps first calls to mind painting and sculpture, it can also be used of music, literature, dance, and architecture. We can even extend the word and (for instance) speak of the art of medicine. Presumably the *science* of medicine is a matter of diligent study of conventional scientific procedures, but the *art* of medicine is a matter of intuition (or of skills developed out of intuitions).

Something of this implication that the arts draw on individual insights is evident, too, in the distinction between *the arts* and *the crafts*. But first we should mention that some people deny that a meaningful distinction can be made. In their view, an elite society snobbishly calls some things that it happens to value "art," and other things that it values less, "craft." Thus, in our society, at least until very recently, an oil painting (probably executed by a man) was a work of art, and a quilt (executed by a woman) was a work of craft; a sculpture of a nude male or female (probably executed by a man) was a work of art, and a clothed doll (executed by a woman) was a work of craft. This view has been called the institutional view of art, or the establishment view of art: Something is a work of art if an important institution says it is. Thus, museums tell us what is and is not art; so long as quilts are not exhibited in museums, they are not works of art, but if major museums exhibit quilts, quilts become art. Similarly, it is argued, educational institutions decree what is literature and what is not. If Alice James's *Diary* is not taught in literature courses in colleges and universities, it is not literature; if it *is* taught, it *is* literature. (Of course other institutions also are part of the game; if a major publishing house publishes a book, the act of publication helps to establish the work as a work of literature.) Is this a cynical view? Or is it in fact a realistic view? After all, we do know that works that were ignored in their own day—let's say the paintings of Vincent van Gogh—have come to be highly regarded as works of art. The works did not change—only the attitudes toward them.

Still, can we say that the distinction between a work of art and a work of craft is in the object itself, and not in the viewer? Let's try. Consider the worker in wood who produces something (let's call it a sculpture) that can be said to be in some degree the product of imagination. Now, on the other hand, let's consider the worker in wood who, following a predictable plan, produces something (for instance a handsome, sturdy coffee table) that is very like countless objects that already exist. The wooden object that is a work of art presumably is valued chiefly as a unique object that (1) *is expressive* (let's say, of power, or lightness, or energy, or tranquility) and that (2) in itself *gives pleasure* by means of its color, its shape, and so on—even though of course we might also stack magazines on it. The wooden object that is a work of craft is, we might say, not essentially expressive and not essentially an object that gives pleasure. Further, it is *made* by technical skill rather than *created* by the imagination. Technical skill, admirable in itself, is possessed by many people, and can be learned by almost all.

Of course works of art also require technical skill—it's not easy to carve (or to write a sonnet)—and there may be widespread disagreement about whether a particular wooden object is a work of art or a work of craft, but the general idea is clear enough. If we ask a carpenter to copy this coffee table, he or she produces a work of craft; if we ask a carpenter to design a table that will somehow go with the rest of the living room and will "make a statement," the table conceivably may be a work of art. Certainly furniture *can* be expressive. For instance, an overstuffed armchair expresses or says something very different from a typist's chair. In short, the line between the arts and the crafts is not always clear. In fact, sculpting has often been thought of as a craft because there is so much physical labor involved in producing a work of sculpture. (Some sculptors, eager to avoid the stigma attached to physical labor, have produced small clay models and then left to stonemasons the job of making a larger copy in stone.) And—to get back to literature—the very word *playwright* implies craft, since a *wright* is a maker; a playwright (*not* "playwrite") is a *maker* of plays, just as a shipwright is a maker of ships.

No one denies that authors must learn their craft, but most people would agree that the enduring writings—the writings that outlive their own generation—are the products of more than technical competence. Still, a case can be made that there is no sharp distinction between the arts and the crafts—just as a case can be made that there is no sharp distinction between literature and the writing that we all produce, for instance letters, diaries, journal entries, lectures. In this view, "literature," "art," and "craft" are social constructs—things constructed (like, say, educational systems or penal systems) by society. Different societies construct different systems; hence, the canon (the body of accepted work called literature, or called art) may change from decade to decade.

Enough of the philosophizing—or almost enough. Artists (in the broad sense, including not only people who produce paintings and sculptures but also those who produce poems, novels, operas, dances, and so forth) are often tempted to think that artists in other fields have some sort of advantage. Thus, writers—casting envious eyes at painters—may fret that their own audiences are limited to persons who can read the language, whereas painters supposedly work in a "universal language" of line and color.

Are there, one may ask, significant correspondences between the arts? If we talk about *rhythm* in a painting, are we talking about a quality similar to *rhythm* in a poem? Are the painter's colors comparable to the poet's images? Does it make sense to say, as Goethe (1749–1832) said, that architecture is frozen music? Or to call architecture music in space? Many artists of one sort have felt that their abilities *ought* to enable them to move into a "sister art," and they have tried their hand at something outside of their specialty, usually with no great success. (William Blake, represented in this book by several poems and pictures, is often said to be the only figure in English history who is significant both as a poet and as a painter.) For instance, the painter Edgar Degas (1834–1917) tried to write sonnets, but he could not satisfy even himself. When he complained to his friend, the poet Stéphane Mallarmé, that he couldn't write poems even though he had plenty of ideas, Mallarmé replied, "You don't write poems with ideas; you write them with words."

Artists (of all kinds) may be pardoned for feeling that there is a kinship between the arts. The idea can be traced back to Simonides (556–468 B.C.), an ancient Greek poet who is reputed to have said that "painting is mute poetry, poetry a speaking picture." The Roman poet Horace (65–8 B.C.) picked up the idea, saying in *The Art of Poetry* that "a poem is like a picture" (*ut pictura poesis*), an assertion that has been disputed ever since.

In John Keats's "Ode on a Grecian Urn" (p. 924) we see one kind of artist, a poet, looking longingly at another form of art. Contemplating a marble urn decorated with a carved woodland ("sylvan") scene, Keats speaks of the urn as a

> Sylvan historian, who [can] thus express
> A flowery tale more sweetly than our rhyme.

A moment later in the poem, referring to the images of musicians depicted on the urn, he says,

> Heard melodies are sweet, but those unheard
> Are sweeter.

Here Keats asserts that the carved scene on the urn is superior not only to a poem but also to a musical work. The urn's *picture* of music excels real music; the *idea* of music, evoked by the picture, is said to be superior to any music that real musicians produce.

Painters have been moved, for many centuries, to illustrate texts—for instance, more than two thousand years ago the painters of Greek vases illustrated the Greek myths, and from the Middle Ages onward artists have illustrated the Bible. In this book we include a mid-twentieth-century painting by Charles Demuth, based on a poem by William Carlos Williams. Conversely, poets have been moved to write about paintings or sculptures. Later in this chapter we reprint several poems about paintings by Botticelli, Brueghel, van Gogh, and others. There are even some poems that themselves are pictures—poems that, printed on the page, *look* like some object. For examples, see two poems by George Herbert, "Easter Wings" (p. 1213) and "The Altar" (p. 1214). Almost in this tradition, too, is Ferlinghetti's "Constantly Risking Absurdity" (p. 934).

THINKING ABOUT POEMS AND PICTURES

Despite Mallarmé's witty remark that poems are not made with ideas but with words (and despite Archibald MacLeish's assertion, on p. 932, that "A poem should not mean / But be"), of course poems use ideas, and of course they have meanings. When you read the poems that we print along with pictures, you might think about some of the following questions:

- What is your own first response to the picture?
- After you have read the poem, do you see the picture in a somewhat different way?
- To what extent does the poem illustrate the picture, and to what extent does it depart from the picture?
- If the picture is based on a poem (see Demuth's painting on p. 904), to what extent does the picture capture the poem?
- Beyond the subject matter, what (if anything) do the two works have in common?

Essays

 PABLO PICASSO

Pablo Picasso (1881–1973) was born in Spain, but after 1900 he lived mostly in Paris. Although he is known chiefly as a painter, he also produced drawings, sculptures, ceramics, and stage designs. He is widely regarded as the most important artist of the twentieth century.

Although Picasso made only a few formal statements about art, he often spoke about art to friends and interviewers. We reproduce some of his comments, and reports of his comments. Although by art he usually means painting or sculpture, the word can of course also refer to works of literature, music, dance, and so on.

Talking about Art

[Art and Truth]

"We all know that Art is not truth. Art is a lie that makes us realize truth, at least the truth that is given us to understand. The artist must know the manner whereby to convince others of the truthfulness of his lies. If he only shows in his work that he has searched, and researched, for the way to put over lies, he would never accomplish anything."

[A Work of Art Changes]

"A picture is not thought out and settled beforehand. While it is being done it changes as one's thoughts change. And when it is finished, it still goes on changing, according to the state of mind of whoever is looking at it. A picture lives a life like a living creature, undergoing the changes imposed on us by our life from day to day. This is natural enough, as the picture lives only through the man who is looking at it."

[On Understanding Art, and Explaining It]

"Everyone wants to understand art. Why not try to understand the songs of a bird? Why does one love the night, flowers, everything around one, without trying to understand them? But in the case of a painting people have to *understand*. If only they would realize above all that an artist works of necessity, that he himself is only a trifling bit of the world, and that no more importance should be attached to him than to plenty of other things which please us in the world, though we can't explain them. People who try to explain pictures are usually barking up the wrong tree. Gertrude Stein joyfully announced to me the other day that she had at last understood what my picture of the three musicians was meant to be. It was a still life!"

[Art as Discovery]

We just left Don Pablo. He was doing a large charcoal drawing of a terrifically dramatic rooster. "Roosters—" he said, "we always have roosters, but like everything else in life we must discover them. Just as Corot discovered the morning and Renoir discovered little girls. Everything must be discovered—this box—a piece of paper. You must always leave the door open, always open—and the main thing is never to turn back once you pass through that door. Never to dismay and never to compromise. Roosters have always been seen but seldom so well as in American weather vanes."

[The Artist's Subject Matter]

"Actually, it's through one's work that one is understood. One must work, work." Then he [Picasso] talks of the difficulties he has in inventing—even in inventing a new subject. "There are, basically, very few subjects. Everybody is repeating them. Venus and Love become the Virgin and Child, then—maternity, but it's always the same subject. It's magnificent to invent new subjects. Take Van Gogh: Potatoes, those shapeless things! To have painted that, or a pair of old shoes! That's really something!"

[Originality]

"The individual who insists on being original wastes his time and deceives himself; if he attains something it is but an imitation of what he likes, and if he goes farther it may be that what he does does not even resemble him. One day I told Angel Ortiz: to make a circle without a compass, try to trace a line always equidistant from the center, but do not think about other forms or about the many people who have traced circles before you. If you kill yourself, you will not make it perfectly round; and in the discrepancy between perfect roundness and your closest approximation to it, you will find your personal expression. If you work in good faith you will try to make it perfect, but each of your circles, in spite of your improved dexterity in drawing them will always suffer from the same defect. Every one of them will bear your mark."

. . .

"What does it mean . . . for a painter to paint in the manner of So-and-So or to actually imitate someone else? What's wrong with that? On the contrary, it's a good idea. You should constantly try to paint like someone else. But the thing is, you can't! You would like to. You try. But it turns out to be a botch. . . .

"And it's at the very moment you make a botch of it that you're yourself.

. . .

"Freedom . . . one must be very careful with that. In painting as in everything else. Whatever you do, you find yourself once more in chains. Freedom not to do one thing requires that you do another, imperatively. And there you have it, chains. That reminds me of a story of Jarry about the anarchist soldiers at drill. They are told: right face. And immediately, since they are anarchists, they all face left . . . Painting is like that. You take freedom and you shut yourself up with your idea, just that particular one and no other. And there you are again, in chains."

[Realism and Pure Form]

"When you start with a portrait and search for a pure form, a clear volume, through successive eliminations, you arrive inevitably at the egg. Likewise, starting with the egg and following the same process in reverse, one finishes with the portrait. But art, I believe, escapes these simplistic exercises which consist in going from one extreme to the other. It's necessary to know when to stop."

 ## TOPICS FOR CRITICAL THINKING AND WRITING

1. Picasso says, in the first paragraph, "Art is a lie that makes us realize truth." Does this make sense? If you think it does, draw on your own experience either as a creator of art or as a consumer of art—for instance, as a reader of a novel, or a visitor to a museum, or a member of the audience at a concert—and clarify the point by giving at least two concrete examples.
2. In the third paragraph Picasso suggests that there is little or no point in trying to "understand art." Drawing on your experience, perhaps in a literature course, an art course, or a music course, consider whether an attempt to understand a work of art led to increased understanding and pleasure.
3. Take any one of Picasso's comments (other than the two just mentioned) and test it against your own experience.

 ## CAMILLE PAGLIA

Camille Paglia, born in Endicott, New York, in 1947, and educated at the State University of New York at Binghamton and at Yale University, teaches humanities at the University of the Arts, in Philadelphia. Paglia achieved fame in 1990 with the publication of a book entitled Sexual Personae, *a study of pornographic, voyeuristic, and sadistic elements in literature. She considers herself a feminist but she has sharply criticized many other feminists, and in turn she has been sharply criticized. As she said in the preface to* Sexual Personae, *"My stress on the truth in sexual stereotypes and on the biologic basis of*

sex difference is sure to cause controversy." We reprint an essay that was first published in the New York Times *in 1990 and was included in a collection of Paglia's essays,* Sex, Art, and American Culture.

Madonna: Animality and Artifice

Madonna, don't preach.

Defending her controversial new video, "Justify My Love," on *Nightline* last week, Madonna stumbled, rambled, and ended up seeming far less intelligent than she really is.

Madonna, 'fess up.

The video is pornographic. It's decadent. And it's fabulous. MTV was right to ban it, a corporate resolve long overdue. Parents cannot possibly control television, with its titanic omnipresence.

5   Prodded by correspondent Forrest Sawyer for evidence of her responsibility as an artist, Madonna hotly proclaimed her love of children, her social activism, and her condom endorsements. Wrong answer. As Baudelaire and Oscar Wilde knew, neither art nor the artist has a moral responsibility to liberal social causes.

"Justify My Love" is truly avant-garde, at a time when that word has lost its meaning in the flabby art world. It represents a sophisticated European sexuality of a kind we have not seen since the great foreign films of the 1950s and 1960s. But it does not belong on a mainstream music channel watched around the clock by children.

On *Nightline,* Madonna bizarrely called the video a "celebration of sex." She imagined happy educational scenes where curious children would ask their parents about the video. Oh, sure! Picture it: "Mommy, please tell me about the tired, tied-up man in the leather harness and the mean, bare-chested lady in the Nazi cap." Okay, dear, right after the milk and cookies.

Sawyer asked for Madonna's reaction to feminist charges that, in the neck manacle and floor-crawling of an earlier video, "Express Yourself," she condoned the "degradation" and "humiliation" of women. Madonna waffled: "But I chained myself! I'm in charge." Well, no. Madonna the producer may have chosen the chain, but Madonna the sexual persona in the video is alternately a cross-dressing dominatrix and a slave of male desire.

But who cares what the feminists say anyhow? They have been outrageously negative about Madonna from the start. In 1985, *Ms.* magazine pointedly feted quirky, cuddly singer Cyndi Lauper as its woman of the year. Great judgment: gimmicky Lauper went nowhere, while Madonna grew, flourished, metamorphosed, and became an international star of staggering dimensions. She is also a shrewd business tycoon, a modern new woman of all-around talent.

10   Madonna is the true feminist. She exposes the puritanism and suffocating ideology of American feminism, which is stuck in an adolescent whining mode. Madonna has taught young women to be fully female and sexual while still exercising control over their lives. She shows girls how to be attractive, sensual, energetic, ambitious, aggressive, and funny—all at the same time.

American feminism has a man problem. The beaming Betty Crockers, hangdog dowdies, and parochial prudes who call themselves feminists want men to be like women. They fear and despise the masculine. The academic feminists think their nerdy bookworm husbands are the ideal model of human manhood.

But Madonna loves real men. She sees the beauty of masculinity, in all its rough vigor and sweaty athletic perfection. She also admires the men who are actually like women: transsexuals and flamboyant drag queens, the heroes of the 1969 Stonewall rebellion, which started the gay liberation movement.

"Justify My Love" is an eerie, sultry tableau of jaded androgynous creatures, trapped in a decadent sexual underground. Its hypnotic images are drawn from such sadomasochistic films as Liliana Cavani's *The Night Porter* and Luchino Visconti's *The Damned.* It's the perverse and knowing world of the photographers Helmut Newton and Robert Mapplethorpe.

Contemporary American feminism, which began by rejecting Freud because of his alleged sexism, has shut itself off from his ideas of ambiguity, contradiction, conflict, ambivalence. Its simplistic psychology is illustrated by the new cliché of the date-rape furor: "'No' always means 'no.'" Will we ever graduate from the Girl Scouts? "No" has always been, and always will be, part of the dangerous, alluring courtship ritual of sex and seduction, observable even in the animal kingdom.

15   Madonna has a far profounder vision of sex than do the feminists. She sees both the animality and the artifice. Changing her costume style and hair color virtually every month, Madonna embodies the eternal values of beauty and pleasure. Feminism says, "No more masks." Madonna says we are nothing but masks.

Through her enormous impact on young women around the world, Madonna is the future of feminism.

[1990]

 TOPICS FOR CRITICAL THINKING AND WRITING

1. In paragraph 5 Paglia says that art and artists do not have "a moral responsibility to liberal social causes." In your opinion, do they have a responsibility to any kinds of causes? To anything at all? If so, why? If not, why not?

2. In paragraph 10 Paglia sums up what she takes to be Madonna's contribution. If you are familiar with Madonna's work, evaluate Paglia's appraisal.

3. As the headnote mentions, this essay originally appeared in the *New York Times.* Write a letter to the newspaper (250 words), expressing your approval or disapproval. Consider the essay as a whole, but call attention to certain passages that you find particularly offensive or particularly praiseworthy, and explain why.

 WILLA CATHER

Willa Cather (1873–1947), born in Virginia but brought up in Nebraska, is chiefly known as a writer of short stories and novels, but she also wrote essays and poems. We reprint a story of hers on page 875 and a poem on page 928.

Light on Adobe Walls

Every artist knows that there is no such thing as "freedom" in art. The first thing an artist does when he begins a new work is to lay down the barriers and limitations; he decides upon a certain composition, a certain key, a certain relation of creatures of objects to each other. He is never free, and the more splendid his imagination, the more intense his feeling, the farther he goes from general truth and general emotion. Nobody can paint the sun, or sunlight. He can only paint the tricks that shadows play with it, or what it does to forms. He cannot even paint those relations of light and shade—he can only paint some emotion they give him, some man-made arrangement of them that happens to give him personal delight—a conception of clouds over distant mesas (or over the towers of St. Sulpice) that makes one nerve in him thrill and tremble. At bottom all he can give you is the thrill of his own poor little nerve—the projection in paint of a fleeting pleasure in a certain combination of form and colour, as temporary and almost as physical as a taste on the tongue. This oft-repeated pleasure in a painter becomes of course a "style," a way of seeing and feeling things, a favourite mood. What could be more different than Leonardo's treatment of daylight, and Velasquez'? Light is pretty much the same in Italy and Spain—southern light. Each man painted what he got out of light—what it did to him.

No art can do anything at all with great natural forces or great elemental emotions. No poet can write of love, hate, jealousy. He can only touch these things as they affect the people in his drama and his story, and unless he is more interested in his own little story and his foolish little people than in the Preservation of the Indian or Sex or Tuberculosis, then he ought to be working in a laboratory or a bureau.

Art is a concrete and personal and rather childish thing after all—no matter what people do to graft it into science and make it sociological and psychological; it is no good at all unless it is let alone to be itself—a game of make-believe, or re-production, very exciting and delightful to people who have an ear for it or an eye for it. Art is too terribly human to be very "great," perhaps. Some very great artists have outgrown art, the men were bigger than the game. Tolstoi did, and Leonardo did. When I hear the last opuses, I think Beethoven did. Shakespeare died at fifty-three, but there is an awful veiled threat in *The Tempest* that he too felt he had outgrown his toys, was about to put them away and free that spirit of Comedy and Lyrical Poetry and all the rest he held captive—quit play-making and verse-making for ever and turn his attention—to what, he did not hint, but it was probably merely to enjoy with all his senses that Warwickshire country which he loved to weakness—with a warm physical appetite. But he died before he had tried to grow old, never became a bitter old man wrangling with abstractions or creeds. . . .

[undated manuscript]

☞ TOPICS FOR CRITICAL THINKING AND WRITING

1. Cather begins by saying that "every artist knows that there is no such thing as 'freedom' in art." Do you believe her? In any case, was this idea a surprise to you, or have you known it for a long time, and do you find

it obvious? Give an example that shows the truth of the idea, or that shows that the idea is unsound.

2. In her last paragraph Cather says that Shakespeare's *The Tempest* seems to indicate that he "felt he had outgrown his toys." If you have read the play—it is in this book—indicate whether you too find such a suggestion in the play. Explain.

Fiction

 ### NATHANIEL HAWTHORNE

Nathaniel Hawthorne (1804-64) was born in Salem, Massachusetts, the son of a sea captain. Two of his ancestors were judges; one had persecuted Quakers, another had served at the Salem witch trials. After graduating from Bowdoin College in Maine he went back to Salem in order to write in relative seclusion. In 1835 he published "Young Goodman Brown" and "The Maypole of Merry Mount"; and in 1844 he published "The Artist of the Beautiful."

From 1839 to 1841 Hawthorne worked in the Boston Customs House and then spent a few months as a member of a communal society, Brook Farm. In 1842 he married. From 1846 to 1849 he was a surveyor at the Salem Customs House; from 1849 to 1850 he wrote The Scarlet Letter, *the book that made him famous. From 1853 to 1857 he served as American consul in Liverpool, England, a plum awarded him in exchange for writing a campaign biography of a former college classmate, President Franklin Pierce. In 1860, after living in England and Italy, he returned to the United States, settling in Concord, Massachusetts.*

The Artist of the Beautiful

An elderly man, with his pretty daughter on his arm, was passing along the street, and emerged from the gloom of the cloudy evening into the light that fell across the pavement from the window of a small shop. It was a projecting window; and on the inside were suspended a variety of watches, pinchbeck,[1] silver, and one or two of gold, all with their faces turned from the streets, as if churlishly disinclined to inform the wayfarers what o'clock it was. Seated within the shop, sidelong to the window, with his pale face bent earnestly over some delicate piece of mechanism on which was thrown the concentrated lustre of a shade lamp, appeared a young man.

"What can Owen Warland be about?" muttered old Peter Hovenden, himself a retired watchmaker, and the former master of this same young man whose occupation he was now wondering at. "What can the fellow be about? These six months past I have never come by his shop without seeing him just as steadily at work as now. It would be a flight beyond his usual foolery to seek for the perpetual motion; and yet I know enough of my old business to be certain that what he is now so busy with is no part of the machinery of a watch."

[1] an alloy used to imitate gold

"Perhaps, father," said Annie, without showing much interest in the question, "Owen is inventing a new kind of timekeeper. I am sure he has ingenuity enough."

"Poh, child! He has not the sort of ingenuity to invent anything better than a Dutch toy," answered her father, who had formerly been put to much vexation by Owen Warland's irregular genius. "A plague on such ingenuity! All the effect that ever I knew of it was to spoil the accuracy of some of the best watches in my shop. He would turn the sun out of its orbit and derange the whole course of time, if, as I said before, his ingenuity could grasp anything bigger than a child's toy!"

5   "Hush, father! He hears you!" whispered Annie, pressing the old man's arm. "His ears are as delicate as his feelings; and you know how easily disturbed they are. Do let us move on."

So Peter Hovenden and his daughter Annie plodded on without further conversation, until in a by-street of the town they found themselves passing the open door of a blacksmith's shop. Within was seen the forge, now blazing up and illuminating the high and dusky roof, and now confining its lustre to a narrow precinct of the coal-strewn floor, according as the breath of the bellows was puffed forth or again inhaled into its vast leathern lungs. In the intervals of brightness it was easy to distinguish objects in remote corners of the shop and the horseshoes that hung upon the wall; in the momentary gloom the fire seemed to be glimmering amidst the vagueness of unenclosed space. Moving about in this red glare and alternate dusk was the figure of the blacksmith, well worthy to be viewed in so picturesque an aspect of light and shade, where the bright blaze struggled with the black night, as if each would have snatched his comely strength from the other. Anon he drew a white-hot bar of iron from the coals, laid it on the anvil, uplifted his arm of might, and was soon enveloped in the myriads of sparks which the strokes of his hammer scattered into the surrounding gloom.

"Now, that is a pleasant sight," said the old watchmaker. "I know what it is to work in gold; but give me the worker in iron after all is said and done. He spends his labor upon a reality. What say you, daughter Annie?"

"Pray don't speak so loud, father," whispered Annie, "Robert Danforth will hear you."

"And what if he should hear me?" said Peter Hovenden. "I say again, it is a good and a wholesome thing to depend upon main strength and reality, and to earn one's bread with the bare and brawny arm of a blacksmith. A watchmaker gets his brain puzzled by his wheels within a wheel, or loses his health or the nicety of his eyesight, as was my case, and finds himself at middle age, or a little after, past labor at his own trade and fit for nothing else, yet too poor to live at his ease. So I say once again, give me main strength for my money. And then, how it takes the nonsense out of a man! Did you ever hear of a blacksmith being such a fool as Owen Warland yonder?"

10   "Well said, uncle Hovenden!" shouted Robert Danforth from the forge, in a full, deep, merry voice, that made the roof reëcho. "And what says Miss Annie to that doctrine? She, I suppose, will think it a genteeler business to tinker up a lady's watch than to forge a horseshoe or make a gridiron."

Annie drew her father onward without giving him time for reply.

But we must return to Owen Warland's shop, and spend more meditation upon his history and character than either Peter Hovenden, or probably his daughter Annie, or Owen's old school-fellow, Robert Danforth, would have thought due to so slight a subject. From the time that his little fingers could grasp a penknife, Owen had been remarkable for a delicate ingenuity, which sometimes produced pretty shapes in wood, principally figures of flowers and birds, and sometimes seemed to aim at the hidden mysteries of mechanism. But it was always for purposes of grace, and never with any mockery of the useful. He did not, like the crowd of school-boy artisans, construct little windmills on the angle of a barn or watermills across the neighboring brook. Those who discovered such peculiarity in the boy as to think it worth their while to observe him closely, sometimes saw reason to suppose that he was attempting to imitate the beautiful movements of Nature as exemplified in the flight of birds or the activity of little animals. It seemed, in fact, a new development of the love of the beautiful, such as might have made him a poet, a painter, or a sculptor, and which was as completely refined from all utilitarian coarseness as it could have been in either of the fine arts. He looked with singular distaste at the stiff and regular processes of ordinary machinery. Being once carried to see a steam-engine, in the expectation that his intuitive comprehension of mechanical principles would be gratified, he turned pale and grew sick, as if something monstrous and unnatural had been presented to him. This horror was partly owing to the size and terrible energy of the iron laborer; for the character of Owen's mind was microscopic, and tended naturally to the minute, in accordance with his diminutive frame and the marvellous smallness and delicate power of his fingers. Not that his sense of beauty was thereby diminished into a sense of prettiness. The beautiful idea has no relation to size, and may be as perfectly developed in a space too minute for any but microscopic investigation as within the ample verge that is measured by the arc of the rainbow. But, at all events, this characteristic minuteness in his objects and accomplishments made the world even more incapable than it might otherwise have been of appreciating Owen Warland's genius. The boy's relatives saw nothing better to be done—as perhaps there was not—than to bind him apprentice to a watchmaker, hoping that his strange ingenuity might thus be regulated and put to utilitarian purposes.

Peter Hovenden's opinion of his apprentice has already been expressed. He could make nothing of the lad. Owen's apprehension of the professional mysteries, it is true, was inconceivably quick; but he altogether forgot or despised the grand object of a watchmaker's business, and cared no more for the measurement of time than if it had been merged into eternity. So long, however, as he remained under his old master's care, Owen's lack of sturdiness made it possible, by strict injunctions and sharp oversight, to restrain his creative eccentricity within bounds; but when his apprenticeship was served out, and he had taken the little shop which Peter Hovenden's failing eyesight compelled him to relinquish, then did people recognize how unfit a person was Owen Warland to lead old blind Father Time along his daily course. One of his most rational projects was to connect a musical operation with the machinery of his watches, so that all the harsh dissonances of life might be rendered tuneful, and each flitting moment fall into the abyss of the past in golden drops of harmony. If a family clock was intrusted to him for repair,—one of those tall, ancient clocks that have grown nearly allied to human nature by measuring out the lifetime of many generations,—he would take upon himself to arrange a dance or funeral procession of figures across its venerable face, representing twelve mirthful or melancholy hours. Several freaks of this kind quite destroyed the young watchmaker's credit with that steady and matter-of-fact class of people who hold the opinion that time is not to be trifled with, whether considered as the medium of advancement and prosperity in this world or preparation for the next. His custom rapidly diminished—a misfortune, however, that was probably reckoned among his better accidents by Owen Warland, who was becoming more and more absorbed in a secret occupation which drew all his science and manual dexterity into itself, and likewise gave full employment to the characteristic tendencies of his genius. This pursuit had already consumed many months.

After the old watchmaker and his pretty daughter had gazed at him out of the obscurity of the street, Owen Warland was seized with a fluttering of the nerves, which made his hand tremble too violently to proceed with such delicate labor as he was now engaged upon.

15   "It was Annie herself!" murmured he. "I should have known it, by this throbbing of my heart, before I heard her father's voice. Ah, how it throbs! I shall scarcely be able to work again on this exquisite mechanism to-night. Annie! dearest Annie! thou shouldst give firmness to my heart and hand, and not shake them thus; for if I strive to put the very spirit of beauty into form and give it motion, it is for thy sake alone. O throbbing heart, be quiet! If my labor be thus thwarted, there will come vague and unsatisfied dreams which will leave me spiritless to-morrow."

As he was endeavoring to settle himself again to his task, the shop door opened and gave admittance to no other than the stalwart figure which Peter Hovenden had paused to admire, as seen amid the light and shadow of the blacksmith's shop. Robert Danforth had brought a little anvil of his own manufacture, and peculiarly constructed, which the young artist had recently bespoken. Owen examined the article and pronounced it fashioned according to his wish.

"Why, yes," said Robert Danforth, his strong voice filling the shop as with the sound of a bass viol, "I consider myself equal to anything in the way of my own trade; though I should have made but a poor figure at yours with such a fist as this," added he, laughing, as he laid his vast hand beside the delicate one of Owen. "But what then? I put more main strength into one blow of my sledge hammer than all that you have expended since you were a 'prentice. Is not that the truth?"

"Very probably," answered the low and slender voice of Owen. "Strength is an earthly monster. I make no pretensions to it. My force, whatever there may be of it, is altogether spiritual."

"Well, but, Owen, what are you about?" asked his old school-fellow, still in such a hearty volume of tone that it made the artist shrink, especially as the question related to a subject so sacred as the absorbing dream of his imagination. "Folks do say that you are trying to discover the perpetual motion."

20   "The perpetual motion? Nonsense!" replied Owen Warland, with a movement of disgust; for he was full of little petulances. "It can never be discovered. It is a dream that may delude men whose brains are mystified with matter, but not me. Besides, if such a discovery were possible, it would not be worth my while to make it only to have the secret turned to such purposes as are now effected by steam and water power. I am not ambitious to be honored with the paternity of a new kind of cotton machine."

"That would be droll enough!" cried the blacksmith, breaking out into such an uproar of laughter that Owen himself and the bell glasses on his work-board quivered in unison. "No, no, Owen! No child of yours will have iron joints and sinews. Well, I won't hinder you any more. Good night, Owen, and success, and if you need any assistance, so far as a downright blow of hammer upon anvil will answer the purpose, I'm your man."

And with another laugh the man of main strength left the shop.

"How strange it is," whispered Owen Warland to himself, leaning his head upon his hand, "that all my musings, my purposes, my passion for the beautiful, my consciousness of power to create it,—a finer, more ethereal power, of which this earthly giant can have no conception,—all, all, look so vain and idle whenever my path is crossed by Robert Danforth! He would drive me mad were I to meet him often. His hard, brute force darkens and confuses the spiritual element within me; but I, too, will be strong in my own way. I will not yield to him."

He took from beneath a glass a piece of minute machinery, which he set in the condensed light of his lamp, and, looking intently at it through a magnifying glass, proceeded to operate with a delicate instrument of steel. In an instant, however, he fell back in his chair and clasped his hands, with a look of horror on his face that made its small features as impressive as those of a giant would have been.

25   "Heaven! What have I done?" exclaimed he. "The vapor, the influence of that brute force,—it has bewildered me and obscured my perception. I have made the very stroke—the fatal stroke—that I have dreaded from the first. It is all over—the toil of months, the object of my life. I am ruined!"

And there he sat, in strange despair, until his lamp flickered in the socket and left the Artist of the Beautiful in darkness.

Thus it is that ideas, which grow up within the imagination and appear so lovely to it and of a value beyond whatever men call valuable, are exposed to be shattered and annihilated by contact with the practical. It is requisite for the ideal artist to possess a force of character that seems hardly compatible with its delicacy; he must keep his faith in himself while the incredulous world assails him with its utter disbelief; he must stand up against mankind and be his own sole disciple, both as respects his genius and the objects to which it is directed.

For a time Owen Warland succumbed to this severe but inevitable test. He spent a few sluggish weeks with his head so continually resting in his hands that the towns-people had scarcely an opportunity to see his countenance. When at last it was again uplifted to the light of day, a cold, dull, nameless change was perceptible upon it. In the opinion of Peter Hovenden, however, and that order of sagacious understandings who think that life should be regulated, like clockwork, with leaden weights, the alteration was entirely for the better. Owen now, indeed, applied himself to business with dogged industry. It was marvellous to witness the obtuse gravity with which he would inspect the wheels of a great old silver watch; thereby delighting the owner, in whose fob it had been worn till he deemed it a portion of his own life, and was accordingly jealous of its treatment. In consequence of the good report thus acquired, Owen Warland was invited by the proper authorities to regulate the clock in the church steeple. He succeeded so admirably in this matter of public interest that the merchants gruffly acknowledged his merits on 'Change;[2] the nurse whispered his praises as she

---

[2]the Exchange, a place of business in a town or city

gave the potion in the sick-chamber; the lover blessed him at the hour of appointed interview; and the town in general thanked Owen for the punctual-
ity of dinner time. In a word, the heavy weight upon his spirits kept everything in order, not merely within his own system, but wheresoever the iron
accents of the church clock were audible. It was a circumstance, though
minute, yet characteristic of his present state, that, when employed to en-
grave names or initials on silver spoons, he now wrote the requisite letters
in the plainest possible style, omitting a variety of fanciful flourishes that had
heretofore distinguished his work in this kind.

One day, during the era of this happy transformation, old Peter Hovenden came to visit his former apprentice.

30   "Well, Owen," said he, "I am glad to hear such good accounts of you
from all quarters, and especially from the town clock yonder, which speaks
in your commendation every hour of the twenty-four. Only get rid altogether of your nonsensical trash about the beautiful, which I nor nobody
else, nor yourself to boot, could ever understand,—only free yourself of
that, and your success in life is as sure as daylight. Why, if you go on in this
way, I should even venture to let you doctor this precious old watch of
mine; though, except my daughter Annie, I have nothing else so valuable in
the world."

"I should hardly dare touch it, sir," replied Owen, in a depressed tone;
for he was weighed down by his old master's presence.

"In time," said the latter,—"In time, you will be capable of it."

The old watchmaker, with the freedom naturally consequent on his former authority, went on inspecting the work which Owen had in hand at the
moment, together with other matters that were in progress. The artist,
meanwhile, could scarcely lift his head. There was nothing so antipodal to
his nature as this man's cold, unimaginative sagacity, by contact with which
everything was converted into a dream except the densest matter of the
physical world. Owen groaned in spirit and prayed fervently to be delivered
from him.

"But what is this?" cried Peter Hovenden abruptly, taking up a dusty bell
glass, beneath which appeared a mechanical something, as delicate and
minute as the system of a butterfly's anatomy. "What have we here? Owen!
Owen! there is witchcraft in these little chains, and wheels, and paddles.
See! with one pinch of my finger and thumb I am going to deliver you from
all future peril."

35   "For Heaven's sake," screamed Owen Warland, springing up with wonderful energy, "as you would not drive me mad, do not touch it! The slightest pressure of your finger would ruin me forever."

"Aha, young man! And is it so?" said the old watchmaker, looking at him
with just enough penetration to torture Owen's soul with the bitterness of
worldly criticism. "Well, take your own course; but I warn you again that in
this small piece of mechanism lives your evil spirit. Shall I exorcise him?"

"You are my evil spirit," answered Owen, much excited,—"you and the
hard, coarse world! The leaden thoughts and the despondency that you fling
upon me are my clogs, else I should long ago have achieved the task that I
was created for."

Peter Hovenden shook his head, with the mixture of contempt and indignation which mankind, of whom he was partly a representative, deem
themselves entitled to feel towards all simpletons who seek other prizes

than the dusty one along the highway. He then took his leave, with an uplifted finger and a sneer upon his face that haunted the artist's dreams for many a night afterwards. At the time of his old master's visit, Owen was probably on the point of taking up the relinquished task; but, by this sinister event, he was thrown back into the state whence he had been slowly emerging.

But the innate tendency of his soul had only been accumulating fresh vigor during its apparent sluggishness. As the summer advanced he almost totally relinquished his business, and permitted Father Time, so far as the old gentleman was represented by the clocks and watches under his control, to stray at random through human life, making infinite confusion among the train of bewildered hours. He wasted the sunshine, as people said, in wandering through the woods and fields and along the banks of streams. There, like a child, he found amusement in chasing butterflies or watching the motions of water insects. There was something truly mysterious in the intentness with which he contemplated these living playthings as they sported on the breeze or examined the structure of an imperial insect whom he had imprisoned. The chase of butterflies was an apt emblem of the ideal pursuit in which he had spent so many golden hours; but would the beautiful idea ever be yielded to his hand like the butterfly that symbolized it? Sweet, doubtless, were these days, and congenial to the artist's soul. They were full of bright conceptions, which gleamed through his intellectual world as the butterflies gleamed through the outward atmosphere, and were real to him, for the instant, without the toil, and perplexity, and many disappointments of attempting to make them visible to the sensual eye. Alas that the artist, whether in poetry, or whatever other material, may not content himself with the inward enjoyment of the beautiful, but must chase the flitting mystery beyond the verge of his ethereal domain, and crush its frail being in seizing it with a material grasp. Owen Warland felt the impulse to give external reality to his ideas as irresistibly as any of the poets or painters who have arrayed the world in a dimmer and fainter beauty, imperfectly copied from the richness of their visions.

40   The night was now his time for the slow progress of re-creating the one idea to which all his intellectual activity referred itself. Always at the approach of dusk he stole into the town, locked himself within his shop, and wrought with patient delicacy of touch for many hours. Sometimes he was startled by the rap of the watchman, who, when all the world should be asleep, had caught the gleam of lamplight through the crevices of Owen Warland's shutters. Daylight, to the morbid sensibility of his mind, seemed to have an intrusiveness that interfered with his pursuits. On cloudy and inclement days, therefore, he sat with his head upon his hands, muffling, as it were, his sensitive brain in a mist of indefinite musings; for it was a relief to escape from the sharp distinctness with which he was compelled to shape out his thoughts during his nightly toil.

From one of these fits of torpor he was aroused by the entrance of Annie Hovenden, who came into the shop with the freedom of a customer, and also with something of the familiarity of a childish friend. She had worn a hole through her silver thimble, and wanted Owen to repair it.

"But I don't know whether you will condescend to such a task," said she, laughing, "now that you are so taken up with the notion of putting spirit into machinery."

"Where did you get that idea, Annie?" said Owen, starting in surprise.

"Oh, out of my own head," answered she, "and from something that I heard you say, long ago, when you were but a boy and I a little child. But come; will you mend this poor thimble of mine?"

45   "Anything for your sake, Annie," said Owen Warland,—"anything, even were it to work at Robert Danforth's forge."

"And that would be a pretty sight!" retorted Annie, glancing with imperceptible slightness at the artist's small and slender frame. "Well; here is the thimble."

"But that is a strange idea of yours," said Owen, "about the spiritualization of matter."

And then the thought stole into his mind that this young girl possessed the gift to comprehend him better than all the world besides. And what a help and strength would it be to him in his lonely toil if he could gain the sympathy of the only being whom he loved! To persons whose pursuits are insulated from the common business of life—who are either in advance of mankind or apart from it—there often comes a sensation of moral cold that makes the spirit shiver as if it had reached the frozen solitudes around the pole. What the prophet, the poet, the reformer, the criminal, or any other man with human yearnings, but separated from the multitude by a peculiar lot, might feel, poor Owen felt.

"Annie," cried he, growing pale as death at the thought, "how gladly would I tell you the secret of my pursuit! You, methinks, would estimate it rightly. You, I know, would hear it with a reverence that I must not expect from the harsh, material world."

50   "Would I not? to be sure I would!" replied Annie Hovenden, lightly laughing. "Come; explain to me quickly what is the meaning of this little whirligig, so delicately wrought that it might be a plaything for Queen Mab.[3] See! I will put it in motion."

"Hold!" exclaimed Owen, "hold!"

Annie had but given the slightest possible touch, with the point of a needle, to the same minute portion of complicated machinery which has been more than once mentioned, when the artist seized her by the wrist with a force that made her scream aloud. She was affrighted at the convulsion of intense rage and anguish that writhed across his features. The next instant he let his head sink upon his hands.

"Go, Annie," murmured he; "I have deceived myself, and must suffer for it. I yearned for sympathy, and thought, and fancied, and dreamed that you might give it me; but you lack the talisman, Annie, that should admit you into my secrets. That touch has undone the toil of months and the thought of a lifetime! It was not your fault, Annie; but you have ruined me!"

Poor Owen Warland! He had indeed erred, yet pardonably; for if any human spirit could have sufficiently reverenced the processes so sacred in his eyes, it must have been a woman's. Even Annie Hovenden, possibly, might not have disappointed him had she been enlightened by the deep intelligence of love.

55   The artist spent the ensuing winter in a way that satisfied any persons who had hitherto retained a hopeful opinion of him that he was, in truth, irrevocably doomed to unutility as regarded the world, and to an evil destiny

---

[3] a fairy, said in *Romeo and Juliet* to create people's dreams (1.4.53)

on his own part. The decease of a relative had put him in possession of a small inheritance. Thus freed from the necessity of toil, and having lost the steadfast influence of a great purpose,—great, at least, to him,—he abandoned himself to habits from which it might have been supposed the mere delicacy of his organization would have availed to secure him. But when the ethereal portion of a man of genius is obscured, the earthly part assumes an influence the more uncontrollable, because the character is now thrown off the balance to which Providence had so nicely adjusted it, and which, in coarser natures, is adjusted by some other method. Owen Warland made proof of whatever show of bliss may be found in riot. He looked at the world through the golden medium of wine, and contemplated the visions that bubble up so gayly around the brim of the glass, and that people the air with shapes of pleasant madness, which so soon grow ghostly and forlorn. Even when this dismal and inevitable change had taken place, the young man might still have continued to quaff the cup of enchantments, though its vapor did but shroud life in gloom and fill the gloom with spectres that mocked at him. There was a certain irksomeness of spirit, which, being real, and the deepest sensation of which the artist was now conscious, was more intolerable than any fantastic miseries and horrors that the abuse of wine could summon up. In the latter case he could remember, even out of the midst of his trouble, that all was but a delusion; in the former, the heavy anguish was his actual life.

From this perilous state he was redeemed by an incident which more than one person witnessed, but of which the shrewdest could not explain or conjecture the operation on Owen Warland's mind. It was very simple. On a warm afternoon of spring, as the artist sat among his riotous companions with a glass of wine before him, a splendid butterfly flew in at the open window and fluttered about his head.

"Ah," exclaimed Owen, who had drank freely, "are you alive again, child of the sun and playmate of the summer breeze, after your dismal winter's nap? Then it is time for me to be at work!"

And, leaving his unemptied glass upon the table, he departed and was never known to sip another drop of wine.

And now, again, he resumed his wanderings in the woods and fields. It might be fancied that the bright butterfly, which had come so spirit-like into the window as Owen sat with the rude revellers, was indeed a spirit commissioned to recall him to the pure, ideal life that had so etheralized him among men. It might be fancied that he went forth to seek this spirit in its sunny haunts; for still, as in the summer time gone by, he was seen to steal gently up wherever a butterfly had alighted, and lose himself in contemplation of it. When it took flight his eyes followed the winged vision, as if its airy track would show the path to heaven. But what could be the purpose of the unseasonable toil, which was again resumed, as the watchman knew by the lines of lamplight through the crevices of Owen Warland's shutters? The towns-people had one comprehensive explanation of all these singularities. Owen Warland had gone mad! How universally efficacious—how satisfactory, too, and soothing to the injured sensibility of narrowness and dulness—is this easy method of accounting for whatever lies beyond the world's most ordinary scope! From St. Paul's days down to our poor little Artist of the Beautiful, the same talisman had been applied to the elucidation of all mysteries in the words or deeds of men who spoke or acted too wisely or too well. In Owen Warland's case the judgment of his towns-people may have been correct. Perhaps he was mad. The lack of sympathy—that contrast between himself and his neighbors which took away the restraint of example—was enough to make him so. Or possibly he had caught just so much of ethereal radiance as served to bewilder him, in an earthly sense, by its intermixture with the common daylight.

60   One evening, when the artist had returned from a customary ramble and had just thrown the luster of his lamp on the delicate piece of work so often interrupted, but still taken up again, as if his fate were embodied in its mechanism, he was surprised by the entrance of old Peter Hovenden. Owen never met this man without a shrinking of the heart. Of all the world he was most terrible, by reason of a keen understanding which saw so distinctly what it did see, and disbelieved so uncompromisingly in what it could not see. On this occasion the old watchmaker had merely a gracious word or two to say.

"Owen, my lad," said he, "we must see you at my house to-morrow night."

The artist began to mutter some excuse.

"Oh, but it must be so," quoth Peter Hovenden, "for the sake of the days when you were one of the household. What, my boy! don't you know that my daughter Annie is engaged to Robert Danforth? We are making an entertainment, in our humble way, to celebrate the event."

"Ah!" said Owen.

65   That little monosyllable was all he uttered; its tone seemed cold and unconcerned to an ear like Peter Hovenden's; and yet there was in it the stifled outcry of the poor artist's heart, which he compressed within him like a man holding down an evil spirit. One slight outbreak, however, imperceptible to the old watchmaker, he allowed himself. Raising the instrument with which he was about to begin his work, he let it fall upon the little system of machinery that had, anew, cost him months of thought and toil. It was shattered by the stroke!

Owen Warland's story would have been no tolerable representation of the troubled life of those who strive to create the beautiful, if, amid all other thwarting influences, love had not interposed to steal the cunning from his hand. Outwardly he had been no ardent or enterprising lover; the career of his passion had confined its tumults and vicissitudes so entirely within the artist's imagination that Annie herself had scarcely more than a woman's intuitive perception of it; but, in Owen's view, it covered the whole field of his life. Forgetful of the time when she had shown herself incapable of any deep response, he had persisted in connecting all his dreams of artistical success with Annie's image; she was the visible shape in which the spiritual power that he worshipped, and on whose altar he hoped to lay a not unworthy offering, was made manifest to him. Of course he had deceived himself; there were no such attributes in Annie Hovenden as his imagination had endowed her with. She, in the aspect which she wore to his inward vision, was as much a creature of his own as the mysterious piece of mechanism would be were it ever realized. Had he become convinced of his mistake through the medium of successful love,—had he won Annie to his bosom, and there beheld her fade from angel into ordinary woman,—the disappointment might have driven him back, with concentrated energy, upon his sole remaining object. On the other hand, had he found Annie what he fancied, his lot would have been so rich in beauty that out of its mere redundancy he might have wrought the beautiful into many a worthier type than he had toiled for; but the guise in which his sorrow came to him, the sense that the angel of his life had been snatched away and given to a rude man of earth and iron, who could neither need nor appreciate her ministrations,—this was the very perversity of fate that makes human existence appear too absurd and contradictory to be the scene of one other hope or one other fear. There was nothing left for Owen Warland but to sit down like a man that had been stunned.

He went through a fit of illness. After his recovery his small and slender frame assumed an obtuser garniture of flesh than it had ever before worn. His thin cheeks became round; his delicate little hand, so spiritually fashioned to achieve fairy task-work, grew plumper than the hand of a thriving infant. His aspect had a childishness such as might have induced a stranger to pat him on the head—pausing, however, in the act, to wonder what manner of child was here. It was as if the spirit had gone out of him, leaving the body to flourish in a sort of vegetable existence. Not that Owen Warland was idiotic. He could talk, and not irrationally. Somewhat of a babbler, indeed, did people begin to think him; for he was apt to discourse at wearisome length of marvels of mechanism that he had read about in books, but which he had learned to consider as absolutely fabulous. Among them he enumerated the Man of Brass, constructed by Albertus Magnus, and the Brazen Head of Friar Bacon;[4] and, coming down to later times, the automata of a little coach and horses, which it was pretended had been manufactured for the Dauphin of France;[5] together with an insect that buzzed about the ear like a living fly, and yet was but a contrivance of minute steel springs. There was a story, too, of a duck that waddled, and quacked, and ate; though, had any honest citizen purchased it for dinner, he would have found himself cheated with the mere mechanical apparition of a duck.

"But all these accounts," said Owen Warland, "I am now satisfied are mere impositions."

Then, in a mysterious way, he would confess that he once thought differently. In his idle and dreamy days he had considered it possible, in a certain sense, to spiritualize machinery, and to combine with the new species of life and motion thus produced a beauty that should attain to the ideal which Nature has proposed to herself in all her creatures, but has never taken pains to realize. He seemed, however, to retain no very distinct perception either of the process of achieving this object or of the design itself.

70   "I have thrown it all aside now," he would say. "It was a dream such as young men are always mystifying themselves with. Now that I have acquired a little common sense, it makes me laugh to think of it."

Poor, poor and fallen Owen Warland! These were the symptoms that he had ceased to be an inhabitant of the better sphere that lies unseen around us. He had lost his faith in the invisible, and now prided himself, as such unfortunates invariably do, in the wisdom which rejected much that even his

[4]Albertus Magnus (1193?-1280) was a German philosopher, alchemist, and saint; Friar Roger Bacon was an English philosopher who was credited with magical powers, including the ability to make a head of brass that could speak   [5]the son of Louis XVI, also known as Louis XVII (1785-95)

eye could see, and trusted confidently in nothing but what his hand could touch. This is the calamity of men whose spiritual part dies out of them and leaves the grosser understanding to assimilate them more and more to the things of which alone it can take cognizance; but in Owen Warland the spirit was not dead nor passed away; it only slept.

How it awoke again is not recorded. Perhaps the torpid slumber was broken by a convulsive pain. Perhaps, as in a former instance, the butterfly came and hovered about his head and reinspired him,—as indeed this creature of the sunshine had always a mysterious mission for the artist,—reinspired him with the former purpose of his life. Whether it were pain or happiness that thrilled through his veins, his first impulse was to thank Heaven for rendering him again the being of thought, imagination, and keenest sensibility that he had long ceased to be.

"Now for my task," said he. "Never did I feel such strength for it as now."

Yet, strong as he felt himself, he was incited to toil the more diligently by an anxiety lest death should surprise him in the midst of his labors. This anxiety, perhaps, is common to all men who set their hearts upon anything so high, in their own view of it, that life becomes of importance only as conditional to its accomplishment. So long as we love life for itself, we seldom dread the losing it. When we desire life for the attainment of an object, we recognize the frailty of its texture. But, side by side with this sense of insecurity, there is a vital faith in our invulnerability to the shaft of death while engaged in any task that seems assigned by Providence as our proper thing to do, and which the world would have cause to mourn for should we leave it unaccomplished. Can the philosopher, big with the inspiration of an idea that is to reform mankind, believe that he is to be beckoned from this sensible existence at the very instant when he is mustering his breath to speak the word of light? Should he perish so, the weary ages may pass away—the world's, whose life sand may fall, drop by drop—before another intellect is prepared to develop the truth that might have been uttered then. But history affords many an example where the most precious spirit, at any particular epoch manifested in human shape, has gone hence untimely, without space allowed him, so far as mortal judgment could discern, to perform his mission on the earth. The prophet dies, and the man of torpid heart and sluggish brain lives on. The poet leaves his song half sung, or finishes it, beyond the scope of mortal ears, in a celestial choir. The painter—as Allston[6] did—leaves half his conception on the canvas to sadden us with its imperfect beauty, and goes to picture forth the whole, if it be no irreverence to say so, in the hues of heaven. But rather such incomplete designs of this life will be perfected nowhere. This so frequent abortion of man's dearest projects must be taken as a proof that the deeds of earth, however etherealized by piety or genius, are without value, except as exercises and manifestations of the spirit. In heaven, all ordinary thought is higher and more melodious than Milton's song. Then, would he add another verse to any strain that he had left unfinished here?

---

[6]Washington Allston (1779–1843), American painter whose picture Belshazzar's Feast was unfinished when he died

75   But to return to Owen Warland. It was his fortune, good or ill, to achieve the purpose of his life. Pass we over a long space of intense thought, yearning effort, minute toil, and wasting anxiety, succeeded by an instant of solitary triumph: let all this be imagined; and then behold the artist, on a winter evening, seeking admittance to Robert Danforth's fireside circle. There he found the man of iron, with his massive substance thoroughly warmed and attempered by domestic influences. And there was Annie, too, now transformed into a matron, with much of her husband's plain and sturdy nature, but imbued, as Owen Warland still believed, with a finer grace, that might enable her to be the interpreter between strength and beauty. It happened, likewise, that old Peter Hovenden was a guest this evening at his daughter's fireside, and it was his well-remembered expression of keen, cold criticism that first encountered the artist's glance.

"My old friend Owen!" cried Robert Danforth, starting up, and compressing the artist's delicate fingers within a hand that was accustomed to gripe bars of iron. "This is kind and neighborly to come to us at last. I was afraid your perpetual motion had bewitched you out of the remembrance of old times."

"We are glad to see you," said Annie, while a blush reddened her matronly cheek. "It was not like a friend to stay from us so long."

"Well, Owen," inquired the old watchmaker, as his first greeting, "how comes on the beautiful? Have you created it at last?"

The artist did not immediately reply, being startled by the apparition of a young child of strength that was tumbling about on the carpet,—a little personage who had come mysteriously out of the infinite, but with something so sturdy and real in his composition that he seemed moulded out of the densest substance which earth could supply. This hopeful infant crawled towards the new-comer, and setting himself on end, as Robert Danforth expressed the posture, stared at Owen with a look of such sagacious observation that the mother could not help exchanging a proud glance with her husband. But the artist was disturbed by the child's look, as imagining a resemblance between it and Peter Hovenden's habitual expression. He could have fancied that the old watchmaker was compressed into this baby shape, and looking out of those baby eyes, and repeating, as he now did, the malicious question:—

80   "The beautiful, Owen! How comes on the beautiful? Have you succeeded in creating the beautiful?"

"I have succeeded," replied the artist, with a momentary light of triumph in his eyes and a smile of sunshine, yet steeped in such depth of thought that it was almost sadness. "Yes, my friends, it is the truth. I have succeeded."

"Indeed!" cried Annie, a look of maiden mirthfulness peeping out of her face again. "And is it lawful, now, to inquire what the secret is?"

"Surely; it is to disclose it that I have come," answered Owen Warland. "You shall know, and see, and touch, and possess the secret! For, Annie,—if by that name I may still address the friend of my boyish years,—Annie, it is for your bridal gift that I have wrought this spiritualized mechanism, this harmony of motion, this mystery of beauty. It comes late, indeed; but it is as we go onward in life, when objects begin to lose their freshness of hue and our souls their delicacy of perception, that the spirit of beauty is most needed. If,—forgive me, Annie,—if you know how to value this gift, it can never come too late."

He produced, as he spoke, what seemed a jewel box. It was carved richly out of ebony by his own hand, and inlaid with a fanciful tracery of pearl, representing a boy in pursuit of a butterfly, which, elsewhere, had become a winged spirit, and was flying heavenward; while the boy, or youth, had found such efficacy in his strong desire that he ascended from earth to cloud, and from cloud to celestial atmosphere, to win the beautiful. This case of ebony the artist opened, and bade Annie place her fingers on its edge. She did so, but almost screamed as a butterfly fluttered forth, and, alighting on her finger's tip, sat waving the ample magnificence of its purple and gold-speckled wings, as if in prelude to a flight. It is impossible to express by words the glory, the splendor, the delicate gorgeousness which were softened into the beauty of this object. Nature's ideal butterfly was here realized in all its perfection; not in the pattern of such faded insects as flit among earthly flowers, but of those which hover across the meads of paradise for child-angels and the spirits of departed infants to disport themselves with. The rich down was visible upon its wings; the lustre of its eyes seemed instinct with spirit. The firelight glimmered around this wonder—the candles gleamed upon it; but it glistened apparently by its own radiance, and illuminated the finger and outstretched hand on which it rested with a white gleam like that of precious stones. In its perfect beauty, the consideration of size was entirely lost. Had its wings overreached the firmament, the mind could not have been more filled or satisfied.

85   "Beautiful! beautiful!" exclaimed Annie. "Is it alive? Is it alive?"

"Alive? To be sure it is," answered her husband. "Do you suppose any mortal has skill enough to make a butterfly, or would put himself to the trouble of making one, when any child may catch a score of them in a summer's afternoon? Alive? Certainly! But this pretty box is undoubtedly of our friend Owen's manufacture; and really it does him credit."

At this moment the butterfly waved its wings anew, with a motion so absolutely lifelike that Annie was startled, and even awestricken; for, in spite of her husband's opinion, she could not satisfy herself whether it was indeed a living creature or a piece of wondrous mechanism.

"Is it alive?" she repeated, more earnestly than before.

"Judge for yourself," said Owen Warland, who stood gazing in her face with fixed attention.

90   The butterfly now flung itself upon the air, fluttered round Annie's head, and soared into a distant region of the parlor, still making itself perceptible to sight by the starry gleam in which the motion of its wings enveloped it. The infant on the floor followed its course with his sagacious little eyes. After flying about the room, it returned in a spiral curve and settled again on Annie's finger.

"But is it alive?" exclaimed she again; and the finger on which the gorgeous mystery had alighted was so tremulous that the butterfly was forced to balance himself with his wings. "Tell me if it be alive, or whether you created it."

"Wherefore ask who created it, so it be beautiful?" replied Owen Warland. "Alive? Yes, Annie; it may well be said to possess life, for it has absorbed my own being into itself; and in the secret of that butterfly, and in its beauty,—which is not merely outward, but deep as its whole system,—is represented the intellect, the imagination, the sensibility, the soul of an Artist of the Beautiful! Yes; I created it. But"—and here his countenance somewhat changed—"this butterfly is not now to me what it was when I beheld it afar off in the daydreams of my youth."

"Be it what it may, it is a pretty plaything," said the blacksmith, grinning with childlike delight. "I wonder whether it would condescend to alight on such a great clumsy finger as mine? Hold it hither, Annie."

By the artist's direction, Annie touched her finger's tip to that of her husband; and, after a momentary delay, the butterfly fluttered from one to the other. It preluded a second flight by a similar, yet not precisely the same, waving of wings as in the first experiment; then, ascending from the blacksmith's stalwart finger, it rose in a gradually enlarging curve to the ceiling, made one wide sweep around the room, and returned with an undulating movement to the point whence it had started.

95   "Well, that does beat all nature!" cried Robert Danforth, bestowing the heartiest praise that he could find expression for; and, indeed, had he paused there, a man of finer words and nicer perception could not easily have said more. "That goes beyond me, I confess. But what then? There is more real use in one downright blow of my sledge hammer than in the whole five years' labor that our friend Owen has wasted on this butterfly."

Here the child clapped his hands and made a great babble of indistinct utterance, apparently demanding that the butterfly should be given him for a plaything.

Owen Warland, meanwhile, glanced sidelong at Annie, to discover whether she sympathized in her husband's estimate of the comparative value of the beautiful and the practical. There was, amid all her kindness towards himself, amid all the wonder and admiration with which she contemplated the marvellous work of his hands and incarnation of his idea, a secret scorn—too secret, perhaps, for her own consciousness, and perceptible only to such intuitive discernment as that of the artist. But Owen, in the latter stages of his pursuit, had risen out of the region in which such a discovery might have been torture. He knew that the world, and Annie as the representative of the world, whatever praise might be bestowed, could never say the fitting word nor feel the fitting sentiment which should be the perfect recompense of an artist who, symbolizing a lofty moral by a material trifle,—converting what was earthly to spiritual gold,—had won the beautiful into his handiwork. Not at this latest moment was he to learn that the reward of all high performance must be sought within itself, or sought in vain. There was, however, a view of the matter which Annie and her husband, and even Peter Hovenden, might fully have understood, and which would have satisfied them that the toil of years had here been worthily bestowed. Owen Warland might have told them that this butterfly, this plaything, this bridal gift of a poor watchmaker to a blacksmith's wife, was, in truth, a gem of art that a monarch would have purchased with honors and abundant wealth, and have treasured it among the jewels of his kingdom as the most unique and wondrous of them all. But the artist smiled and kept the secret to himself.

"Father," said Annie, thinking that a word of praise from the old watch-maker might gratify his former apprentice, "do come and admire this pretty butterfly."

"Let us see," said Peter Hovenden, rising from his chair, with a sneer upon his face that always made people doubt, as he himself did, in every-thing but a material existence. "Here is my finger for it to alight upon. I shall understand it better when once I have touched it."

100   But, to the increased astonishment of Annie, when the tip of her fa-ther's finger was pressed against that of her husband, on which the butterfly still rested, the insect drooped its wings and seemed on the point of falling to the floor. Even the bright spots of gold upon its wings and body, unless her eyes deceived her, grew dim, and the glowing purple took a dusky hue, and the starry lustre that gleamed around the blacksmith's hand became faint and vanished.

"It is dying! it is dying!" cried Annie, in alarm.

"It has been delicately wrought," said the artist, calmly. "As I told you, it has imbibed a spiritual essence—call it magnetism, or what you will. In an atmosphere of doubt and mockery its exquisite susceptibility suffers tor-ture, as does the soul of him who instilled his own life into it. It has already lost its beauty; in a few moments more its mechanism would be irreparably injured."

"Take away your hand, father!" entreated Annie, turning pale. "Here is my child; let it rest on his innocent hand. There, perhaps, its life will revive and its colors grow brighter than ever."

Her father, with an acrid smile, withdrew his finger. The butterfly then appeared to recover the power of voluntary motion, while its hues assumed much of their original lustre, and the gleam of starlight, which was its most ethereal attribute, again formed a halo round about it. At first, when trans-ferred from Robert Danforth's hand to the small finger of the child, this ra-diance grew so powerful that it positively threw the little fellow's shadow back against the wall. He, meanwhile, extended his plump hand as he had seen his father and mother do, and watched the waving of the insect's wings with infantine delight. Nevertheless, there was a certain odd expression of sagacity that made Owen Warland feel as if here were old Pete Hovenden, partially, and but partially, redeemed from his hard scepticism into childish faith.

105   "How wise the little monkey looks!" whispered Robert Danforth to his wife.

"I never saw such a look on a child's face," answered Annie, admiring her own infant, and with good reason, far more than the artistic butterfly. "The darling knows more of the mystery than we do."

As if the butterfly, like the artist, were conscious of something not en-tirely congenial in the child's nature, it alternately sparkled and grew dim. At length it arose from the small hand of the infant with an airy motion that seemed to bear it upward without an effort, as if the ethereal instincts with which its master's spirit had endowed it impelled this fair vision involuntar-ily to a higher sphere. Had there been no obstruction, it might have soared into the sky and grown immortal. But its lustre gleamed upon the ceiling; the exquisite texture of its wings brushed against that earthly medium; and a sparkle or two, as of stardust, floated downward and lay glimmering on the carpet. Then the butterfly came fluttering down, and, instead of returning to the infant, was apparently attracted towards the artist's hand.

"Not so! not so!" murmured Owen Warland, as if his handiwork could have understood him. "Thou has gone forth out of thy master's heart. There is no return for thee."

With a wavering movement, and emitting a tremulous radiance, the butterfly struggled, as it were, towards the infant, and was about to alight upon his finger; but while it still hovered in the air, the little child of strength, with his grandsire's sharp and shrewd expression in his face, made a snatch at the marvellous insect and compressed it in his hand. Annie screamed. Old Peter Hovenden burst into a cold and scornful laugh. The blacksmith, by main force, unclosed the infant's hand, and found within the palm a small heap of glittering fragments, whence the mystery of beauty had fled forever. And as for Owen Warland, he looked placidly at what seemed the ruin of his life's labor, and which was yet no ruin. He had caught a far other butterfly than this. When the artist rose high enough to achieve the beautiful, the symbol by which he made it perceptible to mortal senses became of little value in his eyes while his spirit possessed itself in the enjoyment of the reality.

[1844]

TOPICS FOR CRITICAL THINKING AND WRITING

1. What evidence, if any, supports the view that Hawthorne suggests that Owen, sublimating his sexual desires, turns to the idea as a refuge from his weaknesses?
2. Do you take Owen to be a sympathetic depiction of the dedicated artist, or do you think Hawthorne presents him ironically? Or both, or neither?
3. Near the end of the story we hear that Owen learned "that the reward of all high performance must be sought within itself, or sought in vain." Does this comment strike you as true? Explain.

WILLA CATHER

Willa Cather (1873–1947) was born in Gore, Virginia, but when she was nine her family moved to rural Nebraska. While an undergraduate at the University of Nebraska she published short stories and served as a drama critic for the Nebraska State Journal. *From 1895 to 1906 she lived in Pittsburgh, working first as a journalist and later as a teacher. In 1906 she went to New York to work for Mc-Clure's Magazine; in 1911 she left the magazine in order to devote all of her time to writing. Her most widely known works, novels, include* O Pioneers *(1913),* The Song of the Lark *(1915),* My Antonia *(1918),* A Lost Lady *(1923), and* Death Comes for the Archbishop *(1927).*

"A Wagner Matinée" was originally published in the March 1904 issue of Everybody's Magazine *and was revised for publication in a book of Cather's stories,* The Troll Garden *(1905). She revised it yet*

again when she republished it in another collection of her stories,
Youth and the Bright Medusa *(1920). We reprint the 1920 version.*

A Wagner Matinée

I received one morning a letter, written in pale ink on glassy, blue-lined note-paper, and bearing the postmark of a little Nebraska village. This communication, worn and rubbed, looking as if it had been carried for some days in a coat pocket that was none too clean, was from my uncle Howard, and informed me that his wife had been left a small legacy by a bachelor relative, and that it would be necessary for her to go to Boston to attend to the settling of the estate. He requested me to meet her at the station and render her whatever services might be necessary. On examining the date indicated as that of her arrival, I found it to be no later than tomorrow. He had characteristically delayed writing until, had I been away from home for a day, I must have missed my aunt altogether.

The name of my Aunt Georgiana opened before me a gulf of recollection so wide and deep that, as the letter dropped from my hand, I felt suddenly a stranger to all the present conditions of my existence, wholly ill at ease and out of place amid the familiar surroundings of my study. I became, in short, the gangling farmer-boy my aunt had known, scourged with chilblains and bashfulness, my hands cracked and sore from the corn husking. I sat again before her parlour organ, fumbling the scales with my stiff, red fingers, while she, beside me, made canvas mittens for the huskers.

The next morning, after preparing my landlady for a visitor, I set out for the station. When the train arrived I had some difficulty finding my aunt. She was the last of the passengers to alight, and it was not until I got her into the carriage that she seemed really to recognize me. She had come all the way in a day coach; her linen duster had become black with soot and her black bonnet grey with dust during her journey. When we arrived at my boarding-house the landlady put her to bed at once and I did not see her again until the next morning.

Whatever shock Mrs. Springer experienced at my aunt's appearance, she considerately concealed. As for myself, I saw my aunt's battered figure with that feeling of awe and respect with which we behold explorers who have left their ears and fingers north of Franz-Joseph-Land,[1] or their health somewhere along the Upper Congo. My Aunt Georgiana had been a music teacher at the Boston Conservatory, somewhere back in the latter sixties.[2] One summer, while visiting in the little village among the Green Mountains where her ancestors had dwelt for generations, she had kindled the callow fancy of my uncle, Howard Carpenter, then an idle, shiftless boy of twenty-one. When she returned to her duties in Boston, Howard followed her, and the upshot of this infatuation was that she eloped with him, eluding the reproaches of her family and the criticism of her friends by going with him to the Nebraska frontier. Carpenter, who, of course, had no money, took up a homestead in Red Willow County, fifty miles from the railroad. There they

[1] a group of islands in the Arctic Ocean   [2] 1860s; the story was originally published in 1904

had measured off their land themselves, driving across the prairie in a wagon, to the wheel of which they had tied a red cotton handkerchief, and counting its revolutions. They built a dug-out in the red hillside, one of those cave dwellings whose inmates so often reverted to primitive conditions. Their water they got from the lagoons where the buffalo drank, and their slender stock of provisions was always at the mercy of bands of roving Indians. For thirty years my aunt had not been farther than fifty miles from the homestead.

5   I owed to this woman most of the good that ever came my way in my boyhood, and had a reverential affection for her. During the years when I was riding herd for my uncle, my aunt, after cooking the three meals—the first of which was ready at six o'clock in the morning—and putting the six children to bed, would often stand until midnight at her ironing-board, with me at the kitchen table beside her, hearing me recite Latin declensions and conjugations, gently shaking me when my drowsy head sank down over a page of irregular verbs. It was to her, at her ironing or mending, that I read my first Shakespeare, and her old textbook on mythology was the first that ever came into my empty hands. She taught me my scales and exercises on the little parlour organ which her husband had bought her after fifteen years during which she had not so much as seen a musical instrument. She would sit beside me by the hour, darning and counting, while I struggled with the "Joyous Farmer." She seldom talked to me about music, and I understood why. Once when I had been doggedly beating out some easy passages from an old score of *Euryanthe*[3] I had found among her music books, she came up to me and putting her hands over my eyes, gently drew my head back upon her shoulder, saying tremulously, "Don't love it so well, Clark, or it may be taken from you."

When my aunt appeared on the morning after her arrival in Boston, she was still in a semi-somnambulant state. She seemed not to realize that she was in the city where she had spent her youth, the place longed for hungrily half a lifetime. She had been so wretchedly trainsick throughout the journey that she had no recollection of anything but her discomfort, and, to all intents and purposes, there were but a few hours of nightmare between the farm in Red Willow County and my study on Newbury Street. I had planned a little pleasure for her that afternoon, to repay her for some of the glorious moments she had given me when we used to milk together in the straw-thatched cowshed and she, because I was more than usually tired, or because her husband had spoken sharply to me, would tell me of the splendid performance of the *Huguenots*[4] she had seen in Paris, in her youth.

At two o'clock the Symphony Orchestra was to give a Wagner[5] program, and I intended to take my aunt; though, as I conversed with her, I grew doubtful about her enjoyment of it. I suggested our visiting the Conservatory and the Common before lunch, but she seemed altogether too timid to wish to venture out. She questioned me absently about various changes in the city, but she was chiefly concerned that she had forgotten to leave instructions about feeding half-skimmed milk to a certain weakling calf, "old Maggie's calf, you know, Clark," she explained, evidently having

[3]opera (1823) by Karl Maria von Weber   [4]opera (1836) by Giacomo Meyerbeer
[5]Richard Wagner (1813–83), German composer

forgotten how long I had been away. She was further troubled because she had neglected to tell her daughter about the freshly-opened kit of mackerel in the cellar, which would spoil if it were not used directly.

I asked her whether she had ever heard any of the Wagnerian operas, and found that she had not, though she was perfectly familiar with their respective situations, and had once possessed the piano score of *The Flying Dutchman*. I began to think it would be best to get her back to Red Willow County without waking her, and regretted having suggested the concert.

From the time we entered the concert hall, however, she was a trifle less passive and inert, and for the first time seemed to perceive her surroundings. I had felt some trepidation lest she might become aware of her queer, country clothes, or might experience some painful embarrassment at stepping suddenly into the world to which she had been dead for a quarter of a century. But, again, I found how superficially I had judged her. She sat looking about her with eyes as impersonal, almost as stony, as those with which the granite Rameses in a museum watches the froth and fret that ebbs and flows about his pedestal. I have seen this same aloofness in old miners who drift into the Brown hotel at Denver, their pockets full of bullion, their linen soiled, their haggard faces unshaven; standing in the thronged corridors as solitary as though they were still in a frozen camp on the Yukon.

10   The matinée audience was made up chiefly of women. One lost the contour of faces and figures, indeed any effect of line whatever, and there was only the colour of bodices past counting, the shimmer of fabrics soft and firm, silky and sheer; red, mauve, pink, blue, lilac, purple, écru, rose, yellow, cream, and white, all the colours that an impressionist finds in a sunlit landscape, with here and there the dead shadow of a frock coat. My Aunt Georgiana regarded them as though they had been so many daubs of tube-paint on a palette.

When the musicians came out and took their places, she gave a little stir of anticipation, and looked with quickening interest down over the rail at that invariable grouping, perhaps the first wholly familiar thing that had greeted her eye since she had left old Maggie and her weakling calf. I could feel how all those details sank into her soul, for I had not forgotten how they had sunk into mine when I came fresh from ploughing forever and forever between green aisles of corn, where, as in a treadmill, one might walk from daybreak to dusk without perceiving a shadow of change. The clean profiles of the musicians, the gloss of their linen, the dull black of their coats, the beloved shapes of the instruments, the patches of yellow light on the smooth, varnished bellies of the 'cellos and the bass viols in the rear, the restless, wind-tossed forest of fiddle necks and bows—I recalled how, in the first orchestra I ever heard, those long bow-strokes seemed to draw the heart out of me, as a conjurer's stick reels out yards of paper ribbon from a hat.

The first number was the *Tannhäuser* overture. When the horns drew out the first strain of the Pilgrim's chorus, Aunt Georgiana clutched my coat sleeve. Then it was I first realized that for her this broke a silence of thirty years. With the battle between the two motives, with the frenzy of the Venusberg theme and its ripping of strings, there came to me an overwhelming sense of the waste and wear we are so powerless to combat; and I saw again the tall, naked house on the prairie, black and grim as a wooden fortress; the black pond where I had learned to swim, its margin pitted with sun-dried cattle tracks; the rain-gullied clay banks about the naked house, the four dwarf-ash seedlings where the dish-cloths were always hung to dry before the kitchen door. The world there was the flat world of the ancients; to the east, a cornfield that stretched to daybreak; to the west, a corral that reached to sunset; between, the conquests of peace, dearer-bought than those of war.

The overture closed, my aunt released my coat sleeve, but she said nothing. She sat staring dully at the orchestra. What, I wondered, did she get from it? She had been a good pianist in her day, I knew, and her musical education had been broader than that of most music teachers of a quarter of a century ago. She had often told me of Mozart's operas and Meyerbeer's, and I could remember hearing her sing, years ago, certain melodies of Verdi. When I had fallen ill with a fever in her house she used to sit by my cot in the evening—when the cool, night wind blew in through the faded mosquito netting tacked over the window and I lay watching a certain bright star that burned red above the cornfield—and sing "Home to our mountains, O, let us return!"[6] in a way fit to break the heart of a Vermont boy near dead of homesickness already.

I watched her closely through the prelude to *Tristan and Isolde,* trying vainly to conjecture what that seething turmoil of strings and winds might mean to her, but she sat mutely staring at the violin bows that drove obliquely downward, like the pelting streaks of rain in a summer shower. Had this music any message for her? Had she enough left to at all comprehend this power which had kindled the world since she had left it? I was in a fever of curiosity, but Aunt Georgiana sat silent upon her peak in Darien.[7] She preserved this utter immobility throughout the number from *The Flying Dutchman,* though her fingers worked mechanically upon her black dress, as if, of themselves, they were recalling the piano score they had once played. Poor hands! They had been stretched and twisted into mere tentacles to hold and lift and knead with;—on one of them a thin, worn band that had once been a wedding ring. As I pressed and gently quieted one of those groping hands, I remembered with quivering eyelids their services for me in other days.

15   Soon after the tenor began the "Prize Song,"[8] I heard a quick drawn breath and turned to my aunt. Her eyes were closed, but the tears were glistening on her cheeks, and I think, in a moment more, they were in my eyes as well. It never really died, then—the soul which can suffer so excruciatingly and so interminably; it withers to the outward eye only; like that strange moss which can lie on a dusty shelf half a century and yet, if placed in water, grows green again. She wept so throughout the development and elaboration of the melody.

During the intermission before the second half, I questioned my aunt and found that the "Prize Song" was not new to her. Some years before there had drifted to the farm in Red Willow County a young German, a tramp cow-puncher, who had sung in the chorus at Bayreuth[9] when he was a boy, along with the other peasant boys and girls. Of a Sunday morning he used to sit on his gingham-sheeted bed in the hands' bedroom which opened off the kitchen, cleaning the leather of his boots and saddle, singing

[6]popular song derived from Giuseppe Verdi's *Il Trovatore*   [7]a line from John Keats's "On First Looking into Chapman's Homer"   [8]the courtship song that concludes Wagner's *Die Meistersinger*   [9]a city in Germany, site of an annual Wagner festival

the "Prize Song," while my aunt went about her work in the kitchen. She had hovered over him until she had prevailed upon him to join the country church, though his sole fitness for this step, in so far as I could gather, lay in his boyish face and his possession of this divine melody. Shortly afterward, he had gone to town on the Fourth of July, been drunk for several days, lost his money at a faro table, ridden a saddled Texas steer on a bet, and disappeared with a fractured collar-bone. All this my aunt told me huskily, wanderingly, as though she were talking in the weak lapses of illness.

"Well, we have come to better things than the old *Trovatore* at any rate, Aunt Georgie?" I queried, with a well-meant effort at jocularity.

Her lip quivered and she hastily put her handkerchief up to her mouth. From behind it she murmured, "And you have been hearing this ever since you left me, Clark?" Her question was the gentlest and saddest of reproaches.

The second half of the program consisted of four numbers from the *Ring,* and closed with Siegfried's funeral march. My aunt wept quietly, but almost continuously, as a shallow vessel overflows in a rain-storm. From time to time her dim eyes looked up at the lights, burning softly under their dull glass globes.

20   The deluge of sound poured on and on; I never knew what she found in the shining current of it; I never knew how far it bore her, or past what happy islands.[10] From the trembling of her face I could well believe that before the last number she had been carried out where the myriad graves are, into the grey, nameless burying grounds of the sea; or into some world of death vaster yet, where, from the beginning of the world, hope has lain down with hope and dream with dream and, renouncing, slept.

The concert was over; the people filed out of the hall chattering and laughing, glad to relax and find the living level again, but my kinswoman made no effort to rise. The harpist slipped the green felt cover over his instrument; the flute-players shook the water from their mouthpieces; the men of the orchestra went out one by one, leaving the stage to the chairs and music stands, empty as a winter cornfield.

I spoke to my aunt. She burst into tears and sobbed pleadingly. "I don't want to go, Clark, I don't want to go!"

I understood. For her, just outside the concert hall, lay the black pond with the cattle-tracked bluffs; the tall, unpainted house, with weather-curled boards, naked as a tower; the crook-backed ash seedlings where the dish-cloths hung to dry; the gaunt, moulting turkeys picking up refuse about the kitchen door.

[1904, 1920]

⌧ TOPICS FOR CRITICAL THINKING AND WRITING

1. Look at the third-from-the-last paragraph in the story. When Cather first published "A Wagner Matinée," after the first sentence of this paragraph ("The concert . . . no effort to rise") she went directly to what now begins the next paragraph, "I spoke to my aunt." Do you think the

[10] the Islands of the Blessed, where (according to Greek mythology) noble souls dwell forever

addition in the version we print ("The harpist slipped . . . a winter cornfield") is an improvement or a mistake? Why?

2. How would you characterize Clark? Do you think that he changes during the story? Or, as we go from page to page, do we just get to know
him better?

3. In the middle of the story, before Clark and his aunt attend the concert,
Clark says that he "began to think it would be best to get her back to
Red Willow County without waking her." Does he make a mistake in
taking her to the concert? Explain.

4. Here is a longish quotation from the French anthropologist, Claude
Lévi-Strauss, *The Raw and the Cooked:*

> The musical emotion springs precisely from the fact that at each mo-
> ment the composer withholds or adds more or less than the listener an-
> ticipates on the basis of a pattern that he thinks he can guess, but that
> he is incapable of wholly divining. . . . If the composer withholds more
> than we anticipate, we experience a delicious falling sensation; we feel
> we have been torn from a stable point on the musical ladder and thrust
> into the void. . . . When the composer withholds less, the opposite
> occurs; he forces us to perform gymnastic exercises more skillful than
> our own.

Test this statement against some piece of music that you are deeply attached to, and in about 250 words report your findings.

5. Has any work of art—for instance a song, play, painting, or dance—
deeply moved you? If so, in an essay of about 500 words describe your
emotions during and immediately after the experience. Feel free to extend "art" to include, if you wish, such exhibitions of skill as circus or
rodeo acts and athletic contests.

 KURT VONNEGUT, JR.

*Kurt Vonnegut, Jr., born in Indianapolis in 1922, is the author of sto-
ries, novels, essays, and plays. Among his most widely known novels
are* Cat's Cradle *(1963),* Slaughterhouse Five *(1969), and* Breakfast of
Champions *(1973).*

Who Am I This Time?

The North Crawford Mask and Wig Club, an amateur theatrical society I belong to, voted to do Tennessee Williams's *A Streetcar Named Desire* for the
spring play. Doris Sawyer, who always directs, said she couldn't direct this
time because her mother was so sick. And she said the club ought to develop some other directors anyway, because she couldn't live forever, even
though she'd made it safely to seventy-four.

So I got stuck with the directing job, even though the only thing I'd
ever directed before was the installation of combination aluminum storm
windows and screens I'd sold. That's what I am, a salesman of storm windows and doors, and here and there a bathtub enclosure. As far as acting
goes, the highest rank I ever held on stage was either butler or policeman,
whichever's higher.

I made a lot of conditions before I took the directing job, and the biggest one was that Harry Nash, the only real actor the club has, had to take the Marlon Brando part in the play. To give you an idea of how versatile Harry is, inside of one year he was Captain Queeg in *The Caine Mutiny Court Martial,* then Abe Lincoln in *Abe Lincoln in Illinois* and then the young architect in *The Moon Is Blue.* The year after that, Harry Nash was Henry the Eighth in *Anne of the Thousand Days* and Doc in *Come Back Little Sheba,* and I was after him for Marlon Brando in *A Streetcar Named Desire.* Harry wasn't at the meeting to say whether he'd take the part or not. He never came to meetings. He was too shy. He didn't stay away from meetings because he had something else to do. He wasn't married, didn't go out with women—didn't have any close men friends either. He stayed away from all kinds of gatherings because he never could think of anything to say or do without a script.

So I had to go down to Miller's Hardware Store, where Harry was a clerk, the next day and ask him if he'd take the part. I stopped off at the telephone company to complain about a bill I'd gotten for a call to Honolulu, I'd never called Honolulu in my life.

5   And there was this beautiful girl I'd never seen before behind the counter at the phone company, and she explained that the company had put in an automatic billing machine and that the machine didn't have all the bugs out of it yet. It made mistakes. "Not only did I not call Honolulu," I told her, "I don't think anybody in North Crawford ever has or will."

So she took the charge off the bill, and I asked her if she was from around North Crawford. She said no. She said she just came with the new billing machine to teach local girls how to take care of it. After that, she said, she would go with some other machine to someplace else. "Well," I said, "as long as people have to come along with the machines, I guess we're all right."

"What?" she said.

"When machines start delivering themselves," I said, "I guess that's when the people better start really worrying."

"Oh," she said. She didn't seem very interested in that subject, and I wondered if she was interested in anything. She seemed kind of numb, almost a machine herself, an automatic phone-company politeness machine.

10   "How long will you be in town here?" I asked her.

"I stay in each town eight weeks, sir," she said. She had pretty blue eyes, but there sure wasn't much hope or curiosity in them. She told me she had been going from town to town like that for two years, always a stranger.

And I got it in my head that she might make a good Stella for the play. Stella was the wife of the Marlon Brando character, the wife of the character I wanted Harry Nash to play. So I told her where and when we were going to hold tryouts, and said the club would be very happy if she'd come.

She looked surprised, and she warmed up a little. "You know," she said, "that's the first time anybody ever asked me to participate in any community thing."

"Well," I said, "there isn't any other way to get to know a lot of nice people faster than to be in a play with 'em."

15   She said her name was Helene Shaw. She said she might just surprise me—and herself. She said she just might come.

You would think that North Crawford would be fed up with Harry Nash in plays after all the plays he'd been in. But the fact was that North Crawford probably could have gone on enjoying Harry forever, because he was never Harry on stage. When the maroon curtain went up on the stage in the gymnasium of the Consolidated Junior-Senior High School, Harry, body and soul, was exactly what the script and the director told him to be.

Somebody said one time that Harry ought to go to a psychiatrist so he could be something important and colorful in real life, too—so he could get married anyway, and maybe get a better job than just clerking in Miller's Hardware Store for fifty dollars a week. But I don't know what a psychiatrist could have turned up about him that the town didn't already know. The trouble with Harry was he'd been left on the door-step of the Unitarian Church when he was a baby, and he never did find out who his parents were.

When I told him there in Miller's that I'd been appointed director, that I wanted him in my play, he said what he always said to anybody who asked him to be in a play—and it was kind of sad, if you think about it.

"Who am I this time?" he said.

20   So I held the tryouts where they're always held—in the meeting room on the second floor of the North Crawford Public Library. Doris Sawyer, the woman who usually directs, came to give me the benefit of all her experience. The two of us sat in state upstairs, while the people who wanted parts waited below. We called them upstairs one by one.

Harry Nash came to the tryouts, even though it was a waste of time. I guess he wanted to get that little bit more acting in.

For Harry's pleasure, and our pleasure, too, we had him read from the scene where he beats up his wife. It was a play in itself, the way Harry did it, and Tennessee Williams hadn't written it all either. Tennessee Williams didn't write the part, for instance, where Harry, who weighs about one hundred forty-five, who's about five feet eight inches tall, added fifty pounds to his weight and four inches to his height by just picking up a playbook. He had a short little double-breasted bellows-back grade-school graduation suit coat on and a dinky little red tie with a horsehead on it. He took off the coat and tie, opened his collar, then turned his back to Doris and me, getting up steam for the part. There was a great big rip in the back of his shirt, and it looked like a fairly new shirt too. He'd ripped it on purpose, so he could be that much more like Marlon Brando, right from the first.

When he faced us again, he was huge and handsome and conceited and cruel. Doris read the part of Stella, the wife, and Harry bullied that old, old lady into believing that she was a sweet, pregnant girl married to a sexy gorilla who was going to beat her brains out. She had me believing it too. And I read the lines of Blanche, her sister in the play, and darned if Harry didn't scare me into feeling like a drunk and faded Southern belle.

And then, while Doris and I were getting over our emotional experiences, like people coming out from under ether, Harry put down the playbook, put on his coat and tie, and turned into the pale hardware-store clerk again.

25   "Was—was that all right?" he said, and he seemed pretty sure he wouldn't get the part.

"Well," I said, "for a first reading, that wasn't too bad."

"Is there a chance I'll get the part?" he said. I don't know why he always had to pretend there was some doubt about his getting a part, but he did.

"I think we can safely say we're leaning powerfully in your direction," I told him.

He was very pleased. "Thanks! Thanks a lot!" he said, and he shook my hand.

30   "Is there a pretty new girl downstairs?" I said, meaning Helene Shaw.

"I didn't notice," said Harry.

It turned out that Helene Shaw *had* come for the tryouts, and Doris and I had our hearts broken. We thought the North Crawford Mask and Wig Club was finally going to put a really good-looking, really young girl on stage, instead of one of the beat-up forty-year-old women we generally have to palm off as girls.

But Helene Shaw couldn't act for sour apples. No matter what we gave her to read, she was the same girl with the same smile for anybody who had a complaint about his phone bill.

Doris tried to coach her some, to make her understand that Stella in the play was a very passionate girl who loved a gorilla because she needed a gorilla. But Helene just read the lines the same way again. I don't think a volcano could have stirred her up enough to say, "Oo."

35   "Dear," said Doris, "I'm going to ask you a personal question."

"All right," said Helene.

"Have you ever been in love?" said Doris. "The reason I ask," she said, "remembering some old love might help you put more warmth in your acting."

Helene frowned and thought hard. "Well," she said, "I travel a lot, you know. And practically all the men in the different companies I visit are married and I never stay anyplace long enough to know many people who aren't."

"What about school?" said Doris. "What about puppy love and all the other kinds of love in school?"

40   So Helene thought hard about that, and then she said, "Even in school I was always moving around a lot. My father was a construction worker, following jobs around, so I was always saying hello or good-by to someplace, without anything in between."

"Um," said Doris.

"Would movie stars count?" said Helene. "I don't mean in real life. I never knew any. I just mean up on the screen."

Doris looked at me and rolled her eyes. "I guess that's love of a kind," she said.

And then Helene got a little enthusiastic. "I used to sit through movies over and over again," she said, "and pretend I was married to whoever the man movie star was. They were the only people who came with us. No matter where we moved, movie stars were there."

45   "Uh huh," said Doris.

"Well, thank you, Miss Shaw," I said. "You go downstairs and wait with the rest. We'll let you know."

So we tried to find another Stella. And there just wasn't one, not one woman in the club with the dew still on her. "All we've got are Blanches," I said, meaning all we had were faded women who could play the part of Blanche, Stella's faded sister. "That's life, I guess—twenty Blanches to one Stella."

"And when you find a Stella," said Doris, "it turns out she doesn't know what love is."

Doris and I decided there was one last thing we could try. We could get Harry Nash to play a scene along with Helene. "He just might make her bubble the least little bit," I said.

50   "That girl hasn't got a bubble in her," said Doris.

So we called down the stairs for Helene to come back on up, and we told somebody to go find Harry. Harry never sat with the rest of the people at tryouts—or at rehearsals either. The minute he didn't have a part to play, he'd disappear into some hiding place where he could hear people call him, but where he couldn't be seen. At tryouts in the library he generally hid in the reference room, passing the time looking at flags of different countries in the front of the dictionary.

Helene came back upstairs, and we were very sorry and surprised to see that she'd been crying.

"Oh, dear," said Doris. "Oh, my—now what on earth's the trouble, dear?"

"I was terrible, wasn't I?" said Helene, hanging her head.

55   Doris said the only thing anybody can say in an amateur theatrical society when somebody cries. She said, "Why, no dear—you were marvelous."

"No, I wasn't," said Helene. "I'm a walking icebox, and I know it."

"Nobody could look at you and say that," said Doris.

"When they get to know me, they can say it," said Helene. "When people get to know me, that's what they *do* say." Her tears got worse. "I don't want to be the way I am," she said. "I just can't help it, living the way I've lived all my life. The only experiences I've had have been in crazy dreams of movie stars. When I meet somebody nice in real life, I feel as though I were in some kind of big bottle, as though I couldn't touch that person, no matter how hard I tried." And Helene pushed on air as though it were a big bottle all around her.

"You ask me if I've ever been in love," she said to Doris. "No—but I want to be. I know what this play's about. I know what Stella's supposed to feel and why she feels it. I—I—I—" she said, and her tears wouldn't let her go on.

60   "You what, dear?" said Doris gently.

"I—" said Helene, and she pushed on the imaginary bottle again. "I just don't know how to begin," she said.

There was heavy clumping on the library stairs. It sounded like a deep-sea diver coming upstairs in his lead shoes. It was Harry Nash, turning himself into Marlon Brando. In he came, practically dragging his knuckles on the floor. And he was so much in character that the sight of a weeping woman made him sneer.

"Harry," I said, "I'd like you to meet Helene Shaw. Helene—this is Harry Nash. If you get the part of Stella, he'll be your husband in the play." Harry didn't offer to shake hands. He put his hands in his pockets, and he hunched over, and he looked her up and down, gave her looks that left her naked. Her tears stopped right then and there.

"I wonder if you two would play the fight scene," I said, "and then the reunion scene right after it."

65   "Sure," said Harry, his eyes still on her. Those eyes burned up clothes faster than she could put them on. "Sure," he said, "if Stell's game."

"What?" said Helene. She'd turned the color of cranberry juice.

"Stell—Stella," said Harry. "That's you. Stell's my wife."

I handed the two of them playbooks. Harry snatched his from me without a word of thanks. Helene's hands weren't working very well, and I had to kind of mold them around the book.

"I'll want something I can throw," said Harry.

70   "What?" I said.

"There's one place where I throw a radio out a window," said Harry. "What can I throw?"

So I said an iron paperweight was the radio, and I opened the window wide. Helene Shaw looked scared to death.

"Where you want us to start?" said Harry, and he rolled his shoulders like a prizefighter warming up.

"Start a few lines back from where you throw the radio out the window," I said.

75   "O.K., O.K.," said Harry, warming up, warming up. He scanned the stage directions. "Let's see," he said, "after I throw the radio, she runs off stage, and I chase her, and I sock her one."

"Right," I said.

"O.K., baby," Harry said to Helene, his eyelids drooping. What was about to happen was wilder than the chariot race in *Ben Hur*. "On your mark," said Harry. "Get ready, baby. Go!"

When the scene was over, Helene Shaw was as hot as a hod carrier, as limp as an eel. She sat down with her mouth open and her head hanging to one side. She wasn't in any bottle any more. There wasn't any bottle to hold her up and keep her safe and clean. The bottle was gone.

"Do I get the part or don't I?" Harry snarled at me.

80   "You'll do," I said.

"You said a mouthful!" he said. "I'll be going now. . . . See you around, Stella," he said to Helene, and he left. He slammed the door behind him.

"Helene?" I said. "Miss Shaw?"

"Mf?" she said.

"The part of Stella is yours," I said. "You were great!"

85   "I was?" she said.

"I had no idea you had that much fire in you, dear," Doris said to her.

"Fire?" said Helene. She didn't know if she was afoot or on horseback.

"Skyrockets! Pinwheels! Roman candles!" said Doris.

"Mf," said Helene. And that was all she said. She looked as though she were going to sit in the chair with her mouth open forever.

90   "Stella," I said.

"Huh?" she said.

"You have my permission to go."

So we started having rehearsals four nights a week on the stage of the Consolidated School. And Harry and Helene set such a pace that everybody in the production was half crazy with excitement and exhaustion before we'd rehearsed four times. Usually a director has to beg people to learn their lines, but I had no such trouble. Harry and Helene were working so well together that everybody else in the cast regarded it as a duty and an honor and a pleasure to support them.

I was certainly lucky—or thought I was. Things were going so well, so hot and heavy, so early in the game that I had to say to Harry and Helene after one love scene, "Hold a little something back for the actual performance, would you please? You'll burn yourselves out."

95   I said that at the fourth or fifth rehearsal, and Lydia Miller, who was playing Blanche, the faded sister, was sitting next to me in the audience. In real life, she's the wife of Verne Miller. Verne owns Miller's Hardware Store. Verne was Harry's boss.

"Lydia," I said to her, "have we got a play or have we got a play?"

"Yes," she said, "you've got a play, all right." She made it sound as though I'd committed some kind of crime, done something just terrible. "You should be very proud of yourself."

"What do you mean by that?" I said.

Before Lydia could answer, Harry yelled at me from the stage, asked if I was through with him, asked if he could go home. I told him he could and, still Marlon Brando, he left, kicking furniture out of his way and slamming doors. Helene was left all alone on the stage, sitting on a couch with the same gaga look she'd had after the tryouts. That girl was drained.

100   I turned to Lydia again and I said, "Well—until now, I thought I had every reason to be happy and proud. Is there something going on I don't know about?"

"Do you know that girl's in love with Harry?" said Lydia.

"In the play?" I said.

"What play?" said Lydia. "There isn't any play going on now, and look at her up there." She gave a sad cackle. "You aren't directing this play."

"Who is?" I said.

105   "Mother Nature at her worst," said Lydia. "And think what it's going to do to that girl when she discovers what Harry really is." She corrected herself. "What Harry really isn't," she said.

I didn't do anything about it, because I didn't figure it was any of my business. I heard Lydia try to do something about it, but she didn't get very far.

"You know," Lydia said to Helene one night, "I once played Ann Rutledge, and Harry was Abraham Lincoln."

Helene clapped her hands. "That must have been heaven!" she said.

"It was, in a way," said Lydia. "Sometimes I'd get so worked up, I'd love Harry the way I'd love Abraham Lincoln. I'd have to come back to earth and remind myself that he wasn't ever going to free the slaves, that he was just a clerk in my husband's hardware store."

110   "He's the most marvelous man I ever met," said Helene.

"Of course, one thing you have to get set for, when you're in a play with Harry," said Lydia, "is what happens after the last performance."

"What are you talking about?" said Helene.

"Once the show's over," said Lydia, "whatever you thought Harry was just evaporates into thin air."

"I don't believe it," said Helene.

115   "I admit it's hard to believe," said Lydia.

Then Helene got a little sore. "Anyway, why tell me about it?" she said. "Even if it is true, what do I care?"

"I—I don't know," said Lydia, backing away. "I—I just thought you might find it interesting."

"Well, I don't," said Helene.

And Lydia slunk away, feeling about as frowzy and unloved as she was supposed to feel in the play. After that nobody said anything more to Helene to warn her about Harry, not even when word got around that she'd told the telephone company that she didn't want to be moved around anymore, that she wanted to stay in North Crawford.

120   So the time finally came to put on the play. We ran it for three nights—Thursday, Friday, and Saturday—and we murdered those audiences. They believed every word that was said on stage, and when the maroon curtain came down they were ready to go to the nut house along with Blanche, the faded sister.

On Thursday night the other girls at the telephone company sent Helene a dozen red roses. When Helene and Harry were taking a curtain call together, I passed the roses over the footlights to her. She came forward for them, took one rose from the bouquet to give to Harry. But when she turned to give Harry the rose in front of everybody, Harry was gone. The curtain came down on that extra little scene—that girl offering a rose to nothing and nobody.

I went backstage, and I found her still holding that one rose. She'd put the rest of the bouquet aside. There were tears in her eyes. "What did I do wrong?" she said to me. "Did I insult him some way?"

"No," I said. "He always does that after a performance. The minute it's over, he clears out as fast as he can."

"And tomorrow he'll disappear again?"

125   "Without even taking off his makeup."

"And Saturday?" she said. "He'll stay for the cast party on Saturday, won't he?"

"Harry never goes to parties," I said. "When the curtain comes down on Saturday, that's the last anybody will see of him till he goes to work on Monday."

"How sad," she said.

Helene's performance on Friday night wasn't nearly so good as Thursday's. She seemed to be thinking about other things. She watched Harry take off after curtain call. She didn't say a word.

130   On Saturday she put on the best performance yet. Ordinarily it was Harry who set the pace. But on Saturday Harry had to work to keep up with Helene.

When the curtain came down on the final curtain call, Harry wanted to get away, but he couldn't. Helene wouldn't let go his hand. The rest of the cast and the stage crew and a lot of well-wishers from the audience were all standing around Harry and Helene, and Harry was trying to get his hand back.

"Well," he said, "I've got to go."

"Where?" she said.

"Oh," he said, "home."

135   "Won't you please take me to the cast party?" she said.

He got very red. "I'm afraid I'm not much on parties," he said. All the Marlon Brando in him was gone. He was tongue-tied, he was scared, he was shy—he was everything Harry was famous for being between plays.

"All right," she said. "I'll let you go—if you promise me one thing."

"What's that?" he said, and I thought he would jump out a window if she let go of him then.

"I want you to promise to stay here until I get you your present," she said.

140   "Present?" he said, getting even more panicky.

"Promise?" she said.

He promised. It was the only way he could get his hand back. And he stood there miserably while Helene went down to the ladies' dressing room for the present. While he waited, a lot of people congratulated him on being such a fine actor. But congratulations never made him happy. He just wanted to get away.

Helene came back with the present. It turned out to be a little blue book with a big red ribbon for a place marker. It was a copy of *Romeo and Juliet.* Harry was very embarrassed. It was all he could do to say "Thank you."

"The marker marks my favorite scene," said Helene.

145   "Um," said Harry.

"Don't you want to see what my favorite scene is?" she said.

So Harry had to open the book to the red ribbon.

Helene got close to him, and read a line of Juliet's. "'How cam'st thou hither, tell me, and wherefore?'" she read. "'The orchard walls are high and hard to climb, and the place death, considering who thou art, if any of my kinsmen find thee here.'" She pointed to the next line. "Now, look what Romeo says," she said.

"Um," said Harry.

150   "Read what Romeo says," said Helene.

Harry cleared his throat. He didn't want to read the line, but he had to. "'With love's light wings did I o'erperch these walls,'" he read out loud in his everyday voice. But then a change came over him. "'For stony limits cannot hold love out,'" he read, and he straightened up, and eight years dropped away from him, and he was brave and gay. "'And what love can do, that dares love attempt,'" he read, "'therefore thy kinsmen are no let to me.'"

"'If they do see thee they will murther thee,'" said Helene, and she started him walking toward the wings.

"'Alack!'" said Harry, "'there lies more peril in thine eye than twenty of their swords.'" Helene led him toward the backstage exit. "'Look thou but sweet,'" said Harry, "'and I am proof against their enmity.'"

"'I would not for the world they saw thee here,'" said Helene, and that was the last we heard. The two of them were out the door and gone.

155   They never did show up at the cast party. One week later they were married.

They seem very happy, although they're kind of strange from time to time, depending on which play they're reading to each other at the time.

I dropped into the phone company office the other day, on account of the billing machine was making dumb mistakes again. I asked her what plays she and Harry'd been reading lately.

"In the past week," she said, "I've been married to Othello, been loved by Faust and been kidnaped by Paris. Wouldn't you say I was the luckiest girl in town?"

I said I thought so, and I told her most of the women in town thought so too.

160   "They had their chance," she said.

"Most of 'em couldn't stand the excitement," I said. And I told her I'd been asked to direct another play. I asked if she and Harry would be available for the cast. She gave me a big smile and said, "Who are we this time?"

[1968]

TOPICS FOR CRITICAL THINKING AND WRITING

1. In paragraph 17 the narrator says, "The trouble with Harry was that he'd been left on the door-step of the Unitarian Church when he was a baby, and he never did find out who his parents were." What are the implications of the narrator's remarks concerning the shaping of identity?
2. Do you think it is conceivable that exposure to works of art can help to shape a person's identity? Explain.
3. The narrator says, "For Harry's pleasure, and our pleasure, too, we had him read from the scene where he beats up his wife." Wife-beating is not funny, but do you agree that in works of literature some scenes of violence can give readers or viewers pleasure? How, for instance, do you account for the pleasure that tragedy is supposed to give—or, for that matter, how do you account for the pleasure of horror films?

HISAYE YAMAMOTO

Hisaye Yamamoto was born in 1921, in Redondo Beach, California. At age 21, when she was a student at Compton Junior College in California, she and her family were interned and sent to Poston, Arizona. (Shortly after the Japanese bombed Pearl Harbor, 7 December 1941, more than 110,000 persons of Japanese descent, two-thirds of whom were American-born citizens, were removed from the Pacific states.) While at Poston, Yamamoto wrote for the camp newspaper, and after the war she wrote for the Los Angeles Tribune. *In 1950-51 she received a grant from the John Hay Whitney Foundation, which allowed her to devote herself full time for one year to her creative writing.*

"Seventeen Syllables" was first published in 1949. The title refers to the haiku, a Japanese form of poetry consisting of 3 lines of 5, 7, and 5 syllables. A haiku usually includes a sensory image (especially of hearing or of sight) and a seasonal reference. See page 891 for an example.

Seventeen Syllables

The first Rosie knew that her mother had taken to writing poems was one evening when she finished one and read it aloud for her daughter's approval. It was about cats, and Rosie pretended to understand it thoroughly and appreciate it no end, partly because she hesitated to disillusion her mother about the quantity and quality of Japanese she had learned in all the years now that she had been going to Japanese school every Saturday (and

Wednesday, too, in the summer). Even so, her mother must have been skeptical about the depth of Rosie's understanding, because she explained afterwards about the kind of poem she was trying to write.

See, Rosie, she said, it was a *haiku,* a poem in which she must pack all her meaning into seventeen syllables only, which were divided into three lines of five, seven, and five syllables. In the one she had just read, she had tried to capture the charm of a kitten, as well as comment on the superstition that owning a cat of three colors meant good luck.

"Yes, yes, I understand. How utterly lovely," Rosie said, and her mother, either satisfied or seeing through the deception and resigned, went back to composing.

The truth was that Rosie was lazy; English lay ready on the tongue but Japanese had to be searched for and examined, and even then put forth tentatively (probably to meet with laughter). It was so much easier to say yes, yes, even when one meant no, no. Besides, this was what was in her mind to say: I was looking through one of your magazines from Japan last night, Mother, and towards the back I found some *haiku* in English that delighted me. There was one that made me giggle off and on until I fell asleep—

It is morning, and lo!
I lie awake, comme il faut,[1]
sighing for some dough.

5   Now, how to reach her mother, how to communicate the melancholy song? Rosie knew formal Japanese by fits and starts, her mother had even less English, no French. It was much more possible to say yes, yes.

It developed that her mother was writing the *haiku* for a daily newspaper, the *Mainichi Shimbun,* that was published in San Francisco. Los Angeles, to be sure, was closer to the farming community in which the Hayashi family lived and several Japanese vernaculars were printed there, but Rosie's parents said they preferred the tone of the northern paper. Once a week, the *Mainichi* would have a section devoted to *haiku,* and her mother became an extravagant contributor, taking for herself the blossoming pen name, Ume Hanazono.[2]

So Rosie and her father lived for awhile with two women, her mother and Ume Hanazono. Her mother (Tome Hayashi by name) kept house, cooked, washed, and, along with her husband and the Carrascos, the Mexican family hired for the harvest, did her ample share of picking tomatoes out in the sweltering fields and boxing them in tidy strata in the cool packing shed. Ume Hanazono, who came to life after the dinner dishes were done, was an earnest, muttering stranger who often neglected speaking when spoken to and stayed busy at the parlor table as late as midnight scribbling with pencil on scratch paper or carefully copying characters on good paper with her fat, pale green Parker.

The new interest had some repercussions on the household routine. Before, Rosie had been accustomed to her parents and herself taking their hot baths early and going to bed almost immediately afterwards, unless her parents challenged each other to a game of flower cards or unless company

---

[1]as it should be (French)   [2]Flowering Plum Garden (Japanese)

dropped in. Now if her father wanted to play cards, he had to resort to soli-
taire (at which he always cheated fearlessly), and if a group of friends came
over, it was bound to contain someone who was also writing *haiku,* and the
small assemblage would be split in two, her father entertaining the nonliterary members and her mother comparing ecstatic notes with the visiting
poet.

If they went out, it was more of the same thing. But Ume Hanazono's
life span, even for a poet's, was very brief—perhaps three months at most.

10   One night they went over to see the Hayano family in the neighboring
town to the west, an adventure both painful and attractive to Rosie. It was
attractive because there were four Hayano girls, all lovely and each one
named after a season of the year (Haru, Natsu, Aki, Fuyu),[3] painful because
something had been wrong with Mrs. Hayano ever since the birth of her
first child. Rosie would sometimes watch Mrs. Hayano, reputed to have
been the belle of her native village, making her way about a room, stooped,
slowly shuffling, violently trembling (*always* trembling), and she would be
reminded that this woman, in this same condition, had carried and given
issue to three babies. She would look wonderingly at Mr. Hayano, handsome, tall, and strong, and she would look at her four pretty friends. But it
was not a matter she could come to any decision about.

On this visit, however, Mrs. Hayano sat all evening in the rocker, as motionless and unobtrusive as it was possible for her to be, and Rosie found the
greater part of the evening practically anaesthetic. Too, Rosie spent most of
it in the girls' room, because Haru, the garrulous one, said almost as soon as
the bows and other greetings were over, "Oh, you must see my new coat!"

It was a pale plaid of grey, sand, and blue, with an enormous collar, and
Rosie, seeing nothing special in it, said, "Gee, how nice."

"Nice?" said Haru, indignantly. "Is that all you can say about it? It's gorgeous! And so cheap, too. Only seventeen-ninety-eight, because it was a
sale. The saleslady said it was twenty-five dollars regular."

"Gee," said Rosie. Natsu, who never said much and when she said anything said it shyly, fingered the coat covetously and Haru pulled it away.

15   "Mine," she said, putting it on. She minced in the aisle between the two
large beds and smiled happily. "Let's see how your mother likes it."

She broke into the front room and the adult conversation and went to
stand in front of Rosie's mother, while the rest watched from the door.
Rosie's mother was properly envious. "May I inherit it when you're through
with it?"

Haru, pleased, giggled and said yes, she could, but Natsu reminded
gravely from the door, "You promised me, Haru."

Everyone laughed but Natsu, who shamefacedly retreated into the bedroom. Haru came in laughing, taking off the coat. "We were only kidding,
Natsu," she said. "Here, you try it on now."

After Natsu buttoned herself into the coat, inspected herself solemnly
in the bureau mirror, and reluctantly shed it, Rosie, Aki, and Fuyu got their
turns, and Fuyu, who was eight, drowned in it while her sisters and Rosie
doubled up in amusement. They all went into the front room later, because
Haru's mother quaveringly called to her to fix the tea and rice cakes and

[3] Spring, Summer, Autumn, Winter (Japanese)

open a can of sliced peaches for everybody. Rosie noticed that her mother and Mr. Hayano were talking together at the little table—they were discussing a *haiku* that Mr. Hayano was planning to send to the *Mainichi,* while her father was sitting at one end of the sofa looking through a copy of *Life,* the new picture magazine. Occasionally, her father would comment on a photograph, holding it toward Mrs. Hayano and speaking to her as he always did—loudly, as though he thought someone such as she must surely be at least a trifle deaf also.

20   The five girls had their refreshments at the kitchen table, and it was while Rosie was showing the sisters her trick of swallowing peach slices without chewing (she chased each slippery crescent down with a swig of tea) that her father brought his empty teacup and untouched saucer to the sink and said, "Come on, Rosie, we're going home now."

"Already?" asked Rosie.

"Work tomorrow," he said.

He sounded irritated, and Rosie, puzzled, gulped one last yellow slice and stood up to go, while the sisters began protesting, as was their wont.

"We have to get up at five-thirty," he told them, going into the front room quickly, so that they did not have their usual chance to hang onto his hands and plead for an extension of time.

25   Rosie, following, saw that her mother and Mr. Hayano were sipping tea and still talking together, while Mrs. Hayano concentrated, quivering, on raising the handleless Japanese cup to her lips with both her hands and lowering it back to her lap. Her father, saying nothing, went out the door, onto the bright porch, and down the steps. Her mother looked up and asked, "Where is he going?"

"Where is he going?" Rosie said. "He said we were going home now."

"Going home?" Her mother looked with embarrassment at Mr. Hayano and his absorbed wife and then forced a smile. "He must be tired," she said.

Haru was not giving up yet. "May Rosie stay overnight?" she asked, and Natsu, Aki, and Fuyu came to reinforce their sister's plea by helping her make a circle around Rosie's mother. Rosie, for once having no desire to stay, was relieved when her mother, apologizing to the perturbed Mr. and Mrs. Hayano for her father's abruptness at the same time, managed to shake her head no at the quartet, kindly but adamant, so that they broke their circle and let her go.

Rosie's father looked ahead into the windshield as the two joined him. "I'm sorry," her mother said. "You must be tired." Her father, stepping on the starter, said nothing. "You know how I get when it's *haiku,*" she continued, "I forget what time it is." He only grunted.

30   As they road homeward silently, Rosie, sitting between, felt a rush of hate for both—for her mother for begging, for her father for denying her mother. I wish this old Ford would crash, right now, she thought, then immediately, no, no, I wish my father would laugh, but it was too late: already the vision had passed through her mind of the green pick-up crumpled in the dark against one of the mighty eucalyptus trees they were just riding past, of the three contorted, bleeding bodies, one of them hers.

Rosie ran between two patches of tomatoes, her heart working more rambunctiously than she had ever known it to. How lucky it was that Aunt Taka and Uncle Gimpachi had come tonight, though, how very lucky.

Otherwise she might not have really kept her half-promise to meet Jesus Carrasco. Jesus was going to be a senior in September at the same school she went to, and his parents were the ones helping with the tomatoes this year. She and Jesus, who hardly remembered seeing each other at Cleveland High where there were so many other people and two whole grades between them, had become great friends this summer—he always had a joke for her when he periodically drove the loaded pick-up up from the fields to the shed where she was usually sorting while her mother and father did the packing, and they laughed a great deal together over infinitesimal repartee during the afternoon break for chilled watermelon or ice cream in the shade of the shed.

What she enjoyed most was racing him to see which could finish picking a double row first. He, who could work faster, would tease her by slowing down until she thought she would surely pass him this time, then speeding up furiously to leave her several sprawling vines behind. Once he had made her screech hideously by crossing over, while her back was turned, to place atop the tomatoes in her green-stained bucket a truly monstrous, pale green worm (it had looked more like an infant snake). And it was when they had finished a contest this morning, after she had pantingly pointed a green finger at the immature tomatoes evident in the lugs at the end of his row and he had returned the accusation (with justice), that he had startlingly brought up the matter of their possibly meeting outside the range of both their parents' dubious eyes.

"What for?" she had asked.

"I've got a secret I want to tell you," he said.

35   "Tell me now," she demanded.

"It won't be ready till tonight," he said.

She laughed. "Tell me tomorrow then."

"It'll be gone tomorrow," he threatened.

"Well, for seven hakes, what is it?" she had asked, more than twice, and when he had suggested that the packing shed would be an appropriate place to find out, she had cautiously answered maybe. She had not been certain she was going to keep the appointment until the arrival of mother's sister and her husband. Their coming seemed a sort of signal of permission, of grace, and she had definitely made up her mind to lie and leave as she was bowing them welcome.

40   So as soon as everyone appeared settled back for the evening, she announced loudly that she was going to the privy outside, "I'm going to the *benjo!*" and slipped out the door. And now that she was actually on her way, her heart pumped in such an undisciplined way that she could hear it with her ears. It's because I'm running, she told herself, slowing to a walk. The shed was up ahead, one more patch away, in the middle of the fields. Its bulk, looming in the dimness, took on a sinisterness that was funny when Rosie reminded herself that it was only a wooden frame with a canvas roof and three canvas walls that made a slapping noise on breezy days.

Jesus was sitting on the narrow plank that was the sorting platform and she went around to the other side and jumped backwards to seat herself on the rim of a packing stand. "Well, tell me," she said without greeting, thinking her voice sounded reassuringly familiar.

"I saw you coming out the door," Jesus said. "I heard you running part of the way, too."

"Uh-huh," Rosie said. "Now tell me the secret."

"I was afraid you wouldn't come," he said.

45 Rosie delved around on the chicken-wire bottom of the stall for number two tomatoes, ripe, which she was sitting beside, and came up with a left-over that felt edible. She bit into it and began sucking out the pulp and seeds. "I'm here," she pointed out.

"Rosie, are you sorry you came?"

"Sorry? What for?" she said. "You said you were going to tell me something."

"I will, I will," Jesus said, but his voice contained disappointment, and Rosie fleetingly felt the older of the two, realizing a brand-new power which vanished without category under her recognition.

"I have to go back in a minute," she said. "My aunt and uncle are here from Wintersburg. I told them I was going to the privy."

50 Jesus laughed. "You funny thing," he said. "You slay me!"

"Just because you have a bathroom *inside*," Rosie said. "Come on, tell me."

Chuckling, Jesus came around to lean on the stand facing her. They still could not see each other very clearly, but Rosie noticed that Jesus became very sober again as he took the hollow tomato from her hand and dropped it back into the stall. When he took hold of her empty hand, she could find no words to protest; her vocabulary had become distressingly constricted and she thought desperately that all that remained intact now was yes and no and oh, and even these few sounds would not easily out. Thus, kissed by Jesus, Rosie fell for the first time entirely victim to a helplessness delectable beyond speech. But the terrible, beautiful sensation lasted no more than a second, and the reality of Jesus' lips and tongue and teeth and hands made her pull away with such strength that she nearly tumbled.

Rosie stopped running as she approached the lights from the windows of home. How long since she had left? She could not guess, but gasping yet, she went to the privy in back and locked herself in. Her own breathing deaf-ened her in the dark, close space, and she sat and waited until she could hear at last the nightly calling of the frogs and crickets. Even then, all she could think to say was oh, my, and the pressure of Jesus' face against her face would not leave.

No one had missed her in the parlor, however, and Rosie walked in and through quickly, announcing that she was next going to take a bath. "Your father's in the bathhouse," her mother said, and Rosie, in her room, recalled that she had not seen him when she entered. There had been only Aunt Taka and Uncle Gimpachi with her mother at the table, drinking tea. She got her robe and straw sandals and crossed the parlor again to go outside. Her mother was telling them about the *haiku* competition in the *Mainichi* and the poem she had entered.

55 Rosie met her father coming out of the bathhouse. "Are you through Fa-ther?" she asked. "I was going to ask you to scrub my back."

"Scrub your own back," he said shortly, going toward the main house.

"What have I done now?" she yelled after him. She suddenly felt like doing a lot of yelling. But he did not answer, and she went into the bathhouse. Turning on the dangling light, she removed her denims and T-shirt and threw them in the big carton for dirty clothes standing next to the washing machine. Her other things she took with her into the bath compartment to wash after her bath. After she had scooped a basin of hot water from the square wooden tub, she sat on the grey cement of the floor and soaped herself at exaggerated leisure, singing "Red Sails in the Sunset" at the top of her voice and using da-da-da where she suspected her words. Then, standing up, still singing, for she was possessed by the notion that any attempt now to analyze would result in spoilage and she believed that the larger her volume the less she would be able to hear herself think, she obtained more hot water and poured it on until she was free of lather. Only then did she allow herself to step into the steaming vat, one leg first, then the remainder of her body inch by inch until the water no longer stung and she could move around at will.

She took a long time soaking, afterwards remembering to go around outside to stoke the embers of the tin-lined fireplace beneath the tub and to throw on a few more sticks so that the water might keep its heat for her mother, and when she finally returned to the parlor, she found her mother still talking *haiku* with her aunt and uncle, the three of them on another round of tea. Her father was nowhere in sight.

At Japanese school the next day (Wednesday, it was), Rosie was grave and giddy by turns. Preoccupied at her desk in the row for students on Book Eight, she made up for it at recess by performing wild mimicry for the benefit of her friend Chizuko. She held her nose and whined a witticism or two in what she considered was the manner of Fred Allen; she assumed intoxication and a British accent to go over the climax of the Rudy Vallee recording of the pub conversation about William Ewart Gladstone; she was the child Shirley Temple piping, "On the Good Ship Lollipop"; she was the gentleman soprano of the Four Inkspots trilling, "If I Didn't Care." And she felt reasonably satisfied when Chizuko wept and gasped, "Oh, Rosie, you ought to be in the movies!"

60   Her father came after her at noon, bringing her sandwiches of minced ham and two nectarines to eat while she rode, so that she could pitch right into the sorting when they got home. The lugs were piling up, he said, and the ripe tomatoes in them would probably have to be taken to the cannery tomorrow if they were not ready for the produce haulers tonight. "This heat's not doing them any good. And we've got no time for a break today."

It *was* hot, probably the hottest day of the year, and Rosie's blouse stuck damply to her back even under the protection of the canvas. But she worked as efficiently as a flawless machine and kept the stalls heaped, with one part of her mind listening in to the parental murmuring about the heat and the tomatoes and with another part planning the exact words she would say to Jesus when he drove up with the first load of the afternoon. But when at last she saw that the pick-up was coming, her hands went berserk and the tomatoes started falling in the wrong stalls, and her father said, "Hey, hey! Rosie, watch what you're doing!"

"Well, I have to go to the *benjo,*" she said, hiding panic.

"Go in the weeds over there," he said, only half-joking.

"Oh, Father!" she protested.

65   "Oh, go on home," her mother said. "We'll make out for awhile."

In the privy Rosie peered through a knothole toward the fields, watching as much as she could of Jesus. Happily she thought she saw him look in the direction of the house from time to time before he finished unloading and went back toward the patch where his mother and father worked. As she was heading for the shed, a very presentable black car purred up the dirt driveway to the house and its driver motioned to her. Was this the Hayashi home, he wanted to know. She nodded. Was she a Hayashi? Yes, she said, thinking that he was a good-looking man. He got out of the car with a huge, flat package and she saw that he warmly wore a business suit. "I have something here for your mother then," he said, in a more elegant Japanese than she was used to.

She told him where her mother was and he came along with her, patting his face with an immaculate white handkerchief and saying something about the coolness of San Francisco. To her surprised mother and father, he bowed and introduced himself as, among other things, the *haiku* editor of the *Mainichi Shimbun*, saying that since he had been coming as far as Los Angeles anyway, he had decided to bring her the first prize she had won in the recent contest.

"First prize?" her mother echoed, believing and not believing, pleased and overwhelmed. Handed the package with a bow, she bobbed her head up and down numerous times to express her utter gratitude.

"It is nothing much," he added, "but I hope it will serve as a token of our great appreciation for your contributions and our great admiration of your considerable talent."

70   "I am not worthy," she said, falling easily into his style. "It is I who should make some sign of my humble thanks for being permitted to contribute."

"No, no, to the contrary," he said, bowing again.

But Rosie's mother insisted, and then saying that she knew she was being unorthodox, she asked if she might open the package because her curiosity was so great. Certainly she might. In fact, he would like her reaction to it, for personally, it was one of his favorite *Hiroshiges.*[4]

Rosie thought it was a pleasant picture, which looked to have been sketched with delicate quickness. There were pink clouds, containing some graceful calligraphy, and a sea that was a pale blue except at the edges, containing four sampans with indications of people in them. Pines edged the water and on the far-off beach there was a cluster of thatched huts towered over by pine-dotted mountains of grey and blue. The frame was scalloped and gilt.

After Rosie's mother pronounced it without peer and somewhat prodded her father into nodding agreement, she said Mr. Kuroda must at least have a cup of tea after coming all this way, and although Mr. Kuroda did not want to impose, he soon agreed that a cup of tea would be refreshing and went along with her to the house, carrying the picture for her.

75   "Ha, your mother's crazy!" Rosie's father said, and Rosie laughed uneasily as she resumed judgment on the tomatoes. She had emptied six lugs

---

[4] that is, woodblock prints by Hiroshige Ando (1797–1858)

when he broke into an imaginary conversation with Jesus to tell her to go and remind her mother of the tomatoes, and she went slowly.

Mr. Kuroda was in his shirtsleeves expounding some *haiku* theory as he munched a rice cake, and her mother was rapt. Abashed in the great man's presence, Rosie stood next to her mother's chair until her mother looked up inquiringly, and then she started to whisper the message, but her mother pushed her gently away and reproached, "You are not being very polite to our guest."

"Father says the tomatoes . . ." Rosie said aloud, smiling foolishly.

"Tell him I shall only be a minute," her mother said, speaking the language of Mr. Kuroda.

When Rosie carried the reply to her father, he did not seem to hear and she said again, "Mother says she'll be back in a minute."

80   "All right, all right," he nodded, and they worked again in silence. But suddenly, her father uttered an incredible noise, exactly like the cork of a bottle popping, and the next Rosie knew, he was stalking angrily toward the house, almost running in fact, and she chased after him crying, "Father! Father! What are you going to do?"

He stopped long enough to order her back to the shed. "Never mind!" he shouted, "Get on with the sorting!"

And from the place in the fields where she stood, frightened and vacillating, Rosie saw her father enter the house. Soon Mr. Kuroda came out alone, putting on his coat. Mr. Kuroda got into his car and backed out down the driveway onto the highway. Next her father emerged, also alone, something in his arms (it was the picture, she realized), and, going over to the bathhouse woodpile, he threw the picture on the ground and picked up the axe. Smashing the picture, glass and all (she heard the explosion faintly), he reached over for the kerosene that was used to encourage the bath fire and poured it over the wreckage. I am dreaming, Rosie said to herself, I am dreaming, but her father, having made sure that his act of cremation was irrevocable, was even then returning to the fields.

Rosie ran past him and toward the house. What had become of her mother? She burst into the parlor and found her mother at the back window watching the dying fire. They watched together until there remained only a feeble smoke under the blazing sun. Her mother was very calm.

"Do you know why I married your father?" she said without turning.

85   "No," said Rosie. It was the most frightening question she had ever been called upon to answer. Don't tell me now, she wanted to say, tell me tomorrow, tell me next week, don't tell me today. But she knew she would be told now, that the telling would combine with the other violence of the hot afternoon to level her life, her world to the very ground.

It was like a story out of the magazines illustrated in sepia, which she had consumed so greedily for a period until the information had somehow reached her that those wretchedly unhappy autobiographies, offered to her as the testimonials of living men and women, were largely inventions: Her mother, at nineteen, had come to America and married her father as an alternative to suicide.

At eighteen she had been in love with the first son of one of the well-to-do families in her village. The two had met whenever and wherever they could, secretly, because it would not have done for his family to see him

favor her—her father had no money; he was a drunkard and a gambler besides. She had learned she was with child; an excellent match had already
been arranged for her lover. Despised by her family, she had given premature birth to a stillborn son, who would be seventeen now. Her family
did not turn her out, but she could no longer project herself in any direction
without refreshing in them the memory of her indiscretion. She wrote to
Aunt Taka, her favorite sister in America, threatening to kill herself if
Aunt Taka would not send for her. Aunt Taka hastily arranged a marriage
with a young man of whom she knew, but lately arrived from Japan, a young
man of simple mind, it was said, but of kindly heart. The young man was
never told why his unseen betrothed was so eager to hasten the day of
meeting.

The story was told perfectly, with neither groping for words nor unto-
ward passion. It was as though her mother had memorized it by heart, reciting it to herself so many times over that its nagging vileness had long since
gone.

"I had a brother then?" Rosie asked, for this was what seemed to matter
now; she would think about the other later, she assured herself, pushing
back the illumination which threatened all that darkness that had hitherto
been merely mysterious or even glamorous. "A half-brother?"

90   "Yes."

"I would have liked a brother," she said.

Suddenly, her mother knelt on the floor and took her by the wrists.
"Rosie," she said urgently, "Promise me you will never marry!" Shocked
more by the request than the revelation, Rosie stared at her mother's face.
Jesus, Jesus, she called silently, not certain whether she was invoking the
help of the son of the Carrascos or of God, until there returned sweetly the
memory of Jesus' hand, how it had touched her and where. Still her mother
waited for an answer, holding her wrists so tightly that her hands were
going numb. She tried to pull free. Promise, her mother whispered fiercely,
promise. Yes, yes, I promise, Rosie said. But for an instant she turned away,
and her mother, hearing the familiar glib agreement, released her. Oh, you,
you, you, her eyes and twisted mouth said, you fool. Rosie, covering her
face, began at last to cry, and the embrace and consoling hand came much
later than she expected.

[1949]

 TOPICS FOR CRITICAL THINKING AND WRITING

1. What function, if any, is served by the paragraph reporting how Rosie's
father, looking at *Life* magazine, occasionally shows a photograph to
Mrs. Hayano, whom he mistakenly seems to think is hard of hearing?

2. Is it your impression that Rosie's mother takes up writing haiku simply
as an escape from her difficult life? Explain your position.

3. If your parents are closer to some non-English literature than you are—
as Rosie's mother is closer to Japanese literature than Rosie is—examine your response to this literature. Does it seem utterly remote? Something you want to get to know better? Something you can't imagine
being interested in? Or what?

Poems and Paintings

Vincent Van Gogh, *Vincent's Bed in Arles*. (Oil on canvas, 72 × 90 cm. Vincent van Gogh Foundation/Van Gogh Museum, Amsterdam.)

📖 JANE FLANDERS (born 1940)

Jane Flanders, born in Waynesboro, Pennsylvania, in 1940, and educated at Bryn Mawr College and Columbia University, is the author of three books of poems. Among her awards are poetry fellowships from the National Endowment for the Arts and the New York Foundation for the Arts.

Van Gogh's Bed

is orange,
like Cinderella's coach, like
the sun when he looked it
straight in the eye.   5

is narrow,
he slept alone, tossing
between two pillows, while it carried him
bumpily to the ball

is clumsy,

10

but friendly. A peasant
built the frame; an old wife beat
the mattress till it rose like meringue

is empty,
morning light pours in

15

like wine, melody, fragrance,
the memory of happiness.

[1985]

☞ TOPICS FOR CRITICAL THINKING AND WRITING

Jane Flanders tells us that the poem is indebted not only to the painting of Van
Gogh's bedroom but also to two comments in letters that van Gogh wrote to his
brother, Theo:

I can tell you that for my part I will try to keep a straight course, and
will paint the most simple, the most common things.

(December 1884)

My eyes are still tired, but then I had a new idea in my head and here is
the sketch of it. . . . It's just simply my bedroom, only here color is to do
everything, and giving by its simplification a grander style to things, is
to be suggestive here of *rest* or of sleep in general. In a word, to look at
the picture ought to rest the brain or rather the imagination.

(September 1888)

1. Does the picture convey "rest" to you? If not, has van Gogh failed to
   paint a picture of interest? What *does* the picture convey to you?
2. In an earlier version, the last stanza of the poem went thus:

   empty,
   morning light pours in
   like wine; the sheets are what they are,
   casting no shadows.

   Which version do you prefer? Why?

Charles Demuth, *I Saw the Figure 5 in Gold.* 1928. (Oil on composition
board, 36 × 29 3/4". The Metropolitan Museum of Art, New York,
The Alfred Stieglitz Collection, 1949[49.59.1].)

📖 WILLIAM CARLOS WILLIAMS (1883–1963)

*William Carlos Williams (1883-1963) was the son of an English traveling
salesman and a Basque-Jewish woman. The couple met in Puerto Rico and
settled in Rutherford, New Jersey, where Williams was born. He spent his life
there, practicing as a pediatrician and writing poems in the moments
between seeing patients who were visiting his office.*

In his Autobiography *Williams gives an account of the origin of this poem.
He was walking in New York City, on his way to visit a friend:*

As I approached his number I heard a great clatter of bells and the roar of a
fire engine passing the end of the street down Ninth Avenue. I turned just
in time to see a golden 5 on a red background flash by. The impression was
so sudden and forceful that I took a piece of paper out of my pocket and
wrote a short poem about it.

Several years later his friend Charles Demuth (1883–1939), an American painter who has been called a Cubist-Realist, painted this picture, inspired by the poem. The picture is one of a series of paintings about Demuth's friends.

The Great Figure

Among the rain
and lights
I saw the figure 5
in gold
on a red   5
fire truck
moving
tense
unheeded
to gong clangs   10
siren howls
and wheels rumbling
through the dark city

[1920]

✏ TOPICS FOR CRITICAL THINKING AND WRITING

Williams's draft for the poem runs thus:

Among the rain
and lights
I saw the figure 5
gold on red
moving
to gong clangs
siren howls
and wheels rumbling
tense
unheeded
through the dark city

Do you think the final version is better in all respects, some respects, or no respects? Explain.

Edwin Romanzo Elmer, *Mourning Picture*. (1890. Oil on canvas, 28 × 36 in. [71.1 × 91.5 cm.]. Smith College Museum of Art, Northampton, Massachusetts. Purchased 1953.)

📖 ADRIENNE RICH *(born 1929)*

Adrienne Rich, born in 1929 in Baltimore, was educated at Radcliffe College. Her first book of poems, A Change of World, *published in 1951 when she was still an undergraduate, was selected by W. H. Auden for the Yale Series of Younger Poets.*

Mourning Picture

(The picture was painted by Edwin Romanzo Elmer (1850–1923) as a memorial to his daughter Effie. In the poem, it is the dead girl who speaks.)

They have carried the mahogany chair and the cane rocker
out under the lilac bush,
and my father and mother darkly sit there, in black clothes.
Our clapboard house stands fast on its hill,
my doll lies in her wicker pram   5
gazing at western Massachusetts.
This was our world.
I could remake each shaft of grass
feeling its rasp on my fingers,
draw out the map of every lilac leaf   10
or the net of veins on my father's
grief-tranced hand.

Out of my head, half-bursting,
still filling, the dream condenses—
shadows, crystals, ceilings, meadows, globes of dew.   15
Under the dull green of the lilacs, out in the light
carving each spoke of the pram, the turned porch-pillars,
under high early-summer clouds,
I am Effie, visible and invisible,
remembering and remembered.   20

They will move from the house,
give the toys and pets away.
Mute and rigid with loss my mother
will ride the train to Baptist Corner,
the silk-spool will run bare.   25
I tell you, the thread that bound us lies
faint as a web in the dew.
Should I make you, world, again,
could I give back the leaf its skeleton, the air
its early-summer cloud, the house   30
its noonday presence, shadowless,
and leave *this* out? I am Effie, you were my dream

[1965]

⌐ TOPICS FOR CRITICAL THINKING AND WRITING

1. The poem begins by describing Elmer's picture. In the first stanza, what parts of the picture does it describe? What is missing? Why, do you suppose, are those parts missing?
2. In lines 8 to 12, the speaker names some less concrete or visible signs of the family's life, or her own. What do you think she means when she says "I could remake . . . " and "[I could] draw out . . . " (lines 8 and 10)?
3. In the second stanza, in lines 13–15, the speaker describes her present moment. How does she describe it? What do you think she means by "the dream condenses" (line 14)? If lines 19–20 describe the picture, what do they describe?
4. In the last stanza the speaker foresees the future for her parents. What is her own future? Has she accepted her death?

Kitagawa Utamaro, *Two Women Dressing Their Hair.* (Print Collection, Miriam and Ira D. Wallach Division of Art, Prints and Photographs/ New York Public Library, Astor, Lenox and Tilden Foundations.)

Kitagawa Utamaro (1754-1806) lived in Edo (now called Tokyo). He specialized in designing pictures of courtesans and actors that were then used to make woodblock prints. Brothels and the theater were important parts of what was called the Floating World, that is, the world of transient pleasure.

CATHY SONG (*born 1925*)

Cathy Song was born in Honolulu in 1925 of a Chinese mother and a Korean father. She holds a bachelor's degree from Wellesley College and a master's degree in creative writing from Boston University. A manuscript that she submitted to the Yale Series of Younger Poets was chosen as the winner and in 1983 was published under the title of Picture Bride.

Beauty and Sadness

for Kitagawa Utamaro

He drew hundreds of women
in studies unfolding
like flowers from a fan.
Teahouse waitresses, actresses,
geishas, courtesans and maids.   5
They arranged themselves
before this quick, nimble man
whose invisible presence
one feels in these prints
is as delicate   10
as the skinlike paper
he used to transfer
and retain their fleeting loveliness.

Crouching like cats,
they purred amid the layers of
    kimono   15
swirling around them
as though they were bathing
in a mountain pool with irises
growing in the silken sunlit water.
Or poised like porcelain vases,   20
slender, erect and tall; their heavy
brocaded hair was piled high
with sandalwood combs and blossom
    sprigs
poking out like antennae.
They resembled beautiful iridescent
    insects,   25
creatures from a floating world.

Utamaro absorbed these women of
    Edo
in their moments of melancholy

He captured the wisp of shadows,   30
the half-draped body
emerging from a bath; whatever
skin was exposed
was powdered white as snow.
A private space disclosed.   35
Portraying another girl
catching a glimpse of her own
    vulnerable
face in the mirror, he transposed
the trembling plum lips
like a drop of blood   40
soaking up the white expanse of paper.

At times, indifferent to his inconsolable
eye, the women drifted
through the soft gray feathered light,
maintaining stillness, the moments in
    between.   45
Like the dusty ash-winged moths
that cling to the screens in summer
and that the Japanese venerate
as ancestors reincarnated;
Utamaro graced these women with
    immortality   50
in the thousand sheaves of prints
fluttering into the reverent hands of
    keepers:
the dwarfed and bespectacled painter
holding up to a square of sunlight
what he had carried home beneath his
    coat   55
one afternoon in winter.

                                        [1983]

✐ TOPICS FOR CRITICAL THINKING AND WRITING

1. In the first stanza the women in Utamaro's prints possess a "fleeting loveliness." What does "fleeting" suggest here? What are Utamaro's characteristics in this stanza?

2. In the second stanza would you say that the women are beautiful, or not? And in the third stanza? What do they look like in each stanza?

3. In the last stanza, in the last few lines, we learn that Utamaro was a "dwarfed and bespectacled painter." We might have learned this earlier in the poem, or not at all. Why does Song wait until this late in the poem to tell us?

Sandro Botticelli. *The Birth of Venus.* (About 1480. 5' 8 7/8" × 9' 7/8". Uffizi Gallery, Florence [Scala/Art Resource, New York].)

MARY JO SALTER (born 1954)

Mary Jo Salter, born in 1954 in Grand Rapids, Michigan, was raised in Detroit and Baltimore and was educated at Harvard and at Cambridge University. The author of several books of poetry, Salter has received numerous awards, including a fellowship from the National Endowment for the Arts.

The Rebirth of Venus

He's knelt to fish her face up from the sidewalk

all morning, and at last some shoppers gather
to see it drawn—wide-eyed, and dry as chalk—
whole from the sea of dreams. It's she. None other   4

than the other one who's copied in the book
he copies from, that woman men divined
ages before a painter let them look
into the eyes their eyes had had in mind.   8

Love's called him too, today, though she has taught
him in her beauty to love best
the one who first had formed her from a thought.
One square of pavement, like a headstone (lest   12

anyone mistake where credit lies),
reads BOTTICELLI, but the long-closed dates
suggest, instead, a view of centuries
coming unbracketed, as if the gates   16

might swing wide to admit, here, in the sun,
one humble man into the pantheon
older and more exalted than her own.
    Slow gods of Art, late into afternoon   20

let there be light: a few of us drop the wish
into his glinting coinbox like a well,
remembering the forecast. Yet he won't rush
her finish, though it means she'll have no shell
24

to harbor in; it's clear enough the rain
will swamp her like a tide, and lion-hearted
he'll set off, black umbrella sprung again,
envisioning faces where the streets have parted.   28

[1989]

☞ TOPICS FOR CRITICAL THINKING AND WRITING

1. In the first stanza, what words suggest that Venus, whose portrait is being drawn on the sidewalk, is born in the sea? What medium is the artist using?
2. What do you think Salter means when she says (lines 6–8) that the sidewalk artist's picture is of "that woman men divined/ages before a painter let them look/into the eyes their eyes had had in mind"?
3. According to the Hebrew Bible, "let there be light" (line 21) is what God said in Genesis 1.3. In the context of Salter's poem what do the words mean? Does the poet expect her wish (in line 21) to be granted?
4. If you agree that the poem is lighthearted, what makes it so?
5. Botticelli's painting is a great favorite. Why do you suppose it is so popular?

Vincent van Gogh. *The Starry Night.* (1889. Oil on canvas, 29 × 36 1/4". Collection, The Museum of Modern Art, New York. Acquired through the Lillie P. Bliss Bequest. Photograph © 1995 The Museum of Modern Art.)

📖 ANNE SEXTON (1928–1975)

Anne Sexton (1928-75) was born in Newton, Massachusetts. She attended Garland Junior College, married at 20, and began a life as a housewife. After a mental breakdown at the age of 28 she took up writing poetry on the suggestion of a therapist. She published eight books of poetry, the third of which won a Pulitzer Prize. Despite her literary success, her life was deeply troubled, and she attempted suicide on several occasions. At last she succeeded, by carbon monoxide poisoning.

The Starry Night

That does not keep me from having a terrible need of—shall I say the word—religion. Then I go out at night to paint the stars.

—Vincent van Gogh in a letter to his brother

The town does not exist
except where one black-haired tree slips
up like a drowned woman into the hot sky.
The town is silent. The night boils with eleven stars
Oh starry starry night! This is how   5
I want to die.

It moves. They are all alive.
Even the moon bulges in its orange irons
to push children, like a god, from its eye.
The old unseen serpent swallows up the stars.   10
Oh starry starry night! This is how
I want to die:

into that rushing beast of the night,
sucked up by that great dragon, to split
from my life with no flag,   15
no belly,
no cry.

(1961)

☞ TOPIC FOR CRITICAL THINKING OR WRITING

Sexton calls her poem "The Starry Night" and uses an epigraph from van Gogh. In what ways does her poem *not* describe or evoke van Gogh's painting? In what ways *does* it describe the painting?

Pieter Breughel the Elder, *Landscape with the Fall of Icarus.* (Musées Royaux des Beaux-Arts de Belgique.)

W. H. AUDEN (1907–1973)

Wystan Hugh Auden (1907-73) was born in York, England, and educated at Oxford. In the 1930s his witty left-wing poetry earned him wide acclaim as the leading poet of his generation. He went to Spain during the Spanish Civil War, intending to serve as an ambulance driver for the Republicans in their struggle against Fascism, but he was so distressed by the violence of the Republicans that he almost immediately returned to England. In 1939 he came to America, and in 1946 he became a citizen of the United States, though he spent his last years in England. Much of his poetry is characterized by a combination of colloquial diction and technical dexterity.

In the following poem, Auden offers a meditation triggered by a painting in the Museum of Fine Arts in Brussels. The painting, by Pieter Brueghel (c. 1522-1569), is based on the legend of Icarus, told by the Roman poet Ovid (43 B.C.-A.D. 18) in his Metamorphoses. *The story goes thus: Daedalus, father of Icarus, was confined with his son on the island of Crete. In order to escape, Dedalus made wings for himself and for Icarus by fastening feathers together with wax, but Icarus flew too near the sun, the wax melted, and Icarus fell into the sea. According to Ovid, the event—a boy falling through the sky—was witnessed with amazement by a ploughman, a shepherd, and an angler. In the painting, however, these figures seem to pay no attention to Icarus, who is represented not falling through the sky but already in the water (in the lower right corner, near the ship), with only his lower legs still visible.*

Musée des Beaux Arts

About suffering they were never wrong,
The Old Masters: how well they understood
Its human position; how it takes place
While someone else is eating or opening a window or just walking dully along;
How, when the aged are reverently, passionately waiting
For the miraculous birth, there always must be
Children who did not specially want it to happen, skating
On a pond at the edge of the wood:
They never forgot
That even the dreadful martyrdom must run its course   10
Anyhow in a corner, some untidy spot
Where the dogs go on with their doggy life and the torturer's horse
Scratches its innocent behind on a tree.

In Brueghel's *Icarus,* for instance: how everything turns away
Quite leisurely from the disaster; the plowman may   15
Have heard the splash, the forsaken cry,
But for him it was not an important failure; the sun shone
As it had to on the white legs disappearing into the green
Water; and the expensive delicate ship that must have seen
Something amazing, a boy falling out of the sky,   20
Had somewhere to get to and sailed calmly on

✐ TOPICS FOR CRITICAL THINKING AND WRITING

1. In your own words sum up what, according to the speaker (in lines 1–13), the Old Masters understood about human suffering. (The Old Masters were the great European painters who worked from about 1500 to about 1750.)

2. Suppose the first lines read:

   The Old Masters were never wrong about suffering.
   They understood its human position well.

   What (beside the particular rhymes) would change or be lost?

3. Reread the poem (preferably over the course of several days) a number of times, jotting down your chief responses after each reading. Then, in connection with a final reading, study your notes, and write an essay of 500 words setting forth the history of your final response to the poem. For example, you may want to report that certain difficulties soon were clarified and that your enjoyment increased. Or, conversely, you may want to report that the poem became less interesting (for reasons you will set forth) the more you studied it. Probably your history will be somewhat more complicated than these simple examples. Try to find a chief pattern in your experience, and shape it into a thesis.

4. Consider a picture, either in a local museum or reproduced in a book, and write a 500-word reflection on it. If the picture is not well known, include a reproduction (a postcard from the museum or a photocopy of a page of

Pieter Breughel the Elder, *Two Monkeys*.
(1562. Oil on wood. Gemaldegalerie,
Berlin/Staatliche Museen, Preussicher
Kulturbesitz.)

WISLAWA SZYMBORSKA (*born 1928*)

*Wislawa Szymborska (pronounced "Vislawa Zimborska"), born in 1923, is
one of Poland's leading poets. She published her first book in 1952, and she
has published seven later volumes. Some of her work is available in English,
in* Sounds, Feelings, Thoughts *(1981).*

*Brueghel's Two Monkeys**

This is what I see in my dream about final exams:
two monkeys, chained to the floor, sit on the windowsill,
the sky behind them flutters,
the sea is taking its bath.

The exam is History of Mankind.   5
I stammer and hedge.

One monkey stares and listens with mocking disdain,
the other seems to be dreaming away—
but when it's clear I don't know what to say
he prompts me with a gentle   10
clinking of his chain.

[1933]

TOPICS FOR CRITICAL THINKING AND WRITING

1. What do we know, or guess, about the speaker from the poem's first
   line? Are we willing to listen to him (or her)?
2. We are not likely to be examined on "History of Mankind." Why do you
   suppose the speaker is being quizzed on it? What does the speaker do?
   (Paraphrase line 6.)
3. In the third stanza the speaker again does not know what to say. Do
   we know what the question is? Does the prompting (line 10) help?
4. Write a comment, in prose or verse, on Brueghel's painting.

*Translated, from the Polish, by Stanislaw Baranczak and Clare Cavanagh

Poetry

📖 DANNIE ABSE

Dannie Abse was born in Wales in 1923 and was educated as a physician. The author of novels and plays as well as of poems, Abse continued to practice medicine part time until recently.

Abse's "Brueghel in Naples" begins with an epigraph taken from the poem by W. H. Auden that we print on page 915. Like Abse, Auden derived the story of Icarus from the Roman poet Ovid. (See the biographical introduction to Auden's poem on p. 914.)

Brueghel in Naples

About suffering they were never wrong,
The Old Masters . . .
>   *—W. H. Auden*

Ovid would never have guessed how far
and father's notion about wax melting, bah!
It's ice up there. Freezing.
Soaring and swooping over solitary altitudes
I was breezing along (a record I should think)   5
when my wings began to moult not melt.
These days, workmanship, I ask you.
Appalling.

There's a mountain down there on fire
and I'm falling, falling away from it.   10
Phew, the sun's on the horizon
or am I upside down?

Great Bacchus, the sea is rearing
up. Will I drown? My white legs
the last to disappear? (I have no trousers on)   15
A little to the left the ploughman,
a little to the right a galleon,
a sailor climbing the rigging,
a fisherman casting his line,
and now I hear a shepherd's dog barking.   20
I'm that near.

Lest I have no trace
but a few scattered feathers on the water
show me your face, sailor,
look up, fisherman,   25
look this way, shepherd,
turn around, ploughman.
Raise the alarm! Launch a boat!

My luck. I'm seen
only by a jackass of an artist   30
interested in composition, in the green
tinge of the sea, in the aesthetics
of disaster—not in me.

I drown, bubble by bubble,
(Help! Save me!)   35
while he stands ruthlessly
before the canvas, busy busy,
intent on becoming an Old Master.

                                                                [1991]

TOPICS FOR CRITICAL THINKING AND WRITING

1. In the introduction to his *Collected Poems* Abse says that he wants "to
   write poems which appear translucent but are in fact deceptions. I
   would have a reader enter them, be deceived he could see through
   them like sea-water, and be puzzled when he can not quite touch the
   bottom." Has he succeeded? Explain.
2. Abse says also that as a poet he tries "to look upon the world with the
   eyes of a perpetual convalescent." What do you think he means? Do you
   imagine that all writers have such an aim? Explain.

 ## GWENDOLYN BROOKS

*Gwendolyn Brooks was born in Topeka, Kansas, in 1917 but was
raised in Chicago's South Side, where she has spent most of her life.
Brooks has taught in several colleges and universities and she has
written a novel (*Maud Martha, *1953) and a memoir (*Report from Part
One, *1972), but she is best known as a poet. In 1950, when she won
the Pulitzer Prize for Poetry, she became the first African-American
writer to win a Pulitzer Prize. In 1985 Brooks became Consultant in
Poetry to the Library of Congress.*

The Chicago Picasso, August 15, 1967

*Mayor Daley tugged a white ribon, loosing the blue percale wrap. A hearty
cheer went up as the covering slipped off the big steel sculpture that looks at
once like a bird and a woman.*

                                                   Chicago Sun-Times

*(Seiji Ozawa leads the Symphony.
The Mayor smiles.
And 50,000 See.)*

Does man love Art? Man visits Art, but squirms.
Art hurts. Art urges voyages—
and it is easier to stay at home,
the nice beer ready.

Pablo Picasso, "Chicago Civic Center" (David H. Hamilton / The Image Bank.)

     In commonrooms   5
we belch, or sniff, or scratch.
Are raw.

But we must cook ourselves and style ourselves for Art, who
is a requiring courtesan.
We squirm.   10
We do not hug the Mona Lisa.
We
may touch or tolerate
an astounding fountain, or a horse-and-rider.
At most, another Lion.°   15

[15]**Lion** probably a reference to the realistic bronze lions on the steps of the Art Institute in Chicago

Observe the tall cold of a Flower
which is as innocent and as guilty,
as meaningful and as meaningless as any
other flower in the western field.

[1967]

 ## TOPIC FOR CRITICAL THINKING AND WRITING

Here are several quotations about art. Take two of them, and in an essay of 750 words set forth what you think would be Gwendolyn Brooks's response. If your own response would be different, set forth your view too.

Religion and art spring from the same root and are close kin. Economics and art are strangers.

Willa Cather, American writer

Progressive art can assist people to learn not only about the objective forces at work in the society in which they live, but also about the intensely social character of their interior lives. Ultimately, it can propel people toward social emancipation.

Angela Davis, American political activist

To say that a work of art is good, but incomprehensible to the majority of people, is the same as saying of some kind of food that it is very good but most people can't eat it.

Leo Tolstoy, Russian novelist

The final purpose of art is to intensify, even, if necessary, to exacerbate, the moral consciousness of people.

Norman Mailer, American writer

The history of modern art is the history of the progressive loss of art's audience. Art has increasingly become the concern of the artist, and the bafflement of the public.

Henry Geldzahler, American art critic

There is the falsely mystical view of art that assumes a kind of supernatural inspiration, a possession by universal forces unrelated to questions of power.

Adrienne Rich, American poet and essayist

 ## WILLIAM SHAKESPEARE

William Shakespeare (1564-1616), born in Stratford-upon-Avon in England, is chiefly known as a dramatic poet, but he also wrote non-dramatic poetry. In 1609 a volume of 154 of his sonnets was published, apparently without his permission. Probably he chose to keep his sonnets unpublished not because he thought that they were of little value, but because it was more prestigious to be an amateur poet (unpublished) than a professional (published). Although the sonnets

*were published in 1609, they were probably written in the mid-
1590s, when there was a vogue for sonneteering. A contemporary
writer in 1598 said that Shakespeare's "sugred Sonnets [circulate]
among his private friends."*

Sonnet 55

Not marble, nor the gilded monuments
Of princes, shall outlive this pow'rful rhyme,
But you shall shine more bright in these contents°
Than° unswept stone,° besmeared with sluttish time.   4
When wasteful war shall statues overturn,
And broils° root out the work of masonry,
Nor Mars his sword° nor° war's quick fire shall burn
The living record of your memory.   8
'Gainst death and all oblivious enmity°
Shall you pace forth; your praise shall still find room
Even in the eyes of all posterity
That wear this world out° to the ending doom.   12
  So, till the judgment that° yourself arise,
  You live in this, and dwell in lovers'° eyes.

[c. 1600]

 TOPICS FOR CRITICAL THINKING AND WRITING

1. Line 7 (ten monosyllables) is enjambed—that is, the sense runs over
   into the next line. Speak the lines aloud, and analyze the effect conveyed by the monosyllables and the enjambment.
2. Similarly line 9 is enjambed, and line 10 begins with four stressed mon-
   syllables. What effects do you hear?
3. It is often said that the couplets that end Shakespeare's sonnets merely
   summarize the preceding twelve lines. Does the charge apply to this
   couplet? If not, what does this couplet do?

 WALTER SAVAGE LANDOR

*Walter Savage Landor (1775-1864), a well-to-do Englishman with
an extremely combative temperment—he fought with servants, government officials, and his wife—is especially known for short poems
that seem to reflect serenity. In the following poem he alludes to two
figures from mythology: Helen of Troy, the beautiful woman for
whom the Trojan War was fought, and Alcestis, who gave her life to
save her husband but who was rescued from the underworld (the
"shades" of line 2).*

³**these contents** i.e., the contents of this poem   ⁴**Than** than in   **stone** memorial
tablet in the floor of a church   ⁶**broils** skirmishes   ⁷**Mars his sword** Mars' sword.
Nor . . . nor neither . . . nor   ⁹**all oblivious enmity** all enmity that brings oblivion
(?) enmity that brings oblivion to all (?)   ¹²**wear this world out** outlasts this world
¹³**judgment that** Judgment Day when   ¹⁴**lovers'** admirers'

Past Ruined Ilion

Past ruined Ilion° Helen lives,
  Alcestis rises from the shades;
Verse calls them forth; 'tis verse that gives
  Immortal youth to mortal maids.   4

Soon shall Oblivion's deepening veil
  Hide all the peopled hills you see,
The gay, the proud, while lovers hail
  These many summers you and me.   8

[1831]

 TOPICS FOR CRITICAL THINKING AND WRITING

1. Suppose that in the last line we substitute "winters" for "summers." What is gained or lost?
2. Landor is especially known for poems—such as this one—that almost seem cut into stone. If you agree that this poem conveys this quality, what specifically in the poem produces the effect?
3. When this poem was first published it had a third stanza, later deleted. The stanza ran thus:

   The tear for fading beauty check,
     For passing glory cease to sigh;
   One form shall rise above the wreck,
     One name, Ianthe, shall not die.

   Do you think Landor improved the poem by dropping the stanza? Argue your position.

 WILLIAM WORDSWORTH

William Wordsworth (1770–1850), the son of an attorney, grew up in the Lake District of England. After graduating from Cambridge University in 1791, he spent a year in France, falling in love with a French girl, by whom he had a daughter. His enthusiasm for the French Revolution waned, and he returned alone to England where, with the help of a legacy, he devoted his life to poetry. With his friend, Samuel Taylor Coleridge, in 1798 he published anonymously a volume of poetry, Lyrical Ballads, *which changed the course of English poetry. In 1799 he and his sister Dorothy settled in Grasmere in the Lake District, where he married and was given the office of distributor of stamps. In 1843 he was appointed poet laureate.*

¹**Ilion** Troy

The Solitary Reaper

Behold her, single in the field,
Yon solitary Highland Lass!
Reaping and singing by herself;
Stop here, or gently pass!
Alone she cuts and binds the grain,   5
And sings a melancholy strain;
O listen! for the Vale profound
Is overflowing with the sound.

No Nightingale did ever chant
More welcome notes to weary bands   10
Of travellers in some shady haunt,
Among Arabian sands:
A voice so thrilling ne'er was heard
In spring-time from the Cuckoo-bird,
Breaking the silence of the seas   15
Among the farthest Hebrides.

Will no one tell me what she sings?° —
Perhaps the plaintive numbers flow
For old, unhappy, far-off things,
And battles long ago: 20
Or is it some more humble lay,
Familiar matter of today?
Some natural sorrow, loss, or pain,
That has been, and may be again?

Whate'er the theme, the maiden sang   25
As if her song could have no ending;
I saw her singing at her work,
And o'er the sickle bending;—
I listened, motionless and still;
And, as I mounted up the hill,   30
The music in my heart I bore
Long after it was heard no more.

[1805]

 TOPIC FOR CRITICAL THINKING AND WRITING

Why do people sometimes sing at their work? And why do people sometimes sing *sad* songs?

17**Will . . . sings?** Wordsworth had read an account of a woman reaping. The author had specified that the reaper sang in Erse, hence Wordsworth—imagining himself in the scene—cannot understand the song.

JOHN KEATS

John Keats (1795-1821), son of a London stable keeper, was taken out of school when he was 15 and was apprenticed to a surgeon and apothecary. In 1816 he was licensed to practice as an apothecary-surgeon, but he almost immediately abandoned medicine and decided to make a career as a poet. His progress was amazing; he published books of poems—to mixed reviews—in 1817, 1818, and 1820, before dying of tuberculosis at the age of 25. Today he is esteemed as one of England's greatest poets.

Ode on a Grecian Urn

I

Thou still unravished bride of quietness,
   Thou foster-child of silence and slow time,
Sylvan historian, who canst thus express
   A flowery tale more sweetly than our rhyme:
What leaf-fringed legend haunts about thy shape   5
   Of deities or mortals, or of both,
      In Tempe or the dales of Arcady?
    What men or gods are these? What maidens loth?
What mad pursuit? What struggle to escape?
    What pipes and timbrels? What wild ecstasy?   10

II

Heard melodies are sweet, but those unheard
   Are sweeter; therefore, ye soft pipes, play on;
Not to the sensual° ear, but, more endeared,
   Pipe to the spirit ditties of no tone:
Fair youth, beneath the trees, thou canst not leave   15
   Thy song, nor ever can those trees be bare;
     Bold Lover, never, never canst thou kiss,
Though winning near the goal—yet, do not grieve;
    She cannot fade, though thou hast not thy bliss,
    For ever wilt thou love, and she be fair!   20

III

Ah, happy, happy boughs! that cannot shed
   Your leaves, nor ever bid the Spring adieu;
And, happy melodist, unwearied,
   For ever piping songs for ever new;
More happy love! more happy, happy love!   25
   For ever warm and still to be enjoyed,
    For ever panting, and for ever young;

13**sensual** sensuous

All breathing human passion far above,
   That leaves a heart high-sorrowful and cloyed,
      A burning forehead, and a parching tongue.   30

IV

Who are these coming to the sacrifice?
   To what green altar, O mysterious priest,
Lead'st thou that heifer lowing at the skies,
   And all her silken flanks with garlands drest?
What little town by river or sea shore,   35
   Or mountain-built with peaceful citadel,
      Is emptied of this folk, this pious morn?
And, little town, they streets for evermore
   Will silent be; and not a soul to tell
      Why thou art desolate can e'er return.   40

V

O Attic shape! Fair attitude! with brede°
   Of marble men and maidens overwrought,
With forest branches and the trodden weed;
   Thou, silent form, dost tease us out of thought
As doth eternity: Cold Pastoral!   45
When old age shall this generation waste,
   Thou shalt remain, in midst of other woe
   Than ours, a friend to man, to whom thou say'st,
"Beauty is truth, truth beauty,"—that is all
   Ye know on earth, and all ye need to know.   50
                                                              [1820]

 TOPICS FOR CRITICAL THINKING AND WRITING

1. In the first stanza Keats calls the urn an "unravished bride of quietness,"
   a "foster-child of silence and slow time," and a "Sylvan historian." Paraphrase each of these terms.
2. How much sense does it make to say (lines 11–12) that "Heard melodies
   are sweet, but those unheard / Are sweeter"?
3. In the second stanza Keats says that the youth will forever sing, the
   trees will forever have their foliage, and the woman will forever be
   beautiful. But what words in the stanza suggest that this scene is not entirely happy? Where else in the poem is it suggested that there are
   painful aspects to the images on the urn?
4. What arguments can you offer to support the view that "Beauty is truth,
   truth beauty"?
5. There is much uncertainty about whether everything in the last two
   lines should be enclosed within quotation marks, or only "Beauty is

⁴¹**brede** design

truth, truth beauty." If only these five words from line 49 should be enclosed within quotation marks, does the speaker address the rest of line 49 and the whole of line 50 to the urn, or to the reader of the poem?

 HERMAN MELVILLE

Herman Melville (1819-91) was born into a poor family in New York City. The bankruptcy and death of his father when Melville was 12 forced the boy to leave school. During these early years he worked first as a bank clerk, then as a farm laborer, then as a store clerk and bookkeeper, and then as a schoolmaster. In 1837 he sailed to England as a cabin boy and signed on for other voyages, notably on whalers in the South Pacific, where he spent time in the Marquesas Islands and Tahiti. Out of his maritime adventures he produced commercially successful books, Typee *(1846),* Omoo *(1847),* Mardi *(1849), and* Redburn *(1849), but* Moby Dick *(1851) was a commercial failure, and so was a later book,* Pierre *(1852). Melville next turned to writing short fiction, but, again commercially unsuccessful, he stopped trying to live by his pen. He survived on some inherited money, and on a political appointment as a customs inspector in New York City. The poems that we reprint apparently were written during his last years.*

Art

In placid hours well-pleased we dream
Of many a brave unbodied scheme.
But form to lend, pulsed life create,
What unlike things must meet and mate:
A flame to melt—a wind to freeze;   5
Sad patience—joyous energies;
Humility—yet pride and scorn;
Instinct and study; love and hate;
Audacity—reverence. These must mate,
And fuse with Jacob's° mystic heart,   10
To wrestle with the angel—Art.

[1891]

Greek Architecture

Not magnitude, not lavishness,
But Form—the Site;
Not innovating wilfulness,
But reverence for the Archetype.

[1891]

---

¹⁰**Jacob** In the Hebrew Bible, in Genesis 32.24–29, Jacob wrestles with an angel. The struggle ends with the angel blessing Jacob.

TOPICS FOR CRITICAL THINKING AND WRITING

1. Paraphrase the first four lines of "Art."
2. Suppose someone asked you why the creator of a work of art needs to possess "audacity" and also "reverence." What would you reply?
3. In "Art" Melville is talking about the creative process, but would you say that the finished work of art often reveals apparently contradictory characteristics, for instance a bold statement within an apparently confining form? Take any work of art that you like—perhaps a favorite song or painting or story—and examine it from this point of view.
4. The architecture of ancient Greece is "classic" in the sense that it is ancient, a part of what we call "the classical world," but what other implications do you attribute to the word *classic?* You might begin by thinking not of buildings and of books but of clothing. What do we mean when we speak of a *classic dress* or *classic chinos?*
5. Find a reproduction of an example of Greek architecture (for instance, the Parthenon) and compare it with an example of Gothic architecture (for example, Notre Dame in Paris, or Chartres Cathedral). Does Melville's description of Greek architecture seem accurate, or could it apply equally well to the Gothic building?

 A. E. HOUSMAN

Alfred Edward Housman (1859-1936) was born in rural Shropshire, England, and educated in classics and philosophy at Oxford University. Although he was a brilliant student, his final examination was unexpectedly weak—in fact, he failed—and he did not receive the academic appointment that he had anticipated. He began working as a civil servant at the British Patent Office, but in his spare time he wrote scholarly articles on Latin literature, and these writings in 1892 won him an appointment as Professor of Latin at the University of London. In 1911 he was appointed to Cambridge. During his lifetime he published (in addition to his scholarly writings) only two thin books of poetry, A Shropshire Lad *(1898) and* Last Poems *(1922), and a highly readable lecture called* The Name and Nature of Poetry *(1933). After his death a third book of poems,* More Poems *(1936), was published.*

Loitering with a vacant eye
(A Shropshire Lad #51)

Loitering with a vacant eye
Along the Grecian gallery,°
And brooding on my heavy ill,
I met a statue standing still.
Still in marble stone stood he,   5

²**Grecian gallery** gallery, in a museum, displaying Greek art

And steadfastly he looked at me.
"Well met," I thought the look would say,
"We both were fashioned far away;
We neither knew, when we were young,
These Londoners we live among."   10

  Still he stood and eyed me hard,
An earnest and a grave regard:
"What, lad, drooping with your lot?
I, too, would be where I am not.
I, too, survey that endless line   15
Of men whose thoughts are not as mine.
Years, ere you stood up from rest,
On my neck the collar prest;
Years, when you lay down your ill,
I shall stand and bear it still.   20
Courage, lad, 'tis not for long;
Stand, quit you like stone, be strong."
So I thought his look would say;
And light on me my trouble lay,
And I stept out in flesh and bone   25
Manful like the man of stone.

[Undated]

TOPICS FOR CRITICAL THINKING AND WRITING

1. Some readers find elements of humor in the poem. Do you? If so, what are they?
2. Do you imagine that most viewers of this ancient Greek statue of a male would see in it what Housman sees (and hears)? Explain.
3. If a work of art has ever (so to speak) spoken to you—moved you and in some ways inspired you—describe the work and your response in an essay of 500–750 words.

WILLA CATHER

Willa Cather (1873–1947), born in Virginia but brought up in Nebraska, is chiefly known as a writer of short stories and novels, but she also wrote essays and poems. We reprint an essay of hers on page 857, and a story on page 875.

The Swedish Mother

(Nebraska)

"You shall hear the tale again—
    Hush, my red-haired daughter."
Brightly burned the sunset gold
    On the black pond water.   4

Red the pasture ridges gleamed
  Where the sun was sinking.
Slow the windmill rasped and wheezed
  Where the herd was drinking.   8

On the kitchen doorstep low
  Sat a Swedish mother;
In her arms one baby slept,
  By her sat another.   12

"All time, 'way back in old countree,
Your grandpa, he been good to me.
Your grandpa, he been young man, too,
And I been yust li'l' girl, like you.   16
All time in spring, when evening come,
We go bring sheep an' li'l' lambs home.
We go big field, 'way up on hill,
Ten times high like our windmill.   20
One time your grandpa leave me wait
While he call sheep down. By de gate
I sit still till night come dark;
Rabbits run an' strange dogs bark,   24
Old owl hoot, an' your modder cry,
She been so 'fraid big bear come by.
Last, 'way off, she hear de sheep,
Li'l' bells ring and li'l' lambs bleat.   28
Then all sheep come over de hills,
Big white dust, an' old dog Nils.
Then come grandpa, in his arm
Li'l' sick lamb dat somet'ing harm.   32
He so young then, big and strong,
Pick li'l' girl up, take her 'long,—
Poor li'l' tired girl, yust like you,—
Lift her up an' take her too.   36
Hold her tight an' carry her far,—
Ain't no light but yust one star.
Sheep go 'bah-h,' an' road so steep;
Li'l' girl she go fast asleep."   40

Every night the red-haired child
  Begs to hear the story,
When the pasture ridges burn
  With the sunset glory.   44

She can never understand,
  Since the tale ends gladly,
Why her mother, telling it,
  Always smiles so sadly.   48

Wonderingly she looks away
  Where her mother's gazing;
Only sees the drifting herd,
  In the sunset grazing.   52

[1903]

TOPICS FOR CRITICAL THINKING AND WRITING

1. You probably know from your own experience that many children like to hear the same story told over and over. Why do you suppose this is so? Are there still some works—songs, for instance—that you enjoy hearing again and again? If so, try to account for your pleasure, since there is no longer any suspense or novelty.

2. In lines 45-48 we learn that the mother "smiles so sadly" in telling the tale. Why *does* she smile "sadly" at what seems to be a happy story?

 ROBERT FROST

Robert Frost (1874-1963) was born in California. After his father's death in 1885 Frost's mother brought the family to New England, where she taught in high schools in Massachusetts and New Hampshire. Frost studied for part of one term at Dartmouth College in New Hampshire, then did odd jobs (including teaching), and from 1897 to 1899 was enrolled as a special student at Harvard. He later farmed in New Hampshire, published a few poems in local newspapers, left the farm and taught again, and in 1912 left for England, where he hoped to achieve more popular success as a writer. By 1915 he had won a considerable reputation, and he returned to the United States, settling on a farm in New Hampshire and cultivating the image of the country-wise farmer-poet. In fact he was well read in the classics, in the Bible, and in English and American literature.

Among Frost's many comments about literature, here are three: "Writing is unboring to the extent that it is dramatic"; "Every poem is . . . a figure of the will braving alien entanglements"; and, finally, a poem "begins in delight and ends in wisdom. . . . It runs a course of lucky events, and ends in a clarification of life—not necessarily a great clarification, such as sects and cults are founded on, but in a momentary stay against confusion."

The Aim Was Song

Before man came to blow it right
   The wind once blew itself untaught,
And did its loudest day and night
   In any rough place where it caught.   4

Man came to tell it what was wrong:
   It hadn't found the place to blow;
It blew too hard—the aim was song.
   And listen—how it ought to go!   8

He took a little in his mouth,
   And held it long enough for north
To be converted into south,
   And then by measure blew it forth.   12

By measure. It was word and note,
　The wind the wind had meant to be—
A little through the lips and throat.
　The aim was song—the wind could see.   16

[1923]

TOPICS FOR CRITICAL THINKING AND WRITING

1. Frost is telling a playful fable about the invention of "song." According to the fable, what are the essentials of song?
2. In a journal entry, or in a note of about one typed page, extend Frost's fable to cover some other kind or kinds of art, for instance architecture or music or dance. To what degree, if any, are his comments on "song" relevant to other forms?

ARCHIBALD MACLEISH

Archibald MacLeish (1892-1982) was educated at Harvard and at Yale Law School. His relatively early poetry (say, to about 1930), including "Ars Poetica," often is condensed and allusive, though his later poems and his plays are readily accessible, and MacLeish became a sort of establishment representative of poetry. Under Franklin Delano Roosevelt, he served as librarian of Congress (1939-44) and as assistant secretary of state (1944-45). He then taught at Harvard and at Amherst until he retired in 1967.

Ars Poetica*

A poem should be palpable and mute
As a globed fruit,

Dumb
As old medallions to the thumb,   4

Silent as the sleeve-worn stone
Of casement ledges where the moss has grown—

A poem should be wordless
As the flight of birds.   8

A poem should be motionless in time
As the moon climbs,

Leaving, as the moon releases
Twig by twig the night-entangled trees,   12

Leaving, as the moon behind the winter leaves,
Memory by memory the mind—

*Ars Poetica Latin for "poetic art," or "the art of poetry"

A poem should be motionless in time
As the moon climbs.   16

A poem should be equal to:
Not true.

For all the history of grief
An empty doorway and a maple leaf.   20

For love
The leaning grasses and two lights above the sea—

A poem should not mean
But be.   24

[1926]

TOPICS FOR CRITICAL THINKING AND WRITING

1. A poem uses words. How, then, can it be "mute" (line 1), "dumb" (line 3), "silent" (line 5), and "wordless" (line 7)? What do you think MacLeish means in the first eight lines?
2. MacLeish says that "an empty doorway and a maple leaf" can stand for "all the history of grief." Devise your own images for "grief," and also images for two other emotions, for instance joy and love.
3. What do you take the final two lines to mean? Do they contradict the rest of the poem? If so, is the poem incoherent?

ELIZABETH BISHOP

Elizabeth Bishop (1911–79) was born in Worcester, Massachusetts. Because her father died when she was 8 months old and her mother was confined to a sanitarium four years later, Bishop was raised by relatives in New England and Nova Scotia. After graduating from Vassar College in 1934, where she was co-editor of the student literary magazine, she lived (on a small private income) for a while in Key West, France, and Mexico, and then for much of her adult life in Brazil, before returning to the United States to teach at Harvard. Her financial independence enabled her to write without worrying about the sales of her books and without having to devote energy to distracting jobs.

Poem

About the size of an old-style dollar bill,
American or Canadian,
mostly the same whites, gray greens, and steel grays
—this little painting (a sketch for a larger one?)
has never earned any money in its life.   5
Useless and free, it has spent seventy years

as a minor family relic
handed along collaterally to owners
who looked at it sometimes, or didn't bother to.

It must be Nova Scotia; only there   10
does one see gabled wooden houses
painted that awful shade of brown.
The other houses, the bits that show, are white.
Elm trees, low hills, a thin church steeple
—that gray-blue wisp—or is it? In the foreground   15
a water meadow with some tiny cows,
two brushstrokes each, but confidently cows;
two minuscule white geese in the blue water,
back-to-back, feeding, and a slanting stick.
Up closer, a wild iris, white and yellow,   20
fresh-squiggled from the tube.
The air is fresh and cold; cold early spring
clear as gray glass; a half inch of blue sky
below the steel-gray storm clouds.
(They were the artist's specialty.)   25
A specklike bird is flying to the left.
Or is it a flyspeck looking like a bird?

Heavens, I recognize the place, I know it!
It's behind—I can almost remember the farmer's name.
His barn backed on that meadow. There it is,   30
titanium white, one dab. The hint of steeple,
filaments of brush-hairs, barely there,
must be the Presbyterian church.
Would that be Miss Gillespie's house?
Those particular geese and cows   35
are naturally before my time.

A sketch done in an hour, "in one breath,"
once taken from a trunk and handed over.
*Would you like this? I'll probably never
have room to hang these things again.*   40
*Your Uncle George, no, mine, my Uncle George,
he'd be your great-uncle, left them all with Mother
when he went back to England.
You know, he was quite famous, an R.A.* ° ...

I never knew him. We both knew this place,   45
apparently, this literal small backwater,
looked at it long enough to memorize it,
our years apart. How strange. And it's still loved,
or its memory is (it must have changed a lot).
Our visions coincided—"visions" is   50
too serious a word—our looks, two looks:
art "copying from life" and life itself,

44**R. A.** a member of the Royal Academy

life and the memory of it so compressed
they've turned into each other. Which is which?
Life and the memory of it cramped,   55
dim, on a piece of Bristol board,
dim, but how live, how touching in detail
—the little that we get for free,
the little of our earthly trust. Not much.
About the size of our abidance   60
along with theirs: the munching cows,
the iris, crisp and shivering, the water
still standing from spring freshets,
the yet-to-be-dismantled elms, the geese.

[1976]

 TOPIC FOR CRITICAL THINKING AND WRITING

See how far you can go by thinking about "Poem" as a poem about the arts in
general, and perhaps poetry in particular.

 LAWRENCE FERLINGHETTI

*Lawrence Ferlinghetti (b. 1919) has been much concerned with
bringing poetry to the people. To this end he has not only written poetry but has also been the editor and publisher of City Lights Books in
San Francisco and (since 1953) has operated a bookstore, the City
Lights Bookshop, the first all-paperback bookstore in the United
States. In 1956 Ferlinghetti achieved national fame when, as the publisher of Allen Ginsberg's* Howl, *he was arrested (and later acquitted)
on an obscenity charge.*

Constantly risking absurdity

Constantly risking absurdity
                              and death
              whenever he performs
                     above the heads
                          of his audience   5
        the poet like an acrobat
                    climbs on rime
                        to a high wire of his own making
and balancing on eyebeams
                              above a sea of faces   10
              paces his way
                         to the other side of day
        performing *entrechats*°
                        and sleight-of-foot tricks

¹³**entrechat** a leap in ballet

and other high theatrics   15
              and all without mistaking
      any thing
          for what it may not be
    For he's the super realist
               who must perforce perceive   20
        taut truth
                before the taking of each stance or step

     in his supposed advance
                 toward that still higher perch
where Beauty stands and waits   25
           with gravity
              to start her death-defying leap
   And he
     a little charleychaplin man
               who may or may not catch   30
       her fair eternal form
           spreadeagled in the empty air
      of existence

                              [1958]

TOPICS FOR CRITICAL THINKING AND WRITING

1. According to Ferlinghetti, in what sense is a poet like an acrobat?
2. In this poem, what "tricks" (line 14) does Ferlinghetti engage in?

RICHARD WILBUR

Richard Wilbur, born in New York City in 1921, was educated at Amherst and Harvard. He served in the army during World War II, and in 1947 he published The Beautiful Changes, *a book of poems that reflected some of his experience in Europe. This book and subsequent books of poetry established his literary reputation, but probably his most widely known works are the lyrics that he wrote for Leonard Bernstein's musical version of* Candide.

Museum Piece

The good gray guardians of art
Patrol the halls on spongy shoes,
Impartially protective, though
Perhaps suspicious of Toulouse.°   4

---

⁴**Toulouse** Henri de Toulouse-Lautrec (1864–1901), French painter known especially for his paintings of café life and of prostitutes

Here dozes one against the wall,
Disposed upon a funeral chair.
A Degas° dancer pirouettes°
Upon the parting of his hair.   8

See how she spins! The grace is there,
But strain as well is plain to see.
Degas loved the two together:
Beauty joined to energy.   12

Edgar Degas purchased once
A fine El Greco,° which he kept
Against the wall beside his bed
To hang his pants on while he slept.   16

[1950]

⁷**Degas** Edgar Degas (1834–1917), another French painter, noted for his paintings of ballet dancers   ⁷**pirouette** a full turn of the body on the tip of the toe or the ball of the foot   ¹⁴**a fine El Greco** a painting by Doménikos Theotokópoulos (1541–1614), born in Greece but active chiefly in Spain, where he was known as El Greco (the Greek)

 ## TOPICS FOR CRITICAL THINKING AND WRITING

1. What do people usually mean by "museum piece"? What is meant here?
2. Who are "The good gray guardians of art"? Why are they "good"? Why "gray"? Does the phrase, with the words strung together, have another meaning? (And why do they wear "spongy shoes"?)
3. In lines 9–10 Wilbur says that in Degas's picture of a dancer one sees not only "grace" but also "strain." Where do you find those two qualities together in the poem?
4. The last stanza relates a mildly amusing anecdote. Is there some sort of lesson implied also? If so, what is it?

 ## NIKKI GIOVANNI

Nikki Giovanni was born in Knoxville, Tennessee, in 1943 and educated at Fisk University, the University of Pennsylvania School of Social Work, and Columbia University. She has taught at Queens College, Rutgers University, and The Ohio State University, and she now teaches creative writing at Mt. St. Joseph on the Ohio. Giovanni has published many books of poems, an autobiography (Gemini: An Extended Autobiographical Statement on My First Twenty-Five Years of Being a Black Poet), *a book of essays, and a book consisting of a conversation with James Baldwin.*

For Saundra

i wanted to write
a poem
that rhymes
but revolution doesn't lend
itself to be-bopping   5

then my neighbor
who thinks i hate
asked—do you ever write
tree poems—i like trees
so i thought   10

i'll write a beautiful green tree poem
peeked from my window
to check the image
noticed the school yard was covered
with asphalt   15
no green—no trees grow
in manhattan

then, well, i thought the sky
i'll do a big blue sky poem

but all the clouds have winged   20
low since no-Dick° was elected

so i thought again
and it occurred to me
maybe i shouldn't write
at all   25
but clean my gun
and check my kerosene supply

perhaps these are not poetic
times
at all   30

[1968]

 TOPICS FOR CRITICAL THINKING AND WRITING

1. In a brief paragraph characterize the speaker of the poem.
2. Is the poem about creating a work of art? Or about the contemporary
   scene? Or both, or neither? Explain.

21**no-Dick** Richard Nixon

CHAPTER 21

The Individual and Society

Essays

 JOSEPH BRANT

Joseph Brant (1742–1807), whose Indian name is usually given as Thayendanega, was a Mohawk chief. As a youth Brant was educated at Eleazar Wheelock's Indian School in Connecticut, and he later served the British in the French and Indian War and also during the American Revolution. Brant seems to have moved easily in two worlds; he visited England twice, and after the Revolution he arranged for his people to receive land and subsidies in Canada.

The following remarks were made in a letter, responding to this question: Are Indians (supposedly living in a state of nature) happier than whites (supposedly living in "civilization")? Brant's biographer, Isabel Thompson Kelsay, assumes that the letter was written "with the aid of a secretary" (Joseph Brant [1984], 534).

Indian Civilization vs. White Civilization

I was, sir, born of Indian parents, and lived while a child, among those you are pleased to call savages; I was afterwards sent to live among the white people, and educated at one of your schools; since which period, I have been honoured, much beyond my deserts, by an acquaintance with a number of principal characters both in Europe and America.

After all this experience, and after every exertion to divest myself of prejudice, I am obliged to give my opinion in favour of my own people. . . . I will not enlarge on an idea so singular in civilized life, and perhaps disagreeable to you; and will only observe, that among us, we have no law but that written on the heart of every rational creature by the immediate finger of the great Spirit of the universe himself. We have no prisons—we have no pompous parade of courts; and yet judges are as highly esteemed among us, as they are among you, and their decisions as highly revered; property, to say the least, is as well guarded, and crimes are as impartially punished. We have among us no splendid villains, above the controul of that law, which influences our decisions; in a word, we have no robbery under the colour of law—daring wickedness here is never suffered to triumph over helpless innocence—the estates of widows and orphans are never devoured by enterprising sharpers. Our sachems, and our warriors, eat their own bread, and not the bread of wretchedness. No person, among us, desires any other reward for performing a brave and worthy action, than the consciousness of serving his nation. Our wise men are called fathers—they are truly deserving the character; they are always accessible—I will not say to the meanest of our people—for we have none mean, but such as render themselves so by their vices. . . .

We do not hunger and thirst after those superfluities of life, that are the ruin of thousands of families among you. Our ornaments, in general, are simple, and easily obtained. Envy and covetousness, those worms that destroy the fair flower of human happiness, are unknown in this climate.

The palaces and prisons among you, form a most dreadful contrast. Go to the former places, and you will see, perhaps, a deformed piece of earth swelled with pride, and assuming airs, that become none but the Spirit above. Go to one of your prisons—here description utterly fails!—certainly the sight of an Indian torture, is not half so painful to a well informed mind. Kill them [the prisoners], if you please—kill them, too, by torture; but let the torture last no longer than a day. . . . Those you call savages, relent—the most furious of our tormentors exhausts his rage in a few hours, and dispatches the unhappy victim with a sudden stroke.

5   But for what are many of your prisoners confined? For debt! Astonishing! and will you ever again call the Indian nations cruel?—Liberty, to a rational creature, as much exceeds property, as the light of the sun does that of the most twinkling star: but you put them on a level, to the everlasting disgrace of civilization. . . . And I seriously declare, that I had rather die by the most severe tortures ever inflicted by any savage nation on the continent, than languish in one of your prisons for a single year. Great Maker of the world! and do you call yourselves christians? . . . Does then the religion of him whom you call your Saviour, inspire this conduct, and lead to this practice? Surely no. It was a sentence that once struck my mind with some force, that "a bruised reed he never broke." Cease then, while these practices continue among you, to call yourselves christians, lest you publish to the world your hypocrisy. Cease to call other nations savage, when you are tenfold more the children of cruelty, than they.

[1789]

TOPICS FOR CRITICAL THINKING AND WRITING

1. In his first sentence, Brant says that he was born "among those you are pleased to call savages." Suppose he had left that phrase out, or substituted another phrase such as "and lived among them." How does the phrase he uses help you to anticipate his answer to the question "Are Indians happier than whites?"

2. In his second paragraph Brant says, "We have no law but that written on the heart of every rational creature by the immediate finger of the great Spirit of the universe himself." Judging from the rest of the selection from Brant, what is the law written on the hearts of his fellows? Do you think the behavior he outlines can indeed be characterized as "rational"? Explain.

3. At the end of his second paragraph, what does Brant mean by "meanest" and "mean"? (Check a good dictionary to see which of the several definitions is the most relevant to the context.)

4. In his third paragraph Brant says that "envy and covetousness . . . are unknown" to his people. Do you believe that envy and covetousness are the products of certain kinds of society, and that there may well be societies in which people are free of these qualities? Are you aware of any such society? If not, what *do* you think are the sources of envy and covetousness? Finally, would you say that these qualities play a large role in our society—and is it conceivable that they may play a valuable role? In a paragraph that may run for half a page or a page and a half, begin an essay in which you will attempt to answer these questions— but don't write the essay.

 MARY JEMISON

Mary Jemison (1743–1833) was born at sea while her parents were en route from Ireland to America. Captured in 1758 by a party of Indians in Pennsylvania, she was adopted by two Seneca women. She married twice, to a Delaware and to a Seneca, and she bore several children. Jemison had the opportunity to return to the white world, but she refused, living most of her life in the Genesee country of western New York. In her old age "the white woman of the Genesee" dictated her story—it is reported in J. E. Seaver's The Life of Mrs. Mary Jemison *(1824)—and though the account doubtless is colored by the white man who took it down, the book remains an important source.*

A Narrative of Her Life

At night we arrived at a small Seneca Indian town, at the mouth of a small river, that was called by the Indians, in the Seneca language, She-nan-jee, where the two Squaws to whom I belonged resided. There we landed, and the Indians went on; which was the last I ever saw of them.

Having made fast to the shore, the Squaws left me in the canoe while they went to their wigwam or house in the town, and returned with a suit of

Indian clothing, all new, and very clean and nice. My clothes, though whole and good when I was taken, were now torn in pieces, so that I was almost naked. They first undressed me and threw my rags into the river; then washed me clean and dressed me in the new suit they had just brought, in complete Indian style; and then led me home and seated me in the center of their wigwam.

I had been in that situation but a few minutes, before all the Squaws in the town came in to see me. I was soon surrounded by them, and they immediately set up a most dismal howling, crying bitterly, and wringing their hands in all the agonies of grief for a deceased relative.

Their tears flowed freely, and they exhibited all the signs of real mourning. At the commencement of this scene, one of their number began, in a voice somewhat between speaking and singing, to recite some words to the following purport, and continued the recitation till the ceremony was ended; the company at the same time varying the appearance of their countenances, gestures and tone of voice, so as to correspond with the sentiments expressed by their leader:

5   "Oh our brother! Alas! He is dead—he has gone; he will never return! Friendless he died on the field of the slain, where his bones are yet lying unburied! Oh, who will not mourn his sad fate? No tears dropped around him; oh, no! No tears of his sisters were there! He fell in his prime, when his arm was most needed to keep us from danger! Alas! he has gone! and left us in sorrow, his loss to bewail: Oh where is his spirit? His spirit went naked, and hungry it wanders, and thirsty and wounded it groans to return! Oh helpless and wretched, our brother has gone! No blanket nor food to nourish and warm him; nor candles to light him, nor weapons of war:—Oh, none of those comforts had he! But well we remember his deeds!—The deer he could take on the chase! The panther shrunk back at the sight of his strength! His enemies fell at his feet! He was brave and courageous in war! As the fawn he was harmless: his friendship was ardent: his temper was gentle: his pity was great! Oh! our friend, our companion is dead! Our brother, our brother, alas! he is gone! But why do we grieve for his loss? In the strength of a warrior, undaunted he left us, to fight by the side of the Chiefs! His war-whoop was shrill! His rifle well aimed laid his enemies low: his tomahawk drank of their blood: and his knife flayed their scalps while yet covered with gore! And why do we mourn? Though he fell on the field of the slain, with glory he fell, and his spirit went up to the land of his fathers in war! Then why do we mourn? With transports of joy they received him, and fed him, and clothed him, and welcomed him there! Oh friends, he is happy; then dry up your tears! His spirit has seen our distress, and sent us a helper whom with pleasure we greet. Dickewamis has come: then let us receive her with joy! She is handsome and pleasant! Oh! she is our sister, and gladly we welcome her here. In the place of our brother she stands in our tribe. With care we will guard her from trouble; and may she be happy till her spirit shall leave us."

In the course of that ceremony, from mourning they became serene—joy sparkled in their countenances, and they seemed to rejoice over me as over a long lost child. I was made welcome amongst them as a sister to the two Squaws before mentioned, and was called Dickewamis; which being interpreted, signifies a pretty girl, a handsome girl, or a pleasant, good thing. That is the name by which I have ever since been called by the Indians.

I afterwards learned that the ceremony I at that time passed through, was that of adoption. The two squaws had lost a brother in Washington's war, sometime in the year before, and in consequence of his death went up to Fort Pitt, on the day on which I arrived there, in order to receive a prisoner or an enemy's scalp, to supply their loss.

It is a custom of the Indians, when one of their number is slain or taken prisoner in battle, to give to the nearest relative to the dead or absent, a prisoner, if they have chanced to take one, and if not, to give him the scalp of an enemy. On the return of the Indians from conquest, which is always announced by peculiar shoutings, demonstrations of joy, and the exhibition of some trophy of victory, the mourners come forward and make their claims. If they receive a prisoner, it is at their option either to satiate their vengeance by taking his life in the most cruel manner they can conceive of; or, to receive and adopt him into the family, in the place of him whom they have lost. All the prisoners that are taken in battle and carried to the encampment or town by the Indians, are given to the bereaved families, till their number is made good. And unless the mourners have but just received the news of their bereavement, and are under the operation of a paroxysm of grief, anger and revenge; or, unless the prisoner is very old, sickly, or homely, they generally save him, and treat him kindly. But if their mental wound is fresh, their loss so great that they deem it irreparable, or if their prisoner or prisoners do not meet their approbation, no torture, let it be ever so cruel, seems sufficient to make them satisfaction. It is family, and not national, sacrifices amongst the Indians, that has given them an indelible stamp as barbarians, and identified their character with the idea which is generally formed of unfeeling ferocity, and the most abandoned cruelty.

It was my happy lot to be accepted for adoption; and at the time of the ceremony I was received by the two squaws, to supply the place of their brother in the family; and I was ever considered and treated by them as a real sister, the same as though I had been born of their mother.

10   During my adoption, I sat motionless, nearly terrified to death at the appearance and actions of the company, expecting every moment to feel their vengeance, and suffer death on the spot. I was, however, happily disappointed, when at the close of the ceremony the company retired, and my sisters went about employing every means for my consolation and comfort.

Being now settled and provided with a home, I was employed in nursing the children, and doing light work about the house. Occasionally I was sent out with the Indian hunters, when they went but a short distance, to help them carry their game. My situation was easy; I had no particular hardships to endure. But still, the recollection of my parents, my brothers and sisters, my home, and my own captivity, destroyed my happiness, and made me constantly solitary, lonesome and gloomy.

My sisters would not allow me to speak English in their hearing; but remembering the charge that my dear mother gave me at the time I left her, whenever I chanced to be alone I made a business of repeating my prayer, catechism, or something I had learned in order that I might not forget my own language. By practising in that way I retained it till I came to Genesee flats, where I soon became acquainted with English people with whom I have been almost daily in the habit of conversing.

My sisters were diligent in teaching me their language; and to their great satisfaction I soon learned so that I could understand it readily, and speak it fluently. I was very fortunate in falling into their hands; for they were kind good-natured women; peaceable and mild in their dispositions; temperate and decent in their habits, and very tender and gentle towards me. I have great reason to respect them, though they have been dead a great number of years.

The town where they lived was pleasantly situated on the Ohio, at the mouth of the She-nan-jee: the land produced good corn; the woods furnished a plenty of game, and the waters abounded with fish. Another river emptied itself into the Ohio, directly opposite the mouth of the She-nan-jee. We spent the summer at that place, where we planted, hoed, and harvested a large crop of corn, of an excellent quality.

15   I had then been with the Indians four summers and four winters, and had become so far accustomed to their mode of living, habits and dispositions, that my anxiety to get away, to be set at liberty, and leave them, had almost subsided. With them was my home; my family was there, and there I had many friends to whom I was warmly attached in consideration of the favors, affection and friendship with which they had uniformly treated me, from the time of my adoption. Our labor was not severe; and that of one year was exactly similar, in almost every respect, to that of the others, without that endless variety that is to be observed in the common labor of the white people. Notwithstanding the Indian women have all the fuel and bread to procure, and the cooking to perform, their task is probably not harder than that of white women, who have those articles provided for them; and their cares certainly are not half as numerous, nor as great. In the summer season, we planted, tended and harvested our corn, and generally had all our children with us; but had no master to oversee or drive us, so that we could work as leisurely as we pleased. We had no ploughs on the Ohio; but performed the whole process of planting and hoeing with a small tool that resembled, in some respects, a hoe with a very short handle.

Our cooking consisted in pounding our corn into samp or hommany, boiling the hommany, making now and then a cake and baking it in the ashes, and in boiling or roasting our venison. As our cooking and eating utensils consisted of a hommany block and pestle, a small kettle, a knife or two, and a few vessels of bark or wood, it required but little time to keep them in order for use.

Spinning, weaving, sewing, stocking knitting, and the like, are arts which have never been practised in the Indian tribes generally. After the revolutionary war, I learned to sew, so that I could make my own clothing after a poor fashion; but the other domestic arts I have been wholly ignorant of the application of, since my captivity. In the season of hunting, it was our business, in addition to our cooking, to bring home the game that was taken by the Indians, dress it, and carefully preserve the eatable meat, and prepare or dress the skins. Our clothing was fastened together with strings of deer skin, and tied on with the same.

In that manner we lived, without any of those jealousies, quarrels, and revengeful battles between families and individuals, which have been common in the Indian tribes since the introduction of ardent spirits amongst them.

The use of ardent spirits amongst the Indians, and the attempts which have been made to civilize and christianize them by the white people, has constantly made them worse and worse; increased their vices, and robbed them of many of their virtues; and will ultimately produce their extermination. I have seen, in a number of instances, the effects of education upon some of our Indians, who were taken when young, from their families, and placed at school before they had had an opportunity to contract many Indian habits, and there kept till they arrived to manhood; but I have never seen one of those but what was an Indian in every respect after he returned. Indians must and will be Indians, in spite of all the means that can be used for their cultivation in the sciences and arts.

20   One thing only marred my happiness, while I lived with them on the Ohio; and that was the recollection that I had once had tender parents, and a home that I loved. Aside from that consideration, or, if I had been taken in infancy, I should have been contented in my situation. Notwithstanding all that has been said against the Indians, in consequence of their cruelties to their enemies—cruelties that I have witnessed, and had abundant proof of— it is a fact that they are naturally kind, tender and peaceable towards their friends, and strictly honest; and that those cruelties have been practised, only upon their enemies, according to their idea of justice.

[1824]

 TOPICS FOR CRITICAL THINKING AND WRITING

1. What seem to you to be the chief elements of the ceremony of adoption (paragraph 5)? In what ways is it similar to a ceremony you know, and in what ways is it different?

2. In the last sentence of paragraph 8, Jemison explains the source of the ferocity and cruelty of Indian behavior. What is her explanation? Has her point been demonstrated in the behavior of "Indians" in movies or TV dramas? Try to recall a specific example.

3. In her next-to-last paragraph Jemison says that the introduction of alcohol and Christianity to Indians "increased their vices, and robbed them of many of their virtues." On the basis of her account, what vices and what virtues did the Indians display?

4. In her final sentence Jemison summarizes the behavior of the Indians she lived among. Might her words be said of the people you live among? What would *your* version of her sentence say? In a brief essay (500–750 words) offer an account of instances that exemplify the behavior of the people that you live among. Your sentence can introduce or conclude your discussion. And some fiction may help: Impersonate an adopted member—let's say from another planet—of your group.

 JUDY BRADY

Born in San Francisco in 1937, Judy Brady married in 1960 and two years later earned a bachelor's degree in painting at the University of Iowa. Active in the women's movement and in other political causes, she has worked as an author, an editor, and a secretary. The essay reprinted here, written before she and her husband separated, appeared originally in the first issue of Ms. *in 1971, when the author used her married name, Judy Syfers.*

I Want a Wife

I belong to that classification of people known as wives. I am A Wife. And, not altogether incidentally, I am a mother.

Not too long ago a male friend of mine appeared on the scene fresh from a recent divorce. He had one child, who is, of course, with his ex-wife. He is looking for another wife. As I thought about him while I was ironing one evening, it suddenly occurred to me that I, too, would like to have a wife. Why do I want a wife?

I would like to go back to school so that I can become economically in-dependent, support myself, and, if need be, support those dependent upon me. I want a wife who will work and send me to school. And while I am going to school I want a wife to take care of my children. I want a wife to keep track of the children's doctor and dentist appointments. And to keep track of mine, too. I want a wife to make sure my children eat properly and are kept clean. I want a wife who will wash the children's clothes and keep them mended. I want a wife who is a good nurturant attendant to my chil-dren, who arranges for their schooling, makes sure that they have an ade-quate social life with their peers, takes them to the park, the zoo, etc. I want a wife who takes care of the children when they are sick, a wife who arranges to be around when the children need special care, because, of course, I cannot miss classes at school. My wife must arrange to lose time at work and not lose the job. It may mean a small cut in my wife's income from time to time, but I guess I can tolerate that. Needless to say, my wife will arrange and pay for the care of the children while my wife is working.

I want a wife who will take care of *my* physical needs. I want a wife who will keep my house clean. A wife who will pick up after my children, a wife who will pick up after me. I want a wife who will keep my clothes clean, ironed, mended, replaced when need be, and who will see to it that my personal things are kept in their proper place so that I can find what I need the minute I need it. I want a wife who cooks the meals, a wife who is a *good* cook. I want a wife who will plan the menus, do the necessary gro-cery shopping, prepare the meals, serve them pleasantly, and then do the cleaning up while I do my studying. I want a wife who will care for me when I am sick and sympathize with my pain and loss of time from school. I want a wife to go along when our family takes a vacation so that someone can continue to care for me and my children when I need a rest and change of scene.

5   I want a wife who will not bother me with rambling complaints about a wife's duties. But I want a wife who will listen to me when I feel the need to explain a rather difficult point I have come across in my course of studies. And I want a wife who will type my papers for me when I have written them.

I want a wife who will take care of the details of my social life. When my wife and I are invited out by my friends. I want a wife who will take care of the babysitting arrangements. When I meet people at school that I like and want to entertain, I want a wife who will have the house clean, will pre-pare a special meal, serve it to me and my friends, and not interrupt when I talk about things that interest me and my friends. I want a wife who will have arranged that the children are fed and ready for bed before my guests arrive so that the children do not bother us. I want a wife who takes care of the needs of my guests so that they feel comfortable, who makes sure that they have an ashtray, that they are passed the hors d'oeuvres, that they are offered a second helping of the food, that their wine glasses are replenished when necessary, that their coffee is served to them as they like it. And I want a wife who knows that sometimes I need a night out by myself.

I want a wife who is sensitive to my sexual needs, a wife who makes love passionately and eagerly when I feel like it, a wife who makes sure that I am satisfied. And, of course, I want a wife who will not demand sexual attention when I am not in the mood for it. I want a wife who assumes the complete responsibility for birth control, because I do not want more children. I want a wife who will remain sexually faithful to me so that I do not have to clutter up my intellectual life with jealousies. And I want a wife who understands that *my* sexual needs may entail more than strict adherence to monogamy. I must, after all, be able to relate to people as fully as possible.

If, by chance, I find another person more suitable as a wife than the wife I already have, I want the liberty to replace my present wife with another one. Naturally, I will expect a fresh, new life; my wife will take the children and be solely responsible for them so that I am left free.

When I am through with school and have a job, I want my wife to quit working and remain at home so that my wife can more fully and completely take care of a wife's duties.

10   My God, who *wouldn't* want a wife?

[1971]

TOPICS FOR CRITICAL THINKING AND WRITING

1. Brady uses the word "wife" in sentences where one ordinarily would use "she" or "her." Why? And why does she begin paragraphs 4, 5, 6, and 7 with the same words, "I want a wife"?

2. Drawing on your experience as observer of the world around you (and perhaps as husband, wife, or ex-spouse), do you think Brady's picture of a wife's role is grossly exaggerated? Or is it (allowing for some serious playfulness) fairly accurate, even though it was written in 1971? If grossly exaggerated, is the essay therefore meaningless? If fairly accurate, what attitudes and practices does it encourage you to support? Explain.

3. Whether or not you agree with Brady's vision of marriage in our society, write an essay (500 words) titled "I Want a Husband," imitating her style and approach. Write the best possible essay, and then decide which of the two essays makes a fairer comment on current society. Or, if you believe Brady is utterly misleading, write an essay titled "I Want a Wife," seeing the matter in a different light.

4. If you feel that you have been pressed into an unappreciated, unreasonable role—built-in babysitter, listening post, or girl (or boy or man or woman) Friday—write an essay of 500 words that will help the reader to see both your plight and the injustice of the system. (*Hint:* A little humor will help to keep your essay from seeming to be a prolonged whine.)

NEIL MILLER

Neil Miller was born in Kingston, New York. After graduating in 1967 from Brown University he traveled in the Middle East and for two years taught high school English to the children of Moroccan and Iraqi immigrants in Israel. When he returned to the United States he worked in bookstores, taught English in a Berlitz language school, and in 1975 became the news editor of the Gay Community News, *a nonprofit Boston-based paper. Later he became a feature writer for the* Boston Phoenix, *an alternative newspaper, though he continued to be active in gay causes. In an effort to learn more about gay life in America, in 1987 and 1988 he traveled throughout the United States. He presented his findings in a book,* In Search of Gay America, *from which the following excerpt comes.*

In Search of Gay America: Ogilvie, Minnesota (Population 374)

I missed the Minnesota State Fair by three weeks. As an easterner living in a large urban area, I am not particularly conscious of state fairs. And I never assumed that the beef and poultry barn or the cattle barn of a state fair would be a particularly good place to observe gay and lesbian life.

I was wrong. At the Minnesota State Fair, held at the end of August at the St. Paul fairgrounds, a brown and white fifteen hundred pound bull belonging to Al Philipi and John Ritter was named the 1987 state champion. Al and John are two gay dairy farmers who live sixty-five miles north of the Twin Cities. At the awards ceremony, they received a wooden plaque in the shape of the state of Minnesota with the state seal embossed in gold. Tears were streaming down Al's face, John told me.

In the Twin Cities of Minneapolis and St. Paul, you can't help but be aware of the state's agricultural roots. The farm is always just a generation away, despite the air of urban sophistication, the experimental theatre and the recording studios and the take-out Szechuan restaurants, the punk rockers and the long-haired graduate students pedalling their ten-speeds down Hennepin Avenue as if it were Harvard Square. The connection to the land is as true for gay people as anyone else. Karen Clark, the openly lesbian state representative from an inner-city district of Minneapolis, told me with pride that she had grown up on a farm in southwestern Minnesota; she advertised her rural background in her campaign literature. On the office wall of Allan Spear, the gay state senator and chairman of the Minnesota Senate Judiciary Committee, were large framed photographs of Floyd Olson and Elmer Benson, the two agrarian reforming governors of the thirties elected on the ticket of the Farmer Labor party. So when the managing editor of *Equal Time,* the gay newspaper in Minneapolis, suggested I interview one of their editors who lived on a farm and whose lover was a full-time dairy farmer, I was eager to do so. Orwell[1] had written that the coal miner was second in

---

[1]George Orwell (1903–1950), English writer

importance to the man who plowed the soil. I had found the first after much travail; two genuine dairy farmers were as close as I expected to get to the second.

When I arrived at Al and John's farm, late on a Saturday afternoon, autumn was beginning to wane, though it was only September. The leaves had turned to dull yellows and oranges, the cornfields along the side of the road were a russet brown, the days were crisp and clear, and the nights felt colder. Al and John were in high spirits. They had just returned from an overnight trip to the Guernsey Breeders Association cattle sale in Hutchinson, Minnesota, a few hours' drive away. Their friend Paul Leach, a gay dairy farmer who lived an hour to the north, had come by to do the milking and keep an eye on things. Al and John had bought three new cows in Hutchinson, and their prize-winning bull had been displayed on the cover of the auction catalog. John told me later that Al hadn't slept for the entire week before the auction.

5   Al didn't tend to sleep much anyway. He had put his cows on an unusual schedule, milking and feeding five times in each two-day period, at nine and a half hour intervals, with the schedule changing every other day. The cycle began with a milking at midnight; other milkings followed at nine thirty the next morning and seven in the evening. The next day he milked at four thirty in the morning, at two in the afternoon, and once again at midnight. (Most farmers had a saner schedule, milking regularly at five in the morning and five in the evening.) Al started on this routine to increase cash flow. "Your operation can either get larger and generate more product," he said, "or you can generate more product per unit." Buying more cows was just too expensive, with prices ranging from $750 to $1,600 a head, so Al opted for getting more milk out of the cows he had. The arrangement seemed to work, with production up eighteen percent since they had started on the new schedule. One result was that Al and John had a coffee pot going twenty-four hours a day, and Al took frequent catnaps.

I had never been on a dairy farm before and didn't realize how demanding the work could be. John and Al had fifty cows, twenty of which were milking. Almost all their livestock was brown and white Guernseys, and the two farmers were extremely partial to the breed. Guernsey cattle, they told me, tended to produce higher solids in their milk, which was good for making cheese. Their farm produced six hundred pounds of milk each day, which John and Al sold to a dairy cooperative that resold it to small cheese plants in Wisconsin. Each milking and feeding lasted about two and a half hours.

The evening I arrived, I fell asleep before the midnight milking (or "melking," as John and Al pronounce it) but was at the barn promptly at nine thirty the following morning. There, in a sweatshirt, jeans, and high galoshes, John was lugging a forty-five pound steel milking unit from cow to cow and transferring the milk to a big steel vat at the entrance to the barn; then he washed and cleaned the cows' teats, swept the stalls, and shoveled manure. Paul, the visiting farmer, was in charge of the feeding. Al was shoring up a broken stall and giving the cows a dessert of beet pulp.

Like a proud father, Al introduced me to every cow by name, personality, and production value. First came Lilly, lone Brown Swiss among Guernseys, a cow Al described as "heavy, aggressive, good producing. She will finish with 21,000 to 22,000 pounds of milk this year." Then, Honors: "a people cow." Isabel: "on her first lactation." Teardrop: "Our gay friends love her. She has incredibly beautiful eyes." And so on, through fifty cows, eight crested Polish chickens (whose coloration made them look as if they were wearing hats), sixteen lambs (Al hoped to increase that number to one or two hundred soon; both the wool and lamb market had been up recently), two lavender angora rabbits (whose fur could be spun into yarn), and three horses. Never far away was Nellie, a diminutive white poodle who made a rather humorous farm dog.

Al compared looking after his cows to bringing up fifty children. "They are very dependent on humans and very individual," he said. "With them, there are tremendous difficulties and tremendous disappointments. They can have structural problems, heart attacks. You play doctor and nurse to them. They can lay down and die one day for no apparent reason. In this business, the profit margins are slim, the tension and stress can be awful." The rewards made it all worthwhile, nonetheless: "the renewing experience" of calving, the "tremendous joy" of working with animals.

10   Al was an unusual combination of urban camp sensibility and country style and values. He wore two earrings in his left ear and a bangle on his wrist; his shirt was open almost to his navel. He gave his cows names like "You Tell 'Em Dorothy" and "Fashion Design" and called one sheep "Dottie of Fergus Falls" (after an ice-cream commercial). He divided the cows that weren't milking into three categories: "debs, minnies, and nymphettes." Inside the farmhouse, gay paperback gothics and mysteries filled the shelves. Three movie-theatre seats provided living room furniture, someone's idea of trendy but not particularly comfortable "gay" decor. On the dining room wall was a photograph of someone standing in the barn dressed in black stockings, lace panties, and black jacket, with a cow looking on incredulously in the background. On closer inspection, the person in the photograph turned out to bear a striking resemblance to Al. Also on that wall was the wooden plaque Al and John's bull won at the State Fair. "1987 Minnesota State Fair Grand Champion," it read.

Al, at thirty-seven, was the dreamer, the impractical one, living out his passion—his love of animals. John, at thirty-two, complemented him—he was solid and forthright, bringing sense, balance, and some hard-headed financial realism to the operation and to their life together. When Al described the cows as "a commodity," John assured me, "He doesn't really mean that. He picked up that phrase from me." Unlike Al, John had a life beyond the farm. He commuted five days a week to the Twin Cities, where he worked as a reporter-editor for *The Farmer,* a monthly magazine that covers midwestern agriculture. He also worked part-time as regional news editor for *Equal Time,* the gay and lesbian paper. While Al called dairy farming "my career," John considered himself a journalist first and a farmer second.

Weekdays, John left for work at seven in the morning, often not returning until as late as eleven in the evening, especially if he was doing a story for *Equal Time.* Sometimes he could be gone for days at a stretch covering South Dakota, his beat. John's absences left the management of the farm almost completely in Al's hands. Al became the one to negotiate with the banks and the dairy cooperative and the salesmen who came to the farm to sell feed and semen, to talk to the veterinarian and the county agent. He spent his days like most other dairy farmers in the Midwest: milking and feeding cows, cleaning barns, hauling manure, mowing lawns, confronting crises, and grabbing a few hours of sleep when he could.

Al and John had been dairy farmers for four years and lovers for eight and a half. They leased a five-acre farm near the town of Ogilvie, where the exurbia of Minneapolis gives way to the bait shops and mobile homes of Kanabec County. One demographer recently annointed the county the next area for growth in Minnesota, but there were few signs of development yet, at least in the area where Al and John lived. Ogilvie, the nearest town and where the two did their shopping, looks as if it is out of a painting by Edward Hopper. The country is flat and cheerless, crossed by Highway 65, the route that hunters and fishermen from the Twin Cities take to their cabins on the lakes farther north. The farms are poor and relatively small; the visitor misses the intimacy of the rolling country of Iowa to the south or the dramatic expanses of the wheat belt of the Dakotas to the west.

There was nothing particularly bucolic about John and Al's Blue Spur Farm. They didn't grow their own feed or even have a vegetable garden. The farmhouse, located virtually on the highway, was plain and slightly run-down. Just behind the house, the cattle barn, with its characteristic grey-shingled silo, was badly in need of paint. Connected to it was a tin-roofed, functional structure for the dry cows and baby heifers and a shed for the lambs. A few acres of pasture behind the barn completed the picture.

15   I went off with John and Paul, the visiting farmer, in John's pickup to have dinner at the Sportsman's Cafe, the nearest watering hole, about ten minutes down the road at Mora. Sportsman's was a joint with a large counter in the middle and booths along the side wall. It was open twenty-four hours a day to serve fishermen and hunters and state troopers, and John knew all the waitresses, women in their forties and fifties who have spent their lives standing on their feet. "Where's your friend?" one of them asked John as soon as we walked in. "I haven't seen either one of you in weeks."

At Sportsman's, we ate homemade oyster stew and pecan pie, and John drank several cups of coffee to keep awake for the late-night milking. John told me that he and Al had both grown up on dairy farms—Al in northern Minnesota, sixty miles from the Canadian border, where his father raised Guernseys; John to the west of the Twin Cities, where his family still raised Holsteins. John had always intended to get away from farming; the work was too hard. He met Al at the wedding of a mutual friend in Grand Forks, North Dakota. At the time, John was living in the Twin Cities and working on a newspaper; Al was farming with his father. Soon after, Al moved down to St. Paul to live with John, working in retail clothing stores.

But the attractions of urban life dwindled, and the focus of their lives began to shift back towards the farm. John moved into ag-journalism, writing for *The Farmer*, partly because he was frustrated by the long hours of news writing but also because of Al's continuing interest in the subject. More and more, they began to fantasize about returning to a rural setting, if not to farming itself. Their friends refused to take them seriously, dismissing the idea as "cute" or "a nice little dream." Al and John bought some horses and moved just outside St. Paul. A few cows wouldn't be too much trouble, they decided, and then they moved out even farther. John was somewhat reluctant; he is the cautious one, after all, and also the one who really wanted to get away from farming. But Al pressed, and John gave in.

John stressed that in returning to the farm, he and Al had made a conscious effort to do things differently from most gay farmers in the past. Traditionally, he said, in order to stay in agriculture, gay farmers either married someone of the opposite sex or completely sacrificed any possibility óf a relationship. Whatever their strategy for survival, they remained in the closet. Although John and Al weren't going to advertise their homosexuality, they were determined not to hide it either, letting people draw their own conclusions instead. "I have run into people in town who thought we were brothers, even though our names are different," said John. "They are more comfortable thinking that way." Some people were suspicious, he admitted, and others knew they were gay and didn't approve, sometimes telling them so directly. But he thought that to half of them, the possibility of his and Al's homosexuality "doesn't occur at all."

Al agreed. "Most farmers are more interested in how the livestock in our farming operation performs," he told me later. When a story about them as gay farmers (including photos) appeared on the front page of the daily newspaper in nearby St. Cloud, there was no visible reaction from their neighbors.

20   Their friend Paul had had a more traditionally closeted experience, however. He was a sweet and unassuming man in his late twenties, with curly brown hair and a neatly clipped beard. Four and a half years ago, while living in the Twin Cities, he became the lover of an older man. The two bought a farm together in a predominantly Finnish area about two and a half hours north of Minneapolis. The older man had died of lung cancer a few months before; Paul still spoke of his lover in the present tense. Paul stayed on at the farm with only three small calves, rebuilding a barn and hoping to establish a viable livestock business. Paul said the main issue for the neighbors had not been the couple's homosexuality but the fact that he and his lover were German Catholics, not Finnish Protestants. "First they thought my lover was my father until they realized we didn't have the same last name," he said. "Then they thought I was just his hired man." Now, his neighbors were beginning to wonder. "They are thinking, 'This is weird. The hired man is still living there,'" Paul observed. Just a week before, in the small town nearby, he had heard someone mutter "There goes a queer," as he was leaving a store. "I presume they were talking about me," he said. "I guess I'm 'out' now."

For their part, Al and John had not been particularly active in the organization of local Guernsey farmers, but this was changing. The award their bull received at the state fair and the fact they were advertising their livestock in the Guernsey breeders' magazine had given them increased visibility among local farmers. Now, "people notice us," said John. "The ad gave people an opportunity to say something to us." In fact, the following week Al and John were holding a potluck picnic at their farm for the Northeast District Guernsey Breeders Association. They expected about twenty dairy farmers to attend.

There had been one disturbing episode, however. Al had been coaching the 4-H county dairy cattle judging team, composed of kids aged fourteen to sixteen. One parent complained to the county agent who supervises the 4-H that Al was gay. The agent apparently failed to back Al up, and Al resigned as coach. He hoped to be invited back the following year, noting that the kids involved in the organization had been supportive. But John, always the more realistic one, was doubtful this would happen.

In the process of living in the country, they had increasingly discovered other farmers like themselves—a gay male couple nearby who raised sheep, a lesbian couple who had dairy goats, and two other men with a hog farm. Three years ago, Al and John took out a classified advertisement in *Equal Time,* announcing they would be at the state fair and inviting other gay people to stop by the cattle barn and say hello. They were startled by the constant stream of visitors. This summer, *Equal Time* published John's "Gay Guide to the State Fair" as its cover article. One result was that Paul came by the cattle barn, introduced himself to them, and all three became fast friends.

The fact that John and Al were open about their sexuality put them in a pivotal spot in helping to develop a close-knit rural gay community in Minnesota. (John and Al, it should be noted, were not the first gay farmers in the state to come out publicly. Dick Hanson, farmer, farm activist, and member of the Democratic National Committee, was openly gay and quite well-known. Hanson died of AIDS in late July 1987.) "Unless you are willing to be 'out,' it is hard to connect with people," John observed. "A lot of these gay farmers thought they were the only ones doing this." Now Al and John's social circle was shifting. Although they remained close with many of their urban gay friends, especially those who were interested in what they were doing, only a special occasion could persuade them to trek into the Twin Cities.

25   To me, one of the most interesting aspects of John and Al's return to the farm was that it had brought about a reconciliation with their parents. Several years ago, when John first told his parents he was gay, they were traumatized, he said. But out of seven sons of a farm family, John was the only one currently involved in agriculture. For his father, who was still operating the family farm, the return of his gay son to the land was "the least expected thing," said John. His father had been supportive of their operation and both father and son tried to help each other whenever possible, trading advice and material assistance. As John noted, they were both in the same business and faced the "same questions and troubles."

None of Al's two brothers and two sisters were farming either, and his parents had retired. But family ties to the land remained strong. One sister, who lived in Denver, was "absolutely thrilled," he said, when their bull won the state fair championship. Although she lived in a city, she was eager for her children to have some connection with the family's rural roots. "And it just so happens that in our family Uncle Al and Uncle John are the only ones who are farming," her brother pointed out.

The ability of both sets of parents to identify with Al and John's occupation appeared to provide a counterweight to their difficulties in accepting their sons' homosexuality. If they had lived in the Twin Cities and worked at jobs their parents couldn't identify with, the gay issue might loom larger between the generations, Al and John thought. John noted that from the time he went to college until he began farming, he had had little in common with his family. That certainly wasn't true these days. "As far as sexuality goes, they accept it but they are not supportive," he said. "But they are supportive of the rest of my life."

Al and John maintained that living on the farm had strengthened their own relationship as well, and noted that they had been together the longest in their circle of gay couples. John believed that doing what they wanted to do with their lives—in Al's case, farming, in John's, a combination of farming and journalism—gave their relationship a strength it might not have had if they had sacrificed their aspirations and opted for a more conventional urban gay life. The fact they were business partners as well as lovers provided another tie; it would take months to dissolve their financial bonds. "This is not just a personal relationship, but an economic one, too," Al said.

Although they had left the big city behind, they were reluctant to cut their links to the larger gay world. They had been exploring the notion of combining farming with managing a gay-oriented bed and breakfast. (By the end of my travels, I was convinced that running a B and B is the dream of half the gay men in the United States.) The farm they currently leased wouldn't be appropriate, so they were looking at property slightly closer to the Twin Cities. "It is a dream," John admitted. He also conceded that combining milking cows and raising sheep with changing sheets and cooking breakfast for guests might turn out to be more than they could handle. Nonetheless, they were just not the kind of farmers who want to be "isolated and secluded," as John put it. The presence of a large and active gay community in the Twin Cities offered them a connection and a potential for involvement that other gay farmers who lived farther away didn't have.

30   Few urban gays were following in Al and John's footsteps. The dismal state of the farm economy argued against any major migration back to the farm; large numbers of farmers, both gay and straight, were packing up and leaving the land, as it was. And many gay men and lesbians who grew up on farms and in rural areas didn't necessarily recall their formative years with fondness. "You grow up on the farm and as you realize your sexuality, you feel you just don't fit," Al told me. "You don't fit in at Sunday church dinners or the PTA or picnics. You become frustrated and you search for others like yourself, and they are not real visible in a rural area. So you tend to leave."

But the pull of one's roots is a powerful thing. "As you mature," Al added, "you tend to go back."

[1989]

 TOPICS FOR CRITICAL THINKING AND WRITING

1. In the first paragraph Miller says he had "never assumed" that a state fair "would be a particularly good place to observe gay and lesbian life." What prior assumptions had he presumably made about farmers and state fairs, or about gays and lesbians? How valid do you think these assumptions are? What evidence, if any, can you offer to support your view?

2. The essay, as far as we can discern, has no thesis sentence. Does it have a thesis idea? If so, try to formulate the thesis idea in a sentence or two.

3. "But the pull of one's roots is a powerful thing," Miller tells us in his last paragraph. To which Al adds, "As you mature, . . . you tend to go back." Do these sentiments ring true for your own life? Are you likely at some future time to (or do you now) live a life similar to the one you knew as a child? Do you see yourself in the occupation of either of your parents? Explain in an essay of approximately 750–1000 words.

4. In paragraph 19 we are told that an article about Al and John "as gay farmers" appeared in a daily newspaper. Drawing on Miller's essay, write the article (500 words).

 ANDREW LAM

Andrew Lam is an associate editor of the Pacific News Service. This essay originally appeared as an op-ed piece in the New York Times *in 1993.*

Goodbye, Saigon—Finally

San Francisco

Flipping through my United States passport as if it were a comic book, the customs man at the Noi Bai Airport, near Hanoi, appeared curious. "Brother, when did you leave Vietnam?"

"One day before National Defeat Day," I said without thinking. It was an exile's expression, not his.

"God! When did that happen?"

"The 30th of April, 1975."

5   "But, brother, don't you mean National Liberation Day?"

If this conversation had occurred a decade earlier, the difference would have created a dangerous gap between the Vietnamese and the returning Vietnamese-American. But this happened in 1992, when the walls were down, and as I studied the smiling young official, it occurred to me that there was something about this moment, an epiphany. "Yes, brother, I suppose I do mean liberation day."

Not everyone remembers the date with humor. It marked the Vietnamese diaspora, boat people, refugees.

On April 29, 1975, my family and I escaped from Saigon in a crowded C-130. We arrived in Guam the next day, to hear the BBC's tragic account of Saigon's demise: U.S. helicopters flying over the chaotic city, Vietcong tanks rolling in, Vietnamese climbing over the gate into the U.S. Embassy, boats fleeing down the Saigon River toward the South China Sea.

In time, April 30 became the birth date of an exile's culture built on defeatism and a sense of tragic ending. For a while, many Vietnamese in America talked of revenge, of blood debts, of the exile's anguish. Their songs had nostalgic titles: "The Day When I Return" and "Oh, Mother Vietnam, We Are Still Here."

10   April 30, 1976: A child of 12 with nationalistic fervor, I stood in front of San Francisco City Hall with other refugees. I waved the gold flag with three horizontal red stripes. I shouted (to no one in particular): "Give us back South Vietnam!"

April 30, 1979: An uncle told me there was an American plan to retake our homeland by force: "The way Douglas MacArthur did for the South Koreans in the 50's." My 17-year-old brother declared that he would join the anti-Communist guerrilla movement in Vietnam. My father sighed.

April 30, 1983: I stayed awake all night with Vietnamese classmates from Berkeley to listen to monotonous speeches by angry old men. "National defeat must be avenged by sweat and blood!" one vowed.

But through the years, April 30 has come to symbolize something entirely different to me. Although I sometimes mourn the loss of home and land, it's the American landscape and what it offers that solidify my hyphenated identity. This date of tragic ending, from an optimist's point of view, is also an American rebirth, something close to the Fourth of July.

I remember whispering to a young countryman during one of those monotonous April 30 rallies in the mid-1980's: "Even as the old man speaks of patriotic repatriation, we've already become Americans."

15   Assimilation, education, the English language, the American "I"—these have carried me and many others further from that beloved tropical country than the C-130 ever could. Each optimistic step the young Vietnamese takes toward America is tempered with a little betrayal of Little Saigon's parochialism, its sentimentalities and the old man's outdated passion.

When did this happen? Who knows? One night, America quietly seeps in and takes hold of one's mind and body, and the Vietnamese soul of sorrows slowly fades away. In the morning, the Vietnamese American speaks a new language of materialism: his vocabulary includes terms like career choices, down payment, escrow, overtime.

My brother never made it to the Indochinese jungle. The would-be guerrilla fighter became instead a civil engineer. My talk of endless possibilities is punctuated with favorite verbs—transcend, redefine, become. "I want to become a writer," I declared to my parents one morning. My mother gasped.

April 30, 1975: defeat or liberation?

"It was a day of joyous victory," said a retired Communist official in Hanoi. "We fought and realized Uncle Ho's dream of national independence." Then he asked for Marlboro cigarettes and a few precious dollars.

20   Nhon Nguyen, a real estate salesman in San Jose, a former South Vietnamese naval officer, said: "I could never forget the date. So many people died. So much blood. I could never tolerate Communism, you know."

Mai Huong, a young Vietnamese woman in Saigon, said that, of course, it was National Liberation Day. "But it's the South," she said with a wink, "that liberated the North." Indeed, conservative Uncle Ho has slowly admitted defeat to entrepreneurial and cosmopolitan Miss Saigon. She has taken her meaning from a different uncle, you know, Uncle Sam.

"April 30, 1975?" said Bobby To, my 22-year-old cousin in San Francisco. "I don't know that date. I don't remember Vietnam at all." April 29, 1992, is more meaningful to him, Bobby said. "It's when the race riots broke out all over our country. To me it's more realistic to worry about what's going on over here than there."

Sighing, the customs man, who offered me a ride into Hanoi, said: "In truth, there are no liberators. We are all defeated here." There is no job, no future, no direction, only a sense of collective malaise, something akin to the death of the national soul. He added: "You're lucky, brother. You left Vietnam and became an American."

April 30, 1993: My friends and I plan to watch "Gone with the Wind" for the umpteenth time and look for a scene of our unrequited romantic longings: Scarlett, teary-eyed with wind-blown hair, returning to forlorn Tara. We no longer can. Children of defeat, self-liberating adults, we promise to hug instead and recount to each other our own stories of flight.

[1993]

 TOPICS FOR CRITICAL THINKING AND WRITING

1. Lam sets up at once the distinction between National Defeat Day and National Liberation Day and calls the moment for him "an epiphany." How does he do it? And what is an epiphany?

2. Lam remembers the escape from Vietnam in 1975, and then he tells what he did on April 30 in 1976, in 1979, and in 1983. What techniques does Lam use to make those dates vivid?

3. In paragraph 15 Lam says, "Each optimistic step the young Vietnamese takes toward America is tempered with a little betrayal of Little Saigon's parochialism, its sentimentalities and the old man's outdated passion." What does he mean?

4. At the essay's conclusion Lam says that he and his friends will watch "Gone with the Wind" and "recount to each other our own stories of flight." Why do they watch "Gone with the Wind" (instead of a Vietnamese film)? What does Lam's choice of the film tell us?

5. If you have a story similar to Lam's, or one that in many ways is opposed to Lam's, try to tell it in an essay that begins with a narrative and may end with one too.

Fiction

The Book of Ruth

In the Hebrew Bible, the Book of Ruth appears in the third section, a somewhat miscellaneous collection called the Writings, which includes Psalms, Proverbs, Job, and a later collection called "five scrolls." It is read on the Feast of Weeks (Shabuoth), the harvest festival that occurs seven weeks after Passover. In Christian Bibles, however, Ruth appears between Judges and Samuel, in accordance with the historical setting.

The Book of Ruth is set in the days of the Judges ("Now it came to pass in the days when the judges ruled," 1.1), that is, in the period before the establishment of the monarchy, circa 1020 B.C.E. The date of composition is much disputed; some scholars argue for an early date, not much later than the period in which the story is set, but others argue that it was perhaps based on an early oral tradition and not written down until the sixth century B.C.E., *when part of the Jewish population was exiled to Babylonia. In any case, by including it here in a section called Fiction we do not mean to imply that the story cannot be rooted in history. We mean only that the materials have been shaped into an effective narrative.*

The author is unknown, but almost everyone assumes the author was a male, though one who was remarkably aware of the feelings of women. We give the story in the King James Version (1611). In this version italics are used not *in order to give emphasis, but to indicate words that were not in the original. There are no line numbers or paragraph breaks in the Hebrew text. We follow the line numbers and suggested paragraph breaks of the translators.*

The Book of Ruth

Chapter 1

1 *Elimelech driven by famine into Moab, dieth there.* 4 *Mahlon and Chilion, having married wives of Moab, die also.* 6 *Naomi returning homeward,* 8 *dissuadeth her two daughters in law from going with her.* 14 *Orpah leaveth her, but Ruth with great constancy accompanieth her.* 19 *They two come to Beth-lehem, where they are gladly received.*

Now it came to pass in the days when the judges ruled, that there was a famine in the land. And a certain man of Beth-lehem-judah went to sojourn in the country of Moab,[1] he, and his wife, and his two sons. 2 And the name of the man *was* Elimelech,[2] and the name of his wife Naomi, and the name of his two sons Mahlon and Chilion, Ephrathites[3] of Beth-lehem-judah. And they came into the country of Moab, and continued there. 3 And Elimelech Naomi's husband died; and she was left, and her two sons. 4 And they took them wives of the women of Moab;[4] the name of the one *was* Orpah, and the name of the other Ruth: and they dwelled there about ten years. 5 And Mahlon and Chilion died also both of them; and the woman was left of her two sons and her husband.

6 Then she arose with her daughters in law, that she might return from the country of Moab: for she had heard in the country of Moab how that the LORD had visited his people in giving them bread. 7 Wherefore she went forth out of the place where she was, and her two daughters in law with her; and they went on the way to return unto the land of Judah. 8 And Naomi said unto her two daughters in law, Go, return each to her mother's house: the LORD deal kindly with you, as ye have dealt with the dead, and with me. 9 The LORD grant you that ye may find rest, each *of you* in the house of her husband. Then she kissed them; and they lifted up their voice, and wept. 10 And they said unto her, Surely we will return with thee unto thy people. 11 And Naomi said, Turn again, my daughters: why will ye go

---

[1]**the country of Moab** the plateau east of the Dead Sea; Moabites were traditional enemies of Israel and Judah   [2]**Elimelech** the name means "My God is King"; the other names are of uncertain meaning   [3]**Ephrathites** members of a Judean clan   [4]**the women of Moab** i.e. Gentiles

with me? *are* there yet *any more* sons in my womb°, that they may be your husbands?⁵ 12 Turn again, my daughters, go *your way;* for I am too old to have an husband. If I should say, I have hope, *if* I should have an husband also to night, and should also bear sons; 13 Would ye tarry for them till they were grown? would ye stay for them from having husbands? nay, my daughters; for it grieveth me much for your sakes that the hand of the LORD is gone out against me. 14 And they lifted up their voice, and wept again: and Orpah kissed her mother in law; but Ruth clave unto her. 15 And she said, Behold, thy sister in law is gone back unto her people, and unto her gods: return thou after thy sister in law. 16 And Ruth said, Intreat me not to leave thee, *or* to return from following after thee: for whither thou goest, I will go; and where thou lodgest, I will lodge: thy people *shall be* my people, and thy God my God: 17 Where thou diest, will I die, and there will I be buried: the LORD do so to me, and more also, *if ought* but death part thee and me. 18 When she saw that she was stedfastly minded to go with her, then she left speaking unto her.

19 So they two went until they came to Beth-lehem. And it came to pass, when they were come to Beth-lehem, that all the city was moved about them, and they said, *Is* this Naomi? 20 And she said unto them, Call me not Naomi, call me Mara:⁶ for the Almighty hath dealt very bitterly with me. 21 I went out full, and the LORD hath brought me home again empty: why *then* call ye me Naomi, seeing the LORD hath testified against me, and the Almighty hath afflicted me? 22 So Naomi returned, and Ruth the Moabitess her daughter in law, with her, which returned out of the country of Moab: and they came to Beth-lehem in the beginning of barley harvest.⁷

Chapter 2

1 *Ruth gleaneth in the fields of Boaz. 4 Boaz taking knowledge of her, 8 sheweth her great favour. 18 That which she got, she carrieth to Naomi.*

And Naomi had a kinsman of her husband's, a mighty man of wealth, of the family of Elimelech; and his name *was* Boaz. 2 And Ruth the Moabitess said unto Naomi, Let me now go to the field, and glean ears of corn⁸ after *him* in whose sight I shall find grace. And she said unto her, Go, my daughter. 3 And she went, and came, and gleaned in the field after the reapers: and her hap was to light on a part of the field *belonging* unto Boaz, who *was* of the kindred of Elimelech.

4 And, behold, Boaz came from Beth-lehem, and said unto the reapers, The LORD *be* with you. And they answered him, The LORD bless thee. 5 Then said Boaz unto his servant that was set over the reapers, Whose damsel *is* this?⁹ 6 And the servant that was set over the reapers answered and said, It

---

⁵**sons in my womb . . . your husbands** Naomi is referring to the levirate marriage practice (cf. Deut. 25.5–10), which involved marriage between a childless widow and her deceased husband's brother (or nearest male relative). The firstborn son of this union was considered a son of the deceased.   ⁶**call me Mara** the Hebrew word means "bitter"   ⁷**barley harvest** late April or early May   ⁸**glean ears of corn** pick up the stalks of grain left by the harvesters. Leviticus 19.9–10 commands that something be left in the fields for the poor to glean   ⁹**whose damsel *is* this?** the culture assumed that every woman belonged to some male—a father, husband, brother, oldest son (if she were a widow) or master

is the Moabitish damsel that came back with Naomi out of the country of Moab: 7 And she said, I pray you, let me glean and gather after the reapers among the sheaves: so she came, and hath continued even from the morning until now, that she tarried a little in the house. 8 Then said Boaz unto Ruth, Hearest thou not, my daughter? Go not to glean in another field, neither go from hence, but abide here fast by my maidens: 9 *Let* thine eyes *be* on the field that they do reap, and go thou after them: have I not charged the young men that they shall not touch thee? and when thou art athirst, go unto the vessels, and drink of *that* which the young men have drawn. 10 Then she fell on her face, and bowed herself to the ground, and said unto him, Why have I found grace in thine eyes, that thou shouldest take knowledge of me, seeing I *am* a stranger? 11 And Boaz answered and said unto her, It hath fully been shewed me, all that thou hast done unto thy mother in law since the death of thine husband: and *how* thou hast left thy father and thy mother, and the land of thy nativity, and art come unto a people which thou knewest not heretofore. 12 The LORD recompense thy work, and a full reward be given thee of the LORD God of Israel, under whose wings thou art come to trust. 13 Then she said, Let me find favour in thy sight, my lord; for that thou hast comforted me, and for that thou hast spoken friendly unto thine handmaid, though I be not like unto one of thine handmaidens. 14 And Boaz said unto her, At mealtime come thou hither, and eat of the bread, and dip thy morsel in the vinegar.[10] And she sat beside the reapers: and he reached her parched *corn*,[11] and she did eat, and was sufficed, and left. 15 And when she was risen up to glean, Boaz commanded his young men, saying, Let her glean even among the sheaves,[12] and reproach her not: 16 And let fall also *some* of the handfuls of purpose for her, and leave *them,* that she may glean *them,* and rebuke her not. 17 So she gleaned in the field until even, and beat out that she had gleaned: and it was about an ephah[13] of barley.

18 And she took *it* up, and went into the city: and her mother in law saw what she had gleaned: and she brought forth, and gave to her that she had reserved after she was sufficed. 19 And her mother in law said unto her, Where hast thou gleaned to day? and where wroughtest thou? blessed be he that did take knowledge of thee. And she shewed her mother in law with whom she had wrought, and said, The man's name with whom I wrought to day *is* Boaz. 20 And Naomi said unto her daughter in law, Blessed *be* he of the LORD, who hath not left off his kindness to the living and to the dead. And Naomi said unto her, The man *is* near of kin unto us, one of our next kinsmen. 21 And Ruth the Moabitess said, He said unto me also, Thou shalt keep fast by my young men, until they have ended all my harvest. 22 And Naomi said unto Ruth her daughter in law, *It is* good, my daughter, that thou go out with his maidens, that they meet thee not in any other field. 23 So she kept fast by the maidens of Boaz to glean unto the end of barley harvest and of wheat harvest; and dwelt with her mother in law.

---

[10]**vinegar** a mixture of water, wine, vinegar, and a fermented liquor   [11]**parched corn** lightly roasted barley, somewhat like popcorn or puffed wheat   [12]**even among the sheaves** Ordinarily the reapers, who cut barley stalks, were followed by other laborers, who bound the stalks into sheaves. Normally only after the sheaves had been carted away were the poor allowed to glean the field.   [13]**an ephah** about half a bushel, a large quantity for a gleaner

Chapter 3

1 By Naomi's instruction, 5 Ruth lieth at Boaz's feet. 8 Boaz acknowled-geth the right of a kinsman. 14 He sendeth her away with six measures of barley.

Then Naomi her mother in law said unto her, My daughter, shall I not seek rest for thee, that it may be well with thee? 2 And now *is* not Boaz of our kindred, with whose maidens thou wast? Behold, he winnoweth barley[14] to night in the threshingfloor. 3 Wash thyself therefore, and anoint thee, and put thy raiment upon thee, and get thee down to the floor: *but* make not thyself known unto the man, until he shall have done eating and drinking. 4 And it shall be, when he lieth down, that thou shalt mark the place where he shall lie, and thou shalt go in, and uncover his feet, and lay thee down; and he will tell thee what thou shalt do. 5 And she said unto her, All that thou sayest unto me I will do.

6 And she went down unto the floor, and did according to all that her mother in law bade her. 7 And when Boaz had eaten and drunk, and his heart was merry, he went to lie down at the end of the heap of corn: and she came softly, and uncovered his feet, and laid her down.

8 And it came to pass at midnight, that the man was afraid, and turned himself: and, behold, a woman lay at his feet. 9 And he said, Who *art* thou? And she answered, I *am* Ruth thine handmaid: spread therefore thy skirt over thine handmaid;[15] for thou *art* a near kinsman. 10 And he said, Blessed *be* thou of the Lord, my daughter: *for* thou hast shewed more kindness in the latter end than at the beginning, inasmuch as thou followedst not young men, whether poor or rich. 11 And now, my daughter, fear not; I will do to thee all that thou requirest: for all the city of my people doth know that thou *art* a virtuous woman. 12 And now it is true that I *am thy* near kinsman: howbeit there is a kinsman nearer than I. 13 Tarry this night, and it shall be in the morning, *that* if he will perform unto thee the part of a kinsman, well; let him do the kinsman's part: but if he will not do the part of a kinsman to thee, then will I do the part of a kinsman to thee, *as* the Lord liveth: lie down until the morning.

14 And she lay at his feet until the morning: and she rose up before one could know another. And he said, Let it not be known that a woman came into the floor. 15 Also he said, Bring the vail that *thou hast* upon thee, and hold it. And when she held it, he measured six *measures*[16] of barley, and laid *it* on her: and she went into the city. 16 And when she came to her mother in law, she said, Who *art* thou, my daughter? And she told her all that the man had done to her. 17 And she said, These six *measures* of barley gave he me; for he said to me, Go not empty unto thy mother in law. 18 Then said she, Sit still, my daughter, until thou know how the matter will fall: for the man will not be in rest, until he have finished the thing this day.

---

[14]**he winnoweth barley** in winnowing, crushed sheaves were tossed into the air so that the breeze could blow away blew the chaff (chopped stalks and straw), and the grain would fall back on the floor   [15]**spread thy skirt over thine handmaid** to spread a skirt over someone symbolized marriage   [16]**six measures** probably 1½ bushels

Chapter 4

1 *Boaz calleth into judgment the next kinsman.* 6 *He refuseth the redemption according to the manner in Israel.* 9 *Boaz buyeth the inheritance.* 11 *He marrieth Ruth.* 13 *She beareth Obed the grandfather of
David.* 18 *The generation of Pharez.*

Then went Boaz up to the gate,[17] and sat him down there: and, behold,
the kinsman of whom Boaz spake came by; unto whom he said, Ho, such a
one! turn aside, sit down here. And he turned aside, and sat down. 2 And he
took ten men of the elders of the city, and said, Sit ye down here. And they
sat down. 3 And he said unto the kinsman, Naomi, that is come again out of
the country of Moab, selleth a parcel of land, which *was* our brother Elimelech's: 4 And I thought to advertise thee, saying, Buy *it* before the inhabitants, and before the elders of my people. If thou wilt redeem *it,* redeem *it:*
but if thou wilt not redeem *it, then* tell me, that I may know: for *there is*
none to redeem *it* beside thee; and I *am* after thee. And he said, I will redeem *it.* 5 Then said Boaz, What day thou buyest the field of the hand of
Naomi, thou must buy *it* also of Ruth the Moabitess, the wife of the dead, to
raise up the name of the dead upon his inheritance.

6 And the kinsman said, I cannot redeem *it* for myself, lest I mar mine
own inheritance:[18] redeem thou my right to thyself; for I cannot redeem *it.*
7 Now this *was the manner* in former time in Israel concerning redeeming
and concerning changing, for to confirm all things; a man plucked off his
shoe,[19] and gave *it* to his neighbour: and this *was* a testimony in Israel. 8
Therefore the kinsman said unto Boaz, Buy *it* for thee. So he drew off his
shoe.

9 And Boaz said unto the elders, and *unto* all the people, Ye *are* witnesses this day, that I have bought all that *was* Elimelech's, and all that *was*
Chilion's and Mahlon's, of the hand of Naomi. 10 Moreover Ruth the
Moabitess, the wife of Mahlon, have I purchased to be my wife, to raise up
the name of the dead upon his inheritance, that the name of the dead be not
cut off from among his brethren, and from the gate of his place: ye *are* witnesses this day. 11 And all the people that *were* in the gate, and the elders,
said, *We are* witnesses. The LORD make the woman that is come into thine
house like Rachel and like Leah,[20] which two did build the house of Israel:
and do thou worthily in Ephratah,[21] and be famous in Beth-lehem: 12 And
let thy house be like the house of Pharez,[22] whom Tamar bare unto Judah, of
the seed which the LORD shall give thee of this young woman.

13 So Boaz took Ruth, and she was his wife: and when he went in unto
her, the LORD gave her conception, and she bare a son. 14 And the women

---

[17]**the gate** the city gate was the normal place to transact business   [18]**lest I mar
mine own inheritance** the kinsman refuses to accept the property since if he has
a son by Ruth that son will inherit the land   [19]**shoe** this ceremony of removing a
shoe and presenting it to Boaz indicates that the next of kin is renouncing his right
to Ruth and to Naomi's land, and transferring the right to Boaz   [20]**Rachel and
Leah** these two, with their maidservants, bore twelve sons (and one daughter) to
Jacob, and thus are the ancestors of the twelve tribes of Israel (cf. Gen. 35.23-26)
[21]**Ephratah** Bethlehem   [22]**Pharez** Pharez, son of Tamar, was an ancestor of David.
Tamar, like Ruth a Gentile and a childless widow, later bore Pharez in a relationship
akin to a levirate marriage

said unto Naomi, Blessed *be* the LORD, which hath not left thee this day without a kinsman, that his name may be famous in Israel. 15 And he shall be
unto thee a restorer of *thy* life, and a nourisher of thine old age: for thy
daughter in law, which loveth thee, which is better to thee than seven sons,
hath born him. 16 And Naomi took the child, and laid it in her bosom, and
became nurse unto it. 17 And the women her neighbours gave it a name,
saying, There is a son born to Naomi; and they called his name Obed: he *is*
the father of Jesse, the father of David.

18 Now these *are* the generations of Pharez: Pharez begat Hezron, 19
And Hezron begat Ram, and Ram begat Amminadab, 20 And Amminadab
begat Nahshon, and Nahshon begat Salmon, 21 And Salmon begat Boaz, and
Boaz begat Obed, 22 And Obed begat Jesse, and Jesse begat David.[23]

 TOPICS FOR CRITICAL THINKING AND WRITING

1. Why does Naomi urge her daughters-in-law to return to their mothers'
   houses? What is your attitude toward Orpah?
2. On the basis of 2.4–16, how would you characterize Boaz?
3. Some readers see in the story hints of Providence working through
   faithful mortals. Which passages in the story might be susceptible to
   this interpretation? On the whole, do you find such an interpretation
   plausible? Support your response.
4. Thomas Paine (1737–1809), known as a political leader and a theoreti-
   cian in the American Revolution and known also as the enemy of revealed religion, in *The Age of Man* (1794–95) offers a comment on the
   Book of Ruth:

   Having now shown that every book in the Bible, from Genesis to
   Judges, is without authenticity, I come to the Book of Ruth, an idle,
   bungling story, foolishly told, nobody knows by whom, about a
   strolling country-girl, creeping slyly to bed with her cousin Boaz. Pretty
   stuff indeed, to be called the Word of God. It is, however, one of the
   best books in the Bible, for it is free from murder and rapine.

   Your thoughts on this comment?

 NATHANIEL HAWTHORNE

*Nathaniel Hawthorne (1804–64) was born in Salem, Massachusetts,
the son of a sea captain. Two of his ancestors were judges; one had
persecuted Quakers, and another had served at the Salem witch trials. After graduating from Bowdoin College in Maine he went back to
Salem in order to write in relative seclusion. In 1835 he published
"Young Goodman Brown" and "The Maypole of Merry Mount," and
in 1837 he published "Dr. Heidegger's Experiment."*

*From 1839 to 1841 Hawthorne worked in the Boston Customs
House and then spent a few months as a member of a communal so-*

[23]some commentators believe the genealogy in verses 18–22 is a later addition

ciety, Brook Farm. In 1842 he married. From 1846 to 1849 he was a surveyor at the Salem Customs House; from 1849 to 1850 he wrote The Scarlet Letter, *the book that made him famous. From 1853 to 1857 he served as American consul in Liverpool, England, a plum awarded him in exchange for writing a campaign biography of a former college classmate, President Franklin Pierce. In 1860, after living in England and Italy, he returned to the United States, settling in Concord, Massachusetts.*

In his stories and novels Hawthorne keeps returning to the Puritan past, studying guilt, sin, and isolation.

The Maypole of Merry Mount

There is an admirable foundation for a philosophic romance in the curious history of the early settlement of Mount Wollaston, or Merry Mount. In the slight sketch here attempted, the facts, recorded on the grave pages of our New England annalists, have wrought themselves, almost spontaneously, into a sort of allegory. The masques, mummeries, and festive customs, described in the text, are in accordance with the manners of the age. Authority on these points may be found in Strutt's Book of English Sports and Pastimes.

Bright were the days at Merry Mount, when the Maypole was the banner staff of that gay colony! They who reared it, should their banner be triumphant, were to pour sunshine over New England's rugged hills, and scatter flower seeds throughout the soil. Jollity and gloom were contending for an empire. Midsummer eve had come, bringing deep verdure to the forest, and roses in her lap, of a more vivid hue than the tender buds of Spring. But May, or her mirthful spirit, dwelt all the year round at Merry Mount, sporting with the Summer months, and revelling with Autumn, and basking in the glow of Winter's fireside. Through a world of toil and care she flitted with a dreamlike smile, and came hither to find a home among the lightsome hearts of Merry Mount.

Never had the Maypole been so gayly decked as at sunset on midsummer eve. This venerated emblem was a pine-tree, which had preserved the slender grace of youth, while it equalled the loftiest height of the old wood monarchs. From its top streamed a silken banner, colored like the rainbow. Down nearly to the ground the pole was dressed with birchen boughs, and others of the liveliest green, and some with silvery leaves, fastened by ribbons that fluttered in fantastic knots of twenty different colors, but no sad ones. Garden flowers, and blossoms of the wilderness, laughed gladly forth amid the verdure, so fresh and dewy that they must have grown by magic on that happy pine-tree. Where this green and flowery splendor terminated, the shaft of the Maypole was stained with the seven brilliant hues of the banner at its top. On the lowest green bough hung an abundant wreath of roses, some that had been gathered in the sunniest spots of the forest, and others, of still richer blush, which the colonists had reared from English seed. O, people of the Golden Age, the chief of your husbandry was to raise flowers!

But what was the wild throng that stood hand in hand about the Maypole? It could not be that the fauns and nymphs, when driven from their classic groves and homes of ancient fable, had sought refuge, as all the persecuted did, in the fresh woods of the West. These were Gothic monsters, though perhaps of Grecian ancestry. On the shoulders of a comely youth up-rose the head and branching antlers of a stag; a second, human in all other points, had the grim visage of a wolf; a third, still with the trunk and limbs of a mortal man, showed the beard and horns of a venerable he-goat. There was the likeness of a bear erect, brute in all but his hind legs, which were adorned with pink silk stockings. And here again, almost as wondrous, stood a real bear of the dark forest, lending each of his fore paws to the grasp of a human hand, and as ready for the dance as any in that circle. His inferior nature rose half way, to meet his companions as they stooped. Other faces wore the similitude of man or woman, but distorted or extrava-gant, with red noses pendulous before their mouths, which seemed of awful depth, and stretched from ear to ear in an eternal fit of laughter. Here might be seen the Savage Man, well known in heraldry, hairy as a baboon, and gir-dled with green leaves. By his side, a noble figure, but still a counterfeit, ap-peared an Indian hunter, with feathery crest and wampum belt. Many of this strange company wore foolscaps, and had little bells appended to their gar-ments, tinkling with a silvery sound, responsive to the inaudible music of their gleesome spirits. Some youths and maidens were of soberer garb, yet well maintained their places in the irregular throng by the expression of wild revelry upon their features. Such were the colonists of Merry Mount, as they stood in the broad smile of sunset round their venerated Maypole.

5   Had a wanderer, bewildered in the melancholy forest, heard their mirth, and stolen a half-affrighted glance, he might have fancied them the crew of Comus,[1] some already transformed to brutes, some midway be-tween man and beast, and the others rioting in the flow of tipsy jollity that foreran the change. But a band of Puritans, who watched the scene, invisi-ble themselves, compared the masques to those devils and ruined souls with whom their superstition peopled the black wilderness.

Within the ring of monsters appeared the two airiest forms that had ever trodden on any more solid footing than a purple and golden cloud. One was a youth in glistening apparel, with a scarf of the rainbow pattern cross-wise on his breast. His right hand held a gilded staff, the ensign of high dig-nity among the revellers, and his left grasped the slender fingers of a fair maiden, not less gayly decorated than himself. Bright roses glowed in con-trast with the dark and glossy curls of each, and were scattered round their feet, or had sprung up spontaneously there. Behind this lightsome couple, so close to the Maypole that its boughs shaded his jovial face, stood the fig-ure of an English priest, canonically dressed, yet decked with flowers, in heathen fashion, and wearing a chaplet of the native vine leaves. By the riot of his rolling eye, and the pagan decorations of his holy garb, he seemed the wildest monster there, and the very Comus of the crew.

"Votaries of the Maypole," cried the flower-decked priest, "merrily, all day long, have the woods echoed to your mirth. But be this your merriest hour, my hearts! Lo, here stand the Lord and Lady of the May, whom I, a clerk of Oxford, and high priest of Merry Mount, am presently to join in holy matrimony. Up with your nimble spirits, ye morris-dancers, green men, and glee maidens, bears and wolves, and horned gentlemen! Come; a chorus now, rich with the old mirth of Merry England, and the wilder glee of this fresh forest; and then a dance, to show the youthful pair what life is made

[1]A classical deity of revelry

of, and how airily they should go through it! All ye that love the Maypole, lend your voices to the nuptial song of the Lord and Lady of the May!"

This wedlock was more serious than most affairs of Merry Mount, where jest and delusion, trick and fantasy, kept up a continual carnival. The Lord and Lady of the May, though their titles must be laid down at sunset, were really and truly to be partners for the dance of life, beginning the measure that same bright eve. The wreath of roses, that hung from the lowest green bough of the Maypole, had been twined for them, and would be thrown over both their heads, in symbol of their flowery union. When the priest had spoken, therefore, a riotous uproar burst from the rout of monstrous figures.

"Begin you the stave, reverend Sir," cried they all; "and never did the woods ring to such a merry peal as we of the Maypole shall send up!"

10   Immediately a prelude of pipe, cithern, and viol, touched with practised minstrelsy, began to play from a neighboring thicket, in such a mirthful cadence that the boughs of the Maypole quivered to the sound. But the May Lord, he of the gilded staff, chancing to look into his Lady's eyes, was wonder struck at the almost pensive glance that met his own.

"Edith, sweet Lady of the May," whispered he reproachfully, "is yon wreath of roses a garland to hang above our graves, that you look so sad? O, Edith, this is our golden time! Tarnish it not by any pensive shadow of the mind; for it may be that nothing of futurity will be brighter than the mere remembrance of what is now passing."

"That was the very thought that saddened me! How came it in your mind too?" said Edith, in a still lower tone than he, for it was high treason to be sad at Merry Mount. "Therefore do I sigh amid this festive music. And besides, dear Edgar, I struggle as with a dream, and fancy that these shapes of our jovial friends are visionary, and their mirth unreal, and that we are no true Lord and Lady of the May. What is the mystery in my heart?"

Just then, as if a spell had loosened them, down came a little shower of withering rose leaves from the Maypole. Alas, for the young lovers! No sooner had their hearts glowed with real passion than they were sensible of something vague and unsubstantial in their former pleasures, and felt a dreary presentiment of inevitable change. From the moment that they truly loved, they had subjected themselves to earth's doom of care and sorrow, and troubled joy, and had no more a home at Merry Mount. That was Edith's mystery. Now leave we the priest to marry them, and the masquers to sport round the Maypole, till the last sunbeam be withdrawn from its summit, and the shadows of the forest mingle gloomily in the dance. Meanwhile, we may discover who these gay people were.

Two hundred years ago, and more, the old world and its inhabitants became mutually weary of each other. Men voyaged by thousands to the West: some to barter glass beads, and such like jewels, for the furs of the Indian hunter; some to conquer virgin empires; and one stern band to pray. But none of these motives had much weight with the colonists of Merry Mount. Their leaders were men who had sported so long with life, that when Thought and Wisdom came, even these unwelcome guests were led astray by the crowd of vanities which they should have put to flight. Erring Thought and perverted Wisdom were made to put on masques, and play the fool. The men of whom we speak, after losing the heart's fresh gayety, imagined a wild philosophy of pleasure, and came hither to act out their latest day-dream. They gathered followers from all that giddy tribe whose whole life is like the festal days of soberer men. In their train were minstrels, not unknown in London streets; wandering players, whose theatres had been the halls of noblemen; mummers, rope-dancers, and mountebanks, who would long be missed at wakes, church ales, and fairs; in a word, mirth makers of every sort, such as abounded in that age, but now began to be discountenanced by the rapid growth of Puritanism. Light had their footsteps been on land, and as lightly they came across the sea. Many had been maddened by their previous troubles into a gay despair; others were as madly gay in the flush of youth, like the May Lord and his Lady; but whatever might be the quality of their mirth, old and young were gay at Merry Mount. The young deemed themselves happy. The elder spirits, if they knew that mirth was but the counterfeit of happiness, yet followed the false shadow wilfully, because at least her garments glittered brightest. Sworn triflers of a lifetime, they would not venture among the sober truths of life not even to be truly blest.

15   All the hereditary pastimes of Old England were transplanted hither. The King of Christmas was duly crowned, and the Lord of Misrule bore potent sway. On the Eve of St. John, they felled whole acres of the forest to make bonfires, and danced by the blaze all night, crowned with garlands, and throwing flowers into the flame. At harvest time, though their crop was of the smallest, they made an image with the sheaves of Indian corn, and wreathed it with autumnal garlands, and bore it home triumphantly. But what chiefly characterized the colonists of Merry Mount was their veneration for the Maypole. It has made their true history a poet's tale. Spring decked the hallowed emblem with young blossoms and fresh green boughs; Summer brought roses of the deepest blush, and the perfected foliage of the forest; Autumn enriched it with that red and yellow gorgeousness which converts each wildwood leaf into a painted flower; and Winter silvered it with sleet, and hung it round with icicles, till it flashed in the cold sunshine, itself a frozen sunbeam. Thus each alternate season did homage to the Maypole, and paid it a tribute of its own richest splendor. Its votaries danced round it, once, at least, in every month; sometimes they called it their religion, or their altar; but always, it was the banner staff of Merry Mount.

Unfortunately, there were men in the new world of a sterner faith than those Maypole worshippers. Not far from Merry Mount was a settlement of Puritans, most dismal wretches, who said their prayers before daylight, and then wrought in the forest or the cornfield till evening made it prayer time again. Their weapons were always at hand to shoot down the straggling savage. When they met in conclave, it was never to keep up the old English mirth, but to hear sermons three hours long, or to proclaim bounties on the heads of wolves and the scalps of Indians. Their festivals were fast days and their chief pastime the singing of psalms. Woe to the youth or maiden who did but dream of a dance! The selectman nodded to the constable; and there sat the light-heeled reprobate in the stocks; or if he danced, it was round the whipping-post, which might be termed the Puritan Maypole.

A party of these grim Puritans, toiling through the difficult woods, each with a horseload of iron armor to burden his footsteps, would sometimes draw near the sunny precincts of Merry Mount. There were the silken colonists, sporting round their Maypole; perhaps teaching a bear to dance, or striving to communicate their mirth to the grave Indian; or masquerading in the skins of deer and wolves, which they had hunted for that especial purpose. Often, the whole colony were playing at blindman's buff, magistrates and all, with their eyes bandaged, except a single scapegoat, whom the blinded sinners pursued by the tinkling of the bells at his garments. Once, it is said, they were seen following a flower-decked corpse, with merriment and festive music, to his grave. But did the dead man laugh? In their quietest times, they sang ballads and told tales, for the edification of their pious visitors; or perplexed them with juggling tricks; or grinned at them through horse collars; and when sport itself grew wearisome, they made game of their own stupidity, and began a yawning match. At the very least of these enormities, the men of iron shook their heads and frowned so darkly that the revellers looked up imagining that a momentary cloud had overcast the sunshine, which was to be perpetual there. On the other hand, the Puritans affirmed that, when a psalm was pealing from their place of worship, the echo which the forest sent them back seemed often like the chorus of a jolly catch, closing with a roar of laughter. Who but the fiend, and his bond slaves, the crew of Merry Mount, had thus disturbed them? In due time, a feud arose, stern and bitter on one side, and as serious on the other as anything could be among such light spirits as had sworn allegiance to the Maypole. The future complexion of New England was involved in this important quarrel. Should the grizzly saints establish their jurisdiction over the gay sinners, then would their spirits darken all the clime, and make it a land of clouded visages, of hard toil, of sermon and psalm forever. But should the banner staff of Merry Mount be fortunate, sunshine would break upon the hills, and flowers would beautify the forest, and late posterity do homage to the Maypole.

After these authentic passages from history, we return to the nuptials of the Lord and Lady of the May. Alas! we have delayed too long, and must darken our tale too suddenly. As we glance again at the Maypole, a solitary sunbeam is fading from the summit, and leaves only a faint, golden tinge blended with the hues of the rainbow banner. Even that dim light is now withdrawn, relinquishing the whole domain of Merry Mount to the evening gloom, which has rushed so instantaneously from the black surrounding woods. But some of these black shadows have rushed forth in human shape.

Yes, with the setting sun, the last day of mirth had passed from Merry Mount. The ring of gay masquers was disordered and broken; the stag lowered his antlers in dismay; the wolf grew weaker than a lamb; the bells of the morris-dancers tinkled with tremulous affright. The Puritans had played a characteristic part in the Maypole mummeries. Their darksome figures were intermixed with the wild shapes of their foes, and made the scene a picture of the moment, when waking thoughts start up amid the scattered fantasies of a dream. The leader of the hostile party stood in the centre of the circle, while the route of monsters cowered around him, like evil spirits in the presence of a dread magician. No fantastic foolery could look him in the face. So stern was the energy of his aspect, that the whole man, visage, frame, and soul, seemed wrought of iron, gifted with life and thought, yet all of one substance with his headpiece and breastplate. It was the Puritan of Puritans; it was Endicott himself!

20   "Stand off, priest of Baal!" said he, with a grim frown, and laying no reverent hand upon the surplice. "I know thee, Blackstone![2] Thou art the man who couldst not abide the rule even of thine own corrupted church, and hast come hither to preach iniquity, and to give example of it in thy life. But now shall it be seen that the Lord hath sanctified this wilderness for his peculiar people. Woe unto them that would defile it! And first, for this flower-decked abomination, the altar of thy worship!"

And with his keen sword Endicott assaulted the hallowed Maypole. Nor long did it resist his arm. It groaned with a dismal sound; it showered leaves and rosebuds upon the remorseless enthusiast; and finally, with all its green boughs and ribbons and flowers, symbolic of departed pleasures, down fell the banner staff of Merry Mount. As it sank, tradition says, the evening sky grew darker, and the woods threw forth a more sombre shadow.

"There," cried Endicott, looking triumphantly on his work, "there lies the only Maypole in New England! The thought is strong within me that, by its fall, is shadowed forth the fate of light and idle mirth makers, amongst us and our posterity. Amen, saith John Endicott."

"Amen!" echoed his followers.

But the votaries of the Maypole gave one groan for their idol. At the sound, the Puritan leader glanced at the crew of Comus, each a figure of broad mirth, yet, at this moment, strangely expressive of sorrow and dismay.

25   "Valiant captain," quoth Peter Palfrey, the Ancient of the band, "what order shall be taken with the prisoners?"

"I thought not to repent me of cutting down a Maypole," replied Endicott, "yet now I could find in my heart to plant it again, and give each of these bestial pagans one other dance round their idol. It would have served rarely for a whipping-post!"

"But there are pine-trees enow," suggested the lieutenant.

"True, good Ancient," said the leader. "Wherefore, bind the heathen crew, and bestow on them a small matter of stripes apiece, as earnest of our future justice. Set some of the rogues in the stocks to rest themselves, so soon as Providence shall bring us to one of our own well-ordered settlements where such accommodations may be found. Further penalties, such as branding and cropping of ears, shall be thought of hereafter."

"How many stripes for the priest?" inquired Ancient Palfrey.

30   "None as yet," answered Endicott, bending his iron frown upon the culprit. "It must be for the Great and General Court to determine, whether stripes and long imprisonment, and other grievous penalty, may atone for his transgressions. Let him look to himself! For such as violate our civil order, it may be permitted us to show mercy. But woe to the wretch that troubleth our religion."

---

[2]Did Governor Endicott speak less positively, we should suspect a mistake here. The Rev. Mr. Blackstone, though an eccentric, is not known to have been an immoral man. We rather doubt his identity with the priest of Merry Mount. [Hawthorne's note]

"And this dancing bear," resumed the officer. "Must he share the stripes of his fellows?"

"Shoot him through the head!" said the energetic Puritan. "I suspect witchcraft in the beast."

"Here be a couple of shining ones," continued Peter Palfrey, pointing his weapon at the Lord and Lady of the May. "They seem to be of high station among these misdoers. Methinks their dignity will not be fitted with less than a double share of stripes."

Endicott rested on his sword, and closely surveyed the dress and aspect of the hapless pair. There they stood, pale, downcast, and apprehensive. Yet there was an air of mutual support and of pure affection, seeking aid and giving it, that showed them to be man and wife, with the sanction of a priest upon their love. The youth, in the peril of the moment, had dropped his gilded staff, and thrown his arm about the Lady of the May, who leaned against his breast, too lightly to burden him, but with weight enough to express that their destinies were linked together, for good or evil. They looked first at each other, and then into the grim captain's face. There they stood, in the first hour of wedlock, while the idle pleasures, of which their companions were the emblems, had given place to the sternest cares of life, personified by the dark Puritans. But never had their youthful beauty seemed so pure and high as when its glow was chastened by adversity.

35   "Youth," said Endicott, "ye stand in an evil case thou and thy maiden wife. Make ready presently, for I am minded that ye shall both have a token to remember your wedding day!"

"Stern man," cried the May Lord, "how can I move thee? Were the means at hand, I would resist to the death. Being powerless, I entreat! Do with me as thou wilt, but let Edith go untouched!"

"Not so," replied the immitigable zealot. "We are not wont to show an idle courtesy to that sex, which requireth the stricter discipline. What sayest thou, maid? Shall thy silken bridegroom suffer thy share of the penalty, besides his own?"

"Be it death," said Edith, "and lay it all on me!"

Truly, as Endicott had said, the poor lovers stood in a woeful case. Their foes were triumphant, their friends captive and abased, their home desolate, the benighted wilderness around them, and a rigorous destiny, in the shape of the Puritan leader, their only guide. Yet the deepening twilight could not altogether conceal that the iron man was softened; he smiled at the fair spectacle of early love; he almost sighed for the inevitable blight of early hopes.

40   "The troubles of life have come hastily on this young couple," observed Endicott. "We will see how they comport themselves under their present trials ere we burden them with greater. If, among the spoil, there be any garments of a more decent fashion, let them be put upon this May Lord and his Lady, instead of their glistening vanities. Look to it, some of you."

"And shall not the youth's hair be cut?" asked Peter Palfrey, looking with abhorrence at the lovelock and long glossy curls of the young man.

"Crop it forthwith, and that in the true pumpkin-shell fashion," answered the captain. "Then bring them along with us, but more gently than their fellows. There be qualities in the youth, which may make him valiant to fight, and sober to toil, and pious to pray; and in the maiden, that may fit her to become a mother in our Israel, bringing up babes in better nurture than her own hath been. Nor think ye, young ones, that they are the happiest, even in our lifetime of a moment, who misspend it in dancing round a Maypole!"

And Endicott, the severest Puritan of all who laid the rock foundation of New England, lifted the wreath of roses from the ruin of the Maypole, and threw it, with his own gauntleted hand, over the heads of the Lord and Lady of the May. It was a deed of prophecy. As the moral gloom of the world overpowers all systematic gayety, even so was their home of wild mirth made desolate amid the sad forest. They returned to it no more. But as their flowery garland was wreathed of the brightest roses that had grown there, so, in the tie that united them, were intertwined all the purest and best of their early joys. They went heavenward, supporting each other along the difficult path which it was their lot to tread, and never wasted one regretful thought of the vanities of Merry Mount.

[1835]

 ## TOPICS FOR CRITICAL THINKING AND WRITING

1. In his brief headnote, Hawthorne says that the facts as "recorded on the grave pages of our New England annalists, have wrought themselves, almost spontaneously, into a sort of allegory." In a paragraph or two, explain the allegory.
2. What words or phrases in the first two paragraphs suggest that there is something illusory or insubstantial or transient in the life of Merry Mount?
3. In a paragraph, characterize Endicott.

 ## TILLIE OLSEN

Tillie Olsen was born in 1913 in Omaha of a family that had fled persecution in czarist Russia. She left school after completing the eleventh grade and at 19 began a novel called Yonnonido, *which was not published until 1947. Her first publications, in the* Partisan Review *in 1934, were some poems and a story (the story was the opening chapter of her novel); in the next 20 years, however, when she was wife, mother of four children, office worker, and political activist, she published nothing. In* Silences *(1978), a collection of essays, she comments on the difficulty of working "fulltime on temporary jobs . . . , wandering from office to office, always hoping to manage two, three writing months ahead."*

Her first published book was Tell Me a Riddle *(1961), a collection of six stories, including "I Stand Here Ironing." (This story, written in 1953–54, first appeared in a journal in 1956, under the title "Help Her to Believe.") Her stories are marked by their concentration on what the author obviously feels are immensely important emotions and experiences; she is scarcely concerned with seeming to be objective or with the creation of mere verisimilitude.*

I Stand Here Ironing

I stand here ironing, and what you asked me moves tormented back and forth with the iron.

"I wish you would manage the time to come in and talk with me about your daughter. I'm sure you can help me understand her. She's a youngster who needs help and whom I'm deeply interested in helping."

"Who needs help." . . . Even if I came, what good would it do? You think because I am her mother I have a key, or that in some way you could use me as a key? She has lived for nineteen years. There is all that life that has happened outside of me, beyond me.

And when is there time to remember, to sift, to weigh, to estimate, to total? I will start and there will be an interruption and I will have to gather it all together again. Or I will become engulfed with all I did or did not do, with what should have been and what cannot be helped.

5   She was a beautiful baby. The first and only one of our five that was beautiful at birth. You do not guess how new and uneasy her tenancy in her now-loveliness. You did not know her all those years she was thought homely, or see her poring over her baby pictures, making me tell her over and over how beautiful she had been—and would be, I would tell her—and was now, to the seeing eye. But the seeing eyes were few or non-existent. Including mine.

I nursed her. They feel that's important nowadays. I nursed all the children, but with her, with all the fierce rigidity of first motherhood, I did like the books then said. Though her cries battered me to trembling and my breasts ached with swollenness, I waited till the clock decreed.

Why do I put that first? I do not even know if it matters, or if it explains anything.

She was a beautiful baby. She blew shining bubbles of sound. She loved motion, loved light, loved color and music and textures. She would lie on the floor in her blue overalls patting the surface so hard in ecstasy her hands and feet would blur. She was a miracle to me, but when she was eight months old I had to leave her daytimes with the woman downstairs to whom she was no miracle at all, for I worked or looked for work and for Emily's father, who "could no longer endure" (he wrote in his good-bye note) "sharing want with us."

I was nineteen. It was the pre-relief, pre-WPA world of the depression. I would start running as soon as I got off the streetcar, running up the stairs, the place smelling sour, and awake or asleep to startle awake, when she saw me she would break into a clogged weeping that could not be comforted, a weeping I can hear yet.

10   After a while I found a job hashing at night so I could be with her days, and it was better. But it came to where I had to bring her to his family and leave her.

It took a long time to raise the money for her fare back. Then she got chicken pox and I had to wait longer. When she finally came, I hardly knew her, walking quick and nervous like her father, looking like her father, thin, and dressed in a shoddy red that yellowed her skin and glared at the pockmarks. All the baby loveliness gone.

She was two. Old enough for nursery school they said, and I did not know then what I know now—the fatigue of the long day, and the lacerations of group life in the kinds of nurseries that are only parking places for children.

Except that it would have made no difference if I had known. It was the only place there was. It was the only way we could be together, the only way I could hold a job.

And even without knowing, I knew. I knew the teacher that was evil because all these years it has curdled into my memory, the little boy hunched in the corner, her rasp, "why aren't you outside, because Alvin hits you? that's no reason, go out, scaredy." I knew Emily hated it even if she did not clutch and implore "don't go Mommy" like the other children, mornings.

15   She always had a reason why we should stay home. Momma, you look sick. Momma, I feel sick. Momma, the teachers aren't there today, they're sick. Momma, we can't go, there was a fire there last night. Momma, it's a holiday today, no school, they told me.

But never a direct protest, never rebellion. I think of our others in their three-four-year-oldness—the explosions, the tempers, the denunciations, the demands—and I feel suddenly ill. I put the iron down. What in me demanded that goodness in her? And what was the cost, the cost to her of such goodness?

The old man living in the back once said in his gentle way: "You should smile at Emily more when you look at her." What *was* in my face when I looked at her? I loved her. There were all the acts of love.

It was only with the others I remembered what he said, and it was the face of joy, and not of care or tightness or worry I turned to them—too late for Emily. She does not smile easily, let alone almost always as her brothers and sisters do. Her face is closed and sombre, but when she wants, how fluid. You must have seen it in her pantomimes, you spoke of her rare gift for comedy on the stage that rouses a laughter out of the audience so dear they applaud and applaud and do not want to let her go.

Where does it come from, that comedy? There was none of it in her when she came back to me that second time, after I had had to send her away again. She had a new daddy now to learn to love, and I think perhaps it was a better time.

20   Except when we left her alone nights, telling ourselves she was old enough.

"Can't you go some other time, Mommy, like tomorrow?" she would ask. "Will it be just a little while you'll be gone? Do you promise?"

The time we came back, the front door open, the clock on the floor in the hall. She rigid awake. "It wasn't just a little while. I didn't cry. Three times I called you, just three times, and then I ran downstairs to open the door so you could come faster. The clock talked loud. I threw it away, it scared me what it talked."

She said the clock talked loud again that night I went to the hospital to have Susan. She was delirious with the fever that comes before red measles, but she was fully conscious all the week I was gone and the week after we were home when she could not come near the new baby or me.

She did not get well. She stayed skeleton thin, not wanting to eat, and night after night she had nightmares. She would call for me, and I would rouse from exhaustion to sleepily call back: "You're all right, darling, go to sleep, it's just a dream," and if she still called, in a sterner voice, "now go to sleep, Emily, there's nothing to hurt you." Twice, only twice, when I had to get up for Susan anyhow, I went in to sit with her.

25   Now when it is too late (as if she would let me hold and comfort her like I do the others) I get up and go to her at once at her moan or restless stirring. "Are you awake, Emily? Can I get you something?" And the answer is always the same: "No, I'm all right, go back to sleep, Mother."

They persuaded me at the clinic to send her away to a convalescent home in the country where "she can have the kind of food and care you can't manage for her, and you'll be free to concentrate on the new baby." They still send children to that place. I see pictures on the society page of sleek young women planning affairs to raise money for it, or dancing at the affairs, or decorating Easter eggs or filling Christmas stockings for the children.

They never have a picture of the children so I do not know if the girls still wear those gigantic red bows and the ravaged looks on the every other Sunday when parents can come to visit "unless otherwise notified"—as we were notified the first six weeks.

Oh it is a handsome place, green lawns and tall trees and fluted flower beds. High up on the balconies of each cottage the children stand, the girls in their red bows and white dresses, the boys in white suits and giant red ties. The parents stand below shrieking up to be heard and the children shriek down to be heard, and between them the invisible wall: "Not to Be Contaminated by Parental Germs or Physical Affection."

There was a tiny girl who always stood hand in hand with Emily. Her parents never came. One visit she was gone. "They moved her to Rose Cottage," Emily shouted in explanation. "They don't like you to love anybody here."

30   She wrote once a week, the labored writing of a seven-year-old. "I am fine. How is the baby. If I write my leter nicly I will have a star. Love." There never was a star. We wrote every other day, letters she could never hold or keep but only hear read—once. "We simply do not have room for children to keep any personal possessions," they patiently explained when we pieced one Sunday's shrieking together to plead how much it would mean to Emily, who loved so to keep things, to be allowed to keep her letters and cards.

Each visit she looked frailer. "She isn't eating," they told us.

(They had runny eggs for breakfast or mush with lumps, Emily said later, I'd hold it in my mouth and not swallow. Nothing ever tasted good, just when they had chicken.)

It took us eight months to get her released home, and only the fact that she gained back so little of her seven lost pounds convinced the social worker.

I used to try to hold and love her after she came back, but her body would stay stiff, and after a while she'd push away. She ate little. Food sickened her, and I think much of life too. Oh she had physical lightness and brightness, twinkling by on skates, bouncing like a ball up and down up and down over the jump rope, skimming over the hill: but these were momentary.

35   She fretted about her appearance, thin and dark and foreign-looking at a time when every little girl was supposed to look or thought she should look

a chubby blonde replica of Shirley Temple. The doorbell sometimes rang for her, but no one seemed to come and play in the house or be a best friend. Maybe because we moved so much.

There was a boy she loved painfully through two school semesters. Months later she told me how she had taken pennies from my purse to buy him candy. "Licorice was his favorite and I brought him some every day, but he still liked Jennifer better'n me. Why, Mommy?" The kind of question for which there is no answer.

School was a worry to her. She was not glib or quick in a world where glibness and quickness were easily confused with ability to learn. To her overworked and exasperated teachers she was an overconscientious "slow learner" who kept trying to catch up and was absent entirely too often.

I let her be absent, though sometimes the illness was imaginary. How different from my now-strictness about attendance with the others. I wasn't working. We had a new baby, I was home anyhow. Sometimes, after Susan grew old enough, I would keep her home from school, too, to have them all together.

Mostly Emily had asthma, and her breathing, harsh and labored, would fill the house with a curiously tranquil sound. I would bring the two old dresser mirrors and her boxes of collections to her bed. She would select beads and single earrings, bottle tops and shells, dried flowers and pebbles, old postcards and scraps, all sorts of oddments; then she and Susan would play Kingdom, setting up landscapes and furniture, peopling them with action.

40   Those were the only times of peaceful companionship between her and Susan. I have edged away from it, that poisonous feeling between them, that terrible balancing of hurts and needs I had to do between the two, and did so badly, those earlier years.

Oh there are conflicts between the others too, each one human, needing, demanding, hurting, taking—but only between Emily and Susan, no, Emily toward Susan that corroding resentment. It seems so obvious on the surface, yet it is not obvious. Susan, the second child, Susan, golden- and curly-haired and chubby, quick and articulate and assured, everything in appearance and manner Emily was not; Susan, not able to resist Emily's precious things, losing or sometimes clumsily breaking them; Susan telling jokes and riddles to company for applause while Emily sat silent (to say to me later: that was *my* riddle, Mother, I told it to Susan); Susan, who for all the five years' difference in age was just a year behind Emily in developing physically.

I am glad for that slow physical development that widened the difference between her and her contemporaries, though she suffered over it. She was too vulnerable for that terrible world of youthful competition, of preening and parading, of constant measuring of yourself against every other, of envy, "If I had that copper hair," "If I had that skin . . . ." She tormented herself enough about not looking like the others, there was enough of the unsureness, the having to be conscious of words before you speak, the constant caring—what are they thinking of me? without having it all magnified by the merciless physical drives.

Ronnie is calling. He is wet and I change him. It is rare there is such a cry now. That time of motherhood is almost behind me when the ear is not one's own but must always be racked and listening for the child cry, the child call. We sit for a while and I hold him, looking out over the city spread in charcoal with its soft aisles of light. *"Shoogily,"* he breathes and curls closer. I carry him back to bed, asleep. *Shoogily.* A funny word, a family word, inherited from Emily, invented by her to say: *comfort.*

In this and other ways she leaves her seal, I say aloud. And startle at my saying it. What do I mean? What did I start to gather together, to try and make coherent? I was at the terrible, growing years. War years. I do not remember them well. I was working, there were four smaller ones now, there was not time for her. She had to help be a mother, and housekeeper, and shopper. She had to set her seal. Mornings of crisis and near hysteria trying to get lunches packed, hair combed, coats and shoes found, everyone to school or Child Care on time, the baby ready for transportation. And always the paper scribbled on by a smaller one, the book looked at by Susan then mislaid, the homework not done. Running out to that huge school where she was one, she was lost, she was a drop; suffering over the unpreparedness, stammering and unsure in her classes.

45   There was so little time left at night after the kids were bedded down. She would struggle over books, always eating (it was in those years she developed her enormous appetite that is legendary in our family) and I would be ironing, or preparing food for the next day, or writing V-mail to Bill, or tending the baby. Sometimes, to make me laugh, or out of her despair, she would imitate happenings or types at school.

I think I said once: "Why don't you do something like this in the school amateur show?" One morning she phoned me at work, hardly understandable through the weeping: "Mother, I did it. I won, I won; they gave me first prize; they clapped and clapped and wouldn't let me go."

Now suddenly she was Somebody, and as imprisoned in her difference as she had been in anonymity.

She began to be asked to perform at other high schools, even in colleges, then at city and statewide affairs. The first one we went to, I only recognized her that first moment when thin, shy, she almost drowned herself into the curtains. Then: Was this Emily? The control, the command, the convulsing and deadly clowning, the spell, then the roaring, stamping audience, unwilling to let this rare and precious laughter out of their lives.

Afterwards: You ought to do something about her with a gift like that— but without money or knowing how, what does one do? We have left it all to her, and the gift has as often eddied inside, clogged and clotted, as been used and growing.

50   She is coming. She runs up the stairs two at a time with her light graceful step, and I know she is happy tonight. Whatever it was that occasioned your call did not happen today.

"Aren't you ever going to finish the ironing, Mother? Whistler painted his mother in a rocker. I'd have to paint mine standing over an ironing board." This is one of her communicative nights and she tells me everything and nothing as she fixes herself a plate of food out of the icebox.

She is so lovely. Why did you want me to come in at all? Why were you concerned? She will find her way.

She starts up the stairs to bed. "Don't get me up with the rest in the morning." "But I thought you were having midterms." "Oh, those," she comes back in, kisses me, and says quite lightly, "in a couple of years when we'll all be atom-dead they won't matter a bit."

She has said it before. She *believes* it. But because I have been dredging the past, and all that compounds a human being is so heavy and meaningful in me, I cannot endure it tonight.

55   I will never total it all. I will never come in to say: She was a child seldom smiled at. Her father left me before she was a year old. I had to work her first six years when there was work, or I sent her home and to his relatives. There were years she had care she hated. She was dark and thin and foreign-looking in a world where the prestige went to blondeness and curly hair and dimples, she was slow where glibness was prized. She was a child of anxious, not proud, love. We were poor and could not afford for her the soil of easy growth. I was a young mother, I was a distracted mother. There were other children pushing up, demanding. Her younger sister seemed all that she was not. There were years she did not want me to touch her. She kept too much in herself, her life was such she had to keep too much in herself. My wisdom came too late. She has much to her and probably little will come of it. She is a child of her age, of depression, of war, of fear.

Let her be. So all that is in her will not bloom—but in how many does it? There is still enough left to live by. Only help her to know—help make it so there is cause for her to know—that she is more than this dress on the ironing board, helpless before the iron.

[1954]

TOPICS FOR CRITICAL THINKING AND WRITING

1. Who is the "you" whom the mother speaks of? Do you think the mother will visit the "you"? Why, or why not?
2. What do you make of Emily's telling her mother not to awaken her for the midterm examination on the next morning?
3. If what way(s) did your response toward the mother change as you progressed through the story?
4. What, if anything, has the mother learned about life?

SHIRLEY JACKSON

Shirley Jackson (1919-65) was born in San Francisco but went to college in New York, first at the University of Rochester and then at Syracuse University. Although one of her stories was published in The Best American Short Stories 1944, *she did not receive national attention until 1948, when* The New Yorker *published "The Lottery." The magazine later reported that none of its earlier publications had produced so strong a response.*

In 1962 she experienced a breakdown and was unable to write, but she recovered and worked on a new novel. Before completing the book, however, she died of cardiac arrest at the age of 48. The book was published posthumously under the title Come Along With Me.

Two of her books, Life Among the Savages *(1953) and* Raising Demons *(1957), are engaging self-portraits of a harried mother in a house full of children. But what seems amusing also has its dark un-*

derside. After her breakdown Jackson said, "I think all my books laid end to end would be one long documentary of anxiety."

Her husband, Stanley Edgar Hyman (her college classmate and later a professor of English), said of Jackson, "If she uses the resources of supernatural terror, it was to provide metaphors for the all-too-real terrors of the natural."

The Lottery

The morning of June 27th was clear and sunny, with the fresh warmth of a full-summer day; the flowers were blossoming profusely and the grass was richly green. The people of the village began to gather in the square, between the post office and the bank, around ten o'clock; in some towns there were so many people that the lottery took two days and had to be started on June 26th, but in this village, where there were only about three hundred people, the whole lottery took less than two hours, so it could begin at ten o'clock in the morning and still be through in time to allow the villagers to get home for noon dinner.

The children assembled first, of course. School was recently over for the summer, and the feeling of liberty sat uneasily on most of them; they tended to gather together quietly for a while before they broke into boisterous play, and their talk was still of the classroom and the teacher, of books and reprimands. Bobby Martin had already stuffed his pockets full of stones, and the other boys soon followed his example, selecting the smoothest and roundest stones; Bobby and Harry Jones and Dickie Delacroix—the villagers pronounced this name "Dellacroy"—eventually made a great pile of stones in one corner of the square and guarded it against the raids of the other boys. The girls stood aside, talking among themselves, looking over their shoulders at the boys, and the very small children rolled in the dust or clung to the hands of their older brothers or sisters.

Soon the men began to gather, surveying their own children, speaking of planting and rain, tractors and taxes. They stood together, away from the pile of stones in the corner, and their jokes were quiet and they smiled rather than laughed. The women, wearing faded house dresses and sweaters, came shortly after their menfolk. They greeted one another and exchanged bits of gossip as they went to join their husbands. Soon the women, standing by their husbands, began to call to their children, and the children came reluctantly, having to be called four or five times. Bobby Martin ducked under his mother's grasping hand and ran, laughing, back to the pile of stones. His father spoke up sharply, and Bobby came quickly and took his place between his father and his oldest brother.

The lottery was conducted—as were the square dances, the teenage club, the Halloween program—by Mr. Summers, who had time and energy to devote to civic activities. He was a round-faced, jovial man and he ran the coal business, and people were sorry for him, because he had no children and his wife was a scold. When he arrived in the square, carrying the black wooden box, there was a murmur of conversation among the villagers and he waved and called, "Little late today, folks." The postmaster, Mr. Graves, followed him, carrying a three-legged stool, and the stool was put in the center of the square and Mr. Summers set the black box down on it. The villagers kept their distance, leaving a space between themselves and the stool, and when Mr. Summers said, "Some of you fellows want to give me a hand?" there was a hesitation before two men, Mr. Martin and his oldest son, Baxter, came forward to hold the box steady on the stool while Mr. Summers stirred up the papers inside it.

5   The original paraphernalia for the lottery had been lost long ago, and the black box now resting on the stool had been put into use even before Old Man Warner, the oldest man in town, was born. Mr. Summers spoke frequently to the villagers about making a new box, but no one liked to upset even as much tradition as was represented by the black box. There was a story that the present box had been made with some pieces of the box that had preceded it, the one that had been constructed when the first people settled down to make a village here. Every year, after the lottery, Mr. Summers began talking again about a new box, but every year the subject was allowed to fade off without anything's being done. The black box grew shabbier each year; by now it was no longer completely black but splintered badly along one side to show the original wood color, and in some places faded or stained.

Mr. Martin and his oldest son, Baxter, held the black box securely on the stool until Mr. Summers had stirred the papers thoroughly with his hand. Because so much of the ritual had been forgotten or discarded, Mr. Summers had been successful in having slips of paper substituted for the chips of wood that had been used for generations. Chips of wood, Mr. Summers had argued, had been all very well when the village was tiny, but now that the population was more than three hundred and likely to keep on growing, it was necessary to use something that would fit more easily into the black box. The night before the lottery, Mr. Summers and Mr. Graves made up the slips of paper and put them in the box, and it was then taken to the safe of Mr. Summers's coal company and locked up until Mr. Summers was ready to take it to the square next morning. The rest of the year, the box was put away, sometimes one place, sometimes another; it had spent one year in Mr. Graves's barn and another year underfoot in the post office, and sometimes it was set on a shelf in the Martin grocery and left there.

There was a great deal of fussing to be done before Mr. Summers declared the lottery open. There were lists to make up—of heads of families, heads of households in each family, members of each household in each family. There was the proper swearing-in of Mr. Summers by the postmaster, as the official of the lottery; at one time, some people remembered, there had been a recital of some sort, performed by the official of the lottery, a perfunctory, tuneless chant that had been rattled off duly each year; some people believed that the official of the lottery used to stand just so when he said or sang it, others believed that he was supposed to walk among the people, but years and years ago this part of the ritual had been allowed to lapse. There had been, also, a ritual salute, which the official of the lottery had had to use in addressing each person who came up to draw from the box, but this also had changed with time, until now it was felt necessary only for the official to speak to each person approaching. Mr. Summers was very good at all this; in his clean white shirt and blue jeans, with one hand resting carelessly on the black box, he seemed very proper and important as he talked interminably to Mr. Graves and the Martins.

Just as Mr. Summers finally left off talking and turned to the assembled villagers, Mrs. Hutchinson came hurriedly along the path to the square, her sweater thrown over her shoulders, and slid into place in the back of the crowd. "Clean forgot what day it was," she said to Mrs. Delacroix, who stood next to her, and they both laughed softly. "Thought my old man was out back stacking wood," Mrs. Hutchinson went on, "and then I looked out the window and the kids were gone, and then I remembered it was the twenty-seventh and came a-running." She dried her hands on her apron, and Mrs. Delacroix said, "You're in time, though. They're still talking away up there."

Mrs. Hutchinson craned her neck to see through the crowd and found her husband and children standing near the front. She tapped Mrs. Delacroix on the arm as a farewell and began to make her way through the crowd. The people separated goodhumoredly to let her through; two or three people said, in voices just loud enough to be heard across the crowd, "Here comes your Missus, Hutchinson," and "Bill, she made it after all." Mrs. Hutchinson reached her husband, and Mr. Summers, who had been waiting, said cheerfully, "Thought we were going to have to get on without you, Tessie." Mrs. Hutchinson said, grinning, "Wouldn't have me leave m'dishes in the sink, now would you, Joe?," and soft laughter ran through the crowd as the people stirred back into position after Mrs. Hutchinson's arrival.

10   "Well, now," Mr. Summers said. soberly, "guess we better get started, get this over with, so's we can go back to work. Anybody ain't here?"

"Dunbar," several people said. "Dunbar, Dunbar."

Mr. Summers consulted his list. "Clyde Dunbar," he said. "That's right. He's broke his leg, hasn't he? Who's drawing for him?"

"Me, I guess," a woman said, and Mr. Summers turned to look at her. "Wife draws for her husband," Mr. Summers said. "Don't you have a grown boy to do it for you, Janey?" Although Mr. Summers and everyone else in the village knew the answer perfectly well, it was the business of the official of the lottery to ask such questions formally. Mr. Summers waited with an expression of polite interest while Mrs. Dunbar answered.

"Horace's not but sixteen yet," Mrs. Dunbar said regretfully. "Guess I gotta fill in for the old man this year."

15   "Right," Mr. Summers said. He made a note on the list he was holding. Then he asked, "Watson boy drawing this year?"

A tall boy in the crowd raised his hand. "Here," he said. "I'm drawing for m'mother and me." He blinked his eyes nervously and ducked his head as several voices in the crowd said things like "Good fellow, Jack," and "Glad to see your mother's got a man to do it."

"Well," Mr. Summers said, "guess that's everyone. Old Man Warner make it?"

"Here," a voice said, and Mr. Summers nodded.

A sudden hush fell on the crowd as Mr. Summers cleared his throat and looked at the list. "All ready?" he called. "Now, I'll read the names—heads of families first—and the men come up and take a paper out of the box. Keep the paper folded in your hand without looking at it until everyone has had a turn. Everything clear?"

20   The people had done it so many times that they only half listened to the

directions, most of them were quiet, wetting their lips, not looking around. Then Mr. Summers raised one hand high and said, "Adams." A man disengaged himself from the crowd and came forward. "Hi, Steve," Mr. Summers said, and Mr. Adams said, "Hi, Joe." They grinned at one another humorlessly and nervously. Then Mr. Adams reached into the black box and took out a folded paper. He held it firmly by one corner as he turned and went hastily back to his place in the crowd, where he stood a little apart from his family, not looking down at his hand.

"Allen," Mr. Summers said. "Anderson. . . . Bentham."

"Seems like there's no time at all between lotteries any more," Mrs. Delacroix said to Mrs. Graves in the back row. "Seems like we got through with the last one only last week."

"Time sure goes fast," Mrs. Graves said.

"Clark. . . . Delacroix."

25   "There goes my old man," Mrs. Delacroix said. She held her breath while her husband went forward.

"Dunbar," Mr. Summers said, and Mrs. Dunbar went steadily to the box while one of the women said, "Go on, Janey," and another said, "There she goes."

"We're next," Mrs. Graves said. She watched while Mr. Graves came around from the side of the box, greeted Mr. Summers gravely, and selected a slip of paper from the box. By now, all through the crowd there were men holding the small folded papers in their large hands, turning them over and over nervously. Mrs. Dunbar and her two sons stood together, Mrs. Dunbar holding the slip of paper.

"Harburt. . . . Hutchinson."

"Get up there, Bill," Mrs. Hutchinson said, and the people near her laughed.

30   "Jones."

"They do say," Mr. Adams said to Old Man Warner, who stood next to him, "that over in the north village they're talking of giving up the lottery."

Old Man Warner snorted, "Pack of crazy fools," he said. "Listening to the young folks, nothing's good enough for *them*. Next thing you know, they'll be wanting to go back to living in caves, nobody work any more, live *that* way for a while. Used to be a saying about 'Lottery in June, corn be heavy soon.' First thing you know, we'd all be eating stewed chickweed and acorns. There's *always* been a lottery," he added petulantly. "Bad enough to see young Joe Summers up there joking with everybody."

"Some places have already quit lotteries," Mrs. Adams said.

"Nothing but trouble in *that*," Old Man Warner said stoutly. "Pack of young fools."

35   "Martin." And Bobby Martin watched his father go forward. "Overdyke. . . . Percy."

"I wish they'd hurry," Mrs. Dunbar said to her older son. "I wish they'd hurry," Mrs. Dunbar said to her older son. "I wish they'd hurry."

"They're almost through," her son said.

"You get ready to run tell Dad," Mrs. Dunbar said.

Mr. Summers called his own name and then stepped forward precisely and selected a slip from the box. Then he called, "Warner."

40   "Seventy-seventh year I been in the lottery," Old Man Warner said as he went through the crowd. "Seventy-seventh time."

"Watson." The tall boy came awkwardly through the crowd. Someone said, "Don't be nervous, Jack," and Mr. Summers said, "Take your time, son."

"Zanini."

After that, there was a long pause, a breathless pause, until Mr. Summers, holding his slip of paper in the air, said, "All right, fellows." For a minute, no one moved, and then all the slips of paper were opened. Suddenly, all women began to speak at once, saying, "Who is it?," "Who's got it?," "Is it the Dunbars?," "Is it the Watsons?" Then the voices began to say, "It's Hutchinson. It's Bill." "Bill Hutchinson's got it."

"Go tell your father," Mrs. Dunbar said to her older son.

45   People began to look around to see the Hutchinsons. Bill Hutchinson was standing quiet, staring down at the paper in his hand. Suddenly, Tessie Hutchinson shouted to Mr. Summers, "You didn't give him time enough to take any paper he wanted. I saw you. It wasn't fair!"

"Be a good sport, Tessie," Mrs. Delacroix called, and Mrs. Graves said, "All of us took the same chance."

"Shut up, Tessie," Bill Hutchinson said.

"Well, everyone," Mr. Summers said, "that was done pretty fast, and now we've got to be hurrying a little more to get it done in time." He consulted his next list. "Bill," he said, "you draw for the Hutchinson family. You got any other households in the Hutchinsons?"

"There's Don and Eva," Mrs. Hutchinson yelled. "Make *them* take their chance!"

50   "Daughters draw with their husbands' families, Tessie," Mr. Summers said gently. "You know that as well as anyone else."

"It wasn't fair," Tessie said.

"I guess not, Joe," Bill Hutchinson said regretfully. "My daughter draws with her husband's family, that's only fair. And I've got no other family except the kids."

"Then, as far as drawing for families is concerned, it's you," Mr. Summers said in explanation, "and as far as drawing for households is concerned, that's you, too. Right?"

"Right," Bill Hutchinson said.

55   "How many kids, Bill?" Mr. Summers asked formally.

"Three," Bill Hutchinson said. "There's Bill, Jr., and Nancy, and little Dave. And Tessie and me."

"All right, then," Mr. Summers said. "Harry, you got their tickets back?"

Mr. Graves nodded and held up the slips of paper. "Put them in the box, then," Mr. Summers directed. "Take Bill's and put it in."

"I think we ought to start over," Mrs. Hutchinson said, as quietly as she could. "I tell you it wasn't *fair.* You didn't give him time enough to choose. *Everybody* saw that."

60   Mr. Graves had selected the five slips and put them in the box, and he dropped all the papers but those onto the ground, where the breeze caught them and lifted them off.

"Listen, everybody," Mrs. Hutchinson was saying to the people around her.

"Ready, Bill?" Mr. Summers asked, and Bill Hutchinson, with one quick glance around at his wife and children, nodded.

"Remember," Mr. Summers said, "take the slips and keep them folded until each person has taken one. Harry, you help little Dave." Mr. Graves took the hand of the little boy, who came willingly with him up to the box. "Take a paper out of the box, Davy," Mr. Summers said. Davy put his hand into the box and laughed. "Take just *one* paper," Mr. Summers said. "Harry, you hold it for him." Mr. Graves took the child's hand and removed the folded paper from the tight fist and held it while little Dave stood next to him and looked up at him wonderingly.

"Nancy next," Mr. Summers said. Nancy was twelve, and her school friends breathed heavily as she went forward, switching her skirt, and took a slip daintily from the box. "Bill, Jr.," Mr. Summers said, and Billy, his face red and his feet over-large, nearly knocked the box over as he got a paper out. "Tessie," Mr. Summers said. She hesitated for a minute, looking around defiantly, and then set her lips and went up to the box. She snatched a paper out and held it behind her.

65   "Bill," Mr. Summers said, and Bill Hutchinson reached into the box and felt around, bringing his hand out at last with the slip of paper in it.

The crowd was quiet. A girl whispered, "I hope it's not Nancy," and the sound of the whisper reached the edges of the crowd.

"It's not the way it used to be," Old Man Warner said clearly. "People ain't the way they used to be."

"All right," Mr. Summers said. "Open the papers. Harry, you open little Dave's."

Mr. Graves opened the slip of paper and there was a general sigh through the crowd as he held it up and everyone could see that it was blank. Nancy and Bill, Jr., opened theirs at the same time, and both beamed and laughed, turning around to the crowd and holding their slips of paper above their heads.

70   "Tessie," Mr. Summers said. There was a pause, and then Mr. Summers looked at Bill Hutchinson, and Bill unfolded his paper and showed it. It was blank.

"It's Tessie," Mr. Summers said, and his voice was hushed. "Show us her paper, Bill."

Bill Hutchinson went over to his wife and forced the slip of paper out of her hand. It had a black spot on it, the black spot Mr. Summers had made the night before with the heavy pencil in the coal-company office. Bill Hutchinson held it up, and there was a stir in the crowd.

"All right, folks," Mr. Summers said, "let's finish quickly."

Although the villagers had forgotten the ritual and lost the original black box, they still remembered to use stones. The pile of stones the boys had made earlier was ready; there were stones on the ground with the blowing scraps of paper that had come out of the box. Mrs. Delacroix selected a stone so large she had to pick it up with both hands and turned to Mrs. Dunbar. "Come on," she said. "Hurry up."

75   Mrs. Dunbar had small stones in both hands, and she said, gasping for breath, "I can't run at all. You'll have to go ahead and I'll catch up with you."

The children had stones already, and someone gave little Davy Hutchinson a few pebbles.

Tessie Hutchinson was in the center of a cleared space by now, and she held her hands out desperately as the villagers moved in on her. "It isn't fair," she said. A stone hit her on the side of the head.

Old Man Warner was saying, "Come on, come on, everyone." Steve Adams was in the front of the crowd of villagers, with Mrs. Graves beside him.

"It isn't fair, it isn't right," Mrs. Hutchinson screamed, and then they were upon her.

[1948]

 ## TOPICS FOR CRITICAL THINKING AND WRITING

1. What is the community's attitude toward tradition?
2. Doubtless a good writer could tell this story effectively from the point of view of a participant, but Jackson chose a nonparticipant point of view. What does she gain?
3. Let's say you were writing this story, and you had decided to write it from Tessie's point of view. What would your first paragraph, or your first 250 words, be?
4. Suppose someone claimed that the story is an attack on religious orthodoxy. What might be your response? (Whether you agree or disagree, set forth your reasons.)

 ## ALICE MUNRO

Alice Munroe was born in 1931 in Wingham, Ontario, Canada, a relatively rural community and the sort of place in which she sets much of her fiction. She began publishing stories when she was an undergraduate at the University of Western Ontario. She left Western after two years, worked in a library and in a bookstore, then married, moved to Victoria, British Columbia, and founded a bookstore there. She continued to write while raising three children. She divorced and remarried; much of her fiction concerns marriage or divorce, which is to say it concerns shifting relationships in a baffling world.

Boys and Girls

My father was a fox farmer. That is, he raised silver foxes, in pens; and in the fall and early winter, when their fur was prime, he killed them and skinned them and sold their pelts to the Hudson's Bay Company or the Montreal Fur Traders. These companies supplied us with heroic calendars to hang, one on each side of the kitchen door. Against a background of cold blue sky and black pine forests and treacherous northern rivers, plumed adventurers planted the flags of England or of France; magnificent savages bent their backs to the portage.

For several weeks before Christmas, my father worked after supper in the cellar of our house. The cellar was whitewashed, and lit by a hundred-watt bulb over the worktable. My brother Laird and I sat on the top step and watched. My father removed the pelt inside-out from the body of the fox, which looked surprisingly small, mean and rat-like, deprived of its arrogant weight of fur. The naked, slippery bodies were collected in a sack and buried at the dump. One time the hired man, Henry Bailey, had taken a swipe at me with this sack, saying, "Christmas present!" My mother thought that was not funny. In fact she disliked the whole pelting operation—that was what the killing, skinning, and preparation of the furs was called—and wished it did not have to take place in the house. There was the smell. After the pelt had been stretched inside-out on a long board my father scraped away delicately, removing the little clotted webs of blood vessels, the bubbles of fat; the smell of blood and animal fat, with the strong primitive odor of the fox itself, penetrated all parts of the house. I found it reassuringly seasonal, like the smell of oranges and pine needles.

Henry Bailey suffered from bronchial troubles. He would cough and cough until his narrow face turned scarlet, and his light blue, derisive eyes filled up with tears; then he took the lid off the stove, and, standing well back, shot out a great clot of phlegm—hsss—straight into the heart of the flames. We admired him for this performance and for his ability to make his stomach growl at will, and for his laughter, which was full of high whistlings and gurglings and involved the whole faulty machinery of his chest. It was sometimes hard to tell what he was laughing at, and always possible that it might be us.

After we had been sent to bed we could still smell fox and still hear Henry's laugh, but these things, reminders of the warm, safe, brightly lit downstairs world, seemed lost and diminished, floating on the stale cold air upstairs. We were afraid at night in the winter. We were not afraid of *outside* though this was the time of year when snowdrifts curled around our house like sleeping whales and the wind harassed us all night, coming up from the buried fields, the frozen swamp, with its old bugbear chorus of threats and misery. We were afraid of *inside,* the room where we slept. At this time the upstairs of our house was not finished. A brick chimney went up one wall. In the middle of the floor was a square hole, with a wooden railing around it; that was where the stairs came up. On the other side of the stairwell were the things that nobody had any use for any more—a soldiery roll of linoleum, standing on end, a wicker baby carriage, a fern basket, china jugs and basins with cracks in them, a picture of the Battle of Balaclava, very sad to look at. I had told Laird, as soon as he was old enough to understand such things, that bats and skeletons lived over there; whenever a man escaped from the country jail, twenty miles away, I imagined that he had somehow let himself in the window and was hiding behind the linoleum. But we had rules to keep us safe. When the light was on, we were safe as long as we did not step off the square of worn carpet which defined our bedroom-space; when the light was off no place was safe but the beds themselves. I had to turn out the light kneeling on the end of my bed, and stretching as far as I could to reach the cord.

5   In the dark we lay on our beds, our narrow life rafts, and fixed our eyes on the faint light coming up the stairwell, and sang songs. Laird sang "Jingle Bells," which he would sing any time, whether it was Christmas or not, and I sang "Danny Boy." I loved the sound of my own voice, frail and supplicat-

ing, rising in the dark. We could make out the tall frosted shapes of the windows now, gloomy and white. When I came to the part, *When I am dead, as dead I well may be*—a fit of shivering caused not by the cold sheets but by pleasurable emotion almost silenced me. *You'll kneel and say, an Ave there above me*—What was an Ave? Every day I forgot to find out.

Laird went straight from singing to sleep. I could hear his long, satisfied, bubbly breaths. Now for the time that remained to me, the most perfectly private and perhaps the best time of the whole day, I arranged myself tightly under the covers and went on with one of the stories I was telling myself from night to night. These stories were about myself, when I had grown a little older; they took place in a world that was recognizably mine, yet one that presented opportunities for courage, boldness and self-sacrifice, as mine never did. I rescued people from a bombed building (it discouraged me that the real war had gone on so far away from Jubilee). I shot two rabid wolves who were menacing the schoolyard (the teachers cowered terrified at my back). I rode a fine horse spiritedly down the main street of Jubilee, acknowledging the townspeople's gratitude for some yet-to-be-worked-out piece of heroism (nobody ever rode a horse there, except King Billy in the Orangemen's Day[1] parade). There was always riding and shooting in these stories, though I had only been on a horse twice—bareback because we did not own a saddle—and the second time I had slid right around and dropped under the horse's feet; it had stepped placidly over me. I really was learning to shoot, but I could not hit anything yet, not even tin cans on fence posts.

Alive, the foxes inhabited a world my father made for them. It was surrounded by a high guard fence, like a medieval town, with a gate that was padlocked at night. Along the streets of this town were ranged large, sturdy pens. Each of them had a real door that a man could go through, a wooden ramp along the wire, for the foxes to run up and down on, and a kennel—something like a clothes chest with airholes—where they slept and stayed in winter and had their young. There were feeding and watering dishes attached to the wire in such a way that they could be emptied and cleaned from the outside. The dishes were made of old tin cans, and the ramps and kennels of odds and ends of old lumber. Everything was tidy and ingenious; my father was tirelessly inventive and his favorite book in the world was Robinson Crusoe. He had fitted a tin drum on a wheelbarrow, for bringing water to the pens. This was my job in summer, when the foxes had to have water twice a day. Between nine and ten o'clock in the morning, and again after supper, I filled the drum at the pump and trundled it down through the barnyard to the pens, where I parked it, and filled my watering can and went along the streets. Laird came too, with his little cream and green gardening can, filled too full and knocking against his legs and slopping water on his canvas shoes. I had the real watering can, my father's, though I could only carry it three-quarters full.

The foxes all had names, which were printed on a tin plate and hung beside their doors. They were not named when they were born, but when they survived the first year's pelting and were added to the breeding stock. Those my father had named were called names like Prince, Bob, Wally and

[1]The Orange Society is named for William of Orange, who, as King William III of England, defeated James II of England at the Battle of the Boyne on 12 July 1609. It sponsors an annual procession on 12 July.

Betty. Those I had named were called Star or Turk, or Maureen or Diana. Laird named one Maud after a hired girl we had when he was little, one Harold after a boy at school, and one Mexico, he did not say why.

Naming them did not make pets out of them, or anything like it. Nobody but my father ever went into the pens, and he had twice had blood-poisoning from bites. When I was bringing them their water they prowled up and down on the paths they had made inside their pens, barking seldom—they saved that for night-time, when they might get up a chorus of community frenzy—but always watching me, their eyes burning, clear gold, in their pointed, malevolent faces. They were beautiful for their delicate legs and heavy, aristocratic tails and the bright fur sprinkled on dark down their backs—which gave them their name—but especially for their faces, drawn exquisitely sharp in pure hostility, and their golden eyes.

10   Besides carrying water I helped my father when he cut the long grass, and the lamb's quarter and flowering money-musk, that grew between the pens. He cut with the scythe and I raked into piles. Then he took a pitchfork and threw fresh-cut grass all over the top of the pens to keep the foxes cooler and shade their coats, which were browned by too much sun. My father did not talk to me unless it was about the job we were doing. In this he was quite different from my mother, who, if she was feeling cheerful, would tell me all sorts of things—the name of a dog she had when she was a little girl, the names of boys she had gone out with later on when she was grown up, and what certain dresses of hers had looked like—she could not imagine now what had become of them. Whatever thoughts and stories my father had were private, and I was shy of him and would never ask him questions. Nevertheless I worked willingly under his eyes, and with a feeling of pride. One time a feed salesman came down into the pens to talk to him and my father said, "Like to have you meet my new hired man." I turned away and raked furiously, red in the face with pleasure.

"Could of fooled me," said the salesman. "I thought it was only a girl."

After the grass was cut, it seemed suddenly much later in the year. I walked on stubble in the earlier evening, aware of the reddening skies, the entering silences, of fall. When I wheeled the tank out of the gate and put the padlock on, it was almost dark. One night at this time I saw my mother and father standing on the little rise of ground we called the gangway, in front of the barn. My father had just come from the meathouse; he had his stiff bloody apron on, and a pail of cut-up meat in his hand.

It was an odd thing to see my mother down at the barn. She did not often come out of the house unless it was to do something—hang out the wash or dig potatoes in the garden. She looked out of place, with her bare lumpy legs, not touched by the sun, her apron still on and damp across the stomach from the supper dishes. Her hair was tied up in a kerchief, wisps of it falling out. She would tie her hair up like this in the morning, saying she did not have time to do it properly, and it would stay tied up all day. It was true, too; she really did not have time. These days our back porch was piled with baskets of peaches and grapes and pears, bought in town, and onions and tomatoes and cucumbers grown at home, all waiting to be made into jelly and jam and preserves, pickles and chili sauce. In the kitchen there was a fire in the stove all day, jars clinked in boiling water, sometimes a cheese-cloth bag was strung on a pole between two chairs straining blue-black grape pulp for jelly. I was given jobs to do and I would sit at the table peeling peaches that had been soaked in the hot water, or cutting up onions, my eyes smarting and streaming. As soon as I was done I ran out of the house, trying to get out of earshot before my mother thought of what she wanted me to do next. I hated the hot dark kitchen in summer, the green blinds and the flypapers, the same old oilcloth table and wavy mirror and bumpy linoleum. My mother was too tired and preoccupied to talk to me, she had no heart to tell about the Normal School Graduation Dance; sweat trickled over her face and she was always counting under her breath, pointing at jars, dumping cups of sugar. It seemed to me that work in the house was endless, dreary and peculiarly depressing; work done out of doors, and in my father's service, was ritualistically important.

I wheeled the tank up to the barn, where it was kept, and I heard my mother saying, "Wait till Laird gets a little bigger, then you'll have a real help."

15   What my father said I did not hear. I was pleased by the way he stood listening, politely as he would to a salesman or a stranger, but with an air of wanting to get on with his real work. I felt my mother had no business down here and I wanted him to feel the same way. What did she mean about Laird? He was no help to anybody. Where was he now? Swinging himself sick on the swing, going around in circles, or trying to catch caterpillars. He never once stayed with me till I was finished.

"And then I can use her more in the house," I heard my mother say. She had a dead-quiet, regretful way of talking about me that always made me uneasy. "I just get my back turned and she runs off. It's not like I had a girl in the family at all."

I went and sat on a feed bag in the corner of the barn, not wanting to appear when this conversation was going on. My mother, I felt, was not to be trusted. She was kinder than my father and more easily fooled, but you could not depend on her, and the real reasons for the things she said and did were not to be known. She loved me, and she sat up late at night making a dress of the difficult style I wanted, for me to wear when school started, but she was also my enemy. She was always plotting. She was plotting now to get me to stay in the house more, although she knew I hated it (*because* she knew I hated it) and keep me from working for my father. It seemed to me she would do this simply out of perversity, and to try her power. It did not occur to me that she could be lonely, or jealous. No grown-up could be; they were too fortunate. I sat and kicked my heels monotonously against a feed bag, raising dust, and did not come out till she was gone.

At any rate, I did not expect my father to pay any attention to what she said. Who could imagine Laird doing my work—Laird remembering the padlock and cleaning out the watering dishes with a leaf on the end of a stick, or even wheeling the tank without it tumbling over? It showed how little my mother knew about the way things really were.

I have forgotten to say what the foxes were fed. My father's bloody apron reminded me. They were fed horsemeat. At this time most farmers still kept horses, and when a horse got too old to work, or broke a leg or got down and would not get up, as they sometimes did, the owner would call my father, and he and Henry went out to the farm in the truck. Usually they shot and butchered the horse there, paying the farmer from five to twelve dollars. If they had already too much meat on hand, they would bring the horse back alive, and keep it for a few days or weeks in our stable, until the meat was needed. After the war the farmers were buying tractors and gradually getting rid of horses altogether, so it sometimes happened that we got a good healthy horse, that there was just no use for any more. If this happened in the winter we might keep the horse in our stable till spring, for we had plenty of hay and if there was a lot of snow—and the plow did not always get out road cleared—it was convenient to be able to go to town with a horse and cutter.[2]

20   The winter I was eleven years old we had two horses in the stable. We did not know what names they had had before, so we called them Mack and Flora. Mack was an old black workhorse, sooty and indifferent. Flora was a sorrel mare, a driver. We took them both out in the cutter. Mack was slow and easy to handle. Flora was given to fits of violent alarm, veering at cars and even at other horses, but we loved her speed and high-stepping, her general air of gallantry and abandon. On Saturdays we went down to the stable and as soon as we opened the door on its cosy, animal-smelling darkness Flora threw up her head, rolled her eyes, whinnied despairingly and pulled herself through a crisis of nerves on the spot. It was not safe to go into her stall; she would kick.

This winter also I began to hear a great deal more on the theme my mother had sounded when she had been talking in front of the barn. I no longer felt safe. It seemed that in the minds of the people around me there was a steady undercurrent of thought, not to be deflected, on this one subject. The word *girl* had formerly seemed to me innocent and unburdened, like the word *child;* now it appeared that it was no such thing. A girl was not, as I had supposed, simply what I was; it was what I had to become. It was a definition, always touched with emphasis, with reproach and disappointment. Also it was a joke on me. Once Laird and I were fighting, and for the first time ever I had to use all my strength against him; even so, he caught and pinned my arm for a moment, really hurting me. Henry saw this, and laughed, saying, "Oh, that there Laird's gonna show you, one of these days!" Laird was getting a lot bigger. But I was getting bigger too.

My grandmother came to stay with us for a few weeks and I heard other things. "Girls don't slam doors like that." "Girls keep their knees together when they sit down." And worse still, when I asked some questions, "That's none of girls' business." I continued to slam the doors and sit as awkwardly as possible, thinking by such measures I kept myself free.

When spring came, the horses were let out in the barnyard. Mack stood against the barn wall trying to scratch his neck and haunches, but Flora trotted up and down and reared at the fences, clattering her hooves against the rails. Snow drifts dwindled quickly, revealing the hard gray and brown earth, the familiar rise and fall of the ground, plain and bare after the fantastic landscape of winter. There was a great feeling of opening-out, of release. We just wore rubbers now, over our shoes; our feet felt ridiculously light. One Saturday we went to the stable and found all the doors open, letting in the unaccustomed sunlight and fresh air. Henry was there, just idling around looking at his collection of calendars which were tacked up behind the stalls in a part of the stable my mother had probably never seen.

---

[2] A small sleigh

"Come to say goodbye to your old friend Mack?" Henry said. "Here, you give him a taste of oats." He poured some oats in Laird's cupped hands and Laird went to feed Mack. Mack's teeth were in bad shape. He ate very slowly, patiently shifting the oats around in his mouth, trying to find a stump of a molar to grind it on. "Poor old Mac," said Henry mournfully. "When a horse's teeth's gone, he's gone. That's about the way."

25   "Are you going to shoot him today?" I said. Mack and Flora had been in the stable so long I had almost forgotten they were going to be shot.

Henry didn't answer me. Instead he started to sing in a high, trembly, mocking-sorrowful voice. *Oh, there's no more work, for poor Uncle Ned, he's gone where the good darkies go.* Mack's thick, blackish tongue worked diligently at Laird's hand. I went out before the song was ended and sat down on the gangway.

I had never seen them shoot a horse, but I knew where it was done. Last summer Laird and I had come upon a horse's entrails before they were buried. We had thought it was a big black snake, coiled up in the sun. That was around in the field that ran up beside the barn. I thought that if we went inside the barn, and found a wide crack or a knothole to look through, we would be able to see them do it. It was not something I wanted to see; just the same, if a thing really happened, it was better to see, and know.

My father came down from the house, carrying the gun.

"What are you doing here?" he said.

30   "Nothing."

"Go on up and play around the house."

He sent Laird out of the stable. I said to Laird, "Do you want to see them shoot Mack?" and without waiting for an answer led him around to the front door of the barn, opened it carefully, and went in. "Be quiet or they'll hear us," I said. We could hear Henry and my father talking in the stable; then the heavy, shuffling steps of Mack being backed out of his stall.

In the loft it was cold and dark. Thin crisscrossed beams of sunlight fell through the cracks. The hay was low. It was a rolling country, hills and hollows, slipping under our feet. About four feet up was a beam going around the walls. We piled hay up in one corner and I boosted Laird up and hoisted myself. The beam was not very wide; we crept along it with our hands flat on the barn walls. There were plenty of knotholes, and I found one that gave me the view I wanted—a corner of the barnyard, the gate, part of the field. Laird did not have a knothole and began to complain.

I showed him a widened crack between two boards. "Be quiet and wait. If they hear you you'll get us in trouble."

35   My father came in sight carrying the gun. Henry was leading Mack by the halter. He dropped it and took out his cigarette papers and tobacco; he rolled cigarettes for my father and himself. While this was going on Mack nosed around in the old, dead grass along the fence. Then my father opened the gate and they took Mack through. Henry led Mack way from the path to a patch of ground and they talked together, not loud enough for us to hear. Mack again began searching for a mouthful of fresh grass, which was not to be found. My father walked away in a straight line, and stopped short a distance which seemed to suit him. Henry was walking away from Mack too, but sideways, still negligently holding on to the halter. My father raised the gun and Mack looked up as if he had noticed something and my father shot him.

Mack did not collapse at once but swayed, lurched sideways and fell, first on his side; then he rolled over on his back and, amazingly, kicked his legs for a few seconds in the air. At this Henry laughed, as if Mack had done a trick for him. Laird, who had drawn a long, groaning breath of surprise when the shot was fired, said out loud, "He's not dead." And it seemed to me it might be true. But his legs stopped, he rolled on his side again, his muscles quivered and sank. The two men walked over and looked at him in a business-like way; they bent down and examined his forehead where the bullet had gone in, and now I saw his blood on the brown grass.

"Now they just skin him and cut him up," I said. "Let's go." My legs were a little shaky and I jumped gratefully down into the hay. "Now you've seen how they shoot a horse," I said in a congratulatory way, as if I had seen it many times before. "Let's see if any barn cat's had kittens in the hay." Laird jumped. He seemed young and obedient again. Suddenly I remembered how, when he was little, I had brought him into the barn and told him to climb the ladder to the top beam. That was in the spring, too, when the hay was low. I had done it out of a need for excitement, a desire for something to happen so that I could tell about it. He was wearing a little bulky brown and white checked coat, made down from one of mine. He went all the way up just as I told him, and sat down on the top beam with the hay far below him on one side, and the barn floor and some old machinery on the other. Then I ran screaming to my father, "Laird's up on the top beam!" My father came, my mother came, my father went up the ladder talking very quietly and brought Laird down under his arm, at which my mother leaned against the ladder and began to cry. They said to me, "Why weren't you watching him?" but nobody ever knew the truth. Laird did not know enough to tell. But whenever I saw the brown and white checked coat hanging in the closet, or at the bottom of the rag bag, which was where it ended up, I felt a weight in my stomach, the sadness of unexorcised guilt.

I looked at Laird, who did not even remember this, and I did not like the look on this thin, winter-pale face. His expression was not frightened or upset, but remote, concentrating. "Listen," I said, in an unusually bright and friendly voice, "you aren't going to tell, are you?"

"No," he said absently.

40   "Promise."

"Promise," he said. I grabbed the hand behind his back to make sure he was not crossing his fingers. Even so, he might have a nightmare; it might come out that way. I decided I had better work hard to get all thoughts of what he had seen out of his mind—which, it seemed to me, could not hold very many things at a time. I got some money I had saved and that afternoon we went into Jubilee and saw a show, with Judy Canova,[3] at which we both laughed a great deal. After that I thought it would be all right.

Two weeks later I knew they were going to shoot Flora. I knew from the night before, when I heard my mother ask if the hay was holding out all right, and my father said, "Well, after tomorrow there'll just be the cow, and we should be able to put her out to grass in another week." So I knew it was Flora's turn in the morning.

This time I didn't think of watching it. That was something to see just

[3]American comedian, popular in films in the 1940s

one time. I had not thought about it very often since, but sometimes when I was busy working at school, or standing in front of the mirror combing my hair and wondering if I would be pretty when I grew up, the whole scene would flash into my mind: I would see the easy, practiced way my father raised the gun, and hear Henry laughing when Mack kicked his legs in the air. I did not have any great feeling of horror and opposition, such as a city child might have had; I was too used to seeing the death of animals as a necessity by which we lived. Yet I felt a little ashamed, and there was a new wariness, a sense of holding-off, in my attitude to my father and his work.

It was a fine day, and we were going around the yard picking up tree branches that had been torn off in winter storms. This was something we had been told to do, and also we wanted to use them to make a teepee. We heard Flora whinny, and then my father's voice and Henry's shouting, and we ran down to the barnyard to see what was going on.

45   The stable door was open. Henry had just brought Flora out, and she had broken away from him. She was running free in the barnyard, from one end to the other. We climbed up on the fence. It was exciting to see her running, whinnying, going up on her hind legs, prancing and threatening like a horse in a Western movie, an unbroken ranch horse, though she was just an old driver, an old sorrel mare. My father and Henry ran after her and tried to grab the dangling halter. They tried to work her into a corner, and they had almost succeeded when she made a run between them, wild-eyed, and disappeared around the corner of the barn. We heard the rail clatter down as she got over the fence, and Henry yelled. "She's into the field now!"

That meant she was in the long L-shaped field that ran up by the house. If she got around the center, heading toward the lane, the gate was open; the truck had been driven into the field this morning. My father shouted to me, because I was on the other side of the fence, nearest the lane, "Go shut the gate!"

I could run very fast. I ran across the garden, past the tree where our swing was hung, and jumped across a ditch into the lane. There was the open gate. She had not got out, I could not see her up the road; she must have run to the other end of the field. The gate was heavy. I lifted it out of the gravel and carried it across the roadway. I had it halfway across when she came in sight, galloping straight toward me. There was just time to get the chain on. Laird came scrambling through the ditch to help me.

Instead of shutting the gate, I opened it as wide as I could. I did not make any decision to do this, it was just what I did. Flora never slowed down; she galloped straight past me, and Laird jumped up and down, yelling "Shut it, shut it!" even after it was too late. My father and Henry appeared in the field a moment too late to see what I had done. They only saw Flora heading for the township road. They would think I had not got there in time.

They did not waste any time asking about it. They went back to the barn and got the gun and the knives they used, and put these in the truck; then they turned the truck around and came bouncing up the field toward us. Laird called to them, "Let me go too, let me go too!" and Henry stopped the truck and they took him in. I shut the gate after they were all gone.

50   I supposed Laird would tell. I wondered what would happen to me. I had never disobeyed my father before, and I could not understand why I had

done it. Flora would not really get away. They would catch up with her in the truck. Or if they did not catch her this morning somebody would see her and telephone us this afternoon or tomorrow. There was no wild country here for her to run to, only farms. What was more, my father had paid for her, we needed the meat to feed the foxes, we needed the foxes to make our living. All I had done was make more work for my father who worked hard enough already. And when my father found out about it he was not going to trust me any more; he would know that I was not entirely on his side. I was on Flora's side, and that made me no use to anybody, not even to her. Just the same, I did not regret it; when she came running at me and I held the gate open, that was the only thing I could do.

I went back to the house, and my mother said. "What's all the commotion?" I told her that Flora had kicked down the fence and got away. "Your poor father," she said, "now he'll have to go chasing over the countryside. Well, there isn't any use planning dinner before one." She put up the ironing board. I wanted to tell her, but thought better of it and went upstairs, and sat on my bed.

Lately I had been trying to make my part of the room fancy, spreading the bed with old lace curtains, and fixing myself a dressing table with some leftovers of cretonne for a skirt. I planned to put up some kind of barricade between my bed and Laird's, to keep my section separate from his. In the sunlight, the lace curtains were just dusty rags. We did not sing at night any more. One night when I was singing Laird said, "You sound silly," and I went right on but the next night I did not start. There was not so much need to anyway, we were no longer afraid. We knew it was just old furniture over there, old jumble and confusion. We did not keep to the rules. I still stayed awake after Laird was asleep and told myself stories, but even in these stories something different was happening, mysterious alterations took place. A story might start off in the old way, with a spectacular danger, a fire or wild animals, and for a while I might rescue people; then things would change around, and instead, somebody would be rescuing me. It might be a boy from our class at school, or even Mr. Campbell, our teacher, who tickled girls under the arms. And at this point the story concerned itself at great length with what I looked like—how long my hair was, and what kind of dress I had on; by the time I had these details worked out the real excitement of the story was lost.

It was later than one o'clock when the truck came back. The tarpaulin was over the back, which meant there was meat in it. My mother had to heat dinner up all over again. Henry and my father had changed from their bloody overalls into ordinary working overalls in the barn, and they washed their arms and necks and faces at the sink, and splashed water on their hair and combed it. Laird lifted his arm to show off a streak of blood. "We shot old Flora," he said, "and cut her up in fifty pieces."

"Well I don't want to hear about it," my mother said. "And don't come to my table like that."

55   My father made him go and wash the blood off.

We sat down and my father said grace and Henry pasted his chewing gum on the end of his fork, the way he always did; when he took it off he would have us admire the pattern. We began to pass the bowls of steaming, overcooked vegetables. Laird looked across the table at me and said proudly, distinctly, "Anyway it was her fault Flora got away."

"What?" my father said.

"She could of shut the gate and she didn't. She just open' it up and Flora run out."

"Is that right?" my father said.

60 Everybody at the table was looking at me. I nodded, swallowing food with great difficulty. To my shame, tears flooded my eyes.

My father made a curt sound of disgust. "What did you do that for?"

I did not answer. I put down my fork and waited to be sent from the table, still not looking up.

But this did not happen. For some time nobody said anything, then Laird said matter-of-factly, "She's crying."

"Never mind," my father said. He spoke with resignation, even good humor, the words which absolved and dismissed me for good. "She's only a girl," he said.

65 I didn't protest that, even in my heart. Maybe it was true.

[1968]

 TOPICS FOR CRITICAL THINKING AND WRITING

1. Explain, in a paragraph, what the narrator means when she says (paragraph 21), "The word *girl* had formerly seemed to me innocent and unburdened, like the world *child;* now it appeared that it was no such thing. A girl was not, as I had supposed, simply what I was; it was what I had to become."
2. The narrator says that she "could not understand" why she disobeyed her father and allowed the horse to escape. Can you explain her action to her? If so, do so.
3. In a paragraph, characterize the mother.

 TONI CADE BAMBARA

Toni Cade Bambara was born in 1939 in New York City and grew up in black districts of the city. After studying at the University of Florence in Italy and at City College in New York, where she received a master's degree, she worked for a while as a case investigator for the New York State Welfare Department. Later she directed a recreation program for hospital patients. Now that her literary reputation is established, she spends most of her time writing, though she has also served as writer in residence at Spelman College in Atlanta.

The Lesson

Back in the days when everyone was old and stupid or young and foolish and me and Sugar were the only ones just right, this lady moved on our block with nappy hair and proper speech and no makeup. And quite naturally we laughed at her, laughed the way we did at the junk man who went about his business like he was some big-time president and his sorry-ass horse his secretary. And we kinda hated her too, hated the way we did the winos who cluttered up our parks and pissed on our handball walls and stank up our hallways and stairs so you couldn't halfway play hide-and-seek without a goddamn gas mask. Miss Moore was her name. The only woman on the block with no first name. And she was black as hell, cept for her feet, which were fish-white and spooky. And she was always planning these boring-ass things for us to do, us being my cousin, mostly, who lived on the block cause we all moved North the same time and to the same apartment then spread out gradual to breathe. And our parents would yank our heads into some kinda shape and crisp up our clothes so we'd be presentable for travel with Miss Moore, who always looked like she was going to church, though she never did. Which is just one of the things the grownups talked about when they talked behind her back like a dog. But when she came calling with some sachet she'd sewed up or some gingerbread she'd made or some book, why then they'd all be too embarrassed to turn her down and we'd get handed over all spruced up. She'd been to college and said it was only right that she should take responsibility for the young ones' education, and she not even related by marriage or blood. So they'd go for it. Specially Aunt Gretchen. She was the main gofer in the family. You got some ole dumb shit foolishness you want somebody to go for, you send for Aunt Gretchen. She been screwed into the go-along for so long, it's a blood-deep natural thing with her. Which is how she got saddled with me and Sugar and Junior in the first place while our mothers were in a la-de-da apartment up the block having a good ole time.

So this one day Miss Moore rounds us all up at the mailbox and it's puredee hot and she's knockin herself out about arithmetic. And school suppose to let up in summer I heard, but she don't never let up. And the starch in my pinafore scratching the shit outta me and I'm really hating this nappy-head bitch and her goddamn college degree. I'd much rather go to the pool or to the show where it's cool. So me and Sugar leaning on the mailbox being surly, which is a Miss Moore word. And Flyboy checking out what everybody brought for lunch. And Fat Butt already wasting his peanut-butter-and-jelly sandwich like the pig he is. And Junebug punchin on Q.T.'s arm for potato chips. And Rosie Giraffe shifting from one hip to the other waiting for somebody to step on her foot or ask her if she from Georgia so she can kick ass, preferably Mercedes'. And Miss Moore asking us do we know what money is, like we a bunch of retards. I mean real money, she say, like it's only poker chips or monopoly papers we lay on the grocer. So right away I'm tired of this and say so. And would much rather snatch Sugar and go to the Sunset and terrorize the West Indian kids and take their hair ribbons and their money too. And Miss Moore files that remark away for next week's lesson on brotherhood, I can tell. And finally I say we oughta get to the subway cause it's cooler and besides we might meet some cute boys. Sugar done swiped her mama's lipstick, so we ready.

So we heading down the street and she's boring us silly about what things cost and what our parents make and how much goes for rent and how money ain't divided up right in this country. And then she gets to the part about we all poor and live in the slums, which I don't feature. And I'm ready to speak on that, but she steps out in the street and hails two cabs just like that. Then she hustles half the crew in with her and hands me a five-dollar bill and tells me to calculate 10 percent tip for the driver. And we're off. Me and Sugar and Junebug and Flyboy hangin out the window and hollering to everybody, putting lipstick on each other cause Flyboy a faggot anyway, and making farts with our sweaty armpits. But I'm mostly trying to figure how to spend this money. But they all fascinated with the meter ticking and Junebug starts laying bets to how much it'll read when Flyboy can't hold his breath no more. Then Sugar lays bets as to how much it'll be when we get there. So I'm stuck. Don't nobody want to go for my plan, which is to jump out at the next light and run off to the first bar-b-que we can find. Then the driver tells us to get the hell out cause we there already. And the meter reads eighty-five cents. And I'm stalling to figure out the tip and Sugar say give him a dime. And I decide he don't need it as bad as I do, so later for him. But then he tries to take off with Junebug foot still in the door so we talk about his mama something ferocious. Then we check out that we on Fifth Avenue and everybody dressed up in stockings. One lady in a fur coat, hot as it is. White folks crazy.

"This is the place," Miss Moore say, presenting it to us in the voice she uses at the museum. "Let's look in the windows before we go in."

5   "Can we steal?" Sugar asks very serious like she's getting the ground rules squared away before she plays. "I beg your pardon," say Miss Moore, and we fall out. So she leads us around the windows of the toy store and me and Sugar screamin, "This is mine, that's mine, I gotta have that, that was made for me, I was born for that," till Big Butt drowns us out.

"Hey, I'm goin to buy that there."

"That there? You don't even know what it is, stupid."

"I do so," he say punchin on Rosie Giraffe. "It's a microscope."

"Whatcha gonna do with a microscope, fool?"

10   "Look at things."

"Like what, Ronald?" ask Miss Moore. And Big Butt ain't got the first notion. So here go Miss Moore gabbing about the thousands of bacteria in a drop of water and the somethinorother in a speck of blood and the million and one living things in the air around us is invisible to the naked eye. And what she say that for? Junebug go to town on that "naked" and we rolling. Then Miss Moore ask what it cost. So we all jam into the window smudgin it up and the price tag say $300. So then she ask how long'd take for Big Butt and Junebug to save up their allowances. "Too long," I say. "Yeh," adds Sugar, "outgrown it by that time." And Miss Moore say no, you never outgrow learning instruments. "Why, even medical students and interns and," blah, blah, blah. And we ready to choke Big Butt for bringing it up in the first damn place.

"This here costs four hundred eighty dollars," say Rosie Giraffe. So we pile up all over her to see what she pointin out. My eyes tell me it's a chunk of glass cracked with something heavy, and different-color inks dripped into the splits, then the whole thing put into a oven or something. But for $480 it don't make sense.

"That's a paperweight made of semi-precious stones fused together under tremendous pressure," she explains slowly, and her hands doing the mining and all the factory work.

"So what's a paperweight?" asks Rosie Giraffe.

15   "To weigh paper with, dumbbell," say Flyboy, the wise man from the East.

"Not exactly," say Miss Moore, which is what she say when you warm or way off too. "It's to weigh paper down so it won't scatter and make your desk untidy." So right away me and Sugar curtsy to each other and then to Mercedes who is more the tidy type.

"We don't keep paper on top of the desk in my class," say Junebug, figuring Miss Moore crazy or lyin one.

"At home, then," she say. "Don't you have a calendar and a pencil case and a blotter and a letter-opener on your desk at home where you do your homework?" And she know damn well what our homes look like cause she nosys around in them every chance she gets.

"I don't even have a desk," say Junebug. "Do we?"

20   "No. And I don't get no homework neither," says Big Butt.

"And I don't even have a home," say Flyboy like he do at school to keep the white folks off his back and sorry for him. Send this poor kid to camp posters, is his specialty.

"I do," says Mercedes. "I have a box of stationery on my desk and a picture of my cat. My godmother bought the stationery and the desk. There's a big rose on each sheet and the envelopes smell like roses."

"Who wants to know about your smelly-ass stationery," say Rosie Giraffe fore I can get my two cents in.

"It's important to have a work area all your own so that. . . "

25   "Will you look at this sailboat, please," say Flyboy, cuttin her off and pointin to the thing like it was his. So once again we tumble all over each other to gaze at this magnificent thing in the toy store which is just big enough to maybe sail two kittens across the pond if you strap them to the posts tight. We all start reciting the price tag like we in assembly. "Handcrafted sailboat of fiberglass at one thousand one hundred ninety-five dollars."

"Unbelievable," I hear myself say and am really stunned. I read it again for myself just in case the group recitation put me in a trance. Same thing. For some reason this pisses me off. We look at Miss Moore and she lookin at us, waiting for I dunno what.

"Who'd pay all that when you can buy a sailboat set for a quarter at Pop's, a tube of glue for a dime, and a ball of string for eight cents? It must have a motor and a whole lot else besides," I say. "My sailboat cost me about fifty cents."

"But will it take water?" say Mercedes with her smart ass.

"Took mine to Alley Pond Park once," say Flyboy. "String broke. Lost it. Pity."

30   "Sailed mine in Central Park and it keeled over and sank. Had to ask my father for another dollar."

"And you got the strap," laugh Big Butt. "The jerk didn't even have a string on it. My old man wailed on his behind."

Little Q.T. was staring hard at the sailboat and you could see he wanted it bad. But he too little and somebody'd just take it from him. So what the hell. "This boat for kids, Miss Moore?"

"Parents silly to buy something like that just to get all broke up," say Rosie Giraffe.

"That much money it should last forever," I figure.

35   "My father'd buy it for me if I wanted it."

"Your father, my ass," say Rosie Giraffe getting a chance to finally push Mercedes.

"Must be rich people shop here," say Q.T.

"You are a very bright boy," say Flyboy. "What was your first clue?" And he rap him on the head with the back of his knuckles, since Q.T. the only one he could get away with. Though Q.T. liable to come up behind you years later and get his licks in when you half expect it.

"What I want to know is," I says to Miss Moore though I never talk to her, I wouldn't give the bitch that satisfaction, "is how much a real boat costs? I figure a thousand'd get you a yacht any day."

40   "Why don't you check that out," she says, "and report back to the group?" Which really pains my ass. If you gonna mess up a perfectly good swim day least you could do is have some answers. "Let's go in," she say like she got something up her sleeve. Only she don't lead the way. So me and Sugar turn the corner to where the entrance is, but when we get there I kinda hang back. Not that I'm scared, what's there to be afraid of, just a toy store. But I feel funny, shame. But what I got to be shamed about? Got as much right to go in as anybody. But somehow I can't seem to get hold of the door, so I step away for Sugar to lead. But she hangs back too. And I look at her and she looks at me and this is ridiculous. I mean, damn, I have never ever been shy about doing nothing or going nowhere. But then Mercedes steps up and then Rosie Giraffe and Big Butt crowd in behind and shove, and next thing we all stuffed into the doorway with only Mercedes squeezing past us, smoothing out her jumper and walking right down the aisle. Then the rest of us tumble in like a glued-together jigsaw done all wrong. And people lookin at us. And it's like the time me and Sugar crashed into the Catholic church on a dare. But once we got in there and everything so hushed and holy and the candles and the bowin and the handkerchiefs on all the drooping heads, I just couldn't go through with the plan. Which was for me to run up to the altar and do a tap dance while Sugar played the nose flute and messed around in the holy water. And Sugar kept givin me the elbow. Then later teased me so bad I tied her up in the shower and turned it on and locked her in. And she'd be there till this day if Aunt Gretchen hadn't finally figured I was lyin about the boarder takin a shower.

Same thing in the store. We all walkin on tiptoe and hardly touchin the games and puzzles and things. And I watched Miss Moore who is steady watchin us like she waitin for a sign. Like Mama Drewery watches the sky and sniffs the air and takes note of just how much slant is in the bird formation. Then me and Sugar bump smack into each other, so busy gazing at the toys, 'specially the sailboat. But we don't laugh and go into our fat-lady bumpstomach routine. We just stare at that price tag. Then Sugar run a finger over the whole boat. And I'm jealous and want to hit her. Maybe not her, but I sure want to punch somebody in the mouth.

"Whatcha bring us here for, Miss Moore?"

"You sound angry, Sylvia. Are you mad about something?" Givin me one of them grins like she tellin a grown-up joke that never turns out to be funny. And she's lookin very closely at me like maybe she plannin to do my portrait from memory. I'm mad, but I won't give her that satisfaction. So I slouch around the store bein very bored and say, "Let's go."

Me and Sugar at the back of the train watchin the tracks whizzin by large then small then gettin gobbled up in the dark. I'm thinkin about this tricky toy I saw in the store. A clown that somersaults on a bar then does chin-ups just cause you yank lightly at his leg. Cost $35. I could see me askin my mother for a $35 birthday clown. "You wanna who that costs what?"

she'd say, cocking her head to the side to get a better view of the hole in my head. Thirty-five dollars could buy new bunk beds for Junior and Gretchen's boy. Thirty-five dollars and the whole household could go visit Granddaddy Nelson in the country. Thirty-five dollars would pay for the rent and the piano bill too. Who are these people that spend that much for performing clowns and $1000 for toy sailboats? What kinda work they do and how they live and how come we ain't in on it? Where we are is who we are, Miss Moore always pointin out. But it don't necessarily have to be that way, she always adds then waits for somebody to say that poor people have to wake up and demand their share of the pie and don't none of us know what kind of pie she talkin about in the first damn place. But she ain't so smart cause I still got her four dollars from the taxi and she sure ain't gettin it. Messin up my day with this shit. Sugar nudges me in my pocket and winks.

45   Miss Moore lines us up in front of the mailbox where we started from, seem like years ago, and I got a headache for thinkin so hard. And we lean all over each other so we can hold up under the draggy-ass lecture she always finishes us off with at the end before we thank her for borin us to tears. But she just looks at us like she readin tea leaves. Finally she say, "Well, what do you think of F. A. O. Schwarz?"

Rosie Giraffe mumbles, "White folks crazy."

"I'd like to go there again when I get my birthday money," says Mercedes, and we shove her out the pack so she has to lean on the mailbox by herself.

"I'd like a shower. Tiring day," say Flyboy.

Then Sugar surprises me by sayin, "You know, Miss Moore, I don't think all of us here put together eat in a year what that sailboat costs." And Miss Moore lights up like somebody goosed her. "And?" she say, urging Sugar on. Only I'm standin on her foot so she don't continue.

50   "Imagine for a minute what kind of society it is in which some people can spend on a toy what it would cost to feed a family of six or seven. What do you think?"

"I think," say Sugar pushing me off her feet like she never done before, cause I whip her ass in a minute, "that this is not much of a democracy if you ask me. Equal chance to pursue happiness means an equal crack at the dough, don't it?" Miss Moore is besides herself and I am disgusted with Sugar's treachery. So I stand on her foot one more time to see if she'll shove me. She shuts up, and Miss Moore looks at me, sorrowfully I'm thinkin. And somethin weird is goin on, I can feel it in my chest.

"Anybody else learn anything today?" lookin dead at me. I walk away and Sugar has to run to catch up and don't even seem to notice when I shrug her arm off my shoulder.

"Well, we got four dollars anyway," she says.

"Uh hunh."

55   "We could go to Hascombs and get half a chocolate layer and then go to the Sunset and still have plenty money for potato chips and ice cream sodas."

"Uh hunh."

"Race you to Hascombs," she say.

We start down the block and she gets ahead which is O.K. by me cause I'm going to the West End and then over to the Drive to think this day through. She can run if she want to and even run faster. But ain't nobody gonna beat me at nuthin.

[1972]

TOPICS FOR CRITICAL THINKING AND WRITING

1. What is the point of Miss Moore's lesson? Why does Sylvia resist it?
2. Describe the relationship between Sugar and Sylvia. What is Sugar's function in the story?
3. What does the last line of the story suggest?
4. In a paragraph or two, characterize the narrator. Do not summarize the story—assume that your reader is familiar with it—but support your characterization by some references to episodes in the story and perhaps by a few brief quotations.

ANJANA APPACHANA

Anjana Appachana, a graduate of Delhi University, published "To Rise Above" in 1989, when she was an M.F.A. candidate at Pennsylvania State University.

To Rise Above

Last evening my husband told me that he was tired of seeing me looking so washed out and sick. He said, when I come back from the office, the least I can expect is a smiling face. You don't even give me that. It's bad enough that the house is in a mess, but you don't even seem to have time to entertain my friends properly when they come home. They must be wondering what sort of a wife I have. I tell you, I'm tired of all this. And he walked out of the room, slamming the door behind him.

My baby looked up and went back to her toy. My darling, I told her, my *rani beti,*[1] do you like the toy, do you like it baby? Next time I'll get you a big doll that will open and close its eyes just like you. I nuzzled her and she gurgled with pleasure.

What I say doesn't even affect you, groaned my husband, returning to the room. Look at you, your face unwashed, your hair uncombed, lying on the bed like that. That's not what I married you for. For heaven's sake, get up and prepare something, my friends are coming home for tea. I said, today? He mimicked, yes, today, today. Is the *Maharani*[2] too busy to look after them? I got up and went to the kitchen. O God, where to begin? The dishes had to be washed, the dinner to be made, also snacks for his friends. I put the potatoes to boil, best to make some *aloo sabji* and use the rest of them for *tikkies.* Then I took out the *sooji* to make *halwa.* That should be

---

[1]princess   [2]princess. The other Hindi words in the paragraph designate various foods. For the rest of the story, we annotate only words that are not the names of foods.

enough for them. Why did they have to come today? Even I was tired after a day at the office. The dishes were so dirty. I didn't expect my mother-in-law to wash them, but she could have soaked them in water at least. I suppose I should be thankful she remembered to fill the buckets before the water finished. Please God, I prayed, don't let the electricity go off too, these power cuts will be the death of me. I put the *dal* in the pressure cooker and began the dishes. How could I smile? What was there to smile about?

The bus back home had been so crowded. More so than usual, because the previous bus was held up by some college boys who were protesting about the irregular service. I could hardly get in and once I got in I couldn't move. It was horrible. I don't understand these men. Even if you are sitting they edge closer and closer to you and you can't do a thing. When the bus reached my stop I couldn't get out because I was stuck in the crowd and by the time I reached the door, the bus had started moving again. I told the driver to stop and he said something rude, but did. The air, how fresh it was, and the slight breeze against my face, so cleansing. I walked home slowly. This is the only time I ever get to myself. Sometimes I wished that I didn't know typing so that I didn't have to work, but if I didn't work we couldn't make ends meet. In my husband's matrimonial advertisement his family had insisted that they wanted a working girl, so I suppose it wouldn't be fair at this point to say that I just couldn't cope. When I was working before marriage, Ma would pack me a lunch of soft *parathas* with *sabji*. And when I came back she would make me a cup of hot tea and ask me how her *rani beti* was. Then she would talk to me and give me all the day's gossip—how lazy the *jamardani* was—how Mrs. Sharma next door had a fight with her husband. I always had a good laugh about Mrs. Sharma's fights, she had such a loud voice that very often we could hear her in the house. I wondered what she fought about. Sometimes I wish that I could fight, but I don't know how to, so whenever I'm upset I just go to the bathroom and cry instead. They all think that nothing bothers me. Let them. I long for Ma to come here and stay with me, but when I last wrote to her and asked her to do so she was very angry. Beti, she wrote, now you are a married woman and you must understand that a mother does not stay with her daughters, it is not the right thing to do. I miss her so much. No one talks to me here. Oh, they do in one sense, but not like Ma.

5   My mother-in-law called me, and I went to her room where she was lying down. She is always lying down. What are you doing, she asked me. She always wants to know what I am doing, whether I am in the kitchen or in the bathroom. Cooking, I said. Do you want any help, she asked as she did every day. No, *Mataji*,[3] you rest, I replied as I did every day and returned to the kitchen. I remember once when I had said that I did need some help (some people were coming over for dinner that day) she never let me live it down. She kept telling the guests, the child is still young, she just cannot cope with the housework. She smiled gently as she said this and the guests all looked pityingly at me. Later my husband reproached me for letting her take on so much of my work. I felt so guilty.

The potatoes were ready. I kept half of them for the *sabji* and began to mash the other half for the *tikkies*. Vegetables were so expensive these

---

[3]Mother (the suffix *ji* is a term of respect)

days, not to mention essentials like sugar. One needs another emergency to get our country out of this mess, my husband had said as he cast his vote. But with the new government, prices have gone up still further. Once economy meant buying a *saree*[4] or two less, now we have to cut down on things like fruits and sugar. Household stuff is almost impossible to buy. At the time of my marriage my parents gave me a refrigerator and a T.V. We would never have been able to buy them on our own. In the beginning my family was against giving the T.V., but my husband's side insisted, and as they were not taking any cash, my parents said that they might as well. Still, it was all so expensive, they spent about 50,000 *rupees* on the wedding and even then people said that they could have married me off in better style, considering that there were just my sister and I. Now my husband has taken out a policy for our daughter so that when it matures in another twenty years, we will have one *lakh rupees*[5] for the marriage expenses. The price of gold has gone up so much. My parents gave me three sets of jewelry. I doubt if I can give my daughter even two. God knows how we'll ever have money to build a house after that. And house rents are soaring too, our tiny two-bedroom house costs us 1,500 *rupees* and that is supposed to be cheap! No wonder people are corrupt. How else can they build such huge houses in a city like this? That way my husband isn't bad—he doesn't take bribes, but when he sees other people doing it, he gets mad and takes it out on me.

I put the oil on the gas and began frying the *tikkies*. They should be here any minute. Oh, God, time for baby's milk. I put the milk to heat and got the bottle ready. Is everything ready? asked my husband from the next room. Almost, I replied. He never entered the kitchen. On principle. He can't even heat a glass of milk. That's a woman's job, he said when I once asked him to heat the milk for Baby while I was engaged in some other work. Once, when I was ill and my mother-in-law away, there was no one to look after the house. What chaos. My husband lived for three whole days on bread, butter and cheese, while I, in bed, was given, the same. I had no alternative but to get well and stagger about the house, cleaning up the place and washing the dishes which had mounted alarmingly. During those two days he used twelve mugs, six plates, seven glasses, four knives, eight spoons and two forks—all of which awaited me. Also two trousers, two shirts, four banyans, one pair of *pyjama kurta* and three handkerchiefs. Thank God you're all right, he sighed when he heard me in the kitchen that evening. It is the nearest he has come to paying me a compliment—if you can call it one.

Well, the *tikkies* were ready. Just a few minutes for the *halwa*. I quickly gave Baby her bottle, went back to the kitchen and heard my husband yell that they had come. For heaven's sake, get dressed, he said, coming into the kitchen. You should have finished everything by now. Once you get stuck in the kitchen, you get stuck. Learn to be systematic. I rushed to the bedroom and feverishly washed my face and combed my hair. Should I change my *saree* or not . . . might as well, or he'd say something again. I changed and went to the drawing room with a smile.

Namaste, Bhabiji, Namaste,[6] his friends said, what wonderful smells

---

[4]an outer garment of lightweight cloth, worn draped over one shoulder or covering the head   [5]100,000 rupees   [6]greetings, sister-in-law, greetings (said with folded hands)

coming from the kitchen. Oh, it's nothing, I murmured, what will you have, tea or coffee? Please don't bother, they said. No bother at all, I replied, you must have something. Oh, well, said one, I'll have tea, the other said he would have coffee, but not to bother about anything else, no formality please. No, no, not at all, I said and went to the kitchen. I put one vessel for the tea and another for the coffee. Why couldn't they have asked for the same thing? Sometimes I felt glad that I was working, it provided some variety to this life of cooking and washing and cleaning. In the morning I get up at 5 a.m., make tea for everyone, milk for Baby, then get breakfast ready for the family. Sometimes my husband wants *parathas,* sometimes toast and eggs, sometimes he gets this craving for *dosas.* Then I pack our lunches for the office, make the beds and rush to catch the bus to work. No time to talk to Baby or cuddle her.

10   I took the tea and coffee to the drawing room. Thank you, thank you, they said, perfect weather for hot drinks. I looked out of the window. It was raining . . . I hadn't even known. Yes, perfect weather for tea and *pakodas,* they exclaimed. Good idea, excellent idea, beamed my husband, let us have some *pakodas.* Ah, this is what you would call doing poetic justice to the weather. So I went to the kitchen to do poetic justice to the weather. When they were ready I put the *pakodas, tikkies* and *halwa* on the tray and took it to them. Wonderful, wonderful, they said. What a feast you have laid out for us, you really shouldn't have bothered. No bother, no bother at all, I said. So, they enquired, how is your office? Fine, I smiled. It wasn't. Not now. In the beginning, when I started working, it was all so interesting. I met new people, got a salary, felt independent. But people are so strange. One day I happened to talk to one of my colleagues longer than I usually do. He was telling me about a book he was reading and I got so caught up in what he was saying that I hardly realized how time passed. That evening the girl who sits next to me said, so you had a nice chat did you? Yes, I replied, and then the way she was looking at me made me go red. The next day when he lent me the book I noticed another of my colleagues (male) looking meaningfully at me. Now whenever by chance I happen to talk to him everyone in the office watches and I feel so wretched. The men, especially, gossip so much. At lunchtime they sit among themselves and giggle. They seem to know everything—who is talking to whom, who is wearing what and who the boss favours . . . everything. They never seem to discuss books or music . . . and I miss both. We get bored *yar,*[7] they say, we don't know what to do on weekends. Oh, how I long to be bored. Or just lie in bed with a book and listen to music. That's my idea of heaven.

It's nice to be independent, said my husband's friend, women like you will change the face of this country. Very nice *pakodas,* very nice indeed. Thank you, you're very kind, I murmured. We don't feel like leaving, he added as he settled more comfortably into his chair. Stay for dinner, said my husband at once, then we can all relax and *gup-shup.*[8] That will be too much of a bother for your wife, said his friend. No problem, no problem, said my husband heartily. What is there? The food is ready, there is no such formality in this house. They all looked at me. Of course, I said, it's no bother. I excused myself and went to the kitchen. Would there be enough

---

[7]a somewhat meaningless term, like *you know* or *eh*   [8]gossip

food for them? I felt like flinging the *dal* and *sabji* into their faces and was shocked at the force of the feeling. My husband followed me into the kitchen. Will the food be enough for them? I replied, it had better be. He hissed, what is the matter with you, stop acting difficult. I said, stop breathing down my neck. You invited them, not I. My husband said, this is the limit, I don't understand you. Is this the time to make a scene? Why don't you make another *sabji* and some *khir?* Because there is no other *sabji* and no milk for *khir,* I replied. We stared into each other's faces. I should have expected this, said my husband. Even my friends are not welcome in this house. If you are not prepared to look after them, you should have warned me earlier. This last-minute hysteria I will not stand for. I sank back against the sink. I said, then go and get the milk and *sabji.* Furious, he replied, how do you expect me to go; then who will look after them? I said, that's your problem. We don't have a servant. My husband said, you're always creating problems, this is what comes of being unsystematic. I reminded him, but you told me not to buy more vegetables and milk than was absolutely necessary because of the prices going up. This made him even angrier. What is the matter, can I help you, said my husband's friend, walking into the kitchen. I said, no, no, please. I can manage. I wondered what he would do if I had said yes, please help. The thought made me smile and my husband, seeing my face, gave a sigh of relief and ushered his friend out of the kitchen.

For dinner there were *puris, aloo, dal, karelas,* and mangoes with the cream that I had been collecting for the week's butter. I was so tired by the end of it that I could hardly eat. Then I put Baby to sleep and gave them all coffee. They finished the coffee, and said, *chalo, chalo,*[9] let us go for a movie. Now? I asked. Of course, they replied. If we rush we can get tickets for the night show, *chalo,* let us go. Let us, agreed my husband, these impromptu decisions are always so enjoyable, one shouldn't always plan. I said, I have to wash the dishes. They replied, oh, do that tomorrow, you mustn't always work so hard. I said, but I have to go to the office tomorrow, and I'm tired. My husband replied, don't make a fuss, you are not the only one who has to go to office, even I have to go. That is the trouble with you. You don't know how to enjoy yourself. And *Mataji* will look after the baby. Don't make *her* an excuse now. *Chalo, chalo,* let us hurry.

I put the dishes in the sink, and then we rushed. The tickets were not available so we bought them in black—ten *rupees* each. In spite of that, we were just four rows away from the screen. As the hero and heroine sang their first song to each other I fell asleep. A deep sleep. My husband woke me up when it was over. They were all amused. Even here she sleeps, said my husband indulgently.

We reached our colony at 1 a.m., just managed to get the night service bus back home. I slept in the bus, too. As we walked back home from the bus stop, my husband's mood expanded. What a night, what a night, he exclaimed. He stopped and looked up at the heavens,

> *Palace-roof of cloudless nights!*
> *Paradise of golden lights!*
> *Deep, immeasurable, vast . . .*

[9]let's go, let's go

he quoted dreamily. I leaned sleepily against his arm and he looked at me with something akin to pain. Sleep, always sleep, he said. Why can't you rise above such purely physical reactions? You lack soul.

15   When we reached home, I made the beds and sank into mine with a groan of satisfaction. Heaven. The trouble with you, said my husband, is that your whole attitude to work is wrong. You'll never get tired if you change your attitude to work. Learn from Khalil Gibran, and he quoted:

> *Always you have been told that work is a curse, and labor a misfortune.*
> *But I say to you that when you work you fulfill a part of earth's further dream, assigned to you when that dream was born,*
> *And in keeping yourself with labour you are in truth loving life,*
> *And to love life through labour is to be intimate with life's innermost secret.*

That is poetry, philosophy, truth, mused my husband. So were the *pakodas*, I sighed and slept.

[1989]

TOPICS FOR CRITICAL THINKING AND WRITING

1. Do you find the husband's demands extraordinary? Explain. And what of the mother-in-law, or the bus driver, or the men on the bus, or the husband's friends, or the woman's co-workers? What do they do? In fact, is there anyone in the story who makes reasonable demands?
2. Your answer to the last question should be "No." (If not, reread the story.) Now, why should we be interested in the story? What is the woman who tells us the story like? Does she complain about her husband or not? Do you detect a sense of humor in what she tells us? How much of what she tells us is part of the system in which she lives?
3. Try to imagine this story told in the third person. Can you do it? Or by the mother-in-law? What would have to change?

 DIANA CHANG

Diana Chang, author of several novels and books of poems, teaches creative writing at Barnard College. She identifies herself as an American writer whose background is mostly Chinese.

The Oriental Contingent

Connie couldn't remember whose party it was, whose house. She had an impression of kerosene lamps on brown wicker tables, of shapes talking in doorways. It was summer, almost the only time Connie has run into her since, too, and someone was saying, "You must know Lisa Mallory."

"I don't think so."

"She's here. You must know her."

Later in the evening, it was someone else who introduced her to a figure perched on the balustrade of the steps leading to the lawn where more shapes milled. In stretching out a hand to shake Connie's, the figure almost fell off sideways. Connie pushed her back upright onto her perch and, peering, took in the fact that Lisa Mallory had a Chinese face. For a long instant, she felt nonplussed, and was rendered speechless.

5   But Lisa Mallory was filling in the silence. "Well, now, Connie Sung," she said, not enthusiastically but with a kind of sophisticated interest. "I'm not in music myself, but Paul Wu's my cousin. Guilt by association!" She laughed. "No-tone music, I call his. He studied with John Cage, Varese, and so forth."

Surprised that Lisa knew she was a violinist, Connie murmured something friendly, wondering if she should simply ask outright, "I'm sure I should know, but what do you do?" but she hesitated, taking in her appearance instead, while Lisa went on with, "It's world class composing. Nothing's wrong with the level. But it's hard going for the layman, believe me."

Lisa Mallory wore a one-of-a-kind kimono dress, but it didn't make her look Japanese at all, and her hair was drawn back tightly in a braid which stood out from close to the top of her head horizontally. You could probably lift her off her feet by grasping it, like the handle of a pot.

"You should give a concert here, Connie," she said, using her first name right away, Connie noticed, like any American. "Lots of culturati around." Even when she wasn't actually speaking, she pursued her own line of thought actively and seemed to find herself mildly amusing.

"I'm new to the area," Connie said, deprecatingly. "I've just been a weekend guest, actually, till a month ago."

10   "It's easy to be part of it. Nothing to it. I should know. You'll see."

"I wish it weren't so dark," Connie found herself saying, waving her hand in front of her eyes as if the night were a veil to brush aside. She recognized in herself that intense need to see, to see into fellow Orientals, to fathom them. So far, Lisa Mallory had not given her enough clues, and the darkness itself seemed to be interfering.

Lisa dropped off her perch. "It's important to be true to oneself," she said. "Keep the modern stuff out of your repertory. Be romantic. Don't look like that! You're best at the romantics. Anyhow, take it from me. I know. And *I* like what I like."

Released by her outspokenness, Connie laughed and asked, "I'm sure I should know, but what is it that you do?" She was certain Lisa would say something like, "I'm with a public relations firm." "I'm in city services."

But she replied, "What do all Chinese excel at?" Not as if she'd asked a rhetorical question, she waited, then answered herself. "Well, aren't we all physicists, musicians, architects, or in software?"

15   At that point a voice broke in, followed by a large body which put his arms around both women, "The Oriental contingent! I've got to break this up."

Turning, Lisa kissed him roundly, and said over her shoulder to Connie, "I'll take him away before he tells us we look alike!"

They melted into the steps below, and Connie, feeling put off balance and somehow slow-witted, was left to think over her new acquaintance.

"Hello, Lisa Mallory," Connie Sung always said on the infrequent occasions when they ran into one another. She always said "Hello, Lisa Mallory," with a shyness she did not understand in herself. It was strange, but they had no mutual friends except for Paul Wu, and Connie had not seen him in ages. Connie had no one of whom to ask her questions. But sometime soon, she'd be told Lisa's maiden name. Sometime she'd simply call her Lisa. Sometime what Lisa did with her life would be answered.

Three, four years passed, with their running into one another at receptions and openings, and still Lisa Mallory remained an enigma. Mildly amused herself, Connie wondered if other people, as well, found her inscrutable. But none of her American friends (though, of course, Lisa and she were Americans, too, she had to remind herself), none of their Caucasian friends seemed curious about backgrounds. In their accepting way, they did not wonder about Lisa's background, or about Connie's or Paul Wu's. Perhaps they assumed they were all cut from the same cloth. But to Connie, the Orientals she met were unread books, books she never had the right occasion or time to fully pursue.

20   She didn't even see the humor in her situation—it was such an issue with her. The fact was she felt less, much less, sure of herself when she was with real Chinese.

As she was realizing this, the truth suddenly dawned on her. Lisa Mallory never referred to her own background because it was more Chinese than Connie's, and therefore of a higher order. She was tact incarnate. All along, she had been going out of her way not to embarrass Connie. Yes, yes. Her assurance was definitely uppercrust (perhaps her father had been in the diplomatic service), and her offhand didacticness, her lack of self-doubt, was indeed characteristically Chinese-Chinese. Connie was not only impressed by these traits, but also put on the defensive because of them.

Connie let out a sigh—a sigh that follows the solution to a nagging problem . . . Lisa's mysteriousness. But now Connie knew only too clearly that her own background made her decidedly inferior. Her father was a second-generation gynecologist who spoke hardly any Chinese. Yes, inferior and totally without recourse.

Of course, at one of the gatherings, Connie met Bill Mallory, too. He was simply American, maybe Catholic, possibly lapsed. She was not put off balance by him at all. But most of the time he was away on business, and Lisa cropped up at functions as single as Connie.

Then one day, Lisa had a man in tow—wiry and tall, he looked Chinese from the Shantung area, or perhaps from Beijing, and his styled hair made him appear vaguely artistic.

25   "Connie, I'd like you to meet Eric Li. He got out at the beginning of the *detente,* went to Berkeley, and is assimilating a mile-a-minute," Lisa said, with her usual irony. "Bill found him and is grooming him, though he came with his own charisma."

Eric waved her remark aside. "Lisa has missed her calling. She was born to be in PR," he said, with an accent.

"Is that what she does?" Connie put in at once, looking only at him. "Is that her profession?"

"You don't know?" he asked, with surprise.

Though she was greeting someone else, Lisa turned and answered, "I'm a fabrics tycoon, I think I can say without immodesty." She moved away and continued her conversation with the other friend.

30   Behind his hand, he said, playfully, as though letting Connie in on a secret, "Factories in Hongkong and Taipei, and now he's—Bill, that is—is exploring them on the mainland."

"With her fabulous contacts over there!" Connie exclaimed, now seeing it all. "Of course, what a wonderful business combination they must
make."

Eric was about to utter something, but stopped, and said flatly, "I have
all the mainland contacts, even though I was only twenty when I left, but my
parents. . . "

"How interesting," Connie murmured lamely. "I see," preoccupied as
she was with trying to put two and two together.

Lisa was back and said without an introduction, continuing her line of
thought, "You two look good together, if I have to say so myself. Why don't
you ask him to one of your concerts? And you, Eric, you're in America now,
so don't stand on ceremony, or you'll be out in left field." She walked away
with someone for another drink.

35   Looking uncomfortable, but recovering himself with a smile, Eric said,
"Lisa makes me feel more Chinese than I am becoming—it is her directness,
I suspect. In China, we'd say she is too much like a man."

At which Connie found herself saying, "She makes me feel *less* Chinese."

"Less!"

"Less Chinese than she is."

"That is not possible," Eric said, with a shade of contempt—for whom?
Lisa or Connie? He barely suppressed a laugh, cold as Chinese laughter
could be.

40   Connie blurted out, "I'm a failed Chinese. Yes, and it's to you that I
need to say it." She paused and repeated emphatically, "I am a failed Chinese." Her heart was beating quicker, but she was glad to have got that out,
a confession and a definition that might begin to free her. "Do you know
you make me feel that, too? You've been here only about ten years, right?"

"Right, and I'm thirty-one."

"You know what I think? I think it's harder for a Chinese to do two
things."

At that moment, an American moved in closer, looking pleased somehow to be with them.

She continued, "It's harder for us to become American than, say, for a
German, and it's also harder not to remain residually Chinese, even if you
are third generation."

45   Eric said blandly, "Don't take yourself so seriously. You can't help being
an American product."

Trying to be comforting, the American interjected with, "The young
lady is not a product, an object. She is a human being, and there is no difference among peoples that I can see."

"I judge myself both as a Chinese and as an American," Connie said.

"You worry too much," Eric said, impatiently. Then he looked around
and though she wasn't in sight, he lowered his voice. "She is what she is. I
know what she is. But she avoids going to Hongkong. She avoids it."

Connie felt turned around. "Avoids it?"

50   "Bill's in Beijing right now. She's here. How come?"

"I don't know," Connie replied, as though an answer had been required
of her.

"She makes up many excuses, reasons. Ask her. Ask her yourself," he
said, pointedly.

"Oh, I couldn't do that. By the way, I'm going on a concert tour next year in three cities—Shanghai, Beijing and Nanking," Connie said. "It'll be my first time in China."

"Really! You must be very talented to be touring at your age," he said, genuinely interested for the first time. Because she was going to China, or because she now came across as an over-achiever, even though Chinese American?

"I'm just about your age," she said, realizing then that maybe Lisa Mallory had left them alone purposely.

"You could both pass as teenagers!" the American exclaimed.

Two months later, she ran into Lisa again. As usual, Lisa began in the middle of her own thoughts. "Did he call?"

"Who? Oh. No, no."

"Well, it's true he's been in China the last three weeks with Bill. They'll be back this weekend."

Connie saw her opportunity. "Are you planning to go to China yourself?"

For the first time, Lisa seemed at a loss for words. She raised her shoulders, than let them drop. Too airily, she said, "You know, there's always Paris. I can't bear not to go to Paris, if I'm to take a trip."

"But you're Chinese. You *have* been to China, you came from China originally, didn't you?"

"I could go to Paris twice a year, I love it so," Lisa said. "And then there's London, Florence, Venice."

"But—but your business contacts?"

"*My* contacts? Bill, he's the businessman who makes the contacts. Always has. I take care of the New York office, which is a considerable job. We have a staff of eighty-five."

Connie said, "I told Eric I'll be giving a tour in China. I'm taking Chinese lessons right now."

Lisa Mallory laughed. "Save your time. They'll still be disdainful over there. See, *they* don't care," and she waved her hand at the crowd. "Some of them have been born in Buffalo, too! It's the Chinese you can't fool. They know you're not the genuine article—you and I."

Her face was suddenly heightened in color, and she was breathing as if ready to flee from something. "Yes, you heard right. I was born in Buffalo."

"You were!" Connie exclaimed before she could control her amazement.

"Well, what about you?" Lisa retorted. She was actually shaking and trying to hide it by making sudden gestures.

"Westchester."

"But your parents at least were Chinese."

"Well, so were, so are, yours!"

"I was adopted by Americans. My full name is Lisa Warren Mallory."

Incredulous, Connie said, "I'm more Chinese than you!"

"Who isn't?" She laughed, unhappily. "Having Chinese parents makes all the difference. We're worlds apart."

"And all the time I thought . . . never mind what I thought."

"You have it over me. It's written all over you. I could tell even in the dark that night."

"Oh, Lisa," Connie said to comfort her, "none of this matters to anybody except us. Really and truly. They're too busy with their own problems."

80   "The only time I feel Chinese is when I'm embarrassed I'm not more Chinese—which is a totally Chinese reflex I'd give anything to be rid of!"

"I know what you mean."

"And as for Eric looking down his nose at me, he's knocking himself out to be so American, *but as a secure Chinese!* What's so genuine about that article?"

Both of them struck their heads laughing, but their eyes were not merry.

"Say it again," Connie asked of her, "say it again that my being more Chinese is written all over me."

85   "Consider it said," Lisa said. "My natural mother happened to be there at the time—I can't help being born in Buffalo."

"I know, I know," Connie said with feeling. "If only you had had some say in the matter."

"It's only Orientals who haunt me!" Lisa stamped her foot. "Only them!"

"I'm so sorry," Connie Sung said, for all of them. "It's all so turned around."

"So I'm made in America, so there!" Lisa Mallory declared, making a sniffing sound, and seemed to be recovering her sangfroid.

90   Connie felt tired—as if she'd traveled—but a lot had been settled on the way.

[1989]

TOPICS FOR CRITICAL THINKING AND WRITING

1. In the first paragraph, a person (whose name we don't know) says, "You must know Lisa Mallory." Why does she make that assumption?
2. During their first meeting Connie thinks "she recognized in herself that intense need to see, to see into fellow Orientals, to fathom them" and she waves "her hand in front of her eyes." Does she know what is she looking for?
3. What does Eric do in the story? What is his function? And "the American" (paragraph 43)?
4. In paragraph 88 we read, "'I'm so sorry,' Connie Sung said, for all of them. 'It's all so turned around.'" What does the writer mean by "for all of them"? And what does Connie mean by "It's all so turned around"?

Poetry

 ## RICHARD LOVELACE

Richard Lovelace (1618-57) was born into a prominent English family. Rich, handsome, witty, and favored by King Charles and Queen

Henrietta Maria, he supported the Royalists against the Parliamentarians during the Civil War (1642-52). In 1642 the Parliamentarians imprisoned him, and it was during his stay in prison that he wrote "To Althea, from Prison," a poem that includes his most famous lines: "Stone walls do not a prison make,/Nor iron bars a cage." He was released and exiled, fought in France against the Spanish, returned to England, and in 1648 was again imprisoned. Soon after his release from prison he died, penniless.

"To Lucasta, Going to the Wars," written during his second imprisonment, alludes to his support of the royalist cause.

To Lucasta, Going to the Wars

Tell me not, sweet, I am unkind
That from the nunnery
Of thy chaste breast and quiet mind,
To war and arms I fly.   4

True, a new mistress now I chase,
The first foe in the field;
And with a stronger faith embrace
A sword, a horse, a shield.   8

Yet this inconstancy is such
As you too shall adore;
I could not love thee, dear, so much,
Loved I not honor more.   12

[1649]

 TOPICS FOR CRITICAL THINKING AND WRITING

1. The speaker of this poem explains to his beloved, Lucasta, why he is willing to leave her. What words or lines particularly suggest her presence?
2. In the second stanza, who (or what) is the "new mistress" the speaker chases?
3. How does the speaker justify leaving his beloved? In your answer, take special account of the last two lines.
4. Judging from the tone of this poem, do you assume that his beloved will understand and agree? Explain.

 ALFRED, LORD TENNYSON

Alfred, Lord Tennyson (1809-92), the son of an English clergyman, was born in Lincolnshire, where he began writing verse at five. Educated at Cambridge, he had to leave without a degree when his father died and Alfred had to accept responsibility for bringing up his brothers and sisters. In fact, the family had inherited ample funds, but for some years the money was tied up by litigation. In 1850

Tennyson was made poet laureate following Wordsworth's death. With his government pension he moved with his family to the Isle of Wight, where he lived in vast comfort until his death.

In the poem that we print here, Ulysses has returned to Ithaca as king, after a long absence—ten years at war with Troy and ten years of enforced wandering.

Ulysses

It little profits that an idle king,
By this still hearth, among these barren crags,
Matched with an aged wife, I mete and dole
Unequal laws unto a savage race,
That hoard, and sleep, and feed, and know not me.   5
I cannot rest from travel; I will drink
Life to the lees. All times I have enjoyed
Greatly, have suffered greatly, both with those
That loved me, and alone; on shore, and when
Thro' scudding drifts the rainy Hyades   10
Vext the dim sea. I am become a name;
For always roaming with a hungry heart
Much have I seen and known,—cities of men
And manners, climates, councils, governments,
Myself not least, but honored of them all,—   15
And drunk delight of battle with my peers,
Far on the ringing plains of windy Troy.
I am a part of all that I have met;
Yet all experience is an arch wherethro'
Gleams that untravelled world whose margin fades   20
For ever and for ever when I move.
How dull it is to pause, to make an end,
To rust unburnished, not to shine in use!
As tho' to breathe were life! Life piled on life
Were all too little, and of one to me   25
Little remains; but every hour is saved
From that eternal silence, something more,
A bringer of new things; and vile it were
For some three suns to store and hoard myself,
And this gray spirit yearning in desire   30
To follow knowledge like a sinking star,
Beyond the utmost bound of human thought.

This is my son, mine own Telemachus,
To whom I leave the scepter and the isle,—
Well-loved of me, discerning to fulfill   35
This labor, by slow prudence to make mild
A rugged people, and thro' soft degrees
Subdue them to the useful and the good.
Most blameless is he, centered in the sphere
Of common duties, decent not to fail   40

In offices of tenderness, and pay
Meet adoration to my household gods,
When I am gone. He works his work, I mine.

There lies the port; the vessel puffs her sail;
There gloom the dark, broad seas. My mariners,   45
Souls that have toiled, and wrought, and thought with me,—
That ever with a frolic welcome took
The thunder and the sunshine, and opposed
Free hearts, free foreheads,—you and I are old;
Old age hath yet his honor and his toil.   50
Death closes all; but something ere the end,
Some work of noble note, may yet be done,
Not unbecoming men that strove with Gods.
The lights begin to twinkle from the rocks;
The long day wanes; the slow moon climbs; the deep   55
Moans round with many voices. Come, my friends.
'Tis not too late to seek a newer world.
Push off, and sitting well in order smite
The sounding furrows; for my purpose holds
To sail beyond the sunset, and the baths   60
Of all the western stars, until I die.
It may be that the gulfs will wash us down;
It may be we shall touch the Happy Isles,
And see the great Achilles, whom we knew.
Tho' much is taken, much abides; and tho'   65
We are not now that strength which in old days
Moved earth and heaven, that which we are, we are.
One equal temper of heroic hearts,
Made weak by time and fate, but strong in will
To strive, to seek, to find, and not to yield.   70

[1833]

 ## TOPICS FOR CRITICAL THINKING AND WRITING

1. Ulysses's speech is divided into three sections (lines 1-32, 33-43, 44-70). Do we know to whom he is speaking in the first two sections? In the third? Does it matter whether or not the audience is identified?
2. Tennyson's Ulysses has often been praised for his unconquered spirit, and for his intellectual aspiration. Can a case be made that his departure from his family and his kingdom in order to search for further experience is a rather self-indulgent flight from his responsibilities? Make this case as best you can, and then rebut it, if you wish.
3. Ulysses's voyage is westward. To what extent do you think the west (where the sun sets) here symbolizes death?

 ## ARTHUR HUGH CLOUGH

Arthur Hugh Clough (1819-61), whose name rhymes with "rough," was born into a family of English cotton merchants. He spent five years of his early childhood in South Carolina but was educated in

England, where his teachers and friends, recognizing him as a gifted student and a talented poet, expected him to go on to a promising career. But Clough, deeply troubled both by doubts about the authenticity of the teachings of the Christian church and by the materialism of his age, never fulfilled those expectations.

The Latest Decalogue

Thou shalt have one God only; who
Would be at the expense of two?
No graven images may be
Worshipped, except the currency:
Swear not at all; for for thy curse   5
Thine enemy is none the worse:
At church on Sunday to attend
Will serve to keep the world thy friend:
Honour thy parents; that is, all
From whom advancement may befall: 10

Thou shalt not kill; but needst not strive
Officiously to keep alive:
Do not adultery commit;
Advantage rarely comes of it:
Thou shalt not steal; an empty feat,   15
When it's so lucrative to cheat:
Bear not false witness; let the lie
Have time on its own wings to fly:
Thou shalt not covet; but tradition
Approves all forms of competition.   20

The sum of all is, thou shalt love,
If any body, God above:
At any rate shall never labour
More than thyself to love thy neighbour.

[1847]

 TOPICS FOR CRITICAL THINKING AND WRITING

1. Explain the title.
2. The commandments in this poem (e.g., "Thou shalt have one God only," "Thou shalt not kill") are ancient and they are widely accepted as a guide to our moral life. What is new in the poem?
3. The poem was written in 1847. On the basis of this poem, how would you characterize the period? Does the poem speak to our own period also?

 A. E. HOUSMAN

Alfred Edward Housman (1859-1936) was born in rural Shropshire, England, and educated in classics and philosophy at Oxford University. Although he was a brilliant student, his final examination was

unexpectedly weak—in fact, he failed—and he did not receive the academic appointment that he had anticipated. He began working as a civil servant at the British Patent Office, but in his spare time he wrote scholarly articles on Latin literature, and these writings in 1892 won him an appointment as Professor of Latin at the University of London. In 1911 he was appointed to Cambridge. During his lifetime he published (in addition to his scholarly writings) only two thin books of poetry, A Shropshire Lad *(1898) and* Last Poems *(1922), and a highly readable lecture called* The Name and Nature of Poetry *(1933). After his death a third book of poems,* More Poems *(1936), was published. The poem we reprint here comes from this posthumous volume. Elsewhere in our book, on pages 623 and 927, we print other poems by Housman.*

The laws of God, the laws of man

The laws of God, the laws of man,
He may keep that will and can;
Not I: let God and man decree
Laws for themselves and not for me;
And if my ways are not as theirs   5
Let them mind their own affairs.
Their deeds I judge and much condemn,
Yet when did I make laws for them?
Please yourselves, say I, and they
Need only look the other way.   10
But no, they will not; they must still
Wrest their neighbour to their will,
And make me dance as they desire
With jail and gallows and hell-fire.
And how am I to face the odds   15
Of man's bedevilment and God's?
I, a stranger and afraid
In a world I never made.
They will be master, right or wrong;
Though both are foolish, both are strong.   20
And since, my soul, we cannot fly
To Saturn nor to Mercury,
Keep we must, if keep we can,
These foreign laws of God and man.

[1900]

⌨ TOPICS FOR CRITICAL THINKING AND WRITING

1. Try to recall exactly your response on reading the title and the first line. Did you expect a poem praising the "laws of God"? If so, why did you have this expectation? If you anticipated something else, what was it, and why did you have that expectation?

2. Trace the changes in the speaker's tone, line by line or passage by passage. How would you compare the tone of the first two lines with the tone of the last two?

3. Housman was gay—though that word seems inappropriate, since in conversation he was extremely reserved, and in his published scholarship he was known for his savage denunciations of other scholars. Knowing this, do you think that this poem—not published until after his death—is (at least in part) about his homosexuality? Do you suppose that we respond to it differently from its first readers, in 1936, who did not know of his sexual orientation?

 ROBERT FROST

Robert Frost (1874–1963) was born in California. After his father's death in 1885 Frost's mother brought the family to New England, where she taught in high schools in Massachusetts and New Hampshire. Frost studied for part of one term at Dartmouth College in New Hampshire, then did odd jobs (including teaching), and from 1897 to 1899 was enrolled as a special student at Harvard. He then farmed in New Hampshire, published a few poems in local newspapers, left the farm and taught again, and in 1912 left for England, where he hoped to achieve more popular success as a writer. By 1915 he had won a considerable reputation, and he returned to the United States, settling on a farm in New Hampshire and cultivating the image of the country-wise farmer-poet. In fact he was well read in the classics, the Bible, and English and American literature.

Among Frost's many comments about literature, here are three: "Writing is unboring to the extent that it is dramatic"; "Every poem is . . . a figure of the will braving alien entanglements"; and, finally, a poem "begins in delight and ends in wisdom. . . . It runs a course of lucky events, and ends in a clarification of life—not necessarily a great clarification, such as sects and cults are founded on, but in a momentary stay against confusion."

Mending Wall

Something there is that doesn't love a wall,
That sends the frozen-ground-swell under it,
And spills the upper boulders in the sun;
And makes gaps even two can pass abreast.
The work of hunters is another thing: 5
I have come after them and made repair
Where they have left not one stone on a stone,
But they would have the rabbit out of hiding,
To please the yelping dogs. The gaps I mean,
No one has seen them made or heard them made,   10
But at spring mending-time we find them there.
I let my neighbor know beyond the hill;
And on a day we meet to walk the line

And set the wall between us once again.
We keep the wall between us as we go.   15
To each the boulders that have fallen to each.
And some are loaves and some so nearly balls
We have to use a spell to make them balance:
"Stay where you are until our backs are turned!"
We wear our fingers rough with handling them.   20
Oh, just another kind of outdoor game,
One on a side. It comes to little more:
There where it is we do not need the wall:
He is all pine and I am apple orchard.
My apple trees will never get across   25
And eat the cones under his pines, I tell him.
He only says, "Good fences make good neighbors."
Spring is the mischief in me, and I wonder
If I could put a notion in his head:
"*Why* do they make good neighbors? Isn't it   30
Where there are cows? But here there are no cows.
Before I built a wall I'd ask to know
What I was walling in or walling out,
And to whom I was like to give offense.
Something there is that doesn't love a wall,   35
That wants it down." I could say "Elves" to him,
But it's not elves exactly, and I'd rather
He said it for himself. I see him there
Bringing a stone grasped firmly by the top
In each hand, like an old-stone savage armed.   40
He moves in darkness as it seems to me,
Not of woods only and the shade of trees.
He will not go behind his father's saying,
And he likes having thought of it so well
He says again, "Good fences make good neighbors."   45

[1914]

📖 TOPICS FOR CRITICAL THINKING AND WRITING

1. The poem includes a scene, or action, in which the speaker and a neighbor are engaged. Briefly summarize the scene. What indicates that the scene has been enacted before and will be again?
2. Compare and contrast the speaker and the neighbor.
3. Notice that the speaker, not the neighbor, initiates the business of repairing the wall (line 12). Why do you think he does this?
4. Both the speaker and the neighbor repeat themselves; they each make one point twice in identical language. What do they say? And why does Frost allow the neighbor to have the last word?
5. "Something there is that doesn't love a wall" adds up to "Something doesn't love a wall." Or does it? Within the context of the poem, what is the difference between the two statements?
6. Write an essay of 500 words, telling of an experience in which you came to conclude that "good fences make good neighbors." Or tell of

an experience that led you to conclude that fences (they can be figurative fences, of course) are "like to give offense" (see lines 32-34).

The Road Not Taken

Two roads diverged in a yellow wood,
And sorry I could not travel both
And be one traveler, long I stood
And looked down one as far as I could
To where it bent in the undergrowth;   5

Then took the other, as just as fair,
And having perhaps the better claim,
Because it was grassy and wanted wear
Though as for that the passing there
Had worn them really about the same,   10

And both that morning equally lay
In leaves no step had trodden black.
Oh, I kept the first for another day!
Yet knowing how way leads on to way,
I doubted if I should ever come back.   15

I shall be telling this with a sigh
Somewhere ages and ages hence:
Two roads diverged in a wood, and I—
I took the one less traveled by,
And that has made all the difference.   20

[1916]

 ## TOPICS FOR CRITICAL THINKING AND WRITING

1. Would it make any difference if instead of "yellow" in the first line the poet had written "bright green" (or "dark green")?
2. What reason does the speaker give for choosing the road he takes? Why was it a difficult choice?
3. Frost called the poem "The Road Not Taken." Why didn't he call it "The Road Taken"? Which do you think is the better title, and why?
4. Why do you think the speaker says that he will later be telling this story "with a sigh"? Set forth your response in a paragraph.
5. Consider a choice that you made, perhaps almost unthinkingly, and offer your reflections on how your life might have been different if you had chosen otherwise. Are you now regretful, pleased, puzzled, indifferent, or what? (For instance, what seemed to be a big choice may in retrospect have been a decision of no consequence.)

 ## PAUL LAURENCE DUNBAR

Paul Laurence Dunbar (1872-1906), born in Ohio to parents who had been slaves in Kentucky, achieved fame for his dialect poetry. On

page 1226 we give an example of that kind of poetry, "An Ante-Bellum Sermon." Such poems, popular in their day, later became a source of embarrassment to many African-Americans, who regarded the poems as setting forth demeaning stereotypes. Today, however, they are being reread with renewed interest, and Dunbar's implicit—and sometimes explicit—criticism of society is now perceived.

Dunbar also wrote poems that did not seek to capture what was regarded as a distinctive black idiom. Here is one such poem.

We Wear the Mask

We wear the mask that grins and lies,
   It hides our cheeks and shades our eyes,—
This debt we pay to human guile;
With torn and bleeding hearts we smile,
And mouth with myriad subtleties.   5

Why should the world be over-wise,
In counting all our tears and sighs?
Nay, let them only see us, while
    We wear the mask.

We smile, but, O great Christ, our cries   10
To thee from tortured souls arise.
We sing, but oh the clay is vile
Beneath our feet, and long the mile;
But let the world dream otherwise,
    We wear the mask!   15

[1896]

 TOPICS FOR CRITICAL THINKING AND WRITING

1. What masks—what kinds of behavior—is Dunbar talking about?
2. Some readers think that the poem is more impressive if the second stanza is omitted. Do you agree? Why?
3. Do you associate "masks" with any other racial or ethnic group? If so, what are the masks?

 COUNTEE CULLEN

Countee Cullen (1903–46) was born Countee Porter in New York City, raised by his grandmother, and then adopted by the Reverend Frederick A. Cullen, a Methodist minister in Harlem. Cullen received a bachelor's degree from New York University (Phi Beta Kappa) and a master's degree from Harvard. He earned his living as a high school teacher of French, but his literary gifts were recognized in his own day. Cullen sometimes wrote about black life, but he also wrote

on other topics, insisting that African-Americans need not work only in the literary tradition exemplified by such writers as Langston Hughes.

Incident

(*For Eric Walrond*)

Once riding in old Baltimore,
   Heart-filled, head-filled with glee,
I saw a Baltimorean
   Keep looking straight at me.

Now I was eight and very small,   5
   And he was no whit bigger,
And so I smiled, but he poked out
   His tongue, and called me, "Nigger."

I saw the whole of Baltimore
   From May until December;   10
Of all the things that happened there
   That's all that I remember.

[1925]

🖋 TOPICS FOR CRITICAL THINKING AND WRITING

1. How would you define an "incident"? A serious occurrence? A minor occurrence? Or what? Think about the word, and then think about Cullen's use of it as a title for the event recorded in this poem.
2. What is the tone of the poem? Indifferent? Angry? Or what? What do you think is the speaker's attitude toward the "incident?" What is your attitude?

T. S. ELIOT

Thomas Stearns Eliot (1888–1965) was born into a New England family that had moved to St. Louis. He attended a preparatory school in Massachusetts, then graduated from Harvard and did further study in literature and philosophy in France, Germany, and England. In 1914 he began working for Lloyd's Bank in London, and three years later he published his first book of poems (it included "Prufrock"). In 1925 he joined a publishing firm, and in 1927 he became a British citizen and a member of the Church of England. Much of his later poetry, unlike "The Love Song of J. Alfred Prufrock," is highly religious. In 1948 Eliot received the Nobel Prize for Literature.

The Love Song of J. Alfred Prufrock

S'io credesse che mia risposta fosse
A persona che mai tornasse al mondo,
Questa fiamma staria senza piu scosse.
Ma perciocche giammai di questo fondo
Non torno vivo alcun, s' i' odo il vero,
*Senza tema d'infama ti rispondo.**

Let us go then, you and I,
When the evening is spread out against the sky
Like a patient etherized upon a table;
Let us go, through certain half-deserted streets,
The muttering retreats   5
Of restless nights in one-night cheap hotels
And sawdust restaurants with oyster-shells:
Streets that follow like a tedious argument
Of insidious intent
To lead you to an overwhelming question . . .   10
Oh, do not ask, "What is it?"
Let us go and make our visit.

In the room the women come and go
Talking of Michelangelo.

The yellow fog that rubs its back upon the window-panes,   15
The yellow smoke that rubs its muzzle on the window-panes
Licked its tongue into the corners of the evening,
Lingered upon the pools that stand in drains,
Let fall upon its back the soot that falls from chimneys,
Slipped by the terrace, made a sudden leap,   20
And seeing that it was a soft October night,
Curled once about the house, and fell asleep.

And indeed there will be time
For the yellow smoke that slides along the street,
Rubbing its back upon the window-panes;   25
There will be time, there will be time
To prepare a face to meet the faces that you meet;
There will be time to murder and create,
And time for all the works and days° of hands
That lift and drop a question on your plate;   30
Time for you and time for me,
And time yet for a hundred indecisions,
And for a hundred visions and revisions,
Before the taking of a toast and tea.

*In Dante's *Inferno* XXVII:61–66, a damned soul who had sought absolution before committing a crime addresses Dante, thinking that his words will never reach the earth: "If I believed that my answer were to a person who could ever return to the world, this flame would no longer quiver. But because no one ever returned from his depth, if what I hear is true, without fear of infamy, I answer you."   29 **works and days** "Works and Days" is the title of a poem on farm life by Hesiod (eighth century B.C.).

In the room the women come and go   35
Talking of Michelangelo.

And indeed there will be time
To wonder, "Do I dare?" and, "Do I dare?"
Time to turn back and descend the stair,
With a bald spot in the middle of my hair—   40
[They will say: "How his hair is growing thin!"]
My morning coat, my collar mounting firmly to the chin,
My necktie rich and modest, but asserted by a simple pin—
[They will say: "But how his arms and legs are thin!"]
Do I dare   45
Disturb the universe?
In a minute there is time
For decisions and revisions which a minute will reverse.

For I have known them all already, known them all:—
Have known the evenings, mornings, afternoons,   50
I have measured out my life with coffee spoons;
I know the voices dying with a dying fall°
Beneath the music from a farther room.
    So how should I presume?

And I have known the eyes already, known them all—   55
The eyes that fix you in a formulated phrase,
And when I am formulated, sprawling on a pin,
When I am pinned and wriggling on the wall,
Then how should I begin
To spit out all the butt-ends of my days and ways?   60
    And how should I presume?

And I have known the arms already, known them all—
Arms that are braceleted and white and bare
[But in the lamplight, downed with light brown hair!]

Is it perfume from a dress   65
That makes me so digress?
Arms that lie along a table, or wrap about a shawl.
    And should I then presume?
    And how should I begin?
              . . . . .
Shall I say, I have gone at dusk through narrow streets   70
And watched the smoke that rises from the pipes
Of lonely men in shirt-sleeves, leaning out of windows?. . .

I should have been a pair of ragged claws
Scuttling across the floors of silent seas.
              . . . . .
And the afternoon, the evening, sleeps so peacefully!   75
Smoothed by long fingers,
Asleep . . . tired . . . or it malingers,
Stretched on the floor, here beside you and me.
Should I, after tea and cakes and ices,

52**dying fall** This line echoes Shakespeare's *Twelfth Night* 1.1.4

Have the strength to force the moment to its crisis?   80
But though I have wept and fasted, wept and prayed,
Though I have seen my head [grown slightly bald]
   brought in upon a platter,°
I am no prophet—and here's no great matter;
I have seen the moment of my greatness flicker,
And I have seen the eternal Footman hold my coat, and snicker,   85
And in short, I was afraid.

And would it have been worth it, after all,
After the cups, the marmalade, the tea,
Among the porcelain, among some talk of you and me,
Would it have been worth while,   90
To have bitten off the matter with a smile,
To have squeezed the universe into a ball°
To roll it toward some overwhelming question,
To say: "I am Lazarus,° come from the dead,
Come back to tell you all, I shall tell you all"—   95
If one, settling a pillow by her head,
   Should say: "That is not what I meant at all.
   That is not it, at all."

And would it have been worth it, after all,
Would it have been worth while,   100
After the sunsets and the dooryards and the sprinkled streets,
After the novels, after the teacups, after the skirts
   that trail along the floor—
And this, and so much more?—
It is impossible to say just what I mean!
But as if a magic lantern threw the nerves in patterns
   on a screen: 105
Would it have been worth while
If one, settling a pillow or throwing off a shawl,
And turning toward the window, should say:
   "That is not it at all,
   That is not what I meant, at all."   110

No! I am not Prince Hamlet, nor was meant to be;
Am an attendant lord, one that will do
To swell a progress, start a scene or two,
Advise the prince; no doubt, an easy tool,
Deferential, glad to be of use,   115
Politic, cautious, and meticulous;
Full of high sentence,° but a bit obtuse;°
At times, indeed, almost ridiculous—
Almost, at times, the Fool.

81-83**But . . . platter** These lines allude to John the Baptist (see Matthew 14.1-11).
92**To have . . . ball** this line echoes lines 41-42 of Marvell's "To His Coy Mistress"
(see page 820).   94**Lazarus** see Luke 16 and John 11   117**full of high sentence**
see Chaucer's description of the Clerk of Oxford in the *Canterbury Tales*
112-117**Am . . . obtuse** these lines allude to Polonius and perhaps other figures in
Hamlet

I grow old . . . I grow old . . .   120
I shall wear the bottoms of my trousers rolled.

Shall I part my hair behind? Do I dare to eat a peach?
I shall wear white flannel trousers, and walk upon the beach.
I have heard the mermaids singing, each to each.
I do not think that they will sing to me.   125

I have seen them riding seaward on the waves
Combing the white hair of the waves blown back
When the wind blows the water white and black.

We have lingered in the chambers of the sea
By sea-girls wreathed with seaweed red and brown   130
Till human voices wake us, and we drown.

[1910-11]

 # TOPICS FOR CRITICAL THINKING AND WRITING

1. How does the speaker's name help to characterize him? What suggestions—of class, race, personality—do you find in it? Does the title of this poem strike you as ironic? If so, how or why?
2. What qualities of big-city life are suggested in the poem? How are these qualities linked to the speaker's mood? What other details of the setting—the weather, the time of day—express or reflect his mood? What images do you find especially striking?
3. The speaker's thoughts are represented in a stream-of-consciousness monologue, that is, in what appears to be an unedited flow of thought. Nevertheless, they reveal a story. What is the story?
4. In a paragraph, characterize Prufrock as he might be characterized by one of the women in the poem, and then, in a paragraph or two, offer your own characterization of him.
5. Consider the possibility that the "you" whom Prufrock is addressing is not a listener but is one aspect of Prufrock, and the "I" is another. Given this possibility, in a paragraph characterize the "you," and in another paragraph characterize the "I."
6. Prufrock has gone to a therapist, a psychiatrist, or a member of the clergy for help. Write a 500-word transcript of their session.

 # W. H. AUDEN

Wystan Hugh Auden (1907-73) was born in York, England, and educated at Oxford. In the 1930s his witty left-wing poetry earned him wide acclaim as the leading poet of his generation. He went to Spain during the Spanish Civil War, intending to serve as an ambulance driver for the Republicans in their struggle against Fascism, but he was so distressed by the violence of the Republicans that he almost immediately returned to England. In 1939 he came to America, and in 1946 he became a citizen of the United States, though he spent his last years in England. Much of his poetry is characterized by a combination of colloquial diction and technical dexterity.

The Unknown Citizen

(To JS/07/M/378
This Marble Monument
Is Erected by the State)

He was found by the Bureau of Statistics to be
One against whom there was no official complaint,
And all the reports on his conduct agree
That, in the modern sense of an old-fashioned word, he was a saint,
For in everything he did he served the Greater Community.   5
Except for the War till the day he retired
He worked in a factory and never got fired,
But satisfied his employers, Fudge Motors Inc.
Yet he wasn't a scab or odd in his views,
For his Union reports that he paid his dues.   10
(Our report on his Union shows it was sound)
And our Social Psychology workers found
That he was popular with his mates and liked a drink.
The press are convinced that he bought a paper every day
And that his reactions to advertisements were normal in every way.   15
Policies taken out in his name prove that he was fully insured,
And his Health-card shows he was once in hospital but left it cured.
Both Producers Research and High-Grade Living declare
He was fully sensible to the advantages of the Installment Plan
And had everything necessary to the Modern Man,   20
A phonograph, radio, a car and a frigidaire.
Our researches into Public Opinion are content
That he held the proper opinions for the time of year;
When there was peace, he was for peace; when there was war, he went.
He was married and added five children to the population,   25
Which our Eugenist says was the right number for a parent of his genera-
    tion,
And our teachers report that he never interfered with their education.
Was he free? Was he happy? The question is absurd:
Had anything been wrong, we should certainly have heard.

[1940]

☐ TOPICS FOR CRITICAL THINKING AND WRITING

1. Who is the speaker, and on what occasion is he supposed to be speaking?
2. What do the words "The Unknown Citizen" suggest to you?
3. How does Auden suggest that he doesn't share the attitudes of the
   speaker and is, in fact, satirizing them? What else does he satirize?
4. If Auden were writing the poem today, what might he substitute for "Installment Plan" in line 19 and the items listed in line 21?
5. Explicate the last two lines.
6. *Was* he free? *Was* he happy?

7. Write a tribute to The Unknown Student or The Unknown Professor or Politician or Professional Athlete or some other object of your well-deserved scorn.

 STEVIE SMITH

Stevie Smith (1902–71), christened Florence Margaret Smith, was born in England, in Hull. In addition to writing poems she wrote stories, essays, and three novels. She is the subject of a film, Stevie, *in which Glenda Jackson plays Smith.*

Not Waving but Drowning

Nobody heard him, the dead man,
But still he lay moaning:
I was much further out than you thought
And not waving but drowning.   4

Poor chap, he always loved larking
And now he's dead
It must have been too cold for him his heart gave way,
They said.   8

Oh, no no no, it was too cold always
(Still the dead one lay moaning)
I was much too far out all my life
And not waving but drowning.   12

[1957]

 TOPICS FOR CRITICAL THINKING AND WRITING

1. What sort of man did the friends of the dead man think he was? What sort of man do you think he was?
2. The first line, "Nobody heard him, the dead man," is of course literally true. Dead men do not speak. In what other ways is it true?

 MITSUYE YAMADA

Mitsuye Yamada, the daughter of Japanese immigrants to the United States, was born in Japan in 1923, during her mother's return visit to her native land. Yamada was raised in Seattle, but in 1942 she and her family were incarcerated and then relocated in a camp in Idaho, when Executive Order 9066 gave military authorities the right to remove any and all persons from "military areas." In 1954

she became an American citizen. A professor of English at Cypress Junior College in San Luis Obispo, California, she is the author of poems and stories.

To the Lady

The one in San Francisco who asked:
Why did the Japanese Americans let
the government put them in
those camps without protest?

Come to think of it I   5
    should've run off to Canada
    should've hijacked a plane to Algeria
    should've pulled myself up from my
    bra straps
    and kicked'm in the groin   10
    should've bombed a bank
    should've tried self-immolation
    should've holed myself up in a
    woodframe house
    and let you watch me   15
    burn up on the six o'clock news
    should've run howling down the street
    naked and assaulted you at breakfast
    by AP wirephoto
    should've screamed bloody murder   20
    like Kitty Genovese°

Then
YOU would've
    come to my aid in shining armor
    laid yourself across the railroad track   25
    marched on Washington
    tatooed a Star of David on your arm
    written six million enraged
    letters to Congress

But we didn't draw the line   30
anywhere
law and order Executive Order 9066°
social order moral order internal order

21**Kitty Genovese** In 1964 Kitty Genovese of Kew Gardens, New York, was stabbed to death when she left her car and walked toward her home. Thirty-eight persons heard her screams, but no one came to her assistance.   32**Executive Order 9066** an authorization, signed in 1941 by President Franklin D. Roosevelt, allowing military authorities to relocate Japanese and Japanese-Americans who resided on the Pacific Coast of the United States

YOU let'm
I let'm   35
All are punished.

[1976]

TOPICS FOR CRITICAL THINKING AND WRITING

1. Has the lady's question (lines 2–4) ever crossed your mind? If so, what answers did you think of?
2. What, in effect, is the speaker really saying in lines 5–21? And in lines 22–29?
3. Explain the last line.

ADRIENNE RICH

Adrienne Rich, born in Baltimore in 1929, published her first book of poems while she was an undergraduate at Radcliffe College. In 1953 she married, and she bore three children in rapid succession. In Of Woman Born, a prose work of 1976, she wrote of the conflict she felt between her roles as wife, mother, and writer. Rich was active in opposing the Vietnam War, and she became increasingly interested in feminist issues, including lesbian politics.

Aunt Jennifer's Tigers

Aunt Jennifer's tigers prance across a screen,
Bright topaz denizens of a world of green.
They do not fear the men beneath the tree;
They pace in sleek chivalric certainty.

Aunt Jennifer's fingers fluttering through her wool
Find even the ivory needle hard to pull.
The massive weight of Uncle's wedding band
Sits heavily upon Aunt Jennifer's hand.

When Aunt is dead, her terrified hands will lie
Still ringed with ordeals she was mastered by.
The tigers in the panel that she made
Will go on prancing, proud and unafraid.

[1951]

TOPICS FOR CRITICAL THINKING AND WRITING

1. Exactly what are Aunt Jennifer's tigers?
2. What do you understand Rich to be saying when she speaks of "the massive weight" of the wedding ring?

3. What do we know about Aunt Jennifer? Do you think we should make much of the fact that she created tigers rather than, say, kittens?

Rape

There is a cop who is both prowler and father:
he comes from your block, grew up with your brothers,
had certain ideals.
You hardly know him in his boots and silver badge,
on horseback, one hand touching his gun.   5

You hardly know him but you have to get to know him:
he has access to machinery that could kill you.
He and his stallion clop like warlords among the trash,
his ideals stand in the air, a frozen cloud
from between his unsmiling lips.   10

And so, when the time comes, you have to turn to him,
the maniac's sperm still greasing your thighs,
your mind whirling like crazy. You have to confess
to him, you are guilty of the crime
of having been forced.   15

And you see his blue eyes, the blue eyes of all the family
whom you used to know, grow narrow and glisten,
his hand types out the details
and he wants them all
but the hysteria in your voice pleases him best.   20

You hardly know him but now he thinks he knows you:
he has taken down your worst moment
on a machine and filed it in a file.
He knows, or thinks he knows, how much you imagined;
he knows, or thinks he knows, what you secretly wanted.   25

He has access to machinery that could get you put away;
and if, in the sickening light of the precinct,
your details sound like a portrait of your confessor,
will you swallow, will you deny them, will you lie your way home?

[1972]

TOPIC FOR CRITICAL THINKING OR WRITING

Some critics have suggested that in poems such as "Rape" Adrienne Rich over-simplifies experience, seeing people as utterly innocent or utterly villainous. Do you think that this is true of this poem? And, if so, is the poem therefore a poor poem?

 MARGE PIERCY

Marge Piercy, born in Detroit in 1936, was the first member of her family to attend college. After earning a bachelor's degree from the University of Michigan in 1957 and a master's degree from Northwestern University in 1958, she moved to Chicago. There she worked at odd jobs while writing novels (unpublished) and engaging in action on behalf of women and blacks and against the war in Vietnam. In 1970—the year she moved to Wellfleet, Massachusetts, where she still lives—she published her first book, a novel. Since then she has published other novels, short stories, poems, and essays.

What's That Smell in the Kitchen?

All over America women are burning dinners.
It's lambchops in Peoria; it's haddock
in Providence; it's steak in Chicago;
tofu delight in Big Sur; red
rice and beans in Dallas.   5
All over America women are burning
food they're supposed to bring with calico
smile on platters glittering like wax.
Anger sputters in her brainpan, confined
but spewing out missiles of hot fat.   10
Carbonized despair presses like a clinker
from a barbecue against the back of her eyes.
If she wants to grill anything, it's
her husband spitted over a slow fire.
If she wants to serve him anything   15
it's a dead rat with a bomb in its belly
ticking like the heart of an insomniac.
Her life is cooked and digested,
nothing but leftovers in Tupperware.
Look, she says, once I was roast duck   20
on your platter with parsley but now I am Spam.
Burning dinner is not incompetence but war.

[1980]

 TOPICS FOR CRITICAL THINKING AND WRITING

1. Suppose a friend told you that she didn't understand lines 20–21. How would you paraphrase the lines?
2. Who speaks the title?
3. If a poem begins, "All over America women are . . . ," what words might a reader reasonably expect next?
4. Do you take the poem to be chiefly comic? Superficially but essentially comic but a work with a serious purpose? Or what?

5. If you have ever used apparent incompetence as "war" (line 22), narrate the episode so that the reader understands not only *what* happened but also *why* it happened.

A Work of Artifice

The bonsai tree
in the attractive pot
could have grown eighty feet tall
on the side of a mountain
till split by lightning.   5
But a gardener
carefully pruned it.
It is nine inches high.
Every day as he
whittles back the branches   10
the gardener croons,
It is your nature
to be small and cozy,
domestic and weak;
how lucky, little tree,   15
to have a pot to grow in.
With living creatures
one must begin very early
to dwarf their growth:
the bound feet,   20
the crippled brain,
the hair in curlers,
the hands you
love to touch.

[1973]

 ## TOPICS FOR CRITICAL THINKING AND WRITING

1. Piercy uses a bonsai tree as a metaphor—but a metaphor for what? (If you have never seen a bonsai tree, try to visit a florist or a nursery to take a close look at one. You can find a picture of a bonsai in *The American Heritage Dictionary*.)
2. The gardener "croons" (line 11) a song to the bonsai tree. If the tree could respond, what might it say?
3. Explain lines 17-24 to someone who doesn't get the point. In your response, explain how these lines are connected with "hair in curlers." Explain, too, what "the hands you / love to touch" has to do with the rest of the poem. What tone of voice do you hear in "the hands you / love to touch"?
4. How does the form of the poem suggest its subject?

 JAMES WRIGHT

James Wright (1927-80) was born in Martins Ferry, Ohio, which provided him with the locale for many of his poems. He is often thought of as a poet of the Midwest, but (as in the example that we give) his poems move beyond the scenery. Wright was educated at Kenyon College in Ohio and at the University of Washington. He wrote several books of poetry and published many translations of European and Latin American poetry.

Lying in a Hammock at William Duffy's Farm in Pine Island, Minnesota

Over my head, I see the bronze butterfly,
Asleep on the black trunk,
Blowing like a leaf in green shadow.
Down the ravine behind the empty house,
The cowbells follow one another   5
Into the distances of the afternoon.
To my right,
In a field of sunlight between two pines,
The droppings of last year's horses
Blaze up into golden stones.   10
I lean back, as the evening darkens and comes on.
A chicken hawk floats over, looking for home.
I have wasted my life.

[1963]

 TOPICS FOR CRITICAL THINKING AND WRITING

1. How important is it that the poet is "lying in a hammock"? That he is at some place other than his own home?
2. Do you take the last line as a severe self-criticism, or as a joking remark, or as something in between, or what?
3. Imagine yourself lying in a hammock—perhaps you can recall an actual moment in a hammock—or lying in bed, your eye taking in the surroundings. Write a description ending with some sort of judgment or concluding comment, as Wright does. You may want to parody Wright's poem, but you need not. (Keep in mind the fact that the best parodies are written by people who regard the original with affection.)

 AURORA LEVINS MORALES

Aurora Levins Morales, born in Puerto Rico in 1954, came to the United States with her family in 1967. She has lived in Chicago and

*New Hampshire and now lives in the San Francisco Bay Area. Levins
Morales has published stories, essays, prose poems, and poems.*

Child of the Americas

I am a child of the Americas,
a light-skinned mestiza of the Caribbean,
a child of many diaspora,° born into this continent at a crossroads.

I am a U.S. Puerto Rican Jew,
a product of the ghettos of New York I have never known.   5
An immigrant and the daughter and granddaughter of immigrants.
I speak English with passion: it's the tongue of my consciousness,
a flashing knife blade of crystal, my tool, my craft.

I am Caribeña,° island grown. Spanish is in my flesh,
ripples from my tongue, lodges in my hips: 10
the language of garlic and mangoes,
the singing in my poetry, the flying gestures of my hands.

I am of Latinoamerica, rooted in the history of my continent:
I speak from that body.

I am not african. African is in me, but I cannot return.   15
I am not taína.° Taíno is in me, but there is no way back.
I am not european. Europe lives in me, but I have no home there.

I am new. History made me. My first language was spanglish.°
I was born at the crossroads
and I am whole.   20

[1986]

 TOPICS FOR CRITICAL THINKING AND WRITING

1. In the first stanza, Levins Morales speaks of herself as "a child of many
   diaspora." *Diaspora* often means "a scattering," or "a dispersion of a ho-
   mogeneous people." What does it refer to here?
2. In the second stanza, Levins Morales says that she is "a product of the
   ghettos of New York I have never known." What does she apparently
   refer to?
3. What attitude does "Child of the Americas" have toward the writer's
   ethnicity? What words or lines particularly communicate it?

---

³**diaspora** literally, "scattering"; the term is used especially to refer to the dispersion of the Jews outside of Israel from the sixth century, when they were exiled to
Babylonia, to the present time   ⁹**Caribeña** Caribbean woman   ¹⁶**taína** the Taínos
were the Indian tribe native to Puerto Rico   ¹⁸**spanglish** a mixture of Spanish and
English

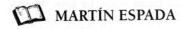 MARTÍN ESPADA

*Martín Espada was born in Brooklyn in 1957. He received a bache-
lor's degree from the University of Wisconsin and a law degree from
Northeastern University. A poet who publishes regularly, Espada is
also Outreach Coordinator and Supervisor of Lawyers of the Arts at
the Artists' Foundation in Boston.*

Bully

Boston, Massachusetts, 1987

In the school auditorium,
the Theodore Roosevelt statue
is nostalgic
for the Spanish-American War,
each fist lonely for a saber   5
or the reins of anguish-eyed horses,
or a podium to clatter with speeches
glorying in the malaria of conquest.

But now the Roosevelt school
is pronounced *Hernández.*   10
Puerto Rico has invaded Roosevelt
with its army of Spanish-singing children
in the hallways,
brown children devouring
the stockpiles of the cafeteria,   15
children painting *Taíno* ancestors
that leap naked across murals.

Roosevelt is surrounded
by all the faces
he ever shoved in eugenic spite   20
and cursed as mongrels, skin of one race,
hair and cheekbones of another.

Once Marines tramped
from the newsreel of his imagination;
now children plot to spray graffiti   25
in parrot-brilliant colors
across the Victorian mustache
and monocle.

                                                          [1990]

 TOPICS FOR CRITICAL THINKING AND WRITING

1. If you're not sure what Theodore Roosevelt was famous for, consult an
   encyclopedia. What *was* he famous for? In the first stanza, what words
   best express Espada's attitude toward him?

2. In the second stanza, what does Espada mean when he says "Puerto Rico has invaded Roosevelt"? What does he mean by an *"army"* of Spanish-singing children"? Who are the *Taino?*

3. What does "bully" mean as a noun? As an adjective?

4. Roosevelt was a great believer in what is called the melting-pot theory of America. What is this theory? Do you think there is a great deal to it, something to it, or nothing to it? Why?

5. Here is a quotation from one of Roosevelt's speeches:

Every immigrant who comes here should be required within five years to learn English or leave the country.

What do you think of this idea? Why? Suppose that for some reason (perhaps political, perhaps economic) you decided to spend the rest of your life in, say, Argentina, or Germany, or Israel, or Nigeria. Do you think the government might reasonably require you to learn the language? Why?

 PAT MORA

Pat Mora, after graduating from Texas Western College earned a master's degree at the University of Texas at El Paso. She is best known for her poems, but she has also published essays on Chicano culture.

Sonrisas*

I live in a doorway
between two rooms. I hear
quiet clicks, cups of black
coffee, *click, click* like facts
   budgets, tenure, curriculum,   5
from careful women in crisp beige
suits, quick beige smiles
that seldom sneak into their eyes.

I peek
in the other room señoras   10
in faded dresses stir sweet
milk coffee, laughter whirls
with steam from fresh *tamales*
   sh, sh, mucho ruido,°
they scold one another,   15
press their lips, trap smiles
in their dark, Mexican eyes.

[1986]

---

*sonrisas smiles (Spanish)   ¹⁴mucho ruido lots of noise

TOPICS FOR CRITICAL THINKING AND WRITING

1. In her first line Pat Mora says, "I live in a doorway." What does she mean?

2. Think about a place where you "live in a doorway" and write two paragraphs, one about each "room." (Living in a doorway can mean, for example, describing two dormitory rooms; or describing the view from a window, morning and evening; or living with separated parents; and so on.) No matter what your topic, keep your descriptions as *specific* as Mora's. If you write about two households, for example, write about a specific time, perhaps breakfast at each.

 CAROLYN FORCHÉ

Carolyn Forché was born in Detroit in 1950. After earning a bachelor's degree from Michigan State University and a master's degree from Bowling Green State University, she traveled widely in the Southwest, living among Pueblo Indians. Between 1978 and 1986 she made several visits to El Salvador, documenting human rights violations for Amnesty International. Her first book of poems, Gathering the Tribes, *won the Yale Younger Poets award in 1975. Her second book of poems,* The Country Between Us *(1981), includes "The Colonel," which has been called a prose poem. (The term prose poem is sometimes applied to a short work that looks like prose but that is highly rhythmical or rich in images, or both.)*

The Colonel

What you have heard is true. I was in his house. His wife carried a tray of coffee and sugar. His daughter filed her nails, his son went out for the night. There were daily papers, pet dogs, a pistol on the cushion beside him. The moon swung bare on its black cord over the house. On the television was a cop show. It was in English. Broken bottles were embedded in the walls around the house to scoop the kneecaps from a man's legs or cut his hands to lace. On the windows there were gratings like those in liquor stores. We had dinner, rack of lamb, good wine, a gold bell was on the table for calling the maid. The maid brought green mangoes, salt, a type of bread. I was asked how I enjoyed the country. There was a brief commercial in Spanish. His wife took everything away. There was some talk then of how difficult it had become to govern. The parrot said hello on the terrace. The colonel told it to shutup, and pushed himself from the table. My friend said to me with his eyes: say nothing. The colonel returned with a sack used to bring groceries home. He spilled many human ears on the table. They were like dried peach halves. There is no other way to say this. He took one of them in his hands, shook it in our faces, dropped it into a water glass. It came alive there. I am tired of fooling around he said. As for the rights of anyone, tell your people they can go fuck themselves. He swept the ears to the floor

with his arm and held the last of his wine in the air. Something for your poetry, no? he said. Some of the ears on the floor caught this scrap of his voice.
Some of the ears on the floor were pressed to the ground.

May 1978

 ## TOPICS FOR CRITICAL THINKING AND WRITING

1. How would you characterize the colonel in a few sentences?
2. We are told that the colonel spoke of "how difficult it had become to
   govern." What do you suppose the colonel assumes is the purpose of
   government? What do *you* assume its purpose is?
3. How much do we know about the narrator? Can we guess the narrator's
   purpose in visiting the colonel? How would you characterize the narrator's tone? Do you believe the narrator?
4. What do you make of the last two lines?

 ## YUSEF KOMUNYAKAA

*Yusef Komunyakaa was born in 1947 in Bogalusa, Louisiana. After
graduating from high school he entered the army and served in Vietnam, where he was awarded the Bronze Star. On his return to the
United States he earned a bachelor's degree at the University of Colorado, and then earned an M.A. at Colorado State University and an
M.F.A. in creative writing at the University of California, Irvine. The
author of several books of poetry, he has been teaching at Indiana
University in Bloomington since 1985. "Facing It" is the last poem in
a book of poems about Vietnam,* Dien Cai Dau *(1988). The title of the
book is a slang term for "crazy."*

Facing It

My black face fades,
hiding inside the black granite.
I said I wouldn't,
dammit: No tears.
I'm stone. I'm flesh.   5
My clouded reflection eyes me
like a bird of prey, the profile of night
slanted against morning. I turn
this way—the stone lets me go.
I turn that way—I'm inside   10
the Vietnam Veterans Memorial
again, depending on the light
to make a difference.
I go down the 58,022 names,
half-expecting to find   15
my own in letters like smoke.
I touch the name Andrew Johnson;

I see the booby trap's white flash.
Names shimmer on a woman's blouse
but when she walks away   20
the names stay on the wall.
Brushstrokes flash, a red bird's
wings cutting across my stare.
The sky. A plane in the sky.
A white vet's image floats   25
closer to me, then his pale eyes
look through mine. I'm a window.
He's lost his right arm
inside the stone. In the black mirror
a woman's trying to erase names: 30
No, she's brushing a boy's hair.

[1988]

 ## TOPICS FOR CRITICAL THINKING AND WRITING

1. The poem's title is "Facing It." What is the speaker facing? How would you describe his attitude?
2. Three people, whose names we don't know, briefly appear on the wall. How might we describe their actions? Try to paraphrase these lines:

   > I'm a window.
   > He's lost his right arm
   > inside the stone.

3. At the poem's end, has the speaker "faced it"? What is your evidence?
4. If you have seen the Vietnam Veterans Memorial, describe it and your reaction to it in a paragraph or two. If you haven't seen it, try to describe it from "Facing It" and any written or photographic accounts you have seen.

Drama

 ## HENRIK IBSEN

Henrik Ibsen (1828–1906) was born in Skien, Norway, of wealthy parents who soon after his birth lost their money. Ibsen worked as a pharmacist's apprentice, but at the age of 22 he had written his first play, a promising melodrama entitled Cataline. *He engaged in theater work first in Norway and then in Denmark and Germany. By 1865 his plays had won him a state pension that enabled him to settle in Rome. After writing romantic, historic, and poetic plays, he*

A Doll's House (Harvard Theatre Collection)

turned to realistic drama with The League of Youth *(1869). Among the major realistic "problem plays" are* A Doll's House *(1879),* Ghosts *(1881), and* An Enemy of the People *(1882). In* The Wild Duck *(1884) he moved toward a more symbolic tragic comedy, and his last plays, written in the nineties, are highly symbolic.* Hedda Gabler *(1890) looks backward to the plays of the eighties rather than forward to the plays of the nineties.*

A Doll's House

Translated by Michael Meyer

LIST OF CHARACTERS

TORVALD HELMER, *a lawyer*
NORA, his wife
DR. RANK
MRS. LINDE
NILS KROGSTAD, *also a lawyer*
The Helmers' three small children
ANNE-MARIE, *their nurse*
HELEN, *the maid*
A Porter

SCENE: *The action takes place in the Helmers' apartment.*

Act 1

A comfortably and tastefully, but not expensively furnished room. Backstage right a door leads out to the hall; backstage left, another door to HELMER*'s study. Between these two doors stands a piano. In the middle of the left-hand wall is a door, with a window downstage of it. Near the window, a round table with armchairs and a small sofa. In the right-hand wall, slightly upstage, is a door, downstage of this, against the same wall, a stove lined with porcelain tiles, with a couple of armchairs and a rocking-chair in front of it. Between the stove and the side door is a small table. Engravings on the wall. A what-not with china and other bric-a-brac; a small bookcase with leather-bound books. A carpet on the floor; a fire in the stove. A winter day.*

A bell rings in the hall outside. After a moment, we hear the front door being opened. NORA *enters the room, humming contentedly to herself. She is wearing outdoor clothes and carrying a lot of parcels, which she puts down on the table right. She leaves the door to the hall open; through it, we can see a* PORTER *carrying a Christmas tree and a basket. He gives these to the* MAID, *who has opened the door for them.*

NORA. Hide that Christmas tree away, Helen. The children mustn't see it before I've decorated it this evening. *[To the* PORTER, *taking out her purse.]* How much—?

PORTER. A shilling.

NORA. Here's half a crown. No, keep it.

The PORTER *touches his cap and goes.* NORA *closes the door. She continues to laugh happily to herself as she removes her coat, etc. She takes from her pocket a bag containing macaroons and eats a couple. Then, she tiptoes across and listens at her husband's door.*

NORA. Yes, he's here. *[Starts humming again as she goes over to the table, right.]*

HELMER *[from his room]*. Is that my skylark twittering out there?

NORA *[opening some of the parcels]*. It is!

HELMER. Is that my squirrel rustling?

NORA. Yes!

HELMER. When did my squirrel come home?

NORA. Just now. *[Pops the bag of macaroons in her pocket and wipes her mouth.]* Come out here, Torvald, and see what I've bought.

HELMER. You mustn't disturb me! *[Short pause; then he opens the door and looks in, his pen in his hand.]* Bought, did you say? All that? Has my little squanderbird been overspending again?

NORA. Oh, Torvald, surely we can let ourselves go a little this year! It's the first Christmas we don't have to scrape.

HELMER. Well, you know, we can't afford to be extravagant.

NORA. Oh yes, Torvald, we can be a little extravagant now. Can't we? Just a tiny bit? You've got a big salary now, and you're going to make lots and lots of money.

HELMER. Next year, yes. But my new salary doesn't start till April.

NORA. Pooh; we can borrow till then.

HELMER. Nora! *[Goes over to her and takes her playfully by the ear.]* What a little spendthrift you are! Suppose I were to borrow fifty pounds today, and you spent it all over Christmas, and then on New Year's Eve a tile fell off a roof onto my head—

NORA *[puts her hand over his mouth]*. Oh, Torvald! Don't say such dreadful things!

HELMER. Yes, but suppose something like that did happen? What then?

NORA. If any thing as frightful as that happened, it wouldn't make much difference whether I was in debt or not.

HELMER. But what about the people I'd borrowed from?

NORA. Them? Who cares about them? They're strangers.

HELMER. Oh, Nora, Nora, how like a woman! No, but seriously, Nora, you know how I feel about this. No debts! Never borrow! A home that is founded on debts can never be a place of freedom and beauty. We two have stuck it out bravely up to now; and we shall continue to do so for the short time we still have to.

NORA *[goes over towards the stove]*. Very well, Torvald. As you say.

HELMER *[follows her]*. Now, now! My little songbird mustn't droop her wings. What's this? Is little squirrel sulking? *[Takes out his purse.]* Nora; guess what I've got here!

NORA *[turns quickly]*. Money!

HELMER. Look. *[Hands her some banknotes.]* I know how these small expenses crop up at Christmas.

NORA *[counts them]*. One—two—three—four. Oh, thank you, Torvald, thank you! I should be able to manage with this.

HELMER. You'll have to.

NORA. Yes, yes, of course I will. But come over here, I want to show you everything I've bought. And so cheaply! Look, here are new clothes for Ivar—and a sword. And a horse and a trumpet for Bob. And a doll and a cradle for Emmy—they're nothing much, but she'll pull them apart in a few days. And some bits of material and handkerchiefs for the maids. Old Anne-Marie ought to have had something better, really.

HELMER. And what's in that parcel?

NORA *[cries]*. No, Torvald, you mustn't see that before this evening!

HELMER. Very well. But now, tell me, you little spendthrift, what do you want for Christmas?

NORA. Me? Oh, pooh, I don't want anything.

HELMER. Oh, yes, you do. Now tell me, what, within reason, would you most like?

NORA. No, I really don't know. Oh, yes—Torvald—!

HELMER. Well?

NORA *[plays with his coat-buttons; not looking at him]*. If you really want to give me something, you could—you could—

HELMER. Come on, out with it.

NORA *[quickly]*. You could give me money, Torvald. Only as much as you feel you can afford; then later I'll buy something with it.

HELMER. But, Nora—

NORA. Oh yes, Torvald dear, please! Please! Then I'll wrap up the notes in pretty gold paper and hang them on the Christmas tree. Wouldn't that be fun?

HELMER. What's the name of that little bird that can never keep any money?

NORA. Yes, yes, squanderbird; I know. But let's do as I say, Torvald; then I'll have time to think about what I need most. Isn't that the best way? Mm?

HELMER *[smiles].* To be sure it would be, if you could keep what I give you and really buy yourself something with it. But you'll spend it on all sorts of useless things for the house, and then I'll have to put my hand in my pocket again.

NORA. Oh, but Torvald—

HELMER. You can't deny it, Nora dear. *[Puts his arm round her waist.]* The squanderbird's a pretty little creature, but she gets through an awful lot of money. It's incredible what an expensive pet she is for a man to keep.

NORA. For shame! How can you say such a thing? I save every penny I can.

HELMER *[laughs].* That's quite true. Every penny you can. But you can't.

NORA *[hums and smiles, quietly gleeful].* Hm. If you only knew how many expenses we larks and squirrels have, Torvald.

HELMER. You're a funny little creature. Just like your father used to be. Always on the look-out for some way to get money, but as soon as you have any it just runs through your fingers, and you never know where it's gone. Well, I suppose I must take you as you are. It's in your blood. Yes, yes, yes, these things are hereditary, Nora.

NORA. Oh, I wish I'd inherited more of Papa's qualities.

HELMER. And I wouldn't wish my darling little songbird to be any different from what she is. By the way, that reminds me. You look awfully—how shall I put it?—awfully guilty today.

NORA. Do I?

HELMER. Yes, you do. Look me in the eyes.

NORA *[looks at him].* Well?

HELMER *[wags his finger].* Has my little sweet-tooth been indulging herself in town today, by any chance?

NORA. No, how can you think such a thing?

HELMER. Not a tiny little digression into a pastry shop?

NORA. No, Torvald, I promise—

HELMER. Not just a wee jam tart?

NORA. Certainly not.

HELMER. Not a little nibble at a macaroon?

NORA. No, Torvald—I promise you, honestly—

HELMER. There, there. I was only joking.

NORA *[goes over to the table, right].* You know I could never act against your wishes.

HELMER. Of course not. And you've given me your word—*[Goes over to her.]* Well, my beloved Nora, you keep your little Christmas secrets to yourself. They'll be revealed this evening, I've no doubt, once the Christmas tree has been lit.

NORA. Have you remembered to invite Dr. Rank?

HELMER. No. But there's no need; he knows he'll be dining with us. Anyway, I'll ask him when he comes this morning. I've ordered some good wine. Oh Nora, you can't imagine how I'm looking forward to this evening.

NORA. So am I. And, Torvald, how the children will love it!

HELMER. Yes, it's a wonderful thing to know that one's position is assured and that one has an ample income. Don't you agree? It's good to know that, isn't it?

NORA. Yes, it's almost like a miracle.

HELMER. Do you remember last Christmas? For three whole weeks you shut yourself away every evening to make flowers for the Christmas tree, and all those other things you were going to surprise us with. Ugh, it was the most boring time I've ever had in my life.

NORA. I didn't find it boring.

HELMER *[smiles]*. But it all came to nothing in the end, didn't it?

NORA. Oh, are you going to bring that up again? How could I help the cat getting in and tearing everything to bits?

HELMER. No, my poor little Nora, of course you couldn't. You simply wanted to make us happy, and that's all that matters. But it's good that those hard times are past.

NORA. Yes, it's wonderful.

HELMER. I don't have to sit by myself and be bored. And you don't have to tire your pretty eyes and your delicate little hands—

NORA *[claps her hands]*. No, Torvald, that's true, isn't it—I don't have to any longer? Oh, it's really all just like a miracle. *[Takes his arm.]* Now, I'm going to tell you what I thought we might do, Torvald. As soon as Christmas is over—*[A bell rings in the hall.]* Oh, there's the doorbell. *[Tidies up one or two things in the room.]* Someone's coming. What a bore.

HELMER. I'm not at home to any visitors. Remember!

MAID *[in the doorway]*. A lady's called, madam. A stranger.

NORA. Well, ask her to come in.

MAID. And the doctor's here too, sir.

HELMER. Has he gone to my room?

MAID. Yes, sir.

> HELMER *goes into his room. The* MAID *shows in* MRS. LINDE, *who is dressed in traveling clothes, and closes the door.*

MRS. LINDE *[shyly and a little hesitantly]*. Good evening, Nora.

NORA *[uncertainly]*. Good evening—

MRS. LINDE. I don't suppose you recognize me.

NORA. No, I'm afraid I—Yes, wait a minute—surely—*[Exclaims.]* Why, Christine! Is it really you?

MRS. LINDE. Yes, it's me.

NORA. Christine! And I didn't recognize you! But how could I—? *[More quietly.]* How you've changed, Christine!

MRS. LINDE. Yes, I know. It's been nine years—nearly ten—

NORA. Is it so long? Yes, it must be. Oh, these last eight years have been such a happy time for me! So you've come to town? All that way in winter! How brave of you!

MRS. LINDE. I arrived by the steamer this morning.

NORA. Yes, of course—to enjoy yourself over Christmas. Oh, how splendid! We'll have to celebrate! But take off your coat. You're not cold, are you? *[Helps her off with it.]* There! Now let's sit down here by the stove and be comfortable. No, you take the armchair. I'll sit here in the rocking-chair. *[Clasps* MRS. LINDE*'s hands.]* Yes, now you look like your old self. It was just at first that—you've got a little paler, though, Christine. And perhaps a bit thinner.

MRS. LINDE. And older, Nora. Much, much older.

NORA. Yes, perhaps a little older. Just a tiny bit. Not much. *[Checks herself suddenly and says earnestly.]* Oh, but how thoughtless of me to sit here and chatter away like this! Dear, sweet Christine, can you forgive me?

MRS. LINDE. What do you mean, Nora?

NORA *[quietly]*. Poor Christine, you've become a widow.

MRS. LINDE. Yes. Three years ago.

NORA. I know, I know—I read it in the papers. Oh, Christine, I meant to write to you so often, honestly. But I always put it off, and something else always cropped up.

MRS. LINDE. I understand, Nora dear.

NORA. No, Christine, it was beastly of me. Oh, my poor darling, what you've gone through! And he didn't leave you anything?

MRS. LINDE. No.

NORA. No children, either?

MRS. LINDE. No.

NORA. Nothing at all, then?

MRS. LINDE. Not even a feeling of loss or sorrow.

NORA *[looks incredulously at her]*. But, Christine, how is that possible?

MRS. LINDE *[smiles sadly and strokes* NORA's *hair]*. Oh, these things happen, Nora.

NORA. All alone. How dreadful that must be for you. I've three lovely children. I'm afraid you can't see them now, because they're out with nanny. But you must tell me everything—

MRS. LINDE. No, no, no. I want to hear about you.

NORA. No, you start. I'm not going to be selfish today, I'm just going to think about you. Oh, but there's one thing I *must* tell you. Have you heard of the wonderful luck we've just had?

MRS. LINDE. No. What?

NORA. Would you believe it—my husband's just been made manager of the bank!

MRS. LINDE. Your husband? Oh, how lucky—!

NORA. Yes, isn't it? Being a lawyer is so uncertain, you know, especially if one isn't prepared to touch any case that isn't—well—quite nice. And of course Torvald's been very firm about that—and I'm absolutely with him. Oh, you can imagine how happy we are! He's joining the bank in the New Year, and he'll be getting a big salary, and lots of percentages too. From now on we'll be able to live quite differently—we'll be able to do whatever we want. Oh, Christine, it's such a relief! I feel so happy! Well, I mean, it's lovely to have heaps of money and not to have to worry about anything. Don't you think?

MRS. LINDE. It must be lovely to have enough to cover one's needs, anyway.

NORA. Not just our needs! We're going to have heaps and heaps of money!

MRS. LINDE *[smiles]*. Nora, Nora, haven't you grown up yet? When we were at school you were a terrible little spendthrift.

NORA *[laughs quietly]*. Yes, Torvald still says that. *[Wags her finger.]* But "Nora, Nora" isn't as silly as you think. Oh, we've been in no position for me to waste money. We've both had to work.

MRS. LINDE. You too?

NORA. Yes, little things—fancy work, crocheting, embroidery and so forth. *[Casually.]* And other things too. I suppose you know Torvald left the Ministry when we got married? There were no prospects of promotion in his department, and of course he needed more money. But the first year he overworked himself quite dreadfully. He had to take on all sorts of extra jobs, and worked day and night. But it was too much for him, and he became frightfully ill. The doctors said he'd have to go to a warmer climate.

MRS. LINDE. Yes, you spent a whole year in Italy, didn't you?

NORA. Yes. It wasn't easy for me to get away, you know. I'd just had Ivar. But of course we had to do it. Oh, it was a marvelous trip! And it saved Torvald's life. But it cost an awful lot of money, Christine.

MRS. LINDE. I can imagine.

NORA. Two hundred and fifty pounds. That's a lot of money, you know.

MRS. LINDE. How lucky you had it.

NORA. Well, actually, we got it from my father.

MRS. LINDE. Oh, I see. Didn't he die just about that time?

NORA. Yes, Christine, just about then. Wasn't it dreadful, I couldn't go and look after him. I was expecting little Ivar any day. And then I had my poor Torvald to care for—we really didn't think he'd live. Dear, kind Papa! I never saw him again, Christine. Oh, it's the saddest thing that's happened to me since I got married.

MRS. LINDE. I know you were very fond of him. But you went to Italy—?

NORA. Yes. Well, we had the money, you see, and the doctors said we mustn't delay. So we went the month after Papa died.

MRS. LINDE. And your husband came back completely cured?

NORA. Fit as a fiddle!

MRS. LINDE. But—the doctor?

NORA. How do you mean?

MRS. LINDE. I thought the maid said that the gentleman who arrived with me was the doctor.

NORA. Oh yes, that's Doctor Rank, but he doesn't come because anyone's ill. He's our best friend, and he looks us up at least once every day. No, Torvald hasn't had a moment's illness since we went away. And the children are fit and healthy and so am I. [*Jumps up and claps her hands.*] Oh God, oh God, Christine, isn't it a wonderful thing to be alive and happy! Oh, but how beastly of me! I'm only talking about myself. [*Sits on a footstool and rests her arms on Mrs. Linde's knee.*] Oh, please don't be angry with me! Tell me, is it really true you didn't love your husband? Why did you marry him, then?

MRS. LINDE. Well, my mother was still alive; and she was helpless and bedridden. And I had my two little brothers to take care of. I didn't feel I could say no.

NORA. Yes, well, perhaps you're right. He was rich then, was he?

MRS. LINDE. Quite comfortably off, I believe. But his business was unsound, you see, Nora. When he died it went bankrupt, and there was nothing left.

NORA. What did you do?

MRS. LINDE. Well, I had to try to make ends meet somehow, so I started a little shop, and a little school, and anything else I could turn my hand to. These last three years have been just one endless slog for me, without a moment's rest. But now it's over, Nora. My poor dear mother doesn't need me any more; she's passed away. And the boys don't need me either; they've got jobs now and can look after themselves.

NORA. How relieved you must feel—

MRS. LINDE. No, Nora. Just unspeakably empty. No one to live for any more. *[Gets up restlessly.]* That's why I couldn't bear to stay out there any longer, cut off from the world. I thought it'd be easier to find some work here that will exercise and occupy my mind. If only I could get a regular job—office work of some kind—

NORA. Oh, but Christine, that's dreadfully exhausting; and you look practically finished already. It'd be much better for you if you could go away somewhere.

MRS. LINDE *[goes over to the window]*. I have no Papa to pay for my holidays, Nora.

NORA *[gets up]*. Oh, please don't be angry with me.

MRS. LINDE. My dear Nora, it's I who should ask you not to be angry. That's the worst thing about this kind of situation—it makes one so bitter. One has no one to work for; and yet one has to be continually sponging for jobs. One has to live; and so one becomes completely egocentric. When you told me about this luck you've just had with Torvald's new job—can you imagine?—I was happy not so much on your account, as on my own.

NORA. How do you mean? Oh, I understand. You mean Torvald might be able to do something for you?

MRS. LINDE. Yes, I was thinking that.

NORA. He will too, Christine. Just you leave it to me. I'll lead up to it so delicately, so delicately; I'll get him in the right mood. Oh, Christine, I do so want to help you.

MRS. LINDE. It's sweet of you to bother so much about me, Nora. Especially since you know so little of the worries and hardships of life.

NORA. I? You say *I* know little of—?

MRS. LINDE *[smiles]*. Well, good heavens—those bits of fancy work of yours—well, really—! You're a child, Nora.

NORA. *[tosses her head and walks across the room]*. You shouldn't say that so patronizingly.

MRS. LINDE. Oh?

NORA. You're like the rest. You all think I'm incapable of getting down to anything serious—

MRS. LINDE. My dear—

NORA. You think I've never had any worries like the rest of you.

MRS. LINDE Nora dear, you've just told me about all your difficulties—

NORA. Pooh—that! *[Quietly.]* I haven't told you about the big thing.

MRS. LINDE. What big thing? What do you mean?

NORA. You patronize me, Christine; but you shouldn't. You're proud that you've worked so long and so hard for your mother.

MRS. LINDE. I don't patronize anyone, Nora. But you're right—I am both proud and happy that I was able to make my mother's last months on earth comparatively easy.

NORA. And you're also proud of what you've done for your brothers.

MRS. LINDE. I think I have a right to be.

NORA. I think so too. But let me tell you something, Christine. I too have done something to be proud and happy about.

MRS. LINDE. I don't doubt it. But—how do you mean?

NORA. Speak quietly! Suppose Torvald should hear! He mustn't, at any price—no one must know, Christine—no one but you.

MRS. LINDE. But what is this?

NORA. Come over here. *[Pulls her down on to the sofa beside her.]* Yes, Christine—I too have done something to be happy and proud about. It was I who saved Torvald's life.

MRS. LINDE. Saved his—? How did you save it?

NORA. I told you about our trip to Italy. Torvald couldn't have lived if he hadn't managed to get down there—

MRS. LINDE. Yes, well—your father provided the money—

NORA *[smiles]*. So Torvald and everyone else thinks. But—

MRS. LINDE. Yes?

NORA. Papa didn't give us a penny. It was I who found the money.

MRS. LINDE. You? All of it?

NORA. Two hundred and fifty pounds. What do you say to that?

MRS. LINDE. But Nora, how could you? Did you win a lottery or something?

NORA *[scornfully]*. Lottery? *[Sniffs.]* What would there be to be proud of in that?

MRS. LINDE. But where did you get it from, then?

NORA *[hums and smiles secretively]*. Hm; tra-la-la-la.

MRS. LINDE. You couldn't have borrowed it.

NORA. Oh? Why not?

MRS. LINDE. Well, a wife can't borrow money without her husband's consent.

NORA *[tosses her head]*. Ah, but when a wife has a little business sense, and knows how to be clever—

MRS. LINDE. But Nora, I simply don't understand—

NORA. You don't have to. No one has said I borrowed the money. I could have got it in some other way. *[Throws herself back on the sofa.]* I could have got it from an admirer. When a girl's as pretty as I am—

MRS. LINDE. Nora, you're crazy!

NORA. You're dying of curiosity now, aren't you, Christine?

MRS. LINDE. Nora dear, you haven't done anything foolish?

NORA *[sits up again]*. Is it foolish to save one's husband's life?

MRS. LINDE. I think it's foolish if without his knowledge, you—

NORA. But the whole point was that he mustn't know! Great heavens, don't you see? He hadn't to know how dangerously ill he was. I was the one they told that his life was in danger and that only going to a warm climate could save him. Do you suppose I didn't try to think of other ways of getting him down there? I told him how wonderful it would be for me to go abroad like other young wives; I cried and prayed; I asked him to remember my condition, and said he ought to be nice and tender to me; and then I suggested he might quite easily borrow the money. But then he got almost angry with me, Christine. He said I was frivolous, and that it was his duty as a husband not to pander to my moods and caprices—I think that's what he called them. Well, well, I thought, you've got to be saved somehow. And then I thought of a way—

MRS. LINDE. But didn't your husband find out from your father that the money hadn't come from him?

NORA. No, never. Papa died just then. I'd thought of letting him into the plot and asking him not to tell. But since he was so ill—! And as things turned out, it didn't become necessary.

MRS. LINDE. And you've never told your husband about this?

NORA. For heaven's sake, no! What an idea! He's frightfully strict about such matters. And besides—he's so proud of being a *man*—it'd be so painful and humiliating for him to know that he owed anything to me. It'd completely wreck our relationship. This life we have built together would no longer exist.

MRS. LINDE. Will you never tell him?

NORA *[thoughtfully, half-smiling]*. Yes—some time, perhaps. Years from now, when I'm no longer pretty. You mustn't laugh! I mean of course, when Torvald no longer loves me as he does now; when it no longer amuses him to see me dance and dress up and play the fool for him. Then it might be useful to have something up my sleeve. *[Breaks off.]* Stupid, stupid, stupid! That time will never come. Well, what do you think of my big secret, Christine? I'm not completely useless, am I? Mind you, all this has caused me a frightful lot of worry. It hasn't been easy for me to meet my obligations punctually. In case you don't know, in the world of business there are things called quarterly installments and interest, and they're a terrible problem to cope with. So I've had to scrape a little here and save a little there as best I can. I haven't been able to save much on the housekeeping money, because Torvald likes to live well; and I couldn't let the children go short of clothes—I couldn't take anything out of what he gives me for them. The poor little angels!

MRS. LINDE. So you've had to stint yourself, my poor Nora?

NORA. Of course. Well, after all, it was my problem. Whenever Torvald gave me money to buy myself new clothes, I never used more than half of it; and I always bought what was cheapest and plainest. Thank heaven anything suits me, so that Torvald's never noticed. But it made me a bit sad sometimes, because it's lovely to wear pretty clothes. Don't you think?

MRS. LINDE. Indeed it is.

NORA. And then I've found one or two other sources of income. Last winter I managed to get a lot of copying to do. So I shut myself away and wrote every evening, late into the night. Oh, I often got so tired, so tired. But it was great fun, though, sitting there working and earning money. It was almost like being a man.

MRS. LINDE. But how much have you managed to pay off like this?

NORA. Well, I can't say exactly. It's awfully difficult to keep an exact check on these kind of transactions. I only know I've paid everything I've managed to scrape together. Sometimes I really didn't know where to turn. *[Smiles.]* Then I'd sit here and imagine some rich old gentleman had fallen in love with me—

MRS. LINDE. What! What gentleman?

NORA. Silly! And that now he'd died and when they opened his will it said in big letters: "Everything I possess is to be paid forthwith to my beloved Mrs. Nora Helmer in cash."

MRS. LINDE. But, Nora dear, who was this gentleman?

NORA. Great heavens, don't you understand? There wasn't any old gentleman, he was just something I used to dream up as I sat here evening after evening wondering how on earth I could raise some money. But what does it matter? The old bore can stay imaginary as far as I'm concerned, because now I don't have to worry any longer! *[Jumps up.]* Oh,

Christine, isn't it wonderful? I don't have to worry any more! No more troubles! I can play all day with the children, I can fill the house with pretty things, just the way Torvald likes. And, Christine, it will soon be spring, and the air will be fresh and the skies blue—and then perhaps we'll be able to take a little trip somewhere. I shall be able to see the sea again. Oh, yes, yes, it's a wonderful thing to be alive and happy! *The bell rings in the hall.*

MRS. LINDE *[gets up].* You've a visitor. Perhaps I'd better go.

NORA. No stay. It won't be for me. It's someone for Torvald—

MAID *[in the doorway].* Excuse me, madam, a gentleman's called who says he wants to speak to the master. But I didn't know—seeing as the doctor's with him—

NORA. Who is this gentleman?

KROGSTAD *[in the doorway].* It's me, Mrs. Helmer.

MRS. LINDE *starts, composes herself; and turns away to the window.*

NORA *[takes a step toward him and whispers tensely].* You? What is it? What do you want to talk to my husband about?

KROGSTAD. Business—you might call it. I hold a minor post in the bank, and I hear your husband is to become our new chief—

NORA. Oh—then it isn't—?

KROGSTAD. Pure business, Mrs. Helmer. Nothing more.

NORA. Well, you'll find him in his study.

Nods indifferently as she closes the hall door behind him. Then she walks across the room and sees to the stove.

MRS. LINDE. Nora, who was that man?

NORA. A lawyer called Krogstad.

MRS. LINDE. It was him, then.

NORA. Do you know that man?

MRS. LINDE. I used to know him—some years ago. He was a solicitor's clerk in our town, for a while.

NORA. Yes, of course, so he was.

MRS. LINDE. How he's changed!

NORA. He was very unhappily married, I believe.

MRS. LINDE. Is he a widower now?

NORA. Yes, with a lot of children. Ah, now it's alight.

She closes the door of the stove and moves the rocking-chair a little to one side.

MRS. LINDE. He does—various things now, I hear?

NORA. Does he? It's quite possible—I really don't know. But don't let's talk about business. It's so boring.

DR. RANK *enters from* HELMER'*s study.*

RANK *[still in the doorway].* No, no, my dear chap, don't see me out. I'll go and have a word with your wife. *[Closes the door and notices* MRS. LINDE.*]* Oh, I beg your pardon. I seem to be *de trop* here too.

NORA. Not in the least. *[Introduces them.]* Dr. Rank. Mrs. Linde.

RANK. Ah! A name I have often heard in this house. I believe I passed you on the stairs as I came up.

MRS. LINDE. Yes. Stairs tire me; I have to take them slowly.

RANK. Oh, have you hurt yourself?

MRS. LINDE. No, I'm just a little run down.

RANK. Ah, is that all? Then I take it you've come to town to cure yourself by a round of parties?

MRS. LINDE. I have come here to find work.

RANK. Is that an approved remedy for being run down?

MRS. LINDE. One has to live, Doctor.

RANK. Yes, people do seem to regard it as a necessity.

NORA. Oh, really, Dr. Rank. I bet you want to stay alive.

RANK. You bet I do. However miserable I sometimes feel, I still want to go on being tortured for as long as possible. It's the same with all my patients; and with people who are morally sick, too. There's a moral cripple in with Helmer at this very moment—

MRS. LINDE *[softly]*. Oh!

NORA. Whom do you mean?

RANK. Oh, a lawyer fellow called Krogstad—you wouldn't know him. He's crippled all right; morally twisted. But even he started off by announcing, as though it were a matter of enormous importance, that he had to live.

NORA. Oh? What did he want to talk to Torvald about?

RANK. I haven't the faintest idea. All I heard was something about the bank.

NORA. I didn't know that Krog—that this man Krogstad had any connection with the bank.

RANK. Yes, he's got some kind of job down there. *[To* MRS. LINDE.*]* I wonder if in your part of the world you too have a species of human being that spends its time fussing around trying to smell out moral corruption? And when they find a case they give him some nice, comfortable position so that they can keep a good watch on him. The healthy ones just have to lump it.

MRS. LINDE. But surely it's the sick who need care most?

RANK *[shrugs his shoulders]*. Well, there we have it. It's that attitude that's turning human society into a hospital.

NORA, *lost in her own thoughts, laughs half to herself and claps her hands.*

RANK. Why are you laughing? Do you really know what society is?

NORA. What do I care about society? I think it's a bore. I was laughing at something else—something frightfully funny. Tell me, Dr. Rank—will everyone who works at the bank come under Torvald now?

RANK. Do you find that particularly funny?

NORA *[smiles and hums]*. Never you mind! Never you mind! *[Walks around the room.]* Yes, I find it very amusing to think that we—I mean, Torvald—has obtained so much influence over so many people. *[Takes the paper bag from her pocket.]* Dr. Rank, would you like a small macaroon?

RANK. Macaroons! I say! I thought they were forbidden here.

NORA. Yes, well, these are some Christine gave me.

MRS. LINDE. What? I—?

NORA. All right, all right, don't get frightened. You weren't to know Torvald had forbidden them. He's afraid they'll ruin my teeth. But, dash it—for once—! Don't you agree, Dr. Rank? Here! *[Pops a macaroon into his mouth.]* You too, Christine. And I'll have one too. Just a little one. Two at the most. *[Begins to walk round again.]* Yes, now I feel really, really happy. Now there's just one thing in the world I'd really love to do.

RANK. Oh? And what is that?

NORA. Just something I'd love to say to Torvald.

RANK. Well, why don't you say it?

NORA. No, I daren't. It's too dreadful.

MRS. LINDE. Dreadful?

RANK. Well, then, you'd better not. But you can say it to us. What is it you'd so love to say to Torvald?

NORA. I've the most extraordinary longing to say: "Bloody hell!"

RANK. Are you mad?

MRS. LINDE. My dear Nora—!

RANK. Say it. Here he is.

NORA *[hiding the bag of macaroons].* Ssh! Ssh!

HELMER, *with his overcoat on his arm and his hat in his hand, enters from his study.*

NORA *[goes to meet him].* Well, Torvald dear, did you get rid of him?

HELMER. Yes, he's just gone.

NORA. May I introduce you—? This is Christine. She's just arrived in town.

HELMER. Christine—? Forgive me, but I don't think—

NORA. Mrs. Linde, Torvald dear. Christine Linde.

HELMER. Ah. A childhood friend of my wife's, I presume?

MRS. LINDE. Yes, we knew each other in earlier days.

NORA. And imagine, now she's traveled all this way to talk to you.

HELMER. Oh?

MRS. LINDE. Well, I didn't really—

NORA. You see, Christine's frightfully good at office work, and she's mad to come under some really clever man who can teach her even more than she knows already—

HELMER. Very sensible, madam.

NORA. So when she heard you'd become head of the bank—it was in her local paper—she came here as quickly as she could and—Torvald, you will, won't you? Do a little something to help Christine? For my sake?

HELMER. Well, that shouldn't be impossible. You are a widow, I take it, Mrs. Linde?

MRS. LINDE. Yes.

HELMER. And you have experience of office work?

MRS. LINDE. Yes, quite a bit.

HELMER. Well then, it's quite likely I may be able to find some job for you—

NORA *[claps her hands].* You see, you see!

HELMER. You've come at a lucky moment, Mrs. Linde.

MRS. LINDE. Oh, how can I ever thank you—?

HELMER. There's absolutely no need. *[Puts on his overcoat.]* But now I'm afraid I must ask you to excuse me—

RANK. Wait. I'll come with you.

He gets his fur coat from the hall and warms it at the stove.

NORA. Don't be long, Torvald dear.

HELMER. I'll only be an hour.

NORA. Are you going too, Christine?

MRS. LINDE *[puts on her outdoor clothes].* Yes, I must start to look round for a room.

HELMER. Then perhaps we can walk part of the way together.

NORA *[helps her].* It's such a nuisance we're so cramped here—I'm afraid we can't offer to—

MRS. LINDE. Oh, I wouldn't dream of it. Goodbye, Nora dear, and thanks for everything.

NORA. *Au revoir.* You'll be coming back this evening, of course. And, you too, Dr. Rank. What? If you're well enough? Of course you'll be well enough. Wrap up warmly, though.

They go out, talking, into the hall. Children's voices are heard from the stairs.

NORA. Here they are! Here they are!

She runs out and opens the door. ANNE-MARIE, *the nurse, enters with the children.*

NORA. Come in, come in! *[Stoops down and kisses them.]* Oh, my sweet darlings—! Look at them, Christine! Aren't they beautiful?

RANK. Don't stand here chattering in this draught!

HELMER. Come, Mrs. Linde. This is for mothers only.

DR. RANK, HELMER, *and* MRS. LINDE *go down the stairs. The* NURSE *brings the children into the room.* NORA *follows, and closes the door to the hall.*

NORA. How well you look! What red cheeks you've got! Like apples and roses! *[The children answer her inaudibly as she talks to them.]* Have you had fun? That's splendid. You gave Emmy and Bob a ride on the sledge? What, both together? I say! What a clever boy you are, Ivar! Oh, let me hold her for a moment, Anne-Marie! My sweet little baby doll! *[Takes the smallest child from the nurse and dances with her.]* Yes, yes, Mummy will dance with Bob too. What? Have you been throwing snowballs? Oh, I wish I'd been there! No, don't—I'll undress them myself, Anne-Marie. No, please let me; it's such fun. Go inside and warm yourself; you look frozen. There's some hot coffee on the stove. *[The nurse goes into the room on the left.* NORA *takes off the children's outdoor clothes and throws them anywhere while they all chatter simultaneously.]* What? A big dog ran after you? But he didn't bite you? No, dogs don't bite lovely little baby dolls. Leave those parcels alone, Ivar. What's in them? Ah, wouldn't you like to know! No, no; it's nothing nice. Come on, let's play a game. What shall we play? Hide and seek. Yes, let's play hide and seek. Bob shall hide first. You want me to? All right, let me hide first.

NORA *and the children play around the room, and in the adjacent room to the left, laughing and shouting. At length* NORA *hides under the table. The children rush in, look, but cannot find her. Then they hear her half-stifled laughter, run to the table, lift up the cloth, and see her. Great excitement. She crawls out as though to frighten them. Further excitement. Meanwhile, there has been a knock on the door leading from the hall, but no one has noticed it. Now the door is half-opened and* KROGSTAD *enters. He waits for a moment; the game continues.*

KROGSTAD. Excuse me, Mrs. Helmer—

NORA *[turns with a stifled cry and half jumps up].* Oh! What do you want?

KROGSTAD. I beg your pardon; the front door was ajar. Someone must have forgotten to close it.

NORA *[gets up]*. My husband is not at home, Mr. Krogstad.

KROGSTAD. I know.

NORA. Well, what do want here, then?

KROGSTAD. A word with you.

NORA. With—? *[To the children, quietly.]* Go inside to Anne-Marie. What? No, the strange gentleman won't do anything to hurt Mummy. When he's gone we'll start playing again.

She takes the children into the room on the left and closes the door behind them.

NORA *[uneasy, tense]*. You want to speak to me?

KROGSTAD. Yes.

NORA. Today? But it's not the first of the month yet.

KROGSTAD. No, it is Christmas Eve. Whether or not you have a merry Christmas depends on you.

NORA. What do you want? I can't give you anything today—

KROGSTAD. We won't talk about that for the present. There's something else. You have a moment to spare?

NORA. Oh, yes. Yes, I suppose so; though—

KROGSTAD. Good. I was sitting in the café down below and I saw your husband cross the street—

NORA. Yes.

KROGSTAD. With a lady.

NORA. Well?

KROGSTAD. Might I be so bold as to ask: was not that lady a Mrs. Linde?

NORA. Yes.

KROGSTAD. Recently arrived in town?

NORA. Yes, today.

KROGSTAD. She is a good friend of yours, is she not?

NORA. Yes, she is. But I don't see—

KROGSTAD. I used to know her too once.

NORA. I know.

KROGSTAD. Oh? You've discovered that. Yes, I thought you would. Well then, may I ask you a straight question: is Mrs. Linde to be employed at the bank?

NORA. How dare you presume to cross-examine me, Mr. Krogstad? You, one of my husband's employees? But since you ask, you shall have an answer. Yes, Mrs. Linde is to be employed by the bank. And I arranged it, Mr. Krogstad. Now you know.

KROGSTAD. I guessed right, then.

NORA *[walks up and down the room]*. Oh, one has a little influence, you know. Just because one's a woman it doesn't necessarily mean that— When one is in a humble position, Mr. Krogstad, one should think twice before offending someone who—hm—

KROGSTAD. —who has influence?

NORA. Precisely.

KROGSTAD *[changes his tone]*. Mrs. Helmer, will you have the kindness to use your influence on my behalf?

NORA. What? What do you mean?

KROGSTAD. Will you be so good as to see that I keep my humble position at the bank?

NORA. What do you mean? Who is thinking of removing you from your position?

KROGSTAD. Oh, you don't need to play innocent with me. I realize it can't be very pleasant for your friend to risk bumping into me; and now I also realize whom I have to thank for being hounded out like this.

NORA. But I assure you—

KROGSTAD. Look, let's not beat about the bush. There's still time, and I'd advise you to use your influence to stop it.

NORA. But, Mr. Krogstad, I have no influence—

KROGSTAD. Oh? I thought you just said—

NORA. But I didn't mean it like that! I? How on earth could you imagine that I would have any influence over my husband?

KROGSTAD. Oh, I've known your husband since we were students together. I imagine he has his weaknesses like other married men.

NORA. If you speak impertinently of my husband, I shall show you the door.

KROGSTAD. You're a bold woman, Mrs. Helmer.

NORA. I'm not afraid of you any longer. Once the New Year is in, I'll soon be rid of you.

KROGSTAD [more controlled]. Now listen to me, Mrs. Helmer. If I'm forced to, I shall fight for my little job at the bank as I would fight for my life.

NORA. So it sounds.

KROGSTAD. It isn't just the money; that's the last thing I care about. There's something else—well, you might as well know. It's like this, you see. You know of course, as every one else does, that some years ago I committed an indiscretion.

NORA. I think I did hear something—

KROGSTAD. It never came into court; but from that day, every opening was barred to me. So I turned my hand to the kind of business you know about. I had to do something; and I don't think I was one of the worst. But now I want to give up all that. My sons are growing up; for their sake, I must try to regain what respectability I can. This job in the bank was the first step on the ladder. And now your husband wants to kick me off that ladder back into the dirt.

NORA. But my dear Mr. Krogstad, it simply isn't in my power to help you.

KROGSTAD. You say that because you don't want to help me. But I have the means to make you.

NORA. You don't mean you'd tell my husband that I owe you money?

KROGSTAD. And if I did?

NORA. That'd be a filthy trick! [Almost in tears.] This secret that is my pride and my joy—that he should hear about it in such a filthy, beastly way— hear about it from you! It'd involve me in the most dreadful unpleasantness—

KROGSTAD. Only—unpleasantness?

NORA [vehemently]. All right, do it! You'll be the one who'll suffer. It'll show my husband the kind of man you are, and then you'll never keep your job.

KROGSTAD. I asked you whether it was merely domestic unpleasantness you were afraid of.

NORA. If my husband hears about it, he will of course immediately pay you whatever is owing. And then we shall have nothing more to do with you.

KROGSTAD *[takes a step closer]*. Listen, Mrs. Helmer. Either you've a bad memory or else you know very little about financial transactions. I had better enlighten you.

NORA. What do you mean?

KROGSTAD. When your husband was ill, you came to me to borrow two hundred and fifty pounds.

NORA. I didn't know anyone else.

KROGSTAD. I promised to find that sum for you—

NORA. And you did find it.

KROGSTAD. I promised to find that sum for you on certain conditions. You were so worried about your husband's illness and so keen to get the money to take him abroad that I don't think you bothered much about the details. So it won't be out of place if I refresh your memory. Well— I promised to get you the money in exchange for an I.O.U., which I drew up.

NORA. Yes, and which I signed.

KROGSTAD. Exactly. But then I added a few lines naming your father as security for the debt. This paragraph was to be signed by your father.

NORA. Was to be? He did sign it.

KROGSTAD. I left the date blank for your father to fill in when he signed this paper. You remember, Mrs. Helmer?

NORA. Yes, I think so—

KROGSTAD. Then I gave you back this I.O.U. for you to post to your father. Is that not correct?

NORA. Yes.

KROGSTAD. And of course you posted it at once; for within five or six days you brought it along to me with your father's signature on it. Whereupon I handed you the money.

NORA. Yes, well. Haven't I repaid the installments as agreed?

KROGSTAD. Mm—yes, more or less. But to return to what we were speaking about—that was a difficult time for you just then, wasn't it, Mrs. Helmer?

NORA. Yes, it was.

KROGSTAD. And your father was very ill, if I am not mistaken.

NORA. He was dying.

KROGSTAD. He did in fact die shortly afterwards?

NORA. Yes.

KROGSTAD. Tell me, Mrs. Helmer, do you by any chance remember the date of your father's death? The day of the month, I mean.

NORA. Papa died on the twenty-ninth of September.

KROGSTAD. Quite correct; I took the trouble to confirm it. And that leaves me with a curious little problem—*[Takes out a paper.]*—which I simply cannot solve.

NORA. Problem? I don't see—

KROGSTAD. The problem, Mrs. Helmer, is that your father signed this paper three days after his death.

NORA. What? I don't understand—

KROGSTAD. Your father died on the twenty-ninth of September. But look at this. Here your father has dated his signature the second of October. Isn't that a curious little problem, Mrs. Helmer? *[NORA is silent.]* Can you suggest any explanation? *[She remains silent.]* And there's another curious thing. The words "second of October" and the year are written in a hand which is not your father's, but which I seem to know. Well, there's a simple explanation to that. Your father could have forgotten to write in the date when he signed, and someone else could have added it before the news came of his death. There's nothing criminal about that. It's the signature itself I'm wondering about. It is genuine, I suppose, Mrs. Helmer? It was your father who wrote his name here?

NORA *[after a short silence, throws back her head and looks defiantly at him].* No, it was not. It was I who wrote Papa's name there.

KROGSTAD. Look, Mrs. Helmer, do you realize this is a dangerous admission?

NORA. Why? You'll get your money.

KROGSTAD. May I ask you a question? Why didn't you send this paper to your father?

NORA. I couldn't. Papa was very ill. If I'd asked him to sign this, I'd have had to tell him what the money was for. But I couldn't have told him in his condition that my husband's life was in danger. I couldn't have done that!

KROGSTAD. Then you would have been wiser to have given up your idea of a holiday.

NORA. But I couldn't! It was to save my husband's life. I couldn't put it off.

KROGSTAD. But didn't it occur to you that you were being dishonest towards me?

NORA. I couldn't bother about that. I didn't care about you. I hated you because of all the beastly difficulties you'd put in my way when you knew how dangerously ill my husband was.

KROGSTAD. Mrs. Helmer, you evidently don't appreciate exactly what you have done. But I can assure you that it is no bigger nor worse a crime than the one I once committed, and thereby ruined my whole social position.

NORA. You? Do you expect me to believe that you would have taken a risk like that to save your wife's life?

KROGSTAD. The law does not concern itself with motives.

NORA. Then the law must be very stupid.

KROGSTAD. Stupid or not, if I show this paper to the police, you will be judged according to it.

NORA. I don't believe that. Hasn't a daughter the right to shield her father from worry and anxiety when he's old and dying? Hasn't a wife the right to save her husband's life? I don't know much about the law but there must be something somewhere that says that such things are allowed. You ought to know about that, you're meant to be a lawyer, aren't you? You can't be a very good lawyer, Mr. Krogstad.

KROGSTAD. Possibly not. But business, the kind of business we two have been transacting—I think you'll admit I understand something about that? Good. Do as you please. But I tell you this. If I get thrown into the gutter for a second time, I shall take you with me.

He bows and goes out through the hall.

NORA [*stands for a moment in thought, then tosses her head*]. What non-sense! He's trying to frighten me! I'm not that stupid. [*Busies herself gathering together the children's clothes; then she suddenly stops.*] But—? No, it's impossible. I did it for love, didn't I?

CHILDREN [*in the doorway, left*]. Mummy, the strange gentleman's gone out into the street.

NORA. Yes, yes, I know. But don't talk to anyone about the strange gentle-man. You hear? Not even to Daddy.

CHILDREN. No, Mummy. Will you play with us again now?

NORA. No, no. Not now.

CHILDREN. Oh but, Mummy, you promised!

NORA. I know, but I can't just now. Go back to the nursery. I've a lot to do. Go away, my darlings, go away. [*She pushes them gently into the other room and closes the door behind them. She sits on the sofa, takes up her embroidery, stitches for a few moments, but soon stops.*] No! [*Throws the embroidery aside, gets up, goes to the door leading to the hall, and calls.*] Helen! Bring in the Christmas tree! [*She goes to the table on the left and opens the drawer in it; then pauses again.*] No, but it's utterly impossible!

MAID [*enters with the tree*]. Where shall I put it, madam?

NORA. There, in the middle of the room.

MAID. Will you be wanting anything else?

NORA. No, thank you, I have everything I need.

The MAID *puts down the tree and goes out.*

NORA [*busy decorating the tree*]. Now—candles here—and flowers here. That loathsome man! Nonsense, nonsense, there's nothing to be fright-ened about. The Christmas tree must be beautiful. I'll do everything that you like. Torvald. I'll sing for you, dance for you—

HELMER, *with a bundle of papers under his arm, enters.*

NORA. Oh—are you back already?

HELMER. Yes. Has anyone been here?

NORA. Here? No.

HELMER. That's strange. I saw Krogstad come out of the front door.

NORA. Did you? Oh yes, that's quite right—Krogstad was here for a few min-utes.

HELMER. Nora, I can tell from your face, he's been here and asked you to put in a good word for him.

NORA. Yes.

HELMER. And you were to pretend you were doing it of your own accord? You weren't going to tell me he'd been here? He asked you to do that too, didn't he?

NORA. Yes, Torvald. But—

HELMER. Nora, Nora! And you were ready to enter into such a conspiracy? Talking to a man like that, and making him promises—and then, on top of it all, to tell me an untruth!

NORA. An untruth?

HELMER. Didn't you say no one had been here? [*Wags his finger.*] My little songbird must never do that again. A songbird must have a clean beak to sing with; otherwise she'll start twittering out of tune. [*Puts his arm round her waist.*] Isn't that the way we want things? Yes, of course it is. [*Lets go of her.*] So let's hear no more about that. [*Sits down in front of the stove.]* Ah, how cozy and peaceful it is here. *[Glances for a few moments at his papers.]*

NORA *[busy with the tree; after a short silence]*. Torvald.

HELMER. Yes.

NORA. I'm terribly looking forward to that fancy dress ball at the Stenborgs on Boxing Day.

HELMER. And I'm terribly curious to see what you're going to surprise me with.

NORA. Oh, it's so maddening.

HELMER. What is?

NORA. I can't think of anything to wear. It all seems so stupid and meaningless.

HELMER. So my little Nora's come to that conclusion, has she?

NORA *[behind his chair, resting her arms on its back]*. Are you very busy, Torvald?

HELMER. Oh—

NORA. What are those papers?

HELMER. Just something to do with the bank.

NORA. Already?

HELMER. I persuaded the trustees to give me authority to make certain immediate changes in the staff and organization. I want to have everything straight by the New Year.

NORA. Then that's why this poor man Krogstad—

HELMER. Hm.

NORA *[still leaning over his chair, slowly strokes the back of his head]*. If you hadn't been so busy, I was going to ask you an enormous favor, Torvald.

HELMER. Well, tell me. What was it to be?

NORA. You know I trust your taste more than anyone's. I'm so anxious to look really beautiful at the fancy dress ball. Torvald, couldn't you help me to decide what I shall go as, and what kind of costume I ought to wear?

HELMER. Aha! So little Miss Independent's in trouble and needs a man to rescue her, does she?

NORA. Yes, Torvald. I can't get anywhere without your help.

HELMER. Well, well, I'll give the matter thought. We'll find something.

NORA. Oh, how kind of you! *[Goes back to the tree. Pause.]* How pretty these red flowers look! But, tell me, is it so dreadful, this thing that Krogstad's done?

HELMER. He forged someone else's name. Have you any idea what that means?

NORA. Mightn't he have been forced to do it by some emergency?

HELMER. He probably just didn't think—that's what usually happens. I'm not so heartless as to condemn a man for an isolated action.

NORA. No, Torvald, of course not!

HELMER. Men often succeed in re-establishing themselves if they admit their crime and take their punishment.

NORA. Punishment?

HELMER. But Krogstad didn't do that. He chose to try and trick his way out of it; and that's what has morally destroyed him.

NORA. You think that would—?

HELMER. Just think how a man with that load on his conscience must always be lying and cheating and dissembling; how he must wear a mask even in the presence of those who are dearest to him, even his own wife and children! Yes, the children. That's the worst danger, Nora.

NORA. Why?

HELMER. Because an atmosphere of lies contaminates and poisons every corner of the home. Every breath that the children draw in such a house contains the germs of evil.

NORA *[comes closer behind him]*. Do you really believe that?

HELMER. Oh, my dear, I've come across it so often in my work at the bar. Nearly all young criminals are the children of mothers who are constitutional liars.

NORA. Why do you say mothers?

HELMER. It's usually the mother; though of course the father can have the same influence. Every lawyer knows that only too well. And yet this fellow Krogstad has been sitting at home all these years poisoning his children with his lies and pretenses. That's why I say that, morally speaking, he is dead. *[Stretches out his hands towards her.]* So my pretty little Nora must promise me not to plead his case. Your hand on it. Come, come, what's this? Give me your hand. There. That's settled, now. I assure you it'd be quite impossible for me to work in the same building as him. I literally feel physically ill in the presence of a man like that.

NORA *[draws her hand from his and goes over to the other side of the Christmas tree]*. How hot it is in here! And I've so much to do.

HELMER *[gets up and gathers his papers]*. Yes, and I must try to get some of this read before dinner. I'll think about your costume too. And I may even have something up my sleeve to hang in gold paper on the Christmas tree. *[Lays his hand on her head.]* My precious little songbird!
He goes into his study and closes the door.

NORA *[softly, after a pause]*. It's nonsense. It must be. It's impossible. It *must* be impossible!

NURSE *[in the doorway, left]*. The children are asking if they can come in to Mummy.

NORA. No, no, no; don't let them in! You stay with them, Anne-Marie.

NURSE. Very good, madam. *[Closes the door.]*

NORA *[pale with fear]*. Corrupt my little children—! Poison my home! *[Short pause. She throws back her head.]* It isn't true! It *couldn't* be true!

Act 2

The same room. In the corner by the piano the Christmas tree stands, stripped and disheveled, its candles burned to their sockets. NORA's outdoor clothes lie on the sofa. She is alone in the room, walking restlessly to and fro. At length she stops by the sofa and picks up her coat.

NORA *[drops the coat again]*. There's someone coming! *[Goes to the door and listens.]* No, it's no one. Of course—no one'll come today, it's Christmas Day. Nor tomorrow. But perhaps—! *[Opens the door and looks out.]* No. Nothing in the letter-box. Quite empty. *[Walks across the room.]* Silly, silly. Of course he won't do anything. It couldn't happen. It isn't possible. Why, I've three small children.

The NURSE, *carrying a large cardboard box, enters from the room on the left.*

NURSE. I found those fancy dress clothes at last, madam.

NORA. Thank you. Put them on the table.

NURSE *[does so]*. They're all rumpled up.

NORA. Oh, I wish I could tear them into a million pieces!

NURSE. Why, madam! They'll be all right. Just a little patience.

NORA. Yes, of course. I'll go and get Mrs. Linde to help me.

NURSE. What, out again? In this dreadful weather? You'll catch a chill, madam.

NORA. Well, that wouldn't be the worst. How are the children?

NURSE. Playing with their Christmas presents, poor little dears. But—

NORA. Are they still asking to see me?

NURSE. They're so used to having their Mummy with them.

NORA. Yes, but, Anne-Marie, from now on I shan't be able to spend so much time with them.

NURSE. Well, children get used to anything in time.

NORA. Do you think so? Do you think they'd forget their mother if she went away from them—for ever?

NURSE. Mercy's sake, madam! For ever!

NORA. Tell me, Anne-Marie—I've so often wondered. How could you bear to give your child away—to strangers?

NURSE. But I had to when I came to nurse my little Miss Nora.

NORA. Do you mean you wanted to?

NURSE. When I had the chance of such a good job? A poor girl what's got into trouble can't afford to pick and choose. That good-for-nothing didn't lift a finger.

NORA. But your daughter must have completely forgotten you.

NURSE. Oh no, indeed she hasn't. She's written to me twice, once when she got confirmed and then again when she got married.

NORA *[hugs her]*. Dear old Anne-Marie, you were a good mother to me.

NURSE. Poor little Miss Nora, you never had any mother but me.

NORA. And if my little ones had no one else, I know you would—no, silly, silly, silly! *[Opens the cardboard box.]* Go back to them, Anne-Marie. Now I must—Tomorrow you'll see how pretty I shall look.

NURSE. Why, there'll be no one at the ball as beautiful as my Miss Nora.

She goes into the room, left.

NORA *[begins to unpack the clothes from the box, but soon throws them down again]*. Oh, if only I dared to go out! If I could be sure no one would come, and nothing would happen while I was away! Stupid, stupid! No one will come. I just mustn't think about it. Brush this muff. Pretty gloves, pretty gloves! Don't think about it, don't think about it! One, two, three, four, five, six—*[Cries.]* Ah—they're coming—!

She begins to run toward the door, but stops uncertainly. MRS. LINDE *enters from the hall, where she has been taking off her outdoor clothes.*

NORA. Oh, it's you, Christine. There's no one else out there, is there? Oh, I'm so glad you've come.

MRS. LINDE. I hear you were at my room asking for me.

NORA. Yes, I just happened to be passing. I want to ask you to help me with something. Let's sit down here on the sofa. Look at this. There's going to be a fancy dress ball tomorrow night upstairs at Consul Stenborg's, and Torvald wants me to go as a Neapolitan fisher-girl and dance the tarantella. I learned it on Capri.

MRS. LINDE. I say, are you going to give a performance?

NORA. Yes, Torvald says I should. Look, here's the dress. Torvald had it made for me in Italy; but now it's all so torn, I don't know—

MRS. LINDE. Oh, we'll soon put that right; the stitching's just come away. Needle and thread? Ah, here we are.

NORA. You're being awfully sweet.

MRS. LINDE *[sews]*. So you're going to dress up tomorrow, Nora? I must pop over for a moment to see how you look. Oh, but I've completely forgotten to thank you for that nice evening yesterday.

NORA *[gets up and walks across the room]*. Oh, I didn't think it was as nice as usual. You ought to have come to town a little earlier, Christine. . . . Yes, Torvald understands how to make a home look attractive.

MRS. LINDE. I'm sure you do, too. You're not your father's daughter for nothing. But, tell me. Is Dr. Rank always in such low spirits as he was yesterday?

NORA. No, last night it was very noticeable. But he's got a terrible disease; he's got spinal tuberculosis, poor man. His father was a frightful creature who kept mistresses and so on. As a result Dr. Rank has been sickly ever since he was a child—you understand—

MRS. LINDE *[puts down her sewing]*. But, my dear Nora, how on earth did you get to know about such things?

NORA *[walks about the room]*. Oh, don't be silly, Christine—when one has three children, one comes into contact with women who—well, who know about medical matters, and they tell one a thing or two.

MRS. LINDE *[sews again; a short silence]*. Does Dr. Rank visit you every day?

NORA. Yes, every day. He's Torvald's oldest friend, and a good friend to me too. Dr. Rank's almost one of the family.

MRS. LINDE. But, tell me—is he quite sincere? I mean, doesn't he rather say the sort of thing he thinks people want to hear?

NORA. No, quite the contrary. What gave you that idea?

MRS. LINDE. When you introduced me to him yesterday, he said he'd often heard my name mentioned here. But later I noticed your husband had no idea who I was. So how could Dr. Rank—?

NORA. Yes, that's quite right, Christine. You see, Torvald's so hopelessly in love with me that he wants to have me all to himself—those were his very words. When we were first married, he got quite jealous if I as much as mentioned any of my old friends back home. So naturally, I stopped talking about them. But I often chat with Dr. Rank about that kind of thing. He enjoys it, you see.

MRS. LINDE. Now listen, Nora. In many ways you're still a child; I'm a bit older than you and have a little more experience of the world. There's something I want to say to you. You ought to give up this business with Dr. Rank.

NORA. What business?

MRS. LINDE. Well, everything. Last night you were speaking about this rich admirer of yours who was going to give you money—

NORA. Yes, and who doesn't exist—unfortunately. But what's that got to do with—?

MRS. LINDE. Is Dr. Rank rich?

NORA. Yes.

MRS. LINDE. And he has no dependents?

NORA. No, no one. But—

MRS. LINDE. And he comes here to see you every day?

NORA. Yes, I've told you.

MRS. LINDE. But how dare a man of his education be so forward?

NORA. NORA. What on earth are you talking about?

MRS. LINDE. Oh, stop pretending, Nora. Do you think I haven't guessed who it was who lent you that two hundred pounds?

NORA. Are you out of your mind? How could you imagine such a thing? A friend, someone who comes here every day! Why, that'd be an impossible situation!

MRS. LINDE. Then it really wasn't him?

NORA. No, of course not. I've never for a moment dreamed of—anyway, he hadn't any money to lend then. He didn't come into that till later.

MRS. LINDE. Well, I think that was a lucky thing for you, Nora dear.

NORA. No, I could never have dreamed of asking Dr. Rank—Though I'm sure that if I ever did ask him—

MRS. LINDE. But of course you won't.

NORA. Of course not. I can't imagine that it should ever become necessary. But I'm perfectly sure that if I did speak to Dr. Rank—

MRS. LINDE. Behind your husband's back?

NORA. I've got to get out of this other business; and *that's* been going on behind his back. I've *got* to get out of it.

MRS. LINDE. Yes, well, that's what I told you yesterday. But—

NORA *[walking up and down]*. It's much easier for a man to arrange these things than a woman—

MRS. LINDE. One's own husband, yes.

NORA. Oh, bosh. *[Stops walking.]* When you've completely repaid a debt, you get your I.O.U. back, don't you?

MRS. LINDE. Yes, of course.

NORA. And you can tear it into a thousand pieces and burn the filthy, beastly thing!

MRS. LINDE *[looks hard at her, puts down her sewing, and gets up slowly]*. Nora, you're hiding something from me.

NORA. Can you see that?

MRS. LINDE. Something has happened since yesterday morning. Nora, what is it?

NORA *[goes toward her]*. Christine! *[Listens.]* Ssh! There's Torvald. Would you mind going into the nursery for a few minutes? Torvald can't bear to see sewing around. Anne-Marie'll help you.

MRS. LINDE *[gathers some of her things together]*. Very well. But I shan't leave this house until we've talked this matter out.

She goes into the nursery, left. As she does so, HELMER *enters from the hall.*

NORA *[runs to meet him]*. Oh, Torvald dear, I've been so longing for you to come back!

HELMER. Was that the dressmaker?

NORA. No, it was Christine. She's helping me mend my costume. I'm going to look rather splendid in that.

HELMER. Yes, that was quite a bright idea of mine, wasn't it?

NORA. Wonderful! But wasn't it nice of me to give in to you?

HELMER [takes her chin in his hand]. Nice—to give in to your husband? All right, little silly, I know you didn't mean it like that. But I won't disturb you. I expect you'll be wanting to try it on.

NORA. Are you going to work now?

HELMER. Yes. [Shows her a bundle of papers.] Look at these. I've been down to the bank—[Turns to go into his study.]

NORA. Torvald.

HELMER [stops]. Yes.

NORA. If little squirrel asked you really prettily to grant her a wish—

HELMER. Well?

NORA. Would you grant it to her?

HELMER. First I should naturally have to know what it was.

NORA. Squirrel would do lots of pretty tricks for you if you granted her wish.

HELMER. Out with it, then.

NORA. Your little skylark would sing in every room—

HELMER. My little skylark does that already.

NORA. I'd turn myself into a little fairy and dance for you in the moonlight, Torvald.

HELMER. Nora, it isn't that business you were talking about this morning?

NORA [comes closer]. Yes, Torvald—oh, please! I beg of you!

HELMER. Have you really the nerve to bring that up again?

NORA. Yes, Torvald, yes, you must do as I ask! You must let Krogstad keep his place at the bank!

HELMER. My dear Nora, his is the job I'm giving to Mrs. Linde.

NORA. Yes, that's terribly sweet of you. But you can get rid of one of the other clerks instead of Krogstad.

HELMER. Really, you're being incredibly obstinate. Just because you thoughtlessly promised to put in a word for him, you expect me to—

NORA. No, it isn't that, Helmer. It's for your own sake. That man writes for the most beastly newspapers—you said so yourself. He could do you tremendous harm. I'm so dreadfully frightened of him—

HELMER. Oh, I understand. Memories of the past. That's what's frightening you.

NORA. What do you mean?

HELMER. You're thinking of your father, aren't you?

NORA. Yes, yes. Of course. Just think what those dreadful men wrote in the papers about Papa! The most frightful slanders. I really believe it would have lost him his job if the Ministry hadn't sent you down to investigate, and you hadn't been so kind and helpful to him.

HELMER. But my dear little Nora, there's a considerable difference between your father and me. Your father was not a man of unassailable reputation. But I am; and I hope to remain so all my life.

NORA. But no one knows what spiteful people may not dig up. We could be so peaceful and happy now, Torvald—we could be free from every worry—you and I and the children. Oh, please, Torvald, please—!

HELMER. The very fact of your pleading his cause makes it impossible for me to keep him. Everyone at the bank already knows that I intend to dismiss Krogstad. If the rumor got about that the new manager had allowed his wife to persuade him to change his mind—

NORA. Well, what then?

HELMER. Oh, nothing, nothing. As long as my little Miss Obstinate gets her way—Do you expect me to make a laughing-stock of myself before my entire staff—give people the idea that I am open to outside influence? Believe me, I'd soon feel the consequences! Besides—there's something else that makes it impossible for Krogstad to remain in the bank while I am its manager.

NORA. What is that?

HELMER. I might conceivably have allowed myself to ignore his moral obloquies—

NORA. Yes, Torvald, surely?

HELMER. And I hear he's quite efficient at his job. But we—well, we were school friends. It was one of those friendships that one enters into over hastily and so often comes to regret later in life. I might as well confess the truth. We—well, we're on Christian name terms. And the tactless idiot makes no attempt to conceal it when other people are present. On the contrary, he thinks it gives him the right to be familiar with me. He shows off the whole time, with "Torvald this," and "Torvald that." I can tell you, I find it damned annoying. If he stayed, he'd make my position intolerable.

NORA. Torvald, you can't mean this seriously.

HELMER. Oh? And why not?

NORA. But it's so petty.

HELMER. What did you say? Petty? You think *I* am petty?

NORA. No, Torvald dear, of course you're not. That's just why—

HELMER. Don't quibble! You call my motives petty. Then I must be petty too. Petty! I see. Well, I've had enough of this. *[Goes to the door and calls into the hall.]* Helen!

NORA. What are you going to do?

HELMER *[searching among his papers]*. I'm going to settle this matter once and for all. *[The* MAID *enters.]* Take this letter downstairs at once. Find a messenger and see that he delivers it. Immediately! The address is on the envelope. Here's the money.

MAID. Very good, sir. *[Goes out with the letter.]*

HELMER *[putting his papers in order]*. There now, little Miss Obstinate.

NORA *[tensely]*. Torvald—what was in that letter?

HELMER. Krogstad's dismissal.

NORA. Call her back, Torvald! There's still time. Oh, Torvald, call her back! Do it for my sake—for your own sake—for the children! Do you hear me, Torvald? Please do it! You don't realize what this may do to us all!

HELMER. Too late.

NORA. Yes. Too late.

HELMER. My dear Nora, I forgive you this anxiety. Though it is a bit of an insult to me. Oh, but it is! Isn't it an insult to imply that I should be frightened by the vindictiveness of a depraved hack journalist? But I forgive you, because it so charmingly testifies to the love you bear me. *[Takes her in his arms.]* Which is as it should be, my own dearest Nora. Let what will happen, happen. When the real crisis comes, you will not find me lacking in strength or courage. I am man enough to bear the burden for us both.

NORA *[fearfully]*. What do you mean?

HELMER. The whole burden, I say—

NORA *[calmly]*. I shall never let you do that.

HELMER. Very well. We shall share it, Nora—as man and wife. And that is as it should be. *[Caresses her.]* Are you happy now? There, there, there; don't look at me with those frightened little eyes. You're simply imagining things. You go ahead now and do your tarantella, and get some practice on that tambourine. I'll sit in my study and close the door. Then I won't hear anything, and you can make all the noise you want. *[Turns in the doorway.]* When Dr. Rank comes, tell him where to find me. *[He nods to her, goes into his room with his papers, and closes the door.]*

NORA *[desperate with anxiety, stands as though transfixed, and whispers]*. He said he'd do it. He will do it. He will do it, and nothing'll stop him. No, never that. I'd rather anything. There must be some escape—Some way out—! *[The bell rings in the hall.]* Dr. Rank—! Anything but that! Anything, I don't care—!

She passes her hand across her face, composes herself, walks across, and opens the door to the hall. DR. RANK *is standing there, hanging up his fur coat. During the following scene, it begins to grow dark.*

NORA. Good evening, Dr. Rank. I recognized your ring. But you mustn't go to Torvald yet. I think he's busy.

RANK. And—you?

NORA *[as he enters the room and she closes the door behind him]*. Oh, you know very well I've always time to talk to you.

RANK. Thank you. I shall avail myself of that privilege as long as I can.

NORA. What do you mean by that? As long as you *can?*

RANK. Yes. Does that frighten you?

NORA. Well, it's rather a curious expression. Is something going to happen?

RANK. Something I've been expecting to happen for a long time. But I didn't think it would happen quite so soon.

NORA *[seizes his arm]*. What is it? Dr. Rank, you must tell me!

RANK *[sits down by the stove]*. I'm on the way out. And there's nothing to be done about it.

NORA *[sighs with relief]*. Oh, it's you—?

RANK. Who else? No, it's no good lying to oneself. I am the most wretched of all my patients, Mrs. Helmer. These last few days I've been going through the books of this poor body of mine, and I find I am bankrupt. Within a month I may be rotting up there in the churchyard.

NORA. Ugh, what a nasty way to talk!

RANK. The facts aren't exactly nice. But the worst is that there's so much else that's nasty to come first. I've only one more test to make. When that's done I'll have a pretty accurate idea of when the final disintegration is likely to begin. I want to ask you a favour. Helmer's a sensitive chap, and I know how he hates anything ugly. I don't want him to visit me when I'm in hospital—

NORA. Oh but, Dr. Rank—

RANK. I don't want him there. On any pretext. I shan't have him allowed in. As soon as I know the worst, I'll send you my visiting card with a black cross on it, and then you'll know that the final filthy process has begun.

NORA. Really, you're being quite impossible this evening. And I did hope you'd be in a good mood.

RANK. With death on my hands? And all this to atone for someone else's sin? Is there justice in that? And in every single family, in one way or another, the same merciless law of retribution is at work—

NORA *[holds her hands to her ears].* Nonsense! Cheer up! Laugh!

RANK. Yes, you're right. Laughter's all the damned thing's fit for. My poor innocent spine must pay for the fun my father had as a gay young lieutenant.

NORA *[at the table, left].* You mean he was too fond of asparagus and *foie gras?*

RANK. Yes, and truffles too.

NORA. Yes, of course, truffles, yes. And oysters too, I suppose?

RANK. Yes, oysters, oysters. Of course.

NORA. And all that port and champagne to wash them down. It's too sad that all those lovely things should affect one's spine.

RANK. Especially a poor spine that never got any pleasure out of them.

NORA. Oh yes, that's the saddest thing of all.

RANK *[looks searchingly at her].* Hm—

NORA *[after a moment].* Why did you smile?

RANK. No, it was you who laughed.

NORA. No, it was you who smiled, Dr. Rank!

RANK *[gets up].* You're a worse little rogue than I thought.

NORA. Oh, I'm full of stupid tricks today.

RANK. So it seems.

NORA *[puts both her hands on his shoulders].* Dear, dear Dr. Rank, you mustn't die and leave Torvald and me.

RANK. Oh, you'll soon get over it. Once one is gone, one is soon forgotten.

NORA *[looks at him anxiously].* Do you believe that?

RANK. One finds replacements, and then—

NORA. Who will find a replacement?

RANK. You and Helmer both will, when I am gone. You seem to have made a start already, haven't you? What was this Mrs. Linde doing here yesterday evening?

NORA. Aha! But surely you can't be jealous of poor Christine?

RANK. Indeed I am. She will be my successor in this house. When I have moved on, this lady will—

NORA. Ssh—don't speak so loud! She's in there!

RANK. Today again? You see!

NORA. She's only come to mend my dress. Good heavens, how unreasonable you are! *[Sits on the sofa.]* Be nice now, Dr. Rank. Tomorrow you'll see how beautifully I shall dance; and you must imagine that I'm doing it just for you. And for Torvald of course; obviously. *[Takes some things out of the box.]* Dr. Rank, sit down here and I'll show you something.

RANK *[sits].* What's this?

NORA. Look here! Look!

RANK. Silk stockings!

NORA. Flesh-colored. Aren't they beautiful? It's very dark in here now, of course, but tomorrow—No, no, no; only the soles. Oh well, I suppose you can look a bit higher if you want to.

RANK. Hm—

NORA. Why are you looking so critical? Don't you think they'll fit me?

RANK. I can't really give you a qualified opinion on that.

NORA *[looks at him for a moment].* Shame on you! *[Flicks him on the ear with the stockings.]* Take that. *[Puts them back in the box.]*

RANK. What other wonders are to be revealed to me?

NORA. I shan't show you anything else. You're being naughty.

She hums a little and looks among the things in the box.

RANK *[after a short silence].* When I sit here like this being so intimate with you, I can't think—I cannot imagine what would have become of me if I had never entered this house.

NORA *[smiles].* Yes, I think you enjoy being with us, don't you?

RANK *[more quietly, looking into the middle distance].* And now to have to leave it all—

NORA. Nonsense. You're not leaving us.

RANK *[as before].* And not to be able to leave even the most wretched token of gratitude behind; hardly even a passing sense of loss; only an empty place, to be filled by the next comer.

NORA. Suppose I were to ask you to—? No—

RANK. To do what?

NORA. To give me proof of your friendship—

RANK. Yes, yes?

NORA. No, I mean—to do me a very great service—

RANK. Would you really for once grant me that happiness?

NORA. But you've no idea what it is.

RANK. Very well, tell me, then.

NORA. No, but, Dr. Rank, I can't. It's far too much—I want your help and advice, and I want you to do something for me.

RANK. The more the better. I've no idea what it can be. But tell me. You do trust me, don't you?

NORA. Oh, yes, more than anyone. You're my best and truest friend. Otherwise I couldn't tell you. Well then, Dr. Rank—there's something you must help me to prevent. You know how much Torvald loves me—he'd never hesitate for an instant to lay down his life for me—

RANK *[leans over towards her].* Nora—do you think he is the only one—?

NORA *[with a slight start].* What do you mean?

RANK. Who would gladly lay down his life for you?

NORA *[sadly].* Oh, I see.

RANK. I swore to myself I would let you know that before I go. I shall never have a better opportunity. . . . Well, Nora, now you know that. And now you also know that you can trust me as you can trust nobody else.

NORA *[rises; calmly and quietly].* Let me pass, please.

RANK *[makes room for her but remains seated].* Nora—

NORA *[in the doorway to the hall].* Helen, bring the lamp. *[Goes over to the stove.]* Oh, dear Dr. Rank, this was really horrid of you.

RANK *[gets up].* That I have loved you as deeply as anyone else has? Was that horrid of me?

NORA. No—but that you should go and tell me. That was quite unnecessary—

RANK. What do you mean? Did you know, then—?

The MAID *enters with the lamp, puts it on the table, and goes out.*

RANK. Nora—Mrs. Helmer—I am asking you, did you know this?

NORA. Oh, what do I know, what did I know, what didn't I know—I really can't say. How could you be so stupid, Dr. Rank? Everything was so nice.

RANK. Well, at any rate now you know that I am ready to serve you, body and soul. So—please continue.

NORA *[looks at him]*. After this?

RANK. Please tell me what it is.

NORA. I can't possibly tell you now.

RANK. Yes, yes! You mustn't punish me like this. Let me be allowed to do what I can for you.

NORA. You can't do anything for me now. Anyway; I don't need any help. It was only my imagination—you'll see. Yes, really. Honestly. *[Sits in the rocking-chair, looks at him, and smiles.]* Well, upon my word you *are* a fine gentleman, Dr. Rank. Aren't you ashamed of yourself, now that the lamp's been lit?

RANK. Frankly, no. But perhaps I ought to say—*adieu?*

NORA. Of course not. You will naturally continue to visit us as before. You know quite well how Torvald depends on your company.

RANK. Yes, but you?

NORA. Oh, I always think it's enormous fun having you here.

RANK. That was what misled me. You're a riddle to me, you know. I'd often felt you'd just as soon be with me as with Helmer.

NORA. Well, you see, there are some people whom one loves, and others whom it's almost more fun to be with.

RANK. Oh yes, there's some truth in that.

NORA. When I was at home, of course I loved Papa best. But I always used to think it was terribly amusing to go down and talk to the servants; because they never told me what I ought to do; and they were such fun to listen to.

RANK. I see. So I've taken their place?

NORA *[jumps up and runs over to him]*. Oh, dear, sweet Dr. Rank, I didn't mean that at all. But I'm sure you understand—I feel the same about Torvald as I did about Papa.

MAID *[enters from the hall]*. Excuse me, madam. *[Whispers to her and hands her a visiting card.]*

NORA *[glances at the card]*. Oh! *[Puts it quickly in her pocket.]*

RANK. Anything wrong?

NORA. No, no, nothing at all. It's just something that—it's my new dress.

RANK. What? But your costume is lying over there.

NORA. Oh—that, yes—but there's another—I ordered it specially—Torvald mustn't know—

RANK. Ah, so that's your big secret?

NORA. Yes, yes. Go in and talk to him—he's in his study—keep him talking for a bit—

RANK. Don't worry. He won't get away from me. *[Goes into* HELMER'S *study.]*

NORA *[to the* MAID*].* Is he waiting in the kitchen?

MAID. Yes, madam, he came up the back way—

NORA. But didn't you tell him I had a visitor?

MAID. Yes, but he wouldn't go.

NORA. Wouldn't go?

MAID. No, madam, not until he'd spoken with you.

NORA. Very well, show him in; but quietly. Helen, you mustn't tell anyone about this. It's a surprise for my husband.

MAID. Very good, madam. I understand. *[Goes.]*

NORA. It's happening. It's happening after all. No, no, no, it can't happen, it mustn't happen.

> *She walks across and bolts the door of* HELMER'*s study. The* MAID *opens the door from the hall to admit* KROGSTAD, *and closes it behind him. He is wearing an overcoat, heavy boots, and a fur cap.*

NORA *[goes towards him].* Speak quietly. My husband's at home.

KROGSTAD. Let him hear.

NORA. What do you want from me?

KROGSTAD. Information.

NORA. Hurry up, then. What is it?

KROGSTAD. I suppose you know I've been given the sack.

NORA. I couldn't stop it, Mr. Krogstad. I did my best for you, but it didn't help.

KROGSTAD. Does your husband love you so little? He knows what I can do to you, and yet he dares to—

NORA. Surely you don't imagine I told him?

KROGSTAD. No. I didn't really think you had. It wouldn't have been like my old friend Torvald Helmer to show that much courage—

NORA. Mr. Krogstad, I'll trouble you to speak respectfully of my husband.

KROGSTAD. Don't worry, I'll show him all the respect he deserves. But since you're so anxious to keep this matter hushed up, I presume you're better informed than you were yesterday of the gravity of what you've done?

NORA. I've learned more than you could ever teach me.

KROGSTAD. Yes, a bad lawyer like me—

NORA. What do you want from me?

KROGSTAD. I just wanted to see how things were with you, Mrs. Helmer. I've been thinking about you all day. Even duns and hack journalists have hearts, you know.

NORA. Show some heart, then. Think of my little children.

KROGSTAD. Have you and your husband thought of mine? Well, let's forget that. I just wanted to tell you, you don't need to take this business too seriously. I'm not going to take any action, for the present.

NORA. Oh, no—you won't, will you? I knew it.

KROGSTAD. It can all be settled quite amicably. There's no need for it to become public. We'll keep it among the three of us.

NORA. My husband must never know about this.

KROGSTAD. How can you stop him? Can you pay the balance of what you owe me?

NORA. Not immediately.

KROGSTAD. Have you any means of raising the money during the next few days?

NORA. None that I would care to use.

KROGSTAD. Well, it wouldn't have helped anyway. However much money you offered me now I wouldn't give you back that paper.

NORA. What are you going to do with it?

KROGSTAD. Just keep it. No one else need ever hear about it. So in case you were thinking of doing anything desperate—

NORA. I am.

KROGSTAD. Such as running away—

NORA. I am.

KROGSTAD. Or anything more desperate—

NORA. How did you know?

KROGSTAD. —just give up the idea.

NORA. How did you know?

KROGSTAD. Most of us think of that at first. I did. But I hadn't the courage—

NORA. *[dully]*. Neither have I.

KROGSTAD. *[relieved]*. It's true, isn't it? You haven't the courage either?

NORA. No. I haven't. I haven't.

KROGSTAD. It'd be a stupid thing to do anyway. Once the first little domestic explosion is over. . . . I've got a letter in my pocket here addressed to your husband—

NORA. Telling him everything?

KROGSTAD. As delicately as possible.

NORA *[quickly]*. He must never see that letter. Tear it up. I'll find the money somehow—

KROGSTAD. I'm sorry, Mrs. Helmer, I thought I'd explained—

NORA. Oh, I don't mean the money I owe you. Let me know how much you want from my husband, and I'll find it for you.

KROGSTAD. I'm not asking your husband for money.

NORA. What do you want, then?

KROGSTAD. I'll tell you. I want to get on my feet again, Mrs. Helmer. I want to get to the top. And your husband's going to help me. For eighteen months now my record's been clean. I've been in hard straits all that time; I was content to fight my way back inch by inch. Now I've been chucked back into the mud, and I'm not going to be satisfied with just getting back my job. I'm going to get to the top, I tell you. I'm going to get back into the bank, and it's going to be higher up. Your husband's going to create a new job for me—

NORA. He'll never do that!

KROGSTAD. Oh, yes he will. I know him. He won't dare to risk a scandal. And once I'm in there with him, you'll see! Within a year I'll be his right-hand man. It'll be Nils Krogstad who'll be running that bank, not Torvald Helmer!

NORA. That will never happen.

KROGSTAD. Are you thinking of—?

NORA. Now I *have* the courage.

KROGSTAD. Oh, you can't frighten me. A pampered little pretty like you—

NORA. You'll see! You'll see!

KROGSTAD. Under the ice? Down in the cold, black water? And then, in the spring, to float up again, ugly, unrecognizable, hairless—?

NORA. You can't frighten me.

KROGSTAD. And you can't frighten me. People don't do such things, Mrs. Helmer. And anyway, what'd be the use? I've got him in my pocket.

NORA. But afterwards? When I'm no longer—?

KROGSTAD. Have you forgotten that then your reputation will be in my hands? *[She looks at him speechlessly.]* Well, I've warned you. Don't do anything silly. When Helmer's read my letter, he'll get in touch with me. And remember, it's your husband who's forced me to act like this. And for that I'll never forgive him. Goodbye, Mrs. Helmer. *[He goes out through the hall.]*

NORA *[runs to the hall door, opens it a few inches, and listens]*. He's going. He's not going to give him the letter. Oh, no, no, it couldn't possibly happen. *[Opens the door a little wider.]* What's he doing? Standing outside the front door. He's not going downstairs. Is he changing his mind? Yes, he—!

A letter falls into the letter-box. KROGSTAD's *footsteps die away down the stairs.*

NORA *[with a stifled cry runs across the room towards the table by the sofa. A pause]*. In the letter-box. *[Steals timidly over towards the hall door.]* There it is! Oh, Torvald, Torvald! Now we're lost!

MRS. LINDE *[enters from the nursery with* NORA's *costume]*. Well, I've done the best I can. Shall we see how it looks—?

NORA *[whispers hoarsely]*. Christine, come here.

MRS. LINDE *[throws the dress on the sofa]*. What's wrong with you? You look as though you'd seen a ghost!

NORA. Come here. Do you see that letter? There—look—through the glass of the letter-box.

MRS. LINDE. Yes, yes, I see it.

NORA. That letter's from Krogstad—

MRS. LINDE. Nora! It was Krogstad who lent you the money!

NORA. Yes. And now Torvald's going to discover everything.

MRS. LINDE. Oh, believe me, Nora, it'll be best for you both.

NORA. You don't know what's happened. I've committed a forgery—

MRS. LINDE. But, for heaven's sake—!

NORA. Christine, all I want is for you to be my witness.

MRS. LINDE. What do you mean? Witness what?

NORA. If I should go out of my mind—and it might easily happen—

MRS. LINDE. Nora!

NORA. Or if anything else should happen to me—so that I wasn't here any longer—

MRS. LINDE. Nora, Nora, you don't know what you're saying!

NORA. If anyone should try to take the blame, and say it was all his fault—you understand—?

MRS. LINDE. Yes, yes—but how can you think?

NORA. Then you must testify that it isn't true, Christine. I'm not mad—I know exactly what I'm saying—and I'm telling you, no one else knows anything about this. I did it entirely on my own. Remember that.

MRS. LINDE. All right. But I simply don't understand—

NORA. Oh, how could you understand? A—miracle—is about to happen.

MRS. LINDE. Miracle?

NORA. Yes. A miracle. But it's so frightening. Christine. It *mustn't* happen, not for anything in the world.

MRS. LINDE. I'll go over and talk to Krogstad.

NORA. Don't go near him. He'll only do something to hurt you.

MRS. LINDE. Once upon a time he'd have done anything for my sake.

NORA. He?

MRS. LINDE. Where does he live?

NORA. Oh, how should I know—? Oh, yes, wait a moment—! *[Feels in her pocket.]* Here's his card. But the letter, the letter—!

HELMER *[from his study, knocks on the door]*. Nora!

NORA *[cries in alarm]*. What is it?

HELMER. Now, now, don't get alarmed. We're not coming in; you've closed the door. Are you trying on your costume?

NORA. Yes, yes—I'm trying on my costume. I'm going to look so pretty for you, Torvald.

MRS. LINDE *[who has been reading the card]*. Why, he lives just around the corner.

NORA. Yes; but it's no use. There's nothing to be done now. The letter's lying there in the box.

MRS. LINDE. And your husband has the key?

NORA. Yes, he always keeps it.

MRS. LINDE. Krogstad must ask him to send the letter back unread. He must find some excuse—

NORA. But Torvald always opens the box at just about this time—

MRS. LINDE. You must stop him. Go in and keep him talking. I'll be back as quickly as I can.

She hurries out through the hall.

NORA *[goes over to* HELMER*'s door, opens it and peeps in]*. Torvald!

HELMER *[offstage]*. Well, may a man enter his own drawing-room again? Come on, Rank, now we'll see what—*[In the doorway.]* But what's this?

NORA. What, Torvald dear?

HELMER. Rank's been preparing me for some great transformation scene.

RANK *[in the doorway]*. So I understood. But I seem to have been mistaken.

NORA. Yes, no one's to be allowed to see me before tomorrow night.

HELMER. But, my dear Nora, you look quite worn out. Have you been practicing too hard?

NORA. No, I haven't practiced at all yet.

HELMER. Well, you must.

NORA. Yes, Torvald, I must, I know. But I can't get anywhere without your help. I've completely forgotten everything.

HELMER. Oh, we'll soon put that to rights.

NORA. Yes, help me, Torvald. Promise me you will? Oh, I'm so nervous. All those people—! You must forget everything except me this evening. You mustn't think of business—I won't even let you touch a pen. Promise me, Torvald?

HELMER. I promise. This evening I shall think of nothing but you—my poor, helpless little darling. Oh, there's just one thing I must see to—*[Goes towards the hall door.]*

NORA. What do you want out there?

HELMER. I'm only going to see if any letters have come.

NORA. No, Torvald, no!

HELMER. Why, what's the matter?

NORA. Torvald, I beg you. There's nothing there.

HELMER. Well, I'll just make sure.

> *He moves towards the door.* NORA *runs to the piano and plays the first bars of the tarantella.*

HELMER *[at the door, turns].* Aha!

NORA. I can't dance tomorrow if I don't practice with you now.

HELMER *[goes over to her].* Are you really so frightened, Nora dear?

NORA. Yes, terribly frightened. Let me start practicing now, at once—we've still time before dinner. Oh, do sit down and play for me, Torvald dear. Correct me, lead me, the way you always do.

HELMER. Very well, my dear, if you wish it.

> *He sits down at the piano.* NORA *seizes the tambourine and a long multi-colored shawl from the cardboard box, wraps the latter hastily around her, then takes a quick leap into the center of the room.*

NORA. Play for me! I want to dance!

> HELMER *plays and* NORA *dances.* DR. RANK *stands behind* HELMER *at the piano and watches her.*

HELMER *[as he plays].* Slower, slower!

NORA. I can't!

HELMER. Not so violently, Nora.

NORA. I must!

HELMER *[stops playing].* No, no, this won't do at all.

NORA *[laughs and swings her tambourine].* Isn't that what I told you?

RANK. Let me play for her.

HELMER *[gets up].* Yes, would you? Then it'll be easier for me to show her.

> RANK *sits down at the piano and plays.* NORA *dances more and more wildly.* HELMER *has stationed himself by the stove and tries repeatedly to correct her, but she seems not to hear him. Her hair works loose and falls over her shoulders; she ignores it and continues to dance.* MRS. LINDE *enters.*

MRS. LINDE *[stands in the doorway as though tongue-tied].* Ah—!

NORA *[as she dances].* Oh, Christine, we're having such fun!

HELMER. But, Nora darling, you're dancing as if your life depended on it.

NORA. It does.

HELMER. Rank, stop it! This is sheer lunacy. Stop it, I say!

> RANK *ceases playing.* NORA *suddenly stops dancing.*

HELMER *[goes over to her].* I'd never have believed it. You've forgotten everything I taught you.

NORA *[throws away the tambourine].* You see!

HELMER. I'll have to show you every step.

NORA. You see how much I need you! You must show me every step of the way. Right to the end of the dance. Promise me you will, Torvald?

HELMER. Never fear. I will.

NORA. You mustn't think about anything but me—today or tomorrow. Don't open any letters—don't even open the letter-box—

HELMER. Aha, you're still worried about that fellow—

NORA. Oh, yes, yes, him too.

HELMER. Nora, I can tell from the way you're behaving, there's a letter from him already lying there.

NORA. I don't know. I think so. But you mustn't read it now. I don't want anything ugly to come between us till it's all over.

RANK *[quietly, to* HELMER*].* Better give her her way.

HELMER *[puts his arm round her]*. My child shall have her way. But tomorrow night, when your dance is over—

NORA. Then you will be free.

MAID *[appears in the doorway, right]*. Dinner is served, madam.

NORA. Put out some champagne, Helen.

MAID. Very good, madam. *[Goes.]*

HELMER. I say! What's this, a banquet?

NORA. We'll drink champagne until dawn! *[Calls.]* And, Helen! Put out some macaroons! Lots of macaroons—for once!

HELMER *[takes her hands in his]*. Now, now, now. Don't get so excited. Where's my little songbird, the one I know?

NORA. All right. Go and sit down—and you too, Dr. Rank. I'll be with you in a minute. Christine, you must help me put my hair up.

RANK *[quietly, as they go]*. There's nothing wrong, is there? I mean, she isn't—er—expecting—?

HELMER Good heavens no, my dear chap. She just gets scared like a child sometimes—I told you before—
They go out right.

NORA. Well?

MRS. LINDE. He's left town.

NORA. I saw it from your face.

MRS. LINDE. He'll be back tomorrow evening. I left a note for him.

NORA. You needn't have bothered. You can't stop anything now. Anyway, it's wonderful really, in a way—sitting here and waiting for the miracle to happen.

MRS. LINDE. Waiting for what?

NORA. Oh, you wouldn't understand. Go in and join them. I'll be with you in a moment.
MRS. LINDE goes into the dining-room.

NORA *[stands for a moment as though collecting herself. Then she looks at her watch]*. Five o'clock. Seven hours till midnight. Then another twenty-four hours till midnight tomorrow. And then the tarantella will be finished. Twenty-four and seven? Thirty-one hours to live.

HELMER *[appears in the doorway, right]*. What's happened to my little songbird?

NORA *[runs to him with her arms wide]*. Your songbird is here!

Act 3

The same room. The table which was formerly by the sofa has been moved into the center of the room; the chairs surround it as before. The door to the hall stands open. Dance music can be heard from the floor above. MRS. LINDE is seated at the table, absent-mindedly glancing through a book. She is trying to read, but seems unable to keep her mind on it. More than once she turns and listens anxiously towards the front door.

MRS. LINDE *[looks at her watch]*. Not here yet. There's not much time left. Please God he hasn't—! *[Listens again.]* Ah, here he is. *[Goes out into the hall and cautiously opens the front door. Footsteps can be heard softly ascending the stairs. She whispers.]* Come in. There's no one here.

KROGSTAD [*in the doorway*]. I found a note from you at my lodgings. What does this mean?

MRS. LINDE. I must speak with you.

KROGSTAD. Oh? And must our conversation take place in this house?

MRS. LINDE. We couldn't meet at my place; my room has no separate entrance. Come in. We're quite alone. The maid's asleep, and the Helmers are at the dance upstairs.

KROGSTAD [*comes into the room*]. Well, well! So the Helmers are dancing this evening? Are they indeed?

MRS. LINDE. Yes, why not?

KROGSTAD. True enough. Why not?

MRS. LINDE. Well, Krogstad. You and I must have a talk together.

KROGSTAD. Have we two anything further to discuss?

MRS. LINDE. We have a great deal to discuss.

KROGSTAD. I wasn't aware of it.

MRS. LINDE. That's because you've never really understood me.

KROGSTAD. Was there anything to understand? It's the old story, isn't it—a woman chucking a man because something better turns up?

MRS. LINDE. Do you really think I'm so utterly heartless? You think it was easy for me to give you up?

KROGSTAD. Wasn't it?

MRS. LINDE. Oh, Nils, did you really believe that?

KROGSTAD. Then why did you write to me the way you did?

MRS. LINDE. I had to. Since I had to break with you, I thought it my duty to destroy all the feelings you had for me.

KROGSTAD [*clenches his fists*]. So that was it. And you did this for money!

MRS. LINDE. You mustn't forget I had a helpless mother to take care of, and two little brothers. We couldn't wait for you, Nils. It would have been so long before you'd had enough to support us.

KROGSTAD. Maybe. But you had no right to cast me off for someone else.

MRS. LINDE. Perhaps not. I've often asked myself that.

KROGSTAD [*more quietly*]. When I lost you, it was just as though all solid ground had been swept from under my feet. Look at me. Now I am a shipwrecked man, clinging to a spar.

MRS. LINDE. Help may be near at hand.

KROGSTAD. It was near. But then you came, and stood between it and me.

MRS. LINDE. I didn't know, Nils. No one told me till today that this job I'd found was yours.

KROGSTAD. I believe you, since you say so. But now you know, won't you give it up?

MRS. LINDE. No—because it wouldn't help you even if I did.

KROGSTAD. Wouldn't it? I'd do it all the same.

MRS. LINDE. I've learned to look at things practically. Life and poverty have taught me that.

KROGSTAD. And life has taught me to distrust fine words.

MRS. LINDE. Then it's taught you a useful lesson. But surely you still believe in actions?

KROGSTAD. What do you mean?

MRS. LINDE. You said you were like a shipwrecked man clinging to a spar.

KROGSTAD. I have good reason to say it.

MRS. LINDE. I'm in the same position as you. No one to care about, no one to care for.

KROGSTAD. You made your own choice.

MRS. LINDE. I had no choice—then.

KROGSTAD. Well?

MRS. LINDE. Nils, suppose we two shipwrecked souls could join hands?

KROGSTAD. What are you saying?

MRS. LINDE. Castaways have a better chance of survival together than on their own.

KROGSTAD. Christine!

MRS. LINDE. Why do you suppose I came to this town?

KROGSTAD. You mean—you came because of me?

MRS. LINDE. I must work if I'm to find life worth living. I've always worked, for as long as I can remember; it's been the greatest joy of my life—my only joy. But now I'm alone in the world, and I feel so dreadfully lost and empty. There's no joy in working just for oneself. Oh, Nils, give me something—someone—to work for.

KROGSTAD. I don't believe all that. You're just being hysterical and romantic. You want to find an excuse for self-sacrifice.

MRS. LINDE. Have you ever known me to be hysterical?

KROGSTAD. You mean you really—? Is it possible? Tell me—you know all about my past?

MRS. LINDE. Yes.

KROGSTAD. And you know what people think of me here?

MRS. LINDE. You said just now that with me you might have become a different person.

KROGSTAD. I know I could have.

MRS. LINDE. Couldn't it still happen?

KROGSTAD. Christine—do you really mean this? Yes—you do—I see it in your face. Have you really the courage—?

MRS. LINDE. I need someone to be a mother to; and your children need a mother. And you and I need each other. I believe in you, Nils. I am afraid of nothing—with you.

KROGSTAD *[clasps her hands]*. Thank you, Christine—thank you! Now I shall make the world believe in me as you do! Oh—but I'd forgotten—

MRS. LINDE *[listens]*. Ssh! The tarantella! Go quickly, go!

KROGSTAD. Why? What is it?

MRS. LINDE. You hear that dance? As soon as it's finished, they'll be coming down.

KROGSTAD. All right, I'll go. It's no good, Christine. I'd forgotten—you don't know what I've just done to the Helmers.

MRS. LINDE. Yes, Nils. I know.

KROGSTAD. And yet you'd still have the courage to—?

MRS. LINDE. I know what despair can drive a man like you to.

KROGSTAD. Oh, if only I could undo this!

MRS. LINDE. You can. Your letter is still lying in the box.

KROGSTAD. Are you sure?

MRS. LINDE. Quite sure. But—

KROGSTAD *[looks searchingly at her]*. Is that why you're doing this? You want to save your friend at any price? Tell me the truth. Is that the reason?

MRS. LINDE. Nils, a woman who has sold herself once for the sake of others doesn't make the same mistake again.

KROGSTAD. I shall demand my letter back.

MRS. LINDE. No, no.

KROGSTAD. Of course I shall. I shall stay here till Helmer comes down. I'll tell him he must give me back my letter—I'll say it was only to do with my dismissal, and that I don't want him to read it—

MRS. LINDE. No, Nils, you mustn't ask for that letter back.

KROGSTAD. But—tell me—wasn't that the real reason you asked me to come here?

MRS. LINDE. Yes—at first, when I was frightened. But a day has passed since then, and in that time I've seen incredible things happen in this house. Helmer must know the truth. This unhappy secret of Nora's must be revealed. They must come to a full understanding; there must be an end of all these shiftings and evasions.

KROGSTAD. Very well. If you're prepared to risk it. But one thing I can do—and at once—

MRS. LINDE *[listens]*. Hurry! Go, go! The dance is over. We aren't safe here another moment.

KROGSTAD. I'll wait for you downstairs.

MRS. LINDE. Yes, do. You can see me home.

KROGSTAD. I've never been so happy in my life before!

He goes out through the front door. The door leading from the room into the hall remains open.

MRS. LINDE *[tidies the room a little and gets her hat and coat]*. What a change! Oh, what a change! Someone to work for—to live for! A home to bring joy into! I won't let this chance of happiness slip through my fingers. Oh, why don't they come? *[Listens.]* Ah, here they are. I must get my coat on.

She takes her hat and coat. HELMER's *and* NORA's *voices become audible outside. A key is turned in the lock and* HELMER *leads* NORA *almost forcibly into the hall. She is dressed in an Italian costume with a large black shawl. He is in evening dress, with a black cloak.*

NORA *[still in the doorway, resisting him]*. No, no, no—not in here! I want to go back upstairs. I don't want to leave so early.

HELMER. But my dearest Nora—

NORA. Oh, please, Torvald, please! Just another hour!

HELMER. Not another minute, Nora, my sweet. You know what we agreed. Come along, now. Into the drawing-room. You'll catch cold if you stay out here.

He leads her, despite her efforts to resist him, gently into the room.

MRS. LINDE. Good evening.

NORA. Christine!

HELMER. Oh, hullo, Mrs. Linde. You still here?

MRS. LINDE. Please forgive me. I did so want to see Nora in her costume.

NORA. Have you been sitting here waiting for me?

MRS. LINDE. Yes. I got here too late, I'm afraid. You'd already gone up. And I felt I really couldn't go back home without seeing you.

HELMER *[takes off* NORA's *shawl]*. Well, take a good look at her. She's worth looking at, don't you think? Isn't she beautiful, Mrs. Linde?

MRS. LINDE. Oh, yes, indeed—

HELMER. Isn't she unbelievably beautiful? Everyone at the party said so. But dreadfully stubborn she is, bless her pretty little heart. What's to be done about that? Would you believe it, I practically had to use force to get her away!

NORA. Oh, Torvald, you're going to regret not letting me stay—just half an hour longer.

HELMER. Hear that, Mrs. Linde? She dances her tarantella—makes a roaring success—and very well deserved—though possibly a trifle too realistic—more so than was aesthetically necessary, strictly speaking. But never mind that. Main thing is—she had a success—roaring success. Was I going to let her stay on after that and spoil the impression? No, thank you. I took my beautiful little Capri signorina—my capricious little Capricienne, what?—under my arm—a swift round of the ballroom, a curtsey to the company, and, as they say in novels, the beautiful apparition disappeared! An exit should always be dramatic, Mrs. Linde. But unfortunately that's just what I can't get Nora to realize. I say, it's hot in here. *[Throws his cloak on a chair and opens the door to his study.]* What's this? It's dark in here. Ah, yes, of course—excuse me. *[Goes in and lights a couple of candles.]*

NORA *[whispers swiftly, breathlessly]*. Well?

MRS. LINDE *[quietly]*. I've spoken to him.

NORA. Yes?

MRS. LINDE. Nora—you must tell your husband everything.

NORA *[dully]*. I knew it.

MRS. LINDE. You've nothing to fear from Krogstad. But you must tell him.

NORA. I shan't tell him anything.

MRS. LINDE. Then the letter will.

NORA. Thank you, Christine. Now I know what I must do. Ssh!

HELMER *[returns]*. Well, Mrs. Linde, finished admiring her?

MRS. LINDE. Yes. Now I must say good night.

HELMER. Oh, already? Does this knitting belong to you?

MRS. LINDE *[takes it]*. Thank you, yes. I nearly forgot it.

HELMER. You knit, then?

MRS. LINDE. Why, yes.

HELMER. Know what? You ought to take up embroidery.

MRS. LINDE. Oh? Why?

HELMER. It's much prettier. Watch me, now. You hold the embroidery in your left hand, like this, and then you take the needle in your right hand and go in and out in a slow, easy movement—like this. I am right, aren't I?

MRS. LINDE. Yes, I'm sure—

HELMER. But knitting, now—that's an ugly business—can't help it. Look—arms all huddled up—great clumsy needles going up and down—makes you look like a damned Chinaman. I say, that really was a magnificent champagne they served us.

MRS. LINDE. Well, good night, Nora. And stop being stubborn. Remember!

HELMER. Quite right, Mrs. Linde!

MRS. LINDE. Good night, Mr. Helmer.

HELMER *[accompanies her to the door]*. Good night, good night! I hope you'll manage to get home all right? I'd gladly—but you haven't far to go, have you? Good night, good night. *[She goes. He closes the door behind her and returns.]* Well, we've got rid of her at last. Dreadful bore that woman is!

NORA. Aren't you very tired, Torvald?

HELMER. No, not in the least.

NORA. Aren't you sleepy?

HELMER. Not a bit. On the contrary, I feel extraordinarily exhilarated. But what about you? Yes, you look very sleepy and tired.

NORA. Yes, I am very tired. Soon I shall sleep.

HELMER. You see, you see! How right I was not to let you stay longer!

NORA. Oh, you're always right, whatever you do.

HELMER *[kisses her on the forehead]*. Now my little songbird's talking just like a real big human being. I say, did you notice how cheerful Rank was this evening?

NORA. Oh? Was he? I didn't have a chance to speak with him.

HELMER. I hardly did. But I haven't seen him in such a jolly mood for ages. *[Looks at her for a moment, then comes closer.]* I say, it's nice to get back to one's home again, and be all alone with you. Upon my word, you're a distractingly beautiful young woman.

NORA. Don't look at me like that, Torvald!

HELMER. What, not look at my most treasured possession? At all this wonderful beauty that's mine, mine alone, all mine.

NORA *[goes round to the other side of the table]*. You mustn't talk to me like that tonight.

HELMER *[follows her]*. You've still the tarantella in your blood, I see. And that makes you even more desirable. Listen! Now the other guests are beginning to go. *[More quietly.]* Nora—soon the whole house will be absolutely quiet.

NORA. Yes, I hope so.

HELMER. Yes, my beloved Nora, of course you do! Do you know—when I'm out with you among other people like we were tonight, do you know why I say so little to you, why I keep so aloof from you, and just throw you an occasional glance? Do you know why I do that? It's because I pretend to myself that you're my secret mistress, my clandestine little sweetheart, and that nobody knows there's anything at all between us.

NORA. Oh, yes, yes, yes—I know you never think of anything but me.

HELMER. And then when we're about to go, and I wrap the shawl round your lovely young shoulders, over this wonderful curve of your neck—then I pretend to myself that you are my young bride, that we've just come from the wedding, that I'm taking you to my house for the first time— that, for the first time, I am alone with you—quite alone with you, as you stand there young and trembling and beautiful. All evening I've had no eyes for anyone but you. When I saw you dance the tarantella, like a huntress, a temptress, my blood grew hot, I couldn't stand it any longer! That was why I seized you and dragged you down here with me—

NORA. Leave me, Torvald! Get away from me! I don't want all this.

HELMER. What? Now, Nora, you're joking with me. Don't want, don't want—? Aren't I your husband—?

There is a knock on the front door.

NORA *[starts]*. What was that?

HELMER *[goes towards the hall]*. Who is it?

RANK *[outside]*. It's me. May I come in for a moment?

HELMER *[quietly, annoyed]*. Oh, what does he want now? *[Calls.]* Wait a moment. *[Walks over and opens the door.]* Well! Nice of you not to go by without looking in.

RANK. I thought I heard your voice, so I felt I had to say goodbye. *[His eyes travel swiftly around the room.]* Ah, yes—these dear rooms, how well I know them. What a happy, peaceful home you two have.

HELMER. You seemed to be having a pretty happy time yourself upstairs.

RANK. Indeed I did. Why not? Why shouldn't one make the most of this world? As much as one can, and for as long as one can. The wine was excellent—

HELMER. Especially the champagne.

RANK. You noticed that too? It's almost incredible how much I managed to get down.

NORA. Torvald drank a lot of champagne too, this evening.

RANK. Oh?

NORA. Yes. It always makes him merry afterwards.

RANK. Well, why shouldn't a man have a merry evening after a well-spent day?

HELMER. Well-spent? Oh, I don't know that I can claim that.

RANK *[slaps him across the back]*. I can though, my dear fellow!

NORA. Yes, of course, Dr. Rank—you've been carrying out a scientific experiment today, haven't you?

RANK. Exactly.

HELMER. Scientific experiment! Those are big words for my little Nora to use!

NORA. And may I congratulate you on the finding?

RANK. You may indeed.

NORA. It was good, then?

RANK. The best possible finding—both for the doctor and the patient. Certainty.

NORA *[quickly]*. Certainty?

RANK. Absolute certainty. So aren't I entitled to have a merry evening after that?

NORA. Yes, Dr. Rank. You were quite right to.

HELMER. I agree. Provided you don't have to regret it tomorrow.

RANK. Well, you never get anything in this life without paying for it.

NORA. Dr. Rank—you like masquerades, don't you?

RANK. Yes, if the disguises are sufficiently amusing.

NORA. Tell me. What shall we two wear at the next masquerade?

HELMER. You little gadabout! Are you thinking about the next one already?

RANK. We two? Yes, I'll tell you. You must go as the Spirit of Happiness—

HELMER. You try to think of a costume that'll convey that.

RANK. Your wife need only appear as her normal, everyday self—

HELMER. Quite right! Well said! But what are you going to be? Have you decided that?

RANK. Yes, my dear friend. I have decided that.

HELMER. Well?

RANK. At the next masquerade, I shall be invisible.

HELMER. Well, that's a funny idea.

RANK. There's a big, black hat—haven't you heard of the invisible hat? Once it's over your head, no one can see you any more.

HELMER *[represses a smile]*. Ah yes, of course.

RANK. But I'm forgetting what I came for. Helmer, give me a cigar. One of your black Havanas.

HELMER. With the greatest pleasure. *[Offers him the box.]*

RANK *[takes one and cuts off the tip]*. Thank you.

NORA *[strikes a match]*. Let me give you a light.

RANK. Thank you. *[She holds out the match for him. He lights his cigar.]* And now—goodbye.

HELMER. Goodbye, my dear chap, goodbye.

NORA. Sleep well, Dr. Rank.

RANK. Thank you for that kind wish.

NORA. Wish me the same.

RANK. You? Very well—since you ask. Sleep well. And thank you for the light. *[He nods to them both and goes.]*

HELMER *[quietly]*. He's been drinking too much.

NORA *[abstractedly]*. Perhaps.

HELMER *takes his bunch of keys from his pocket and goes out into the hall.*

NORA. Torvald, what do you want out there?

HELMER. I must empty the letter-box. It's absolutely full. There'll be no room for the newspapers in the morning.

NORA. Are you going to work tonight?

HELMER. You know very well I'm not. Hullo, what's this? Someone's been at the lock.

NORA. At the lock—?

HELMER. Yes, I'm sure of it. Who on earth—? Surely not one of the maids? Here's a broken hairpin. Nora, it's yours—

NORA *[quickly]*. Then it must have been the children.

HELMER. Well, you'll have to break them of that habit. Hm, hm. Ah, that's done it. *[Takes out the contents of the box and calls into the kitchen.]* Helen! Put out the light on the staircase. *[Comes back into the drawing-room with the letters in his hand and closes the door to the hall.]* Look at this! You see how they've piled up? *[Glances through them.]* What on earth's this?

NORA *[at the window]*. The letter! Oh, no, Torvald, no!

HELMER. Two visiting cards—from Rank.

NORA. From Dr. Rank?

HELMER *[looks at them]*. Peter Rank, M.D. They were on top. He must have dropped them in as he left.

NORA. Has he written anything on them?

HELMER. There's a black cross above his name. Look. Rather gruesome, isn't it? It looks just as though he was announcing his death.

NORA. He is.

HELMER. What? Do you know something? Has he told you anything?

NORA. Yes. When these cards come, it means he's said goodbye to us. He wants to shut himself up in his house and die.

HELMER. Ah, poor fellow. I knew I wouldn't be seeing him for much longer. But so soon—! And now he's going to slink away and hide like a wounded beast.

NORA. When the time comes, it's best to go silently. Don't you think so, Torvald?

HELMER *[walks up and down]*. He was so much a part of our life. I can't realize that he's gone. His suffering and loneliness seemed to provide a kind of dark background to the happy sunlight of our marriage. Well, perhaps it's best this way. For him, anyway. *[Stops walking.]* And perhaps for us too, Nora. Now we have only each other. *[Embraces her.]* Oh, my beloved wife—I feel as though I could never hold you close enough. Do you know, Nora, often I wish some terrible danger might threaten you, so that I could offer my life and my blood, everything, for your sake.

NORA *[tears herself loose and says in a clear, firm voice].* Read your letters now, Torvald.

HELMER. No, no. Not tonight. Tonight I want to be with you, my darling wife—

NORA. When your friend is about to die—?

HELMER. You're right. This news has upset us both. An ugliness has come between us; thoughts of death and dissolution. We must try to forget them. Until then—you go to your room; I shall go to mine.

NORA *[throws her arms around his neck].* Good night, Torvald! Good night!

HELMER *[kisses her on the forehead].* Good night, my darling little songbird. Sleep well, Nora. I'll go and read my letters.

He goes into the study with the letters in his hand, and closes the door.

NORA *[wild-eyed, fumbles around, seizes* HELMER's *cloak, throws it round herself and whispers quickly, hoarsely].* Never see him again. Never. Never. Never. *[Throws the shawl over her head.]* Never see the children again. Them too. Never. Never. Oh—the icy black water! Oh—that bottomless—that—! Oh, if only it were all over! Now he's got it—he's reading it. Oh, no, no! Not yet! Goodbye, Torvald! Goodbye, my darlings!

She turns to run into the hall. As she does so, HELMER *throws open his door and stands there with an open letter in his hand.*

HELMER. Nora!

NORA *[shrieks].* Ah—!

HELMER. What is this? Do you know what is in this letter?

NORA. Yes, I know. Let me go! Let me go!

HELMER *[holds her back].* Go? Where?

NORA *[tries to tear herself loose].* You mustn't try to save me, Torvald!

HELMER *[staggers back].* Is it true? Is it true, what he writes? Oh, my God! No, no—it's impossible, it can't be true!

NORA. It *is* true. I've loved you more than anything else in the world.

HELMER. Oh, don't try to make silly excuses.

NORA *[takes a step towards him].* Torvald—

HELMER. Wretched woman! What have you done?

NORA. Let me go! You're not going to suffer for my sake. I won't let you!

HELMER. Stop being theatrical. *[Locks the front door.]* You're going to stay here and explain yourself. Do you understand what you've done? Answer me! Do you understand?

NORA *[looks unflinchingly at him and, her expression growing colder, says].* Yes. Now I am beginning to understand.

HELMER *[walking around the room].* Oh, what a dreadful awakening! For eight whole years—she who was my joy and my pride—a hypocrite, a liar—worse, worse—a criminal! Oh, the hideousness of it! Shame on you, shame!

NORA *is silent and stares unblinkingly at him.*

HELMER *[stops in front of her].* I ought to have guessed that something of this sort would happen. I should have foreseen it. All your father's recklessness and instability—be quiet!—I repeat, all your father's recklessness and instability he has handed on to you. No religion, no morals, no sense of duty! Oh, how I have been punished for closing my eyes to his faults! I did it for your sake. And now you reward me like this.

NORA. Yes. Like this.

HELMER. Now you have destroyed all my happiness. You have ruined my whole future. Oh, it's too dreadful to contemplate! I am in the power of a man who is completely without scruples. He can do what he likes with me, demand what he pleases, order me to do anything—I dare not disobey him. I am condemned to humiliation and ruin simply for the weakness of a woman.

NORA. When I am gone from this world, you will be free.

HELMER. Oh, don't be melodramatic. Your father was always ready with that kind of remark. How would it help me if you were "gone from this world," as you put it? It wouldn't assist me in the slightest. He can still make all the facts public; and if he does, I may quite easily be suspected of having been an accomplice in your crime. People may think that I was behind it—that it was I who encouraged you! And for all this I have to thank you, you whom I have carried on my hands through all the years of our marriage! Now do you realize what you've done to me?

NORA *[coldly calm].* Yes.

HELMER. It's so unbelievable I can hardly credit it. But we must try to find some way out. Take off that shawl. Take it off, I say! I must try to buy him off somehow. This thing must be hushed up at any price. As regards our relationship—we must appear to be living together just as before. Only *appear,* of course. You will therefore continue to reside here. That is understood. But the children shall be taken out of your hands. I dare no longer entrust them to you. Oh, to have to say this to the woman I once loved so dearly—and whom I still—! Well, all that must be finished. Henceforth there can be no question of happiness; we must merely strive to save what shreds and tatters—*[The front door bell rings.* HELMER *starts.]* What can that be? At this hour? Surely not—? He wouldn't—? Hide yourself, Nora. Say you're ill.

NORA *does not move.* HELMER *goes to the door of the room and opens it. The* MAID *is standing half-dressed in the hall.*

MAID. A letter for madam.

HELMER. Give it to me. *[Seizes the letter and shuts the door.]* Yes, it's from him. You're not having it. I'll read this myself.

NORA. Read it.

HELMER *[by the lamp].* I hardly dare to. This may mean the end for us both. No, I must know. *[Tears open the letter hastily; reads a few lines; looks at a piece of paper which is enclosed with it; utters a cry of joy.]* Nora! *[She looks at him questioningly.]* Nora! No—I must read it once more. Yes, yes, it's true! I am saved! Nora, I am saved!

NORA. What about me?

HELMER. You too, of course. We're both saved, you and I. Look! He's returning your I.O.U. He writes that he is sorry for what has happened—a
happy accident has changed his life—oh, what does it matter what he
writes? We are saved, Nora! No one can harm you now. Oh, Nora,
Nora—no, first let me destroy this filthy thing. Let me see—! *[Glances
at the I.O.U.]* No, I don't want to look at it. I shall merely regard the
whole business as a dream. *[He tears the I.O.U. and both letters into
pieces, throws them into the stove, and watches them burn.]* There.
Now they're destroyed. He wrote that ever since Christmas Eve you've
been—oh, these must have been three dreadful days for you, Nora.

NORA. Yes. It's been a hard fight.

HELMER. It must have been terrible—seeing no way out except—no, we'll
forget the whole sordid business. We'll just be happy and go on telling
ourselves over and over again: "It's over! It's over!" Listen to me. Nora.
You don't seem to realize. It's over! Why are you looking so pale? Ah,
my poor little Nora, I understand. You can't believe that I have forgiven
you. But I have, Nora. I swear it to you. I have forgiven you everything.
I know that what you did you did for your love of me.

NORA. That is true.

HELMER. You have loved me as a wife should love her husband. It was simply
that in your inexperience you chose the wrong means. But do you think
I love you any the less because you don't know how to act on your own
initiative? No, no. Just lean on me. I shall counsel you. I shall guide you.
I would not be a true man if your feminine helplessness did not make
you doubly attractive in my eyes. You mustn't mind the hard words I
said to you in those first dreadful moments when my whole world
seemed to be tumbling about my ears. I have forgiven you, Nora. I
swear it to you; I have forgiven you.

NORA. Thank you for your forgiveness.

She goes out through the door, right.

HELMER. No, don't go—*[Looks in.]* What are you doing there?

NORA *[offstage]*. Taking off my fancy dress.

HELMER *[by the open door]*. Yes, do that. Try to calm yourself and get your
balance again, my frightened little songbird. Don't be afraid. I have
broad wings to shield you. *[Begins to walk around near the door.]*
How lovely and peaceful this little home of ours is, Nora. You are safe
here; I shall watch over you like a hunted dove which I have snatched
unharmed from the claws of the falcon. Your wildly beating little heart
shall find peace with me. It will happen, Nora; it will take time, but it
will happen, believe me. Tomorrow all this will seem quite different.
Soon everything will be as it was before. I shall no longer need to remind you that I have forgiven you; your own heart will tell you that it is
true. Do you really think I could ever bring myself to disown you, or
even to reproach you? Ah, Nora, you don't understand what goes on in
a husband's heart. There is something indescribably wonderful and satisfying for a husband in knowing that he has forgiven his wife—forgiven her unreservedly, from the bottom of his heart. It means that she
has become his property in a double sense; he has, as it were, brought
her into the world anew; she is now not only his wife but also his child.

From now on that is what you shall be to me, my poor, helpless, bewildered little creature. Never be frightened of anything again, Nora. Just open your heart to me. I shall be both your will and your conscience. What's this? Not in bed? Have you changed?

NORA *[in her everyday dress]*. Yes, Torvald. I've changed.

HELMER. But why now—so late—?

NORA. I shall not sleep tonight.

HELMER. But, my dear Nora—

NORA *[looks at her watch]*. It isn't that late. Sit down here, Torvald. You and I have a lot to talk about.
She sits down on one side of the table.

HELMER. Nora, what does this mean? You look quite drawn—

NORA. Sit down. It's going to take a long time. I've a lot to say to you.

HELMER *[sits down on the other side of the table]*. You alarm me, Nora. I don't understand you.

NORA. No, that's just it. You don't understand me. And I've never understood you—until this evening. No, don't interrupt me. Just listen to what I have to say. You and I have got to face facts, Torvald.

HELMER. What do you mean by that?

NORA *[after a short silence]*. Doesn't anything strike you about the way we're sitting here?

HELMER. What?

NORA. We've been married for eight years. Does it occur to you that this is the first time that we two, you and I, man and wife, have ever had a serious talk together?

HELMER. Serious? What do you mean, serious?

NORA. In eight whole years—no, longer—ever since we first met—we have never exchanged a serious word on a serious subject.

HELMER. Did you expect me to drag you into all my worries—worries you couldn't possibly have helped me with?

NORA. I'm not talking about worries. I'm simply saying that we have never sat down seriously to try to get to the bottom of anything.

HELMER. But, my dear Nora, what on earth has that got to do with you?

NORA. That's just the point. You have never understood me. A great wrong has been done to me, Torvald. First by Papa, and then by you.

HELMER. What? But we two have loved you more than anyone in the world!

NORA *[shakes her head]*. You have never loved me. You just thought it was fun to be in love with me.

HELMER. Nora, what kind of a way is this to talk?

NORA. It's the truth, Torvald. When I lived with Papa, he used to tell me what he thought about everything, so that I never had any opinions but his. And if I did have any of my own, I kept them quiet, because he wouldn't have liked them. He called me his little doll, and he played with me just the way I played with my dolls. Then I came here to live in your house—

HELMER. What kind of a way is that to describe our marriage?

NORA *[undisturbed]*. I mean, then I passed from Papa's hands into yours. You arranged everything the way you wanted it, so that I simply took over your taste in everything—or pretended I did—I don't really know—I think it was a little of both—first one and then the other. Now I look back on it, it's as if I've been living here like a pauper, from hand to mouth. I performed tricks for you, and you gave me food and drink. But that was how you wanted it. You and Papa have done me a great wrong. It's your fault that I have done nothing with my life.

HELMER. Nora, how can you be so unreasonable and ungrateful? Haven't you been happy here?

NORA. No; never. I used to think I was; but I haven't ever been happy.

HELMER. Not—not happy?

NORA. No. I've just had fun. You've always been very kind to me. But our home has never been anything but a playroom. I've been your doll-wife, just as I used to be Papa's doll-child. And the children have been my dolls. I used to think it was fun when you came in and played with me, just as they think it's fun when I go in and play games with them. That's all our marriage has been, Torvald.

HELMER. There may be a little truth in what you say, though you exaggerate and romanticize. But from now on it'll be different. Playtime is over. Now the time has come for education.

NORA. Whose education? Mine or the children's?

HELMER. Both yours and the children's, my dearest Nora.

NORA. Oh, Torvald, you're not the man to educate me into being the right wife for you.

HELMER. How can you say that?

NORA. And what about me? Am I fit to educate the children?

HELMER. Nora!

NORA. Didn't you say yourself a few minutes ago that you dare not leave them in my charge?

HELMER. In a moment of excitement. Surely you don't think I meant it seriously?

NORA. Yes. You were perfectly right. I'm not fitted to educate them. There's something else I must do first. I must educate myself. And you can't help me with that. It's something I must do by myself. That's why I'm leaving you.

HELMER *[jumps up]*. What did you say?

NORA. I must stand on my own feet if I am to find out the truth about myself and about life. So I can't go on living here with you any longer.

HELMER. Nora, Nora!

NORA. I'm leaving you now, at once. Christine will put me up for tonight—

HELMER. You're out of your mind! You can't do this! I forbid you!

NORA. It's no use your trying to forbid me any more. I shall take with me nothing but what is mine. I don't want anything from you, now or ever.

HELMER. What kind of madness is this?

NORA. Tomorrow I shall go home—I mean, to where I was born. It'll be easiest for me to find some kind of a job there.

HELMER. But you're blind! You've no experience of the world—

NORA. I must try to get some, Torvald.

HELMER. But to leave your home, your husband, your children! Have you thought what people will say?

NORA. I can't help that. I only know that I must do this.

HELMER. But this is monstrous! Can you neglect your most sacred duties?

NORA. What do you call my most sacred duties?

HELMER. Do I have to tell you? Your duties towards your husband, and your children.

NORA. I have another duty which is equally sacred.

HELMER. You have not. What on earth could that be?

NORA. My duty towards myself.

HELMER. First and foremost you are a wife and a mother.

NORA. I don't believe that any longer. I believe that I am first and foremost a human being, like you—or anyway, that I must try to become one. I know most people think as you do, Torvald, and I know there's something of the sort to be found in books. But I'm no longer prepared to accept what people say and what's written in books. I must think things out for myself, and try to find my own answer.

HELMER. Do you need to ask where your duty lies in your own home? Haven't you an infallible guide in such matters—your religion?

NORA. Oh, Torvald, I don't really know what religion means.

HELMER. What are you saying?

NORA. I only know what Pastor Hansen told me when I went to confirmation. He explained that religion meant this and that. When I get away from all this and can think things out on my own, that's one of the questions I want to look into. I want to find out whether what Pastor Hansen said was right—or anyway, whether it is right for me.

HELMER. But it's unheard of for so young a woman to behave like this! If religion cannot guide you, let me at least appeal to your conscience. I presume you have some moral feelings left? Or—perhaps you haven't? Well, answer me.

NORA. Oh, Torvald, that isn't an easy question to answer. I simply don't know. I don't know where I am in these matters. I only know that these things mean something quite different to me from what they do to you. I've learned now that certain laws are different from what I'd imagined them to be; but I can't accept that such laws can be right. Has a woman really not the right to spare her dying father pain, or save her husband's life? I can't believe that.

HELMER. You're talking like a child. You don't understand how society works.

NORA. No, I don't. But now I intend to learn. I must try to satisfy myself which is right, society or I.

HELMER. Nora, you're ill; you're feverish. I almost believe you're out of your mind.

NORA. I've never felt so sane and sure in my life.

HELMER. You feel sure that it is right to leave your husband and your children?

NORA. Yes. I do.

HELMER. Then there is only one possible explanation.

NORA. What?

HELMER. That you don't love me any longer.

NORA. No, that's exactly it.

HELMER. Nora! How can you say this to me?

NORA. Oh, Torvald, it hurts me terribly to have to say it, because you've always been so kind to me. But I can't help it. I don't love you any longer.

HELMER *[controlling his emotions with difficulty]*. And you feel quite sure about this too?

NORA. Yes, absolutely sure. That's why I can't go on living here any longer.

HELMER. Can you also explain why I have lost your love?

NORA. Yes, I can. It happened this evening, when the miracle failed to happen. It was then that I realized you weren't the man I'd thought you to be.

HELMER. Explain more clearly. I don't understand you.

NORA. I've waited so patiently, for eight whole years—well, good heavens, I'm not such a fool as to suppose that miracles occur every day. Then this dreadful thing happened to me, and then I *knew:* "Now the miracle will take place!" When Krogstad's letter was lying out there, it never occurred to me for a moment that you would let that man trample over you. I *knew* that you would say to him: "Publish the facts to the world." And when he had done this—

HELMER. Yes, what then? When I'd exposed my wife's name to shame and scandal—

NORA. Then I was certain that you would step forward and take all the blame on yourself, and say: "I am the one who is guilty!"

HELMER. Nora!

NORA. You're thinking I wouldn't have accepted such a sacrifice from you? No, of course I wouldn't! But what would my word have counted for against yours? That was the miracle I was hoping for, and dreading. And it was to prevent it happening that I wanted to end my life.

HELMER. Nora, I would gladly work for you night and day, and endure sorrow and hardship for your sake. But no man can be expected to sacrifice his honor, even for the person he loves.

NORA. Millions of women have done it.

HELMER. Oh, you think and talk like a stupid child.

NORA. That may be. But you neither think nor talk like the man I could share my life with. Once you'd got over your fright—and you weren't frightened of what might threaten me, but only of what threatened you—once the danger was past, then as far as you were concerned it was exactly as though nothing had happened. I was your little songbird just as before—your doll whom henceforth you would take particular care to protect from the world because she was so weak and fragile. *[Gets up.]* Torvald, in that moment I realized that for eight years I had been living here with a complete stranger, and had borne him three children—! Oh, I can't bear to think of it! I could tear myself to pieces!

HELMER *[sadly]*. I see it, I see it. A gulf has indeed opened between us. Oh, but Nora—couldn't it be bridged?

NORA. As I am now, I am no wife for you.

HELMER. I have the strength to change.

NORA. Perhaps—if your doll is taken from you.

HELMER. But to be parted—to be parted from you! No, no, Nora, I can't conceive of it happening!

NORA [*goes into the room, right*]. All the more necessary that it should happen.

She comes back with her outdoor things and a small traveling-bag, which she puts down on a chair by the table.

HELMER. Nora, Nora, not now! Wait till tomorrow!

NORA [*puts on her coat*]. I can't spend the night in a strange man's house.

HELMER. But can't we live here as brother and sister, then—?

NORA [*fastens her hat*]. You know quite well it wouldn't last. [*Puts on her shawl.*] Goodbye, Torvald. I don't want to see the children. I know they're in better hands than mine. As I am now, I can be nothing to them.

HELMER. But some time, Nora—some time—?

NORA. How can I tell? I've no idea what will happen to me.

HELMER. But you are my wife, both as you are and as you will be.

NORA. Listen, Torvald. When a wife leaves her husband's house, as I'm doing now, I'm told that according to the law he is freed of any obligations towards her. In any case, I release you from any such obligations. You mustn't feel bound to me in any way, however small, just as I shall not feel bound to you. We must both be quite free. Here is your ring back. Give me mine.

HELMER. That too?

NORA. That too.

HELMER. Here it is.

NORA. Good. Well, now it's over. I'll leave the keys here. The servants know about everything to do with the house—much better than I do. Tomorrow, when I have left town, Christine will come to pack the things I brought here from home. I'll have them sent on after me.

HELMER. This is the end then! Nora, will you never think of me any more?

NORA. Yes, of course. I shall often think of you and the children and this house.

HELMER. May I write to you, Nora?

NORA. No, never. You mustn't do that.

HELMER. But at least you must let me send you—

NORA. Nothing. Nothing.

HELMER. But if you should need help?—

NORA. I tell you, no. I don't accept things from strangers.

HELMER. Nora—can I never be anything but a stranger to you?

NORA [*picks up her bag*]. Oh, Torvald! Then the miracle of miracles would have to happen.

HELMER. The miracle of miracles?

NORA. You and I would both have to change so much that—oh, Torvald, I don't believe in miracles any longer.

HELMER. But I want to believe in them. Tell me. We should have to change so much that—?

NORA. That life together between us two could become a marriage. Goodbye.

She goes out through the hall.

HELMER [*sinks down on a chair by the door and buries his face in his hands*]. Nora! Nora! [*Looks round and gets up.*] Empty! She's gone! [*A hope strikes him.*] The miracle of miracles—?

The street door is slammed shut downstairs.

[1879]

TOPICS FOR CRITICAL THINKING AND WRITING

1. Near the beginning of the play, how does Mrs. Linde's presence help to define Nora's character? How does Nora's response to Krogstad's entrance tell us something about Nora?

2. What does Dr. Rank contribute to the play? If he were eliminated, what would be lost?

3. Can it be argued that although at the end Nora goes out to achieve self-realization, her abandonment of her children—especially to Torvald's loathsome conventional morality—is a crime? (By the way, exactly why does Nora leave the children? She seems to imply, in some passages, that because she forged a signature she is unfit to bring them up. But do you agree with her?)

4. Michael Meyer, in his splendid biography *Henrik Ibsen,* says that the play is not so much about women's rights as about "the need of every individual to find out the kind of person he or she really is, and to strive to become that person." What evidence can you offer to support or refute this interpretation?

5. In *The Quintessence of Ibsenism* Bernard Shaw says that Ibsen, reacting against a common theatrical preference for strange situations, "saw that . . . the more familiar the situation, the more interesting the play. Shakespear had put ourselves on the stage but not our situations. Our uncles seldom murder our fathers and . . . marry our mothers. . . . Ibsen . . . gives us not only ourselves, but ourselves in our own situations. The things that happen to his stage figures are things that happen to us. One consequence is that his plays are much more important to us than Shakespear's. Another is that they are capable both of hurting us cruelly and of filling us with excited hopes of escape from idealistic tyrannies, and with visions of intenser life in the future." How much of this do you believe?

 AUGUST WILSON

August Wilson was born in Pittsburgh in 1945, the son of a black woman and a white man. After dropping out of school at the age of 15, Wilson took various odd jobs, such as stock clerk and short-order cook, in his spare time educating himself in the public library, chiefly by reading works by such black writers as Richard Wright, Ralph Ellison, Langston Hughes, and Amiri Baraka (LeRoi Jones). In 1978 the director of a black theater in St. Paul, Minnesota, who had known Wilson in Pittsburgh, invited him to write a play for the theater. Six months later Wilson moved permanently to St. Paul.

The winner of the Pulitzer Prize for drama in 1987, Wilson's Fences *was first presented as a staged reading in 1983 and was later performed in Chicago, Seattle, Rochester (New York), and New Haven (Connecticut) before reaching New York City in 1987. An earlier play,* Ma Rainey's Black Bottom, *was voted Best Play of the Year 1984-85 by the New York Drama Critics' Circle. In 1981 when* Ma Rainey *was first read at the O'Neill Center in Waterford, Connecticut, Wilson met Lloyd Richards, a black director with whom he has continued to work closely.* The Piano Lesson, *directed by Richards, won Wilson a second Pulitzer Prize in 1990.*

Fences in the Seattle Reperatory Theatre production with (left to right) Frances Foster as Rose, Keith Amos as Cory, William Jay as Gabriel, and Gilbert Lewis as Troy. (Photo © Chris Bennion)

Fences

for Lloyd Richards,
who adds to whatever he touches

> *When the sins of our fathers visit us*
> *We do not have to play host.*
> *We can banish them with forgiveness*
> *As God, in His Largeness and Laws.*

> —*August Wilson*

LIST OF CHARACTERS

TROY MAXSON
JIM BONO, *Troy's friend*
ROSE, *Troy's wife*
LYONS, *Troy's oldest son by previous marriage*
GABRIEL, *Troy's brother*
CORY, *Troy and Rose's son*
RAYNELL, *Troy's daughter*

SETTING: *The setting is the yard which fronts the only entrance to the Maxson household, an ancient two-story brick house set back off a small alley in a big-city neighborhood. The entrance to the house is gained by two or three steps leading to a wooden porch badly in need of paint.*

A relatively recent addition to the house and running its full width, the porch lacks congruence. It is a sturdy porch with a flat roof. One or two chairs of dubious value sit at one end where the kitchen window opens onto the porch. An old-fashioned icebox stands silent guard at the opposite end.

The yard is a small dirt yard, partially fenced, except for the last scene, with a wooden saw horse, a pile of lumber, and other fence-building equipment set off to the side. Opposite is a tree from which hangs a ball made of rags. A baseball bat leans against the tree. Two oil drums serve as garbage receptacles and sit near the house at right to complete the setting.

THE PLAY: *Near the turn of the century, the destitute of Europe sprang on the city with tenacious claws and an honest and solid dream. The city devoured them. They swelled its belly until it burst into a thousand furnaces and sewing machines, a thousand butcher shops and bakers' ovens, a thousand churches and hospitals and funeral parlors and money-lenders. The city grew. It nourished itself and offered each man a partnership limited only by his talent, his guile, and his willingness and capacity for hard work. For the immigrants of Europe, a dream dared and won true.*

The descendants of African slaves were offered no such welcome or participation. They came from places called the Carolinas and the Virginias, Georgia, Alabama, Mississippi, and Tennessee. They came strong, eager, searching. The city rejected them and they fled and settled along the riverbanks and under bridges in shallow, ramshackle houses made of sticks and tarpaper. They collected rags and wood. They sold the use of their muscles and their bodies. They cleaned houses and washed clothes, they shined shoes, and in quiet desperation and vengeful pride, they stole, and lived in pursuit of their own dream. That they could breathe free, finally, and stand to meet life with the force of dignity and whatever eloquence the heart could call upon.

By 1957, the hard-won victories of the European immigrants had solidified the industrial might of America. War had been confronted and won with new energies that used loyalty and patriotism as its fuel. Life was rich, full, and flourishing. The Milwaukee Braves won the World Series, and the hot winds of change that would make the sixties a turbulent, racing, dangerous, and provocative decade had not yet begun to blow full.

Act 1

Scene 1

It is 1957. TROY *and* BONO *enter the yard, engaged in conversation.* TROY *is fifty-three years old, a large man with thick, heavy hands; it is this largeness that he strives to fill out and make an accommodation with. To-*

gether with his blackness, his largeness informs his sensibilities and the choices he has made in his life.

Of the two men, BONO *is obviously the follower. His commitment to their friendship of thirty-odd years is rooted in his admiration of* TROY'S *honesty, capacity for hard work, and his strength, which* BONO *seeks to emulate.*

It is Friday night, payday, and the one night of the week the two men engage in a ritual of talk and drink. TROY *is usually the most talkative and at times he can be crude and almost vulgar, though he is capable of rising to profound heights of expression. The men carry lunch buckets and wear or carry burlap aprons and are dressed in clothes suitable to their jobs as garbage collectors.*

BONO. Troy, you ought to stop that lying!

TROY. I ain't lying! The nigger had a watermelon this big. *[He indicates with his hands.]* Talking about . . . "What watermelon, Mr. Rand?" I liked to fell out! "What watermelon, Mr. Rand?" . . . And it sitting there big as life.

BONO. What did Mr. Rand say?

TROY. Ain't said nothing. Figure if the nigger too dumb to know he carrying a watermelon, he wasn't gonna get much sense out of him. Trying to hide that great big old watermelon under his coat. Afraid to let the white man see him carry it home.

BONO. I'm like you . . . I ain't got no time for them kind of people.

TROY. Now what he look like getting mad cause he see the man from the union talking to Mr. Rand?

BONO. He come to me talking about . . . "Maxson gonna get us fired." I told him to get away from me with that. He walked away from me calling you a troublemaker. What Mr. Rand say?

TROY. Ain't said nothing. He told me to go down the Commissioner's office next Friday. They called me down there to see them.

BONO. Well, as long as you got your complaint filed, they can't fire you. That's what one of them white fellows tell me.

TROY. I ain't worried about them firing me. They gonna fire me cause I asked a question? That's all I did. I went to Mr. Rand and asked him, "Why? Why you got the white mens driving and the colored lifting?" Told him, "what's the matter, don't I count? You think only white fellows got sense enough to drive a truck. That ain't no paper job! Hell, anybody can drive a truck. How come you got all whites driving and the colored lifting?" He told me "take it to the union." Well, hell, that's what I done! Now they wanna come up with this pack of lies.

BONO. I told Brownie if the man come and ask him any questions . . . just tell the truth! It ain't nothing but something they done trumped up on you cause you filed a complaint on them.

TROY. Brownie don't understand nothing. All I want them to do is change the job description. Give everybody a chance to drive the truck. Brownie can't see that. He ain't got that much sense.

BONO. How you figure he be making out with that gal be up at Taylor's all the time . . . that Alberta gal?

TROY. Same as you and me. Getting just as much as we is. Which is to say nothing.

BONO. It is, huh? I figure you doing a little better than me . . . and I ain't saying what I'm doing.

TROY. Aw, nigger, look here . . . I know you. If you had got anywhere near that gal, twenty minutes later you be looking to tell somebody. And the first one you gonna tell . . . that you gonna want to brag to . . . is me.

BONO. I ain't saying that. I see where you be eyeing her.

TROY. I eye all the women. I don't miss nothing. Don't never let nobody tell you Troy Maxson don't eye the women.

BONO. You been doing more than eyeing her. You done bought her a drink or two.

TROY. Hell yeah, I bought her a drink! What that mean? I bought you one, too. What that mean cause I buy her a drink? I'm just being polite.

BONO. It's all right to buy her one drink. That's what you call being polite. But when you wanna be buying two or three . . . that's what you call eyeing her.

TROY. Look here, as long as you known me . . . you ever known me to chase after women?

BONO. Hell yeah! Long as I done known you. You forgetting I knew you when.

TROY. Naw, I'm talking about since I been married to Rose?

BONO. Oh, not since you been married to Rose. Now, that's the truth, there. I can say that.

TROY. All right then! Case closed.

BONO. I see you be walking up around Alberta's house. You supposed to be at Taylors' and you be walking up around there.

TROY. What you watching where I'm walking for? I ain't watching after you.

BONO. I seen you walking around there more than once.

TROY. Hell, you liable to see me walking anywhere! That don't mean nothing cause you see me walking around there.

BONO. Where she come from anyway? She just kinda showed up one day.

TROY. Tallahassee. You can look at her and tell she one of them Florida gals. They got some big healthy women down there. Grow them right up out the ground. Got a little bit of Indian in her. Most of them niggers down in Florida got some Indian in them.

BONO. I don't know about that Indian part. But she damn sure big and healthy. Woman wear some big stockings. Got them great big old legs and hips as wide as the Mississippi River.

TROY. Legs don't mean nothing. You don't do nothing but push them out of the way. But them hips cushion the ride!

BONO. Troy, you ain't got no sense.

TROY. It's the truth! Like you riding on Goodyears!

ROSE *enters from the house. She is ten years younger than* TROY, *her devotion to him stems from her recognition of the possibilities of her life without him: a succession of abusive men and their babies, a life of partying and running the streets, the Church, or aloneness with its attendant pain and frustration. She recognizes* TROY's *spirit as a fine and illuminating one and she either ignores or forgives his faults, only some of which she recognizes. Though she doesn't drink, her presence is an integral part of the Friday night rituals. She alternates between the porch and the kitchen, where supper preparations are under way.*

ROSE. What you all out here getting into?

TROY. What you worried about what we getting into for? This is men talk, woman.

ROSE. What I care what you all talking about? Bono, you gonna stay for supper?

BONO. No, I thank you, Rose. But Lucille say she cooking up a pot of pigfeet.

TROY. Pigfeet! Hell, I'm going home with you! Might even stay the night if you got some pigfeet. You got something in there to top them pigfeet, Rose?

ROSE. I'm cooking up some chicken. I got some chicken and collard greens.

TROY. Well, go on back in the house and let me and Bono finish what we was talking about. This is men talk. I got some talk for you later. You know what kind of talk I mean. You go on and powder it up.

ROSE. Troy Maxson, don't you start that now!

TROY. *[puts his arm around her].* Aw, woman . . . come here. Look here, Bono . . . when I met this woman . . . I got out that place, say, "Hitch up my pony, saddle up my mare . . . there's a woman out there for me somewhere. I looked here. Looked there. Saw Rose and latched on to her." I latched on to her and told her—I'm gonna tell you the truth—I told her, "Baby, I don't wanna marry, I just wanna be your man." Rose told me . . . tell him what you told me, Rose.

ROSE. I told him if he wasn't the marrying kind, then move out the way so the marrying kind could find me.

TROY. That's what she told me. "Nigger, you in my way. You blocking the view! Move out the way so I can find me a husband." I thought it over two or three days. Come back—

ROSE. Ain't no two or three days nothing. You was back the same night.

TROY. Come back, told her . . . "Okay, baby . . . but I'm gonna buy me a banty rooster and put him out there in the backyard . . . and when he see a stranger come, he'll flap his wings and crow. . . ." Look here, Bono, I could watch the front door by myself . . . it was that back door I was worried about.

ROSE. Troy, you ought not talk like that. Troy ain't doing nothing but telling a lie.

TROY. Only thing is . . . when we first got married . . . forget the rooster . . . we ain't had no yard!

BONO. I hear you tell it. Me and Lucille was staying down there on Logan Street. Had two rooms with the outhouse in the back. I ain't mind the outhouse none. But when that goddamn wind blow through there in the winter . . . that's what I'm talking about! To this day I wonder why in the hell I ever stayed down there for six long years. But see, I didn't know I could do no better. I thought only white folks had inside toilets and things.

ROSE. There's a lot of people don't know they can do no better than they doing now. That's just something you got to learn. A lot of folks still shop at Bella's.

TROY. Ain't nothing wrong with shopping at Bella's. She got fresh food.

ROSE. I ain't said nothing about if she got fresh food. I'm talking about what she charge. She charge ten cents more than the A&P.

TROY. The A&P ain't never done nothing for me. I spends my money where I'm treated right. I go down to Bella, say, "I need a loaf of bread, I'll pay you Friday." She give it to me. What sense that make when I got money to go and spend it somewhere else and ignore the person who done right by me? That ain't in the Bible.

ROSE. We ain't talking about what's in the Bible. What sense it make to shop there when she overcharge?

TROY. You shop where you want to. I'll do my shopping where the people been good to me.

ROSE. Well, I don't think it's right for her to overcharge. That's all I was saying.

BONO. Look here . . . I got to get on. Lucille going be raising all kind of hell.

TROY. Where you going, nigger? We ain't finished this pint. Come here, finish this pint.

BONO. Well, hell, I am . . . if you ever turn the bottle loose.

TROY *[hands him the bottle].* The only thing I say about the A&P is I'm glad Cory got that job down there. Help him take care of his school clothes and things. Gabe done moved out and things getting tight around here. He got that job. . . . He can start to look out for himself.

ROSE. Cory done went and got recruited by a college football team.

TROY. I told that boy about that football stuff. The white man ain't gonna let him get nowhere with that football. I told him when he first come to me with it. Now you come telling me he done went and got more tied up in it. He ought to go and get recruited in how to fix cars or something where he can make a living.

ROSE. He ain't talking about making no living playing football. It's just something the boys in school do. They gonna send a recruiter by to talk to you. He'll tell you he ain't talking about making no living playing football. It's a honor to be recruited.

TROY. It ain't gonna get him nowhere. Bono'll tell you that.

BONO. If he be like you in the sports . . . he's gonna be all right. Ain't but two men ever played baseball as good as you. That's Babe Ruth and Josh Gibson.[1] Them's the only two men ever hit more home runs than you.

TROY. What it ever get me? Ain't got a pot to piss in or a window to throw it out of.

ROSE. Times have changed since you was playing baseball, Troy. That was before the war. Times have changed a lot since then.

TROY. How in hell they done changed?

ROSE. They got lots of colored boys playing ball now. Baseball and football.

BONO. You right about that, Rose. Times have changed, Troy. You just come along too early.

TROY. There ought not never have been no time called too early! Now you take that fellow . . . what's that fellow they had playing right field for the Yankees back then? You know who I'm talking about, Bono. Used to play right field for the Yankees.

ROSE. Selkirk?

TROY. Selkirk! That's it! Man batting .269, understand? .269. What kind of sense that make? I was hitting .432 with thirty-seven home runs! Man batting .269 and playing right field for the Yankees! I saw Josh Gibson's

[1] African-American ballplayer (1911–47), known as the Babe Ruth of the Negro leagues

daughter yesterday. She walking around with raggedy shoes on her feet. Now I bet you Selkirk's daughter ain't walking around with raggedy shoes on the feet! I bet you that!

ROSE. They got a lot of colored baseball players now. Jackie Robinson[2] was the first. Folks had to wait for Jackie Robinson.

TROY. I done seen a hundred niggers play baseball better than Jackie Robinson. Hell, I know some teams Jackie Robinson couldn't even make! What you talking about Jackie Robinson. Jackie Robinson wasn't nobody. I'm talking about if you could play ball then they ought to have let you play. Don't care what color you were. Come telling me I come along too early. If you could play . . . then they ought to have let you play.

TROY *takes a long drink from the bottle.*

ROSE. You gonna drink yourself to death. You don't need to be drinking like that.

TROY. Death ain't nothing. I done seen him. Done wrassled with him. You can't tell me nothing about death. Death ain't nothing but a fastball on the outside corner. And you know what I'll do to that! Lookee here, Bono . . . am I lying? You get one of them fastballs, about waist high, over the outside corner of the plate where you can get the meat of the bat on it . . . and good god! You can kiss it goodbye. Now, am I lying?

BONO. Naw, you telling the truth there. I seen you do it.

TROY. If I'm lying . . . that 450 feet worth of lying! *[Pause.]* That's all death is to me. A fastball on the outside corner.

ROSE. I don't know why you want to get on talking about death.

TROY. Ain't nothing wrong with talking about death. That's part of life. Everybody gonna die. You gonna die, I'm gonna die. Bono's gonna die. Hell, we all gonna die.

ROSE. But you ain't got to talk about it. I don't like to talk about it.

TROY. You the one brought it up. Me and Bono was talking about baseball . . . you tell me I'm gonna drink myself to death. Ain't that right, Bono? You know I don't drink this but one night out of the week. That's Friday night. I'm gonna drink just enough to where I can handle it. Then I cuts it loose. I leave it alone. So don't you worry about me drinking myself to death. 'Cause I ain't worried about Death. I done seen him. I done wrestled with him.

Look here, Bono . . . I looked up one day and Death was marching straight at me. Like Soldiers on Parade! The Army of Death was marching straight at me. The middle of July, 1941. It got real cold just like it be winter. It seem like Death himself reached out and touched me on the shoulder. He touch me just like I touch you. I got cold as ice and Death standing there grinning at me.

ROSE. Troy, why don't you hush that talk.

TROY. I say . . . what you want, Mr. Death? You be wanting me? You done brought your army to be getting me? I looked him dead in the eye. I

---

[2]In 1947 Robinson (1919–72) became the first African-American to play baseball in the major leagues.

wasn't fearing nothing. I was ready to tangle. Just like I'm ready to tangle now. The Bible say be ever vigilant. That's why I don't get but so drunk. I got to keep watch.

ROSE. Troy was right down there in Mercy Hospital. You remember he had pneumonia? Laying there with a fever talking plumb out of his head.

TROY. Death standing there staring at me . . . carrying that sickle in his hand. Finally he say, "You want bound over for another year?" See, just like that . . . "You want bound over for another year?" I told him, "Bound over hell! Let's settle this now!"

It seem like he kinda fell back when I said that, and all the cold went out of me. I reached down and grabbed that sickle and threw it just as far as I could throw it . . . and me and him commenced to wrestling.

We wrestled for three days and three nights. I can't say where I found the strength from. Everytime it seemed like he was gonna get the best of me, I'd reach way down deep inside myself and find the strength to do him one better.

ROSE. Everytime Troy tell that story he find different ways to tell it. Different things to make up about it.

TROY. I ain't making up nothing. I'm telling you the facts of what happened. I wrestled with Death for three days and three nights and I'm standing here to tell you about it. *[Pause.]* All right. At the end of the third night we done weakened each other to where we can't hardly move. Death stood up, throwed on his robe . . . had him a white robe with a hood on it. He throwed on that robe and went off to look for his sickle. Say, "I'll be back." Just like that. "I'll be back." I told him, say, "Yeah, but . . . you gonna have to find me!" I wasn't no fool. I wasn't going looking for him. Death ain't nothing to play with. And I know he's gonna get me. I know I got to join his army . . . his camp followers. But as long as I keep my strength and see him coming . . . as long as I keep up my vigilance . . . he's gonna have to fight to get me. I ain't going easy.

BONO. Well, look here, since you got to keep up your vigilance . . . let me have the bottle.

TROY. Aw hell, I shouldn't have told you that part. I should have left out that part.

ROSE. Troy be talking that stuff and half the time don't even know what he be talking about.

TROY. Bono know me better than that.

BONO. That's right. I know you. I know you got some Uncle Remus[3] in your blood. You got more stories that the devil got sinners.

TROY. Aw hell, I done seen him too! Done talked with the devil.

ROSE. Troy, don't nobody wanna be hearing all that stuff.

LYONS *enters the yard from the street. Thirty-four years old,* TROY'S *son by a previous marriage, he sports a neatly trimmed goatee, sport coat, white shirt, tieless and buttoned at the collar. Though he fancies himself a musician, he is more caught up in the rituals and "idea" of*

---

[3]Narrator of traditional black tales in a book by Joel Chandler Harris

being a musician than in the actual practice of the music. He has come to borrow money from TROY, *and while he knows he will be successful, he is uncertain as to what extent his lifestyle will be held up to scrutiny and ridicule.*

LYONS. Hey, Pop.

TROY. What you come "Hey, Popping" me for?

LYONS. How you doing, Rose? *[He kisses her.]* Mr. Bono. How you doing?

BONO. Hey, Lyons . . . how you been?

TROY. He must have been doing all right. I ain't seen him around here last week.

ROSE. Troy, leave your boy alone. He come by to see you and you wanna start all that nonsense.

TROY. I ain't bothering Lyons. *[Offers him the bottle.]* Here . . . get you a drink. We got an understanding. I know why he come by to see me and he know I know.

LYONS. Come on, Pop . . . I just stopped by to say hi . . . see how you was doing.

TROY. You ain't stopped by yesterday.

ROSE. You gonna stay for supper, Lyons? I got some chicken cooking in the oven.

LYONS. No, Rose . . . thanks. I was just in the neighborhood and thought I'd stop by for a minute.

TROY. You was in the neighborhood all right, nigger. You telling the truth there. You was in the neighborhood cause it's my payday.

LYONS. Well, hell, since you mentioned it . . . let me have ten dollars.

TROY. I'll be damned! I'll die and go to hell and play blackjack with the devil before I give you ten dollars.

BONO. That's what I wanna know about . . . that devil you done seen.

LYONS. What . . . Pop done seen the devil? You too much, Pops.

TROY. Yeah, I done seen him. Talked to him too!

ROSE. You ain't seen no devil. I done told you that man ain't had nothing to do with the devil. Anything you can't understand, you want to call it the devil.

TROY. Look here, Bono . . . I went down to see Hertzberger about some furniture. Got three rooms for two-ninety-eight. That what it say on the radio. "Three rooms . . . two-ninety-eight." Even made up a little song about it. Go down there . . . man tell me I can't get no credit. I'm working every day and can't get no credit. What to do? I got an empty house with some raggedy furniture in it. Cory ain't got no bed. He's sleeping on a pile of rags on the floor. Working every day and can't get no credit. Come back here—Rose'll tell you—madder than hell. Sit down . . . try to figure what I'm gonna do. Come a knock on the door. Ain't been living here but three days. Who know I'm here? Open the door . . . devil standing there bigger than life. White fellow . . . white fellow . . . got on good clothes and everything. Standing there with a clipboard in his hand. I ain't had to say nothing. First words come out of his mouth was . . . "I understand you need some furniture and can't get no credit." I liked to fell over. He say, "I'll give you all the credit you want, but you got to pay the interest on it." I told him, "Give me three rooms worth and charge whatever you want." Next day a truck pulled up here and two men unloaded them three rooms. Man what drove the truck give me a book. Say send ten dollars, first of every month to the address in the book and every thing will be all right. Say if I miss a payment the devil was coming back and it'll be hell to pay. That was fifteen years ago. To this day . . . the first of the month I send my ten dollars, Rose'll tell you.

ROSE. Troy lying.

TROY. I ain't never seen that man since. Now you tell me who else that could have been but the devil? I ain't sold my soul or nothing like that, you understand. Naw, I wouldn't have truck with the devil about nothing like that. I got my furniture and pays my ten dollars the first of the month just like clockwork.

BONO. How long you say you been paying this ten dollars a month?

TROY. Fifteen years!

BONO. Hell, ain't you finished paying for it yet? How much the man done charged you?

TROY. Ah hell, I done paid for it. I done paid for it ten times over! The fact is I'm scared to stop paying it.

ROSE. Troy lying. We got that furniture from Mr. Glickman. He ain't paying no ten dollars a month to nobody.

TROY. Aw hell, woman. Bono know I ain't that big a fool.

LYONS. I was just getting ready to say . . . I know where there's a bridge for sale.

TROY. Look here, I'll tell you this . . . it don't matter to me if he was the devil. It don't matter if the devil give credit. Somebody has got to give it.

ROSE. It ought to matter. You going around talking about having truck with the devil . . . God's the one you gonna have to answer to. He's the one gonna be at the Judgment.

LYONS. Yeah, well, look here, Pop . . . Let me have that ten dollars. I'll give it back to you. Bonnie got a job working at the hospital.

TROY. What I tell you, Bono? The only time I see this nigger is when he wants something. That's the only time I see him.

LYONS. Come on, Pop, Mr. Bono don't want to hear all that. Let me have the ten dollars. I told you Bonnie working.

TROY. What that mean to me? "Bonnie working." I don't care if she working. Go ask her for the ten dollars if she working. Talking about "Bonnie working." Why ain't you working?

LYONS. Aw, Pop, you know I can't find no decent job. Where am I gonna get a job at? You know I can't get no job.

TROY. I told you I know some people down there. I can get you on the rubbish if you want to work. I told you that the last time you came by here asking me for something.

LYONS. Naw, Pop . . . thanks. That ain't for me. I don't wanna be carrying nobody's rubbish. I don't wanna be punching nobody's time clock.

TROY. What's the matter, you too good to carry people's rubbish? Where you think that ten dollars you talking about come from? I'm just supposed to haul people's rubbish and give my money to you cause you too lazy to work. You too lazy to work and wanna know why you ain't got what I got.

ROSE. What hospital Bonnie working at? Mercy?

LYONS. She's down at Passavant working in the laundry.

TROY. I ain't got nothing as it is. I give you that ten dollars and I got to eat beans the rest of the week. Naw . . . you ain't getting no ten dollars here.

LYONS. You ain't got to be eating no beans. I don't know why you wanna say that.

TROY. I ain't got no extra money. Gabe done moved over to Miss Pearl's paying her the rent and things done got tight around here. I can't afford to be giving you every payday.

LYONS. I ain't asked you to give me nothing. I asked you to loan me ten dollars. I know you got ten dollars.

TROY. Yeah, I got it. You know why I got it? Cause I don't throw my money away out there in the streets. You living the fast life . . . wanna be a musician . . . running around in them clubs and things . . . then, you learn to take care of yourself. You ain't gonna find me going and asking nobody for nothing. I done spent too many years without.

LYONS. You and me is two different people, Pop.

TROY. I done learned my mistake and learned to do what's right by it. You still trying to get something for nothing. Life don't owe you nothing. You owe it to yourself. Ask Bono. He'll tell you I'm right.

LYONS. You got your way of dealing with the world . . . I got mine. The only thing that matters to me is the music.

TROY. Yeah, I can see that! It don't matter how you gonna eat . . . where your next dollar is coming from. You telling the truth there.

LYONS. I know I got to eat. But I got to live too. I need something that gonna help me to get out of the bed in the morning. Make me feel like I belong in the world. I don't bother nobody. I just stay with the music cause that's the only way I can find to live in the world. Otherwise there ain't no telling what I might do. Now I don't come criticizing you and how you live. I just come by to ask you for ten dollars. I don't wanna hear all that about how I live.

TROY. Boy, your mamma did a hell of a job raising you.

LYONS. You can't change me, Pop. I'm thirty-four years old. If you wanted to change me, you should have been there when I was growing up. I come by to see you . . . ask for ten dollars and you want to talk about how I was raised. You don't know nothing about how I was raised.

ROSE. Let the boy have ten dollars, Troy.

TROY *[to* LYONS*]*. What the hell you looking at me for? I ain't got no ten dollars. You know what I do with my money. *[To* ROSE.*]* Give him ten dollars if you want him to have it.

ROSE. I will. Just as soon as you turn it loose.

TROY *[handing* ROSE *the money]*. There it is. Seventy-six dollars and forty-two cents. You see this, Bono? Now, I ain't gonna get but six of that back.

ROSE. You ought to stop telling that lie. Here, Lyons. *[She hands him the money.]*

LYONS. Thanks, Rose. Look . . . I got to run . . . I'll see you later.

TROY. Wait a minute. You gonna say, "thanks, Rose" and ain't gonna look to see where she got that ten dollars from? See how they do me, Bono?

LYONS. I know she got it from you, Pop. Thanks. I'll give it back to you.

TROY. There he go telling another lie. Time I see that ten dollars . . . he'll be owing me thirty more.

LYONS. See you, Mr. Bono.

BONO. Take care, Lyons!

LYONS. Thanks, Pop. I'll see you again.

LYONS exits the yard.

TROY. I don't know why he don't go and get him a decent job and take care of that woman he got.

BONO. He'll be all right, Troy. The boy is still young.

TROY. The *boy* is thirty-four years old.

ROSE. Let's not get off into all that.

BONO. Look here . . . I got to be going. I got to be getting on. Lucille gonna be waiting.

TROY *[puts his arm around* ROSE*].* See this woman, Bono? I love this woman. I love this woman so much it hurts. I love her so much . . . I done run out of ways of loving her. So I got to go back to basics. Don't you come by my house Monday morning talking about time to go to work . . . 'cause I'm still gonna be stroking!

ROSE. Troy! Stop it now!

BONO. I ain't paying him no mind, Rose. That ain't nothing but gin-talk. Go on, Troy. I'll see you Monday.

TROY. Don't you come by my house, nigger! I done told you what I'm gonna be doing.

The lights go down to black.

Scene 2

The lights come up on ROSE *hanging up clothes. She hums and sings softly to herself. It is the following morning.*

ROSE *[sings].* Jesus, be a fence all around me every day

Jesus, I want you to protect me as I travel on my way.

Jesus, be a fence all around me every day.

TROY *enters from the house.*

Jesus, I want you to protect me

As I travel on my way.

[To TROY*.]* 'Morning. You ready for breakfast? I can fix it soon as I finish hanging up these clothes?

TROY. I got the coffee on. That'll be all right. I'll just drink some of that this morning.

ROSE. That 651 hit yesterday. That's the second time this month. Miss Pearl hit for a dollar . . . seem like those that need the least always get lucky. Poor folks can't get nothing.

TROY. Them numbers don't know nobody. I don't know why you fool with them. You and Lyons both.

ROSE. It's something to do.

TROY. You ain't doing nothing but throwing your money away.

ROSE. Troy, you know I don't play foolishly. I just play a nickel here and a nickel there.

TROY. That's two nickels you done thrown away.

ROSE. Now I hit sometimes . . . that makes up for it. It always comes in handy when I do hit. I don't hear you complaining then.

TROY. I ain't complaining now. I just say it's foolish. Trying to guess out of six hundred ways which way the number gonna come. If I had all the money niggers, these Negroes, throw away on numbers for one week— just one week—I'd be a rich man.

ROSE. Well, you wishing and calling it foolish ain't gonna stop folks from playing numbers. That's one thing for sure. Besides . . . some good things come from playing numbers. Look where Pope done bought him that restaurant off of numbers.

TROY. I can't stand niggers like that. Man ain't had two dimes to rub together. He walking around with his shoes all run over bumming money for cigarettes. All right. Got lucky there and hit the numbers . . .

ROSE. Troy, I know all about it.

TROY. Had good sense, I'll say that for him. He ain't throwed his money away. I seen niggers hit the numbers and go through two thousand dollars in four days. Man bought him that restaurant down there . . . fixed it up real nice . . . and then didn't want nobody to come in it! A Negro go in there and can't get no kind of service. I seen a white fellow come in there and order a bowl of stew. Pope picked all the meat out of the pot for him. Man ain't had nothing but a bowl of meat! Negro come behind him and ain't got nothing but the potatoes and carrots. Talking about what numbers do for people, you picked a wrong example. Ain't done nothing but make a worser fool out of him than he was before.

ROSE. Troy, you ought to stop worrying about what happened at work yesterday.

TROY. I ain't worried. Just told me to be down there at the Commissioner's office on Friday. Everybody think they gonna fire me. I ain't worried about them firing me. You ain't got to worry about that. *[Pause.]* Where's Cory? Cory in the house? *[Calls.]* Cory?

ROSE. He gone out.

TROY. Out, huh? He gone out 'cause he know I want him to help me with this fence. I know how he is. That boy scared of work.

GABRIEL *enters. He comes halfway down the alley and, hearing* TROY'*s voice, stops.*

TROY *[continues].* He ain't done a lick of work in his life.

ROSE. He had to go to football practice. Coach wanted them to get in a little extra practice before the season start.

TROY. I got his practice . . . running out of here before he get his chores done.

ROSE. Troy, what is wrong with you this morning? Don't nothing set right with you. Go on back in there and go to bed . . . get up on the other side.

TROY. Why something got to be wrong with me? I ain't said nothing wrong with me.

ROSE. You got something to say about everything. First it's the numbers . . . then it's the way the man runs his restaurant . . . then you done got on Cory. What's it gonna be next? Take a look up there and see if the weather suits you . . . or is it gonna be how you gonna put up the fence with the clothes hanging in the yard.

TROY. You hit the nail on the head then.

ROSE. I know you like I know the back of my hand. Go on in there and get you some coffee . . . see if that straighten you up. 'Cause you ain't right this morning.

TROY *starts into the house and sees* GABRIEL. GABRIEL *starts singing.* TROY'*s brother, he is seven years younger than* TROY. *Injured in World*

War II, he has a metal plate in his head. He carries an old trumpet tied around his waist and believes with every fiber of his being that he is the Archangel Gabriel. He carries a chipped basket with an assortment of discarded fruits and vegetables he has picked up in the strip district and which he attempts to sell.

GABRIEL *[singing].* Yes, ma'am I got plums

You ask me how I sell them

Oh ten cents apiece

Three for a quarter

Come and buy now

'Cause I'm here today

And tomorrow I'll be gone

GABRIEL *enters.*

Hey, Rose!

ROSE. How you doing Gabe?

GABRIEL. There's Troy . . . Hey, Troy!

TROY. Hey, Gabe.

Exit into kitchen.

ROSE *[to GABRIEL].* What you got there?

GABRIEL. You know what I got, Rose. I got fruits and vegetables.

ROSE *[looking in basket].* Where's all these plums you talking about?

GABRIEL. I ain't got no plums today, Rose. I was just singing that. Have some tomorrow. Put me in a big order for plums. Have enough plums tomorrow for St. Peter and everybody.

TROY *reenters from kitchen, crosses to steps.*

[To ROSE.] Troy's mad at me.

TROY. I ain't mad at you. What I got to be mad at you about? You ain't done nothing to me.

GABRIEL. I just moved over to Miss Pearl's to keep out from in your way. I ain't mean no harm by it.

TROY. Who said anything about that? I ain't said anything about that.

GABRIEL. You ain't mad at me, is you?

TROY. Naw . . . I ain't mad at you, Gabe. If I was mad at you I'd tell you about it.

GABRIEL. Got me two rooms. In the basement. Got my own door too. Wanna see my key? *[He holds up a key.]* That's my own key! My two rooms!

TROY. Well, that's good, Gabe. You got your own key . . . that's good.

ROSE. You hungry, Gabe? I was just fixing to cook Troy his breakfast.

GABRIEL. I'll take some biscuits. You got some biscuits? Did you know when I was in heaven . . . every morning me and St. Peter would sit down by the gate and eat some big fat biscuits? Oh, yeah! We had us a good time. We'd sit there and eat us them biscuits and then St. Peter would go off to sleep and tell me to wake him up when it's time to open the gates for the judgment.

ROSE. Well, come on . . . I'll make up a batch of biscuits.

ROSE *exits into the house.*

GABRIEL. Troy . . . St. Peter got your name in the book. I seen it. It say . . . Troy Maxson. I say . . . I know him! He got the same name like what I got. That's my brother!

TROY. How many times you gonna tell me that, Gabe?

GABRIEL. Ain't got my name in the book. Don't have to have my name. I done died and went to heaven. He got your name though. One morning St. Peter was looking at his book . . . marking it up for the judgment . . . and he let me see your name. Got it in there under M. Got Rose's name . . . I ain't seen it like I seen yours . . . but I know it's in there. He got a great big book. Got everybody's name what was ever been born. That's what he told me. But I seen your name. Seen it with my own eyes.

TROY. Go on in the house there. Rose going to fix you something to eat.

GABRIEL. Oh, I ain't hungry. I done had breakfast with Aunt Jemimah. She come by and cooked me up a whole mess of flapjacks. Remember how we used to eat them flapjacks?

TROY. Go on in the house and get you something to eat now.

GABRIEL. I got to sell my plums. I done sold some tomatoes. Got me two quarters. Wanna see? *[He shows* TROY *his quarters.]* I'm gonna save them and buy me a new horn so St. Peter can hear me when it's time to open the gates. *[GABRIEL stops suddenly. Listens.]* Hear that? That's the hellhounds. I got to chase them out of here. Go on get out of here! Get out!

GABRIEL *exits singing.*

Better get ready for the judgment
Better get ready for the judgment
My Lord is coming down

ROSE *enters from the house.*

TROY. He's gone off somewhere.

GABRIEL *[offstage].* Better get ready for the judgment
Better get ready for the judgment morning
Better get ready for the judgment
My God is coming down

ROSE. He ain't eating right. Miss Pearl say she can't get him to eat nothing.

TROY. What you want me to do about it, Rose? I done did everything I can for the man. I can't make him get well. Man got half his head blown away . . . what you expect?

ROSE. Seem like something ought to be done to help him.

TROY. Man don't bother nobody. He just mixed up from that metal plate he got in his head. Ain't no sense for him to go back into the hospital.

ROSE. Least he be eating right. They can help him take care of himself.

TROY. Don't nobody wanna be locked up, Rose. What you wanna lock him up for? Man go over there and fight the war . . . messin' around with them Japs, get half his head blow off . . . and they give him a lousy three thousand dollars. And I had to swoop down on that.

ROSE. Is you fixing to go into that again?

TROY. That's the only way I got a roof over my head . . . cause of that metal plate.

ROSE. Ain't no sense you blaming yourself for nothing. Gabe wasn't in no condition to manage that money. You done what was right by him. Can't nobody say you ain't done what was right by him. Look how long you took care of him . . . till he wanted to have his own place and moved over there with Miss Pearl.

TROY. That ain't what I'm saying, woman! I'm just stating the facts. If my brother didn't have that metal plate in his head . . . I wouldn't have a pot to piss in or a window to throw it out of. And I'm fifty-three years old. Now see if you can understand that!

TROY *gets up from the porch and starts to exit the yard.*

ROSE. Where you going off to? You been running out of here every Saturday for weeks. I thought you was gonna work on this fence?

TROY. I'm gonna walk down to Taylor's. Listen to the ball game. I'll be back in a bit. I'll work on it when I get back.

He exits the yard. The lights go to black.

Scene 3

The lights come up on the yard. It is four hours later. ROSE *is taking down the clothes from the line.* CORY *enters carrying his football equipment.*

ROSE. Your daddy like to had a fit with you running out of here this morning without doing your chores.

CORY. I told you I had to go to practice.

ROSE. He say you were supposed to help him with this fence.

CORY. He been saying that the last four or five Saturdays, and then he don't never do nothing, but go down to Taylors'. Did you tell him about the recruiter?

ROSE. Yeah, I told him.

CORY. What he say?

ROSE. He ain't said nothing too much. You get in there and get started on your chores before he gets back. Go on and scrub down them steps before he gets back here hollering and carrying on.

CORY. I'm hungry. What you got to eat, Mama?

ROSE. Go on and get started on your chores. I got some meat loaf in there. Go on and make you a sandwich . . . and don't leave no mess in there.

CORY *exits into the house.* ROSE *continues to take down the clothes.* TROY *enters the yard and sneaks up and grabs her from behind.*

Troy! Go on, now. You liked to scared me to death. What was the score of the game? Lucille had me on the phone and I couldn't keep up with it.

TROY. What I care about the game? Come here, woman. *[He tries to kiss her.]*

ROSE. I thought you went down Taylors' to listen to the game. Go on, Troy! You supposed to be putting up this fence.

TROY *[attempting to kiss her again].* I'll put it up when I finish with what is at hand.

ROSE. Go on, Troy. I ain't studying you.

TROY *[chasing after her].* I'm studying you . . . fixing to do my homework!

ROSE. Troy, you better leave me alone.

TROY. Where's Cory? That boy brought his butt home yet?

ROSE. He's in the house doing his chores.

TROY *[calling].* Cory! Get your butt out here, boy!

ROSE *exits into the house with the laundry.* TROY *goes over to the pile of wood, picks up a board, and starts sawing.* CORY *enters from the house.*

TROY. You just now coming in here from leaving this morning?

CORY. Yeah, I had to go to football practice.

TROY. Yeah, what?

CORY. Yessir.

TROY. I ain't but two seconds off you noway. The garbage sitting in there overflowing . . . you ain't done none of your chores . . . and you come in here talking about "Yeah."

CORY. I was just getting ready to do my chores now, Pop . . .

TROY. Your first chore is to help me with this fence on Saturday. Everything else come after that. Now get that saw and cut them boards.

CORY *takes the saw and begins cutting the boards.* TROY *continues working. There is a long pause.*

CORY. Hey, Pop . . . why don't you buy a TV?

TROY. What I want with a TV? What I want one of them for?

CORY. Everybody got one. Earl, Ba Bra . . . Jesse!

TROY. I ain't asked you who had one. I say what I want with one?

CORY. So you can watch it. They got lots of things on TV. Baseball games and everything. We could watch the World Series.

TROY. Yeah . . . and how much this TV cost?

CORY. I don't know. They got them on sale for around two hundred dollars.

TROY. Two hundred dollars, huh?

CORY. That ain't that much, Pop.

TROY. Naw, it's just two hundred dollars. See that roof you got over your head at night? Let me tell you something about that roof. It's been over ten years since that roof was last tarred. See now . . . the snow come this winter and sit up there on that roof like it is . . . and it's gonna seep inside. It's just gonna be a little bit . . . ain't gonna hardly notice it. Then the next thing you know, it's gonna be leaking all over the house. Then the wood rot from all that water and you gonna need a whole new roof. Now, how much you think it cost to get that roof tarred?

CORY. I don't know.

TROY. Two hundred and sixty-four dollars . . . cash money. While you thinking about a TV, I got to be thinking about the roof . . . and whatever else go wrong here. Now if you had two hundred dollars, what would you do . . . fix the roof or buy a TV?

CORY. I'd buy a TV. Then when the roof started to leak . . . when it needed fixing . . . I'd fix it.

TROY. Where you gonna get the money from? You done spent it for a TV. You gonna sit up and watch the water run all over your brand new TV.

CORY. Aw, Pop. You got money. I know you do.

TROY. Where I got it at, huh?

CORY. You got it in the bank.

TROY. You wanna see my bankbook? You wanna see that seventy-three dollars and twenty-two cents I got sitting up in there?

CORY. You ain't got to pay for it all at one time. You can put a down payment on it and carry it on home with you.

TROY. Not me. I ain't gonna owe nobody nothing if I can help it. Miss a payment and they come and snatch it right out of your house. Then what you got? Now, soon as I get two hundred dollars clear, then I'll buy a TV. Right now, as soon as I get two hundred and sixty-four dollars, I'm gonna have this roof tarred.

CORY. Aw . . . Pop!

TROY. You go on and get you two hundred dollars and buy one if ya want it. I got better things to do with my money.

CORY. I can't get no two hundred dollars. I ain't never seen two hundred dollars.

TROY. I'll tell you what . . . you get you a hundred dollars and I'll put the other hundred with it.

CORY. All right, I'm gonna show you.

TROY. You gonna show me how you can cut them boards right now.

CORY *begins to cut the boards. There is a long pause.*

CORY. The Pirates won today. That makes five in a row.

TROY. I ain't thinking about the Pirates. Got an all-white team. Got that boy . . . that Puerto Rican boy . . . Clemente. Don't even half-play him. That boy could be something if they give him a chance. Play him one day and sit him on the bench the next.

CORY. He gets a lot of chances to play.

TROY. I'm talking about playing regular. Playing every day so you can get your timing. That's what I'm talking about.

CORY. They got some white guys on the team that don't play every day. You can't play everybody at the same time.

TROY. If they got a white fellow sitting on the bench . . . you can bet your last dollar he can't play! The colored guy got to be twice as good before he get on the team. That's why I don't want you to get all tied up in them sports. Man on the team and what it get him? They got colored on the team and don't use them. Same as not having them. All them teams the same.

CORY. The Braves got Hank Aaron and Wes Covington. Hank Aaron hit two home runs today. That makes forty-three.

TROY. Hank Aaron ain't nobody. That what you supposed to do. That's how you supposed to play the game. Ain't nothing to it. It's just a matter of timing . . . getting the right follow-through. Hell, I can hit forty-three home runs right now!

CORY. Not off no major-league pitching, you couldn't.

TROY. We had better pitching in the Negro leagues. I hit seven home runs off of Satchel Paige.[4] You can't get no better than that!

CORY. Sandy Koufax. He's leading the league in strikeouts.

TROY. I ain't thinking of no Sandy Koufax.

CORY. You got Warren Spahn and Lew Burdette. I bet you couldn't hit no home runs off of Warren Spahn.

TROY. I'm through with it now. You go on and cut them boards. *[Pause.]* Your mama tell me you done got recruited by a college football team? Is that right?

CORY. Yeah. Coach Zellman say the recruiter gonna be coming by to talk to you. Get you to sign the permission papers.

TROY. I thought you supposed to be working down there at the A&P. Ain't you suppose to be working down there after school?

CORY. Mr. Stawicki say he gonna hold my job for me until after the football season. Say starting next week I can work weekends.

[4]Paige (1906–82) was a pitcher in the Negro leagues

TROY. I thought we had an understanding about this football stuff? You suppose to keep up with your chores and hold that job down at the A&P. Ain't been around here all day on a Saturday. Ain't none of your chores done . . . and now you telling me you done quit your job.

CORY. I'm going to be working weekends.

TROY. You damn right you are! And ain't no need for nobody coming around here to talk to me about signing nothing.

CORY. Hey, Pop . . . you can't do that. He's coming all the way from North Carolina.

TROY. I don't care where he coming from. The white man ain't gonna let you get nowhere with that football noway. You go on and get your book-learning so you can work yourself up in that A&P or learn how to fix cars or build houses or something, get you a trade. That way you have something can't nobody take away from you. You go on and learn how to put your hands to some good use. Besides hauling people's garbage.

CORY. I get good grades, Pop. That's why the recruiter wants to talk with you. You got to keep up your grades to get recruited. This way I'll be going to college. I'll get a chance . . .

TROY. First you gonna get your butt down there to the A&P and get your job back.

CORY. Mr. Stawicki done already hired somebody else 'cause I told him I was playing football.

TROY. You a bigger fool than I thought . . . to let somebody take away your job so you can play some football. Where you gonna get your money to take out your girlfriend and whatnot? What kind of foolishness is that to let somebody take away your job?

CORY. I'm still gonna be working weekends.

TROY. Naw . . . naw. You getting your butt out of here and finding you another job.

CORY. Come on, Pop! I got to practice. I can't work after school and play football too. The team needs me. That's what Coach Zellman say . . .

TROY. I don't care what nobody else say. I'm the boss . . . you understand? I'm the boss around here. I do the only saying what counts.

CORY. Come on, Pop!

TROY. I asked you . . . did you understand?

CORY. Yeah . . .

TROY. What?!

CORY. Yessir.

TROY. You go on down there to that A&P and see if you can get your job back. If you can't do both . . . then you quit the football team. You've got to take the crookeds with the straights.

CORY. Yessir. *[Pause.]* Can I ask you a question?

TROY. What the hell you wanna ask me? Mr. Stawicki the one you got the questions for.

CORY. How come you ain't never liked me?

TROY. Liked you? Who the hell say I got to like you? What law is there say I got to like you? Wanna stand up in my face and ask a damn foolass question like that. Talking about liking somebody. Come here, boy, when I talk to you.

CORY *comes over to where* TROY *is working. He stands slouched over and* TROY *shoves him on his shoulder.*

Straighten up, goddammit! I asked you a question . . . what law is there say I got to like you?

CORY. None.

TROY. Well, all right then! Don't you eat every day? *[Pause.]* Answer me when I talk to you! Don't you eat every day?

CORY. Yeah.

TROY. Nigger, as long as you in my house, you put that sir on the end of it when you talk to me.

CORY. Yes . . . sir.

TROY. You eat every day.

CORY. Yessir!

TROY. Got a roof over your head.

CORY. Yessir!

TROY. Got clothes on your back.

CORY. Yessir.

TROY. Why you think that is?

CORY. Cause of you.

TROY. Ah, hell I know it's cause of me . . . but why do you think that is?

CORY *[hesitant].* Cause you like me.

TROY. Like you? I go out of here every morning . . . bust my butt . . . putting up with them crackers every day . . . cause I like you? You are the biggest fool I ever saw. *[Pause.]* It's my job. It's my responsibility! You understand that? A man got to take care of his family. You live in my house . . . sleep you behind on my bedclothes . . . fill you belly up with my food . . . cause you my son. You my flesh and blood. Not cause I like you! Cause it's my duty to take care of you. I owe a responsibility to you! Let's get this straight right here . . . before it go along any further . . . I ain't got to like you. Mr. Rand don't give me my money come payday cause he likes me. He gives me cause he owe me. I done give you everything I had to give you. I gave you your life! Me and your mama worked that out between us. And liking your black ass wasn't part of the bargain. Don't you try and go through life worrying about if somebody like you or not. You best be making sure they doing right by you. You understand what I'm saying boy?

CORY. Yessir.

TROY. Then get the hell out of my face, and get on down to that A&P.

ROSE *has been standing behind the screen door for much of the scene. She enters as* CORY *exits.*

ROSE. Why don't you let the boy go ahead and play football, Troy? Ain't no harm in that. He's just trying to be like you with the sports.

TROY. I don't want him to be like me! I want him to move as far away from my life as he can get. You the only decent thing that ever happened to me. I wish him that. But I don't wish him a thing else from my life. I decided seventeen years ago that boy wasn't getting involved in no sports. Not after what they did to me in the sports.

ROSE. Troy, why don't you admit you was too old to play in the major leagues? For once . . . why don't you admit that?

TROY. What do you mean too old? Don't come telling me I was too old. I just wasn't the right color. Hell, I'm fifty-three years old and can do better than Selkirk's .269 right now!

ROSE. How's was you gonna play ball when you were over forty? Sometimes I can't get no sense out of you.

TROY. I got good sense, woman. I got sense enough not to let my boy get hurt over playing no sports. You been mothering that boy too much. Worried about if people like him.

ROSE. Everything that boy do . . . he do for you. He wants you to say "Good job, son." That's all.

TROY. Rose, I ain't got time for that. He's alive. He's healthy. He's got to make his own way. I made mine. Ain't nobody gonna hold his hand when he get out there in that world.

ROSE. Times have changed from when you was young, Troy. People change. The world's changing around you and you can't even see it.

TROY [slow, methodical]. Woman . . . I do the best I can do. I come in here every Friday. I carry a sack of potatoes and a bucket of lard. You all line up at the door with your hands out. I give you the lint from my pockets. I give you my sweat and my blood. I ain't got no tears. I done spent them. We go upstairs in that room at night . . . and I fall down on you and try to blast a hole into forever. I get up Monday morning . . . find my lunch on the table. I go out. Make my way. Find my strength to carry me through to the next Friday. [Pause.] That's all I got, Rose. That's all I got to give. I can't give nothing else.

TROY exits into the house. The lights go down to black.

Scene 4

It is Friday. Two weeks later. CORY *starts out of the house with his football equipment. The phone rings.*

CORY [calling]. I got it! [He answers the phone and stands in the screen door talking.] Hello? Hey, Jesse. Naw . . . I was just getting ready to leave now.

ROSE [calling]. Cory!

CORY. I told you, man, them spikes is all tore up. You can use them if you want, but they ain't no good. Earl got some spikes.

ROSE [calling]. Cory!

CORY [calling to ROSE]. Mam? I'm talking to Jesse. [Into phone.] When she say that? [Pause.] Aw, you lying, man. I'm gonna tell her you said that.

ROSE [calling]. Cory, don't you go nowhere!

CORY. I got to go to the game, Ma! [Into the phone.] Yeah, hey, look, I'll talk to you later. Yeah, I'll meet you over Earl's house. Later. Bye, Ma.

CORY *exits the house and starts out the yard.*

ROSE. Cory, where you going off to? You got that stuff all pulled out and thrown all over your room.

CORY [in the yard]. I was looking for my spikes. Jesse wanted to borrow my spikes.

ROSE. Get up there and get that cleaned up before your daddy get back in here.

CORY. I got to go to the game! I'll clean it up *when I get back.*

CORY *exits.*

ROSE. That's all he need to do is see that room all messed up.

ROSE *exits into the house.* TROY *and* BONO *enter the yard.* TROY *is dressed in clothes other than his work clothes.*

BONO. He told him the same thing he told you. Take it to the union.

TROY. Brownie ain't got that much sense. Man wasn't thinking about nothing. He wait until I confront them on it . . . then he wanna come crying seniority. *[Calls.]* Hey, Rose!

BONO. I wish I could have seen Mr. Rand's face when he told you.

TROY. He couldn't get it out of his mouth! Liked to bit his tongue! When they called me down there to the Commissioner's office . . . he thought they was gonna fire me. Like everybody else.

BONO. I didn't think they was gonna fire you. I thought they was gonna put you on the warning paper.

TROY. Hey, Rose! *[To* BONO.*]* Yeah, Mr. Rand like to bit his tongue.

TROY *breaks the seal on the bottle, takes a drink, and hands it to* BONO.

BONO. I see you run right down to Taylors' and told that Alberta gal.

TROY *[calling]*. Hey Rose! *[To* BONO.*]* I told everybody. Hey, Rose! I went down there to cash my check.

ROSE *[entering from the house]*. Hush all that hollering, man! I know you out here. What they say down there at the Commissioner's office?

TROY. You supposed to come when I call you, woman. Bono'll tell you that. *[To* BONO.*]* Don't Lucille come when you call her?

ROSE. Man, hush your mouth. I ain't no dog . . . talk about "come when you call me."

TROY *[puts his arm around* ROSE*]*. You hear this, Bono? I had me an old dog used to get uppity like that. You say, "C'mere, Blue!" . . . and he just lay there and look at you. End up getting a stick and chasing him away trying to make him come.

ROSE. I ain't studying you and your dog. I remember you used to sing that old song.

TROY *[he sings]*. Hear it ring! Hear it ring! I had a dog his name was Blue.

ROSE. Don't nobody wanna hear you sing that old song.

TROY *[sings]*. You know Blue was mighty true.

ROSE. Used to have Cory running around here singing that song.

BONO. Hell, I remember that song myself.

TROY *[sings]*. You know Blue was a good old dog.
Blue treed a possum in a hollow log.
That was my daddy's song. My daddy made up that song.

ROSE. I don't care who made it up. Don't nobody wanna hear you sing it.

TROY *[makes a song like calling a dog]*. Come here, woman.

ROSE. You come in here carrying on, I reckon they ain't fired you. What they say down there at the Commissioner's office?

TROY. Look here, Rose . . . Mr. Rand called me into his office today when I got back from talking to them people down there . . . it come from up top . . . he called me in and told me they was making me a driver.

ROSE. Troy, you kidding!

TROY. No I ain't. Ask Bono.

ROSE. Well, that's great, Troy. Now you don't have to hassle them people no more.

LYONS *enters from the street.*

TROY. Aw hell, I wasn't looking to see you today. I thought you was in jail.

Got it all over the front page of the *Courier* about them raiding Sefus's place . . . where you be hanging out with all them thugs.

LYONS. Hey, Pop . . . that ain't got nothing to do with me. I don't go down there gambling. I go down there to sit in with the band. I ain't got nothing to do with the gambling part. They got some good music down there.

TROY. They got some rogues . . . is what they got.

LYONS. How you been, Mr. Bono? Hi, Rose.

BONO. I see where you playing down at the Crawford Grill tonight.

ROSE. How come you ain't brought Bonnie like I told you? You should have brought Bonnie with you, she ain't been over in a month of Sundays.

LYONS. I was just in the neighborhood . . . thought I'd stop by.

TROY. Here he come . . .

BONO. Your daddy got a promotion on the rubbish. He's gonna be the first colored driver. Ain't got to do nothing but sit up there and read the paper like them white fellows.

LYONS. Hey, Pop . . . if you knew how to read you'd be all right.

BONO. Naw . . . naw . . . you mean if the nigger knew how to drive he'd be all right. Been fighting with them people about driving and ain't even got a license. Mr. Rand know you ain't got no driver's license?

TROY. Driving ain't nothing. All you do is point the truck where you want it to go. Driving ain't nothing.

BONO. Do Mr. Rand know you ain't got no driver's license? That's what I'm talking about. I ain't asked if driving was easy. I asked if Mr. Rand know you ain't got no driver's license.

TROY. He ain't got to know. The man ain't got to know my business. Time he find out, I have two or three driver's licenses.

LYONS *[going into his pocket]*. Say, look here, Pop . . .

TROY. I knew it was coming. Didn't I tell you, Bono? I know what kind of "Look here, Pop" that was. The nigger fixing to ask me for some money. It's Friday night. It's my payday. All them rogues down there on the avenue . . . the ones that ain't in jail . . . and Lyons is hopping in his shoes to get down there with them.

LYONS. See, Pop . . . if you give somebody else a chance to talk sometimes, you'd see that I was fixing to pay you back your ten dollars like I told you. Here . . . I told you I'd pay you when Bonnie got paid.

TROY. Naw . . . you go ahead and keep that ten dollars. Put it in the bank. The next time you feel like you wanna come by here and ask me for something . . . you go on down there and get that.

LYONS. Here's your ten dollars, Pop. I told you I don't want you to give me nothing. I just wanted to borrow ten dollars.

TROY. Naw . . . you go on and keep that for the next time you want to ask me.

LYONS. Come on, Pop . . . here go your ten dollars.

ROSE. Why don't you go on and let the boy pay you back, Troy?

LYONS. Here you go, Rose. If you don't take it I'm gonna have to hear about it for the next six months. *[He hands her the money.]*

ROSE. You can hand yours over here too, Troy.

TROY. You see this, Bono. You see how they do me.

BONO. Yeah, Lucille do me the same way.

GABRIEL *is heard singing off stage. He enters.*

GABRIEL. Better get ready for the Judgment! Better get ready for . . . Hey! . . . Hey! . . . There's Troy's boy!

LYONS. How are you doing, Uncle Gabe?

GABRIEL. Lyons . . . The King of the Jungle! Rose . . . hey, Rose. Got a flower for you. *[He takes a rose from his pocket.]* Picked it myself. That's the same rose like you is!

ROSE. That's right nice of you, Gabe.

LYONS. What you been doing, Uncle Gabe?

GABRIEL. Oh, I been chasing hellhounds and waiting on the time to tell St. Peter to open the gates.

LYONS. You been chasing hellhounds, huh? Well . . . you doing the right thing, Uncle Gabe. Somebody got to chase them.

GABRIEL. Oh, yeah . . . I know it. The devil's strong. The devil ain't no pushover. Hellhounds snipping at everybody's heels. But I got my trumpet waiting on the judgment time.

LYONS. Waiting on the Battle of Armageddon, huh?

GABRIEL. Ain't gonna be too much of a battle when God get to waving that Judgment sword. But the people's gonna have a hell of a time trying to get into heaven if them gates ain't open.

LYONS *[putting his arm around GABRIEL].* You hear this, Pop. Uncle Gabe, you all right!

GABRIEL *[laughing with LYONS].* Lyons! King of the Jungle.

ROSE. You gonna stay for supper, Gabe? Want me to fix you a plate?

GABRIEL. I'll take a sandwich, Rose. Don't want no plate. Just wanna eat with my hands. I'll take a sandwich.

ROSE. How about you, Lyons? You staying? Got some short ribs cooking.

LYONS. Naw, I won't eat nothing till after we finished playing. *[Pause.]* You ought to come down and listen to me play, Pop.

TROY. I don't like that Chinese music. All that noise.

ROSE. Go on in the house and wash up, Gabe . . . I'll fix you a sandwich.

GABRIEL *[to LYONS, as he exits].* Troy's mad at me.

LYONS. What you mad at Uncle Gabe for, Pop?

ROSE. He thinks Troy's mad at him cause he moved over to Miss Pearl's.

TROY. I ain't mad at the man. He can live where he want to live at.

LYONS. What he move over there for? Miss Pearl don't like nobody.

ROSE. She don't mind him none. She treats him real nice. She just don't allow all that singing.

TROY. She don't mind that rent he be paying . . . that's what she don't mind.

ROSE. Troy, I ain't going through that with you no more. He's over there cause he want to have his own place. He can come and go as he please.

TROY. Hell, he could come and go as he please here. I wasn't stopping him. I ain't put no rules on him.

ROSE. It ain't the same thing, Troy. And you know it.

GABRIEL *comes to the door.*

Now, that's the last I wanna hear about that. I don't wanna hear nothing else about Gabe and Miss Pearl. And next week . . .

GABRIEL. I'm ready for my sandwich, Rose.

ROSE. And next week . . . when that recruiter come from that school . . . I want you to sign that paper and go on and let Cory play football. Then that'll be the last I have to hear about that.

TROY [*to* ROSE *as she exits into the house*]. I ain't thinking about Cory nothing.

LYONS. What . . . Cory got recruited? What school he going to?

TROY. That boy walking around here smelling his piss . . . thinking he's grown. Thinking he's gonna do what he want, irrespective of what I say. Look here, Bono . . . I left the Commissioner's office and went down to the A&P . . . that boy ain't working down there. He lying to me. Telling me he got his job back . . . telling me he working weekends . . . telling me he working after school . . . Mr. Stawicki tell me he ain't working down there at all!

LYONS. Cory just growing up. He's just busting at the seams trying to fill out your shoes.

TROY. I don't care what he's doing. When he get to the point where he wanna disobey me . . . then it's time for him to move on. Bono'll tell you that. I bet he ain't never disobeyed his daddy without paying the consequences.

BONO. I ain't never had a chance. My daddy came on through . . . but I ain't never knew him to see him . . . or what he had on his mind or where he went. Just moving on through. Searching out the New Land. That's what the old folks used to call it. See a fellow moving around from place to place . . . woman to woman . . . called it searching out the New Land. I can't say if he ever found it. I come along, didn't want no kids. Didn't know if I was gonna be in one place long enough to fix on them right as their daddy. I figured I was going searching too. As it turned out I been hooked up with Lucille near about as long as your daddy been with Rose. Going on sixteen years.

TROY. Sometimes I wish I hadn't known my daddy. He ain't cared nothing about no kids. A kid to him wasn't nothing. All he wanted was for you to learn how to walk so he could start you to working. When it come time for eating . . . he ate first. If there was anything left over, that's what you got. Man would sit down and eat two chickens and give you the wing.

LYONS. You ought to stop that, Pop. Everybody feed their kids. No matter how hard times is . . . everybody care about their kids. Make sure they have something to eat.

TROY. The only thing my daddy cared about was getting them bales of cotton in to Mr. Lubin. That's the only thing that mattered to him. Sometimes I used to wonder why he was living. Wonder why the devil hadn't come and got him. "Get them bales of cotton in to Mr. Lubin" and find out he owe him money . . .

LYONS. He should have just went on and left when he saw he couldn't get nowhere. That's what I would have done.

TROY. How he gonna leave with eleven kids? And where he gonna go? He ain't knew how to do nothing but farm. No, he was trapped and I think he knew it. But I'll say this for him . . . he felt a responsibility toward us. Maybe he ain't treated us the way I felt he should have . . . but without that responsibility he could have walked off and left us . . . made his own way.

BONO. A lot of them did. Back in those days what you talking about . . . they walk out their front door and just take on down one road or another and keep on walking.

LYONS. There you go! That's what I'm talking about.

BONO. Just keep on walking till you come to something else. Ain't you never heard of nobody having the walking blues? Well, that's what you call it when you just take off like that.

TROY. My daddy ain't had them walking blues! What you talking about? He stayed right there with his family. But he was just as evil as he could be. My mama couldn't stand him. Couldn't stand that evilness. She run off when I was about eight. She sneaked off one night after he had gone to sleep. Told me she was coming back for me. I ain't never seen her no more. All his women run off and left him. He wasn't good for nobody.

When my turn come to head out, I was fourteen and got to sniffing around Joe Canewell's daughter. Had us an old mule we called Grey-boy. My daddy sent me out to do some plowing and I tied up Greyboy and went to fooling around with Joe Canewell's daughter. We done found us a nice little spot, got real cozy with each other. She about thirteen and we done figured we was grown anyway . . . so we down there enjoying ourselves . . . ain't thinking about nothing. We didn't know Greyboy had got loose and wandered back to the house and my daddy was looking for me. We down there by the creek enjoying ourselves when my daddy come up on us. Surprised us. He had them leather straps off the mule and commenced to whupping me like there was no tomorrow. I jumped up, mad and embarrassed. I was scared of my daddy. When he commenced to whupping on me . . . quite naturally I run to get out of the way. *[Pause.]* Now I thought he was mad cause I ain't done my work. But I see where he was chasing me off so he could have the gal for himself. When I see what the matter of it was, I lost all fear of my daddy. Right there is where I become a man . . . at fourteen years of age. *[Pause.]* Now it was my turn to run him off. I picked up them same reins that he had used on me. I picked up them reins and commenced to whupping on him. The gal jumped up and run off . . . and when my daddy turned to face me, I could see why the devil had never come to get him . . . cause he was the devil himself. I don't know what happened. When I woke up, I was laying right there by the creek, and Blue . . . this old dog we had . . . was licking my face. I thought I was blind. I couldn't see nothing. Both my eyes were swollen shut. I laid there and cried. I didn't know what I was gonna do. The only thing I knew was the time had come for me to leave my daddy's house. And right there the world suddenly got big. And it was a long time before I could cut it down to where I could handle it.

Part of that cutting down was when I got to the place where I could feel him kicking in my blood and knew that the only thing that separated us was the matter of a few years.

GABRIEL *enters from the house with a sandwich.*

LYONS. What you got there, Uncle Gabe?

GABRIEL. Got me a ham sandwich. Rose gave me a ham sandwich.

TROY. I don't know what happened to him. I done lost touch with every-body except Gabriel. But I hope he's dead. I hope he found some peace.

LYONS. That's a heavy story, Pop. I didn't know you left home when you was fourteen.

TROY. And didn't know nothing. The only part of the world I knew was the forty-two acres of Mr. Lubin's land. That's all I knew about life.

LYONS. Fourteen's kinda young to be out on your own. *[Phone rings.]* I don't even think I was ready to be out on my own at fourteen. I don't know what I would have done.

TROY. I got up from the creek and walked on down to Mobile. I was through with farming. Figured I could do better in the city. So I walked the two hundred miles to Mobile.

LYONS. Wait a minute . . . you ain't walked no two hundred miles, Pop. Ain't nobody gonna walk no two hundred miles. You talking about some walking there.

BONO. That's the only way you got anywhere back in them days.

LYONS. Shhh. Damn if I wouldn't have hitched a ride with somebody!

TROY. Who you gonna hitch it with? They ain't had no cars and things like they got now. We talking about 1918.

ROSE *[entering]*. What you all out here getting into?

TROY *[to* ROSE*]*. I'm telling Lyons how good he got it. He don't know nothing about this I'm talking.

ROSE. Lyons, that was Bonnie on the phone. She say you supposed to pick her up.

LYONS. Yeah, okay, Rose.

TROY. I walked on down to Mobile and hitched up with some of them fel-lows that was heading this way. Got up here and found out . . . not only couldn't you get a job . . . you couldn't find no place to live. I thought I was in freedom. Shhh. Colored folks living down there on the river-banks in whatever kind of shelter they could find for themselves. Right down there under the Brady Street Bridge. Living in shacks made of sticks and tarpaper. Messed around there and went from bad to worse. Started stealing. First it was food. Then I figured, hell, if I steal money I can buy me some food. Buy me some shoes too! One thing led to an-other. Met your mama. I was young and anxious to be a man. Met your mama and had you. What I do that for? Now I got to worry about feed-ing you and her. Got to steal three times as much. Went out one day looking for somebody to rob . . . that's what I was, a robber. I'll tell you the truth. I'm ashamed of it today. But it's the truth. Went to rob this fel-low . . . pulled out my knife . . . and he pulled out a gun. Shot me in the chest. I felt just like somebody had taken a hot branding iron and laid it on me. When he shot me I jumped at him with my knife. They told me I killed him and they put me in the penitentiary and locked me up for fifteen years. That's where I met Bono. That's where I learned how to play baseball. Got out that place and your mama had taken you and went on to make life without me. Fifteen years was a long time for her to wait. But that fifteen years cured me of that robbing stuff. Rose'll tell you. She asked me when I met her if I had gotten all that foolishness out of my system. And I told her, "Baby, it's you and baseball all what count with me." You hear me, Bono? I meant it too. She say, "Which one comes first?" I told her, "Baby, ain't no doubt it's baseball . . . but you stick and get old with me and we'll both outlive this baseball." Am I right, Rose? And it's true.

ROSE. Man, hush your mouth. You ain't said no such thing. Talking about, "Baby you know you'll always be number one with me." That's what you was talking.

TROY. You hear that, Bono. That's why I love her.

BONO. Rose'll keep you straight. You get off the track, she'll straighten you up.

ROSE. Lyons, you better get on up and get Bonnie. She waiting on you.

LYONS [gets up to go]. Hey, Pop, why don't you come on down to the Grill and hear me play?

TROY. I ain't going down there. I'm too old to be sitting around in them clubs.

BONO. You got to be good to play down at the Grill.

LYONS. Come on, Pop . . .

TROY. I got to get up in the morning.

LYONS. You ain't got to stay long.

TROY. Naw, I'm gonna get my supper and go on to bed.

LYONS. Well, I got to go. I'll see you again.

TROY. Don't you come around my house on my payday.

ROSE. Pick up the phone and let somebody know you coming. And bring Bonnie with you. You know I'm always glad to see her.

LYONS. Yeah, I'll do that, Rose. You take care now. See you, Pop. See you, Mr. Bono. See you, Uncle Gabe.

GABRIEL. Lyons! King of the Jungle!

LYONS *exits.*

TROY. Is supper ready, woman? Me and you got some business to take care of. I'm gonna tear it up too.

ROSE. Troy, I done told you now!

TROY [puts his arm around BONO]. Aw hell, woman . . . this is Bono. Bono like family. I done known this nigger since . . . how long I done know you?

BONO. It's been a long time.

TROY. I done know this nigger since Skippy was a pup. Me and him done been through some times.

BONO. You sure right about that.

TROY. Hell, I done know him longer than I known you. And we still standing shoulder to shoulder. Hey, look here, Bono . . . a man can't ask for no more than that. [Drinks to him.] I love you, nigger.

BONO. Hell, I love you too . . . I got to get home see my woman. You got yours in hand. I got to get mine.

BONO *starts to exit as* CORY *enters the yard, dressed in his football uniform. He gives* TROY *a hard, uncompromising look.*

CORY. What you do that for, Pop?

He throws his helmet down in the direction of TROY.

ROSE. What's the matter? Cory . . . what's the matter?

CORY. Papa done went up to the school and told Coach Zellman I can't play football no more. Wouldn't even let me play the game. Told him to tell the recruiter not to come.

ROSE. Troy . . .

TROY. What you Troying me for. Yeah, I did it. And the boy know why I did it.

CORY. Why you wanna do that to me? That was the one chance I had.

ROSE. Ain't nothing wrong with Cory playing football, Troy.

TROY. The boy lied to me. I told the nigger if he wanna play football . . . to keep up his chores and hold down that job at the A&P. That was the conditions. Stopped down there to see Mr. Stawicki . . .

CORY. I can't work after school during the football season, Pop! I tried to tell you that Mr. Stawicki's holding my job for me. You don't never want to listen to nobody. And then you wanna go and do this to me!

TROY. I ain't done nothing to you. You done it to yourself.

CORY. Just cause you didn't have a chance! You just scared I'm gonna be better than you, that's all.

TROY. Come here.

ROSE. Troy . . .

CORY *reluctantly crosses over to* TROY.

TROY. All right! See. You done made a mistake.

CORY. I didn't even do nothing!

TROY. I'm gonna tell you what your mistake was. See . . . you swung at the ball and didn't hit it. That's strike one. See, you in the batter's box now. You swung and you missed. That's strike one. Don't you strike out!

Lights fade to black.

Act 2

Scene 1

The following morning. CORY *is at the tree hitting the ball with the bat. He tries to mimic* TROY, *but his swing is awkward, less sure.* ROSE *enters from the house.*

ROSE. Cory, I want you to help me with this cupboard.

CORY. I ain't quitting the team. I don't care what Poppa say.

ROSE. I'll talk to him when he gets back. He had to go see about your Uncle Gabe. The police done arrested him. Say he was disturbing the peace. He'll be back directly. Come on in here and help me clean out the top of this cupboard.

CORY *exits into the house.* ROSE *sees* TROY *and* BONO *coming down the alley.*

Troy . . . what they say down there?

TROY. Ain't said nothing. I give them fifty dollars and they let him go. I'll talk to you about it. Where's Cory?

ROSE. He's in there helping me clean out these cupboards.

TROY. Tell him to get his butt out here.

TROY *and* BONO *go over to the pile of wood.* BONO *picks up the saw and begins sawing.*

TROY *[to* BONO*]*. All they want is the money. That makes six or seven times I done went down there and got him. See me coming they stick out their hands.

BONO. Yeah. I know what you mean. That's all they care about . . . that money. They don't care about what's right. *[Pause.]* Nigger, why you got to go and get some hard wood? You ain't doing nothing but building a little old fence. Get you some soft pine wood. That's all you need.

TROY. I know what I'm doing. This is outside wood. You put pine wood inside the house. Pine wood is inside wood. This here is outside wood. Now you tell me where the fence is gonna be?

BONO. You don't need this wood. You can put it up with pine wood and it'll stand as long as you gonna be here looking at it.

TROY. How you know how long I'm gonna be here, nigger? Hell, I might just live forever. Live longer than old man Horsely.

BONO. That's what Magee used to say.

TROY. Magee's damn fool. Now you tell me who you ever heard of gonna pull their own teeth with a pair of rusty pliers.

BONO. The old folks . . . my granddaddy used to pull his teeth with pliers. They ain't had no dentists for the colored folks back then.

TROY. Get clean pliers! You understand? Clean pliers! Sterilize them! Besides we ain't living back then. All Magee had to do was walk over to Doc Goldblum's.

BONO. I see where you and that Tallahassee gal . . . that Alberta . . . I see where you all done got tight.

TROY. What you mean "got tight"?

BONO. I see where you be laughing and joking with her all the time.

TROY. I laughs and jokes with all of them, Bono. You know me.

BONO. That ain't the kind of laughing and joking I'm talking about.

CORY *enters from the house.*

CORY. How you doing. Mr. Bono?

TROY. Cory? Get that saw from Bono and cut some wood. He talking about the wood's too hard to cut. Stand back there, Jim, and let that young boy show you how it's done.

BONO. He's sure welcome to it.

CORY *takes the saw and begins to cut the wood.*

Whew-e-e! Look at that. Big old strong boy. Look like Joe Louis. Hell, must be getting old the way I'm watching that boy whip through that wood.

CORY. I don't see why Mama want a fence around the yard noways.

TROY. Damn if I know either. What the hell she keeping out with it? She ain't got nothing nobody want.

BONO. Some people build fences to keep people out . . . and other people build fences to keep people in. Rose wants to hold on to you all. She loves you.

TROY. Hell, nigger, I don't need nobody to tell me my wife loves me. Cory . . . go on in the house and see if you can find that other saw.

CORY. Where's it at?

TROY. I said find it! Look for it till you find it!

CORY *exits into the house.*

What's that supposed to mean? Wanna keep us in?

BONO. Troy . . . I done known you seem like damn near my whole life. You and Rose both. I done know both of you all for a long time. I remember when you met Rose. When you was hitting them baseball out the park. A lot of them old gals was after you then. You had the pick of the litter. When you picked Rose, I was happy for you. That was the first time I knew you had any sense. I said . . . My man Troy knows what he's doing . . . I'm gonna follow this nigger . . . he might take me somewhere. I been following you too. I done learned a whole heap of things about life watching you. I done learned how to tell where the shit lies. How to tell it from the alfalfa. You done learned me a lot of things. You showed me how to not make the same mistakes . . . to take life as it comes along and keep putting one foot in front of the other. *[Pause.]* Rose a good woman, Troy.

TROY. Hell, nigger, I know she a good woman. I been married to her for eighteen years. What you got on your mind, Bono?

BONO. I just say she a good woman. Just like I say anything. I ain't got to have nothing on my mind.

TROY. You just gonna say she a good woman and leave it hanging out there like that? Why you telling me she a good woman?

BONO. She loves you, Troy. Rose loves you.

TROY. You saying I don't measure up. That's what you trying to say. I don't measure up cause I'm seeing this other gal. I know what you trying to say.

BONO. I know what Rose means to you, Troy. I'm just trying to say I don't want to see you mess up.

TROY. Yeah, I appreciate that, Bono. If you was messing around on Lucille I'd be telling you the same thing.

BONO. Well, that's all I got to say. I just say that because I love you both.

TROY. Hell, you know me . . . I wasn't out there looking for nothing. You can't find a better woman than Rose. I know that. But seems like this woman just stuck onto me where I can't shake her loose. I done wrestled with it, tried to throw her off me . . . but she just stuck on tighter. Now she's stuck on for good.

BONO. You's in control . . . that's what you tell me all the time. You responsible for what you do.

TROY. I ain't ducking the responsibility of it. As long as it sets right in my heart . . . then I'm okay. Cause that's all I listen to. It'll tell me right from wrong every time. And I ain't talking about doing Rose no bad turn. I love Rose. She done carried me a long ways and I love and respect her for that.

BONO. I know you do. That's why I don't want to see you hurt her. But what you gonna do when she find out? What you got then? If you try and juggle both of them . . . sooner or later you gonna drop one of them. That's common sense.

TROY. Yeah, I hear what you saying, Bono. I been trying to figure a way to work it out.

BONO. Work it out right, Troy. I don't want to be getting all up between you and Rose's business . . . but work it so it come out right.

TROY. Ah hell, I get all up between you and Lucille's business. When you gonna get that woman that refrigerator she been wanting? Don't tell me you ain't got no money now. I know who your banker is. Mellon don't need that money bad as Lucille want that refrigerator. I'll tell you that.

BONO. Tell you what I'll do . . . when you finish building this fence for Rose . . . I'll buy Lucille that refrigerator.

TROY. You done stuck your foot in your mouth now!

TROY *grabs up a board and begins to saw.* BONO *starts to walk out the yard.*

Hey, nigger . . . where you going?

BONO. I'm going home. I know you don't expect me to help you now. I'm protecting my money. I wanna see you put that fence up by yourself. That's what I want to see. You'll be here another six months without me.

TROY. Nigger, you ain't right.

BONO. When it comes to my money . . . I'm right as fireworks on the Fourth of July.

TROY. All right, we gonna see now. You better get out your bankbook.

BONO *exits, and* TROY *continues to work.* ROSE *enters from the house.*

ROSE. What they say down there? What's happening with Gabe?

TROY. I went down there and got him out. Cost me fifty dollars. Say he was disturbing the peace. Judge set up a hearing for him in three weeks. Say to show cause why he shouldn't be recommitted.

ROSE. What was he doing that cause them to arrest him?

TROY. Some kids was teasing him and he run them off home. Say he was howling and carrying on. Some folks seen him and called the police. That's all it was.

ROSE. Well, what's you say? What'd you tell the judge?

TROY. Told him I'd look after him. It didn't make no sense to recommit the man. He stuck out his big greasy palm and told me to give him fifty dollars and take him on home.

ROSE. Where's he at now? Where'd he go off to?

TROY. He's gone about his business. He don't need nobody to hold his hand.

ROSE. Well, I don't know. Seem like that would be the best place for him if they did put him into the hospital. I know what you're gonna say. But that's what I think would be best.

TROY. The man done had his life ruined fighting for what? And they wanna take and lock him up. Let him be free. He don't bother nobody.

ROSE. Well, everybody got their own way of looking at it I guess. Come on and get your lunch. I got a bowl of lima beans and some cornbread in the oven. Come and get something to eat. Ain't no sense you fretting over Gabe.

ROSE *turns to go into the house.*

TROY. Rose . . . got something to tell you.

ROSE. Well, come on . . . wait till I get this food on the table.

TROY. Rose!

She stops and turns around.

I don't know how to say this. *[Pause.]* I can't explain it none. It just sort of grows on you till it gets out of hand. It starts out like a little bush . . . and the next thing you know it's a whole forest.

ROSE. Troy . . . what is you talking about?

TROY. I'm talking, woman, let me talk. I'm trying to find a way to tell you . . .
I'm gonna be a daddy. I'm gonna be somebody's daddy.

ROSE. Troy . . . you're not telling me this? You're gonna be . . . what?

TROY. Rose . . . now . . . see . . .

ROSE. You telling me you gonna be somebody's daddy? You telling your *wife*
this?

GABRIEL *enters from the street. He carries a rose in his hand.*

GABRIEL. Hey, Troy! Hey, Rose!

ROSE. I have to wait eighteen years to hear something like this.

GABRIEL. Hey, Rose . . . I got a flower for you. *[He hands it to her.]* That's a
rose. Same rose like you is.

ROSE. Thanks, Gabe.

GABRIEL. Troy, you ain't mad at me is you? Them bad mens come and put me
away. You ain't mad at me is you?

TROY. Naw, Gabe, I ain't mad at you.

ROSE. Eighteen years and you wanna come with this.

GABRIEL *[takes a quarter out of his pocket].* See what I got? Got a brand new
quarter.

TROY. Rose . . . it's just . . .

ROSE. Ain't nothing you can say, Troy. Ain't no way of explaining that.

GABRIEL. Fellow that give me this quarter had a whole mess of them. I'm
gonna keep this quarter till it stop shining.

ROSE. Gabe, go on in the house there. I got some watermelon in the
Frigidaire. Go on and get you a piece.

GABRIEL. Say, Rose . . . you know I was chasing hellhounds and them bad
mens come and get me and take me away. Troy helped me. He come
down there and told them they better let me go before he beat them
up. Yeah, he did!

ROSE. You go on and get you a piece of watermelon, Gabe. Them bad mens
is gone now.

GABRIEL. Okay, Rose . . . gonna get me some watermelon. The kind with the
stripes on it.

GABRIEL *exits into the house.*

ROSE. Why, Troy? Why? After all these years to come dragging this in to me
now. It don't make no sense at your age. I could have expected this ten
or fifteen years ago, but not now.

TROY. Age ain't got nothing to do with it, Rose.

ROSE. I done tried to be everything a wife should be. Everything a wife could
be. Been married eighteen years and I got to live to see the day you tell
me you been seeing another woman and done fathered a child by her.
And you know I ain't never wanted no half nothing in my family. My
whole family is half. Everybody got different fathers and mothers . . . my
two sisters and my brother. Can't hardly tell who's who. Can't never sit
down and talk about Papa and Mama. It's your papa and your mama and
my papa and my mama . . .

TROY. Rose . . . stop it now.

ROSE. I ain't never wanted that for none of my children. And now you wanna
drag your behind in here and tell me something like this.

TROY. You ought to know. It's time for you to know.

ROSE. Well, I don't want to know, goddamn it!

TROY. I can't just make it go away. It's done now. I can't wish the circumstance of the thing away.

ROSE. And you don't want to either. Maybe you want to wish me and my boy away. Maybe that's what you want? Well, you can't wish us away. I've got eighteen years of my life invested in you. You ought to have stayed upstairs in my bed where you belong.

TROY. Rose . . . now listen to me . . . we can get a handle on this thing. We can talk this out . . . come to an understanding.

ROSE. All of a sudden it's "we." Where was "we" at when you was down there rolling around with some godforsaken woman? "We" should have come to an understanding before you started making a damn fool of yourself. You're a day late and a dollar short when it comes to an understanding with me.

TROY. It's just . . . She gives me a different idea . . . a different understanding about myself. I can step out of this house and get away from the pressures and problems . . . be a different man. I ain't got to wonder how I'm gonna pay the bills or get the roof fixed. I can just be a part of myself that I ain't never been.

ROSE. What I want to know . . . is do you plan to continue seeing her. That's all you can say to me.

TROY. I can sit up in her house and laugh. Do you understand what I'm saying. I can laugh out loud . . . and it feels good. It reaches all the way down to the bottom of my shoes. *[Pause.]* Rose, I can't give that up.

ROSE. Maybe you ought to go on and stay down there with her . . . if she's a better woman than me.

TROY. It ain't about nobody being a better woman or nothing. Rose, you ain't the blame. A man couldn't ask for no woman to be a better wife than you've been. I'm responsible for it. I done locked myself into a pattern trying to take care of you all that I forgot about myself.

ROSE. What the hell was I there for? That was my job, not somebody else's.

TROY. Rose, I done tried all my life to live decent . . . to live a clean . . . hard . . . useful life. I tried to be a good husband to you. In every way I knew how. Maybe I come into the world backwards, I don't know. But . . . you born with two strikes on you before you come to the plate. You got to guard it closely . . . always looking for the curve ball on the inside corner. You can't afford to let none get past you. You can't afford a call strike. If you going down . . . you going down swinging. Everything lined up against you. What you gonna do. I fooled them, Rose. I bunted. When I found you and Cory and a halfway decent job . . . I was safe. Couldn't nothing touch me. I wasn't gonna strike out no more. I wasn't going back to the penitentiary. I wasn't gonna lay in the streets with a bottle of wine. I was safe. I had me a family. A job. I wasn't gonna get that last strike. I was on first looking for one of them boys to knock me in. To get me home.

ROSE. You should have stayed in my bed, Troy.

TROY. Then when I saw that gal . . . she firmed up my backbone. And I got to thinking that if I tried . . . I just might be able to steal second. Do you understand after eighteen years I wanted to steal second.

ROSE. You should have held me tight. You should have grabbed me and held on.

TROY. I stood on first base for eighteen years and I thought . . . well, god-damn it . . . go on for it!

ROSE. We're not talking about baseball! We're talking about you going off to lay in bed with another woman . . . and then bring it home to me. That's what we're talking about. We ain't talking about no baseball.

TROY. Rose, you're not listening to me. I'm trying the best I can to explain it to you. It's not easy for me to admit that I been standing in the same place for eighteen years.

ROSE. I been standing with you! I been right here with you, Troy. I got a life too. I gave eighteen years of my life to stand in the same spot with you. Don't you think I ever wanted other things? Don't you think I had dreams and hopes? What about my life? What about me. Don't you think it ever crossed my mind to want to know other men? That I wanted to lay up somewhere and forget about my responsibilities? That I wanted someone to make me laugh so I could feel good? You not the only one who's got wants and needs. But I held on to you, Troy. I took all my feelings, my wants and needs, my dreams . . . and I buried them inside you. I planted a seed and watched and prayed over it. I planted myself inside you and waited to bloom. And it didn't take me no eigh-teen years to find out the soil was hard and rocky and it wasn't never gonna bloom.

But I held on to you, Troy. I held you tighter. You was my husband. I owed you everything I had. Every part of me I could find to give you. And upstairs in that room . . . with the darkness falling in on me . . . I gave everything I had to try and erase the doubt that you wasn't the finest man in the world. And wherever you was going . . . I wanted to be there with you. Cause you was my husband. Cause that's the only way I was gonna survive as your wife. You always talking about what you give . . . and what you don't have to give. But you take too. You take . . . and don't even know nobody's giving!

ROSE *turns to exit into the house;* TROY *grabs her arm.*

TROY. You say I take and don't give!

ROSE. Troy! You're hurting me!

TROY. You say I take and don't give!

ROSE. Troy . . . you're hurting my arm! Let go!

TROY. I done give you everything I got. Don't you tell that lie on me.

ROSE. Troy!

TROY. Don't you tell that lie on me!

CORY *enters from the house.*

CORY. Mama!

ROSE. Troy. You're hurting me.

TROY. Don't you tell me about no taking and giving.

CORY *comes up behind* TROY *and grabs him.* TROY, *surprised, is thrown off balance just as* CORY *throws a glancing blow that catches him on the chest and knocks him down.* TROY *is stunned, as is* CORY.

ROSE. Troy. Troy. No!

TROY *gets to his feet and starts at* CORY.

Troy . . . no. Please! Troy!

ROSE *pulls on* TROY *to hold him back.* TROY *stops himself.*

TROY [to CORY]. All right. That's strike two. You stay away from around me, boy. Don't you strike out. You living with a full count. Don't you strike out.

TROY *exits out the yard as the lights go down.*

Scene 2

It is six months later, early afternoon. TROY *enters from the house and starts to exit the yard.* ROSE *enters from the house.*

ROSE. Troy, I want to talk to you.

TROY. All of a sudden, after all this time, you want to talk to me, huh? You ain't wanted to talk to me for months. You ain't wanted to talk to me last night. You ain't wanted no part of me then. What you wanna talk to me about now?

ROSE. Tomorrow's Friday.

TROY. I know what day tomorrow is. You think I don't know tomorrow's Friday? My whole life I ain't done nothing but look to see Friday coming and you got to tell me it's Friday.

ROSE. I want to know if you're coming home.

TROY. I always come home, Rose. You know that. There ain't never been a night I ain't come home.

ROSE. That ain't what I mean . . . and you know it. I want to know if you're coming straight home after work.

TROY. I figure I'd cash my check . . . hang out at Taylors' with the boys . . . maybe play a game of checkers . . .

ROSE. Troy, I can't live like this. I won't live like this. You livin' on borrowed time with me. It's been going on six months now you ain't been coming home.

TROY. I be here every night. Every night of the year. That's 365 days.

ROSE. I want you to come home tomorrow after work.

TROY. Rose . . . I don't mess up my pay. You know that now. I take my pay and I give it to you. I don't have no money but what you give me back. I just want to have a little time to myself . . . a little time to enjoy life.

ROSE. What about me? When's my time to enjoy life?

TROY. I don't know what to tell you, Rose. I'm doing the best I can.

ROSE. You ain't been home from work but time enough to change your clothes and run out . . . and you wanna call that the best you can do?

TROY. I'm going over to the hospital to see Alberta. She went into the hospital this afternoon. Look like she might have the baby early. I won't be gone long.

ROSE. Well, you ought to know. They went over to Miss Pearl's and got Gabe today. She said you told them to go ahead and lock him up.

TROY. I ain't said no such thing. Whoever told you that is telling a lie. Pearl ain't doing nothing but telling a big fat lie.

ROSE. She ain't had to tell me. I read it on the papers.

TROY. I ain't told them nothing of the kind.

ROSE. I saw it right there on the papers.

TROY. What it say, huh?

ROSE. It said you told them to take him.

TROY. Then they screwed that up, just the way they screw up everything. I ain't worried about what they got on the paper.

ROSE. Say the government send part of his check to the hospital and the other part to you.

TROY. I ain't got nothing to do with that if that's the way it works. I ain't made up the rules about how it work.

ROSE. You did Gabe just like you did Cory. You wouldn't sign the paper for Cory . . . but you signed for Gabe. You signed that paper.

The telephone is heard ringing inside the house.

TROY. I told you I ain't signed nothing, woman! The only thing I signed was the release form. Hell, I can't read, I don't know what they had on that paper! I ain't signed nothing about sending Gabe away.

ROSE. I said send him to the hospital . . . you said let him be free . . . now you done went down there and signed him to the hospital for half his money. You went back on yourself, Troy. You gonna have to answer for that.

TROY. See now . . . you been over there talking to Miss Pearl. She done got mad cause she ain't getting Gabe's rent money. That's all it is. She's liable to say anything.

ROSE. Troy, I seen where you signed the paper.

TROY. You ain't seen nothing I signed. What she doing got papers on my brother anyway? Miss Pearl telling a big fat lie. And I'm gonna tell her about it too! You ain't seen nothing I signed. Say . . . you ain't seen nothing I signed.

ROSE *exists into the house to answer the telephone. Presently she returns.*

ROSE. Troy . . . that was the hospital. Alberta had the baby.

TROY. What she have? What is it?

ROSE. It's a girl.

TROY. I better get on down to the hospital to see her.

ROSE. Troy . . .

TROY. Rose . . . I got to go see her now. That's only right . . . what's the matter . . . the baby's all right, ain't it?

ROSE. Alberta died having the baby.

TROY. Died . . . you say she's dead? Alberta's dead?

ROSE. They said they done all they could. They couldn't do nothing for her.

TROY. The baby? How's the baby?

ROSE. They say it's healthy. I wonder who's gonna bury her.

TROY. She had family, Rose. She wasn't living in the world by herself.

ROSE. I know she wasn't living in the world by herself.

TROY. Next thing you gonna want to know if she had any insurance.

ROSE. Troy, you ain't got to talk like that.

TROY. That's the first thing that jumped out your mouth. "Who's gonna bury her?" Like I'm fixing to take on that task for myself.

ROSE. I am your wife. Don't push me away.

TROY. I ain't pushing nobody away. Just give me some space. That's all. Just give me some room to breathe.

ROSE *exists into the house.* TROY *walks about the yard.*

TROY. *[with a quiet rage that threatens to consume him].* All right . . . Mr. Death. See now . . . I'm gonna tell you what I'm gonna do. I'm gonna

take and build me a fence around this yard. See? I'm gonna build me a fence around what belongs to me. And then I want you to stay on the other side. See? You stay over there until you're ready for me. Then you come on. Bring your army. Bring your sickle. Bring your wrestling clothes. I ain't gonna fall down on my vigilance this time. You ain't gonna sneak up on me no more. When you ready for me . . . when the top of your list say Troy Maxson . . . that's when you come around here. You come up and knock on the front door. Ain't nobody else got nothing to do with this. This is between you and me. Man to man. You stay on the other side of that fence until you ready for me. Then you come up and knock on the front door. Anytime you want. I'll be ready for you.
The lights go down to black.

Scene 3

The lights come up on the porch. It is late evening three days later. ROSE *sits listening to the ball game waiting for* TROY. *The final out of the game is made and* ROSE *switches off the radio.* TROY *enters the yard carrying an infant wrapped in blankets. He stands back from the house and calls.*

ROSE *enters and stands on the porch. There is a long, awkward silence, the weight of which grows heavier with each passing second.*

TROY. Rose . . . I'm standing here with my daughter in my arms. She ain't but a wee bittie little old thing. She don't know nothing about grownups' business. She innocent . . . and she ain't got no mama.

ROSE. What you telling me for, Troy?

She turns and exits into the house.

TROY. Well . . . I guess we'll just sit out here on the porch.

He sits down on the porch. There is an awkward indelicateness about the way he handles the baby. His largeness engulfs and seems to swallow it. He speaks loud enough for ROSE *to hear.*

A man's got to do what's right for him. I ain't sorry for nothing I done. It felt right in my heart. *[To the baby.]* What you smiling at? Your daddy's a big man. Got these great big old hands. But sometimes he's scared. And right now your daddy's scared cause we sitting out here and ain't got no home. Oh, I been homeless before. I ain't had no little baby with me. But I been homeless. You just be out on the road by your lonesome and you see one of them trains coming and you just kinda go like this . . .

He sings as a lullaby.

> Please, Mr. Engineer let a man ride the line
> Please, Mr. Engineer let a man ride the line
> I ain't got no ticket please let me ride the blinds.

ROSE *enters from the house.* TROY, *hearing her steps behind him, stands and faces her.*

She's my daughter, Rose. My own flesh and blood. I can't deny her no more than I can deny them boys. *[Pause.]* You and them boys is my family. You and them and this child is all I got in the world. So I guess what I'm saying is . . . I'd appreciate it if you'd help me take care of her.

ROSE. Okay, Troy . . . you're right. I'll take care of your baby for you . . .

cause . . . like you say . . . she's innocent . . . and you can't visit the sins of the father upon the child. A motherless child has got a hard time. *[She takes the baby from him.]* From right now . . . this child got a mother. But you a womanless man.

ROSE *turns and exits into the house with the baby. Lights go down to black.*

Scene 4

It is two months later. LYONS *enters the street. He knocks on the door and calls.*

LYONS. Hey, Rose! *[Pause.]* Rose!

ROSE *[from inside the house].* Stop that yelling. You gonna wake up Raynell. I just got her to sleep.

LYONS. I just stopped by to pay Papa this twenty dollars I owe him. Where's Papa at?

ROSE. He should be here in a minute. I'm getting ready to go down to the church. Sit down and wait on him.

LYONS. I got to go pick up Bonnie over her mother's house.

ROSE. Well, sit it down there on the table. He'll get it.

LYONS *[enters the house and sets the money on the table].* Tell Papa I said thanks. I'll see you again.

ROSE. All right, Lyons. We'll see you.

LYONS *starts to exit as* CORY *enters.*

CORY. Hey, Lyons.

LYONS. What's happening, Cory? Say man, I'm sorry I missed your graduation. You know I had a gig and couldn't get away. Otherwise, I would have been there, man. So what you doing?

CORY. I'm trying to find a job.

LYONS. Yeah I know how that go, man. It's rough out here. Jobs are scarce.

CORY. Yeah, I know.

LYONS. Look here, I got to run. Talk to Papa . . . he know some people. He'll be able to help get you a job. Talk to him . . . see what he say.

CORY. Yeah . . . all right, Lyons.

LYONS. You take care. I'll talk to you soon. We'll find some time to talk.

LYONS *exits the yard.* CORY *wanders over to the tree, picks up the bat, and assumes a batting stance. He studies an imaginary pitcher and swings. Dissatisfied with the result, he tries again.* TROY *enters. They eye each other for a beat.* CORY *puts the bat down and exits the yard.* TROY *starts into the house as* ROSE *exits with* RAYNELL. *She is carrying a cake.*

TROY. I'm coming in and everybody's going out.

ROSE. I'm taking this cake down to the church for the bake sale. Lyons was by to see you. He stopped by to pay you your twenty dollars. It's laying in there on the table.

TROY *[going into his pocket].* Well . . . here go this money.

ROSE. Put it in there on the table, Troy. I'll get it.

TROY. What time you coming back?

ROSE. Ain't no use in you studying me. It don't matter what time I come back.

TROY. I just asked you a question, woman. What's the matter . . . can't I ask you a question?

ROSE. Troy, I don't want to go into it. Your dinner's in there on the stove. All you got to do is heat it up. And don't you be eating the rest of them cakes in there. I'm coming back for them. We having a bake sale at the church tomorrow.

>   ROSE *exits the yard.* TROY *sits down on the steps, takes a pint bottle from his pocket, opens it, and drinks. He begins to sing.*

TROY. Hear it ring! Hear it ring!

>   Had an old dog his name was Blue
>   You know Blue was mighty true
>   You know Blue as a good old dog
>   Blue trees a possum in a hollow log
>   You know from that he was a good old dog.

>   BONO *enters the yard.*

BONO. Hey, Troy.

TROY. Hey, what's happening, Bono?

BONO. I just thought I'd stop by to see you.

TROY. What you stop by and see me for? You ain't stopped by in a month of Sundays. Hell, I must owe you money or something.

BONO. Since you got your promotion I can't keep up with you. Used to see you every day. Now I don't even know what route you working.

TROY. They keep switching me around. Got me out in Greentree now . . . hauling white folks' garbage.

BONO. Greentree, huh? You lucky, at least you ain't got to be lifting them barrels. Damn if they ain't getting heavier. I'm gonna put in my two years and call it quits.

TROY. I'm thinking about retiring myself.

BONO. You got it easy. You can drive for another five years.

TROY. It ain't the same, Bono. It ain't like working the back of the truck. Ain't got nobody to talk to . . . feel like you working by yourself. Naw, I'm thinking about retiring. How's Lucille?

BONO. She all right. Her arthritis get to acting up on her sometime. Saw Rose on my way in. She going down to the church, huh?

TROY. Yeah, she took up going down there. All them preachers looking for somebody to fatten their pockets. *[Pause.]* Got some gin here.

BONO. Naw, thanks. I just stopped by to say hello.

TROY. Hell, nigger . . . you can take a drink. I ain't never known you to say no to a drink. You ain't got to work tomorrow.

BONO. I just stopped by. I'm fixing to go over to Skinner's. We got us a domino game going over his house every Friday.

TROY. Nigger, you can't play no dominoes. I used to whup you four games out of five.

BONO. Well, that learned me. I'm getting better.

TROY. Yeah? Well, that's all right.

BONO. Look here . . . I got to be getting on. Stop by sometime, huh?

TROY. Yeah, I'll do that, Bono. Lucille told Rose you bought her a new refrigerator.

BONO. Yeah, Rose told Lucille you had finally built your fence . . . so I figured we'd call it even.

TROY. I knew you would.

BONO. Yeah . . . okay. I'll be talking to you.

TROY. Yeah, take care, Bono. Good to see you. I'm gonna stop over.

BONO. Yeah. Okay, Troy.

> BONO *exits.* TROY *drinks from the bottle.*

TROY.   Old Blue died and I dig his grave
>   Let him down with a golden chain
>   Every night when I hear old Blue bark
>   I know Blue treed a possum in Noah's Ark.
>   Hear it ring! Hear it ring!

> CORY *enters the yard. They eye each other for a beat.* TROY *is sitting in the middle of the steps.* CORY *walks over.*

CORY. I got to get by.

TROY. Say what? What's you say?

CORY. You in my way. I got to get by.

TROY. You got to get by where? This is my house. Bought and paid for. In full. Took me fifteen years. And if you wanna go in my house and I'm sitting on the steps . . . you say excuse me. Like your mama taught you.

CORY. Come on, Pop . . . I got to get by.

> CORY *starts to maneuver his way past* TROY. TROY *grabs his leg and shoves him back.*

TROY. You just gonna walk over top of me?

CORY. I live here too!

TROY [*advancing toward him*]. You just gonna walk over top of me in my own house?

CORY. I ain't scared of you.

TROY. I ain't asked if you was scared of me. I asked you if you was fixing to walk over top of me in my own house? That's the question. You ain't gonna say excuse me? You just gonna walk over top of me?

CORY. If you wanna put it like that.

TROY. How else am I gonna put it?

CORY. I was walking by you to go into the house cause you sitting on the steps drunk, singing to yourself. You can put it like that.

TROY. Without saying excuse me???

> CORY *doesn't respond.*

I asked you a question. Without saying excuse me???

CORY. I ain't got to say excuse me to you. You don't count around here no more.

TROY. Oh, I see . . . I don't count around here no more. You ain't got to say excuse me to your daddy. All of a sudden you done got so grown that your daddy don't count around here no more . . . Around here in his own house and yard that he done paid for with the sweat of his brow. You done got so grown to where you gonna take over. You gonna take over my house. Is that right? You gonna wear my pants. You gonna go in there and stretch out on my bed. You ain't got to say excuse me cause I don't count around here no more. Is that right?

CORY. That's right. You always talking this dumb stuff. Now, why don't you just get out my way?

TROY. I guess you got someplace to sleep and something to put in your belly. You got that, huh? You got that? That's what you need. You got that, huh?

CORY. You don't know what I got. You ain't got to worry about what I got.

TROY. You right! You one hundred percent right! I done spent the last seventeen years worrying about what you got. Now it's your turn, see? I'll tell you what to do. You grown . . . we done established that. You a man. Now, let's see you act like one. Turn your behind around and walk out this yard. And when you get out there in the alley . . . you can forget about this house. See? Cause this is my house. You go on and be a man and get your own house. You can forget about this. Cause this is mine. You go on and get yours cause I'm through with doing for you.

CORY. You talking about what you did for me . . . what'd you ever give me?

TROY. Them feet and bones! That pumping heart, nigger! I give you more than anybody else is ever gonna give you.

CORY. You ain't never gave me nothing! You ain't never done nothing but hold me back. Afraid I was gonna be better than you. All you ever did was try and make me scared of you. I used to tremble every time you called my name. Every time I heard your footsteps in the house. Wondering all the time . . . what's Papa gonna say if I do this? . . . What's he gonna say if I do that? . . . What's Papa gonna say if I turn on the radio? And Mama, too . . . she tries . . . but she's scared of you.

TROY. You leave your mama out of this. She ain't got nothing to do with this.

CORY. I don't know how she stand you . . . after what you did to her.

TROY. I told you to leave your mama out of this!

He advances toward CORY.

CORY. What you gonna do . . . give me a whupping? You can't whup me no more. You're too old. You just an old man.

TROY *[shoves him on his shoulder]*. Nigger! That's what you are. You just another nigger on the street to me!

CORY. You crazy! You know that?

TROY. Go on now! You got the devil in you. Get on away from me!

CORY. You just a crazy old man . . . talking about I got the devil in me.

TROY. Yeah, I'm crazy! If you don't get on the other side of that yard . . . I'm gonna show you how crazy I am! Go on . . . get the hell out of my yard.

CORY. It ain't your yard. You took Uncle Gabe's money he got from the army to buy this house and then you put him out.

TROY *[advances on* CORY*]*. Get your black ass out of my yard!

TROY*'s advance backs* CORY *up against the tree.* CORY *grabs up the bat.*

CORY. I ain't going nowhere! Come on . . . put me out! I ain't scared of you.

TROY. That's my bat!

CORY. Come on!

TROY. Put my bat down!

CORY. Come on, put me out.

CORY *swings at* TROY, *who backs across the yard.*

What's the matter? You so bad . . . put me out!

TROY *advances toward* CORY.

CORY *[backing up]*. Come on! Come on!

TROY. You're gonna have to use it! You wanna draw that bat back on me . . . you're gonna have to use it.

CORY. Come on! . . . Come on!

> CORY *swings the bat at* TROY *a second time. He misses.* TROY *continues to advance toward him.*

TROY. You're gonna have to kill me! You wanna draw that bat back on me. You're gonna have to kill me.

> CORY, *backed up against the tree, can go no farther.* TROY *taunts him. He sticks out his head and offers him a target.*

Come on! Come on!

> CORY *is unable to swing the bat.* TROY *grabs it.*

TROY. Then I'll show you.

> CORY *and* TROY *struggle over the bat. The struggle is fierce and fully engaged.* TROY *ultimately is the stronger and takes the bat from* CORY *and stands over him ready to swing. He stops himself.*

Go on and get away from around my house.

> CORY, *stung by his defeat, picks himself up, walks slowly out of the yard and up the alley.*

CORY. Tell Mama I'll be back for my things.

TROY. They'll be on the other side of that fence.

> CORY *exits.*

TROY. I can't taste nothing. Helluljah! I can't taste nothing no more. *[TROY assumes a batting posture and begins to taunt Death, the fastball on the outside corner.]* Come on! It's between you and me now! Come on! Anytime you want! Come on! I be ready for you . . . but I ain't gonna be easy.

> *The lights go down on the scene.*

Scene 5

> *The time is 1965. The lights come up in the yard. It is the morning of* TROY's *funeral. A funeral plaque with a light hangs beside the door. There is a small garden plot off to the side. There is noise and activity in the house as* ROSE, LYONS, *and* BONO *have gathered. The door opens and* RAYNELL, *seven years old, enters dressed in a flannel nightgown. She crosses to the garden and pokes around with a stick.* ROSE *calls from the house.*

ROSE. Raynell!

RAYNELL. Mam?

ROSE. What you doing out there?

RAYNELL. Nothing.

> ROSE *comes to the door.*

ROSE. Girl, get in here and get dressed. What you doing?

RAYNELL. Seeing if my garden growed.

ROSE. I told you it ain't gonna grow overnight. You got to wait.

RAYNELL. It don't look like it never gonna grow. Dag!

ROSE. I told you a watched pot never boils. Get in here and get dressed.

RAYNELL. This ain't even no pot, Mama.

ROSE. You just have to give it a chance. It'll grow. Now you come on and do what I told you. We got to be getting ready. This ain't no morning to be playing around. You hear me?

RAYNELL. Yes, mam.

> ROSE *exits into the house.* RAYNELL *continues to poke at her garden with a stick.* CORY *enters. He is dressed in a Marine corporal's uniform, and carries a duffelbag. His posture is that of a military man, and his speech has a clipped sternness.*

CORY *[to* RAYNELL*].* Hi. *[Pause.]* I bet your name is Raynell.

RAYNELL. Uh huh.

CORY. Is your mama home?

> RAYNELL *runs up on the porch and calls through the screen door.*

RAYNELL. Mama . . . there's some man out here. Mama?

> ROSE *comes to the door.*

ROSE. Cory? Lord have mercy! Look here, you all!

> ROSE *and* CORY *embrace in a tearful reunion as* BONO *and* LYONS *enter from the house dressed in funeral clothes.*

BONO. Aw, looka here . . .

ROSE. Done got all grown up!

CORY. Don't cry, Mama. What you crying about?

ROSE. I'm just so glad you made it.

CORY. Hey Lyons. How you doing, Mr. Bono.

> LYONS *goes to embrace* CORY.

LYONS. Look at you, man. Look at you. Don't he look good, Rose. Got them Corporal stripes.

ROSE. What took you so long?

CORY. You know how the Marines are, Mama. They got to get all their paperwork straight before they let you do anything.

ROSE. Well, I'm sure glad you made it. They let Lyons come. Your Uncle Gabe's still in the hospital. They don't know if they gonna let him out or not. I just talked to them a little while ago.

LYONS. A Corporal in the United States Marines.

BONO. Your daddy knew you had it in you. He used to tell me all the time.

LYONS. Don't he look good, Mr. Bono?

BONO. Yeah, he remind me of Troy when I first met him. *[Pause.]* Say, Rose, Lucille's down at the church with the choir. I'm gonna go down and get the pallbearers lined up. I'll be back to get you all.

ROSE. Thanks, Jim.

CORY. See you, Mr. Bono.

LYONS *[with his arm around* RAYNELL*].* Cory . . . look at Raynell. Ain't she precious? She gonna break a whole lot of hearts.

ROSE. Raynell, come and say hello to your brother. This is your brother, Cory. You remember Cory.

RAYNELL. No, Mam.

CORY. She don't remember me, Mama.

ROSE. Well, we talk about you. She heard us talk about you. *[To* RAYNELL*]* This is your brother, Cory. Come on and say hello.

RAYNELL. Hi.

CORY. Hi. So you're Raynell. Mama told me a lot about you.

ROSE. You all come on into the house and let me fix you some breakfast. Keep up your strength.

CORY. I ain't hungry, Mama.

LYONS. You can fix me something, Rose. I'll be in there in a minute.

ROSE. Cory, you sure you don't want nothing? I know they ain't feeding you right.

CORY. No, Mama . . . thanks. I don't feel like eating. I'll get something later.

ROSE. Raynell . . . get on upstairs and get that dress on like I told you.

ROSE *and* RAYNELL *exit into the house.*

LYONS. So . . . I hear you thinking about getting married.

CORY. Yeah, I done found the right one, Lyons. It's about time.

LYONS. Me and Bonnie been split up about four years now. About the time Papa retired. I guess she just got tired of all them changes I was putting her through. *[Pause.]* I always knew you was gonna make something out yourself. Your head was always in the right direction. So . . . you gonna stay in . . . make it a career . . . put in your twenty years?

CORY. I don't know. I got six already, I think that's enough.

LYONS. Stick with Uncle Sam and retire early. Ain't nothing out here. I guess Rose told you what happened with me. They got me down the work-house. I thought I was being slick cashing other people's checks.

CORY. How much time you doing?

LYONS. They give me three years. I got that beat now. I ain't got but nine more months. It ain't so bad. You learn to deal with it like anything else. You got to take the crookeds with the straights. That's what Papa used to say. He used to say that when he struck out. I seen him strike out three times in a row . . . and the next time up he hit the ball over the grandstand. Right out there in Homestead Field. He wasn't satisfied hitting in the seats . . . he want to hit it over everything! After the game he had two hundred people standing around waiting to shake his hand. You got to take the crookeds with the straights. Yeah, Papa was something else.

CORY. You still playing?

LYONS. Cory . . . you know I'm gonna do that. There's some fellows down there we got us a band . . . we gonna try and stay together when we get out . . . but yeah, I'm still playing. It still helps me to get out of bed in the morning. As long as it do that I'm gonna be right there playing and trying to make some sense out of it.

ROSE *[calling].* Lyons, I got these eggs in the pan.

LYONS. Let me go on and get these eggs, man. Get ready to go bury Papa. *[Pause.]* How you doing? You doing all right?

CORY *nods.* LYONS *touches him on the shoulder and they share a moment of silent grief.* LYONS *exits into the house.* CORY *wanders about the yard.* RAYNELL *enters.*

RAYNELL. Hi.

CORY. Hi.

RAYNELL. Did you used to sleep in my room?

CORY. Yeah . . . that used to be my room.

RAYNELL. That's what Papa call it. "Cory's room." It got your football in the closet.

ROSE *comes to the door.*

ROSE. Raynell, get in there and get them good shoes on.

RAYNELL. Mama, can't I wear these? Them other one hurt my feet.

ROSE. Well, they just gonna have to hurt your feet for a while. You ain't said they hurt your feet when you went down to the store and got them.

RAYNELL. They didn't hurt then. My feet done got bigger.

ROSE. Don't you give me no backtalk now. You get in there and get them shoes on.

RAYNELL *exits into the house.*

Ain't too much changed. He still got that piece of rag tied to that tree. He was out here swinging that bat. I was just ready to go back in the house. He swung that bat and then he just fell over. Seem like he swung it and stood there with this grin on his face . . . and then he just fell over. They carried him on down to the hospital, but I knew there wasn't no need . . . why don't you come on in the house?

CORY. Mama . . . I got something to tell you. I don't know how to tell you this . . . but I've got to tell you . . . I'm not going to Papa's funeral.

ROSE. Boy, hush your mouth. That's your daddy you talking about. I don't want hear that kind of talk this morning. I done raised you to come to this? You standing there all healthy and grown talking about you ain't going to your daddy's funeral?

CORY. Mama . . . listen . . .

ROSE. I don't want to hear it, Cory. You just get that thought out of your head.

CORY. I can't drag Papa with me everywhere I go. I've got to say no to him. One time in my life I've got to say no.

ROSE. Don't nobody have to listen to nothing like that. I know you and your daddy ain't seen eye to eye, but I ain't got to listen to that kind of talk this morning. Whatever was between you and your daddy . . . the time has come to put it aside. Just take it and set it over there on the shelf and forget about it. Disrespecting your daddy ain't gonna make you a man, Cory. You got to find a way to come to that on your own. Not going to your daddy's funeral ain't gonna make you a man.

CORY. The whole time I was growing up . . . living in his house . . . Papa was like a shadow that followed you everywhere. It weighed on you and sunk into your flesh. It would wrap around you and lay there until you couldn't tell which one was you anymore. That shadow digging in your flesh. Trying to crawl in. Trying to live through you. Everywhere I looked, Troy Maxson was staring back at me . . . hiding under the bed . . . in the closet. I'm just saying I've got to find a way to get rid of that shadow, Mama.

ROSE. You just like him. You got him in you good.

CORY. Don't tell me that, Mama.

ROSE. You Troy Maxson all over again.

CORY. I don't want to be Troy Maxson. I want to be me.

ROSE. You can't be nobody but who you are, Cory. That shadow wasn't nothing but you growing into yourself. You either got to grow into it or cut it down to fit you. But that's all you got to make life with. That's all you got to measure yourself against that world out there. Your daddy wanted you to be everything he wasn't . . . and at the same time he tried to make you into everything he was. I don't know if he was right or wrong . . . but I do know he meant to do more good than he meant to do harm. He wasn't always right. Sometimes when he touched he bruised. And sometimes when he took me in his arms he cut.

When I first met your daddy I thought . . . Here is a man I can lay down with and make a baby. That's the first thing I thought when I seen him. I was thirty years old and had done seen my share of men. But when he walked up to me and said, "I can dance a waltz that'll make you dizzy," I thought, Rose Lee, here is a man that you can open yourself up to and be filled to bursting. Here is a man that can fill all them empty spaces you been tipping around the edges of. One of them empty spaces was being somebody's mother.

I married your daddy and settled down to cooking his supper and keeping clean sheets on the bed. When your daddy walked through the house he was so big he filled it up. That was my first mistake. Not to make him leave some room for me. For my part in the matter. But at that time I wanted that. I wanted a house that I could sing in. And that's what your daddy gave me. I didn't know to keep up his strength I had to give up little pieces of mine. I did that. I took on his life as mine and mixed up the pieces so that you couldn't hardly tell which was which anymore. It was my choice. It was my life and I didn't have to live it like that. But that's what life offered me in the way of being a woman and I took it. I grabbed hold of it with both hands.

By the time Raynell came into the house, me and your daddy had done lost touch with one another. I didn't want to make my blessing off of nobody's misfortune . . . but I took on to Raynell like she was all them babies I had wanted and never had.

The phone rings.

Like I'd been blessed to relive a part of my life. And if the Lord see fit to keep up my strength . . . I'm gonna do her just like your daddy did you . . . I'm gonna give her the best of what's in me.

RAYNELL *[entering, still with her old shoes]*. Mama . . . Reverend Tollivier on the phone.

ROSE *exits into the house.*

RAYNELL. Hi.

CORY. Hi.

RAYNELL. You in the Army or the Marines?

CORY. Marines.

RAYNELL. Papa said it was the Army. Did you know Blue?

CORY. Blue? Who's Blue?

RAYNELL. Papa's dog what he sing about all the time.

CORY *[singing]*. Hear it ring! Hear it ring!

    I had a dog his name was Blue
    You know Blue was mighty true
    You know Blue was a good old dog
    Blue treed a possum in a hollow log
    You know from that he was a good old dog.
    Hear it ring! Hear it ring!

RAYNELL *joins in singing.*

CORY AND RAYNELL. Blue treed a possum out on a limb
    Blue looked at me and I looked at him
    Grabbed that possum and put him in a sack

Blue stayed there till I came back
Old Blue's feets was big and round
Never allowed a possum to touch the ground.

Old Blue died and I dug his grave
I dug his grave with a silver spade
Let him down with a golden chain
And every night I call his name
Go on Blue, you good dog you
Go on Blue, you good dog you.

RAYNELL.   Blue laid down and died like a man
Blue laid down and died . . .

BOTH.   Blue laid down and died like a man
Now he's treeing possums in the Promised Land
I'm gonna tell you this to let you know
Blue's gone where the good dogs go
When I hear old Blue bark
When I hear old Blue bark
Blue treed a possum in Noah's Ark
Blue treed a possum in Noah's Ark.

ROSE *comes to the screen door.*

ROSE.   Cory, we gonna be ready to go in a minute.

CORY *[to RAYNELL].*   You go on in the house and change them shoes like Mama
told you so we can go to Papa's funeral.

RAYNELL.   Okay, I'll be back.

RAYNELL *exits into the house.* CORY *gets up and crosses over to the tree.*
ROSE *stands in the screen door watching him.* GABRIEL *enters from the*
alley.

GABRIEL *[calling].*   Hey, Rose!

ROSE.   Gabe?

GABRIEL.   I'm here, Rose. Hey Rose, I'm here!

ROSE *enters from the house.*

ROSE.   Lord . . . Look here, Lyons!

LYONS.   See, I told you, Rose . . . I told you they'd let him come.

CORY.   How you doing, Uncle Gabe?

LYONS.   How you doing, Uncle Gabe?

GABRIEL.   Hey, Rose. It's time. It's time to tell St. Peter to open the gates.
Troy, you ready? You ready, Troy. I'm gonna tell St. Peter to open the
gates. You get ready now.

GABRIEL, *with great fanfare, braces himself to blow. The trumpet is*
without a mouthpiece. He puts the end of it into his mouth and blows
with great force, like a man who has been waiting some twenty-odd
years for this single moment. No sound comes out of the trumpet. He
braces himself and blows again with the same result. A third time he
blows. There is a weight of impossible description that falls away and
leaves him bare and exposed to a frightful realization. It is a trauma
that a sane and normal mind would be unable to withstand. He be-
gins to dance. A slow, strange dance, eerie and life-giving. A dance of
atavistic signature and ritual. LYONS *attempts to embrace him.* GABRIEL
pushes LYONS *away. He begins to howl in what is an attempt at song,*
or perhaps a song turning back into itself in an attempt at speech. He

finishes his dance and the gates of heaven stand open as wide as God's closet.

That's the way that go!

(BLACKOUT)

[1987]

TOPICS FOR CRITICAL THINKING AND WRITING

1. What do you think Bono means when he says, early in Act 2 (page 1119), "Some people build fences to keep people out . . . and other people build fences to keep people in"? Why is the play called *Fences?* What is Troy fencing in? (You'll want to take account of Troy's last speech in 2.2, but don't limit your response to this speech.)

2. Would you agree that Troy's refusal to encourage his son's aspirations is one of the "fences" of the play? What do you think Troy's reasons are— conscious and unconscious—for not wanting Cory to play football at college?

3. Compare and contrast Cory and Lyons. Consider, too, in what ways they resemble Troy, and in what ways they differ from him.

4. In what ways is Troy like his father, and in what ways unlike?

5. What do you make of the prominence given to the song about Blue?

6. There is a good deal of anger in the play, but there is also humor. Which passages do you find humorous, and why?

7. Characterize Rose Maxson.

8. Some scenes begin by specifying that "the lights come up." Others do not, presumably beginning with an illuminated stage. All scenes except the last one—which ends with a sudden blackout—end with the lights slowly going down to blackness. How would you explain Wilson's use of lighting?

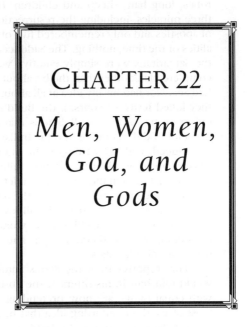

CHAPTER 22

Men, Women, God, and Gods

Essays

 **JILL TWEEDIE**

Jill Tweedie was born in 1936 of an English family in the Middle East. She grew up in England and then lived ten years in Canada before returning to England. The author of a novel and of books of essays (some of the essays have been collected under the title It's Only Me*), she now lives in London and writes articles for the* Guardian.

God the Mother Rules—OK?

Recently I read a snippet about women in the United States who were altering prayers and hymns by substituting Her for Him, Mother for Father and Goddess for God. Oh ho ho, did you ever, sniggered the writer. Put them in straitjackets and take them off to the funny farm.

    One of the continuing small surprises for the enquiring atheist is the widespread ignorance of believers about their belief. A viewpoint peculiarly limited—parochial is, I suppose, the *mot juste*.[1] Is it wildly unfair to say that if you picked the first avowed Christian off any pew and set him the religious equivalent of the 11-plus,[2] he would fail?

    The one I picked was quite hot on the Church version of Jesus's life: who he was born to, where he was born, how he died and where he died, though in between was a bit of a blank, apart from a vague image of white

[1]exact word (French)   [2]school examination

robes, long hair, sheep and children. He knew about Judas and he listed three miracles, including the resurrection, but he didn't know the number of apostles and only remembered five of their names. As to any historical realities of the time, nothing. The Sadducees, the Philistines, the Pharisees and the Samaritans were simply emotive words, the Old Testament an almost complete blank other than the bit about Moses in the cradle and parting the Red Sea. Nor had he any idea at all about the beliefs of the Jews (except that they killed Jesus, of course), the Buddhists, Islam, Taoism, Shintoism, Hinduism or any other ism. Religions that preceded Christianity? The Greeks had a lot of different gods and the Indians (Red) had the totem pole.

Indeed, without wishing to be unduly critical, my experience even of those who have taken up religion fulltime, priests and vicars, monks and nuns, is that though they may have a detailed knowledge of the mystical side of things, the mysteries, the ritual, the dogma, they are almost as ignorant as my random sample of historical realities. Which is, of course, not entirely accidental. Historical realities and, worse, historical perspectives, have a frightening way of shedding light and reason on corners that, to the believer, are best left dark.

5   That reporter from the States automatically assumed that his readers would join him in his titters at the absurdity of women who, not content with equal rights, are now pretending God could be female. He has, like most of us, the comforting idea that history started yesterday and will stay that way for ever. Because God and God's son are male today, so they always were and always will be, amen.

Brother, you couldn't be wronger. Slowly but surely a vast and ancient international jig-saw is being pieced together: antique temples here, swollen statues there, papyri drawings, carvings and writings from all over. And already the puzzle, half-finished though it is, is as exciting and significant as would be the revelation of a mother to a child who supposed itself an orphan from birth. Because it appears increasingly certain that a male God is an *arriviste,* a mere *nouveau riche*[3] upon the contemporary scene. Before Him, for literally thousands of years, disappearing back into the trackless wastes of pre-history, the people of the world shared one central figure of worship. A She, a Her, a Mother. The Goddess.

Merlin Stone, sculptor and art historian, has spent over 10 years on the trail of the Goddess and the results of her detective work in museums and ancient sites in the Near and Middle East have been published in *The Paradise Papers.* It makes a beautiful whole of many scattered clues until now undiscovered, ignored, misinterpreted, or—shamefully often—unacknowledged; an anthology of archaeological material that fairly bellows Ms Stone's central thesis. The impulse to worship came from the mystery of birth and the performer of that mystery, apparently entirely on her own, was woman.

So the explanation of a Goddess, the original Mother of humanity, came about as naturally and, when you think about it, as obviously as all the other apparent miracles of life and the Goddess was made manifest in the millions of statues, large and small, of big-bellied women. Statues we all know about and we have all been encouraged to dismiss as unimportant, mere fertility

---

[3]upstart . . . one who has lately become rich (French)

symbols, evidence only of cults, of strange rites practised in corners by heretics instead of what they surely are—endless variations of the same central belief held by many peoples over anything up to 25,000 years.

The face behind the clouds is a woman's face, women are her chosen priestesses and handmaidens and unto women shall go all kinship lines and rights of inheritance. Call her Ishtar in Babylon, Ashtoreth in Israel, Astarte in Phoenicia, Athar in Syria or Ate in Cicilia, call her what you will in the Mediterranean, the Near or the Middle East, even in old Ireland—by any other name she is the Goddess, the Queen of Heaven.

10   Ms Stone opines that the core of all theological thought is the quest for the ultimate source of life and ancestry worship occurs (and occurred) among tribal people the world over. Add that fact to the observations of anthropologists like Margaret Mead and James Frazer—that in the most ancient human societies coitus was not linked with reproduction—and you have woman the life-giver, the sex that gives birth.

What, then, more logical than to posit a First Ancestress in the sky? Robertson Smith, writing of the precedence of the female deity among the Arab and Hebrew peoples, says: "It was the mother's, not the father's, blood which formed the original bond of kinship among the Semites as among other early people and in this stage of society, if the tribal deity was thought of as the parent of the stock, a goddess, not a god, would necessarily have been the object of worship."

How did women fare when the Goddess reigned in their lands? Merlin Stone brings together the researches of many archaeologists and anthropologist to find out and the answer is as predictable as it is revealing of the purpose of religion. If you have a God in heaven, men rule on earth. If you have a Goddess, women take charge. Diodorus of Sicily, observant traveller BC, reported that the ladies of Ethiopia carried arms, practised communal marriage and raised their children communally. Of the warrier women in Libya he says: "All authority was vested in the woman, who discharged every kind of public duty. The men looked after domestic affairs and did as they were told by their wives.

"They were not allowed to undertake war service or to exercise any functions of government or to fill any public office, such as might have given them more spirit to set themselves up against the women. The children were handed over immediately after birth to the men." Are you listening, Colonel Gaddafi?

Professor Cyrus Gordon, writing of life in ancient Egypt, says: "In family life women had a peculiarly important position for inheritance passed through the mother . . . this system may well hark back to prehistoric times when only the obvious relationship between mother and child was recognized." The message is as clear and as apposite today as ever. Though you gain power through error (the misunderstanding about the father's part in reproduction), once the system is working for you (matrilineal descent) you can hang on for a very long time in the face of the most damning facts. Patriarchal gods know all about this, too.

15   Mind you, in spite of probable male suppression under a goddess, there is a plethora of evidence that the goddess made it well worth their while and that under her sexually permissive reign there were more tempting compensations for being a mere man than ever there were for a mere

woman in a god's world. Subjugation, says the God, is your punishment. Subjugation, said the Goddess, can be fun. Because one thing is certain. It took eons of bloody struggle to put the Goddess down. They came out of the northern countries, those eventual victors, migrating in waves over perhaps a thousand, even three thousand years, to the lands of the Goddess, armed with their God and the realization that power for men could only come when a man knew his own son. And how could a man know his own son? By caging women, by making her male property, by scaring her into believing that all hell would break loose if *she* did, that only by cleaving to one man from virginity to death could she hope to save her soul by a male God's intervention.

So battle commenced, fought as much against the desires of many men as against the sexual freedom of women. All over the territories of the Goddess are the myths that mark the traces of that battle. For years I have wondered at the stories of men fighting dragons—what did a dragon represent, what was its factual origin? Merlin Stone drops in another piece of the puzzle. The snake (serpent, dragon) was the widespread Goddess symbol and the living companion of her priestesses. So what was St. George doing, fighting his dragon? He was the new religion fighting the old, the male squaring off with the female, an historical reality told in snake/man struggles in hundreds of nations and tribes from India to Turkey, from Babylon to Assyria, from Ireland to Israel and Jehovah's battle with the serpent Leviathan.

"But it was upon the last assaults by the Hebrews and eventually by the Christians of the first centuries after Christ that the religion was finally suppressed and nearly forgotten," says Merlin Stone. The struggle rages still in the pages of the Bible, pages that as a girl amazed and fascinated me, with their constant emphasis on whores; whores of Babylon, whores of Sodom and Gomorrah, whores like Lilith and Jezebel, painted whores to be spurned by the sons and daughters of Israel. I had thought it then a sort of kink, a kind of mental aberration common to Jews and Christians. Not at all. The truth is far more tangible. The whore was the Garden, the old religion. The sin—adherence to the old religion. The real sin—ignorance of paternity, female promiscuity.

And that whole battle, so bitterly fought over so many years, produced as its apogee the fable of the Garden of Eden. There is the serpent, creature of the Goddess, of the old religion. There is Eve, the woman, handmaiden to the Goddess and traitress at the heart of the new religion, potentially promiscuous and, therefore, potentially the underminer of male power, of patrilineal descent. She must be warned, threatened, terrified in order to save Adam from the temptations of the Goddess. If she will not accept a male God and reject the Goddess, if she will not accept one man and one man only, all her life, she will be thrown out of Paradise and bear her children in agony.

It is all there in *The Paradise Papers* and, for me at least, Merlin Stone crystallizes what has all along been obvious, however submerged. Even today, in the dour Protestant religions, the last lingering trace of the Goddess (Mary, carefully a virgin) is hardly allowed to surface. The Catholics, always more opportunist, gave Mary her place in the sun but exacted from the ordinary women a terrible price for this concession.

20   Yesterday, I thought the leaders of all contemporary religions a blind

and prejudiced lot for their refusal to allow women any more power within their churches than the arrangement of flowers upon the altars. Now I know they are simply afraid, afraid that the Goddess may return from her long exile and take over again, and that is curiously comforting, an explanation from weakness rather than strength.

This, then, was the original battle of the sexes. A Goddess reigned for thousands of years, a God for two thousand. Shall we soon, perhaps, learn to do without either?

[1976]

 ## TOPICS FOR CRITICAL THINKING AND WRITING

1. In paragraph 3 Tweedie ridicules a Christian who didn't know the number of the apostles and could name only five. If you are a Christian, could you pass Tweedie's test? If you are a Christian and couldn't pass, would you agree that you are deficient in essential knowledge of the faith—or, on the other hand, would you argue that her test is invalid? (If you are a member of some faith other than Christianity, apply a comparable test to yourself.)
2. Drawing on the writing of Merlin Stone, in paragraph 7 Tweedie asserts that "The impulse to worship came from the mystery of birth and the performer of that mystery, apparently entirely on her own, was woman." Given the rest of Tweedie's essay, in an essay of 500 words explain why you are willing or not willing to accept this assertion.

 ## W. E. B. DU BOIS

W. E. B. Du Bois (1868–1963) was born in Massachusetts, where he seems to have had a relatively happy early childhood—though in grade school he was shocked to learn that his classmates considered him different because of his color. In 1885 he went to Fisk University in Nashville, Tennessee, and then, for doctoral work, to Harvard University where he studied history and to the University of Berlin where he studied sociology. His doctoral dissertation, The Suppression of the Slave Trade in the United States of America, *was published in* Harvard Historical Studies *in 1896.*

Although Du Bois had embarked on a scholarly career, he became increasingly concerned with the injustices of contemporary society, and his writings were now directed at a general public. In 1903 he published The Souls of Black Folk, *a book challenging Booker T. Washington's more resigned position. From 1910 to the mid-1930s he edited* The Crisis, *the journal of the National Association for the Advancement of Colored People; although he energetically solicited the writings of other people, he wrote so many essays for the journal that he can almost be said to be its author as well as its editor. Eventually Du Bois joined the Communist Party, and in 1963 he left the United States for Ghana, where he died.*

We reprint part of chapter 14 from The Souls of Black Folk.

Of the Sorrow Songs

I walk through the churchyard
  To lay this body down;
I know moon-rise, I know star-rise;
I walk in the moonlight, I walk in the starlight;
I'll lie in the grave and stretch out my arms,
I'll go to judgment in the evening of the day,
And my soul and thy soul shall meet that day,
  When I lay this body down.

Negro Song

They that walked in darkness sang songs in the olden days—Sorrow Songs—
for they were weary at heart. And so before each thought that I have written
in this book I have set a phrase, a haunting echo of these weird old songs in
which the soul of the black slave spoke to men. Ever since I was a child
these songs have stirred me strangely. They came out of the South unknown
to me, one by one, and yet at once I knew them as of me and of mine. Then
in after years when I came to Nashville I saw the great temple builded of
these songs towering over the pale city. To me Jubilee Hall seemed ever
made of the songs themselves, and its bricks were red with the blood and
dust of toil. Out of them rose for me morning, noon, and night, bursts of
wonderful melody, full of the voices of my brothers and sisters, full of the
voices of the past.

Little of beauty has America given the world save the rude grandeur
God himself stamped on her bosom; the human spirit in this new world has
expressed itself in vigor and ingenuity rather than in beauty. And so by fateful chance the Negro folk-song—the rhythmic cry of the slave—stands today
not simply as the sole American music, but as the most beautiful expression
of human experience born this side the seas. It has been neglected, it has
been, and is, half despised, and above all it has been persistently mistaken
and misunderstood; but notwithstanding, it still remains as the singular spiritual heritage of the nation and the greatest gift of the Negro people.

Away back in the thirties the melody of these slave songs stirred the nation, but the songs were soon half forgotten. Some, like "Near the lake
where dropped the willow," passed into current airs and their source was
forgotten; others were caricatured on the "minstrel" stage and their memory
died away. Then in war-time came the singular Port Royal experiment after
the capture of Hilton Head, and perhaps for the first time the North met the
Southern slave face to face and heart to heart with no third witness. The Sea
Islands of the Carolinas, where they met, were filled with a black folk of
primitive type, touched and moulded less by the world about them than any
others outside the Black Belt. Their appearance was uncouth, their language
funny, but their hearts were human and their singing stirred men with a
mighty power. Thomas Wentworth Higginson hastened to tell of these
songs, and Miss McKim and others urged upon the world their rare beauty.
But the world listened only half credulously until the Fisk Jubilee Singers
sang the slave songs so deeply into the world's heart that it can never wholly
forget them again.

There was once a blacksmith's son born at Cadiz, New York, who in the
changes of time taught school in Ohio and helped defend Cincinnati from
Kirby Smith. Then he fought at Chancellorsville and Gettysburg and finally

served in the Freedman's Bureau at Nashville. Here he formed a Sunday-school class of black children in 1866, and sang with them and taught them to sing. And then they taught him to sing, and when once the glory of the Jubilee songs passed into the soul of George L. White, he knew his life-work was to let those Negroes sing to the world as they had sung to him. So in 1871 the pilgrimage of the Fisk Jubilee Singers began. North to Cincinnati they rode,—four half-clothed black boys and five girl-women,—led by a man with a cause and a purpose. They stopped at Wilberforce, the oldest of Negro schools, where a black bishop blessed them. Then they went, fighting cold and starvation, shut out of hotels, and cheerfully sneered at, ever northward; and ever the magic of their song kept thrilling hearts, until a burst of applause in the Congregational Council at Oberlin revealed them to the world. They came to New York and Henry Ward Beecher dared to welcome them, even though the metropolitan dailies sneered at his "Nigger Minstrels." So their songs conquered till they sang across the land and across the sea, before Queen and Kaiser, in Scotland and Ireland, Holland and Switzerland. Seven years they sang, and brought back a hundred and fifty thousand dollars to found Fisk University. . . .

5   The words that are left to us are not without interest, and, cleared of evident dross, they conceal much of real poetry and meaning beneath conventional theology and unmeaning rhapsody. Like all primitive folk, the slave stood near to Nature's heart. Life was a "rough and rolling sea" like the brown Atlantic of the Sea Islands; the "Wilderness" was the home of God, and the "lonesome valley" led to the way of life. "Winter'll soon be over" was the picture of life and death to a tropical imagination. The sudden wild thunder-storms of the South awed and impressed the Negroes,—at times the rumbling seemed to them "mournful," at times imperious:

> "My Lord calls me,
> He calls me by the thunder,
> The trumpet sounds it in my soul."

The monotonous toil and exposure is painted in many words. One sees the ploughmen in the hot, moist furrow, singing:

> "Dere's no rain to wet you,
> Dere's no sun to burn you,
> Oh, push along, believer,
> I want to go home."

The bowed and bent old man cries, with thrice-repeated wail:

> "O Lord, keep me from sinking down,"

and he rebukes the devil of doubt who can whisper:
> "Jesus is dead and God's gone away."

Yet the soul-hunger is there, the restlessness of the savage, the wail of the wanderer, and the plaint is put in one little phrase:

> My soul wants something that's new, that's new.

                          . . .

Of death the Negro showed little fear, but talked of it familiarly and even fondly as simply a crossing of the waters, perhaps—who knows?—back to his ancient forests again. Later days transfigured his fatalism, and amid the dust and dirt the toiler sang:

> "Dust, dust and ashes, fly over my grave,
> But the Lord shall bear my spirit home."

The things evidently borrowed from the surrounding world undergo characteristic change when they enter the mouth of the slave. Especially is this true of Bible phrases. "Weep, O captive daughter of Zion," is quaintly turned into "Zion, weep-a-low," and the wheels of Ezekiel are turned every way in the mystic dreaming of the slave, till he says:

> "There's a little wheel a-turnin' in-a-my heart."

10   As in olden time, the words of these hymns were improvised by some leading minstrel of the religious band. The circumstances of the gathering, however, the rhythm of the songs, and the limitations of allowable thought, confined the poetry for the most part to single or double lines, and they seldom were expanded to quatrains or longer tales, although there are some few examples of sustained efforts, chiefly paraphrases of the Bible. Three short series of verses have always attracted me,—the one that heads this chapter, of one line of which Thomas Wentworth Higginson has fittingly said, "Never, it seems to me, since man first lived and suffered was his infinite longing for peace uttered more plaintively." The second and third are descriptions of the Last Judgment,—the one a late improvisation, with some traces of outside influence:

> "Oh, the stars in the elements are falling,
> And the moon drips away into blood,
> And the ransomed of the Lord are returning unto God,
> Blessed be the name of the Lord."

And the other earlier and homelier picture from the low coast lands:

> "Michael, haul the boat ashore,
> Then you'll hear the horn they blow,
> Then you'll hear the trumpet sound,
> Trumpet sound the world around,
> Trumpet sound for rich and poor,
> Trumpet sound for Jubilee,
> Trumpet sound for you and me."

Through all the sorrow of the Sorrow Songs there breathes a hope—a faith in the ultimate justice of things. The minor cadences of despair change often to triumph and calm confidence. Sometimes it is faith in life, sometimes a faith in death, sometimes assurance of boundless justice in some fair world beyond. But whichever it is, the meaning is always clear: that sometime, somewhere, men will judge men by their souls and not by their skins. Is such a hope justified? Do the Sorrow Songs sing true?

The silently growing assumption of this age is that the probation of races is past, and that the backward races of to-day are of proven inefficiency and not worth the saving. Such an assumption is the arrogance of peoples irreverent toward Time and ignorant of the deeds of men. A thousand years ago such an assumption, easily possible, would have made it difficult for the Teuton to prove his right to life. Two thousand years ago such dogmatism, readily welcome, would have scouted the idea of blond races ever leading civilization. So wofully unorganized is sociological knowledge that the meaning of progress, the meaning of "swift" and "slow" in human doing, and the limits of human perfectability, are veiled, unanswered sphinxes on the shores of science. Why should Aeschylus have sung two thousand years before Shakespeare was born? Why has civilization flourished in Europe, and flickered, flamed, and died in Africa? So long as the world stands meekly dumb before such questions, shall this nation proclaim its ignorance and unhallowed prejudices by denying freedom of opportunity to those who brought the Sorrow Songs to the Seats of the Mighty?

Your country? How came it yours? Before the Pilgrims landed we were here. Here we have brought our three gifts and mingled them with yours: a gift of story and song—soft, stirring melody in an ill-harmonized and unmelodious land; the gift of sweat and brawn to beat back the wilderness, conquer the soil, and lay the foundations of this vast economic empire two hundred years earlier than your weak hands could have done it; the third, a gift of the Spirit. Around us the history of the land has centred for thrice a hundred years; out of the nation's heart we have called all that was best to throttle and subdue all that was worst; fire and blood, prayer and sacrifice, have billowed over this people, and they have found peace only in the altars of the God of Right. Nor has our gift of the Spirit been merely passive. Actively we have woven ourselves with the very warp and woof of this nation,—we fought their battles, shared their sorrow, mingled our blood with theirs, and generation after generation have pleaded with a headstrong, careless people to despise not Justice, Mercy, and Truth, lest the nation be smitten with a curse. Our song, our toil, our cheer, and warning have been given to this nation in blood-brotherhood. Are not these gifts worth the giving? Is not this work and striving? Would America have been America without her Negro people?

Even so is the hope that sang in the songs of my fathers well sung. If somewhere in this whirl and chaos of things there dwells Eternal Good, pitiful yet masterful, then anon in His good time America shall rend the Veil and the prisoned shall be free. Free, free as the sunshine trickling down the morning into these high windows of mine, free as yonder fresh young voices welling up to me from the caverns of brick and mortar below—welling with song, instinct with life, tremulous treble and darkening bass. My children, my little children, are singing to the sunshine, and thus they sing:

> Let us cheer the weary traveller,
> Cheer the weary traveller,
> Let us cheer the weary traveller
> Along the heavenly way.

15   And the traveller girds himself, and sets his face toward the Morning, and goes his way.

[1903]

 TOPICS FOR CRITICAL THINKING AND WRITING

1. Du Bois uses some terms that may disconcert a reader, such as "primitive" and "backward races." Look especially closely at the passages in which these terms occur, and then summarize Du Bois's view of the

African-Americans of his time. Look closely, too, at passages in which he discusses whites' attitudes toward African-Americans, and summarize his views of these whites also.

2. Read the spirituals on pages 1208–1210, or, better, hear a performance of spirituals. To what extent, if any, has Du Bois helped you to understand and enjoy these works?

3. Alain Locke (1886–1954), African American educator and literary critic and historian, in *The Negro and His Music,* says this of the spirituals:

> Over-emphasize the melodic elements of a spiritual, and you get a sentimental ballad à la Stephen Foster. Stress the harmony and you get a cloying glee or "barber-shop" chorus. Over-emphasize, on the other hand, the rhythmic idiom and instantly you secularize the product and it becomes a syncopated shout, with the religious tone and mood completely evaporated.

If you are familiar with performances of spirituals, test the performances against Locke's words—or test Locke's words against the performances.

 FLANNERY O'CONNOR

Flannery O'Connor (1925–64)—her first name was Mary but she did not use it—was born in Savannah, Georgia, but spent most of her life in Milledgeville, Georgia, where her family moved when she was 12. She was educated in parochial schools and at the local college and then went to the School for Writers at the University of Iowa where she earned an M.F.A. in 1946. For a few months she lived at a writers' colony in Saratoga Springs, New York, and then for a few weeks she lived in New York City, but most of her life was spent back in Milledgeville, where she tended her peacocks and wrote stories, novels, essays (posthumously published as Mystery and Manners *[1970]), and letters (posthumously published under the title of* The Habit of Being *[1979]). A devout Catholic, O'Connor forthrightly summarized the relation between her belief and her writing:*

> *I see from the standpoint of Christian orthodoxy. This means that for me the meaning of life is centered in our Redemption by Christ and what I see in the world I see in its relation to that.*

We print, immediately below, a letter that O'Connor wrote to a young poet who had heard her lecture in an English class at Emory University (too shy to speak to her after the talk, he had written to her). Later in the chapter we print two stories by O'Connor.

A Letter to Alfred Corn

30 May 62

I think that this experience you are having of losing your faith, or as you think, of having lost it, is an experience that in the long run belongs to faith;

or at least it can belong to faith if faith is still valuable to you, and it must be or you would not have written me about this.

I don't know how the kind of faith required of a Christian living in the 20th century can be at all if it is not grounded on this experience that you are having right now of unbelief. This may be the case always and not just in the 20th century. Peter said, "Lord, I believe. Help my unbelief." It is the most natural and most human and most agonizing prayer in the gospels, and I think it is the foundation prayer of faith.

As a freshman in college you are bombarded with new ideas, or rather pieces of ideas, new frames of reference, an activation of the intellectual life which is only beginning, but which is already running ahead of your lived experience. After a year of this, you think you cannot believe. You are just beginning to realize how difficult it is to have faith and the measure of a commitment to it, but you are too young to decide you don't have faith just because you feel you can't believe. About the only way we know whether we believe or not is by what we do, and I think from your letter that you will not take the path of least resistance in this matter and simply decide that you have lost your faith and that there is nothing you can do about it.

One result of the stimulation of your intellectual life that takes place in college is usually a shrinking of the imaginative life. This sounds like a paradox, but I have often found it to be true. Students get so bound up with difficulties such as reconciling the clashing of so many different faiths such as Buddhism, Mohammedanism, etc., that they cease to look for God in other ways. Bridges once wrote Gerard Manley Hopkins and asked him to tell him how he, Bridges, could believe. He must have expected from Hopkins a long philosophical answer. Hopkins wrote back, "Give alms." He was trying to say to Bridges that God is to be experienced in Charity (in the sense of love for the divine image in human beings). Don't get so entangled with intellectual difficulties that you fail to look for God in this way.

5   The intellectual difficulties have to be met, however, and you will be meeting them for the rest of your life. When you get a reasonable hold on one, another will come to take its place. At one time, the clash of the different world religions was a difficulty for me. Where you have absolute solutions, however, you have no need of faith. Faith is what you have in the absence of knowledge. The reason this clash doesn't bother me any longer is because I have got, over the years, a sense of the immense sweep of creation, of the evolutionary process in everything, of how incomprehensible God must necessarily be to be the God of heaven and earth. You can't fit the Almighty into your intellectual categories. I might suggest that you look into some of the works of Pierre Teilhard de Chardin (*The Phenomenon of Man* et al.). He was a paleontologist—helped to discover Peking man—and also a man of God. I don't suggest you go to him for answers but for different questions, for that stretching of the imagination that you need to make you a sceptic in the face of much that you are learning, much of which is new and shocking but which when boiled down becomes less so and takes its place in the general scheme of things. What kept me a sceptic in college was precisely my Christian faith. It always said: wait, don't bite on this, get a wider picture, continue to read.

If you want your faith, you have to work for it. It is a gift, but for very few is it a gift given without any demand for equal time devoted to its cultivation. For every book you read that is anti-Christian, make it your business to read one that presents the other side of the picture; if one isn't satisfactory read others. Don't think that you have to abandon reason to be a Christian. A book that might help you is *The Unity of Philosophical Experience* by Etienne Gilson. Another is Newman's *The Grammar of Assent.* To find out about faith, you have to go to the people who have it and you have to go to the most intelligent ones if you are going to stand up intellectually to agnostics and the general run of pagans that you are going to find in the majority of people around you. Much of the criticism of belief that you find today comes from people who are judging it from the standpoint of another and narrower discipline. The Biblical criticism of the 19th century, for instance, was the product of historical disciplines. It has been entirely revamped in the 20th century by applying broader criteria to it, and those people who lost their faith in the 19th century because of it, could better have hung on in blind trust.

Even in the life of a Christian, faith rises and falls like the tides of an invisible sea. It's there, even when he can't see it or feel it, if he wants it to be there. You realize, I think, that it is more valuable, more mysterious, altogether more immense than anything you can learn or decide upon in college. Learn what you can, but cultivate Christian scepticism. It will keep you free—not free to do anything you please, but free to be formed by something larger than your own intellect or the intellects of those around you.

I don't know if this is the kind of answer that can help you, but any time you care to write me, I can try to do better.

[1962]

 TOPICS FOR CRITICAL THINKING AND WRITING

1. What is the assumption in O'Connor's first paragraph? Do you agree with it?
2. In paragraph 3 O'Connor says, "About the only way we know whether we believe or not is by what we do." On the whole, she intends this to be comforting. Is it?
3. In paragraph 5 O'Connor explains how Corn might become a sceptic. What does she mean?
4. How would you characterize O'Connor's last sentence? What other qualities would you ascribe to her writing?

Fiction

 NATHANIEL HAWTHORNE

Nathaniel Hawthorne (1804–64) was born in Salem, Massachusetts, the son of a sea captain. Two of his ancestors were judges; one had persecuted Quakers, and another had served at the Salem witch trials. After graduating from Bowdoin College in Maine he went back to

Salem in order to write in relative seclusion. In 1831 he published "My Kinsman, Major Molineux"; in 1835 he published "Young Goodman Brown" and "The Maypole of Merry Mount"; and in 1837 he published "Dr. Heidegger's Experiment."

From 1839 to 1841 Hawthorne worked in the Boston Customs House and then spent a few months as a member of a communal society, Brook Farm. In 1842 he married. From 1846 to 1849 he was a surveyor at the Salem Customs House; from 1849 to 1850 he wrote The Scarlet Letter, *the book that made him famous. From 1853 to 1857 he served as American consul in Liverpool, England, a plum awarded him in exchange for writing a campaign biography of a former college classmate, President Franklin Pierce. In 1860, after living in England and Italy, he returned to the United States, settling in Concord, Massachusetts.*

In his stories and novels Hawthorne keeps returning to the Puritan past, studying guilt, sin, and isolation.

Young Goodman Brown

Young Goodman Brown came forth at sunset into the street at Salem village; but put his head back, after crossing the threshold, to exchange a parting kiss with his young wife. And Faith, as the wife was aptly named, thrust her own pretty head into the street, letting the wind play with the pink ribbons of her cap while she called to Goodman Brown.

"Dearest heart," whispered she, softly and rather sadly, when her lips were close to his ear, "prithee put off your journey until sunrise and sleep in your own bed to-night. A lone woman is troubled with such dreams and such thoughts that she's afeared of herself sometimes. Pray tarry with me this night, dear husband, of all nights in the year."

"My love and my Faith," replied young Goodman Brown, "of all nights in the year, this one night must I tarry away from thee. My journey, as thou callest it, forth and back again, must needs be done 'twixt now and sunrise. What, my sweet, pretty wife, dost thou doubt me already, and we but three months married?"

"Then God bless you!" said Faith, with the pink ribbons; "and may you find all well when you come back."

5   "Amen!" cried Goodman Brown. "Say thy prayers, dear Faith, and go to bed at dusk, and no harm will come to thee."

So they parted; and the young man pursued his way until, being about to turn the corner by the meeting-house, he looked back and saw the head of Faith still peeping after him with a melancholy air, in spite of her pink ribbons.

"Poor little Faith!" thought he, for his heart smote him. "What a wretch am I to leave her on such an errand! She talks of dreams, too. Methought as she spoke there was trouble in her face, as if a dream had warned her what work is to be done to-night. But no, no; 'twould kill her to think it. Well, she's a blessed angel on earth; and after this one night I'll cling to her skirts and follow her to heaven."

With this excellent resolve for the future, Goodman Brown felt himself justified in making more haste on his present evil purpose. He had taken a dreary road, darkened by all the gloomiest trees of the forest, which barely stood aside to let the narrow path creep through, and closed immediately behind. It was all as lonely as could be; and there is this peculiarity in such a solitude, that the traveler knows not who may be concealed by the innumerable trunks and the thick boughs overhead; so that with lonely footsteps he may yet be passing through an unseen multitude.

"There may be a devilish Indian behind every tree," said Goodman Brown to himself; and he glanced fearfully behind him as he added, "What if the devil himself should be at my very elbow!"

10   His head being turned back, he passed a crook of the road, and, looking forward again, beheld the figure of a man, in grave and decent attire, seated at the foot of an old tree. He arose at Goodman Brown's approach and walked onward side by side with him.

"You are late, Goodman Brown," said he. "The clock of the Old South was striking as I came through Boston, and that is full fifteen minutes agone."

"Faith kept me back a while," replied the young man, with a tremor in his voice, caused by the sudden appearance of his companion, though not wholly unexpected.

It was now deep dusk in the forest, and deepest in that part of it where these two were journeying. As nearly as could be discerned, the second traveller was about fifty years old, apparently in the same rank of life as Goodman Brown, and bearing a considerable resemblance to him, though perhaps more in expression than features. Still they might have been taken for father and son. And yet, though the elder person was as simply clad as the younger, and as simple in manner too, he had an indescribable air of one who knew the world, and who would not have felt abashed at the governor's dinner table or in King William's court, were it possible that his affairs should call him thither. But the only thing about him that could be fixed upon as remarkable was his staff, which bore the likeness of a great black snake, so curiously wrought that it might almost be seen to twist and wriggle itself like a living serpent. This, of course, must have been an ocular deception, assisted by the uncertain light.

"Come, Goodman Brown," cried his fellow-traveller, "this is a dull pace for the beginning of a journey. Take my staff, if you are so soon weary."

15   "Friend," said the other, exchanging his slow pace for a full stop, "Having kept covenant by meeting thee here, it is my purpose now to return whence I came. I have scruples touching the matter thou wot'st of."

"Sayest thou so?" replied he of the serpent, smiling apart. "Let us walk on, nevertheless, reasoning as we go; and if I convince thee not thou shalt turn back. We are but a little way in the forest yet."

"Too far! too far!" exclaimed the goodman, unconsciously resuming his walk. "My father never went into the woods on such an errand, not his father before him. We have been a race of honest men and good Christians since the days of the martyrs; and shall I be the first of the name of Brown that ever took this path and kept—"

"Such company, thou wouldst say," observed the elder person, interpreting his pause. "Well said, Goodman Brown! I have been as well acquainted with your family as with ever a one among the Puritans; and that's no trifle to say. I helped your grandfather, the constable, when he lashed the Quaker woman so smartly through the streets of Salem; and it was I that brought your father a pitch-pine knot, kindled at my own hearth, to set fire to an Indian village, in King Philip's war. They were my good friends, both; and many a pleasant walk have we had along this path, and returned merrily after midnight. I would fain be friends with you for their sake."

"If it be as thou sayest," replied Goodman Brown, "I marvel they never spoke of these matters; or, verily, I marvel not, seeing that the least rumor of the sort would have driven them from New England. We are a people of prayer, and good works to boot, and abide no such wickedness."

20   "Wickedness or not," said the traveller with the twisted staff, "I have a very general acquaintance here in New England. The deacons of many a church have drunk the communion wine with me; the selectmen of divers towns make me their chairman; and a majority of the Great and General Court are firm supporters of my interest. The governor and I, too—But these are state secrets."

"Can this be so?" cried Goodman Brown, with a stare of amazement at his undisturbed companion. "Howbeit, I have nothing to do with the governor and council; they have their own ways, and are no rule for a simple husbandman like me. But, were I to go on with thee, how should I meet the eye of that good old man, our minister, at Salem village? Oh, his voice would make me tremble both Sabbath day and lecture day."

Thus far the elder traveller had listened with due gravity; but now burst into a fit of irrepressible mirth, shaking himself so violently that his snake-like staff actually seemed to wriggle in sympathy.

"Ha! ha! ha!" shouted he again and again; then composing himself, "Well, go on, Goodman Brown, go on; but, prithee, don't kill me with laughing."

"Well, then, to end the matter at once," said Goodman Brown, considerably nettled, "there is my wife, Faith. It would break her dear little heart; and I'd rather break my own."

25   "Nay, if that be the case," answered the other, "e'en go thy ways, Goodman Brown. I would not for twenty old women like the one hobbling before us that Faith should come to any harm."

As he spoke he pointed his staff at a female figure on the path, in whom Goodman Brown recognized a very pious and exemplary dame, who had taught him his catechism in youth, and was still his moral and spiritual adviser, jointly with the minister and Deacon Gookin.

"A marvel, truly, that Goody Cloyse should be so far in the wilderness at nightfall," said he. "But with your leave, friend, I shall take a cut through the woods until we have left this Christian woman behind. Being a stranger to you, she might ask whom I was consorting with and whither I was going."

"Be it so," said his fellow-traveller. "Betake you the woods, and let me keep the path."

Accordingly the young man turned aside, but took care to watch his companion, who advanced softly along the road until he had come within a staff's length of the old dame. She, meanwhile, was making the best of her way, with singular speed for so aged a woman, and mumbling some indistinct words—a prayer, doubtless—as she went. The traveller put forth his staff and touched her withered neck with what seemed the serpent's tail.

30   "The devil!" screamed the pious old lady.

"Then Good Cloyse knows her old friend?" observed the traveller, confronting her and leaning on his writhing stick.

"Ah, forsooth, and is it your worship indeed?" cried the good dame. "Yea, truly is it, and in the very image of my old gossip, Goodman Brown, the grandfather of the silly fellow that now is. But—would your worship believe it?—my broomstick hath strangely disappeared, stolen, as I suspect, by that unhanged witch, Goody Cory, and that, too, when I was all anointed with the juice of smallage, and cinquefoil, and wolf's bane—"

"Mingled with fine wheat and the fat of a new-born babe," said the shape of old Goodman Brown.

"Ah, your worship knows the recipe," cried the old lady, cackling aloud. "So, as I was saying, being all ready for the meeting, and no horse to ride on, I made up my mind to foot it; for they tell me there is a nice young man to be taken into communion to-night. But now your good worship will lend me your arm, and we shall be there in a twinkling."

35   "That can hardly be," answered her friend. "I may not spare you my arm, Goody Cloyse; but here is my staff, if you will."

So saying, he threw it down at her feet, where, perhaps, it assumed life, being one of the rods which its owner had formerly lent to the Egyptian magi. Of this fact, however, Goodman Brown could not take cognizance. He had cast up his eyes in astonishment, and, looking down again, beheld neither Goody Cloyse nor the serpentine staff, but his fellow-traveller alone, who waited for him as calmly as if nothing had happened.

"That old woman taught me my catechism," said the young man; and there was a world of meaning in this simple comment.

They continued to walk onward, while the elder traveller exhorted his companion to make good speed and persevere in the path, discoursing so aptly that his arguments seemed rather to spring up in the bosom of his auditor than to be suggested by himself. As they went, he plucked a branch of maple to serve for a walking stick, and began to strip it of the twigs and the little boughs, which were wet with evening dew. The moment his fingers touched them they became strangely withered and dried up as with a week's sunshine. Thus the pair proceeded, at a good free pace, until suddenly, in a gloomy hollow of the road, Goodman Brown sat himself down on the stump of a tree and refused to go any farther.

"Friend," said he, stubbornly, "my mind is made up. Not another step will I budge on this errand. What if a wretched old woman do choose to go to the devil when I thought she was going to heaven: is that any reason why I should quit my dear Faith and go after her?"

40   "You will think better of this by and by," said his acquaintance, composedly. "Sit here and rest yourself a while; and when you feel like moving again, there is my staff to help you along."

Without more words, he threw his companion the maple stick, and was as speedily out of sight as if he had vanished into the deepening gloom. The young man sat a few moments by the roadside, applauding himself greatly, and thinking with how clear a conscience he should meet the minister in his morning walk, nor shrink from the eye of good old Deacon Gookin. And what calm sleep would be his that very night, which was to have been spent so wickedly, but so purely and sweetly now, in the arms of Faith! Amidst these pleasant and praiseworthy meditations, Goodman Brown heard the tramp of horses along the road, and deemed it advisable to conceal himself within the verge of the forest, conscious of the guilty purpose that had brought him thither, though now so happily turned from it.

On came the hoof tramps and the voices of the riders, two grave old voices, conversing soberly as they drew near. These mingled sounds appeared to pass along the road, within a few yards of the young man's hiding-place; but, owing doubtless to the depth of the gloom at that particular spot, neither the travellers nor their steeds were visible. Though their figures brushed the small boughs by the wayside, it could not be seen that they intercepted, even for a moment, the faint gleam from the strip of bright sky athwart which they must have passed. Goodman Brown alternately crouched and stood on tiptoe, pulling aside the branches and thrusting forth his head as far as he durst without discerning so much as a shadow. It vexed him the more, because he could have sworn, were such a thing possible, that he recognized the voices of the minister and Deacon Gookin, jogging along quietly, as they were wont to do, when bound to some ordination or ecclesiastical council. While yet within hearing, one of the riders stopped to pluck a switch.

"Of the two, reverend sir," said the voice like the deacon's, "I had rather miss an ordination dinner than to-night's meeting. They tell me that some of our community are to be here from Falmouth and beyond, and others from Connecticut and Rhode Island, besides several of the Indian powwows, who, after their fashion, know almost as much deviltry as the best of us. Moreover, there is a goodly young woman to be taken into communion."

"Mighty well, Deacon Gookin!" replied the solemn old tones of the minister. "Spur up, or we shall be late. Nothing can be done, you know, until I get on the ground."

45   The hoofs clattered again; and the voices, talking so strangely in the empty air, passed on through the forest, where no church had ever been gathered or solitary Christian prayed. Whither, then, could these holy men be journeying so deep into the heathen wilderness? Young Goodman Brown caught hold of a tree for support, being ready to sink down on the ground, faint and overburdened with the heavy sickness of his heart. He looked up to the sky, doubting whether there really was a heaven above him. Yet there was the blue arch, and the stars brightening in it.

"With heaven above and Faith below, I will yet stand firm against the devil!" cried Goodman Brown.

While he still gazed upward into the deep arch of the firmament and had lifted his hands to pray, a cloud, though no wind was stirring, hurried across the zenith and hid the brightening stars. The blue sky was still visible, except directly overhead, where this black mass of cloud was sweeping swiftly northward. Aloft in the air, as if from the depths of the cloud, came a confused and doubtful sound of voices. Once the listener fancied that he could distinguish the accents of townspeople of his own, men and women, both pious and ungodly, many of whom he had met at the communion table, and had seen others rioting at the tavern. The next moment, so indistinct were the sounds, he doubted whether he had heard aught but the murmur of the old forest, whispering without a wind. Then came a stronger swell of those familiar tones, heard daily in the sunshine at Salem village, but never until now from a cloud of night. There was one voice, of a young woman, uttering lamentations, yet with an uncertain sorrow, and entreating for some favor, which, perhaps, it would grieve her to obtain; and all the unseen multitude, both saints and sinners, seemed to encourage her onward.

"Faith!" shouted Goodman Brown, in a voice of agony and desperation;

and the echoes of the forest mocked him, crying, "Faith! Faith!" as if bewildered wretches were seeking her all through the wilderness.

The cry of grief, rage, and terror was yet piercing the night, when the unhappy husband held his breath for a response. There was a scream, drowned immediately in a louder murmur of voices, fading into far-off laughter, as the dark cloud swept away, leaving the clear and silent sky above Goodman Brown. But something fluttered lightly down through the air and caught on the branch of a tree. The young man seized it, and beheld a pink ribbon.

50   "My Faith is gone!" cried he, after one stupefied moment. "There is no good on earth; and sin is but a name. Come, devil; for to thee is this world given."

And, maddened with despair, so that he laughed loud and long, did Goodman Brown grasp his staff and set forth again, at such a rate that he seemed to fly along the forest path rather than to walk or run. The road grew wilder and drearier and more faintly traced, and vanished at length, leaving him in the heart of the dark wilderness, still rushing onward with the instinct that guides mortal man to evil. The whole forest was peopled with frightful sounds—the creaking of the trees, the howling of wild beasts, and the yell of Indians; while sometimes the wind tolled like a distant church bell, and sometimes gave a broad roar around the traveller, as if all Nature were laughing him to scorn. But he was himself the chief horror of the scene, and shrank not from its other horrors.

"Ha! ha! ha!" roared Goodman Brown when the wind laughed at him. "Let us hear which will laugh loudest. Think not to frighten me with your deviltry. Come witch, come wizard, come Indian powwow, come devil himself, and here comes Goodman Brown. You may as well fear him as he fear you."

In truth, all through the haunted forest there could be nothing more frightful than the figure of Goodman Brown. On he flew among the black pines, brandishing his staff with frenzied gestures, now giving vent to an inspiration of horrid blasphemy, and now shouting forth such laughter as set all the echoes of the forest laughing like demons around him. The fiend in his own shape is less hideous than when he rages in the breast of man. Thus sped the demoniac on his course, until, quivering among the trees, he saw a red light before him, as when the felled trunks and branches of a clearing have been set on fire, and throw up their lurid blaze against the sky, at the hour of midnight. He paused, in a lull of the tempest that had driven him onward, and heard the swell of what seemed a hymn, rolling solemnly from a distance with the weight of many voices. He knew the tune; it was a familiar one in the choir of the village meeting-house. The verse died heavily away, and was lengthened by a chorus, not of human voices, but of all the sounds of the benighted wilderness pealing in awful harmony together. Goodman Brown cried out, and his cry was lost to his own ear by its unison with the cry of the desert.

In the interval of silence he stole forward until the light glared full upon his eyes. At one extremity of an open space, hemmed in by the dark wall of the forest, arose a rock, bearing some rude, natural resemblance either to an altar or a pulpit, and surrounded by four blazing pines, their tops aflame, their stems untouched, like candles at an evening meeting. The mass of foliage that had overgrown the summit of the rock was all on fire, blazing high into the night and fitfully illuminating the whole field. Each pendent twig and leafy festoon was in a blaze. As the red light arose and fell, a numerous congregation alternately shone forth, then disappeared in shadow, and again grew, as it were, out of the darkness, peopling the heart of the solitary woods at once.

55   "A grave and dark-clad company," quoth Goodman Brown.

In truth they were such. Among them, quivering to and fro between gloom and splendor, appeared faces that would be seen next day at the council board of the province, and others which, Sabbath after Sabbath, looked devoutly heavenward, and benignantly over the crowded pews, from the holiest pulpits in the land. Some affirm that the lady of the governor was there. At least three were high dames well known to her, and wives of honored husbands, and widows, a great multitude, and ancient maidens, all of excellent repute, and fair young girls, who trembled lest their mothers should espy them. Either the sudden gleams of light flashing over the obscure field bedazzled Goodman Brown, or he recognized a score of the church members of Salem village famous for their especial sanctity. Good old Deacon Gookin had arrived, and waited at the skirts of that venerable saint, his revered pastor. But, irreverently consorting with these grave, reputable, and pious people, these elders of the church, these chaste dames and dewy virgins, there were men of dissolute lives and women of spotted fame, wretches given over to all mean and filthy vice, and suspected even of horrid crimes. It was strange to see that the good shrank not from the wicked, nor were the sinners abashed by the saints. Scattered also among their pale-faced enemies were the Indian priests, or powwows, who had often scared their native forest with more hideous incantations than any known to English witchcraft.

"But where is Faith?" thought Goodman Brown; and, as hope came into his heart, he trembled.

Another verse of the hymn arose, a slow and mournful strain, such as the pious love, but joined to words which expressed all that our nature can conceive of sin, and darkly hinted at far more. Unfathomable to mere mortals is the lore of fiends. Verse after verse was sung; and still the chorus of the desert swelled between like the deepest tone of a mighty organ; and with the final peal of that dreadful anthem there came a sound, as if the roaring wind, the rushing streams, the howling beasts, and every other voice of the unconcerted wilderness were mingling and according with the voice of guilty man in homage to the prince of all. The four blazing pines threw up a loftier flame, and obscurely discovered shapes and visages of horror on the smoke wreaths above the impious assembly. At the same moment the fire on the rock shot redly forth and formed a glowing arch above its base, where now appeared a figure. With reverence be it spoken, the figure bore no slight similitude, both in garb and manner, to some grave divine of the New England churches.

"Bring forth the converts!" cried a voice that echoed through the field and rolled into the forest.

60   At the word, Goodman Brown stepped forth from the shadow of the trees and approached the congregation, with whom he felt a loathful brotherhood by the sympathy of all that was wicked in his heart. He could have well-nigh sworn that the shape of his own dead father beckoned him to advance, looking downward from a smoke wreath, while a woman, with dim

features of despair, threw out her hand to warn him back. Was it his mother? But he had no power to retreat one step, nor to resist, even in thought, when the minister and good old Deacon Gookin seized his arms and led him to the blazing rock. Thither came also the slender form of a veiled female, led between Goody Cloyse, that pious teacher of the catechism, and Martha Carrier, who had received the devil's promise to be queen of hell. A rampant hag was she. And there stood the proselytes beneath the canopy of fire.

"Welcome, my children," said the dark figure, "to the communion of your race. Ye have found thus young your nature and your destiny. My children, look behind you!"

They turned; and flashing forth, as it were, in a sheet of flame, the fiend worshippers were seen; the smile of welcome gleamed darkly on every visage.

"There," resumed the sable form, "are all whom ye have reverenced from youth. Ye deemed them holier than yourselves, and shrank from your own sin, contrasting it with their lives of righteousness and prayerful aspirations heavenward. Yet here are they all in my worshipping assembly. This night it shall be granted you to know their secret deeds: how hoary-bearded elders of the church have whispered wanton words to the young maids of their households; how many a woman, eager for widows' weeds, has given her husband a drink at bedtime and let him sleep his last sleep in her bosom; how beardless youths have made haste to inherit their fathers' wealth; and how fair damsels—blush not, sweet ones—have dug little graves in the garden, and bidden me, the sole guest, to an infant's funeral. By the sympathy of your human hearts for sin ye shall scent out all the places—whether in church, bedchamber, street, field, or forest—where crime has been committed, and shall exult to behold the whole earth one stain of guilt, one mighty blood spot. Far more than this. It shall be yours to penetrate, in every bosom, the deep mystery of sin, the fountain of all wicked arts, and which inexhaustibly supplies more evil impulses than human power—than my power at its utmost—can make manifest in deeds. And now, my children, look upon each other."

They did so; and, by the blaze of the hell-kindled torches, the wretched man beheld his Faith, and the wife her husband, trembling before that unhallowed altar.

65   "Lo, there ye stand, my children," said the figure, in a deep and solemn tone, almost sad with its despairing awfulness, as if his once angelic nature could yet mourn for our miserable race. "Depending upon one another's hearts, ye had still hoped that virtue were not all a dream. Now are ye undeceived. Evil is the nature of mankind. Evil must be your only happiness. Welcome again, my children, to the communion of your race."

"Welcome," repeated the fiend worshippers, in one cry of despair and triumph.

And there they stood, the only pair, as it seemed, who were yet hesitating on the verge of wickedness in this dark world. A basin was hollowed, naturally, in the rock. Did it contain water, reddened by the lurid light? or was it blood? or, perchance, a liquid flame? Herein did the shape of evil dip his hand and prepare to lay the mark of baptism upon their foreheads, that they might be partakers of the mystery of sin, more conscious of the secret guilt of others, both in deed and thought, than they could now be of their own. The husband cast one look at his pale wife, and Faith at him. What polluted wretches would the next glance show them to each other, shuddering alike at what they disclosed and what they saw!

"Faith! Faith!" cried the husband, "look up to heaven, and resist the wicked one."

Whether Faith obeyed he knew not. Hardly had he spoken when he found himself amid calm night and solitude, listening to a roar of the wind which died heavily away through the forest. He staggered against the rock, and felt it chill and damp; while a hanging twig, that had been all on fire, besprinkled his cheek with the coldest dew.

70   The next morning young Goodman Brown came slowly into the street of Salem village, staring around him like a bewildered man. The good old minister was taking a walk along the graveyard to get the appetite for breakfast and meditate his sermon, and bestowed a blessing, as he passed, on Goodman Brown. He shrank from the venerable saint as if to avoid an anathema. Old Deacon Gookin was at domestic worship, and the holy words of his prayer were heard through the open window. "What God doth the wizard pray to?" quoth Goodman Brown. Goody Cloyse, that excellent old Christian, stood in the early sunshine at her own lattice, catechizing a little girl who had brought her a pint of morning's milk. Goodman Brown snatched away the child as from the grasp of the fiend himself. Turning the corner by the meeting-house, he spied the head of Faith, with the pink ribbons, gazing anxiously forth, and bursting into such joy at sight of him that she skipped along the street and almost kissed her husband before the whole village. But Goodman Brown looked sternly and sadly into her face, and passed on without a greeting.

Had Goodman Brown fallen asleep in the forest and only dreamed a wild dream of a witch-meeting?

Be it so if you will; but alas! it was a dream of evil omen for young Goodman Brown. A stern, a sad, a darkly meditative, a distrustful, if not a desperate man did he become from the night of that fearful dream. On the Sabbath day, when the congregation were singing a holy psalm, he could not listen because an anthem of sin rushed loudly upon his ear and drowned all the blessed strain. When the minister spoke from the pulpit and power and fervid eloquence, and, with his hand on the open Bible, of the sacred truths of our religion, and of saint-like lives and triumphant deaths, and of future bliss or misery unutterable, then did Goodman Brown turn pale, dreading lest the roof should thunder down upon the gray blasphemer and his hearers. Often, awaking suddenly at midnight, he shrank from the bosom of Faith; and at mourning or eventide, when the family knelt down at prayer, he scowled and muttered to himself, and gazed sternly at his wife, and turned away. And when he had lived long, and was borne to his grave a hoary corpse, followed by Faith, an aged woman, and children and grandchildren, a goodly procession, besides neighbors not a few, they carved no hopeful verse upon his tombstone, for his dying hour was gloom.

[1835]

 ## TOPICS FOR CRITICAL THINKING AND WRITING

1. What do you think Hawthorne gains (or loses) by the last sentence?
2. Evaluate the view that when Young Goodman Brown enters the dark forest he is really entering his own evil mind. Why, by the way, does he

go into the forest at night? (Hawthorne gives no explicit reason, but you may want to offer a conjecture.)

3. In a sentence or two summarize the plot, and then in another sentence or two state the theme of the story. (On theme, see pages 149-50.)

4. If you have undergone a religious experience, write an essay discussing your condition before, during, and after the experience.

 I. L. PERETZ

Isaac Loeb Peretz (1852-1915) was born in Poland and educated as a lawyer. He was active as a political radical—he was imprisoned as a socialist agitator—but he devoted most of his professional life to writing fiction, poetry, and plays. He wrote his early work in Hebrew, but he then turned to writing in Yiddish, and it is as a Yiddish writer that he is remembered.

If Not Higher*

Early every Friday morning, at the time of the Penitential Prayers,[1] the Rabbi of Nemirov would vanish.

He was nowhere to be seen—neither in the synagogue nor in the two Houses of Study nor at a *minyan.*[2] And he was certainly not at home. His door stood open; whoever wished could go in and out; no one would steal from the rabbi. But not a living creature was within.

Where could the rabbi be? Where should he be? In heaven, no doubt. A rabbi has plenty of business to take care of just before the Days of Awe. Jews, God bless them, need livelihood, peace, health, and good matches. They want to be pious and good, but our sins are so great, and Satan of the thousand eyes watches the whole earth from one end to the other. What he sees he reports; he denounces, informs. Who can help us if not the rabbi!

That's what the people thought.

5   But once a Litvak[3] came, and he laughed. You know the Litvaks. They think little of the Holy Books but stuff themselves with Talmud and law. So this Litvak points to a passage in the *Gemarah*[4]—it sticks in your eyes— where it is written that even Moses, our Teacher, did not ascend to heaven during his lifetime but remained suspended two and a half feet below. Go argue with a Litvak!

So where can the rabbi be?

"That's not my business," said the Litvak, shrugging. Yet all the while— what a Litvak can do!—he is scheming to find out.

That same night, right after the evening prayers, the Litvak steals into the rabbi's room, slides under the rabbi's bed, and waits. He'll watch all

---

* Translated by Marie Syrkin
[1] prayers recited in the days preceding the Days of Awe. The Days of Awe extend from the New Year's days (Rosh Hashanah) to the Day of Atonement (Yom Kippur), a period of ten days   [2] the quorum of ten men needed to conduct Jewish public worship   [3] a Lithuanian Jew   [4] part of the Talmud, a commentary on Jewish law

night and discover where the rabbi vanishes and what he does during the Penitential Prayers.

Someone else might have got drowsy and fallen asleep, but a Litvak is never at a loss; he recites a whole tractate of the Talmud by heart.

10   At dawn he hears the call to prayers.

The rabbi has already been awake for a long time. The Litvak has heard him groaning for a whole hour.

Whoever has heard the Rabbi of Nemirov groan knows how much sorrow for all Israel, how much suffering, lies in each groan. A man's heart might break, hearing it. But a Litvak is made of iron; he listens and remains where he is. The rabbi, long life to him, lies on the bed, and the Litvak under the bed.

Then the Litvak hears the beds in the house begin to creak; he hears people jumping out of their beds, mumbling a few Jewish words, pouring water on their fingernails, banging doors. Everyone has left. It is again quiet and dark; a bit of light from the moon shines through the shutters.

(Afterward the Litvak admitted that when he found himself alone with the rabbi a great fear took hold of him. Goose pimples spread across his skin, and the roots of his earlocks pricked him like needles. A trifle: to be alone with the rabbi at the time of the Penitential Prayers! But a Litvak is stubborn. So he quivered like a fish in water and remained where he was.)

15   Finally the rabbi, long life to him, arises. First he does what befits a Jew. Then he goes to the clothes closet and takes out a bundle of peasant clothes: linen trousers, high boots, a coat, a big felt hat, and a long wide leather belt studded with brass nails. The rabbi gets dressed. From his coat pocket dangles the end of a heavy peasant rope.

The rabbi goes out, and the Litvak follows him.

On the way the rabbi stops in the kitchen, bends down, takes an ax from under the bed, puts it in his belt, and leaves the house. The Litvak trembles but continues to follow.

The hushed dread of the Days of Awe hangs over the dark streets. Every once in a while a cry rises from some *minyan* reciting the Penitential Prayers, or from a sickbed. The rabbi hugs the sides of the streets, keeping to the shade of the houses. He glides from house to house, and the Litvak after him. The Litvak hears the sound of his heartbeats mingling with the sound of the rabbi's heavy steps. But he keeps on going and follows the rabbi to the outskirts of the town.

A small wood stands behind the town.

20   The rabbi, long life to him, enters the wood. He takes thirty or forty steps and stops by a small tree. The Litvak, overcome with amazement, watches the rabbi take the ax out of his belt and strike the tree. He hears the tree creak and fall. The rabbi chops the tree into logs and the logs into sticks. Then he makes a bundle of the wood and ties it with the rope in his pocket. He puts the bundle of wood on his back, shoves the ax back into his belt, and returns to the town.

He stops at a back street beside a small broken-down shack and knocks at the window.

"Who is there?" asks a frightened voice. The Litvak recognizes it as the voice of a sick Jewish woman.

"I," answers the rabbi in the accent of a peasant.

"Who is I?"

25   Again the rabbi answers in Russian. "Vassil."

"Who is Vassil, and what do you want?"

"I have wood to sell, very cheap." And, not waiting for the woman's reply, he goes into the house.

The Litvak steals in after him. In the gray light of the early morning he sees a poor room with broken, miserable furnishings. A sick woman, wrapped in rags, lies on the bed. She complains bitterly, "Buy? How can I buy? Where will a poor widow get money?"

"I'll lend it to you," answers the supposed Vassil. "It's only six cents."

30   "And how will I ever pay you back?" said the poor woman, groaning.

"Foolish one," says the rabbi reproachfully. "See, you are a poor sick Jew, and I am ready to trust you with a little wood. I am sure you'll pay. While you, you have such a great and mighty God and you don't trust him for six cents."

"And who will kindle the fire?" said the widow. "Have I the strength to get up? My son is at work."

"I'll kindle the fire," answers the rabbi.

As the rabbi put the wood into the oven he recited, in a groan, the first portion of the Penitential Prayers.

35   As he kindled the fire and the wood burned brightly, he recited, a bit more joyously, the second portion of the Penitential Prayers. When the fire was set he recited the third portion, and then he shut the stove.

The Litvak who saw all this became a disciple of the rabbi.

And ever after, when another disciple tells how the Rabbi of Nemirov ascends to heaven at the time of the Penitential Prayers, the Litvak does not laugh. He only adds quietly, "If not higher."

[1900]

TOPICS FOR CRITICAL THINKING AND WRITING

1. According to the third paragraph, why would a rabbi go to heaven "just before the Days of Awe"? Why does the rabbi of this story *not* go to heaven during this period?

2. In a paragraph characterize the Litvak, taking account of his final speech.

KATHERINE ANNE PORTER

Katherine Anne Porter (1890–1980) had the curious habit of inventing details in her life, but it is true that she was born in a log cabin in Indian Creek, Texas, that she was originally named Callie Russell Porter, that her mother died when the child was 2 years old, and that Callie was brought up by her maternal grandmother in Kyle, Texas. She was sent to convent schools, where, in her words, she received a "strangely useless and ornamental education." When she was 16 she left school, married (and soon divorced), and worked as a reporter, first in Texas and later in Denver and Chicago. She moved around a good deal, both within the United States and abroad; she lived for a while in Mexico, Belgium, Switzerland, France, and Germany.

*Even as a child she was interested in writing, but she did not publish her first story until she was 33. She wrote essays and one novel (*Ship of Fools*), but she is best known for her stories. Porter's* Collected Stories *won the Pulitzer Prize and the National Book Award in 1965.*

The Jilting of Granny Weatherall

She flicked her wrist neatly out of Doctor Harry's pudgy careful fingers and pulled the sheet up to her chin. The brat ought to be in knee breeches. Doctoring around the country with spectacles on his nose! "Get along now, take your schoolbooks and go. There's nothing wrong with me."

Doctor Harry spread a warm paw like a cushion on her forehead where the forked green vein danced and made her eyelids twitch. "Now, now, be a good girl, and we'll have you up in no time."

"That's no way to speak to a woman nearly eighty years old just because she's down. I'd have you respect your elders, young man."

"Well, Missy, excuse me." Doctor Harry patted her cheek. "But I've got to warn you, haven't I? You're a marvel, but you must be careful or you're going to be good and sorry."

5   "Don't tell me what I'm going to be. I'm on my feet now, morally speaking. It's Cornelia. I had to go to bed to get rid of her."

Her bones felt loose, and floated around in her skin, and Doctor Harry floated like a balloon around the foot of the bed. He floated and pulled down his waistcoat and swung his glasses on a cord. "Well, stay where you are, it certainly can't hurt you."

"Get along and doctor your sick," said Granny Weatherall. "Leave a well woman alone. I'll call for you when I want you. . . . Where were you forty years ago when I pulled through milk-leg and double pneumonia? You weren't even born. Don't let Cornelia lead you on," she shouted, because Doctor Harry appeared to float up to the ceiling and out. "I pay my own bills, and I don't throw my money away on nonsense!"

She meant to wave good-bye, but it was too much trouble. Her eyes closed of themselves, it was like a dark curtain drawn around the bed. The pillow rose and floated under her, pleasant as a hammock in a light wind. She listened to the leaves rustling outside the window. No, somebody was swishing newspapers: no, Cornelia and Doctor Harry were whispering together. She leaped broad awake, thinking they whispered in her ear.

"She was never like this, *never* like this!" "Well, what can we expect?" "Yes, eighty years old. . . ."

10   Well, and what if she was? She still had ears. It was like Cornelia to whisper around doors. She always kept things secret in such a public way. She was always being tactful and kind. Cornelia was dutiful; that was the trouble with her. Dutiful and good: "So good and dutiful," said Granny, "and I'd like to spank her." She saw herself spanking Cornelia and making a fine job of it.

"What'd you say, Mother?"

Granny felt her face tying up in hard knots.

"Can't a body think, I'd like to know?"

"I thought you might want something."

15   "I do. I want a lot of things. First off, go away and don't whisper."
        She lay and drowsed, hoping in her sleep that the children would keep out and let her rest a minute. It had been a long day. Not that she was tired. It was always pleasant to snatch a minute now and then. There was always so much to be done, let me see: tomorrow.
        Tomorrow was far away and there was nothing to trouble about. Things were finished somehow when the time came; thank God there was always a little margin over for peace; then a person could spread out the plan of life and tuck in the edges orderly. It was good to have everything clean and folded away, with the hair brushes and tonic bottles sitting straight on the white embroidered linen: the day started without fuss and the pantry shelves laid out with rows of jelly glasses and brown jugs and white stone-china jars and blue whirligigs and words painted on them: coffee, tea, sugar, ginger, cinnamon, allspice: and the bronze clock with the lion on top nicely dusted off. The dust that lion could collect in twenty-four hours! The box in the attic with all those letters tied up, she'd have to go through that tomorrow. All those letters—George's letters and John's letters and her letters to them both—lying around for the children to find afterwards made her uneasy. Yes, that would be tomorrow's business. No use to let them know how silly she had been once.
        While she was rummaging around she found death in her mind and it felt clammy and unfamiliar. She had spent so much time preparing for death there was no need for bringing it up again. Let it take care of itself now. When she was sixty she had felt very old, finished, and went around making farewell trips to see her children and grandchildren, with a secret in her mind: This is the very last of your mother, children! Then she made her will and came down with a long fever. That was all just a notion like a lot of other things, but it was lucky too, for she had once for all got over the idea of dying for a long time. Now she couldn't be worried. She hoped she had better sense now. Her father had lived to be one hundred and two years old and had drunk a noggin of strong hot toddy at his last birthday. He told the reporters it was his daily habit, and he owed his long life to that. He had made quite a scandal and was very pleased about it. She believed she'd just plague Cornelia a little.
        "Cornelia! Cornelia!" No footsteps, but a sudden hand on her cheek. "Bless you, where have you been?"
20   "Here, Mother."
        "Well, Cornelia, I want a noggin of hot toddy."
        "Are you cold, darling?"
        "I'm chilly, Cornelia. Lying in bed stops the circulation. I must have told you that a thousand times."
        Well, she could just hear Cornelia telling her husband that Mother was getting a little childish and they'd have to humor her. The thing that most annoyed her was that Cornelia thought she was deaf, dumb, and blind. Little hasty glances and tiny gestures tossed around her and over her head saying, "Don't cross her, let her have her way, she's eighty years old," and she sitting there as if she lived in a thin glass cage. Sometimes Granny almost made up her mind to pack up and move back to her own house where nobody could remind her every minute that she was old. Wait, wait, Cornelia, till your own children whisper behind your back!

25   In her day she had kept a better house and had got more work done. She wasn't too old yet for Lydia to be driving eighty miles for advice when one of the children jumped the track, and Jimmy still dropped in and talked things over: "Now, Mammy, you've a good business head, I want to know what you think of this?. . . " Old. Cornelia couldn't change the furniture around without asking. Little things, little things! They had been so sweet when they were little. Granny wished the old days were back again with the children young and everything to be done over. It had been a hard pull, but not too much for her. When she thought of all the food she had cooked, and all the clothes she had cut and sewed, and all the gardens she had made— well, the children showed it. There they were, made out of her, and they couldn't get away from that. Sometimes she wanted to see John again and point to them and say, Well, I didn't do so badly, did I? But that would have to wait. That was for tomorrow. She used to think of him as a man, but now all the children were older than their father, and he would be a child beside her if she saw him now. It seemed strange and there was something wrong in the idea. Why, he couldn't possibly recognize her. She had fenced in a hundred acres once, digging the post holes herself and clamping the wires with just a negro boy to help. That changed a woman. John would be look-ing for a young woman with the peaked Spanish comb in her hair and the painted fan. Digging post holes changed a woman. Riding country roads in the winter when women had their babies was another thing: sitting up nights with sick horses and sick negroes and sick children and hardly ever losing one. John, I hardly ever lost one of them! John would see that in a minute, that would be something he could understand, she wouldn't have to explain anything!

It made her feel like rolling up her sleeves and putting the whole place to rights again. No matter if Cornelia was determined to be everywhere at once, there were a great many things left undone on this place. She would start tomorrow and do them. It was good to be strong enough for every-thing, even if all you made melted and changed and slipped under your hands, so that by the time you finished you almost forgot what you were working for. What was it I set out to do? she asked herself intently, but she could not remember. A fog rose over the valley, she saw it marching across the creek swallowing the trees and moving up the hill like an army of ghosts. Soon it would be at the near edge of the orchard, and then it was time to go in and light the lamps. Come in, children, don't stay out in the night air.

Lighting the lamps had been beautiful. The children huddled up to her and breathed like little calves waiting at the bars in the twilight. Their eyes followed the match and watched the flame rise and settle in a blue curve, then they moved away from her. The lamp was lit, they didn't have to be scared and hang on to mother any more. Never, never, never more. God, for all my life I thank Thee. Without Thee, my God, I could never have done it. Hail, Mary, full of grace.

I want you to pick all the fruit this year and see that nothing is wasted. There's always someone who can use it. Don't let good things rot for want of using. You waste life when you waste good food. Don't let things get lost. It's bitter to lose things. Now, don't let me get to thinking, not when I am tired and taking a little nap before supper. . . .

The pillow rose about her shoulders and pressed against her heart and the memory was being squeezed out of it: oh, push down that pillow, somebody: it would smother her if she tried to hold it. Such a fresh breeze blowing and such a green day with no threats in it. But he had not come, just the same. What does a woman do when she has put on the white veil and set out the white cake for a man and he doesn't come? She tried to remember. No, I swear he never harmed me but in that. He never harmed me but in that . . . and what if he did? There was the day, the day, but a whirl of dark smoke rose and covered it, crept up and over into the bright field where everything was planted so carefully in orderly rows. That was hell, she knew hell when she saw it. For sixty years she had prayed against remembering him and against losing her soul in the deep pit of hell, and now the two things were mingled in one and the thought of him was a smoky cloud from hell that moved and crept in her head when she had just got rid of Doctor Harry and was trying to rest a minute. Wounded vanity, Ellen, said a sharp voice in the top of her mind. Don't let your wounded vanity get the upper hand of you. Plenty of girls get jilted. You were jilted, weren't you? Then stand up to it. Her eyelids wavered and let in streamers of blue-gray light like tissue paper over her eyes. She must get up and pull the shades down or she'd never sleep. She was in bed again and the shades were not down. How could that happen? Better turn over, hide from the light, sleeping in the light gave you nightmares. "Mother, how do you feel now?" and a stinging wetness on her forehead. But I don't like having my face washed in cold water!

30   Hapsy? George? Lydia? Jimmy? No, Cornelia, and her features were swollen and full of little puddles. "They're coming, darling, they'll all be here soon." Go wash your face, child, you look funny.

Instead of obeying, Cornelia knelt down and put her head on the pillow. She seemed to be talking but there was no sound. "Well, are you tongue-tied? Whose birthday is it? Are you going to give a party?"

Cornelia's mouth moved urgently in strange shapes. "Don't do that, you bother me, daughter."

"Oh, no, Mother. Oh, no. . . ."

Nonsense. It was strange about children. They disputed your every word. "No what, Cornelia?"

35   "Here's Doctor Harry."

"I won't see that boy again. He just left five minutes ago."

"That was this morning, Mother. It's night now. Here's the nurse."

"This is Doctor Harry, Mrs. Weatherall. I never saw you look so young and happy!"

"Ah, I'll never be young again—but I'd be happy if they'd let me lie in peace and get rested."

40   She thought she spoke up loudly, but no one answered. A warm weight on her forehead, a warm bracelet on her wrist, and a breeze went on whispering, trying to tell her something. A shuffle of leaves in the everlasting hand of God. He blew on them and they danced and rattled. "Mother, don't mind, we're going to give you a little hypodermic." "Look here, daughter, how do ants get in this bed? I saw sugar ants yesterday." Did you send for Hapsy too?

It was Hapsy she really wanted. She had to go a long way back through a great many rooms to find Hapsy standing with a baby on her arm. She seemed to herself to be Hapsy also, and the baby on Hapsy's arm was Hapsy and himself and herself, all at once, and there was no surprise in the meeting. Then Hapsy melted from within and turned flimsy as gray gauze and the baby was a gauzy shadow, and Hapsy came up close and said, "I thought you'd never come," and looked at her very searchingly and said, "You haven't changed a bit!" They leaned forward to kiss, when Cornelia began whispering from a long way off, "Oh, is there anything you want to tell me? Is there anything I can do for you?"

Yes, she had changed her mind after sixty years and she would like to see George. I want you to find George. Find him and be sure to tell him I forgot him. I want him to know I had my husband just the same and my children and my house like any other woman. A good house too and a good husband that I loved and fine children out of him. Better than I hoped for even. Tell him I was given back everything he took away and more. Oh, no, oh, God, no, there was something else besides the house and the man and the children. Oh, surely they were not all? What was it? Something not given back. . . . Her breath crowded down under her ribs and grew into a monstrous frightening shape with cutting edges; it bored up into her head, and the agony was unbelievable: Yes, John, get the doctor now, no more talk, my time has come.

When this one was born it should be the last. The last. It should have been born first, for it was the one she had truly wanted. Everything came in good time. Nothing left out, left over. She was strong, in three days she would be as well as ever. Better. A woman needed milk in her to have her full health.

"Mother, do you hear me?"

45   "I've been telling you—"

"Mother, Father Connolly's here."

"I went to Holy Communion only last week. Tell him I'm not so sinful as all that."

"Father just wants to speak to you."

He could speak as much as he pleased. It was like him to drop in and inquire about her soul as if it were a teething baby, and then stay on for a cup of tea and a round of cards and gossip. He always had a funny story of some sort, usually about an Irishman who made his little mistakes and confessed them, and the point lay in some absurd thing he would blurt out in the confessional showing his struggles between native piety and original sin. Granny felt easy about her soul. Cornelia, where are your manners? Give Father Connolly a chair. She had her secret comfortable understanding with a few favorite saints who cleared a straight road to God for her. All as surely signed and sealed as the papers for the new Forty Acres. Forever . . . heirs and assigns forever. Since the day the wedding cake was not cut, but thrown out and wasted. The whole bottom dropped out of the world, and there she was blind and sweating and nothing under her feet and the walls falling away. His hand had caught her under the breast, she had not fallen, there was the freshly polished floor with the green rug on it, just as before. He had cursed like a sailor's parrot and said, "I'll kill him for you." Don't lay a hand on him, for my sake leave something to God. "Now, Ellen, you must believe what I tell you. . . ."

50   So there was nothing, nothing to worry about any more, except sometimes in the night one of the children screamed in a nightmare, and they both hustled out shaking and hunting for the matches and calling, "There,

wait a minute, here we are!" John, get the doctor now, Hapsy's time has come. But there was Hapsy standing by the bed in a white cap. "Cornelia, tell Hapsy to take off her cap. I can't see her plain."

Her eyes opened very wide and the room stood out like a picture she had seen somewhere. Dark colors with the shadows rising toward the ceiling in long angles. The tall black dresser gleamed with nothing on it but John's picture, enlarged from a little one, with John's eyes very black when they should have been blue. You never saw him, so how do you know how he looked? But the man insisted the copy was perfect, it was very rich and handsome. For a picture, yes, but it's not my husband. The table by the bed had a linen cover and a candle and a crucifix. The light was blue from Cornelia's silk lampshades. No sort of light at all, just frippery. You had to live forty years with kerosene lamps to appreciate honest electricity. She felt very strong and she saw Doctor Harry with a rosy nimbus around him.

"You look like a saint, Doctor Harry, and I vow that's as near as you'll ever come to it."

"She's saying something."

"I heard you, Cornelia. What's all this carrying on?"

55   "Father Connolly's saying—"

Cornelia's voice staggered and bumped like a cart in a bad road. It rounded corners and turned back again and arrived nowhere. Granny stepped up in the cart very lightly and reached for the reins, but a man sat beside her and she knew him by his hands, driving the cart. She did not look in his face, for she knew without seeing, but looked instead down the road where the trees leaned over and bowed to each other and a thousand birds were singing a Mass. She felt like singing too, but she put her hand in the bosom of her dress and pulled out a rosary, and Father Connolly murmured Latin in a very solemn voice and tickled her feet. My God, will you stop that nonsense? I'm a married woman. What if he did run away and leave me to face the priest by myself? I found another a whole world better. I wouldn't have exchanged my husband for anybody except St. Michael himself, and you may tell him that for me with a thank you in the bargain.

Light flashed on her closed eyelids, and a deep roaring shook her. Cornelia, is that lightning? I hear thunder. There's going to be a storm. Close all the windows. Call the children in. . . . "Mother, here we are, all of us." "Is that you, Hapsy?" "Oh, no, I'm Lydia. We drove as fast as we could." Their faces drifted above her, drifted away. The rosary fell out of her hands and Lydia put it back. Jimmy tried to help, their hands fumbled together, and Granny closed two fingers around Jimmy's thumb. Beads wouldn't do, it must be something alive. She was so amazed her thoughts ran round and round. So, my dear Lord, this is my death and I wasn't even thinking about it. My children have come to see me die. But I can't, it's not time. Oh, I always hated surprises. I wanted to give Cornelia the amethyst set—Cornelia, you're to have the amethyst set, but Hapsy's to wear it when she wants, and, Doctor Harry, do shut up. Nobody sent for you. Oh, my dear Lord, do wait a minute. I meant to do something about the Forty Acres, Jimmy doesn't need it and Lydia will later on, with that worthless husband of hers. I meant to finish the altar cloth and send six bottles of wine to Sister Borgia for her dyspepsia. I want to send six bottles of wine to Sister Borgia, Father Connolly, now don't let me forget.

Cornelia's voice made short turns and tilted over and crashed. "Oh, Mother, oh, Mother, oh, Mother. . . ."

"I'm not going, Cornelia. I'm taken by surprise. I can't go."

60   You'll see Hapsy again. What about her? "I thought you'd never come." Granny made a long journey outward, looking for Hapsy. What if I don't find her? What then? Her heart sank down and down, there was no bottom to death, she couldn't come to the end of it. The blue light from Cornelia's lampshade drew into a tiny point in the center of her brain, it flickered and winked like an eye, quietly it fluttered and dwindled. Granny lay curled down within herself, amazed and watchful, starting at the point of light that was herself; her body was now only a deeper mass of shadow in an endless darkness and this darkness would curl around the light and swallow it up, God, give a sign!

For the second time there was no sign. Again no bridegroom and the priest in the house. She could not remember any other sorrow because this grief wiped them all away. Oh, no, there's nothing more cruel than this—I'll never forgive it. She stretched herself with a deep breath and blew out the light.

[1929]

TOPICS FOR CRITICAL THINKING AND WRITING

1. In a paragraph, characterize Granny Weatherall. In another paragraph, evaluate her claim that the anguish of the jilting has been compensated for by her subsequent life.

2. The final paragraph alludes to Christ's parable of the bridegroom (Matthew 25.1-13). With this allusion in mind, write a paragraph explaining the title of the story.

ERNEST HEMINGWAY

Ernest Hemingway (1899-1961) was born in Oak Park, Illinois. After graduating from high school in 1917 he worked on the Kansas City Star, *but left to serve as a volunteer ambulance driver in Italy, where he was wounded in action. He returned home, married, and then served as European correspondent for the Toronto* Star, *but he soon gave up journalism for fiction. In 1922 he settled in Paris, where he moved in a circle of American expatriates that included Ezra Pound, Gertrude Stein, and F. Scott Fitzgerald. He served as a journalist during the Spanish Civil War and during the Second World War, but he was also something of a private soldier.*

After the Second World War his reputation sank, though he was still active as a writer (for instance, he wrote The Old Man and the Sea *in 1952). In 1954 he was awarded the Nobel Prize in Literature, but in 1961, depressed by a sense of failing power, he took his own life.*

A Clean, Well-Lighted Place

It was late and every one had left the café except an old man who sat in the shadow the leaves of the tree made against the electric light. In the day time the street was dusty, but at night the dew settled the dust and the old man liked to sit late because he was deaf and now at night it was quiet and he felt the difference. The two waiters inside the café knew that the old man was a little drunk, and while he was a good client they knew that if he became too drunk he would leave without paying, so they kept watch on him.

"Last week he tried to commit suicide," one waiter said.

"Why?"

"He was in despair."

5   "What about?"

"Nothing."

"How do you know it was nothing?"

"He has plenty of money."

They sat together at a table that was close against the wall near the door of the café and looked at the terrace where the tables were all empty except where the old man sat in the shadow of the leaves of the tree that moved slightly in the wind. A girl and a soldier went by in the street. The street light shone on the brass number on his collar. The girl wore no head covering and hurried beside him.

10   "The guard will pick him up," one waiter said.

"What does it matter if he gets what he's after?"

"He had better get off the street now. The guard will get him. They went by five minutes ago."

The old man sitting in the shadow rapped on his saucer with his glass. The younger waiter went over to him.

"What do you want?"

15   The old man looked at him. "Another brandy," he said.

"You'll be drunk," the waiter said. The old man looked at him. The waiter went away.

"He'll stay all night," he said to his colleague. "I'm sleepy now. I never get into bed before three o'clock. He should have killed himself last week."

The waiter took the brandy bottle and another saucer from the counter inside the café and marched out to the old man's table. He put down the saucer and poured the glass full of brandy.

"You should have killed yourself last week," he said to the deaf man. The old man motioned with his finger. "A little more," he said. The waiter poured on into the glass so that the brandy slopped over and ran down the stem into the top saucer of the pile. "Thank you," the old man said. The waiter took the bottle back inside the café. He sat down at the table with his colleague again.

20   "He's drunk now," he said.

"He's drunk every night."

"What did he want to kill himself for?"

"How should I know."

"How did he do it?"

25   "He hung himself with a rope."

"Who cut him down?"

"His niece."

"Why did they do it?"

"Fear for his soul."

30   "How much money has he got?"

"He's got plenty."

"He must be eighty years old."

"Anyway I should say he was eighty."

"I wish he would go home. I never get to bed before three o'clock. What kind of hour is that to go to bed?"

35   "He stays up because he likes it."

"He's lonely. I'm not lonely. I have a wife waiting in bed for me."

"He had a wife once too."

"A wife would be no good to him now."

"You can't tell. He might be better with a wife."

40   "His niece looks after him. You said she cut him down."

"I know."

"I wouldn't want to be that old. An old man is a nasty thing."

"Not always. This old man is clean. He drinks without spilling. Even now, drunk. Look at him."

"I don't want to look at him. I wish he would go home. He has no regard for those who must work."

45   The old man looked from his glass across the square, then over at the waiters.

"Another brandy," he said, pointing to his glass. The waiter who was in a hurry came over.

"Finished," he said, speaking with that omission of syntax stupid people employ when talking to drunken people or foreigners. "No more tonight. Close now."

"Another," said the old man.

"No. Finished." The waiter wiped the edge of the table with a towel and shook his head.

50   The old man stood up, slowly counted the saucers, took a leather coin purse from his pocket and paid for the drinks, leaving half a peseta[1] tip.

The waiter watched him go down the street, a very old man walking unsteadily but with dignity.

"Why didn't you let him stay and drink?" the unhurried waiter asked. They were putting up the shutters. "It is not half-past two."

"I want to go home to bed."

"What is an hour?"

55   "More to me than to him."

"An hour is the same."

"You talk like an old man yourself. He can buy a bottle and drink at home."

"It's not the same."

"No, it is not," agreed the waiter with a wife. He did not wish to be unjust. He was only in a hurry.

60   "And you? You have no fear of going home before your usual hour?"

"Are you trying to insult me?"

"No, hombre, only to make a joke."

"No," the waiter who was in a hurry said, rising from pulling down the metal shutters. "I have confidence. I am all confidence."

"You have youth, confidence, and a job," the old waiter said. "You have everything."

65   "And what do you lack?"

[1]Spanish coin

"Everything but work."

"You have everything I have."

"No. I have never had confidence and I am not young."

"Come on. Stop talking nonsense and lock up."

70   "I am of those who like to stay late at the café," the older waiter said. "With all those who do not want to go to bed. With all those who need a light for the night."

"I want to go home and into bed."

"We are of two different kinds," the older waiter said. He was now dressed to go home. "It is not only a question of youth and confidence although those things are very beautiful. Each night I am reluctant to close up because there may be some one who needs the café."

"Hombre,² there are bodegas³ open all night long."

"You do not understand. This is a clean and pleasant café. It is well lighted. The light is very good and also, now, there are shadows of the leaves."

75   "Good night," said the younger waiter.

"Good night," the other said. Turning off the electric light he continued the conversation with himself. It is the light of course but it is necessary that the place be clean and pleasant. You do not want music. Certainly you do not want music. Nor can you stand before a bar with dignity although that is all that is provided for these hours. What did he fear? It was not fear or dread. It was a nothing that he knew too well. It was all a nothing and a man was nothing too. It was only that and light was all it needed and a certain cleanness and order. Some lived in it and never felt it but he knew it all was nada y pues nada y pues nada.⁴ Our nada who art in nada, nada be thy name thy kingdom nada thy will be nada in nada as it is in nada. Give us this nada our daily nada and nada us our nada as we nada our nadas and nada us not into nada but deliver us from nada; pues nada. Hail nothing full of nothing, nothing is with thee. He smiled and stood before a bar with a shining steam pressure coffee machine.

"What's yours?" asked the barman.

"Nada."

"Otro loco más,"⁵ said the barman and turned away.

80   "A little cup," said the waiter.

The barman poured it for him.

"The light is very bright and pleasant but the bar is unpolished," the waiter said.

The barman looked at him but did not answer. It was too late at night for conversation.

"You want another copita?"⁶ the barman asked.

85   "No, thank you," said the waiter and went out. He disliked bars and bodegas. A clean, well-lighted café was a very different thing. Now, without thinking further, he would go home to his room. He would lie in the bed and finally, with daylight, he would go to sleep. After all, he said to himself, it is probably only insomnia. Many must have it.

[1933]

---

²man   ³wineshops   ⁴nothing and then nothing   ⁵another madman   ⁶little cup

TOPICS FOR CRITICAL THINKING AND WRITING

1. In an essay of 500 words compare and contrast the two waiters. What does the young waiter believe in? Does the older waiter believe in anything? In your answer devote some space to each waiter's view of the café.

2. What is the point of the parody of the Lord's Prayer? In this context, note, too, the setting in which it is spoken: a bar in a bodega equipped with a steam-pressure coffee machine.

3. In 250 words explain why, if the older waiter is a nihilist (Latin *nihil*, like Spanish *nada,* means "nothing"), he is concerned that there be a clean, well-lighted place.

4. Reread the story, draw some conclusions about Hemingway's style, and then write a paragraph or a short dialogue in his style. Or write a parody of Hemingway's style. (The writing of a parody usually employs the style of the victim, but in circumstances that make the language amusing. For example, you might have two infants, or two duchesses, talking like Hemingway's waiters.)

 FLANNERY O'CONNOR

Flannery O'Connor (1925-1964)—her first name was Mary but she did not use it—was born in Savannah, Georgia, but spent most of her life in Milledgeville, Georgia, where her family moved when she was 12. She was educated at parochial schools and at the local college and then went to School for Writers at the University of Iowa, where she earned an M.F.A. in 1946. For a few months she lived at a writers' colony in Saratoga Springs, New York and then spent a few weeks in New York City, but she lived most of her life in Milledgeville, where she tended her peacocks and wrote stories, novels, essays (posthumously published as Mystery and Manners *[1970]), and letters (posthumously published under the title of* The Habit of Being *[1979]).*

In 1951, when she was 25, Flannery O'Connor discovered that she was a victim of lupus erythematosus, an incurable degenerative blood disease that had crippled and then killed her father ten years before. She died at the age of 39. O'Connor faced her illness with stoic courage and Christian fortitude and tough humor. Here is a glimpse, from one of her letters, of how she dealt with those who pitied her:

> *An old lady got on the elevator behind me and as soon as I turned around she fixed me with a moist gleaming eye and said in a loud voice, "Bless you, darling!" I felt exactly like the Misfit [in "A Good Man Is Hard To Find"] and I gave her a weakly lethal look, whereupon greatly encouraged she grabbed my arm and whispered (very loud) in my ear, "Remember what they said to John at the gate, darling!" It was not my floor but I got off and I suppose the old lady was astounded at how quick I could get away on crutches. I have a one-legged friend and I asked*

*her what they said to John at the gate. She said she reck-
oned they said, "The lame shall enter first." This may be
because the lame will be able to knock everybody else
aside with their crutches.*

A Good Man Is Hard to Find

The grandmother didn't want to go to Florida. She wanted to visit some of
her connections in east Tennessee and she was seizing at every chance to
change Bailey's mind. Bailey was the son she lived with, her only boy. He
was sitting on the edge of his chair at the table, bent over the orange sports
section of the *Journal.* "Now look here, Bailey," she said, "see here, read
this," and she stood with one hand on her thin hip and the other rattling the
newspaper at his bald head. "Here this fellow that calls himself The Misfit is
aloose from the Federal Pen and headed toward Florida and you read here
what it says he did to these people. Just you read it. I wouldn't take my children in any direction with a criminal like that aloose in it. I couldn't answer
to my conscience if I did."

Bailey didn't look up from his reading so she wheeled around then and
faced the children's mother, a young woman in slacks, whose face was as
broad and innocent as a cabbage and was tied round with a green headker-
chief that had two points on the top like rabbit's ears. She was sitting on the
sofa, feeding the baby his apricots out of a jar. "The children have been to
Florida before," the old lady said. "You all ought to take them somewhere
else for a change so they would see different parts of the world and be
broad. They never have been to east Tennessee."

The children's mother didn't seem to hear her but the eight-year-old
boy, John Wesley, a stocky child with glasses, said, "If you don't want to go
to Florida, why dontcha stay at home?" He and the little girl, June Star, were
reading the funny papers on the floor.

"She wouldn't stay at home to be queen for a day," June Star said without raising her yellow head.

5   "Yes and what would you do if this fellow, The Misfit, caught you?" the
grandmother asked.

"I'd smack his face," John Wesley said.

"She wouldn't stay at home for a million bucks," June Star said. "Afraid
she'd miss something. She has to go everywhere we go."

"All right, Miss," the grandmother said. "Just remember that the next
time you want me to curl you hair."

June Star said her hair was naturally curly.

10   The next morning the grandmother was the first one in the car, ready to
go. She had her big black valise that looked like the head of a hippopotamus
in one corner, and underneath it she was hiding a basket with Pitty Sing, the
cat, in it. She didn't intend for the cat to be left alone in the house for three
days because he would miss her too much and she was afraid he might
brush against one of the gas burners and accidentally asphyxiate himself.
Her son, Bailey, didn't like to arrive at a motel with a cat.

She sat in the middle of the back seat with John Wesley and June Star on
either side of her. Bailey and the children's mother and the baby sat in the

front and they left Atlanta at eight forty-five with the mileage on the car at 55890. The grandmother wrote this down because she thought it would be interesting to say how many miles they had been when they got back. It took them twenty minutes to reach the outskirts of the city.

The old lady settled herself comfortably, removing her white cotton gloves and putting them up with her purse on the shelf in front of the back window. The children's mother still had on slacks and still had her head tied up in a green kerchief, but the grandmother had on a navy blue straw sailor hat with a bunch of white violets on the brim and a navy blue dress with a small white dot in the print. Her collar and cuffs were white organdy trimmed with lace and at her neckline she had pinned a purple spray of cloth violets containing a sachet. In case of an accident, anyone seeing her dead on the highway would know at once that she was a lady.

She said she thought it was going to be a good day for driving, neither too hot nor too cold, and she cautioned Bailey that the speed limit was fifty-five miles an hour and that the patrolmen hid themselves behind billboards and small clumps of trees and sped out after you before you had a chance to slow down. She pointed out interesting details of the scenery: Stone Mountain; the blue granite that in some places came up to both sides of the highway; the brilliant red clay banks slightly streaked with purple; and the various crops that made rows of green lace-work on the ground. The trees were full of silver-white sunlight and the meanest of them sparkled. The children were reading comic magazines and their mother had gone back to sleep.

"Let's go through Georgia fast so we won't have to look at it much," John Wesley said.

15   "If I were a little boy," said the grandmother, "I wouldn't talk about my native state that way. Tennessee has the mountains and Georgia has the hills."

"Tennessee is just a hillbilly dumping ground," John Wesley said, "and Georgia is a lousy state too."

"You said it," June Star said.

"In my time," said the grandmother, folding her thin veined fingers, "children were more respectful of their native states and their parents and everything else. People did right then. Oh look at the cute little pickaninny!" she said and pointed to a Negro child standing in the door of a shack. "Wouldn't that make a picture, now?" she asked and they all turned and looked at the little Negro out of the back window. He waved.

"He didn't have any britches on," June Star said.

20   "He probably didn't have any," the grandmother explained. "Little niggers in the country don't have things like we do. If I could paint, I'd paint that picture," she said.

The children exchanged comic books.

The grandmother offered to hold the baby and the children's mother passed him over the front seat to her. She set him on her knee and bounced him and told him about the things they were passing. She rolled her eyes and screwed up her mouth and stuck her leathery thin face into his smooth bland one. Occasionally he gave her a faraway smile. They passed a large cotton field with five or six graves fenced in the middle of it, like a small island. "Look at the graveyard!" the grandmother said, pointing it out. "That was the old family burying ground. That belonged to the plantation."

"Where's the plantation?" John Wesley asked.

"Gone with the Wind," said the grandmother. "Ha. Ha."

25   When the children finished all the comic books they had brought, they opened the lunch and ate it. The grandmother ate a peanut butter sandwich and an olive and would not let the children throw the box and the paper napkins out the window. When there was nothing else to do they played a game by choosing a cloud and making the other two guess what shape it suggested. John Wesley took one the shape of a cow and June Star guessed a cow and John Wesley said, no, an automobile, and June Star said he didn't play fair, and they began to slap each other over the grandmother.

The grandmother said she would tell them a story if they would keep quiet. When she told a story, she rolled her eyes and waved her head and was very dramatic. She said once when she was a maiden lady she had been courted by a Mr. Edgar Atkins Teagarden from Jasper, Georgia. She said he was a very good-looking man and a gentleman and that he brought her a watermelon every Saturday afternoon with his initials cut in it. E. A. T. Well, one Saturday, she said, Mr. Teagarden brought the watermelon and there was nobody at home and he left it on the front porch and returned in his buggy to Jasper, but she never got the watermelon, she said, because a nigger boy ate it when he saw the initials, E. A. T.! This story tickled John Wesley's funny bone and he giggled and giggled but June Star didn't think it was any good. She said she wouldn't marry a man that just brought her a watermelon on Saturday. The grandmother said she would have done well to marry Mr. Teagarden because he was a gentleman and had bought Coca-Cola stock when it first came out and that he had died only a few years ago, a very wealthy man.

They stopped at The Tower for barbecued sandwiches. The Tower was a part stucco and part wood filling station and dance hall set in a clearing outside of Timothy. A fat man named Red Sammy Butts ran it and there were signs stuck here and there on the building and for miles up and down the highway saying, TRY RED SAMMY'S FAMOUS BARBECUE. NONE LIKE FAMOUS RED SAMMY'S! RED SAM! THE FAT BOY WITH THE HAPPY LAUGH. A VETERAN! RED SAMMY'S YOUR MAN!

Red Sammy was lying on the bare ground outside The Tower with his head under a truck while a gray monkey about a foot high, chained to a small chinaberry tree, chattered nearby. The monkey sprang back into the tree and got on the highest limb as soon as he saw the children jump out of the car and run toward him.

Inside, The Tower was a long dark room with a counter at one end and tables at the other and dancing space in the middle. They all sat down at a broad table next to the nickelodeon and Red Sam's wife, a tall burnt-brown woman with hair and eyes lighter than her skin, came and took their order. The children's mother put a dime in the machine and played "The Tennessee Waltz," and the grandmother said that tune always made her want to dance. She asked Bailey if he would like to dance but he only glared at her. He didn't have a naturally sunny disposition like she did and trips made him nervous. The grandmother's brown eyes were very bright. She swayed her head from side to side and pretended she was dancing in her chair. June Star said play something she could tap to so the children's mother put in another dime and played a fast number and June Star stepped out onto the dance floor and did her tap routine.

30   "Ain't she cute?" Red Sam's wife said, leaning over the counter. "Would you like to come be my little girl?"

"No I certainly wouldn't," June Star said. "I wouldn't live in a broken-down place like this for a million bucks!" and she ran back to the table.

"Ain't she cute?" the woman repeated, stretching her mouth politely.

"Aren't you ashamed?" hissed the grandmother.

Red Sam came in and told his wife to quit lounging on the counter and hurry up with these people's order. His khaki trousers reached just to his hip bones and his stomach hung over them like a sack of meal swaying under his shirt. He came over and sat down at a table nearby and let out a combination sigh and yodel. "You can't win," he said. "You can't win," and he wiped his sweating red face off with a gray handkerchief. "These days you don't know who to trust," he said. "Ain't that the truth?"

35   "People are certainly not nice like they used to be," said the grandmother.

"Two fellers come in here last week," Red Sammy said, "driving a Chrysler. It was a old beat-up car but it was a good one and these boys looked all right to me. Said they worked at the mill and you know I let them fellers charge the gas they bought? Now why did I do that?"

"Because you're a good man!" the grandmother said at once.

"Yes'm, I suppose so," Red Sam said as if he were struck with the answer.

His wife brought the orders, carrying the five plates all at once without a tray, two in each hand and one balanced on her arm. "It isn't a soul in this green world of God's that you can trust," she said. "And I don't count anybody out of that, not nobody," she repeated, looking at Red Sammy.

40   "Did you read about that criminal, The Misfit, that's escaped?" asked the grandmother.

"I wouldn't be a bit surprised if he didn't attact this place right here," said the woman. "If he hears about it being here, I wouldn't be none surprised to see him. If he hears it's two cent in the cash register, I wouldn't be a tall surprised if he. . . "

"That'll do," Red Sam said. "Go bring these people their Co'Colas," and the woman went off to get the rest of the order.

"A good man is hard to find," Red Sammy said. "Everything is getting terrible. I remember the day you could go off and leave your screen door unlatched. Not no more."

He and the grandmother discussed better times. The old lady said that in her opinion Europe was entirely to blame for the way things were now. She said the way Europe acted you would think we were made of money and Red Sam said it was no use talking about it, she was exactly right. The children ran outside into the white sunlight and looked at the monkey in the lacy chinaberry tree. He was busy catching fleas on himself and biting each one carefully between his teeth as if it were a delicacy.

45   They drove off again into the hot afternoon. The grandmother took cat naps and woke up every few minutes with her own snoring. Outside of Toombsboro she woke up and recalled an old plantation that she had visited

in this neighborhood once when she was a young lady. She said the house had six white columns across the front and that there was an avenue of oaks leading up to it and two little wooden trellis arbors on either side in front where you sat down with your suitor after a stroll in the garden. She recalled exactly which road to turn off to get to it. She knew that Bailey would not be willing to lose any time looking at an old house, but the more she talked about it, the more she wanted to see it once again and find out if the little twin arbors were still standing. "There was a secret panel in this house," she said craftily, not telling the truth but wishing that she were, "and the story went that all the family silver was hidden in it when Sherman came through but it was never found. . . "

"Hey!" John Wesley said. "Let's go see it! We'll find it! We'll poke all the woodwork and find it! Who lives there? Where do you turn off at? Hey, Pop, can't we turn off there?"

"We never have seen a house with a secret panel!" June Star shrieked. "Let's go to the house with the secret panel! Hey, Pop, can't we go see the house with the secret panel!"

"It's not far from here, I know," the grandmother said. "It wouldn't take over twenty minutes."

Bailey was looking straight ahead. His jaw was as rigid as a horseshoe. "No," he said.

50   The children began to yell and scream that they wanted to see the house with the secret panel. John Wesley kicked the back of the front seat and June Star hung over her mother's shoulder and whined desperately into her ear that they never had any fun even on their vacation, and that they could never do what THEY wanted to do. The baby began to scream and John Wesley kicked the back of the seat so hard that his father could feel the blows in his kidney.

"All right!" he shouted, and drew the car to a stop at the side of the road. "Will you all shut up? Will you all just shut up for one second? If you don't shut up, we won't go anywhere."

"It would be very educational for them," the grandmother murmured.

"All right," Bailey said, "but get this: this is the only time we're going to stop for anything like this. This is the one and only time."

"The dirt road that you have to turn down is about a mile back," the grandmother directed. "I marked it when we passed."

55   "A dirt road," Bailey groaned.

After they had turned around and were headed toward the dirt road, the grandmother recalled other points about the house, the beautiful glass over the front doorway and the candle-lamp in the hall. John Wesley said that the secret panel was probably in the fireplace.

"You can't go inside this house," Bailey said. "You don't know who lives there."

"While you all talk to the people in front, I'll run around behind and get in a window," John Wesley suggested.

"We'll all stay in the car," his mother said.

60   They turned onto the dirt road and the car raced roughly along in a swirl of pink dust. The grandmother recalled the times when there were no paved roads and thirty miles was a day's journey. The dirt road was hilly and there were sudden washes in it and sharp curves on dangerous embank-

ments. All at once they would be on a hill, looking down over the blue tops of trees for miles around, then the next minute they would be in a red depression with the dust-coated trees looking down on them.

"This place had better turn up in a minute," Bailey said, "or I'm going to turn around."

The road looked as if no one had traveled on it in months.

"It's not much farther," the grandmother said and just as she said it, a horrible thought came to her. The thought was so embarrassing that she turned red in the face and her eyes dilated and her feet jumped up, upsetting her valise in the corner. The instant the valise moved, the newspaper top she had over the basket under it rose with a snarl and Pitty Sing, the cat, sprang onto Bailey's shoulder.

The children were thrown to the floor and their mother, clutching the baby, was thrown out of the door onto the ground, the old lady was thrown into the front seat. The car turned over once and landed rightside up in a gulch on the side of the road. Bailey remained in the driver's seat with the cat—gray-striped with a broad white face and an orange nose—clinging to his neck like a caterpillar.

65   As soon as the children saw they could move their arms and legs, they scrambled out of the car, shouting, "We've had an ACCIDENT!" The grandmother was curled up under the dashboard, hoping she was injured so that Bailey's wrath would not come down on her all at once. The horrible thought she had had before the accident was that the house she remembered so vividly was not in Georgia but in Tennessee.

Bailey removed the cat from his neck with both hands and flung it out the window against the side of a pine tree. Then he got out of the car and started looking for the children's mother. She was sitting against the side of a red gutted ditch, holding the screaming baby, but she only had a cut down her face and a broken shoulder. "We've had an ACCIDENT!" the children screamed in a frenzy of delight.

"But nobody's killed," June Star said with disappointment as the grandmother limped out of the car, her hat still pinned to her head but the broken front brim standing up at a jaunty angle and the violet spray hanging off the side. They all sat down in the ditch, except the children, to recover from the shock. They were all shaking.

"Maybe a car will come along," said the children's mother hoarsely.

"I believe I have injured an organ," said the grandmother, pressing her side, but no one answered her. Bailey's teeth were clattering. He had on a yellow sport shirt with bright blue parrots designed in it and his face was as yellow as the shirt. The grandmother decided that she would not mention that the house was in Tennessee.

70   The road was about ten feet above and they could see only the tops of the trees on the other side of it. Behind the ditch they were setting in there were more woods, tall and dark and deep. In a few minutes they saw a car come some distance away on top of a hill, coming slowly as if the occupants were watching them. The grandmother stood up and waved both arms dramatically to attract their attention. The car continued to come on slowly, disappeared around a bend and then appeared again, moving even slower, on top of the hill they had gone over. It was a big black battered hearselike automobile. There were three men in it.

It came to a stop just over them and for some minutes, the driver looked down with a steady expressionless gaze to where they were sitting, and didn't speak. Then he turned his head and muttered something to the other two and they got out. One was a fat boy in black trousers and a red sweat shirt with a silver stallion embossed on the front of it. He moved around on the right side of them and stood staring, his mouth partly open in a kind of loose grin. The other had on khaki pants and a blue striped coat and a gray hat pulled down very low, hiding most of his face. He came around slowly on the left side. Neither spoke.

The driver got out of the car and stood by the side of it, looking down at them. He was an older man than the other two. His hair was just beginning to gray and he wore silver-rimmed spectacles that gave him a scholarly look. He had a long creased face and didn't have on any shirt or undershirt. He had on blue jeans that were too tight for him and was holding a black hat and a gun. The two boys also had guns.

"We've had an ACCIDENT!" the children screamed.

The grandmother had the peculiar feeling that the bespectacled man was someone she knew. His face was so familiar to her as if she had known him all her life, but she could not recall who he was. He moved away from the car and began to come down the embankment, placing his feet carefully so that he wouldn't slip. He had on tan and white shoes and no socks, and his ankles were red and thin. "Good afternoon," he said. "I see you all had you a little spill."

75   "We turned over twice!" said the grandmother.

"Oncet," he corrected. "We seen it happen. Try their car and see will it run, Hiram," he said quietly to the boy with the gray hat.

"What you got that gun for?" John Wesley asked. "Whatcha gonna do with that gun?"

"Lady," the man said to the children's mother, "would you mind calling them children to set down by you? Children make me nervous. I want all you all to sit down right together there where you're at."

"What are you telling us what to do for?" June Star asked.

80   Behind them the line of woods gaped like a dark open mouth. "Come here," said their mother.

"Look here now," Bailey began suddenly, "we're in a predicament! We're in. . . ."

The grandmother shrieked. She scrambled to her feet and stood staring. "You're The Misfit!" she said. "I recognized you at once."

"Yes'm," the man said, smiling slightly as if he were pleased in spite of himself to be known, "but it would have been better for all of you, lady, if you hadn't of recognized me."

Bailey turned his head sharply and said something to his mother that shocked even the children. The old lady began to cry and The Misfit reddened.

85   "Lady," he said, "don't you get upset. Sometimes a man says things he don't mean. I don't reckon he meant to talk to you thataway."

"You wouldn't shoot a lady, would you?" the grandmother said and removed a clean handkerchief from her cuff and began to slap at her eyes with it.

The Misfit pointed the toe of his shoe into the ground and made a little hole and then covered it up again. "I would hate to have to," he said.

"Listen," the grandmother almost screamed, "I know you're a good man. You don't look a bit like you have common blood. I know you must come from nice people!"

"Yes ma'm," he said, "finest people in the world." When he smiled he showed a row of strong white teeth. "God never made a finer woman than my mother and my daddy's heart was pure gold," he said. The boy with the red sweat shirt had come around behind them and was standing with his gun at his hip. The Misfit squatted down on the ground. "Watch them children, Bobby Lee," he said. "You know they make me nervous." He looked at the six of them huddled together in front of him and he seemed to be embarrassed as if he couldn't think of anything to say. "Ain't a cloud in the sky," he remarked, looking up at it. "Don't see no sun but don't see no cloud neither."

90   "Yes, it's a beautiful day," said the grandmother. "Listen," she said, "you shouldn't call yourself The Misfit because I know you're a good man at heart. I can just look at you and tell."

"Hush!" Bailey yelled. "Hush! Everybody shut up and let me handle this!" He was squatting in the position of a runner about to sprint forward but he didn't move.

"I pre-chate that, lady," The Misfit said and drew a little circle in the ground with the butt of his gun.

"I'll take a half a hour to fix this here car," Hiram called, looking over the raised hood of it.

"Well, first you and Bobby Lee get him and that little boy to step over yonder with you," The Misfit said, pointing to Bailey and John Wesley. "The boys want to ask you something," he said to Bailey. "Would you mind stepping back in them woods there with them?"

95   "Listen," Bailey began, "we're in a terrible predicament. Nobody realizes what this is," and his voice cracked. His eyes were as blue and intense as the parrots on his shirt and he remained perfectly still.

The grandmother reached up to adjust her hat brim as if she were going to the woods with him but it came off in her hand. She stood staring at it and after a second she let if fall on the ground. Hiram pulled Bailey up by the arm as if he were assisting an old man. John Wesley caught hold of his father's hand and Bobby Lee followed. They went off toward the woods and just as they reached the dark edge, Bailey turned and supporting himself against a gray naked pine trunk, he shouted, "I'll be back in a minute, Mamma, wait on me!"

"Come back this instant!" his mother shrilled but they all disappeared into the woods.

"Bailey Boy!" the grandmother called in a tragic voice but she found she was looking at The Misfit squatting on the ground in front of her. "I just know you're a good man," she said desperately. "You're not a bit common!"

"Nome, I ain't a good man," The Misfit said after a second as if he had considered her statement carefully, "but I ain't the worst in the world neither. My daddy said I was a different breed of dog from my brothers and sisters. 'You know,' Daddy said, 'it's some that can live their whole life out without asking about it and it's others has to know why it is, and this boy is one of the latters. He's going to be into everything!'" He put on his black hat and looked up suddenly and then away deep into the woods as if he were embarrassed again. "I'm sorry I don't have on a shirt before you ladies," he said, hunching his shoulders slightly. "We buried our clothes that we had on when we escaped and we're just making do until we can get better. We borrowed these from some nice folks we met," he explained.

100   "That's perfectly all right," the grandmother said. "Maybe Bailey has an extra shirt in his suitcase."

"I'll look and see terrectly," The Misfit said.

"Where are they taking him?" the children's mother screamed.

"Daddy was a card himself," The Misfit said. "You couldn't put anything over on him. He never got in trouble with the Authorities though. Just had the knack of handling them."

"You could be honest too if you'd only try," said the grandmother. "Think how wonderful it would be to settle down and live a comfortable life and not have to think about somebody chasing you all the time."

105   The Misfit kept scratching in the ground with the butt of his gun as if he were thinking about it. "Yes'm, somebody is always after you," he murmured.

The grandmother noticed how thin his shoulder blades were just behind his hat because she was standing up looking down on him. "Do you ever pray?" she asked.

He shook his head. All she saw was the black hat wiggle between shoulder blades. "Nome," he said.

There was a pistol shot from the woods, followed closely by another. Then silence. The old lady's head jerked around. She could hear the wind move through the tree tops like a long satisfied insuck of breath. "Bailey Boy!" she called.

"I was a gospel singer for a while," The Misfit said. "I been most everything. Been in the arm service, both land and sea, at home and abroad, been twict married, been an undertaker, been with the railroads, plowed Mother Earth, been in a tornado, see a man burnt alive oncet," and he looked up at the children's mother and the little girl who were sitting close together, their faces white and their eyes glassy; "I even seen a woman flogged," he said.

110   "Pray, pray," the grandmother began, "pray, pray. . . ."

"I never was a bad boy that I remember of," The Misfit said in an almost dreamy voice, "but somewhere along the line I done something wrong and got sent to the penitentiary. I was buried alive," and he looked up and held her attention to him by a steady stare.

"That's when you should have started to pray," she said. "What did you do to get sent to the penitentiary that first time?"

"Turn to the right, it was a wall," The Misfit said, looking up again at the cloudless sky. "Turn to the left, it was a wall. Look up it was a ceiling, look down it was a floor. I forgot what I done, lady. I set there and set there, trying to remember what it was I done and I ain't recalled it to this day. Oncet in a while, I would think it was coming to me, but it never come."

"Maybe they put you in by mistake," the old lady said vaguely.

115   "Nome," he said. "It wasn't no mistake. They had the papers on me."

"You must have stolen something," she said.

The Misfit sneered slightly. "Nobody had nothing I wanted," he said. "It was a head-doctor in the penitentiary said what I had done was kill my daddy but I know that for a lie. My daddy died in nineteen ought nineteen of an epidemic flu and I never had a thing to do with it. He was buried in the

Mount Hopewell Baptist churchyard and you can go there and see for yourself."

"If you would pray," the old lady said, "Jesus would help you."

"That's right," The Misfit said.

120   "Well then, why don't you pray?" she asked trembling with delight suddenly.

"I don't want no help," he said. "I'm doing all right by myself."

Bobby Lee and Hiram came ambling back from the woods. Bobby Lee was dragging a yellow shirt with bright blue parrots in it.

"Throw me that shirt, Bobby Lee," The Misfit said. The shirt came flying at him and landed on his shoulder and he put it on. The grandmother couldn't name what the shirt reminded her of. "No, lady," The Misfit said while he was buttoning it up. "I found out the crime don't matter. You can do one thing or you can do another, kill a man or take a tire off his car, because sooner or later you're going to forget what it was you done and just be punished for it."

The children's mother had begun to make heaving noises as if she couldn't get her breath. "Lady," he asked, "would you and that little girl like to step off yonder with Bobby Lee and Hiram and join your husband?"

125   "Yes, thank you," the mother said faintly. Her left arm dangled helplessly and she was holding the baby, who had gone to sleep, in the other. "Hep that lady up, Hiram," The Misfit said as she struggled to climb out of the ditch, "and Bobby Lee, you hold onto that little girl's hand."

"I don't want to hold hands with him," June Star said. "He reminds me of a pig."

The fat boy blushed and laughed and caught her by the arm and pulled her off into the woods after Hiram and her mother.

Alone with The Misfit, the grandmother found that she had lost her voice. There was not a cloud in the sky nor any sun. There was nothing around her but woods. She wanted to tell him that he must pray. She opened and closed her mouth several times before anything came out. Finally she found herself saying, "Jesus, Jesus," meaning Jesus will help you, but the way she was saying it, it sounded as if she might be cursing.

"Yes'm," The Misfit said as if he agreed. "Jesus thrown everything off balance. It was the same case with Him as with me except He hadn't committed any crime and they could prove I had committed one because they had the papers on me. Of course," he said, "they never shown me my papers. That's why I sign myself now. I said long ago, you get you a signature and sign everything you do and keep a copy of it. Then you'll know what you done and you can hold up the crime to the punishment and see do they match and in the end you'll have something to prove you ain't been treated right. I call myself The Misfit," he said, "because I can't make what all I done wrong fit with all I gone through in punishment."

130   There was a piercing scream from the woods, followed closely by a pistol report. "Does it seem right to you, lady, that one is punished a heap and another ain't punished at all?"

"Jesus!" the old lady cried. "You've got good blood! I know you wouldn't shoot a lady! I know you come from nice people! Pray! Jesus, you ought not to shoot a lady. I'll give you all the money I've got!"

"Lady," The Misfit said, looking beyond her into the woods, "there never was a body that give the undertaker a tip."

There were two more pistol reports and the grandmother raised her head like a parched old turkey hen crying for water and called, "Bailey Boy, Bailey Boy!" as if her heart would break.

"Jesus was the only One that ever raised the dead," The Misfit continued, "and He shouldn't have done it. He thrown everything off balance. If He did what He said, then it's nothing for you to do but thow away everything and follow Him, and if He didn't, then it's nothing for you to do but enjoy the few minutes you got left the best way you can—by killing somebody or burning down his house or doing some other meanness to him. No pleasure but meanness," he said and his voice had become almost a snarl.

135   "Maybe He didn't raise the dead," the old lady mumbled, now knowing what she was saying and feeling so dizzy that she sank down in the ditch with her legs twisted under her.

"I wasn't there so I can't say He didn't," The Misfit said. "I wisht I had of been there," he said, hitting the ground with his fist. "It ain't right I wasn't there because if I had of been there I would of known. Listen lady," he said in a high voice, "if I had of been there I would of known and I wouldn't be like I am now." His voice seemed about to crack and the grandmother's head cleared for an instant. She saw the man's face twisted close to her own as if he were going to cry and she murmured, "Why you're one of my babies. You're one of my own children!" She reached out and touched him on the shoulder. The Misfit sprang back as if a snake had bitten him and shot her three times through the chest. Then he put his gun down on the ground and took off his glasses and began to clean them.

Hiram and Bobby Lee returned from the woods and stood over the ditch, looking down at the grandmother who half sat and half lay in a puddle of blood with her legs crossed under her like a child's and her face smiling up at the cloudless sky.

Without his glasses, The Misfit's eyes were red-rimmed and pale and defenseless-looking. "Take her off and throw her where you thown the others," he said, picking up the cat that was rubbing itself against his leg.

"She was a talker, wasn't she?" Bobby Lee said, sliding down the ditch with a yodel.

140   "She would of been a good woman," The Misfit said, "if it had been somebody there to shoot her every minute of her life."

"Some fun!" Bobby Lee said.

"Shut up, Bobby Lee," The Misfit said. "It's no real pleasure in life."

[1953]

 # TOPICS FOR CRITICAL THINKING AND WRITING

1. What are the associations of the names June Star, John Wesley, and Bobby Lee?

2. What are the values of the members of the family?

3. Flannery O'Connor, a Roman Catholic, wrote, "I see from the standpoint of Christian orthodoxy. This means that for me the meaning of life is centered in our Redemption by Christ and what I see in the world I see is its relation to that." In the light of this statement and drawing on "A Good Man Is Hard to Find," explain what O'Connor saw in the world.

4. Let's assume that a reader, unlike O'Connor, does *not* "see from the standpoint of Christian orthodoxy." In an essay of 500 words, explain what interest "A Good Man Is Hard to Find" can have for such a reader.

5. The Misfit says, "I can't make what all I done wrong fit what all I gone through in punishment." What would O'Connor's explanation (i.e., the orthodox Christian explanation) be? In 250 to 500 words, explain what the Misfit means by saying that Jesus has "thrown everything off balance."

Revelation

The doctor's waiting room, which was very small, was almost full when the Turpins entered and Mrs. Turpin, who was very large, made it look even smaller by her presence. She stood looming at the head of the magazine table set in the center of it, a living demonstration that the room was inadequate and ridiculous. Her little bright black eyes took in all the patients as she sized up the seating situation. There was one vacant chair and a place on the sofa occupied by a blond child in a dirty blue romper who should have been told to move over and make room for the lady. He was five or six, but Mrs. Turpin saw at once that no one was going to tell him to move over. He was slumped down in the seat, his arms idle at his sides and his eyes idle in his head; his nose ran unchecked.

Mrs. Turpin put a firm hand on Claud's shoulder and said in a voice that included everyone that wanted to listen, "Claud, you sit in that chair there," and gave him a push down into the vacant one. Claud was florid and bald and sturdy, somewhat shorter than Mrs. Turpin, but he sat down as if he were accustomed to doing what she told him to.

Mrs. Turpin remained standing. The only man in the room besides Claud was a lean stringy old fellow with a rusty hand spread out on each knee, whose eyes were closed as if he were asleep or dead or pretending to be so as not to get up and offer her his seat. Her gaze settled agreeably on a well-dressed gray-haired lady whose eyes met hers and whose expression said: If that child belonged to me, he would have some manners and move over—there's plenty of room there for you and him too.

Claud looked up with a sigh and made as if to rise.

5   "Sit down," Mrs. Turpin said, "You know you're not supposed to stand on that leg. He has an ulcer on his leg," she explained.

Claud lifted his foot onto the magazine table and rolled his leg up to reveal a purple swelling on a plump marble-white calf.

"My!" the pleasant lady said. "How did you do that?"

"A cow kicked him," Mrs. Turpin said.

"Goodness!" said the lady.

10   Claud rolled his trouser leg down.

"Maybe the little boy would move over," the lady suggested, but the child did not stir.

"Somebody will be leaving in a minute," Mrs. Turpin said. She could not understand why a doctor—with as much money as they made charging five dollars a day just to stick his head in the hospital door and look at you—couldn't afford a decent-sized waiting room. This one was hardly bigger than a garage. The table was cluttered with limp-looking magazines and at one end of it there was a big green ash tray full of cigaret butts and cotton wads with little blood spots on them. If she had had anything to do with the running of the place, that would have been emptied every so often. There were no chairs against the wall at the head of the room. It had a rectangular-shaped panel in it that permitted a view of the office where the nurse came and went and the secretary listened to the radio. A plastic fern in a gold pot sat in the opening and trailed its fronds down almost to the floor. The radio was softly playing gospel music.

Just then the inner door opened and a nurse with the highest stack of yellow hair Mr. Turpin had ever seen put her face in the crack and called for the next patient. The woman sitting beside Claud grasped the two arms of her chair and hoisted herself up; she pulled her dress free from her legs and lumbered through the door where the nurse had disappeared.

Mrs. Turpin eased into the vacant chair, which held her tight as a corset. "I wish I could reduce," she said, and rolled her eyes and gave a comic sigh.

15   "Oh, *you* aren't fat," the stylish lady said.

"Oooo I am too," Mrs. Turpin said. "Claud he eats all he wants to and never weighs over one hundred and seventy-five pounds, but me I just look at something good to eat and gain some weight," and her stomach and shoulders shook with laughter. "You can eat all you want to, can't you, Claud?" she asked turning to him.

Claud only grinned.

"Well, as long as you have a good disposition," the stylish lady said, "I don't think it makes a bit of difference what size you are. You just can't beat a good disposition."

Next to her was a fat girl of eighteen or nineteen, scowling into a thick blue book which Mrs. Turpin saw was entitled *Human Development.* The girl raised her head and directed her scowl at Mrs. Turpin as if she did not like her looks. She appeared annoyed that anyone should speak while she tried to read. The poor girl's face was blue with acne and Mrs. Turpin thought how pitiful it was to have a face like that at any age. She gave the girl a friendly smile but the girl only scowled the harder. Mrs. Turpin herself was fat but she always had good skin, and, though she was forty-seven years old, there was not a wrinkle in her face except around her eyes from laughing too much.

20   Next to the ugly girl was the child, still in exactly the same position, and next to him was a thin leathery old woman in a cotton print dress. She and Claud had three sacks of chicken feed in their pump house that was in the same print. She had seen from the first that the child belonged with the old woman. She could tell by the way they sat—kind of vacant and white-trashy, as if they would sit there until Doomsday if nobody called and told them to get up. And at right angles but next to the well-dressed pleasant lady was a lank-faced woman who was certainly the child's mother. She had on a yellow sweat shirt and wine-colored slacks, both gritty-looking, and the rims of her lips were stained with snuff. Her dirty yellow hair was tied behind with a little piece of red paper ribbon. Worse than niggers any day, Mrs. Turpin thought.

The gospel hymn playing was, "When I looked up and He looked down," and Mrs. Turpin, who knew it, supplied the last line mentally, "And wona these days I know I'll we-eara crown."

Without appearing to, Mrs. Turpin always noticed people's feet. The well-dressed lady had on red and grey suede shoes to match her dress. Mrs. Turpin had on her good black patent leather pumps. The ugly girl had on Girl Scout shoes and heavy socks. The old woman had on tennis shoes and the white-trashy mother had on what appeared to be bedroom slippers, black straw with gold braid threaded through them—exactly what you would have expected her to have on.

Sometimes at night when she couldn't go to sleep, Mrs. Turpin would occupy herself with the question of who she would have chosen to be if she couldn't have been herself. If Jesus had said to her before he made her, "There's only two places available for you. You can either be a nigger or white-trash," what would she have said? "Please, Jesus, please," she would have said, "just let me wait until there's another place available," and he would have said, "No, you have to go right now and I have only those two places so make up your mind." She would have wiggled and squirmed and begged and pleaded but it would have been no use and finally she would have said, "All right, make me a nigger then—but that don't mean a trashy one." And he would have made her a neat clean respectable Negro woman, herself but black.

Next to the child's mother was a red-headed youngish woman, reading one of the magazines and working a piece of chewing gum, hell for leather, as Claud would say. Mrs. Turpin could not see the woman's feet. She was not white-trash, just common. Sometimes Mrs. Turpin occupied herself at night naming the classes of people. On the bottom of the heap were most colored people, not the kind she would have been if she had been one, but most of them; then next to them—not above, just away from—were the white-trash; then above them were the homeowners, and above them the home-and-land owners, to which she and Claud belonged. Above she and Claud were people with a lot of money and much bigger houses and much more land. But here the complexity of it would begin to bear in on her, for some of the people with a lot of money were common and ought to be below she and Claud and some of the people who had good blood had lost their money and had to rent and then there were colored people who owned their homes and land as well. There was a colored dentist in town who had two red Lincolns and a swimming pool and farm with registered white-faced cattle on it. Usually by the time she had fallen asleep all the classes of people were moiling and roiling around in her head, and she would dream they were all crammed in together in a box car, being ridden off to be put in a gas oven.

25   "That's a beautiful clock," she said and nodded to her right. It was a big wall clock, the face encased in a brass sunburst.

"Yes, it's very pretty," the stylish lady said agreeably. "And right on the dot too," she added, glancing at her watch.

The ugly girl beside her cast an eye upward at the clock, smirked, then looked directly at Mrs. Turpin and smirked again. Then she returned her eyes to her book. She was obviously the lady's daughter because, although they didn't look anything alike as to disposition, they both had the same shape of face and the same blue eyes. On the lady they sparkled pleasantly but in the girl's seared face they appeared alternately to smolder and to blaze.

What if Jesus had said, "All right, you can be white-trash or a nigger or ugly"!

Mrs. Turpin felt an awful pity for the girl, though she thought it was one thing to be ugly and another to act ugly.

30   The woman with the snuff-stained lips turned around in her chair and looked up at the clock. Then she turned back and appeared to look a little to the side of Mrs. Turpin. There was a cast in one of her eyes. "You want to know wher you can get one of themther clocks?" she asked in a loud voice.

"No, I already have a nice clock," Mrs. Turpin said. Once somebody like her got a leg in the conversation, she would be all over it.

"You can get you one with green stamps," the woman said. "That's most likely wher he got hisn. Save you up enough, you can get you most anythang. I got me some joo'ry."

Ought to have got you a wash rag and some soap, Mrs. Turpin thought.

"I get contour sheets with mine," the pleasant lady said.

35   The daughter slammed her book shut. She looked straight in front of her, directly through Mrs. Turpin and on through the yellow curtain and the plate glass window which made the wall behind her. The girl's eyes seemed lit all of a sudden with a peculiar light, an unnatural light like night road signs give. Mrs. Turpin turned her head to see if there was anything going on outside that she should see, but she could not see anything. Figures passing cast only a pale shadow through the curtain. There was no reason the girl should single her out for her ugly looks.

"Miss Finely," the nurse said, cracking the door. The gum-chewing woman got up and passed in front of her and Claud and went into the office. She had on red high-heeled shoes.

Directly across the table, the ugly girl's eyes were fixed on Mrs. Turpin as if she had some very special reason for disliking her.

"This is wonderful weather, isn't it?" the girl's mother said.

"It's good weather for cotton if you can get the niggers to pick it," Mrs. Turpin said, "but niggers don't want to pick cotton any more. You can't get the white folks to pick it and now you can't get the niggers—because they got to be right up there with the white folks."

40   "They gonna *try* anyways," the white-trash woman said, leaning forward.

"Do you have one of those cotton-picking machines?" the pleasant lady asked.

"No," Mrs. Turpin said, "they leave half the cotton in the field. We don't have much cotton anyway. If you want to make it farming now, you have to have a little of everything. We got a couple of acres of cotton and a few hogs and chickens and just enough white-face that Claud can look after them himself."

"One thang I don't want," the white-trash woman said, wiping her mouth with the back of her hand. "Hogs. Nasty stinking things, a-gruntin and a-rootin all over the place."

Mrs. Turpin gave her the merest edge of attention. "Our hogs are not dirty and they don't stink," she said. "They're cleaner than some children I've seen. Their feet never touch the ground. We have a pig-parlor—that's where you raise them on concrete," she explained to the pleasant lady, "and Claud scoots them down with the hose every afternoon and washes off the floor." Cleaner by far than that child right there, she thought. Poor nasty little thing. He had not moved except to put the thumb of his dirty hand into his mouth.

45   The woman turned her face away from Mrs. Turpin. "I know I wouldn't scoot down no hog with no hose," she said to the wall.

You wouldn't have no hog to scoot down, Mrs. Turpin said to herself.

"A-gruntin and a-rootin and a-groanin," the woman muttered.

"We got a little of everything," Mrs. Turpin said to the pleasant lady. "It's no use in having more than you can handle yourself with help like it is. We found enough niggers to pick our cotton this year but Claud he has to go after them and take them home again in the evening. They can't walk that half a mile. No they can't. I tell you," she said and laughed merrily, "I sure am tired of buttering up niggers, but you got to love em if you want em to work for you. When they come in the morning, I run out and I say, 'Hi yawl this morning?' and when Claud drives them off to the field I just wave to beat the band and they just wave back." And she waved her hand rapidly to illustrate.

"Like you read out of the same book," the lady said, showing she understood perfectly.

50   "Child, yes," Mrs. Turpin said. "And when they come in from the field, I run out with a bucket of icewater. That's the way it's going to be from now on," she said. "You may as well face it."

"One thang I know," the white-trash woman said. "Two thangs I ain't going to do: love no niggers or scoot down no hog with no hose." And she let out a bark of contempt.

The look that Mrs. Turpin and the pleasant lady exchanged indicated they both understood that you had to *have* certain things before you could *know* certain things. But every time Mrs. Turpin exchanged a look with the lady, she was aware that the ugly girl's peculiar eyes were still on her, and she had trouble bringing her attention back to the conversation.

"When you got something," she said, "you got to look after it." And when you ain't got a thing but breath and britches, she added to herself, you can afford to come to town every morning and just sit on the Court House coping and spit.

A grotesque revolving shadow passed across the curtain behind her and was thrown palely on the opposite wall. Then a bicycle clattered down against the outside of the building. The door opened and a colored boy glided in with a tray from the drug store. It had two large red and white paper cups on it with tops on them. He was a tall, very black boy in discolored white pants and a green nylon shirt. He was chewing gum slowly, as if to music. He set the tray down in the office opening next to the fern and stuck his head through to look for the secretary. She was not in there. He rested his arms on the ledge and waited, his narrow bottom stuck out, swaying slowly to the left and right. He raised a hand over his head and scratched the base of his skull.

55   "You see that button there, boy?" Mrs. Turpin said. "You can punch that and she'll come. She's probably in the back somewhere."

"Is that right?" the boy said agreeably, as if he had never seen the button before. He leaned to the right and put his finger on it. "She sometime out," he said and twisted around to face his audience, his elbows behind him on the counter. The nurse appeared and he twisted back again. She handed him a dollar and he rooted in his pocket and made the change and counted it out to her. She gave him fifteen cents for a tip and he went out with the empty tray. The heavy door swung to slowly and closed at length with the sound of suction. For a moment no one spoke.

"They ought to send all them niggers back to Africa," the white-trash woman said. "That's wher they come from in the first place."

"Oh, I couldn't do without my good colored friends," the pleasant lady said.

"There's a heap of things worse than a nigger," Mrs. Turpin agreed. "It's all kinds of them just like it's all kinds of us."

60   "Yes, and it takes all kinds to make the world go round," the lady said in her musical voice.

As she said it, the raw-complexioned girl snapped her teeth together. Her lower lip turned downwards and inside out, revealing the pale pink inside of her mouth. After a second it rolled back up. It was the ugliest face Mrs. Turpin had ever seen anyone make and for a moment she was certain that the girl had made it at her. She was looking at her as if she had known and disliked her all her life—all of Mrs. Turpin's life, it seemed too, not just all the girl's life. Why, girl, I don't even know you, Mrs. Turpin said silently.

She forced her attention back to the discussion. "It wouldn't be practical to send them back to Africa," she said. "They wouldn't want to go. They got it too good here."

"Wouldn't be what they wanted—if I had anythang to do with it," the woman said.

"It wouldn't be a way in the world you could get all the niggers back over there," Mrs. Turpin said. "They'd be hiding out and lying down and turning sick on you and wailing and hollering and raring and pitching. It wouldn't be a way in the world to get them over there."

65   "They got over here," the trashy woman said. "Get back like they got over."

"It wasn't so many of them then," Mrs. Turpin explained.

The woman looked at Mrs. Turpin as if here was an idiot indeed but Mrs. Turpin was not bothered by the look, considering where it came from.

"Nooo," she said, "they're going to stay here where they can go to New York and marry white folks and improve their color. That's what they all want to do, every one of them, improve their color."

"You know what comes of that, don't you?" Claud asked.

70   "No, Claud, what?" Mrs. Turpin said.

Claud's eyes twinkled. "White-faced niggers," he said with never a smile.

Everybody in the office laughed except the white-trash and the ugly girl. The girl gripped the book in her lap with white fingers. The trashy woman looked around her from face to face as if she thought they were all idiots. The old woman in the feed sack dress continued to gaze expressionless across the floor at the high-top shoes of the man opposite her, the one who had been pretending to be asleep when the Turpins came in. He was laughing heartily, his hands still spread out on his knees. The child had fallen to the side and was lying now almost face down in the old woman's lap.

While they recovered from their laughter, the nasal chorus on the radio kept the room from silence.

> *You go to blank blank*
> *And I'll go to mine*
> *But we'll all blank along*
> *To-geth-ther*
> *And all along the blank*
> *We'll hep each other out*
> *Smile-ling in any kind of*
> *Weath-ther!*

Mrs. Turpin didn't catch every word but she caught enough to agree with the spirit of the song and it turned her thoughts sober. To help anybody out that needed it was her philosophy of life. She never spared herself when she found somebody in need, whether they were white or black, trash or decent. And of all she had to be thankful for, she was most thankful this was so. If Jesus had said, "You can be high society and have all the money you want and be thin and svelte-like, but you can't be a good woman with it," she would have had to say, "Well don't make me that then. Make me a good woman and it don't matter what else, how fat or how ugly or how poor!" Her heart rose. He had not made her a nigger or white-trash or ugly! He had made her herself and given her a little of everything. Jesus, thank you! she said. Thank you thank you thank you! Whenever she counted her blessings she felt as buoyant as if she weighed one hundred and twenty-five pounds instead of one hundred and eighty.

75   "What's wrong with your little boy?" the pleasant lady asked the white-trashy woman.

"He has an ulcer," the woman said proudly. "He ain't give me a minute's peace since he was born. Him and her are just alike," she said, nodding at the old woman, who was running her leather fingers through the child's pale hair. "Look like I can't get nothing down them two but Co'Cola and candy."

That's all you try to get down em, Mrs. Turpin said to herself. Too lazy to light the fire. There was nothing you could tell her about people like them that she didn't know already. And it was not just that they didn't have anything. Because if you gave them everything, in two weeks it would all be broken or filthy or they would have chopped it up for lightwood. She knew all this from her own experience. Help them you must, but help them you couldn't.

All at once the ugly girl turned her lips inside out again. Her eyes were fixed like two drills on Mrs. Turpin. This time there was no mistaking that there was something urgent behind them.

Girl, Mrs. Turpin exclaimed silently, I haven't done a thing to you! The girl might be confusing her with somebody else. There was no need to sit by and let herself be intimidated. "You must be in college," she said boldly, looking directly at the girl. "I see you reading a book there."

80   The girl continued to stare and pointedly did not answer.

Her mother blushed at this rudeness. "The lady asked you a question, Mary Grace," she said under her breath.

"I have ears," Mary Grace said.

The poor mother blushed again. "Mary Grace goes to Wellesley College," she explained. She twisted one of the buttons on her dress. "In Massachusetts," she added with a grimace. "And in the summer she just keeps right on studying. Just reads all the time, a real book worm. She's done real well at Wellesley; she's taking English and Math and History and Psychology and Social Studies," she rattled on, "and I think it's too much. I think she ought to get out and have fun."

The girl looked as if she would like to hurl them all through the plate glass window.

85 "Way up north," Mrs. Turpin murmured and thought, well, it hasn't done much for her manners.

"I'd almost rather to have him sick," the white-trash woman said, wrenching the attention back to herself. "He's so mean when he ain't. Look like some children just take natural to meanness. It's some gets bad when they get sick but he was the opposite. Took sick and turned good. He don't give me no trouble now. It's me waitin to see the doctor," she said.

If I was going to send anybody back to Africa, Mrs. Turpin thought, it would be your kind, woman. "Yes, indeed," she said aloud, but looking up at the ceiling, "it's a heap of things worse than a nigger." And dirtier than a hog, she added to herself.

"I think people with bad dispositions are more to be pitied than anyone on earth," the pleasant lady said in a voice that was decidely thin.

"I thank the Lord he has blessed me with a good one," Mrs. Turpin said. "The day has never dawned that I couldn't find something to laugh at."

90 "Not since she married me anyways," Claud said with a comical straight face.

Everybody laughed except the girl and the white-trash.

Mrs. Turpin's stomach shook. "He's such a caution," she said, "that I can't help but laugh at him."

The girl made a loud ugly noise through her teeth.

Her mother's mouth grew thin and tight. "I think the worst thing in the world," she said, "is an ungrateful person. To have everything and not appreciate it. I know a girl," she said, "who has parents who would give her anything, a little brother who loves her dearly, who is getting a good education, who wears the best clothes, but who can never say a kind word to anyone, who never smiles, who just criticizes and complains all day long."

95 "Is she too old to paddle?" Claud asked.

The girl's face was almost purple.

"Yes," the lady said, "I'm afraid there's nothing to do but leave her to her folly. Some day she'll wake up and it'll be too late."

"It never hurt anyone to smile," Mrs. Turpin said. "It just makes you feel better all over."

"Of course," the lady said sadly, "but there are just some people you can't tell anything to. They can't take criticism."

100 "If it's one thing I am," Mrs. Turpin said with feeling, "it's grateful. When I think who all I could have been besides myself and what all I got, a little of everything, and a good disposition besides, I just feel like shouting, 'Thank you, Jesus for making everything the way it is!' It could have been different!" For one thing, somebody else could have got Claud. At the thought of this, she was flooded with gratitude and a terrible pang of joy ran through her. "Oh thank you, Jesus, Jesus, thank you!" she cried aloud.

The book struck her directly over the left eye. It struck almost at the same instant that she realized the girl was about to hurl it. Before she could utter a sound, the raw face came crashing across the table toward her, howling. The girl's fingers sank like clamps into the soft flesh of her neck. She heard the mother cry out and Claud shout, "Whoa!" There was an instant when she was certain that she was about to be in an earthquake.

All at once her vision narrowed and she saw everything as if it were happening in a small room far away, or as if she were looking at it through the wrong end of a telescope. Claud's face crumpled and fell out of sight. The nurse ran in, then out, then in again. Then the gangling figure of the doctor rushed out of the inner door. Magazines flew this way and that as the table turned over. The girl fell with a thud and Mrs. Turpin's vision suddenly reversed itself and she saw everything large instead of small. The eyes of the white-trashy woman were staring hugely at the floor. There the girl, held down on one side by the nurse and on the other by her mother, was wrenching and turning in their grasp. The doctor was kneeling astride her, trying to hold her arm down. He managed after a second to sink a long needle into it.

Mrs. Turpin felt entirely hollow except for her heart which swung from side to side as if it were agitated in a great empty drum of flesh.

"Somebody that's not busy call for the ambulance," the doctor said in the off-hand voice young doctors adopt for terrible occasions.

105   Mrs. Turpin could not have moved a finger. The old man who had been sitting next to her skipped nimbly into the office and made the call, for the secretary still seemed to be gone.

"Claud!" Mrs. Turpin called.

He was not in his chair. She knew she must jump up and find him but she felt like some one trying to catch a train in a dream, when everything moves in slow motion and the faster you try to run the slower you go.

"Here I am," a suffocated voice, very unlike Claud's, said.

He was doubled up in the corner on the floor, pale as paper, holding his leg. She wanted to get up and go to him but she could not move. Instead, her gaze was drawn slowly downward to the churning face on the floor, which she could see over the doctor's shoulder.

110   The girl's eyes stopped rolling and focused on her. They seemed a much lighter blue than before, as if a door that had been tightly closed behind them was now open to admit light and air.

Mrs. Turpin's head cleared and her power of motion returned. She leaned forward until she was looking directly into the fierce brilliant eyes. There was no doubt in her mind that the girl did know her, knew her in some intense and personal way, beyond time and place and condition. "What you got to say to me?" she asked hoarsely and held her breath, waiting, as for a revelation.

The girl raised her head. Her gaze locked with Mrs. Turpin's. "Go back to hell where you came from, you old wart hog," she whispered. Her voice was low but clear. Her eyes burned for a moment as if she saw with pleasure that her message had struck its target.

Mrs. Turpin sank back in her chair.

After a moment the girl's eyes closed and she turned her head wearily to the side.

115   The doctor rose and handed the nurse the empty syringe. He leaned

over and put both hands for a moment on the mother's shoulders, which were shaking. She was sitting on the floor, her lips pressed together, holding Mary Grace's hand in her lap. The girl's fingers were gripped like a baby's around her thumb. "Go on to the hospital," he said. "I'll call and make the arrangements."

"Now let's see that neck," he said in a jovial voice to Mrs. Turpin. He became to inspect her neck with his first two fingers. Two little moon-shaped lines like pink fish bones were indented over her windpipe. There was the beginning of an angry red swelling above her eye. His fingers passed over this also.

"Lea' me be," she said thickly and shook him off. "See about Claud. She kicked him."

"I'll see about him in a minute," he said and felt her pulse. He was a thin grey-haired man, given to pleasantries. "Go home and have yourself a vacation the rest of the day," he said and patted her on the shoulder.

Quit your pattin me, Mrs. Turpin growled to herself.

120   "And put an ice pack over that eye," he said. Then he went and squatted down beside Claud and looked at his leg. After a moment he pulled him up and Claud limped after him into the office.

Until the ambulance came, the only sounds in the room were the tremulous moans of the girl's mother, who continued to sit on the floor. The white-trash woman did not take her eyes off the girl. Mrs. Turpin looked straight ahead at nothing. Presently the ambulance drew up, a long dark shadow, behind the curtain. The attendants came in and set the stretcher down beside the girl and lifted her expertly onto it and carried her out. The nurse helped the mother gather up her things. The shadow of the ambulance moved silently away and the nurse came back in the office.

"That ther girl is going to be a lunatic, ain't she?" the white-trash woman asked the nurse, but the nurse kept on to the back and never answered her.

"Yes, she's going to be a lunatic," the white-trash woman said to the rest of them.

"Po' critter," the old woman murmured. The child's face was still in her lap. His eyes looked idly out over her knees. He had not moved during the disturbance except to draw one leg up under him.

125   "I thank Gawd," the white-trash woman said fervently, "I ain't a lunatic."

Claud came limping out and the Turpins went home.

As their pick-up truck turned into their own dirt road and made the crest of the hill, Mrs. Turpin gripped the window ledge and looked out suspiciously. The land sloped gracefully down through a field dotted with lavender weeds and at the start of the rise their small yellow frame house, with its little flower beds spread out around it like a fancy apron, sat primly in its accustomed place between two giant hickory trees. She would not have been startled to see a burnt wound between two blackened chimneys.

Neither of them felt like eating so they put on their house clothes and lowered the shade in the bedroom and lay down, Claud with his leg on a pillow and herself with a damp washcloth over her eye. The instant she was flat on her back the image of a razor-backed hog with warts on its face and horns coming out behind its ears snorted into her head. She moaned, a low quiet moan.

"I am not," she said tearfully, "a wart hog. From hell." But the denial had no force. The girl's eyes and her words, even the tone of her voice, low but clear, directed only to her, brooked no repudiation. She had been singled out for the message, though there was trash in the room to whom it might justly have been applied. The full force of this fact struck her only now. There was a woman there who was neglecting her own child but she had been overlooked. The message had been given to Rudy Turpin, a respectable, hardworking, church-going woman. The tears dried. Her eyes began to burn instead with wrath.

130   She rose on her elbow and the washcloth fell into her hand. Claud was lying on his back, snoring. She wanted to tell him what the girl had said. At the same time, she did not wish to put the image of herself as a wart hog from hell into his mind.

"Hey, Claud," she muttered and pushed his shoulder.

Claud opened one pale baby blue eye.

She looked into it warily. He did not think about anything. He just went his way.

"Wha, whasit?" he said and closed the eye again.

135   "Nothing," she said. "Does your leg pain you?"

"Hurts like hell," Claud said.

"It'll quit terreckley," she said and lay back down. In a moment Claud was snoring again. For the rest of the afternoon they lay there. Claud slept. She scowled at the ceiling. Occasionally she raised her fist and made a small stabbing motion over her chest as if she was defending her innocence to invisible guests who were like the comforters of Job,[1] reasonable-seeming but wrong.

About five-thirty Claud stirred. "Got to go after those niggers," he sighed, not moving.

She was looking straight up as if there were unintelligible handwriting on the ceiling. The protuberance over her eye had turned a greenish-blue. "Listen here," she said.

140   "What?"

"Kiss me."

Claud leaned over and kissed her loudly on the mouth. He pinched her side and their hands interlocked. Her expression of ferocious concentration did not change. Claud got up, groaning and growling, and limped off. She continued to study the ceiling.

She did not get up until she heard the pick-up truck coming back with the Negroes. Then she rose and thrust her feet in her brown oxfords, which she did not bother to lace, and stumped out onto the back porch and got her red plastic bucket. She emptied a tray of ice cubes into it and filled it half full of water and went out into the back yard. Every afternoon after Claud brought the hands in, one of the boys helped him put out hay and the rest waited in the back of the truck until he was ready to take them home. The truck was parked in the shade under one of the hickory trees.

---

[1]In the Book of Job, in the Hebrew Bible, Job was afflicted terribly. Friends seek to comfort him, but they insist that he must have sinned and offended God. Job rejects their view, insisting on his sinlessness, but at the end, when God addresses him in a whirlwind, Job is humbled and he says, "I abhor myself, and repent in dust and ashes."

"Hi yawl this evening?" Mrs. Turpin asked grimly, appearing with the bucket and the dipper. There were three women and a boy in the truck.

145   "Us doing nicely," the oldest woman said. "Hi you doin?" and her gaze stuck immediately on the dark lump on Mrs. Turpin's forehead. "You done fell down, ain't you?" she asked in a solicitous voice. The old woman was dark and almost toothless. She had on an old felt hat of Claud's set back on her head. The other two women were younger and lighter and they both had new bright green sun hats. One of them had hers on her head; the other had taken hers off and the boy was grinning beneath it.

Mrs. Turpin set the bucket down on the floor of the truck. "Yawl hep youselves," she said. She looked around to make sure Claud had gone. "No. I didn't fall down," she said, folding her arms. "It was something worse than that."

"Ain't nothing bad happen to you!" the old woman said. She said it as if they all knew that Mrs. Turpin was protected in some special way by Divine Providence. "You just had you a little fall."

"We were in town at the doctor's office for where the cow kicked Mr. Turpin," Mrs. Turpin said in a flat tone that indicated they could leave off their foolishness. "And there was this girl there. A big fat girl with her face all broke out. I could look at that girl and tell she was peculiar but I couldn't tell how. And me and her mama were just talking and going along and all of a sudden WHAM! She throws this big book she was reading at me and. . ."

"Naw!" the old woman cried out.

150   "And then she jumps over the table and commences to choke me."

"Naw!" they all exclaimed, "naw!"

"Hi come she do that?" the old woman asked. "What ail her?"

Mrs. Turpin only glared in front of her.

"Somethin ail her," the old woman said.

155   "They carried her off in an ambulance," Mrs. Turpin continued, "before she went she was rolling on the floor and they were trying to hold her down to give her a shot and she said something to me." She paused. "You know what she said to me?"

"What she say?" they asked.

"She said," Mrs. Turpin began, and stopped, her face very dark and heavy. The sun was getting whiter and whiter, blanching the sky overhead so that the leaves of the hickory tree were black in the face of it. She could not bring forth the words. "Something real ugly," she muttered.

"She sho shouldn't say nothing ugly to you," the old woman said. "You so sweet. You the sweetest lady I know."

"She pretty too," the one with the hat on said.

160   "And stout," the other one said. "I never knowed no sweeter white lady."

"That's the truth befo' Jesus," the old woman said. "Amen! You des as sweet and pretty as you can be."

Mrs. Turpin knew just exactly how much Negro flattery was worth and it added to her rage. "She said," she began again and finished this time with a fierce rush of breath, "that I was an old wart hog from hell."

There was an astounded silence.

"Where she at?" the youngest woman cried in a piercing voice.

165   "Lemme see her. I'll kill her!"

"I'll kill her with you!" the other one cried.

"She b'long in the sylum," the old woman said emphatically. "You the sweetest white lady I know."

"She pretty too," the other two said. "Stout as she can be and sweet. Jesus satisfied with her!"

"Deed he is," the old woman declared.

170 Idiots! Mrs. Turpin growled to herself. You could never say anything intelligent to a nigger. You could talk at them but not with them. "Yawl ain't drunk your water," she said shortly. "Leave the bucket in the truck when you're finished with it. I got more to do than just stand around and pass the time of day," and she moved off and into the house.

She stood for a moment in the middle of the kitchen. The dark protuberance over her eye looked like a miniature tornado cloud which might any moment sweep across the horizon of her brow. Her lower lip protruded dangerously. She squared her massive shoulders. Then she marched into the front of the house and out the side door and started down the road to the pig parlor. She had the look of a woman going single-handed, weaponless, into battle.

The sun was a deep yellow now like a harvest moon and was riding westward very fast over the far tree line as if it meant to reach the hogs before she did. The road was rutted and she kicked several good-sized stones out of her path as she strode along. The pig parlor was on a little knoll at the end of a lane that ran off from the side of the barn. It was a square of concrete as large as a small room, with a board fence about four feet high around it. The concrete floor sloped slightly so that the hog wash could drain off into a trench where it was carried to the field for fertilizer. Claud was standing on the outside, on the edge of the concrete, hanging onto the top board, hosing down the floor inside. The hose was connected to the faucet of a water trough nearby.

Mrs. Turpin climbed up beside him and glowered down at the hogs inside. There were seven long-snouted bristly shoats in it—tan with liver-colored spots—and an old sow a few weeks off from farrowing. She was lying on her side grunting. The shoats were running about shaking themselves like idiot children, their little slit pig eyes searching the floor for anything left. She had read that pigs were the most intelligent animal. She doubted it. They were supposed to be smarter than dogs. There had even been a pig astronaut. He had performed his assignment perfectly but died of a heart attack afterwards because they left him in his electric suit, sitting upright throughout his examination when naturally a hog should be on all fours.

A-gruntin and a-rootin and a-groanin.

175 "Gimme that hose," she said, yanking it away from Claud. "Go on and carry them niggers home and then get off that leg."

"You look like you might have swallowed a mad dog," Claud observed, but he got down and limped off. He paid no attention to her humors.

Until he was out of earshot, Mrs. Turpin stood on the side of the pen, holding the hose and pointing the stream of water at the hind quarter of any shoat that looked as if it might try to lie down. When he had had time to get over the hill, she turned her head slightly and her wrathful eyes scanned the path. He was nowhere in sight. She turned back again and seemed to gather herself up. Her shoulders rose and she drew in her breath.

"What do you send me a message like that for?" she said in a low fierce voice, barely above a whisper but with the force of a shout in its concentrated fury. "How am I a hog and me both? How am I saved and from hell too?" Her free fist was knotted and with the other she gripped the hose, blindly pointing the stream of water in and out of the eye of the old sow whose outraged squeal she did not hear.

The pig parlor commanded a view of the back pasture where their twenty beef cows were gathered around the hay-bales Claud and the boy had put out. The freshly cut pasture sloped down to the highway. Across it was their cotton field and beyond that a dark green dusty wood which they owned as well. The sun was behind the wood, very red, looking over the paling of trees like a farmer inspecting his own hogs.

180   "Why me?" she rumbled. "It's no trash around here, black or white, that I haven't given to. And break my back to the bone every day working. And do for the church."

She appeared to be the right size woman to command the arena before her. "How am I a hog?" she demanded. "Exactly how am I like them?" and she jabbed the stream of water at the shoats. "There was plenty of trash there. It didn't have to be me."

"If you like trash better, go get yourself some trash then," she railed. "You could have made me trash. Or a nigger. If trash is what you wanted why didn't you make me trash?" She shook her fist with the hose in it and a watery snake appeared momentarily in the air. "I could quit working and take it easy and be filthy," she growled. "Lounge about the sidewalks all day drinking root beer. Dip snuff and spit in every puddle and have it all over my face. I could be nasty."

"Or you could have made me a nigger. It's too late for me to be a nigger," she said with deep sarcasm, "but I could act like one. Lay down in the middle of the road and stop traffic. Roll on the ground."

In the deepening light everything was taking on a mysterious hue. The pasture was growing a peculiar glassy green and the streak of highway had turned lavender. She braced herself for a final assault and this time her voice rolled out over the pasture. "Go on," she yelled, "call me a hog! Call me a hog again. From hell. Call me a wart hog from hell. Put that bottom rail on top. There'll still be a top and bottom!"

185   A garbled echo returned to her.

A final surge of fury shook her and she roared, "Who do you think you are?"

The color of everything, field and crimson sky, burned for a moment with a transparent intensity. The question carried over the pasture and across the highway and the cotton field and returned to her clearly like an answer from beyond the wood.

She opened her mouth but no sound came out of it.

A tiny truck, Claud's, appeared on the highway, heading rapidly out of sight. Its gears scraped thinly. It looked like a child's toy. At any moment a bigger truck might smash into it and scatter Claud's and the niggers' brains all over the road.

190   Mrs. Turpin stood there, her gaze fixed on the highway, all her muscles rigid, until in five or six minutes the truck reappeared, returning. She waited until it had had time to turn into their own road. Then like a monumental statue coming to life, she bent her head slowly and gazed, as if through the very heart of the mystery, down into the pig parlor at the hogs. They had

settled all in one corner around the old sow who was grunting softly. A red glow suffused them. They appeared to pant with a secret life.

Until the sun slipped finally between the tree line, Mrs. Turpin remained there with her gaze bent to them as if she were absorbing some abysmal life-giving knowledge. At last she lifted her head. There was only a purple streak in the sky, cutting through a field of crimson and leading, like an extension of the highway, into the descending dusk. She raised her hands from the side of the pen in a gesture hieratic and profound. A visionary light settled in her eyes. She saw the streak as a vast swinging bridge extending upward from the earth through a field of living fire. Upon it a vast horde of souls were rumbling toward heaven. There were whole companies of white-trash, clean for the first time in their lives, and bands of black niggers in white robes, and battalions of freaks and lunatics shouting and clapping and leaping like frogs. And bringing up the end of the procession was a tribe of people whom she recognized at once as those who, like herself and Claud, had always had a little of everything and the God-given wit to use it right. She leaned forward to observe them closer. They were marching behind the others with great dignity, accountable as they had always been for good order and common sense and respectable behavior. They alone were on key. Yet she could see by their shocked and altered faces that even their virtues were being burned away. She lowered her hands and gripped the rail of the hog pen, her eyes small but fixed unblinkingly on what lay ahead. In a moment the vision faded but she remained where she was, immobile.

At length she got down and turned off the faucet and made her slow way on the darkening path to the house. In the woods around the invisible cricket choruses had struck up, but what she heard were the voices of the souls climbing upward into the starry field and shouting hallelujah.

[1964]

TOPICS FOR CRITICAL THINKING AND WRITING

1. When Mrs. Turpin goes toward the pig parlor, she has "the look of a woman going single-handed, weaponless, into battle" (paragraph 171). Once there, she dismisses Claud, uses the hose as a weapon against the pigs, and talks to herself "in a low fierce voice." What is she battling, besides the pigs?
2. In 500 words, characterize Mrs. Turpin before her revelation.
3. If you have read Flannery O'Connor's "A Good Man Is Hard to Find," compare and contrast the grandmother and Mrs. Turpin, paying special attention to their attitudes toward other people and their concepts of religion.

 ## LESLIE MARMON SILKO

Leslie Marmon Silko—part Laguna Pueblo Indian, part Mexican, part Anglo—was born in 1948 in Albuquerque, New Mexico, and grew up on the Laguna Pueblo Reservation. After attending the Bureau of Indian Affairs school, she went to the University of New Mexico and graduated cum laude in 1969. She has taught at Navajo Community College and at the University of Arizona. In 1981 the

MacArthur Foundation, recognizing Silko as an "exceptionally talented individual," granted her five years of financial support.

The Man to Send Rain Clouds

One

They found him under a big cottonwood tree. His Levi jacket and pants were faded light-blue so that he had been easy to find. The big cottonwood tree stood apart from a small grove of winterbare cottonwoods which grew in the wide, sandy arroyo. He had been dead for a day or more, and the sheep had wandered and scattered up and down the arroyo. Leon and his brother-in-law, Ken, gathered the sheep and left them in the pen at the sheep camp before they returned to the cottonwood tree. Leon waited under the tree while Ken drove the truck through the deep sand to the edge of the arroyo. He squinted up at the sun and unzipped his jacket—it sure was hot for this time of year. But high and northwest the blue mountains were still deep in snow. Ken came sliding down the low, crumbling bank about fifty yards down, and he was bringing the red blanket.

Before they wrapped the old man, Leon took a piece of string out of his pocket and tied a small gray feather in the old man's long white hair. Ken gave him the paint. Across the brown wrinkled forehead he drew a streak of white and along the high cheekbones he drew a strip of blue paint. He paused and watched Ken throw pinches of corn meal and pollen into the wind that fluttered the small gray feather. Then Leon painted with yellow under the old man's broad nose, and finally, when he had painted green across the chin, he smiled.

"Send us rain clouds, Grandfather." They laid the bundle in the back of the pickup and covered it with a heavy tarp before they started back to the pueblo.

They turned off the highway onto the sandy pueblo road. Not long after they passed the store and post office they saw Father Paul's car coming toward them. When he recognized their faces he slowed his car and waved for them to stop. The young priest rolled down the car window.

5   "Did you find old Teofilo?" he asked loudly.

Leon stopped the truck. "Good morning, Father. We were just out to the sheep camp. Everything is O.K. now."

"Thank God for that. Teofilo is a very old man. You really shouldn't allow him to stay at the sheep camp alone."

"No, he won't do that any more now."

"Well, I'm glad you understand. I hope I'll be seeing you at Mass this week—we missed you last Sunday. See if you can get old Teofilo to come with you." The priest smiled and waved at them as they drove away.

Two

10   Louise and Teresa were waiting. The table was set for lunch, and the coffee was boiling on the black iron stove. Leon looked at Louise and then at Teresa.

"We found him under a cottonwood tree in the big arroyo near sheep camp. I guess he sat down to rest in the shade and never got up again." Leon walked toward the old man's bed. The red plaid shawl had been shaken and spread carefully over the bed, and a new brown flannel shirt and pair of stiff new Levis were arranged neatly beside the pillow. Louise held the screen door open while Leon and Ken carried in the red blanket. He looked small and shriveled, and after they dressed him in the new shirt and pants he seemed more shrunken.

It was noontime now because the church bells rang the Angelus. They ate the beans with hot bread, and nobody said anything until after Teresa poured the coffee.

Ken stood up and put on his jacket. "I'll see about the gravediggers. Only the top layer of soil is frozen. I think it can be ready before dark."

Leon nodded his head and finished his coffee. After Ken had been gone for a while, the neighbors and clanspeople came quietly to embrace Teofilo's family and to leave food on the table because the gravediggers would come to eat when they were finished.

Three

15   The sky in the west was full of pale-yellow light. Louise stood outside with her hands in the pockets of Leon's green army jacket that was too big for her. The funeral was over, and the old men had taken their candles and medicine bags and were gone. She waited until the body was laid into the pickup before she said anything to Leon. She touched his arm, and he noticed that her hands were still dusty from the corn meal that she had sprinkled around the old man. When she spoke, Leon could not hear her.

"What did you say? I didn't hear you."

"I said that I had been thinking about something."

"About what?"

"About the priest sprinkling holy water for Grandpa. So he won't be thirsty."

20   Leon stared at the new moccasins that Teofilo had made for the ceremonial dances in the summer. They were nearly hidden by the red blanket. It was getting colder, and the wind pushed gray dust down the narrow pueblo road. The sun was approaching the long mesa where it disappeared during the winter. Louise stood there shivering and watching his face. Then he zipped up his jacket and opened the truck door. "I'll see if he's there."

Four

Ken stopped the pickup at the church, and Leon got out; and then Ken drove down the hill to the graveyard where people were waiting. Leon knocked at the old carved door with its symbols of the Lamb. While he waited he looked up at the twin bells from the king of Spain with the last sunlight pouring around them in their tower.

The priest opened the door and smiled when he saw who it was. "Come in! What brings you here this evening?"

The priest walked toward the kitchen, and Leon stood with his cap in his hand, playing with the earflaps and examining the living room—the brown sofa, the green armchair, and the brass lamp that hung down from the ceiling by links of chain. The priest dragged a chair out of the kitchen and offered it to Leon.

"No thank you, Father. I only came to ask you if you would bring your holy water to the graveyard."

25   The priest turned away from Leon and looked out the window at the patio full of shadows and the dining-room windows of the nuns' cloister across the patio. The curtains were heavy, and the light from within faintly penetrated; it was impossible to see the nuns inside eating supper. "Why didn't you tell me he was dead? I could have brought the Last Rites anyway."

Leon smiled. "It wasn't necessary, Father."

The priest stared down at his scuffed brown loafers and the worn hem of his cassock. "For a Christian burial it was necessary."

His voice was distant, and Leon thought that his blue eyes looked tired.

"It's O.K., Father, we just want him to have plenty of water."

30   The priest sank down in the green chair and picked up a glossy missionary magazine. He turned the colored pages full of lepers and pagans without looking at them.

"You know I can't do that, Leon. There should have been the Last Rites and a funeral Mass at the very least."

Leon put on his green cap and pulled the flaps down over his ears. "It's getting late, Father. I've got to go."

When Leon opened the door Father Paul stood up and said, "Wait." He left the room and came back wearing a long brown overcoat. He followed Leon out the door and across the dim churchyard to the adobe steps in front of the church. They both stooped to fit through the low adobe entrance. And when they started down the hill to the graveyard only half of the sun was visible above the mesa.

The priest approached the grave slowly, wondering how they had managed to dig into the frozen ground; and then he remembered that this was New Mexico, and saw the pile of cold loose sand beside the hole. The people stood close to each other with little clouds of steam puffing from their faces. The priest looked at them and saw a pile of jackets, gloves, and scarves in the yellow, dry tumbleweeds that grew in the graveyard. He looked at the red blanket, not sure that Teofilo was so small, wondering if it wasn't some perverse Indian trick—something they did in March to ensure a good harvest—wondering if maybe old Teofilo was actually at sheep camp corraling the sheep for the night. But there he was, facing into a cold dry wind and squinting at the last sunlight, ready to bury a red wool blanket while the faces of the parishioners were in shadow with the last warmth of the sun on their backs.

35   His fingers were stiff, and it took them a long time to twist the lid off the holy water. Drops of water fell on the red blanket and soaked into dark icy spots. He sprinkled the grave and the water disappeared almost before it touched the dim, cold sand; it reminded him of something—he tried to remember what it was, because he thought if he could remember he might understand this. He sprinkled more water; he shook the container until it was empty, and the water fell through the light from sundown like August rain that fell while the sun was still shining, almost evaporating before it touched the wilted squash flowers.

The wind pulled at the priest's brown Franciscan robe and swirled away the corn meal and pollen that had been sprinkled on the blanket. They lowered the bundle into the ground, and they didn't bother to untie the stiff pieces of new rope that were tied around the ends of the blanket. The sun was gone, and over on the highway the eastbound lane was full of headlights. The priest walked away slowly. Leon watched him climb the hill, and when he had disappeared within the tall, thick walls, Leon turned to look up at the high blue mountains in the deep snow that reflected a faint red light from the west. He felt good because it was finished, and he was happy about the sprinkling of the holy water; now the old man could send them big thunderclouds for sure.

[1969]

 ## TOPICS FOR CRITICAL THINKING AND WRITING

1. How would you describe the response of Leon, Ken, Louise, and Teresa to Teofilo's death? To what degree does it resemble or differ from responses to death that you are familiar with?
2. How do the funeral rites resemble or differ from those of your community?
3. How well does Leon understand the priest? How well does the priest understand Leon?
4. At the end of the story we are told that Leon "felt good." Do you assume that the priest also felt good? Why, or why not?
5. From what point of view is the story told? Mark the passages where the narrator enters a character's mind, and then explain what, in your opinion, Silko gains (or loses?) by doing so.

Poetry

A NOTE ON THE PSALMS

The Book of Psalms (*psalm* is from the Greek *psalmoi,* "songs of praise"), or the Psalter (Greek *psalterion,* a stringed instrument), contains about 150 songs, prayers, and meditations. The number is a bit imprecise for several reasons: for instance, in the Hebrew Bible the numbering from Psalm 10 to Psalm 148 is one digit ahead of the numbering in Bibles used in the Christian church, which joins 9 and 10 and 114 and 115 but divides both 116 and 147 into two. It is also a bit imprecise to call the psalms "songs"; although some of them are entitled songs and some were certainly sung—the texts include references to instruments and to singing—it is by no means certain that all were sung.

The Hebrew text attributes 73 of the psalms to David, who reigned circa 1010-970 B.C.E., and the Greek text attributes 82 to him. David is said to have been a musician (1 Samuel 16.23, Amos 6.5), but these attributions are not taken very seriously by scholars; some of the psalms may indeed go back to the tenth century B.C.E., though some others may be as late as 200 B.C.E. The book in fact is a compilation of earlier collections from hundreds of years of Hebrew history.

We give the psalms in the King James Version (1611) but we also give Psalm 23 in a modern version from the Revised English Bible (1989) to allow for a comparison.

Psalm 1

1 Blessed *is* the man that walketh not in the counsel of the ungodly, nor standeth in the way of sinners,° nor sitteth in the seat of the scornful.

2 But his delight *is* in the law° of the LORD; and in his law doth he meditate day and night.

3 And he shall be like a tree planted by the rivers of water, that bringeth forth his fruit in his season; his leaf also shall not wither; and whatsoever he doeth shall prosper.

4 The ungodly *are* not so: but *are* like the chaff° which the wind driveth away.

5 Therefore the ungodly shall not stand in the judgment, nor sinners in the congregation of the righteous.

6 For the LORD knoweth the way of the righteous: but the way of the ungodly shall perish.°

¹**standeth in the way of sinners** stands in the road with sinners, i.e., consorts with sinners (the *way* is literally a road or path, figuratively a manner of life)   ²**the law** the Torah (first five books of the Hebrew Bible)   ⁴**chaff** worthless material (in threshing, the crushed sheaves were tossed into the air, allowing the wind to blow away the chaff—the inedible material enclosing the grain)   ⁶**perish** disappear, i.e., the path will peter out

Psalm 19

To the chief Musician, A Psalm of David.

1 The heavens declare the glory of God; and the firmament° sheweth his handywork.

2 Day unto day uttereth speech, and night unto night sheweth knowledge.

3 *There is* no speech nor language, *where* their voice is not heard.

4 Their line is gone out through all the earth, and their words to the end of the world. In them hath he set a tabernacle for the sun,

5 Which *is* as a bridegroom coming out of his chamber, *and* rejoiceth as a strong man to run a race.

6 His going forth *is* from the end of the heaven, and his circuit unto the ends of it: and there is nothing hid from the heat thereof.

7 The law of the LORD *is* perfect, converting the soul: the testimony of the LORD *is* sure, making wise the simple.

8 The statutes of the LORD *are* right, rejoicing the heart: the commandment of the LORD *is* pure, enlightening the eyes.

9 The fear° of the LORD *is* clean, enduring for ever: the judgments of the LORD *are* true *and* righteous altogether.

¹**firmament** dome of the sky   ⁹**fear** often emended in later translations to *word*

10 More to be desired *are they* than gold, yea, than much fine gold: sweeter also than honey and the honeycomb.

11 Moreover by them is thy servant warned: *and* in keeping of them *there is* great reward.

12 Who can understand *his* errors? cleanse thou me from secret *faults.*°

13 Keep back thy servant also from presumptuous *sins;* let them not have dominion over me: then shall I be upright, and I shall be innocent from the great transgression.

14 Let the words of my mouth, and the meditation of my heart, be acceptable in thy sight, O Lord, my strength, and my redeemer.

12**secret faults** unconscious violations of God's will

Psalm 23

1 The Lord *is* my shepherd; I shall not want.

2 He maketh me to lie down in green pastures: he leadeth me beside the still waters.

3 He restoreth my soul: he leadeth me in the paths of righteousness for his name's sake.°

4 Yea, though I walk through the valley of the shadow of death,° I will fear no evil: for thou *art* with me; thy rod° and thy staff° they comfort me.

5 Thou preparest a table° before me in the presence of mine enemies: thou anointest my head with oil; my cup runneth over.

6 Surely goodness and mercy shall follow me° all the days of my life: and I will dwell in the house of the Lord for ever.

3**for his name's sake** because he is that kind of God (the *name* reveals the nature of a person or a god); or in order to exalt his name   4**valley of the shadow of death** a mistranslation—but most readers will not willingly give it up. Modern translations give something like *dark valley* or *valley of deep shadow* (metaphoric for "deep distress").   **rod** a cudgel, to ward off wild animals.   **staff** a pole, probably with a hook at the end, to guide timid sheep   5**table** probably a table in the temple, prepared for a sacrificial meal   6**shall follow me** the goodness and mercy experienced in the temple will continue in daily life

Psalm 23 (Revised English Bible, 1989)

1 The Lord is my shepherd; I lack for nothing.

2 He makes me lie down in green pastures,
   he leads me to water where I may rest;

3 he revives my spirit
   for his name's sake he guides me in the right paths.

4 Even were I to walk through a valley of deepest darkness
   I should fear no harm, for you are with me;
   your shepherd's staff and crook afford me comfort.

5 You spread a table for me in the presence of my enemies;

you have richly anointed my head with oil,
and my cup brims over.
6 Goodness and love unfailing will follow me all the days of my life,
and I shall dwell in the house of the Lord hroughout the years to come.

Psalm 23 (version by an adolescent on probation)

The following version is from God Is For Real, Man *(1966), a book of
"interpretations of Bible passages and stories" by adolescents who
had had run-ins with the law. In writing this material they were assisted by Carl F. Burke, chaplain of Erie County Jail in Buffalo, New
York. Burke explains, in his preface, that the boy who wrote this version felt that only his probation officer—whom the boy admired—
was interested in the boy. According to Burke, by composing this version the boy "was able to express his feelings and establish a
relationship with a person, which he could then translate into a relationship with our Lord" (15).*

The Lord Is Like My Probation Officer

The Lord is like my Probation Officer,
  He will help me,
    He tries to help me make it every day.
      He makes me play it cool
        And feel good inside of me.

He shows me the right path
  So I'll have a good record,
    And he'll have one too.

Because I trust him,
  And that ain't easy,
    I don't worry too much about
      What's going to happen.
        Just knowing he care about
          Me helps me.

He makes sure I have my food
  And that Mom fixes it.
    He helps her stay sober
      And that makes me feel good
        All over.

He's a good man, I think,
  And he is kind
    And these things will stay
      With me.

And when I'm kind and good
  Then I know the Lord
    Is with me like the Probation Officer.

Psalm 121

1 I will lift up mine eyes unto the hills, from
whence cometh my help.

2 My help *cometh* from the Lord, which made
heaven and earth.

3 He will not suffer thy foot to be moved: he that
keepeth thee will not slumber.

4 Behold, he that keepeth Israel shall neither slumber
nor sleep.

5 The Lord *is* thy keeper: the Lord *is* thy shade
upon thy right hand.

6 The sun shall not smite thee by day, nor the
moon° by night.

7 The Lord shall preserve thee from all evil: he shall
preserve thy soul.

8 The Lord shall preserve thy going out and thy coming in
from this time forth, and even for evermore.

 ## TOPICS FOR CRITICAL THINKING AND WRITING

1. In Psalm 1, verse 1, "walketh not in the counsel of the ungodly" contains a metaphor since people do not literally *walk* in advice. How
   would you explain the metaphor? And what do you make of "the seat of
   the scornful"?
2. Examine other metaphors in Psalm 1, especially the tree in verse 3 and
   the chaff in verse 4. Try to paraphrase them. What is gained or lost in
   the paraphrases? What connection (or contrast) can you make between
   these two metaphors?
3. Probably most readers will agree about the structure of Psalm 19: verses
   1–6 are on nature, 7–11 are on the Law, and 12–14 are a prayer. Do you
   think these units cohere into a whole? For instance, does it make sense
   to say that the second unit is connected to the first by the idea that just
   as nothing is hidden from the heat of the sun (6), in like manner "the
   law of the Lord" is everywhere? Is such a reading appropriate, or is it
   strained. Explain.
4. In Psalm 23, line 1 (King James Version), the speaker says, "I shall not
   want," that is, "I shall not lack anything." Judging from the rest of the
   psalm, what does the speaker hope to be granted?
5. Some scholars consider Psalm 121 to contain a question by a pilgrim
   (in their view, the pilgrim's question is "From whence cometh my
   help?") and an answer by a priest (in this view, the answer is that help
   comes not from the hills, with their pagan sanctuaries, but from the
   Lord). Since the scholars are divided, we may offer our own opinions.
   Do you think the poem gains or loses by being read as a dialogue?
   Explain.

⁶**the sun . . . the moon** the sun can cause sunstroke; the moon was thought to
cause lunacy

A NOTE ON SPIRITUALS

Spirituals, or sorrow songs, by slaves in the United States, seem to have been created chiefly in the first half of the nineteenth century. Their origins are still a matter of some dispute, but probably most students of the subject agree that the songs represent a distinctive fusion of African rhythms with white hymns, and of course many of the texts derive ultimately from Biblical sources. One of the chief themes is the desire for release, sometimes presented with imagery drawn from ancient Israel. Examples include references to crossing the River Jordan (a river that runs from north of the Sea of Galilee to the Dead Sea), the release of the Israelites from slavery in Egypt (Exodus), Jonah's release from the whale (Book of Jonah), and Daniel's deliverance from the fiery furnace and from the lions' den (Book of Daniel, chapters 3 and 6).

The texts were collected and published especially in the 1860s, for instance in *Slave Songs of the United States* (1867). These books usually sought to reproduce the singers' pronunciation, and we have followed the early texts here.

Deep River

Deep river, my home is over Jordan, Deep river,
Lord, I want to cross over into campground,
Lord, I want to cross over into campground,
Lord, I want to cross over into campground.
Oh, chillun, Oh, don't you want to go to that gospel feast,   5
That promised land, that land, where all is peace?
Walk into heaven, and take my seat,
And cast my crown at Jesus feet,
Lord, I want to cross over into campground,
Lord, I want to cross over into campground,   10
Lord, I want to cross over into campground.
Deep river, my home is over Jordan, Deep river,
Lord, I want to cross over into campground,
Lord, I want to cross over into campground,
Lord, I want to cross over into campground, Lord!   15

Go Down, Moses

When Israel was in Egypt's land,
  Let my people go;
Oppressed so hard they could not stand,
  Let my people go.

Chorus:
Go down, Moses, way down in Egypt's land;   5
Tell old Pharoah, to let my people go.

Thus saith the Lord, bold Moses said,
  Let my people go;
If not I'll smite your first born dead,
  Let my people go.   10

No more shall they in bondage toil,
    Let my people go;
Let them come out with Egypt's spoil,
    Let my people go.

O 'twas a dark and dismal night,   15
    Let my people go;
When Moses led the Israelites,
    Let my people go.

The Lord told Moses what to do,
    Let my people go;   20
To lead the children of Israel through,
    Let my people go.

O come along, Moses, you won't get lost,
    Let my people go;
Stretch our your rod and come across,   25
    Let my people go.

As Israel stood by the water side,
    Let my people go;
At the command of God it did divide,
    Let my people go.   30

And when they reached the other side,
    Let my people go;
They sang a song of triumph o'er,
    Let my people go.

You won't get lost in the wilderness,   35
    Let my people go;
With a lighted candle in your breast,
    Let my people go.

O let us all from bondage flee,
    Let my people go;   40
And let us all in Christ be free,
    Let my people go.

We need not always weep and moan,
    Let my people go;
And wear these slavery chains forlorn,   45
    Let my people go.

What a beautiful morning that will be,
    Let my people go;
When time breaks up in eternity,
    Let my people go.   50

Didn't My Lord Deliver Daniel

Didn't my Lord deliver Daniel, deliver Daniel, deliver Daniel,
Didn't my Lord deliver Daniel,
    An' why not every man.
He delivered Daniel from de lion's den,

Jonah from de belly of de whale,   5
An' de Hebrew chillun from de fiery furnace,
An' why not every man.
   Didn't my Lord deliver Daniel, deliver Daniel, deliver Daniel,
   Didn't my Lord deliver Daniel,
   An' why not every man.   10
De moon run down in a purple stream,
De sun forbear to shine,
An' every star disappear,
King Jesus shall-a be mine.
(Refrain)
De win' blows eas' an' de win' blows wes',   15
It blows like de judgament day,
An' every po' soul dat never did pray
'll be glad to pray dat day.
(Refrain)
I set my foot on de Gospel ship,
An de ship begin to sail,   20
It landed me over on Canaan's shore,°
An' I'll never come back no mo'.
(Refrain)

[21]**Canaan's shore** Canaan is the ancient name of a territory that included part of
what is now Israel

TOPIC FOR CRITICAL THINKING OR WRITING

As we mention in our introductory note, we give the texts of the songs as they
were printed in the second half of the nineteenth century, when an effort to indicate pronunciation was made (e.g., *chillun* for *children*). If you were printing
the songs, would you retain these attempts to indicate pronunciation? What, if
anything, is gained by keeping them? What, if any, unintentional side effects are
produced?

WILLIAM SHAKESPEARE

William Shakespeare (1564–1616), born in Stratford-upon-Avon in
England, is chiefly known as a dramatic poet, but he also wrote non-
dramatic poetry. In 1609 a volume of 154 of his sonnets was pub-
lished, apparently without his permission. Probably he chose to keep
his sonnets unpublished not because he thought that they were of lit-
tle value, but because it was more prestigious to be an amateur poet
(unpublished) than a professional (published). Although the sonnets
were published in 1609, they were probably written in the mid-
1590s, when there was a vogue for sonneteering. A contemporary
writer in 1598 said that Shakespeare's "sugred Sonnets [circulate]
among his private friends."

Sonnet 146

Poor soul, the center of my sinful earth,
My sinful earth these rebel pow'rs that thee array,
Why doest thou pine within and suffer dearth,
Painting thy outward walls so costly gay?   4
Why so large cost,° having so short a lease,
Dost thou upon thy fading mansion spend?
Shall worms, inheritors of this excess,
Eat up thy charge? Is this thy body's end?   8
Then, soul, live thou upon thy servant's loss,
And let that pine to aggravate thy store;
Buy terms divine° in selling hours of dross;
Within be fed, without be rich no more.   12
    So shalt thou feed on Death, that feeds on men,
    And death once dead, there's no more dying then.

⁵**cost** expense   ¹¹**buy terms divine** buy ages of immortality

 TOPICS FOR CRITICAL THINKING AND WRITING

1. "My sinful earth," in line 2, is doubtless an error made by the printer of
   the first edition (1609), who mistakenly repeated the end of the first
   line. Among suggested replacements are "Thrall to," "Fooled by," "Rebuke," "Leagued with," and "Feeding." If you wish, suggest your own
   corrections. Which do you prefer?
2. In what tone of voice would you speak the first line? The last line? Trace
   the speaker's shifts in emotion throughout the poem.

 JOHN DONNE

*John Donne (1572–1631) was born into a Roman Catholic family in
England, but in the 1590s he abandoned that faith. In 1615 he became an Anglican priest and soon was known as a great preacher.
One hundred sixty of his sermons survive, including one with the famous line "No man is an island, entire of itself; every man is a piece
of the continent, a part of the main; if a clod be washed away by the
sea, Europe is the less . . . ; and therefore never send to know for whom
the bell tolls; it tolls for thee." From 1621 until his death he was dean
of St. Paul's Cathedral in London. His love poems (often bawdy and
cynical) are said to be his early work, and his "Holy Sonnets" (among
the greatest religious poems written in English) his later work.*

Holy Sonnet IV

At the round earth's imagined corners, blow
Your trumpets, angels, and arise, arise
From death, you numberless infinities

Of souls, and to your scattered bodies go,   4
All whom the flood did, and fire shall o'erthrow,
All whom war, dearth, age, agues, tyrannies,
Despair, law, chance, hath slain, and you whose eyes,
Shall behold God, and never taste death's woe.   8
But let them sleep, Lord, and me mourn a space,
For, if above all these, my sins abound,
'Tis late to ask abundance of thy grace,
When we are there; here on this lowly ground,   12
Teach me how to repent; for that's as good
As if thou hadst sealed° my pardon, with thy blood.

[1633]

¹⁴**sealed** confirmed, with a seal

🗒 TOPICS FOR CRITICAL THINKING AND WRITING

1. What is the speaker envisioning in the first four lines? Put into your own words the meaning of line 5.
2. What is the effect of piling up nouns in lines 6-7?
3. In which line is there the most marked change of tone? Why does the change occur?

Holy Sonnet XIV

Batter my heart, three-personed God; for you
As yet but knock, breathe, shine, and seek to mend;
That I may rise and stand, o'erthrow me, and bend
Your force, to break, blow, burn, and make me new.   4
I, like an usurped town, to another due,
Labor to admit you, but oh, to no end.
Reason, your viceroy in me, me should defend,
But is captived, and proves weak or untrue.   8
Yet dearly I love you, and would be loved fain,
But am betrothed unto your enemy:
Divorce me, untie, or break that knot again,
Take me to you, imprison me, for I   12
Except you enthrall me, never shall be free,
Nor ever chaste, except you ravish me.

[1633]

🗒 TOPICS FOR CRITICAL THINKING AND WRITING

1. Explain the paradoxes (apparent contradictions) in lines 1, 3, 13, and 14. Explain the double meanings of "enthrall" (line 13) and "ravish" (line 14).
2. In lines 1-4, what is god implicitly compared to (considering especially lines 2 and 4)? How does this comparison lead into the comparison that dominates lines 5-8? What words in lines 9-12 are especially related to the earlier lines?

3. What is gained by piling up verbs in lines 2–4?
4. Are sexual references necessarily irreverent in a religious poem? (Donne, incidentally, was an Anglican priest.)

 GEORGE HERBERT

George Herbert (1593–1633) served two years as a member of Parliament in England, but most of his adult life was spent as a clergyman. His poems were published posthumously a few months after his death, in a volume piously called THE TEMPLE.

We give two examples of a form known as SHAPED VERSE *or* PATTERNED POETRY. *The form originated in the ancient world; it was revived in the sixteenth century, chiefly by scholarly authors who imitated not only the forms but also the languages (Latin and Greek) of the originals. Poems in the shape of an altar were fairly common; other forms included a column, an egg, a heart, a boat, and a bottle.*

Easter Wings

Lord, who createdst man in wealth and store,°
Though foolishly he lost the same,
Decaying more and more
Till he became
Most poor: 5
With thee
O let me rise
As larks, harmoniously,
And sing this day thy victories:
Then shall the fall further the flight in me.   10

My tender age in sorrow did begin:
And still with sicknesses and shame
Thou didst so punish sin,
That I became
Most thin.   15
With thee
Let me combine,
And feel this day thy victory;
For, if I imp° my wing on thine,
Affliction shall advance the flight in me.   20

[1633]

 TOPICS FOR CRITICAL THINKING AND WRITING

1. In what ways is the shape—the form—relevant to the content? (Hint: Notice especially lines 5 and 15.)
2. Do you find the poem too cute? Explain

¹**store** abundance   ¹⁹**imp** gaft (a term from falconry)

The Altar

A broken A L T A R , Lord, thy servant rears,
Made of a heart, and cemented with tears:
  Whose parts are as thy hand did frame;
  No workman's tool hath touched the same.°
        A   H E A R T   alone   5
        Is   such   a   stone,
        As   nothing   but
        Thy power doth cut.
        Wherefore each part
        Of my hard heart   10
        Meets in this frame,
        To praise thy Name:
  That, if I chance to hold my peace,°
  These stones to praise thee may not cease.°
Oh let thy blessed S A C R I F I C E be mine,   15
And sanctify this   A L T A R   to be thine.

[1633]

4**No . . . same** Herbet has in mind a passage from the Hebrew Bible, in which God tells Moses to build an altar without using any tools: "And if thou wilt make me an altar of stone, thou shalt not build it of hewn stone: for if thou lift up thy tool upon it, thou hast polluted it" (Exodus 20.25)   13-14**That . . . cease** Herbert says that his poem praises God even when it is not being read or spoken

☞ TOPIC FOR CRITICAL THINKING OR WRITING

In what sense is the speaker's heart "cut" (5-9)?

Discipline

  Throw away thy rod,
Throw away thy wrath.
    O my God,
Take the gentle path.

  For my heart's desire   5
Unto thine is bent;
    I aspire
To a full consent.

  Not a word or look
I affect to own,   10
    But by book,
And thy book alone.

  Though I fail, I weep.
Though I halt in pace,
    Yet I creep   15
To the throne of grace.

Then let wrath remove;
Love will do the deed,
      For with love
Stony hearts will bleed.   20

Love is swift of foot,
Love's a man of war,
      And can shoot,
And can hit from far.

Who can 'scape his bow?   25
That which wrought on thee,
      Brought thee low,
Needs must work on me.

Throw away thy rod.
Though man frailties hath,   30
      Thou art God.
Throw away thy wrath.

[1633]

 ## TOPICS FOR CRITICAL THINKING AND WRITING

1. What do you think is the effect of the short third line in each stanza? Is the line prolonged in reading?
2. Is the poem "disciplined"? What do the lengths of the lines and the emphatic rhymes contribute?
3. How would you explain the paradox (lines 19–28) that love is warlike? What figure of speech is used in lines 21–24? Explain lines 26–27. Would "Love" be a better title than "Discipline"? Why?
4. Compare the tone of the last stanza with that of the first. Do you think the poem would be more effective if the last stanza were identical with the first? Why?
5. The Christian usually petitions God rather than commands Him. Do you find this poem offensively imperious? Explain.

 ## JOHN MILTON

John Milton (1608–74) was born into a well-to-do family in London, where from childhood he was a student of languages, mastering at an early age Latin, Greek, Hebrew, and most modern languages. Instead of becoming a minister in the Anglican Church, he resolved to become a poet and spent five years at his family's country home, reading. His attacks against the monarchy secured him a position in Oliver Cromwell's Puritan government as Latin secretary for foreign affairs. He became totally blind, but he continued his work through secretaries, one of whom was Andrew Marvell, author of "To His Coy Mistress" (page 820). With the restoration of the monarchy in 1660, Milton was for a time confined but was later pardoned in the general amnesty. Until his death he continued to work on many subjects, including his greatest poem, the epic Paradise Lost.

When I consider how my light is spent

When I consider how my light is spent
  Ere half my days, in this dark world and wide,
  And that one talent which is death to hide°
  Lodged with me useless,° though my soul more bent   4
To serve therewith my Maker, and present
  My true account, lest he returning chide;
  "Doth God exact day-labor, light denied?"
  I fondly° ask; but Patience to prevent°   8
That murmur, soon replies, "God doth not need
  Either man's work or his own gifts; who best
  Bear his mild yoke, they serve him best. His state
Is kingly. Thousands at his bidding speed   12
  And post o'er land and ocean without rest:
  They also serve who only stand and wait."

[1655]

³There is a pun in *talent,* relating Milton's literary talent to Christ's Parable of the Talents (Matthew 25:14 ff.), in which a servant is rebuked for not putting his talent (a unit of money) to use   ⁴**useless** a pun on *use,* i.e., usury, interest   ⁸**fondly** foolishly.   **prevent** forestall

 ## TOPICS FOR CRITICAL THINKING AND WRITING

1. This sonnet is sometimes called "On His Blindness," though Milton never gave it a title. Do you think this title gets toward the heart of the poem? Explain. If you were to give it a title, what would the title be?
2. Read the parable in Matthew 25.14–30, and then consider how close the parable is to Milton's life as Milton describes it in this poem.

 ## WILLIAM BLAKE

William Blake (1757–1827) was born in London and at 14 was apprenticed for seven years to an engraver. A Christian visionary poet, he made his living by giving drawing lessons and by illustrating books, including his own Songs of Innocence *(1789) and* Songs of Experience *(1794). These two books represent, he said, "two contrary states of the human soul." ("The Lamb" come from Innocense and "The Tyger" comes from* Experience.*) In 1809 Blake exhibited his art, but the show was a failure. Not until he was in his sixties, when he stopped writing poetry, did he achieve any public recognition—and then it was as a painter.*

The Lamb

  Little Lamb, who made thee?
  Dost thou know who made thee?
Gave thee life, and bid thee feed

By the stream and o'er the mead;
Gave thee clothing of delight,   5
Softest clothing, wooly, bright;
Gave thee such a tender voice,
Making all the vales rejoice?
   Little Lamb, who made thee?
   Dost thou know who made thee?   10

   Little Lamb, I'll tell thee,
   Little Lamb, I'll tell thee:
He is callèd by thy name,
For he calls himself a Lamb.
He is meek, and he is mild;   15
He became a little child.
I a child, and thou a lamb,
We are callèd by his name.
   Little Lamb, God bless thee!
   Little Lamb, God bless thee!   20

[1789]

The Tyger

Tyger! Tyger! burning bright
In the forests of the night,
What immortal hand or eye
Could frame thy fearful symmetry?   4

In what distant deeps or skies
Burnt the fire of thine eyes?
On what wings dare he aspire?
What the hand dare seize the fire?   8

And what shoulder, and what art,
Could twist the sinews of thy heart?
And, when thy heart began to beat,
What dread hand? and what dread feet?   12

What the hammer? what the chain?
In what furnace was thy brain?
What the anvil? what dread grasp
Dare its deadly terrors clasp?   16

When the stars threw down their spears,
And watered heaven with their tears,
Did he smile his work to see?
Did he who made the lamb make thee?   20

Tyger! Tyger! burning bright
In the forests of the night,
What immortal hand or eye,
Dare frame thy fearful symmetry?   24

[1794]

TOPICS FOR CRITICAL THINKING AND WRITING

1. Why do you suppose Blake answers the question in "The Lamb" but does not answer the questions in "The Tyger"?
2. Read aloud, two or three times, the first two lines of each poem. Of course the words are different, but don't you also find yourself reading in a somewhat different way? How can you account for this change?
3. As our introductory note says, "The Lamb" was first published in *Songs of Innocence* (1789), "The Tyger" in *Songs of Experience* (1794). Blake characterized the volumes as "Showing contrary states of the Human Soul." What do you think he meant by this?

 EMILY DICKINSON

Emily Dickinson (1830-86) was born into a proper New England family in Amherst, Massachusetts. Although she spent her seventeenth year a few miles away, at Mount Holyoke Seminary (now Mount Holyoke College), in her twenties and thirties she left Amherst only five or six times, and in her last twenty years she may never have left her house. Her brother was probably right when he said that having seen something of the rest of the world—she had visited Washington with her father when he was a member of Congress— "she could not resist the feeling that it was painfully hollow. It was to her so thin and unsatisfying in the face of the Great Realities of Life."

Dickinson lived with her parents (a somewhat reclusive mother and an austere, remote father) and a younger sister; a married brother lived in the house next door. She did, however, form some passionate attachments, to women as well as men, but there is no evidence that they found physical expression.

By the age of 12 Dickinson was writing witty letters, but she apparently did not write more than an occasional poem before her late twenties. At her death—she died in the house where she was born— she left 1,775 poems, only seven of which had been published (anonymously) during her lifetime.

Those—dying then

Those—dying then,
Knew where they went
They went to God's Right Hand—
The Hand is amputated now
And God cannot be found—   5

The abdication of Belief
Makes the Behavior small—
Better an ignis fatuus
Than no illume at all—

[1882]

TOPICS FOR CRITICAL THINKING AND WRITING

1. In a sentence or two, state the point of the poem.
2. Is the image in line 4 in poor taste? Explain.
3. What is an "ignis fatuus?" In what ways does it connect visually with traditional images of hell and heaven?

There's a certain Slant of light

There's a certain Slant of light,
Winter Afternoons—
That oppresses, like the Heft°
Of Cathedral Tunes—   4

Heavenly Hurt, it gives us—
We can find no scar,
But internal difference,
Where the Meanings, are—   8

None may teach it—Any—
'Tis the Seal Despair—
An imperial affliction
Sent us of the Air—   12

When it comes, the Landscape listens—
Shadows—hold their breath—
When it goes, 'tis like the Distance
On the look of Death—   16

[c. 1861]

TOPICS FOR CRITICAL THINKING AND WRITING

1. In the first stanza, what kind or kinds of music does "Cathedral Tunes" suggest? In what ways might they (and the light to which they are compared) be oppressive?
2. In the second stanza, the effect on us of the light is further described. Try to paraphrase Dickinson's lines, or interpret them. Compare your paraphrase or interpretation with that of a classmate or someone else who has read the poem. Are your interpretations similar? If not, can you account for some of the differences?
3. In the third stanza, how would you interpret "None may teach it"? Is the idea "No one can instruct (or tame) the light to be different"? Or "No one can teach us what we learn from the light"? Or do you have a different reading of this line?
4. "Death" is the last word of the poem. Rereading the poem, how early (and in what words or images) do you think "death" is suggested or foreshadowed?

3 **Heft** heaviness, weight

5. Try to describe the rhyme scheme. Then, a more difficult business, try to describe the effect of the rhyme scheme. Does it work with or against the theme, or meaning, of the poem?

6. What is the relationship in the poem between the light as one might experience it in New England on a winter afternoon and the experience of despair? To put it crudely, does the light itself cause despair, or does Dickinson see the light as an image or metaphor for human despair? And how is despair related to death?

7. Overall, how would you describe the tone of the poem? Anguished? Serene? Resigned?

This World is not Conclusion

This World is not Conclusion.
A Species stands beyond—
Invisible, as Music—
But positive, as Sound—   4
It beckons, and it baffles—
Philosophy—dont know—
And through a Riddle, at the last—
Sagacity, must go—   8
To guess it, puzzles scholars—
To gain it, Men have borne
Contempt of Generations
And Crucifixion, shown—   12
Faith slips—and laughs, and rallies—
Blushes, if any see—
Plucks at a twig of Evidence—
And asks a Vane, the way—   16
Much Gesture, from the Pulpit—
Strong Hallelujahs roll—
Narcotics cannot still the Tooth
That nibbles at the soul—   20

[c. 1862]

✏ TOPICS FOR CRITICAL THINKING AND WRITING

1. Given the context of the first two lines, what do you think "Conclusion" means in the first line?

2. Although white spaces are not used to divide the poem into stanzas, the poem seems to be constructed in units of four lines each. Summarize each four-line unit in a sentence or two.

3. Compare your summaries with those of a classmate. If you substantially disagree, reread the poem to see if, on reflection, one or the other of you seems in closer touch with the poem. Or does the poem (or some part of it) allow for two very different interpretations?

4. In the first four lines the speaker seems (to use a word from line 4) quite "positive." Do some or all of the following stanzas seem less positive? If so, which—and what makes you say so?
5. Would you agree with a reader who said that "Much Gesture, from the Pulpit" (line 17) suggests—by its vigorous action—*a lack* of deep conviction?

 ## CHRISTINA ROSSETTI

Christina Rossetti (1830-94) was the daughter of an exiled Italian patriot who lived in London and the sister of the poet and painter Dante Gabriel Rossetti. After her father became an invalid, she led an extremely ascetic life, devoting most of her life to doing charitable work. Her first and best-known volume of poetry, Goblin Market and Other Poems, *was published in 1862.*

Amor Mundi*

"Oh where are you going with your love-locks flowing,
　On the west wind blowing along this valley track?"
"The downhill path is easy, come with me an it please ye,
　We shall escape the uphill by never turning back."　　　　4

So they two went together in glowing August weather,
　The honey-breathing heather lay to their left and right;
And dear she was to doat on, her swift feet seemed to float on
　The air like soft twin pigeons too sportive to alight.　　　8

"Oh what is that in heaven where grey cloud-flakes are seven,
　Where blackest clouds hang riven just as the rainy skirt?"
"Oh that's a meteor sent us, a message dumb, portentous,
　An undeciphered solemn signal of help or hurt."　　　　12

"Oh what is that glides quickly where velvet flowers grow thickly,
　Their scent comes rich and sickly?" "A scaled and hooded worm."
"Oh what's that in the hollow, so pale I quake to follow?"
　"Oh that's a thin dead body which waits the eternal term."　16

"Turn again, O my sweetest,—turn again, false and fleetest:
　This beaten way thou beatest, I fear, is hell's own track."
"Nay, too steep for hill mounting; nay, too late for cost counting:
　This downhill path is easy, but there's no turning back."　20

[1865]

*****Amor Mundi** Latin for "love of the world." *World* here has the sense, common in the New Testament, of an arena of sin, or of human alienation from God.

TOPICS FOR CRITICAL THINKING AND WRITING

1. Taking into account "she" in line 7, try to assign all of the quoted passages, giving some to this "she" and the others to (presumably) a "he." Is it clear whether the seducer is male or female?
2. The speaker of the last line of the poem says, "There's no turning back." Do you assume that the reader is to believe this assertion? Why, or why not? Christina Rossetti was a devout Anglo Catholic, but could one use this poem as evidence that she sometimes had moments of doubt about the possibility of free will and of salvation?
3. The poem uses anapests, feminine rhymes, and internal rhymes (on these terms, see the glossary at the rear of this book). What is their cumulative effect here?

Uphill

Does the road wind uphill all the way?
   Yes, to the very end.
Will the day's journey take the whole long day?
   From morn to night, my friend.   4

But is there for the night a resting-place?
   A roof for when the slow dark hours begin.
May not the darkness hide it from my face?
   You cannot miss that inn.   8

Shall I meet other wayfarers at night?
   Those who have gone before.
Then must I knock, or call when just in sight?
   They will not keep you standing at that door.   12

Shall I find comfort, travel-sore and weak?
   Of labor you shall find the sum.
Will there be beds for me and all who seek?
   Yea, beds for all who come.   16

[1858]

TOPICS FOR CRITICAL THINKING AND WRITING

1. Suppose that someone told you this poem is about a person preparing to go on a hike. The person is supposedly making inquiries about the road and the possible hotel arrangements. What would you reply?
2. Who is the questioner? A woman? A man? All human beings collectively? "Uphill," unlike Rossetti's "Amor Mundi" (see the previous poem), does not use quotation marks to distinguish between two speakers. Can one say that in "Uphill" the questioner and the answerer are the same person?

3. Are the answers unambiguously comforting? Or can it, for instance, be argued that the "roof" is (perhaps among other things) the lid of a coffin—hence the questioner will certainly not be kept "standing at that door"? If the poem can be read along these lines, is it chilling rather than comforting?

 ## GERARD MANLEY HOPKINS

Gerard Manly Hopkins (1844-89) was born near London and was educated at Oxford, where he studied Classics. A convert from Anglicanism to Roman Catholicism, he was ordained a Jesuit priest in 1877. After serving as a parish priest and teacher, he was appointed Professor of Greek at the Catholic University in Dublin.

Hopkins published only a few poems during his lifetime, partly because he believed that the pursuit of literary fame was incompatible with his vocation as a priest, and partly because he was aware that his highly individual style might puzzle readers.

God's Grandeur

The world is charged with the grandeur of God.
  It will flame out, like shining from shook foil;
  It gathers to a greatness, like the ooze of oil
Crushed. Why do men then now not reck his rod?   4
Generations have trod, have trod, have trod;
  And all is seared with trade; bleared, smeared with toil;
  And wears man's smudge and shares man's smell: the soil
Is bare now, nor can foot feel, being shod.   8

And for all this, nature is never spent;
  There lives the dearest freshness deep down things;
And though the last lights off the black West went
  Oh, morning, at the brown brink eastward, springs—   12
Because the Holy Ghost over the bent
  World broods with warm breast and with ah! bright wings.

[1877]

 ## TOPICS FOR CRITICAL THINKING AND WRITING

1. Hopkins, a Roman Catholic priest, lived in England during the last decades of the nineteenth century—that is, in an industrialized society. Where in the poem do you find him commenting on his setting? Circle the words in the poem that can refer both to England's physical appearance and to the sinful condition of human beings.

2. What is the speaker's tone in the first three and one-half lines (through "Crushed")? In the rest of line 4? In lines 5–8? Is the second part of the

sonnet (the next six lines) more unified in *tone* or less? In an essay of 500 words describe the shifting tones of the speaker's voice. Probably after writing a first draft you will be able to form a thesis that describes an overall pattern. As you revise your drafts, make sure that (1) the thesis is clear to the reader, and (2) it is adequately supported by brief quotations.

Pied* Beauty

Glory be to God for dappled things—
    For skies of couple-colour as a brinded° cow;
      For rose-moles all in stipple° upon trout that swim;
Fresh-firecoal chestnut-falls°; finches' wings;   4
    Landscape plotted and pieced—fold, fallow, and plough;°
      And áll trádes, their gear and tackle and trim.°
All things counter, original, spare° strange;
    Whatever is fickle, freckled (who knows how?)   8
      With swift, slow; sweet, sour; adazzle, dim;
He fathers-forth whose beauty is past change:
                Praise him.

[1877]

📓 TOPICS FOR CRITICAL THINKING AND WRITING

1. The poem begins by praising God and then quickly introduces landscape elements and the animal and vegetable worlds. Why do you suppose Hopkins introduced these before human elements? By the way, exactly where in the poem do you find the first implication of the human world?

2. What might be some specific examples of the "gear and tackle and trim" (line 6) that Hopkins would have seen in the late nineteenth century? What "gear and tackle and trim" have you seen that appeals to you?

3. What is the connection between the first line and line 10? Do you find the relationship contradictory? Or *apparently* contradictory rather than truly contradictory?

4. Read the poem aloud, at least twice. Do certain phrases or even whole lines especially appeal to you? If so, try to explain why they give pleasure.

5. As the introductory biographical note says, Hopkins was a Roman Catholic priest. Do you think that a reader has to be a Roman Catholic—or any sort of Christian—to enjoy the poem? Explain.

***Pied** of two or more colors   ²**brinded** brindled, brownish-orange steaked with gray   ³**stipple** dots, colored specks   ⁴**chestnut-falls** freshly fallen chestnuts, which look like glowing coals   ⁵**fold, fallow, and plough** i.e, fields (1) fenced to contain animals, (2) lying fallow, (3) cultivated   ⁶**tackle and trim** equipment
⁷**spare** rare

The Windhover:*

To Christ our Lord

I caught this morning morning's minion, king-
    dom of daylight's dauphin,° dapple-dawn-drawn Falcon, in
      his riding
    Of the rolling level underneath him steady air, and striding
High there, how he rung° upon the rein of a wimpling° wing
In his ecstasy! then off, off forth on swing,   5
    As a skate's heel sweeps smooth on a bow-bend: the hurl
      and gliding
    Rebuffed the big wind. My heart is hiding
Stirred for a bird,—the achieve of, the mastery of the thing!

Brute beauty and valour and act, oh, air, pride, plume, here
    Buckle!° AND the fire that breaks from thee° then, a billion   10
Times told lovelier, more dangerous, O my chevalier!

    No wonder of it: shéer plód makes plough down sillion°
Shine, and blue-break embers, ah my dear,
    Fall, gall° themselves, and gash gold-vermillion.

[1877]

*Windhover a small hawk, a kestrel   ²dauphin the heir to the French throne
⁴rung a term from horsemanship (the horse is trained, on a long rein, to make a circle).   wimpling wing rippling wing   ¹⁰Buckle suggested meanings include "join"
or "fasten together" and "collapse" or "crumple"   thee Christ, called "my chevalier" in the next line   ¹²sillion a furrow

📋 TOPICS FOR CRITICAL THINKING AND WRITING

1. The poem is either dedicated to Christ or addressed to Christ. How does this influence your reading of the last line, or the last two lines?
2. The footnotes suggest alternative readings for "Buckle" (line 10). Which of the readings do you prefer—or do you think both meanings, and perhaps others too, are appropriate here? Explain.
3. What connections does Hopkins seem to make between the bird and Christ? And, judging from this poem, what is Hopkins's view of God?

Thou Art Indeed Just, Lord

Justus quidem tu es, Domine, si disputem tecum: verumtamen justa
loquar ad te: Quare via impiorum prosperatur? etc.
          (Jeremiah 12:1, translated in lines 1-3)

Thou art indeed just, Lord, if I contend
With thee; but, sir, so what I plead is just.
Why do sinners' ways prosper? and why must
Disappointment all I endeavor end?

Wert thou my enemy, O thou my friend,   5
How wouldst thou worse, I wonder, than thou dost
Defeat, thwart me? Oh, the sots and thralls of lust
Do in spare hours more thrive than I that spend,
Sir, life upon thy cause. See, banks and brakes
Now, leavèd how thick! lacèd they are again   10
With fretty chervil, look, and fresh wind shakes
Them; birds build—but not I build; no, but strain,
Time's eunuch, and not breed one work that wakes
Mine, O thou lord of life, send my roots rain.

                                                                [1889]

 ## TOPICS FOR CRITICAL THINKING AND WRITING

1. How would you describe the tone of the first part of the first line, up
   through "Lord"? How would you describe the tone of "sir," in the second line? (Speak the lines aloud a few times, until you feel that you have
   a good grasp of the speaker's mental state.)
2. A critic, Yvor Winters, in *Of Modern Poetry* complains that in lines
   9–12 Hopkins "goes into a trivial passage about [nature]; the birds and
   blossoms which he describes are outside of the moral order and are irrelevant to the problems which he has posed." Do you agree or disagree? Why?

 ## PAUL LAURENCE DUNBAR

*Paul Laurence Dunbar (1872–1906), born in Ohio to parents who
had been slaves in Kentucky, achieved fame for his dialect poetry. He
published early—even while in high school—and by 1896, with the
publication of* Lyrics of Lowly Life, *he had three books to his credit.*
Lyrics of Lowly Life *was equipped with a preface by William Dean
Howells, a leading man of literature of the day.*

*Because Dunbar often used African-American speech patterns
and pronunciation, as in "An Ante-Bellum Sermon" (from* Lyrics of
Lowly Life), *his work was sometimes thought to present demeaning
racial stereotypes and to glorify plantation life, but in recent years
critics have seen the protest beneath the quaint surface.*

An Ante-Bellum Sermon*

We is gathahed hyeah, my brothahs,
  In dis howlin' wildaness,
Fu' to speak some words of comfo't
  To each othah in distress.   4

---

*A sermon preached before the Civil War

An' we chooses fu' ouah subjic'
  Dis—we'll 'splain it by an' by;
"An' de Lawd said, 'Moses, Moses,'
  An' de man said, 'Hyeah am I.'"°   8

Now ole Pher'oh, down in Egypt,
  Was de wuss man evah bo'n,
An' he had de Hebrew chillun
  Down dah wukin' in his co'n;   12
'T well de Lawd got tiahed o' his foolin',
  An' sez he: "I'll let him know—
Look hyeah, Moses, go tell Pher'oh
  Fu' to let dem chillun go."   16

"An' ef he refuse to do it,
  I will make him rue de houah,
Fu' I'll empty down on Egypt
  All de vials of my powah."   20
Yes, he did—an' Pher'oh's ahmy
  Was n't wuth a ha'f a dime;
Fu' de Lawd will he'p his chillun,
  You kin trust him evah time.   24

An' yo' enemies may 'sail you
  In de back an' in de front;
But de Lawd is all aroun' you,
  Fu' to ba' de battle's brunt.   28
Dey kin fo'ge yo' chains an' shackles
  F'om de mountains to de sea;
But de Lawd will sen' some Moses
  Fu' to set his chillun free.   32

An' de lan' shall hyeah his thundah,
  Lak a blas' f'om Gab'el's ho'n,
Fu' de Lawd of hosts is mighty
  When he girds his ahmor on.   36
But fu' feah some one mistakes me,
  I will pause right hyeah to say,
Dat I'm still a-preachin' ancient,
  I ain't talkin' 'bout to-day.   40

But I tell you, fellah christuns,
  Things 'll happen mighty strange;
Now, de Lawd done dis fu' Isrul,
  An' his ways don't nevah change,   44
An' de love he showed to Isrul
  Was n't all on Isrul spent;
Now don't run an' tell yo' mastahs
  Dat I's preachin' discontent.   48

'Cause I is n't; I'se a-judgin'
  Bible people by deir ac's;
I'se a-givin' you de Scriptuah,
  I'se a-handin' you de fac's.   52

7-8**Lawd . . . am I** in Exodus 3.4 God calls Moses, and Moses responds, "Here am I"

Cose ole Pher'oh b'lieved in slav'ry,
  But de Lawd he let him see,
Dat de people he put bref in,—
  Evah mothah's son was free.   56

An' dahs othahs thinks lak Pher'oh,
  But dey calls de Scriptuah liar,
Fu' de Bible says "a servant
  Is a-worthy of his hire."   60
An' you cain't git roun' nor thoo dat,
  An' you cain't git ovah it,
Fu' whatevah place you git in,
  Dis hyeah Bible too 'll fit.   64

So you see de Lawd's intention,
  Evah sence de worl' began,
Was dat His almighty freedom
  Should belong to evah man,   68
But I think it would be bettah,
  Ef I'd pause agin to say,
Dat I'm talkin' 'bout ouah freedom
  In a Bibleistic way.   72

But de Moses is a-comin',
  An' he's comin', suah and fas'
We kin hyeah his feet a-trompin',
  We kin hyeah his trumpit blas'.   76
But I want to wa'n you people,
  Don't you git too brigity;
An' don't you git to braggin'
  'Bout dese things, you wait an' see.   80

But when Moses wif his powah
  Comes an' sets us chillun free,
We will praise de gracious Mastah
  Dat has gin us liberty;   84
An' we'll shout ouah halleluyahs,
  On dat mighty reck'nin' day,
When we'se reco'nised ez citiz'—
  Huh uh! Chillun, let us pray!   88

[1896]

TOPICS FOR CRITICAL THINKING AND WRITING

1. Who is the "gracious Mastah" mentioned in line 83?
2. The biographical headnote mentions that some readers disapprove of the use of dialect. What is your position on this issue?

ROBERT FROST

*Robert Frost (1874–1963) was born in California. After his father's
death in 1885 Frost's mother brought the family to New England,*

where she taught in high schools in Massachusetts and New Hampshire. Frost studied for part of one term at Dartmouth College in New Hampshire, then did odd jobs (including teaching), and from 1897 to 1899 was enrolled as a special student at Harvard. He then farmed in New Hampshire, published a few poems in local newspapers, left the farm and taught again, and in 1912 left for England, where he hoped to achieve more popular success as a writer. By 1915 he had won a considerable reputation, and he returned to the United States, settling on a farm in New Hampshire and cultivating the image of the country-wise farmer-poet. In fact he was well read in the classics, the Bible, and English and American literature.

Design

I found a dimpled spider, fat and white,
On a white heal-all, holding up a moth
Like a white piece of rigid satin cloth—
Assorted characters of death and blight   4
Mixed ready to begin the morning right,
Like the ingredients of a witches' broth—
A snow-drop spider, a flower like froth,
And dead wings carried like a paper kite.   8

What had that flower to do with being white,
The wayside blue and innocent heal-all?
What brought the kindred spider to that height,
Then steered the white moth thither in the night?   12
What but design of darkness to appall?—
If design govern in a thing so small.

[1936]

 TOPICS FOR CRITICAL THINKING AND WRITING

1. Do you find the spider as described in line 1, cute or disgusting? Why?
2. What is the effect of "If" in the last line?
3. The word "design" can mean "pattern" (as in "a pretty design"), or it can mean "intention," especially an evil intention (as in "He had designs on her"). Does Frost use the word in one sense or in both? Explain.

The Most of It

He thought he kept the universe alone;
For all the voice in answer he could wake
Was but the mocking echo of his own
From some tree-hidden cliff across the lake.
Some morning from the boulder-broken beach   5
He would cry out on life, that what it wants
Is not its own love back in copy speech,
But counter-love, original response.

And nothing ever came of what he cried
Unless it was the embodiment that crashed   10
In the cliff's talus on the other side,
And then in the far distant water splashed,
But after a time allowed for it to swim,
Instead of proving human when it neared
And someone else additional to him,   15
As a great buck it powerfully appeared,
Pushing the crumpled water up ahead,
And landed pouring like a waterfall,
And stumbled through the rocks with horny tread,
And forced the underbrush—and that was all.   20

[1942]

 TOPICS FOR CRITICAL THINKING AND WRITING

1. What do you think the first line means? And (given the rest of the
   poem) what sort of person is "he"?
2. Frost originally called the poem "Making the Most of It." Which title do
   you prefer, and why?
3. If wherever in the poem we have "he," "his," and "him" Frost had instead written "I," "my," and "me," how different would the poem be?

 T. S. ELIOT

*Thomas Stearns Eliot (1888-1965) was born into a New England
family that had moved to St. Louis. He attended a preparatory school
in Massachusetts; then graduated from Harvard and did further
study in literature and philosophy in France, Germany, and England.
In 1914 he began working for Lloyd's Bank in London, and three
years later he published his first book of poems. In 1925 he joined a
publishing firm, and in 1927 he became a British citizen and a member of the Church of England. In 1948 Eliot received the Nobel Prize
for Literature.*

*"Journey of the Magi," published shortly before Eliot announced
his conversion, is spoken by one of the Magi, that is, by one of the
Wise Men who, according to Matthew 2.1-2, 9-10, followed a star to
Bethlehem, where they paid homage to the infant Jesus. The first five
lines are enclosed within quotation marks because they are derived,
with slight changes, from a sermon on the Nativity by Bishop
Lancelot Andrewes (1555-1626), preached at Christmas in 1622. In
line 24 the three trees prefigure the three crosses of Matthew 27.38.
The white horse in line 25 is indebted to Revelation 6.2 and 19.11,
and perhaps it is also indebted to G. K. Chesterton's* The Ballad of the
White Horse, *in which the disappearance of the horse represents the
disappearance of paganism at the advent of Christianity. The vine
(line 26) is often associated with Christ; see, for example, John
15.1-6. Line 27 ("dicing for pieces of silver") may allude to Matthew*

27.3-6 (Judas is paid in silver) and 35 (the soldiers cast lots for Jesus's clothes).

Journey of the Magi

'A cold coming we had of it,
Just the worst time of the year
For a journey, and such a long journey:
The ways deep and the weather sharp,
The very dead of winter.'   5
And the camels galled, sore-footed, refractory,
Lying down in the melting snow.
There were times we regretted
The summer palaces on slopes, the terraces,
And the silken girls bringing sherbet.   10
Then the camel men cursing and grumbling
And running away, and wanting their liquor and women,
And the night-fires going out, and the lack of shelters,
And the cities hostile and the towns unfriendly
And the villages dirty and charging high prices: 15
A hard time we had of it.
At the end we preferred to travel all night,
Sleeping in snatches,
With the voices singing in our ears, saying
That this was all folly.   20

Then at dawn we came down to a temperate valley,
Wet, below the snow line, smelling of vegetation;
With a running stream and a water-mill beating the darkness,
And three trees on the low sky,
And an old white horse galloped away in the meadow.   25
Then we came to a tavern with vine-leaves over the lintel,
Six hands at an open door dicing for pieces of silver,
And feet kicking the empty wine-skins.
But there was no information, and so we continued
And arrived at evening, not a moment too soon   30
Finding the place; it was (you may say) satisfactory.

All this was a long time ago, I remember,
And I would do it again, but set down
This set down
This: were we led all that way for   35
Birth or Death? There was a Birth, certainly,
We had evidence and no doubt. I had seen birth and death,
But had thought they were different; this Birth was
Hard and bitter agony for us, like Death, our death.
We returned to our places, these Kingdoms,   40
But no longer at ease here, in the old dispensation,
With an alien people clutching their gods.
I should be glad of another death.

                                                              [1927]

TOPIC FOR CRITICAL THINKING AND WRITING

In the first stanza, what is the speaker's attitude toward the palaces he has left behind? What is his attitude in the last stanza? How do you explain the difference?

 ## KRISTINE BATEY

We have been unable to find any biographical information about Ms. Batey.

Lot's Wife

While Lot, the conscience of a nation,
struggles with the Lord,
she struggles with the housework.
The City of Sin is where
she raises the children.   5
Ba'al or Adonai—
Whoever is God—
the bread must still be made
and the doorsill swept.
The Lord may kill the children tomorrow,   10
but today they must be bathed and fed.
Well and good to condemn your neighbor's religion;
but weren't they there
when the baby was born,
and when the well collapsed?   15
While her husband communes with God—
she tucks the children into bed.
In the morning, when he tells her of the judgment,
she puts down the lamp she is cleaning
and calmly begins to pack.   20
In between bundling up the children
and deciding what will go,
she runs for a moment
to say goodbye to the herd,
gently patting each soft head   25
with tears in her eyes for the animals that will not understand.
She smiles blindly to the woman
who held her hand at childbed.
It is easy for eyes that have always turned to heaven
not to look back;   30
those that have been—by necessity—drawn to earth
cannot forget that life is lived from day to day.
Good, to a God, and good in human terms
are two different things.

On the breast of the hill, she chooses to be human,   35
and turns, in farewell—
and never regrets
the sacrifice.

[1978]

 TOPICS FOR CRITICAL THINKING AND WRITING

1. The story of the pious Lot, his wife, and the destruction of the wicked
   city of Sodom is told in the Old Testament, in Genesis 19.1–28. Briefly,
   Lot sheltered two angels who, in the form of men, visited him in
   Sodom. The townspeople sought to rape the angels, and the city was
   marked for destruction, but the angels warned Lot's family and urged
   them to flee and not to look back. Lot's wife, however, looked back and
   was turned into a pillar of salt. What was the message of the biblical
   tale? What does Batey see in the original tale? Do you find her interpretation compelling? Why?
2. In line 35, why "breast" instead of, say "crest" or "foot"?
3. Exactly what is "the sacrifice" Lot's wife makes in the last line?

 JUDITH ORTIZ COFER

*Born in Puerto Rico in 1952 of a Puerto Rican mother and a United
States mainland father who served in the Navy, Judith Ortiz Cofer
was educated both in Puerto Rico and on the mainland. After earning a bachelor's and a master's degree in English, she did further
graduate work at Oxford and then taught English in Florida. She has
published seven volumes of poetry.*

Latin Women Pray

Latin women pray
In incense sweet churches
They pray in Spanish to an Anglo God
With a Jewish heritage.   4
And this Great White Father
Imperturbable in his marble pedestal
Looks down upon his brown daughters
Votive candles shining like lust   8
In his all seeing eyes
Unmoved by their persistent prayers.

Yet year after year
Before his image they kneel   12
Margarita Josefina Maria and Isabel

All fervently hoping
That if not omnipotent
At least he be bilingual   16

                                                        [1987]

 ## TOPICS FOR CRITICAL THINKING AND WRITING

1. Explain Cofer's assertion that Latin women pray "to an Anglo God /
   With Jewish heritage," and that this God is a "Great White Father."
2. Is the poem only a joke? If it is more than a joke, explain what the
   "more" is.

Drama

A NOTE ON GREEK TRAGEDY

Little or nothing is known for certain of the origin of Greek tragedy. The most
common hypothesis holds that it developed from improvised speeches during
choral dances honoring Dionysos, a Greek nature god associated with spring,
fertility, and wine. Thespis (who perhaps never existed) is said to have introduced an actor into these choral performances in the sixth century B.C. Aeschylus (525–456 B.C.), Greece's first great writer of tragedies, added the second
actor, and Sophocles (496?–406 B.C.) added the third actor and fixed the size of
the chorus at fifteen. (Because the chorus leader often functioned as an additional actor, and because the actors sometimes doubled in their parts, a Greek
tragedy could have more characters than might at first be thought.)

All of the extant great Greek tragedy is of the fifth century B.C. It was performed at religious festivals in the winter and early spring, in large outdoor am-
phitheaters built on hillsides. Some of these theaters were enormous; the one at
Epidaurus held about fifteen thousand people. The audience sat in tiers, looking
down on the *orchestra* (a dancing place), with the acting area behind it and the
skene (the scene building) yet farther back. The scene building served as dressing room, background (suggesting a palace or temple), and place for occasional
entrances and exits. Furthermore, this building helped to provide good
acoustics, for speech travels well if there is a solid barrier behind the speaker
and a hard, smooth surface in front of him, and if the audience sits in tiers. The
wall of the scene building provided the barrier; the orchestra provided the surface in front of the actors; and the seats on the hillside fulfilled the third requirement. Moreover, the acoustics were somewhat improved by slightly elevating
the actors above the orchestra, but it is not known exactly when this platform
was first constructed in front of the scene building.

A tragedy commonly begins with a *prologos* (prologue), during which the
exposition is given. Next comes the *parodos,* the chorus's ode of entrance, sung
while the chorus marches into the theater, through the side aisles and onto the
orchestra. The *epeisodion* (episode) is the ensuing scene; it is followed by a

Greek theater of Epidaurus on the Peloponnesus east of Nauplia.
(Frederick Ayer, Photo Researchers)

stasimon (choral song, ode). Usually there are four or five *epeisodia,* alternating
with *stasima.* Each of these choral odes has a *strophe* (lines presumably sung
while the chorus dances in one direction) and an *antistrophe* (lines presumably
sung while the chorus retraces its steps). Sometimes a third part, an *epode,* concludes an ode. (In addition to odes that are *stasima,* there can be odes within
episodes; the fourth episode of *Antigonê* (here called Scene IV) contains an ode
complete with *epode.*) After the last part of the last ode comes the *exodos,* the
epilogue or final scene.

The actors (all male) wore masks, and they seem to have chanted much of
the play. Perhaps the total result of combining speech with music and dancing
was a sort of music-drama roughly akin to opera with some spoken dialogue, like
Mozart's *Magic Flute.*

SOPHOCLES

*One of the three great writers of tragedies in ancient Greece, Sopho-
cles (496?–406 B.C.) was born in Colonus, near Athens, into a well-to-
do family. Well educated, he first won public acclaim as a tragic poet*

Laurence Olivier in *Oedipus Rex* (Photograph by John Vickers)

*at the age of 27, in 468 B.C., when he defeated Aeschylus in a compe-
tition for writing a tragic play. He is said to have written some 120
plays, but only 7 tragedies are extant; among them are* Oedipus Rex,
Antigonê, *and* Oedipus at Colonus. *He died, much honored, in his
ninetieth year, in Athens, where he had lived his entire life.*

Oedipus Rex

An English Version by Dudley Fitts and Robert Fitzgerald

LIST OF CHARACTERS

OEDIPUS
A PRIEST
CREON
TEIRESIAS
IOCASTÊ
MESSENGER
SHEPHERD OF LAÏOS
SECOND MESSENGER
CHORUS OF THEBAN ELDERS

SCENE: *Before the palace of* OEDIPUS, *King of Thebes. A central door and
two lateral doors open onto a platform which runs the length of the facade. On the platform, right and left, are altars; and three steps lead down
into the "orchestra," or chorus-ground. At the beginning of the action
these steps are crowded by* SUPPLIANTS *who have brought branches and
chaplets of olive leaves and who lie in various attitudes of despair.* OEDIPUS
enters.

Prologue

OEDIPUS. My children, generations of the living
    In the line of Kadmos,° nursed at his ancient hearth;
    Why have you strewn yourselves before these altars
    In supplication, with your boughs and garlands?
    The breath of incense rises from the city   5
    With a sound of prayer and lamentation.
                             Children,
    I would not have you speak through messengers,
    And therefore I have come myself to hear you—
    I, Oedipus, who bear the famous name.
    [To a PRIEST.*]* You, there, since you are eldest in the company,   10
    Speak for them all, tell me what preys upon you,
    Whether you come in dread, or crave some blessing:
    Tell me, and never doubt that I will help you
    In every way I can; I should be heartless
    Were I not moved to find you suppliant here.   15
PRIEST. Great Oedipus, O powerful King of Thebes!
    You see how all the ages of our people
    Cling to your altar steps: here are boys
    Who can barely stand alone, and here are priests
    By weight of age, as I am a priest of God,   20
    And young men chosen from those yet unmarried;
    As for the others, all that multitude,
    They wait with olive chaplets in the squares,
    At the two shrines of Pallas,° and where Apollo°
    Speaks in the glowing embers.
                       Your own eyes   25
    Must tell you: Thebes is in her extremity
    And cannot lift her head from the surge of death.
    A rust consumes the buds and fruits of the earth;
    The herds are sick; children die unborn,
    And labor is vain. The god of plague and pyre   30
    Raids like detestable lightning through the city,
    And all the house of Kadmos is laid waste,
    All emptied, and all darkened: Death alone
    Battens upon the misery of Thebes.
    You are not one of the immortal gods, we know;   35
    Yet we have come to you to make our prayer
    As to the man of all men best in adversity
    And wisest in the ways of God. You saved us
    From the Sphinx,° that flinty singer, and the tribute

---

2 Kadmos mythical founder of Thebes   **24 Pallas** Athena, goddess of wisdom,
protectress of Athens   **Apollo** god of light and healing   **39 Sphinx** a monster
(body of a lion, wings of a bird, face of a woman) who asked the riddle, "What goes
on four legs in the morning, two at noon, and three in the evening?" and who killed
those who could not answer. When Oedipus responded correctly that man crawls
on all fours in infancy, walks upright in maturity, and uses a staff in old age, the
Sphinx destroyed herself.

We paid to her so long; yet you were never   40
Better informed than we, nor could we teach you:
It was some god breathed in you to set us free.

Therefore, O mighty King, we turn to you:
Find us our safety, find us a remedy,
Whether by counsel of the gods or the men.   45
A king of wisdom tested in the past
Can act in a time of troubles, and act well.
Noblest of men, restore
Life to your city! Think how all men call you
Liberator for your triumph long ago;   50
Ah, when your years of kingship are remembered,
Let them not say *We rose, but later fell—*
Keep the State from going down in the storm!
Once, years ago, with happy augury,
You brought us fortune; be the same again!   55
No man questions your power to rule the land:
But rule over men, not over a dead city!
Ships are only hulls, citadels are nothing,
When no life moves in the empty passageways.
OEDIPUS. Poor children! You may be sure I know   60
All that you longed for in your coming here.
I know that you are deathly sick; and yet,
Sick as you are, not one is as sick as I.
Each of you suffers in himself alone
His anguish, not another's; but my spirit   65
Groans for the city, for myself, for you.

I was not sleeping, you are not waking me.
No, I have been in tears for a long while
And in my restless thought walked many ways.
In all my search, I found one helpful course,   70
And that I have taken: I have sent Creon,
Son of Menoikeus, brother of the Queen,
To Delphi, Apollo's place of revelation,
To learn there, if he can,
What act or pledge of mine may save the city.   75
I have counted the days, and now, this very day,
I am troubled, for he has overstayed his time.
What is he doing? He has been gone too long.
Yet whenever he comes back, I should do ill
To scant whatever hint the god may give.   80
PRIEST. It is a timely promise. At this instant
They tell me Creon is here.
OEDIPUS.   O Lord Apollo!
May his news be fair as his face is radiant!
PRIEST. It could not be otherwise: he is crowned with bay,
The chaplet is thick with berries.
OEDIPUS.   We shall soon know;   85
He is near enough to hear us now.
Enter CREON.

O Prince:

Brother: son of Menoikeus:
What answer do you bring us from the god?
CREON. It is favorable. I can tell you, great afflictions
    Will turn out well, if they are taken well.   90
OEDIPUS. What was the oracle? These vague words
    Leave me still hanging between hope and fear.
CREON. Is it your pleasure to hear me with all these
    Gathered around us? I am prepared to speak,
    But should we not go in?
OEDIPUS.   Let them all hear it.   95
    It is for them I suffer, more than myself.
CREON. Then I will tell you what I heard at Delphi.

    In plain words
    The god commands us to expel from the land of Thebes
    An old defilement that it seems we shelter.   100
    It is a deathly thing, beyond expiation.
    We must not let it feed upon us longer.
OEDIPUS. What defilement? How shall we rid ourselves of it?
CREON. By exile or death, blood for blood. It was
    Murder that brought the plague-wind on the city.   105
OEDIPUS. Murder of whom? Surely the god has named him?
CREON. My lord: long ago Laïos was our king,
    Before you came to govern us.
OEDIPUS.   I know;
    I learned of him from others; I never saw him.
CREON. He was murdered; and Apollo commands us now   110
    To take revenge upon whoever killed him.
OEDIPUS. Upon whom? Where are they? Where shall we find a clue
    To solve that crime, after so many years?
CREON. Here in this land, he said.
                  If we make enquiry,
    We may touch things that otherwise escape us.   115
OEDIPUS. Tell me: Was Laïos murdered in his house,
    Or in the fields, or in some foreign country?
CREON. He said he planned to make a pilgrimage.
    He did not come home again.
OEDIPUS.   And was there no one,
    No witness, no companion, to tell what happened?   120
CREON. They were all killed but one, and he got away
    So frightened that he could remember one thing only.
OEDIPUS. What was that one thing? One may be the key
    To everything, if we resolve to use it.
CREON. He said that a band of highwaymen attacked them,   125
    Outnumbered them, and overwhelmed the King.
OEDIPUS. Strange, that a highwayman should be so daring—
    Unless some faction here bribed him to do it.
CREON. We thought of that. But after Laïos' death
    New troubles arose and we had no avenger.   130
OEDIPUS. What troubles could prevent your hunting down the killers?
CREON. The riddling Sphinx's song

Made us deaf to all mysteries but her own
OEDIPUS. Then once more I must bring what is dark to light.
It is most fitting that Apollo shows,   135
As you do, this compunction for the dead.
You shall see how I stand by you, as I should,
To avenge the city and the city's god,
And not as though it were for some distant friend,
But for my own sake, to be rid of evil.   140
Whoever killed King Laïos might—who knows?—
Decide at any moment to kill me as well.
By avenging the murdered king I protect myself.
Come, then, my children: leave the altar steps,
Lift up your olive boughs!
                    One of you go   145
And summon the people of Kadmos to gather here.
I will do all that I can; you may tell them that.

                                        [Exit a PAGE*]*

So, with the help of God,
We shall be saved—or else indeed we are lost.
PRIEST. Let us rise, children. It was for this we came,   150
And now the King has promised it himself.
Phoibos° has sent us an oracle; may he descend
Himself to save us and drive out the plague.
    Exeunt OEDIPUS *and* CREON *into the palace by the central door. The*
    PRIEST *and the* SUPPLIANTS *disperse right and left. After a short*
    pause the CHORUS *enters the orchestra.*

                         Párodos

CHORUS. What is God singing in his profound   *Strophe 1*
Delphi of gold and shadow?
What oracle for Thebes, the sunwhipped city?
Fear unjoints me, the roots of my heart tremble.
Now I remember, O Healer, your power, and wonder;   5
Will you send doom like a sudden cloud, or weave it
Like nightfall of the past?
Speak, speak to us, issue of holy sound:
Dearest to our expectancy: be tender!

Let me pray to Athenê, the immortal daughter of Zeus, *Antistrophe 1*   10
And to Artemis her sister
Who keeps her famous throne in the market ring,
And to Apollo, bowman at the far butts of heaven—

O gods, descend! Like three streams leap against
The fires of our grief, the fires of darkness;   15
Be swift to bring us rest!

As in the old time from the brilliant house
Of air you stepped to save us, come again!

    152 **Phoibos** Phoebus Apollo, the sun god

Now our afflictions have no end,   *Strophe 2*
Now all our stricken host lies down   20
And no man fights off death with his mind;

The noble plowland bears no grain,
And groaning mothers cannot bear—
See, how our lives like birds take wing,
Like sparks that fly when a fire soars,   25
To the shore of the god of evening.

The plague burns on, it is pitiless   *Antistrophe 2*
Though pallid children laden with death
Lie unwept in the stony ways,
And old gray women by every path   30
Flock to the strand about the altars

There to strike their breasts and cry
Worship of Phoibos in wailing prayers:
Be kind, God's golden child!

There are no swords in this attack by fire,   *Strophe 3*   35
No shields, but we are ringed with cries.
Send the besieger plunging from our homes
Into the vast sea-room of the Atlantic
Or into the waves that foam eastward of Thrace—
For the day ravages what the night spares—   40

Destroy our enemy, lord of the thunder!
Let him be riven by lightning from heaven!

Phoibos Apollo, stretch the sun's bowstring,   *Antistrophe 3*
That golden cord, until it sing for us,
Flashing arrows in heaven!
                                   Artemis, Huntress,   45
Race with flaring lights upon our mountains!
O scarlet god, O golden-banded brow,
O Theban Bacchos° in a storm of Maenads,°
Enter OEDIPUS, *center.*
Whirl upon Death, that all the Undying hate!
Come with blinding cressets, come in joy!   50

Scene I

OEDIPUS. Is this your prayer? It may be answered. Come,
      Listen to me, act as the crisis demands,
      And you shall have relief from all these evils.

      Until now I was a stranger to this tale,
      As I had been a stranger to the crime.   5
      Could I track down the murderer without a clue?
      But now, friends,

48 **Bacchos** Dionysos, god of wine, thus scarlet-faced   48 **Maenads** Dionysos's
female attendants

As one who became a citizen after the murder,
I make this proclamation to all Thebans:
If any man knows by whose hand Laïos, son of Labdakos,   10
Met his death, I direct that man to tell me everything,
No matter what he fears for having so long withheld it.
Let it stand as promised that no further trouble
Will come to him, but he may leave the land in safety.

Moreover: If anyone knows the murderer to be foreign,   15
Let him not keep silent: he shall have his reward from me.
However, if he does conceal it, if any man
Fearing for his friend or for himself disobeys this edict,
Hear what I propose to do:

I solemnly forbid the people of this country,   20
Where power and throne are mine, ever to receive that man
Or speak to him, no matter who he is, or let him
Join in sacrifice, lustration, or in prayer.
I decree that he be driven from every house,

Being, as he is, corruption itself to us: the Delphic   25
Voice of Zeus has pronounced this revelation.
Thus I associate myself with the oracle
And take the side of the murdered king.

As for the criminal, I pray to God—
Whether it be a lurking thief, or one of a number—   30
I pray that that man's life be consumed in evil and wretchedness.
And as for me, this curse applies no less
If it should turn out that the culprit is my guest here,
Sharing my hearth.
                    You have heard the penalty.
I lay it on you now to attend to this   35
For my sake, for Apollo's, for the sick
Sterile city that heaven has abandoned.
Suppose the oracle had given you no command:
Should this defilement go uncleansed for ever?
You should have found the murderer: your king,   40
A noble king, had been destroyed!
                    Now I,
Having the power that he held before me,
Having his bed, begetting children there
Upon his wife, as he would have, had he lived—
Their son would have been my children's brother,   45
If Laïos had had luck in fatherhood!
(But surely ill luck rushed upon his reign)—
I say I take the son's part, just as though
I were his son, to press the fight for him
And see it won! I'll find the hand that brought   50
Death to Labdakos' and Polydoros' child,
Heir of Kadmos' and Agenor's line.
And as for those who fail me,
May the gods deny them the fruit of the earth,

Fruit of the womb, and may they rot utterly!   55
Let them be wretched as we are wretched, and worse!

For you, for loyal Thebans, and for all
Who find my actions right, I pray the favor
Of justice, and of all the immortal gods.
CHORAGOS.° Since I am under oath, my lord, I swear   60
    I did not do the murder, I cannot name
    The murderer. Might not the oracle
    That has ordained the search tell where to find him?
OEDIPUS. An honest question. But no man in the world
    Can make the gods do more than the gods will.   65
CHORAGOS. There is one last expedient—
OEDIPUS.   Tell me what it is.
    Though it seem slight, you must not hold it back.
CHORAGOS. A lord clairvoyant to the lord Apollo,
    As we all know, is the skilled Teiresias.
    One might learn much about this from him, Oedipus.   70
OEDIPUS. I am not wasting time:
    Creon spoke of this, and I have sent for him—
    Twice, in fact; it is strange that he is not here.
CHORAGOS. The other matter—that old report—seems useless.
OEDIPUS. Tell me. I am interested in all reports.   75
CHORAGOS. The King was said to have been killed by highwaymen.
OEDIPUS. I know. But we have no witnesses to that.
CHORAGOS. If the killer can feel a particle of dread,
    Your curse will bring him out of hiding!
OEDIPUS.   No.
    The man who dared that act will fear no curse.   80

Enter the blind seer TEIRESIAS *led by a* PAGE.

CHORAGOS. But there is one man who may detect the criminal.
    This is Teiresias, this is the holy prophet
    In whom, alone of all men, truth was born.
OEDIPUS. Teiresias: seer: student of mysteries,
    Of all that's taught and all that no man tells,   85
    Secrets of Heaven and secrets of the earth:
    Blind though you are, you know the city lies
    Sick with plague; and from this plague, my lord,
    We find that you alone can guard or save us.

Possibly you did not hear the messengers?   90
Apollo, when we sent to him,
Sent us back word that this great pestilence
Would lift, but only if we established clearly
The identity of those who murdered Laïos.
They must be killed or exiled.
                          Can you use   95
Birdflight or any art of divination
To purify yourself, and Thebes, and me
From this contagion? We are in your hands.

---

⁶⁰ **Choragos** leader of the Chorus

> There is no fairer duty
> Than that of helping others in distress.   100

TEIRESIAS. How dreadful knowledge of the truth can be
> When there's no help in truth! I knew this well,
> But did not act on it: else I should not have come.

OEDIPUS. What is troubling you? Why are your eyes so cold?

TEIRESIAS. Let me go home. Bear your own fate, and I'll   105
> Bear mine. It is better so: trust what I say.

OEDIPUS. What you say is ungracious and unhelpful
> To your native country. Do not refuse to speak.

TEIRESIAS. When it comes to speech, your own is neither temperate
> Nor opportune. I wish to be more prudent.   110

OEDIPUS. In God's name, we all beg you—

TEIRESIAS.   You are all ignorant.
> No; I will never tell you what I know.
> Now it is my misery; then, it would be yours.

OEDIPUS. What! You do know something, and will not tell us?
> You would betray us all and wreck the State?   115

TEIRESIAS. I do not intend to torture myself, or you.
> Why persist in asking? You will not persuade me.

OEDIPUS. What a wicked man you are! You'd try a stone's
> Patience! Out with it! Have you no feeling at all?

TEIRESIAS. You call me unfeeling. If you could only see   120
> The nature of your feelings . . .

OEDIPUS.   Why,
> Who would not feel as I do? Who could endure
> Your arrogance toward the city?

TEIRESIAS.   What does it matter!
> Whether I speak or not, it is bound to come.

OEDIPUS. Then, if "it" is bound to come, you are bound to tell me.   125

TEIRESIAS. No, I will not go on. Rage as you please

OEDIPUS. Rage? Why not!
>   And I'll tell you what I think:
> You planned it, you had it done, you all but
> Killed him with your own hands: if you had eyes,
> I'd say the crime was yours, and yours alone.   130

TEIRESIAS. So? I charge you, then,
> Abide by the proclamation you have made.
> From this day forth
> Never speak again to these men or to me;
> You yourself are the pollution of this country.   135

OEDIPUS. You dare say that! Can you possibly think you have
> Some way of going free, after such insolence?

TEIRESIAS. I have gone free. It is the truth sustains me.

OEDIPUS. Who taught you shamelessness? It was not your craft.

TEIRESIAS. You did. You made me speak. I did not want to.   140

OEDIPUS. Speak what? Let me hear it again more clearly.

TEIRESIAS. Was it not clear before? Are you tempting me?

OEDIPUS. I did not understand it. Say it again.

TEIRESIAS. I say that you are the murderer whom you seek.

OEDIPUS. Now twice you have spat out infamy. You'll pay for it!   145

TEIRESIAS. Would you care for more? Do you wish to be really angry?

OEDIPUS. Say what you will. Whatever you say is worthless.

TEIRESIAS. I say you live in hideous shame with those
Most dear to you. You cannot see the evil.

OEDIPUS. It seems you can go on mouthing like this for ever.   150

TEIRESIAS. I can, if there is power in truth.

OEDIPUS.   There is:
But not for you, not for you,
You sightless, witless, senseless, mad old man!

TEIRESIAS. You are the madman. There is no one here
Who will not curse you soon, as you curse me.   155

OEDIPUS. You child of endless night! You cannot hurt me
Or any other man who sees the sun.

TEIRESIAS. True: it is not from me your fate will come.
That lies within Apollo's competence,
As it is his concern.

OEDIPUS.   Tell me: 160
Are you speaking for Creon, or for yourself?

TEIRESIAS. Creon is no threat. You weave your own doom.

OEDIPUS. Wealth, power, craft of statesmanship!
Kingly position, everywhere admired!
What savage envy is stored up against these,   165
If Creon, whom I trusted, Creon my friend,
For this great office which the city once
Put in my hands unsought—if for this power
Creon desires in secret to destroy me!

He has brought this decrepit fortune-teller, this   170
Collector of dirty pennies, this prophet fraud—
Why, he is no more clairvoyant than I am!
                                        Tell us:
Has your mystic mummery ever approached the truth?
When that hellcat the Sphinx was performing here,
What help were you to these people?   175
Her magic was not for the first man who came along:
It demanded a real exorcist. Your birds—
What good were they? or the gods, for the matter of that?
But I came by,
Oedipus, the simple man, who knows nothing—   180
I thought it out for myself, no birds helped me!
And this is the man you think you can destroy,
That you may be close to Creon when he's king!
Well, you and your friend Creon, it seems to me,
Will suffer most. If you were not an old man,   185
You would have paid already for your plot.

CHORAGOS. We cannot see that his words or yours
Have spoken except in anger, Oedipus,
And of anger we have no need. How can God's will
Be accomplished best? That is what most concerns us.   190

TEIRESIAS. You are a king. But where argument's concerned
I am your man, as much a king as you.

I am not your servant, but Apollo's.
I have no need of Creon to speak for me.

Listen to me. You mock my blindness, do you?   195
But I say that you, with both your eyes, are blind:
You cannot see the wretchedness of your life,
Not in whose house you live, no, nor with whom.
Who are your father and mother? Can you tell me?
You do not even know the blind wrongs   200
That you have done them, on earth and in the world below.
But the double lash of your parents' curse will whip you
Out of this land some day, with only night
Upon your precious eyes.
Your cries then—where will they not be heard?   205
What fastness of Kithairon° will not echo them?
And that bridal-descant of yours—you'll know it then,
The song they sang when you came here to Thebes
And found your misguided berthing.
All this, and more, that you cannot guess at now,   210
Will bring you to yourself among your children.
Be angry, then. Curse Creon. Curse my words.
I tell you, no man that walks upon the earth
Shall be rooted out more horribly than you.

OEDIPUS. Am I to bear this from him?—Damnation   215
    Take you! Out of this place! Out of my sight!
TEIRESIAS. I would not have come at all if you had not asked me.
OEDIPUS. Could I have told that you'd talk nonsense, that
    You'd come here to make a fool of yourself, and of me?
TEIRESIAS. A fool? Your parents thought me sane enough.   220
OEDIPUS. My parents again!—Wait: who were my parents?
TEIRESIAS. This day will give you a father, and break your heart.
OEDIPUS. Your infantile riddles! Your damned abracadabra!
TEIRESIAS. You were a great man once at solving riddles.
OEDIPUS. Mock me with that if you like; you will find it true. 225
TEIRESIAS. It was true enough. It brought about your ruin.
OEDIPUS. But if it saved this town.
TEIRESIAS [to the PAGE].   Boy, give me your hand.
OEDIPUS. Yes, boy; lead him away.
                        —While you are here
    We can do nothing. Go; leave us in peace.
TEIRESIAS. I will go when I have said what I have to say.   230
    How can you hurt me? And I tell you again:
    The man you have been looking for all this time,
    The damned man, the murderer of Laïos,
    That man is in Thebes. To your mind he is foreignborn,
    But it will soon be shown that he is a Theban,   235
    A revelation that will fail to please
                        A blind man
    Who has his eyes now; a penniless man, who is rich now;

206 **fastness of Kithairon** stronghold in a mountain near Thebes

And he will go tapping the strange earth with his staff;
To the children with whom he lives now he will be
Brother and father—the very same; to her   240
Who bore him, son and husband—the very same
Who came to his father's bed, wet with his father's blood.

Enough. Go think that over.
If later you find error in what I have said,
You may say that I have no skill in prophecy.   245
Exit TEIRESIAS, *led by his* PAGE. OEDIPUS *goes into the palace.*

Ode 1

CHORUS. The Delphic stone of prophecies   *Strophe 1*
    Remembers ancient regicide
    And a still bloody hand.
    That killer's hour of flight has come.
    He must be stronger than riderless   5
    Coursers of untiring wind,
    For the son of Zeus° armed with his father's thunder
    Leaps in lightning after him;
    And the Furies° follow him, the sad Furies.

    Holy Parnossos' peak of snow   *Antistrophe 1* 10
    Flashes and blinds that secret man,
    That all shall hunt him down:
    Though he may roam the forest shade
    Like a bull gone wild from pasture
    To rage through glooms of stone.   15
    Doom comes down on him; flight will not avail him;
    For the world's heart calls him desolate,
    And the immortal Furies follow, for ever follow.

    But now a wilder thing is heard   *Strophe 2*
    From the old man skilled at hearing Fate in the wingbeat of a bird.   20
    Bewildered as a blown bird, my soul hovers and cannot find
    Foothold in this debate, or any reason or rest of mind.
    But no man ever brought—none can bring
    Proof of strife between Thebes' royal house,
    Labdakos' line,° and the son of Polybos;°   25
    And never until now has any man brought word
    Of Laïos dark death staining Oedipus the King.

    Divine Zeus and Apollo hold   *Antistrophe 2*
    Perfect intelligence alone of all tales ever told;
    And well though this diviner works, he works in his own night;   30
    No man can judge that rough unknown or trust in second sight,
    For wisdom changes hands among the wise.
    Shall I believe my great lord criminal.
    At a raging word that a blind old man let fall?

Ode 1 7 son of Zeus Apollo   **9 Furies** avenging deities   **25 Labdakos' line** family of Laïos   **son of Polybos** Oedipus (so the Chorus believes)

I saw him, when the carrion woman faced him of old,   35
Prove his heroic mind! These evil words are lies.

Scene II

CREON. Men of Thebes:
I am told that heavy accusations
Have been brought against me by King Oedipus.
I am not the kind of man to bear this tamely.

If in these present difficulties   5
He holds me accountable for any harm to him
Through anything I have said or done—why, then,
I do not value life in this dishonor.
It is not as though this rumor touched upon
Some private indiscretion. The matter is grave.   10
The fact is that I am being called disloyal
To the State, to my fellow citizens, to my friends.
CHORAGOS. He may have spoken in anger, not from his mind.
CREON. But did you hear him say I was the one
Who seduced the old prophet into lying?   15
CHORAGOS. The thing was said; I do not know how seriously.
CREON. But you were watching him! Were his eyes steady?
Did he look like a man in his right mind?
CHORAGOS.   I do not know.
I cannot judge the behavior of great men.
But here is the King himself.
Enter OEDIPUS.
OEDIPUS.   So you dared come back.   20
Why? How brazen of you to come to my house,
You murderer!
                    Do you think I do not know
That you plotted to kill me, plotted to steal my throne?
Tell me, in God's name: am I coward, a fool,
That you should dream you could accomplish this?   25
A fool who could not see your slippery game?
A coward, not to fight back when I saw it?
You are the fool, Creon, are you not? hoping
Without support or friends to get a throne?
Thrones may be won or bought: you could do neither.   30
CREON. Now listen to me. You have talked; let me talk, too.
You cannot judge unless you know the facts.
OEDIPUS. You speak well: there is one fact; but I find it hard
To learn from the deadliest enemy I have.
CREON. That above all I must dispute with you.   35
OEDIPUS. That above all I will not hear you deny.
CREON. If you think there is anything good in being stubborn
Against all reason, then I say you are wrong.
OEDIPUS. If you think a man can sin against his own kind
And not be punished for it, I say you are mad.   40
CREON. I agree. But tell me: what have I done to you?

OEDIPUS. You advised me to send for that wizard, did you not?

CREON. I did. I should do it again.

OEDIPUS.   Very well. Now tell me:

How long has it been since Laïos—

CREON.   What of Laïos?

OEDIPUS. Since he vanished in that onset by the road?   45

CREON. It was long ago, a long time.

OEDIPUS.   And this prophet,

Was he practicing here then?

CREON.   He was; and with honor, as now.

OEDIPUS. Did he speak of me at that time?

CREON.   He never did;

At least, not when I was present.

OEDIPUS.   But . . . the enquiry?

I suppose you held one?

CREON.   We did, but we learned nothing.   50

OEDIPUS. Why did the prophet not speak against me then?

CREON. I do not know; and I am the kind of man

Who holds his tongue when he has no facts to go on.

OEDIPUS. There's one fact that you know, and you could tell it.

CREON. What fact is that? If I know it, you shall have it.   55

OEDIPUS. If he were not involved with you, he could not say

That it was I who murdered Laïos.

CREON. If he says that, you are the one that knows it!—

But now it is my turn to question you.

OEDIPUS. Put your questions. I am no murderer.   60

CREON. First, then: You married my sister?

OEDIPUS.   I married your sister.

CREON. And you rule the kingdom equally with her?

OEDIPUS. Everything that she wants she has from me.

CREON. And I am the third, equal to both of you?

OEDIPUS. That is why I call you a bad friend.   65

CREON. No. Reason it out, as I have done.

Think of this first. Would any sane man prefer

Power, with all a king's anxieties,

To that same power and the grace of sleep?

Certainly not I.   70

I have never longed for the king's power—only his rights.

Would any wise man differ from me in this?

As matters stand, I have my way in everything

With your consent, and no responsibilities.

If I were king, I should be a slave to policy.   75

How could I desire a scepter more

Than what is now mine—untroubled influence?

No, I have not gone mad; I need no honors,

Except those with the perquisites I have now.

I am welcome everywhere; every man salutes me,   80

And those who want your favor seek my ear,

Since I know how to manage what they ask.

Should I exchange this ease for that anxiety?

Besides, no sober mind is treasonable.
I hate anarchy   85
And never would deal with any man who likes it.

Test what I have said. Go to the priestess
At Delphi, ask if I quoted her correctly.
And as for this other thing: if I am found
Guilty of treason with Teiresias,   90
Then sentence me to death! You have my word
It is a sentence I should cast my vote for—
But not without evidence!
                            You do wrong
When you take good men for bad, bad men for good.
A true friend thrown aside—why, life itself   95
Is not more precious!
                            In time you will know this well:
For time, and time alone, will show the just man,
Though scoundrels are discovered in a day.

CHORAGOS. This is well said, and a prudent man would ponder it.
    Judgments too quickly formed are dangerous.   100
OEDIPUS. But is he not quick in his duplicity?
    And shall I not be quick to parry him?
    Would you have me stand still, hold my peace, and let
    This man win everything, through my inaction?
CREON. And you want—what is it, then? To banish me?   105
OEDIPUS. No, not exile. It is your death I want,
    So that all the world may see what treason means.
CREON. You will persist, then? You will not believe me?
OEDIPUS. How can I believe you?
CREON.   Then you are a fool.
OEDIPUS. To save myself?
CREON.   In justice, think of me.   110
OEDIPUS. You are evil incarnate.
CREON.   But suppose that you are wrong?
OEDIPUS. Still I must rule.
CREON.   But not if you rule badly.
OEDIPUS. O city, city!
CREON.   It is my city, too!
CHORAGOS. Now, my lords, be still. I see the Queen,
    Iocastê, coming from her palace chambers;   115
    And it is time she came, for the sake of you both.
    This dreadful quarrel can be resolved through her.
    Enter IOCASTÊ.
IOCASTÊ. Poor foolish men, what wicked din is this?
    With Thebes sick to death, is it not shameful
    That you should rake some private quarrel up?   120
    [To OEDIPUS.*]* Come into the house.
                            —And you, Creon, go now:
    Let us have no more of this tumult over nothing.
CREON. Nothing? No, sister: what your husband plans for me
    Is one of two great evils: exile or death.

OEDIPUS.   He is right.
    Why, woman, I have caught him squarely   125
    Plotting against my life.

CREON.   No! Let me die
    Accurst if ever I have wished you harm!

IOCASTÊ. Ah, believe it, Oedipus!
    In the name of the gods, respect this oath of his
    For my sake, for the sake of these people here!   130

CHORAGOS. Open your mind to her, my lord. Be ruled   *Strophe 1*
    by her, I beg you!

OEDIPUS. What would you have me do?

CHORAGOS. Respect Creon's word. He has never spoken like a fool,
    And now he has sworn an oath.

OEDIPUS. You know what you ask?

CHORAGOS.   I do.

OEPIDUS.   Speak on, then.

CHORAGOS. A friend so sworn should not be baited so,   135
    In blind malice, and without final proof.

OEDIPUS. You are aware, I hope, that what you say
    Means death for me, or exile at the least.

CHORAGOS. No, I swear by Helios,° first in Heaven!   *Strophe 2*
    May I die friendless and accurst,   140
    The worst of deaths, if ever I meant that!
      It is the withering fields
        That hurt my sick heart:
      Must we bear all these ills,
        And now your bad blood as well?   145

OEDIPUS. Then let him go. And let me die, if I must,
    Or be driven by him in shame from the land of Thebes.
    It is your unhappiness, and not his talk,
    That touches me.
        As for him—
    Wherever he is, I will hate him as long as I live.   150

CREON. Ugly in yielding, as you were ugly in rage!
    Natures like yours chiefly torment themselves.

OEDIPUS. Can you not go? Can you not leave me?

CREON.   I can.
    You do not know me; but the city knows me,
    And in its eyes I am just, if not in yours.   155

                              [Exit CREON.*]*

CHORAGOS. Lady Iocastê, did you not ask the King   *Antistrophe 1*
    to go to his chambers?

IOCASTÊ. First tell me what has happened.

CHORAGOS. There was suspicion without evidence; yet it rankled
    As even false charges will.

IOCASTÊ.   On both sides?

CHORAGOS.   On both.

139 **Helios** sun god

IOCASTÊ.   But what was said?

CHORAGOS. Oh let it rest, let it be done with!   160
    Have we not suffered enough?

OEDIPUS. You see to what your decency has brought you:
    You have made difficulties where my heart saw none.

CHORAGOS. Oedipus, it is not once only I have told you—   *Antistrophe 2*
    You must know I should count myself unwise   165
    To the point of madness, should I now forsake you—
      You, under whose hand,
        In the storm of another time,
      Our dear land sailed out free,
        But now stand fast at the helm!   170

IOCASTÊ. In God's name, Oedipus, inform your wife as well:
    Why are you so set in this hard anger?

OEDIPUS. I will tell you, for none of these men deserves
    My confidence as you do. It is Creon's work,
    His treachery, his plotting against me.   175

IOCASTÊ. Go on, if you can make this clear to me.

OEDIPUS. He charges me with the murder of Laïos.

IOCASTÊ. Has he some knowledge? Or does he speak from hearsay?

OEDIPUS. He would not commit himself to such a charge,
    But he has brought in that damnable soothsayer   180
    To tell his story.

IOCASTÊ.   Set your mind at rest.
    If it is a question of soothsayers, I tell you
    That you will find no man whose craft gives knowledge
    Of the unknowable.

              Here is my proof.

An oracle was reported to Laïos once   185
(I will not say from Phoibos himself, but from
His appointed ministers, at any rate)
That his doom would be death at the hands of his own son—
His son, born of his flesh and of mine!

Now, you remember the story: Laïos was killed   190
By marauding strangers where three highways meet;
But his child had not been three days in this world
Before the King had pierced the baby's ankles
And left him to die on a lonely mountainside.

Thus, Apollo never caused that child   195
To kill his father, and it was not Laïos fate
To die at the hands of his son, as he had feared.
This is what prophets and prophecies are worth!
Have no dread of them.
             It is God himself
Who can show us what he wills, in his own way.   200

OEDIPUS. How strange a shadowy memory crossed my mind,
    Just now while you were speaking; it chilled my heart.

IOCASTÊ. What do you mean? What memory do you speak of?

OEDIPUS. If I understand you, Laïos was killed

At a place where three roads meet.

IOCASTÊ.   So it was said;   205
We have no later story.

OEDIPUS.   Where did it happen?

IOCASTÊ. Phokis, it is called: at a place where the Theban Way
Divides into the roads towards Delphi and Daulia.

OEDIPUS. When?

IOCASTÊ.   We had the news not long before you came
And proved the right to your succession here.   210

OEDIPUS. Ah, what net has God been weaving for me?

IOCASTÊ. Oedipus! Why does this trouble you?

OEDIPUS.   Do not ask me yet.
First, tell me how Laïos looked, and tell me
How old he was.

IOCASTÊ.   He was tall, his hair just touched
With white; his form was not unlike your own.   215

OEDIPUS. I think that I myself may be accurst
By my own ignorant edict.

IOCASTÊ.   You speak strangely.
It makes me tremble to look at you, my King.

OEDIPUS. I am not sure that the blind man cannot see.
But I should know better if you were to tell me—   220

IOCASTÊ. Anything—though I dread to hear you ask it.

OEDIPUS. Was the King lightly escorted, or did he ride
With a large company, as a ruler should?

IOCASTÊ. There were five men with him in all: one was a herald;
And a single chariot, which he was driving.   225

OEDIPUS. Alas, that makes it plain enough!
                          But who—
Who told you how it happened?

IOCASTÊ.   A household servant,
The only one to escape.

OEDIPUS.   And is he still
A servant of ours?

IOCASTÊ.   No; for when he came back at last
And found you enthroned in the place of the dead king,   230
He came to me, touched my hand with his, and begged
That I would send him away to the frontier district
Where only the shepherds go—
As far away from the city as I could send him.
I granted his prayer; for although the man was a slave,   235
He had earned more than this favor at my hands.

OEDIPUS. Can he be called back quickly?

IOCASTÊ.   Easily.
But why?

OEDIPUS.   I have taken too much upon myself
Without enquiry; therefore I wish to consult him.

IOCASTÊ. Then he shall come.
                          But am I not one also   240
To whom you might confide these fears of yours!

OEDIPUS. That is your right; it will not be denied you,

Now least of all; for I have reached a pitch
Of wild foreboding. Is there anyone
To whom I should sooner speak?   245
Polybos of Corinth is my father.
My mother is a Dorian: Meropê.
I grew up chief among the men of Corinth
Until a strange thing happened—
Not worth my passion, it may be, but strange.   250

At a feast, a drunken man maundering in his cups
Cries out that I am not my father's son!

I contained myself that night, though I felt anger
And a sinking heart. The next day I visited
My father and mother, and questioned them. They stormed,   255
Calling it all the slanderous rant of a fool;
And this relieved me. Yet the suspicion
Remained always aching in my mind;
I knew there was talk; I could not rest;
And finally, saying nothing to my parents,   260
I went to the shrine at Delphi.
The god dismissed my question without reply;
He spoke of other things.
                        Some were clear,
Full of wretchedness, dreadful, unbearable:
As, that I should lie with my own mother, breed   265
Children from whom all men would turn their eyes;
And that I should be my father's murderer.

I heard all this, and fled. And from that day
Corinth to me was only in the stars
Descending in that quarter of the sky,   270
As I wandered farther and farther on my way
To a land where I should never see the evil
Sung by the oracle. And I came to this country
Where, so you say, King Laïos was killed.
I will tell you all that happened there, my lady.   275

There were three highways
Coming together at a place I passed;
And there a herald came towards me, and a chariot
Drawn by horses, with a man such as you describe
Seated in it. The groom leading the horses   280
Forced me off the road at his lord's command;
But as this charioteer lurched over toward me
I struck him in my rage. The old man saw me
And brought his double goad down upon my head
As I came abreast.
                    He was paid back, and more!   285
Swinging my club in this right hand I knocked him
Out of his car, and he rolled on the ground.
                                    I killed him.
I killed them all.

Now if that stranger and Laïos were—kin,
Where is a man more miserable than I?   290
More hated by the gods? Citizen and alien alike
Must never shelter me or speak to me—
I must be shunned by all.
                              And I myself
Pronounced this malediction upon myself!

Think of it: I have touched you with these hands,   295
These hands that killed your husband. What defilement!

Am I all evil, then? It must be so,
Since I must flee from Thebes, yet never again
See my own countrymen, my own country,
For fear of joining my mother in marriage   300
And killing Polybos, my father.
                              Ah,
If I was created so, born to this fate,
Who could deny the savagery of God?

O holy majesty of heavenly powers!
May I never see that day! Never!   305
Rather let me vanish from the race of men
Than know the abomination destined me!
CHORAGOS. We too, my lord, have felt dismay at this.
     But there is hope: you have yet to hear the shepherd.
OEDIPUS. Indeed, I fear no other hope is left me.   310
IOCASTÊ. What do you hope from him when he comes?
OEDIPUS.   This much:
     If his account of the murder tallies with yours,
     Then I am cleared.
IOCASTÊ.   What was it that I said
     Of such importance?
OEDIPUS.   Why, "marauders," you said,
     Killed the King, according to this man's story.   315
     If he maintains that still, if there were several,
     Clearly the guilt is not mine: I was alone.
     But if he says one man, singlehanded, did it,
     Then the evidence all points to me.
IOCASTÊ. You may be sure that he said there were several; 320
     And can he call back that story now? He cannot.
     The whole city heard it as plainly as I.
     But suppose he alters some detail of it:
     He cannot ever show that Laïos' death
     Fulfilled the oracle: for Apollo said   325
     My child was doomed to kill him; and my child—
     Poor baby!—it was my child that died first.

     No. From now on, where oracles are concerned,
     I would not waste a second thought on any.
OEDIPUS. You may be right.
                              But come: let someone go 330
     For the shepherd at once. This matter must be settled.

IOCASTÊ. I will send for him.
　　　I would not wish to cross you in anything,
　　　And surely not in this.—Let us go in.　　*[Exeunt into the palace.]*

Ode II

CHORUS. Let me be reverent in the ways of right,　　　　　　*Strophe 1*
　　　Lowly the paths I journey on;
　　　Let all my words and actions keep
　　　The laws of the pure universe
　　　From highest Heaven handed down.　　　　　　　　　　　　5
　　　For Heaven is their bright nurse,
　　　Those generations of the realms of light;
　　　Ah, never of mortal kind were they begot,
　　　Nor are they slaves of memory, lost in sleep:
　　　Their Father is greater than Time, and ages not.　　　　10

　　　The tyrant is a child of Pride　　　　　　　　　*Antistrophe 1*
　　　Who drinks from his great sickening cup
　　　Recklessness and vanity,
　　　Until from his high crest headlong
　　　He plummets to the dust of hope.　　　　　　　　　　　15
　　　That strong man is not strong.
　　　But let no fair ambition be denied;
　　　May God protect the wrestler for the State
　　　In government, in comely policy,
　　　Who will fear God, and on His ordinance wait.　　　　20

　　　Haughtiness and the high hand of disdain　　　　　*Strophe 2*
　　　Tempt and outrage God's holy law;
　　　And any mortal who dares hold
　　　No immortal Power in awe
　　　Will be caught up in a net of pain:　　　　　　　　　25
　　　The price for which his levity is sold.
　　　Let each man take due earnings, then,
　　　And keep his hands from holy things,
　　　And from blasphemy stand apart—
　　　Else the crackling blast of heaven　　　　　　　　　30
　　　Blows on his head, and on his desperate heart;
　　　Though fools will honor impious men,
　　　In their cities no tragic poet sings.

　　　Shall we lose faith in Delphi's obscurities,　　　*Antistrophe 2*
　　　We who have heard the world's core　　　　　　　　　35
　　　Discredited, and the sacred wood
　　　Of Zeus at Elis praised no more?
　　　The deeds and the strange prophecies
　　　Must make a pattern yet to be understood.
　　　Zeus, if indeed you are lord of all,　　　　　　　　40
　　　Throned in light over night and day,
　　　Mirror this in your endless mind:
　　　Our masters call the oracle

Words on the wind, and the Delphic vision blind!
Their hearts no longer know Apollo,   45
And reverence for the gods has died away.

Scene III

Enter IOCASTÊ.

IOCASTÊ. Princes of Thebes, it has occurred to me
    To visit the altars of the gods, bearing
    These branches as a suppliant, and this incense.
    Our King is not himself: his noble soul
    Is overwrought with fantasies of dread,   5
    Else he would consider
    The new prophecies in the light of the old.
    He will listen to any voice that speaks disaster,
    And my advice goes for nothing.
    She approaches the altar, right.
                            To you, then, Apollo,
    Lycean lord, since you are nearest, I turn in prayer.   10
    Receive these offerings, and grant us deliverance
    From defilement. Our hearts are heavy with fear
    When we see our leader distracted, as helpless sailors
    Are terrified by the confusion of their helmsman.
    Enter MESSENGER

MESSENGER. Friends, no doubt you can direct me: 15
    Where shall I find the house of Oedipus,
    Or, better still, where is the King himself?

CHORAGOS. It is this very place, stranger; he is inside.
    This is his wife and mother of his children.

MESSENGER. I wish her happiness in a happy house,   20
    Blest in all the fulfillment of her marriage.

IOCASTÊ. I wish as much for you: your courtesy
    Deserves a like good fortune. But now, tell me:
    Why have you come? What have you to say to us?

MESSENGER. Good news, my lady, for your house and your husband.   25

IOCASTÊ. What news? Who sent you here?

MESSENGER.   I am from Corinth.
    The news I bring ought to mean joy for you,
    Though it may be you will find some grief in it.

IOCASTÊ. What is it? How can it touch us in both ways?

MESSENGER. The people of Corinth, they say,   30
    Intend to call Oedipus to be their king.

IOCASTÊ. But old Polybos—is he not reigning still?

MESSENGER. No. Death holds him in his sepulchre.

IOCASTÊ. What are you saying? Polybos is dead?

MESSENGER. If I am not telling the truth, may I die myself.   35

IOCASTÊ *[to a* MAIDSERVANT*]*. Go in, go quickly; tell this to your master.

    O riddlers of God's will, where are you now!
    This was the man whom Oedipus, long ago,
    Feared so, fled so, in dread of destroying him—
    But it was another fate by which he died.   40

Enter OEDIPUS, *center.*

OEDIPUS. Dearest Iocastê, why have you sent for me?

IOCASTÊ. Listen to what this man says, and then tell me
What has become of the solemn prophecies.

OEDIPUS. Who is this man? What is his news for me?

IOCASTÊ. He has come from Corinth to announce your father's death!   45

OEDIPUS. Is it true, stranger? Tell me in your own words.

MESSENGER. I cannot say it more clearly: the King is dead.

OEDIPUS. Was it by treason? Or by an attack of illness?

MESSENGER. A little thing brings old men to their rest.

OEDIPUS. It was sickness, then?

MESSENGER.   Yes, and his many years.   50

OEDIPUS. Ah!
Why should a man respect the Pythian hearth,° or
Give heed to the birds that jangle above his head?
They prophesied that I should kill Polybos,
Kill my own father; but he is dead and buried,   55
And I am here—I never touched him, never,
Unless he died in grief for my departure,
And thus, in a sense, through me. No Polybos
Has packed the oracles off with him underground.
They are empty words.

IOCASTÊ.   Had I not told you so?   60

OEDIPUS. You had; it was my faint heart that betrayed me.

IOCASTÊ. From now on never think of those things again.

OEDIPUS. And yet—must I not fear my mother's bed?

IOCASTÊ. Why should anyone in this world be afraid,
Since Fate rules us and nothing can be foreseen?   65
A man should live only for the present day.
Have no more fear of sleeping with your mother
How many men, in dreams, have lain with their mothers!
No reasonable man is troubled by such things.

OEDIPUS. That is true; only—   70
If only my mother were not still alive!
But she is alive. I cannot help my dread.

IOCASTÊ. Yet this news of your father's death is wonderful.

OEDIPUS. Wonderful. But I fear the living woman.

MESSENGER. Tell me, who is this woman that you fear?   75

OEDIPUS. It is Meropê, man; the wife of King Polybos.

MESSENGER. Meropê? Why should you be afraid of her?

OEDIPUS. An oracle of the gods, a dreadful saying.

MESSENGER. Can you tell me about it or are you sworn to silence?

OEDIPUS. I can tell you, and I will.   80
Apollo said through his prophet that I was the man
Who should marry his own mother, shed his father's blood
With his own hands. And so, for all these years
I have kept clear of Corinth, and no harm has come—
Though it would have been sweet to see my parents again.   85

52 **Pythian hearth** Delphi (also called Pytho because a great snake had lived
there), where Apollo spoke through a priestess

MESSENGER. And is this the fear that drove you out of Corinth?

OEDIPUS. Would you have me kill my father?

MESSENGER.   As for that

    You must be reassured by the news I gave you.

OEDIPUS. If you could reassure me, I would reward you.

MESSENGER. I had that in mind, I will confess: I thought   90

    I could count on you when you returned to Corinth.

OEDIPUS. No: I will never go near my parents again.

MESSENGER. Ah, son, you still do not know what you are doing—

OEDIPUS. What do you mean? In the name of God tell me!

MESSENGER. —If these are your reasons for not going home—   95

OEDIPUS. I tell you, I fear the oracle may come true.

MESSENGER. And guilt may come upon you through your parents?

OEDIPUS. That is the dread that is always in my heart.

MESSENGER. Can you not see that all your fears are groundless?

OEDIPUS. How can you say that? They are my parents, surely?   100

MESSENGER. Polybos was not your father.

OEDIPUS.   Not my father?

MESSENGER. No more your father than the man speaking to you.

OEDIPUS. But you are nothing to me!

MESSENGER.   Neither was he.

OEDIPUS. Then why did he call me son?

MESSENGER.   I will tell you:

    Long ago he had you from my hands, as a gift.   105

OEDIPUS. Then how could he love me so, if I was not his?

MESSENGER. He had no children, and his heart turned to you.

OEDIPUS. What of you? Did you buy me? Did you find me by chance?

MESSENGER. I came upon you in the crooked pass of Kithairon.

OEDIPUS. And what were you doing there?

MESSENGER.   Tending my flocks.   110

OEDIPUS. A wandering shepherd?

MESSENGER.   But your savior, son, that day.

OEDIPUS. From what did you save me?

MESSENGER.   Your ankles should tell you that.

OEDIPUS. Ah, stranger, why do you speak of that childhood pain?

MESSENGER. I cut the bonds that tied your ankles together.

OEDIPUS. I have had the mark as long as I can remember.   115

MESSENGER. That was why you were given the name you bear.°

OEDIPUS. God! Was it my father or my mother who did it?

    Tell me!

MESSENGER. I do not know. The man who gave you to me

    Can tell you better than I.   120

OEDIPUS. It was not you that found me, but another?

MESSENGER. It was another shepherd gave you to me.

OEDIPUS. Who was he? Can you tell me who he was?

MESSENGER. I think he was said to be one of Laïos' people.

OEDIPUS. You mean the Laïos who was king here years ago?   125

MESSENGER. Yes; King Laïos; and the man was one of his herdsmen.

OEDIPUS. Is he still alive? Can I see him?

---

116 **name you bear** *Oedipus* means "swollen-foot"

MESSENGER.   These men here
    Know best about such things.
OEDIPUS.   Does anyone here
    Know this shepherd that he is talking about?
    Have you seen him in the fields, or in the town?   130
    If you have, tell me. It is time things were made plain.
CHORAGOS. I think the man he means is that same shepherd
    You have already asked to see. Iocastê perhaps
    Could tell you something.
OEDIPUS.   Do you know anything
    About him, Lady? Is he the man we have summoned?   135
    Is that the man this shepherd means?
IOCASTÊ.   Why think of him?
    Forget this herdsman. Forget it all.
    This talk is a waste of time.
OEDIPUS.   How can you say that,
    When the clues to my true birth are in my hands?
IOCASTÊ. For God's love, let us have no more questioning!   140
    Is your life nothing to you?
    My own is pain enough for me to bear.
OEDIPUS. You need not worry. Suppose my mother a slave,
    And born of slaves: no baseness can touch you.
IOCASTÊ. Listen to me, I beg you: do not do this thing!   145
OEDIPUS. I will not listen; the truth must be made known.
IOCASTÊ. Everything that I say is for your own good!
OEDIPUS.   My own good
    Snaps my patience, then: I want none of it.
IOCASTÊ. You are fatally wrong! May you never learn who you are!
OEDIPUS. Go, one of you, and bring the shepherd here.   150
    Let us leave this woman to brag of her royal name.
IOCASTÊ. Ah, miserable!
    That is the only word I have for you now.
    That is the only word I can ever have.

                             Exit into the palace.
CHORAGOS. Why has she left us, Oedipus? Why has she gone   155
    In such a passion of sorrow? I fear this silence:
    Something dreadful may come of it.
OEDIPUS.   Let it come!
    However base my birth, I must know about it.
    The Queen, like a woman, is perhaps ashamed
    To think of my low origin. But I   160
    Am a child of luck; I cannot be dishonored.
    Luck is my mother; the passing months, my brothers,
    Have seen me rich and poor. If this is so,
    How could I wish that I were someone else?
    How could I not be glad to know my birth?   165

Ode III

CHORUS. If ever the coming time were known   *Strophe*
    To my heart's pondering,

Kithairon, now by Heaven I see the torches
At the festival of the next full moon,
And see the dance, and hear the choir sing   5
A grace to your gentle shade:
Mountain where Oedipus was found,
O mountain guard of a noble race!
May the god who heals us lend his aid,
And let that glory come to pass   10
For our king's cradling-ground.

Of the nymphs that flower beyond the years.   *Antistrophe*
Who bore you, royal child,
To Pan of the hills or the timberline Apollo,
Cold in delight where the upland clears.   15
Or Hermês for whom Kyllenês° heights are piled?
Or flushed as evening cloud,
Great Dionysos, roamer of mountains,
He—was it he who found you there,
And caught you up in his own proud   20
Arms from the sweet god-ravisher°
Who laughed by the Muses' fountains?

Scene IV

OEDIPUS. Sirs: though I do not know the man,
    I think I see him coming, this shepherd we want:
    He is old, like our friend here, and the men
    Bringing him seem to be servants of my house.
    But you can tell, if you have ever seen him.   5
    Enter SHEPHERD *escorted by servants.*
CHORAGOS. I know him, he was Laïos' man. You can trust him.
OEDIPUS. Tell me first, you from Corinth: is this the shepherd
    We were discussing?
MESSENGER.   This is the very man.
OEDIPUS *[to* SHEPHERD*]*. Come here. No, look at me. You must answer
    Everything I ask.—You belonged to Laïos?   10
SHEPHERD. Yes: born his slave, brought up in his house.
OEDIPUS. Tell me: what kind of work did you do for him?
SHEPHERD. I was a shepherd of his, most of my life.
OEDIPUS. Where mainly did you go for pasturage?
SHEPHERD. Sometimes Kithairon, sometimes the hills near-by.   15
OEDIPUS. Do you remember ever seeing this man out there?
SHEPHERD. What would he be doing there? This man?
OEDIPUS. This man standing here. Have you ever seen him before?
SHEPHERD. No. At least, not to my recollection.
MESSENGER. And that is not strange, my lord. But I'll refresh   20
    His memory: he must remember when we two
    Spent three whole seasons together, March to September,

16 **Hermês . . . Kyllenê's** Hermês, messenger of the gods, was said to have been
born on Mt. Kyllenê   21 **the sweet god-ravisher**   the presumed mother, the
nymph whom the god found irresistible

On Kithairon or thereabouts. He had two flocks;
I had one. Each autumn I'd drive mine home
And he would go back with his to Laïos' sheepfold.—   25
Is this not true, just as I have described it?
SHEPHERD. True, yes; but it was all so long ago.
MESSENGER. Well, then: do you remember, back in those days
    That you gave me a baby boy to bring up as my own?
SHEPHERD. What if I did? What are you trying to say?   30
MESSENGER. King Oedipus was once that little child.
SHEPHERD. Damn you, hold your tongue!
OEDIPUS.   No more of that!
    It is your tongue needs watching, not this man's.
SHEPHERD. My King, my Master, what is it I have done wrong?
OEDIPUS. You have not answered his question about the boy.   35
SHEPHERD. He does not know . . . He is only making trouble . . .
OEDIPUS. Come, speak plainly, or it will go hard with you.
SHEPHERD. In God's name, do not torture an old man!
OEDIPUS. Come here, one of you; bind his arms behind him.
SHEPHERD. Unhappy king! What more do you wish to learn?   40
OEDIPUS. Did you give this man the child he speaks of?
SHEPHERD.   I did.
    And I would to God I had died that very day.
OEDIPUS. You will die now unless you speak the truth.
SHEPHERD. Yet if I speak the truth, I am worse than dead.
OEDIPUS. Very well; since you insist upon delaying—   45
SHEPHERD. No! I have told you already that I gave him the boy.
OEDIPUS. Where did you get him? From your house?
    From somewhere else?
SHEPHERD. Not from mine, no. A man gave him to me.
OEDIPUS. Is that man here? Do you know whose slave he was?
SHEPHERD. For God's love, my King, do not ask me any more!   50
OEDIPUS. You are a dead man if I have to ask you again.
SHEPHERD. Then . . . Then the child was from the palace of Laïos.
OEDIPUS. A slave child? or a child of his own line?
SHEPHERD. Ah, I am on the brink of dreadful speech!
OEDIPUS. And I of dreadful hearing. Yet I must hear.   55
SHEPHERD. If you must be told, then . . .
                            They said it was Laïos' child,
    But it is your wife who can tell you about that.
OEDIPUS. My wife!—Did she give it to you?
SHEPHERD.   My lord, she did.
OEDIPUS. Do you know why?
SHEPHERD.   I was told to get rid of it.
OEDIPUS. An unspeakable mother!
SHEPHERD.   There had been prophecies . . .   60
OEDIPUS. Tell me.
SHEPHERD.   It was said that the boy would kill his own father.
OEDIPUS. Then why did you give him over to this old man?
SHEPHERD. I pitied the baby, my King,
    And I thought that this man would take him far away
    To his own country.

He saved him—but for what a fate!   65
For if you are what this man says you are,
No man living is more wretched than Oedipus.
OEDIPUS. Ah God!
It was true!
All the prophecies!
—Now,

O Light, may I look on you for the last time!   70
I, Oedipus,
Oedipus, damned in his birth, in his marriage damned,
Damned in the blood he shed with his own hand!
He rushes into the palace.

Ode IV

CHORUS. Alas for the seed of men.   *Strophe 1*

What measure shall I give these generations
That breathe on the void and are void
And exist and do not exist?

Who bears more weight of joy   5
Than mass of sunlight shifting in images,
Or who shall make his thought stay on
That down time drifts away?

Your splendor is all fallen.

O naked brow of wrath and tears,   10
O change of Oedipus!
I who saw your days call no man blest—
Your great days like ghósts góne.

That mind was a strong bow.   *Antistrophe 1*
Deep, how deep you drew it then, hard archer,   15
At a dim fearful range,
And brought dear glory down!

You overcame the stranger—
The virgin with her hooking lion claws—
And though death sang, stood like a tower   20
To make pale Thebes take heart.

Fortress against our sorrow!

Divine king, giver of laws,
Majestic Oedipus!
No prince in Thebes had ever such renown,   25
No prince won such grace of power.

And now of all men ever known   *Strophe 2*
Most pitiful is this man's story:
His fortunes are most changed, his state
Fallen to a low slave's   30
Ground under bitter fate.

O Oedipus, most royal one!
The great door that expelled you to the light
Gave it night—ah, gave night to your glory:
As to the father, to the fathering son.   35

All understood too late.

How could that queen whom Laïos won,
The garden that he harrowed at his height,
Be silent when that act was done?

But all eyes fail before time's eye,   *Antistrophe 2*   40
All actions come to justice there.
Though never willed, though far down the deep past,
Your bed, your dread sirings,
Are brought to book at last.
Child by Laïos doomed to die,   45
Then doomed to lose that fortunate little death,
Would God you never took breath in this air
That with my wailing lips I take to cry:

For I weep the world's outcast.

I was blind, and now I can tell why: 50
Asleep, for you had given ease of breath
To Thebes, while the false years went by.

Exodos

Enter, from the palace, SECOND MESSENGER.
SECOND MESSENGER. Elders of Thebes, most honored in this land,
     What horrors are yours to see and hear, what weight
     Of sorrow to be endured, if, true to your birth,
     You venerate the line of Labdakos!
     I think neither Istros nor Phasis, those great rivers,   5
     Could purify this place of the corruption
     It shelters now, or soon must bring to light—
     Evil not done unconsciously, but willed.

     The greatest griefs are those we cause ourselves.
CHORAGOS. Surely, friend, we have grief enough already;   10
     What new sorrow do you mean?
SECOND MESSENGER.   The Queen is dead.
CHORAGOS. Iocastê? Dead? But at whose hand?
SECOND MESSENGER.   Her own.
     The full horror of what happened you cannot know,
     For you did not see it; but I, who did, will tell you
     As clearly as I can how she met her death.   15

     When she had left us,
     In passionate silence, passing through the court,
     She ran to her apartment in the house,
     Her hair clutched by the fingers of both hands.
     She closed the doors behind her; then, by that bed   20
     Where long ago the fatal son was conceived—

That son who should bring about his father's death—
We heard her call upon Laïos, dead so many years,
And heard her wail for the double fruit of her marriage,
A husband by her husband, children by her child.   25

Exactly how she died I do not know:
For Oedipus burst in moaning and would not let us
Keep vigil to the end: it was by him
As he stormed about the room that our eyes were caught.
From one to another of us he went, begging a sword,   30
Cursing the wife who was not his wife, the mother
Whose womb had carried his own children and himself.
I do not know: it was none of us aided him,
But surely one of the gods was in control!
For with a dreadful cry   35
He hurled his weight, as though wrenched out of himself,
At the twin doors: the bolts gave, and he rushed in.
And there we saw her hanging, her body swaying
From the cruel cord she had noosed about her neck.
A great sob broke from him heartbreaking to hear,   40
As he loosed the rope and lowered her to the ground.

I would blot out from my mind what happened next!
For the King ripped from her gown the golden brooches
That were her ornament, and raised them, and plunged them down
Straight into his own eyeballs, crying, "No more,   45
No more shall you look on the misery about me,
The horrors of my own doing! Too long you have known
The faces of those whom I should never have seen,
Too long been blind to those for whom I was searching!
From this hour, go in darkness!" And as he spoke,   50
He struck at his eyes—not once, but many times;
And the blood spattered his beard,
Bursting from his ruined sockets like red hail.

So from the unhappiness of two this evil has sprung,
A curse on the man and woman alike. The old   55
Happiness of the house of Labdakos
Was happiness enough: where is it today?
It is all wailing and ruin, disgrace, death—all
The misery of mankind that has a name—
And it is wholly and for ever theirs.   60
CHORAGOS. Is he in agony still? Is there no rest for him?
SECOND MESSENGER. He is calling for someone to lead him to the gates
So that all the children of Kadmos may look upon
His father's murderer, his mother's—no,
I cannot say it!
                    And then he will leave Thebes,   65
Self-exiled, in order that the curse
Which he himself pronounced may depart from the house.
He is weak, and there is none to lead him,
So terrible is his suffering.
                    But you will see:

Look, the doors are opening; in a moment   70
You will see a thing that would crush a heart of stone.
The central door is opened; OEDIPUS, *blinded, is led in.*
CHORAGOS. Dreadful indeed for men to see.
  Never have my own eyes
  Looked on a sight so full of fear.

  Oedipus!   75
  What madness came upon you, what daemon°
  Leaped on your life with heavier
  Punishment than a mortal man can bear?
  No: I cannot even
  Look at you, poor ruined one.   80
  And I would speak, question, ponder,
  If I were able. No.
  You make me shudder.
OEDIPUS. God. God.
  Is there a sorrow greater?   85
  Where shall I find harbor in this world?
  My voice is hurled far on a dark wind.
  What has God done to me?
CHORAGOS. Too terrible to think of, or to see.

OEDIPUS. O cloud of night,   *Strophe 1*   90
  Never to be turned away: night coming on,
  I cannot tell how: night like a shroud!
  My fair winds brought me here.
      Oh God. Again
  The pain of the spikes where I had sight,
  The flooding pain   95
  Of memory, never to be gouged out.
CHORAGOS. This is not strange.
  You suffer it all twice over, remorse in pain,
  Pain in remorse.

OEDIPUS. Ah dear friend   *Antistrophe 1* 100
  Are you faithful even yet, you alone?
  Are you still standing near me, will you stay here,
  Patient, to care for the blind?
      The blind man!
  Yet even blind I know who it is attends me,
  By the voice's tone—   105
  Though my new darkness hide the comforter.
CHORAGOS. Oh fearful act!
  What god was it drove you to rake black
  Night across your eyes?

OEDIPUS. Apollo. Apollo. Dear   *Strophe 2*   110
  Children, the god was Apollo.
  He brought my sick, sick fate upon me.
  But the blinding hand was my own!

76 **daemon** a spirit, not necessarily evil

How could I bear to see
When all my sight was horror everywhere?   115
CHORAGOS. Everywhere; that is true.
OEDIPUS. And now what is left?
      Images? Love? A greeting even,
      Sweet to the senses? Is there anything?
      Ah, no, friends: lead me away.   120
      Lead me away from Thebes.
                              Lead the great wreck
      And hell of Oedipus, whom the gods hate.
CHORAGOS. Your fate is clear, you are not blind to that.
      Would God you had never found it out!

OEDIPUS. Death take the man who unbound   *Antistrophe 2*   125
      My feet on that hillside
      And delivered me from death to life! What life?
      If only I had died,
      This weight of monstrous doom
      Could not have dragged me and my darlings down.   130
CHORAGOS. I would have wished the same.
OEDIPUS. Oh never to have come here
      With my father's blood upon me! Never
      To have been the man they call his mother's husband!
      Oh accurst! O child of evil,   135
      To have entered that wretched bed—
                              the selfsame one!
      More primal than sin itself, this fell to me.
CHORAGOS. I do not know how I can answer you.
      You were better dead than alive and blind.
OEDIPUS. Do not counsel me any more. This punishment   140
      That I have laid upon myself is just.
      If I had eyes,
      I do not know how I could bear the sight
      Of my father, when I came to the house of Death,
      Or my mother: for I have sinned against them both   145
      So vilely that I could not make my peace
      By strangling my own life.
                              Or do you think my children,
      Born as they were born, would be sweet to my eyes?
      Ah never, never! Nor this town with its high walls,
      Nor the holy images of the gods.
                              For I,   150
      Thrice miserable—Oedipus, noblest of all the line
      Of Kadmos, have condemned myself to enjoy
      These things no more, by my own malediction
      Expelling that man whom the gods declared
      To be a defilement in the house of Laïos.   155
      After exposing the rankness of my own guilt,
      How could I look men frankly in the eyes?
      No, I swear it,
      If I could have stifled my hearing at its source,
      I would have done it and made all this body   160

A tight cell of misery, blank to light and sound:
So I should have been safe in a dark agony
Beyond all recollection.

Ah Kithairon!

Why did you shelter me? When I was cast upon you,
Why did I not die? Then I should never   165
Have shown the world my execrable birth.

Ah Polybos! Corinth, city that I believed
The ancient seat of my ancestors: how fair
I seemed, your child! And all the while this evil
Was cancerous within me!

For I am sick   170

In my daily life, sick in my origin.

O three roads, dark ravine, woodland and way
Where three roads met: you, drinking my father's blood,
My own blood, spilled by my own hand: can you remember
The unspeakable things I did there, and the things   175
I went on from there to do?

O marriage, marriage!

The act that engendered me, and again the act
Performed by the son in the same bed—

Ah, the net

Of incest, mingling fathers, brothers, sons,
With brides, wives, mothers: the last evil   180
That can be known by men: no tongue can say
How evil!

No. For the love of God, conceal me

Somewhere far from Thebes; or kill me; or hurl me
Into the sea, away from men's eyes for ever.
Come, lead me. You need not fear to touch me.   185
Of all men, I alone can bear this guilt.

Enter CREON.

CHORAGOS. We are not the ones to decide; but Creon here
    May fitly judge of what you ask. He only
    Is left to protect the city in your place.

OEDIPUS. Alas, how can I speak to him? What right have I   190
    To beg his courtesy whom I have deeply wronged?

CREON. I have not come to mock you, Oedipus,
    Or to reproach you, either.

    [To ATTENDANTS.*]*   —You, standing there:
    If you have lost all respect for man's dignity,
    At least respect the flame of Lord Helios: 195
    Do not allow this pollution to show itself
    Openly here, an affront to the earth
    And Heaven's rain and the light of day. No, take him
    Into the house as quickly as you can.
    For it is proper   200
    That only the close kindred see his grief.

OEDIPUS. I pray you in God's name, since your courtesy
    Ignores my dark expectation, visiting

With mercy this man of all men most execrable:
Give me what I ask—for your good, not for mine.   205
CREON. And what is it that you would have me do?
OEDIPUS. Drive me out of this country as quickly as may be
To a place where no human voice can ever greet me.
CREON. I should have done that before now—only,
God's will had not been wholly revealed to me.   210
OEDIPUS. But his command is plain: the parricide
Must be destroyed. I am that evil man.
CREON. That is the sense of it, yes; but as things are,
We had best discover clearly what is to be done.
OEDIPUS. You would learn more about a man like me?   215
CREON. You are ready now to listen to the god.
OEDIPUS. I will listen. But it is to you.
That I must turn for help. I beg you, hear me.

The woman in there—
Give her whatever funeral you think proper: 220
She is your sister.
                     —But let me go, Creon!
Let me purge my father's Thebes of the pollution
Of my living here, and go out to the wild hills,
To Kithairon, that has won such fame with me,
The tomb my mother and father appointed for me,   225
And let me die there, as they willed I should.
And yet I know
Death will not ever come to me through sickness
Or in any natural way: I have been preserved
For some unthinkable fate. But let that be.   230
As for my sons, you need not care for them.
They are men, they will find some way to live.
But my poor daughters, who have shared my table,
Who never before have been parted from their father—
Take care of them, Creon; do this for me.   235
And will you let me touch them with my hands
A last time, and let us weep together?
Be kind, my lord,
Great prince, be kind!
                         Could I but touch them,
They would be mine again, as when I had my eyes.   240
Enter ANTIGONÊ *and* ISMENÊ, *attended.*
Ah, God!
Is it my dearest children I hear weeping?
Has Creon pitied me and sent my daughters?
CREON. Yes, Oedipus: I knew that they were dear to you
In the old days, and know you must love them still.   245
OEDIPUS. May God bless you for this—and be a friendlier
Guardian to you than he has been to me!

Children, where are you?
Come quickly to my hands: they are your brother's—
Hands that have brought your father's once clear eyes   250

To this way of seeing—
                Ah dearest ones,
I had neither sight nor knowledge then, your father
By the woman who was the source of his life!
And I weep for you—having no strength to see you—,
I weep for you when I think of the bitterness   255
That men will visit upon you all your lives.
What homes, what festivals can you attend
Without being forced to depart again in tears?
And when you come to marriageable age,
Where is the man, my daughters, who would dare   260
Risk the bane that lies on all my children?
Is there any evil wanting? Your father killed
His father; sowed the womb of her who bore him;
Engendered you at the fount of his own existence!
That is what they will say of you.
                          Then, whom   265
Can you ever marry? There are no bridegrooms for you,
And your lives must wither away in sterile dreaming.
O Creon, son of Menoikeus!
You are the only father my daughters have,
Since we, their parents, are both of us gone forever.   270
They are your own blood: you will not let them
Fall into beggary and loneliness;
You will keep them from the miseries that are mine!
Take pity on them; see, they are only children,
Friendless except for you. Promise me this,   275
Great Prince, and give me your hand in token of it.
CREON *clasps his right hand.*
Children:
I could say much, if you could understand me,
But as it is, I have only this prayer for you:
Live where you can, be as happy as you can—   280
Happier, please God, than God has made your father!
CREON. Enough. You have wept enough. Now go within.
OEDIPUS. I must; but it is hard.
CREON.   Time eases all things.
OEDIPUS. But you must promise—
CREON.   Say what you desire.
OEDIPUS. Send me from Thebes!
CREON.   God grant that I may!   285
OEDIPUS. But since God hates me . . .
CREON.   No, he will grant your wish.
OEDIPUS. You promise?
CREON.   I cannot speak beyond my knowledge.
OEDIPUS. Then lead me in.
CREON.   Come now, and leave your children.
OEDIPUS. No! Do not take them from me!
CREON.   Think no longer
That you are in command here, but rather think   290
How, when you were, you served your own destruction.

Exeunt into the house all but the CHORUS; *the* CHORAGOS *chants directly to the audience.*

CHORAGOS. Men of Thebes: look upon Oedipus.
    This is the king who solved the famous riddle
    And towered up, most powerful of men.
    No mortal eyes but looked on him with envy,   295

    Yet in the end ruin swept over him.
    Let every man in mankind's frailty
    Consider his last day; and let none
    Presume on his good fortune until he find
    Life, at his death, a memory without pain.   300

[c. 430 B.C.]

 # TOPICS FOR CRITICAL THINKING AND WRITING

1. On the basis of the Prologue, characterize Oedipus. What additional traits are revealed in Scene I and Ode I?
2. How fair is it to say that Oedipus is morally guilty? Does he argue that he is morally innocent because he did not intend to do immoral deeds? Can it be said that he is guilty of hubris but that hubris has nothing to do with his fall?
3. Oedipus says that he blinds himself in order not to look upon people he should not. What further reasons can be given? Why does he not (like his mother) commit suicide?
4. How fair is it to say that the play shows the contemptibleness of man's efforts to act intelligently?
5. How fair is it to say that in *Oedipus* the gods are evil?
6. Are the choral odes lyrical interludes that serve to separate the scenes, or do they advance the dramatic action?
7. Matthew Arnold said that Sophocles saw life steadily and saw it whole. But in this play is Sophocles facing the facts of life, or, on the contrary, is he avoiding life as it usually is and presenting a series of unnatural and outrageous coincidences?
8. Can you describe your emotions at the end of the play? Do they include pity for Oedipus? Pity for all human beings, including yourself? Fear that you might be punished for some unintended transgression? Awe, engendered by a perception of the interrelatedness of things? Relief that the story is only a story? Exhilaration?

Antigonê

An English Version by Dudley Fitts and Robert Fitzgerald

LIST OF CHARACTERS

ANTIGONÊ
ISMENÊ
EURYDICÊ
CREON

Jane Lapotaire in *Antigone,* National Theater, London, 1984 (Donald Cooper/Photostage)

HAIMON
TEIRESIAS
A SENTRY
A MESSENGER
CHORUS

SCENE: *Before the palace of* CREON, *king of Thebes. A central double door, and two lateral doors. A platform extends the length of the façade, and from this platform three steps lead down into the "orchestra," or chorus-ground.*

TIME: *Dawn of the day after the repulse of the Argive army from the assault on Thebes.*

Prologue

ANTIGONÊ *and* ISMENÊ *enter from the central door of the palace.*
ANTIGONÊ. Ismenê, dear sister,
    You would think that we had already suffered enough
    For the curse on Oedipus.°
    I cannot imagine any grief
    That you and I have not gone through. And now—   5
    Have they told you of the new decree of our King Creon?

3 Oedipus, once King of Thebes, was the father of Antigonê and Ismenê, and of their brothers Polyneicês and Eteoclês. Oedipus unwittingly killed his father, Laïos, and married his own mother Iocastê. When he learned what he had done, he blinded himself and left Thebes. Eteoclês and Polyneicês quarreled; Polyneicês was driven out but returned to assault Thebes. In the battle each brother killed the other; Creon became king and ordered that Polyneicês be left to rot unburied on the battlefield as a traitor.

ISMENÊ. I have heard nothing: I know
    That two sisters lost two brothers, a double death
    In a single hour; and I know that the Argive army
    Fled in the night; but beyond this, nothing.   10
ANTIGONÊ. I thought so. And this is why I wanted you
    To come out here with me. There is something we must do.
ISMENÊ. Why do you speak so strangely?
ANTIGONÊ. Listen, Ismenê:
    Creon buried our brother Eteoclês   15
    With military honors, gave him a soldier's funeral,
    And it was right that he should; but Polyneicês,
    Who fought as bravely and died as miserably,—
    They say that Creon has sworn
    No one shall bury him, no one mourn for him,   20
    But his body must lie in the fields, a sweet treasure
    For carrion birds to find as they search for food.
    That is what they say, and our good Creon is coming here
    To announce it publicly; and the penalty—
    Stoning to death in the public square!
                                    There it is,   25
    And now you can prove what you are:
    A true sister, or a traitor to your family.
ISMENÊ. Antigonê, you are mad! What could I possibly do?
ANTIGONÊ. You must decide whether you will help me or not.
ISMENÊ. I do not understand you. Help you in what?   30
ANTIGONÊ. Ismenê. I am going to bury him. Will you come?
ISMENÊ. Bury him! You have just said the new law forbids it.
ANTIGONÊ. He is my brother. And he is your brother, too.
ISMENÊ. But think of the danger! Think what Creon will do!
ANTIGONÊ. Creon is not strong enough to stand in my way.   35
ISMENÊ. Ah sister!
    Oedipus died, everyone hating him
    For what his own search brought to light, his eyes
    Ripped out by his own hand; and Iocastê died,
    His mother and wife at once: she twisted the cords   40
    That strangled her life; and our two brothers died,
    Each killed by the other's sword. And we are left:
    But oh, Antigonê,
    Think how much more terrible than these
    Our own death would be if we should go against Creon   45
    And do what he has forbidden! We are only women,
    We cannot fight with men, Antigonê!
    The law is strong, we must give in to the law
    In this thing, and in worse. I beg the Dead
    To forgive me, but I am helpless: I must yield   50
    To those in authority. And I think it is dangerous business
    To be always meddling.
ANTIGONÊ.   If that is what you think,
    I should not want you, even if you asked to come.
    You have made your choice, you can be what you want to be.
    But I will bury him; and if I must die,   55

I say that this crime is holy: I shall lie down
With him in death, and I shall be as dear
To him as he to me.
                              It is the dead,
Not the living, who make the longest demands:
We die for ever. . . .
                              You may do as you like.   60
Since apparently the laws of the gods mean nothing to you.
ISMENÊ. They mean a great deal to me; but I have no strength
    To break laws that were made for the public good.
ANTIGONÊ. That must be your excuse, I suppose. But as for me,
    I will bury the brother I love.
ISMENÊ.   Antigonê,   65
    I am so afraid for you!
ANTIGONÊ.   You need not be:
    You have yourself to consider, after all.
ISMENÊ. But no one must hear of this, you must tell no one!
    I will keep it a secret, I promise!
ANTIGONÊ.   O tell it! Tell everyone!
    Think how they'll hate you when it all comes out   70
    If they learn that you knew about it all the time!
ISMENÊ. So fiery! You should be cold with fear.
ANTIGONÊ. Perhaps. But I am doing only what I must.
ISMENÊ. But can you do it? I say that you cannot.
ANTIGONÊ. Very well: when my strength gives out,
    I shall do no more.   75
ISMENÊ. Impossible things should not be tried at all.
ANTIGONÊ. Go away, Ismenê:
    I shall be hating you soon, and the dead will too,
    For your words are hateful. Leave me my foolish plan:
    I am not afraid of the danger; if it means death,   80
    It will not be the worst of deaths—death without honor.
ISMENÊ. Go then, if you feel that you must.
    You are unwise,
    But a loyal friend indeed to those who love you.
    Exit into the palace. ANTIGONÊ *goes off, left. Enter the* CHORUS.

Párodos

CHORUS. Now the long blade of the sun, lying   *Strophe 1*
    Level east to west, touches with glory
    Thebes of the Seven Gates. Open, unlidded
    Eye of golden day! O marching light
    Across the eddy and rush of Dircê's stream,°   5
    Striking the white shields of the enemy
    Thrown headlong backward from the blaze of morning!
CHORAGOS.° Polyneicês their commander
    Roused them with windy phrases,
    He the wild eagle screaming   10

Prodos   5 Dircê's stream a stream west of Thebes   **8 Choragos** leader of the
Chorus

Insults above our land,
His wings their shields of snow,
His crest their marshalled helms.

CHORUS. Against our seven gates in a yawning ring   *Antistrophe 1*
The famished spears came onward in the night: 15
But before his jaws were sated with our blood,
Or pinefire took the garland of our towers,
He was thrown back; and as he turned, great Thebes—
No tender victim for his noisy power—
Rose like a dragon behind him, shouting war.   20
CHORAGOS. For God hates utterly
The bray of bragging tongues;
And when he beheld their smiling,
Their swagger of golden helms,
The frown of his thunder blasted   25
Their first man from our walls.
CHORUS. We heard his shout of triumph high in the air   *Strophe 2*
Turn to a scream; far out in a flaming arc
He fell with his windy torch, and the earth struck him.
And others storming in fury no less than his   30
Found shock of death in the dusty joy of battle.
CHORAGOS. Seven captains at seven gates
Yielded their clanging arms to the god
That bends the battle-line and breaks it.
These two only, brothers in blood,   35
Face to face in matchless rage.
Mirroring each the other's death,
Clashed in long combat.
CHORUS. But now in the beautiful morning of victory   *Antistrophe 2*
Let Thebes of the many chariots sing for joy!   40
With hearts for dancing we'll take leave of war:
Our temples shall be sweet with hymns of praise,
And the long nights shall echo with our chorus.

Scene I

CHORAGOS. But now at last our new King is coming:
Creon of Thebes, Menoikeus' son.
In this auspicious dawn of his reign
What are the new complexities
That shifting Fate has woven for him?   5
What is his counsel? Why has he summoned
The old men to hear him?
Enter CREON *from the palace, center. He addresses the* CHORUS *from
the top step.*
CREON. Gentlemen: I have the honor to inform you that our Ship of
State, which recent storms have threatened to destroy, has come
safely to harbor at last, guided by the merciful wisdom of Heaven. I   10
have summoned you here this morning because I know that I can
depend upon you: your devotion to King Laïos was absolute; you
never hesitated in your duty to our late ruler Oedipus; and when

Oedipus died, your loyalty was transferred to his children. Unfortunately, as you know, his two sons, the princes Eteoclês and Poly-   15
neicês, have killed each other in battle; and I, as the next in blood,
have succeeded to the full power of the throne.

I am aware, of course, that no Ruler can expect complete loyalty from his subjects until he has been tested in office. Nevertheless, I say to you at the very outset that I have nothing but con-   20
tempt for the kind of Governor who is afraid, for whatever reason,
to follow the course that he knows is best for the State; and as for
the man who sets private friendship above the public welfare,—I
have no use for him, either. I call God to witness that if I saw my
country headed for ruin, I should not be afraid to speak out plainly;   25
and I need hardly remind you that I would never have any dealings
with an enemy of the people. No one values friendship more
highly than I: but we must remember that friends made at the risk
of wrecking our Ship are not real friends at all.

These are my principles, at any rate, and that is why I have   30
made the following decision concerning the sons of Oedipus: Eteoclês, who died as a man should die, fighting for his country, is to be
buried with full military honors, with all the ceremony that is usual
when the greatest heroes die; but his brother Polyneicês, who
broke his exile to come back with fire and sword against his native   35
city and the shrines of his fathers' gods, whose one idea was to spill
the blood of his blood and sell his own people into slavery—
Polyneicês, I say, is to have no burial: no man is to touch him or say
the least prayer for him; he shall lie on the plain, unburied; and the
birds and the scavenging dogs can do with him whatever they like.   40
This is my command, and you can see the wisdom behind it.
As long as I am King, no traitor is going to be honored with the
loyal man. But whoever shows by word and deed that he is on the
side of the State—he shall have my respect while he is living and
my reverence when he is dead.   45

CHORAGOS. If that is your will, Creon son of Menoikeus,
    You have the right to enforce it: we are yours.
CREON. That is my will. Take care that you do your part.
CHORAGOS. We are old men: let the younger ones carry it out.
CREON. I do not mean that: the sentries have been appointed.   50
CHORAGOS. Then what is it that you would have us do?
CREON. You will give no support to whoever breaks this law.
CHORAGOS. Only a crazy man is in love with death!
CREON. And death it is; yet money talks, and the wisest
    Have sometimes been known to count a few coins too many.   55
    Enter SENTRY *from left.*
SENTRY. I'll not say that I'm out of breath from running, King, because
    every time I stopped to think about what I have to tell you, I felt
    like going back. And all the time a voice kept saying, "You fool,
    don't you know you're walking straight into trouble?"; and then an-
    other voice: "Yes, but if you let somebody else get the news to   60
    Creon first, it will be even worse than that for you!" But good sense
    won out, at least I hope it was good sense, and here I am with a

story that makes no sense at all; but I'll tell it anyhow, because, as
they say, what's going to happen's going to happen and—

CREON. Come to the point. What have you to say?   65

SENTRY. I did not do it. I did not see who did it. You must not punish me
for what someone else has done.

CREON. A comprehensive defense! More effective, perhaps, if I knew its
purpose. Come: what is it?

SENTRY. A dreadful thing . . . I don't know how to put it—   70

CREON. Out with it!

SENTRY.   Well, then;

The dead man—

                     Polyneicês—

Pause. The SENTRY *is overcome, fumbles for words.* CREON *waits*
impassively.

                              out there—

                                     someone,—

New dust on the slimy flesh!

Pause. No sign from CREON.

Someone has given it burial that way, and

Gone. . . .   75

Long pause. CREON *finally speaks with deadly control.*

CREON. And the man who dared do this?

SENTRY.   I swear I

Do not know! You must believe me!

                              Listen:

The ground was dry, not a sign of digging, no,

Not a wheeltrack in the dust, no trace of anyone.

It was when they relieved us this morning: and one of them,   80

The corporal, pointed to it.

                         There it was,

The strangest—

             Look:

The body, just mounded over with light dust: you see?

Not buried really, but as if they'd covered it

Just enough for the ghost's peace. And no sign   85

Of dogs or any wild animal that had been there.

And then what a scene there was! Every man of us

Accusing the other: we all proved the other man did it,

We all had proof that we could not have done it.

We were ready to take hot iron in our hands,   90

Walk through fire, swear by all the gods,

It was not I!

I do not know who it was, but it was not I!

CREON'S *rage has been mounting steadily, but the* SENTRY *is too in-*
tent upon his story to notice it.

And then, when this came to nothing, someone said

A thing that silenced us and made us stare   95

Down at the ground: you had to be told the news,

And one of us had to do it! We threw the dice,

And the bad luck fell to me. So here I am,
No happier to be here than you are to have me:
Nobody likes the man who brings bad news.   100

CHORAGOS. I have been wondering, King: can it be that the gods have
done this?

CREON [*furiously*]. Stop!
    Must you doddering wrecks
Go out of your heads entirely? "The gods"!   105
Intolerable!
The gods favor this corpse? Why? How had he served them?
Tried to loot their temples, burn their images,
Yes, and the whole State, and its laws with it!
Is it your senile opinion that the gods love to honor bad men?   110
A pious thought!—
                No, from the very beginning
There have been those who have whispered together,
Stiff-necked anarchists, putting their heads together,
Scheming against me in alleys. These are the men,
And they have bribed my own guard to do this thing.   115
[*Sententiously.*] Money!
There's nothing in the world so demoralizing as money.
Down go your cities,
Homes gone, men gone, honest hearts corrupted.
Crookedness of all kinds, and all for money!
[*To* SENTRY.]   But you—!   120
I swear by God and by the throne of God,
The man who has done this thing shall pay for it!
Find that man, bring him here to me, or your death
Will be the least of your problems: I'll string you up
Alive, and there will be certain ways to make you   125
Discover your employer before you die;
And the process may teach you a lesson you seem to have missed:
The dearest profit is sometimes all too dear:
That depends on the source. Do you understand me?
A fortune won is often misfortune.   130

SENTRY. King, may I speak?
CREON.   Your very voice distresses me.
SENTRY. Are you sure that it is my voice, and not your conscience?
CREON. By God, he wants to analyze me now!
SENTRY. It is not what I say, but what has been done, that hurts you.
CREON. You talk too much.
SENTRY.   Maybe; but I've done nothing.   135
CREON. Sold your soul for some silver: that's all you've done.
SENTRY. How dreadful it is when the right judge judges wrong!
CREON. Your figures of speech
May entertain you now; but unless you bring me the man,
You will get little profit from them in the end.   140
    Exit CREON *into the palace.*
SENTRY. "Bring me the man"—!
I'd like nothing better than bringing him the man!

But bring him or not, you have seen the last of me here.
At any rate, I am safe!   *[Exit* SENTRY.*]*

Ode I

CHORUS. Numberless are the world's wonders, but not   *Strophe 1*
    More wonderful than man; the stormgray sea
    Yields to his prows, the huge crests bear him high;
    Earth, holy and inexhaustible, is graven
    With shining furrows where his plows have gone   5
    Year after year, the timeless labor of stallions.

    The lightboned birds and beasts that cling to cover,   *Antistrophe 1*
    The lithe fish lighting their reaches of dim water,
    All are taken, tamed in the net of his mind;
    The lion on the hill, the wild horse windy-maned,   10
    Resign to him; and his blunt yoke has broken
    The sultry shoulders of the mountain bull.

    Words also, and thought as rapid as air,   *Strophe 2*
    He fashions to his good use; statecraft is his,
    And his the skill that deflects the arrows of snow,   15
    The spears of winter rain: from every wind
    He has made himself secure—from all but one:
    In the late wind of death he cannot stand.

    O clear intelligence, force beyond all measure!   *Antistrophe 2*
    O fate of man, working both good and evil!   20
    When the laws are kept, how proudly his city stands!
    When the laws are broken, what of his city then?
    Never may the anarchic man find rest at my hearth,
    Never be it said that my thoughts are his thoughts.

Scene II

    Reenter SENTRY *leading* ANTIGONÊ.
CHORAGOS. What does this mean? Surely this captive woman
    Is the Princess, Antigonê. Why should she be taken?
SENTRY. Here is the one who did it! We caught her
    In the very act of burying him.—Where is Creon?
CHORAGOS. Just coming from the house.
    Enter CREON, *center.*
CREON.   What has happened?   5
    Why have you come back so soon?
SENTRY *[expansively].*   O King,
    A man should never be too sure of anything:
    I would have sworn
    That you'd not see me here again: your anger
    Frightened me so, and the things you threatened me with; 10
    But how could I tell then
    That I'd be able to solve the case so soon?
    No dice-throwing this time: I was only too glad to come!
    Here is this woman. She is the guilty one:

We found her trying to bury him.   15
Take her, then; question her; judge her as you will.
I am through with the whole thing now, and glad of it.
CREON. But this is Antigonê! Why have you brought her here?
SENTRY. She was burying him, I tell you!
CREON *[severely].*   Is this the truth?
SENTRY. I saw her with my own eyes. Can I say more?   20
CREON. The details: come, tell me quickly!
SENTRY.   It was like this:
After those terrible threats of yours, King,
We went back and brushed the dust away from the body.
The flesh was soft by now, and stinking,
So we sat on a hill to windward and kept guard.   25
No napping this time! We kept each other awake.
But nothing happened until the white round sun
Whirled in the center of the round sky over us:
Then, suddenly,
A storm of dust roared up from the earth, and the sky   30
Went out, the plain vanished with all its trees
In the stinging dark. We closed our eyes and endured it.
The whirlwind lasted a long time, but it passed;
And then we looked, and there was Antigonê!
I have seen   35
A mother bird come back to a stripped nest, heard
Her crying bitterly a broken note or two
For the young ones stolen. Just so, when this girl
Found the bare corpse, and all her love's work wasted,
She wept, and cried on heaven to damn the hands   40
That had done this thing.
                          And then she brought more dust
And sprinkled wine three times for her brother's ghost.

We ran and took her at once. She was not afraid,
Not even when we charged her with what she had done.
She denied nothing.
                    And this was a comfort to me,   45
And some uneasiness: for it is a good thing
To escape from death, but it is no great pleasure
To bring death to a friend.
                          Yet I always say
There is nothing so comfortable as your own safe skin!
CREON *[slowly, dangerously].* And you, Antigonê,   50
You with your head hanging,—do you confess this thing?
ANTIGONÊ. I do. I deny nothing.
CREON *[to* SENTRY*].*   You may go.

                                          [Exit SENTRY.*]*

[To ANTIGONÊ.*]* Tell me, tell me briefly:
Had you heard my proclamation touching this matter?
ANTIGONÊ. It was public. Could I help hearing it?   55
CREON. And yet you dared defy the law.
ANTIGONÊ.   I dared.

It was not God's proclamation. That final Justice
That rules the world below makes no such laws.

Your edict, King, was strong.
But all your strength is weakness itself against   60
The immortal unrecorded laws of God.
They are not merely now: they were, and shall be,
Operative for ever, beyond man utterly.
I knew I must die, even without your decree:
I am only mortal. And if I must die   65
Now, before it is my time to die,
Surely this is no hardship: can anyone
Living, as I live, with evil all about me,
Think Death less than a friend? This death of mine
Is of no importance; but if I had left my brother   70
Lying in death unburied, I should have suffered.
Now I do not.
                    You smile at me. Ah Creon,
Think me a fool, if you like; but it may well be
That a fool convicts me of folly.

CHORAGOS. Like father, like daughter: both headstrong, deaf to reason!   75
She has never learned to yield.

CREON.   She has much to learn.
The inflexible heart breaks first, the toughest iron
Cracks first, and the wildest horses bend their necks
At the pull of the smallest curb.
                                Pride? In a slave?
This girl is guilty of a double insolence,   80
Breaking the given laws and boasting of it.
Who is the man here,
She or I, if this crime goes unpunished?
Sister's child, or more than sister's child,
Or closer yet in blood—she and her sister   85
Win bitter death for this!
[To SERVANTS.*]*   Go, some of you,
Arrest Ismenê. I accuse her equally.
Bring her: you will find her sniffling in the house there.

Here mind's a traitor: crimes kept in the dark
Cry for light, and the guardian brain shudders;   90
But how much worse than this
Is brazen boasting of barefaced anarchy!

ANTIGONÊ. Creon, what more do you want than my death?

CREON.   Nothing.
That gives me everything.

ANTIGONÊ.   Then I beg you: kill me.
This talking is a great weariness: your words   95
Are distasteful to me, and I am sure that mine
Seem so to you. And yet they should not seem so:
I should have praise and honor for what I have done.
All these men here would praise me
Were their lips not frozen shut with fear of you.   100

[Bitterly.] Ah the good fortune of kings,
    Licensed to say and do whatever they please!
CREON. You are alone here in that opinion.
ANTIGONÊ. No, they are with me. But they keep their tongues in leash.
CREON. Maybe. But you are guilty, and they are not.   105
ANTIGONÊ. There is no guilt in reverence for the dead.
CREON. But Eteoclês—was he not your brother too?
ANTIGONÊ. My brother too.
CREON.   And you insult his memory?
ANTIGONÊ *[softly]*. The dead man would not say that I insult it.
CREON. He would: for you honor a traitor as much as him.   110
ANTIGONÊ. His own brother, traitor or not, and equal in blood.
CREON. He made war on his country. Eteoclês defended it.
ANTIGONÊ. Nevertheless, there are honors due all the dead.
CREON. But not the same for the wicked as for the just.
ANTIGONÊ. Ah Creon, Creon,   115
    Which of us can say what the gods hold wicked?
CREON. An enemy is an enemy, even dead.
ANTIGONÊ. It is my nature to join in love, not hate.
CREON. *[finally losing patience]*. Go join them then; if you must have
      your love,
    Find it in hell!   120
CHORAGOS. But see, Ismenê comes:
    Enter ISMENÊ, *guarded.*
    Those tears are sisterly, the cloud
    That shadows her eyes rains down gentle sorrow.
CREON. You too, Ismenê,
    Snake in my ordered house, sucking my blood   125
    Stealthily—and all the time I never knew
    That these two sisters were aiming at my throne!
                        Ismenê,
    Do you confess your share in this crime, or deny it?
    Answer me.
ISMENÊ. Yes, if she will let me say so. I am guilty.   130
ANTIGONÊ *[coldly]*. No, Ismenê. You have no right to say so.
    You would not help me, and I will not have you help me.
ISMENÊ. But now I know what you meant; and I am here
    To join you, to take my share of punishment.
ANTIGONÊ. The dead man and the gods who rule the dead   135
    Know whose act this was. Words are not friends.
ISMENÊ. Do you refuse me, Antigonê? I want to die with you:
    I too have a duty that I must discharge to the dead.
ANTIGONÊ. You shall not lessen my death by sharing it.
ISMENÊ. What do I care for life when you are dead?   140
ANTIGONÊ. Ask Creon. You're always hanging on his opinions.
ISMENÊ. You are laughing at me. Why, Antigonê?
ANTIGONÊ. It's a joyless laughter, Ismenê.
ISMENÊ.   But can I do nothing?
ANTIGONÊ. Yes. Save yourself. I shall not envy you.
    There are those who will praise you; I shall have honor, too.   145
ISMENÊ. But we are equally guilty!

ANTIGONÊ.   No more, Ismenê.
    You are alive, but I belong to Death.
CREON *[to the* CHORUS*].* Gentlemen, I beg you to observe these girls:
    One has just now lost her mind; the other,
    It seems, has never had a mind at all.   150
ISMENÊ. Grief teaches the steadiest minds to waver, King.
CREON. Yours certainly did, when you assumed guilt with the guilty!
ISMENÊ. But how could I go on living without her?
CREON.   You are.
    She is already dead.
ISMENÊ.   But your own son's bride!
CREON. There are places enough for him to push his plow.   155
    I want no wicked women for my sons!
ISMENÊ. O dearest Haimon, how your father wrongs you!
CREON. I've had enough of your childish talk of marriage!
CHORAGOS. Do you really intend to steal this girl from your son?
CREON. No; Death will do that for me.
CHORAGOS.   Then she must die?   160
CREON *[ironically].* You dazzle me.
              —But enough of this talk!
[To GUARDS*.]* You, there, take them away and guard them well:
For they are but women, and even brave men run
When they see Death coming.
              Exeunt ISMENÊ, ANTIGONÊ, *and* GUARDS.

Ode II

CHORUS. Fortunate is the man who has never tasted   *Strophe 1*
    God's vengeance!
Where once the anger of heaven has struck, that house is shaken
For ever: damnation rises behind each child
Like a wave cresting out of the black northeast,
When the long darkness under sea roars up   5
And bursts drumming death upon the windwhipped sand.

I have seen this gathering sorrow from time long past   *Antistrophe 1*
Loom upon Oedipus' children: generation from generation
Takes the compulsive rage of the enemy god.
So lately this last flower of Oedipus' line   10
Drank the sunlight! but now a passionate word
And a handful of dust have closed up all its beauty.

What mortal arrogance   *Strophe 2*
Transcends the wrath of Zeus?
Sleep cannot lull him nor the effortless long months   15
Of the timeless gods: but he is young for ever,
And his house is the shining day of high Olympos.
All that is and shall be,
And all the past, is his.
No pride on earth is free of the curse of heaven.   20

The straying dreams of men   *Antistrophe 2*
May bring them ghosts of joy:

But as they drowse, the waking embers burn them;
Or they walk with fixed eyes, as blind men walk.
But the ancient wisdom speaks for our own time: 25
    Fate works most for woe
    With Folly's fairest show.
Man's little pleasure is the spring of sorrow.

Scene III

CHORAGOS. But here is Haimon, King, the last of all your sons.
    Is it grief for Antigonê that brings him here,
    And bitterness at being robbed of his bride?
    Enter HAIMON.
CREON. We shall soon see, and no need of diviners.

                         —Son,
    You have heard my final judgment on that girl: 5
    Have you come here hating me, or have you come
    With deference and with love, whatever I do?
HAIMON. I am your son, father. You are my guide.
    You make things clear for me, and I obey you.
    No marriage means more to me than your continuing wisdom.   10
CREON. Good. That is the way to behave: subordinate
    Everything else, my son, to your father's will.
    This is what a man prays for, that he may get
    Sons attentive and dutiful in his house,
    Each one hating his father's enemies,   15
    Honoring his father's friends. But if his sons
    Fail him, if they turn out unprofitably,
    What has he fathered but trouble for himself
    And amusement for the malicious?
                      So you are right
    Not to lose your head over this woman.   20
    Your pleasure with her would soon grow cold, Haimon,
    And then you'd have a hellcat in bed and elsewhere.
    Let her find her husband in Hell!
    Of all the people in this city, only she
    Has had contempt for my law and broken it.   25

    Do you want me to show myself weak before the people?
    Or to break my sworn word? No, and I will not.
    The woman dies.
    I suppose she'll plead "family ties." Well, let her.
    If I permit my own family to rebel,   30
    How shall I earn the world's obedience?
    Show me the man who keeps his house in hand,
    He's fit for public authority.
                    I'll have no dealings
    With lawbreakers, critics of the government:
    Whoever is chosen to govern should be obeyed—   35
    Must be obeyed, in all things, great and small,
    Just and unjust! O Haimon,
    The man who knows how to obey, and that man only,

Knows how to give commands when the time comes.
You can depend on him, no matter how fast   40
The spears come: he's a good soldier, he'll stick it out.

Anarchy, anarchy! Show me a greater evil!
This is why cities tumble and the great houses rain down,
This is what scatters armies!
No, no: good lives are made so by discipline.   45
We keep the laws then, and the lawmakers,
And no woman shall seduce us. If we must lose,
Let's lose to a man, at least! Is a woman stronger than we?
CHORAGOS. Unless time has rusted my wits,
What you say, King, is said with point and dignity.   50
HAIMON [boyishly earnest]. Father:
Reason is God's crowning gift to man, and you are right
To warn me against losing mine. I cannot say—
I hope that I shall never want to say!—that you
Have reasoned badly. Yet there are other men   55
Who can reason, too; and their opinions might be helpful.
You are not in a position to know everything
That people say or do, or what they feel:
Your temper terrifies—everyone
Will tell you only what you like to hear.   60
But I, at any rate, can listen; and I have heard them
Muttering and whispering in the dark about this girl.
They say no woman has ever, so unreasonably,
Died so shameful a death for a generous act:
"She covered her brother's body. Is this indecent?   65
She kept him from dogs and vultures. Is this a crime?
Death?—She should have all the honor that we can give her!"

This is the way they talk out there in the city.

You must believe me:
Nothing is closer to me than your happiness.   70
What could be closer? Must not any son
Value his father's fortune as his father does his?
I beg you, do not be unchangeable:
Do not believe that you alone can be right.
The man who thinks that,   75
The man who maintains that only he has the power
To reason correctly, the gift to speak, the soul—
A man like that, when you know him, turns out empty.

It is not reason never to yield to reason!

In flood time you can see how some trees bend,   80
And because they bend, even their twigs are safe,
While stubborn trees are torn up, roots and all.
And the same thing happens in sailing:
Make your sheet fast, never slacken,—and over you go,
Head over heels and under: and there's your voyage.   85
Forget you are angry! Let yourself be moved!
I know I am young; but please let me say this:

The ideal condition
Would be, I admit, that men should be right by instinct;
But since we are all too likely to go astray,   90
The reasonable thing is to learn from those who can teach.
CHORAGOS. You will do well to listen to him, King,
If what he says is sensible. And you, Haimon,
Must listen to your father.—Both speak well.
CREON. You consider it right for a man of my years and experience   95
To go to school to a boy?
HAIMON.   It is not right
If I am wrong. But if I am young, and right,
What does my age matter?
CREON. You think it right to stand up for an anarchist?
HAIMON. Not at all. I pay no respect to criminals.   100
CREON. Then she is not a criminal?
HAIMON. The City would deny it, to a man.
CREON. And the City proposes to teach me how to rule?
HAIMON. Ah. Who is it that's talking like a boy now?
CREON. My voice is the one voice giving orders in this City!   105
HAIMON. It is no City if it takes orders from one voice.
CREON. The State is the King!
HAIMON.   Yes, if the State is a desert.
    Pause.
CREON. This boy, it seems, has sold out to a woman.
HAIMON. If you are a woman: my concern is only for you.
CREON. So? Your "concern"! In a public brawl with your father!   110
HAIMON. How about you, in a public brawl with justice?
CREON. With justice, when all that I do is within my rights?
HAIMON. You have no right to trample on God's right.
CREON *[completely out of control].* Fool, adolescent fool! Taken in by a
    woman!
HAIMON. You'll never see me taken in by anything vile.   115
CREON. Every word you say is for her!
HAIMON *[quietly, darkly].*   And for you.
    And for me. And for the gods under the earth.
CREON. You'll never marry her while she lives.
HAIMON. Then she must die.—But her death will cause another.
CREON. Another?   120
Have you lost your senses? Is this an open threat?
HAIMON. There is no threat in speaking to emptiness.
CREON. I swear you'll regret this superior tone of yours!
    You are the empty one!
HAIMON.   If you were not my father,
    I'd say you were perverse.   125
CREON. You girlstruck fool, don't play at words with me!
HAIMON. I am sorry. You prefer silence.
CREON.   Now, by God—
    I swear, by all the gods in heaven above us,
    You'll watch it, I swear you shall!
    [To the SERVANTS.*]*   Bring her out!
    Bring the woman out! Let her die before his eyes!   130

Here, this instant, with her bridegroom beside her!

HAIMON. Not here, no; she will not die here, King.

And you will never see my face again.

Go on raving as long as you've a friend to endure you.

Exit HAIMON.

CHORAGOS. Gone, gone.   135

Creon, a young man in a rage is dangerous!

CREON. Let him do, or dream to do, more than a man can.

He shall not save these girls from death.

CHORAGOS.   These girls?

You have sentenced them both?

CREON.   No, you are right.

I will not kill the one whose hands are clean.   140

CHORAGOS. But Antigonê?

CREON. *[somberly].*   I will carry her far away

Out there in the wilderness, and lock her

Living in a vault of stone. She shall have food,

As the custom is, to absolve the State of her death.

And there let her pray to the gods of hell: 145

They are her only gods:

Perhaps they will show her an escape from death,

Or she may learn,

though late,

That piety shown the dead is piety in vain.

[Exit CREON.*]*

Ode III

CHORUS. Love, unconquerable   *Strophe*

Waster of rich men, keeper

Of warm lights and all-night vigil

In the soft face of a girl:

Sea-wanderer, forest-visitor!   5

Even the pure Immortals cannot escape you,

And the mortal man, in his one day's dusk,

Trembles before your glory.

Surely you swerve upon ruin   *Antistrophe*

The just man's consenting heart,   10

As here you have made bright anger

Strike between father and son—

And none has conquered by Love!

A girl's glánce wórking the will of heaven:

Pleasure to her alone who mocks us,   15

Merciless Aphroditê.°

Scene IV

CHORAGOS *[as* ANTIGONÊ *enters guarded].* But I can no longer stand in awe

of this,

Ode III 16 Aphroditê goddess of love

Nor, seeing what I see, keep back my tears.
Here is Antigonê, passing to that chamber
Where all find sleep at last.

ANTIGONÊ. Look upon me, friends, and pity me   *Strophe 1*   5
    Turning back at the night's edge to say
    Good-by to the sun that shines for me no longer;
    Now sleepy Death
    Summons me down to Acheron,° that cold shore:
    There is no bridesong there, nor any music.   10
CHORUS. Yet not unpraised, not without a kind of honor,
    You walk at last into the underworld;
    Untouched by sickness, broken by no sword.
    What woman has ever found your way to death?

ANTIGONÊ. How often I have heard the story of Niobê,°   *Antistrophe 1*   15
    Tantalos' wretched daughter, how the stone
    Clung fast about her, ivy-close: and they say
    The rain falls endlessly
    And sifting soft snow; her tears are never done.
    I feel the loneliness of her death in mine.   20
CHORUS. But she was born of heaven, and you
    Are woman, woman-born. If her death is yours,
    A mortal woman's, is this not for you
    Glory in our world and in the world beyond?

ANTIGONÊ. You laugh at me. Ah, friends, friends   *Strophe 2*   25
    Can you not wait until I am dead? O Thebes,
    O men many-charioted, in love with Fortune,
    Dear springs of Dircê, sacred Theban grove,
    Be witnesses for me, denied all pity,
    Unjustly judged! and think a word of love   30
    For her whose path turns
    Under dark earth, where there are no more tears.
CHORUS. You have passed beyond human daring and come at last
    Into a place of stone where Justice sits.
    I cannot tell   35
    What shape of your father's guilt appears in this.
ANTIGONÊ. You have touched it at last: *Antistrophe 2*
    That bridal bed
    Unspeakable, horror of son and mother mingling:
    Their crime, infection of all our family!
    O Oedipus, father and brother!   40
    Your marriage strikes from the grave to murder mine.
    I have been a stranger here in my own land:
    All my life
    The blasphemy of my birth has followed me.

---

9 Acheron a river of the underworld, which was ruled by Hades   **15 Niobê** (Niobê
boasted of her numerous children, provoking Leto, the mother of Apollo, to destroy
them. Niobê wept profusely, and finally was turned to stone on Mount Sipylus,
whose streams are her tears).

CHORUS. Reverence is a virtue, but strength
    Lives in established law: that must prevail.
    You have made your choice,
    Your death is the doing of your conscious hand.

ANTIGONÊ. Then let me go, since all your words are bitter,   *Epode*
    And the very light of the sun is cold to me.   50
    Lead me to my vigil, where I must have
    Neither love nor lamentation; no song, but silence.
    CREON *interrupts impatiently.*

CREON. If dirges and planned lamentations could put off death,
    Men would be singing for ever.
    [To the SERVANTS.*]*   Take her, go!
    You know your orders: take her to the vault   55
    And leave her alone there. And if she lives or dies,
    That's her affair, not ours: our hands are clean.

ANTIGONÊ. O tomb, vaulted bride-bed in eternal rock,
    Soon I shall be with my own again
    Where Persephonê° welcomes the thin ghosts underground: 60
    And I shall see my father again, and you, mother,
    And dearest Polyneicês—
                dearest indeed
    To me, since it was my hand
    That washed him clean and poured the ritual wine:
    And my reward is death before my time!   65

    And yet, as men's hearts know, I have done no wrong,
    I have not sinned before God. Or if I have,
    I shall know the truth in death. But if the guilt
    Lies upon Creon who judged me, then, I pray,
    May his punishment equal my own.

CHORAGOS.   O passionate heart,   70
    Unyielding, tormented still by the same winds!

CREON. Her guards shall have good cause to regret their delaying.

ANTIGONÊ. Ah! That voice is like the voice of death!

CREON. I can give you no reason to think you are mistaken.

ANTIGONÊ. Thebes, and you my fathers' gods,   75
    And rulers of Thebes, you see me now, the last
    Unhappy daughter of a line of kings,
    Your kings, led away to death. You will remember
    What things I suffer, and at what men's hands,
    Because I would not transgress the laws of heaven.   80
    [To the GUARDS, *simply.]* Come: let us wait no longer.
                             [Exit ANTIGONÊ, *left, guarded.]*

Ode IV

CHORUS. All Danaê's beauty was locked away   *Strophe 1*
    In a brazen cell where the sunlight could not come:

60 Persephonê queen of the underworld

A small room still as any grave, enclosed her.
Yet she was a princess too,
And Zeus in a rain of gold poured love upon her.   5
O child, child,
No power in wealth or war
Or tough sea-blackened ships
Can prevail against untiring Destiny!

And Dryas' son° also, that furious king,   *Antistrophe 1*   10
Bore the god's prisoning anger for his pride:
Sealed up by Dionysos in deaf stone,
His madness died among echoes.
So at the last he learned what dreadful power
His tongue had mocked: 15
For he had profaned the revels,
And fired the wrath of the nine
Implacable Sisters° that love the sound of the flute.

And old men tell a half-remembered tale   *Strophe 2*
Of horror where a dark ledge splits the sea   20
And a double surf beats on the gráy shóres:
How a king's new woman,° sick
With hatred for the queen he had imprisoned,
Ripped out his two sons' eyes with her bloody hands
While grinning Arês° watched the shuttle plunge   25
Four times: four blind wounds crying for revenge,

Crying, tears and blood mingled.—Piteously born,   *Antistrophe 2*
Those sons whose mother was of heavenly birth!
Her father was the god of the North Wind
And she was cradled by gales,   30
She raced with young colts on the glittering hills
And walked untrammeled in the open light:
But in her marriage deathless Fate found means
To build a tomb like yours for all her joy.

Scene V

Enter blind TEIRESIAS, *led by a boy. The opening speeches of*
TEIRESIAS *should be in singsong contrast to the realistic lines of*
CREON.

TEIRESIAS. This is the way the blind man comes, Princes, Princes,
    Lock-step, two heads lit by the eyes of one.
CREON. What new thing have you to tell us, old Teiresias?
TEIRESIAS. I have much to tell you: listen to the prophet, Creon.
CREON. I am not aware that I have ever failed to listen.   5

---

10 Dryas' son Lycurgus, King of Thrace   **18 Sisters** the Muses   **22 king's new
woman** Eidothea, second wife of King Phineus, blinded her stepsons. Their
mother, Cleopatra, had been imprisoned in a cave. Phineus was the son of a king,
and Cleopatra, his first wife, was the daughter of Boreas, the North wind, but this
illustrious ancestry could not protect his sons from violence and darkness.
25 Arês god of war

TEIRESIAS. Then you have done wisely, King, and ruled well.
CREON. I admit my debt to you. But what have you to say?
TEIRESIAS. This, Creon: you stand once more on the edge of fate.
CREON. What do you mean? Your words are a kind of dread.
TEIRESIAS. Listen, Creon: 10
    I was sitting in my chair of augury, at the place
    Where the birds gather about me. They were all a-chatter,
    As is their habit, when suddenly I heard
    A strange note in their jangling, a scream, a
    Whirring fury; I knew that they were fighting,   15
    Tearing each other, dying
    In a whirlwind of wings clashing. And I was afraid.
    I began the rites of burnt-offering at the altar,
    But Hephaistos° failed me: instead of bright flame,
    There was only the sputtering slime of the fat thigh-flesh   20
    Melting: the entrails dissolved in gray smoke,
    The bare bone burst from the welter. And no blaze!

    This was a sign from heaven. My boy described it,
    Seeing for me as I see for others.

    I tell you, Creon, you yourself have brought   25
    This new calamity upon us. Our hearths and altars
    Are stained with the corruption of dogs and carrion birds
    That glut themselves on the corpse of Oedipus' son.
    The gods are deaf when we pray to them, their fire
    Recoils from our offering, their birds of omen   30
    Have no cry of comfort, for they are gorged
    With the thick blood of the dead.
                      O my son,
    These are no trifles! Think: all men make mistakes,
    But a good man yields when he knows his course is wrong,
    And repairs the evil. The only crime is pride.   35

    Give in to the dead man, then: do not fight with a corpse—
    What glory is it to kill a man who is dead?
    Think, I beg you:
    It is for your own good that I speak as I do.
    You should be able to yield for your own good.   40
CREON. It seems that prophets have made me their especial province.
    All my life long
    I have been a kind of butt for the dull arrows
    Of doddering fortune-tellers!
                      No, Teiresias:
    If your birds—if the great eagles of God himself   45
    Should carry him stinking bit by bit to heaven,
    I would not yield. I am not afraid of pollution:
    No man can defile the gods.
                    Do what you will,
    Go into business, make money, speculate

19 Hephaistos god of fire

In India gold or that synthetic gold from Sardis,   50
    Get rich otherwise than by my consent to bury him.
    Teiresias, it is a sorry thing when a wise man
    Sells his wisdom, lets out his words for hire!
TEIRESIAS. Ah Creon! Is there no man left in the world—
CREON. To do what?—Come, let's have the aphorism!   55
TEIRESIAS. No man who knows that wisdom outweighs any wealth?
CREON. As surely as bribes are baser than any baseness.
TEIRESIAS. You are sick, Creon! You are deathly sick!
CREON. As you say: it is not my place to challenge a prophet.
TEIRESIAS. Yet you have said my prophecy is for sale.   60
CREON. The generation of prophets has always loved gold.
TEIRESIAS. The generation of kings has always loved brass.
CREON. You forget yourself! You are speaking to your King.
TEIRESIAS. I know it. You are a king because of me.
CREON. You have a certain skill; but you have sold out.   65
TEIRESIAS. King, you will drive me to words that—
CREON.   Say them, say them!
    Only remember: I will not pay you for them.
TEIRESIAS. No, you will find them too costly.
CREON.   No doubt. Speak:
    Whatever you say, you will not change my will.
TEIRESIAS. Then take this, and take it to heart!   70
    The time is not far off when you shall pay back
    Corpse for corpse, flesh of your own flesh.
    You have thrust the child of this world into living night,
    You have kept from the gods below the child that is theirs:
    The one in a grave before her death, the other,   75
    Dead, denied the grave. This is your crime:
    And the Furies and the dark gods of Hell
    Are swift with terrible punishment for you.

    Do you want to buy me now, Creon?

                       Not many days,
    And your house will be full of men and women weeping,   80
    And curses will be hurled at you from far
    Cities grieving for sons unburied, left to rot
    Before the walls of Thebes.

    These are my arrows, Creon: they are all for you.

[To BOY.*]* But come, child: lead me home.   85
    Let him waste his fine anger upon younger men.
    Maybe he will learn at last
    To control a wiser tongue in a better head.   *[Exit* TEIRESIAS.*]*
CHORAGOS. The old man has gone, King, but his words
    Remain to plague us. I am old, too,   90
    But I cannot remember that he was ever false.
CREON. That is true. . . . It troubles me.
    Oh it is hard to give in! but it is worse
    To risk everything for stubborn pride.

CHORAGOS. Creon: take my advice.

CREON.   What shall I do?   95

CHORAGOS. Go quickly: free Antigonê from her vault
    And build a tomb for the body of Polyneicês.

CREON. You would have me do this!

CHORAGOS.   Creon, yes!
    And it must be done at once: God moves
    Switftly to cancel the folly of stubborn men.   100

CREON. It is hard to deny the heart! But I
    Will do it: I will not fight with destiny.

CHORAGOS. You must go yourself, you cannot leave it to others.

CREON. I will go.
                —Bring axes, servants:
    Come with me to the tomb. I buried her, I   105
    Will set her free.
                    Oh quickly!
    My mind misgives—
    The laws of the gods are mighty, and a man must serve them
    To the last day of his life!

                                                    [*Exit* CREON.]

                        Paean°

CHORAGOS. God of many names   *Strophe 1*

CHORUS.   O Iacchos
                                son
        of Kadmeian Sémelê
                        O born of the Thunder!
        Guardian of the West
                            Regent
        of Eleusis' plain
                        O Prince of maenad Thebes
        and the Dragon Field by rippling Ismenós:°   5

CHORAGOS. God of many names   *Antistrophe 1*

CHORUS.   the flame of torches
        flares on our hills
                        the nymphs of Iacchos
        dance at the spring of Castalia:°
        from the vine-close mountain
                                come ah come in ivy:
        Evohé evohé! sings through the streets of Thebes   10

CHORAGOS. God of many names   *Strophe 2*

CHORUS.   Iacchos of Thebes
        heavenly Child
                    of Sémelê bride of the Thunderer!

Paean a hymn (here dedicated to Iacchos, also called Dionysos. His father was
Zeus, his mother was Sémelê, daughter of Kadmos. Iacchos's worshipers were the
Maenads, whose cry was "*Evohé evohé*")   **5 Ismenós** a river east of Thebes (from
a dragon's teeth, sown near the river, there sprang men who became the ancestors
of the Theban nobility)   **8 Castalia** a spring on Mount Parnassos

The shadow of plague is upon us:

come

with clement feet

oh come from Parnassos

down the long slopes

across the lamenting water   15

CHORAGOS. Iô Fire! Chorister of the throbbing stars!   *Antistrophe 2*
O purest among the voices of the night!
Thou son of God, blaze for us!
CHORUS. Come with choric rapture of circling Maenads
Who cry *Iô Iacche!*

God of many names!   20

Exodos

Enter MESSENGER *from left.*
MESSENGER. Men of the line of Kadmos,° you who live
Near Amphion's citadel,°

I cannot say
Of any condition of human life "This is fixed,
This is clearly good, or bad." Fate raises up,
And Fate casts down the happy and unhappy alike: 5
No man can foretell his Fate.

Take the case of Creon:
Creon was happy once, as I count happiness:
Victorious in battle, sole governor of the land,
Fortunate father of children nobly born.
And now it has all gone from him! Who can say   10
That a man is still alive when his life's joy fails?
He is a walking dead man. Grant him rich,
Let him live like a king in his great house:
If his pleasure is gone, I would not give
So much as the shadow of smoke for all he owns.   15
CHORAGOS. Your words hint at sorrow: what is your news for us?
MESSENGER. They are dead. The living are guilty of their death.
CHORAGOS. Who is guilty? Who is dead? Speak!
MESSENGER.   Haimon.
Haimon is dead; and the hand that killed him
Is his own hand.
CHORAGOS. His father's? or his own?   20
MESSENGER. His own, driven mad by the murder his father had done.
CHORAGOS. Teiresias, Teiresias, how clearly you saw it all!
MESSENGER. This is my news: you must draw what conclusions you can from
it.
CHORAGOS. But look: Eurydicê, our Queen:
Has she overheard us?   25
Enter EURYDICÊ *from the palace, center.*
EURYDICÊ. I have heard something, friends:
As I was unlocking the gate of Pallas'° shrine,

1 **Kadmos,** who sowed the dragon's teeth, was founder of Thebes   2 **Amphion's
citadel** Amphion played so sweetly on his lyre that he charmed stones to form a
wall around Thebes   27 **Pallas** Pallas Athene, goddess of wisdom

For I needed her help today, I heard a voice
Telling of some new sorrow. And I fainted
There at the temple with all my maidens about me.   30
But speak again: whatever it is, I can bear it:
Grief and I are no strangers.
MESSENGER.   Dearest Lady,
     I will tell you plainly all that I have seen.
     I shall not try to comfort you: what is the use,
     Since comfort could lie only in what is not true?   35
     The truth is always best.
                              I went with Creon
     To the outer plain where Polyneicês was lying,
     No friend to pity him, his body shredded by dogs.
     We made our prayers in the place to Hecatê
     And Pluto,˚ that they would be merciful. And we bathed   40
     The corpse with holy water, and we brought
     Fresh-broken branches to burn what was left of it,
     And upon the urn we heaped up a towering barrow
     Of the earth of his own land.
                              When we were done, we ran
     To the vault where Antigonê lay on her couch of stone.   45
     One of the servants had gone ahead,
     And while he was yet far off he heard a voice
     Grieving within the chamber, and he came back
     And told Creon. And as the King went closer,
     The air was full of wailing, the words lost,   50
     And he begged us to make all haste. "Am I a prophet?"
     He said, weeping, "And must I walk this road,
     The saddest of all that I have gone before?
     My son's voice calls me on. Oh quickly, quickly!
     Look through the crevice there, and tell me   55
     If it is Haimon, or some deception of the gods!"

     We obeyed; and in the cavern's farthest corner
     We saw her lying:
     She had made a noose of her fine linen veil
     And hanged herself. Haimon lay beside her,   60
     His arms about her waist, lamenting her,
     His love lost under ground, crying out
     That his father had stolen her away from him.

     When Creon saw him the tears rushed to his eyes
     And he called to him: "What have you done, child?
     Speak to me.   65
     What are you thinking that makes your eyes so strange?
     O my son, my son, I come to you on my knees!"
     But Haimon spat in his face. He said not a word,
     Staring—
                    And suddenly drew his sword
     And lunged. Creon shrank back, the blade missed; and the boy, 70

---

40 **Hecatê / And Pluto** Hecatê and Pluto (also known as Hades) were deities of the
underworld

Desperate against himself, drove it half its length
Into his own side, and fell. And as he died
He gathered Antigonê close in his arms again,
Choking, his blood bright red on her white cheek.
And now he lies dead with the dead, and she is his   75
At last, his bride in the house of the dead.

Exit EURYDICÊ *into the palace.*

CHORAGOS. She has left us without a word. What can this mean?
MESSENGER. It troubles me, too; yet she knows what is best,
Her grief is too great for public lamentation,
And doubtless she has gone to her chamber to weep   80
For her dead son, leading her maidens in his dirge.
Pause.
CHORAGOS. It may be so: but I fear this deep silence.
MESSENGER. I will see what she is doing. I will go in.

Exit MESSENGER *into the palace.*
Enter CREON *with attendants, bearing* HAIMON's *body.*

CHORAGOS. But here is the king himself: on look at him,
Bearing his own damnation in his arms.   85
CREON. Nothing you say can touch me any more.
My own blind heart has brought me
From darkness to final darkness. Here you see
The father murdering, the murdered son—
And all my civic wisdom!   90

Haimon my son, so young, so young to die,
I was the fool, not you; and you died for me.
CHORAGOS. That is the truth; but you were late in learning it.
CREON. This truth is hard to bear. Surely a god
Has crushed me beneath the hugest weight of heaven,   95
And driven me headlong a barbaric way
To trample out the thing I held most dear.

The pains that men will take to come to pain!
Enter MESSENGER *from the palace.*
MESSENGER. The burden you carry in your hands is heavy,
But it is not all: you will find more in your house.   100
CREON. What burden worse than this shall I find there?
MESSENGER. The Queen is dead.
CREON. O port of death, deaf world,
Is there no pity for me? And you, Angel of evil,
I was dead, and your words are death again.   105
Is it true, boy? Can it be true?
Is my wife dead? Has death bred death?
MESSENGER. You can see for yourself.
The doors are opened and the body of EURYDICÊ *is disclosed within.*
CREON. Oh pity!
All true, all true, and more than I can bear!   110
O my wife, my son!
MESSENGER. She stood before the altar, and her heart
Welcomed the knife her own hand guided,

And a great cry burst from her lips for Megareus° dead,
    And for Haimon dead, her sons; and her last breath   115
    Was a curse for their father, the murderer of her sons.
    And she fell, and the dark flowed in through her closing eyes.
CREON. O God, I am sick with fear.
    Are there no swords here? Has no one a blow for me?
MESSENGER. Her curse is upon you for the deaths of both.   120
CREON. It is right that it should be. I alone am guilty.
    I know it, and I say it. Lead me in,
    Quickly, friends.
    I have neither life nor substance. Lead me in.
CHORAGOS. You are right, if there can be right in so much wrong.   125
    The briefest way is best in a world of sorrow.
CREON. Let it come,
    Let death come quickly, and be kind to me.
    I would not ever see the sun again.
CHORAGOS. All that will come when it will; but we, meanwhile,   130
    Have much to do. Leave the future to itself.
CREON. All my heart was in that prayer!
CHORAGOS. Then do not pray any more: the sky is deaf.
CREON. Lead me away. I have been rash and foolish.
    I have killed my son and my wife.   135
    I look for comfort; my comfort lies here dead.
    Whatever my hands have touched has come to nothing.
    Fate has brought all my pride to a thought of dust.
    As CREON *is being led into the house, the* CHORAGOS *advances and*
    speaks directly to the audience.
CHORAGOS. There is no happiness where there is no wisdom;
    No wisdom but in submission to the gods.   140
    Big words are always punished,
    And proud men in old age learn to be wise.

[c. 441 B.C.]

 TOPICS FOR CRITICAL THINKING AND WRITING

1. Would you use masks for some (or all) of the characters? If so, would they be masks that fully cover the face, Greek style, or some sort of half-masks? (A full mask enlarges the face, and conceivably the mouthpiece can amplify the voice, but only an exceptionally large theater might require such help. Perhaps half-masks are enough if the aim is chiefly to distance the actors from the audience and from daily reality, and to force the actors to develop resources other than facial gestures. One director, arguing in favor of half-masks, has said that an actor who wears even a half-mask learns to act not with his eyes but with his neck.)

2. How would you costume the players? Would you dress them as the Greeks might have? Why? One argument sometimes used by those who hold the modern productions of Greek drama should use classical

114 **Megareus** Megareus, brother of Haimon, had died in the assault on Thebes

costumes is that Greek drama *ought* to be remote and ritualistic. Evaluate this view. What sort of modern dress might be effective?

3. If you were directing a college production of *Antigone*, how large a chorus would you use? (Sophocles is said to have used a chorus of 15.) Would you have the chorus recite (or chant) the odes in unison, or would you assign lines to single speakers?

4. If you have read *Oedipus Rex*, compare and contrast the Creon of *Antigone* with the Creon of *Oedipus*.

5. Although Sophocles called his play *Antigone*, many critics say that Creon is the real tragic hero, pointing out that Antigone is absent from the last third of the play. Evaluate this view.

6. In some Greek tragedies, fate plays a great role in bringing about the downfall of the tragic hero. Though there are references to the curse on the House of Oedipus in *Antigone*, do we feel that Antigone goes to her death as a result of the workings of fate? Do we feel that fate is responsible for Creon's fall? Are both Antigone and Creon the creators of their own tragedy?

7. Are the words *hamartia* (page 205) and *hubris* (page 204) relevant to Antigone? To Creon?

8. Why does Creon, contrary to the Chorus's advice, bury the body of Polyneices before he releases Antigone? Does his action show a zeal for piety as short-sighted as his earlier zeal for law? Is his action plausible, in view of the facts that Teiresias has dwelt on the wrong done to Polyneices and that Antigone has ritual food to sustain her? Or are we not to worry about Creon's motive?

9. A *foil* is a character who, by contrast, sets off or helps define another character. To what extent is Ismene a foil to Antigone? Is she entirely without courage?

10. What function does Eurydice serve? How deeply do we feel about her fate?

APPENDIX A

Remarks about Manuscript Form

BASIC MANUSCRIPT FORM

Much of what follows is nothing more than common sense.

- Use **8½" × 11" paper** of good weight. Make a photocopy, or, if you have written on a word processor, print out a second copy, in case the instructor's copy goes astray.
- If you write on a typewriter or a word processor, use a reasonably fresh ribbon, **double-space,** and type on one side of the page only. If you submit handwritten copy, used lined paper and write on one side of the page only in black or dark blue ink, on every other line.
- Use **1" margins** on all sides.
- Within the top margin, put your last name and then (after hitting the space bar twice) the **page number** (in arabic numerals), so that the number is flush with the right-hand margin.
- On the first page, below the top margin and flush with the left-hand margin, put **your full name,** your **instructor's name,** the **course number** (including the section), and the **date,** one item per line, double-spaced.
- **Center the title** of your essay. Remember that the title is important—it gives the readers their first glimpse of your essay. **Create your own title**—one that reflects your topic or thesis. For example, a paper on Shirley Jackson's "The Lottery" should not be called "The Lottery" but might be called

```
        Suspense in Shirley Jackson's "The Lottery"
```

or

```
        Is "The Lottery" Rigged?
```

or

```
        Jackson's "The Lottery" and Scapegoat Rituals
```

These titles do at least a little in the way of rousing a reader's interest.

- **Capitalize the title thus:** Begin the first word of the title with a capital letter, and capitalize each subsequent word except articles (*a, an, the*), conjunctions (*and, but, if, when,* etc.), and prepositions (*in, on, with,* etc.):

```
        A Word on Behalf of Mrs. Mitty
```

Notice that you do *not* enclose your title within quotation marks, and you do not underline it—though if it includes the title of a story, *that* is enclosed within quotation marks, or if it includes the title of a novel or play, *that* is underlined (to indicate italics), thus:

```
Jackson's "The Lottery" and the Scapegoat Tradition
```

and

```
        Gender Stereotypes in Macbeth
```

- **After writing your title, double space,** indent five spaces, and begin your first sentence.
- Unless your instructor tells you otherwise, **use a paper clip** to hold the pages together. (Do not use a stiff binder; it will only add to the bulk of the instructor's stack of papers.)
- Extensive revisions should have been made in your drafts, but minor **last-minute revisions** may be made—neatly—on the finished copy. Proofreading may catch some typographical errors, and you may notice some small weaknesses. You can make corrections with the proofreader's symbols described in the following section.

CORRECTIONS IN THE FINAL COPY

Changes in wording may be made by crossing through words and rewriting them:

```
                                            has
    The influence of Poe and Hawthorne  have  greatly
                                            ∧
diminished.
```

Additions should be made above the line, with a caret below the line at the appropriate place:

```
                                        greatly
    The influence of Poe and Hawthorne has diminished.
                                          ∧
```

Transpositions of letters may be made thus:

```
    The influence of Poe and Hawthorne has greatly
diminished.
```

Deletions are indicated by a horizontal line through the word or words to be deleted. Delete a single letter by drawing a vertical or diagonal line through it; then indicate whether the letters on either side are to be closed up by drawing a connecting arc:

```
The influence of Poe and Hawthorne has great͟ly

diminished.
```

Separation of words accidentally run together is indicated by a vertical line, **closure** by a curved line connecting the letters to be closed up:

```
The influence|of Poe and Hawthorne has g reatly

diminished.
```

Paragraphing may be indicated by the symbol ¶ before the word that is to begin the new paragraph:

```
The influence of Poe and Hawthorne has greatly

diminished. ¶  The influence of Borges has very

largely replaced that of earlier writers of fantasy.
```

QUOTATIONS AND QUOTATION MARKS

First, a word about the *point* of using quotations. Don't use quotations to pad the length of a paper. Rather, give quotations from the work you are discussing so that your readers will see the material you are discussing and (especially in a research paper) so that your readers will know what some of the chief interpretations are and what your responses to them are.

Note: The next few paragraphs do *not* discuss how to include citations of pages, a topic discussed in Appendix B under the heading "How to Document: Footnotes and Internal Parenthetical Citations."

The Golden Rule: If you quote, *comment on* the quotation. Let the reader know what you make of it and why you quote it.

Additional principles:

1. **Identify the speaker or writer of the quotation** so that the reader is not left with a sense of uncertainty. Usually, in accordance with the principle of letting readers know where they are going, this identification precedes the quoted material, but occasionally it may follow the quotation, especially if it will provide something of a pleasant surprise. For instance, in a discussion of Flannery O'Connor's stories, you might quote a disparaging comment on one of the stories and then reveal that O'Connor herself was the speaker.

2. If the quotation is part of your own sentence, **be sure to fit the quotation grammatically and logically into your sentence.**

Incorrect: Holden Caulfield tells us very little about "what my lousy childhood was like."

Correct: Holden Caulfield tells us very little about what his "lousy childhood was like."

3.   **Indicate any omissions or additions.** The quotation must be exact. Any material that you add—even one or two words—must be enclosed within square brackets, thus:

```
Hawthorne tells us that "owing doubtless to the depth

of the gloom at that particular spot [in the forest],

neither the travellers nor their steeds were

visible."
```

If you wish to omit material from within a quotation, indicate the ellipsis by three spaced periods. If your sentence ends in an omission, add a closed-up period and then three spaced periods to indicate the omission. The following example is based on a quotation from the sentences immediately above this one:

```
The instructions say, "If you . . . omit material from

within a quotation, [you must] indicate the

ellipsis. . . . If your sentence ends in an omission,

add a closed-up period and then three spaced

periods. . . .
```

Notice that although material preceded "If you," periods are not needed to indicate the omission because "If you" began a sentence in the original. Customarily, initial and terminal omissions are indicated only when they are part of the sentence you are quoting. Even such omissions need not be indicated when the quoted material is obviously incomplete—when, for instance, it is a word or phrase.

4.   **Distinguish between short and long quotations,** and treat each appropriately. *Short quotations* (usually defined as no more than four lines of typed prose or two lines of poetry) are enclosed within quotation marks and run into the text (rather than being set off, without quotation marks), as in the following example:

```
Hawthorne begins the story by telling us that "Young

Goodman Brown came forth at sunset into the street at

Salem village," thus at the outset connecting the

village with daylight. A few paragraphs later, when

Hawthorne tells us that the road Brown takes was

"darkened by all of the gloomiest trees of the

forest," he begins to associate the forest with

darkness--and a very little later with evil.
```

If your short quotation is from a poem, be sure to follow the capitalization of the original, and use a slash mark (with a space before and after it) to indicate separate lines. Give the line numbers, if your source gives them, in parentheses, immediately after the closing quotation marks and before the closing punctuation, thus:

> In Adrienne Rich's "Aunt Jennifer's Tigers," Rich
> says that "Uncle's wedding band / Sits heavily upon
> Aunt Jennifer's hand" (7-8). The band evidently is a
> sign of her oppression.

To set off a *long quotation* (more than four typed lines of prose or more than two lines of poetry), indent the entire quotation ten spaces from the left margin. Usually, a long quotation is introduced by a clause ending with a colon—for instance, "The following passage will make this point clear:" or "The closest we come to hearing an editorial voice is a long passage in the middle of the story:" or some such lead-in. After typing your lead-in, double-space, and then type the quotation, indented and double-spaced.

5.   Commas and periods go inside the quotation marks.

> Chopin tells us in the first sentence that "Mrs.
> Mallard was afflicted with heart trouble," and in the
> last sentence the doctors say that Mrs. Mallard "died
> of heart disease."

Exception: If the quotation is immediately followed by material in parentheses or in square brackets, close the quotation, then give the parenthetic or bracketed material, and then—after closing the parenthesis or bracket—put the comma or period.

> Chopin tells us in the first sentence that "Mrs.
> Mallard was afflicted with heart trouble" (12), and
> in the last sentence the doctors say that Mrs.
> Mallard "died of heart disease" (13).

Semicolons, colons, and dashes go outside the closing quotation marks.

Question marks and exclamation points go inside if they are part of the quotation, outside if they are your own.

In the following passage from a student's essay, notice the difference in the position of the question marks. The first is part of the quotation, so it is enclosed within the quotation marks. The second question mark, however, is the student's, so it comes after the closing quotation mark.

> The older man says to Goodman Brown, "Sayest thou
> so?" Doesn't a reader become uneasy when the man

immediately adds, "We are but a little way in the
forest yet"?

Quotation Marks or Underlining?

Use quotation marks around titles of short stories and other short works—that is, titles of chapters in books, essays, and poems that might not be published by themselves. Underline (to indicate italics) titles of books, periodicals, collections of essays, plays, and long poems such as *The Rime of the Ancient Mariner.* If you are using a word processor, your software probably will let you use italic type (instead of underlining) if you wish.

APPENDIX B

Writing a Research Paper

WHAT RESEARCH IS NOT, AND WHAT RESEARCH IS

Jeff, in a "Mutt and Jeff" cartoon, sells jars of honey. He includes in each jar a dead bee as proof that the product is genuine. Some writers—even some professionals—seem to think that a hiveful of dead quotations or footnotes is proof of research. But research requires much more than the citation of authorities. What it requires, briefly, is informed, *thoughtful* analysis.

Because a research paper requires its writer to collect and interpret evidence—usually including the opinions of earlier investigators—one sometimes hears that a research paper, unlike a critical essay, is not the expression of personal opinion. Such a view is unjust both to criticism and to research. A critical essay is not a mere expression of personal opinions; if it is any good, it offers evidence that supports the opinions and thus persuades the reader of their objective rightness. A research paper is in the final analysis largely personal because the author continuously uses his or her own judgment to evaluate the evidence, deciding what is relevant and convincing. A research paper is not the mere presentation of what a dozen scholars have already said about a topic; it is a thoughtful evaluation of the available evidence, and so it is, finally, an expression of what the author thinks the evidence adds up to.

Research can be a tedious and frustrating business; hours are spent reading books and articles that prove to be irrelevant, pieces of evidence contradict themselves, and time is always short.

Still, even though research is time-consuming, those who engage in it feel (at least sometimes) an exhilaration, a sense of triumph at having studied a problem thoroughly and arrived at conclusions that—for the moment, anyway—seem objective and irrefutable. Later, new evidence may turn up and require a new conclusion, but until that time one has built something that will endure wind and weather.

PRIMARY AND SECONDARY MATERIALS

The materials of literary research may be conveniently divided into two sorts, primary and secondary. The *primary materials* or sources are the real subject of study; the *secondary materials* are critical and historical accounts already written about these primary materials. For example, if you want to know whether Shakespeare's attitude toward Julius Caesar was highly traditional or highly original (or a little of each), you read the primary materials (*Julius Caesar* and other Elizabethan writings about Caesar); and, since research requires that you be informed about the present state of thought on your topic, you also read the secondary materials (post-Elizabethan essays, books on Shakespeare, and books on Elizabethan attitudes toward Caesar, or, more generally, on Elizabethan attitudes toward Rome and toward monarchs).

FROM TOPIC TO THESIS

Almost every literary work lends itself to research. As has already been mentioned, a study of Shakespeare's attitude toward Julius Caesar would lead to a study of other Elizabethan works and of modern critical works. Similarly, a study of the ghost of Caesar—does it have a real, objective existence, or is it merely a figment of Brutus's imagination?—could lead to a study of Shakespeare's other ghosts (for instance, those in *Hamlet* and *Macbeth*), and a study of Elizabethan attitudes toward ghosts. Or, to take an example from our own century, a reader of Edward Albee's *The Sandbox* might want to study the early critical reception of the play. Did the reviewers like it? More precisely, did the reviewers in relatively highbrow journals evaluate it differently from those in popular magazines and newspapers? Or, what has Albee himself said about the play in the decades that have passed since he wrote it? Do his comments in essays and interviews indicate that he now sees the play as something different from what he saw when he wrote it? Or, to take yet another example of a work from the middle of our century, a reader might similarly study George Orwell's *1984*, looking at its critical reception, or Orwell's own view of it, or, say, at the sources of Orwell's inspiration. Let's look, for a few minutes, at this last topic.

Assume that you have read George Orwell's *1984* and that, in preparing to do some research on it, browsing through *The Collected Essays, Journalism, and Letters*, you come across a letter (17 February 1944) in which Orwell says that he has been reading Evgenii Zamyatin's *We* and that he himself has been keeping notes for "that kind of book." And in *The Collected Essays, Journalism, and Letters* you also come across a review (4 January 1946) Orwell wrote of *We*, from which it is apparent that *We* resembles *1984*. Or perhaps you learned in a preface to an edition of *1984* that Orwell was influenced by *We*, and you have decided to look into the matter. You want to know exactly how great the influence is.

You borrow *We* from the library, read it, and perceive resemblances in plot, character, and theme. But it's not simply a question of listing resemblances between the two books. Your topic is: What do the resemblances add up to? After all, Orwell in the letter said he had already been working in Zamyatin's direction without even knowing Zamyatin's book, so your investigation may find, for example, that the closest resemblances are in relatively trivial details and that everything really important in *1984* was already implicit in Orwell's earlier books; or your investigation may find that Zamyatin gave a new depth to Orwell's thought; or it may find that though Orwell borrowed heavily from Zamyatin, he missed the depth of *We*.

In the earliest stage of your research, then, you don't know what you will find, so you cannot yet formulate a thesis (or, at best, you can formulate only a tentative thesis). But you know that there is a topic, that it interests you, and that you are ready to begin the necessary legwork.

LOCATING MATERIAL

First Steps

First, prepare a working bibliography, that is, a list of books and articles that must be looked at. The **library catalog** is an excellent place to begin. If your topic is Orwell and Zamyatin, you'll want at least to glance at whatever books by and about these two authors are available. When you have looked over the most promising portions of this material (in secondary sources, chapter headings and indexes will often guide you), you will have found some interesting things. But you want to get a good idea of the state of current scholarship on your topic, and you realize that you must go beyond the catalog's listings under *Orwell, Zamyatin,* and such obviously related topics as *utopian literature.* Doubtless there are pertinent articles in journals, but you cannot start thumbing through them at random.

MLA International Bibliography   The easiest way to locate articles and books on literature written in a modern language—that is, on a topic other than literature of the ancient world—is to consult the *MLA International Bibliography* (1922–   ), which until 1969 was published as part of *PMLA* (*Publications of the Modern Language Association*) and since 1969 has been published separately. It is also available on CD-ROM through WILSONDISC, and in fact the disc is preferable since it is updated quarterly, whereas the print version is more than a year behind the times.

The *MLA International Bibliography* lists scholarly studies—books as well as articles in academic journals—published in a given year. Because the number of items listed is very great, the print version of the bibliography runs to more than one volume, but material written in English (including, for instance, South African authors who write in English) is in one volume. To see what has been published on Orwell in a given year, then, in this volume you turn to the section on English literature (as opposed to American, Canadian, Irish, and so forth), and then to the subsection labeled 1900–1999, to see if anything is listed that sounds relevant. But to find material on Zamyatin you will have to turn to the volume that lists publications on Russian writing.

Because your time is severely limited, you probably cannot read everything published on your topic. At least for the moment, therefore, you will use only the last five or ten years of this bibliography. Presumably, any important earlier material will have been incorporated into some of the recent studies listed, and if, when you come to read these recent studies, you find references to an article of, say, 1975 that sounds essential, of course you will read that article too.

American Literary Scholarship   Although the *MLA International Bibliography* includes works on American literature, if you are doing research on an aspect of American literature you may want to begin with *American Literary Scholarship* (1965–   ), an annual publication noted for its broad coverage of articles and books on major and minor American writers, and perhaps especially valuable for its frank comments on the material that it lists.

Readers' Guide   On some recent topics, for instance the arguments for and against dropping *Huckleberry Finn* from high school curricula, there may be few or no books, and there may not even be material in the learned journals indexed in the *MLA International Bibliography*. Popular magazines, however, such as *The Atlantic Monthly, Ebony,* and *Newsweek*—not listed in *MLA*—may include some useful material. These magazines, and about 200 others, are indexed in the *Readers' Guide to Periodical Literature* (1900–   ). If, for example, you want to write a research paper on the controversy over *Huckleberry Finn,* or, say, on the popular reception given to Kenneth Branagh's recent films of Shakespeare's *Henry V* and *Much Ado about Nothing,* you can locate material (for instance, reviews of Branagh's films) through the *Readers' Guide.* For that matter, you can also locate reviews of older films, let's say Olivier's films of Shakespeare's plays, by consulting the volumes for the years in which the films were issued.

Computer Indexes   On many campuses the *Readers' Guide* has been supplanted by *InfoTrac* (1985), a CD-ROM system that searches publications of the last four years. The disc is preinstalled in a microcomputer that can be accessed from a computer terminal with a printer, and the instructions are easy to follow. *InfoTrac,* an index to authors and subjects in popular and scholarly magazines and in newspapers, provides access to several database indexes, including

1. The *General Periodicals Index,* available in an academic library edition (about 1,100 general and scholarly periodicals) and in a public library edition (about 1,100 popular magazines).
2. The *Academic Index* (400 general-interest publications, all of which are also available in the Academic Library Edition of the *General Periodicals Index*).
3. The *Magazine Index Plus* (the four most recent years of *The New York Times,* the two most recent months of *The Wall Street Journal,* and 400 popular magazines, all of which are included in the public library edition of the *General Periodicals Index*).

4. The *National Newspaper Index* (the four most recent years of *The New York Times, The Christian Science Monitor, The Washington Post,* and *The Los Angeles Times*).

Other Bibliographic Aids

There are hundreds of guides to publications and to reference works. For instance, *American Women Writers: Bibliographical Essays* (1983), edited by Maurice Duke, Jackson R. Bryer, and M. Thomas Inge, includes scholarship through 1981 on 24 authors, including Anne Bradstreet, Sarah Orne Jewett, Kate Chopin, Gertrude Stein, Flannery O'Connor, Zora Neale Hurston, and Sylvia Plath. *Black American Writers: Bibliographical Essays* (1978), edited by M. Thomas Inge, Maurice Duke, and Jackson R. Bryer, covers slave narratives, as well as such later African-American writers as Langston Hughes, Ralph Ellison, and James Baldwin.

How do you find such books? Two invaluable guides to reference works (that is, to bibliographies and to such helpful compilations as handbooks of mythology, place names, and critical terms) are

James L. Harner, *Literary Research Guide: A Guide to Reference Sources for the Study of Literatures in English and Related Topics,* 2nd ed. (1993)

and

Michael J. Marcuse, *A Reference Guide for English Studies* (1990).

And there are guides to these guides: reference librarians. If you don't know where to turn to find something, turn to the librarian.

TAKING NOTES

Let's assume now that you have checked some bibliographies and that you have a fair number of references you must read to have a substantial knowledge of the evidence and the common interpretations of the evidence. Most researchers find it convenient, when examining bibliographies and the library catalog, to write down each reference on a 3″ × 5″ index card—one title per card. On the card put the author's full name (last name first), the exact title of the book or of the article, and the name of the journal (with dates and pages). Titles of books and periodicals (publications issued periodically—for example, monthly or four times a year) are underlined; titles of articles and of essays in books are put within quotation marks. It's also a good idea to put the library catalog number on the card to save time if you need to get the item for a second look.

Next, start reading or scanning the materials whose titles you have collected. Some of these items will prove irrelevant or silly; others will prove valuable in themselves and also in the leads they give you to further references, which you should duly record on 3″ × 5″ cards. Notes—aside from these bibliographic notes—are best taken on 4″ × 6″ cards. Smaller cards do not provide enough space for summaries of useful materials, but 4″ × 6″ cards—rather than larger cards—will serve to remind you that you should not take notes on every-thing. Be selective in taking notes.

Two Mechanical Aids: The Photocopier and the Word Processor

The photocopier of course enables you to take home from the library, with very little effort, lots of material (including material that does not circulate) that you might otherwise have to copy laboriously by hand. If, for instance, you are writing a paper on feminist responses to Faulkner's "A Rose for Emily," you can simply scan the material to locate the relevant pages, then photocopy the essays in journals or the appropriate passages in books. Later, at your convenience, without making another trip to the library you can read or reread the photocopied material, highlighting or underlining the chief points. But (and this point is so important that it will be made again, in a moment) because it is easy to highlight or underline, you may mark almost everything. That is, you may not *think* about the material, as you would if you were taking notes by hand, where you would have a powerful incentive to think about whether the material really is noteworthy.

The great advantages of using a word processor have already been discussed in Chapter 2, but it is worth repeating here that a word processor is useful not only in the final stage, to produce a neat copy, but also in the early stages of research, when you are getting ideas and are taking notes.

If you take notes on the word processor, print them out and then scissor them apart. Although the slips will not be identical in size, you can still arrange them into appropriate packets, and (as with index cards) you can then arrange the packets into an appropriate sequence. At this point you can begin to draft your paper, working from your organized notes, or—and this is probably a better method—you can rearrange the sequence of notes in your word processor. That is, guided by the sequence of slips, you can move blocks of notes in the word processor into the sequence that you have tentatively settled on. After you have done this, you can start drafting your paper, writing a lead-in to the first quotation, printing the quotation (or part of it, or a summary of it), and commenting on it. *Caution:* Do not feel that you must use all of your notes. Your reader does not want to read a series of notes that are linked by thin connectives.

A Guide to Note Taking

1. **In the upper left-hand corner of the card specify the source in an abbreviated form.** The author's last name, or the name and the first word of the title, will usually be enough (unless the first word is *A, An,* or *The*).

2. **Write summaries, not paraphrases** (that is, write abridgments rather than restatements which in fact may be as long as or longer than the original). There is rarely any point to paraphrasing. Generally speaking, either quote exactly (and put the passage in quotation marks, with a notation of the source, including the page number or numbers) or summarize, reducing a page or even an entire article or chapter of a book to a single $4'' \times 6''$ card. Even when you summarize, indicate your source (including the page numbers) on the card, so that you can give appropriate credit in your paper.

3. **Quote sparingly.** Of course in your summary you will sometimes quote a phrase or a sentence—putting it in quotation marks—but don't over-use quotation. You are not doing stenography; rather you are assimilating knowledge and you are thinking, and so for the most part your source should be digested rather than engorged whole. Thinking now, while taking notes, will also help you later to avoid plagiarism. If, on the other hand, when you take notes you mindlessly copy material at length, later when you are writing the paper you may be tempted to copy it yet again, perhaps without giving credit. Similarly, if you photocopy pages from articles or books, and then merely underline some passages, you probably will not be thinking; you will just be underlining. But if you make a terse summary on a note card you will be forced to think and to find your own words for the idea. Quote directly only those passages that are particularly effective, or crucial, or memorable. In your finished paper these quotations will provide authority and emphasis.

4. **Quote accurately.** After copying a quotation, check your card against the original, correct any misquotation, and then put a checkmark after your quotation to indicate that it is accurate. Verify the page number also, and then put a checkmark on your card after the page number. If a quotation runs from the bottom of, say, page 306 to the top of 307, on your card put a distinguishing mark (for instance two parallel vertical lines after the last word of the first page), so that if you later use only part of the quotation, you will know the page on which it appeared.

Use ellipses (three spaced periods) to indicate the omission of any words within a sentence. If the omitted words are at the end of the quoted sentence, put a period where you end the sentence, and then add three spaced periods to indicate the omission:

```
If the . . . words were at the end of the quoted

sentence, put a period where you end. . . .
```

Use square brackets to indicate your additions to the quotation. Here is an example:

```
Here is an [uninteresting] example.
```

5. **Never copy a passage by changing an occasional word,** under the impression that you are thereby putting it into your own words. Notes of this sort may find their way into your paper, your reader will sense a style other than yours, and suspicions of plagiarism may follow. (For a detailed discussion of plagiarism, see pages 1313-14.)

6. **Write on one side of the card only.** Because when you set out to draft your paper you will probably want to spread out your notes so that you can see all of the material simultaneously, notes on the rear of a card are of little use and they will probably get overlooked. If a note won't fit on one side of a card, continue the note on a second card (and a third, if necessary), and put the appropriate number on each card.

7. **Comment on your notes.** Feel free to jot down your responses to the note. Indeed, consider it your obligation to *think* about the material, evaluating it and using it as a stimulus to further thought. For example, you may want to say "Gold seems to be generalizing from insufficient evidence," or "Corsa made the same point five years earlier"; but make certain that later you will be able to dis-

tinguish between these comments and the notes summarizing or quoting your source. A suggestion: surround all comments recording your responses with double parentheses, thus: ((. . .)).

8. In the upper right-hand corner of each note card write a brief key—for example, "Orwell's first reading of *We*" or "Characterization" or "Thought control"—so that later you can tell at a glance what is on the card.

As you work, you'll find yourself returning again and again to your primary materials—and you'll probably find to your surprise that a good deal of the secondary material is unconvincing or even wrong, despite the fact that it is printed in a handsome book or a scholarly journal. At times, under the weight of evidence, you will have to abandon some of your earlier views, but at times you will have your own opinions reinforced, and at times you will feel that your ideas have more validity than those you are reading. One of the things we learn from research is that not everything in print is true; this discovery is one of the pleasures we get from research.

DRAFTING THE PAPER

The difficult job of writing up your findings remains, but if you have taken good notes and have put useful headings on each card, you are well on your way. Read through the cards and sort them into packets of related material. Discard all notes, however interesting, that you now see are irrelevant to your paper. Go through the cards again and again, sorting and resorting, putting together what belongs together. Probably you will find that you have to do a little additional research—somehow you aren't quite clear about this or that—but after you have done this additional research, you should be able to arrange the packets into a reasonable and consistent sequence. You now have a kind of first draft, or at least a tentative organization for your paper. Two further pieces of advice:

1. Beware of the compulsion to include every note card in your essay; that is, beware of telling the reader, "*A* says. . . ; *B* says. . . ; *C* says. . . ."
2. You must have a point, a thesis.

Remember: As you studied the evidence, you increasingly developed or documented or corrected a thesis. You may, for example, have become convinced that the influence of Zamyatin was limited to a few details of plot and character and that Orwell had already developed the framework and the chief attitudes that are implicit in *1984*. Similarly, now, as you write and revise your paper, you will probably still be modifying your thesis to some extent, discovering what in fact the evidence implies.

The final version of the paper, however, should be a finished piece of work, without the inconsistencies, detours, and occasional dead ends of an early draft. Your readers should feel that they are moving toward a conclusion (by means of your thoughtful evaluation of the evidence) rather than merely reading an anthology of commentary on the topic. And so we should get some such structure as "There are three common views on. . . . The first two are represented by A and B; the third, and by far the most reasonable, is C's view that. . . . A argues . . . but. . . . The second view, B's, is based on . . . but. . . . Although the third view,

C's, is not conclusive, still. . . . Moreover, C's point can be strengthened when we consider a piece of evidence that he does not make use of. . . ."

Be sure, when you quote, to *write a lead-in,* such as "X concisely states the common view" or "Z, without offering any proof, asserts that. . . ." Let the reader know where you are going, or, to put it a little differently, let the reader know how the quotation fits into your argument.

Quotations and summaries, in short, are accompanied by judicious analyses of your own so that by the end of the paper your readers not only have read a neatly typed paper (see page 1299-1304) and have gained an idea of what previous writers have said, but also are persuaded that under your guidance they have seen the evidence, heard the arguments justly summarized, and reached a sound conclusion.

A bibliography or list of works consulted (see pages 1320-26) is usually appended to a research paper so that readers may easily look further into the primary and secondary material if they wish; but if you have done your job well, readers will be content to leave the subject where you left it, grateful that you have set matters straight.

DOCUMENTATION

What to Document: Avoiding Plagiarism

Honesty requires that you acknowledge your indebtedness for material, not only when you quote directly from a work, but also when you appropriate an idea that is not common knowledge. Not to acknowledge such borrowing is plagiarism. If in doubt whether to give credit, give credit.

You ought, however, to develop a sense of what is considered **common knowledge.** Definitions in a dictionary can be considered common knowledge, so there is no need to say, "According to Webster, a novel is. . . ." (This is weak in three ways: It's unnecessary, it's uninteresting, and it's unclear, since "Webster" appears in the titles of several dictionaries, some good and some bad.) Similarly, the date of first publication of *The Scarlet Letter* can be considered common knowledge. Few can give it when asked, but it can be found out from innumerable sources, and no one need get the credit for providing you with the date. The idea that Hamlet delays is also a matter of common knowledge. But if you are impressed by So-and-so's argument that Claudius has been much maligned, you should give credit to So-and-so.

Suppose you happen to come across Frederick R. Karl's statement in the revised edition of *A Reader's Guide to the Contemporary English Novel* (New York: Farrar, Straus & Giroux, 1972) that George Orwell was "better as a man than as a novelist." This is an interesting and an effectively worded idea. You cannot use these words without giving credit to Karl. And you cannot retain the idea but alter the words, for example, to "Orwell was a better human being than he was a writer of fiction," presenting the idea as your own, for here you are simply lifting Karl's idea—and putting it less effectively. If you want to use Karl's point, give him credit and—since you can hardly summarize so brief a statement—use his exact words and put them within quotation marks.

What about a longer passage that strikes you favorably? Let's assume that in reading Alex Zwerdling's *Orwell and the Left* (New Haven: Yale UP, 1974) you find the following passage from page 105 interesting:

> *1984* might be said to have a predominantly negative goal, since it is much more concerned to fight *against* a possible future society than *for* one. Its tactics are primarily defensive. Winston Smith is much less concerned with the future than with the past—which is of course the reader's present.

You certainly *cannot* say:

```
The goal of 1984 can be said to be chiefly negative

because it is devoted more to opposing some future

society than it is to fighting for a future society.

Smith is more concerned with the past (our present)

than he is with the future.
```

This passage is simply a theft of Zwerdling's property: The writer has stolen Zwerdling's automobile and put a different color paint on it. How, then, can a writer use Zwerdling's idea? (1) Give Zwerdling credit and quote directly, or (2) give Zwerdling credit and summarize his point in perhaps a third of the length, or (3) give Zwerdling credit and summarize the point but include—within quotation marks—some phrase you think is especially quotable. Thus:

1. *Direct quotation.* In a study of Orwell's politics, Alex Zwerdling says, "*1984* might be said to have a predominantly negative goal, since it is much more concerned to fight *against* a possible future society than *for* one" (105).
2. *Summary.* The goal of *1984*, Zwerdling points out, is chiefly opposition to, rather than advocacy of, a certain kind of future society (105).
3. *Summary with selected quotation.* Zwerdling points out that the goal of *1984* is "predominantly negative," opposition to, rather than advocacy of, a certain kind of future society (105).

If for some reason you do not wish to name Zwerdling in your lead-in, you will have to give his name with the parenthetical citation so that a reader can identify the source:

```
The goal of 1984, one critic points out, is

"predominantly negative" (Zwerdling 105), opposition

to, rather than advocacy of, a certain kind of future

society.
```

But it is hard to imagine why the writer preferred to say "one critic," rather than to name Zwerdling immediately, since Zwerdling sooner or later must be identified.

How to Document: Footnotes and Internal Parenthetical Citations

Documentation tells your reader exactly what your sources are. Until recently, the standard form was the footnote, which, for example, told the reader that the source of such-and-such a quotation was a book by so-and-so. But in 1984 the Modern Language Association, which had established the footnote form used in hundreds of journals, university presses, and classrooms, substituted a new form. It is this new form—parenthetical citations within the text (rather than at the foot of the page or the end of the essay)—that we will discuss at length. Keep in mind, though, that footnotes still have their uses.

Footnotes If you are using only one source, your instructor may advise you to give the source in a footnote. (Check with your instructors to find out their preferred forms of documentation.)

Let's say that your only source is a textbook. Let's say, too, that all of your quotations will be from a single story—Kate Chopin's "The Story of an Hour"—printed in this book on pages 12-13. The simplest way to cite your source is (if you are using a typewriter rather than a computer) to type the digit 1 (elevated, and *without* a period after it) after your first reference to (or quotation from) the story and then to put a footnote at the bottom of the page, explaining where the story can be found. After the last line of type on the page, triple-space, indent five spaces from the left-hand margin, raise the typewriter carriage half a line, and type the arabic number 1. Do *not* put a period after it. Then lower the carriage half a line, and type a statement (double-spaced) to the effect that all references are to this book. Notice that although the footnote begins by being indented five spaces, if the note runs to more than one line the subsequent lines are typed flush left.

[1]Chopin's story appears in Sylvan Barnet, ed., The

Harper Anthology of Fiction (New York:

HarperCollins, 1991), 25-27.

If you use a word processor, your software may do the job for you. It probably will automatically indent, elevate the footnote number, and print the note on the appropriate page.

If a book has two or three editors, give all the names but with the abbreviation "eds." instead of "ed." (*not* within quotation marks). If it has more than three editors, give the name of only the first editor, followed by "et al." (the Latin abbreviation for "and others") and "eds." See the next example.

Even if you are writing a comparison of, say, two stories in a book, you may use a note of this sort. It might run thus:

[1]All page references, given parenthetically

within the essay, refer to stories in Sylvan Barnet

et al., eds., Literature for Composition, 4th ed.

(New York: HarperCollins, 1995).

If you use such a note, do not put a footnote after each quotation that follows. Give the citations right in the body of the paper, by putting the page references in parentheses after the quotations.

Internal Parenthetical Citations   Information on page 1302 distinguishes between embedded quotations (which are short, are run right into your own sentence, and are enclosed within quotation marks) and quotations that are set off on the page (for example, three or more lines of poetry, or five or more lines of typed prose that are not enclosed within quotation marks).

For an embedded quotation, put the page reference in parentheses immediately after the closing quotation mark, *without* any intervening punctuation. Then, after the parenthesis that follows the number, put the necessary punctuation (for instance, a comma or a period).

Woolf says that there was "something marvelous as

well as pathetic" about the struggling moth (122).

She goes on to explain . . .

Notice that the period comes *after* the parenthetical citation. Notice, similarly, that in the next example *no* punctuation comes after the first citation—because none is needed—and a comma comes *after* (not before or within) the second citation, because a comma is needed in the sentence.

This is ironic because almost at the start of the

story, in the second paragraph, Richards with the

best of motives "hastened" (63) to bring his sad

message; if he had at the start been "too late" (64),

Mallard would have arrived at home first.

For a quotation that is not embedded within the text but is set off (indented ten spaces), put the parenthetical citation on the last line of the quotation, two spaces *after* the period that ends the quoted sentence.

Long sentences are not necessarily hard to follow.

For instance, a reader has no trouble with this

sentence, from Juanita Miranda's essay:

    The Philistine's scorn when he sees David,

    David's reply (a mixture of scorn and pity,

    for David announces that he comes "in the

    name of the Lord"), the observation that

    David was eager to do battle (he "ran

    toward the army to meet the Philistine"),

the explanation that David cut off
Goliath's head with Goliath's own sword--
all of these details help us to see the
scene, to believe in the characters, and
yet of course the whole story is, on the
literal level, remote from our experience.
(249)

Why is the sentence easy to follow? Partly because it
uses parallel constructions ("The Philistine's
scorn. . ., David's reply"; "the observation that. . .,
the explanation that"; "to see, . . . to believe"), and
partly because Miranda does not hesitate to repeat
the names of David and Goliath. In certain places if
she had (as we might normally expect) substituted the
pronoun he, the passage probably would have become
muddled. For instance, we have no trouble with "David
cut off Goliath's head with Goliath's own sword," but
we might have been at least briefly uncertain if
Miranda had written "David cut off Goliath's head
with his own sword."

Notice that the indented quotation ends with a period. After the period there are
two spaces and then the citation in parentheses.

Four additional points:

1. The abbreviations "p." "pg.," and "pp." are *not* used in citing pages.
2. If a **story** is very short—perhaps running for only a page or two—your
   instructor may tell you not to cite the page reference for each quotation. Simply mention in the footnote that the story appears on, say,
   pages 200-202.
3. If you are referring to a **poem,** your instructor may tell you to use parenthetical citations of line numbers rather than of page numbers. But,
   again, your footnote will tell the reader that the poem can be found in
   this book, and on what page.
4. If you are referring to a **play** with numbered lines, your instructor may
   prefer that in your parenthetical citations you give act, scene, and line,
   rather than page numbers. Use arabic (not roman) numerals, separating
   the act from the scene, and the scene from the line, by periods. Here,

then, is how a reference to act three, scene two, line 118 would be given:

```
(3.2.118)
```

Parenthetical Citations and List of Works Cited   Footnotes have fallen into disfavor. Parenthetical citations are now usually clarified not by means of a footnote but by means of a list, headed Works Cited, given at the end of the essay. In this list you give alphabetically (last name first) the authors and titles that you have quoted or referred to in the essay.

Briefly, the idea is that the reader of your paper encounters an author's name and a parenthetical citation of pages. By checking the author's name in Works Cited, the reader can find the passage in the book. Suppose you are writing about Kate Chopin's "The Story of an Hour." Let's assume that you have already mentioned the author and the title of the story—that is, you have let the reader know the subject of the essay—and now you introduce a quotation from the story in a sentence such as this. (Notice the parenthetical citation of page numbers immediately after the quotation.)

```
True, Mrs. Mallard at first expresses grief when she
hears the news, but soon (unknown to her friends) she
finds joy in it. So, Richards's "sad message" (12),
though sad in Richards's eyes, is in fact a happy
message.
```

Turning to Works Cited, the reader, knowing the quoted words are by Chopin, looks for Chopin and finds the following:

```
Chopin, Kate. "The Story of an Hour." Literature for
    Composition, 4th ed. Eds. Sylvan Barnet et al.
    New York: HarperCollins, 1995.
```

Thus the essayist is informing the reader that the quoted words ("sad message") are to be found on page 12 of this anthology.

If you have not mentioned Chopin's name in some sort of lead-in, you will have to give her name within the parentheses so that the reader will know the author of the quoted words:

```
What are we to make out of a story that ends by
telling us that the leading character has died "of
joy that kills" (Chopin 13)?
```

(Notice, by the way, that the closing quotation marks come immediately after the last word of the quotation; the citation and the final punctuation—in this case, the essayist's question mark—come *after* the closing quotation marks.)

If you are comparing Chopin's story with Hurston's "Sweat," in Works Cited you will give a similar entry for Hurston—her name, the title of the story, the book in which it is reprinted, and the page numbers that the story occupies.

If you are referring to several works reprinted within one volume, instead of listing each item fully, it is acceptable in Works Cited to list each item simply by giving the author's name, the title of the work, then a period, two spaces, and the name of the anthologist, followed by the page numbers that the selection spans. Thus a reference to Chopin's "The Story of an Hour" would be followed only by: Barnet, 12-13. This form requires that the anthology itself be cited under the name of the first-listed editor, thus:

```
Barnet, Sylvan, et al., eds. Literature for

     Composition, 4th ed. New York: HarperCollins,

     1995.
```

If you are writing a research paper, you will use many sources. Within the essay itself you will mention an author's name, quote or summarize from this author, and follow the quotation or summary with a parenthetical citation of the pages. In Works Cited you will give the full title, place of publication, and other bibliographic material.

Here are a few examples, all referring to an article by Joan Templeton, "The *Doll House* Backlash: Criticism, Feminism, and Ibsen." The article appeared in *PMLA* 104 (1989): 28-40, but this information is given only in Works Cited, not within the text of the student's essay.

If in the text of your essay you mention the author's name, the citation following a quotation (or a summary of a passage) is merely a page number in parentheses, followed by a period, thus:

```
In 1989 Joan Templeton argued that many critics,

     unhappy with recognizing Ibsen as a feminist, sought

     "to render Nora inconsequential" (29).
```

Or:

```
In 1989 Joan Templeton noted that many critics,

     unhappy with recognizing Ibsen as a feminist, have

     sought to make Nora trivial (29).
```

If you don't mention the name of the author in a lead-in, you will have to give the name within the parenthetic citation:

```
Many critics, attempting to argue that Ibsen was not

     a feminist, have tried to make Nora trivial

     (Templeton 29).
```

Notice in all of these examples that the final period comes after the parenthetic citation. *Exception:* If the quotation is longer than four lines and, therefore, is set off by being indented ten spaces from the left margin, end the quotation with the appropriate punctuation (period, question mark, or exclamation mark), hit the space bar twice, and type (in parentheses) the page number. In this case, do not put a period after the citation.

Another point: If your list of Works Cited includes more than one work by an author, in your essay when you quote or refer to one or the other you'll have to identify *which* work you are drawing on. You can provide the title in a lead-in, thus:

In "The <u>Doll House</u> Backlash: Criticism, Feminism, and

Ibsen," Templeton says, "Nora's detractors have often

been, from the first, her husband's defenders" (30).

Or you can provide the information in the parenthetic citation, giving a shortened version of the title—usually the first word, unless it is *A, An,* or *The,* in which case the second word usually will do, though certain titles may require still another word or two, as in this example:

According to Templeton, "Nora's detractors have often

been, from the first, her husband's defenders" ("<u>Doll</u>

<u>House</u> Backlash" 30).

Forms of Citation in Works Cited   In looking over the following samples of entries in Works Cited, remember:

1. The list of Works Cited appears at the end of the paper. It begins on a new page, and the page continues the numbering of the text.
2. The list of Works Cited is arranged alphabetically by author (last name first).
3. If a work is anonymous, list it under the first word of the title unless the first word is *A, An,* or *The,* in which case list it under the second word.
4. If a work is by two authors, although the book is listed alphabetically under the first author's last name, the second author's name is given in the normal order, first name first.
5. If you list two or more works by the same author, the author's name is not repeated but is represented by three hyphens followed by a period and two spaces.
6. Each item begins flush left, but if an entry is longer than one line, subsequent lines in the entry are indented five spaces.

For details about almost every imaginable kind of citation, consult Joseph Gibaldi and Walter S. Achtert, *MLA Handbook for Writers of Research Papers,* 4th. ed. (New York: MLA, 1995). We give here, however, information concerning the most common kinds of citations.

Here are samples of the kinds of citations you are most likely to include in your list of Works Cited.

Entries (arranged alphabetically) begin flush with the left margin. If an entry runs more than one line, indent the subsequent line or lines five spaces from the left margin.

A book by one author:

Douglas, Ann. <u>The Feminization of American Culture</u>. New

York: Knopf, 1977.

Notice that the author's last name is given first, but otherwise the name is given as on the title page. Do not substitute initials for names written out on the title page, but you may shorten the publisher's name—for example, from Little, Brown and Company to Little.

Take the title from the title page, not from the cover or the spine, but disregard unusual typography—for instance, the use of only capital letters or the use of & for *and.* Underline the title and subtitle with one continuous underline, but do not underline the period. The place of publication is indicated by the name of the city. If the city is not well known or if several cities have the same name (for instance, Cambridge, Massachusetts, and Cambridge, England) the name of the state is added. If the title page lists several cities, give only the first.

A book by more than one author:

Gilbert, Sandra, and Susan Gubar. <u>The Madwoman in the</u>

    <u>Attic: The Woman Writer and the Nineteenth-Century</u>

    <u>Literary Imagination</u>. New Haven: Yale UP 1979.

Notice that the book is listed under the last name of the first author (Gilbert) and that the second author's name is then given with first name (Susan) first. *If the book has more than three authors,* give the name of the first author only (last name first) and follow it with "et al." (Latin for "and others.")

A book in several volumes:

McQuade, Donald, et al., eds. <u>The Harper American</u>

    <u>Literature</u>. 2nd ed. 2 vols. New York:

    HarperCollins, 1994.

Pope, Alexander. <u>The Correspondence of Alexander Pope</u>. 5

    vols. Ed. George Sherburn. Oxford: Clarendon, 1955.

Notice that the total number of volumes is given after the title, regardless of the number that you have used.

If you have used more than one volume, within your essay you will parenthetically indicate a reference to, for instance, page 30 of volume 3 thus: (3:30). If you have used only one volume of a multivolume work—let's say you used only volume 2 of McQuade's anthology—in your entry in Works Cited write, after the period following the date, Vol. 2. In your parenthetical citation within the essay you will therefore cite only the page reference (without the volume number), since the reader will (on consulting Works Cited) understand that in this example the reference is in volume 2.

If, instead of using the volumes as whole, you used only an independent work within one volume—say an essay in volume 2—in Works Cited omit the abbreviation "Vol." Instead, give an arabic 2 (indicating volume 2) followed by a colon, a space, and the page numbers that encompass the selection you used:

McPherson, James Alan. "Why I Like Country Music." <u>The</u>

    <u>Harper American Literature</u>. 2nd ed. 2 vols. New

    York: HarperCollins, 1994. 2: 2304-15.

Notice that this entry for McPherson specifies not only that the book consists of two volumes, but also that only one selection ("Why I Like Country Music," occupying pages 2304-15 in volume 2) was used. If you use this sort of citation in Works Cited, in the body of your essay a documentary reference to this work will be only to the page; the volume number will *not* be added.

A book with a separate title in a set of volumes:

Churchill, Winston. The Age of Revolution. Vol. 3 of A
    History of the English-Speaking Peoples. New York:
    Dodd, 1957.

Jonson, Ben. The Complete Masques. Ed. Stephen Orgel.
    Vol. 4 of The Yale Ben Jonson. New Haven: Yale UP,
    1969.

A revised edition of a book:

Ellmann, Richard. James Joyce. Rev. ed. New York: Oxford
    UP, 1982.

Chaucer, Geoffrey. The Works of Geoffrey Chaucer. Ed.
    F. N. Robinson. 2nd ed. Boston: Houghton, 1957.

A reprint, such as a paperback version of an older clothbound book:

Rourke, Constance. American Humor. 1931. Garden City,
    New York: Doubleday, 1953.

Notice that the entry cites the original date (1931) but indicates that the writer is using the Doubleday reprint of 1953.

An edited book other than an anthology:

Keats, John. The Letters of John Keats. Ed. Hyder Edward
    Rollins. 2 vols. Cambridge, MA: Harvard UP, 1958.

An anthology: You can list an anthology either under the editor's name or under the title.

A work in a volume of works by one author:

Sontag, Susan. "The Aesthetics of Silence." In Styles of
    Radical Will. New York: Farrar, 1969. 3-34.

This entry indicates that Sontag's essay, called "The Aesthetics of Silence," appears in a book of hers entitled *Styles of Radical Will.* Notice that the page numbers of the short work are cited (not page numbers that you may happen to refer to, but the page numbers of the entire piece).

A work in an anthology, that is, in a collection of works by several authors: Begin with the author and the title of the work you are citing, not with the name of the anthologist or the title of the anthology. The entry ends with the pages occupied by the selection you are citing:

Ng, Fae Myenne. "A Red Sweater." <u>Charlie Chan Is Dead:</u>

<u>An Anthology of Contemporary Asian American</u>

<u>Fiction</u>. Ed. Jessica Hagedorn. New York: Penguin,

1993. 358-68.

Porter, Katherine Anne. "The Jilting of Granny

Weatherall." <u>Literature for Composition</u>. Ed. Sylvan

Barnet, et al. 4th ed. New York: HarperCollins,

1995. 1163-69.

Normally, you will give the title of the work you are citing (probably an essay, short story, or poem) in quotation marks. If you are referring to a book-length work (for instance, a novel or a full-length play), underline it to indicate italics. If the work is translated, after the period that follows the title, write "Trans." and give the name of the translator, followed by a period and the name of the anthology.

If the collection is a multivolume work and you are using only one volume, in Works Cited you will specify the volume. Because the list of Works Cited specifies the volume, your parenthetical documentary reference within your essay will specify (as mentioned earlier) only the page numbers, not the volume. Thus, although an essay appears on pages 2198-2210 in the second volume of a two-volume work, a parenthetical citation will refer only to the page numbers because the citation in Works Cited specifies the volume.

Remember that the pages specified in the entry in your list of Works Cited are to the *entire selection,* not simply to pages you may happen to refer to within your paper.

If you are referring to a *reprint of a scholarly article,* give details of the original publication, as in the following example:

Mack, Maynard. "The World of Hamlet." <u>Yale Review</u> 41

(1952): 502-23. Rpt. in <u>Hamlet</u>. By William

Shakespeare. Ed. Edward Hubler. New York: New

American Library, 1963. 234-56.

Two or more works in an anthology: If you are referring to more than one work in an anthology (for example, in this book), in order to avoid repeating all the information about the anthology in each entry in Works Cited, under each author's name (in the appropriate alphabetical place) give the author and title of the work, then a period, one space, and the name of the anthologist, followed by the page numbers that the selection spans. Thus, a reference to Shakespeare's *Hamlet* would be followed only by

Barnet 628-735

rather than by a full citation of this book. This form requires that the anthology itself also be listed, under Barnet.

Two or more works by the same author: Notice that the works are given in alphabetical order (*Fables* precedes *Fools*) and that the author's name is not repeated but is represented by three hyphens followed by a period and one space. If the author is the translator or editor of a volume, the three hyphens are followed not by a period but by a comma, then a space, then the appropriate abbreviation (trans. or ed.), then (one space after the period) the title:

Frye, Northrop. <u>Fables of Identity: Studies in Poetic

Mythology</u>. New York: Harcourt, 1963.

---. <u>Fools of Time: Studies in Shakespearean Tragedy</u>.

Toronto: U of Toronto P, 1967.

A translated book:

Gogol, Nikolai. <u>Dead Souls</u>. Trans. Andrew McAndrew. New

York: New American Library, 1961.

If you are discussing the translation itself, as opposed to the book, list the work under the translator's name. Then put a comma, a space, and "trans." After the period following "trans." skip one space, then give the title of the book, a period, one space, and then "By" and the author's name, first name first. Continue with information about the place of publication, publisher, and date, as in any entry to a book.

An introduction, foreword, or afterword, or other editorial apparatus

Fromm, Erich. Afterword. <u>1984</u>. By George Orwell. New

American Library, 1961.

Usually a book with an introduction or some such comparable material is listed under the name of the author of the book rather than the name of the author of the editorial material (see the citation to Pope on page 1321). But if you are referring to the editor's apparatus rather than to the work itself, use the form just given.

Words such as *preface, introduction, afterword,* and *conclusion* are capitalized in the entry but are neither enclosed within quotation marks nor underlined.

A book review: First, an example of a review that does not have a title:

Vendler, Helen. Rev. of <u>Essays on Style</u>. Ed. Roger

Fowler. <u>Essays in Criticism</u> 16 (1966): 457-63.

If the review has a title, give the title after the period following the reviewer's name, before "Rev." If the review is unsigned, list it under the first word of the title, or the second word if the first word is *A, An,* or *The.* If an unsigned review has no title, begin the entry with "Rev. of" and alphabetize it under the title of the work being reviewed.

An encyclopedia: The first example is for a signed article, the second for an unsigned article:

Lang, Andrew. "Ballads." Encyclopaedia Britannica. 1910

ed.

"Metaphor." The New Encyclopaedia Britannica:

Micropaedia. 1974 ed.

An article in a scholarly journal: Some journals are paginated consecutively; that is, the pagination of the second issue picks up where the first issue left off. Other journals begin each issue with a new page 1. The forms of the citations in Works Cited differ slightly.

First, the citation of *a journal that uses continuous pagination:*

Burbick, Joan. "Emily Dickinson and the Economics

of Desire." American Literature 58 (1986): 361-78.

This article appeared in volume 58, which was published in 1986. (Notice that the volume number is followed by a space, then by the year, in parentheses, then by a colon, a space, and the page numbers of the entire article.) Although each volume consists of four issues, you do *not* specify the issue number when the journal is paginated continuously.

For a journal that paginates each issue separately (a quarterly journal will have four page 1's each year), give the issue number directly after the volume number and a period, with no spaces before or after the period:

Spillers, Hortense J. "Martin Luther King and the Style

of the Black Sermon." The Black Scholar 3.1 (1971):

14-27.

An article in a weekly, biweekly, or monthly publication:

McCabe, Bernard. "Taking Dickens Seriously." Commonweal

14 May 1965: 24.

Notice that the volume number and the issue number are omitted for popular weeklies or monthlies such as *Time* and *The Atlantic Monthly.*

An article in a newspaper: Because newspapers usually consist of several sections, a section number may precede the page number. The example indicates that an article begins on page 3 of section 2 and is continued on a later page:

Wu, Jim. "Authors Praise New Forms." The New York Times

8 March 1987, sec. 2: 3+.

You may also have occasion to cite something other than a printed source, for instance a lecture. Here are the forms for the chief nonprint sources:

An interview

Howard Saretta. Personal interview. 3 Nov. 1994.

A lecture

Seamus Heaney. Tufts University. 15 Oct. 1994.

A television or radio program

<u>Sixty Minutes</u>. CBS. 30 Jan. 1994.

A film or videotape

<u>Modern Times</u>. Dir. Charles Chaplin. United Artists,

    1936.

A recording

Frost, Robert. "The Road Not Taken." <u>Robert Frost Reads</u>

    <u>His Poetry</u>. Caedmon, TC 1060, 1956.

A performance

<u>The Cherry Orchard</u>. By Anton Chekhov. Dir. Ron Daniels.

    American Repertory Theatre, Cambridge, MA. 3 Feb.

    1994.

✔ A Checklist for Reading Drafts

1. Is the tentative title informative and focused?
2. Does the paper make a point, or does it just accumulate other people's ideas?
3. Does it reveal the thesis early?
4. Are generalizations supported by evidence?
5. Are quotations introduced adequately?
6. Are all of the long quotations necessary, or can some of them be effectively summarized?
7. Are quotations discussed adequately?
8. Are all sources given, including sources for paraphrased material?
9. Does the paper advance in orderly stages? Can your imagined reader easily follow your thinking?
10. Is the documentation in the correct form?

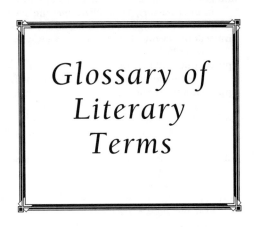

Glossary of Literary Terms

The terms briefly defined here are for the most part more fully defined earlier in the text. Hence many of the entries below are followed by page references to the earlier discussions.

Absurd, Theater of the plays, especially written in the 1950s and 1960s, that call attention to the incoherence of character and of action, the inability of people to communicate, and the apparent purposelessness of existence

accent stress given to a syllable (350)

act a major division of a play

action (1) the happenings in a narrative or drama, usually physical events (*B* marries *C*, *D* kills *E*), but also mental changes (*F* moves from innocence to experience); in short, the answer to the question, "What happens?" (2) less commonly, the theme or underlying idea of a work (207–08)

allegory a work in which concrete elements (for instance, a pilgrim, a road, a splendid city) stand for abstractions (humanity, life, salvation), usually in an unambiguous, one-to-one relationship. The literal items (the pilgrim, and so on) thus convey a meaning, which is usually moral, religious, or political. To take a nonliterary example: The Statue of Liberty holds a torch (enlightenment, showing the rest of the world the way to freedom), and at her feet are broken chains (tyranny overcome). A caution: Not all of the details in an allegorical work are meant to be interpreted. For example, the hollowness of the Statue of Liberty does not stand for the insubstantiality or emptiness of liberty.

alliteration repetition of consonant sounds, especially at the beginnings of words (*f*ree, *f*orm, *ph*antom) (354)

allusion an indirect reference; thus when Lincoln spoke of "a nation dedicated to the proposition that all men are created equal," he was making an allusion to the Declaration of Independence

ambiguity multiplicity of meaning, often deliberate, that leaves the reader uncertain about the intended significance

anagnorisis a recognition or discovery, especially in tragedy—for example, when the hero understands the reason for his or her fall (205)

analysis an examination, which usually proceeds by separating the object of study into parts (28, 44–58, 70–71)

anapest a metrical foot consisting of two unaccented syllables followed by an accented one. Example, showing three anapests: "As I came / to the edge / of the wood." (352)

anecdote a short narrative, usually reporting an amusing event in the life of an important person

antagonist   a character or force that opposes (literally, "wrestles") the protagonist (the main character). Thus, in *Hamlet* the antagonist is King Claudius, the protagonist Hamlet; in *Antigonê,* the antagonist is Creon, the protagonist Antigonê.

antecedent action   happenings (especially in a play) that occurred before the present action (208)

apostrophe   address to an absent figure or to a thing as if it were present and could listen. Example: "O rose, thou art sick!" (340)

approximate rhyme   only the final consonant-sounds are the same, as in *crown/alone,* or *pail/fall*

archetype   a theme, image, motive, or pattern that occurs so often in literary works it seems to be universal. Examples: a dark forest (for mental confusion), the sun (for illumination).

aside   in the theater, words spoken by a character in the presence of other characters, but directed to the spectators, i.e., understood by the audience to be inaudible to the other characters

assonance   the repetition of similar vowel sounds in a string of stressed syllables. Example: *light/bride* (354)

atmosphere   the emotional tone (for instance, joy or horror) in a work, most often established by the setting (145)

ballad   a short narrative poem, especially one that is sung or recited, often in a stanza of four lines, with 8, 6, 8, 6 syllables, with the second and fourth lines rhyming. A **popular ballad** is a narrative song that has been transmitted orally by what used to be called "the folk"; a **literary ballad** is a conscious imitation (without music) of such a work, often with complex symbolism.

blank verse   unrhymed iambic pentameter, that is, unrhymed lines of ten syllables, with every second syllable stressed (356)

cacophony   an unpleasant combination of sounds

caesura   a strong pause within a line of verse (353)

canon   a term originally used to refer to those books accepted as Holy Scripture by the Christian church. The term has come to be applied to literary works thought to have a special merit by a given culture, for instance the body of literature traditionally taught in colleges and universities. Such works are sometimes called "classics" and their authors are "major authors." As conceived in the United States until recently, the canon consisted chiefly of works by dead white European and American males—partly, of course, because middle-class and upper-class white males were in fact the people who did most of the writing in the western hemisphere, but also because white males—for instance college professors—were the people who chiefly established the canon. Not surprisingly the canon makers valued (or valorized or "privileged") writings that revealed, asserted, or reinforced the canon makers' own values. From about the 1960s feminists and Marxists and others argued that these works had been regarded as central not because they were inherently better than other works but because they reflected the interests of the dominant culture, and that other work, such as slave narratives and the diaries of women, had been "marginalized."

   In fact, the literary canon has never been static (in contrast to the biblical canon, which has not changed for more than a thousand years), but it is true that certain authors, such as Homer, Chaucer, and Shakespeare, have been permanent fixtures. Why? Partly because they do indeed support the values of those who in large measure control the purse strings for the "high culture," and perhaps partly because these books are rich enough to invite constant reinterpretation from age to age, that is, to allow each generation to find its needs and its values in them. (400–01)

catastrophe   the concluding action, especially in a tragedy

catharsis   Aristotle's term for the purgation or purification of the pity and terror supposedly experienced while witnessing a tragedy

character   (1) a person in a literary work (Romeo); (2) the personality of such a figure (sentimental lover, or whatever). Characters (in the first sense) are sometimes classified as either "flat" (one-dimensional) or "round" (fully realized, complex). (142–43, 150, 210, 214-15)

characterization   the presentation of a character, whether by direct description, by showing the character in action, or by the presentation of other characters who help to define each other

cliché   an expression that through overuse has ceased to be effective. Examples: acid test, sigh of relief, the proud possessor.

climax   the culmination of a conflict; a turning point, often the point of greatest tension in a plot (207)

comedy   a literary work, especially a play, characterized by humor and by a happy ending (206)

comparison and contrast   to compare is strictly to note similarities; to contrast is to note differences. But *compare* is now often used for both activities. (49–51)

complication   an entanglement in a narrative or dramatic work that causes a conflict

conflict   a struggle between a character and some obstacle (for example, another character or fate) or between internal forces, such as divided loyalties (208, 214)

connotation   the associations (suggestions, overtones) of a word or expression. Thus *seventy* and *three score and ten* both mean "one more than sixty-nine," but because *three score and ten* is a biblical expression, it has an association of holiness; see *denotation*. (340)

consistency building   the process engaged in during the act of reading, of reevaluating the details that one has just read in order to make them consistent with the new information that the text is providing (6)

consonance   repetition of consonant sounds, especially in stressed syllables. Also called half rhyme or slant rhyme. Example: *arouse/doze*. (354)

convention   a pattern (for instance, the 14-line poem, or sonnet) or motif (for instance, the bumbling police officer in detective fiction) or other device occurring so often that it is taken for granted. Thus it is a convention that actors in a performance of *Julius Caesar* are understood to be speaking Latin, though in fact they are speaking English. Similarly, the soliloquy (a character alone on the stage speaks his or her thoughts aloud) is a convention, for in real life sane people generally do not talk aloud to themselves.

couplet   a pair of lines of verse, usually rhyming (355)

crisis   a high point in the conflict that leads to the turning point (207)

criticism   the analysis or evaluation of a literary work (432–52)

cultural criticism   criticism that sets literature in a social context, often of economics or politics or gender. Borrowing some of the methods of anthropology, cultural criticism usually extends the canon to include popular material, for instance comic books and soap operas

dactyl   a metrical foot consisting of a stressed syllable followed by two unstressed syllables. Example: *underwear* (352)

deconstruction   a critical approach assuming that language is unstable and ambiguous and is therefore inherently contradictory. Because authors cannot control their language, texts reveal more than their authors are aware of. For instance, texts (like such institutions as the law, the churches, and the schools) are likely, when closely scrutinized, to reveal connections to a society's economic system, even though the authors may have believed they were outside the system.

denotation   the dictionary meaning of a word. Thus *soap opera* and *daytime serial* have the same denotation, but the connotations (associations, emotional overtones) of *soap opera* are less favorable. (340)

dénouement   the resolution or the outcome (literally, the "unknotting") of a plot (207)

deus ex machina   literally, "a god out of a machine"; any unexpected and artificial way of resolving the plot—for example, by introducing a rich uncle, thought to be dead, who arrives on the scene and pays the debts that otherwise would overwhelm the young hero

dialogue   exchange of words between characters; speech

diction   the choice of vocabulary and of sentence structure. There is a difference in diction between "One never knows" and "You never can tell." (334-35)

didactic   pertaining to teaching; having a moral purpose

dimeter   a line of poetry containing two feet (352)

discovery   see *anagnorisis* (205)

drama   (1) a play; (2) conflict or tension, as in "The story lacks drama" (197-214)

dramatic irony   see *irony*

dramatic monologue   a poem spoken entirely by one character but addressed to one or more other characters whose presence is strongly felt (1322)

effaced narrator   a narrator who reports but who does not editorialize or enter into the minds of any of the characters in the story

elegy   a lyric poem, usually a meditation on a death

elision   omission (usually of a vowel or unstressed syllable), as in *o'er* (for *over*) and in "Th' inevitable hour"

end rhyme   identical sounds at the ends of lines of poetry (354)

end-stopped line   a line of poetry that ends with a pause (usually marked by a comma, semicolon, or period) because the grammatical structure and the sense reach (at least to some degree) completion. It is contrasted with a *run-on line.* (353)

English (or Shakespearean) sonnet   a poem of 14 lines (three quatrains and a couplet), rhyming *ababcdcdefefgg* (355)

enjambment   a line of poetry in which the grammatical and logical sense run on, without pause, into the next line or lines (353)

epic   a long narrative, especially in verse, that usually records heroic material in an elevated style

epigram   a brief, witty poem or saying

epigraph   a quotation at the beginning of the work, just after the title, often giving a clue to the theme

epiphany   a "showing forth," as when an action reveals a character with particular clarity

episode   an incident or scene that has unity in itself but is also a part of a larger action

epistle   a letter, in prose or verse

essay   a work, usually in prose and usually fairly short, that purports to be true and that treats its subject tentatively. In most literary essays the reader's interest is as much in the speaker's personality as in any argument that is offered. (101-04)

euphony   literally, "good sound," a pleasant combination of sounds

explication   a line-by-line unfolding of the meaning of a text (39-44, 346-50)

exposition   a setting forth of information. In fiction and drama, introductory material introducing characters and the situation; in an essay, the presentation of information, as opposed to the telling of a story or the setting forth of an argument (208)

eye rhyme   words that look as though they rhyme, but do not rhyme when pronounced. Example: *come/home.* (354)

fable   a short story (often involving speaking animals) with an easily grasped moral

farce   comedy based not on clever language or on subtleties of characters but on broadly humorous situations (for instance, a man mistakenly enters the ladies' locker room)

feminine rhyme   a rhyme of two or more syllables, with the stress falling on a syllable other than the last. Examples: *fatter/batter; tenderly/slenderly.* (354)

feminist criticism   an approach especially concerned with analyzing the depiction of women in literature—what images do male authors present of female characters?—and also with the reappraisal of work by female authors (443-45, 452)

fiction   an imaginative work, usually a prose narrative (novel, short story), that reports incidents that did not in fact occur. The term may include all works that invent a world, such as a lyric poem or a play.

figurative language   words intended to be understood in a way that is other than literal. Thus *lemon* used literally refers to a citrus fruit, but *lemon* used figuratively refers to a defective machine, especially a defective automobile. Other examples:

"He's a beast," "She's a witch," "A sea of troubles." Literally, such expressions are nonsense, but writers use them to express meanings inexpressible in literal speech. Among the commonest kinds of figures of speech are *apostrophe, metaphor,* and *simile* (see the discussions of these words in this glossary). (338–41)

flashback   an interruption in a narrative that presents an earlier episode

flat character   a one-dimensional character (for instance, the figure who is only and always the jealous husband or the flirtatious wife) as opposed to a round or many-sided character. (142–43)

fly-on-the-wall narrator   a narrator who never editorializes and never enters a character's mind but reports only what is said and done (147)

foil   a character who makes a contrast with another, especially a minor character who helps to set off a major character (210)

foot   a metrical unit, consisting of two or three syllables, with a specified arrangement of the stressed syllable or syllables. Thus the iambic foot consists of an unstressed syllable followed by a stressed syllable. (352–54)

foreshadowing   suggestions of what is to come (143–45, 208)

formal (or formalist) criticism   an approach that assumes that the work of art is a carefully constructed artifact with a meaning that can be perceived, and agreed on, by all competent readers. literary criticism, in this view, is an objective description and analysis of the work. (432–33, 450)

free verse   poetry in lines of irregular length, usually unrhymed (356)

gap   a term from reader-response criticism, referring to a reader's perception that something is unstated in the text, requiring the reader to fill in the material—for instance, to draw a conclusion as to why a character behaves as she does. Filling in the gaps is a matter of "consistency building." Different readers of course may fill the gaps differently, and readers may even differ as to whether a gap exists at a particular point in the text.

gender criticism   criticism concerned especially with alleged diffeences in the ways that males and females read and write, and also with the representations of gender in literature (443–48, 452)

genre   kind or type, roughly analogous to the biological term *species.* The four chief literary genres are nonfiction, fiction, poetry, and drama, but these can be subdivided into further genres. Thus fiction obviously can be divided into the short story and the novel, and drama obviously can be divided into tragedy and comedy. But these can be still further divided—for instance, tragedy into heroic tragedy and bourgeois tragedy, comedy into romantic comedy and satirical comedy.

gesture   physical movement, especially in a play (209)

haiku   a Japanese lyric verse form of three unrhymed lines of five, seven, and five syllables

half rhyme   repetition in accented syllables of the final consonant sound but without identity in the preceding vowel sound; words of similar but not identical sound. Also called near rhyme, slant rhyme, approximate rhyme, and off-rhyme. See *consonance.* Examples: *light/bet; affirm/perform* (354)

hamartia   a flaw in the tragic hero, or an error made by the tragic hero (205)

heptameter   a metrical line of seven feet (352)

hero, heroine   the main character (not necessarily heroic or even admirable) in a work; cf. *protagonist*

heroic couplet   an end-stopped pair of rhyming lines of iambic pentameter (355)

hexameter   a metrical line of six feet (352)

historical criticism   the attempt to illuminate a literary work by placing it in its historical context (439, 451)

hubris, hybris   a Greek word, usually translated as "overweening pride," "arrogance," "excessive ambition," and often said to be characteristic of tragic figures (204)

hyperbole   figurative language using overstatement, as in "He died a thousand deaths" (342)

iamb, iambic   a poetic foot consisting of an unaccented syllable followed by an accented one. Example: *alone.* (352)

image, imagery   imagery is established by language that appeals to the senses, especially sight ("deep blue sea") but also other senses ("tinkling bells," "perfumes of Arabia") (340–41)

indeterminacy   a passage that careful readers agree is open to more than one interpretation. According to some poststructural critics, because language is unstable and because contexts can never be objectively viewed, all texts are indeterminate. (436)

innocent eye   a naive narrator in whose narration the reader sees more than the narrator sees

internal rhyme   rhyme within a line (354)

interpretation   the exposition or assignment of meaning to a text, chiefly by means of analysis (404–09)

intertextuality   all works show the influence of other works. If an author writes (say) a short story, no matter how original she thinks she is, she inevitably brings to her own story a knowledge of other stories, e.g., a conception of what a short story is, and, speaking more generally, an idea of what a story (long or short, written or oral) is. In opposition to formalist critics, who see a literary work as an independent whole containing a fixed meaning, some contemporary critics emphasize the work's *intertextuality,* that is, its connections with a vast context of writings and indeed of all aspects of culture, and in part depending also on what the reader brings to the work. Because different readers bring different things, meaning is thus ever-changing. In this view, then, no text is self-sufficient, and no writer fully controls the meaning of the text. Because we are talking about connections of which the writer is unaware, and because *meaning* is in part the creation of the reader, the author is by no means an authority. Thus, the critic should see a novel (for instance) in connection not only with other novels, past and present, but also in connection with other kinds of narratives, such as TV dramas and films, even though the author of the book lived before the age of film and TV. See Jay Clayton and Eric Rothstein, eds., *Influences and Intertextuality in Literary History* (1991).

irony   a contrast of some sort. For instance, in **verbal irony** or **Socratic irony** the contrast is between what is said and what is meant ("You're a great guy," meant bitterly). In **dramatic irony** or **Sophoclean irony** (205) the contrast is between what is intended and what is accomplished (Macbeth usurps the throne, thinking he will then be happy, but the action leads him to misery), or between what the audience knows (a murderer waits in the bedroom) and what a character says (the victim enters the bedroom, innocently saying, "I think I'll have a long sleep").

Italian (or Petrarchan) sonnet   a poem of 14 lines, consisting of an octave (rhyming *abbaabba*) and a sestet (usually *cdecde* or *cdccdc*) (355)

litotes   a form of understatement in which an affirmation is made by means of a negation; thus "He was not underweight," meaning "He was grossly overweight"

lyric poem   a short poem, often songlike, with the emphasis not on narrative but on the speaker's emotion or reverie

Marxist criticism   the study of literature in the light of Karl Marx's view that economic forces, controlled by the dominant class, shape the literature (as well as the law, philosophy, religion, etc.) of a society (439–40, 451)

masculine rhyme   rhyme of one-syllable words (*lies/cries*) or, if more than one syllable, words ending with accented syllables (*behold/foretold*) (354)

mask   a term used to designate the speaker of a poem, equivalent to *persona* or *voice* (332–33)

meaning   critics seek to interpret *meaning,* variously defined as what the writer intended the work to say about the world and human experience, or as what the work says to the reader irrespective of the writer's intention. Both versions imply that a literary work is a nut to be cracked, with a kernel that is to be extracted. Because few critics today hold that meaning is clear and unchanging, the tendency now is to say that a critic offers "an interpretation" or "a reading" rather than a "statement of the meaning of a work." Many critics today would say that an alleged interpretation is really a creation of meaning. (5, 397-400, 404-09)

melodrama a narrative, usually in dramatic form, involving threatening situations but ending happily. The characters are usually stock figures (virtuous heroine, villainous landlord).

metaphor a kind of figurative language equating one thing with another: "This novel is garbage" (a book is equated with discarded and probably inedible food), "a piercing cry" (a cry is equated with a spear or other sharp instrument) (339)

meter a pattern of stressed and unstressed syllables (351-53)

metonymy a kind of figurative language in which a word or phrase stands not for itself but for something closely related to it: *saber rattling* means "militaristic talk or action"

monologue a relatively long, uninterrupted speech by a character

monometer a metrical line consisting of only one foot (352)

mood the atmosphere, usually created by descriptions of the settings and characters

motif a recurrent theme within a work, or a theme common to many works

motivation grounds for a character's action (210)

myth (1) a traditional story reflecting primitive beliefs, especially explaining the mysteries of the natural world (why it rains, or the origin of mountains); (2) a body of belief, not necessarily false, especially as set forth by a writer. Thus one may speak of William Butler Yeats or Alice Walker as mythmakers, referring to the visions of reality that they set forth in their works.

narrative, narrator a narrative is a story (an anecdote, a novel); a narrator is one who tells a story (not the author, but the invented speaker of the story). On kinds of narrators, see *point of view*. (146-49)

New Criticism a mid-twentieth-century movement (also called *formal criticism*) that regarded a literary work as an independent, carefully constructed object—hence it made little or no use of the author's biography or of historical context and it relied chiefly on explication (432-33, 450)

New Historicism a school of criticism holding that the past cannot be known objectively. According to this view, because historians project their own "narrative"— their own invention or "construction"—on the happenings of the past, historical writings are not objective but are, at bottom, political statements (440-41, 451)

novel a long work of prose fiction, especially one that is relatively realistic

novella a work of prose fiction longer than a short story but shorter than a novel, say about 40 to 80 pages

objective point of view a narrator reports but does not editorialize or enter into the minds of any of the characters in the story (147)

octave, octet an eight-line stanza, or the first eight lines of a sonnet, especially of an Italian sonnet (355)

octosyllabic couplet a pair of rhyming lines, each line with four iambic feet (355)

ode a lyric exalting someone (for instance, a hero) or something (for instance, a season)

omniscient narrator a speaker who knows the thoughts of all of the characters in the narrative (146-47)

onomatopoeia words (or the use of words) that sound like what they mean. Examples: *buzz, whirr* (354-55)

open form poetry whose form seems spontaneous rather than highly patterned

oxymoron a compact paradox, as in "a mute cry," "a pleasing pain," "proud humility"

parable a short narrative that is at least in part allegorical and that illustrates a moral or spiritual lesson

paradox an apparent contradiction, as in Jesus' words: "Whosoever will save his life shall lose it; but whosoever will lose his life for my sake, the same shall save it" (342)

paraphrase a restatement that sets forth an idea in diction other than that of the original (86-88, 347, 395-96)

parody a humorous imitation of a literary work, especially of its style (92-94)

pathos   pity, sadness

pentameter   a line of verse containing five feet (352)

peripeteia   a reversal in the action (205)

persona   literally, a mask; the "I" or speaker of a work, sometimes identified with the author but usually better regarded as the voice or mouthpiece created by the author (102-04, 112, 332-33)

personification   a kind of figurative language in which an inanimate object, animal, or other nonhuman is given human traits. Examples: "the creeping tide" (the tide is imagined as having feet), "the cruel sea" (the sea is imagined as having moral qualities) (339-40)

plot   the episodes in a narrative or dramatic work—that is, what happens. (But even a lyric poem can be said to have a plot; for instance, the speaker's mood changes from anger to resignation.) Sometimes *plot* is defined as the author's particular arrangement (sequence) of these episodes, and *story* is the episodes in their chronological sequence. Until recently it was widely believed that a good plot had a logical structure: A caused B (B did not simply happen to follow A), but in the last few decades some critics have argued that such a concept merely represents the white male's view of experience. (142-43, 150, 207-09, 214)

poem   an imaginative work in meter or in free verse, usually employing figurative language

point of view   the perspective from which a story is told—for example, by a major character or a minor character or a fly on the wall; see also *narrative, narrator, omniscient narrator* (146-49, 151)

post-modernism   the term came into prominence in the 1960s, to distinguish the contemporary experimental writing of such authors as Samuel Beckett and Jorge Luis Borges from such early-twentieth-century classics of modernism as James Joyce's *Ulysses* (1922) and T. S. Eliot's *The Waste Land* (1922). Although the classic modernists had been thought to be revolutionary in their day, after World War II they seemed to be conservative, and their works seemed remote from today's society with its new interests in such things as feminism, gay and lesbian rights, and pop culture. Postmodernist literature, though widely varied and not always clearly distinct from modernist literature, usually is more politically concerned, more playful—it is given to parody and pastiche—and more closely related to the art forms of popular culture than is modernist literature.

prosody   the principles of versification (350-56)

protagonist   the chief actor in any literary work. The term is usually preferable to *hero* and *heroine* because it can include characters—for example, villainous or weak ones—who are not aptly called heroes or heroines.

psychological criticism   a form of analysis especially concerned both with the ways in which authors unconsciously leave traces of their inner lives in their works and with the ways in which readers respond, consciously and unconsciously, to works. (441-43, 452)

pyrrhic foot   in poetry, a foot consisting of two unstressed syllables (352)

quatrain   a stanza of four lines (355)

reader-response criticism   criticism emphasizing the idea that various readers respond in various ways and therefore that readers as well as authors "create" meaning (435-38, 451)

realism   presentation of plausible characters (usually middle-class) in plausible (usually everyday) circumstances, as opposed, for example, to heroic characters engaged in improbable adventures. Realism in literature seeks to give the illusion of reality.

recognition   see *anagnorisis* (205)

refrain   a repeated phrase, line, or group of lines in a poem, especially in a *ballad*

resolution   the dénouement or untying of the complication of the plot

reversal   a change in fortune, often an ironic twist (205)

rhetorical question a question to which no answer is expected or to which only one answer is plausible. Example: "Do you think I am unaware of your goings-on?"

rhyme similarity or identity of accented sounds in corresponding positions, as, for example, at the ends of lines: *love/dove; tender/slender* (354)

rhythm in poetry, a pattern of stressed and unstressed sounds; in prose, some sort of recurrence (for example, of a motif) at approximately identical intervals (350-54)

rising action in a story or play, the events that lead up to the climax (207-08)

rising meter a foot (for example, iambic or anapestic) ending with a stressed syllable

romance narrative fiction, usually characterized by improbable adventures and love

round character a many-sided character, one who does not always act predictably, as opposed to a "flat" or one-dimensional, unchanging character (142-43)

run-on line a line of verse whose syntax and meaning require the reader to go on, without a pause, to the next line; an enjambed line (353)

sarcasm crudely mocking or contemptuous language; heavy verbal irony

satire literature that entertainingly attacks folly or vice; amusingly abusive writing

scansion description of rhythm in poetry; metrical analysis (353)

scene (1) a unit of a play, in which the setting is unchanged and the time continuous; (2) the setting (locale, and time of the action); (3) in fiction, a dramatic passage, as opposed to a passage of description or of summary

selective omniscience a point of view in which the author enters the mind of one character and for the most part sees the other characters only from the outside

sentimentality excessive emotion, especially excessive pity, treated as appropriate rather than as disproportionate

sestet a six-line stanza, or the last six lines of an Italian sonnet

sestina a poem with six stanzas of six lines each and a concluding stanza of three lines. The last word of each line in the first stanza appears as the last word of a line in each of the next five stanzas but in a different order. In the final (three-line) stanza, each line ends with one of these six words, and each line includes in the middle of the line one of the other three words.

setting the time and place of a story, play, or poem (for instance, a Texas town in winter, about 1900) (145, 151, 210)

short story a fictional narrative, usually in prose, rarely longer than 30 pages and often much briefer

simile a kind of figurative language explicitly making a comparison—for example, by using *as, like,* or a verb such as *seems* (339)

soliloquy a speech in a play, in which a character alone on the stage speaks his or her thoughts aloud

sonnet a lyric poem of 14 lines; see *English sonnet, Italian sonnet* (355-56)

speaker see *persona* (332-33, 356-57)

spondee a metrical foot consisting of two stressed syllables (352)

stage direction a playwright's indication to the actors or readers—for example, offering information about how an actor is to speak a line

stanza a group of lines forming a unit that is repeated in a poem (355-56)

stereotype a simplified conception, especially an oversimplification—for example, a stock character such as the heartless landlord, the kindly old teacher, the prostitute with a heart of gold. Such a character usually has only one personality trait, and this is boldly exaggerated.

stream of consciousness the presentation of a character's unrestricted flow of thought, often with free associations, and often without punctuation (147)

stress relative emphasis on one syllable as compared with another (350)

structuralism a critical theory holding that a literary work consists of conventional elements that, taken together by a reader familiar with the conventions, give the work its meaning. Thus, just as a spectator must know the rules of a game (e.g., three strikes and you're out) in order to enjoy the game, so a reader must know the rules of, say, a novel (coherent, realistic, adequately motivated characters, a plausible plot, for instance *The Color Purple*) or of a satire (caricatures of contemptible figures in amusing situations that need not be at all plausible, for instance *Gulliver's Travels*). Structuralists normally have no interest in the origins of a work (i.e., in the historical background, or in the author's biography), and no interest in the degree to which a work of art seems to correspond to reality. The interest normally is in the work as a self-sufficient construction. Consult Robert Scholes, *Structuralism in Literature: An Introduction,* and two books by Jonathan Culler, *Structuralist Poetics* (1976) and (for the critical shift from structuralism to poststructuralism) *On Deconstruction* (1982).

structure   the organization of a work, the relationship between the chief parts, the large-scale pattern—for instance, a rising action or complication followed by a crisis and then a resolution (342, 356)

style   the manner of expression, evident not only in the choice of certain words (for instance, colloquial language) but in the choice of certain kinds of sentence structure, characters, settings, and themes (148-49)

subplot   a sequence of events often paralleling or in some way resembling the main story

summary   a synopsis or condensation

symbol   a person, object, action, or situation that, charged with meaning, suggests another thing (for example, a dark forest may suggest confusion, or perhaps evil), though usually with less specificity and more ambiguity than an allegory. A symbol usually differs from a metaphor in that a symbol is expanded or repeated and works by accumulating associations. (145-46, 152, 340-41)

synecdoche   a kind of figurative language in which the whole stands for a part ("the law," for a police officer), or a part ("all hands on deck," for all persons) stands for the whole

tale   a short narrative, usually less realistic and more romantic than a short story; a yarn

tercet   a unit of three lines of verse (355)

tetrameter   a verse line of four feet (352)

theme   what the work is about; an underlying idea of a work; a conception of human experience suggested by the concrete details. Thus the theme of *Macbeth* is often said to be that "Vaulting ambition o'erleaps itself." (149-50, 152, 206-07)

thesis   the point or argument that a writer announces and develops. A thesis differs from a *topic* by making an assertion. "The fall of Oedipus" is a topic, but "Oedipus falls because he is impetuous" is a thesis, as is "Oedipus is impetuous, but his impetuosity has nothing to do with his fall." (9, 19-20, 57-58, 104)

thesis sentence   a sentence summarizing, as specifically as possible, the writer's chief poing (argument and perhaps purpose) (57, 109-10)

third-person narrator   the teller of a story who does not participate in the happenings (146-47)

tone   the prevailing attitude (for instance, ironic, genial, objective) as perceived by the reader. Notice that a reader may feel that the tone of the persona of the work is genial while the tone of the author of the same work is ironic. (103-04, 334-35)

topic   a subject, such as "Hamlet's relation to Horatio." A topic becomes a *thesis* when a predicate is added to this subject, thus: "Hamlet's relation to Horatio helps to define Hamlet." (56-57)

tragedy   a serious play showing the protagonist moving from good fortune to bad and ending in death or a deathlike state (204-06)

tragic flaw   a supposed weakness (for example, arrogance) in the tragic protagonist. If the tragedy results from an intellectual error rather than from a moral weakness it is better to speak of "a tragic error." (205)

transition   a connection between one passage and the next

trimeter   a verse line with three feet (352)

triplet   a group of three lines of verse, usually rhyming (355)

trochee   a metrical foot consisting of a stressed syllable followed by an unstressed sylla-ble. Example: garden. (352)

understatement   a figure of speech in which the speaker says less than what he or she means; an ironic minimizing, as in "You've done fairly well for yourself" said to the winner of a multimillion-dollar lottery

unity   harmony and coherence of parts, absence of irrelevance

unreliable narrator   a narrator whose report a reader cannot accept at face value, per-haps because the narrator is naive or is too deeply inplicated in the action to report it objectively

verse   (1) a line of poetry; (2) a stanza of a poem (355)

vers libre   free verse, unrhymed poetry (356)

villanelle   a poem with five stanzas of three lines rhyming *aba,* and a concluding stanza of four lines, rhyming *abaa.* The first and third lines of the first stanza rhyme. The entire first line is repeated as the third line of the second and fourth stanzas; the en-tire third line is repeated as the third line of the third and fifth stanzas. These two lines form the final two lines of the last (four-line) stanza.

voice   see *persona, style,* and *tone* (332-33)

Credits

Charles R. Anderson, "Stairway of Surprise," Emily Dickinson's Poetry by Charles R. Anderson. Copyright 1963, 1982 by Charles R. Anderson. Reprinted by permission.

Maya Angelou, "Graduation" from *I Know Why the Caged Bird Sings* by Maya Angelou. Copyright © 1969 by Maya Angelou. Reprinted by permission of Random House, Inc.

Anjana Appachana, "To Rise Above" by Anjana Appachana is reprinted by permission of the publisher from *The Forbidden Stitch: An Asian American Women's Anthology* (Calyx Books, © 1989) edited by Shirley Geok-lin Lim et al.

Max Apple, "Bridging" pages 16–27 from *Free Agents* by Max Apple. Copyright © 1984 by Max Apple. Reprinted by permission of HarperCollins Publishers, Inc.

José Armas, "El Tonto del Barrio" originally published in Pajarito Publications, 1979, from *Cuentos Chicanos*, Revised Edition, 1984, edited by Rudolfo A. Anaya and Antonio Marques, University of New Mexico Press. Reprinted by permission of José Armas.

W. H. Auden, "Musée des Beaux Arts" and "The Unknown Citizen" from *W. H. Auden: Collected Poems* by W. H. Auden, ed. by E. Mendelson. Copyright © 1976 by Edward Mendelson, William Meredith, and Monroe K. Spears, Executors of the Estate of W. H. Auden. Reprinted by permission of Random House, Inc. and Faber and Faber Ltd.

Toni Cade Bambara, "The Lesson" and "My Man Bovanne" from *Gorilla, My Love* by Toni Cade Bambara. Copyright © 1971 by Toni Cade Bambara. Reprinted by permission of Random House, Inc.

Linda Bamber, "The Tempest and the Traffic in Women" by Linda Bamber. Reprinted by permission of the author.

Kristine Batey, "Lot's Wife" from *Jam Today #6* (1978). Copyright © 1978 by Jam Today.

Paula Bennett, "Emily Dickinson" by Paula Bennett from *Woman Poet.* Copyright © 1991 by Paula Bennett. Reprinted by permission of the University of Iowa Press.

Ralph Berry, "A Production of *The Tempest*" from *On Directing Shakespeare* by Ralph Berry. Copyright © 1990 by Ralph Berry. Used by permission of Viking Penguin, a division of Penguin Books USA Inc.

Elizabeth Bishop, "Filling Station," "Poem," and "The Fish" from *The Complete Poems, 1927–1979* by Elizabeth Bishop. Copyright © 1940 by Elizabeth Bishop. Copyright © 1979, 1983 by Alice Helen Methfessel. Reprinted by permission of Farrar, Straus and Giroux, Inc.

Susan Blake, "Racism and the Classics: Teaching *Heart of Darkness*" by Susan Blake, *CLA Journal*, Volume 25, Number 4, June 1982. Reprinted by permission of College Language Association Journal.

Index of Authors, Titles, and First Lines of Poems

Index of Terms